Human Resource Management

Uday Kumar Haldar

Principal

Swami Vivekananda Institute of Management and Computer Science

Kolkata

Juthika Sarkar

HR practitioner

OXFORD

UNIVERSITY PRESS

OXFORD
UNIVERSITY PRESS

Oxford University Press is a department of the University of Oxford.
It furthers the University's objective of excellence in research, scholarship,
and education by publishing worldwide. Oxford is a registered trade mark of
Oxford University Press in the UK and in certain other countries.

Published in India by
Oxford University Press
YMCA Library Building, 1 Jai Singh Road, New Delhi 110001, India

First published in 2012

ISBN-13: 978-0-19-807668-1
ISBN-10: 0-19-807668-1

Typeset in Garamond
by iPlus Knowledge Solutions Private Limited, Chennai
Printed in India by Adage Printers (P) Ltd., Noida 201301 U.P.

To the loving memory of Late Prof. Udai Pareek
who was the driving force behind the conception and realization of this book
His vision and beliefs continue to guide us in all our endeavours.

Preface

With the advent of globalization, organizations today are seen to be increasingly operating in the global village. Markets have been seen to expand tremendously where older products have undergone a makeover and the new ones are showing a marked dependence on technology. The struggle for limited resources at the global level seems to be a perennial concern being faced by organizations. This has made the competition between organizations, to survive and excel in the market, more acute than ever before. Thus, it has become essential for organizations to have a proper system in place that can deal with achieving results for, with, and through people.

Managing business organizations requires an integrated approach among its several functional areas—marketing, finance, operations, information, and human resources. In spite of increased dependence on technology, human beings can surely make a difference to the way organizations work. Hence among all the disciplines, human resource management (HRM) will be the one of the most critical functions in the organizations of tomorrow.

Human resource management is the art of making people more effective than they would have been without a manager, and a science for having a systematic approach behind every action. It is the study and practice of increasing the enabling capacities of individuals, groups, collectives, work force, and organizations through the development and application of managerial interventions for the purpose of organizational growth and effectiveness. Activities involved in managing human beings are pervasive throughout every organization. Irrespective of the size of the company and nature of the business, the presence of a formal system of managing the human resources (HR) has become mandatory today.

ABOUT THE BOOK

Since HRM has become an essential aspect in every organization as well as a manager's life, this book has been developed to help the potential managers understand and appreciate various HR functions. Written in a student friendly manner, this comprehensive textbook is designed to meet the needs of postgraduate and graduate management students. It focuses on theoretical fundamentals and applications of HR related concepts. It attempts to discuss every sphere of HRM along with a presentation of industry-oriented case studies and researches that would complement the academic and professional interest of the readers.

The book follows a unique feature of each chapter beginning with an opening case study. These cases are specifically based on organizations facing some crisis specifically pertaining to the topics discussed in the chapter, and the solutions to these are dealt with in the closing case. This feature helps make the topics more interesting and augments the process of learning.

Faculty members will find the cases and exhibits of this book—particularly the opening cases—useful while introducing any new topic to the students. They may introduce the opening cases to the students, discuss the learning points, and emphasise the necessities of the content of the chapter. This approach would make the topics more interesting and useful. In chapters where the same organization has been discussed in both the opening and the closing cases, teachers are appealed to elucidate the importance of a strong knowledge base to the students.

Keeping the students' interest in mind, critical thinking questions, assignments, and, manager's insights have been provided at the end of every chapter. These would facilitate them to gain insight and more clarity on the concept discussed.

Research scholars and training organizations will also find this book useful for developing and implementing HR development programmes. Students are recommended to visit the web resources given at the end of the chapters for furthering their knowledge.

PEDAGOGICAL FEATURES

Special pedagogical features used throughout the book are as follows:

- *Extensive coverage* Provides in-depth discussion on the various facets of the HR system including acquiring, retaining, and developing talents
- *Researches in HR* Dedicates a chapter exclusively to the contemporary researches carried out in the field of HRM
- *HR in different sectors* Discusses different strategies and experiences of HR personnel in different sectors such as manufacturing, service, and knowledge industries
- *Exhibits and examples* Chapters contain glimpses of HR practices drawn mainly from the Indian context practised in organizations in the form of various exhibits and examples
- *Case studies* Each chapter begins with an opening case with learning points and ends with a case study with discussion questions based on it. These in-depth discussions help students in gaining insight and clarity of concepts
- *Chapter-end exercises* Concept review questions help students recollect the principal concepts learnt therein; critical thinking questions and project assignments facilitate in applying the knowledge in real-life situations
- *Manager's insight* Provides specific organizational situations and questions to develop analytical thinking of the students
- *HR mantra* Every chapter ends with a mantra giving an essence of the chapter
- *Biographies* Provides details of noted academicians and organizational stalwarts at the end of each chapter, primarily to convey their contributions in the arena of HR management and development, which will definitely motivate and encourage the students

ORGANIZATION OF THE BOOK

The book is divided into 4 parts and each begins with an overview to facilitate the readers to take a glance and obtain a general idea of the content discussed in that section.

Part I: Inception

Chapter 1, *Understanding Organizations*, provides an understanding of an organization, helps to gain an insight about the role and importance of people, and emphasizes the significance of leadership and most importantly the changing role of HR managers.

Chapter 2, *Business Focus of HRM*, discusses the changing business scenario, laying focus on the HRM functions. Classification of business environments including technological and international environments are discussed. The relationship between an organization and the environment is also discussed.

Chapter 3, *Human Resource Management—An Overview*, brings out the various facets of HRM including topics such as HRM during economic recession and boom. Thereafter, the dependence of HRM on culture, organization, people, and systems are discussed with checklists for each.

Chapter 4, *Talent Management and Employee Engagement*, talks about various aspects such as talent, talent management, and relevant survey, and then switches over to employee engagement, taking into account the extent of promoting engagement.

Chapter 5, *Competency Framework for Talent Management*, details about competence, its types, organizational practices on developing competencies, and competency approaches in a few HRM functions.

Part II: HR Systems

Chapter 6, *Manpower Planning and Recruitment*, deals with sources of manpower (human resource), forecasting (demand and supply), types of recruitment, job analysis and evaluation, selection tools and methods, and a model of attracting prospective talents. The inclusion of recruitment and selection is a distinctive feature of this chapter.

Chapter 7, *Induction and Placement*, highlights the importance of inducting new recruits into an organization, the role of buddy, and checklists for induction. It also examines the mandatory learning contents of an induction programme.

Chapter 8, *Performance Management System*, discusses various aspects of performance management including system theory and human performance, basic purpose of performance appraisal and associated methods, means of achieving superior performances, and means adopted by organizations directed towards managing performances.

Chapter 9, *Training and Development*, discusses all facets of training including pre-training work, designing curriculum, appropriate pedagogy, evaluating training, and post-training work for making the training effective.

Chapter 10, *Multi-source Feedback*, emphasizes the utmost need of appraisal of an employee by all those with whom the employee is required to interact almost every day. This system also discusses the softer dimensions of performance that are essential for employee development.

Chapter 11, *Potential Appraisal and Career System*, throws light on the necessity of identifying the inner potential or latent talent of employees in order to make the best use of their capability. This, in turn, promotes employee engagement and reduces the probability of attrition.

Chapter 12, *Reward System and Compensation Management*, explains the different modes of compensating employees including rewards, incentives, and wage administration.

Chapter 13, *Separation and Beyond*, presents separation as a social and organizational concept, and means of handling it with sensitivity and utmost care without injuring the sentiment of the employees being separated.

Chapter 14, *Developing Workers and Sub-staff*, discusses developing the workforce including labourers, managing knowledge workers, and tools to help the workers to lead a productive life.

Part III: Contemporary Issues in HRM

Chapter 15, *Managing Change*, discusses the changing business scenario, dynamics of change, sources of resistance vis-à-vis coping mechanisms, key roles in organizational change, and other aspects of change. Considering the importance of this chapter, multiple choice questions have been provided to help readers acquire clear conception.

Chapter 16, *Knowledge Management*, deals with knowledge management practices, processes, and the tools used. Framing a knowledge strategy and managing knowledge workers are also discussed.

Chapter 17, *HRD Audit*, explains the various facets of HRD audits and the utmost need for verifying and using good HR practices.

Chapter 18, *Ethics and Corporate Social Responsibility*, discusses ethics and its importance in companies. Following this, it deliberates on corporate social responsibility (CSR) and its practices in diverse and reputed companies.

Chapter 19, *Managing Globalization*, deals with the conceptual framework, themes, facets benefits, and threats of globalization along with culture management elements.

Chapter 20, *Technology and HRM*, highlights technological changes, technology management, relevant HR initiatives, and developing the change mindset.

Chapter 21, *Work–Life Balance*, discusses the impacts and consequences of an imbalanced work life, interventions to enhance the work–life balance, and explains the checklist of the International Labour Organization (ILO) concerning family-friendly policies.

Chapter 22, *Quality Management and HRM*, emphasizes on quality management tools such as JIT, 5S, Kaizen, and six-sigma and the related role of HR.

Chapter 23, *HRM Strategy*, draws attention to organizational goals, corresponding HRM goals, and the strategies to achieve the set goals.

Chapter 24, *HRM in Various Sectors*, entails discussion on HRM in various sectors such as manufacturing, service, and knowledge industries. It pays special attention to the role of an HR manager in Panchayats to benefit the people.

Part IV: Research in HRM

Chapter 25, *Research in HRM*, includes objectives, motivation, types and areas of researches, glimpses of statistical tools and packages, and guidance to preparing a thesis. Students must read and conceptualize the learning points at the end of the opening case.

The book concludes with the following appendices:

Appendix A, *Stress Management*, details the consequence of stress, and the utmost need for managing stress for the benefit of both individuals and organizations.

Appendix B, *Organizational Climate and Organizational Role Stress*, sketches the importance of improving the organizational climate, consequences of organizational role stress, their reciprocal dependency with each other with the help of a conceptual model, and proposes the need for an internal research cell.

Appendix C, *Leadership Styles in Organization*, discusses the roles of leaders, leadership styles in organizations, and their influences on organizational functioning.

Acknowledgements

Many have contributed towards the development of this book. We wish to thank all those who have encouraged and given us their valuable inputs during its development.

We would like to express our gratitude to Prof. Sushma Khanna, Director of EMPI, New Delhi, for providing us the biography of Prof. Udai Pareek.

We express our gratitude to Mr Arun Ray Chaudhuri, General Manager (HR), Ericsson, for providing his valuable inputs across various chapters. Mr Bimalendu Saha, General Manager, Gun and Shell Factory (Cossipore) and Mr Vinod Kumar Singh, General Manager, Ordnance Factory (Dum Dum) have consistently encouraged us throughout the development of this book. We are indebted to Prof. Paul Spector, Department of Psychology, University of South Florida and Dr Rabindra Kumar Pradhan, IIT Kharagpur, who extended their helps towards the completion of this book.

We are grateful to everyone who contributed to the closing cases in the chapters—Dr T.S. Kuckrejja, President, AMRI Hospital, Salt Lake; Mr Indranil Bhattacharya, Regional HR, Titan; Mr Partha Pratim Dhara, CMRI Hospital, Dhakuria, Kolkata; Ms Poonam Sharda; Mr Abhishek Banerjee; Mr Ravi Prakash; Ms Saswati Chatterjee; Ms Rima Patra; Mr P.S. Sukumar, Deputy General Manager, Knowledge Management, Eureka Forbes Limited, Bangalore; and Mr Biplab Biswas, Directorate of Panchayat and Rural Development Offices, West Bengal. Mr Sanjoy Shaw, General Manager (HR), PepsiCo India, Kolkata Plant was instrumental in finalizing the closing case of Chapter 18. We would also like to thank his seniors, Ayan Das, Rikhia Basu, Devraj Sharma, Vivek Bharati, and Rohini Seth, for their immense support while developing this case study.

We also thank the officials of Ericsson; Dr Samta Jain, IBS Mumbai, and Dr Namrata Mehta, J.N.V. University, Jodhpur, for sharing their valuable inputs for Chapter 19.

We are grateful to Prof. D.M. Pestonjee, Prof. T.V. Rao, Prof. B.R. Virmani, Prof. Avinash Srivastav, Prof. Sharu S. Rangnekar, Mr Sanjeev Himachalli, and many others who have provided their biographies for use in the book.

We received immense support from our families during the development of this manuscript. Dr Haldar specifically acknowledges his wife Sikha, children Amlan and Sonali, and daughter-in-law Mitil for being his constant sources of motivation and encouragement.

Dr Haldar pays tributes to the departed souls of Dr Labanya Kumar Haldar (father), Mrs Durga Rani Devi (mother), Mr Pravat Kumar Haldar (elder brother), Mr Krishendu Haldar (younger brother), and Mr Mridul Kanti Das (brother-in-law).

Ms Sarkar is grateful to Mrs Jamuna Sarkar (mother), Mr Sricharan Sarkar (elder brother), Mr Biplab Biswas (husband), and daughter Adrita for their support and encouragement towards fulfilling her academic endeavour. She pays tributes to the departed souls of her father Dr Chandi Charan Sarkar and grandmother Mrs Jogmaya Mondal.

We would also like to thank all other family members for making the experience of writing this book memorable.

We extend our thanks to all the scholars, writers, and managers who have helped us directly and indirectly. Last but not least, we are indebted to the editorial team at Oxford University Press, India, for providing useful inputs throughout the development of the manuscript.

We welcome suggestions and feedback about the book to improve the future editions. Readers may contact us at ukhaldar@rediffmail.com and juthika_sarkar@yahoo.co.in.

Uday Kumar Haldar and Juthika Sarkar

Features of the Book

Opening Case and Chapter-end Case
Each chapter begins and ends with a detailed case study that is designed to consolidate your understanding of the concepts studied and broaden your decision-making skills.

OPENING CASE

Manpower Planning, Recruitment, and Selection

Seamless Engineering Limited (SEL) came into existence in 1993. It initially focused on manufacturing and marketing spare parts for hydraulic and pneumatic pumps, automobiles, and other engineering products. These products were low-technology products. SEL planned to enhance its product range by

HRM INITIATIVES DURING TECHNOLOGY UPGRADATION

About the organization

OFDC is a public sector enterprise, located in north Kolkata. It was established in 1846 as Ammunition Factory, and following restructuring, it changed its name to OFDC in 1964. The organization manufactures high precision engineering components. It received an ISO 9002:1994

OFDC duly considered the increasing knowledge intensity of production, quality aspirations of customers, skills and other human attributes required to run the sophisticated CNC machines, the essential deskilling and reskilling, and the financial impact with regard to wages. Workers were paid on the basis of individual piece work (IPW) and gang

Box 9.1 Organizational drives to involve people

1. The vision for the future of the organization
2. The organization's policies and objectives
3. Organizational change and development

Exhibit 7.1 Roles in induction

1. Line manager/supervisor explains his/her jurisdiction—the departmental organization, the requirements of the job, the purpose and operation of any probationary period, and the appraisal system.
2. HR personnel cover the general aspects of the day of joining for a new recruit such as completing employee formats, taking bank details, and explaining the induction programme.
5. Senior manager(s) and/or HR give an overview of the organization, its history, products and services, quality system, and culture.
6. Training officer (or line manager) describes available training services, and helps develop a personalized training plan. He/She also provides details of other sources of information during induction such as the company's intranet or interactive learning facilities.

Boxed Items and Exhibits
Every chapter provides boxed items and exhibits that will help you relate to and enhance your ability to apply the theory discussed.

Sidebars
Sidebars included in every chapter highlight the important points discussed in the text. This will help you to remember and recollect easily, the key takeaways from each chapter.

The seven engagement elements or levers that matter the most are shared values, effective leadership, motivational recognition, contribution to success, employee involvement or engagement, personal development, and economic self-interest.

HR initiatives such as job description, role clarity, flexi time, no meetings after core working hours, forced annual leave, maternity and paternity leave, shopping at work, crèche, disincentives to overtime, gym and good food facility, no late sitting culture, help in achieving work–life balance.

Cartoons
More than 40 cartoons have been provided throughout the book to visually depict important HR concepts.

MANAGER'S INSIGHT

Ahuja and Ahuja, a famous company for manufacturing bags and shoes, has been into the business for the last two decades. With a modest beginning, the company has grown steadily over the years. Its reputation for product innovation and customer service has enabled the company to remain competitive and increase its product and customer base. The employees in the company were also very happy with the company and management. Due to some personal reasons, the senior manager of the product development department had to leave the and effectiveness that they used to show pı fact, there was a visible downfall in the pı of the company. The HR realized that th could be attributed to the sudden depar senior manager.

Questions:

1. What would be the best way for the HR the situation?
2. Do you think the company could have kep

Manager's Insight
Manager's insight, provided at the end of every chapter, explains a typical real-life situation and asks you to find the best feasible solution that can be applied by a manager. This will aid you in polishing your managerial skills.

Biographies
Biographies of eminent personalities have been included at the end of every chapter to give you an insight into the lives and work of prominent HR practioners.

PETER DRUCKER

Peter Drucker was born on 19 November 1909 in a small village called Kaasgraben in Vienna, Austria. He was a business thinker, an influential business author, a strategist, and a consultant. His ideas on management, operating large corporations, and leadership have been published in more than 30 books.

Drucker's paternal and maternal relations were Jewish. His parents were converted to Christianity and lived in what he referred to

Over the years, Drucker's writings were marked by a focus on relationships among human beings, as opposed to the crunching of numbers. Drucker's books were filled with lessons on how organizations can bring out the best in people, and how workers can find a sense of community and dignity in a modern society organized around large institutions. As a business consultant, he disliked the term 'guru', though it was often applied to him. "I have been saying

HR MANTRA Your actions will speak

A rich man purchased a healthy cow and a poor man purchased a sickly cow from the same market. The rich man displayed his cow at the entrance to his house, while the poor man invested a lot of money on his sickly cow. In course of time, the rich man's cow became weak, while the poor man's cow gained health.

People are the most vital and valuable resources of any organization. Material resources depreciate, while human resources appreciate.

The mantra: Understand and nurture people

HR Mantras
Mantras included at the end of every chapter capture the essence of the chapter, in the form of an interesting story or incident.

Brief Contents

Detailed Contents

PART ONE

Overview—Inception

Before independence, India was an agriculture-based economy. Over the years, it has gradually shifted from an agricultural economy to an industrial and knowledge-based economy. Indian doctors, scientists, and engineers have made their presence felt in countries across the globe. The contribution made by the information technology (IT) sector is extremely significant. This is one of the main reasons why India is at the forefront of the IT outsourcing and off-shoring revolution. Indians are considered competent with regard to knowledge, talent, and skills.

Boosting productivity, enhancing distinctive competence, gaining competitive advantages, acquiring excellence, identifying new ways of processing, winning in cutthroat competition, discovering and benchmarking innovative organizational practices, managing changes, and utilizing the most valuable human resources need talent and continue to be the principal concerns of any organization. Anyone joining the organization, especially the human resources (HR) department, needs to understand the organization, its people, and the leadership styles.

Big business tycoons express their voracious appetite through mergers, acquisitions, and takeovers. Whatever be the size of an organization, its success depends upon the goodness of its people. An act of Parliament cannot make people virtuous. Similarly, good philosophy, administrative quality, environmental policies, objectives, or structured systems cannot guarantee organizational effectiveness. The people (human capital) are the most valued assets of the organization and they significantly impact the organizational transformation. Focusing on the people waves the shape and responsibilities of the traditional human resources function. When competent people are empowered, they become self-propelled.

In today's rapidly-changing business scenario, the shift from industrial-era models to knowledge-era models is very evident. Furthermore, in many companies, talents or knowledge assets have emerged as their real assets. To effectively utilize this asset, companies need to develop superior teaming skills in order to continually team and reteam the core talents of the organization. One has to consider teaming beyond domain. Human resources significantly contribute in the change process.

Organizational leaders also devote adequate attention to make people innovative and 'total-quality persons'.

Leaders are committed, maintain administrative transparency, keep the processes visible, provide the necessary support, hold people accountable for results, and practice what they preach. At its best, human resources have a significant contribution to advance an organization. Top management must lead, facilitate, and coach in the creation of organizational environments and cultures that support flexibility. They further have to develop core competencies, a culture of mutual trust and shared vision necessary to move forward. Only people can make or mar the organization. The technology, system, process or machineries, can only help the concerted and orchestrated efforts of the people. In doing so, the quality of work life gets enriched, and in turn, improves the quality of life. The society also benefits with the perking up of our 'quality of life'. In short, one can say that in order to be successful in business, one has to understand the business by focusing onto the human resource management.

Human resource management excellence has helped many companies rebound and turnaround. With the passing of time, a person's knowledge, skills, experience, maturity, pragmatism, and wisdom enhance. Of the many resources, only human resource appreciates. Also, human resource differs from all other resources from many standpoints. An organization under making or transformation is comparable with an unformatted hard disk which must be formatted using software. Human resources can offer leadership which solves the purpose of the software. Organizational learning occurs when members of an organization act as learning agents. A learning organization is skilled at creating, acquiring, and transferring knowledge and modifying its behaviour to reflect new knowledge and insights. It is the workforce that can create, acquire, stretch,, transfer knowledge, suggest changes, offer leadership, and so forth. The management and nurturing of the people can take an organization to great heights.

Contextually, Jack Welch, former chairman and chief executive officer of General Electric, said that an organization's ability to learn and translate learning rapidly into action forms the ultimate competitive advantage. We can gain competitive advantage by transforming people. The tenets of human resource management should ideally be aimed at developing people, grooming future people, ensuring employee deployment, building employee communities, and turning managers into coaches. Human resource management should not be viewed as a specialized and standalone function. Human resource managers and the line managers must build partnerships to gain competitive advantage and achieve overall business goals. The need of the day is 'transformational human resource management'. It stands established that managing human resources should be the primary concern of any organization.

Human resource management traditionally refers to the organizational policies, practices and norms, and systems that influence employee behaviours, attitudes, and performance. The recruitment or 'talent acquisition' policy should be such that the right people, with the aptitude and abilities to meet current and future organizational needs, get into the bus. Thereafter, they have to undertake a long journey. After attracting the talent, the top management makes a conscious and deliberate approach to develop and retain them. A dynamic management must recognize the contributions of human capital, develop them into balanced human beings in order to use their real potentials, and thus offers a new set of opportunities to the human resource in the organization.

The historical, environmental, strategic, political, and interpersonal perspectives must be considered in HRM. Contextually, it must be mentioned that people management emphasizes building the best team and driving it, building bridges of relationship, focusing on delivery, seeking and considering feedback, developing people, defining accountability, setting standards, laying emphasis on value creation, and trusting the people. From the standpoint of people management, human resource management may be described as encompassing all the managerial decisions and actions that directly affect or influence people as members of the organization rather than as job-holders. The human resource should not be defined as by what is does but what it delivers. We have to consider and judge the results that enrich the organization's value to customers, investors, and employees. The HR must be a partner with senior and line managers, link HR activities with the business goals, must build an image as the 'champion of employees', and should strive to become driving force behind continuous transformation removing all sort of organizational barriers.

Talent is another important requirement in organizations. It refers to persons with higher degree of aptitude having the innate and instinctive ability to contribute to organizational excellence. It is hard to search and get talented people for an organization, and even harder to retain them. Hence, the main focus of human resource management should invariably be talent management. Talent management is a conscious, deliberate approach to attract, develop and retain people with the aptitude and abilities to meet current and future organizational needs. It involves individual and organizational development in response to a changing and complex business environment. It demands the creation and maintenance of a supportive and people-oriented organizational culture.

The human resource management profession and practices have undergone a sea change. The HRM services should not merely be mired down in managing trivial and traditional administrative functions; the services should provide value to the organization by way of acquiring, nurturing, multiplying, and developing talents in the organization. The services must be directed to identify the people and positions of all levels performing activities that are critical to the organization. Many organizations have lost huge amounts of 'organizational knowledge' in the downsizing exercises. The impact of the loss may not be immediately apparent. It has also been evidenced that those who left the organization mostly comprised talented people who could easily find a position in the competitors' house. Acquiring talents must be followed by engaging them and assigning them with challenging assignments so that they are satisfied, involved, and are committed to the work assignments. Otherwise, they may quit and there are many examples to prove the same.

It is obvious that organizations should identify the people and positions of all levels performing activities that are critical to the organization. They must have certain means to recognize the people and ascertain the critical activities; examine the activities to identify the skills and competencies essentially needed for successful execution or completion of an activity or cluster of activities. Some jobs might need specialized skills. Talent management has emerged as a new avatar of the HR managers. It is the core element of human capital management. People generate capital for an organization through their competencies, behaviour, and intellectual energies. Knowledge-intensive organizations are now dominating the commercial world. Intellectual capacity of talents is more crucial for the survival of knowledge-intensive organizations.

However, in any organization, people must be competent to undertake and complete a job. An organization has to identify the competency framework containing several aptitudes which might be logically arranged in a few clusters. An organization's competency framework should capture the behaviour of its top performers. Competency framework also supports administrative functions and legal obligations such as recruitment, performance management, and redundancy. First of all, an organization has to identify the job profiles, followed by the key job functions and competencies for each profile. For example, some of the key functions and competencies for IT personnel include corporate function analysis, business unit support, data management, technology development, IT infrastructure library (ITIL) creation, infrastructure management, systems management, architecture, etc. Competency framework for talent management is the basic need of any business house.

In view of the foregoing discussions, this part of the book has been structured in five chapters:

1. Understanding Organizations
2. Changing Business Scenario—Focus on Human Resource Management
3. Human Resource Management: An Overview
4. Talent Management and Employee Engagement
5. Competency Framework for Talent Management

CHAPTER 1

Understanding Organizations

LEARNING OBJECTIVES

After studying this chapter, you will be able to

- Understand the role of an organization
- Gain an insight into the role and importance of people in the organization
- Appreciate the importance of leadership and recognize the various leadership styles practised in an organization
- Understand the concept of job attitudes

OPENING CASE

A Perplexed Entrepreneur

M/s Agrawal Enterprises

Agrawal was a non-resident Indian (NRI) based in Canada. A graduate in engineering, he also held a post-graduate degree in production engineering from an institute of international repute. Although he received several lucrative offers from various organizations in his campus interviews, he rejected them as he had a strong drive to be his own boss and function independently. He decided to launch his own consultancy firm, Agrawal Consultants. Within a short span of time, he became famous and reaped the benefits of a thriving practice in New Jersey. However, despite the success of his operations, Agrawal harboured thoughts of returning to India.

During the period 1981–82, the Government of India appealed to NRIs to invest in various businesses in their home country. Many NRIs responded to the request and Agrawal foresaw an opportunity in this idea. He found it hard to resist and invested a substantial sum in a few businesses that offered high rates of return on investment at that point of time. After conducting lengthy discussions with an Indian businessman, he passed on his decision of returning to India to his clients in New Jersey. Despite consistent persuasion from his clients to continue in New Jersey with his well-established practice, Agrawal returned to India after a 15-year stint in the US.

After his return to India, he established contacts with the companies in which he had invested, and studied all the related financial documents carefully. Earlier, in New Jersey, many firms had benefited from his consultancy services. A majority of those clients were producing special-purpose hydraulic and pneumatic pumps. He had advised them with regard to design and manufacture of components. He also assisted them with assembly and quality control parameters. He lived up to the expectations of consumers and the clients never received any complaints.

In due course of time, he wanted to start his own venture. Having gained confidence in his field of expertise, Agrawal decided to start an organization that aimed to design, manufacture, and sell hydraulic and pneumatic pumps. Accordingly, he chose the location in an industrial area located in his native state. He applied for a trade license, registered his firm, and appointed technical and administrative personnel. During the next six months, he procured the machines, and spent four months in erecting and commissioning them. He appointed an expert mechanical engineer to look after the quality control department. Meanwhile, he secured orders for the pumps. Once all the necessary equipment was in place, he began producing and selling the products in the domestic market.

To take his initiative forward, Agrawal recruited salespersons, who were fresh diploma holders in sales management from a local management institute. They were assigned the job of delivering the pumps directly to customers without the intervention of distributors or dealers. Gradually, pressure began building up, and customers wanted him to expedite delivery. Agrawal, in turn, advised his team to act upon the orders with immediate effect. His team strived hard to cope with the demands.

In order to meet the urgent need for increasing production, Agrawal appointed a production manager. For the sake of the study, we shall address him as PM. PM was a qualified, disciplined manager, and a hard taskmaster. Towards the end of each day, he would collect the production figures. While most operators strived hard to meet their targets, some operators tried to express their difficulties and grievances. However, PM did not pay attention to their grievances.

There was one noteworthy incident that occurred, when a team of three officials visited Agrawal's firm for capacity assessment. During inspection, they enquired with a line supervisor about his duties and responsibilities. The supervisor could not give a clear answer as the employees were not clear about their roles in the firm. Soon after the inspection, the officials met Agrawal in his office, where PM was already present. Agrawal very politely postponed the discussion with PM until the next day. When PM left the office, Agrawal began the discussion with the team. He did not introduce PM to the team members, who later learnt about PM's position. The team discussed issues pertaining to the product being manufactured in the firm. However, despite being aware of Agrawal's technical expertise from interviews in a leading business periodical that highlighted several of his success stories in New Jersey, the team did not place the order.

On another occasion, a customer had complained about the malfunctioning of some pumps and some others had expressed dissatisfaction. Agrawal replaced the defective pumps with an equal number of new pumps from the assembly line. However, customers continued to complain about the product and the situation was becoming serious, with one customer threatening to file a lawsuit.

Despite being a renowned consultant and entrepreneur, Agrawal was utterly confused. In order to solve the impending issues, he discussed the situation with his friend, a successful organizational leader and stalwart in a multinational company. His friend underlined the difference between the business scenarios in India and the US, and advised Agrawal to take assistance from an Indian human resources (HR) expert. Eventually, Agrawal selected Mr M.S. Menon, an HR expert, to advise him.

Mr Menon studied the situation and decided to execute organizational diagnostics. However, he advised Agrawal to arrange for a trust-building workshop for his supervisory employees immediately.

Learning points

- Organizations should develop their workforce and ensure that their roles are clearly specified.
- Adhering to the appropriate leadership styles will produce the desired results.
- Understanding people is imperative for organizational growth.
- Mutual trust between people leads to organizational effectiveness.

(Based on a case from Haldar, U.K., *Human Resource Development*, Oxford University Press, New Delhi, 2010.)

INTRODUCTION TO ORGANIZATION

An organization, be it a government, a corporation, or a private enterprise, is a social unit with certain specific objectives. A broader definition of an organization may also include a family, school, football team, temple, church, mosque, etc. Organizations fulfil a large variety of our societal and personal needs and affect a large segment of our society. Parsons (1979) perceives organizations as 'a social unit which is deliberately constructed and reconstructed to seek specific goals'. The structure of the organization is created and maintained through a process comprising the following steps:

1. Determining specific activities essential to accomplish the organizational objectives
2. Clustering activities into 'activity packages' and assigning them to competent personnel
3. Creating a network or organizational hierarchy for the purpose of planning, motivating, communicating, coordinating, and controlling

Thus, an organization is a social entity that is directed by goals, with a consciously structured activity system and a relatively identifiable boundary.

Organizational leaders strive for sustenance and growth of the organization. In a competitive business scenario, organizations need talents and creative personnel to enhance their growth through innovations. Creativity is the ability to discover new relationships and ideas. Innovation refers to the practical implementation of new ideas in the workplace. Finding out the causal relation that exists between the assertiveness of a person and his/her performance level is a creative task. It can be measured to enhance the level of assertiveness of the people in the workplace by suitable means, thereby enhancing their performance. Thus, the idea is implemented in real life and is called innovation. If an organization does not encourage innovation, it is likely to perish eventually.

Innovation is an ongoing process. In a changing business environment, organizations need to cope with changes. Thus, organizations must transform or change themselves in order to survive and grow in the society.

It is also important to know that these changes should be accommodated as early as possible. The law of the jungle was 'survival of the fittest'. In today's business scenario, the rule has changed to 'survival of the fastest'. In addition, the maxim 'slow and steady' has changed to 'fast and consistent'. Although though transformation is considered a major undertaking with a high price, when implemented, the rewards surpass the painstaking efforts. Prior to transformation, it is important to understand the culture and values of an organization. The culture of the organization speaks about the norms, beliefs, and behaviours that are shared by the members of the organization. Values indicate greater awareness, including those testable in the physical environment and those testable only by social consensus (Pareek 2008).

The maxim 'slow and steady' has changed to 'fast and consistent' in today's time.

Core beliefs drive an organization towards success. Positive core beliefs combine to create an organization's formula for success. For instance, the core values and beliefs of Tata Consultancy Services are integrity, understanding, excellence, unity, and responsibility. Exhibit 1.1 shows the same for a famous brand, Lijjat.

Exhibit 1.1 Core beliefs of Lijjat

Mahila Griha Udyog Lijjat Papad, popularly known as Lijjat, is an organization comprising women employees. Lijjat was the brain child of seven semi-literate Mumbai-based Gujarati housewives. Lijjat believes in the philosophy of *sarvodaya* and collective ownership. It accepts all its working members as owners who take part in both profits and losses equally. Consumers of Lijjat products consider the products as their own house-hold products. Members are also co-owners of the company and are fondly referred to as *bahena* or sisters. The organization's decisions are based on the consensus of every member who has the right to veto a decision. Its work culture is based on values and mutual trust.

Over the years, Lijjat's members have expanded from seven to over 42,000 throughout India. In 2005, Lijjat received the Brand Equity Award from the then President of India, Dr A.P. J. Abdul Kalam.

(Contd)

Exhibit 1.1 (Contd)

Today, Lijjat has diversified into various activities. Apart from its world-famous *papads*, it also comprises the following:

1. A flour division at Vashi in Mumbai where flour is milled from *urad* dal and *moong* dal
2. A masala division and a quality control laboratory at Cottongreen where different spice powders such as turmeric, chillies, coriander and ready mix masalas such as *garam* masala, tea masala, *pav bhaji* masala, Punjabi *chole* masala are prepared and sealed into packets
3. A printing division, along with a labelling and packaging unit
4. An advertising division at Bandra in Mumbai
5. A *khakhra* division at Buhari in Valod
6. *Chapati* divisions at Wadala, Borivali, Mulund and Kandivali
7. A polypropylene unit at Kashi-Mira Road
8. A *vadi*-producing factory and a bakery division at Valod
9. A detergent powder and cake-manufacturing unit at Pune and Hyderabad

Source: www.lijjat.com, last accessed on 8 January 2010.

Culture also plays a dominant role in organizations and societies. Moreover, organizational culture and social culture are relevant to change management. Generally, a team undertakes the responsibility of planning, designing, and implementing a change. The members come from diverse cultures and are dictated by their social and economic backgrounds. They possess a variety of values and attitudes. In an organization, certain prevailing values must be preserved. If a change agent who is an impatient reformer, attempts to introduce a change in a society or an organization by disregarding the prevailing values, problems will definitely arise. This necessitates a proactive approach to change.

Organizational culture can be positive or negative. A positive organizational culture reinforces the core beliefs and behaviours desired by a leader. Organizational leaders strive to achieve the business goals that create a positive culture conducive to effective work culture. A negative culture, on the other hand, becomes toxic, poisons the life of the organizational members, and hinders any future potential for growth of the organization. Obviously, there is an inevitable bridge joining organizational culture and the level of success that it enjoys (Peters and Waterman 1982).

The organizational culture can be influenced by the business environment as well. The impact of external variables cannot be seen or felt directly, but is critical to the understanding of organizational culture and therefore, must not be ignored. For instance, industry and government systems impact an organization's internal culture. Leaders in any organization must be prepared to face these transformations and stand up to them.

A 'culture of commitment' takes an organization to a win–win situation.

In other words, to survive, grow, and march towards excellence, organizations need competent leaders. Leadership skills must be developed within managers as different situations need different styles of leadership.

ORGANIZATIONS AND LEADERSHIP

Q 1 Leadership drives an organization and can make or mar it. Any deficiency in leadership can simply create a culture of compliance rather than a culture of commitment. A leader can become a true learner only though personal development. He must learn, unlearn, and relearn. Once created, this 'culture of commitment', can take an organization to a win–win situation.

People's mindsets cannot be forcefully changed. Any attempt to forcefully change their mindset may simply lead to disaster. However, organizational transformation imposed on followers is first resisted and then resented by them. To be successful, leaders should first impose change on themselves and then cultivate it in others. Generally, exemplary leadership is most effective in cases where leaders slowly change the mindset of members of the organization. It is important to understand that transformation must begin within the heart and mind of the leader.

The members of the organization aim to serve its mission and significantly impact its culture. Organizations rely more on the transformation of its leaders rather than on the transformation of subordinates or systems.

THE ORGANIZATION AND ITS PEOPLE

According to Kaufman (2002), 'An organization is only as good as its people.' People are the most valued resource in any organization. One has to create the organizational culture that is marked by a culture of commitment and nurture people to make them effective. The elements of McKinsey's 7-S framework could be considered during the course of development of human resources. This concept will be taken up later in the chapter.

Kaufman (2002) highlights the contribution and role of people in an organization. As discussed, an organization is a framework where people operate or work together for a common goal. Consultants at McKinsey developed the 7-S framework with seven aspects—strategy, structure, system, staff, skill, style, and 'super ordinate goal' at the core. A company may possess excellent technology, strategy, structure, and systems; yet it may not be able to achieve success. Present day organizations rely heavily on technology while they inadvertently ignore the people (staff), employee proficiency (skill), and the pattern of interaction of the organizational members (style). In the McKinsey 7-S framework, the term 'style' bears a special connotation and refers to the way organizations introduce young recruits into the mainstream of activities. It also denotes the manner in which they manage their careers as the new recruits develop into future managers.

Apart from the new recruits, long-standing employees also need renewal. The experienced employees need to keep themselves updated with the latest happenings and cope with the new surroundings and strategies.

On the other hand, for organizations to develop, people must undergo significant changes at various points in their development. It is the people who develop the organization and not the technology, system, or infrastructure. Thus, people management is the most vital consideration. However, the policies followed in various situations seem to be contradicting this view.

> The term 'style' bears a special connotation, referring to the way organizations introduce young recruits into the mainstream of activities.

Today, the role of HR functions is changing. Customer focus and customer satisfaction are the buzzwords. Organizations are emphasizing on teamwork, and thinking in terms of 'teaming beyond domain'. With regard to leadership, visionary leadership is getting importance.

THE CHANGING ROLE OF HR FUNCTIONS

Q 2 The business scenario is ever-changing. There are several reasons that generally affect and invite changes in organizations, such as multiple and fast-paced technological innovations. Products, processes, and know-how are fast becoming obsolete and there is scarcity of natural resources. The costs of basic resources have increased and there is rising cost sensitivity and quality consciousness among customers. Competition has multiplied and there are frequent changes in regulatory mechanisms, and socio-economic structures. Besides, the onslaught of liberalization, privatization, and globalization have led to the growth and popularity of information technology, proliferation of environmental and consumer interest groups. The last decade has witnessed a shift from industrial-era models to knowledge-era models among organizations.

Customers are more demanding, quality-conscious, and cost-sensitive. Hence, organizations have begun to shift from the traditional platforms to total quality management (TQM) organizations. They no longer view employees as the source of the problem; on the contrary, they try to identify the problems in the processes. The benchmark for measurement has shifted from individuals to processes. While motivating people, more emphasis is laid on removal of barriers. With respect to employees, development has replaced control. 'Prevention of errors' has replaced 'reduce variation' and 'correct errors'. Furthermore, the product market is more competitive than ever before.

Though organizations belonging to different industries vary in size and nationality, there are four common themes that characterize the process of and ultimately shape the organizational transformations. These comprise the following:

1. Focusing on the customer
2. Teaming and supporting non-hierarchical and informal structures
3. Visionary leadership
4. Change in language and style

Focusing on the Customer

Times have changed and present-day organizations depend on their customers. Therefore, it is important to understand their customers' current and future needs, meet their requirements, and strive to surpass customer expectations. Many organizations carry out research to unveil customer needs and expectations in order to ensure that the objectives of the organization are linked to customer needs and expectations. It must be realized that crucial activities measure and enhance both customer satisfaction and customer relationship management. Contextually, communicating relevant information to employees (the internal customers) throughout the organization is also an essential requirement.

These activities are essential in order to increase revenue and market share, boost effectiveness, execute fast responses to market opportunities, improve customer loyalty, and eventually, lead to more business opportunities. In one way or another, most organizations have made significant changes in the way they think about their business and their customers. The focus of business has changed from 'working with money' to 'working with the customer'. The corporate vision and credo must illustrate the magnitude of this redefinition of the business. The employees (the human capital) are required to be developed to perform tasks related to customer orientation, satisfy and delight the customers, and convert prospective customers to actual customers.

Crucial activities measure and enhance customer satisfaction and CRM

In order to develop customer focus, the following activities are unavoidable:

1. Understanding customer orientation
2. Identifying the intrinsic needs of customers

3. Satisfying and delighting customers
4. Increasing certain competencies such as logical thinking and teamwork
5. Enhancing interpersonal communication
6. Reinstating mental balance and stability
7. Encouraging continuous learning

Converting prospective customers to actual customers requires knowledge about the business, persuasiveness, and negotiating skills. These competencies may be developed through training and development, which comes within the purview of human resource management (HRM). These topics would be discussed in greater detail in further chapters.

Teaming and Supporting Non-hierarchical and Informal Structures

The functioning of formal organizations differs from that of informal organizations. While informal organizations rely heavily on working in voluntarily-formed teams, formal organizations also encourage working in teams for improved performance. Non-hierarchical and informal structures also enable faster working and decision-making, which in turn, ensure organizational effectiveness. In the transformation process, teaming across organizational boundaries appears to be a hallmark of successful companies. In fact, a number of companies have eliminated many traditional organizational boundaries completely. Besides eliminating job titles, some companies have also done away with functional departments. Project teams are seen to organize work, and people join teams based on their competencies and interest. Consequently, HR functions have been shifted to the 'functional departments'. As such, in most organizations, HR functions have now become 'line functions' and not 'staff functions'. Added to this, organizations today are foregoing departmental affiliation and encouraging working in teams.

> In most organizations, HR functions are now 'line functions' and not 'staff functions'.

It is also believed that shifting of HR functions to line is an organizational transformation and transformational leadership can ease out this transfer and enable smooth transition. Knowledge of transformational leadership styles may be instilled through leadership development.

Visionary Leadership

A visionary leader must possess spontaneous dynamism and respect for others, make sacrifices for teammates, and foster creative thinking. Visionary leaders must also have qualities such as good communication skills, decision-making skills, human relation skills, and commitment to achieving goals. Inspiration and a practical vision of the future are the basis of visionary leadership. The vision should encourage and invite others to participate as partners. The followers are instilled with a sense of vigour, energy, and optimism that influences and motivates others. Obviously then, when the role of HR functions changes, visionary leaders need to discharge certain predominant added responsibilities as well.

The other contemporary leadership styles practised in organizations are transactional, transformational, charismatic leadership, value-based leadership, ethical and servant leadership, and boundary spanning leadership. All these leadership styles will be discussed in Appendix C of this book.

Change in Language and Style

> Indian companies that were operating within our national border are now operating across it.

The business scenario is constantly changing. The focus, as discussed earlier, should be on the customers, encouraging working in teams, supporting non-hierarchical and informal structures, and striving for visionary leadership. 'Managing new India' is the current rage. This topic has some dimensions, (a) The Indian MNCs, (b) emerging leadership, (c) India and the Asia Pacific regions, (d) striving for inclusive growth, (e) challenging the change, and (f) connecting across generations. Indian companies were doing businesses 'within borders', and are now operating 'across borders'. They will also be doing business when there will be no borders or in a 'borderless' environment. The designation of chief controlling officer has changed to chief executive officer, which in turn, has further changed to chief people empowerment officer.

Indian companies that resembled 'sleeping giants' in the past have become 'challengers' and are striving to become 'global leaders'. The challenges to change are being characterized by distinct shift from 'rigid' to 'reactive' and further to 'agility'. In the changing scenario, both language and style need consideration.

> Top management of companies consciously change the language and the rhetoric as a way of reinforcing changes.

In one sense, language defines reality. It also helps to shape the mindset of the people and plays an essential role in transforming organizations. Top management of companies consciously changes the language and the rhetoric as a way of reinforcing actions to be performed during the changes. The change in language also reinforces and strengthens the interpersonal relationship among management, employers, employees and customers.

Style is one of the seven levers of the McKinsey 7-S framework. The style of an organization becomes evident through the actions taken by the top management over a period of time. Style does not mean only the top management style. Organizational style includes reporting relationships, self-certification with regard to quality, and making the research and development (R&D) department, a part of the engineering department.

Hence, language and style play a predominant role in achieving the all-round success of an organization. Change management manifests its importance at this stage. Organizational culture should be conducive to accepting changes essential for growth. We are now evidencing a distinct shift of functional responsibilities to the line. These shifts characterized by treating HR personnel as business partners and focusing on career and competency development shall be discussed in Chapter 15 on managing change.

EGALITARIAN ORGANIZATION

It is believed that open organizations perform better than closed or conservative organizations. An open organization receives inputs from the environment. Organizations need the collective efforts of its people which are backed by inter-human logic leading instrumental or techno-economic rationality. Contextually, Srivastav and Cooperrider (1986) opine that '*Egalitarian or classless theory of organization is premised on the emergence of an inter-human logic that transcends instrumental or techno-economic rationality and forms a basis for collective action*'. The inter-human logic seeks to create and maintain socio-organizational arrangements to heighten or maximize the ideal membership situation for all members of an organization.

Organizational citizenship behaviour (OCB) is a human behavioural technique used across many institutions globally. It is a tried and tested approach employed by many Fortune 500 companies for improvization. It has also become a popular study in the field of HRM and has been of increasing interest to both scholars and organizational stalwarts.

Organizational citizenship behaviour is one way of establishing direct involvement of business leaders with employees. There is an open communication channel and also a clear understanding in every individual with regard to their role in the organization. This human behavioural technique underlines the principle of OCTAPACE—the acronym for openness, collaboration, trust, authenticity, proactivity, autonomy, confrontation, and experimenting. Companies that follow the principle of OCTAPACE progress faster. Some companies have flattened their hierarchies, reduced their work levels to become more unrestricted, uncensored, and egalitarian. At present, organizational environments that are more egalitarian are more successful at growing faster and competing in the industry. In this aspect, the egalitarian concept is similar to OCB.

ORGANIZATIONAL BEHAVIOUR AND JOB ATTITUDES

Feelings of the employees about the organization and their attitudes need utmost consideration. Organizational behaviour refers to the understanding, prediction, and management of human behaviour in the organizational context. The topic lays emphasis on the job attitudes of the personnel to enhance organizational effectiveness. Attitude surveys conducted with the help of questionnaires help in determining the attitude of members of the organization about their job, work groups, supervisor, and the organization. Fred Luthans (1977) says that major job attitudes include job satisfaction, job involvement, and organizational commitment. These characteristics are discussed here:

1. Job satisfaction—positive feelings about one's job resulting from an evaluation
2. Job involvement—degree to which an employee identifies himself psychologically with the job. A high degree of involvement results in psychological empowerment, which is, the employees' beliefs in the degree to which they impact the work environment.
3. Organizational commitment—This is a state in which an employee identifies with a particular organization, its mission, policies, objectives, goals, and wishes to continue as a member of the organization. The three separate dimensions of organizational commitment are affective commitment (emotional attachment), continuance commitment (perceived economic value), and normative commitment (employees wanting to remain with the organization for their moral or ethical value).

People who are satisfied with and involved in their jobs and are committed to their organization are the ones who can contribute their best to the organization. These attributes need periodical measurement in order to initiate remedial actions.

SUMMARY

The business scenario today is very competitive. Organizations must make the best use of employee capabilities and potential. Organizations basically depend upon the characteristics of the people they employ. An Act of the Parliament cannot make men virtuous. The people are the most valued asset of the organization and they significantly impact the organizational transformations.

Leadership drives an organization and can make or mar it. Visionary leaders significantly contribute to the smooth running and growth of an organization. Human resource function responsibilities are shifting to the line managers as they know their people best. Some companies have redefined the role of human resource personnel and are treating them as business partners and empowering them. Open organizations perform better than closed or conservative organizations. Egalitarian or classless theory of organization is premised on the emergence of an inter-human logic. Organizational behaviour and job attitudes are intertwined. Job attitudes include job satisfaction, job involvement, and organizational commitment.

KEY TERMS

Attitude of a person is identified from the evaluative statements or judgments concerning objects, people, or events; job attitudes include job satisfaction, job involvement and organizational commitment.

Egalitarian or classless organization is characterized by its inter-human logic that transcends instrumental or techno-economic rationality and forms the basis for collective actions.

Job involvement refers to degree to which people identify themselves psychologically with the job; a high degree of involvement results in psychological empowerment.

Job satisfaction refers to positive feelings about one's job resulting from an evaluation.

Organizational commitment is a state when an employee wishes to continue his/her membership of the organization as he/she is akin to the organization's mission, policies, objectives, and goals.

EXERCISES

Concept Review Questions

1. 'People are the most-valued assets of an organization.' Discuss with examples.
2. Consider the changing role of the HR functions and discuss the themes that characterize the process, and ultimately shape the organizational transformations.
3. What do you understand by 'visionary leadership'? Discuss the role of visionary leadership in present-day organizations.

Critical Thinking Questions

4. 'An organization is only as good as its people.' Do you subscribe to this view? Critically review the statement with examples from the organization you are working in or any organization you know.
5. The role of the HR department is changing. Some organizations have shifted the responsibilities to the individual departments. Do you think this shift will strengthen HR activities? Also comment on the extent to which it should be shifted. Do you feel the need for having an HR cell to coordinate? Justify your answer with examples.

Assignments

6. Visit three or four organizations, and try to collect information about their core beliefs.
7. Take appointments from two or three organizations, and discuss with the HR managers the changing role of HR functions. Make a note of their responses and present them to your college professor.

MANAGER'S INSIGHT

Workers at the shop floor of Ramsons and Co. demanded immediate replacement of the floor's chief supervisor. They alleged that he was responsible for the breakdown of the main boiler. The chief supervisor was informed about the malfunctioning of the boiler a week ago. He apparently had not done taken any measures to correct the situation. It is alleged that the mechanic who was instructed to look at the boiler could not identify the root cause and used a trial-and-error approach. This ultimately led to the breakdown of the boiler. The workers had also complained about the chief supervisor not attending to their needs. The chief supervisor decided to confront the situation head on.

Questions:

1. Which leadership style do you think would be most appropriate for the chief supervisor to follow?
2. What could the chief supervisor have done to avoid the situation?

BIBLIOGRAPHY AND WEB RESOURCES

Bass, B.M., 'Does the Transactional–Transformational Paradigm Transcend Organizational and National Boundaries?', *American Psychologist*, 1997, pp. 52, 130–139.

Fry, Louis and Melanie Cohen, 'Spiritual Leadership as a Paradigm for Organizational Transformation and Recovery from Extended Work Hours Cultures', *Journal of Business Ethics*, Supplement 2, Vol. 84, 2009, pp. 265–278, search.ebscohost.com, last accessed on 10 February 2009.

Haldar, U.K., *Leadership and Teambuilding*, Oxford Higher Education, Oxford University Press, New Delhi, 2010.

Howell, Jon P. and Costley, Dan. L., *Understanding Behaviors for Effective Leadership*, Prentice Hall of India Private Limited, New Delhi, 2008.

Kaufman, R.S., *Promethean Builds a Company Culture That Serves, Sizzles & Succeeds*, last accessed through www.leadingtoday.org/weleadinlearning/bb-oct02.htm, accessed on 6 June 2008, 2002.

Lancourt, Joan and Charles Savage, *Organizational Transformation and the Changing Role of the Human Resource Function*, Oticon and Johnsonville Foods, Denmark, 1995, www.kee-inc.com/article.htm, last accessed on 16 September 2007.

Louis. W, *Toward a Theory of Spiritual Leadership*, Tarleton State University, Central Texas.Killeen, USA, 2003, www.tarleton.edu/~fry/SLTTheory.pdf, last accessed on 27 February 2009.

Parsons, Talcott, 'An Approach to the Theory of Organizations', *Organizational Science*, Vol. 13. No. 1, 1979.

Peters, J. Thomas and Waterman, Jr, *In Search of Excellence, Lessons from America's Best Run Companies*, Harper & Row, London, (Reprint 2004), 1982.

Robbins, Stephen, *Management*, Prentice-Hall of India, New Delhi, 2001.

Stoner, James. A.F., Freeman, R. Edward, and Gilbert, Jr Daniel. R., *Management*, Prentice Hall India, New Delhi, 2006.

Haldar, Uday Kumar, *Human Resource Development*, Oxford Higher Education, Oxford University Press, New Delhi, 2009.

Pareek, Udai, *Understanding Organisational Behaviour*, Oxford Higher Education, Oxford University Press, New Delhi, 2008.

Luthans, Fred, *Organizational Behaviours* (Special Indian Edition), McGraw-Hill, New Delhi, 1997.

Srivastval, S. and Cooperrider, D.L., *The Emergence of Egalitarian Organization*, Williams Custom Printing, Euclid, Ohio, 1986, www.appriciativeinquiry.case.edu/research/, last accessed on 17 September 2008.

Web Resources

www.rediff.com/money/2007/jan/22murthy.htm, last accessed on 10 March 2009.

www.iispiritualleadership.com, last accessed on 27 February 2009.

www.lijjat.com, last accessed on 20 March 2011.

DEVELOPING ORGANIZATIONAL RESOURCES

M/s Agrawal Enterprises (Year 2000)

(This case is a continuation of the opening case)

Mr M.S. Menon, the appointed HR expert, adopted the management by walking around (MBWA) style. While on the rounds, he stopped to talk and discuss issues with personnel of various levels engaged in different functional areas. He studied the anatomy of the organization. He discovered the managerial style of the production manager and recorded the same. Menon also requested Agrawal to arrange separate meetings with the suppliers and customers. Agrawal questioned the purpose and usefulness of the meeting, and was reluctant to convene such meetings initially. However, he agreed to the proposal after repeated persuasion by Menon.

Following this, there were repeated requests from Menon. However, Agrawal did not want any other official of his company to attend the meeting. In the meetings, Menon was not very vocal; he meticulously scribbled notes in his diary. Of course, he did ask a few questions. He obtained the consent of Agrawal to access the contact details of some of the suppliers and customers and presumably contacted some of them. After a week, he submitted an interim report to Agrawal recommending action programmes that laid emphasis on the following:

1. Interpersonal relations
2. Customer satisfaction measurement
3. Leadership development
4. Organizational culture

When Agrawal sought clarification, Menon explained as follows.

'Interpersonal relationships involve social associations, connections, or affiliations between two or more people. These people may interact overtly, covertly, face-to-face, or may remain effectively unknown to each other, such as those in a virtual community who maintain ambiguity and do not socialize together outside a chat room. Communication is best achieved through simple planning and control. Performance appraisal is essential for performance monitoring.'

Menon also emphasized the need for potential appraisal and development for the progress of the organization. Furthermore, he stressed upon the need for 'customer satisfaction measurement' in order to analyse, and improvement as means for sustenance and growth in the acute competitive environment. He also opined that as an organizational leader, a manager must be aware of the appropriate leadership style with respect to specific situations and target persons. He further emphasized the need for developing a good organizational culture.

Agrawal was convinced and directed Menon to proceed in a phased manner. He also sanctioned some initial funds and requested Menon to submit a detailed plan with associated expenditure. Menon corrected Agrawal by saying that he must treat the amount sanctioned as an investment and not as expenditure. Menon took it as a challenge, was committed to rejuvenating the enterprise, and began his course of action.

Discussion Questions

1. Agrawal was always trying to avoid involving others in meetings. Is this approach correct for leadership in an organization? What might be the consequences?
2. In his interim report, Menon mentioned about customer satisfaction measurement. What is the importance and necessity of this measurement? Do you feel there is a need to measure customer satisfaction in order to enhance employee satisfaction?
3. In the interim report, Menon mentioned four action programmes. Narrate the possible reasons behind the selection of the programmes. Your discussion should be programme-wise.
4. Had you been the HR expert and advisor to Agrawal, how you would have gone about developing the enterprise and its people?

HR MANTRA Your actions will speak

A rich man purchased a healthy cow and a poor man purchased a sickly cow from the same market. The rich man displayed his cow at the entrance to his house, while the poor man invested a lot of money on his sickly cow. In course of time, the rich man's cow became weak, while the poor man's cow gained health.

People are the most vital and valuable resources of any organization. Material resources depreciate, while human resources appreciate.

The mantra: Understand and nurture people.

N.R. NARAYANA MURTHY

N.R. Narayana Murthy, the chief mentor of Infosys technologies limited, was born on 20 August 1946. He obtained his B.E. in electrical engineering in 1967 from the University of Mysore, followed by M.Tech in 1969 from IIT, Kanpur. He began his career with Patni Computer Systems in Pune.

In 1981, he founded Infosys in Mumbai with six other software professionals. In 1987, Infosys opened its first international office in the United States. In 1993, the company came up with its initial public offering (IPO). Infosys set up development centres across several cities in India in 1995. The company established its first office in Europe in Milton Keynes, UK. In 1999, Infosys became the first Indian company to be listed on the NASDAQ. The success of Infosys is built on the twin pillars of strong business model and sound corporate governance.

Narayana Murthy propounds faith and hope in the future, and believes that life is all about hope. He is the embodiment of transparency, moral integrity, dynamism, spirit, and honesty. This is evidenced from his activities and excerpts.

After serving for 21 years as the company's chief executive officer, Murthy handed over the reins to cofounder, Nandan M. Nilekani, in March 2002. He now operates as the non-executive chairman and chief mentor of Infosys. He has set new standards in corporate governance, and is a living legend and an epitome of the fact that honesty is the prime need for business acumen.

Along with the growth of Infosys, Narayana Murthy has grown in stature and has been the recipient of many honours and awards.

Narayana Murthy's words of wisdom are worth mentioning. He has many success *mantras*, some of which reflect his life's philosophy and the values of Infosys. The value system of Infosys is its true strength and is similar to the British Constitution—'all unwritten but extremely well-practised'. Unless the company can sell well, it cannot create jobs, pay good salaries, and satisfy investors. Right from the beginning, the company realized that it has to focus on selling better in the marketplace.

Narayana Murthy believes, 'Truth is God. Our success at Infosys depends on our continual learning'. He says, 'Entrepreneurship is about running a marathon, not a 100-metre dash. Anyone must dream and plan to realize it'. In this context, he adds, 'We were huddled together in a small room in Bombay (now Mumbai) in the hope of creating a brighter future for ourselves, for the Indian society, and perhaps, we dreamed, even for the world'.

He further emphasizes, 'Leadership is an action, not a word'. He is an institution builder and believes in leadership development. He advises employees to build a climate of honesty, hard work, and excellence; construct a social conscience, benchmark oneself with the best in the world, be honest and true to the profession, and act fearlessly. His vision upholds IT as the force that can help alleviate many problems that rural India faces. He believes that health care, education, and environment conservation can be comprehensively brought to villages.

In his opinion, working extended hours over the long term is harmful for the employee. One's mindset and imagination are more critical than other resources. He says, 'Beyond a certain level of comfort, I think one's wealth should be seen as an opportunity to make a difference to society'. He believes that events keep occurring round the clock and advises people to take a nap; things will happen while one is asleep, but one will have the energy to catch up when once awake. Narayana Murthy's dictum is that performance leads to recognition; recognition brings respect; respect enhances power, and humility and grace in one's moments of power enhances the majesty of an organization. He advocates that a value system is the protocol for behaviour that enhances the trust, confidence, and commitment of members of the community. An organization must feel responsible to develop the society. Mutual trust is the essence behind all-round organizational success. Such foundations create great organizations and take them to great heights.

He has great respect for people and believes in the power of talent. He says, 'Our core corporate assets walk out every evening. It is our duty to make sure that these assets return the next morning, mentally and physically enthusiastic and energetic'. People must aspire for higher achievements. Aspiration is the main fuel for progress and transforms a set of ordinary people into extraordinary achievers.

His inclination and capacity to develop organizations and leaders for tomorrow have made him the visionary that he is.

References

en.wikipedia.org/wiki/N._R._Narayana_Murthy, last accessed on 8 October 2011.

Haldar, Uday Kumar, *Leadership and Team Building*, Oxford Higher Education, Oxford University Press, New Delhi, 2010.

CHAPTER 2

Changing Business Scenario—Focus on Human Resource Management

LEARNING OBJECTIVES

After studying this chapter, you will be able to

- Understand a business environment
- Comprehend organizational boundaries and the boundary-spanning process
- Understand business development and link it with organizational performance
- Define accountability
- Appreciate the roles of HRM in a dynamic business environment

OPENING CASE

Computech Services Limited

Computech Services Limited (CSL) is a family-owned business venture that came into existence in 1998 when the demand for assembled personal computers (PCs) was high. In the late 1990s, people were excited about working on computers, and also encouraged their children to do so. Owning a PC was treated as a status symbol.

Mr Gera headed CSL as its director; his wife looked after the public relations activities and customer queries; their son, Suneel, and daughter, Diya, offered technical assistance. The family managed the entire business with a couple of support staff. In order to attract clients, CSL advertised on local cable television and obtained a reasonably good clientele. During that time, competitors were few and the business was growing fast. CSL desired to expand its business, and shifted to a bigger place. It also recruited computer mechanics who had undergone short-term training on computer hardware. CSL further started contacting companies to extend their computer maintenance services through an 'annual maintenance contract'.

After five years, in 2003, CSL increased its number of customers by nearly ten times since its inception. Its profit multiplied, and the business had considerably expanded. Gera now planned for further expansion, and grabbed more market share with the existing products and services. During this time, companies similar to CSL mushroomed all over the country and capitalized on the high rate of return on investment.

Meanwhile, laptops began gaining entry into the market. The price of the laptops was competitive and many people started purchasing them instead of desktops. Offices also purchased them to be distributed to their managerial personnel. The market of laptops grew higher than the market for desktops and the sale of PCs showed a decreasing trend.

There was another major development as large organizations took a decision to conclude the existing computer maintenance services or annual maintenance contracts and continue them with larger companies that possessed ISO 9001 certification. This decision impacted CSL and many similar smaller companies. CSL customers also started discussing about ISO certifications. However, Gera was not bothered about ISO certification as he believed that their product and service standards were world-class. Some customers approached Mrs Gera and discussed this issue as she was looking after public relations and customer complaints. She was also not convinced about the certification. Gradually, CSL customers began discontinuing the service contract. Consequentlys, CSL lost many customers.

Learning points

- Top management needs to keep a watch on the business environment.
- Organizations need to adapt themselves to changes in the environment.

INTRODUCTION

Business is an organization comprising people who strive together to achieve common objectives and goals. It is important for a business organization to have a vision that implies what it intends to achieve in the future and values that represent the organization's integrity. Organizations need to create an environment where people want to work and concurrently develop themselves through coaching, feedback, and information sharing. A business house should work in partnership with its employees, customer, suppliers, community, and the media. In order to enhance the image, it should communicate the key messages, both internally and externally, and gain commitment to its principal goals.

A reputed business house often prefers to share its best practices with its competitors as it believes in networking, partnering, and informal collaboration. It should even undertake a practice of rewarding its employees when they perform well. It should establish a process to learn, grow, and measure its successes. Thus, the primers of an organization include vision, values, behaviours/competencies/standards, coaching, information sharing, networking, rewarding, and continuous learning.

UNDERSTANDING BUSINESS

A business organization is a commercial, industrial, or mercantile enterprise, and comprises the people who constitute it. Business is a legally-recognized organization which provides goods, services, or both to the consumers. In order to develop an understanding of business organizations, one should be able to identify the differences between the private and public sectors of the economy, state the traditional examples of business organizations in the private sector (sole trader, partnership, and private limited and public limited companies), understand the difference in terms of liability among these business types, and identify two non-traditional business types (co-operatives and franchises).

The fundamental idea regarding business is that it is an economic activity and business decision-making is an economic process. The principal aim of any business is to make profit. An HR manager must have the ability to understand the changes in an environment, and the direction and speed of those changes. He/she should be able to develop an action plan that is essential to cope with the changes, involve employee representatives, gain their confidence, implement the changes, and finally measure the benefits of these changes.

> Understanding an organization encompasses understanding its structures, behaviours, cultures, resources, and functions, and also how it learns to manage its external environment.

Understanding an organization encompasses understanding its structures, behaviours, cultures, resources, and functions, and how it learns to manage the external environment. Once the business environment has been understood, all the activities taking place inside and outside it are also easily understood.

BUSINESS ENVIRONMENT

A business house in general, functions broadly under three kinds of environment—general environment, task environment, and competitive environment—along with the cooperation of its business associates. The various other environments in which a business operates are—social, cultural, economic, technological, political, and international. All these environments are interdependent. The business is required to conform to certain societal and cultural norms, consider the national economic system at the macro level, and decide upon the pricing mechanism at the micro level. Existing or emerging competitors, their strategies, markets, reputation, and product costs sway and influence the business tactics of an organization.

Environment consists of forces or institutions that are outside the business organization, but substantially affect its performance. Business environment affects business management; particularly HRM and must be subjected to analysis based on different criteria. For convenience of analysis, environment may be classified based on the following parameters:

1. Space—It encompasses the local, regional, national, and international environment.
2. Time—It speaks about the past, present, and future environment.
3. Forces—This includes the market as well as the non-market environment.
4. Factors—This spreads over economic and non-economic environment.

The environmental factors may be exogenous or endogenous. Moreover, the factors are interrelated, interactive, and interdependent. A business needs to adapt to the environment and adopt suitable HRM initiatives in addition to strategic management drives. The adaptation to a particular environment, obviously, also needs consideration of space, time, forces, and factors. Usually, it becomes a little difficult for companies to keep a tab on all these factors. Therefore, in order to overcome this hassle, questionnaires are framed to aid an organization in framing a strategy. Exhibit 2.1 gives an idea of such a questionnaire.

Exhibit 2.1 Measuring preparedness

In recent times, the concepts of merger and acquisition have been gaining popularity. To cope with this trend and derive maximum benefits, many companies are now keen on looking for ways to improve their skills in these areas, especially their ability to assess and integrate target companies successfully. To excel in this regard, companies understand the need to focus on scanning the business environment and evaluating themselves, before actually entering into a merger or an acquisition.

To ensure a successful integration, certain questions have been framed for companies to answer, in order for them to know if they are fully prepared. If answers to the questions on six distinct organizational aspects are 'Yes', there would be room for improvement to smooth post-merger efforts.

The questions that arise are as follows:

1. Applications and technology structure—Do you rely heavily on custom or proprietary technologies?
2. IT infrastructure—Do you have many small data centres in expensive locations?
3. Labour productivity—Are your processes different in different locations?
4. Sourcing—Do you have many vendors providing materials that could be sourced from fewer, larger vendors?
5. Demand management—Do business leaders fail to prioritize IT needs and assert that *everything* is important?
6. Organization and governance—Does IT management spend a lot of time putting out fires?

Answers to these questions help a company in evaluating its own preparedness with regard to space, time, forces, and factors of the business environment.

Source: The questions were formulated by Gautam Thapar, President, AIMA, and Chairman and CEO of the Avanta Group, in the article, 'M&A Trends and Expectations in 2011', *Indian Management*, February 2011, Volume 50, Issue 2, p. 26.

The general environment comprises socio-cultural environment, economic environment, politico-legal environment, and technological environment.

General Environment

The general environment comprises socio-cultural environment, economic and non-economic environment, politico-legal environment, technological, and international environment. Human resource management has a predominant role in shaping and moulding the behaviour of the people to work effectively in diverse environments. In the following sections, we shall discuss these types of environments and the role of an HR manager.

Q 1 Socio-cultural Environment

The socio-cultural environment includes mobility of labour, customs and convention, caste structure, cultural heritage, respect for elders, ethics and values, view towards scientific methods, and deference for seniority. All these conjointly determine the choice of the people, which in turn would govern the goods or services, and product range of the business houses. Thus, the business venture and the kind of people working in the organization depend on the environment. Socio-cultural environment contributes to work ethics and work culture too.

Work ethics, as defined by the Webster International Dictionary, is a discipline that deals with moral duty and obligation. It is a group of moral principles or a set of values. It is a principle of conduct governing an individual or a profession. It is a standard of behaviour for social and professional well-being. In short, ethics can be defined as a science of moral principles and rules of conduct.

Culture is the integrated pattern of human behaviour that includes thought, speech, action and artifacts, and depends on man's capacity for learning and transmitting knowledge to the succeeding generation (Webster Dictionary). A business is affected by the prevailing culture. In the organizational context, Marvin Bower, former managing director of Mckinsey and Company, defines culture as 'the way we do things around here.' Therefore, the way we carry out our multifarious activities in the business organization indicates our work culture. The work culture depends on the ethical values and beliefs of the management and the employees. These values and beliefs guide their activities and behaviour patterns in the business organization. Values such as responsibility, fairness, justice, integrity, commitment, and patriotism are universal and eternal. The need for the values is time-tested and will exist forever. These values have the same meaning in any country, developed or undeveloped, such as America, India, Africa, and so on. Environment, experience, and education are the three factors that determine our attitudes towards the values.

Culture is the integrated pattern of human behaviour that includes thought, speech, action and artifacts and depends on man's capacity for learning and transmitting knowledge.

Socio-cultural environments are usually seen to be changing frequently. To cope with the changes, a business house needs to follow a guiding principle that balances adaptation, and change its organizational culture to design the HR function accordingly in an organization. Fifteen guiding principles for designing the HR function are discussed in this chapter.

Q 1 Economic Environment

The business sector shares economic relations with the government, the capital market, the household sector, and the foreign sector. The different sectors conjointly influence the trends and structure of the economy and the business as well. The form and functioning of the economy varies from one country to another. In a democratic setup, people exercise an influence, either directly or indirectly.

Some critical elements of this environment are the economic system, nature, anatomy, and functioning of the economy, economic planning, programmes, policy statements, proposals, controls, regulations, legislations, trends, structure, problems, and prospects. Obviously, economic environment influences both business management and the HRM initiatives that are required. Managers need to be aware of the economic factors and analyse them to drive the business in the right direction.

As mentioned earlier, all the factors in an environment impact each other. The sociological environment affects and gets affected by the economic environment of business. Added to this, the educational-cultural, politico-legal, and historical environments are closely knit with the economic environment. Moreover, the educational environment greatly impacts a business. The rate of return approach of HR planning (discussed in Chapter 6) supports this view as the approach treats education as a contributor to productivity.

Educational and Cultural Environment

The status of economic development of a place is a determinant of the choice of the system of education. For example, only a few high income countries can afford to impart expensive higher education and fundamental researches in science and technology. Again, the system of education may be responsible for a given economic environment. Vocational courses and training elevate the economic status of a country. Business houses acquire human resources, particularly from academia through campus interviews, and these resources are capable of directly contributing to their organizations.

The interdependence between educational and economic factors at the corporate level takes the form of a vicious circle. For example, a low-profit business concern may not find the resources required for finance management training or management development programmes, though it may feel the utmost need for the training and programme. As a result, there would be a shortage of highly qualified and trained management personnel in the business concern. Subsequently, lack of competent managers may lead to business inefficiency.

Politico-legal Environment

The form and structure of the economy is also conditioned by the socio-political arrangements; the two environments are intertwined and interlocked. In a parliamentary setup, most decisions are formulated, processed, and finalized by the cabinet ministers. Under a presidential form of government, the President acts as the real manager of the state—it is he/she who takes the decisions. Political organizations, political stability, and strengths of the political parties lead to the political-economy. In case of political instability, business uncertainties develop and multiply, and businessmen may opt for initiating new business ventures.

As discussed earlier, a business operates under external forces in the environment. A series of political legislations such as the Monopolistic and Trade Practices Act (MRTP), Foreign Exchange Regulation Act (FERA), General Agreement on Tariffs and Trade (GATT), import policy, foreign exchange policy, and Urban Land Ceiling Act, may be necessary to cope with the economic environment. The various acts represent the politico-economic characteristics of a country. The government's intervention in business must be taken into account for its smooth running. The role of the World Trade Organization (WTO), the World Bank, and the business policies of other countries contribute to the international economic environment and impact the businesses operating in a country.

In the changing politico-legal environment, the guiding principle, *continuous review and self-renewal*, is an indispensable requirement for sustenance and growth. Hence, it is important for the HR manager to keep a check and be ready with a plan to tackle all the possibilities that might come his/her way. One such example where the scenario of business changed because of the political reasons is given in Exhibit 2.2.

Exhibit 2.2 Back to farming in Singur, Tata training goes waste

Singur, in West Bengal, is a place where people depend mostly on agriculture. Tata Motors took great efforts to industrialize the area and trained several people. The youth of Singur who had gone to industrial training institutes had been absorbed as technical hands in the Tata Motors project in town. Their fathers were farmers. They had dreamt of a life different from their fathers'—a life protected from the cruelties of the weather and shaped by their own hard work and abilities. They thought that their dreams would be translated into reality. However, their dreams lasted for a very short time.

Tata Motors had to leave Singur because of various political issues. Many people trained by Tata Motors lamented that their job opportunities had vanished and that their entire training had become useless.

Several trained people restarted harvesting on their agricultural lands. The dream of the West Bengal chief minister, Buddhadeb Bhattacharjee, was to make the car plant possible and he extended all legal support from the government's side. However, his dream did not materialize as the politico-legal environment influenced and impacted the business environment, in this instance.

Source: The Telegraph, Tuesday, 29 December 2009, Report by Uttam Dutta.

Technological Environment

Over the past few decades, science and technology have been advancing at a fast pace. The quality of goods depends on the plant and equipment, state of the technology employed to produce those, and the skill of the people. Computer numerical control (CNC), dual numerical control (DNC), horizontal machining centre (HMC), vertical numerical centre (VMC), and flexible manufacturing system (FMS) are some of the state-of-the-art technologies being used today. These machines are precise in nature and are hence capable of manufacturing components with a high degree of accuracy. Moreover, these machines produce results faster as the cycle time is much lesser than in conventional machines. It is also important to keep in mind that the choice of technology depends on its availability and affordability by the business organization.

Advancements in automation and information technology has created challenging situations for the organizations. Large organizations are engaged in technological forecasting. During periods of such technological innovations, organizations need to consider the role of HRM. This is because, technological upgradation leads to developing a workforce that is able to work on the computer-enabled machines, managing changes, carrying out attitude surveys to assess the effect of the upgraded technology, etc. It is in these areas that HRM interventions become inescapable. These issues are discussed in detail in the chapter, 'Technology and HRM'.

International Environment

There are a number of forces in the international environment, which may have either favourable or unfavourable effects on a business. Following the GATT in 1993, liberalization of industrial licensing by developing countries and reduction of economic barriers has brought significant changes in business scenario. The multilateral trade among the nations has also improved. If a country is disintegrated, then the exporters to that country are negatively affected. In the early 1990s, the disintegration of the USSR had adversely affected exporters in those countries.

Several multinational corporations have entered India with their expertise—know-how, values, and cultures. The inflow of expertise and know-how have contributed to the Indian business organizations and economy. Further, the presence of many players in one domain of business has forced organizations to be competitive. People need to be trained to understand the forces favourable to the business organization, and derive the best possible benefits from them. The most crucial need is that of recognizing the forces that may produce unfavourable effects to the business, identifying the tactical moves, converting threats into opportunities, and implementing the remedial measures when HR development and management manifest their importance.

Box 2.1 Impact of liberalization

The government of India liberalized the Indian economy to decontrol the economy and opened Indian markets to the rest of the world. Though the need for liberalization was debated and re-debated for long by everyone in the intelligentsia, the intention of the government was to gain faster economic progress for the country. All those who considered themselves as custodians of values, culture, and nationalism, voiced its likely impact.

The visible outcomes of liberalization are as follows:

1. Accelerated movement of the workforce to new economies and different geographic locations
2. More choices and options to save, spend, or store
3. Higher speed of change in products, people, or possibilities
4. Survival of the powerful (money, manipulation, muscle); here, the word 'powerful' has replaced 'fittest'
5. More hype over personalities, companies, desires, or even calamities
6. Higher degree of information

Each one of these areas and their visible outcomes has impacted the workforce both positively and adversely in the following areas:

1. Competency level
2. Work habits
3. Disappearing habit of reinventing the wheel of excellence
4. Psychological impact

Source: www.itpeopleindia.com/20040920/careers.shtml

Globalization is another term used when one talks about the international environment. It refers to the tendency of firms to expand their business territory, extend their sales, ownership, and/or manufacturing into new zones abroad. For instance, in the automotive industry, Mercedes Benz has established its market share all over the world. Similarly, Sony, Apple, Nike, etc., have markets around the world. Infosys, TCS, and Wipro, are some Indian software companies serving customers around the world by developing software codes and providing support services.

Following globalization, business houses now operate in a global village. Globalization has brought in both benefits and threats. The benefits are that products of better quality are made available to consumers at comparatively lower costs. Globalization has posed the threat of investing more on labour and employees who are feeling increasingly insecure about their jobs. This applies to various products from computers to cars. In the post-globalization environment, the texture of the workforce has changed in India as well as in many other countries. The change in this texture is exhibited in Box 2.2.

Box 2.2 Impact of globalization

1. Indian IT companies plan to increase the number of foreign employees posted in countries other than India by 10–20 per cent over three to five years. Hiring locals abroad where they have 'near shore' development centres will help them tap local markets, serve local clients better, and win more deals and goodwill in those countries.
2. Over the last five years, TCS has set up operations in 14 countries including major centres in Argentina, Brazil, Chile and Uruguay, thus employing over 5000 employees.

Source: *Indian Management*, April 2008, Volume No. 47, Issue 4.

Task Environment

The task environment typically includes the industry to which an organization belongs, its competitors, customers of the products or services, techniques of production, suppliers of all types of inputs, stock market, raw materials, market sectors, and also the human resources and international sectors. An organization interacts directly with the task environment. Any change in the task environment produces a direct impact on an organization's structure and its goals. It mainly impacts the suppliers, employees and customers, regulating bodies and agencies, and business associates. Some of these impacts are discussed in this section.

Suppliers include providers of capital such as shareholders, debenture holders, banks, and financial institutions. Providers of materials in any form are also suppliers. Suppliers of capital look for return on investments. Suppliers of material require timely payments. Both these tasks are vital for an organization. Suppliers are a critical part of the task environment because organizations must have a continuous source of resources in order to serve their customers. Organizations need to maintain a healthy relationship with the suppliers using HRM tools and techniques.

Employees are included in the payroll of the organization. Some employees may be members of trade unions, associations, collective bargaining forums, works committee, joint consultative machinery, etc. Employees need a work environment conducive for efficient working.

Customers include distributors, dealers, retailers, and consumers. Customer satisfaction is the ultimate aim of all business activities. The level of satisfaction of the end-user or the consumer must be measured through market surveys. Business houses operate under the regulations of designated agencies. Some of these designated agencies are exhibited in Box 2.3.

Box 2.3 Regulating bodies and agencies

Some regulating bodies and agencies include the following:

1. Pollution control board
2. Revenue department (Central excise, Income tax, Sales tax, etc.)
3. Consumer forums
4. Quality certification (Bureau of Indian Standards)
5. Professional bodies (All India Institute of Chartered Accountants, Institute of Company Secretaries)

(Contd)

Box 2.3 (Contd)

The roles and responsibilities of these bodies are as follows:

1. Chemical factories are required to conform to requirements stated by the pollution control board.
2. Revenue department bears responsibilities for direct and indirect taxes.
3. The consumer forum protects the interests of the general customers.
4 The Bureau of Indian Standards tests and certifies the quality of products.
5. Professional bodies are responsible for verification of accounts.

A business must discharge its social responsibility. Social values, social institutions, social order, social contracts, social conflicts, and social problems—everything changes along with the business culture.

Competitors' policies and practices directly influence a business unit. For example, the reduction of price of a product by one competitor produces a threat to another organization manufacturing the same product. Similarly, improvement in quality features of a product or set of similar products compels a competitor to give attention to quality improvement. Both the actions are directed to protect declining sales.

By collaborating with a business associate, one can gain the advantage of knowing the other's tools, techniques, technology, best practices, and can benchmark the other. In case of shortage of capital, financial or non-financial, one can easily borrow from the other. Finding the collaborating partner needs knowledge about that company, and skills of assessing their strengths and weaknesses. After collaboration, the firms are better prepared to face potential and strong competitors as they possess a combined strength.

SOCIAL RESPONSIBILITY OF BUSINESS

In traditional pre-industrial societies, business houses did not feel the need to contribute to the society; even though a few businesses contributed, the extent of contributions was negligible. Today, the business scenario has significantly changed. In a modern industrial society, business grows by leaps and bounds; products of any type are meant for the market; exchange transactions multiply. The complexities of businesses have grown manifold. Social values, social institutions, social order, social contracts, social conflicts, and social problems change along with the business culture. Obviously, business must be socially responsible too.

The elements of the 'public' in any business comprise shareholders, promoters, the owner, managers and employees at all levels, suppliers and service providers, distributors, dealers, retailers, customers and end users, government officials, regulatory bodies, watch dogs, conservationists, and environmentalists. Every social group has a very definite expectation from the business. Shareholders, promoters, and owners expect a fair rate of return on investment; managers need attractive salary packages and perquisites; employees need fair wages and bonus; government officials look for conformance to rules and regulations; customers desire quality goods or services having high utility value and durability.

In today's competitive business environment, discharging social responsibilities is of paramount importance. Hence, it is equally important for the organization to keep a check on its social responsibilities while planning its strategies. Needless to say, HR has to play a vital role here, too. We shall discuss more about social responsibilities of business in the chapter, 'Corporate social responsibility and ethics'.

DIMENSIONS OF ENVIRONMENT

A business environment has three dimensions—capacity, volatility, and complexity.

Singh and Chhabra (2005) have mentioned about three dimensions of environment—capacity, volatility, and complexity.

Q 2

Capacity Business environments are changing, and organizations need to survive and grow in changing environments. Capacity refers to the extent to which an organization can support. It needs to have a reserve of raw materials to keep the wheel of production revolving in times of scarcity. However, overstocking of raw material blocks money, and also increases the carrying cost. Therefore, an organization has to strike a balance. The stock should neither be abundant nor scarce.

Volatility In a volatile business environment, the extent of change is never predictable. An organization needs to watch the speed and direction of the environmental change. Many organizations have perished due to their inabilities to watch these changes. If the change is insignificant, the environment may be said to be static; but if the change is sudden, as in the case of the government imposing a policy without prior warning, then that is an unpredictable change. From the standpoint of volatility, the dimension may range from stable to dynamic.

Complexity The number of forces may be few or many and they may be favourable or unfavourable to the business. The complexity is more if the number of unfavourable or unbalancing forces is more and vice versa.

After duly taking into consideration the dimensions of the environment, an organization is required to reassess its capacity to grow to meet the market demands. The organization must watch the speed and direction of change using HR development and management initiatives to prevent its disappearance. Finally, the complexity dimension demands scanning and predicting the environment to initiate proactive steps.

Singh and Chhabra (2005) also mention the classification of environment as explained by Emery and Trist. Each type of the environment needs different HRM practices that are specific to the organization to be effective. The form of typology is presented as follows:

1. Placid-randomized environment—This is the simplest type of environment. When the situation is placid/calm, external forces are minimal, changes occur slowly, the environment does not impact the organization, and can operate independently. The problem of complexity is low, and the outcome of uncertainty is also low in this environment. In such cases, the organizational structure can be traditional and mechanistic. In order to survive in such an environment, an organization needs to follow the rules framed by it.
2. Placid-clustered environment—An environment where changes occur slowly, causal relationship can be predicted and based on this prediction, the organizations can revise their plans. It must be noted that an organization's survival depends on the correct prediction and hence planning is of paramount importance. The problem of complexity is low, and the outcome of uncertainty is also low in a placid-clustered environment. As such, in this situation, the organizational structure can be traditionally mechanistic. HR needs to interact with the strategic management department/cell or the department responsible to formulate the strategies, to cope up with the changes. Later, it has to develop the relevant human resources to execute the strategies.

3. Disturbed-reactive environment—An organization cannot always initiate proactive actions. When many organizations produce similar products, the market is oligopolistic. Obviously, the situation in this case, is complex and uncertain to some extent. In such a situation, organic and flexible organizational structure can perform better, and can accommodate some changes. Hence, the HR should concentrate on attitudinal changes of the people, and make it possible for them to adapt to the changes in the organization.
4. Turbulent-field environment—This is the most critical form of an environment. Dynamic processes are seen to arise from this field and are merely not a result of the interactions of competitors. This complex and rapidly-changing environment arises as a result of interconnectedness of organizations, interdependency of the society and economic organization, and acute competition in the market. A turbulent-field environment necessitates the increased use of research and development to remain competent. In order to function in such an environment successfully, the management should adopt an organic structure. The role of an HR cannot be the sole prescription in such a situation. In such situations, an organization needs to adapt to crisis management as no other proactive action can be taken.

In other words, it is important to understand that the environment is not stable, and is highly prone to change. In fact, it passes through a set of stages. Since HR plays a prominent role in the success of any organization, their proposals need to be planned and clarified much before any strategy can be implemented. In short, HRM tools and techniques are required to be identified and cautiously applied in all the stages.

With regard to change management, HR initiatives in the unfreezing (initial) stages must include expressing the need for changes, communicating the potential benefits, protecting the interest of the people concerned, getting people involved, communicating the progress of change, using a respected change agent, and reinforcing earlier changes. While implementing the change, the change agent must get an opportunity to build new patterns of behaviour. In the refreezing or final phase of the change process, new parts of one's total perspective is required to be established and integrated into the whole. Thereafter, the individuals or groups can begin to enjoy the rewards for the new behaviour in the changed situation. *Note*: Singh and Chhabra (2005) have mentioned the Emery and Trist typology of environment.

NATURE OF ENVIRONMENT

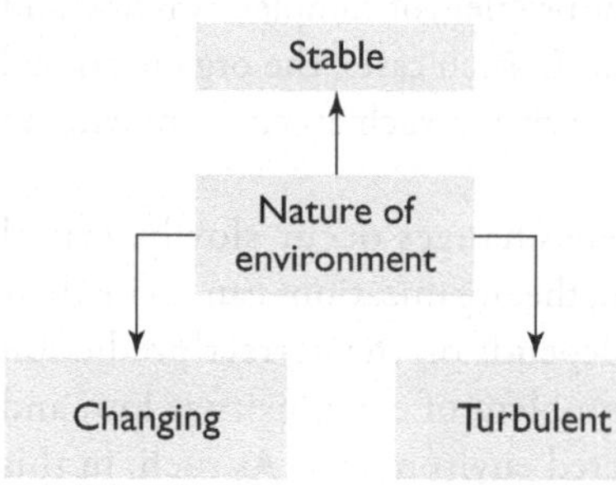

Fig. 2.1 Nature of environment

Organizations operate in a stable, changing, or turbulent environment.

The environment in which organizations operate may be stable, changing, or turbulent, as shown in Figure 2.1.

Stable environment—Changes in a stable environment are inevitable but are minor. Customer demands are not very dynamic, and therefore, product changes occur infrequently. The fluctuation in the market is infrequent and predictable. The rate of advancement of technology is slow and government regulations are not so relevant to the organization.

Changing environment—This environment is characterized by technological innovations, changes in market dynamics, amendments in relevant laws and regulations, and technology obsolescence.

Turbulent environment—This environment is categorized as turbulent due to unforeseen events such as sudden intrusion by competitors and rapidly changing technology. In a turbulent environment, an organization is required to consider the changes essential for its survival. It has to pass through the phases of unfreezing, moving, and refreezing as enunciated by Kurt Lewin (1947). Managing changes emerges as the inescapable step for survival and growth.

ORGANIZATIONAL BOUNDARIES

Organizational boundaries are barriers to the flow of energy, materials, and information. The boundaries of an organization are invisible, but they filter the outputs of organizations. All the levels of an organization—strategic, coordinating, and operating—are affected by boundaries. The strategic level decides policy and direction, and makes decisions.

Organizational boundaries offer barriers to the flow of energy, materials, and information.

Organizations must establish links with the external environment to anticipate the alteration in customer choices, availability of inputs, and emergence of new players in the industry, with the ultimate aim of necessary preparedness. Knowledge of organizational boundaries sets the foundation for organizational development and research, and balancing internal and external help, which are the guiding principles of HRM.

Boundary-spanning Process

Boundary spanners link an organization with the environment.

Organizations link with their external environment through boundary spanning activities and functions. The most common boundary spanners in organizations are the following:

Q 4

1. Public relation officer, who endeavours to uplift the image of the organization.
2. Spokesperson, who informs the outsiders of important events in the organization.
3. Market research officer, who collects information on customer needs and expectations.
4. Material procurement officer, who gathers information regarding suppliers' abilities.
5. HR department, which collects information about B-schools providing quality education suitable for campus recruitment.
6. Finance department, which collects information about capital providers.

Boundary spanners or boundary role persons build reciprocal relationships between an organization and its environment. These people require stress management as their role is highly stressful. Selectively-chosen HRD instruments or sub-systems help to strengthen the boundary spanners and in turn, the organizational activities.

ORGANIZATIONS AND ENVIRONMENT INTERFACE

An organization's environment comprises forces that are outside the organization, and can potentially affect its performance. An organization is linked with the environment in terms of certain flows and

An organization's environment relationship is studied through exchange of resources, information, and influence.

processes. It receives resources into the system, and gives output information to the environment. Thus, an organization may be viewed as an input–output system. We can study the relationship of an organization and its environment through the exchange of resources, information, and influence, as illustrated in Figure 2.2.

Exchange of resources—This includes the flow of input and output resources. Faculty exchange by educational institutions is a very common example.

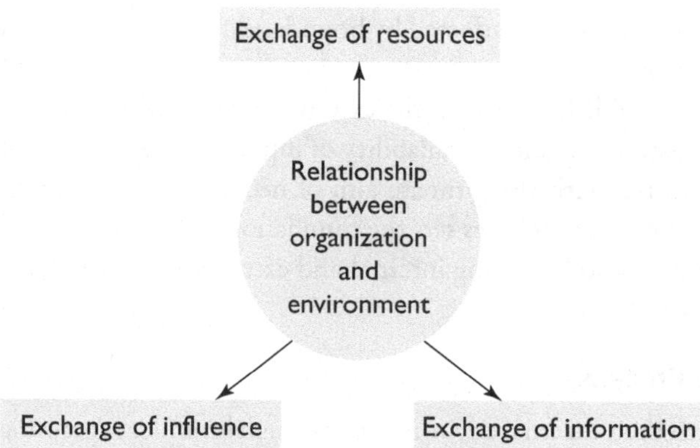

FIG. 2.2 Organization and environment relationship

Exchange of information—The person who possesses information from various sources is mightier. He/she must be very observant in order to understand what the organization communicates, and how the organization views him/her.

Exchange of influence—When two organizations collaborate, each of them gains the strength of the other and in the process, both of them are strengthened. Organizations exchange influence through networking.

It should be remembered that interdependence and influence are reciprocal as they bear causal relationships.

Strategy to Deal with Environment

The most common strategies for organizations to deal with the environment are buffering, smoothing or levelling, anticipating and adapting, and rationing. Managers need to try any one or a combination of these strategies based on the result of scanning of the environment. Managers must carry out the cost-benefit analysis prior to selecting any particular initiative. These strategies are briefly discussed in this section.

Buffering It refers to stockpiling, creating reserves, enriching the HR database with knowledge of available experts, alternate processes and technologies, and retaining information about the initiatives.

Smoothing or levelling A product's demand varies over the seasons. This strategy is adopted while it is required to initiate remedial measures for fluctuating demands across the seasons. A common practice that is followed involves increasing the price when the demand is more, and giving discounts when it is less. For example, room heaters and geysers are high-priced during winter, whereas they are sold at lower prices during the off-season. By doing so, a manufacturer avoids holding costs.

Anticipating and adapting Managers need to visualize forthcoming changes and plan ahead for adjusting to the change. Anticipating the changes needs visionary skills. Visionary leaders are dynamic, communicate well, inspire people, and can foresee the future. With the information gleaned from forecasting, managers can initiate the necessary steps so that the organization can adapt internally to the anticipated environmental demands.

Buffering, smoothing or leveling, anticipating and adapting, and rationing are common strategies to deal with the environment.

Rationing This refers to the practice of exercising control on scarce resources and products. Dairies allocate more milk to general public during times of high demand, and less for production of milk products (butter, ghee, etc).

Human resource management and development sub-systems enable understanding the situation, selecting suitable strategies, and implementing them to deal with the environment.

BUSINESS DEVELOPMENT

Businesses can develop through the process of simplification, integration, and transformation. Simplification refers to removing redundant tasks, superfluous variety, and complexity. Variety reduction has to be a principal consideration of any business. Integration refers to launching multiple types of products, establishing a few strategic business units, connecting separate processes, and promoting interaction among the process steps. Altering business relationships and reconfiguring the business are part of transformation. Simplification and integration enable reduction in cycle time whereas integration and transformation lead to business successes.

Factors such as selecting the right business strategy, conducting a detailed HR analysis, determining the critical issues affecting people, and so on, enhance the scope of business development. The strategy for HRM will be discussed in Chapter 3.

Dimensions of organizational performance are output or result, input, time, quality, cost, and focus.

Organizational Performance

The various dimensions of organizational performance are output or result, input, time, quality, cost, and focus. These are illustrated in Figure 2.3.

1. Output or result dimension considers the ultimate profit gain of the organization.
2. Input dimensions encompass the resources utilized to achieve the output.
3. Time dimension refers to the time taken to convert raw materials into finished products in the manufacturing sectors, or to translate ideas into actions in the service sectors.
4. Quality dimension takes into account the durability, longevity, esteem value, reusability, ease of maintenance, interchangeability, conformance to specification, fitness for purpose, and ease of operation of the product. This is the most important dimension.
5. Cost dimension is vital from the standpoint of competitiveness and affordability by consumers.
6. Focus dimension varies for different people. For a sales director, it can be profit, market share, and penetrating into new markets. For a salesperson, the focus may be on enhancing the sales. The focus of a production director may be commissioning new technologies and producing more at lesser costs. The focus of the HR director may be centered on enhancing the enabling capacities of the people of the organization.

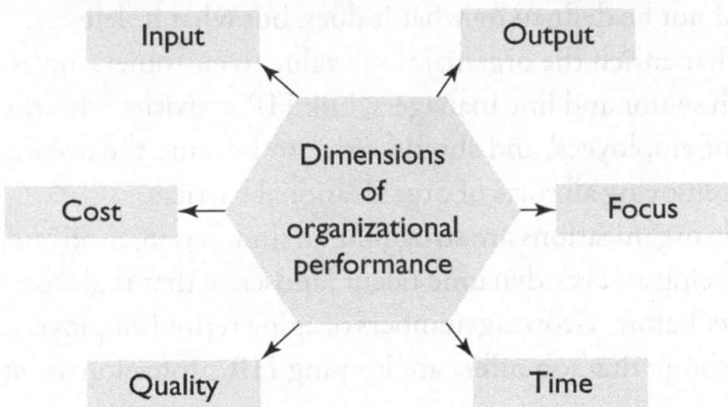

FIG. 2.3 Dimensions of organizational performance

FOCUS OF HRM

The business environment and its dimensions, organizational boundaries, organization and environmental interface, and the result of scanning a business environment, all demand effective management of business. The choice of strategy to deal with the environment and to develop the business further dictates the need of talents to sustain and advance a business. Values need to be created in organizations. People are the most valuable assets, as they create value. The values created by them are the lifeblood of an organization. Organizations need talent and persons capable of producing results. They must be identified, nurtured, and managed for the survival and growth of the organization.

Managing businesses in India poses challenges and many complex problems. One of the most complex problems is to understand and manage the international business environment. It is also vital to remember that the forces that act on people may not be purely internal to an organization; rather they could be external too. So, apart from HRM, factors outside a company's control will also affect its business results.

A business has to survive and grow within the economic turbulence and cultural diversity. Designing HR initiatives to combat both external and internal crises, and incorporating leadership skills at all levels of management should be a part of the core people initiatives.

It must be remembered that people management emphasizes building the best team and driving it, building bridges of relationship, focussing on delivery, seeking and considering feedback, developing the people, defining accountability, setting standards, laying emphasis on value creation, and trusting the people. From the standpoint of people management, HRM may be described as encompassing all the managerial decisions and actions that directly affect or influence people as members of the organization rather than merely as job-holders. HRD should not be defined by what it does, but what it delivers.

We have to consider and judge the results that enrich the organization's value to customers, investors, and employees. The HR must partner with senior and line managers, link HR activities with the business goals, build its image as a 'champion of employees', and should strive to become the driving force behind continuous transformation, thus removing all sorts of organizational barriers.

The global talent war is now upon us. While organizations are struggling to find, retain, motivate, and develop their people adequately, they are facing an ever-dynamic talent landscape that is globally competitive, demanding, and expensive than ever before. Growing numbers of aging retired employees, shifting business requirements, and attractive competing job offers are keeping HR professionals on their toes.

The main focus of HRM across many organizations is talent management. Talent management is a conscious, deliberate approach to attract, develop, and retain people with the aptitude and abilities to meet the current and future organizational needs. It involves individual and organizational development in response to a changing and complex business environment. It demands the creation and maintenance of a supportive and people-oriented organizational culture.

> From the standpoint of people management, HRM may be described as all the managerial decisions and actions that directly affect or influence people as members of the organization rather than as mere job-holders.

The HRM profession and practices have undergone a sea change. The HRM services should not merely be mired down in managing trivial and traditional administrative functions; rather, the services should provide value to the organization by way of acquiring, retaining, nurturing, multiplying, developing, advancing, promoting, recognizing, networking, and engaging talents in the organization. The HRM services must be directed to identify the people and positions at all levels of activities that are critical to the organization. The talent war is discussed in Chapter 4.

Accountability

> Establishing accountability is essential for the ultimate success of an organization.

In the arena of people management, accountability manifests the utmost importance for the ultimate success of the organization. Accountability is the obligation of an individual, firm, or institution to account for its activities, accept responsibility for them, and to disclose the results in a transparent manner. It also includes the responsibility for money or other entrusted property. Unless people are made accountable, the probability of achieving the business goals becomes less. In the absence of accountability, it is practically impossible to achieve the business goals.

HRM IN A DYNAMIC ENVIRONMENT

Q 7 **Q 5** In the dwindling business environment, HRM needs to play a vital role. Organizational leaders, including HR managers, need to scan the environment and identify the external threats and opportunities that may be crucial to the organization's survival and growth in line with strategic planning process. Further, the strengths and weaknesses, in the context of the prevailing scenario, need identification.

Thereafter, the HR manager should plan the necessary HR interventions to achieve the corporate strategy. HR professionals must be the strategic partners of the company. As strategic partners of an organization, they should develop an appropriate HRM system and deal with the effects of the changing world of work. For them, this means understanding the implications of globalization, work-force diversity, changing skill requirements, corporate downsizing, total quality management, reengineering the contingent work force, decentralizing work sites, and enhancing employee involvement. Let us **Q 6** examine how these changes affect HRM goals and practices in Exhibit 2.3.

Exhibit 2.3 Impact of globalization

Globalization has its implications on HRM. In the early 1970s, US businesses realized the impact of international force on profit and loss statements. The world was changing rapidly; oil-rich countries had made significant inroads into traditional US markets. Unfortunately, US businesses did not adapt to this changing environment as quickly or skillfully as they should have. The results were that US businesses lost out in world markets and had to fight much harder to get in. Only by the late 1980s did the US businesses begin to get the message. However, when they did, they aggressively began to improve the production standards by concentrating more on quality and preparing their employees for a global village. It is on this latter point that human resources will have the biggest effect.

Hence, HR professionals should be on the lookout for the changes in the environment. In the aftermath of globalization, many foreign intruders have started their operations in India. Many multinational companies transfer personnel to other countries. They carry their culture, beliefs, ethnicity, to other countries, thus, often leading to cultural shocks and contrasts.

On the whole, the roles of HRM should be as follows:

1. HR personnel design and redesign HRD interventions in tangible terms to eliminate the weaknesses in the system.
2. They initiate measures to add to the strengths of the organization.
3. They understand work-force diversity, changing skill requirements, and plan and execute steps to keep the wheel of production revolving even in the case of downsizing.
4. HR professionals translate business strategies into HR practices.

5. The HR department does not confine itself only to regular training programmes.
6. HR personnel must be all-rounders.
7. They watch the changes in the environment.
8. They should involve themselves during the environment-scanning stage.
9. HR personnel need to take care of the cultural differences and instigate proactive actions to prevent the effects due to cultural shocks and contrasts.
10. They must be able to fit the organization in the dynamic environment.

These actions by HR professionals will not only save and help the organizations grow, but also facilitate enhancing the image of the HR department, and treat the HR professionals as icons of the organizations.

SUMMARY

Business, commercial, industrial, or mercantile organizations are groups of people who strive to achieve the stated goals. Business environment comprises general and task environments. General environment consists of the socio-cultural, economic and non-economic, politico-legal, and technological environments. Task environment includes competitors, suppliers, and customers. Business houses should contribute to the society as part of their corporate social responsibility. Capacity, volatility, and complexity are the three dimensions of business environment. Organizations operate in stable, changing or turbulent environments.

Organizational boundaries are barriers to the flow of energy, materials, and information. Boundary spanners link an organization with the environment. The relationship between an organization and its environment is studied through the exchange of resources, information, and influence. Buffering, smoothing or levelling, anticipating and adapting, and rationing are the common strategies to deal with environmental changes.

A business develops through the process of simplification, integration, and transformation. Dimensions of organizational performance include output or result, input dimension, time, quality, cost, and focus. HRM needs sharper focus in a dwindling business environment. Accountability of personnel is essential for the ultimate success of the organization. The role of HRM should be predominant in a dynamic business environment.

KEY TERMS

Accountability refers to the obligation of an individual, firm, or institution to account for its activities, and accept responsibility for them. In the arena of people management, accountability manifests utmost importance for the ultimate success of the organization.

Boundary spanning is the process that helps organizations link with their external environment through specific activities/functions.

Environment refers to the forces or institutions that are outside the organization, but substantially affect their performance.

Ethics can be defined as a science of morals, moral principles, and rules of conduct.

Task environment is the ways and means through which the general environment influences an organization's working.

EXERCISES

Concept Review Questions

1. Discuss the socio-cultural, economic, and non-economic components of a business environment.
2. What do you understand by dimensions of environment and nature of environment? How does the Emery and Trist typology of environment differ from traditional classification of environment?
3. What do you mean by a task environment? Name the agencies that are affected by the task environment.

4. How do you interpret organizational boundaries? What do mean by the boundary spanning process? Discuss with examples.
5. What roles should HRM discharge in the dynamic business environment? Discuss how HRD can intervene in such a scenario.

Critical Thinking Questions

6. 'Human resource management should be in sharper focus in the dwindling business environment'. Do you agree with the statement? Define the role of accountability by citing examples in a business context.
7. 'HR has vital roles to play in managing an organization during days of uncertainty and unpredictability.' Critically discuss the statement citing examples from organizations.
8. Explain the role of HR in strategy formulation in an organization. How can HR strategies be linked with the organizational strategies? Explain by citing examples.

Assignments

9. Take the help of a resourceful person at your college. Make a planned visit to at least five organizations. Collect information on the scanning environment and examine if they have any systematic procedure in this regard. Discuss your findings with your professor.
10. Take an appointment with the HR managers of five organizations, and discuss about the persons performing boundary spanning roles. Approach them, and question them about the activities they perform. Interrogate them regarding the hurdles they face and the modes in which they overcome them.

MANAGER'S INSIGHT

Ahuja and Ahuja, a famous company for manufacturing bags and shoes, has been into the business for the last two decades. With a modest beginning, the company has grown steadily over the years. Its reputation for product innovation and customer service has enabled the company to remain competitive and increase its product and customer base. The employees in the company were also very happy with the company and management. Due to some personal reasons, the senior manager of the product development department had to leave the company. This created chaos in the department, and the workers could not work with the same efficiency and effectiveness that they used to show previously. In fact, there was a visible downfall in the profit margin of the company. The HR realized that the slowdown could be attributed to the sudden departure of the senior manager.

Questions:

1. What would be the best way for the HR to deal with the situation?
2. Do you think the company could have kept themselves prepared for a situation like this? If yes, explain the alternatives.

BIBLIOGRAPHY AND WEB RESOURCES

Agarwala, Tanuja, *Strategic Human Resource Management*, Oxford University Press, New Delhi, 2008.

Singh, B.P., and T.N. Chhabra, *Organization Theory and Behaviour*, Dhanpat Rai & Co. (P) Ltd, New Delhi, 2005.

Thorne, Kaye and Andy Pellant, *The Essential Guide to Managing Talent (First South Asian Edition)*, Kogan Page, New Delhi, 2007.

Dutta Uttam, *The Telegraph*, Tuesday, 29 December, 2009.

Indian Management, Volume 47, Issue 4, April 2008.

Lewin, Kurt, 'Frontiers in Group Dynamics—Concept, Method, and Reality in Social Science, Social Equilibria, and Social Change', *Human Relations*, Volume 1, Issue 1, Sage Publications, 1947, pp. 5–41.

www.itpeopleindia.com/20040920/careers1.shtml, last accessed on 16 February, 2011.

Report by Uttam Dutta, *The Telegraph*, Tuesday, 29 December, 2009.

Questions for the questionnaire were formulated by Gautam Thapar, President, AIMA and Chairman and Chief Executive Officer of the Avanta Group in the article, 'M & A Trends and Expectations in 2011', *Indian Management*, February 2011, Volume 50, Issue 2, p. 26.

LEADERSHIP CHANGE IN VICTOR ELECTRONICS LIMITED

Mr Victor was a dynamic, vibrant, enthusiastic person who was always eager to perform challenging tasks. After completing his post graduation in computer technology, he joined an entrepreneurship development programme (EDP). While pursuing the course, he meticulously studied the processes of obtaining industrial loans. He collected data from relevant sources, obtained suggestions from key people in the government, and discussed with industry people to understand the entire mechanism. His report was admired while being presented to the faculty members of the EDP.

After finishing the program, he established his own firm, named Victor Electronics Limited in 1992, and began operations with an initial corpus of ₹7 million. The business involved assembling and marketing computers. The foresightedness of Mr Victor made his company one of the most sought-after suppliers in his state. Mr Victor, by virtue of his unique capacity of building relationships with people, including significant personalities, could grab considerable clients, and enter new markets as well.

Software development was a booming business at that time. Mr Victor thought it imperative to venture into providing software solutions in 1997. Victor Electronics succeeded and emerged as a leading software service provider by 1999.

The beginning of the millennium witnessed some downfall in the software development sector. The business of Victor Electronics Limited also suffered. Mr Victor planned to recruit a general manager (GM) and a manager for operations. As the proprietor and owner of the company, he felt the utmost need to distance himself from the direct management of the company. He thus withdrew himself from direct management and became the chairman of his company. The newly appointed GM recruited a HR manager to look after the HR and IR activities.

The chairman, general manager, manager (operations), and the HR manager decided to jointly review the HR activities and efforts, with the aim to operationalize certain HR strategies to regain the lost market.

The HR strategies comprised the following:

1. To identify and enhance employee competencies
2. To establish career planning for all employees
3. To establish a reward and compensation system to boost employee morale
4. To carry out manpower analysis and recruit people
5. To establish a training and development system
6. To establish the organization's own learning and development center

Questions

1. Do you feel the formulated HR strategies are likely to meet the purpose?
2. Is the HR department proactive and professional?
3. Which strategy is aligned with the current business?

HR MANTRA Your observational skill and actions

Changes are taking place continuously in the environment. The dinosaur, a gigantic animal, could not cope up with the changes in the environment, and finally the species became extinct. However, there were many small animals that survived.

It is not the size or shape, but the capacity to withstand the change that matters. We have to accept the changes as we do not have any control over them. We need to recall that, 'It is wise to ride a horse in the direction it's going.'

The mantra: Predict changes and prepare to accept them.

PETER DRUCKER

Peter Drucker was born on 19 November 1909 in a small village called Kaasgraben in Vienna, Austria. He was a business thinker, an influential business author, a strategist, and a consultant. His ideas on management, operating large corporations, and leadership have been published in more than 30 books.

Drucker's paternal and maternal relations were Jewish. His parents were converted to Christianity and lived in what he referred to as a 'liberal' Lutheran Protestant household in Austria-Hungary. Drucker grew up in a home where many intellectuals, high government officials, and scientists would meet to discuss new ideas.

In 1933, Drucker left Germany for England where he worked for an insurance company, and later, as a chief economist at a private bank. Drucker got married in 1934 to an acquaintance from the University of Frankfurt. The couple permanently stayed in the US, where he became a university professor as well as a freelance writer and a business consultant.

Drucker had a distinguished career as a teacher; initially as a professor of politics and philosophy at Bennington College from 1942 to 1949, and then as a professor of management from 1950 to 1971 at the New York University.

Drucker came to California in 1971, where he developed one of the country's first executive MBA programmes for working professionals at Claremont Graduate University (formerly known as Claremont Graduate School). From 1971 till his last days, Drucker worked as the Clarke professor of social science and management at the Claremont Graduate University. The university's management school was named 'Peter F. Drucker Graduate School of Management' in his honour in 1987. It was later renamed 'Peter F. Drucker and Masatoshi Ito Graduate School of Management'. He taught his last class in 2002 when he was 92 years. Drucker also continued to work as a consultant to businesses and non-profit organizations well into his 90s.

Over the years, Drucker's writings were marked by a focus on relationships among human beings, as opposed to the crunching of numbers. Drucker's books were filled with lessons on how organizations can bring out the best in people, and how workers can find a sense of community and dignity in a modern society organized around large institutions. As a business consultant, he disliked the term 'guru', though it was often applied to him. 'I have been saying for many years,' Drucker once remarked, 'that we are using the word 'guru' only because 'charlatan' is too long to fit into a headline.'

Drucker's career in business started in 1942, when his initial writings on politics and society won him access to the internal workings of General Motors (GM); one of the largest companies in the world at that time. He shared his fascination with the mastermind, Donaldson Brown, who was behind the administrative control at GM. In 1943, when invited by Brown, Drucker carried out a 'two-year social-scientific analysis' of the corporation, which was called a 'political audit'.

Drucker published the book, *Concept of the Corporation*, which popularized GM's multidivisional structure. The book has been referred in numerous articles. Drucker taught that management is 'a liberal art', and he infused his management advice along with interdisciplinary lessons from history, sociology, psychology, philosophy, culture, and religion. He also believed strongly that all institutions, including those in the private sector, have a responsibility to the whole society. In his 1973 book, *Management: Tasks, Responsibilities, Practices*, Drucker said, 'The fact is that in modern society, there is no other leadership group but managers. If the managers of our major institutions, and especially of business, do not take responsibility for the common good, no one else can or will.'

Drucker always encouraged people who worked with their minds rather than their hands. He was intrigued by employees who knew more about certain subjects or topics than their bosses or colleagues and yet, had to cooperate with others in a large organization. Drucker never glorified or adored the phenomenon as the epitome of human progress. He rather analysed it and explained how the phenomenon challenged the common thinking about how organizations should be run.

In the second half of the 20th century, Drucker's approach worked well in the increasingly mature business world. By that time, large corporations had developed the basic manufacturing efficiencies and managerial hierarchies of mass production. Executives thought they knew how to run companies. Drucker ventured to correct their beliefs in a sympathetic manner. He assumed that his readers were intelligent, rational, and hardworking people of good will. If organizations struggled, Drucker believed it was usually because of outdated ideas, a narrow conception of problems, or internal misunderstandings.

The great business thinker expired on November 11 2005.

References

www.woopidoo.com/biography/peter-drucker/index.htm, last accessed on 12 October 2011.

www.google.co.in/imgres?q=peter+drucker, last accessed on 12 October 2011.

en.wikipedia.org/wiki/Peter_Drucker , last accessed on 12 October 2011.

CHAPTER 3

Human Resource Management: An Overview

LEARNING OBJECTIVES

After studying this chapter, you will be able to

- Understand the scope of personnel management
- Comprehend industrial relations, the issues related to contract labour, and the functioning of HRM systems
- Differentiate HRM from personnel management
- Define the roles and responsibilities of HR managers
- Appreciate the turnaround strategies for HRM
- Differentiate between traditional and strategic HRM

OPENING CASE

Importance of Direct Communication

Perfect Engineering Works is an organization with a few thousand employees, headed by a chairman and a managing director. It also has vice presidents for each department—production, maintenance, finance and accounts, personnel, etc. The vice president is the coordinating head for his department, and has two executive directors—one responsible for administration and policy, and the other for industrial relations (IR). The executive directors have a few directors to help them at the policy level, and for certain purposes of administration, these directors are vested with independent powers.

The IR executive director has a couple of directors to help him to deal with union matters and the legal aspects of the company. He coordinates meetings with the managing director and the unions. He is accountable to the managing director and answerable to the unions regarding agreements. One day, the personnel vice president received a note from the IR executive director stating that the personnel director had been indifferent to the IR problems of the company, irregular in attending the union meetings, and had not attended any of the important meetings fixed by the IR executive director. The personnel vice president marked the note to the administration executive director, who gave a copy to the personnel director, and called for an explanation by a specified date. The personnel director, a qualified and experienced man, tried to discuss the matter, but was asked to give a written explanation.

The vice president was designated his position in the personnel department by choice and he liked the function, whereas the executive directors of IR and administration departments were deputed on a temporary basis. The personnel director was very unhappy and upset over the manner in which the episode was handled; nonetheless, he explained in writing that he had not been irregular, but could not attend the meetings that were fixed at short notice as he had prior engagements for the selection of candidates for senior posts from among several employees from all over the country. He also sounded a word of caution that unless there is better camaraderie and understanding, particularly in personnel aspects that are human-centered, achieving the organizational goals would be difficult. The director also felt harassed and offered to resign. The administration executive director passed on this explanation to the personnel vice president.

The director later realized that on the day of the meeting, when he was busy with the selection, the IR executive director had asked his counterpart in the administration department to attend the meeting in his place, but the latter had expressed his inabitily to do so. Although the assistant to the personnel director had ably handled the situation, the IR executive director felt let down.

Learning points

- Open communication leads to clarity regarding issues.
- Organizational culture should foster and encourage openness.
- Misunderstanding shows the way to conflict.
- Suitable HRD instruments should be chosen to manage a situation.

INTRODUCTION

Human resource management (HRM) traditionally referred to the organizational policies, practices, norms, and systems that influence employee behaviour, attitudes, and performance. Today, HRM practices are considered essential for achieving business objectives and goals. With liberalization, privatization, globalization, and increased career opportunities, there are a number of factors that have made the traditional approach to personnel management obsolete. The present situation demands a complete, holistic, and strategic approach to HRM. An organization's HRM strategy must fit in the overall organizational strategy because it involves long-term implications.

The modern approach to management acknowledges the interest of the employees who are the major stakeholders in an organization. Thus, a knowledge of the group dynamics is crucial for success. In addition to the interest of the employees, process and performance are the other requirements. An organization cannot function without the application of information technology, strategic management, competency development, total quality management, leadership and team building, managing change for success, etc. For all these processes to run smoothly, HRM has to manifest its importance.

However, with the introduction of HRM, the usual practice of personnel management (PM) cannot be ignored. It is important to consider the various aspects of PM along with the new practices of HRM for the organization to run smoothly.

In this regard, this chapter has been structured with sections on PM, industrial relations, a comparison of PM and HRM, group and group dynamics, roles and responsibilities of HR managers, turnaround strategies for HRM, and strategic HRM. HR, today, definitely needs a re-look.

PERSONNEL MANAGEMENT

It is clear from the previous chapters that an organization can be a manufacturing firm, an insurance company, a government agency, a social organization, a hospital, a university, a public school system, or even a religious trust. Whatever be the organization, it needs people to perform tasks. The changing business environment and the role of HR in the dynamic environment were discussed in Chapter 2.

The duties and responsibilities of each person differ significantly in an organization. Organizational objectives are multiple, and each department strives to accomplish the departmental objectives to achieve the business goals of the organization. In order to achieve these goals, a well-run establishment needs to work out a set of rules and regulations, policies, programmes, procedures, instructions, etc., common to all the departments. These are developed to assist the members of the organization in accomplishing the organizational goals effectively in a systematic manner.

It has already been said that people are the principal component of an organization, and one needs to invest considerable effort in them. This is important for using the manpower effectively and efficiently. Thus, managers need to plan, organize, lead, and control various activities. Personnel management is concerned with the effective use of the skills of people. They may be salespeople in a store, clerks in an office, operators in a factory, technicians in a research laboratory, or a software developer in an information company. In a business, PM starts with the recruiting, hiring, and engaging of qualified people, and directing and taking control of the problems and tensions that arise in working towards established goals.

To summarize, the various PM functions are as follows:

1. Preparing the job description
2. Recruiting and selecting personnel
3. Induction and placement
4. Classifying jobs and preparing wage and salary scales
5. Counselling employees
6. Dealing with disciplinary problems
7. Negotiating with labour unions and service union contracts
8. Developing safety standards and practices
9. Managing benefit programmes, such as group insurance, health, and retirement plans
10. Providing for periodic reviews of the performance of each individual employee, recognition of his/her strengths and need for further development
11. Assisting individuals in their efforts to develop and qualify for more advanced jobs
12. Planning and supervising training programs
13. Keeping abreast of developments in the area of personnel management

The scope of PM is pervasive. However, more pervasive and enveloping is the scope of HRM, which would be taken up later in this chapter. Industrial relations is a vital element of PM, which is discussed in the following section.

INDUSTRIAL RELATIONS

As mentioned earlier, industrial relations is an integral part of PM. It is the composite result of the attitudes and approaches of employers and employees towards each other with regard to planning, supervision, direction, and coordination of all the activities of an organization. Industrial relations refer to the relations and interactions in the industry between the workers and the management. Both employees and employers need to look after the well-being of all members of the organization. This denotes the collective relationship between the management and the workers, and between the unions and the management. Traditionally, the term industrial relations encompassed all aspects of industrial life such as trade unionism, collective bargaining, workers' participation in management, industrial discipline, grievance handling, industrial disputes, and interpretation of labour laws, rules, and code of conduct.

In any industry, conflicting interests are bound to exist as workers and management view issues from different perspectives. As such, IR involves attempts at arriving at solutions between conflicting objectives and values. The issues may be based on profit motive and social gain; conflicts between discipline and freedom, authority and industrial democracy, bargaining and cooperation, or conflicting interests of an individual worker or group and the worker community.

Flexibility in the workplace has increased. Globalization has brought many major changes in the IR policy in India.

Prior to 1991, the IR system in India sought to control conflicts and disputes through excessive labour legislations. These labour laws were protective in nature, and covered a wide range of workplace aspects such as wages, working hours, health and safety of workers, layoffs and retrenchment policies, and industrial disputes. The basic purpose of these laws was to protect the workers. However, these protective policies created an atmosphere that led to decreased efficiency in companies, over employment, and inability to introduce effectiveness. With the onset of globalization, the four-decade old policy of protectionism proved inadequate for the Indian industry to remain competitive as the lack of flexibility posed a serious threat to the manufacturers because they had to compete in the international market.

Hence, the Government of India announced the liberalization policy. With the beginning of liberalization in 1992, the IR policy began to change. Now, the policy was tilted towards employers. Employers opted for workforce reduction, introduced policies of voluntary retirement schemes, and flexibility in workplace also increased. The distinct changes are enumerated as follows (http://industrialrelations.naukrihub.com):

1. In India, collective bargaining has mostly been decentralized. Those sectors where this has not been effected are facing mounting pressures, and hence are currently involved in the process of decentralization.
2. Industries are reducing employees to a significant extent to reduce costs and remain competitive in the domestic and foreign markets. The reverse scenario of increasing employee growth in some other industries is also seen.
3. In the expanding economy there is a clear dearth of managers and skilled labour.
4. There is a significant reduction in the influence of the unions though the number of local and enterprise level unions has increased.
5. Some unions and federations are coming together to have a united front when faced with issues. One example is the banking sector.
6. It is further evidenced that the employers have started to push for internal unions, without outside affiliation. Unions are encouraged without having any affiliation to any political parties.
7. Practices such as multi-skilling, multi-tasking, variable compensation packages, job rotation, and other HR practices are emerging, especially in multinational companies. However, old organizations are finding it difficult to replace the old HR practices with the new emerging ones.
8. Human resource management is seen as a key component of business strategy.
9. Training and skill development is also receiving attention in a number of industries, especially banking, information technology, and information technology-enabled services.

Industrial relations advocate industrial democracy in organizations.

INDUSTRIAL DEMOCRACY

Major policy decisions are taken by a body in a forum comprising representatives from all unions/associations, each having an equal say in an environment that enables free and frank expression of power. The purpose of industrial democracy is to give workers a sense of belonging, enhance their commitment, encourage involvement, reduce wastages, and inculcate a sense of increased productivity. In other words, industrial democracy advocates that every citizen should be treated as a human being, equal treatment

Industrial democracy underscores workers' participation in management.
Industrial democracy results in many benefits to the organization.

must be meted out to all, irrespective of nationality, caste, religion, gender, or ethnic groups; every citizen should have freedom of speech, be empowered to contribute to the community, and most importantly, leadership should not be restricted only to political parties.

Industrial democracy works towards workers' participation in management for the purpose of better understanding, reduced industrial unrest, enhanced organizational balance, transparency in organizational problems, developmental issues, reduced absenteeism, promoted organizational learning, etc. Participation further promotes communication with regard to shift timings, payment dates, suggestion schemes, grievance handling, and other similar areas. It leads to higher productivity, increased commitment, development in individuals, reduced resistance to change, and obviously, improved quality of work life. Participation may be effected through the formation and functioning of a works committee, joint management council, and worker directors in the private sector.

Application areas of participative forums include operational areas, economic and financial issues, personnel issues, welfare issues, and environmental issues. Operational areas stretch over multiple activities encompassing various issues as displayed in Box 3.1.

Box 3.1 Operational areas of industrial democracy

1. Evolution of productivity schemes (considering local conditions)
2. Planning, implementation, and review of monthly targets and schedules
3. Material supply and its shortfall
4. Storage and inventories
5. Housekeeping
6. Improvements in productivity
7. Encouragement to and consideration of suggestions
8. Quality and technological improvements
9. Machine utilization and development of new products
10. Operational performance figures
11. Matters not resolved at shop level or concerning more than one shop
12. Review of the works of shop level bodies

INDUSTRIAL RELATIONS ISSUES RELATED TO CONTRACT LABOUR

Many organizations are seen to engage contract labour in different occupations including skilled and semi-skilled jobs. This system of employing people on a contractual basis is also prevalent in agricultural and allied operations, and to some extent, in the services sector.

While economic factors such as cost effectiveness may justify the system of contract labour, considerations of social justice call for its abolition or regulation.

A workman is deemed to be employed as a contract labour when he is hired in connection with the work of an establishment by or through a contractor. Contract workmen are indirect employees; persons who are hired, supervised, and remunerated by a contractor who is compensated by the establishment. Contract labour has to be employed for work that is specific and for a definite duration. The major characteristics of contract labour are inferior labour status, casual nature of employment, lack of job security, and poor economic conditions. While economic factors such as cost effectiveness may justify the system of

Principal employers are the establishments who engage contract labourers. Principal employers must be registered with the appropriate authorities.

contract labour, considerations of social justice call for its abolition or regulation. Contract labourers can be employed if the work is not perennial but only for a short duration; is incidental to and necessary for the work of the factory; and there is no need for employing whole time workmen.

Establishments that engage the contract labourers are the principal employers, and they must be registered with the appropriate authorities. Every contractor is required to obtain a license and not undertake or execute any work through contract labour except under, and in accordance with, the license issued in that behalf by the licensing officer. The license granted is subject to conditions such as hours of work, fixation of wages, and other essential amenities with respect to contract labour as laid down in the rules.

The Central Industrial Relations Machinery (CIRM), in the national central sphere, has been entrusted with the responsibility of enforcing the provisions of the Contract Labour (Regulation and Abolition) Act of 1970, and the rules made there under, through inspectors, licensing officers, registering officers and appellate authorities appointed under the act. CIRM looks after issues pertaining to IR (www.labour.nic.in).

Contract Labour (Regulation and Abolition) Act, 1970

Contract Labour Act is not applicable to an establishment in which work of an intermittent or casual nature is performed.

The Act aims to regulate the employment of contract labourers in certain establishments and provides for its abolition in certain circumstances, and for matters connected herewith. This Act applies to every establishment where 20 or more workmen are currently employed or were employed in any of the preceding 12 months. However, the government is empowered to extend the application of this act to any establishment or contractor employing less than 20 workmen, after giving not less than 2 months notice of its intention to do so, by means of a notification in the official gazette. This Act is not applicable to an establishment in which work of an intermittent or casual nature is performed (www.labour.nic.in).

Evolution of Trade Unions

In the pre-industrial revolution scenario, industrial disputes were settled by the disputing parties through a simple discussion. During that time, the economy was fluctuating violently, and the proprietors or owners treated people as bonded labourers or even slaves. Wage cuts, closures, retrenchments, and illogical demands from the workmen were the greatest nightmares of the time. These owners economized by increasing the work load, reducing labour, and cutting wages. The owners used authoritarian leadership style and power motive.

Trade unions were the first fruit of the industrial revolution. They possessed opposing views with regard to contracting of services in jobs. The reasons stated are as follows:

1. Contracting will reduce regular employment.
2. The contract labourers, generally belonging to weaker sections of the society, will be deprived of the benefits that accrue to regular employees.
3. The efficiency of the establishment may decrease due to a shortage of experienced staff.
4. The coordination of activities by a large number of contractors and sub-contractors is likely to consume more time, and be costlier than in-house activity.
5. In-house improvements and restructuring are required, whereas, privatization is not required.

6. Outsourcing may lead to a type of employment based on discrimination, and exploitation of contract labourers with regard to wages paid, working conditions, etc.

Some registered trade unions in India are as follows:

1. All India Trade Union Congress (AITUC)
2. Bharatiya Mazdoor Sangh (BMS)
3. Centre of Indian Trade Unions (CITU)
4. Hind Mazdoor Kisan Panchayat (HMKP)
5. Hind Mazdoor Sabha (HMS)
6. Indian Federation of Free Trade Unions (IFFTU)
7. Indian National Trade Union Congress (INTUC)
8. National Front of Indian Trade Unions (NFITU)
9. National Labour Organization (NLO)
10. Trade Unions Coordination Centre (TUCC)
11. United Trade Union Congress (UTUC)

INDUSTRIAL DISPUTES

Industrial disputes are a part of organizational life and arise out of various economic or non-economic causes. The economic causes relate to compensation such as wages, bonus, allowances, conditions of work, working hours, leave, holidays without pay, unjust layoffs, and retrenchments. The non-economic factors include victimization of workers, ill-treatment by staff members, sympathetic strikes, political factors, indiscipline, etc. Trade unions and other forums generally bargain for higher wages and allowances to meet the rising cost of living and to increase their standards of living. Differences of opinion in these issues lead to disputes. Retrenchment and layoffs also continue to be important factors that give rise to industrial disputes. Indiscipline, unruliness, disorderliness, disruptive behaviour, aggression, hostility, violence, etc., jeopardize the normal working in any type of organization. Industrial disputes also revolve around the number of leaves and working hours though they have not been so important causes.

Industrial Disputes Act, 1947

The preamble of this Act states that it aims at settling conflicts between the employer and the employee by reaching an amicable solution, and at the same time, making provisions for some of the other problems that may arise from time to time in an industrial or commercial undertaking which arise within the purview of the industry. This Act does not discourage collective bargaining so long as industrial peace is not disturbed. The Industrial Disputes Act is a benign and gentle measure which seeks to pre-empt industrial tension, provide the mechanisms for dispute resolution, and set up the necessary infrastructure so that the energies of the partners in production may not be dissipated in counter-productive battles, and assurance of industrial justice may create a congenial climate.

> Industrial Disputes Act is a benign and gentle measure which seeks to pre-empt industrial tension, provide the mechanisms for dispute resolution, and set up the necessary infrastructure.

The Act mentions some statutory authorities, vests in them the necessary powers to investigate the disputes, and brings about the settlement of such disputes. The statutory authorities include the works committee, conciliation officer, boards of conciliation, courts of inquiry, labour courts, industrial tribunals, and national tribunals.

The Act has defined the term 'industry' in Section 2(j) as, 'industry means any business, trade, undertaking, manufacture, or calling of employers and includes any calling, service, employment, handicraft, industrial occupation, or avocation of workmen'.

As discussed earlier, an organization is a collection of people who work to achieve some common objectives. In the following section, we shall discuss about group and group dynamics, which are equally important for an HR to understand for the smooth working of an organization.

GROUP AND GROUP DYNAMICS

Organizations are a collection of people who socialize with one another, and prefer to work in groups. Thus, it is important to understand the concept of groups. However, the most important reason for studying groups, apart from their role in helping individuals achieve difficult goals is that, it is essential to understand the psychology of the individuals in a group. A person can work as an individual or as a member of a group. However, it is believed that the human nature is developed and expressed best in groups. By studying human behaviour in groups, we can better understand larger social units such as organizations, communities, institutions, and societies. These larger units are composed of many overlapping smaller groups. Hence, it is important for the HR department to have a clear idea about the groups working in the organizations.

Group dynamics, a general term for group processes, is the study of groups. It is the way through which people interact and relate to one another while in a group. It helps in developing group cohesiveness and problem-solving skills, and encourages collaboration and creativity.

Tuckman (1965) propounded his 'forming-storming-norming-performing' model to explain team development and behaviour. He elucidated that maturity, ability, and interpersonal relationships are established as a team develops. Consequently, the team leader changes the leadership style. The leader begins with a directing style, progresses through coaching, then moves onto participating, finishes by delegating, and slowly becomes detached to take over and develop a new team. At this point, the team may produce a successive leader, and the previous leader can move on to develop a new team.

We discuss the four stages of the model in detail as follows:

Forming This is the stage where members meet and form teams. They learn about what the team's opportunities and challenges would be. During this stage, individual members may be confused about their role, or may not understand the need for a team. After understanding their roles, members are assigned tasks on which they prefer working independently. Slowly, the ground rules or team guidelines are established.

In the beginning, the team leader may be the only member of the group. At this stage, leaders facilitate the team-building process, and help the members define their roles. The leader needs to be commanding, and understand the requirements for the team's training to move from this stage to the next one.

Storming During this stage, the members express their ideas about various ways of performing their respective tasks. This sometimes leads to an open conflict among them. Members tend to focus on details rather than on the issues, and start competing with each other for influence. Furthermore, conflict arises due to the non-homogeneous contribution towards the group. One member might notice that another one is not taking the group activities too seriously, whereas the second member might be passionate to respond to activities of his/her likings. Individual differences of this type 'storm' the group when the episode of conflict starts. This feeling leads to low trust among team members which becomes very obvious.

At this stage, it is important for the team to select its desired leadership style and decision methodology. The team leader can employ endurance and tolerance to help the team. The leader should further guide the team towards clearly-stated goals, defined individual roles, acceptable team behaviour, and a mutual feedback process for team communication.

Norming This is the stage when the team develops certain work habits that support the group rules and values. The team members use established tools and methods, and exhibit the desired team behaviour. Mutual trust and motivation also develops among the members. Open communication among the members increases, and is accompanied by positive teamwork and group focus. Individual characteristics are understood better, and this improves the relationship between the members. During this stage, the leader continues to encourage participation, involvement, and professionalism among the team members.

Performing The fourth stage is characterized by high levels of loyalty, participation, motivation, concerted efforts, and group decision-making. Knowledge sharing, mutual trust, and interdependence is also on the rise. The team becomes self-directing in developing plans and strategies to achieve its goals, and accomplishes its work. Personal growth and sharing is encouraged through membership. The leader becomes a facilitator, aiding the team in communication processes, and helping if it reverts to a prior stage.

Later, Tuckman added the fifth stage implying the dissolution of the group on completion of the task.

At the adjourning stage, the members wrap up activities.
Some groups form, storm, and reach the adjourning stage.

Adjourning During this stage, everyone moves on to new avenues and feels good about the achievements. However, the adjourning step also applies in the case of temporary groups such as a task force. At the adjourning stage, the members wrap up activities. With disbandment in mind, the group's focus shifts from high-task performance to closure. The attitude of the members varies from excitement to depression.

Tuckman's theory is an elegant and helpful explanation of team development and behaviour. Understanding groups and their working eases out management of the group members.

Knowledge of group and group dynamics is important for the HR department to manage its employees more effectively. It not only provides details to the HR about the individual characteristics, but also about the group as a whole. It enables the HR team to take charge and deal with the issues being faced by individuals and groups head on. On a similar note, we also need to know about the development and strategy of HRM, steps in developing an HRM strategy, and the scope of HRM.

HUMAN RESOURCE MANAGEMENT

It is needless to mention that out of all the resources, human resource is the only living resource in an organization. As time passes, though the material resources depreciate, human resource is the only one that appreciates. This is because, the knowledge, experience, pragmatism, skill, and wisdom of an individual increase over a period of time.

Let us recall the maxim, 'People are our most valuable asset'. It is a cliché, a maxim, or a platitude in the organizational context. It is true that no member of any senior management team would disagree with this maxim. Yet, the reality in many organizations is that their people are generally characterized as follows:

Undervalued They do not get the deserved returns for their efforts, recognition, or rewards, and gradually become frustrated.

> People are the most valuable asset.
> Yet in reality they remain undervalued, undertrained, underutilized, poorly motivated, and perform well below their true capability.

Undertrained Everyone needs training to bridge the knowledge gap. A person cannot perform to the extent expected unless he/she is trained.

Underutilized Identifying the inner potential of a person and assigning him/her work based on his/her capability is an essential task of the HR personnel. If a person does not get the opportunity of working based on his/her aptitude and potential, he/she is being under utilized.

Poorly motivated An underutilized person is poorly motivated and therefore unable to deliver his/her best.

Underperformers These factors result in them performing way below their true capability.

History abounds with examples that show that only if people are valued, trained, and motivated, can they contribute their best to the organization. Some organizations are not very inclined to train their resources; presumably, they are of the opinion that training is costly. They forget that training is costly; but, lack of training is costlier. Lack of training greatly impedes achieving excellence.

Human resource (or personnel) management involves the concept of getting things done through people. Although it is an essential part of every manager's responsibilities, modern organizations find it easier to have a division especially dedicated to human resource functions.

The rate of change in organizations has never been as high as it is at present. Organizations must be able to absorb and manage these changes at a much faster rate than in the past. In order to implement a successful business strategy to face these challenges, organizations of any size, large or small, must ensure that they have the right people who are capable of translating these strategies into actions, and delivering the products. The market place for talented and skilled people is competitive and expensive. Taking on new staff can be disruptive to the existing employees as it takes time for them to develop cultural awareness, experience, and knowledge of the product, process, and organization.

As discussed in earlier chapters, organizations vary in size, aims, functions, complexity, construction, the nature of their products, and appeal. Similarly, the emphasis on HR values and practices also vary in organizations. However, the ultimate aim of the function is to ensure that the business is always correctly staffed by the right number of people with the skills relevant to the business needs. They must not be overstaffed or understaffed in total or with respect to any one discipline or work grade.

Q 2 Exhibit 3.1 gives a brief outline of how the systems of HRM were developed.

Exhibit 3.1 Development of HRM

It has been more than three decades since the term 'human resource development' became popular in India. In 1975, a decision was taken to dedicate a department entirely to promoting human resources, at Larsen & Toubro Limited.

Pareek and Rao (1975) outlined a philosophy for the new HRD system. They outlined 14 principles to be kept in mind while designing an HRD system. These principles dealt with both the purpose of HRD systems and the process of their implementation. This saga of the development of HRM in India can be traced back to the write-up by Rao and Pareek in their paper, 'From a Sapling to the Forest'. They shared 15 guiding principles for designing the HR function for Larsen & Toubro. The guiding principles are as follows:

1. Focusing on enabling capacity
2. Integrating the development of the people with organizational development
3. Maximizing individual autonomy and growth through increased responsibility

(Contd)

Exhibit 3.1 (Contd)

4. Decentralization through delegation and shared responsibility
5. Participatory decision-making
6. Balancing adaptation to and changing the organizational culture
7. Balancing differentiation and integration
8. Balancing specialization and diffusion of functions
9. Ensuring responsibility for the functions
10. Balancing linkages within and with other functions
11. Building feedback and reinforcing mechanisms
12. Balancing quantification and qualitative decisions
13. Balancing internal and external help
14. Planning evaluation of the function
15. Continuous review and self-renewal

Later, Rao and Pareek (1975) reassigned 11 systems; six in human resource administration, four in human resource development, and one for industrial relations. This breakup is described as follows:

Human resource administration

1. Manpower planning
2. Recruitment and placement
3. Performance and potential appraisal
4. Promotion salary administration
5. Staff administration
6. Information and data processing

Human resource development

7. Training
8. Organization development and research
9. Employee feedback and counselling
10. Career development and career planning

Industrial relations

11. Worker affairs

Following this breakup, a lot of attention was paid to the structure of the HR function. Detailed recommendations were developed for implementation of the system and functions. To help the organization take the right decisions, a detailed description of the HR functions were prepared, and this included critical attributes for each function. These were carried out through interviews and discussions.

PERSONNEL MANAGEMENT VS HRM

Personnel management and human resource management can be compared based on several dimensions.

Personnel management and HRM can be compared based on several dimensions such as focus, philosophy, function, pervasiveness, motivation, orientation, and tools and techniques. With regard to focus, PM cares for profit maximization and controlling people, whereas HRM is development-oriented and attempts to fulfill the needs and aspirations, finding out ways and means for employees to contribute their best. A detailed comparison of some dimensions is shown in Table 3.1.

Table 3.1 Personnel management vs human resource management

Dimension	Personnel management	Human resource management
Focus	• Profit maximization • Aims at controlling people	• Development oriented • Attempts to fulfil needs and aspirations of people • Aims to make employees contribute their best
Philosophy	• Functional area of management	• Primarily a philosophy • Can be variously described as an attitude, a policy, an approach, or a practice • Aims at a more humane management
Function	• A traditional staff function • Deals with procurement, compensation, training, and appraisal	• A part and parcel of each line function • Helps to lead active managers
Pervasiveness	• Concern of personnel manager	• Concern of all managers

(Contd)

Table 3.1 (Contd)

Dimension	Personnel management	Human resource management
Motivation	• Primarily concentrates on recruitment, selection, and appraisal	• Primarily concentrates on morale boosting, motivation, and getting more work from people
Orientation	• Administration • Individual performance	• Synergy • Teambuilding • Team performance
Tools and techniques	• Rules • Procedures • Pressure tactics • Coercive measures	• Integrated approach

STRATEGY FOR HRM

As discussed earlier, HRM is basically a management tool for the employees of an organization. It concerns issues such as employment and arbitration in accordance with the law, and with the company's directives, compensation, performance, and technology. Hence, it is vital for HRM to possess a strategy and a policy, for smooth functioning of the organization.

A policy is an overall intention of the top management with regard to an issue that needs to be formally expressed. HR policies are versatile and encompass many issues such as recruitment and selection, career planning, performance management, training and development, communication, organizational culture, human resource accounting and audit, compensation and benefits, and so forth. The policy statement must be documented and percolated at all levels of the organization in such a way that it can be understood by all. The policy of an organization, as an example, is reproduced as follows:

1. We commit to fulfil the training needs of our customers by providing effective training services.
2. We also commit to enhance customer satisfaction and continually improve the standard of training.

Framing objectives to achieve a policy, is also being used widely by companies. Time-bound goals or targets are being framed in order to work towards the achievement of policies framed. Certain steps need to be followed in order to be able to develop an effective HRM strategy.

Steps in Developing HRM Strategy

The HRM strategy needs to be developed in a methodical and strict manner. The steps are generic in nature. However, depending on the nature of the business, an organization may lay more emphasis on any of the following seven steps:

Step 1: Get the 'Business Picture'

Human resource management strategy needs to be developed methodically by strictly following seven steps.

In order to grasp the business picture, one has to know the key driving and restraining forces which may include technology, vendor development, resource procurement, distribution channels, competitors, markets (existing and prospective), and other parameters. One must also know the implications of these driving and restraining forces and values of contribution of the people.

Step 2: Develop a Mission Statement or Statement of Intent

After the factors responsible for affecting the process in a business have been identified, the mission and the statement of intent have to be finalized. The statement of intent relates to the people's side of the business. The mission statement guides the people to march and accomplish the stated and implied goals.

Step 3: Conduct a SWOT Analysis of the Organization

While conducting a SWOT analysis, one should focus on the internal strengths and weaknesses of the people in the business. One should consider the current skills and capability issues. It is essential to vigorously identify the external business and market environment, and highlight the opportunities and threats relating to the people side of the business. This helps one formulate a better strategy.

Step 4: Conduct a Detailed Human Resources Analysis

It is necessary to concentrate on the organization's culture, organization, people, and systems (COPS). One needs to consider the present state and the future state (where one wants to be) to identify the gaps. This is how one can be sure of framing the right plan of action.

Step 5: Determine Critical People Issues

At this stage, one needs to examine the business strategy against the SWOT and COPS analyses. Critical issues pertaining to people that have a key impact on the delivery of business strategy need to be identified. Thereafter, these key people issues need to be prioritized and the consequences if any one remains unattended needs to be analysed.

Step 6: Develop Consequences and Solutions

For each critical issue identified at the previous stage, the options for managerial actions are highlighted—generate, elaborate, and create. The various courses of actions could be any of the HR functions such as communication, motivation, training, performance review, pay, and so on. Organizations need to identify the right mix of the HR systems required in specific situations, and set time-bound targets to achieve the objectives.

Step 7: Implement and Evaluate the Action Plans

The ultimate purpose of developing an HR strategy is to ensure that the objectives are mutually supportive and collectively exhaustive. The aim is to integrate a reward and payment system with employee training and career development plans. However, effectiveness of any training programme should be ascertained and the return on investment must be considered.

Unless the steps are followed in a sequential order, it may be difficult for an organization to define the strategies essentially required to achieve business goals. Refer to Exhibit 3.2 to understand the kind of questions that an HR can ask himself to check his effectiveness.

SCOPE OF HRM

As a key source, HRM utilizes other resources for effective designing and implementation of various policies, procedures, and programs. Human resource management has its gamut over the 3Ps of an organization, information technology (IT), strategic management, competency development, total quality management (TQM), performance management, leadership, change management, and other organizational phenomena such as economic boom or recession. This is shown in Figure 3.1.

Exhibit 3.2 Indicators of ineffective HRM functioning

> Effectiveness of the functioning of the HRM system may be assessed through the use of certain indicators.

Once the systems and strategies of HRM have been acquainted with, the managers should become vigilant to diagnose the effectiveness of the systems formulated and the strategies finalized. For this purpose, they need to observe the responsiveness of the workforce and symptoms in their organization. In case the systems/mechanisms/schemes do not function effectively, they can use certain indicators; some of which are listed as follows:

1. Increased grievances and labour disputes jeopardize smooth working of the orgnization
2. Unsettled inter-group and inter-departmental conflicts lead to employee dissatisfaction
3. Underperformance of skilled operators causes lowering of productivity
4. Increasing absenteeism
5. Dissatisfaction with pay and working conditions
6. Deterioration in the quality of products
7. Increasing number of customer complaints

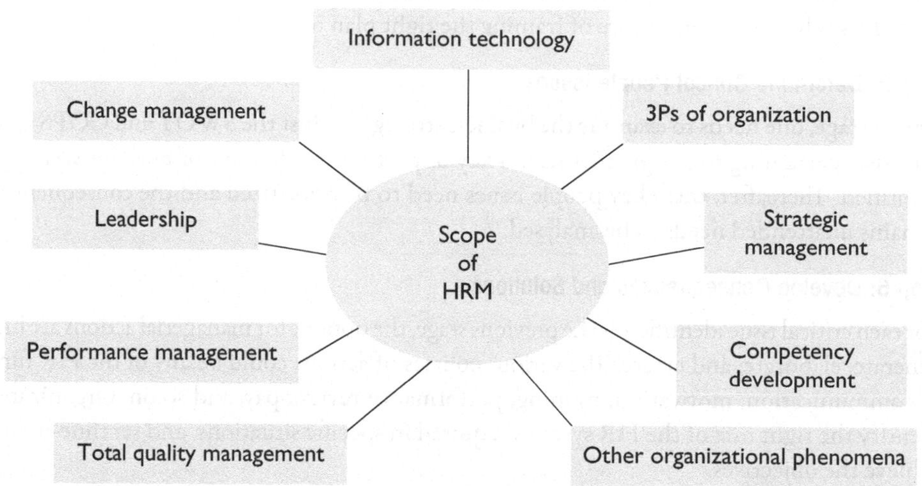

FIG. 3.1 Scope of HRM

HRM and 3Ps

People, process, and performance are the three pillars of HRM, and are also termed as the 3Ps. The 3Ps are described as follows:

People It stands established that people are the core strength of an organization and that they are the only resources that appreciate unlike others, which depreciate. It is also known that all resources, except the human resource can be replaced. We all know that people are guided by their emotions, and on nurturing, developing, and leading, they contribute their best. It is the human resource that can make or mar an organization. An organization is identified by its people, their behaviour, concerted efforts, team spirit, and helping attitude towards others. Thus, they must be carefully handled.

> HRM includes IT, strategic management, competency development, TQM, performance management, leadership, change management, and other organizational management concepts.

Process Organizational processes are a set of interrelated activities which evolve over a period of time. Each process yields a product or a service. In a changing business environment, more emphasis is laid on flexibility and adaptability of any process.

In today's times, product orientation has changed to process orientation. Products are manufactured through a process. If we concentrate on the process, the products are likely to be right. Engineers are required to design and develop these processes through which a product is manufactured or a service is delivered. HRM manifests its importance in equipping people to follow the process to achieve the business goals.

Performance An organization must create value and enhance its rate of return on investment (ROI) to move towards growth. It is a known fact that value creation and ROI enhancement are the two pillars of supporting performance in an organization. Manufacturing technology and information technology aid in marching towards excellence. Management of knowledge workers is different from that of managing other employees. This is because, knowledge workers, due to their intelligence and maturity, expect a greater degree of flexibility. They further deserve and prefer to work without interference as their independence motives are dominant. Their expectations are fulfilled through the requisite HRM tools. The HR needs to look at the performance of various workers from different perspectives for different functions.

HRM and IT

Management information system (MIS) has four levels, namely, office automation system (OAS), transaction processing system (TPS), MIS, and decision support system (DSS). Generally, the operating core of an organization works on OAS and TPS, managerial personnel use MIS, whereas the top management or strategic apex utilizes DSS for decision making. Advancement of science and technology has paved the way for intensive use of information technology, which in turn has revolutionized the working of organizations. Business organizations are no exception to these phenomena.

IT is seen to be influencing and dominating the corporate world from three viewpoints, which are discussed in this section. As everyone is using IT these days, it has become very important for any organization's success. The HR departments need to update themselves with the latest IT tools and techniques.

Information technology practices This refers to the extent of adoption and implementation of IT at various levels of managerial functions and the extent of infrastructure created to spread IT in order to support the business processes and operations.

Information management practices Raw data is processed to yield information, which is then used for decision making. Once the decision has been taken and implemented, the information may or may not be referred back. Some of this information is retained for legal purposes. In a nutshell, information has its lifecycle. Information management practices denote the organizational capabilities to manage the entire information life cycle.

Information behaviour/values In organizations, willing acceptance of IT depends on the attitude and qualification of people, dimensions of organizational climate, motivation, and the age group of people. Attitude and qualification are subjective and general terms. The twelve dimensions of organizational climate are orientation, interpersonal relationship, supervision, problem management, management of mistakes, conflict management, communication, decision making, trust, management of rewards, risk taking, innovation, and change. The six motives are achievement, expert influence, extension, control, dependency, and affiliation. Higher-age groups generally tend to avoid the use of IT. Organizations where the average age of the people is less do not face this problem. However, HR personnel still need to work in close coordination with the IT personnel. The key challenge of the HR managers lies in identifying the information behaviour/values expected from the employees and in defining and communicating these to the employees. Unless this is done, achieving results from the implementation of IT may remain unachieved or only partially achieved.

Another major factor common between HRM and the IT sector is the high rate of attrition. The most common causes of attrition in the IT sector (Haldar 2006) are as follows:

1. Inability to use one's competencies
2. Lack of challenging tasks
3. Mismatch of one's expectations with the prevailing management style
4. Lack of scope of growth in terms of salary, status, and other factors
5. Absence of role clarity
6. Lack of sense of belongingness
7. Rust out stress syndrome (ROSS)
8. Lack of learning opportunities
9. Low levels of motivation
10. Unfulfilled 'occupational values'
11. Lifestyle inventory unmatched with the task
12. Lack of excitement and innovation in the job

The prime function of HR managers in the IT sector is identifying the causes behind attrition in that organization and initiating measures to prevent them.

HRM and Strategic Management

Strategic management is the process by which an organization formulates its strategies and implements them. Strategy is the route from the origin to the destination; the origin may be choosing a predefined objective and fulfilling the objective would be the destination. Strategic management encompasses the study of internal and external environments with a view to unearth and assess the relevant threats and opportunities. This is clubbed with relentless appraisal of the organization's strength and weaknesses, a thorough analysis of the strategic choices, and evaluation of each strategy. It allows an organization to base its decisions on long-range forecasts, and therefore benefits the organization with consistency of actions, thereby preventing a drift in different directions. Furthermore, strategic management creates an opportunity of involving different levels of management in the process.

Strategic management processes rely heavily on the leadership of organizational stalwarts. The managers responsible for implementing strategic management processes and the HR manager need to exhibit a requisite leadership style suitable for that situation. Some commonly exhibited leadership styles have been discussed in Chapter 1. A leader effectively builds his/her team as a cohesive group and develops every member of the team to give his/her best. Leaders integrate the task needs and human needs, as their moral and organizational responsibilities. Hence, HR managers need to concentrate on leadership development. They are required to work in association with the learning and development division, leadership development personnel to plan leadership development methods and techniques appropriate to the organizational situation. Organizations formulate short-term and long-term strategies. For the long-term strategies, HR managers should consider the leadership passage and be instrumental in developing an appropriate leadership pipeline (Haldar 2010).

HRM and Competency Enhancement

Competencies refer to the managerial characteristics which are demonstrated and observable; these lead to effective and superior performance. Competency embodies the capacity to transfer skills and abilities to a person from one functional area to another. It also refers to exhibiting good performance more consistently.

Core competence is a bundle of skills and technologies that represents the enduring strength of a company and cannot be easily copied. The core competence of Larsen & Toubro is construction. Infosys has the capabilities of retaining people, developing leadership potential, and providing software solutions. Haldia Petrochemical Limited has capabilities to provide polymers (polyethylene and polypropylene) and chemicals (products for energy segments and other industries) to the utmost satisfaction of the customers. It is the distinctive competence of people that helps the organization gain competitive advantages. Various aspects of competency are discussed at length in Chapter 5.

As an all-rounder, the HR manager needs to scan the business environment, finalize the business strategies, consider the available technology and infrastructure, and assess the competencies required for various positions. He/she needs to evaluate the employees, identify the competency gaps, and conduct development programmes to impart those competencies as well. This will help the organization to develop a suitable core competence and excel in the same.

HRM and TQM

Total quality management is a systematic customer-focused approach that is aimed at continuous performance improvement. It is a philosophy and a set of guiding principles, which represents the foundation for continuously improving the organization through employee involvement. It is also an application of quantitative methods where human resources work towards improving the materials and services supplied to and by an organization. It also takes care of all the processes within the organization and the degree to which the needs of the customers can be met.

TQM advocates the integration of fundamental management techniques, existing improvement efforts, and technical tools under a disciplined approach, thus resulting in continuous improvement. It emphasizes that the expectations of all the stakeholders must be met. Some of these expectations are listed in Table 3.2.

TQM is a company-wide perspective that strives for customer satisfaction by seeking zero defects in products and services. Making quality improvements was once thought to be the sole responsibility of specialists such as the quality engineers, product designers, and process engineers. Over the years, the concept has undergone a sea change. Today, developing quality across the entire company is an important function of the HRM department. TQM embarks upon the 'total quality person', and to procure, develop, and retain them, one has to consider certain issues as follows:

1. Organizational chart and reporting
2. Selection and recruitment
3 Induction, grooming, and mentoring
4. Setting goals and key result areas (KRAs)
5. Appraisal and performance measurement
6. Growth, promotion, and compensation
7. Impact of employee turnover
8. Psychological contracts

Table 3.2 Expectations of stakeholders

Stakeholder	Expectation
Customers	Product quality or service quality
Employees	Career growth, satisfaction
Owners	Investment performance
Sub-suppliers	Continuing business opportunities
Society	Responsible stewardship

HR professionals perform many activities to enrich the quality movements of organizations and enhance the quality indices. At this juncture, HR manifests its importance to lend its helping hand to organizations and get the total quality from the people involved (http://www.ijric.org).

HRM and Performance Management

Performance concerns the behaviour directed towards achieving an organization's missions and business goals, and manufacturing the products or services resulting from it. It refers to only that behaviour which is related to the production of goods or services maintaining the qualitative requirements. Performance differs from effectiveness, which generally involves making judgements about the adequacy of the behaviour with respect to certain criteria such as a work group or an organizational goal (Hughes et al. 2008).

Performance is also considered to be a multidimensional variable (MacKinney 1967) being a conglomerate of several dimensions. Hence, people high on one dimension may not be high on the other, and such standings may change over time. Performance is effective and efficient work which also considers personal data such as measures of accidents, turnover, absence, and tardiness. Performance index is the measure to determine if an executive's salary is commensurate with the organization's performance. Each employee of the organization is evaluated through a formal process on a regular basis.

The top individual strengths identified by Ramusson (1999) include ego strength, assertiveness, willingness to take risks, sociable and abstract reasoning, healthy sense of skepticism, creativity, and empathy. Many psychologists and behavioural scientists are engaged in fundamental research to investigate the determinants of performance. Pestonjee (1991) has mentioned about the global acceptance of high positive correlation between job satisfaction and performance. An organization cannot excel unless it focusses on the actions and behaviour of the human resources. Performance excellence is characterized by team-work, group cohesiveness, values, and value systems. These factors should be looked into for boosting productivity and attracting customers. Performance excellence is also the congruence of employee output with the organizational goal. Job performance has causal relationships with factors such as assertiveness, job satisfaction, job involvement, and organizational commitment.

Assertiveness is social boldness; saying 'no' if the situation demands it. It also refers to the ability to express one's own viewpoints without trampling upon others' interests. Satisfaction in the workplace is just a constellation of attitudes about the job; the extent to which people like or dislike the various aspects of the work and the fulfillment of the requirement of an individual by the work environment. Job involvement is the degree to which people identify themselves psychologically with the job; a high degree of involvement results in psychological empowerment. Organizational commitment is a state in which an employee identifies with a particular organization, its mission, policies, objectives, goals, and wishes to maintain membership in the organization.

HR managers should hold programmes in the organization to develop assertiveness. They should keep working towards measuring levels of satisfaction, involvement, and commitment, identify areas, and initiate actions for improvement.

HRM and Leadership Development

In organizations, there are administrators, managers, and leaders who perform various roles. Among them, leaders are usually the ones who excel, apply creativity, set trends, push benchmarks, engage in boundary management, extend vision, effectively network, are proactive, build culture, mentor followers, extend helping hands, multiply concepts of power, and empower the followers. Of course, administrators and managers also do these jobs. Not all of us are born with the same potential to lead. However, it is important to remember that different characteristics can help or hinder in developing leadership competencies. Leaders have to be cognitive tuners, people catalysers, and efficacy builders.

Everyone in an organization can develop his/her leadership skills and effectiveness. Classroom-style training, workshops, and associated reading can also contribute to leadership skills, to know more about what he/she has in possession, what else is needed, and what is involved in leading efficiently.

Based on these perceptions and notions, organizations arrange leadership development programmes with objectives such as to provide the organization with the required number of leaders having the ability to meet the present and future organizational needs, to instill leadership capabilities among the managers, to inculcate a sense of self-dependency, achievement, and affiliation to team members, to encourage the leaders to keep themselves up to date, and grow to meet the challenges, cope up with the changes, handle complex situations and greater problems, to discharge their responsibilities with improved performance, and to sustain good performance and gain distinctive competence.

The HR professionals need to organize leadership development programmes to meet the organizational needs. The programmes may be organized in phases and consist of project works between two phases. Different situations and different persons function and work better under different leadership styles. HRM plays a predominant role in identifying the leadership styles that would be best suited for getting the work done by others. The contemporary leadership styles practiced in organizations are transactional, transformational, and charismatic leadership. Value-based leadership, spiritual and servant leadership, boundary spanning, and team leadership are the other styles.

Human resource management especially helps in building the leadership pipeline in organizations. Furthermore, succession planning is an essential need when a significant person approaches superannuation.

HRM and Change

Business scenarios have been changing continuously due to multiple reasons such as changes in social, economic, and cultural settings. There are a number of similar factors that affect organizations, compel them to anticipate changes and implement relevant actions to cope with them, survive, and grow. Change management has become the most vital area while running a business or managing an organization; it is probably the most difficult one too. One needs to identify the change, ascertain the state to be moved to, initiate proactive steps, manage resistance, move to accommodate change, and refreeze again to gain

> Many reasons affect organizations, compelling them to anticipate changes and implement relevant actions to cope with them, survive, and grow.

competitive advantages. For many, the general tendency is to be complacent with policies and practices that have been successful in the past.

A cursory glance at the history of many of the successful organizations indicates that organizations that have been adaptive and change-oriented continue to be successful. Organizations need to continuously scan the environment, study the changes, analyse their pace and direction, interpret them in the context of the organization, and plan the changes essential to survive and grow. Many organizations have perished as they could not study the changes or could not implement the changes in a planned manner.

Organizations today are facing challenges due to reasons that have emerged from new business needs such as the following:

1. Technology facilitating working of virtual teams
2. Customers demanding round-the-clock service
3. Working in a global village requires 24 × 7 support to attend to queries
4. Blurring of the geographical borders with the formation of the virtual world

HRD was originally only a staff function. Following strategic shifts, it has now become a line function. As a strategic function, it has to coordinate with other functional areas and gear up the human resources to meet the future challenges. Therefore, HR bears the arduous task of convincing the top management to support, initiate, and sustain change management programmes. Jyothi and Venkatesh (2008) have mentioned certain challenges faced by an HR with regard to change management as follows:

1. Facilitating the work–life balance for employees
2. Facilitating culture change for employees
3. Competence mapping and building
4. Preparing career plans
5. Managing attritions
6. Managing cultural diversity
7. Sustaining and improving the productivity and creativity
8. Reorienting the organizational practices and policies to suit the new generation employees

In the context of work–life balance, the employees have to achieve a balance among work, home, and community. In such cases, the HR personnel have to intervene to discharge the responsibility of facilitating these employees through pragmatic awareness programmes, facilitating their thinking about organizational work and non-organizational work life, educating the managerial personnel to coach, mentor, and counsel their employees, and extending professional counselling directly by the trained HR personnel for struggling employees.

In the arena of change management, HR professionals have to act as change champions. They have to convince the people by explaining the need for the changes, the consequence if the change is not implemented, and the expected benefits out of the changes. They are required to constantly evaluate the effectiveness of the results of the organizational efforts. Both knowledge and distinctive ability to execute successful change strategies make the HR professional exceptionally valued. They need to know how to link change to the strategic needs of the organization with minimal employee dissatisfaction and resistance to change. When they start implementing changes, they no more remain 'change agents'; they become 'change champions'.

HRM during Other Organizational Phenomenon

This millennium has witnessed an acute economic recession. The business situation has observed an economic boom as well. Different companies have had to adopt diverse HRM practices in the various situations to survive and grow.

HRM during Economic Recession

Tough times call for tough measures; HR managers need to figure out ways to deal with their employees and hold on to them. They have to make sure that they stay within the budget at all times. It has already been established that an organization is as good as its people. The driving force behind one's business is good employees who perform and contribute to the organization. In the period of recession, the performers are not expendable. Thus during tough economic times, an organization has to retain its performing people with itself and away from its competitors.

At this juncture, HR managers need to adopt some practices. These are described as follows:

Discriminate among star, good, and average employees The HR manager needs to check the performance and potential of all the employees. This is required in order to identify the capabilities of all the employees and categorize them as shown in the Table 3.3.

Deadwood In any organization, one will find that 80% of the employees (passengers) do 20% of the work, and the rest 20% (performers) do the remaining 80% of the work. The passengers are incompetent, unsatisfactory, and unsuitable occupants of their positions, and are unable to perform their roles.

Problem child There are examples of persons with great potential to work and capable of contributing significantly to the organization, but do not use their genuine capacities; rather they work below their capacity or only with mixed results. It must be evidenced that in some instances, they divert their energies to make mischief, indulge in harmful activities, and get easily influenced by external agencies. They are simply wasting their talents. This type of employee is called the problem child.

Work horse The work horses have limited capacity but they invest a lot of efforts and try to accomplish the tasks entrusted to them. These are the people who actually reach the peak of their performances. Reddy (2005) found in his study that 75% out of more than 200 managers at the Kerala state level public enterprises belonged to this category.

Star These members of the organization have high potential and high performance levels. They are performers responsible for the growth of the organization. Around 15% of the employees in the managerial cadre belong to this classification (Reddy 2005).

During recession, an organization needs the star employees to brave out the recessionary storm, and for that one will have to use the most valuable weapons from one's arsenal. The weapons may be organization-specific. The bad ones, particularly those in the problem child category, will turn out to be bigger liabilities once the pressure to perform inevitably increases.

Table 3.3 Categorization of employees

Job performance	Potential	Combination
Low	Low	Deadwood
Low	High	Problem child
High	Low	Work horse
High	High	Star

Redirect employees to other departments One of the best ways to retain employees is through job rotation. Considering their competencies and the job attributes, they can be transferred to other departments. One central benefit of job rotation is to understand the processes. In the case of executives, job rotation facilitates understanding the business.

This can be done periodically and the frequency can be defined in the company's administrative manual to avoid resistance from employees. For example, if there are too many sales people handling too few sales in a week in an area, then they can be redirected to another area. The employees will acquire additional skills while working in different departments. However, the best salespeople of the star category would be required in the sales department, as sales strategy would still need attention in order to enhance sales. Job rotation is required at all functional areas of an organization.

Listen to the employees This is a very important aspect that every HR manager must be good at. By listening to the grievances of the employees, one not only gains their trust and confidence but also encourages them to do the tasks efficiently.

Keep them motivated and engaged During lean times, employees feel insecure. There arises a need to keep all the employees occupied and busy. Many companies organize training sessions and outstation trips for the employees to make them feel busy, motivated, and happy.

Highlight the company's position One must lay your cards on the table to show up the company's position. During meetings with the employees, the HR manager should paint a clear picture. Explain to them that the recession has forced the organization to take some harsh steps and their cooperation is required. Their concerted efforts are inescapable for the survival and growth of the company. Being open and upfront with the staff from the very beginning will help prevent the key employees to jump from the ship.

All the steps mentioned here are likely to enable an HR manager to hold his/her team together during a recession, to make the interpersonal bond stronger, and to inculcate team spirit. The employees will be motivated and their commitment will enhance. It is necessary to be understanding during tough times and put in the extra efforts required for the business to come out of the storm unscathed.

Exhibit 3.3 discusses some HR-related instances during acute recession.

Exhibit 3.3 Measures to deal with economic recession

The diverse measures adopted by several companies for their survival during an economic recession are listed here.

Shoppers Stop

1. Until a few months before the recession, the company was busy chasing headhunters to find candidates who are willing to join. This situation took a sharp turn.
2. The then managing director of the company, B.S. Nagesh, decided to be very selective in filling up new vacancies.
3. Shoppers Stop would recruit only when new stores came up.

Future Group

1. Companies owning large retail chains such as Pantaloons and Big Bazaar cut people cost by 1% by linking salaries with performance.
2. Future Group's chairman, Kishore Biyani said, 'Human capability is infinite and multitasking is the order of the day'.

Jet Airways

1. The company initially sacked 800 employees and announced to further sack 1150 employees.
2. However, it retreated within 24 hours after public and political outcry.
3. The company was still reeling under experiments.

Kingfisher Airlines

The company slashed the salaries of the copilots by 90%.

Estimates of workers by McKinsey consultancy

1. Just a few years ago, consultancy firm McKinsey estimated that India's factories would need 73 million workers by 2015 (50% more than that today's numbers).
2. India's airlines were projected to add 440 new planes by 2010.
3. About 40,000 vacancies were expected in the coming three to four years.
4. The situation later changed from plenty to paltry.

(Contd)

Exhibit 3.3 (Contd)

Impact on academia

1. On campus, companies recruiting from IITs and IIMs were offering lucrative packages and perquisites, prior to the recession.
2. Several multinational companies withdrew job offers they had offered the students of IITs and IIMs.

Wipro Technologies

1. Wipro had placed 4–5% of its employees under the scanner for non-performance.
2. Corporate vice-president of Wipro, Pratik Kumar said, 'This is a regular annual exercise'.
3. Wipro has issued 6,000 offer letters as against 12,000 in the previous year.

MphasiS, an HP company

MphasiS is a Bangalore-based IT outsourcing service provider.

1. It has reduced its hiring plans by almost 50%.
2. Prior to recession, it had announced that it would recruit 8,000 people.
3. According to the company's chief executive officer, Jeya Kumar, the figure is down to 4,000.

Teamlease, the largest Indian staffing solution company

1. Teamlease's chairman, Mr Manish Sabharwal, said that companies were earlier recruiting anybody with a pair of hands just to stock up the manpower, in case the growth story continued. However, this feeling drastically changed during recession.

Source: Indian Management (2008)

HRM during Economic Boom

During an economic boom, some companies may become complacent. A company may even initiate special ventures. For example, it can analyse the competition in the market, launch new products to enlarge the product range, penetrate into new markets, assess the organization for change and development, concentrate on people development, talent acquisition, and retention, and perform many such activities. The company can also do so by investing a major share of the profit earned in the business itself. In a booming economy, a company can further think of reviewing and redesigning the compensation packages.

Presently, HR is treated as a business partner. In the time of economic boom, HRM should function by taking into consideration the following points for better results:

1. Business expansion—new and specific skills can be imparted to employees.
2. Fund availability—a major share of the profit can be reinvested in the business for modernization.
3. Compensation packages—the existing system can be reviewed and innovative systems can be launched.
4. Companies can carry out SWOT analysis and identify strategies to beat competitors.
5. Funds in developing human resources can be utilized to impart need-based training and conducting management development programmes.
6. Employee retention can be ensured by attitude surveys, satisfaction measurement, and initiating remedial measures (even if retention cannot be eliminated, it can be greatly reduced).

Tremendous attention, of course, is required to increase the talent pool available in the marketplace through various options as follows:

1. Hiring foreign workers
2. Supporting vocational courses
3. Encouraging greater enrollment in apprenticeship programs
4. Extending the work–life span by delaying retirement of older workers

All these options are unparalleled and inevitably bear fruit in the long term. In the short term, however, an employer can still face crisis.

Out of these, acquiring and retaining talents must be an on-going exercise, during this period. For retaining valuable employees, a company has to pay utmost attention. The probability of poaching by competitors is likely to be more during the time of economic boom. Retaining one's existing employees, if they are adjudged right, is one of the most critical ways to accelerate the growth during the economic boom. If employees can be retained, huge savings can be made on recruitment costs, valuable time, and energy, and these resources can be redirected back to the core business, thus truly taking advantage of the booming economy.

Apart from financial packages, companies can adopt certain non-financial means, both to attract and retain people. There are numerous strategies that companies can undertake, a few of which are discussed here.

1. Creating a convincing vision, mission, and purpose—A structured and documented vision statement helps a company to attract talent. Furthermore, it aids to enhance their continuous commitment. The vision and mission greatly reduces employee attrition. Employees should also know the purpose of existence of the company. The vision, mission, and, purpose statements must be communicated and explained to all employees.
2. Providing opportunities for training, learning, and development—Stagnant employees who get bored and are unchallenged tend to leave the organization. Opportunities for continuous learning and development motivate them and bring out the best in them.
3. Managing to focus on individual strengths—Employees' strengths and weaknesses may widely differ and hence they must periodically be identified. Employees must be helped to take care of their weaknesses in addition to focussing on their strong points.
4. Managing stress—A stressed employee cannot contribute his best to the company. Various types of organizational role stresses need identification and suitable remedial actions.

An organization's greatest asset is its employees, and hence, it is important to take care of their needs. A few questions that arise in this context are as follows:

1. What would it take for them to recommend their friends and acquaintances to work for this company?
2. What can be improved to make this company a better place to work?

FUNCTIONING OF HRM SYSTEMS

HRM systems vary from organization to organization. They need to be commissioned according to the various factors that are responsible for the success or failure of an organization. Some of these systems are discussed in the following sections.

Culture, Organization, People, Systems

The HRM system depends on the culture prevailing in an organization, the organizational structure, the people working there, and the structured HR systems. They can make or mar an organization. In other words, the functioning of HRM systems depends on the culture, organization, people, and systems (COPS) in an organization. The reasons behind failure may be attributed to any one or a combination of these factors and they must be ascertained.

Checklists have been used to review the COPS status of the organization. Website 'accel team' has emphasized the need for using checklists for this purpose. These checklists are provided here for better understanding.

Checklist for Culture

1. Do the organizational leaders share success to enthuse followers?
2. Do the staff members feel pride while working in the organization?
3. Do the staff members prefer working in teams?
4. Are decisions made by seniors and circulated to the departments for conformance?
5. Does the senior management use power bases for problem solving?
6. Are juniors involved in the decision-making process on technical matters?
7. Do the people stay beyond normal office hours in case of emergency without any financial benefits?
8. Do the organizational leaders use participative styles to achieve organizational goals?
9. Do people accept changes without much resistance?
10. In a group discussion, can juniors freely express their ideas, opinions, beliefs, etc?
11. Does the organization encourage creativity and innovation among juniors?
12. Do staff members feel a sense of personal responsibility for their work?
13. Is quality emphasized in all aspects of the organization?

Checklist for Organization

1. Does the structure of the organization encourage quality performance?
2. Is the organization structure flexible to accommodate changing demands?
3. Is the structure too complex in certain areas? If so, what are the areas?
4. Do the staff members have role clarity in terms of clear roles and responsibilities?
5. Does the organizational structure tend to push problems rather than resolve them at the point of generation?
6. Do the procedures and management practices facilitate accomplishment of tasks?
7. Do people constantly seek to challenge the organizational structure?

Checklist for People

1. Do the people have the necessary knowledge and requisite competencies to perform the jobs assigned to them in the most effective manner?
2. Do the people understand their jobs and the processes to be followed?
3. Do the people have clear goals and objectives, and contribute to the overall business performance?
4. Do the people understand the concept of internal customer?
5. Do they have a customer orientation?
6. Do the people believe in interdependency of tasks?
7. Have people with potential been spotted and developed for the future?
8. Are the people encouraged to perform well through recognition, feedback, etc.?
9. Do the people know what is expected of them with regard to organizational performance?

Checklist for System

1. Do the organization's systems such as recruitment, selection, promotion, planning, management, information, and control, encourage effective performance?

2. Are the HR systems consistent across the organization?
3. Are there clear reward systems for effective performance within the work group?
4. Are the organizational systems reviewed periodically at predetermined intervals?
5. Do the various reward systems have objectivity to avoid any sort of bias, favouritism, or nepotism?

Having studied the various aspects of HRM, one needs to know how an organization can gain competitive advantage.

VRIO FRAMEWORK

> An organization gains competitive advantage and can sustain it when four criteria—value, rarity, imitability, and organization—are met.

The manner in which the human resources are managed determines their value as intangible assets of the organization.

Employees of the organization must understand the role of the HR function. Further, it is also important for organizations to understand the potential of human assets in providing competitive advantages. This is the reason why scholars are applying a resource-based view (RBV) that was originally proposed by Barney in 1991. According to the RBV, human resources contribute to sustain the competitive advantage for an organization only when they are valuable, non-tradable, non-imitable, and non-sustainable. Popularly referred to as the VRIO framework, the RBV of an organization determines the value of human resources for the organization on the basis of four criteria—value, rarity, imitability, and organization (VRIO). Only when these four criteria are met, people become a source for sustained competitive advantage for an organization. Figure 3.2 illustrates the VRIO framework.

Value The value of a product is created or enhanced by decreasing the costs of the product or services, adding features to the products without increasing costs, or even by delivering unique products to the consumers at a premium price which customers do not hesitate to pay. Since employees actually undertake innovations that can positively contribute to an organization's revenues, the HR department needs to be instrumental to energize, encourage them, and also enhance employee commitment and involvement. Hence, it is said that it is only the HRD that can create or enhance the value using creativity and innovation.

Rarity Distinctiveness or distinctive competence of a human being makes him/her perform tasks differently. Management personnel are required to enhance their enabling capacities through constant efforts such as competency building, shaping behavioural patterns, increasing proneness to accept changes, moulding attitudes, and so on. Products with unique features are considered valuable in the market.

Imitability Imitating or benchmarking organizational practices is a common exercise. People can provide competitive advantage to their organization when the HR characteristics of a company cannot be easily imitated by its competitors. An organization's unique history or culture is difficult to imitate and can be used to extract high levels of performance and commitment from the employees (Agarwala 2007). A specially-blended leadership style used by a leader while working on a challenging assignment of a team may be cited as an example of a unique HR characteristic that cannot be easily imitated by others.

FIG. 3.2 VRIO framework

Organization A dynamic manager can blend a few leadership styles, and develop a unique one which he may be willing to apply in an organizational scenario for task accomplishment. It is important for the organization to have the system and practice to allow the differentiable and unique HR practice to be used for success. Thus, innovative persons must be exploited and allowed to implement singular distinguishable ideas in the workplace for the benefit of the organization. Organizations need not consider much about the probability of successes from the implementation of the idea. It is organizational culture that promotes innovations in all facets of organizational life.

Hence, it can be said that the VRIO framework helps recognize the significant contribution of HR in achieving competitive advantages.

ROLES AND RESPONSIBILITIES OF HR MANAGERS

We have already dicussed the importance of HRM in IT, strategic management, competency enhancement, TQM, performance management, and leadership. At this stage, one should be aware of the roles and responsibilities of the managers who hold and steer the HR functions.

It is important for the HR manager to place his role on the same lines as that of the organization. Within this environment, the HR professional has to be a strategic partner, an employee advocate, and a change mentor to be able to survive the changing environment. Depending on the size of the organization, an HR manager has the responsibility of looking at all the functions that deal with the needs and activities essential for people management. Some of roles and responsibilities are as follows:

1. Recruiting and hiring—It is a process of discovering sources of manpower and employing effective measures for attracting that manpower in adequate numbers to facilitate the selection of an efficient working force in an organization.
2. Training and development—These processes help in enhancing and enabling the capacities of people to build their strengths and confidence in order for them to deliver more effectively.
3. Competency development—Competency is a cluster of related knowledge, skills, and attitude that affect a major part of one's job. It can be improved by means of training and development.
4. Organization development—It is an organization-wide effort to increase its effectiveness and viability, and move towards growth.
5. Communication—It is an activity that involves conveying meaningful information. At all times, the HR must convey all relevant information to the employees.
6. Performance management—It focusses on improving the performance of the organization, employees, and various other services.

> The role of the HR manager must be congruent with the organizational needs. The HR manager has responsibility for all the functions that deal with the needs and activities essential for people management.

7. Employee relations—This is a concept that works towards bettering the relations among the employees, as well as between the employee and the management.
8. Coaching, mentoring, and counselling—It is a practice of supporting an individual and helping him overcome all his issues in order to perform better.
9. Policy recommendation—Policy recommendations help to streamline management practices and reduce employee grievances. For example, a manager who is more than 35 years and, who possesses a minimum experience of 7 years, is entitled to receive the benefits stated in the company's administrative manual.

10. Wages, salary, and compensation benefits—These benefits are provided to the employees to keep them motivated towards their work and the organization.
11. Talent management and employee engagement—It is a management concept that works towards retaining the talent by engaging the person in a way which would further the organization's interest.
12. Leadership development—This activity refers to enhancing the quality and efficiency of a leader in an organization.
13. Team building—It focusses on bringing out the best in a team to ensure development of an organization, and the ability to work together closely to achieve goals.
14. Networking and partnering—It is also important to build relations with the external stakeholders, including the customers and suppliers for better business.

All these roles would be taken up separately in individual chapters in detail. We would now be concentrating on understanding the two main roles of HR managers with respect to the organization and the employee.

Role as Business Partner to Organizations

In today's times, HR managers in organizations function as strategic partners working closely with others to be able to contribute to the development and the accomplishment of the organization's business plan and objectives. The HR business objectives need to be aligned to the overall strategic business plan and objectives. The tactical HR representative needs to be deeply knowledgeable about the design and redesign of work systems to make the organization a better and a more efficient place to work in. This strategic partnership impacts all the HR services including hiring, rewarding, recognizing, developing appraisal systems, and many more.

To be an effective business manager, the HR personnel should be business-minded, knowledgeable about finance and accounting, and accountable and responsible for cost reductions and the measurement of all other HR programs and processes.

Role as Employee Advocate

As an employee advocate, the HR manager utilizes his knowledge and skills to promote people's interests for organizational successes. This advocacy includes expertise in creating a work environment in which people choose to be motivated and happy. It conforms to the maxim—live happily and work happily.

An HR professional fosters effective methods of goal setting, communication, empowerment through responsibility, and builds employee ownership of the organization. Apart from these functions, he also helps in establishing a suitable organizational culture and environment in which people have the competency, concern, and commitment to serve customers well.

STRATEGIC HRM

> SHRM deals with strategic assets, managing human resources from investment perspectives, and aligns human resource development strategy with the business strategy.

Strategic human resource management (SHRM) explores the strategic role of human resources in the arena of human resource environment, human resource evaluation and accounting, measuring and improving human performances, coaching, mentoring, counselling, and career management. SHRM deals with strategic assets, manages human resources from an investment perspective, and aligns the HR development strategy with the business strategy. SHRM focusses on people as the primary source of competitive advantage in the organization, and it is considered critical for a company's success. It has many perspectives such as fit (congruity), functional, economic, typological, inducement, investment, and involvement perspectives. These are described as follows:

Q 5

1. Fit or congruity perspective emphasizes that HRM practices should be integrated with the strategic planning process of the organization.
2. The functional perspective relies on the principle that an organization performs best when each departmental unit maximizes its contribution.
3. The economic perspective views HR as a unique and distinguishable source of competitive advantage.
4. The typology perspective helps in developing systematic comprehensive theories for the study of new innovations.
5. Inducement refers to supporting a highly competitive business environment.
6. Investment is likely to be found in firms where the business strategy is based on differentiation.
7. Involvement strategy is found in companies with a business strategy based on innovation and flexibility when they are confronted with a market that is characterized by highly competitive price.

It is necessary to understand the differences between traditional HRM and SHRM, and between SHRM and HR strategy, before we proceed further.

Q 8

Traditional HRM vs Strategic HRM

Agarwala (2007) has drawn differences between traditional HRM and SHRM mentioning the publication of J.A.Mellow. The approaches differ based on many dimensions. This is given in Table 3.4.

Strategic HRM vs HR Strategy

Although these two terms are used interchangeably, some distinction between SHRM and HR strategy can be drawn. Both describe an approach adopted by the management, focus on the long-term issues, and provide directions to the organization. Business strategies are outcomes of strategic management; human resource strategies are the outcomes of SHRM.

Agarwala (2007) has adopted the differences between SHRM and HR strategies from M. Armstrong, which is reproduced in Table 3.5.

Table 3.4 Traditional HRM vs Strategic HRM

Dimension	Traditional HRM	Strategic HRM
Responsibility for HR programmes	Staff personnel in the HR department	Line manager is responsible for people as HR manager
Focus of activities	Employee relations—ensuring employee motivation, productivity, and compliance with law	Partnerships with internal (employees) and external (customers, stakeholders, public interest groups) groups
Role of HR	Reactive and transactional	Proactive and transformational, functions as a change leader
Initiative for change	Slow, piecemeal, and fragmented, not integrated with larger issues	Fast, flexible, and systemic, change initiatives implemented in line with other HR systems
Time horizon	Short term	Considers various time frames as necessary (short, medium, or long term
Control	Bureaucratic control rules, procedures, and policies	Organic control through flexibility, as few restrictions on employee behaviour as possible
Job design	Focus on scientific management principles—division of labour, independence, and specialization	Broad job design, flexibility, teams and groups, and cross-training
Important investments	Capital, products, technology, and finance	People and their knowledge, skills, and abilities
Accountability	Cost centre	Investment centre

Table 3.5 Strategic HRM and HR Strategies

Strategic HRM	HR strategies
A general approach in strategic management of human resources	Outcome (manifestation) of the general SHRM approach
Aligned with the organizational intention about its future direction	Focus on specific organizational intentions about what needs to be done
Focus on long-term people issues; define the areas in which specific HR strategies need to be developed; focus on macro concerns such as structure, culture	Focus on specific issues that facilitate the achievement of corporate strategy
Strategic HRM decisions are built into the strategic business plan	Human resource strategy decisions derived from SHRM

TURNAROUND STRATEGIES FOR HRM

The activities performed by HR professionals have undergone a sea change. Over the years, particularly in the last decade, HR has witnessed a remarkable makeover in the way it has functioned. In the late nineties and early 2000s, the overhaul of HRM has transformed it into human capital management. In many cases, HR has assumed the role of an entrepreneur to put a structure in place to support innovative human resource practices and also to prop up entrepreneurs. The year 2010 is

Three stages of the turnaround strategy:
- Pre-turnaround
- Period of crisis
- Period of recovery

considered as the 'Entrepreneurial HR' (Gaurav 2010). The HR is also viewed as 'the silent turnaround specialist'.

Managing people is the key to survival and growth in the highly competitive global business environment. Prasad et al. (2007) argue that innovative practices in HR have revealed the best practices that can be used to reduce costs of employees and improve their quality. Based on their research findings, researchers also corroborate that HR managers must endeavour to streamline processes, lower their overhead costs, and enhance organizational transactions with strategic business partners.

The business scenario is turbulent like an ocean at the time of a tsunami. Businesses are like ships floating in the sea; some sink due to leakage. In order to save the vessel, the captain has to repair the leakage. Similarly, in order to save the business, the HR professional, as the captain of the ship, has to identify the loopholes and initiate the remedial measures, plan the turnaround strategies, and ultimately execute them. Prasad et al. (2007) prescribe three stages of the turnaround strategy—pre-turnaround, period of crisis, and period of recovery.

Pre-turnaround stage The first stage is the period before the profitability begins to decline. The company is still considered as profitable though it has started to lose ground.

Period of crisis This is the stage when the company has lost some market or customers, market share, and profitability starts declining as is evidenced by the company's poor cash share.

Q 7 **Period of recovery** This is the stage when the company starts implementing planned turnaround strategies, which may include scaling back production, adding features to products as identified through market reports, reengineering the processes, commissioning of new technology, aggressive marketing, and so forth. This is actually the recovering stage or the turning point of the business.

Whatever be the turnaround strategies, they need to be implemented by following certain steps. The steps are classified as changing the leadership, redefining the strategic focus, selling or divesting unnecessary assets, improving profitability, and making careful acquisitions.

Changing the leadership It is very important to analyse the effectiveness of leadership styles in an organization during its early days. These styles generate follower satisfaction to ease out performing the assigned task to them by way of motivation, role clarity, and most importantly, willingness, to contribute.

Redefining the strategic focus During the pre-turnaround stage, different companies adopt different strategies such as diversification, reengineering, quality improvement, new market penetration, customer satisfaction measurement for enhancement, launching new products, and so forth. This should be decided based on the kind of situation.

Selling or divesting unnecessary assets There may be some company assets that may be profitable, yet some others that may be required to be sold out. Depending on the balance sheet status, the cash received may be used to repay debts or any other purposes.

Improving profitability A big company that is in line with the cost centre can define a profit centre after which the company can assign responsibilities to the profit centre chiefs. All overhead expenditures need a thorough review to curtail avoidable and unnecessary expenditures by keeping the output targets unaltered. The company can also undertake zero-base manpower budgeting and plan layoffs by duly taking the industrial unrest into account. The company can pursue work redesign through engineering techniques. Another essential step is to relook the inventory management system to classify the items as fast-moving, slow-moving, and non-moving items, and dispose all those stores which cannot otherwise be used either in maintenance or in production systems.

Making careful acquisitions A company might be interested to acquire some other company to enhance its strengths. While doing so, it should consider its core products and business so as to quickly rebuild and replace its weak divisions.

Role of HR during Turnaround

During times of turnaround, HR professionals have to discharge some unique roles. To this effect, Prasad et al. (2007) mentioned about benchmarking results from 67 companies worldwide following innovative practices in HRM. They submitted a report with the best practices that could be used and technologies that can be adopted to reduce the costs of employees and improve their quality. Some of these practices are as follows:

1. Setting up a communication system—This system is set up with the help of the Internet and/or intranets and help to march towards paperless offices, quick retrieval of information, and highly reduced storage space.
2. Centralized HR department and call centres—The central HR department will frame policy and procedures; the call centre personnel will provide information based on the framed policy and procedures.
3. Introducing a 360-degree performance system—The system has multiple advantages over the traditional performance management system. It considers the opinions of both the internal and the external groups.
4. Implementing a human resource information system (HRIS)—This system is used to acquire, store, manipulate, analyse, retrieve, and distribute information to the related company's HR. HRIS supports strategic decision making to avoid litigations, to evaluate programmes or policies, or to support daily operating concerns (discussed in detail in Chapter 17).
5. Setting up a voice response system—This is a system that responds to voice commands, rather than input from a keystroke or a mouse. The uses for this kind of system range from necessity to convenience and security.
6. Fostering the e-recruitment practice—This involves recruiting through the Internet, following the explosion of information technology.
7. Introducing automated time keeping systems—The time and attendance system (generally SQL-based) application is designed for middle to large organizations.
8. Outsourcing non-core functions—This comprises employee leave, attendance system, payments based on salary system, etc.
9. Business process reengineering—This includes the fundamental rethinking and radical redesign of business processes to achieve dramatic improvements in critical existing measures of performance, such as quality, cost, service, and speed.

By implementing some of the innovative HR practices, the quality of internal organizational practices can improve, and in addition, possible risks and obstacles can be avoided. The costs associated with the tools are insignificant when compared to the benefits. Research findings further revealed that Fortune 500 companies have experienced phenomenal financial savings by introducing the new HR tools.

MOTIVATION

Without inspiration, the best powers of the mind remain dormant. There is a fuel within and it needs to be ignited with sparks (Johann Gottfried Von Herder). Human beings need motivation in both traditional and strategic HRM. Human relations encompass the important reactions of a person to other people in the society, club, organization, or anywhere else. The relations among individuals, between individuals and groups, and between groups constitute a critical phase of industrial psychology. Motivation cuts across all topics in industrial psychology. Employee motivation and attitudes to an event may vary from positive to negative. An employer wishes to hire positively-motivated people who want to work, and will continue to work hard throughout the years of employment.

There are four phases in the process of motivated behaviour—a need is aroused in the organism, behaviour is directed towards satisfying the need, the need is satisfied, and the organism relaxes (Pestonjee 1991). During the period between arousal and satisfaction of the need, the organism is in a state of tension, or a condition of unrest or uneasiness. The organism can only relax after the need is satisfied because the equilibrium has been restored. Equilibrium is defined as the state or condition in which no pressure (need) compels the organism to become active.

Motivating the employees should be an ongoing activity, though during good times when a company is growing and energy is high, this often seems unnecessary. Employees show up for work, work is done, activities progress, and business is good. However, if people start suffering from complacency, then the results may be serious and may invite disaster for the organization. In times of uncertainty, however, employee motivation becomes not only more important as a general principle, but is often critical for survival. In reality, employee motivation underlies success during all market cycles, but problems with employee motivation become even more apparent in times of uncertainty and change (Kennedy 2001).

People come to work in an organization from different cultural, social, and economic backgrounds. They come with diverse aspirations and work because they need something from the organization. Some might need money to provide for the family, others might need power, social status, and prestige, and someone else might need self-respect for accomplishing a work in an exemplary manner. Sometimes, for the same person, the needs change from time to time.

As discussed here, needs occur when there is a perceived discrepancy between an actual state and a desired state of being. Motivation is an activated state within a person that leads to goal-directed behaviour. Motivation comes in many forms, and what motivates one individual may not motivate the other. Therefore, it is important to understand how motivation differs among individuals, and how these differences affect the overall drive and determination of a team toward a goal. Motive is a construct representing an unobservable force that stimulates and compels a behavioural response, and provides specific direction to that response.

People are considered the functional instruments of an organization. Unless their behaviour and elemental attributes are fully understood, it is difficult to plan and execute any action. There is no better method of understanding human nature than by actually handling the person. However, it takes a long time to understand human behaviour. The second method of acquiring knowledge about a person is through study, but one should know what to study, how to study, and how much to study. It is the moral responsibility of the organization to create a proper motivational climate by adopting the following steps:

1. Creating an environment where the workforce can work freely, and apply their creativity and innovative skills.

2. Creating an organizational climate that facilitates interdependent work.
3. Establishing a competitive, but healthy climate through reward systems.
4. Generating a productive climate through personal examples.
5. Setting up an environment to encourage problem solving rather than avoidance.
6. Motivating individuals through coaching, counselling, and mentoring.

In an industrial set-up, motivation may be intrinsic or extrinsic. Intrinsic motivation is related to the job one is doing, and constitutes the job content. When a skilled operative performs a job well, he derives a sense of satisfaction. Intrinsic motivation satisfies the creative instinct in man. Thus, intrinsic motivation has its relevance in performance improvement and boosting productivity.

On the other hand, extrinsic motivation is external to the job and the job context. For example, financial incentives for a job well done may motivate the workers. Other external motivators could include the following:

1. Praise from the superior for good work
2. Recognition of good performance by the company in the form of public citation and award
3. Admiration of fellow workers
4. Improved working conditions and other facilities

Now, a few theories of motivations are briefly discussed such that you can refresh your knowledge.

Theories of Motivation

The most common theories of motivation are the following:

1. Abraham H. Maslow's Need Hierarchy or Deficient Theory of Motivation
2. Alderfer's ERG Theory of Motivation
3. Herzberg's Two Factor or Hygiene/Maintenance Theory
4. Mcclelland's Three Needs Theory

Maslow's Need Hierarchy (or Deficient Theory of Motivation)

The crux of Abraham H. Maslow's theory, which was propounded in 1943, states that human needs are arranged in a hierarchy composed of five categories. Maslow began his theory based on the assumption that man is an animal with a hierarchy of needs. Of these needs, there are some that are lower on the scale of necessity and others that are higher. According to the theory, as and when the lower needs are satisfied, higher needs emerge and are required to be satisfied. Higher needs cannot be satisfied unless the lower needs are fulfilled.

This resembles the standard economic theory of diminishing returns. The hierarchy of needs at work in the individual is a routine tool of the personnel trade, and when these needs are active, they act as powerful conditioners of behaviour in the form of motivators. From the lowest level to the highest level, the needs are physiological or body needs, safety and security needs, social or affiliation needs, ego or esteem needs, and self-realization or self-actualization needs. These are briefly discussed here:

Physiological or body needs This is the lowest level need, which has to be fulfilled before an individual craves for any of the other needs. An individual moves up the ladder responding first to the physiological needs for nourishment, clothing, and shelter. These physical needs must be equated with pay rate, pay practices, and to an extent with the physical conditions of the job.

Safety and security needs The next in order of needs is safety. This is the need to be free from any danger, either from other people or from the environment. The individual wants to be assured that he/she is secure, once his/her bodily needs are satisfied. The safety needs may also take the form of job security, security against disease, misfortune, old age, etc., as also against industrial injury. Such needs are generally met by safety laws, measures of social security, protective labour laws, and collective agreements.

Social or affiliation needs The next need is to be able to work in a group, be identified as a member of that group, and belong to it. This need also involves the need to love and be loved. In a large organization, it is not easy to build social relations.

Ego or esteem needs These needs reflect an individual's desire to achieve a certain status and recognition, respect, and prestige in the workplace. Some of these needs are also related to one's self-esteem, such as the need for achievement, self confidence, knowledge, competence, etc.

Self-realization or self-actualization needs After fulfilling all the other needs, an individual reaches this stage, as per Maslow's theory. The individual becomes growth-oriented, self-directed, detached, and creative. To quote Maslow, 'A musician must make music, an artist must paint, a poet must write, if he is to be ultimately happy. What a man wants to be, he must be. This need we may call self-actualization'.

The creativity of a man in producing new and practical ideas, and in bringing about productivity, innovation, and reducing costs might satisfy some of these needs.

Alderfer's ERG Theory of Motivation

Taking Maslow's theory as the starting point, Clayton Alderfer (1969) built a theory which he claims has realistic application to a work organization. According to him, Maslow's five levels of needs can be amalgamated into three—existence, relatedness, and growth—resulting in his approach being termed as the ERG Theory.

Existence needs These include all forms of physiological and safety needs or the first two levels of Maslow's hierarchy.

Related needs These include relationship with other people (social needs of Maslow's third level) and the need for recognition and respect that forms the part of Maslow's fourth level (esteem needs).

Growth needs Similar to Maslow's notion of self-actualization, these are concerned with the desire to be creative and to achieve full potential in the existing environment.

The novelty of Alderfer's theory lies not in the regrouping of the needs but in doing away with the hierarchy of human needs. He conceived the ERG theory, thereby avoiding the implication that the higher up an individual is in the hierarchy, the better he is. According to him, different types of needs can operate simultaneously, and if a particular path towards satisfaction is blocked, the individual will both persist along that path and at the same time regress towards more easily satisfied needs. In this way, he distinguishes between chronic needs which persist over a period and episode needs which are situational and can change according to the environment.

Table 3.6 Motivation and hygiene factors

Motivation factors	Hygiene factors
1. Achievement	1. Pay and benefits
2. Recognition	2. Company policy and administration
3. Work itself	3. Relationships with co-workers
4. Responsibility	4. Supervision
5. Promotion	5. Status
6. Growth	6. Job security
	7. Working conditions
	8. Personal life

Herzberg's Two Factor or Hygiene Theory

According to Herzberg (1968), every human has two different categories of needs, which are essentially independent of each other and affect his/her behaviour in different ways. When people are dissatisfied with their jobs, they are possibly concerned about the environment in which they are working. On the other hand, when people feel good about their jobs, this has to do with the work itself.

Herzberg's Two Factor, Hygiene, or Motivation Theory calls the first category of needs 'hygiene factors' because they describe a man's environment and serve the primary purpose of job satisfaction. Hygiene factors include company policies, administration, supervision, working conditions, interpersonal relations, wages and allowances, status, and security.

He calls the second category of needs 'motivators' since they seem to be effective in motivating the people to superior performance. Motivators or job content factors include achievement, recognition, increased responsibility, challenging work, growth, and development.

According to Herzberg, both the sets of factors work in only one direction. The absence of hygiene factors may dissatisfy the workers, but will not demotivate them. Similarly, in the absence of motivation factors, workers may remain motivated, but their absence does not make them dissatisfied. Table 3.6 gives a list of motivation and hygiene factors.

McClelland's Three Needs Theory

According to this theory, every individual gets motivated by a bundle of particular needs. It also posits that certain needs act more strongly on some individuals than the others.

In early studies that attempted to understand the qualities of leadership, one of the first types of personality traits to be observed was an apparent need by some people to excel without any external rewards. When asked to play a ring toss game without the imposition of any rules, some people would stand so close that they would never miss and some would stand so far away that winning or losing would be greatly due to chance. Others, however, would be very calculative in their distance to ensure that winning or losing was due in large part to their own skill. If they missed the toss, they would move a little closer; if they won the toss, they would step back a bit.

The idea of the theory is that we all have the drive to excel or achieve to some degree, but some people have a lesser amount of this drive than others. This theory proposes that each of us has these three needs, to a varying degree. The needs that are proposed in McClelland's theory are shown in Table 3.7.

Table 3.7 McClelland's theory

Need	Description
n_{ACH}	The need for achievement and the drive to excel; the drive to achieve in relation to a set of standards; the need to strive to succeed
n_{POW}	The need for power and the need to make others behave in a way in which they would not have behaved otherwise
n_{AFF}	The need for affiliation and the desire for friendly and close interpersonal relationships

Exhibit 3.4 gives an insight into how an internationally acclaimed HR personality motivated juniors.

Exhibit 3.4 Motivating juniors

Late Prof. Udai Pareek not only envisioned and initiated this book, but also made significant contributions to it. In fact, he was initially one of the co-authors of this book.

The bond between Prof. Pareek and the authors of this book was not merely academic but also emotional. He first met Dr Haldar in 1993, at the 35th annual convention of the Indian Institution of Industrial Engineering (Mumbai), in Hyderabad. Prof. Pareek's association with Ms. Juthika Sarkar, though not for many years, is invaluable. Prof. Pareek had complete faith in Juthika's academic potential and encouraged her to co-author this book.

In one of her mails to Prof. Pareek, Ms Sarkar addressed herself as 'Your disciple'. Prof. Pareek politely refused the honour. In his reply, he said, 'Dear Juthika, Thanks for your nice sentiment which I value, but I urge you to feel and correspond like a colleague. When you are a co-author, we are all colleagues. Best wishes, Udai'.

In spite of his towering academic achievements, his humility and sense of camaraderie continue to motivate everyone who was associated with him, to this date. Such an open attitude helped all his juniors, especially Dr Haldar and Ms Sarkar, in many ways to re-discover themselves and have more faith in their own potential both as academicians and, more importantly, as human beings.

One major strength of Prof. Pareek was his unending hope. He taught his juniors that to hope was not only to expect a certain occurrence but also to apply every conceivable effort to make it possible. This book is but one such hope that Prof. Pareek inspired the authors to realize.

While working on this book, Prof. Pareek fell sick. He stayed in the hospital for a long time before succumbing to his illness. The authors fondly recollect the memories they shared with this legend.

'Looking back, we treasure our conversations and correspondences with Prof. Pareek. He did not preach ethics in work, he practiced them. As his soul rests in heaven, his thoughts and beliefs continue to be the driving force in our day-to-day lives. We are fortunate to have been a part of his legacy and hope to pass on the values that we have inherited from him, to the future generations.

In fond memory of a mentor, colleague, and a friend,
Uday Kumar Haldar and Juthika Sarkar'

A NEW LOOK AT HR

Intellectual capital is a product of competence multiplied by commitment where competence represents the 'can-do potential' and commitment indicates the 'will-do potential' of an individual (Ulrich 2005). It depends on the HR manager to optimize the competence and commitment factors of individuals. The purpose of HRM is to achieve organizational effectiveness through individual effectiveness, and as such, it strives to create an enabling work environment in an organization which facilitates employees to achieve organizational effectiveness through individual effectiveness.

It stands established that HR is not merely a number game; rather it is the sum total of the inherited intelligence, acquired knowledge, learned skill, and accumulated experience over the years. Backed with commitment, human resources can sail an organization to excellence. HR is the greatest asset of an organization, and assumes highest importance since it constitutes the organization's intangible, irreplaceable, and inimitable resource.

> Intellectual capital is a product of competence and commitment. Competence represents the 'can-do potential'. Commitment indicates the 'will-do potential'.

After studying the whole chapter, it can be said that human resources are required to discharge four basic roles—strategic partner, administrative expert, employee champion, and change agent. These four roles need to be integrated into a coherent whole, and that too in a sequential manner, which would sound logical and produce results. Let us assume that an individual takes up an assignment as an HR manager. It is futile for the incumbent to talk about changes unless the rank and file believes the veracity and sanctity of such a prediction. In any organization, a sensible approach would be to start working shoulder-to-shoulder with people and developing a team spirit. This is where the concept of 'strategic partner' comes in. The HR practitioner has to transcend from a thinker to a doer.

Following this, the HR manager needs to win the confidence of one and all. He/she can do this once he/she emerges as the darling of the team. This can be realized if the HR manager exhibits the role of an 'employee champion'. Here, he/she acts as an emissary of the people to top management. Once this is accomplished, only then that the HR person can profess change. The role of 'change agent', therefore, comes eventually (Chattopadhyay 2009). In this capacity, the HR person acts as a facilitator who catalyses metamorphosis and ushers in the change process. Needless to mention, such a dovetailed approach would help elevate the HR's esteem in front of others.

In today's time, many visible transformations have taken place in most of the organizations. HR, a facilitatory function, is now a line function; and line functionaries are responsible to perform the HR functions. Hence, it is repeatedly said that HR needs to solve problems as administrative experts, behave like employee champions, effect changes, and act as strategic partners in an organization, to be successful in the market.

SUMMARY

Personnel management is concerned with the effective use of the skills of people. In any industry, conflicting interests are bound to exist between the working class and the management and understanding industrial relations are of vital importance. Industrial democracy provides workers with a sense of belongingness, enhances their commitment, encourages involvement, reduces wastages, and inculcates a sense of production and productivity. Organizations today engage contract labour under conditions stipulated in the Contract Labour (Regulation and Abolition) Act of 1970. Trade unions and management possess conflicting views about engaging contract labourers. Industrial disputes arise out of economic and non-economic causes. The Industrial Dispute Act of 1947 aims to maintain peace in industries.

HRM advocates working in groups. It helps to identify people who are under-valued, under-utilized, under-trained, and de-motivated and initiate remedial measures. Personnel management and HRM differ over several dimensions. HRM strategy must be developed systematically by following certain steps. It has its gamut spread over many areas of the organizations including IT, strategic management, competency development, TQM, PM, leadership, change management, and other organizational phenomena. Functioning of the HRM systems depends on the factors of culture, organization, people, and systems (COPS). The four criteria of value, rarity, imitability, and organization (VRIO) determine the worth of human resources in an organization.

The roles of the HR manager must be congruent with the organizational needs; and he/she should discharge responsibilities accordingly. HR managers should be treated as business partners and also as employee advocates. The activities performed by HR professionals have undergone a sea change in recent times. In the turbulent business scenario, HR managers need to contribute while finalizing the turnaround strategy in three stages, namely, pre-turnaround, period of crisis, and period of recovery. Innovative HR practices help to improve the quality of people and reduce possible risks and obstacles. Traditional HRM and strategic HRM differ on certain aspects. Intellectual capital is a product of competence and commitment.

KEY TERMS

Assertiveness is social boldness; saying 'no' if the situation demands it, and the ability to express one's own viewpoints without trampling upon others interests.

Contract labour refers to an indirect employee; a person hired, supervised, and remunerated by a contractor, hired in connection with a specific work of an establishment. Contract labourers can be hired directly by an establishment.

Information behaviour mainly means sharing of information. Organizational learning leads to enhanced information behaviour.

Information value refers to the integrity, uprightness, and reliability of information.

Job involvement is the degree to which people identify themselves psychologically with the job; high degree of involvement results in psychological empowerment.

Organizational commitment is a state in which an employee identifies with a particular organization, its mission, policies, objectives, goals, and wishes to maintain membership of the organization.

Satisfaction or job satisfaction in the workplace is just a constellation of attitudes about the job; the extent to which people like or dislike the various aspects of the work and fulfillment of the requirement of an individual by the work environment.

Strategic management is the process by which an organization formulates its strategies and implements them.

EXERCISES

Concept Review Questions

1. Explain the importance of HRM in the prevailing business scenario.
2. Elucidate the guiding principles of HRM.
3. Describe the systems under the purview of human resource administration.
4. What do you understand by the VRIO framework? Elucidate the last two components of the framework.
5. Define strategic human resource management. Clearly highlight the points of the differences between SHRM and human resource strategies.

Critical Thinking Questions

6. Discuss the steps in developing an HRM strategy in the context of the organization you are familiar with. Describe the organization in brief.
7. Narrate your understanding of the turnaround strategies for HRM. Discuss the stages in the context of an organization. Define the role of HR during turnaround.
8. Study any business magazine or visit any organization, and collect information on the dimensions of strategic HRM. Discuss the benefits those would have on the growth of the business.

Assignments

9. Take the help of a resourceful person of your college. Make a planned visit to at least two organizations. Collect information on how are they developing their HRM strategy. Discuss your findings with your professor and share with your classmates.
10. Take the help of your professor to visit at least two organizations, administer the checklists on COPS and comment on the functioning of the HRM system. Discuss your findings with the HR managers of the respective organizations

MANAGER'S INSIGHT

Perfect Security Systems has grown consistently since its inception 11 years back. The small team of around 30 to 40 has now grown to more than 130. This has prompted Mr Kapoor, the owner, to take HR activities seriously and establish a separate department with a team of four to five full-time staff members.

Perfect Security Systems wanted to employ training from time to time.

Since the market had become more demanding and competitive, Perfect Security Systems felt the extreme importance to upgrade of the skills of its employees, both behavioural and technical, on a regular basis. Of course, other functions of HR such as recruitment, selection, induction and job specifications also needed to be looked at more carefully.

Question:

Suggest an action plan for Kapoor.

BIBLIOGRAPHY AND WEB RESOURCES

Agarwala, Tanuja, *Strategic Human Resource Management*, Oxford University Press, New Delhi, 2008.

Barney, J., 'Firm Resources and Sustained Competitive Advantage', *Journal of Management*, Vol. 17, pp. 99–120, 1991.

Gaurav, Sunny, 'HR—The Silent Turnaround Specialist', *HRD Newsletter*, Vol. 25, Issue 10, pp. 30–31, January 2010.

Haldar, Uday Kumar, *Total Quality Management in IT Industry*, Proceedings, 46th National Convention organized by The Indian Institution of Industrial Engineering, Bangalore, 2006.

Haldar, Uday Kumar, *Human Resource Development*, Oxford University Press, New Delhi, 2009.

Haldar, Uday Kumar, *Leadership and Team Building*, Oxford University Press, New Delhi, 2010.

Hughes, Richard L., Robert C. Ginnett, and Gordon J. Curphy, *Leadership Enhancing the Lessons of Experience*, Tata McGraw-Hill Publishing Company Limited, New Delhi, 2008.

Lakshmi, S., Shyamal Mazumdar, and George Skaria, 'Building Future Leaders', *Indian Management*, Vol. 47, Issue 1, January 2008.

MacKinney, A., *The Assessment of Performance Change: An Inductive Example, Organizational Behaviour, and Human Performance*, Vol. 2, pp. 56–72, 1967.

Pareek, U. and Rao, T.V., *HRD System in Larsen &Toubro, Ahmedabad*, Indian Institute of Management, Unpublished Consultancy Report.

Pestonjee, D.M., *Motivation and Job Satisfaction*, Macmillan India Limited, New Delhi, 1991.

Rama Prasad, M.V., K. Sivarama Krishna, and K. Krishnaiah Chowdhary, 'Turnaround Strategy for Human Resource Management', *Indian Journal for Training and Development—Journal of Indian Society for Training and Development*, Vol. XXXVII, No. 3, July–September 2007.

Ramusson, Erika, *The 10 Traits of Top Salespeople, Sales, and Marketing Management*, Vol. 152, pp 34–37, August 1999.

Reddy, B. Rathan, *Effective Human Resource Training and Development Strategy*, Himalaya Publishing House, New Delhi, 2005.

Ulrich, Dave and Wayne Brockbank, *The HR Value Proposition*, Harvard Business Press, USA, 2006.

Web Resources

http://industrialrelations.naukrihub.com/industrial-relation-policy.html, last accessed on 31 August 2011.

http://www.ijric.org/volumes/Vol4/2Vol4.pdf, last accessed on 31August 2011.

http://www.vikalpa.com/pdf/articles/2001/2001_jan_mar_49_63.pdf, last accessed on 4 July 2011.

www.accel-team.com/human_resources/hrm_08a.html, last accessed on 25 December 2009.

www.labour.nic.in, last accessed on 31 August 2011.

A DEMORALIZED TRAINEE ENGINEER

Magna Industries Limited

Bangalore-based Magna Industries Limited (MIL) is an automobile ancillary industry with a turnover of ₹150 million, and has about 4,000 employees.

The company is professionally managed. A dynamic managing director heads the management team. He expects performance of high orders at every level. This is more so at the supervisory and managerial levels. Usually people of high calibre are selected through open advertisements to meet the personnel requirements at higher levels. However, the company fills the junior level vacancies by recruiting and providing in-house training.

The company has various training schemes; it offers one year training for fresh engineering graduates. During the first six months of training, the trainees are exposed to different functional areas, which are considered to be the core training for this category of trainees. By then, the trainees are identified for placement against the available or projected vacancies. Their further training in the next quarter is planned according to individual placement requirements. The last quarter consists of on-the-job training. After the training is completed, the trainee is required to perform the jobs expected of him/her after being placed.

MIL is a manufacturing industry. A majority of the technical graduates, who are appointed as trainees, happen to be mechanical engineering graduates. However, depending upon requirements, sometimes a few graduates from other disciplines are also recruited. The training is broadly structured, mainly keeping in mind the training scheme of mechanical engineering graduates. The company has a reasonably good system of manpower planning. The intake of trainees is generally planned on the basis of projected requirements.

Rakesh Sharma joined the company in the year 1983, after completing his graduation in paint technology from a reputed institute. He was taken as a trainee against a projected vacancy in the paint application department.

In MIL, there are only a few areas of interest for trainees in paint technology. Hence, Sharma's core training was planned only for the first three months. Thereafter, he was sent for on-the-job training to the paint application department. He took interest and showed enthusiasm in his work there. The report from the shop manager was quite satisfactory.

The performance of the trainee is normally reviewed once at the end of every quarter. The training manager personally talked to the trainee about his progress, strengths, and weaknesses. He also suggested ways to overcome the shortcomings.

At the end of the second quarter, the training manager called Sharma for his performance review. He appreciated his good performance. A month later, Sharma met with the training manager, and requested him to curtail the training period to seven months only, and to absorb him as an engineer. He argued that he has been performing like a regular employee in the department for the last quarter. As such, there was no justification for him to continue training any longer. Further, he indicated that by doing so, he could be more effective in the department as a regular engineer. He would gain seniority as well as monetary benefits, as trainees were only eligible for stipend. Regular employees were eligible for many other benefits such as dearness allowance, house rent, medical, conveyance, and education allowances, and so on, which was a substantial amount as compared to the stipend paid to a trainee. Sharma would remain more dedicated and motivated to fulfill his tasks.

The training manager turned down his request and informed him that this was not the company policy. He told him that any good performance or contribution made by the trainees during this period would be rewarded at the time of placement, on completion of the one year training. Further, he told Sharma that it would be a wrong precedence. Thereafter, Sharma's behaviour in the department changed. Initially, his change of attitude did not receive much attention. However, by the end of the third quarter, his behaviour had become erratic and unacceptable. When he was asked by the department manager to attend to a particular task, he replied that he was still on training and such tasks should not be assigned to a trainee. According to him, those jobs were meant to be attended by full-time employees and not by trainees.

The paint shop manager complained to the training manager about Sharma's behaviour and the training manager summoned him. During the discussions, Sharma complained that while all the remaining trainees were having a comfortable time as trainees, he was the only one who was put under a lot of stress and strain; the department was expecting too much from him. He felt that he should be duly rewarded for such hard work; otherwise, it was not appropriate to expect similar output from him.

The training manager assured Sharma that his good performance as a trainee would be appropriately taken into account, and rewarded when the right occasion arose. He tried to convince him that he should not harp on rewards right away, and being a trainee, his sole concern should be to learn as much as possible and to improve his abilities. He explained that he should have a long-term perspective rather than a narrow-minded approach. The training manager cautioned and warned Sharma stating that he was exhibiting a negative attitude, which would be viewed seriously. His demand for earlier placement was illogical and should not be expected. As he had already completed eight months, he would have to wait for only four more months. He advised Sharma that the career of an individual had to be seen with a long-term perspective, and that he should not resort to such childish behaviour as it would affect his career and image in the company.

Sharma seemed to have been convinced by the assurance given by the training manager and remained positive for sometime. However, when feedback was sought after a month, the report stated that he had become more averse to his work. He was again called for a counselling session and was given two weeks to show improvement. At the end of those two weeks, the training manager met the department manager to have a discussion about Sharma. It was found that there was absolutely no reason for him to nurture a grievance regarding poor rewards. It was decided that he be given a warning letter as per the practice of the company and accordingly this was done.

Rather than bring about any improvement, this further aggravated the situation. Sharma felt offended and retaliated by thoroughly disobeying any instruction given to him. The situation further deteriorated the relationship between the manager of the department and the trainee.

In the case of a rupture of relationship, the practice was normally to shift the trainee from the department where he was not getting along well so that he would be tried in some other department where he could have another opportunity for striking a better rapport. Unfortunately, in the case of Sharma, there was no other department to which he could be transferred, as that was the only department where his specialization could have been of proper use. By the time he completed his training, he turned out to be the one who was not at all acceptable in the department for placement. His behaviour and involvement were lacking. In view of this, the department manager recommended that he be taken out of that department. When Sharma was informed about this, he was thoroughly depressed.

One of the primary objectives of the training department is to recruit fresh graduates who have a good potential, and train them to be effective persons in different departments. They are taken after a rigorous selection process, which includes a written test, a preliminary, and a final interview. During the training period, their aptitudes, strengths, and weaknesses are identified. Their placements in departments are decided primarily on the basis of their overall effectiveness there.

Here is a case where the person happened to be hard working in the beginning, but turned out to be a failure in the end. The training manager was conscious of this serious lapse and was not inclined to recommend his termination. However, at the same time, it was difficult to retain a person whose track record was not satisfactory. He still felt that a fresh look could be given into the case, but was unable to find a way out. He was now faced with the dilemma of whether to terminate Sharma's service or not.

Questions

1. Where did things go wrong?
2. What are the options available to the training manager other than termination of Sharma's service?
3. Did the paint shop manager handle the trainee properly?
4. How would you put Sharma back on the right track?
5. Identify the relevant IR issue.

Source: Haldar, U.K., *Human Resource Development*, Oxford Higher Education, Oxford University Press, New Delhi, 2009.

HR MANTRA Organizational resources

An organization uses many resources, namely, men, machines, material, time, money, etc., to manufacture and market its products. Of these resources, the value of machines and material depreciates. Time is spent at the uniform rate of 60 seconds per minute, 60 minutes per hour, and 24 hours per day. Decisions on selection and utilization of machines and purchase of materials are taken by human beings. Decisions on productive utilization of time are also taken by human beings. They are the decision-makers. Being a type of resource, men are the source for all other types of resources. The quality of decisions is the root cause behind the success or failure of any organization. As time passes, knowledge, skills, maturity, pragmatism, experience, and wisdom also increase. With the passage of time, material resources depreciate, but human resources appreciate.

The mantra: Human beings can make or mar an organization.

UDAI PAREEK

Born on 21 January 1925 in Jaipur, Dr Udai Pareek completed his schooling in his home town. He did his BA from St. John's College, Agra University in 1944; B.T. at Teachers' Training college, in Ajmer from the Agra University in 1945; and secured an MA in psychology from Calcutta University in 1950. He also obtained his MA in philosophy from Agra University in 1952, and Ph D. in psychology from the University of Delhi in 1956. Besides, he also got his diploma certificate in research methods from Italy. As his biography would indicate, Dr Pareek travelled widely and experienced living in most countries representing the modern world ranging from USA to Europe to Asian and South Asian countries such as Thailand, Indonesia, Singapore, and Malaysia. His students are spread across the world. He admired all cultures and people from different countries, and for the same reason he also had close friends in all parts of the world.

Any history of the human resource development (HRD) movement of India or any book on HR issues would be incomplete and irrelevant without mentioning the contributions of late Dr Udai Pareek. Popularly known as the 'pioneer of HRD in India' and 'father of HRD movement of India', Dr Pareek changed the thought process of many organizations and individuals. He influenced the life of thousands of HR professionals as a mentor, coach, and a scholar, who kept in touch with diverse worlds of academic, industrial, and management and research.

He could foresee the changing role of HR functions. Accordingly, he always shared his concern about the image of HR professionals in the country and the growing need of HR professionals to become a strategic partner in business, and so on. A survey report was published in *Business Manager's* November 2006 issue about the image of HR people amongst the employees. The results showed that 53 per cent of employees dislike HR. He got really concerned by this information and took up this issue at the national level during conferences and also wrote about the same on his blog. All his life, he lived every moment for the progress of the HR profession.

During his study at the University of Calcutta, the strong traditions of psychoanalysis and experimental psychology had a great impact on him. He was deeply influenced by his exposure to Marxism as a student, his extensive readings, and his participation in the student movement. His encounter with Mahatma Gandhi, a living apostle of humanism, and resistance to oppression led to the development of 'transformational leadership' (electrifying traditionally helpless people into mass movement and action).

After completing his doctoral work, he worked as a psychologist for several years in 'basic education', a name given by Gandhi to education that was designed to make students self-sufficient by giving them an education more relevant to Indian society. During this period of work with teachers and headmasters, he became interested in the work of Kurt Lewin and his associates, and began to see action research as a key to help them help themselves to solve their problems. Interestingly, this idea was also inspired by Gandhi.

In 1965, the technical cooperation mission (the forerunner of the US agency for international development) brought Stephen M. Corey, the then dean of Teachers College of Columbia University, to India. Max Corey introduced Dr Pareek to the 'T-Group' experience at his home in New Delhi. Dr Pareek's thirst for knowledge made him arrange a visit to the US to learn more about action research, social change, and group dynamics. Among other things, he did an internship at the National Training Laboratories and later, became a Fellow there as well.

While working with the small industry extension training institute, he worked with Rolf Lynton and David McClelland. Lynton had done extensive work in Southeast Asia with groups of Asian leaders on issues of dependency, leadership, competition, and collaboration, using the Tavistock approach. With McClelland, he worked on developing entrepreneurs through enhancing their achievement motivation. This involved changing the motivational pattern of key persons in a community. This initial work influenced national strategies of small industry development in India, as well as the practices of government agencies, financial institutions, and development projects.

In addition to the five needs or motivation as suggested by David McClelland, he proposed the concept of a 'need for extension', a need to relate to a larger group or cause. He interviewed a number of Indian managers and collected information about critical incidents that shed light on the effectiveness of management with different motives. This resulted in an approach avoidance concept of motivation and an instrument to measure both the approach and avoidance aspects of six motives: achievement, affiliation, influence, extension, control, and dependency.

Dr Pareek's biggest contribution to HR is the concept of 'role'. Based on in-depth interviews with managers about why they worked or felt demotivated, Dr Pareek developed a concept of 'role efficacy' with regard to the potential effectiveness of an organizational role. He developed an instrument to analyse 10 aspects of role efficacy such as self-role integration, proactivity, creativity, confrontation, centrality, influence, growth, inter-role linkage, helping, and superordination. He then designed some organizational development work to increase role efficacy as a way of motivating roles rather than individuals.

His concern for the development of persons through their organizational roles led him to redesign the personnel function by following the concept of HRD, which differed from the western concept in three ways. It was value-based (focusing on values of openness, confrontation, trust, authenticity, proactive measures, autonomy, collaboration, and experimentation); it included all human units in an organization (person, role, dyad, team, inter-team, and organization), and it dealt not only with training and education, but with all systems of development (work systems, appraisal systems, career systems, training systems, cultural systems, self-renewal systems).

During his lifetime, Dr Pareek served and provided guidance to several organizations, institutions, and professional bodies in the area of HR. He was the chairperson of the Human Resource Laboratory of the Applied Behavioral Sciences at EMPI Business School, New Delhi, chairperson of the governing board of the Institute of Developmental Research and Statistics, Jaipur; advisory member for Asia and the Middle East of Human Resource Development International; member of the academic advisory board of the Global Committee on the Future of Organization Development (OD) (sponsored by the OD institute in collaboration with the OD Network and the International OD Association); chairperson of the governing boards of the Institute of Development Studies, Academy of Human Resource Development (promoted by the National HRD Network of India), the South Asian Association of Psychologists (SAAP); founder president of the National HRD Network and the Indian Society of Applied Behavioural Science; Chairperson of the Scientific Advisory Committee and vice president of the management board of IIHMR.

He was on the governing boards of several institutes and companies, including Globarena, Hyderabad; National HRD Network; GGS Indraprastha University, Delhi; Banasthali Vidyapeeth; FORE School of Management, New Delhi; IILM Academy of Higher Learning, Jaipur; State Institute of Health and Family Welfare, Rajasthan. He was the only Asian to become Fellow of the National Training Laboratories (NTL), and the only Fellow from India of the Society for the Study of Social Issues (SPSSI). He was a Fellow of the Indian Society of Extension Education.

Some of the organizations he worked for are USAID Organization Development advisor, Ministry of health of the Republic of Indonesia; USAID Management Training System Development advisor, Ministry of health; professor of Organizational Behaviour, Indian Institute of Management, Ahmedabad; director, School of Basic Sciences and Humanities, and chairperson, Director of School of Social Sciences, University of Udaipur; professor and head of the department of social sciences, National Institute of Health Administration and Education, New Delhi; visiting professor of psychology (with joint appointment in Carolina Population Center), University of North Carolina, Chapel Hill, N.C. USA; director, Small Industry Extension Training Institute, Hyderabad; education psychologist, Indian Agricultural Research Institute, New Delhi; psychologist, National Institute of Basic Education, New Delhi, etc.

Some of his consultation/professional activities are: team development of holding companies of Egypt and Alexandria; UNIDO organization development consultant to the Institute of Computer Development of Hungary, Budapest; UNIDO consultant on transfer of training technology, MIDF, Malaysia; organization development consultant to Bank Pertanian, Malaysia; USAID Organization Development advisor, Rural Development Program of NTT, Province of the Republic of Indonesia; organization designing (and restructuring) of some Indian organizations, including Bharat Coking Coal Ltd, Kothari Industries Ltd, Bharat Earth Movers Ltd, State Bank of India, Industrial Development Bank of India, Punjab & Sind Bank, Unit Trust of India, Petrofils Ltd, CASP-PLAN, organization development in several Indian organizations, including State Bank of India, Indian Airlines, HMT, Larsen & Toubro, BCCL, ICI, Holy Family Hospital, Medical Mission Sisters RPG Transmission, team building in several companies such as Rickett & Coleman,

Swed Forest, Red Barna (Sri Lanka), Kidavari (an NGO working for out-of-school adolescents) and a group in Malaysia (with NTL of USA and ORI of Malaysia).

He has authored and edited about 60 books and more than 360 papers. He has been given several national and international awards and has been cited in a large number of national and international biographical reference books. Some of these are: *India's Who's Who*, Delhi; *Who's Who in the World*; *Dictionary of International Biography*, London; *Writers Directory*, London; *Men of Achievement*, Cambridge, England; *All India Educational Directory*, Chandigarh; *Contemporary Authors*, USA; *Famous India*; *Reference Asia*; *Leaders of India* etc.

His contributions to the arena of HRD are infinite, immeasurable, and invaluable. Above all, he loved humankind and always endeavored to encourage and uplift new faces. With due respect to the departed soul, the biography of the eminent and legendary personality is presented here.

References

Email from Prof. Dr Sushma Khanna, dated 24 September 2011.

HRD Newsletter, National HRD Network, Volume 26, Issue 1, June 2010.

CHAPTER 4

Talent Management and Employee Engagement

LEARNING OBJECTIVES

After studying this chapter, you will be able to

- Understand the concept of talent management and its various facets
- Identify talent management as an HR function and understand talent mapping
- Recognize the pillars of the talent mapping programme
- Distinguish between hiring and engagement
- Comprehend talent wars

OPENING CASE

Managing Talent in Public Sector Banks

About Canara Bank

The Canara Bank Hindu Permanent Fund was founded by late Mr Ammembal Subba Rao Pai, a philanthropist, in 1906. It was converted into a limited company and was named Canara Bank Ltd in 1910. In 1969, after nationalization, it came to be called Canara Bank. The bank has many significant milestones to its credit.

Rewards for talents

Staff members of public sector banks get rewards; however, the rewards are not comparable with those given by private sector banks and foreign banks. Nevertheless, things are constantly improving in the public sector banks.

Challenges faced by public sector banks

Attrition and poaching have made things difficult for public sector banks. The banks' ability to hire fresh talent has been constrained by structured compensation packages with limited flexibility. Additionally, for public sector banks, talent nurturing has also become a major issue.

Actions needed to retain talent by public sector banks

Banks need to find ways to provide incentives to the available talent. This needs a relook at the compensation packages commensurate with the paying capacity, differentiation of the performers and non-performers, and the institution of a reward mechanism.

Talent management requires the following actions:

1. Restructuring the organization by building business capability through excellent programmes to attract, engage, and retain the most valued employees
2. Underlining the importance of talent differentiation
3. Aligning the talent management strategy to the overall business plan

4. Implementing a 'nuance' approach towards the most-valued employees with a paradigm shift from uniform service regulations and compensation package structure to flexible compensation package and service conditions

The roadmap

Banks should put in place appropriate talent audits that could play a vital role in instilling a sense of confidence in the management and HR functions in the organization. There is an urgent need to address the key drivers in attracting and retaining the right talents. Building an ideal work environment, and cultivating and retaining talents in these difficult times requires effective management and leadership. It involves maintaining a talent-friendly environment, and ensuring alignment of talent expectation with core business strategy.

Change in management systems

The alignment of talent expectation with the core business strategy necessitates periodical revisiting of the dynamics of compensation management, performance measurement, organizational change, employee relation management, employer branding, talent development, and succession planning. However, the ultimate requirement is that employee rewards and recognition move beyond compensation and benefits. In the world of flux and flow, turbulence and volatility, attrition and organizational dynamics, employers need to offer a holistic package to their employees. While monetary aspects should be an integral part of this package, organizations must not ignore the non-monetary incentives. Both monetary and non-monetary incentives impact and positively contribute to the structural transformation of any organization.

Succession planning

Succession planning (management succession planning is a key concern for all organizations, wherein a senior executive identifies his successor) is necessary to prevent losses of any technical or corporate knowledge. It helps in driving business growth, by retaining valued persons. For public sector banks, succession planning requires linking the planning model to the overall strategic plan of the banks. Succession planning enables harnessing the power of talent management.

Succession planning has emerged as a predominant need for all public sector banks to develop their second line of senior executives. As part of succession planning, Canara Bank had formed a 2020 club, wherein the bank identified and inducted potential leaders for the future. A cross-section of the bank officers helped the bank in enhancing awareness among officers about the importance accorded to them by the organization. The bank developed employee expertise by relentless skill upgradation.

Competency mapping

The bank further felt the need for competency mapping and put requisite action plans in place, in order to develop identified personnel to take the organization forward in the next decade.

Streamlining policy

Within the constraints of functions and working of public sector banks, Canara Bank attempted to streamline the human resource management policies and procedures in conformity with the needs of the present and the expectations of the future.

Source: Rao, *Business Manager*, Vol. 16, No. 9, March 2008.

Learning points

- There is a need to nurture talent in the organization.
- Expectations of organizational members should be aligned with organizational goals.
- Every organization has to find ways of growth through proper HR processes.

INTRODUCTION

Today, the business scenario is seen to be unremittingly changing. There are many players in the competitive market. Boosting productivity, augmenting distinctive competence, gaining competitive advantages, acquiring excellence, identifying new ways of processing, winning against cutthroat competition, discovering innovative organizational practices and benchmarking them, managing changes, and utilizing the most valuable human resources need talent and continue to be the principal concern of any organization.

Employees can be divided into four categories—stars, lone wolves, corporate citizens, and apathetic employees—based on their extent of job involvement and affective commitment.

Blau and Boal (1987) categorized the employees of an organization on the basis of the extent (high and low) of their job involvement and affective commitment. The employees were divided into four categories—stars, lone wolves, corporate citizens, and apathetic employees.

Employees having high affective commitment and high job involvement fall under the category of 'stars'. For this category of people, work is more important than anything else. Their work is important to their self-image. Behaviourally, they exert a high level of personal task-related effort and a high level of group maintenance effort to help maintain their commitment to the organization (Blau and Boal 1987).

Star Star employees are upwardly mobile in the organization and are supported by powerful coalitions or individuals within the organization. They are often even considered as role models for other employees. Star employees possess the potential to contribute greatly to the organization.

Lone wolves They form the group of employees that has high job involvement, but low affective commitment. They are workaholics. Work and/or jobs are important to them, but they do not identify strongly with their organization. They only relate with factors that are directly related to their work. They are low on organizational loyalty.

Corporate citizens These employees love their organizations, prefer to highlight the achievements of the organization, and thus, have high affective commitment. However, their job involvement is low; hence, they are unable to relate to their jobs. Behaviourally, these people are seen as employees who are always ready to work towards achieving organizational goals.

Apathetic employees These are employees with low job involvement and low affective commitment. At one point of time, they might have been highly motivated by their jobs and strongly committed to their organization, but for some reason are now indifferent to both aspects. Behaviourally, they are prone to calculative behaviour. They exert minimal work effort, just enough to maintain organizational membership, and try to leave the organization at the earliest opportunity, as they look for high extrinsic rewards.

The four categories of employees are shown in Figure 4.1.

Organizations are always looking out for new talent. Talent refers to people with a high degree of aptitude, having the innate and instinctive ability to contribute to organizational excellence. It is hard to search and get talented people for an organization; it is even harder to retain them. From this standpoint, HRM has received a new dimension of responsibility. Organizations always need employees who are capable of achieving business goals. Talent is 'an identifiable ability that is perceived to add immediate or future value to any prescribed activity, discipline, or enterprise' (Maurice 2003).

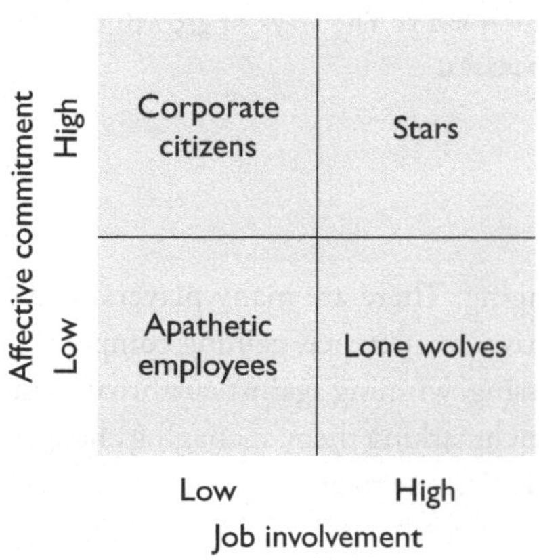

FIG. 4.1 Employee categorization

As organizations struggle to find, retain, motivate, and develop their people adequately, they face an ever-dynamic talent landscape that is globally more competitive, demanding, and expensive than ever before. Growing numbers of aging retiree employees, shifting business requirements, and attractive competing job offers are keeping HR professionals on their toes.

FOCUS OF HRM

As per the discussion in the previous section, the main focus of HRM in many organizations is talent management. Talent management is a

Talent management is a conscious, deliberate approach to attract, develop, and retain people with the aptitude and ability to meet current and future organizational needs.

conscious and deliberate approach to attract, develop, and retain people with the right aptitude and abilities to meet current and future organizational needs. It involves development of an individual and an organization in response to the changing and complex business environment. Organizations demand the creation and maintenance of a supportive and people-oriented organizational culture to succeed. The HRM profession and practices have undergone a sea change.

HRM services should not merely be mired down into managing trivial and traditional administrative functions; rather, the services should look at providing value to the organization by way of acquiring, retaining, nurturing, multiplying, developing, advancing, promoting, recognizing, networking, and engaging talents in the organization. They must be directed towards identifying people of all levels, who perform activities that are critical to the organization. The need to focus on HRM will be further dealt with in the section, 'Talent Management—An Essential HR Function'.

TALENT MANAGEMENT

A talented employee with high potential can make a significant difference to the current and future performance of the organization. In fact, talent management is considered as a driver to organizational success. According to the Society of Human Resource Management's (SHRM) glossary of terms, talent management is 'the implementation of integrated strategies of systems designed to increase workplace productivity by developing improved processes for attracting, developing, retaining, and utilizing people with the required skills and aptitude to meet current and future needs'. In other words, talent management is an integrated system to attract, develop, retain, and utilize people having the requisite knowledge, skills, aptitude, and attitude to contribute towards the achievement of an organization's present and future objectives and goals.

SHRM undertook a survey to gather views on some aspects of talent management from the HR professionals from different types of industries scattered over different territories of the USA. SHRM surveyed a total of 388 HR professionals who shared their views with the SHRM team. The key findings are interesting and are displayed in Exhibit 4.1.

Exhibit 4.1 Talent management survey SHRM 2006

1. Overall, 53% of HR professionals indicated that their organizations had specific talent management initiatives in place.
2. Around 47% reported that their organizations did not have such initiatives in place.
3. Large organizations consisting of 500 or more employees that were profit-oriented and having five or more staff members in their HR departments, were more likely to have talent management plans in place.
4. Among respondents who reported that their organizations had specific talent management systems in place, 76% of HR professionals indicated that talent management was a top priority for their organizations.
5. The top four areas in which organizations needed improvement in talent management practices were building a deeper reservoir of successors at every level, creating a culture that made employees want to stay with the organization, identifying gaps in current employee and candidate competency levels, and creating policies that encouraged career growth and development opportunities.
6. Only 20% of the employees indicated that their organizations adequately prepared their junior or mid-level employees to step into senior leadership positions.
7. Although employee retention may be the biggest talent management concern that organizations will confront in the next decade, less than 31% of HR professionals indicated that their organizations had formal budgets in place for retaining employees. Most of all, they

(Contd)

Exhibit 4.1 (Contd)

were not viewing this phase of the talent management process seriously. Overall, the employee retention budgets in these companies were significantly lower in comparison with the budgets for recruitment and employee development.

Source: Emre Kavukcuogu Zaman 2008

The key to talent management should start with talent searching and recognizing individuals for their unique strengths.

In simple terms, talent management is simply the art and science of attracting, developing, and retaining talents. These are the three key deliverables of the HR function. Talent management describes the process through which employers of all kinds anticipate their human capital needs and set about meeting them. Procuring the right people with the requisite knowledge and right skills for the right jobs is the main purpose of talent management. The focus of talent management tends to be more on management and executive positions. It has a direct and a quantifiable connection to the overall business risk management, business improvement, and cost management.

Talent management involves individual and organizational development in response to a changing and complex operating environment. It includes the creation and maintenance of a supportive and people-oriented organizational culture. Decisions about talent management shape and mould the competencies of organizations and their ultimate success. From the perspective of individuals, these decisions determine the path and pace of their careers. Talent management practices, in the long run, can have a crucial impact on the society as well.

The key to talent management begins with talent searching and recognizing individuals for their unique strengths. Managers need this skill at observing the unique differences between individuals and their talents. Organizations have to ensure that this talent is provided with the environment to flourish. In order to spot talent at a recruitment interview or at work, one has to keep an open mind and go
Q 1 beyond the accepted norms of the pedigree, academic credentials, and social impression. The mantra is to see beyond the first impression and beyond the existing knowledge, skills, and attitude and look for passion. Once managers discover the applicant's edge, they should give them a chance to serve the organization even if they do not fit the 'norms'; they should believe in them and support them.

Talent management encompasses manpower planning and recruitment, induction and placement, performance management system, development system, multi-source feedback, potential appraisal and career system, compensation management, reward system, separation and beyond, and developing workers and sub-staff. All these would be discussed in detail in the forthcoming chapters.

Acquiring Talent—Manpower Planning and Recruitment

In order to recruit the right people, an organization has to structure its manpower planning and recruitment process. Manpower or human resource planning forms the core of HRM, and deals with the acquiring of human resources of an organization. Planning consists of the process of knowing how to select appropriate individuals as employees based on their skills, knowledge, pragmatism, maturity, etc., and making sure that they are smoothly fitted into their assigned roles as well as the overall system. Thus, smooth functioning of the organization to achieve its business objectives and goals is ensured. Planning further refers to using the available assets for the effective implementation of the production plans.

After the preparation of plans, people are grouped together to achieve the organizational objectives. Apart from selecting suitable employees, manpower planning also deals with the process of upgrading the existing employees. The human resources are the most valuable assets of any organization and are the only resource that appreciates. This is because they contribute to the realization of its business objectives. Human resources also contribute their time and expertise to the overall functioning of their organization. Thus, the process of manpower planning and staffing is crucial to the business development of an organization.

The recruitment and selection activities are by far the major functions of the HR department as they create the competitive strength of the company. Recruitment process must be based on a strategy formulated by the company. The company has to decide the positions to be filled through manpower planning, carrying out job analysis, developing the job description and job specifications, followed by finalizing the man specification. Obviously, the company must utilize a band of people accustomed for this job. This is followed by designing the advertisement by conforming to the attract-interest-desire-action (AIDA) model strictly in that order to attract talent for the company, selecting suitable selection tools to facilitate background investigations, job specifications, tests for screening, etc.

Selection tools that are meticulously used also help a company to avoid 'select error' and 'reject error'. *Select error* refers to the situation when a person is selected and cannot perform the assigned tasks or contribute anything to achieve the goals. This happens either due to choice of wrong selection tools or some defects in administering the tool. On the other hand, *reject error* refers to the mistake when the attributes of a well-qualified person remain unidentified during the selection process and he/she is rejected. Being rejected by the interviewers of one company, he/she may join some other company at the same or higher position and is seen to perform there.

There are a few more points that managers must keep in mind to avoid problems or mistakes at this level:

1. Focus recruiting efforts on young talent from small towns and cities, and base their compensation packages on the job role and skill sets rather than only on their qualifications. Remember that youth from villages, small towns, and cities are likely to be more ethical. Probabilities of attrition will be less, too.
2. Performance reviews should be conducted at close intervals, say at six-month intervals rather than annually. They can even design and provide certain innovative reward programs over the more traditional ones of recognizing employee performance.
3. Allow the employees to identify their developmental needs. Place learning and educational responsibilities solely on them. It is advisable to forego conventional company-mandated training. Provide employees with professional development opportunities.
4. Offer skill-based and performance-based compensation and long-term incentives to employees.
5. Try to identify and eliminate as many routine and tedious processes and jobs as possible.
6. Allocate human resources to vigorous entry-level training.

Scarcity of resources might be an issue in India and the rest of the world in the years to come. However, we can continue to be optimistic for many reasons. India has a rich source of educated young talent base. It is important to understand that they can be developed to be readily usable for industries through macro level planning.

Manpower planning and recruitment is discussed in greater detail in Chapter 6.

Retaining Talent—Induction and Placement

Every organization conducts an induction programme for new recruits. During this programme, the organization tries to identify the inner potential of the recruits such as their likes and dislikes, motives, personality attributes, lifestyle inventories, and attempts to place them accordingly to derive the best from them. Placement based on psychological attributes reduces attrition.

Once the selection and administrative formalities are complete, an employee is placed in an appropriate job. He then needs to be familiarized with the job and the organization by way of induction. Induction is the process of receiving and welcoming an employee when he first joins the company and the basic information to settle down is shared with him, after which he is able to start work.

Induction of new recruits helps in building a two-way channel of communication between management and employees, and facilitates creating an informal atmosphere and building team work. Effective induction helps to integrate the new employee into the organization and to develop a sense of belonging. A formal induction programme makes it easier for the recruits to have a good start. Familiarization of the recruits with the organization is the main concern during induction, as a lot of information about the organization is supplied to the recruits.

The curriculum of an induction should include genesis and evolution of the organization, operations, organization structure, policies and procedures, products and services, infrastructure, safety measures, benefits and services of employees, standing orders and disciplinary procedures, opportunities for training, promotions, transfer, suggestion schemes, rules and regulations, grievance redressal system, etc.

After the stage of induction is completed, the process of placement begins. It is a process of assigning a specific job to each of the new recruits. It involves assigning a specific task and responsibility to an individual, considering the prerequisites of the task and knowledge base and skills possessed by the new recruit. This process of matching is vital for organizational effectiveness and satisfaction of the recruit.

A carefully-designed placement system can improve employee morale, helps in reducing employee turnover and absenteeism, helps in diminishing accident rates, avoids misfit between the employee and the job, and finally helps the employee to work as per the predetermined objectives of the organization.

> A carefully designed placement system improves employee morale, which in turn reduces employee turnover and absenteeism.

To remain competitive, companies need performers or talents. After attracting and placing them at appropriate job profiles, companies need to develop methods to retain the new talent. Some views on talent retention are shown in Exhibit 4.2.

Exhibit 4.2 View on talent retention by a reputed IT service company

The general manager of a global IT services company, a fully-owned subsidiary of a reputed company, possesses a distinctive view with regard to talent retention. The company is rated among the 'world's most reputed companies' by *Forbes* magazine and among 'India's most valuable companies' by *Business Today*. The manager believes that the talent retention initiative should start from the talent acquisition stage.

During the selection process, the interviewer should attempt to identify the cultural background of the prospective talent and the compatibility or like-mindedness with the culture prevailing in the company.

He emphasizes that after joining a company the first three to seven days is comparable with one's honeymoon period. It must be clearly understood and the manager should organize the induction to inculcate and develop a positive image about the company.

To make their stay longer in the company, employees need continuous mentoring. Personal development plans must

(*Contd*)

Exhibit 4.2 (Contd)

be organized to ensure learning and growth. In addition, they need challenging assignments that can be accomplished by utilizing their creative potential.

He strongly emphasizes and accentuates that attractive compensation packages alone cannot help in retaining talents in an organization.

Induction and placement will be discussed more extensively in Chapter 7.

Q 8 Nurturing Talent—Performance Management System

Potential capabilities of human resources must be honed through a structured performance management system. Nurturing talent refers to managing and developing employees to achieve business goals. Performance management system focuses on every employee because each of them has a bearing on business performance. Performance concerns the behaviour directed towards achieving an organization's missions and business goals, and manufacturing products or services resulting from that behaviour. In other words, it refers to only the behaviour related to the production of goods or services by maintaining the qualitative requirements.

Performance is a multidimensional variable (MacKinney 1967) and is a conglomerate of several dimensions. Hence, people high on one dimension may not be high on the other, and such standings may change over time.

Performance management is the means through which managers ensure that employees' activities and output are congruent with the organization's goal. It is central to gaining competitive advantage, and comprises three phases—defining performance, measuring performance, and taking a feedback on the performance.

Managing performance is interactive, interrelated, and interdependent with managing people. History is littered with examples of poor performance management. It has been evidenced that organizations could not excel as they focused only on results and not actions. It is important for companies to define their long-term and short-term goals, rigidly apply a single doctrinaire approach, involve the use of jargons, and install suitable support measures to excel. The goals and targets of successful performance management are very specific and quantifiable, easy to understand, and consist of continuous and ongoing activities concerned with the results. Performance management system will be discussed in Chapter 8.

Q 3 Multiplying Talent—Development System

In today's world, it has become important to multiply the talent of an organization to succeed in the market. Training and development, performance management system, and performance appraisal are some of the processes that are used to multiply talent in an organization. Besides these, members of the organizations also need professional development through coaching, mentoring, and counselling. Coaching is organized for employees to develop skills to perform their roles better, mentoring is meant to aid development in work leadership, and counselling is carried out to cope with the stress. These will be discussed in greater detail in Chapter 9.

Training is an HRD mechanism that improves the knowledge, skills, and performance of an employee. Most of the organizations identify specific training needs prior to training its people. Once the training needs are identified, development of the training objectives should be carried out. This involves designing the syllabus, framing the training curriculum, and selecting the training methodology considering the profile of the participants. Trained and developed talents have a greater probability of staying and growing in a company.

Performance appraisal is another form of multiplying talent. It is a written formal assessment of the employee showing his strengths and weaknesses, achievements, degree of various attributes, etc., which organizations perform annually. It is a part of performance management system.

Developing Talent—Multi-source Feedback

Q 4 Multi-source assessment and feedback system (MAFS) is also known as '360-degree feedback' or 'multi-raters appraisal system'. This system has gained great popularity and manifests its importance for developing talent. Almost every Fortune 500 company has implemented MAFS in some form or the other. MAFS enables multiple raters to measure employee behaviour critical to performance; at the same time, questionnaires designed by the HR department could also be used.

Traditionally, an appraisal was done only by one's immediate senior colleague. This type of an appraisal/assessment could be biased due to interpersonal relations. Keeping this point in view, presently, appraisals are carried out by many persons including the immediate superior, internal customers, external customers, suppliers, colleagues, seniors of cross-functional areas, and immediate subordinates.

The all-round capability of a person can only be judged if the views of all the persons regularly interacting with him are gathered. It is also important that the raters' or appraisers' identity is kept confidential. Thus, in this system the content of the remark is more important than the person marking it. To eliminate any sort of bias, external consultants are engaged to collect the assessment sheets and analyse the comments of different appraisers in order to identify different competencies of different employees. MAFS lays emphasis on softer dimensions of performance such as leadership, creativity, originality, innovation, teamwork, initiative, entrepreneurship, and emotional intelligence, which have emerged as crucial organizational needs in recent times. The principal objectives are performance-linked pay or rewards, culture building, leadership development, team building, succession planning, and development.

In order to make this system more successful, top management needs to the build the confidence of its employees on the appraisal methodology, create opportunities for employees, invest time and effort, take the current appraisal system seriously, conduct performance reviews, and agree to be assessed by subordinates. Employees or candidates must be ready to welcome the MAFS. There are certain indicators to assess the readiness of the candidate, such as the candidates intent to be better, are receptive and respect the views of others, are learning-oriented individuals, have an aptitude for healthy competition, etc. The candidate should have a direct relationship with at least six individuals who can rate him.

The values of 360-degree feedback are manifold. The set of feedbacks enables an organization to focus on developmental efforts. A carefully-designed questionnaire helps to get a realistic feedback. An appraisee, on accepting the views of the raters, gains acceptance of the multiple stakeholders. Most managers are surprised and delighted by the amount of positive feedback on introspection.

T. V. Rao learning system (TVRLS) was developed using the RSDQ model (roles, styles, delegation, and qualities) for Indian top and senior management levels to measure the managerial and leadership competencies (www.tvrls.com).

Roles are the extent to which individuals play various leadership and managerial roles and activities.

Style, an element of McKinsey's 7S framework, is the way in which managers discharge their leadership roles. The model envisages that managers may play most roles well, and devote time and effort, but could be insensitive to the style with which they carry out these activities. The model mentions three styles—benevolent or paternalistic leadership style, critical leadership style, and developmental leadership style.

Delegation is an important part of a senior executive's effectiveness as he/she delegates not only for offloading oneself but also diverting the time in performing creative higher order tasks. The model envisages that managers should exhibit qualities of leaders and world-class managers (e.g., proaction, listening, communication, positive approach, participative nature, quality orientation, etc.).

Such *qualities* not only affect the effectiveness with which top level managers perform various roles, but also have an impact on the leadership style, and hence are very critical. Multi-source system will be discussed in Chapter 10.

Advancing Talent—Potential Appraisal and Career System

Potential appraisal and career system help to advance the talents in an organization.

Potential Appraisal

Potential appraisal refers to the identification and exploration of an employee's potential and capabilities, hitherto unknown, to perform new roles and responsibilities in view of changing customer demands. Thus, identifying the hidden capability is known as potential appraisal. An employee tries to perform the tasks assigned to him to the utmost satisfaction of his superiors. The company keeps growing continuously because of the contribution of all the employees at all levels. A dynamic organization reviews, structures systems, creates new roles, and assigns new responsibilities at all possible times to explore hidden potential.

Career System

Career denotes all the jobs that one holds in one's working life. Career planning is a process that fixes career goals and lays down the path to meet these goals, provides answers to questions such as 'Where shall I be after five, 10, or 15 years?'. The purpose of career planning is to provide continuity, order, and meaning to a person's work life. It is not an event or an end in itself. It tells the employees/prospects about the ways in which they can advance in the company. A career aims to integrate individual and organizational goals.

Career planning system manifests its importance in attracting competent persons providing suitable promotional and advancement opportunities, challenging work, and enabling development, boosting morale, increasing motivation, utilizing managerial reserves, and retaining talent.

Career planning has many terms related to it, some of which are career goals, career cycle, career paths, career anchors, career progression, career development, and career counselling. Career goals represent the future positions one may want to occupy. Career cycle involves the stages through which a person's career evolves. Career paths are the flexible lines of progression through which an employee moves. Career anchors are distinct patterns of self-perceived talents, attitudes, motives, and values that guide and stabilize a person's career. Career progression refers to the progress made by an individual in one's career through a series of right moves. Career development means actions undertaken by a person to achieve the career goals. Career counselling is the process of advising employees in setting career goals, and assisting them to find suitable career paths.

Career planning system manifests its importance in attracting competent persons, providing suitable promotional and advancement opportunities, providing

Top management commitment is essential for successful career planning.

challenging work, enabling them to develop, boosting their morale, increasing their motivation, utilizing their managerial reserves, and retaining talent.

Career counselling helps employees to understand the job more clearly, identify strengths and weaknesses, develop an outlook, achieve and enjoy greater satisfaction, and realize the forces and dynamics in the system.

Career planning has certain limitations too as it is more suitable for small organizations, and not so effective for a large number of employees. It is not appropriate for illiterate employees, the workforce, and the backward classes. As expectations of organizational members are growing, it is not effective for a longer period of time such as 10 years or more. Changes in environment, political interventions, nepotism, and favouritism are also responsible behind limitations of career planning.

The success of career planning depends on certain factors. Top management's commitment is essential for successful career planning. The enterprise should be expanding and must have clear corporate goals. The workforce should be motivated and jobs should be assigned to the right people. There must be a balance of age in the organization. Fair promotion policy and management of career or occupational stress further smoothens out the career planning system. Potential appraisal and career system will be discussed at length in Chapter 11.

Recognizing Talent—Reward System

Rewarding an employee for the good work done by him/her is extremely essential. This can be done by recognizing his/her splendid contribution towards the organization. Rewards and recognition play a crucial role in developing the levels of motivation, commitment, and loyalty of employees towards the organization. Talents are no exception to this. Rewards are often linked with performance. Rewards also help to promote the desired values, attitudes, and behaviour. Rewards are further linked to the quality of work and improvement. Rewards need not always be of a high cost. They can also be of a low cost value such as a token appreciation reward.

There are many companies where rewards are linked to career advancement or development. It is important that the rewards system must be structured, documented, and communicated to the employees. The system should be unambiguous and objective. This is essential to avoid demotivation of those who aspired, but did not receive any reward. Reward system will be discussed in Chapter 12.

Promoting Talent—Compensation Management

Presently, compensation management is a strategic issue and includes all forms of pay and rewards given to employees. Compensation includes both direct financial payments and indirect financial payments that employees receive during their employment period. A sound and effective compensation management system is the key driver of motivation, employee retention, and enhanced quality of work life. The term compensation refers to the disbursement of incentives with regard to salary and wage administration.

The compensation system considers both intrinsic components covering monetary and non-monetary rewards, and extrinsic components reflecting the employee's emotional satisfaction through accomplishment of the job.

The compensation system considers both intrinsic (intangible) and extrinsic (tangible) components. Extrinsic compensation covers both monetary and non-monetary rewards, whereas intrinsic compensation reflects an employee's emotional satisfaction through accomplishment of the job.

Designing and administering compensation needs certain legal considerations such as acts relating to the framework for remuneration of the top management of Indian companies, conformance to minimum pay, maximum hours, and overtime pay. Other considerations are child labour protection, ensuring equal pay for women doing the same work as men, and unemployment compensation for workers. Compensation management and reward system will be discussed in Chapter 12.

Q 7 Networking Talent—Separation and Beyond

Adequate care must be taken to ensure that during separation, the separating employee does not feel harassed or embarrassed.

Separation is a term used to refer to the resignation or termination of service. It is generally classified as layoff, voluntary resignation, or discharge. The entire separation process is conducted in such a way that the separating employee does not feel harassed or embarrassed. Smooth transitions and return of company property is ensured. A departing employee naturally feels emotional and can also share valuable insights about the organization. Keeping this in view, an organization arranges an exit interview that helps the organization reduce future attrition.

Employee departures are a natural part of the employee life cycle. Whether caused by voluntary resignation, retirement, or company induced termination, employee separations need to be efficiently managed by the HR. The separation needs to be handled with sensitivity, discretion, and speed so that exits can happen without burning bridges with the employee. After all, it is also important to remember that a leaving employee can be the most effective brand ambassador of the company.

Departing employees present an opportunity for the organization to gather a wealth of valuable feedback and insights on its strengths and weaknesses. However, all separations are not similar. Sometimes, it is worthwhile to go an extra mile in trying to retain a separating employee. The end of an employment relationship is frequently associated with emotional distress. Separation management will be discussed in Chapter 13.

Engaging Talent—Developing Workers and Sub-staff

Employee engagement is a measure of their commitment or loyalty to the organization, and the degree of their willingness to perform tasks to achieve quantitative targets and conform to the qualitative requirements. Employees must work above and beyond the expectations of the organization. An organization and its employees should conduct day-to-day business based on a common set of shared values.

Managers of the organization should effectively communicate and be emphatic listeners for effective leadership. Recognition, both extrinsic and intrinsic, is essential for a job well-done and, the doer should be recognized spontaneously. The organization must develop a proper mechanism to let the employees understand how their work contributes to the organization's overall success.

The seven engagement elements or levers that matter the most are shared values, effective leadership, motivational recognition, contribution to success, employee involvement or engagement, personal development, and economic self-interest.

Employees must be involved in decision-making that affects their work. Each employee should get opportunities to advance and grow in his/her professional career by means of personal development. Employees must be made to understand that their pay and benefits are fair and competitive in the marketplace. Thus, the seven engagement elements or levers that matter the most are shared values, effective leadership, motivational recognition, contribution to success, employee involvement or engagement, personal development, and economic self-interest. Developing workers and sub-staff will be discussed in Chapter 14. Exhibit 4.3 describes the steps followed by Tata for managing talent.

Exhibit 4.3 Managing talent—the Tata way

The following are some initiatives taken by Tata:

1. Launching of the talent identification and development process across the group—Senior group leadership annually conducts reviews with the company management about its talent banks. The company management, in turn, takes steps to strengthen the talent nurturing processes in its own units.
2. Strengthening, coaching, and mentoring—The group companies initiate programmes to hone the coaching skills of the senior managers. Many of them mentor young talent inducted in the companies.
3. Tata Management Training Centre (TMTC) has instituted a three-tier leadership development programme—These are prestigious courses, meant for developing better managers, where they also get an opportunity to socialize with group managers of the companies.
4. Differentiation is integral to effective talent management—More sophisticated use of market indexing of salaries for high potential as well as larger population is being used to refine and tweak the competitiveness of the salaries.
5. Emphasis on mobility, first within the company and then within the group—TCS, the most populated Tata company, is an excellent example in this regard. The company has benefitted immensely in performance as well as in consistently experiencing attrition rates lower than the industry average.
6. Use of structure design tools such as 'Work Level' to create large and challenging jobs for managers—Management research literature has shown that talent development happens by handling large and challenging jobs.
7. Recognition programme in companies such as Taj and TCS have significant impact—They build and encourage appropriate behaviour and signal a positive message of values to the huge benefit of the organization.

Source: Satish Pradhan (2008)

TALENT MANAGEMENT—AN ESSENTIAL HR FUNCTION

Q 5 HR is one of the most misunderstood and misinterpreted functions in an organization. Other functions such as production, maintenance, quality control, marketing, and sales do not have this problem. However, HR plays the role of the guardian of human capital.

In today's competitive business scenario, organizations seek to hire and engage talents. It is seen that since the 1990s, the HR personnel have been trying their best to align HR efforts with the business objectives. Many journals of repute have addressed HR professionals as players of the business, strategic partners, and other similar terms.

The HR Proposition, Ulrich and Brockbank et al. (2005), mentions the following:

'For the last decade, HR professionals have aspired to be the most complete players relative to the core issues of the businesses, as described in a number of business roles—business partners, strategic partners, full contributors, players in the business, and so forth. These aspirations are appropriate and desirable, but the fact that HR professionals continue to frame aspirations in these terms communicates a continuing concern.'

The concerns of the HR professionals force them to contribute in the arena of talent management as well. Thorne and Pellant (2007) highlight the HR's credibility debate and mention a roadmap and guidelines as follows:

Q 9

1. The HR director and the head of learning and development need to establish strong relationship with the business.
2. Both the HR director and learning and development professionals need to develop sound understanding of the business—its overall goals, the business strategy, and associated functions.
3. Audit is a verification of activities. An audit of services and products, quality of response, solutions, and most importantly, the expertise of HR staff should be organized for finding facts that cannot otherwise be identified.

4. Conversations need to take place with all business relations to identify likely future requirements with the ultimate aim of improvement.
5. Change is an inevitable need and as such, people must be committed to accept changes, which should be sequentially undertaken—unfreezing, moving, and refreezing. Unfreezing is the stage to loosen emotional and intellectual forces, and recognizing and enhancing the driving forces to reduce the resistance to change. The moving stage indicates readiness of the individuals for new behaviour and the change perspective. Refreezing is the final phase of the change process leading to the reinforcement of the new desirable behaviour.
6. Using the knowledge base, the HR and the learning and development professionals can really start to build a meaningful relationship with the business.
7. Sometimes, people development processes (PDP) appear somewhat similar to the corporate agenda such as business process reengineering (BPR), introduction of new technology, modernization, or IT implementation. During this phase, the HR might feel frustrated and isolated. This is quite natural when one should not feel isolated, as it is merely a temporary phase.
8. With the growing realization that people are operators of various systems, focusing on the enhancement of the capabilities of individuals to transform their performances is a critical role of all training, learning, and development professionals.
9. HR as well as learning and development strategies and visions need to be built considering the overall business strategy and vision. Thus, these strategies must address the business requirements and be based on key business deliverables.
10. The HR should constantly strive to develop a pool of talents exercising ownership of the talent agenda. They should seek a response to the question, 'How much of what we need have we currently got?'

Box 4.1 identifies a questionnaire that helps in judging if a HR manager is truly contributing towards talent management and growth in business.

Box 4.1 HR—A business partner: Self-assessment questions

An HR professional is a business partner who is closely associated with the business functions. One can assess the extent of their association through the use of a self-assessment questionnaire.

Some of the questions are as follows:

1. Do I know the business vision, objectives, and key result areas?
2. Can I precisely describe the current business success of the company I am working in?
3. Do I know the major competitors?
4. Do I know the people with whom my company should maintain relationships with?
5. Do I have the ability to identify the strengths and weaknesses of the key players?
6. Have I identified the key manufacturing processes?
7. Have I identified the competencies required for critical manufacturing processes?

As already discussed, trends happening in talent management among organizations are an area of interest that one should be aware of. BPM Forum and Success Factors together with Human Capital Institute carried out a collaborative survey on talent management trends in organizations. The survey covered more than 725 performance and HR professionals' responses, mainly from North America. The project aimed to have a year-end audit and assessment of talent management trends and projections for 2007. The important findings are shown in Exhibit 4.4.

Exhibit 4.4 Talent management trend survey 2007

1. Around 73% of respondents indicated that talent management is a high or very high priority.
2. Some 88% of the respondents stated that critical competencies are changing or evolving in their organizations. The most valued competencies are listed as management leadership (62%), technical knowledge (42%), and people skills (43%).
3. The top talent management challenges are listed as talent development (63%), talent retention, and turnover (60%), followed by talent acquisition (49%).
4. Around 98% of the survey participants noted that competition for talent is heating up in their industries.
5. The impact of intensified war for talent on overall business results in talent search for a longer period of time, the need for better internal development, and the need to pay higher salaries.
6. Some 77% of the respondents said that global factors are making a significant difference in their talent management and acquisition strategies.
7. Despite the need for talent management strategies, only 26% of the participants have talent scorecards in place. Over 70%, either did not know or were not sure as to how they measure people performance and productivity in terms of business value creation.

Source: Emre Kavukcuogu Zaman (2008)

TALENT MAPPING

Q 2 Organizations should develop talent mapping programmes to facilitate assessing the effectiveness of people management. It is essential to critically evaluate the working of an organization's talent mapping and performance management programme. Sheth (2008) suggests the need for examining a few factors.

1. Does the business environment facilitate optimal performance management?
2. What is the organization-wide perception of a performance management programme?
3. What are the monitoring methodologies and who are the stakeholders?
4. Are the right people implementing these programmes?

The purpose of answering these questions is to create an alignment between performance management processes and strategic priorities. Consistency, identity, and genuineness of a talent management programme ensure its longevity.

Talent Mapping Programme

It is vital to assess an organization's talent management programme and partners. Certain pillars of assessment are clarity and communication, design, implementation, assessment and rewards, reviews, environment and culture, cost, impact, deployability, and objectivity. These pillars must be given proper attention during the process of talent mapping.

Clarity and communication The purpose of performance management system should be clear and it should be communicated to all in the organization.

Q 10 ***Design*** One has to identify the way in which the performance management system was designed and check whether the system reflects company vision and values, whether it is simple and scientific, etc. One must ensure that the system is free from amalgamation of complex HR jargons and concepts. It should be user-friendly.

Some typical career anchors for talents in the organizations are technical/ functional competence, general managerial competency, autonomy or independence, entrepreneurial zeal and creativity, etc.

Implementation Organizations must assign the responsibility of implementing the performance management system to a responsible person. He/she has to verify to what extent the performance evaluation is linked to the success of the talent mapping programme.

Assessment and rewards Measurability of the success of performance management needs assessment. Further, it is required to check the availability of monetary and non-monetary rewards for performance.

Reviews Along with the changing business environment, the business strategy also changes. Periodical reviews are also essential in redefining talent management strategies so that they align with the business strategies.

Environment and culture Management needs to foster an environment and culture to support the talent mapping programme.

Cost The performance management system should be cost-effective. One has to ensure that it does not need a higher budget.

Impact It is necessary to ascertain the impact of the performance management system; it should be applicable for the whole organization and its applicability should not be confined only to limited departments.

Deployability The performance management system should be deployable at all levels and in all geographies.

Objectivity It is wiser to collect objective third-party views about an organization's performance management system. The views should neither be biased nor emotional as the purpose of gathering third-party views would then be useless.

EMPLOYEE ENGAGEMENT

People are the primary source of competitive advantage. If the people or employees of the organization can be effectively 'engaged', then achieving the organizational goals becomes an easy task. The widely-used term 'employee engagement', embraces two attempts of management—motivating the employees and focusing their commitment to achieve the organizational objectives. Employee engagement further emphasizes the willingness to help out colleagues at par with organizational citizenship behaviour. In the broader sense, employee engagement goes beyond job satisfaction, job involvement, motivation, etc.

Henderson (2009) mentions that, 'engagement is something the employee has to be offered, it cannot be 'required' as part of the employee contract'. We can hire employees and we need to motivate them. Motivated employees are crucial to an organization's success; this has never been more apppli-cable than today, particularly when margins are thin (or nonexistent) and economic recovery remains elusive. These hard bottom-line realities also mean that managers cannot rely, as much as they might have in the past two decades, only on using financial incentives to drive employee engagement. We need to make employees feel valued. Understanding the levels of employee engagement has become crucial to organizational success.

To strengthen the communication process and promote employee engagement in the levels of associates/employees and top management personnel, TCS has introduced the PEEP programme where PEEP stands for proactive employee engagement program.

Some typical career anchors for talent engagement in organizations are technical/functional competency, general managerial competency, autonomy or independence, entrepreneurial zeal, and creativity. A person desires to excel in his/her career in the chosen line of work. As such, the organization must be instrumental to enhance the person's technical/functional competency. In order to move along the traditional career path, a person needs general managerial competency. A talented person always looks for working independently and craves autonomy, and therefore, the anchor of autonomy/independence is vital. Security and stability refers to a predictable environment. A creative person backed by entrepreneurial zeal wants to create something of his/her own and derive pleasure from the creation.

There are three organizational forces that enhance employee engagement as follows:

Lower attrition rate An employee who engages in his assignments is unlikely to leave the organization. High attrition rate causes loss of huge amount of talents that could have been well-groomed and retained if provided the required environment . The probability of retention, in such a case, is high.

Better productivity The quality of work is more relevant than quantity of work. An involved person has to have an understanding of what is expected of him and what goes far ahead for him to perform his/her best in the company.

Enhanced profitability Every company desires to enhance profitability, for which the organization must enhance its employees' abilities. A person with complete dedication and commitment, and who is more engaged, can contribute to a greater extent to organizational profitability.

Employee Engagement—Relationship with Talent Management

Effective talent management policies and practices demonstrate commitment to human capital, which results in more engaged employees, and lower turnover. Consequently, employee engagement has a substantial impact on employee productivity and talent retention. Employee engagement, in fact, can make or break the bottom line. Employees who are committed the most perform 20% better and are 87% less likely to resign. In addition, the foundation for an engaged workforce is established by the quality, depth, and authenticity of communication by HR and senior management.

The role of the manager as the most important enabler of employee commitment to the job, organization, and teams cannot be overemphasized. Furthermore, when implemented well, practices that support talent management also support employee engagement (e.g., work-life balance programs such as flexible time, telecommuting, compressed workweeks, reward programs, performance management systems). Rewards and recognition also help retain talent and improve performance. A Carlson/Gallup study on employee engagement and business success showed that employees who were extremely satisfied with work were four times more likely than unsatisfied employees to have a formal measurement process in place and receive regular recognition.

Means to Promote Employee Engagement

Each employee has a reservoir of knowledge and skill base to his/her credit, which must be fruitfully utilized. An organization should not have any negative feeling or opinion about the people who are striving for its profit. It is impossible to work and produce results, if the resources are inadequate. The employees must be provided with all that is required. The resources include both tangible and intangible benefits, including intellectual properties. The senior management has to communicate to the employees about their role, expectation from them with regard to the assigned work, the organization's values, vision, mission, and other relevant information, to energize them and to keep the wheel of production moving. It is equally important to identify the right kind of job profile for an individual, keeping in mind the person's aptitude and capability.

Furthermore, it is essential to identify their shortcomings, knowledge, and skill gaps, and conduct training programmes and workshops to bridge those gaps. A manager also needs to assess oneself through the subordinates' eyes; though difficult, it is not impossible. One should not feel shy to ask them questions such as, 'How can I improve as a manager? How should I contribute to make your work simpler and easier?' An empathetic behaviour will help a manager understand himself/herself from their viewpoints. One must share the organizations' success stories with the subordinates. It is advisable to treat one's subordinates as junior colleagues. This view will help remove the status symbol and in turn be closer to them.

All individuals need motivation; be it intrinsic or extrinsic. It is important to recognize the good work done by one's junior colleagues. Even positive sensory gratification is a way of recognizing their efforts. One must remember to praise in public, and criticize in private; reward them in the opportune moments; and most importantly, celebrate both accomplishments and praiseworthy efforts, even those that could not bring a tangible profit, but created an avenue for success in future. One must not forget to share failure stories as lessons can be learnt from them. Employee engagement initiatives, once started, should be continued; any break or delay in recognizing the talent is not desirable, as it may cause unfavourable results. Consistency in recognizing the talent over a long period of time leads to organizational success.

In summary, following the principle of forgive and forget, providing adequate resources, communicating unambiguously what is expected of employees, sharing values and vision, considering employee organizational roles, continuous conversation, sharing success and failure stories, reward and recognition, and so forth, are essential in effectively engaging them and managing the talent.

TALENT WAR

The business scenario is changing rapidly. Success in achieving business objectives requires talented resources who are capable of thinking and doing things differently. Identifying and acquiring talent has become difficult; it is more difficult to retain them because talents are very mobile. The cause of attrition and mechanisms for retaining employees must be devised.

Tymon et al. (2010) developed and tested a model of talent management across 28 Indian firms involving 4,811 professional-level employees. They observed that intrinsic rewards experienced were a critical element in employee retention, satisfaction with the organization, and career success. They also explored four antecedents of intrinsic rewards—the social responsibility of the employer, pride in the organization, manager support, and performance management. The researchers found support for the importance of intrinsic rewards as a mediating variable, as well as for the moderating role of certain hygiene factors. Their research suggested that multinational, international, and national employers may have non-pecuniary mechanisms to promote retention and employee satisfaction, even in challenging labour market environments.

The globalization of information technology (IT), in which developing countries play a major role, has caused a war for talent. In order to meet the challenging growth targets, service providers find that recruitment and retention are of key importance. For developing countries, globalization offers the opportunity for economic development. Beulen (2008) pursued a research in the company Accenture to find an answer to the question, 'How can IT be used to support service providers?'. He observed that Accenture's industrialized approach makes effective and efficient HRM processes possible and concludes that the HRM applications working in tandem will ultimately converge into a fully integrated application suite.

India, once a major exporter of unskilled manpower, has turned into a source of highly-skilled expertise. Developed countries are facing shortages of specific skills, and hence, are instrumental in importing people meeting these requirements and procuring persons with the requisite skills to their credit.

The World Economic Forum and Boston Consulting Group study indicates that in the years, 2020 and 2030, India will face a shortage of right-skills talents in sectors such as IT and leisure, and a more pronounced gap in manufacturing and engineering construction. The study unambiguously points out, 'The talent shock is coming. It will arrive in years, not decades, regardless of the current economic crisis. It is time for all involved stakeholders to ally forces and prepare for an era of extreme labour scarcity, significant talent mobility, and a truly global workforce.' Even today, there are shortages in many areas of technology, teaching/research, and in industry.

Thousands of candidates are competing for jobs everyday; similarly, organizations are competing with plenty of other organizations to hire the most qualified and competent persons with the requisite aptitude. At this juncture, one needs to recall the maxim—in the workplace, human attitude overrides aptitude. Thus, when the talent war is in progress, one needs to find the right mix of knowledge, skills, aptitude, attitude, and capability to fit in the organizational culture to enhance the probability of retention.

Tomorrow's world is not going to be about capturing ever-depleting natural resources, but about a more scarce commodity—the top-flight talent. A global war of talent is already underway. The HR manager and the learning and development manager need to be dynamic warrios in the era of talent war.

SUMMARY

Talent acquisition and management have emerged as inescapable steps to boost productivity, augment distinctive competence, gain competitive advantages, achieve excellence, identify new ways of processing, survive and win the cutthroat competitions, and so forth. In view of the fact that the global talent war is upon us, organizations are searching for talents or performers. Talent management has many facets. Reports of talent management surveys indicate the utmost importance of talent management.

Organizations need to undertake talent-mapping programmes to facilitate assessment of the effectiveness of people management. After being hired, employees need to be engaged for organizational excellence. There are soft means to promote employee engagement. The depth and breadth of the talent war intensifies the need for talent, talent management, talent mapping, etc. Organizations need talents and prospective performers to survive, grow, and excel.

KEY TERMS

Employee engagement refers to the concept of using the capabilities to the fullest extent by applying certain techniques.

Talent management is an integrated system to attract, develop, retain, and utilize people having the requisite knowledge, skills, aptitude, and attitude to contribute to achieve the organization's present and future objectives and goals.

Talent mapping is a procedure of assessing the effectiveness of people management.

Talent mapping programme is the application of talent mapping using pillars of assessment such as clarity and communication, design, implementation, assessment and rewards, reviews, environment and culture, cost, impact, deployability, and objectivity.

EXERCISES

Concept Review Questions

1. What are the various facets of talent management? Discuss each facet in brief providing an example each.
2. Name the pillars of a talent management programme. Discuss any three of them with examples in an organizational context.
3. What are the tools and techniques of enhancing the capabilities of employees? Discuss briefly.
4. Mention the uniqueness of multi-source feedback and assessment. Discuss the roles of top management in adopting this system.
5. Do you feel that talent management is an essential HR function? Suggest a roadmap and some guidelines to promote talent management.

Critical Thinking Questions

6. Distinguish between employee hiring and employee engagement citing an example in the organizational context.
7. Do you feel that an attractive compensation management system can promote talent retention?
8. 'Performance is a multidimensional variable and is a conglomerate of several dimensions. Hence, people high on one dimension may not be high on the other, and such standings may change over time' (MacKinney 1967). Identify the dimensions of performance in the context of a service organization.

Assignments

9. You have been assigned the task of recording the talent managing initiatives taken by 10 organizations. How will you go about it? Your report must contain briefs of the organizations, questionnaires you will administer, findings, recommendations to the organizations surveyed, and hurdles faced, if any, and the ways in which you tackled the hurdles, and other information you feel appropriate.
10. Talent management is the talk of the day. You have been asked to assess the talent management programmes of the organization you are working in. Prior to starting the work, you must meticulously plan such that your findings are useful to your organization and are appreciated by superiors. Discuss your plan in detail.

MANAGER'S INSIGHT

Elite Enterprises is a 500-member organization providing financial solutions to its clients. The employees, in general, were considered to be one of the most talented groups in the industry. Recently, during a meeting, the managing director of the company expressed that he felt that the turnover in the company had enormously increased and was much greater than that of the competitors. He suggested that the HR takes some serious actions such as arranging for training sessions or increasing the salaries of the employees to control the situation. He also asked the research department to survey and research to find out more on this.

The HR department, on the other hand, expressed apprehensions in this regard. Investing more on people development, they pointed out, could be critical, as poaching is rampant in the industry. They, however, came up with a suggestion of enriching the job profiles and responsibilities of the employees.

Questions:

1. Do you agree with what the HR department feels at Elite Enterprises?
2. What would be a smart approach to retain the talent at Elite Enterprises?

BIBLIOGRAPHY AND WEB RESOURCES

A summer internship project pursued by Poonam Sharda titled, 'Talent Acquisition Procedures and its comparative analyses at Wipro Ltd (Infotech), Kolkata'. The SIP was submitted to Indian Institute of Social Welfare and Business Management (IISWBM) for evaluation by University of Calcutta, 2009.

Banerjee, Anirban. R, 'Leveraging Talent for Growth,' *HRD Newsletter*, Vol. 25, Issue: 6, p. 20, 2009.

Beulen, Erik, *Information Technology for Development*, Vol. 14 Issue 3, p. 213, 2008.

Blau G.J. and Boal K.B., 'Conceptualizing How Job Involvement and Organizational Commitment Affect Turnover and Absenteeism,' *Academy of Management Review*, pp. 288–300, 1987.

Lain, Henderson, *Human Resource Management*, University Press, Talent Management pp. 86–87, Hyderabad, 2009.

MacKinney, A., *The Assessment of Performance Change: An Inductive Example, Organizational Behavior and Human Performance*, 2, pp. 56–72, 1967.

Pradhan, Satish, 'Managing Talent: The Tata Way', *Business Manager*, Vol. 10, No. 9, p. 19, Alwar, 2008.

Rao, *Business Manager*, Vol. 16, No. 9, March 2008.

Rao, M.B.N, 'Managing Talent in Public Sector Banks by CMD, Canara Bank', *Business Manager*, Vol. 16, No. 9, March 2008.

Rawal, Priyanka, 'Employee Retention—An Art of Keeping the People Who Keep You in the Business', *HRM Review*, April 2011.

Sheth, Purvi, 'Is Your Talent Mapping Programme Working?', *Business Manager*, Vol. 10, No. 9, pp. 23–24, Alwar, March 2008.

Thorne, Kaye, and Andy, Pellant, *The Essential Guide to Managing Talent*, Kogan Page India, New Delhi, 2007.

Tymon, Walter G., Stephen A. Stumpf, and Jonathan P. Doh, 'Exploring Talent Management in India: The Neglected Role of Intrinsic Rewards,' *Journal of World Business*, Vol. 45, Issue 2, pp. 109–121, p. 13, 2010.

Ulrich, D., Brockbank, W., Yeung, A., and Lake, D., 'Human Resource Competencies: An Empirical Approach', *Human Resource Management Journal*, Vol. 34, pp. 4–14, 1995.

Zaman, Emre. Kavukcuogu., 'Talent Management', *Business Manager*, Vol. 10, No. 9, pp. 16–22, Alwar, March 2008.

Web Resources

www.learndirect.co.uk/media/pdfs/nurturing_talent.pdf, last accessed on 19 October 2009.

www.talentmgt.com/assessment_evaluation/2007/August/391/index.php, last accessed on 24 November 2009.

www.talentmgt.com/assessment_evaluation/2007/August/391/index.php, last accessed on 24 November 2009.

www.talentmgt.com/assessment_evaluation/2007/August/391/index.php, last accessed on 24 November 2009.

BPM Survey, www.successfactors.com/articles/performance-management-trends/2007/, last accessed on 24 November 2009.

TALENT ACQUISITION PROCEDURES AT WIPRO LTD (INFOTECH)

About Wipro Ltd (Infotech)

Wipro Ltd is a global provider of IT services, one of the Fortune 500 companies, and a multi-business entity that provides high-end IT solutions to leading companies worldwide. It has profitable businesses in niche markets such as India. Wipro currently employs more than 97,000 personnel across 54 countries. Wipro is driven by a passion for quality and commitment to customers. This drive has catapulted Wipro to be among the 10 most-admired companies in India. Through constant innovation and a people-first attitude, it aims to be a world leader in providing comprehensive and world class IT services.

Talent acquisition system

Wipro has a very robust recruitment and staffing methodology for hiring the right talent. The company has a dedicated talent acquisition team, in all global delivery centers who can recruit from within or outside India. This team is responsible to build up a large pool of quality hires, which are the best in class, and maintain a cost per hire model. Their productivity is measured in terms of reduced turnaround time and customer satisfaction. Wipro also has a pool of resource suppliers who are trained in recruiting associates specific to company requirements.

Steps in the acquisition process

During the acquisition process, Wipro follows typical steps such as resource request, sourcing the curriculum vitae (CV), matching the skills set, CV screening, telephone interview, technical interviews, HR interview, final interview, and on-boarding.

Resource request—This is the step where the business team puts forth a hiring requisition-request for resource (RR) to the personnel department. This step includes the involvement of the business heads. The RR contains job design, job specification, CTC on offer etc. The job specifications are communicated to the extensive internal databank source called the central staffing team (CST) headquartered in Bangalore, and several other external resourcing partners (RPs). The recruiting team needs concrete information with no ambiguity. Once the RR is approved, it is allotted a number and the position is considered open.

Sourcing the CV—Sourcing candidates is a way to identify and attract those job candidates who are actively looking for new opportunities and passive candidates, qualified individuals, who are not seeking a new job opportunity.

Matching the skills set—The first resource matching is done within the existing resources. In the case of matching of skill set with existing resources, on-the-job-training is provided.

CV screening—CV is received against a job opening and screened.

Telephone interview—In the initial telephonic interview, the candidate is given a brief about the job opening to assess the interest of the candidate in the position.

Technical interview—The technical round of interview is conducted by a board formed with certified line managers to judge the specific technical skill set. These interviews are mostly conducted within the company premises. In case of extremely critical skills, a second round of technical interview is organized.

HR interview—Once the candidate clears the technical round, he has to go through an HR interview. The HR panel assesses the personal attributes of the candidate in terms of written and spoken communication skills, energy levels exhibited, initiative, result orientation, breadth of interest, culture fit, interpersonal skills, and other attributes.

Final interview—After a candidate clears all the previous rounds of interviews and is deemed appropriate for the position, he/she undergoes the final round of interview, called the client interview. Here, he may face another round of technical interview. Once he clears this round, he may be considered for the position.

On-boarding—The process of on-boarding includes background verification (BGV). After receiving a green (clear) report and on completion of other pre-joining formalities, medical tests etc. are conducted.

Skill metrics tracker—Since CVs are expensive to source, a lot of care and effort needs to be spent on making sure that every candidate's CV is received and processed. This helps in improving the number of hires made from a given advertisement. Keeping this in mind, the skill metrics tracker was developed. Many candidates pass through the technical and HR interview stage, but often they are rejected at the client round. This may or may not be because of any deficiency in the candidate that could not be detected in the earlier stages.

A database of such CVs needs to be maintained and shared across all regions. Each time a new requisition for the skill is made by a different client or in a different region, the skill metrics tracker can be searched. This tracker can be updated at a regular interval of time with all the details of such candidates along with a recommendation by the project workers.

Note: Talent acquisition process is not different from the traditional recruitment and selection process. Meticulous identification of the competency sets (intellectual, personal, communication, interpersonal, leadership, and result-oriented) for various positions followed by verification and availability of the competencies within the candidates/interviewees in multiple stages ensures talent acquisition by the organization.

A flowchart on talent acquisition followed by Wipro Infotech is exhibited in Figure 4.2.

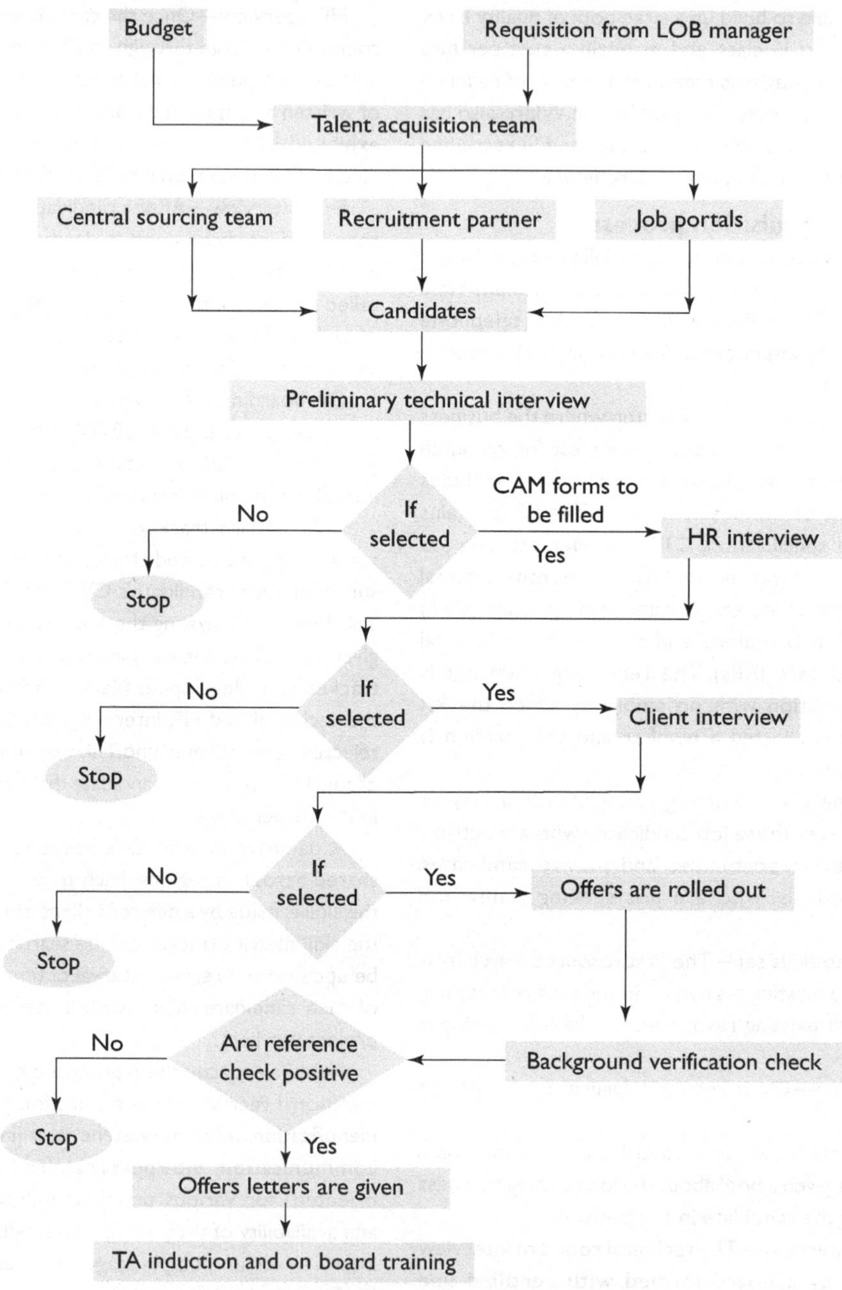

FIG. 4.2 Talent acquisition process at Wipro Infotech [Based on a summer internship project (SIP) pursued by Poonam Sharda titled, 'Talent Acquisition Procedures and its Comparative Analyses at Wipro Ltd (Infotech), Kolkata. The SIP (2009) was submitted to Indian Institute of Social Welfare and Business Management (IISWBM) for evaluation by University of Calcutta.]

Discussion Questions

1. Wipro has a structured talent acquisition system. Suggest whether the system can be further strengthened. Discuss the ways and means of doing the same.
2. After acquisition, what else can Wipro do to promote retention of the acquired talents?

HR MANTRA A folk story

A boatman was entrusted with the task of transferring a tiger, a goat, and a bundle of grass from one side (the eastern bank) to the other side of a river (the western bank). The limitation is that the boatman can carry only one item per trip in either direction. There are also some conditions:

1. The tiger should not eat the boatman.
2. The tiger can eat the goat if alone, but not in presence of the boatman.
3. The goat can eat the grass if left alone on a bank, but not in presence of the boatman.
4. The boatman has to complete the transfer in a minimum number of trips.

The boatman performed the task successfully, following this sequence of steps:

Trip 1: To take the goat to the western bank
Trip 2: To return empty to the eastern bank
Trip 3: To take the tiger to the western bank
Trip 4: To bring back the goat (condition 2 applies)
Trip 5: To take the grass bundle to the western bank
Trip 6: To return empty to the eastern bank
Trip 7: To take the goat to the western bank

Thus, it is possible to accomplish the task in seven trips.

The mantra: Think out of the box; every problem has a solution.

ROBERT OWEN

Robert Owen was born on 14 May 1771 in Newtown, Wales. His father was a saddler and ironmonger. As a boy, Robert was intelligent and performed very well at school. However, at the age of ten, his father sent him to work in large drapers in Stamford, Lincolnshire.

The market term, 'talent management' has been around for the last two decades or so. Only recently have companies realized that people are their greatest assets. Owen had foreseen the need for developing children, identifying prospective persons, and managing them as important resources to develop the society. Robert Owen propounded the concept of talent management and is regarded as the *father of talent management*.

He was one of the earliest pioneers of modern companies. Owen was the Jim Goodnight of his time and became a successful textile entrepreneur by the age of 30. He was against engaging children in industries, particularly in the unorganized sector. In fact, he was berated in the business community as he believed eight-year olds should not work 13 hours a day. Here is an excerpt from a historian

(O'Toole 1995) who studied him. 'Owen provided clean and decent housing for his workers and their families in a community free from contagious disease, crime, and gin shops. He took young children out of the factories, founded a school for them, and enrolled them in it. He provided preschool, day care, the first adult night school, and a brand of progressive education that stressed learning as a pleasurable experience.The entire business world was shocked and dumbfounded when he prohibited corporal punishment in his factory when he retrained his supervisors in human disciplinary practices. He offered his workers an extremely high standard of living compared to other workers of the era. Owen was making a fortune.'

Owen tried to convince his fellow capitalists that an investment in people provides greater return than an investment in tangible assets. He was 150 years ahead of his time. Today, numerous studies conclude that an investment in people yields long-term success in any company.

Owen's philosophy was based on three intellectual pillars:

1. First, no one was responsible for one's will and actions because one's whole character is formed independently; people are products of their heredity and environment, hence his support for education and labour reform, rendered him a pioneer in human capital investment.
2. Second, all religions are based on the same ridiculous imagination, that make man a weak and an imbecile animal; a furious bigot and fanatic; or a miserable hypocrite (though in his later years he embraced spiritualism).
3. Third, he was in favour of the putting-out system instead of the factory system.

While working in Manchester, Owen learned about the success story of Richard Arkwright, a leading entrepreneur of the industrial revolution. Arkwright was owned a textile factory in Cromford and was quick to see the potential of manufacturing cloth. At the age of 19, he borrowed £100, established a business of manufacturing spinning mules along with John Jones, an engineer. In 1792, the partnership with Jones came to an end and Owen began working as a manager of Peter Drinkwater's large spinning factory in Manchester.

As a manager at the Drinkwater's factory, Owen met a lot of businessmen involved in the textile industry. Some of them included David Dale, the owner of Chorton Twist Company in New Lanark, Scotland, which was the largest cotton-spinning business in Britain. Soon, the two became good friends. In 1799, Robert married Dale's daughter, Caroline.

With the financial support of several businessmen from Manchester, Owen purchased Dale's four textile factories in New Lanark for £60,000. Under Owen's control, the Chorton Twist Company expanded rapidly. However, Owen was not solely concerned with making money; he was also interested in creating a new type of community at New Lanark. He believed that a person's character is formed by the effect of their environment. He believed and was convinced that if he created the right environment, he could produce rational, good, and humane people. Owen argued that people were naturally good, but were corrupted by the harsh ways in which they were treated. For example, Owen was a strong opponent of physical punishment in schools and factories, and immediately banned its use in New Lanark.

Dale had originally built a large number of houses close to his factories in New Lanark. By the time Owen arrived, over 2,000 people lived in New Lanark village. When he became owner of New Lanark, Owen ordered the building of a school in the area. Furthermore, Owen was convinced that education was crucially important in developing the desired type of personality.

When Owen arrived at New Lanark, he was utterly astonished to see children as young as five years of age working for 13 hours a day in the textile mills. He stopped employing children under 10 and reduced their labour to 10 hours a day. Owen arranged to send the children to nursery and infant schools. Older children worked in the factory, but also had to attend his secondary school for a part of the day.

Owen's partners were concerned that these reforms would reduce profits. Unable to convince them of the wisdom of these reforms, Owen decided to borrow money from Archibald Campbell, a local banker, in order to buy their share of the business. Later, Owen sold the shares in the business to men who agreed with his modes of running his factory.

References

www.grandmaslaw.com/?p=148, last accessed on 1 October 2011.

en.wikipedia.org/wiki/Robert_Owen, last accessed on 1 October 2011.

www.spartacus.schoolnet.co.uk/IRowen.htm, last accessed on 1 October 2011.

CHAPTER 5

Competency Framework for Talent Management

LEARNING OBJECTIVES

After studying this chapter, you will be able to

- Define competency and competence
- Recognize the need, objectives, and advantages of competency mapping
- Comprehend the differences between competency mapping and competency framework
- Chart out competency categories such as managerial, technical, behavioural, and conceptual
- Appreciate competency mapping processes and practices
- Understand the methods of developing competencies
- Realize the competency approach in recruitment and retention
- Be able to map competencies

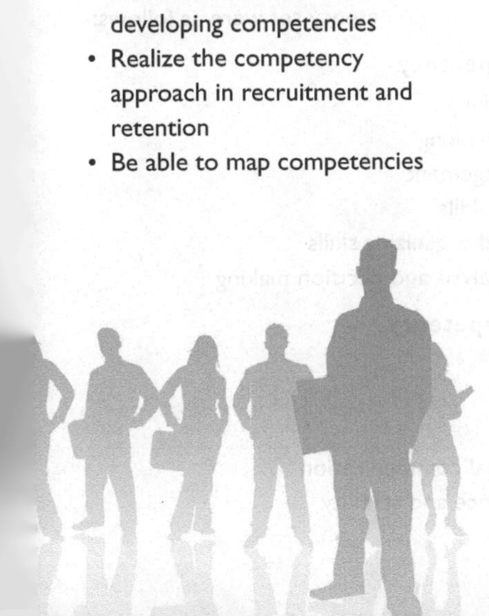

OPENING CASE

Competency Framework at Reliance Communications

About the organization

Reliance Infocomm offers a complete range of telecom services covering mobile and fixed line telephones including broadband, national, and international long distance services, and data services. It also covers a wide range of value-added services and applications that enhance the productivity of enterprises and individuals.

The birth of Reliance–ADAG (Anil Dhirubhai Ambani Group) created an unprecedented value for over two million Reliance shareholders and generated an incremental wealth of over $16 billion. On the basis of financial and other major parameters, the company emerged as one of the top three business houses in the country.

It has a business presence that extends to over 4,500 towns and 3,00,000 villages in India and five continents across the globe. Reliance started with the mantra 'Think Big, Think Fast, Think Ahead, and Think Better'. The revised mantra is, 'Think Bigger, Think Better'. The new corporate colours, blue and red, convey the values of integrity, confidence, energy, and passion.

Value addition for the organization

The company desires to improve further by following the adoption of competency mapping and keeping in mind certain desired outcomes as follows:

1. Identifying the need for obtaining quality certification as a business requirement
2. Enhancing the organization's stature and competitive position
3. Improving the profiles of sales officers/sales executives
4. Selecting the right people for the right job through placements
5. Developing manpower in time, according to the organizational needs
6. Boosting overall performance by capturing the market share, improving customer service, innovation, improving efficiency, and decreasing decision-making time

Developing competency framework at Reliance Infocomm

Objectives of the study

1. To find out the existing competency level of Reliance employees (with respect to certain roles for evaluation) and analyse the gap between the desired and the actual levels
2. To determine certain job-based personality attributes that relate to the competency levels of each role or job

Competency mapping process

The competency mapping process at Reliance Infocomm involves the following steps:

1. Developing competency models to facilitate competency profiling for each job/role
2. Identifying competencies required for a given job/role or a set of tasks to be performed successfully at a given point of time
3. Assessing competency to measure the extent to which a particular individual or a group of individuals possess the competencies required to perform a given role or set of roles

These are shown in Figure 5.1.

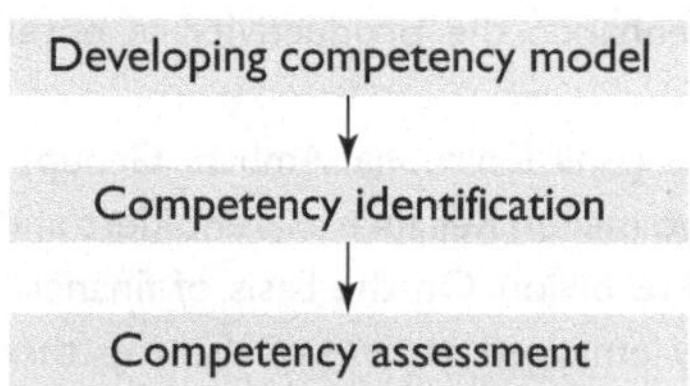

FIG. 5.1 Competency mapping process

Competency model

The company preferred to use the managerial, behavioural, and functional competency (MBF) model, shown in Figure 5.2.

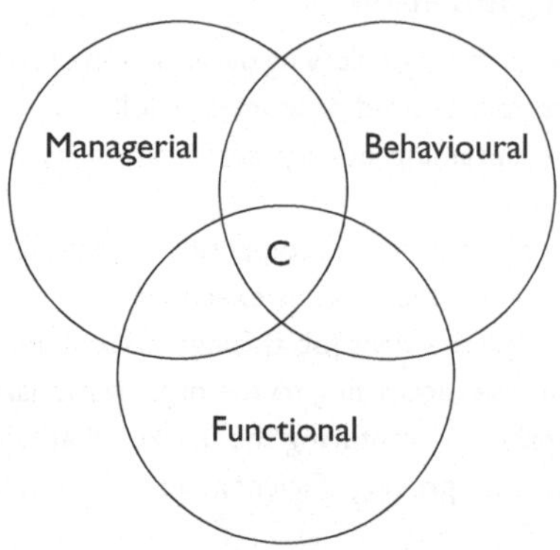

FIG. 5.2 MBF competency model

Competency assessment begins with identifying the competency required for the job/role assigned to an employee. The various steps are shown in Figure 5.3.

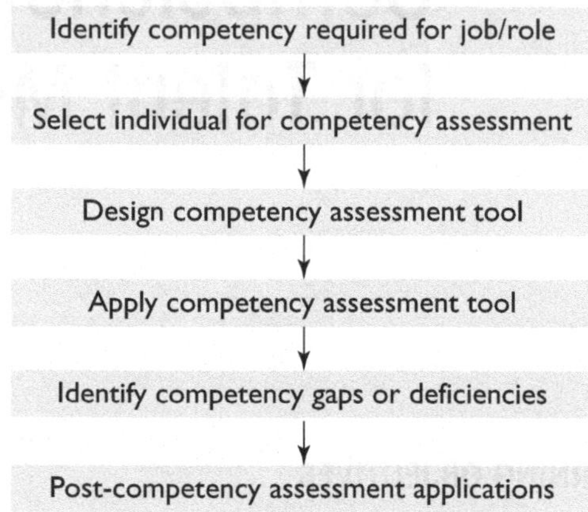

FIG. 5.3 Steps for competency assessment

Competency assessment

The company preferred to use the following assessment tools:

1. Self and superior assessment
2. Interviews

Primary data was collected from six departments (RF engineering, web world, commercial, fixed access, sales, and broadband).

The scholar used the questionnaire and interview schedules.

About the questionnaire

The researcher used a questionnaire covering managerial, behavioural, and functional competencies. The competencies mentioned in each competency set were as follows:

Managerial competency

1. Logical thinking
2. Analytical thinking
3. Stress management
4. Leadership skills
5. Planning and organizing skills
6. Problem analysis and decision making

Behavioural competency

7. Teamwork
8. Initiative
9. Innovation
10. Interpersonal communication
11. Mental balance and stability

12. Continuous learning
13. Timely completion of the job
14. Commitment to quality improvement
15. Adaptability to change

Functional competency

16. Knowledge of the job and its application
17. Business knowledge
18. Customer orientation
19. Knowledge of equipment standards
20. Knowledge of process standards
21. Computer skills (hardware and software)

Analysis of data

Each competency was rated on a five-point scale, followed by calculation of the scores for each of the three sets and the total score. The scholar found the job-dependent personality attributes and the profiling of characteristics such as tiger, chameleon, eagle, turtle, and salmon, of the 'life-style inventory'. The project concluded with the following:

1. Competency analysis score card
2. Personality inventory interpretation sheet

Learning points

The following observations were made from this exercise:

• Organizational growth and developing competencies go hand in hand.
• Competencies need to be assessed periodically.
• Assessment of competencies requires a scientific procedure

(Case study based on a project report titled 'Competency Evaluation of Reliance Communications Personnel' at Reliance Infocom, Kolkata, prepared by Mr Rajnish Sood and submitted to Indian Institute of Social Welfare and Business Management, 2007, for evaluation by the University of Kolkata.)

INTRODUCTION

The term 'competency mapping' has gained a wider circulation and importance among academicians and businesses in recent times. In a competitive business scenario, organizations have felt the utmost need for procuring and retaining competent employees and developing distinct competencies. Most of the jobs contain some critical elements or parts. To perform or fulfill these parts, it is important for the employees to have special competencies. It is also natural that some people perform a particular job more effectively than others. This difference exists because a particular individual may have certain competencies that other individuals might lack. This might help him/her to have an edge over the other in a particular job.

An organization examines every job to ascertain the component parts and the work environment in which it is performed. The process of examining a job is termed as job analysis. Job analysis comprises two functions, namely, job description and job specification. These are interrelated, interactive, and interdependent. Job description comprises job orientation, whereas job specification is oriented towards the jobholder. In other words, job description is a broad statement, which consists of the purpose, duties, and responsibilities of a job, all taken together. Job specification, on the other hand, is also a broad statement, which specifies only the qualities required for a jobholder.

It is evidenced that in earlier days, people in an organization were convinced that technical skills of the people in the research and development team was primarily responsible for the increased performance/output. On further exploration and extended study, it was revealed much to their surprise, that one of the most important differentiators between top performers and all others was their presentation skills. The key to validate these competencies is to determine the competencies (technical or interpersonal skills) and differentiate the best from the rest. Otherwise, one ends up with a very subjective data.

Let us recall the saying, 'Winners do not do different things, they do things differently'. Past experience shows that exceptional performers use a variety of approaches to get their job done. These approaches and behaviour chosen by these exceptional performers differ from those who perform at specified levels.

If one thinks about the teachers and doctors who are renowned in their fields, it can be observed that sound technical knowledge and skills are not the only basis of their distinctive competence. It is also their behaviour that has made them excellent, exceptional, and distinguished in their respective areas. One definitely believes that a doctor who cured an ailing relative is 'next to God'. Competencies provide a means of looking at the behaviour that differentiates the best from the rest, and a common language for talking about critical on-the-job behaviour.

In today's business scenario, which is characterized by mergers, acquisitions, growing competition, constant threats, and high degrees of uncertainties, most managers constantly face stressful situations. One must agree that a manager has to cope with all these challenges and yet, perform well. A complex combination of competencies comes into play to achieve success.

To some extent, competencies are also believed to be a result of academic training and experience. Learning and development takes place at three separate levels—knowledge, skill, and competency. Sanghi (2004) elucidates the conceptual difference among the three with the following example. Knowledge comes through reading (a person understands the meaning of driving a car). Skill develops through practicing (the person is shown how to drive a car and is allowed to practice in a non-traffic area). Competence refers to applying the skill (the person exhibits the ability to drive in traffic).

COMPETENCY

Competency is a concept that gives an indication to the employee about the areas and levels of performance that he would be expected to do. It is like a map that shows the employee the kind of behaviour that would be valued, recognized, and in some organizations, rewarded as well.

Competency is a cluster of related knowledge, skill, and attitude that affects a major part of one's job (a role or responsibility), and correlates with performance on the job. It can be measured against accepted standards, and can be improved through training and development (Parry 1996).

Often, the meaning of talent and competency are interchanged; they are different as discussed in Box 5.1.

Box 5.1 Talent and competency—a comparison

Talent is a particular strength or instinct that cannot be learned, at least, not easily. Talent is something innate, inborn, and inherent. Talent directs the mindset and governs the way of looking at things. Talent is stable within an individual. While working with a talented person, a team gets encouraged about the way it can complete the task assigned to it. Talent is a passion or excitement of doing a thing better.

On the other hand, competency refers to the ability that one possesses and refers to something that has been learned, studied, or practised, and ultimately mastered. Competency relates to a task required to be accomplished by one. Different persons take time to learn a thing in varying degrees. The level of talent is a determinant of the time required to accomplish a task. During a selection interview, interviewers use requisite tools to identify the competency. Hence, the term 'competency-based interview' has come into practice.

Talent is an additional aspect that should be encouraged and cultivated. Usually this is where an organization's performers or star employees exist with unique combinations of talent and competency.

The terms competency, talent, and skill are alternatively used. The iceberg model of competency provides clarification about these terms.

ICEBERG MODEL OF COMPETENCIES

The iceberg model of competencies (web.mit.edu) highlights the visible (iceberg that remains above the surface of water) and the less visible (iceberg that remains below the surface of water) competencies. A person demonstrates his skill and knowledge in the work area, and these are easily observable in his daily work and are evidenced from his outcomes. Obviously then, skill and knowledge represent the visible part of the competency. On the other hand, his interpersonal skills, attitudes, values, and motivation cannot be evidenced so easily and constitute the invisible part. Refer to Figure 5.4.

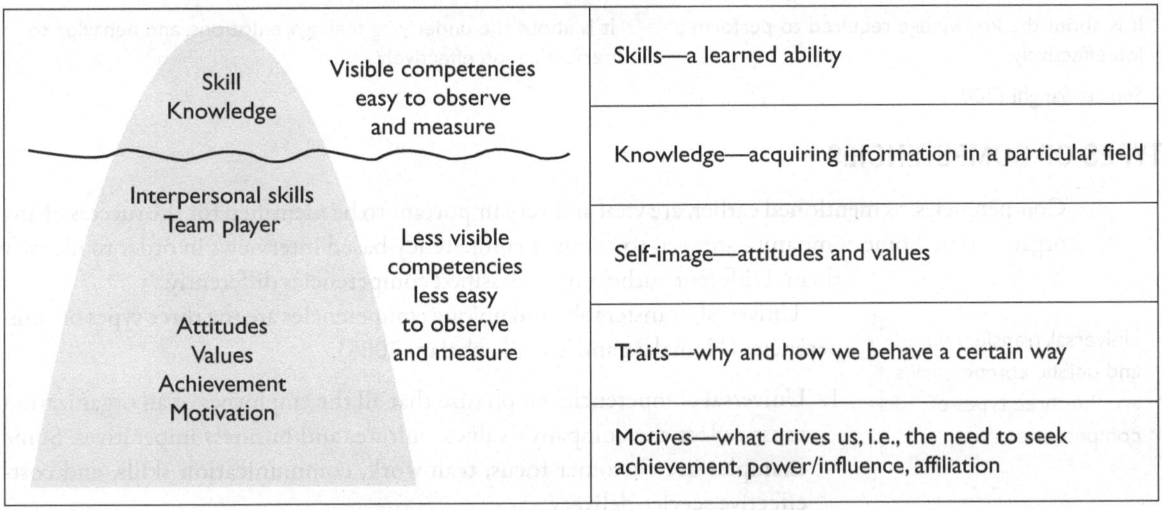

Fig. 5.4 Iceberg model of competencies

Contextually, it is mentioned that skills are the learned abilities;, knowledge is the information acquired in a particular field; attitudes and values constitute self-image; traits refer to the reasons as to why and how one behaves in a certain way; and motive is what drives us (for example, achievement, power/influence, affiliation) towards completing a task.

COMPETENCE VS COMPETENCY

Q 2 Many people in the organizations interchangeably use the terms competence and competency. Both these words are related, but do not convey the same meaning and are not synonyms of each other. HR professionals, especially those involved in performance management, distinguish these terms very well.

Competency is the behaviour that employees must have or acquire as input for a situation in order to achieve high levels of performance, whereas competence relates to a system of minimum standards of an organization or is demonstrated by its performance and outputs. Some of the differences are mentioned in Table 5.1.

Table 5.1 Differences between competence and competency

Competence	Competency
Ability to perform a job	Behavioural competencies
Skill and standard of performance reached	The behaviour by which competence has been achieved

(Contd)

Table 5.1 (Contd)

Competence	Competency
Skill-based	Behaviour-based
Standard attained	Manner of behaviour
What is measured?	How the standard is achieved?
Result of intelligence quotient	Result of emotional quotient
Refers to aptitude	Refers to attitude
It is about the knowledge required to perform a job effectively.	It is about the underlying feelings, emotions, and behavior to perform a job effectively.

Source: Sanghi (2004)

TYPES OF COMPETENCIES

Competencies, as mentioned earlier, are vital and very important to be identified for the success of any organization. Some companies are seen to conduct competency-based interviews in order to identify them. Different authors have classified competencies differently.

Universal, transferable, and unique competencies are the three types of competencies.

Universal, transferable, and unique competencies are the three types of competencies (Hemalata and Thanikachalam 2005).

1. Universal competencies emphasize that all the employees of an organization must reflect the company's values, culture, and business imperatives. Some examples are customer focus, teamwork, communication skills, and cost-effective service delivery.
2. Transferable competencies include skills and abilities needed to perform several roles in varying degrees of importance and mastery. Examples are leadership skills and managerial skills.
3. Unique competencies refer to specialized know-how or abilities required within a specific role or job.

Many academicians have mentioned five types of competency characteristics such as motives, traits, self-concept, knowledge, and skills. Out of these, the characteristics, motives, traits, and self-concept are invisible, whereas knowledge and skills are visible.

Motives Something that a person constantly thinks about or wants and drives him to take actions

Traits Physical characteristics and an individual's consistent responses to situations or information

Self-concept A person's attitudes, values, or self-image

Knowledge Information that a person has in a specific content area

Skills Ability to perform a certain mental or physical task

General Competency

There are some competencies that are essentially required by all human beings irrespective of the type of the organization, position in the organizational hierarchy, nature of products and services, whether it is operating in mild or tough competition, national or multinational, functioning in placid or turbulent environment, and so on. These are generic competencies which are also termed as 'skeleton competencies'.

Competencies which are essentially required by all human beings irrespective of the type of the organization, position in the organizational hierarchy, nature of products and services, etc., are termed as general or skeleton competencies.

Generic competencies include ambition, career aspirations, creativity, originality, compassion, peer relationship, organizing ability, personal learning, interpersonal savvy, self-knowledge, self-development, time management, urge to be a self-starter, etc.

Just as no person can stand without a skeleton, an individual cannot succeed in his/her professional career without having the generic or skeleton competencies.

Research scholars and organizational stalwarts have expressed their views and have defined competency, top competency, core competence, and competency mapping from different angles. Some of these definitions formulated by different academicians are given in Exhibit 5.1.

Exhibit 5.1 Definitions and interpretations

1. **Competency** refers to the underlying characteristics of a person, which results in an effective and/or superior performance on the job. This is widely accepted among HR specialists in the corporate environment.
2. **Competence** at work represents the underlying characteristics of an individual that is causally related to criterion such as referenced effecting and/or superior performance in job situations.
3. **Core competence** represents the enduring strength of a company that cannot be easily imitated. It is 'a bundle of skills and technologies that enable a company to provide a particular benefit to customers (Prahalad and Hamel 1996). It is a fundamental, unique, and inimitable strength of the firm. It is a centralized knowledge and skill base capable of producing a variety of products with differential features.
4. **Competencies** are behaviours that excellent performers exhibit more consistently than average performers.
5. **Competency map** is a comprehensive list of an individual's competencies that represent the factors most critical to success in given jobs, departments, organizations, or industries that are part of the individual's current career plan.
6. **Competency mapping** is a process followed by an organization or an individual to identify and describe competencies that are most critical to success in a work situation or work role. The process consists of breaking the job or role into its constituent elements or activities and identifying the competencies essentially required to perform the job successfully.
7. **Top competencies** are those few competencies (generally four to seven, on an average) that are most important to an individual in his ongoing career management process. 'Important to the individual' is an intuitive decision, based on the combination of three factors that comprise past demonstrated excellence in using the competency, inner passion for using the competency, and the current or likely future demand for the competency in the individual's current position or targeted career field.

If one analyses the definitions, the following can be interpreted:

1. Competencies are managerial characteristics.
2. Competencies must be demonstrated, and hence are observable.
3. Competencies lead to effective and superior performance.
4. Competency embodies the capacity to transfer skills and abilities to other persons and from one area to another.
5. Competency refers to exhibiting performance much more consistently.
6. Competence at work is causally related to criterion and affects superior performance in job situations.
7. Core competence is a bundle of skills and technologies that represents the enduring strength of a company that can't be easily copied.

Functional Competency

Q 1 Functional competencies are specific to a specific department or a type of job. Today's business scenario is very demanding and considers competency mapping very important for its survival and growth.

Competency identification skill is, in itself, a competency, which falls under the category of *technical competency*. The advent of information technology has resulted in the inclusion of computer competencies and electronic system skills in the technical competency set as well. Selecting the facilities required to perform a task and prepare objectives in measurable terms require skills, which also belong to this set. Developing a system of documentation, capacity of coaching, gaining negotiation skills, and managing knowledge have emerged as essential requirements in organizations. These need requisite competencies for the success of any organization.

In the changing scenario, a complete understanding of the business is vital. In the competitive environment, cost benefit analysis is an essential requirement in view of resource crunch, and hence, developing a delegation of junior colleagues is inescapable. Information and its supporting medium is a document that includes specifications, procedure documents, drawings, reports, standards, etc. Records are special types of documents. Documents and records are required to preserve information legibly and in a properly-indexed format to facilitate easy retrieval. Thus, documents and record management has also emerged as an essential requirement. These kinds of skills belong to the category of *business competencies*.

Coaching is another aspect that has become really important for the candidates to go through in order to achieve high efficiency from the employees. It helps in facilitating the enhancement of work performance of individuals. The coach can either be a manager or an external consultant. The coach can help anyone who wants to get better at their work. Coaching can be offered through designated coaching sessions.

Feedback is a HRD mechanism that helps a person understand his/her own strengths and weaknesses. The supervisors need to take the responsibility of observing, identifying and providing feedback to the junior colleagues about their strengths and weaknesses. In specific organizational situations, the feedback system emerges as an indispensable tool.

All of us negotiate in various spheres of our lives. In an organization, everyone negotiates informally at all times without even being aware of it. However, formal negotiation is a skill that can be learnt through experience and practice. A man who has never participated in formal negotiation is unlikely to have the skill. People who negotiate a lot tend to be much more skilled. Negotiation skills can be induced within junior colleagues. Also, one has knowledge about a process, procedure, or system. Enhancement of presentation skills might help him to disseminate his knowledge. These types of skills form the set of *interpersonal competencies*.

The scope of knowledge management emphasizes on data, information, knowledge, and wisdom. Acquisition and use of knowledge needs intellectual versatility. Organizational phenomena and their interrelationship require presentation through models, and thus model building skills and observation skills manifest their importance. Knowledge of self is an essential requirement. Additionally, a senior organizational leader must have vision and visionary skills. *Intellectual competencies* include all these skills.

Therefore, we can summarize the various visible parts of competencies (knowledge and skills) under the categories of competencies discussed so far.

Let us now study other competency sets comprising technical competencies, business competencies, interpersonal competencies, and intellectual competencies.

Technical Competencies

This category includes the underlying knowledge and skills (the portion of the iceberg that remains above the surface of water), described in observable and measurable terms that are necessary in order to perform a particular task assigned to a person achieving quantitative target and conforming to qualitative requirement. These competencies include the following:

1. Competency identification skill
2. Computer competencies
3. Career development theories and techniques understanding
4. Electronic system skill
5. Facilities selection skill
6. Objectives preparation skill
7. Performance observation skill
8. Training and development theories and techniques skill
9. Research skill

Business Competencies

Business competencies include knowledge and skills essentially required for decision-making and to run a business. Some business competencies are

1. Business understanding skill
2. Cost benefit analysis skill
3. Delegation skill
4. Organization behaviour understanding
5. Organization understanding
6. Project management skill
7. Marketing skill
8. Concept selling skill
9. Documents and records management skill

Interpersonal Competencies

The interpersonal competencies comprise knowledge and skills to develop the workforce, maintain relationship, understand others, and to communicate effectively.

1. Coaching skill
2. Feedback skill
3. Group process skill
4. Negotiation skill
5. Presentation skill
6. Questioning skill
7. Relationship building skill
8. Writing skill

Intellectual Competencies

These competencies need to be possessed by the organizational leaders for survival, and growth of the business in the complex and turbulent business environment.

1. Data reduction skill
2. Information search skill

3. Intellectual versatility
4. Model building skill
5. Observing skill
6. Self-knowledge
7. Visioning skill
8. Performance management skills

COMPETENCY SET

Now that we have discussed about competency and its types, let us look at the six competency sets—intellectual, personal, communication, interpersonal, leadership, and result-oriented competencies (Sanghi 2004). Refer to Table 5.2.

Table 5.2 Competency set

1. Intellectual	2. Personal	3. Communication
1. Information collection	13. Adaptability	21. Reading
2. Problem analysis	14. Independence	22. Written communication
3. Numerical interpretation	15. Integrity	23. Listening
4. Judgement	16. Stress tolerance	24. Oral expression
5. Critical faculty	17. Resilience	25. Oral presentation
6. Creativity	18. Detail consciousness	
7. Planning	19. Self-management	
8. Perspective	20. Change-oriented	
9. Organizational awareness		
10. External awareness		
11. Learning orientated		
12. Technical expertise		

4. Interpersonal	5. Leadership	6. Result-oriented
26. Impact	32. Organizing	38. Risk taking
27. Persuasiveness	33. Empowering	39. Decisiveness
28. Sensitivity	34. Appraising	40. Business sense
29. Flexibility	35. Motivating others	41. Energy
30. Ascendancy	36. Developing others	42. Concern for excellence
31. Negotiating	37. Leading	43. Tenacity
		44. Initiative
		45. Customer-oriented

Exhibit 5.2 gives a brief explanation on the competency set essential for HRD practioners.

Exhibit 5.2 Competency sets for HRD practitioners

In his article entitled, 'Competencies for Human Resource Development Practitioners', Barney Erasmus of Business University of South Africa, mentions business competencies, interpersonal competencies, and personal competencies as essential competencies for HRD practitioners. He has mentioned the specific attributes of these competencies.

The category of business competencies includes analysing needs and proposing solutions, applying business acumen, driving results, planning and implementing assignments, and thinking strategically.

The category of interpersonal competencies encompasses building trust, communicating effectively, influencing stakeholders, leveraging diversity, and networking and partnering.

However, demonstrating adaptability and modeling personal development are contributors to the personal competencies.

Source: www.cluteinstitute.com/proceedings/2010, last accessed on 24 January 2011

COMPETENCY MAPPING

Q 2 Competency mapping refers to the process of identifying the key skills required for accomplishing tasks at a particular position. On completion of this process, the map becomes an input for several other HR processes such as job-evaluation; recruitment; training and development; performance management; and succession planning.

The mapping process starts with the understanding of the vision and mission of the organization, followed by translating them into specific, measurable, and time-bound business goals. It then goes on to clearly outlining an organization's structure, identifying various levels and positions, as well as reporting relationships obtained within the structure.

HR professionals initially draw a distinction between competencies and competences. Though, it has already been discussed that these two terms are often used interchangeably, competency more precisely refers to employee behaviour whereas competence highlights on employee performances, skills, or their results.

Need for Competency Mapping

Competency mapping has gained commonness, momentum, and popularity. The old maxim, 'Slow and steady wins the race' has lost its validity in view of the fast changing business environment. In order to cope with the changing world economy and keeping in view that the world is becoming a global village, companies have become more aware of the need for having competent employees and developing distinguished competencies for every organization. In terms of quality of people, organizations need fast and consistent manpower. As such, in the sharper focus of management, competency mapping is engaged in the collection and constellation of information about the appropriate talent in various levels. The needs for competency mapping are enumerated here:

1. The cost of manpower is becoming increasingly high
2. Realization of the truth that people can transform an organization
3. Getting more from the people rather than getting more people.
4. Increased customer focus; identifying and fulfilling implied customer needs and expectations.
5. Recognizing the fact that the right kind of human resources can monitor and manage the technology, finance, market, customers, customer relationship, processes, procedures, and the system effectively.
6. Importance of role performer vis-à-vis time management.

Today, organizations need fast and consistent manpower as against slow and steady.

In the era of competitive business, hunting for talent and managing them properly is a crucial task for HR professionals. As a result, the top management and HRD directors or managers are paying attention to competencies of the workforce. Hence, competency and competency mapping are important and essential exercises.

Objectives of Competency Mapping

The concept of competency mapping now exists in organizations with well-developed HR practices. HR directors and their top management have always paid attention to consider competencies and incorporated them in the appraisal forms in order to improve the performance management system. Companies such as Larsen & Toubro, National Dairy Development Board, Life Insurance Corporation of India, Hindustan Lever Ltd (presently Hindustan Unilever Ltd), NOCIL Ltd, Bharat Petroleum, and so on, have felt the utmost need for management of competencies and revised their performance appraisal systems (SAIL 2009). Some of their objectives while performing their competency mapping are as follows:

1. Identifying the key success factors
2. Pinpointing triggers for each role
3. Laying direction for superior performance
4. Setting defined expectations from employees
5. Serving means for communicating performance expectations
6. Ensuring that the employees obtain greater transparency about their roles
7. Providing opportunities for development
8. Creating a more empowered workforce
9. Employing the workforce effectively

Therefore, from the discussion, it is clear that competency mapping is important. Box 5.2 lists some applications of the same.

Box 5.2 Applications of competency mapping

Competency mapping is a process. The outcomes of competency mapping are applied in many activities in the organization. These include the following:

1. Performance management and appraisal
2. Personal development plans
3. Career and succession planning
4. Job descriptions
5. Person specifications
6. Management selection
7. Recruitment, selection, induction and placement
8. Management development programmes
9. Training and development

(Contd)

Box 5.2 (Contd)

Mapping at these levels helps in knowing exactly the kind of competencies that are required for those particular jobs. In other words, standardizing the required characteristics of employees to successfully finish a task is finalized. It also helps in judging the capacity of the individual currently holding the position and makes him responsible.

BENEFITS OF COMPETENCY APPROACH

The benefits of the competency approach are manifold. Competency approaches and analysis, if done correctly, leads to great benefits for the organization. Some of these are as follows:

1. Increases productivity
2. Enhances perfection in quality of work
3. Improves work performance
4. Helps in designing the training process focused on the company objectives
5. Empowers the workforce
6. Treats the employees as partners in their own performance development
7. Builds trust between employees and managing interpersonal relationships
8. Improves control over delivering the metrics to evaluate staff performance against competency frameworks and organizational objectives.
9. Monitors the training and development budget—cost reduction and rigorous management, once a clear picture of business needs and individual skills are assessed
10. Improves and develops good processes as a result of which members of organizations produce better output
11. Enhances resource utilization where natural resources are scarce

Chatterjee (2007) pursued a study on competency framework of some selected organizations organizations at their initial stage. The companies developed their competency frameworks and undertook competency mapping practices of ITC Ltd (Kolkata), Shoppers Stop Ltd, UB Group, and Ananda Bazar Patrika Ltd. Exhibit 5.3 gives an idea on the type of competencies these organizations finalized for themselves.

Exhibit 5.3 Competency mapping practices

ITC Ltd (Kolkata)

The marketing practices of the organization include competencies relating to the following:

1. *Brand*—Brand is just an identity of a specific product, which can take the form of a name, logo, symbol, colour, or any combination. Brand management refers to the application of specific techniques where competencies are required.
2. *Sales and distribution*—It means designing a multi-channel system to reach customers, selling products or services, providing after sales services, collecting feedback to provide to product design department, etc.
3. *Product and development*—It involves the process of developing a new product considering the customer needs, bringing the new product into the market, and arranging a method of collecting feedback for incorporation in future design.
4. *Exports*—This means shipping of goods or commodities from one country to another country in a legitimate fashion. Typically, this term is used for business and is the reverse meaning of import.

The company defines its sales and distribution competencies in the state of West Bengal, in certain categories such as

(Contd)

Exhibit 5.3 (Contd)

1. Market knowledge
2. Sales forecasting
3. West Bengal state pricing
4. Work processes, procedures, and systems
5. Stick control
6. Logistics management
7. Distribution management
8. Trade relationship management
9. Portfolio management

The company has personnel at nine levels, L–9 (the lowest level) to L–1 (executive vice president), in the sales departments. The company defines competencies relating to the categories mentioned earlier for each of the nine levels.

1. L–9: Sales operation manager
2. L–8: Area executive
3. L–7: Area manager
4. L–6: Assistant manager
5. L–5: Branch manager
6. L–4: Regional sales manager
7. L–3: National sales manager
8. L–2: General manager
9. L–1: Executive vice president

For all the levels the company rates the competencies on a five-point scale based on which decisions regarding training, development, and promotion, are taken.

Shoppers Stop Ltd

Even though this organization does not have any competency model, it lays emphasis on the following attributes of competencies:

1. Communication skills
2. Presentable
3. Customer service orientation
4. Focused people—those who want to make a career in retail sales
5. Stress management ability
6. Good selling skill
7. Product knowledge

United Breweries Group

The group does not have any competency model as such, but it looks into some attributes of competencies for the frontline sales officer and those in the managerial cadre. The attributes are as follows:

1. Sound business knowledge
2. Analytical skills
3. Ability to convince
4. Negotiating skills
5. Job knowledge
6. Trade relationship management
7. Competitor tracking

The competency requirements for managerial cadres include the following:

1. Problem-solving ability
2. Ability to work in teams
3. Leadership quality—the ability to motivate, set directions, and maintain the morale of the group in a crisis situation
4. Coordination skills
5. Foresight—the ability to visualize changes, its speed, and direction
6. Networking and partnering

Ananda Bazar Patrika

The competency model is simple and includes the following seven winning competencies:

1. Leading teamwork and change—working in teams and accommodating change is beneficial to the members and to the organization as well.
2. Practical creativity—creativity that can be applied in organizational context
3. Initiative and achievement orientation—propensity to take initiative and orientation to achieve goals
4. Self-confidence and integrity—fumbling leads to mistake; one should gain confidence through mentoring and work in harmony with others
5. Self-development and watching others—one should continuously develop and should not hesitate to learn from others
6. Customer focus—refers to knowing the stated and implicated needs of customers
7. Business insight—anticipating the direction and speed of change, initiating proactive steps for sustenance and growth of business

COMPETENCY FRAMEWORK

Competency framework refers to the conceptual structure in an organization relating to the behavioural elements of employees. It is an illustration of the softer skills that are essential for effective performance. The frameworks have slowly become broader and more ambitious in scope and include more technical

Competency framework refers to conceptual structure relating to the behavioural elements of employees.

competencies. This development has been given an even greater momentum by the use of personal computers and the intranet.

While designing a competency framework, care must be taken that only measurable components are included. It is advised to restrict the number and complexity of competencies in a framework, typically aiming for no more than 12 for any particular role (preferably less), and arranging them into clusters to make the framework more accessible to the users. The definitions and examples for each competency must also be provided.

When supporting talent management, the competency framework is an essential resource for understanding the current performance of the employees. Of course, it is a recognized fact that talent management is a future-focused activity, and it measures an individual's future potential and motivation that are also embraced in the decision-making process.

Competency framework refers to a conceptual framework and it plays an important role in all aspects of talent management, including talent acquisition, talent development, performance management, and talent separation. For studying the use of competency framework in an organization, one would need to glance into the detailed aspects of these processes. However, there might be one area where the linkage between competency framework and a process is visible, partially, or fully.

Job descriptions are prepared considering the position in an organization, the associated nature of duty, and the competency framework developed for that particular position. We find job descriptions everywhere, in newspapers, on job search portals, and on a company's website as well. Nowadays, one can search job openings on the company's website by giving keywords, location, etc.

By adopting and applying a consistent competency framework across their organization, employers can ensure that they recruit the most suitable candidates, identify high potentials at an early stage, promote the right individuals, and increase retention through structured performance management and career development planning.

The competency framework holds many separate competencies that may be arranged into five core clusters—thinking, relating, leading, self-managing, and achieving.

1. *Thinking*—cognitive and intellectual competencies. This cluster includes competency identification skill, business understanding skill, organization behaviour understanding skill, project management skill, electronic system skill, facilities selection skill, etc.
2. *Relating*—social or interpersonal competencies. This cluster demands building bridges of relationship; creating networking and partnering.
3. *Leading*—managerial competencies (logical thinking, analytical thinking, stress management, leadership skills, planning and organizing skills, and problem analysis and decision-making). It comprises several skills—building a strong team of people, creating a learning environment, monitoring and reviewing business situations periodically, attracting talent, preventing attrition, recognizing innovative work done, sharing ideas regarding organizational growth, etc.
4. *Self-managing*—competencies relating to emotions, stimulation, motivation, driving forces, and reactions; the degree of influences on effectiveness and efficiency, and analysing how these influence effectiveness and efficiency.
5. *Achieving*—result-focused competencies relating to achievement of business goals. Negotiation skill, presentation skill, visioning skills, etc. are all essential to achieve business results.

Competency framework holds five core clusters—thinking, relating, leading, self-managing, and achieving.

Exhibit 5.4 shows the established framework followed at the Chartered Institute of Personnel and Development (CIPD).

Exhibit 5.4 Competency framework at CIPD

The Chartered Institute of Personnel and Development mentions certain simple steps, based on research findings, to develop the competency framework. The steps ensure to check whether a competency framework is fit for the purpose. These steps are as follows:

1. Communicating the purpose
2. Identifying key themes
3. Getting conditions right
4. Being realistic
5. Tackling the root cause
6. Keeping it simple
7. Training, not blaming

Communicating the purpose—This step is by far the most important one. The framework should be established only after a proper mapping of the position is carried out. The purpose of a particular position elucidates the importance of behaviour as contributor to personal and organizational successes.

Identifying the key themes—Aspirations of an organization include achievement of goals, values, business plans, and so on. Staff members might be clear about the purpose of the competency framework. The efforts of individuals might not be synchronous, and in such cases, coordination manifests its importance. People must exert concerted efforts to achieve the aspirations. In order to translate the aspiration to actions, they need competencies.

Getting conditions right—The various procedures of an organization need to support the framework; including the culture, resourcing and management structures. Hence, after the purpose and the theme are identified, the next step for the organization is to create the right conditions for the framework to be the most effective.

Being realistic—While setting the conditions, it is important to keep in mind the behaviour/element that might inhibit or slow up the process. If the situation demands, such elements should be modified.

Tackling the root cause—It is important to unearth the right factors responsible for affecting the business. Suppose in an organization, poor communication between teams is the main factor jeopardizing the business. In such a case, if the organization starts working towards the improving the behaviour of its employee, it would be futile. Hence, the root cause must be identified and tackled.

Keeping it simple—Language and structure are the two key elements that make the competency framework user-friendly and easy to use. A 'perfect' but complicated and lengthy framework is quite likely to be misinterpreted. Hence, it is best to make the framework simple with language being meaningful and non-ambiguous.

Training, not blaming—Training manifests its importance at this stage. People need to be trained with respect to the working of the framework. A framework is a tool. A user manual is given in a tool kit in order to acquaint the user. Training is comparable with the user manual. Users must know how to use the framework. Otherwise, the framework will fall into disuse or fail to meet its full potential.

CIPD conducted a learning and development survey in 2007. The following are the most popular steps or actions found in employer competency frameworks:

1. Communication skills
2. People management skills
3. Team building/leading skills
4. Customer service skills
5. Results-orientation skills
6. Problem-solving skills

Q 3 Developing a Competency Framework

An organization can develop its competency framework in different ways. Generally, companies draw their competency framework keeping in view their occupational standards. Frameworks developed in this way are often linked with progression towards recognized qualifications. Many organizations develop their competency frameworks through an internal research programme for which they engage advisers from consultancy services. The method of developing a framework ranges from importing an existing and available package to developing the entire framework from scratch by departmental experts.

The best solution usually lies between these two extremes, namely, internally generating a framework that builds relevance in business and done by adapting the existing models that have already been widely used and have been proved successful.

It is evident that many organizations develop a competency/behaviour framework with a view to effectively manage performance and progression. However, many managers find it difficult to use the frameworks and as such, fail to achieve their individual goals. Thus, the goals of the organization remain unachieved. The most common reason for this failure is that people are not adequately trained and they do not see the benefit of the framework. In addition to this, people must be clear about the framework. In fact, many frameworks are a mix of different concepts. There are not clear links as to what the business is aiming to achieve; many frameworks are a mix of different concepts, which makes them clumsy and cumbersome.

Exhibit 5.5 lists the key job functions and competencies in different industries.

Exhibit 5.5 Key job functions and competencies

IT personnel

Information technology personnel are required to perform some key job functions. Persons associated with information technology need a set of competencies to successfully accomplish the tasks they are assigned. Some of the key job functions and competencies they must have are

1. Application services
2. Business unit support
3. Computer operations
4. Corporate function analysis
5. Data management
6. IT infrastructure library (ITIL)
7. Infrastructure management
8. Information technology security
9. VIRUS protection
10. IT service management
11. Network services
12. Program/project management
13. Systems management
14. Technology development
15. Architecture
16. Web services

Corporate personnel

The key job functions and competencies for corporate personnel are different from those of the IT personnel due to the nature of the job they perform. You can evidence the differences by comparing the job functions of IT and corporate personnel. The following are some of the key functions of corporate personnel:

1. Administration
2. Application services
3. Business unit support
4. Computer operations
5. Corporate communications
6. Corporate functions
7. Customer support
8. Data management
9. Executive
10. Finance and accounting
11. Human resources
12. Infrastructure management
13. IT security and IT service management
14. Legal services
15. Marketing
16. Network services
17. Program/project management
18. Purchasing
19. Research and development
20. Sales
21. Systems management
22. Technology development and architecture
23. Training and development

Let us now concentrate on the competencies of an HR professional.

1. HR expertise
2. Understand and contribute to advance the business
3. Take calculated risks
4. Understand team behaviour and provide leadership
5. Build up followers, develop and maintain a trusting relationship
6. Knowing industrial relation mechanisms
7. Acting as an internal change agent
8. Acquaintance with the HR principles
9. Be customer orientated
10. Select HRD mechanisms
11. Appreciate the organization's mission
12. Be a strategic planner
13. Develop innovative systems

COMPETENCY MAPPING METHODOLOGY

Q 4 Identification of all the competencies required to accomplish a job is not easy. Managers commonly use some techniques to identify the competencies. These comprise the following:

1. Assessment centre
2. Critical incident method
3. Interview techniques
4. Questionnaires
5. Psychometric tests

These would now be taken up individually and discussed in detail.

Assessment Centre

Organizations are now seen to be investing in assessment centres that are into the business of mapping/diagnosing competencies. This, in turn, has led to a job–person–organization fit and alignment to HR systems, namely talent management, recruitment and selection, retention, management development, career, and succession planning. In 1960, American Telephone and Telegraph (AT&T) initiated the assessment centre method while promoting its line personnel to supervisory positions.

Q 5 Assessment centre is a procedural mechanism to identify the potential for the growth of the company. It is very often misperceived as a location. Assessment centre is strictly a procedure (and not a location) to evaluate employees for manpower planning and decisions. The procedure uses a 'situational test' to observe specific job behaviour characteristics. Assessment centre procedure is used to determine the suitability of a person for a specific job. As such, elements related to the job are simulated through a variety of tests. The assessors observe the behavioural disposition and make independent evaluations of the observation. This results in the identification of the strengths and weaknesses of the attributes being studied. The company can initiate remedial measures such as eliminating or reducing the weaknesses and enhancing the strengths.

Based on large bodies of academic research, the assessment centre is treated as the most valid predictor of performance. It comprises of a number of exercises such as the following:

1. Assessment centre elements
2. Group discussion
3. In tray
4. Interview, simulation/role plays
5. Case studies/analysis exercises

Assessment Centre Elements

There are certain elements that are essential if an assessment centre is to be considered as a process. In this regard, the International Personnel Management Association (IPMA) identified elements, some of which are as follows:

1. Job analysis is meant to determine attributes, skills, ability, etc., required for effective job performance, and to define the scope of evaluation of the assessment centre.
2. One must validate the technique or techniques to be used to assess the dimensions of skills and abilities.
3. One must not stick to a particular technique; rather, multiple techniques should be used.

4. The assessment technique must include job-related simulations.
5. Multiple assessors must be engaged for each assessment to control any possible human errors.
6. Before assigning the task of assessment, the assessors should be thoroughly trained.
7. The observations must be classified into some meaningful categories of attributes, skills, and abilities.
8. The observations conforming to a systematic procedure must be recorded.
9. Assessors must prepare a report.
10. The information must be integrated through discussion or by applying statistical techniques.

Group Discussion

A team is formed with candidates and they are given one or more agendas (such as management of a problem, improvement initiative) on which they are required to make a recommendation. Each member is assigned a specific role in the group. As a ground rule, they are all provided the same basic information. The discussion allows the candidates to share and exchange ideas and information, based on their knowledge and experience. It enables the management to draw on the ideas and expertise about the members, and make decisions. Some of the advantages of group discussions are enumerated as follows:

1. Additional ideas can be generated.
2. Ideas (of one member) can be shared with other members.
3. New ideas can be tried out.
4. It can facilitate a member to think and contribute innovative ideas.
5. Group dynamics and synergy are restored.
6. Group discussion skills have multifaceted professional applications.
7. Boredom is relieved and work becomes enjoyable.

Group discussion is applied in the identification of task and maintenance roles that members can take up. From the participation and exchanged dialogues of the members, the observers can identify positive task roles, positive maintenance roles, as well as negative roles. These roles give a clearer idea to the examiners about whom to select.

Positive Task Roles

Possession of these roles helps one reach the decision faster and ensures more effectiveness. Identification and recognition of the following roles—initiator, information seeker, information giver, opinion seeker, opinion giver, clarifier, and summarizer—can be easily judged.

1. *Initiator*—initiates the discussion by providing new ways to approach the problem; recommends novel ideas pertaining to the problem
2. *Information seeker*—accentuates 'getting the facts' and invites background information from others
3. *Information giver*—supplies facts and figures collected from different sources, provides data to make decisions, and offers own expertise
4. *Opinion seeker*—ensures involvement seeking qualitative data, such as aptitude, attitude, values, traits, and feelings
5. *Opinion giver*—discloses himself/herself, provides an opinion and feelings
6. *Clarifier*—takes an analytical approach, gives additional information, uses examples, rephrases wherever required, and pays attention
7. *Summarizer*—provides a summary of the discussions

Positive Maintenance Roles

This role helps the group discussion to continue definitely, in a positive direction. Opposing points and comments may emerge as roadblocks. At this point of time, the maintenance role carried out by some participating members settles the group discussion environment. This is the individual who comes in the notice of the examiners. Some of the maintenance roles are the following:

1. *Social supporter*—expresses compliments, extends warmth, offers rewards, respects others comments, behaves assertively, and praises to enthuse group members.
2. *Harmonizer*—synchronizes the situation, regularizes the issues, manages interpersonal conflicts, and promotes a healthy situation.
3. *Tension reliever*—rationally explains the merits and demerits of an idea, and approaches informally to bring out the positive and negative aspects of group dynamics.
4. *Energizer*—Sometimes the group discussion slows down and members lose the tempo of offering ideas. The energizing role stimulates the candidates and facilitates to continue the discussion in its rhythm.
5. *Compromiser*—adjusts oneself to accommodate others' viewpoint on an issue and shifts his/her own stand thus reducing conflicts.
6. *Gatekeeper*—sets up procedures (such as structured brainstorming) to smooth out communication and also to ensure equal participation of all members. In the absence of any such procedure, a few members dominate the discussion while others are not able to express their viewpoint, ideas, and plans.

Negative Roles

There are a number of negative roles, which are often taken up by some members that adversely affect the discussion. These roles should be avoided. The discussion group may adopt the ground rule prohibiting the use of these negative rules. In fact, at the beginning of the discussion, the group must censure the negative roles. Some negative roles are the following:

1. *Attacker*—behaving aggressively, expressing disapproval rudely, and criticizing the personality and intellect of others
2. *Passivity*—possessing tortoise characteristics, withdrawing from the group, and not contributing ideas; their presence retards the active participation of other members; members emerge as disgruntled non-participants
3. *Dominator*—trying to take control over others during the discussion, talking a great deal about own expertise and background, and interrupting other members.
4. *Clown*—not participating seriously, adopting a haughty attitude, disrupting others, and becoming inappropriately humorous.

In Tray

Assessors undertake this type of exercise individually when a person is required to replace somebody else. The requirement of positioning may be undertaken for replacing his predecessor, and assuming new assignments at short notice. He has to deal with pending papers and correspondence received by the candidate, by post or through courier or electronic media such as e-mail. The candidate may take guidance from the annotations (marginal notes) of his predecessor, but he has to act effectively. The accumulated correspondences cannot be just dealt with. An experienced senior manager goes through the annotations. The candidate's decision-making ability and his approach to managerial problems are judged through his/her ways of dealing with the papers.

Interview, Simulation/Role Plays

In these exercises, a resource person (or role player) executes a vital role. Each member of a team (employees of the company) individually meets the resource person. After having discussions on some specific aspect or issue of dispute with the resource person, the candidate is asked to take part in a meeting. Of course, the employees are allowed to prepare for the meeting within a short time of 15–30 minutes. During the meeting, the conduct of the candidates is observed by the assessors as a part of the assessment process. Preparatory notes are also considered for the purpose of evaluation.

Case Studies/Analysis Exercises

The main task of managers is decision-making. The success of an organization depends on the strategy, structure, system, and style of the managers. Cases are prepared reflecting the status of an organization covering some functional areas. The case contains a large amount of factual information. In some cases, the information may be ambiguous or even contradictory. Candidates generally do the case analysis independently. They are asked to submit a brief written report or to communicate the findings or decisions by way of a presentation. During the presentation, the thought process gets articulated to the audience (the assessors). The case analysis, findings, and decisions taken are followed by a presentation, and when taken as a system, they assume paramount importance.

CRITICAL INCIDENTS TECHNIQUE

Q 6 This technique was developed by Flanagan (1954). In the literal sense, critical means serious, vital, crucial, derogatory, and precarious. But in an organizational context, it is difficult to define critical incidents. Nevertheless, we can definitely opine that critical incidents can contribute to the growth or decay of an organizational system, and of the organization as a whole. The critical incidents technique uses a set of procedures to systematically identify behaviour that contributes to the success or failure of individuals or the organizations in specific situations. Supervisors, clients, peers, or subordinates are better suited for using this technique as they are good observers. The observers should have adequate exposure to the critical incident method. Observers are interrogated to describe the incidents of effective and ineffective behaviour of a person over a long period of time. Organizations initially prepare an exhaustive list of good or bad job behaviour. The panel of experts helps to rate how good or bad the behaviours are. Next, the organization finalizes the checklist of the good or bad behaviour.

Supervisors take notes based on direct observations. The junior colleagues also take part in discussions with the respective superior, particularly when the result is adverse to the organization. In this way, the subordinates are involved and trained simultaneously, and a balance sheet for each employee is generated. These records help to review the performance of the employees at the end of the financial year. In addition to this, the balance sheets are further used while assigning tasks to new individuals in the future. This technique is useful around a particular role or set of tasks.

There are certain criteria for the successful use of the critical incidents technique. Some of these are the following:

1. Data is collected by direct observations of real critical incidents that occurred while accomplishing a task in a real-life situation.

2. The actual jobholders perform tasks.
3. Users are located in a real work environment from whom the data is collected.
4. Users are required to report the critical incidents after they have occurred.
5. Direct interaction between the users and the evaluators does not take place.
6. Qualitative data can be gathered by the users at a very low cost.

Steps Involved in Critical Incidents Technique

There are three steps involved in this technique, namely, gathering facts, content analysis, and creating feedback.

Step 1: Gathering facts Retrospective data is captured through an open-minded questionnaire. One must ensure that there is much of a gap between the occurrence of the events and capturing the data. In case of a longer time period, it becomes difficult to gather the true responses as imagined stereotyped responses replace the true responses.

For gathering facts, generally two approaches are adopted—unstructured approach and moderate structured approach.

1. Unstructured approach—Individuals are asked to submit two good things and two bad things while performing a given task or set of activities.
2. Moderate structured approach—In this approach, the individuals are requested to respond to certain questions on the happenings relating to the activity he/she was performing. The questions may be of the following types:
   (a) What exactly happened?
   (b) What might be the reason behind the happenings?
   (c) How did the happening affect the outcome or result?

Step 2: Content analysis This step facilitates identification of particular incidents that are capable of representing content dimensions or categories. Recording of incidents is an ongoing process. Several incidents are recorded and submitted to the analysts who study the cluster of incidents, categorize, and sort them into content dimensions. This process groups the incidents based on the dimensions. The sorted incidents resemble the affinity diagram of total quality management.

The basis of grouping is 'identical', 'quite similar' or 'could be similar'. Each category is assigned a name and the number of incidents are counted and recorded. The number of incidents in a category is expressed as a percentage of the total number of incidents. The categories are often arranged in descending order of the percentage counts and the report is compiled.

Step 3: Creating feedback Every individual has his/her own strengths and weaknesses, which often remain unidentified. These could be useful in specific organizational situations. The supervisors in the HRD system bear the responsibility of observing, identifying, and providing feedback to the junior colleagues about their strengths and weaknesses. Added to this, they should have the guidance to improve enabling capacities and performance capabilities. It is important to provide both positive and negative feedback to the juniors. They have to arrange the poor features as well as the good features in a descending order using the frequencies in each category. At this point it is advisable take the help of some software. Each poor and good feature can be hyperlinked to examine the specific circumstance that led to each category of critical incident. It is possible that more than one aspect has led to the critical incident. Thus, they should concentrate on all the aspects that might have been combined to make the incident critical.

After understanding the steps of the technique, they must also be aware of certain precautions that need to be kept in mind to work it smoothly.

Human error can always occur in any activity. However, error that is unconsciously committed can be traced back in the critical incident technique, and the analyst can also rectify it.

For instance, a person possessing a learner's driving license proceeded on a long road drive. His wife, an MBA graduate, had read an article on the critical incident method in a journal. She recorded a few critical incidents on driving and casually discussed these with an analyst working in her organization. The experienced analyst pointed out the mistakes. If an inadequately-trained person is assigned the task of recording critical incidents of a pilot relating to reading and interpreting the aircraft instruments, the recordings may lead to disaster.

The recorder of critical incidents must be an experienced person. This job should not be assigned to a person with superficial knowledge in the subject. The analyst must have knowledge of the critical incident technique. In addition to this, he/she should have a fair degree of knowledge in software engineering, which is required to use the technique in mapping.

With knowledge in both the fields, he/she will be able to identify the critical incidents, and report and rate the severity level.

There are certain disadvantages in this technique.

1. This technique focuses only on critical incidents and overlooks routine and regular incidents. However, lapses in routine incidents may sometimes lead to disaster.
2. It is evidenced that interviewees give stereotyped replies which do not relate to the actual events. The analyst must be careful in this regard. He should not just record whatever they say.
3. Error may occur due to the lack of ability of the end users in recognizing and reporting the critical incidents effectively. It should never be believed that all the end users have this ability. The analyst must be meticulous.

INTERVIEW TECHNIQUE

As a method of competency mapping, the interview technique is considered unique because it involves direct interaction between the interviewer and interviewee. The interviewer can observe the body language of the interviewee from which he can record his readings. An interview is the most commonly used personal contact method and many organizations use this technique for competency mapping. The following steps must be observed for successful mapping:

Step 1 Preparation of a checklist of questions to identify the judging ability and skills. The questions are to be framed based on the critical areas. The responses may be rated on five-point or ten-point rating scales.

Step 2 The responsible person scrutinizes the information provided to him to identify the skills, incidents, and experiences in the career of the candidate. He gets the answers to the questions raised on critical areas. This procedure ensures that the interview is 'to the point' without digressing from reality. The interviewee feels comfortable because the questions are focused on his experiences.

Step 3 The interviewer must use tact and sensitivity to create a sense of ease and informality so that the interviewees can get rid of tension, nervousness, and be at ease. If tensed and afraid, they lose their creativity and originality. The interviewers should create an environment where the interviewees are relaxed and open. They should also honour the interviewee's motivation, attitude, feelings, temperament, etc.

Step 4 The interviewer must cautiously build rapport with the interviewee. The initial questions must be based on the interviewee's fields of interest. Otherwise, one may start discussions on the weather, tourism, sports and games, and similar subjects or any other unrelated topic.

Step 5 After creating an environment conducive to the fruitful interaction, the interviewer may start asking questions about the critical areas. Asking difficult and complex questions at the beginning should be avoided. Gradually, after the confidence level builds up, the interviewee may be able to answer complex questions. Thus, the pattern should range from simple to complex questions.

Step 6 Disapproval or disagreement of answers inhibits the interviewee from responding spontaneously. The interviewer must try to examine the viewpoint of the interviewee. However, disagreement can definitely be expressed tactfully.

Step 7 The interviewer must avoid leading questions as the interviewee may feel that a certain stereotyped response is expected. At the same time, the interviewer is alerted that he must not allow the interview to get out of hand. He should check if the interviewee tries to lead the discussion in areas in which he has mastery and feels competent of himself.

Note: The interviewer should keep a list of questions ready prior to beginning the interview.

QUESTIONNAIRE

Q 7 Sir Francis Galton (1822–1911) developed the format for the questionnaire. This questionnaire helps in analysing a job by collecting information from respondents. Of course, the responses collected are subjected to analysis, including statistical analysis, for the final interpretation. The questionnaire may contain multiple choice questions, and true or false statements. However, such standardized answers often frustrate the respondents. Questionnaires are limited to only the literates but can be circulated across a large sample in less time. Question construction seems to be one of the major hurdles in using this technique.

The questionnaire includes the following:

1. Common metric questionnaire (CMQ)
2. Functional job analysis (FJA)
3. Multipurpose occupational system analysis inventory (MOSAIC)
4. Occupational analysis inventory (OAI)
5. Positional analysis inventory (PAQ)
6. Work profiling system (WPS)

Common Metric Questionnaire

Different tasks need different types of competencies. However, it has been evidenced that work performance needs some common competencies. The common metric questionnaire has been field tested on

4,552 positions representing over 900 occupations in the Dictionary of Occupational Titles (DOT), and has yielded reasonably-high reliabilities (Harvey 1993). The CMQ comprises the following five distinct sections:

1. *Background*—helps to identify different requirements of the work
2. *Contacts with people*—embarks upon building bridges of relationship like corporate contacts, customer relationship management, and the extent of internal and external contacts
3. *Decision making*—focuses on measuring an employee's abilities (knowledge and skill), language and sensory requirements, and managerial and business decision making skills
4. *Physical and mechanical activities*—ergonomics to take care of minimum fatigue, physical activities, equipment, machineries, and tools
5. *Work setting*—aims at finding the environmental conditions conducive to effective working along with other job characteristics

Section	No. of items
Background	41
Contacts with people	62
Decision making	80
Physical and mechanical activities	53
Work setting	47

Functional Job Analysis

Functional job analysis is a methodology or a type of questionnaire that is used for collecting job-related information. The US employment service first used FJA during early 1940s. According to Sanghi (2004), the following are the various techniques of job analysis:

1. Observation
2. Interviews
3. Diaries
4. Questionnaire
5. Critical incident technique
6. Repertory grid techniques
7. Customer contact maps

The most recent version of FJA uses seven scales to describe what workers do in jobs, namely things, data, people, worker instructions, reasoning, math, and language. Each scale has several levels that are anchored with specific behavioural statements and illustrative tasks.

Multipurpose Occupational System Analysis Inventory

The personnel management department maintains a variety of job descriptions. In MOSAIC, the analyst collects data from the office of personnel management. The US government mostly uses MOSAIC for job analysis. It involves tasks and competencies as the two major descriptors in this questionnaire. Here, the tasks are rated on the basis of importance while the competencies are rated on several scales including the importance and requirements for performing the tasks.

Occupational Analysis Inventory

In real-life situations, one wants specific job-related information. At the same time, one intends to capture work requirements for almost all types of occupations as well. The occupational analysis inventory (OAI) helps to examine some of the competencies of work performance. The OAI is designed to yield more specific job information for virtually all occupations. OAI provides the following:

1. Conceptual structure
2. Work elements with widespread applicability

3. Tests in the cognitive, psychomotor, and affective domains
4. Scaling procedures providing for quantitative job descriptions.

OAI describes occupations in terms of work activities and conditions, and attribute–requirement estimates, characterizing occupation in terms of various human requirements. This inventory contains both worker-oriented tasks and job-oriented tasks. The worker-oriented tasks include categories such as information received, mental activities, and work behaviour whereas, job-oriented tasks include output indicators such as work goals and work content.

The OAI comprises a total of 622 work elements in the following five major categories of items:

1. Information received
2. Mental activities
3. Work behaviour
4. Work goals
5. Work content

Most of the 622 work elements are rated by the following three dimensions—significance to the job, extent of occurrence, and applicability. Some elements have special rating dimensions and scales.

Respondents perform each job element on the basis of one of the four rating scales—part-of-job, extent, applicability, or a special scale designed for the specific job element. Finally, the assessors perform a comparison between competencies and work requirements. The huge number of items present in the inventory prohibits its use.

Riccobono and Cunningham (1971) performed a study representing the phase of a broader research project designed to develop and test the occupation analysis inventory. The main objective of the investigative study was to systematically obtain a comprehensive set of work dimensions. These dimensions were to be used for describing and classifying jobs for educational purposes. It was applied to a sample of 400 jobs that were representative of the percentages of jobs in the major occupational categories of the Dictionary of Occupational Titles. The researchers obtained duplicate ratings on a sub-sample of 134 jobs for reliability purposes. They performed factor analyses on seven separate principal components within groups of items corresponding to the following sections of the OAI:

1. Information received
2. Mental activities
3. Physical work behaviour
4. Representational work behaviour
5. Interpersonal work behaviour
6. Work goals
7. Work content

They obtained acceptable reliabilities for most part and found meaningful results of the seven sectional factor analyses. The total number is 617. Respondents do the rating of each job element on one of four rating scales, part-of-job, extent, applicability, or a special scale designed for the specific job element. Finally, the assessors compare the competencies and work requirements.

Positional Analysis Inventory

The position analysis questionnaire is a structured job analysis instrument used to measure job characteristics and relate them with human characteristics. McCormick, Jeanneret, and Mecham (1989) developed the PAQ. It consists of 195 job elements that represent the domain of human behaviour involved in work activities in a comprehensive manner. The items fall under the following five categories:

1. Information input (where and how the worker gets information)
2. Mental processes (reasoning and other processes that workers use)
3. Work output (physical activities and tools used on the job)

4. Relationships with other persons, and
5. Job context (the physical and social contexts of work)

Over the course of many studies, PAQ researchers have aggregated PAQ data for hundreds of jobs; the database is maintained by Purdue University.

Work Profiling System

The work profiling system helps employers to accomplish various human resource functions. The job analysis approach to competency mapping yields reports. The reports are inputs to the decision-making process in the area of functions such as developing job specifications, deciding the selection tools, employee selection, planning individual development, framing job description, and other HR functions. There are three versions of the WPS tied to types of occupations—managerial, service, and technical.

Companies make use of a computer-administered job analysis system, which contains a structured questionnaire that measures ability and personality attributes in areas such as hearing skills, sight, taste, smell, touch, body coordination, verbal skills, number skills, complex management skills, personality, and team role.

PSYCHOMETRIC TESTS

Q 8 The British Psychological Society has defined a psychometric test as 'an instrument designed to produce a quantitative assessment of some psychological attribute or attributes' (Lewis and Crozier 2002). A psychometric test talks about a capacity, propensity or liability to act, react, experience, or to structure or order thoughts, or behaviour in particular ways. In general, they relate to two distinct (but overlapping) kinds of performance—maximum performance and habitual performance. Every organization uses some form of psychometric assessment as a part of their selection process. Some applicants view psychometric tests as comfortable and as such welcome this test.

The main objective of a psychometric test is to measure a sample of behaviour. The procedure of administering the test, the environment in which the test is to be taken, and the scoring technique are uniformly applied, and hence, the test is also termed as standardized. The test is objective in nature too. It measures dimensions using an unbiased method without getting affected by any human factors. Each question or statement has only one correct answer.

In some tests, you get multiple options out of which, any one might describe your characteristic. For example, Rathus assertiveness schedule is a schedule used to measure the assertiveness of a person. The number of options per item is six.

The job involvement scale designed by Lodahl and Kejner is used to measure the degree of job involvement in a four-option scale.

Similarly, Paul Spector's job satisfaction survey is used to measure the job satisfaction of a person and is also a six-option questionnaire.

A scale may be single-faceted or multi-faceted. The job satisfaction survey designed by Paul Spector is a nine-faceted scale, as follows:

1. Pay and remuneration
2. Promotion opportunities
3. Immediate supervisor
4. Monetary and non-monetary fringe benefits
5. Appreciation, recognition, and rewards for good work
6. Operating policies and procedures
7. People one works with
8. Job tasks
9. Communication within the organization

The total score of all the facets gives the measure for job satisfaction. Most of the tests are time- bound. The questionnaires contain both positive and negative items. The scoring is done based on a preset methodology. The markings of negative items are reversed.

Most psychometric tests are classified into two categories, aptitude test and achievement test.

Aptitude test Aptitude tests measure the potentiality of a person and how much he has to contribute to an organization. Responses to an aptitude test helps one to analyse how well a person will perform after training, irrespective of his/her performance in the present task. The purpose of aptitude tests is to identify individuals with special inclinations and abilities to perform the tasks that would be given to him. As such, aptitude tests cover more concrete, clearly defined, or practical abilities like mechanical aptitude, clinical aptitude, artistic aptitude, working in stressful conditions, etc.

Achievement test This tests measures the level of proficiency that a person has been able to achieve, and measures what one has contributed to the organization. Most of the tests measure aspects such as language usage, reasoning, arithmetic computation, and the like.

For every competency mapping approach, one needs to consider the factors that might affect it as well as its purpose and application areas. The tools of mapping comprise competency identification and competency assessment. All the factors are represented in Figure 5.5.

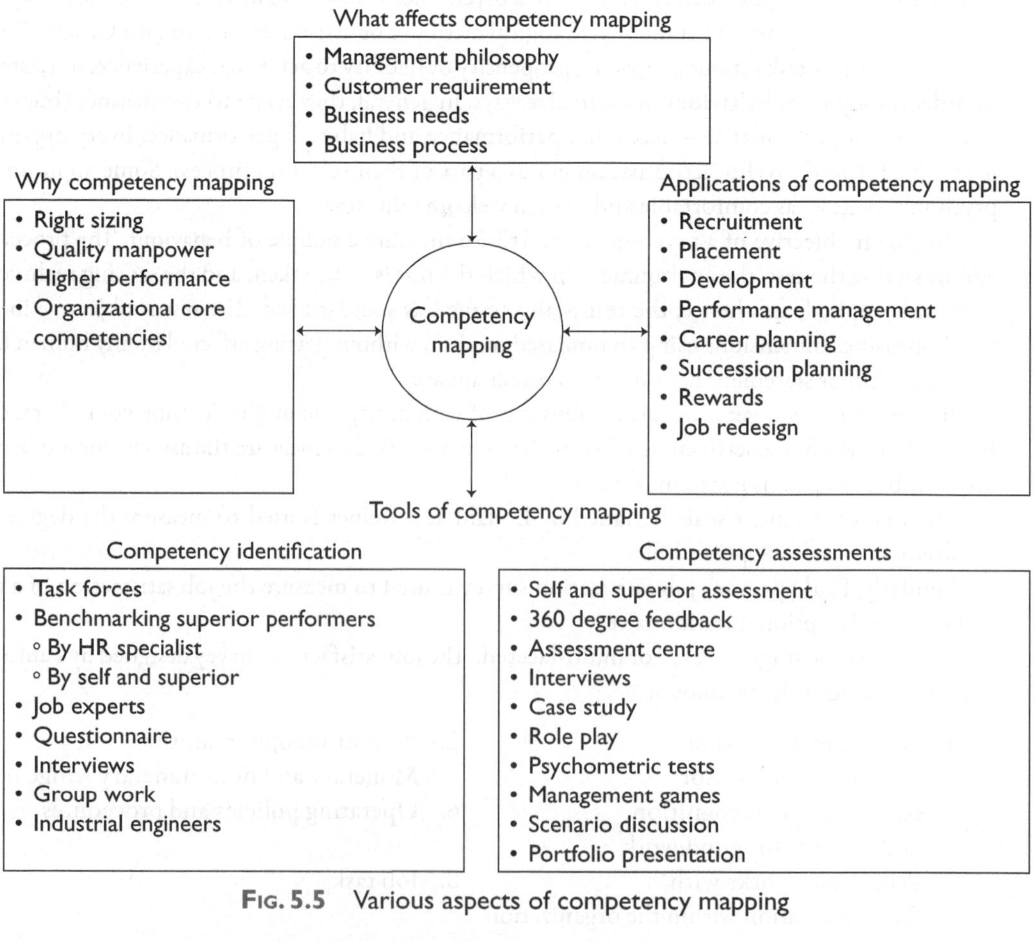

FIG. 5.5 Various aspects of competency mapping

PROCESS OF DEVELOPING COMPETENCY

Hemalata and Thanikachalam (2005) illustrate the process for developing a competency set comprising the following tasks:

1. Synthesizing business vision, mission, policy, objectives, goals, and strategies
2. Defining performance effectiveness criteria
3. Identity
4. Data collection and analysis
5. Proposing competencies
6. Validating competency model
7. Application using tools
8. Factors to be considered for generating competencies

We now study each process in detail.

Synthesizing business vision, mission, policy, objectives, goals, and strategies While synthesizing business strategies, the mission should be focused, organizational needs need to be defined or refined, and business objectives and goals, in measurable terms, must be considered.

Defining performance effectiveness criteria To define the performance effectiveness, you have to collect hard data of the company (including projects, domains, clients, deadlines, financial limits, products, and quality standards), production centres, project managers and associates, executive ratings, peer ratings, subordinate ratings, and client ratings.

Identity Identity refers to the criterion sample including star performers and average performers. Workforce comprises various types of people whose performances greatly vary. Some people who work with dedication and are backed by their knowledge and skills become 'star performers'. This category of workforce consists of achievers who strive to achieve individual as well as company's goals. But, a majority of the workforce invests their efforts to achieve the required targets. Competency sets need to be identified for total workforce.

Data collection and analysis This step incorporates occupational groups or work units, identification of jobs, identification of tasks, selecting a data collection method comprising behavioural event interviews, panels, surveys, and 360-degree ratings, expert system databases, etc. Thereafter, you are required to analyse the data, identify the competencies, and describe the behavioural indicators for each competency.

Proposing competencies This process emphasizes that you need to identify characteristics of the people who are competent to undertake the work.

Validating competency model You must get the competency model validated by way of behavioural event interviews, tests, and assessment centre ratings.

Application using tools This step of the process includes selection of personnel, training of the personnel, professional development, performance appraisal, succession planning, and compensation or rewards.

Factors to be considered for generating competencies In order to generate competencies, you must focus on the personal characteristics needed for success in a broader job role, focus on outstanding performance, and the underlying personal characteristics.

METHODS OF DEVELOPING COMPETENCY SETS

Professional managers working in organizations and HRD consultants have developed a variety of approaches to develop competencies. Four widely used sources of data for preparing competency sets leading to developing competencies are the following:

1. Resource panel or focus groups with subject matter experts
2. Critical event interviews with superior performers
3. Competency-based interview
4. Generic competency dictionaries

Resource Panel or Focus Groups

Resource panel generally includes job incumbents and HR training staff, who have worked closely with the job incumbents. The resource panel follows a structured process to get participants to think systematically about the job and the personal characteristics essential for effectiveness. The facilitator administers a series of standard questions to capture respondents' answers, generally recorded on flipcharts. The contents of the questions include main responsibilities and tasks, formal and informal performance measures, most challenging types of situations encountered, and personal characteristics required for effectiveness. A key section, sometimes called future scan, involves asking participants about the following areas:

1. Emerging issues
2. Changes in business scenario
3. Changes needed in the organization and industry
4. Surfacing market dynamics
5. New technologies
6. Likely impact of the market dynamics and new technologies on the organization.

It is a common practice to use multiple resource panels with different stakeholders rather than only one. This practice is generally employed for developing a leadership model for the middle and the upper middle level managers. There can be as many as four focus groups.

Critical Event Interviews

Reports of critical event interviews with superior performers form the second potential source of data. While preparing competency sets, some, research scholars use behavioural event interviews. The researchers carry out in-depth probing a small number of broad events or experiences. Conducting this interview necessitates mastering the sophisticated probing strategy. You should preferably record the discussion of critical event interviews on audio or employ audio-visual media for replaying. These interviews are time-consuming and need more investment.

Competency-based Interviews

Through campus interviews, organizations recruit candidates who are pursuing master degrees in engineering or management. Their suitability for a job role of the candidates, without any experience, cannot be judged based on their curriculum vitae only. They are screened through group discussion, personal interviews, and/or psychometric tests. However, to identify the right candidates, the application of competency-based interview has gained popularity. Questions in competency-based interviews usually refer to the events or activities in which the candidate had participated in his/her school, college or university, or any other activity that effectively displays a particular competency or a set of competencies.

A typical question in a competency-based interview could be, 'Describe two situations where you had to work as a team member'. A candidate should be able talk for several minutes to answer this type of a question. He/she is expected to highlight his/her participation in a strong team; the task achieved or project completed by the team, and the leadership role played by him/her as a contribution to the teamwork. The candidate should narrate how his/her teamwork helped achieving the target, the synergy of working in a team, the psychological closeness and fellow feelings of team members, pride of accomplishment, and so forth. His/her body language shall very much be noted by the interviewers.

Unless a student prepares for such a situation, it is difficult to respond in a structured and systematic manner. A student should visit the company's website, study about the nature of business and product range, try to know the strategy for growth, etc., to understand the key competencies of the company to which he/she is applying for. He/she should exhibit the competency needed in the company. Big organizations recruiting graduate trainees generally use competency-based interviews. In general, motivation and commitment to one's career are the two generic key competencies any organization looks for in addition to other specific competencies.

Generic Competency Dictionaries

Generic competency dictionaries are used when an organization needs to develop multiple competency sets. This is done to ensure that common skills and characteristics are always described with a unique competency head. The competency sets derived and decided by using this technique are used across various organizations uniformly. In fact, these become the base for any organization when it goes into finalizing individual competencies required for particular jobs. The use of a generic competency dictionary set helps as follows:

1. It helps the management by giving them a starting point for preparing a framework for the competencies.
2. The jobs or the roles of a particular employee can be easily rated.
3. It aids the HR in analysing the individual capabilities during interviews.

COMPETENCY APPROACH IN RECRUITMENT AND RETENTION

As discussed in earlier sections, competency mapping is significantly useful in recruitment, selection, induction, placement of employees, and all the other important HR functions. It helps in providing a precise analysis of the job requirements and the candidate's capability. On similar lines, when an individual has certain aspirations of working in a certain field and position, the HR can give them details on the exact skills and capabilities required. This approach satisfies the intrinsic needs of employees.

ELEMENTS OF RECRUITMENT AND RETENTION

Attrition continues to be a regular problem in organizations; particularly in knowledge organizations. Sometimes, people are unsatisfied with the work assignment. This has been because there have been many instances where organizations could not extract the best from the recruits. There have been studies which have revealed that organizations fail to identify the competencies essentially required to perform the scheduled tasks.

Recruiting people with the requisite competencies ensures their job satisfaction and prevents or reduces attrition. This correlates recruitment and the use of competency framework leading to attrition management.

Some of the key attrition factors are listed in Box 5.3.

Box 5.3 Key attrition factors

From the studies pursued by many academicians, industrial stalwarts, and the author's personal interactions with HR personnel, a set of factors, which can be treated as key attrition factors, is listed as follows:

1. Inability to use one's competencies
2. Lack of challenge in the work
3. Lack of role clarity
4. Rust-out stress syndrome (ROSS)
5. Burn-out stress syndrome (BOSS)
6. Lack of learning opportunity
7. Levels of motivations
8. Lack of excitement and innovation in the job
9. Work environment—not conducive or effective
10. Lack of scope of growth in terms of salary, status, and other factors
11. Lack of sense of belonging
12. Unfulfilled occupational values
13. Lifestyle inventory—unmatched with the task
14. Boss and his management style

Talented employees desire to perform challenging tasks and derive joy from the work. The competency approach enables an organization to assign challenging tasks to an employee. The employee, in turn, derives pleasure in accomplishing those tasks and contributing to the organization. If the role is clear, one performs one's assignments better and derives intrinsic satisfaction.

In general, the competency approach helps to remove the 'rust out stress syndrome' (ROSS), and 'burnout stress syndrome' (BOSS). Once an employee knows his task and has the right competency for finishing that job, the stress level automatically reduces, accompanied by the removal of stress syndromes.

Based on the advantages of the competency framework in various functions of an organization, many organizations have actually developed their own competencies. These are developed through many processes. Most of the processes for developing competencies begin with the understanding of the business perspective and short and long-term goals of the organization. Refer to Exhibit 5.6 which gives details on developing competencies by various organizations.

Exhibit 5.6 Developing competencies by organizations

Moser Baer initially examined the organization's strategy and goals, identified the core priority areas, and then converted them into both expected and non-expected behaviour. Moser Baer identified common themes through affinity exercises, and then grouped them into broad clusters. The organization developed the total competency model formulating the definitions, based on behaviour for these clusters. The validation of the model was then obtained from HR operational teams, and senior leaders of the organization.

(Contd)

Exhibit 5.6 (Contd)

Jindal Steel and Power Ltd (JSPL) adopted a two-step approach to develop competencies. One technology partner identified and listed 18 competencies appropriate for JSPL. The first phase included discussion with top management and handing over list of competencies to a group of consultants. The second phase consisted of identifying the appropriate tool for measuring the set of competencies. The methodology of mapping was designed with due knowledge and agreement of top management of JSPL. It was decided to assess each competency using at least two tools; assessing each competency by at least two assessors, and assessing each individual by at least two assessors.

JSPL used nine tools—three psychological tests, two paper-pencil exercises, one interview session, and three individual and group activities. JSPL carried the mapping exercise of skill gap analysis. Descriptions of the tools used by JSPL are as follows:

1. *Psychometric tests*—FIRO-B, smart skill test, and executive initiative test.
2. *In-basket exercise*—The exercise exposes the managers to a series of real-life situations in a short period of time just to assess his ability to handle these situations. The exercise comprises simulation of reality.
3. *Case analysis*—Involves reading and analysing of a problem situation and identifying probable and solutions; prioritizing the solutions based on techno-economic feasibility analysis to arrive at a final solution.
4. *Behavioural event interview*—Motives or skills as thought by people about a person may not be credible. But, the attributes can be assessed observing what they actually do in the most critical incidents they have faced. In the course of discussion, when a person narrates his/her experience and actions are taken, the different competencies can be assessed with more perfection.
5. *Role play*—A practice or a modus operandi where an individual enacts a particular role given to him/her. He/she is expected to perform in a desired manner. He/she is evaluated based on his/her performance or behaviour exhibited while performing the role.
6. *Management games*—The games involve group activity, and a simulation of real-life situations faced by managers in their every day life. A task is designed involving all the behaviours that a manager is expected to exhibit in a specific situation. A manager is assessed based on the exhibition of the expected behaviours.
7. *Leadership group discussion*—Normally, members of a team work under the guidance of a leader. In a leaderless group, any member gets an equal and ample opportunity to express one's view, opinions, and leadership potential. Leadership group discussion is a particular type of behavioural interview. Each member is provided with 'Personal Assessment Questionnaire' and a 'Competency Tool Kit' to get relevant background details of the behavioural interview and to know about their own needs for personal growth.

Subsequent to this exercise JSPL initiated a functional competency framework and assessment programme.

ITW Signode operates its business in North America, Latin America, Europe, Middle East and Africa, Australia, New Zealand, India, and some Asian countries. ITW sought the help of external consultants who worked with the senior management. They derived 12 core competencies intrinsic to ITW business. Thereafter, they mapped the various roles to these 12 competencies. ITW followed the following steps in developing the competency framework:

1. Identification of the role to be played
2. Understanding his/her existing roles to achieve the business objectives
3. Identifying the 'linchpin roles' in every function of the company to recruit key players
4. On identifying the 'linchpin positions', depending on the role, ITW Signode made out the 12 behavioural competencies linked to the roles
5. The company further classified the behavioural competencies into four proficiency levels
6. Lastly, these were mapped accordingly to the roles

TALENT MANAGEMENT

Talent refers to the identifiable ability that is perceived to add immediate or future value to any prescribed activity, discipline, or enterprise. A talented employee with high potential can make a significant difference to the current and future performance of the organization. Talents are acquired, developed, nurtured, and should be retained. Attracting, developing, and retaining talents are the three key deliverables of the HR function. Talent management is an art and also a science. Talent management has been discussed in the previous chapter.

Competency Framework for Talent Management

We are familiar with the maxim, 'what gets measured gets monitored and done'. Similarly, we must identify organizational needs, meet, and fulfill those needs in order to develop the organization. An organization strives to achieve the business goals for the purpose of which it must identify the competencies and develop competency framework. The most important aspects of talent management are talent acquisition and talent retention. Talent management emphasizes that an organization must identify the competencies necessary for success of the business. Talent management focused on HRM and has been discussed in Chapter 4. However, from the standpoint of competency framework for talent management, the essential tasks are as follows:

1. Ensuring that your people demonstrate sufficient expertise
2. Recruiting and selecting new staff more effectively through structured processes
3. Evaluating performance periodically
4. Identifying skill and competency gaps more methodically
5. Providing more customized training and professional development
6. Planning sufficient scope for succession
7. Making change management processes work more efficiently

Talent Acquisition through Competency Framework

Douglas and Conger (2008) surveyed 40 companies around the world in the year 2005 and found that their high-potential employees were insufficient in fulfilling the strategic management role. The survey revealed two primary reasons—(a) the formal procedure for identifying and developing next-generation leaders have fallen out of sync, and (b) HR managers are facing trouble in getting attention of top organizational leaders.

However, the company needs to grow, and without competent leaders it cannot grow. On economic considerations, while working on budget cuts, some companies have eliminated positions that would expose high-potential employees to a broad range of problems. By doing so, they have sacrificed their future development opportunities. At the juncture of economic downturn, any company needs to acquire the best available people from the market. For this purpose, a company needs a procedure and a set of tools, and the procedure must be structured to avoid 'select error'. For this purpose, a proactive company always uses competency framework for talent acquisition.

Competency framework, once developed, can be used for multiple purposes. During talent acquisition, competency framework plays an important role. Organizations use competency framework to develop job specification. Competency framework further helps job-seekers to search jobs of their likings by giving keywords on the job search portals or on company's websites as well. This is the linkage between competency framework and talent acquisition. Competency framework will improve the efficiency and quality of recruitment. A certain framework for a competency management programme is shown in Box 5.4.

> A proactive company always uses competency framework for talent acquisition.

Box 5.4 Programme on competency management

A company might be interested to develop competency framework, implement competency mapping, and derive benefits from the mapped competencies. The company may opt to invite an external agency for this purpose. Tentatively the programme might cover the following points:

(Contd)

Box 5.4 (Contd)

1. Awareness of competency
2. Promoting competency culture
3. Historical perspective of competency
4. Competency—global debates and contradictions
5. Competency framework and model
6. Business and role analysis
7. Competency mapping
8. Competency dictionary development
9. Developing competency framework
10. Basics of competency assessment
11. Basics of tool development
12. Competency assessment technique
13. Preparation for assessment process
14. Report writing and feedback facilitation
15. Application of competency profiling
16. Competency initiative and business/HR certification
17. Implementation planning and strategies
18. Use of technology in competency management

SUMMARY

A good competency framework should strengthen various talent management processes including talent acquisition. Managers should leverage the competency framework while bringing out job descriptions. This helps in improving efficiency and quality of recruitment. Competency is the ability to perform one's role in the job. The two terms 'competence' and 'competency', though interchangeably used, carry different meanings. Competency framework is a concept, whereas competency mapping is a process. Before assigning tasks, considering the competency framework and mapped competencies lead to success. There are a number of competencies and competency sets. Competency mapping is a process, which an organization follows in order to identify and describe competencies that are most critical to succeed in a work situation or work role.

Organizations use various methods for competency mapping. Each method has its own advantages and disadvantages. The field of application includes many HR functions such as recruitment and selection, placement, employee development, training, management development, performance management, career planning, succession planning, reward policy, job redesign, etc. The competency approach also helps an organization to manage retention of its employees. It takes care of the key attrition factors, thus helping the organization to promote the retention of manpower. Competency approaches and analysis provide benefits such as increase in productivity, enhancing perfection in quality work, improving the work performance, promoting mutual trust, and effective resource utilization. Competency approaches are a passion of the organizations striving to reach the goal.

KEY TERMS

Assessment centre is a procedural mechanism to ascertain the suitability of a person for a specific job using a situational test and observing the behavioural disposition, and to identify the potential for the growth of individuals.

Competency framework refers to a conceptual structure relating to the behavioural elements of employees.

Competency set means a bundle of competencies in a particular category, for example, a result-oriented competency comprises risk taking, decisiveness, business sense, energy, concern for excellence, tenacity, initiative, and customer orientation.

Core competence is a bundle of skills and technologies that enables a company to provide a particular benefit to the customers. It represents the enduring strength of a company that cannot be easily copied.

Critical incidents contribute to the growth or decay of an organizational system or the organization as a whole. The critical incidents technique uses a set of procedures to systematically identify behaviours that contribute to the success or failure of individuals or the organizations in specific situations.

Leadership competency is a set of competencies encompassing organizing, involving, empowering, appraising, motivating and developing, leading, planning, directing, controlling, and managing change, etc.

Exercises

Concept Review Questions

1. Define and explain competency. Mention the different types of competencies. What is meant by competency set?
2. Distinguish between competency and competence. In view of today's competitive business scenario, discuss the need for competency mapping. How does it really contribute to organizational excellence?
3. How should an organization ensure that the competency framework is fit for purpose? Discuss the various steps.
4. What are the different methodologies of competency mapping? What might be the consequences if the prescribed steps of a particular method are not adhered to? Justify your answer.
5. What do you mean by assessment centre? Discuss in detail about the various task roles pertaining to the assessment centre method.
6. Discuss the critical incidents technique and the various criteria of this method.
7. What are the sections of common metric questionnaire (CMQ)? Compare CMQ with positional analysis inventory (PAQ).
8. What are psychometric tests? Why do organizations conduct this test? Discuss certain psychometric tests. What do you mean by multi-facet scale? Explain with examples. Mention the broad classifications of this test.

Critical Thinking Questions

9. 'My company is undertaking a job evaluation exercise, along with competency mapping. Competency mapping is an area, which has been least explored in my company. I would like relevant information on competency mapping along with references, so as to develop skills of the people in my organization. I have contacted you and expressed a desire to appoint you as my consultant. I have requested you to submit a brief report prior to concluding a contract for a period of three years.' How would you go about compiling the report?
10. 'People need competencies to perform tasks. Without continuous development of competencies, an organization is not likely to achieve its goals. Competent and motivated employees are essential for organizational survival, growth and excellence.' Comment on this statement and discuss the underlying issues, with suitable examples.
11. You have been assigned the task of conducting an interview for the post of 'marketing executive' of your company. How would you go ahead? Detail out the steps and their necessities.

Assignments

12. Visit five companies of medium or large sizes, and inquire how they are developing competency framework. You must gather information with regard to their organizational structure, levels of management, attributes of competencies, and other information you feel relevant. Have they identified winning competencies?
13. A medium-scale automobile company has design, planning, purchase, material control, four production sections (machining section, press shop, fabrication, and finishing shop), heat treatment and surface treatment plants, and maintenance (mechanical,

electrical, building and vehicles) sections. In addition to this, the company has a store, labour welfare, a dispensary, and security. The proprietor attended a three-day management development programme and hence, has some knowledge on competency mapping. Immediately after joining as an HRD manager, you have been assigned the task of developing competency sets for all positions, identifying the gaps, and proposing training needs. You are also required to identify the institutes where employees may be sent for knowledge input. Finally, you are required to evaluate the training. Explain the steps you would follow in detail. (You may like to develop a flow diagram in this regard).

MANAGER'S INSIGHT

Aston International was established in 1995 to provide insurance- related services to the corporate world. Since then, it has enjoyed a good market share and has been able to boast about a long list of satisfied customers.

Recently, the top management has started thinking about venturing into providing HR-related services to its existing as well as other companies. They had conducted a survey and it was identified that such a service was required in the market. Now, the company needs to form a suitable and an appropriate team who would be working towards achieving the same. The top management came to the conclusion that conducting a SWOT analysis and a competency assessment of their employees was their first requirement.

Questions:

1. Please suggest skills and qualities that the management must look for to come out successfully?
2. How should Aston International proceed to identify a group of employees suitable for developing and marketing HR services?

BIBLIOGRAPHY AND WEB RESOURCES

Chatterjee, Saswati, *Competency Mapping at Titan Industries Ltd*, Unpublished project report submitted to the Indian Institute of Social Welfare and Business Management in partial fulfillment of the requirements of the two-year Masters degree in HRM, 2007.

Douglas. A. Ready, and Jay. A. Conger, 'Making Your Company a Talent Factory', *Harvard Business Review* on Talent Management, Harvard Business Press, USA, 2008.

Flippo, E.B., *Principles of Personnel Management*, Tata McGraw Hill, New Delhi, 1994.

Harvey, Robert. J., *Research Monograph: The Development of the CMQ Monograph Describing the Development and Field-testing of the Common Metric Questionnaire (CMQ)*, 1993.

Haldar, U.K., *Human Resource Development*, Oxford University Press, New Delhi, 2009.

Hemalata, M. and Dr V. Thanikachalam, 'Developing a Competency Set for Integrating the Human Resource Management in a Manufacturing Industry', *Indian Journal for Training Development (IJTD)*, Vol. XXXV, No. 2, April–June, pp. 88–155, 2005.

Lewis, Gareth. and Gene Crozier, *Psychometric Testing In a Week*, Hodder & Stoughton, UK, 2002.

McCormick, E.J., P.R. Jeanneret, and R.C. Mecham, *Position Analysis Questionnaire*, PAQ Services, Bellingham, 1989.

Miller, L., N. Rankin, and F. Neathy, *Competency Frameworks in UK Organizations: Key Issues in Employers' Use of Competencies*, Chartered Institute of Personnel and Development, London, 2001.

Prahalad, C.K. and Gary Hamel, *Competing For the Future*, Harvard Business School Press, 1996.

SAIL, HR Best Practices, Steel Authority of India Ltd, New Delhi, 2009.

Saiyadin, M.S., *Human Resource Management*, Tata McGraw Hill, New Delhi, 2003.

Saiyadin, M.S., *Organisational Behaviour*, Tata McGraw Hill, New Delhi, 2003.

Sanghi, Seema, *The Handbook of Competency Mapping: Understanding, Designing and Implementing Competency Models in Organizations*, Sage Publications Inc. London, 2004.

Sood, Rajnish, *Competency Evaluation of Reliance Communications Personnel* Reliance Infocom, Reliance House, Kolkata, Unpublished project report submitted to the 'Indian Institute of Social Welfare and Business Management' in partial fulfillment of masters degree in HRM, 2007.

Spencer, L. M., and S.M. Spencer, *Competency at Work*, Wiley, New York, 1993.

Wilson, John. P., *Human Resource Development*, First South Asian Edition, Kogan page, London, 2005.

Web Resources

www.hr-guide.com, last accessed on 26 October 2007.

www.salary.com/ITG/layoutscripts/itgl_default.asp?tab=itg&cat=cat021&ser=ser060&part=par851, last accessed on 2 October 2009.

www.cipd.co.uk/subjects/perfmangmt/competnces/comptfrmwk.htm, last accessed on 8 November 2009 (*Competency Frameworks in UK Organisations: Key Issues in Employers' Use of Competencies*).

web.mit.edu/career/www/workshops/competencies/model.html, last accessed on 31 July 2010 (Iceberg Model of Competencies).

www.cluteinstitute.com/proceedings/2010_Dublin_EABR_Articles/Article%20146.pdf, last accessed on 1 August 2010 (Barney Erasmus).

www.paq.com/index.cfm?FuseAction=bulletins.job-analysis, last accessed on 15 March 2010.

www.cipd.co.uk/subjects/perfmangmt/competnces/comptfrmwk.htm>, last accessed on 8 November 2009.

COMPETENCY MAPPING AT TITAN INDUSTRIES LTD

About the organization

Titan Industries Ltd was incorporated in 1984 as a joint venture between Tata Group and TIDCO Ltd, a government of Tamil Nadu undertaking. The company has been manufacturing and marketing quartz watches since 1987. In 1995, the company diversified into manufacturing and marketing 18-carat studded jewellery. It expanded its business sphere by entering into two more businesses, namely licensed brands and accessories to leverage the marketing and retailing skills by launching Fastrack eye gear and entering into an agreement for marketing Tommy Hilfiger watches, and a precision engineering division to leverage the precision engineering capabilities in Titan.

These business units attract customers in multiple areas such as automobiles, clock and plastic components, precision engineered components, automobiles, and aerospace solutions. The company has its outlets for watches throughout the country. The divisions for watches and jewellery are the two main strategic business units.

Human resources

Titan Industries has about 3,000 employees in its factories, regional offices, and corporate office. The members of the factory workforce are technocrats with a high level of technical skills, while the personnel of corporate and regional offices belong to sales and marketing, retailing, finance, and administration background. The HR personnel perform support functions.

Hierarchy of positions

1. Sales channel—The regional sales manager (RSM) heads the channel. Other positions include area sales manager (ASM), sales executive (SE), and sales officer (SO).
2. Retail sales watch division—The regional retail executive (RTE) heads this division, where the other two levels are store manager (SM) and customer relationship officer (CRO).
3. Jewellery division (Tanishq boutique)—The regional business manager (RBM) is the head and other levels include regional business executive (RBE), boutique manager (BM), assistant boutique manager (ABM), and retail sales officer (RSO).

The competency profile for the position of sales officers or sales executives requires consideration at two levels—at the entry level and differential level. Both the levels need knowledge competency, skill competency, and behavioural competency. At the entry level, the retail sales officers and customer relationship officers need knowledge, skill, and behavioural competencies.

The regional sales manager and area sales manager must have managerial competencies translated to functional competencies. The managerial competencies include 'human resource cluster', 'goal and action cluster' (leadership cluster), and 'directing subordinates cluster'.

Mapped competencies

Competency profiles for the position of sales officer or sales executive at entry level, sales officer or sales executive at differential levels as they move up along the organizational hierarchy, and retail sales officer or customer relationship officer at entry level are as shown in Table 5.3.

Table 5.3 Competency profiles

Levels \ Competency	Knowledge competency	Skill competency	Behavioural competency
1. Entry level competency profile for the position of sales officer/sales executive	• Basic marketing and selling concept • Channel functions and flows • Product and branding strategies • Analysing consumer market and buying behaviour • Basic commercial and analytical skill	• Basic selling and communication skill • Problem solving skills • Quantitative reasoning • Follow up and maintenance • Overcoming objections • Stress tolerance	• Positive attitude • Knowledge • High emotional stamina • Assertiveness • Focus • Ego drive • Helpful
2. Differential level competency profile of sales officer/sales executive	• Market knowledge • Customer knowledge • Product knowledge • Brand knowledge • Competitor knowledge	• Relationship building • Relationship maintenance • Decisiveness • Organization • Initiative	• Positive attitude • Personal integrity • Focus • High energy level • Assertiveness • Self-confidence • Knowledgeable • Helpful • Ego drive
3. Entry level competency profile for the position of retail sales officer/customer relationship officer	• Goal orientation • Customer • Customer perception and information gathering • Value driven	• Communication skills • Basic selling skills • Understanding needs • Problem solving skills • Stress tolerance • Customized services	• Positive attitude • Knowledgeable • High emotional stamina • Assertiveness • Focus • Ego drive • Helpful

Competency profiles for the position of regional sales manager and area sales manager are as shown in Table 5.4.

Table 5.4 Managerial competency profiles

Managerial competency	Functional competency
1. Human resource cluster	1.1 Marketing knowledge 1.2 Leading both in terms of business and team
2. Goal and action cluster (Leadership cluster)	2.1 Sales and process driven 2.2 Foresight and planning 2.3 Trade relationship management
3. Directing subordinates cluster	3.1 Strong analytical knowledge

Discussion Questions

1. Why does the company consider the competency profile of sales personnel at two levels. Why does the company place emphasis on behavioural competencies?
2. Study the mapped competencies and analyse to what extent the competencies of the regional sales manager differ from those of sales officers/executives, retail sales officer, and customer relationship officer.
3. Study the competencies in each competency set for each level. Do you feel that the competencies will differ for the same positions in a company manufacturing different goods?

(Case study taken from 'Human Resource Development' (2009), Uday Kumar Haldar, published by Oxford Higher Education, Oxford University Press, New Delhi, pages 113–116. The case was written based on an unpublished project submitted to the Indian Institute of Social Welfare and Business Management for evaluation by University of Calcutta by Ms Saswati Chatterjee).

HR MANTRA Empowering individuals

A production supervisor was known for his outstanding work efficiency, skills, attitude, values, and behaviour. He was always trying to help others in solving their problems. His superiors treated him as an asset to the company. Soon, he was promoted to the position of junior manager of a small department, where about 30 employees were working.

A year passed after his promotion. He preferred to perform the duties he was doing prior to his promotion, thus confining to a small group of the department. In periodic meetings, he was unable to reply to the queries of the chairperson of the meeting. He seldom acted as a manager and exercised his managerial competencies.

He was trying to solve all the departmental problems on his own, became overburdened, and started suffering from work role stress. As a manager, he could not develop a credible relationship with his juniors. He also never tried to uncover the abilities of people around him.

The mantra: Empower competent people.

C.K. PRAHALAD

Coimbatore Krishnao or C.K. Prahalad, as he was popularly known, was born on 8 August 1941 in Coimbatore, Tamil Nadu. He studied physics at the University of Madras (now Chennai), and worked as a manager in a branch of the Union Carbide Battery company, before continuing his further education in the United States. He earned his PhD from Harvard. He has taught in both India and America, and eventually joined the faculty of the University of Michigan's Business School, where he was holding the Harvey C. Fruehauf Chair of Business Administration. Prahalad was a distinguished university professor of corporate strategy at the Stephen M. Ross School of Business in the university.

At Ann Arbor, Prahalad met Gary Hamel, who was then a young international business student. Their collaboration ultimately resulted in the bestseller, *Competing for the Future* (1994). In his book, *The Future of Competition* (2004), Prahalad (with Venkat Ramaswamy as coauthor), argued that companies have not made enough use of the opportunities provided by globalization. They emphasized that along with the change in the rules of the game, the role of the players has also been transformed. They highlighted that the customer is a more powerful and a proactive figure. Customers are no longer meant to be merely satisfied. They are agents who create and participate in transactions. The concept of value has also changed; values are no more inherent in products or services; they cannot be instilled by producers or providers. Values have to be co-created with consumers. They build the same by using and experiencing the products. The authors said that the only way companies can compete successfully is through building new strategic capital.

While wrestling with the perplexingly complex and political issue of poverty, Prahalad identified the world's poor (the 'bottom of the pyramid') as a potential untapped market for companies, worth anything up to $13 trillion a year. He mentioned these in his book, *The Fortune at the Bottom of the Pyramid* in 2004.

Further, he advocated, the real source of market promise is not the wealthy few in the developing world, or even the emerging middle-income consumers. It is the billions of aspiring poor who are joining the market economy for the first time. He stressed that market at the bottom of the pyramid could be co-created by multinationals and domestic industries, non-governmental organizations and, most importantly, the poor themselves. The poor would then have choice over their lives and the products they use. He pointed to Hindustan Lever's success in marketing soap powder and detergents in smaller, cheaper units. This created prosperity downstream through new distribution mechanisms. Very often, poor people are patronized; Prahalad wanted them to have real power in the marketplace.

Prahlad and Hamel (1990) argued that core competence provides distinct competitive advantage to the organizations, and they provide the baseline for renewal and expansion. Managing core competence has proved to be difficult and challenging. Core competence represents the enduring strength of a company that cannot be easily copied. It is a bundle of skills and technologies that enables a company to provide a particular benefit to the customers (Prahalad and Hamel 1990). It is a fundamental, unique, and inimitable strength of the firm. It is a centralized knowledge base and skill base capable of producing a variety of products with differential features.

Organizational capabilities can also be described as an organization's core competence. The HRD literature has tended to associate core competence or capabilities with the concept of human capital and this strengthens a wide range of HRD interventions (for example, induction, skills training, management development etc).

After contributing to the HR fraternity for more than four decades, Prahalad left us on 16 April 2010.

References

Prahalad, C.K. and G. Hamel, 'The Core Competence of the Corporation', *Harvard Business Review*, Vol. 68, No. 3, pp. 79–91, 1990.

www.thinkers50.com/biographies/1/2009, last accessed on 12 October 2011.

PART TWO
Overview—HR Systems

Organizations today need a variety of resources, including efficient human resources, for their manpower to be productive. It has become important for organizations to plan the requirements of HR well in advance to meet the fluctuating demands of customers. Taking care of the needs of HR helps organizations, as it is human resource planning that leads to recruitment and selection of manpower from internal or external sources.

New recruits acquired from any source need to understand the organization and its people, the culture and management styles, the work procedures and systems, responsiveness, and so forth, to settle in the organization. Further, new entrants need to recognize the organizational climate. They must also understand their roles without any ambiguity; and the limitations of discretions they can apply. All the organizational aspects can be fruitfully conveyed to them after joining by means of an organized programme. The programme, if effective, contributes a lot towards achieving organizational objectives.

Organizational performance depends on technology, systems, procedures, etc. Nevertheless, to a great extent, organizational performance is influenced by responsibilities, accountabilities, and performances of individual. Employees must be given feedback about their performances—achievement of quantitative targets and conformance to qualitative requirements. They get opportunities to set right their weaknesses only if they know about the same. Suitable performance evaluation methods must be utilized by organizations. Both organization and employees are stakeholders of performance system. Thus, performances of the employees and performance of the organization are intertwined.

Employees join an organization with some background knowledge and skill sets. However, for tasks to be completed in the organization, they may require additional skills. The skills required have to be imparted through training programmes. Training and development programmes motivate employees and stimulate most of them to undertake new and challenging tasks. Any organization should maintain training-related documents and records for effectiveness.

In the workplace, an employee receives instructions from his immediate supervisor. Actually, an employee of any level is required to interact with many persons in the organization. The immediate supervisor would be interested for target achievement; the junior colleagues seek guidance and

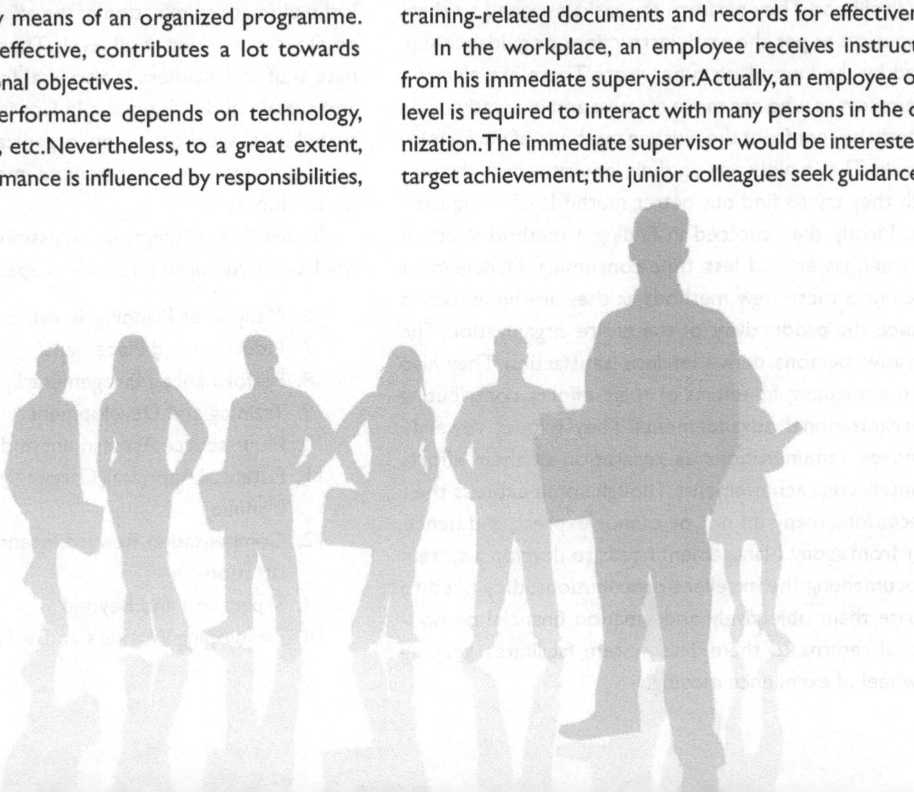

leadership, colleagues need mutual help, dependent departments need information and smooth flow of materials, and so on. Every stakeholder possesses different views about the employee from their respective perspectives. Thus, an employee should preferably be assessed by all the stakeholders with whom he is required to contact on a daily basis.

Evaluating and monitoring performance is obviously required. Concurrently, it is also essential to identify qualities in employees that may be hidden and unearthed, and hence, unutilized. Any employee possesses some extent of brilliance, talent, and aptitude. Advancing talents in an organization is the moral responsibility of management, which, in turn, contributes to enhancing organizational effectiveness. Employees aspire to grow in their careers at close intervals. Employees should not only be satisfied; they should be engaged. Employee engagement is a way of managing and retaining talent in an organization. Organizations execute, evaluate, and monitor performances of every employee. Organizations should attempt to determine the latent talents of employees. Otherwise, the employee potentials are likely to remain unrealized. Organizations must develop suitable means to determine and identify the employee potentials and capabilities to assign new and challenging tasks which also affect their performance along the organizational hierarchy. This, in turn, promotes employee retention and engagement.

Employees work for organizations primarily to earn their livelihood. They perform the tasks assigned to them by superiors as per the work instructions or guidance suggested by the immediate supervisors. There are always a few employees who are more creative and innovative than the rest; they confront the existing methods of performing the tasks. They mainly rely on their inquisitiveness through which they try to find out better methods of doing their tasks. Mostly, they succeed in finding a method which is smoother, faster, and less time-consuming. Management implements these new methods as they are beneficial to enhance the productivity of the entire organization. The innovative persons derive intrinsic satisfaction. They also desire something in return of their efforts contributing to organizational advancements. They expect rewards, incentives, remunerations as reparation of their efforts and intellectual achievements. Though some express their expectations; many do not or cannot express, and hence, suffer from agony. Management needs to develop a system of documenting the excellent contributions; they need to evaluate them objectively, and sanction financial or non-financial returns to them. This system facilitates keeping the wheel of excellence moving.

Human beings come on the earth, perform some duties, and demise. Similarly, in organizations, people join, perform some duties, and move up the organizational hierarchy, and on attaining the retirement age, they superannuate. This is a natural and unavoidable separation. Many employees intend to advance in their careers faster and prefer to change the employer, thus leading to separation. In case of multi-unit companies, transfer from one unit to another is ordered either in an existing grade or on promotion, which also results in a type of separation. Employees need to conform to the various standing rules and instructions, and follow different systems and procedures while achieving the targets. Some may even fail to follow the rules and regulations inadvertently or willfully. Companies initiate disciplinary actions which may lead to layoffs, discharge, or dismissal, leading to forced separation. There might be variety of causes behind separation. Whatever be the cause, employee separation needs to be handled with sensitivity, and with utmost care, without injuring the sentiments of the separating employees. Prior to separation, companies may plan to collect their views about the company and other vital information using suitable means.

It is seen that companies generally organize developmental programmes for personnel working in managerial positions as a means for overall organizational development. It is true that organizational development is intertwined with individual development. Organizational development is the ultimate culmination of the effective contributions of employees working at all levels. Thus, developing subordinate staff and workers is also vital for companies' growth and sustained development. In fact, in the days of business turbulence, workers of an organization need all-round development—technical, general, moral, and other types of development.

In view of the foregoing discussion, this part of the book has been structured into nine chapters.

6. Manpower Planning, Recruitment, and Selection
7. Induction and Placement
8. Performance Management System
9. Training and Development
10. Multi-source Assessment and Feedback System
11. Potential Appraisal, Career System, and Succession Planning
12. Compensation, Reward, Incentives, and wage Administration
13. Separation and Beyond
14. Developing Workers and Subordinate Staff

CHAPTER 6

Manpower Planning, Recruitment, and Selection

LEARNING OBJECTIVES

After studying this chapter, you will be able to

- Realize the importance of manpower planning
- Recognize the sources of recruitment
- Understand job analysis, its importance, and products
- Use job analysis reports during the selection of candidates
- Differentiate between recruitment and selection
- Appreciate the need for credential verification (reference check)
- Generate accounting records related to manpower planning
- Compute recruitment, selection, and hiring costs

OPENING CASE

Manpower Planning and Recruitment

Seamless Engineering Limited (SEL) came into existence in 1993. It initially focused on manufacturing and marketing spare parts for hydraulic and pneumatic pumps, automobiles, and other engineering products. These products were low-technology products. SEL planned to enhance its product range by diversification. Hence, it recruited people by means of employee referrals. An advertisement was displayed in the company's notice board seeking applications for various positions in the prescribed format. SEL also placed a drop box to receive applications for various positions. The personnel department sorted the applications according to their positions. There were vacant positions for both skilled and highly skilled machine operators, maintenance mechanics for different types of machines, crane operators, security personnel, data entry operators, and some other positions. SEL prepared the list of requisite qualifications and experience for each type of vacancy. For each post, the estimated vacancy was as shown in Table 6.1.

Table 6.1 Estimated vacancies at Seamless Engineering Limited

Post	Vacancy
Machine operators—skilled	12
Machine operators—highly skilled	3
Maintenance mechanics	4
Crane operators	2
Security personnel	3
Data entry operators	4
Total	28

Soon after, the company formed a board, interviewed, and selected the candidates. Later, the selected candidates were examined for medical fitness. In fact, the selected candidates were asked to produce a medical certificate of fitness from a private practitioner. All the new recruits were taken on roll, their details were included in the employee database, the finance and accounts section was instructed to make payments, and all relevant formalities were completed.

After one month of induction, all the new recruits were placed in the respective departments according to their trade and grade. They were also assigned regular tasks. Of the 12 skilled machine operators, two operators were unable to achieve their targets, and the achievements of the remaining 10 operators were satisfactory. A few incidents are mentioned here:

1. One maintenance mechanic faced difficulty in diagnosing the problems in machines that had broken down. However, with the help of a senior and experienced mechanic, he could undertake the repairing component of the maintenance work effectively after diagnosing the problem.
2. In another case, while operating the jib crane, a crane operator met with an accident while hitting the load with a machine in the shop floor.
3. One data entry operator was slow and committed mistakes frequently.

After such incidents, SEL constituted a board of inquiry, with an external member, to investigate the root causes behind underperformance of the two skilled machine operators, diagnose the problem of the maintenance mechanics, probe into the accident caused by the crane operator, and identify the reason for the slow working of the data entry operator. The findings of the board were as follows:

1. The two skilled machine operators did not know how to select the object under observation, and did not look at the object being moved and the obstacles in its way. Thus, the probability of accidents increased manifold.
2. Data entry operators need finger dexterity, which the underperforming operator lacked; without agility and liveliness of fingers, a data entry operator cannot feed data in the database, and he/she is treated as an underperformer.

The board of inquiry then referred to the job specifications of the four positions under investigation. Most astonishingly, the board observed and noted with concern the following points:

1. In the specifications for the post of skilled operators, the essential attributes were not mentioned. It was simply mentioned that 'the candidates must have two years of experience; they must produce certificates to this regard.' Practical tests were not conducted.
2. The credentials of the maintenance mechanic were not verified by the recruitment committee.
3. The personnel specification for crane operators was not prepared at all.
4. The personnel specification for data entry operators did not have any mention about characters to be typed/inserted, or formatting and aligning documents needed, which are essential for data entry personnel.

Learning points

- Job specifications need to be developed carefully, considering all human attributes required for performing the scheduled tasks.
- Practical tests are essential to adjudge the capability of machine operators (A company should not rely only on experience certificates provided).
- The ability to read, write, and interpret information from the given text are essential prerequisites for a maintenance mechanic.
- A company should identify the suitable selection tool to avoid choosing a person unfit for the job—this will result in a 'select error'.

INTRODUCTION

An organization always looks out for manpower that is capable of performing and achieving its business goals. It is the manpower that shows the capacity to achieve its production targets and sustain productivity. Requirement of manpower depends on the variable workload of an organization. As the load of an organization fluctuates, at some point of time, it may appear that the available manpower is adequate enough to achieve the target. Considering the consistency of load, an organization goes in for recruitment. In order to make the recruitment and selection process perfect, and to get the right man for the right job, an organization should preferably have its own recruitment philosophy. It has to decide on the right selection tool for the purpose of screening and select the best out of all the applicants.

After selection, the credentials need verification along with completion of other administrative formalities. This chapter discusses manpower planning and its importance, recruitment philosophy, policy, objectives, strategy, different sources of recruitment, selection tools, and possible errors in the process of manpower acquisition and accounting of recruitment and selection functions.

HUMAN RESOURCE PLANNING

> Planning is a process of developing a set of decisions for action in future.

Planning is a process of developing a set of decisions for action in future. Human resource (HR) planning is also termed 'manpower planning' by many authors. It is the process of preparing a set of decisions with regard to HR development and deployment. The actions required to be initiated are exogenous to HR planning and are generally categorized as (a) employment opportunity and (b) economic development.

HR planning comprises putting the right number and kind of people at the right place, at the right time, and making them do things for which they are suited, to achieve business goals. In the era of industrialization, structured HR planning has become a really important aspect. It is carried out in a particular sequence of steps which begins with analysing the current inventory of manpower available. The managers need to suitably make plans for future requirements, by forecasting along with developing employment and training programmes.

Employment opportunity originates from technology upgration, innovation, and continuous search for newer scope and ideas. For example, after launching CNC machines, the use of old conventional machines has mostly been discontinued in large companies. The new generation machines have opened up opportunities for employment for software engineers, growth of air conditioner manufacturers, etc. In fact, modern technology explosion has made our lives hassle-free. This is directly related to economic development. Obviously, employment opportunity and technology advancement are interdependent.

HR planning also calls for deciding the position to be filled based on the workload for a considerable period of time by means of personnel planning and forecasting, building a pool of potential candidates who are capable of performing the required tasks through internal and external recruitment, using the most suitable selection tools tailor-made for the position, and populating the HR inventory/information system. While negotiating during an interview, the financial as well as the non-financial offers must be discussed openly to prevent attrition at a later stage. HR planning manifests its importance as the key to managerial functions, efficient utilization, motivation, better industrial relations, and higher productivity.

Manpower planning is an important aspect of manpower management and administration. A large pool of manpower exists, but utilizing them for the right job at the right time is a major managerial task. Manpower is the quantity of productive people who can be used in any organization as human capital and as assets to achieve the common goal. Manpower planning is a process that comprises forecasting, developing, and controlling by an organization to ensure that it has the right number and kind of people with regard to their skills and competencies.

HUMAN RESOURCE

The term HR planning has gained popularity and is also used by academicians and people from organizations all over the world. Let us discuss the term human resource, its rate of growth, quantitative and qualitative dimensions, and other facets.

The quantity of human resource has four determining variables:
1. Population policy
2. Population structure
3. Migration
4. Labour force participation

Resource refers to the productive power of natural goods. Human resource means human beings with productive power. Human beings are both participants and beneficiaries of economic development of a country. The demographic profile, migration, mobility, and participation patterns in economic activity determine the quantitative aspects of actual and potential human resources.

The rate of growth of HR has two dimensions—quantity and quality. The quantity of human resource has four determining variables:

1. Population policy
2. Population structure
3. Migration
4. Labour force participation

Three influencing variables of the quality of human resource are as follows:

1. Education and training
2. Health and nutrition
3. Equality of opportunity

Quantitative dimensions of HR planning consider human beings (a) with productive power and (b) without productive power.

The definitions of population used may be categorized into two groups—*de facto* and *de jure*.

The *de facto* (present-in-area) concept refers to residents and non-residents physically present at the time of enumeration.

The *de jure* concept necessitates a complete count of all persons—normal residents of the country, irrespective of where each person is located, at the time of the census.

Strict conformity to either can never be possible because of difficulties in enumeration due to the following types of people:

1. Nationals living abroad
2. Nomadic (roaming) population
3. Jungle inhabitants
4. Population in disturbed areas

Box 6.1 describes the objectives of human resource planning.

Box 6.1 Objective of human resource planning

Human resource planning is a process that organizations adopt to ensure that they have the right number and kind of people, at the right places, at the right time, and that these people are capable of performing their tasks effectively and efficiently conforming to the organizational norms. HR planning facilitates the organization to achieve its overall objectives.

The principal objective of HR planning is to ensure the optimum use of existing HR, to forecast future skill requirement, to search for HR with requisite skills, and to ensure availability as and when required. Manpower planning has always been an important function. However, at present, HR planning is associated with organizational requirements used to ascertain recruitment levels, anticipate redundancy, determine levels of training, identify need-based training, and provide a basis of management development programmes.

Furthermore, HR planning assists in productivity bargaining, study cost of overhead, and helps to decide whether certain activities can be subcontracted. As such, HR planning has emerged as a crucial organizational function in the arena of human resource.

MAJOR ACTIVITIES IN HUMAN RESOURCE PLANNING

Forecasting, inventorying, and anticipating are the three major activities in HR planning. Forecasting may be conducted in terms of mathematical projections or judgmental estimates considering (a) economic trends and (b) industry development. Inventorying refers to preparing the HR database and ascertaining the extent of manpower utilization. Anticipating means considering the career progression of existing human resources, and the future loads to determine the adequacy or redundancy of manpower, both quantitatively and qualitatively.

APPROACHES TO HUMAN RESOURCE PLANNING

HR planning follows three distinct approaches—(a) social demand approach, (b) rate of return approach, and (c) HR requirement approach.

Social Demand Approach

The social demand approach relies on the assessment of the society's requirement of education. In principle, it is an aggregate of individuals' demand for education in respect to all individuals within the society. The approach is capable of revealing the number of students with different types of professional preparations that may be expected by a given target date. Projections of social demand for education depend on aspects such as the following:

> HR planning follows three distinct approaches:
> 1. Social demand approach
> 2. Rate of return approach
> 3. HR requirement approach

1. Incomes of educated people
2. Tastes and preferences of households for education
3. Preferences of domestic circles for education
4. Demographic characteristics such as fertility and mortality
5. Direct costs of education
6. Student grants
7. Existing standards of entrance to institutes

Social demand approach has certain persistent problems associated with it. The main problem is associated with the database on demographic aspects such as district, block, village, wastage of education, stagnation and break in education, intensity of utilization of existing educational facilities, and difficulties in predicting the future.

Rate of Return Approach

The rate of return approach is a critic of the social demand approach. This approach argues that after crossing the school-learning age, people attach positive values to present and future benefits of education, and their careers on considerations. The rate of return approach treats education as a contributor to productivity, prompts students to decide whether to receive more education, and facilitates investment decisions to in education.

Three parameters of rate of return approach are cost of education, returns to education, and present net worth (used in discounting future return to arrive at present value).

Conceptual issues involved in the rate of return approach are as follows:

1. Investment in education has two-element taxonomy—direct and indirect cost
2. Direct cost has two components—private expenditure and public expenditure in education
3. Private expenditure is incurred by individuals (fees, hostel, books, etc.)

4. Public expenditure comprises (a) creating, expanding, maintaining facilities, (b) publicizing need of education, (c) recurring expenditure in affiliating institutes, (d) expenditures towards students' welfare, (e) non-recurring costs in developing building, plant and equipment, library, sports complex, etc.
5. Indirect cost may be viewed from both private and social angles. From a private angle, it includes earnings foregone for studying. The social viewpoint of indirect costs comprises opportunity cost of public expenditure on education.

In the rate of return approach, returns to education are generally split into three categories: direct monetary benefits, indirect monetary benefits, and non-monetary benefits.

Manpower Requirement Approach

Manpower requirement approach rests on the maxim or axiom that a definite link exists between education and economic growth; lack of skilled manpower hinders the growth of a nation. In manpower requirement approach, a future target of gross national product (GNP) or specific targets of industrial production is achieved by forecasting the needs that could be required in the future. Based on this approach, planners indicate the directions of development of the education sector over the forthcoming years. The basic steps in the manpower requirement approach are shown in Box 6.2.

Box 6.2 Steps in manpower requirement approach

1. Anticipating the direction and magnitude of development of each individual sector in the economy
2. Evolving norms for engaging manpower in each individual sector duly considering the technological options, both present and future
3. Translating the physical targets for the development into manpower requirements using specific manpower norms
4. Estimating the educational equivalents of manpower requirements
5. Analysing the propositions of estimates of educated manpower requirements for educational developments; based on assumptions regarding enrolment rates, transition probabilities, and wastage and stagnation rates at each level of education

Source: http://www.egyankosh.ac.in/bitstream/123456789/35830/1/MTM2-01.pdf

HUMAN RESOURCE FORECASTING

Human resource forecasting refers to the predictions that the managers need to make for demand and supply of workers and skills at organizational, regional, or national levels. Human resource forecasting forms a part of the HR planning process. A number of techniques are used for human resource forecasting, including statistical analysis of current trends along with the use of mathematical models.

Types of Forecasts

Human resource forecasts are categorized differently depending on the purpose of the forecast. These are short-term, medium-term, and long-term forecasts, policy conditional forecast, onlookers forecast, and macro and micro forecasts.

Short-term forecasts Short-term forecasts are made to facilitate the estimation of financial provisions for wage or salary for programmes or projects to be initiated in the near future. These forecasts are generally made for a period not exceeding two years.

Medium-term forecasts Medium-term forecasts are made for a period of two to five years. These forecasts are made while preparing contingency plans to meet twists and turns of the economic circumstances.

Long-term forecasts If forecasting is done for a period more than five years, it is termed as long-term forecast. The length actually varies from situation to situation. Forecasting relating to educational planning or highly-skilled professional categories is generally termed as long-term forecasting.

Policy conditional forecasts Governments frame policies towards factors that influence the demand of HR and the forecasts are generally based on rule of thumb, professional judgements, on the basis of explicitly specified model, or combination of them. These forecasts are called policy conditional forecasts.

Onlookers forecasts Some planners assume that the factors that influence HR demand will behave in the future in the way as they did in the past. Forecasts made on this assumption are termed onlookers forecasts and are obtained based on rule of thumb, professional judgements, on the basis of explicitly specified models, or a combination of them.

Macro forecasts Macro forecasts are done at the national, industry/sector, and region/state levels. Macro forecasts are done while planning for education and training facilities, decision making for choice of industry for development, choice of industry and location, and determining order of priorities for creating and/or for expanding economic and social infrastructure employed.

Micro forecasts Micro forecasting is done at an enterprise or department level. Human resource forecasts are needed while planning recruitment, promotion, and training for the development of enterprise or department.

Demand Forecasting

Human resource demand forecasting is influenced by two important factors—the volume of output and the level of productivity. Human resource requirements may change due to change in output volume, productivity, or mix, and may necessitate analysis of performance. However, economists view demand for a particular category of HR as a schedule of relationships between quantities of that particular category of HR demanded and a series of possible wage rates. They conceive that HR demand varies with wage rates.

In the area of forecasting, 'need' refers to the number of people required to provide an ideal level of contribution or service. Of course, the ideal level depends on technological, structural, and socio-cultural constraints. 'Requirements' are the functional composition of employment adequate enough to produce goods products or service offerings within the framework of social, cultural, economic, and technological targets.

Supply Forecasting

The terms 'manpower' and 'labour force' are interchangeably used, though there is a slight difference between the two. Labour force includes all persons in the population who are economically active; manpower refers to all persons in the population or labour force, excluding the purely unskilled ones.

In the area of HR planning, the four dimensions of HR supply are stock and flow, quantity and flow, occupation and education, and macro and micro.

1. Flow dimension refers to HR supply over a period of time, whereas stock dimension means HR supply at a particular point of time.
2. Quantity dimension of HR indicates number of persons available with requisite qualification and experience. Qualitative dimension manifests its importance when characteristics of HR supply such as specialization, quality of training, length of directional experience, and the necessary aptitude and requisite attitude and motivation are being considered.
3. Occupation and education—Occupation is a description of the functional role to be played in the workplace. Physicians, engineers, accountants are some examples of occupation. These occupational groups are uniquely related to an education programme. Human resource supply of such an occupation is related to graduates of the relevant educational programme. For example, HR supply in case of engineers would be as follows:
   (a) Number of engineers with a degree from engineering colleges
   (b) Number of engineering graduates in other occupations
   (c) Number of experienced persons without an engineering degree

In the absence of reliable occupation and education data, the forecasting of human resource becomes extremely difficult. Human resource supply forecasts are generally made by broad categories of educational qualification.

4. Macro and micro supply forecasting—Macro-level HR forecasting is a complex and dynamic process. Two methods, direct and indirect, are used. The direct method relies on census count of persons belonging to category for which supply is being estimated. The limitation of the direct method arises from infrequent census counts. In the indirect method, estimation of HR involves steps such as estimating actual life span, determining base period, forecasting annual institutional out-turn, obtaining cumulative out-turn adjusted for attrition, and estimating HR supply.

Micro-level HR supply forecasting comprises internal and external supplies. The internal supply within an organization is governed by two factors—outward movement from the organization caused by voluntary resignation, death or superannuation, and internal movement resulting from transfer and promotions.

Human Resource Forecasting Techniques

At the macro level, manpower planning model is concerned more with the demand for jobs than with the supply side of the employment equation (Bhattacharyya 2006). During macro-level manpower planning, planners try to understand the number of people coming from the labour market, their education and training levels, their ages, etc. These input information facilitate an organization to determine the induction training needs to transform the labour supply to meet the demands of the economy. Thus, macro-level and micro-level planning are interdependent and interrelated. Macro-level HR planning is reinforced through educational planning. There are certain well-known models and techniques used in forecasting, some of which are described briefly:

1. Social demand approach
2. Manpower requirement approach (MRA)
3. Rate of return approach (RRA)

Social demand approach This is a leading model of HR planning that contains three major steps: (a) assessing the demand for manpower, (b) assessing the supply of manpower, and (c) balancing the supply and demand.

The demand side of the model deals with the estimation of future level of gross domestic product (GDP), estimation of structural change of the economy in terms of distribution of output by economic sector over time, and estimation of labour productivity by economic sector and its evolution over time.

The supply side refers to the estimation of population and educational level, age, and sex; the number of graduates, dropouts by age, gender, and education level; distribution of labour force with age, sex, and educational level.

Balancing labour supply and demand The labour demand may be very different from labour supply due to poor quality of data collected during enumeration. In such cases, the planners tend to use an ad-hoc adjustment mechanism revising one or more of the key assumptions. While developing a human resource plan, if the planner is too optimistic about labour productivity, the forecasting may fall short of the actual labour demand. On the contrary, optimistic labour force participation rate can also increase the actual supply of labour. In such paradoxical situations, reconciliation of labour supply and labour demand emerge to be imperative.

Manpower requirement approach National planners adopt this approach during macro-level manpower planning. A linear relationship is established between the manpower category in different industry groups and their outputs. MRA helps to project the demand for manpower at the macro-level. This approach manifests its importance for the purpose of educational planning at the national level.

Rate of return approach This is another well-recognized approach that planners adopt during macro-level manpower planning. RRA is based on the calculation of the net returns on educational expenditure. Earning of any individual is likely to increase on receiving education. RRA is measured considering the net increase in income on receiving education. The present value of the flow of future net income in calculated through this approach.

Educational programmes, which have positive returns, are promoted, while programmes showing negative or zero net present value (NPV) are reduced or even discontinued.

IMPORTANCE OF HUMAN RESOURCE PLANNING

We are acquainted with the objectives, approaches, forecasting, and techniques of HR planning. Obviously the importance of HR planning is manifold. It serves as a key to managerial functions, efficient utilization of men, identifying and motivating them, promoting industrial relations, and boosting productivity.

Key to Managerial Functions

Planning, organizing, leading, directing, and controlling (POLDC) are the five managerial functions that need HR for their execution. Human resources help in the accomplishment of all these managerial activities effectively and efficiently. Therefore, staffing becomes a key to all managerial functions.

Efficient Utilization

With the emergence of the concept of the global village, handling HR efficiently has become an important function in the industry. Large organizations need huge HR to execute their job effectively. As such, the staffing function has emerged as a critical organization process.

Motivation

Irrespective of their levels, organizational citizens need motivation. The staffing function, in addition to putting the right men on the right job, also comprises various motivational programmes. It is essential to launch financial and non-financial motivational schemes, including incentive plans. Therefore, all types of incentive plans become an integral part of staffing function to satisfy both intrinsic and extrinsic motivation.

Better Industrial Relations

Stability, smooth running, and growth of a concern depend on the quality of interpersonal relations; especially on the relation between the management and unions. Members from the unions and associations form a collective bargaining forum. A strong relation between them helps taking decisions collectively. Furthermore, human relations can become even stronger through effective control, clear communication, and effective supervision and leadership.

Higher Productivity

Productivity levels increase with the efficient utilization of resources in the best possible manner. Productivity is enhanced by minimizing wastage of time, money, efforts, and energies. Alternatively, cost reduction, value engineering, method study and work measurement, and other techniques help to enhance productivity. Human resource and its related activities/systems such as performance appraisal, training and development, remuneration, further settle on productivity.

RESPONSIBILITY AND ACCOUNTABILITY

Managers are responsible for hiring and accountable for recruitment; the HR manager has to actively help line managers in the process, provide support and extend specialist advice, and further ensure that all proper steps are initiated. The compliance regarding international policies in addition to applicable local rules and regulations are required to be set in consultation with the hiring manager and HR manager. Of course, it is difficult when the hiring manager is unfamiliar with the country's legal framework. In such cases, the local HR manager needs to cooperate with the hiring manager, and provide him with all the local policies at the beginning of the hiring process.

After discussing the various aspects of manpower planning, approaches to HR planning, and forecasting techniques, key managerial functions, etc., one should now understand job analysis and related topics.

JOB ANALYSIS, JOB DESCRIPTION, AND JOB SPECIFICATION

Job analysis is the basis on which all the HR activities are based. Job analysis, job description, and job specification play dominant roles in the recruitment process. There are a number of steps, which are generally used to define and set out the nature of particular jobs for recruitment purposes. Job description provides a clear idea about the activities and job specification underlines the mental and physical attributes required. Job description and job specification will be discussed after discussing job analysis.

> Job analysis, job description, and job specification provide inputs for the recruitment process.

Job analysis provides information about the job and the characteristics required in an employee to carry out these activities. The information, in the form of job descriptions and job specifications, helps managers decide what sort of people to recruit and hire (Dessler and Varkkey, 2009). Job analysis, its importance, and products are discussed next.

Job Analysis

Q 2 Job analysis, also referred to as work analysis, is the process of examining the jobs to identify the key requirements of each job. In simpler terms, it is the procedure for determining the duties and skill requirements of a job and the kind of person who should be hired for it (Dessler and Varkkey 2009). Before beginning the process of recruitment through job analysis, a number of important questions are explored and need to be answered. These include the following:

1. Title of the job
2. Whom the employee is supposed to report to
3. What the employee is responsible for
4. Simple description of the role and duties of the employee within the organization

In simple words, job analysis can be referred to as a systematic approach that helps to describe and clearly identify the job role, description, requirements, and responsibilities. It also aids in identifying the level of qualifications, skills, knowledge, training, etc. required for any individual to successfully accomplish a task or a job. It helps in understanding the worth of a job on the basis of which compensation packages and related fields can easily be decided upon. The information can be either gathered through direct observation of the workers working or through interviews, records etc.

To be able to do the job analysis well, a lot of organizations employ 'job analysts'. In many companies, job analysis is expected to be a part of the general skills of a training or personnel officer. Job analysis for two positions—purchase manager and training and development manager—is illustrated in Annexures 6.1 and 6.2, respectively.

Importance of Job Analysis

Job analysis helps in analysing the resources and establishing strategies to achieve the business goals and strategic objectives. In fact, it is the basis for demand–supply analysis, recruitments, compensation management, and needs identification and performance appraisal. Job analysis focuses on getting job-related information (tasks, duties, and required qualifications). The inputs of job analysis are detailed in Box 6.3.

Box 6.3 Significance of job analysis

1. Choosing candidates either from internal employees or from the recruitment of new staff through advertisement
2. Setting out the training requirements to perform a particular job effectively and efficiently
3. Providing information about the type of equipment and materials to be employed with the job, to help in decision making
4. Identifying and profiling the experiences of employees in their tasks; this is information that can be fruitfully used as evidence for staff development and promotion
5. Identifying areas of risk and danger at work
6. Helping in setting rates of pay for job tasks, and developing compensation packages

Job analysis information supports several HR management activities such as recruitment and selection, compensation, training, performance appraisal, discovering unassigned duties, and legal compliance (Dessler and Varkkey 2009).

Job Analysis Data

Job analysts chart out the actual duties and responsibilities of job holders. Essential functions of the job are determined during analysis. The job analysts gather information about the job or work-related activities, job holder oriented activities, and the utilities and facilities. The utilities and facilities include machines, tools, and work aids and equipments. With regard to the job, the job analysts study financial and nonfinancial incentives, working conditions necessary for effective working, the qualifications, and experience pertinent to the job.

Exhibit 6.1 lists the type of data that job analysts generally collect through job analysis.

Exhibit 6.1 Job analysis data

1. **Activities**
   (a) Activities and processes
   (b) Documentation (hard copy, or on electronic or other media)
   (c) Systems, procedures, and instructions
   (d) Individual responsibilities
2. **Operator-oriented activities**
   (a) Operator behaviours (physical actions, communication, etc.)
   (b) Method of study and work measurement
   (c) Energy required to be expended
3. **Machines, tools, equipments**
   (a) Knowledge of handling
   (b) Controlling the speed, feed, and depth of cut
   (c) Engaging the probe for automatic adjustment of tools
4. **Work performance**
   (a) Defect analysis
   (b) Conformance to set standards
5. **Job-related information**
   (a) Common sense (or sixth sense of a human being)
   (b) Knowledge essential to perform the job
   (c) Input materials to be used
   (d) The outcome: product or service
   (e) Necessary quality control parameters
6. **Job context**
   (a) Work environment
   (b) Reward and compensation management scheme
   (c) Organizational culture
7. **Personality attributes**
   (a) Patience and tolerance essential to perform
   (b) Perfection, mental ability, etc.
   (c) Level of education
   (d) Experience, skills, and training

Products of Job Analysis

Job analysis yields multiple products; the most important of them are job description and job specification. However, other products of job analysis include job classification, job design/structuring, job evaluation, performance appraisal, training and development, succession planning, improving efficiency, safety, HR planning, and legal and quasi-legal requirements. These are represented in Figure 6.1.

Job description Job description helps to anticipate the suitability of a particular employee into the organization for a particular job. Job description will be discussed in a separate section.

Job specification A job specification underlines the mental and physical attributes required of the job holder, and it goes beyond the job description. Job specification will be discussed in a separate section.

Job classification Different jobs are arranged into classes or groups based on their characteristics and according to some systematic scheme, which may be technology-based job/task content, human behaviour-based job content, or on the basis of criticality.

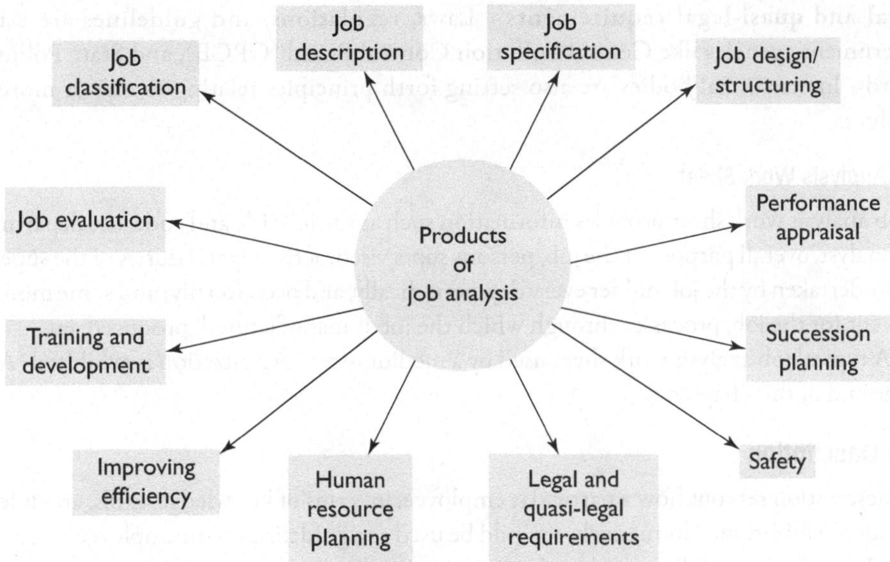

Fig. 6.1 Products of job analysis

Job design/structuring A job constitutes multiple work activities. Job design refers to allocation and arrangement of organizational work activities and tasks into sets where a singular set of activities is a 'job' and the job is assigned to a job incumbent.

Job evaluation Job evaluation refers to systematically classifying the jobs in accordance to their relative worth both within the organization and within the related labour market. Job evaluation provides vital inputs to the designing of compensation management. Job evaluation will be discussed in a separate section.

Performance appraisal In some companies, employees and their immediate line managers discuss personal goals and targets for the forthcoming time period (say, for the next three or six months). The appraisal will then involve a review of performance during the previous three or six months, and new targets will be set. Job details can serve as a useful basis for establishing dialogue and targets.

Training and development Training needs are identified and provided to abridge the specific skill gaps. Development is generic in nature.

Succession planning Succession planning refers to searching for high potential managers who are capable of assuming higher managerial positions.

Improving efficiency Efficiency of a person can be improved through carefully selected HRD mechanisms and applying the same.

Safety Safety refers to protection that enhances the wellbeing of employees.

Q 6 **Human resource planning** Human resource planning is a significant part of HRM. A large number of human resources exist but utilizing them for the right job at the right time is the major task. Human resource is the quantity of people,that can be used in any organization as capital and in the form of assets to achieve the common goal. HR planning encompasses career planning, HR information system, HR valuation and accounting, HR audit, etc. HR planning will be discussed in a separate section.

Legal and quasi-legal requirements Laws, regulations, and guidelines are established by government agencies like Central Pollution Control Board (CPCB), and State Pollution Control Boards. International bodies are also setting forth principles relating to one or more job analysis products.

Job Analysis Work Sheet

A job analysis work sheet provides information such as the job title and code, the department, name of the analyst, overall purpose of the job, persons supervised, activities and duties of the supervisor, activities undertaken by the job holder every day, periodically, and occasionally; and some more information relevant for the job, processes through which the job is manufactured/produced, etc.

A typical job analysis work sheet used by a medium-scale organization is exhibited (Annexure 6.4) at the end of this chapter.

Job Description

Job description sets out how a particular employee, in terms of knowledge, skills, attitudes, etc., can fit into an organization. Alternatively, it could be used as a guideline for an employee to get an idea about his roles and responsibilities within the organization.

A job description incorporates the following:

1. Title of the job
2. Whom the new recruit reports to
3. Job overview
4. Key tasks that the employee is responsible for accomplishing
5. Simple description of the roles, duties, and responsibilities of the employee within the organization
6. Tools and technology used
7. Physical working environment

Job description, as discussed, provides a clear idea about the activities and the responsibilities required for a job to be completed successfully. This makes it easy for the recruitment manager to recruit candidates. Obviously then, job analysis is an early step in the recruitment process. The accuracy of the individual's specification and all the subsequent stages in selection will depend on the quality of the job analysis. Refer to Exhibits 6.2 and 6.3 for two examples of job description.

Exhibit 6.2 Job description—maintenance manager

Reporting authority—general manager

Job overview

The maintenance manager is responsible to organize preventive maintenance, upkeep the machines and equipments, reduce 'mean time between failures', and attend breakdown machines, with the ultimate aim to enhance productive time of machines.

Key activities

1. Conducting periodic reviews to promote services and repairs
2. Managing emergency and regular repairs
3. Coordinating maintenance and repairs to mechanical and electronic machines
4. Directing maintenance and repairs of air conditioners, heating systems, generators, and other similar appliances
5. Preparing budgets for running maintenance operations
6. Arranging all maintenance manuals methodically

Tools and technology used

Computers, printers, telephones, faxes, and other office hardware

(Contd)

Exhibit 6.2 (Contd)

Physical working environment

1. Nine-hour shifts or more in emergency
2. Salary as per administrative manual

Performance standard

Quality performance is subject to annual appraisal

Exhibit 6.3 Job description—sales manager

Reporting authority—general manager

Job overview

The sales manager is responsible for the actual distribution or movement to the customers, coordination of sales distribution by establishing sales territories, quotas, and goals, and organizing training programmes for skill enhancement for sales representatives. The job also involves collecting sales data to analyse sales statistics, determining marketwise sale potential and inventory requirements, and monitoring the preferences of customers.

Key activities

1. Monitoring customer preferences to determine focus of sales efforts
2. Measuring and enhancing customer satisfaction
3. Developing sales teams to lead and coordinate sales activities
4. Determining price schedule, discount rates for bulk purchases
5. Developing the sales force by imparting need-based training
6. Evaluating performances to develop and control sales and service programmes
7. Resolving customer complaints
8. Coordinating sales distribution through establishing sales territories, quotas, and goals
9. Preparing sales budgets and approving budget expenditures

Tools and technology used

Computers, printers, telephones, faxes, and other office hardware

Physical working environment

1. Nine-hour shifts or more in emergency
2. Salary as per administrative manual

Performance standard

Quality performance is subject to annual appraisal

Selection involves procedures to identify the most appropriate candidates to fill posts. Therefore, it is important for an effective selection procedure to take into consideration the following:

1. Keeping the costs of selection low
2. Making sure that the skills and qualities being sought have been identified
3. Developing a process for identifying these qualities in candidates
4. Making sure that the candidates selected will want the job and will stay with the company

Job Specification

A job specification goes beyond job description. It underlines the mental and physical attributes required of the job holder to carry out the job effectively. A job specification is a combination of statements of employee characteristics including qualifications required for successful accomplishments of the tasks, leading to satisfactory performance of defined duties, comprising a specific job or functions. It is basically derived from job analysis and is a conglomeration of knowledge, skills, and abilities, and the requisite education, training, and experience required to perform a job conforming to the quantitative target and qualitative requirements. These also constitute the minimum recruiting criteria or minimum qualifications for the job. Refer to Figure 6.2.

Job specifications are used when a company advertises in mass media for hunting talents, recruitment, and selection. Job specifications are different from job description. While a person focuses on

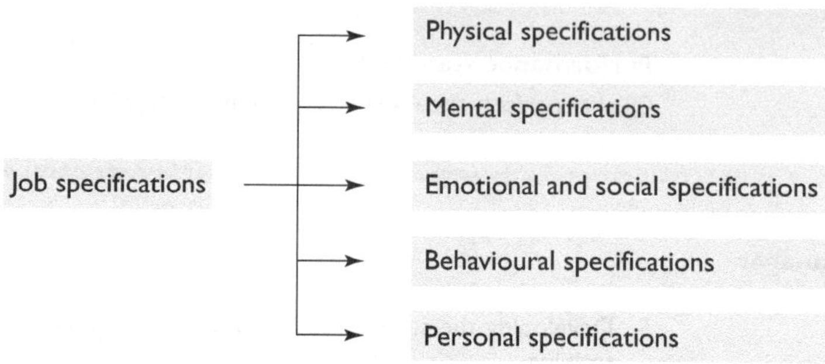

FIG. 6.2 Components of job specification

job specifications, the organization is responsible for developing and documenting job descriptions. The various elements of job specifications are physical specifications, mental specifications, behavioural specifications, and personal specifications. Of course, some jobs need licenses or certifications. For example, an electrical mechanic needs certification by the competent authority. An auditor of environmental management system needs certification with regard to ISO 14000 EMS, and a quality auditor should preferably have 'lead assessor' certification to his credit.

Physical specifications Some specific physical features may be essential to perform a particular job. The physical abilities and skills must be specified. The kind of physical effort required and the duration of such exertion are the points discussed here. For example, continuous walking, standing, or lifting of heavy objects is essential for certain jobs. The features include height, weight, vision, finger dexterity, voice, hand and foot coordination, motor coordination, colour discrimination, age, gender, etc.

Aircraft pilots essentially need eye-hand-foot coordination, which must be specified in advertisements. While recruiting them, these physical attributes must be judged. Presently, in most companies, computer monitors and a joystick are employed to test these attributes. The coordination makes a pilot capable of multitasking. Fulfillment of this criterion makes an aspirant capable of being selected, provided he possesses the requisite aptitude. The ambitious person having flair for flying can only reach his coveted desire if he possesses the unique skill of eye-hand-foot coordination.

Mental specifications Intelligence, memory, judgement, ability to plan, ability to estimate, to read, to write, to think, concentrate and conceptualize, and analytical ability come within the purview of mental specifications. Intelligence test measures the over-all intelligence quotient (IQ) of a candidate.

Emotional and social specifications Individuals are required to discharge duties in work environment that demand particular behavioural disposition. A person working in the reception of an organization or a public relations department needs to interact with many unknown people throughout the day. His/her personal appearance must be conducive to the work situation. Visitors need realistic information with regard to various aspects of production, purchase, cost, availability, presence of any dignitary, etc.

For instance, the person in the reception must have a high degree of emotional stability, should be reasonably submissive, and be an extrovert. Their social adaptability, public relation skills, cooperativeness, leadership, initiative and drive, manners, and most importantly, helping attitude, etc., are the essential prerequisites for success in the profession.

Behavioural specifications While executing and performing the duties and responsibilities, a person needs to execute a set of manners, behavioural disposition, etiquette, and conform to norms. Accomplishing the task is not an end in itself. It is the employee behaviour that constitutes the organizational culture. Juniors learn from the demonstrated behaviours of organizational superiors. When persons are recruited, either through campus interviews or experience, they need to be acclimatized with the organizational culture. Otherwise, cultural contrast may jeopardize the functioning of the organization.

Seniors are expected to behave in a particular manner. There cannot be a written document in this aspect. It is largely a matter of feeling. However, these are to be kept in mind during the recruitment, selection and placement process.

Personal specifications Personal specifications include attributes of the person essential to perform the job correctly and adequately. The person's characteristics must be relevant, independent, and assessable.

1. Relevant—Only those characteristics, connected demonstrably with the success or failure of the job, should be specified. For example, a salesperson must have a high degree of tolerance and be a good listener, be smiling and communicative, and have in possession full knowledge of the product.
2. Independent—Overlapping elements should be avoided.
3. Assessable—Only those attributes that can be assessed with the selection tools that are available (usually application form and interviews) should be included.

JOB EVALUATION

Job evaluation is a systematic process of evaluating and determining the value or worth of jobs performed and the worth or contribution of the employee's efforts within the organization. Job evaluation is done for the purpose of establishing the wage and salary credentials. Look at Box 6.4 to understand the factors that affect the process of job evaluation.

Box 6.4 Factors in job evaluation

Factors that job evaluators generally consider while evaluating a job are as follows:

1. Specific training need or qualifications and requirements to perform the assigned tasks better
2. Requisite knowledge and skills for successful accomplishment of the job
3. Complexity or intricacy of tasks demanding special skills
4. Interaction with different departments of the organization to promote interaction
5. Problem-solving skills and independent judgement for promptness
6. Accountability and responsibility for fault-free activities
7. Decision-making authority to develop leadership skills
8. Degree of supervision required for the task
9. Cross-training requirements for multi-skilling and multitasking
10. Working conditions such as lighting, noise, ventilation, etc., in which the job is performed

Methods of Job Evaluation

The four major methods of job evaluation are job ranking, job classification, factor comparison, and the point method.

Job Ranking Method

This method is perhaps the simplest method in which jobs are ranked from highest to lowest, in order of their values or merit to the organization. Jobs are often arranged according to the relative difficulty in performing them. Jobs are examined as a whole, rather than on the basis of important factors contained by the job. The evaluator just ranks the jobs on the basis of his/her perception. This method can be easily adopted in small organizations, but gets more and more difficult as different jobs exist within the company. In the Table 6.2, jobs ranked for six designations based on their contribution to the organization and corresponding monthly salaries are exhibited.

Table 6.2 Job ranking and salary

S. no.	Designation	Monthly salary
1.	Production manager	₹55,000
2.	Production supervisor	₹30,000
3.	High skilled operator	₹25,000
4.	Skilled operator	₹20,000
5.	Semi-skilled operator	₹15,000
6.	Labourer (unskilled)	₹12,000

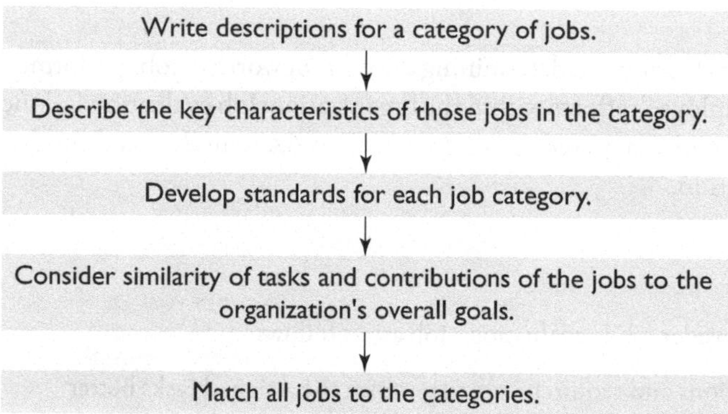

FIG. 6.3 Job classification

Job Classification Method

The general purpose of a job classification method is to create and maintain pay grades for comparable work across your organization (heathfield-office.microsoft.com). The job classification method uses job classes that does a more customized evaluation. This method also uses scales to measure performance rather than simply comparing and ranking employee performances.

To carry out a job classification, you are required to write descriptions for the different categories of jobs; after which you need to develop standards for each job category by describing the key characteristics of those jobs in the category; finally consider similarities among tasks and contributions of the jobs to the organization's overall goals, and match the jobs to the categories.

The flowchart in Figure 6.3 lists the steps.

Government and non-government organizations, universities and institutes, and other large organizations typically use job classification systems. Organizations that have many types of jobs and have their offices across the globe must make sure to maintain fair standards across all work settings.

The advantage of job classification method is that it is very simple once you have established your categories. Job classification is subjective and the jobs fall into several categories. This is a disadvantage. It is also important for the job evaluators to be careful while evaluating jobs.

Factor Method or Factor Comparison Method

The factor comparison method is more scientific and complex than the qualitative methods of ranking and classification. The factor comparison method of job evaluation assumes that there are five universal factors consisting of mental requirements, skills, physical requirements, responsibilities, and working conditions. The evaluator makes decisions on these factors independently (Mondy 2009). The five universal factors are discussed briefly.

> The factor comparison method determines the absolute value of the job, after which the jobs can be ranked like most other job evaluation methods.

Mental requirements—this reflects mental traits such as inquisitiveness, intelligence, reasoning, imagination, and innovation.

Skills—this factor pertains to facility in muscular coordination and training in the interpretation of sensory impressions (Mondy 2009).

Physical requirements—these requirements involves sitting, standing, walking, lifting, and so on.

Responsibilities—covers the areas of collecting input materials, arranging funds, generating, maintaining, retrieving, and analysing records for decision making; and leading and supervising.

Working condition—highlights environmental factors such as noise, suffocation, illumination, smell, ventilation, hazards, and length of working hours.

After classifying the factors, the evaluators create a monetary scale, containing each of the five universal factors. Thereafter, the evaluator ranks the jobs according to the value for each factor. The factor comparison method determines the absolute value of the job. Then jobs can be ranked like most other job evaluation methods.

Point Method

A rater using this method first identifies specific job factors; such as knowledge, and skills required to perform the job. Thereafter, he/she assigns numerical values to each factor. The algebraic sum of the points provides a quantitative assessment of a job's relative worth. This method measures performance through scales and job factors rather than focusing on the entire job functions and ranking employees against each other. The point method is usually seen as the most reliable and valid job evaluation method by employees compared to more subjective methods such as the job ranking method. This is the most commonly-used method.

The key elements of each job are referred to as 'factors'. These factors are identified by the organization and then broken down into smaller components. Each factor is assessed separately and points are allocated according to the level needed for the job. The more demanding the job, the higher are the 'points value'. Factors usually assessed include knowledge and skills, people management, communication and networking, freedom to act, decision-making, working environment, impact and influence, and financial responsibility (www.cipd.co.uk). Refer to Exhibit 6.4.

Exhibit 6.4 Point method factors

1. **Knowledge and skills**
   (a) Work experience (b) External qualifications
   (c) Qualifications (d) Specialist training
2. **People management**
   (a) Human relations skills
   (b) Ability to deal with work pressure
   (c) Supervisory responsibility
3. **Communication and networking**
   (a) Social skills (b) Presentation skills
   (c) Diplomacy
4. **Freedom to act**
   (a) Depth of control (b) Supervision received
5. **Decision making**
   (a) Judgement (b) Initiative
   (c) Analytical ability
6. **Working environment**
   (a) Knowledge of special working practices
   (b) Breadth of management skill required
7. **Impact and influence**
   (a) Efficiency (b) Impact on customers
   (c) Responsibility (d) Results of errors
8. **Financial responsibility**
   (a) Budgeting

Comparison of the Job Evaluation Methods

Anderson (1997) studied all the 'pluses' and 'minuses' of the various methods of job evaluation, and advocated that the ranking method was simpler (for smaller jobs), cheaper, and easy to explain. On the other hand, he stated that the result of ranking method could be superficial, having the possibility of perpetuation.

The classification method might suffer from the subjectivity of evaluators or raters and job overlaps. The factor comparison methods, though not complex, could discriminate between the jobs better because they are objective.

Despite being expensive, the point rating system, has difficulty in weightage fixing, and was identified to be scientific, logical, and objective.

While comparing two jobs, certain points are allotted to them. CIPD suggests allotting the following:

1. Two points if it is considered to be of higher value
2. One point if it is regarded as equal worth
3. No point if it is less important

Job Evaluation vs Personal Specifications

The human resource flow is managed and developed through a particular process. The first step of this process is forming a decision about the job and the qualities essential for its successful accomplishment. Job analysis may reveal that the requirements of the job are possessed by many employable persons with initial training. In such cases, the selection process does not pose any problem. However, job analysis may also reveal that the requirements and the set of qualities, for a job like that of an astronaut are rarely found in a single person within the population. Such situation demands highly sophisticated selection process that consumes appreciable time.

Prior to hiring, for any position, organizations need to identify the criteria for job success and the characteristics required of the job-holder to achieve the success. The list of the various attributes and the personnel qualification which candidates should possess in order to achieve job success can be usefully structured to help and guide the interviewers during selection. Rodger (1952) and Fraser (1972), identified plans for personal specification. Apart from these two plans, another eight-point plan is also used. The plans are exhibited in Table 6.3.

Table 6.3 Plans for personal specifications

Seven-point plan by Alec Rodger (1952)	Five-point grading system by Munro Fraser (1972)	Eight-point plan
1. Physical make-up	1. Impact	1. First impression
2. Attainments	2. Qualification	2. Education and qualification
3. General intelligence	3. Brain and abilities	3. General intelligence and special aptitudes
4. Special aptitudes	4. Motivation	4. Personal background
5. Interests	5. Adjustment	5. Experiences
6. Disposition		6. Interests
7. Circumstances		7. Personality
		8. Motivation

For example, a job specification for a trainee manager's post in a retail store of a reputed company includes the following: The company is looking for people who are tough and talented. They should have a flair for business, know how to sell, and work as a member of a team and merely not as an individual.

RECRUITMENT

Recruitment is the process of attracting individuals on a timely basis, in sufficient numbers, and with appropriate qualifications, to apply for jobs with an organization (Mondy 2009).

Recruitment is the process through which the organization seeks applicants for potential employment. (Noe, et al. 2008).

The term recruitment may be defined as the process to discover sources of manpower to meet the requirements or the staffing schedule and to employ effective measures for attracting that manpower in adequate number to facilitate the selection of an efficient working force (Bhattacharyya 2006).

Thus, recruitment is a process of attracting job seekers with appropriate qualifications who are capable of meeting the organizational staffing needs and are likely to achieve the business goals. They should be recruited in sufficient numbers on a timely basis. The recruitment process is followed by selection, induction, and placement.

Recruitment Philosophy

An organization's values and beliefs are reflected through its philosophy. Often, an organization circulates its 'philosophy' in the form of a statement.

Recruitment is not an exception and also has its philosophy. The main slogan of recruitment philosophy is to, 'Hire the right people, for the right job, in the right time.' Most multinational organizations use this philosophy to strengthen themselves. It helps in filling up the vacant positions by duly considering the job-related competencies and values. The prime objective is to fill the position with the best talents available either within the organization or in the market. Firstly, it offers the unique opportunity of internal employees to the current workforce (to leverage existing talent), and secondly, by recruiting top external talents. This philosophy is common and is followed in principle by all organizations.

Recruitment Policy

> The recruitment policy statement ensures a sound recruitment process.

This recruitment policy outlines the principles and processes related to the recruitment of both internal and external candidates to position new recruits within a firm. The recruitment process may be ineffective in the absence of a structured policy. A well-defined recruitment policy helps organizations to respond to its HR requirements in time. The policy statement should be clear and concise. Developing a suitable recruitment policy is the first step in the efficient hiring process. The policy statement helps to ensure a sound recruitment process.

Recruitment Policy Components

A recruitment policy has some vital components, which essentially contribute to the recruitment process, and make it effective and error-free.

1. Finalizing the general policies and terms regarding recruitment
2. Recruitment services of consultants, if sought
3. Filling of temporary vacancies
4. Crash recruitment in demanding situations
5. Drafting the selection process
6. Developing job descriptions
7. Defining employment terms and conditions

The recruitment policy of an organization needs

1. to focus on recruiting the best available talents;
2. to ensure that every candidate, internal or external, is treated equally with dignity and respect;
3. to make an unbiased policy;
4. to encourage employees and help to unearth their hidden full potential;
5. to ensure transparency, task orientation, and merit based selection;
6. to decide upon the weightage of factors that suit organizational needs during the selection process;
7. to optimize HR needs at the time of selection;
8. to define the competent authority to approve the selection process and tools;
9. to conform to applicable public policy and legislation on hiring and employment relationship; and
10. to establish congruency between employee needs with the organizational needs.

Recruitment Objectives

An organization must develop its recruitment objectives. The objectives of recruitment of an organization may be the following:

1. Creating an open and fair process
2. Identifying prospective candidates with qualifications, competencies, experience, and requisite attributes, in line with the organization's business objectives, the requirements of the position and its values, in a cost-efficient and timely manner
3. Ensuring that selected candidates are well-suited for the organization and the position
4. Using proper selection tools including interviewing, assessment, reference checking, and where appropriate, background clearance
5. Building balanced teams and allowing inclusion of diverse applicants
6. Reflecting the brand, employer's image, and values through the recruitment communication material. The recruitment advertising should be consistent and conform to the global guidelines of the organization.

Recruitment Strategy

The recruitment process needs adequate care with regard to the use of selection tools to avoid 'select error'. An organization must develop its recruitment strategy after addressing certain elements. The elements of the strategy must include the primary goals of the recruitment, priority of the positions, expected levels of performance, targeted experience levels, category of candidates such as previously unemployed or employed, time of beginning the search for candidates, the source of HR, recruitment agency primary sourcing tool, priority skills, methods of recruitment, and principal attracting methods. Refer to Exhibit 6.5.

Exhibit 6.5 Twelve elements of recruitment strategy

1. The company must decide the primary objective of hiring outside people. The recruitment must be linked with the business goal to be achieved, and how the recruitment shall contribute to the objective. The reasons behind hiring should specify (a) whether the recruitment is made to compensate

(Contd)

Exhibit 6.5 (Contd)

a turnover, (b) for business diversification, (c) need of talent to meet the business volume, (d) to meet the challenges due to emergence of a new competitor, (e) benchmarking, and (f) enhancing the capability of the company adding talents with new skill sets.

2. It is impossible to hire people for all the positions at a time. As such, priority must be fixed, based on HR planning. However, priority may be assigned on considering whether the recruitment is for a key strategic business unit, or for a key job, and so forth.
3. Recruitment is done to achieve a business objective, and therefore, the level of performance must be predetermined and the target is set. Performance targets focus on average performers and top performers in all the jobs. In addition, emphasis must be laid on top performers in key jobs.
4. Some employment strategies are framed keeping in view long-term HR needs. For example, developing own talent pool, while another approach may be employed to recruit persons experienced in similar organizations. In the first case, a fresher learns and grows in the organization. But in the second case, an experienced person joins a new one with in-built values, ethics, prejudices, etc. and is induced in the earlier organization. As a result, cultural shock may develop from the cultural contrast and diversity between the two organizations.
5. A sound recruitment strategy must mention the class of candidates—experienced or fresher or employed—and if they are satisfied in their current job against the position. The strategy may have a tremendous impact on the quality of hiring.
6. It is wiser for any organization to continuously search, develop a talent pool, and maintain the database of candidates. It is not possible to locate the suitable talent by searching only after receipt of a requisition. This practice can be implemented for evergreen jobs that have a constant need, and where attrition is higher.
7. The source of HR is a decisive factor. Three common decisions are internal versus external, inside or outside the industry, and geographic focus. Of these three factors, internal versus external recruitment has already been discussed in this chapter. The management may decide to target within the industry only or may decide to apportion a fixed proportion outside the industry. Depending on the position, it is decided whether the candidate will be searched locally, in the region or country, or truly globally.
8. Recruitment is done either by the recruitment section of the organization or any agency on behalf of the organization. Sometimes, the line management of an organization does the recruitment in consultation with the HR department. Use of employee referrals is not an uncommon practice. External agencies are used in case of hard-to-fill jobs. However, some organizations outsource the entire recruiting function.
9. The primary sourcing tools must be carefully decided. The focus may be traditional media (electronic media, newspapers, walk-ins), sourcing events (job fairs and industry events), Internet sourcing (large and niche job boards), and employment branding (a long-term sourcing strategy to build a steady long-term supply of candidates). Acquiring intact teams and a large amount of talent through mergers and acquisitions is also a common practice.
10. Different jobs need diverse skills and competencies. A public relations officer needs a strong network with influential persons. In an academic institution, a placement should have a network with organizations. A position in a research and development department needs brain and intelligence. Keeping inter-departmental transfers in view, the company-wide competency needs (present and future) may be a consideration. The target skills and competencies must be prioritized.
11. Depending on the position, skills, and competencies required, the selection tools are used. For example, interviews, personality tests, skills tests, job simulations, etc., are some selection tools. The use of the tools is an essential part of any recruiting strategy to assess the right candidates. References (business, personal, or educational), grades, or academic performance (primarily for college hires) are also some considerations.
12. Attracting the talents for prospective candidates needs a strategic approach. An organization may highlight various aspects in the advertisement. For example, compensation and retirement benefits, available opportunities for promotion, fringe benefits and perquisites, stock option opportunities, challenging assignments, growth and learning opportunities are some aspects that attract talents. This will be discussed under the section on the AIDA model in this chapter.

Source: www.citehr.com

RECRUITMENT STRATEGY VIS-À-VIS CORPORATE STRATEGY

Q 8 Based on the mission and policies of a corporate house, it formulates its strategy to achieve the, business goals. The plan of different corporates may be diverse as given in Box 6.5.

Box 6.5 Plans of different corporate houses

1. Merging and acquiring
2. Fast growth in competitive market and change
3. Market penetration
4. Business process reengineering
5. Sustainable growth
6. Expansion of its business through diversification
7. Broadening the product range
8. Entering into new and foreign markets

The corporate strategy and recruitment strategy of an organization must be compatible.

In view of acute competition, a corporate may decide to merge with similar businesses to enhance each other's strengths or acquire some other business. Again, in the changing environment, a corporate may strategize for fast growth and change. A company launching a new product might adopt the loss leadership pricing policy to penetrate in the market. Differentiation and integration might also be planned. Above all, customer focus and orientation by way of super customer service may be used as a strategy.

When a corporate intends to expand business by way of diversification, it needs human resources with a variety of skills. At this point of time, the corporate needs to recruit persons having multiple skills. A corporate may naturally be interested and find it imperative to increase its market share by overseas ventures. But the culture differs widely from one country to another. Thus, a candidate with an understanding of multi-cultural backgrounds is quite suitable. Mergers and acquisitions are common phenomena. In such cases, while recruiting candidates, one should look to hire multi-skilled personnel with a multicultural background.

If a corporate strategizes to grow fast, then outsourcing of select activities becomes essential. Corporates need highly skilled and smart candidates if they opt for a 'low cost leadership' marketing strategy to grab more market share. A differentiated corporate strategy needs candidates with entrepreneurial skills. Candidates' positive attitude towards customers and emotional feelings enables a corporate to understand the intrinsic needs of the customers and, as such, provide excellent customer service.

Business process reengineering (BPR) is used to initiate radical business process change focused upon the use of information technology to facilitate a shift away from linear/sequential work organization towards parallel processing and multidisciplinary team working. It is important for the HR managers to be able to identify and react to the complexities associated with BPR. The leaders need to be always ready to take on the responsibilities of being change agents. They should possess transformational leadership skills in addition to transactional and visionary leadership.

A company planning to enter into foreign markets needs senior executives capable of handling cross-cultural issues.

Obviously then, corporate strategy is a major determinant behind formulating recruitment strategies. Whatever be the corporate strategy, it must develop its corresponding recruitment strategy aimed at achieving the corporate strategy. Corporate strategy and recruitment strategy must be compatible to one another. Refer to Table 6.4.

Table 6.4 Recruitment strategy vis-à-vis corporate strategy

Corporate Strategy	Recruitment Strategy
Sustainable growth	Centralized recruitment
Expansion	Decentralized recruitment
Diversification	Candidates with multiple skills
Entry into foreign markets	Candidates with multi-cultural background
Mergers and acquisitions	Outsourcing
Fast growth and change	Highly skilled and smart candidates
Low-cost leadership	Candidates with entrepreneurial skills
Differentiation	
Super customer service	Candidates with positive attitude and emotional feelings

RECRUITMENT PROCESS

The recruitment process starts with defining and approving vacant positions required to be filled in. The hiring manager is responsible for defining the vacant position and preparing a clear description of the job content, the requirements of the position, and the necessary competencies. The HR needs to be consulted for the content of the job description.

It is equally important to describe the working and business environment, networks, and organizational entity. While defining the position, it is necessary to take into account the existing team composition and consider factors relating to the impact of this recruitment on the team's composition including competencies, skills, work experience, working styles, background, and diversity. It is the hiring manager's responsibility to obtain and document the necessary approvals to recruit for the position prior to initiating the recruitment process. After requisition approval, the hiring manager should work with the local HR to develop a recruiting plan.

SOURCES OF RECRUITMENT

Broadly, the sources of recruitment are internal and external. With the explosion of information technology, many organizations adopt e-recruitment. Recruitment from each of these sources has its advantages and disadvantages.

Internal Recruitment

Q 1 Recruiting individuals need to fill particular posts within a business and it can be done internally by declaring the vacancy in the notice board. Internal recruitment happens when the business organization desires to fill the vacancy from within its existing workforce. Internal recruitment refers to the internal mobility of employees.

Internal Mobility of Employees

Internal mobility of employees is a part of internal recruitment. Internal mobility of personnel at higher position in organizational hierarchy is referred to as succession planning. Providing adequate internal career development opportunities is a key factor in employee motivation and job satisfaction. Promoting internal recruitment is also critical for any organization; helps retaining top talent and ensures future business success. Internal mobility provides an opportunity for personal development and thus employees are encouraged to take personal responsibility for their own professional growth and competence development. Internal mobility has the components like time in one position, open communication, transfer period, internal transfer within a country, and internal transfer between countries. Refer to Exhibit 6.6.

Internal mobility at higher positions is termed as succession planning.

Exhibit 6.6 Components of internal mobility

Time in one position An appropriate time in a position depends on the nature of the job, but in general, it is recommended that an appointed candidate remains in the position for a period of about 2–3 years. This period is long enough to realize the results of his/her own effort and endeavours for the business unit and to gain the most benefit from learning opportunities. A company should periodically review the time in the position, document the same, preferably in performance management discussions. A company must have a policy defining the approximate time in each position. However, in case of the need of certain prerequisites, the company may use the 'eligibility bar' before promoting and assigning higher responsibility to an individual. As a person moves up in the organizational hierarchy, he/she needs leadership skills, variety of personality traits, motives, etc. These need to be verified prior to the movement.

Open communication Present-day organizations characterised by participative management, workers' intervention, and OCTAPACE culture, industrial organizations resort to open communication. It is important that an employee and a manager have a trusted relationship for discussing the employee's career development that leads to organizational growth. The wishes of the person who desires transfer (regular, short term, international) should preferably be discussed openly with his/her manager as part of the performance management process. Employees must notify their manager if they aspire to attend the final interview for the higher position, especially if they are in responsible positions vacating which may result in premature termination of an international assignment.

In such cases, customer commitment or an agreed upon long-term field assignment might be affected and may deteriorate the image of the organization. The manager can support the employee's career development by expressing his/her view with regard to transfer possibilities. For the avoidance of doubt and ensuring clarity, a manager may not prevent an employee from moving to another role and higher responsibility. Organizations face resistances even during internal mobility of employees. Open communication reduces resistance. In fact, an employee should be told about his/her possible movement to other departments, (internal mobility) even prior to issuing the formal transfer order.

Transfer period Consideration must be given to the employee between the transfer period of the old and new positions to ensure good knowledge transfer to the successor and to ensure clear responsibilities over the old tasks. As a part of career progression, an appropriate transfer period has to be agreed between the employee and management. Management must take into account the employee's motivation and workload. The transfer period should generally be around one month, and, unless otherwise agreed by both the parties.

Internal transfer within a country For a national organization having multiple units within the country, employees of all levels may be transferred from one unit to another. In such cases of transfer within the same country in a similar level position, the salary remains the same. If the new job has a higher grade, the salary needs review commensurate to the higher responsibility of the new job grade. In these cases, hiring managers must consult HR for advice.

Internal transfer between countries For a multinational organization having units in different countries, the framework of local terms and conditions will apply in each country. However, for specific business reasons and/or if the competencies in question cannot be found locally, the manager in the host country may apply for approval to have an expatriate or deportee in the job. The local approval procedure for agreeing on salaries and costs must be followed in accordance with the transfer policy of the organization.

Advantages and Disadvantages of Internal Recruitment

The advantages of internal recruitment are manifold:

1. A firm can save substantial recruitment cost during the recruitment process. Individuals with knowledge of the firm will need shorter periods of training and time for 'fitting in'. The process of induction is not required at all. They only need to be given a brief about the higher position.
2. Disruption in the organization will be minimal as the promoted or the transferred individual is used to work with others in the organization.
3. Internal promotion acts as an incentive to all staff to work harder within the organization.

4. From the point of view of the firm, the strengths and weaknesses of an employee are assessed. There is always a risk attached to employing an outsider who may only be a success 'on paper,' without actually having a good track record.

The disadvantages of internal recruitment are as follows:

1. The firm will have to replace the person who has been promoted. In other words, the promotion can create a ripple effect in the organization.
2. An insider may be less likely to make the essential criticisms required to get the firm working more effectively.
3. Sometimes, promoting an individual may upset someone else. This happens when one competent person expects promotion but does not get that due to shortage of vacancies.

The advantages and disadvantages of internal recruitment are tabled in Table 6.5.

Table 6.5 Advantages and disadvantages of internal recruitment

Advantages	Disadvantages
1. Cost of recruitment is less.	1. It limits the number of potential candidates.
2. The process is quicker.	2. Outsiders can bring new ideas for the business.
3. The recruits are familiar with the organization.	3. It may cause resentment amongst candidates who are rejected.
4. Employees get opportunity for promotion, and derive motivation.	4. It creates another vacancy which needs to be filled; produces ripple effect.
5. Strengths and weaknesses of the candidates are known.	

External Recruitment

External recruitment makes it possible to draw upon a wider range of talents from the markets. This source provides the opportunity to bring in new experience and ideas in to the business. The disadvantages are that it is more costly and the company may end up with someone who proves to be less effective or an underperformer in practice than they did on paper and in the interview situation. This happens due to the occurrence of 'select error' during the selection process. External recruitment is used when the business looks to fill the vacancy by a suitable applicant outside the business.

Advantages and Disadvantages of External Recruitment

Similar to internal recruitment, external recruitment has its advantages and disadvantages as well. These are displayed in Table 6.6.

Table 6.6 Advantages and disadvantages of external recruitment

Advantages	Disadvantages
1. External people may propose new ideas for the organization.	1. The process is longer.
2. It provides a larger pool of workforce from which best candidates can be identified.	2. It is more expensive due to the need for advertisements and interviews.

ELECTRONIC RECRUITMENT (E-RECRUITMENT)

> E-recruitment is an evolving face of recruitment, and it may possibly replace traditional advertising.

With the intensification and popularization of information technology, electronic recruitment (e-recruitment) has become a common and popular practice of recruitment. The extensive growth of information technology has opened up a panorama for organizations trying to acquire talents through an entirely different gateway. There are many ways to use the Internet, and organizations are largely inclining and refining their use of this medium. In fact, e-recruitment is an evolving face of recruitment, and may possibly replace the advertising in newspapers.

According to a study by NASSCOM (National Association of Software and Services Companies), 'Jobs are among the top reasons why new users will come on to the internet, besides e-mail'. There are more than 18 million resumes floating online across the world. This penetration of e-recruitment is seen to be increasing in India at a very rapid rate.

The two popular kinds of e-recruitment used by companies in India are

Job portals Companies post their requirements along with job description and job specifications on these portals. These portals help in shortlisting suitable resumes too.

Creating a complete online recruitment section Some companies have their own websites specifically for recruitments. Job seekers can submit their resumes directly into this database, from where the organization chooses a suitable candidate.

Resume scanners, widely popular among the recruitment agencies, are a big help to them as they aid in screening and filtering the resumes.

Monster (www.monster.com), HotJobs (www.hotjobs.com), and CareerBuilder (www.careerbuilder.co.in) are some well-known job sites which attract a vast array of applicants, who submit standardized resumes that can be electronically searched using key terms. Organization can search for suitable candidates and job seekers can search organizations in the same way.

Techniques of Online Recruitment

A particular method or modus operandi needs to be followed for online recruitment. Otherwise, the process may not achieve the desired purpose.

1. Giving a detailed job description and job specifications in the job postings
2. Furnishing evolution, growth vectors, achievements, and other aspects to attract candidates with the right competencies and qualifications at the entry stage
3. Incorporating e-recruitment into the overall recruitment strategy of the organization
4. Enabling applicant tracking through a well-defined and structured system, and integrating the system having a back-end support

5. Developing a comprehensive website. Along with the back-office support, the website should receive and process job applications. The website may receive the applications either direct or through online advertising.

SOURCES OF HUMAN RESOURCE AND MEANS OF ATTRACTING THEM

We have studied that internal, external, and e-recruitment are sources used by organizations for recruitment, depending on whichever they find appropriate for the situation in which they want to add manpower. After decided the same, attention should be given to attract them. In fact, at present, there are abundant sources of human resources; though getting the right persons from them continues to be a problem. Hence, multiple sources must be exploited.

Most Common Sources of Human Resource

The source of HR or manpower depends on the level at which employees are being recruited. For lower levels, internal recruitment is conducted. However, for recruitment at the upper level, companies generally take on external recruitment when they search for talents from the open market with requisite qualifications, experiences, and proven track records in their present companies. For recruitment, the most common sources of HR are notice boards, employment exchanges, state and union public service commissions, educational institutions, recommendations of present employees, labour unions, etc.

Notice board A company's notice board is used for putting up notices showing the appraisals of the employees so that they can inform family members, friends, and other known persons about the position that has fallen vacant. The applications are received; scrutinized, short-listed, and eligible candidates are called for selection tests. In this case, the recruitment is the minimal.

Internal job market The internal job market (IJM) is another tool to search for potential candidates within the same family for various lucrative positions. It is an electronic tool extensively used by multinational companies. The IJM facilitates worldwide search for talent. The principal purpose of IJM is to help the internal mobility system and the process of career development of the employees.

Q 7 **Employee referral** Some companies ask their present employees to recommend prospective candidates. This mode is widely practised in information technology companies such as Yahoo, Google, and Microsoft. The recommended candidate undergoes a screening process. On selection, the recommended employee gets some honorarium as he/she saves the recruitment cost for the company.

Employment exchange As per public policy, employment exchanges established in various cities act as an important source of recruitment.

Service commissions The Union Public Service Commission (UPSC), state PSC, and College Service Commission (CSC), serve as a point of recruitment for professional and managerial positions.

Placement agencies Some recruitment agencies and associations establish and maintain a database of job seekers. When a company approaches such an agency, it refers to the database, fetches the candidates with requisite backgrounds, and provides the list to the company who carries out the selection process. In some cases, companies desire the agency to recruit on their behalf and agencies do that. This is also a good source for recruitment as the process is smooth and the lead time for recruitment is minimum.

Educational institutions The placement cell of B-schools and engineering colleges/institutions approach organizations and invite them for campus recruitment. Some companies make special efforts to establish and maintain constructive relationships with management and engineering colleges, universities, and institutes to get the suitable, qualified HR.

Labour unions Unions look after the welfare of the employees. As a part of the welfare measure, many organizations provide employment to the next-of-kin of the deceased person on compassionate grounds in consultation with the labour unions after due verification about the movable and immovable assets.

Nepotism In family-owned organizations, there may not be definite recruitment policy. Rather they recruit family members having the capacity to perform the tasks.

Leasing To meet short-term requirements, persons can be taken on 'lien' or 'lease' basis for a period of one, two, or three years. The organization gets experienced persons and is not required to bear any obligation. People working in the government sector are seen to frequently proceed to some government organization on lien. The main advantage is that if the person finds the new organization not very promising for some considerations, he/she may return back to the parent organization within the lien period.

Attracting Human Resource

Q 3 Getting more applicants makes it possible to get good candidates. Through a multi-stage selection process, candidates get screened, and only a few extremely good and suitable candidates reach the interview level. Finally, the board selects the best of the lot, and prepares the panel of selected candidates.

To obtain a large number of applicants, an organization must initiate a proactive approach. Like any other advertisements, these advertisements compete with one another for attention. You must remember that the readers of the advertisement may become your prospective employees. Marketing professionals follow a simple and effective method called AIDA (attention, interest, desire, action) for creating superior advertisements. AIDA emphasizes the following:

A: Attract the reader's *attention*.
I: Generate *interest* in the vacancy.
D: Create *desire* for the job.
A: Stimulate the reader to take *action*.

In order to attract *attention*, an organization should briefly mention in the advertisement about the evolution of the company, the group of dependable suppliers, its potential customers, share value and belief, image, technology in use, awards it bagged, strategy of development, etc. In order to attract employees, it should communicate the essential (appealing and relevant) points quickly and clearly.

Interest in the vacancy may be generated by mentioning the career growth and progression, career anchors, succession planning, etc. You must also communicate a very clear and a realistic picture of the organization to ensure that the organization's values match those of potential candidates. Moreover, this would reduce the probability of attrition.

> To get more applicants, the prescribed application format may be uploaded on the website, facilitating the filling up of the form. The provision for remitting the requisite application fees online using debit card or credit card may be provided.

The *desire* of prospective candidates or talents may be created by mentioning a few challenging projects which they would be required to manage, mention chances of visiting abroad, scope of attending management development programmes in reputed institutes, opportunity for self-development, and so forth.

Government departments generally advertise by specifying the job requirements, and ask candidates to collect the form by sending a postal order, pay order, or any other mode of remittance. Many prospective candidates feel lethargic going through this process. On the contrary, the prescribed application format may be uploaded to the website, thus facilitating filling the form. Further, the provision for remitting the requisite amount online may also be provided using debit card or credit card. Providing the facility of uploading the photograph would further help the selection process.

One should have a general idea as to where potential candidates will be coming from, so that one can choose appropriate strategies to target them and select the appropriate media of advertising to reach them.

SELECTION

Recruitment has been defined earlier as a process of attracting job seekers who will be capable to meet the organizational staffing needs and who would be likely to achieve the business goals with appropriate qualifications in sufficient numbers on a timely basis. Selection is the process of screening the applicants to find those with the right attitude, aptitude, and qualifications.

Selection follows the recruitment process and may vary from one organization to another. This process starts with the scrutiny of applications, a preliminary screening test, written test, preliminary interview, final interview, background and reference checks, selection decision, medical examination, and police verification. Some companies start selection with 'walk-in interviews' also.

Selection is a process of choosing the right candidates, having the right attitude and aptitude, from a group of aspirants for a particular position in the organization. The goal of selection extends to matching people with the jobs and the organization.

As selection is about choosing the right person, it affects all other HR functions. For example, a person with inadequate credibility may not be able to fulfill the performance criteria. A highly-qualified person, on the other hand, would not be happy with the standard compensation packages that may lead to attrition. Some positions such as marketing, sales, public relations, etc., need specific behavioural norms. Behaviour is a manifestation of human attitudes. Moreover, the absence of 'right attitude' disturbs smooth working and harmony. Thus, one without the 'right attitude' would be a source of disturbance.

For selecting the right candidates, an organization should develop a database of eligible aspirants and draw them from different sources. In today's competitive business scenario, attrition is a common phenomenon. In such cases, the database facilitates saving time and keeping the wheel of operation moving.

Thus, organizations must use appropriate selection tools when selecting a candidate, keeping in mind the position and the job requirements.

Selection Tests

There is a maxim, 'Where recruitment ends, selection starts'. Selection is a stage that follows the recruitment process wherein the applications are screened. The selection process also includes organizing screening tests, selection interviews, and finalizing selection decisions. Screening of application forms encompasses assessing the quantifiable data and checking for consistency. The selection process employs a number of tests to identify whether or not the candidates have to their credit the qualities essential to accomplish the tasks assignable to them.

The process includes tests of intelligence, aptitude, ability and interest. Tests in intellectual ability, spatial and mechanical ability, perceptual ability and motor ability are considered to be moderately valid predictors for many semi-skilled and unskilled operative jobs in industrial organizations. There are two sets of tests—performance and psychological.

The following are some such tests used extensively in selecting candidates:

Tests for cognitive ability Cognitive tests include tests of general reasoning ability (intelligence) and tests of specific mental ability such as memory, personality, or achievement (Dessler and Varkey 2009).

Intelligence tests These tests measure general intellectual abilities and assist to assess capacity of comprehension and reasoning. Managers depend highly on the results of these types of psychological tests.

Intelligence quotient (IQ) is a procedure adopted to divide a child's mental age (as measured by intelligence tests) by his/her chronological age, and then multiply the result by 100.

Special cognitive abilities or aptitude tests These tests measure special cognitive abilities and are often called aptitude tests. Their purpose is to measure aptitude for the job in question. Aptitude tests are conducted to measure whether an individual has the capacity or latent ability to learn a given job, if adequate training is given.

Aptitude tests include management trial exercise (MATRIX) developed by Proctor and Gamble, clerical aptitude test (CAT) to assess vocabulary, spelling, arithmetical ability, etc., pilot aptitude test (PAT) to assess coordination between the hand and feet, and computer aptitude test to assess power of reasoning and analysis.

Interest tests help to evaluate interest and curiosity of candidates in the job he/she has applied for.

Performance simulation test In this test, the candidate is asked to perform an actual job. It enables the management to find out if the candidate is capable of doing that job successfully or not. Performance simulation tests include work sampling and assessment center.

Work sampling is an effort to create a miniature replica of a job or its prototype. The applicants need to demonstrate that they possess the necessary skills by actually performing the tasks assigned to them. The assessment center is not a location but a process by which psychologists evaluate candidates. Candidates are invited to appear for interviews or other tests through a letter (a format is given in Annexure 6.3).

Personality test Thematic apperception test (TAT), which is a type of personality test, is a projective test wherein candidates are shown a series of pictures (one at a time) and asked to write a story for each picture. For example, a few scenes from this test are an old man being knocked down by a car, a schoolboy sleeping under a tree with his school bag and a knife lying beside him, a good-looking girl standing at the door of a train, a policeman viewing a crowd, etc.

Preference record test by Kuder This questionnaire helps in testing the interest of a candidate in the field of mechanical, scientific, clerical, social service, computation, persuasive, artistic, literary, and musical abilities. Kuder designed techniques to differentiate between honest answers and those which are responded to make a good impression. Emphasis is laid on detecting the dishonest answers. Kuder reported that the system was 90 per cent accurate in detecting dishonest answers.

Psychological tests These tests are considered extremely beneficial in providing an objective measure of human characteristics and abilities. Untrained people can misuse and misinterpret these tests; hence, only the trained ones should use them. These unbiased tests used for selections. Psychological tests include intelligence tests.

Rorschach ink blot test In this test, a candidate is asked to organize unstructured ink blots into meaningful concepts; the integration by the candidate helps to predict and formulate his/her personality.

Strong vocational interest blank In these tests, an applicant is asked whether he/she likes, dislikes, or is indifferent to his/her occupation, certain peculiarities of people, and particular activities. The answers given are compared with the answers given by successful people in specific professions and occupations.

Selection Interview

Interviews are the most common form of selection tools used by organizations. During an interview, organizations should treat the interviewee as their guest. They should portray a positive image of their company in front of the interviewee so that he gets a good impression about the organization. Interviewing the candidates is the last stage of the screening process. Data furnished in the application forms or results of tests, done before the interview session, cannot address some areas. Ability to work under stress, inter-personal skills, ability to fit in the organization, grasping capacity, style of interaction, etc., are some of these aspects that are judged by means of interview by the board members.

The interview board should welcome the interviewees with a warm greeting, and exchange information to create a homely environment. Interviewers should begin with general questions like areas of interests. A candidate interested in cricket may be interrogated about the results of a cricket match so that he/she feels comfortable. Interviewees must be encouraged to respond positively. Interviews are considered good when the flow of information is smooth between the interviewer and the candidate. The board should take notes during interview. In order to get an accurate assessment of a candidate's ability, the interviewers should be specifically cautious when resorting to competency-based interviews. A candidate can be nervous, uncommunicative, or even talkative.

Nervous candidates In order to ascertain the knowledge content to the extent possible, nervous candidates should be greeted warmly, engaged in more small talks than usual, spoken to about their areas of interest, and pointed out facilities available within the organization. To such candidates, the chairperson should start with specific and fact-based questions that are easy for the candidate to answer and unlikely to be stressful. Gradually, his/her confidence will be strengthened. It is advisable to speak slowly in a relaxed and informal manner to such candidates.

Uncommunicative candidates There are many individuals who are reserved or uncommunicative by nature. These candidates simply need to be encouraged to share their thoughts. It has also been evidenced that they can be made vocal using silence. If the interviewers become silent for some time, the candidate starts answering the question asked earlier. The candidate may not be able to state his strengths and weaknesses. If the candidate has trouble in answering a particular question, he/she may be asked some other question. The same question could be asked again later. These types of candidates may be given some time to think, before responding to the questions.

Talkative candidates Talkative employees can be very good performers, and should not be neglected. Candidates, who talk too much, often narrate about events unrelated to the job or interview question and move out of the track. They should not be neglected but managed. Such candidates may be reminded about the time constraints. They should be told that the interviewer will be following a structure, and stress on the time available for each section of the interview. The conversation can be redirected.

As in every organizational event, the cost of selection process needs to be controlled. This can be achieved by holding the interviews in one location, accessible to the interviewing panel, and to those being interviewed. Most of the companies reimburse the return travel fare to the candidates. In order to utilize the cost of selection in the best possible way, care must be taken to ensure that the necessary documents like application forms, results of previously held selection tests, etc., are available to the interview board before the start of the interview. This is of utmost importance in the case of a mobile interview board.

Interview Assessment

After interviewing the candidates, the board members need to sit together to assess all the candidates, one by one. There can be varied opinions about a candidate's performance. Each candidate is assessed based on multiple parameters such as appearance and attitude, personality, communication style, education, work experience, technical competence, ambition, potential, and many such aspects. In fact, an interviewer uses a pre-designed format to facilitate quick decision-making. A model interview assessment form is exhibited in Annexure 6.4 at the end of the chapter.

Interview Question Bank

The interview board members discuss the attributes essential for the task accomplishment, before finalizing the question bank. At present, to avoid or reduce, 'accept error' or 'select error', board members develop and use a question bank before the start of the interview. Some companies also develop a tailor-made question bank for the position to present to the board members. While interviewing candidates, they generally ask questions from the bank. However, in demanding situations, they can deter from the question bank and ask any other question as well. This might happen in cases where the interviewee might express his experience from a unique area of specialization. The question bank basically deals with questions about achievements (past and/or present), motivation, sense of defining self, strength and weaknesses, depth of knowledge, leadership ability, analytical thinking, knowledge about the company, sales or marketing ability, capacity to work in stress, self-esteem, and many such aspects.

For the selection of candidates for various positions, organizations develop a different question bank. The interviewers and invited external experts are provided with the question for the particular position. The question bank also helps to standardize the interview process and procure potential talents. It categorically protects the interview process from undesirable factors such as duplication and repetition. Most importantly, in a campus interview, interviewers ask questions for the summer internship project (SIP). A question bank generally used by employers during campus recruitment from B-schools is given in Annexure 6.5.

Selection Decision

Members of the interview board make judgmental decisions to select the right candidates. In order to minimize subjectivity, each candidate should be evaluated against the same selection criteria and factors. To facilitate evaluating and comparing candidates at a glance, the board may design a grid or spreadsheet, with the selection criteria and factors listed along one axis, and the candidates' names along the other. It is important to take some time, say one or two days, to consider all of the decision factors. They should avoid making on the spot or quick selection decisions.

Possible Selection Errors

As discussed earlier, it is vital to take a correct decision with respect to selection. However, in some cases, certain errors may occur. Some of these errors are as follows:

Select errors This error is also referred to as 'accept error', 'false positive', or 'erroneous acceptance', where the selected candidates fail to perform the tasks, cannot attain the quantitative target, or conform to the qualitative requirements or both. They continue to be underperformers as can be evidenced from their poor performance.

Reject errors These errors arise when we reject a candidate who would have otherwise performed successfully on the job. This is termed as 'reject error'. Sometimes, during selection for a higher post, one is selected and the rest of the candidates are rejected. Later, we find that a candidate, who was rejected, is performing exceedingly well in some other organization. In such cases, the reject error comes to limelight. Refer to Table 6.7.

Table 6.7 Possible selection errors

	Management decision	
	Candidate rejected	**Candidate accepted**
Candidate should have been rejected.	Correct decision	Accept error
Candidate should have been accepted.	Reject error	Correct decision

Both the select and reject errors can be minimized, if the selection system is impartial, has a degree of objectivity, and follows a fairly uniform standard of assessment.

One possible reason behind wrong selection may be attributed to the unverifiable skills. The 'Iceberg Model of Competencies' (web.mit.edu) highlights visible (portion of the iceberg that remains above the surface of water) and less visible (portion of the iceberg that remains below the surface of water) competencies. Skills and knowledge constitute the visible part of competency, which can be verified during the interview. The interpersonal skills, attitudes and values, and motivation constitute the invisible part.

Contextually, it is mentioned that skills are learned ability, knowledge is information acquired in a particular field, attitudes and values constitute self-image, trait refers to why and how we behave in a certain way, and motive is what drives us (for example, achievement, power/influence, affiliation).

RECRUITMENT VS SELECTION

Q 1 Recruitment and selection are intertwined. These two processes can be compared over dimensions such as meaning, nature, aim, procedure, and contract of services. Refer to Table 6.8.

Table 6.8 Recruitment vs selection

Dimension	Recruitment	Selection
Meaning	The process of searching for prospective employees and stimulating them to apply for jobs	The process of selecting the right candidate
Nature	A positive process	A negative process
Aim	Attracting more candidates to apply for vacant jobs	Identifying and rejecting unsuitable candidates
Procedure	Company notifies vacancy and specifications	Company asks candidates to pass through a number of stages
Contract of service	No contractual relation	Leads to a contract of service between employer and employee

ISSUES OF GENDER IN RECRUITMENT AND SELECTION

Issues of diversity must get attention in the recruitment and selection process. The most serious diversity may arise from gender issues. During selection, the following points must be considered.

1. Do not discard applicants who took a break from work to provide care for a child or for childbirth.
2. Consider the dynamics of the interview—whether the candidate is being interviewed in an environment that is comparable with the office environment.
3. Understand questions that cannot be asked regarding family, children, pregnancy, and other matters that cannot be disclosed.
4. Provide medical insurance that covers the full range of medical needs and benefits of women employees, including reproductive health care facilities.
5. Provide and share paid sick leave policies for employees' illness and illness of spouses, lifetime partners, dependent children, and elderly parents.
6. Announce life insurance, disability and pension programmes that are nondiscriminatory on the basis of gender.
7. Develop clear and vigorously enforced sex, race and sexual orientation discrimination and sexual harassment policies, and include a statement about these policies in the advertisement of the position.
8. Female candidates should not be discarded unless the job description prohibits hiring of female candidates.

RATIONALE FOR RECRUITMENT AND SELECTION POLICY

Recruitment and selection should include procedures directed to analyse the need and purpose of a vacancy, the culture of the company, and ultimately, to select and hire the person that best fits the position. The recruitment and selection policy should then be directed towards the following objectives:

1. Hire the right person for the job specification
2. Conduct an extensive search for candidates for the potential position
3. Recruit staff members who are compatible with the company's environment and culture
4. Hire individuals by using a model that focuses on employee learning
5. Place individuals in positions with responsibilities that will enhance their personal development and growth
6. The selection process should not have any gender bias

A typical example of recruitment and selection policy statement is given in Exhibit 6.7 below. The policy statement of a hospital is also furnished in Exhibit 6.8.

Exhibit 6.7 Recruitment and selection policy statement—A typical example

Every vacancy position will be filled based upon a thorough position analysis regardless of the level of the position or the extent of the search. The diversity goals of the institution, division of student affairs, and the unit will be addressed in all recruitment and selection processes.

Units may use different processes for recruitment, depending upon the prevailing circumstances and the

(Contd)

Exhibit 6.7 (Contd)

need to fill the position. However, the unit must take steps to ensure that the values of the profession are applied in all procedures that are used. Recruitment and selection committee members should be properly trained to assume the important responsibilities of recruitment and selection and discharge their roles.

Exhibit 6.8 Recruitment and selection policy of AMRI Hospital, Kolkata

It is the policy of the organization to select employees possessing the required qualification for a particular position. All posts can be contested by both internal and external candidates. It will be the management's internal policy to give preference to the internal candidates when both internal and external candidates are equal in all respects.

CREDENTIAL VERIFICATION OR REFERENCE CHECKING

Q 4 When a person having directional experience in some other concern of the same industry is recruited, his/her credentials, contribution, and track record in that organization should preferably be verified. At present, a system of 'exit interview' exists. During the exit interview, the person discloses his new employer, nature of duties, along with other information that may be asked. Thus, there cannot be a hide and seek game. An organization designs the credential verification format considering the aspects it intends to verify. Credential verification or conducting reference checks is an essential part of the recruitment process; reference checking is a proactive action to maintain the sound health of the organization in various ways. The objectives of reference checking signify the following:

1. Proactive action to protect the organization in future from the costly mistakes of 'select error' and to select only the right people.
2. Sound reference checking saves the organization from duplicity of candidate's choice.
3. It helps the organization to understand a candidate better by knowing his/her motive, skills, work habits, and requisite personality traits tailored for the position.
4. 'Negligent hiring' generally creates a common legal claim against the employer. Reference checking is often not done while recruiting from colleges/institutes through campus interviews.

> Credential verification or conducting reference checks is an essential part of the recruitment process.

Reference checks should be made only for those candidates who have advanced to the final stage and who are under serious consideration for the job. Refer to Box 6.6.

Box 6.6 Exit interview

The following is a sample set of questions asked to an employee (senior software engineer) leaving a software organization and the concluding remarks of the country head:

1. How long did you serve this company?
2. Were you able to learn something while working in this company?
3. Were you satisfied with the job and the role here?
4. Were you able to work satisfactorily with your team?
5. Were you satisfied with your immediate superior?
6. What was the role of your team in the overall success of the company?

(Contd)

Box 6.6 (Contd)

7. Which company are you going to join?

Concluding remarks: I am sure that you will do well in your new organization, just as you did here. However, this company will always remain ready to welcome you back.

Improving Reference Checking

The following are some ways to improve reference checking:

1. One of the most popular ways of improving reference checking is to inform the candidates about the hiring supervisor conducting a reference check, in case the candidates are advanced as a finalist for the position. They should be told that it is an obligatory requirement. This information should encourage candidates to be frank and honest in their responses to questions.
2. While getting the forms filled, the candidates must be asked to provide at least five reference names with their professional associations and their contact details. The list must contain names of immediate supervisors too.
3. It is important for the supervisor to call these reference names himself. This can help to collect only the related information.
4. A few references may not be too willing to discuss a candidate's qualifications and skills. In such cases, open-ended questions in the proper order should be asked to get the best possible answers from them.
5. One can avoid inquiring about the candidate's marital status, age, disabilities, religion, ethnicity, gender, or other personal issues and information that is not used in hiring.

With a view to achieve the recruitment and selection objectives, a reference check is done and the credentials are verified. A typical format of the reference check form (alternatively known as credential verification form) to collect the previous employer's view has been exhibited in Annexure 6.6 at the end of this chapter.

MAKING THE OFFER

On completion of the use of a selection tool, members evaluate the records. After this, the interview board is constituted. The board members evaluate, prepare, and sign the panel in order of merit. The board submits the panel to the hiring manager. The committee may submit one of the following types of recommendations. This is dependent upon the charge that was originally given to the search committee. It includes

1. the name of one candidate;
2. the names of two or more candidates in order of hiring preference; and
3. the names of two or more candidates in no particular order.

Once a qualified candidate has been recommended to the hiring manager, he/she should strongly consider the recommendation that has been presented. The manager may accept a hiring recommendation or request the search committee to continue the search in case of disagreement. In case of acceptance of the hiring recommendation, the manager should contact the preferred candidate and make the job offer. Some important issues that should be addressed in the job offer are as follows:

1. Starting salary
2. Starting date
3. Length of contract

4. Employee benefits
5. Moving expenses (if applicable)
6. Living accommodations (if applicable)
7. Any other points of negotiation

The candidate should be given sufficient time to either accept or reject the offer. At the same time, the authority should not compromise by allowing them too much time between the offer and the decision. In this case, the authority should look at other candidates.

However, the hiring authority should not compromise on the availability of other candidates, if the candidate of choice declines the offer by allowing too much time to pass between the offer and the decision.

If the candidate accepts the position, the offer and the conditions of hiring should be sent to him in writing (two forms) as soon as possible. The candidate needs to authenticate one copy of the offer by signing it and returning it to the hiring manager. In case the candidate declines the position, the hiring manager should make the offer to the next candidate of choice or should reconvene the search committee to make other arrangements. Once an individual has joined the company, all relevant departments should be intimated immediately, requesting them to close the records. It is also important for the management to dissolve the search committee after properly acknowledging their time and service.

It is only proper to notify those candidates who were interviewed but not selected, either by telephone or email. In this entire process, the skills required to fill this position are collected. The format for this is provided in Annexure 6.8.

ACCOUNTING OF RECRUITMENT AND SELECTION

Human resource is the most fundamental of all available resources to an economy or an organization. The cost incurred by an organization on the recruitment, selection, induction, training, and development of its employees reflects the amount of investment to build up its HR. We need to identify and accumulate such costs separately for managerial accounting, planning, and control. The cost of elements in the total recruitment and selection process builds up the total investments, which must be subjected to analysis to judge their effectiveness. Building up such costs for the recruitment, selection, induction, and other functions would involve an identification of relevant costs, and inputting them from facts and figures.

Relevant costs need to be allocated and apportioned using traditional overhead absorption methods as well as other accounting methods (Koley 2005). The various elements of costs essential to maintain the recruitment section are as follows:

1. Salaries and benefits of human resources
2. Office establishment expenses
3. Burden of general overhead charges

Besides the cost of maintaining the recruitment section and its personnel, some elements of costs in the recruitment and selection processes are as follows:

1. Advertisements for locating and attracting candidates
2. Traveling allowances paid to candidates and selection committee members
3. Support services of recruitment agents, selection committee experts, etc.
4. Joining and relocation provisions for new recruits

The following solved problems will give an idea about recording and retrieving data, which can be used to compute information necessary to exercise managerial control. In all the problems, 'mu' stands for monetary unit.

Problem 6.1 A common advertisement was circulated by an organization at a cost of 18,000 mu for the recruitment of six employees in the junior officer grade in three functional areas of marketing, production, and finance. The column space utilized in the advertisement for a response in the different functional areas was in the ratio 2:3:4 relating to finance, production, and marketing respectively. Find the relevant recruitment cost of junior officers in each area of specialization.

Solution

Let the constant of proportionality be x.

Cost of advertisement shall be proportional to the column space used.

Respective cost of advertising for marketing, production, and finance = $2x$, $3x$, $4x$

Total cost = $2x + 3x + 4x = 9x$ mu $\Rightarrow 9x =$ 18,000 mu, $x =$ 20,000 mu

Cost of advertisement for marketing ($2x$) = 2 × 20000 = 40,000 mu

Cost of advertisement for production ($3x$) = 3 × 20000 = 60,000 mu

Cost of advertisement for finance ($4x$) = 4 × 20000 = 80,000 mu

Answer: Costs of advertisement for marketing, production, and finance respectively are 40,000 mu, 60,000 mu, and 80,000 mu.

Problem 6.2 A common advertisement was circulated at a cost of 1,20,000 mu for the recruitment of 24 management graduates with a specialization in three functional areas—production, marketing, and accounts. The space distribution in the advertisement was designed as follows—a 36-line column space to introduce the organization in general; while remaining 40% of the advertisement space was allotted to the three areas of specialization providing a two line-column space more to marketing, and four line-column spaces more to production area as compared to that of accounts. Find the relevant recruitment cost for management graduates belonging to each area of specialization.

Solution

After utilizing 36-line column space to introduce the organization, 40% was left. This implies that 36 lines were occupied (100 – 40) = 60% of the total space.

40% of total space = (36/60) × 40 = 24 lines

For accounts, the organization used x lines.

For marketing, it used (x + 2) lines. For production, it used (x + 4) lines.

Total lines used for accounts, marketing, and production = $x + (x + 2) + (x + 4) = 3x + 6$ lines.

The equation is $3x + 6 = 24$ or $x = 6$.

So lines for accounts = 6, marketing = 8, and production = 10.

Common space is apportioned equally: 36/3 = 12 lines for each specialization.

Total space for accounts = 12 + 6 = 18

Total space for marketing = 12 + (6 + 2) = 20. Total space for production = 12 + (6 + 4) = 22

The advertisement cost can now be proportionately distributed for the specialization.

Cost of advertisement for accounts = 1,20,000/(18 + 20 + 22) × 18 = 36,000 mu

Cost of advertisement for marketing = 1,20.000/(18 + 20 + 22) × 20 = 40,000 mu

Cost of advertisement for production = 1,20,000/(18 + 20 + 22) × 22 = 44,000 mu

Answer: Recruitment cost for management graduates in production, marketing and accounts: 44,000 mu, 40,000 mu, and 36,000 mu.

Problem 6.3 The total salary and office establishment expenses of the recruitment section have been 3,00,000 mu in the current year. During the year, 300 new employees have been hired—150 in the supervisory grade, 100 in the officer grade, and 50 in the senior officer grade. While recruiting 300 employees, a total of 10,000 applications have been processed—6,500 in the supervisory grade, 2,500 in the officer grade, and 1,000 in the senior officer grade.

The following points are further noted:

(a) Man-days spent by the recruitment section on the locating and selection activities together correspond to 75%, and the remaining 25% on the activity of hiring new employees;

(b) Man-days spent on locating and selecting candidates for different grades being proportional to the number of applications handled;

(c) Man-days spent on hiring activity for different grades being proportional to the number of candidates hired;

(d) The scope of locating and selection activities have been so defined in the organization. The locating activities take on an average of 80% of the total time spent on locating and selection, irrespective of the grade in which the employees are recruited.

Find the relevant cost of recruitment in terms of the elemental costs of the three activities, locating, selecting, and hiring of employees in each grade.

Solution

Given:

Grade	Hired (in number)	Applications processed
Supervisory grade	150	6500
Officer grade	100	2500
Senior officer grade	50	1000

Man-days spent on:

Locating and selection activities	75%	3,00,000 × 0.75	= 2,25,000 mu
Hiring activities	25%	3,00,000 × 0.25	= 75,000 mu

Locating activities take an average of 80% of locating and selection activities.
Thus, the remaining 20% is consumed in selection activities.
Expenditure in locating: 2,25,000 × 0.80 = 1,80,000 mu
Expenditure in selecting: 2,25,000 × 0.20 = 45,000 mu
Man-days spent on locating and selecting for different grades are proportional to the number of applications handled. Thus, costs for both locating and selection are also proportional to the number of applications handled.

Apportioned costs for locating

Supervisory grade	= 1,80,000 × 6,500/10,000 mu	= 1,17,000
Officer grade	= 1,80,000 × 2,500/10,000 mu	= 45,000
Senior officer grade	= 1,80,000 × 1,000/10,000 mu	= 18,000

Similarly, apportioned costs for selection

Supervisory grade	= 45,000 × 6,500/10,000 mu	= 29,250
Officer grade	= 45,000 × 2,500/10,000 mu	= 11,250
Senior officer grade	= 45,000 × 1,000/10,000 mu	= 4,500

Apportioned costs for hiring

Supervisory grade	= 75,000 × 150/300 mu	= 37,500 mu
Officer grade	= 75,000 × 100/300 mu	= 25,000 mu
Senior officer grade	= 75,000 × 50/300 mu	= 12,500 mu

We now combine the figures as follows:

Grade	Locating cost (mu)	Selection cost (mu)	Hiring cost (mu)	Total (mu)
Supervisory grade	1,17,000	29,250	37,500	1,83,750
Officer grade	45,000	11,250	25,000	81,250
Senior officer grade	18,000	4,500	12,500	35,000
Total cost	1,80,000	45,000	75,000	3,00,000

SUMMARY

Manpower or HR planning is a process of developing a set of decisions for action with regard to the need of people in an organization commensurate with the workload. At the micro or organizational level, HR planning depends on macro level manpower planning. At macro level, HR planning has three approaches. Availability of quality people for organizations depends on both supply and demand forecasting. HR planning leads to recruitment and selection. An organization should have its recruitment philosophy, policy, and objectives. Corporate strategy influences the recruitment strategy. E-recruitment is becoming increasingly popular.

Job analysis or work analysis is the process of examining the jobs to identify the key requirements of each job. Job analysis yields multiple products such as job description, job specification, etc. There are many selection tools and an organization selects the tools considering the position and job specification. There may be two types of errors in selecting. Issues of diversity must get attention in the recruitment and selection processes. In order to attract talent, an organization may use the AIDA (attention, interest, desire, action) model during advertising. After selection and prior to offering appointment, the credentials (or reference check) may be verified from the previous organization. Interviewers may use question banks for convenience. Accounting of recruitment and selection is essential to exercise managerial control.

KEY TERMS

E-recruitment is online recruitment and has gained popularity due to intensification and extensive growth of information technology; it is an evolving face of recruitment that may possibly replace traditional advertising.

Job description sets out how a particular employee will fit into the organization and could be used as a job indicator for applicants for a job.

Job evaluation is systematically classifying the jobs in accordance to their relative worth both within the organization and within the related labour market; it provides vital inputs to the designing of compensation management.

Job or work analysis is the process of examining the jobs to identify the key requirements of each job.

Job specification is derived from job analysis and underlines the mental and physical attributes required of the job holder; it comprises statements of employee characteristics and is a conglomeration of knowledge, skills, and abilities.

Manpower or HR planning is a process of developing a set of decisions for action with regard to the need of people in an organization and commensurate with the workload.

Selection is a process of choosing the right candidates, having the right attitude and aptitude, from a group of aspirants for a particular position in the organization. The goal of selection extends to matching people with the jobs and the organization.

EXERCISES

Concept Review Questions

1. Define recruitment and differentiate it from selection. Discuss different methods of recruitment.
2. Define job analysis, job description and job specification. Discuss the relationship between the three. Explain the process for evaluating jobs, with suitable examples.
3. For filling vacancies, human resources can be searched from many sources. Discuss the relative advantages and disadvantages. How can an organization attract human resource?
4. Discuss the importance and means of credential verification or reference checking. Discuss in detail.
5. 'In future e-recruitment is likely to replace the conventional paper-based recruitment methods.' Critically discuss the statement mentioning the plus and minus points of the recruitment methods.

Critical Thinking Questions

6. 'An organization should first do thorough job analysis and then human resource planning as a part of restructuring processes. Critically discuss the statement.
7. Employee referral is a popular source of human resource while recruiting candidates. Mention the possible advantages and disadvantages.
8. An organization has high attrition in the front line sales staff. On analysis, the HR manager has noted that this attrition is due to mismatch of job specification and person specifications. Explain how you would go about it if you have to recruit in large numbers without diluting the quality of recruitment. (ISTD 12/2009).
9. An organization has recruited 100 sales people during the year 2008. However, in the current economic scenario, the company wants to redeploy these recruits. If you are the HR manager, explain how you would identify the positions to which these personnel can be redeployed (ISTD 6/2009).

Assignments

10. Contact five medium-sized (whose employee strength is less than 2000) companies. Discuss with the HR managers of the companies whether they are using job analysis reports as an input to the selection process. Study in detail about the step-by-step method of collecting data to prepare the job analysis report.
11. Suppose you are employed in a large and reputed organization as a manager of a department. A key employee has just submitted his resignation and the exit interview is due. You have placed requisition to the HR department for a suitable replacement. How could you help the recruiter find the best replacement?

MANAGER'S INSIGHT

Jain and Jain Co., a famous FMCG company, was on the lookout for a senior marketing executive. After screening several candidates, the HR manager finally zeroed on an employee, Savita, based solely on her qualifications. She seemed to be a reasonable choice for the post as she had performed well during her interview. In the eyes of the members of the interview board, there was no controversy involved in her appointment.

However, it was not long before the first worrying signs began to appear. There was nothing specific but one could spot a general lack of urgency and commitment in her work. She was taking much longer than the other members of the team to complete her work assignments and showed absolutely no evidence of self motivation. Clients had called up the organization to complain about the slackness in the style with which she worked with them. It seemed now to the HR manager that Savita had absolutely no interest in her profile.

The HR manager tried to meet with Savita to understand if there was anything wrong, that concerned her in particular. However, there was no specific outcome from the meeting.

Questions:

1. How should the HR manager handle the situation? Should he replace her?

2. What selection shortcuts might have been made by the HR during the recruitment process?
3. Devise a strategy plan for recruitment that could be used by the HR manager to avoid any such problems.
4. Devise a strategy plan for recruitment that could be used by the HR manager to avoid any such problems.

BIBLIOGRAPHY AND WEB RESOURCES

Anderson, Charles, H., *Developing a Framework for a factor-ranking benchmark system of Job Evaluation*, Civil Service Commission, Personnel Research and Development Center, Research Section, 1973.

Anderson, N. and Herriot, P., *International Handbook of Selection and Assessment*, Vol. 13, Chichester, UK, pp. 652, 1997.

Anderson N. and Ostroff. C., *Selection as Socialization*, Anderson & Herriot, pp. 413–40, 1997.

Bhattacharyya, Dipak Kumar., *Human Resource Management*, Excel Books, New Delhi, 2006.

Chhabra, T.N., *Human Resource Management Concepts and Issues*, Dhanpat Rai & Co., New Delhi, 2005.

Dessler, Gary and Biju Varkkey, *Dorling Kindersley* (India), New Delhi, 2009.

Henderson, Lain, *Human Resource Management*, University Press (India) Private Limited, Hyderabad, 2009.

Koley, M.K., *Accounting Applied to Human Resource Management*, Allied Publishers Orivate Limited, New Delhi, 2005.

Mondy, R. Wayne, *Human Resource Management*, Pearson Education, New Delhi, 2009.

Noe, A.N., John R. Hollenback, Barry Gerhart, and Patric M. Wright., *Human Resource Management Gaining A Competitive Advantage*, Tata McGraw-Hill, New Delhi, 2008.

Pattanayak, Biswajeet, *Human Resource Management*, Prentice-Hall of India Private Limited, New Delhi, 2005.

Pratim Dhara, Partha, *Recruitment, Selection, and Retention Strategy in AMRI Hospital,* Submitted to Indian Institute of Social Welfare and Business Management (IISWBM) for evaluation by University of Calcutta.

Web Resources

www.citehr.com/58471-12-elements-recruitment-strategy.html, last accessed on 20 January 2010.

www.cipd.co.uk/subjects/pay/general/jobeval.htm, last accessed on 30 July 2008.

recruitment.naukrihub.com/e-recruitment.html, last accessed on 3 April 2010.

Heathfield, Susan M., office.microsoft.com/en-us/infopath-help/conduct-a-job-evaluation-HA001189535.aspx, last accessed on 30 July 2010.

RECRUITMENT AND SELECTION AT AMRI HOSPITAL

About the hospital

Advanced Medicare and Research Institute Limited (AMRI), the first state-of-the-art hospital in Kolkata, is a collaboration with the healthcare sector between EMAMI group, SHRACHI group, and the Government of West Bengal. With 530 beds available for patients, AMRI has its branches in different locations of Kolkata and a branch at Bhubaneswar too. Every branch has multifarious facilities for diagnosis and treatment. The hospital is planning to expand further.

AMRI hospital is a center for training of radiology and medical imaging courses as well. The hospital's M. Pharm course is affiliated to Jadavpur University, Kolkata. Moreover, the hospital is ISO 9001:2000 certified and has tie-ups with many leading corporates. AMRI hospitals and diagnostic centers are present in many places.

The hospital follows a structured recruitment procedure and recruits at all levels conforming to its recruitment policy.

Recruitment policy at AMRI

It is the policy of the organization to select employees from candidates possessing the required qualification for a position. All posts can be contested by both internal and external candidates. The management gives preference to the internal candidates when both internal and external candidates are found equal in all respects.

Recruitment procedure

1. Any request for human resource for filling up a vacant position either for replacement or a new position created will be made in the prescribed human resource requisition form (HREF).
2. The functional department submits its requisition to HR department.
3. The HR department will examine the requirement, project queries (if any), and the head of the respective department will settle the same within seven days.

4. When requisition crosses the sanctioned strength, the HR department shall submit it to the appropriate authority for approval.
5. Approval or rejection is obtained within seven days and it has to be communicated within the next two working days to the respective department.

Scope

The policy and procedure apply to all recruitments for all departments and positions.

Accountability

1. All head of the departments (HODs) are accountable for identifying and initiating the staffing needs of their departments and qualifications of each position within their departments. Deviation/alteration, if any, proposed by the HOD has to be justified and sanctioned by the management committee.
2. In consultation with the respective HOD, the HR is accountable for obtaining the qualified candidates, conducting credential checks, negotiating compensation, and providing all necessary forms to implement this policy and procedure.

Manpower planning and recruitment

AMRI periodically carries out manpower planning to assess the HR required with different skills and competencies. Then, it conducts a gap analysis to initiate hiring of new employees. The recruitment process starts with a requisition from the department.

Manpower requisition

AMRI uses a manpower requisition form. The form contains fields such as department, designation (for which requisition is raised), nature of vacancy, number of posts sanctioned and date of sanctioning, number of employees existing in the post, number of posts vacant, and reasons behind the vacancy (resignation, retirement, transfer, etc.). The form also contains a description about the position (brief description of job and the duties/responsibilities involved) and person specification (education, experiences, attributes, etc.).

Post approval action

1. Within 15 days of the receipt of approval, the HR department looks for candidates through internal and external sources.
2. HR submits the application and resumes along with a summary of the candidates to the relevant HOD for review.

Recruitment practice

The HR department receives applications and sorts to file them according to the departments. Initially, they shortlist the candidates. These shortlisted candidates are invited to attend the selection process where selection tools are used. The general manager, HRM&D, along with other members, interviews the candidates; and immediately after the interview, evaluates the candidates for suitability based on records (interview appraisal form). While evaluating, both experience and qualification are given weightage.

All selected candidates are required to undergo a pre-employment medical check up in AMRI hospital. Appointment is offered only after a candidate is certified medically fit.

Salary and grade fixation

Matters connected to salary and grade level proposal of the unit are cleared by the HR department and finally, by the management committee board, after considering all the relevant factors.

AMRI hospital duly considers qualification, experience and track record, existing compensation structure, etc. to give maximum effort to sanction the best possible compensation package to the new recruits.

Offer of appointment

The medical superintendent issues all offers of appointment. A selected candidate is normally given 15 days time to join, unless the need is very pressing. However, some employers also allow a maximum of one month's time.

SWOT analysis of recruitment

AMRI also considers its strengths, weaknesses, opportunities, and threats with regard to recruitment.

Strengths

1. Exclusive contract with its channel partners to meet manpower requirement
2. Both internal and external sources are used.
3. Generally, the recruitment procedure is completed within 10 days.

Weaknesses

1. Huge employee turnover
2. High vacancy rate (for nurses)
3. Huge investment of time
4. Huge recruitment cost
5. Long absent cases in nursing department

Opportunities

1. Campus recruitments have huge potential for compensating manpower recruitment cost
2. Tie up with recruitment agencies for supplying fixed number of candidates when needed.
3. Strengthening the exclusive contract with its channel partners to meet manpower requirement

Threats

1. Increasing number of private hospitals create ample choices, frequent and easy mobility for employees, specially for nurses.
2. Same channel partners are handling all private hospitals. This leads to same pool of candidates being circulated to all partners.
3. Increasing spillover as a candidate has more than one offer at the time of making a job shift

(Based on a project report titled, 'Recruitment, Selection, and Retention Strategy in AMRI Hospital' submitted by Partha Pratim Dhara, to Indian Institute of Social Welfare and Business Management (IISWBM) for evaluation by University of Calcutta)

Discussion Questions

1. AMRI carries out a SWOT analysis for recruitment. Justify the necessity of this analysis.
2. How can AMRI further strengthen and attain speed in recruitment?
3. Suggest post-recruitment activities that AMRI should adopt.

HR MANTRA The king and the painter

An artist painted the portrait of the king of a great kingdom. With extreme humility, he sought permission to enter the palace, brought the portrait, and presented it to the king. The painting of the emperor was so lively that the minister and all those present there were overwhelmed. The king expressed his utmost satisfaction and thanked the artist. The king further desired to uncover the portrait in front of all the countrymen and declare a prize to recognize the artist's talent and efforts in a special ceremony. The king himself invited the artist to attend the ceremony.

After about a fortnight, the ceremony was organized. The king uncovered the painting in the presence of many invitees. All those present admired and applauded the splendid painting. The king announced the prize—'Today, in the presence of all the courtiers, ministers, and others, I am appointing this painter as the chief minister of my ministry.' With the passing of time, the painter naturally proved his gross inability and worthlessness, and the king was left frustrated.

The mantra: While acquiring new blood, examine the blood group.

JACK WELCH

Jack Welch was born in 1935 in Salem, Massachusetts. His parents were John, an Irish American railroad conductor with Boston & Maine Railroad, and Grace, a housewife. Welch, the only son of the family, attended the Salem High School and later the University of Massachusetts. In 1957, he secured a Bachelor of Science degree in chemical engineering. Welch went on to receive his MS and PhD at the University of Illinois in 1960.

Welch joined General Electric (GE) in 1960 as a junior engineer when he was 24 years old. He joined as a fresher from a PhD programme with a salary of $10,500 annually and wanted to earn $30,000 at the age of 30. Soon, he started getting promoted and his stature rose. By the mid-1970s, Welch began thinking, 'Maybe I could run the place one day.' Welch had many odds against him. Many of his peers regarded him as the round peg in a square hole, and found him very different from the others. In his words, 'I was brutally honest and outspoken. I was impatient and, to many, abrasive. My behaviour wasn't the norm, especially the frequent parties at local bars to celebrate victories, large or small'.

Welch knew the key to hiring smart people. 'The smartest people in the world hire the smartest people in the world,' declared Welch. Presumably, due to his belief in employing people, he could appoint and engage people, and transformed GE from a lumbering manufacturing behemoth into one of the world's most agile enterprises that had 'change in the blood.' Welch and his handpicked team of 4E (energy, energize, edge, and execute) leaders transformed GE. GE saw immense growth and expansion under Welch's leadership. He streamlined operations, acquired new businesses, and ensured that each business under the GE umbrella was one of the best in its field.

Jack Welch is the most admired, copied, and studied chief executive officer of the 20th century. His visionary initiatives, concepts, and adaptive management strategies have earned him the title of the most effective CEO in history. Michael D. Eisner, Chairman and CEO, Walt Disney Company, said, 'Jack Welch gave team leadership a new meaning as he took an industrial giant and turned it into an industrial colossus with a heart and a soul and a brain'. Jack Welch grew to fame in the business world through his management success and skills during his many years at GE. Welch turned the struggling 'slow moving giant' of a company into a dynamic growth company revered by many. During his 20 years of leadership at GE, Welch increased the value of the company from $13 billion to several hundred billion.

Welch strived to eradicate inefficiencies by trimming inventories and disregarding the bureaucracy. The bureaucratic style of management had almost led Welch to leave GE in the past, but a colleague Gutoff counselled and retained him in GE. He always pushed his business managers to become more productive. He shut down factories, reduced payrolls, and cut lacklustre old-line units. Welch's philosophy was that a company should be either ranked first or second in a particular industry, or leave it completely. Welch's strategy was later adopted by other CEOs across corporate America.

His chariot of advancement followed a unique path. Welch was named vice president of GE in 1972. He moved up the ranks to become senior vice president in 1977, vice chairman in 1979, and chairman and CEO in 1981. He was the youngest chairman in GE's history. In 1981, he made a memorable speech in New York city titled 'Growing fast in a slow-growth economy'. During his reign, GE acquired National Broadcasting Corporation and many financial services. GE was also modernized by shifting from manufacturing to financial services.

Every year, Welch would fire the bottom 10 per cent of his managers. He earned a reputation for brutal candour in his meetings with executives. He would push his managers to perform, but he would reward those in the top 20 per cent with bonuses and stock options. Welch is also known for obliterating the nine-layer management hierarchy and bringing a sense of informality to the company. He led GE to massive revenues. In 1999 he was named 'manager of the century' by *Fortune* magazine.

Welch had little time for bureaucracy and archaic business ways. If managers did not change, they were replaced with someone who could change. Managers were given free reign as long as they followed the GE ethics of constant change and striving to do better. He ran GE like a small dynamic business that was able to change as opportunities arose or profitability reduced.

During his 20-year reign at GE, Welch's management skills became almost legendary. His no-nonsense leadership style gave him a reputation of being hard, even ruthless, and also fair when making business decisions. At the time of his retirement, Welch received a salary of $4 million a year, followed by his record retirement plan of $8 million a year.

Retiring from his role as GE's chairman in 2001, Welch wrote a bestselling memoir, *Jack, Straight from the Gut*, and consults with several Fortune 500 businesses.

References

en.wikipedia.org/wiki/Jack_Welch, last accessed on 8 October 2011.

Haldar, Uday Kumar, *Leadership and Team Building*, Oxford Higher Education, Oxford University Press, New Delhi, 2010.

ANNEXURE 6.1

Job Analysis—Purchase Manager

	Job title	**Purchase manager**
Job description	Reporting authority	General manager
	Job overview	Plan, lead, coordinate the activities of purchasing in the company, coordinate with departments to cater to their material needs.
	Key activities	1. Preparing and processing requisitions and purchase orders for materials and equipment 2. Developing vendors 3. Establishing vendor rating system 4. Maintaining records of goods ordered and received 5. Resolving vendor grievances and settling claims 6. Developing and implementing purchasing and contract management instructions, policies and procedures
Job description	Tools and technology used	Computer, printer, telephone, fax, and other facilities
	Physical working environment	In company: Nine hours or more Salary: As per administrative manual
	Performance standards	Quality performance is subject to annual appraisal
Job specification	Education	MBA from renowned institute
	Knowledge	Production, economics and accounting, mathematics, computer operations, English, and other local languages
	Experience	Five to eight years in a similar position
	Skills	Organizing, planning, team building, ascertaining using quality parameters of materials, decision making, problem solving, time management
	Personality traits	Leadership, integrity, tolerance, stress management, persistence, initiative

ANNEXURE 6.2

Job Analysis—Training and Development Manager

Job description	**Job title**	**Training and development manager**
	Reporting authority	General manager
	Job overview	Plan, lead, coordinate all training and development activities. Identify training needs.
	Key activities	1. Preparing and processing training budgets 2. Establishing training procedures and maintaining records 3. Organizing training programmes conforming to procedure 4. Collecting participant feedbacks 5. Evaluating training programme and trainers

Job description		6. Conferring with top management and conducting surveys to identify training needs based on projected production processes, change, and other factors 7. Anticipating changes in the business environment and helping people to cope
	Tools and technology used	Computer, printer, telephone, fax, LCD and OHP, projectors, other facilities
	Physical working environment	In company: Nine hours or more Salary: As per administrative manual
	Performance standards	Quality performance is subject to annual appraisal
Job specification	Education	MBA from renowned institute
	Knowledge	Education and training, administration and management, environment scanning, psychology, HRD, quality standards for services, training methods, mathematics, computer operations, English, and other local languages
	Experience	Five to eight years in similar position
	Skills	Communication, motivation, critical thinking, active learning, empathic listening, and innovation
	Personality traits	Leadership, originality, creativity, adaptability, organizing, planning, perfection, problem solving, time management, desire to learn, knowledge dissemination

ANNEXURE 6.3

Invitation for Interview

Ref. No. .... From ....

Dated .... HR Manager

To
Interviewee's name ....
Address ....

Sub: Personal interview for the post of ....

The following candidates are advised to appear for personal interview on .... (date) at ....

Candidates name:
1. Abc
2. Pqr
3. Xyz

The above candidates are also advised to carry with them all documents in original pertaining to their eligibility, for verification before interview. It may be noted that their candidature is purely provisional on the basis of details furnished by them in their application form and that they are being called for personal interview does not, in any way, establish their eligibility for the post.

Further, at any stage, if found that they do not possess the laid-down qualification or do not fulfil the stipulated eligibility criteria as enumerated in the aforesaid staff employment notice issued for the post, their candidatures are liable to be rejected without any intimation to them.

No TA/DA admissible to appear at this interview.

Canvassing in any form will disqualify a candidate.

Sd/-..........................
HRManager—Operations

ANNEXURE 6.4

Job Analysis Work Sheet

PQR Corporation

Department

....

Job title

....

Observation: Started at .... Completed at ....

Name of analyst: ....

1. Overall purpose of the job ....
   ....
2. If the job holder is a supervisor, name of the persons supervised by him.
   ....
   ....

Activities that are part of the duties of the supervisor:

(a) Training and development
(b) Performance appraisal and management
(c) Quality control
(d) Coaching, mentoring, and counselling
(e) Preparation of departmental budget
(f) Miscellaneous duties (Elaborate) ....

3. Nature of the job: What does the job holder do daily, periodically, and occasionally?
   (a) Daily or routine activities: ....
   ....
   (b) Duties he/she does periodically (mention periodicity): ....
   ....
   (c) Duties he/she does occasionally, including the 'must do' activities, which may be assigned by superior: ....
4. What does the job holder do that he/she feels is beyond the scope of duties?
   ....
5. Checklist of education: An organization should stratify the educational levels; to tick the level required to perform the job
6. Experience: To specify the type and length of experience or trade and grade
7. Environmental condition: To specify the dirt, noise, vibration, etc., that may affect the quantity and/or quality of performance
8. Occupational hazards and diseases: To specify the hazards and occupational diseases that may develop while performing the job, chemical or other processes, etc. Medical practitioners must be consulted while identifying these.
9. Pollution: To identify the environmental pollution aspects and specify the pollution control measures
10. Waste analysis: Solid, liquid, or gaseous waste likely to pollute the environment must be identified and specified. Company must also mention the neutralization measures.
11. Any other special information (not covered above):

ANNEXURE 6.5
Interview Assessment Form

Interview Assessment Form

Position							DIV/UNIT	
Name of candidate							Interviewers	
Date:								
	RATING	0	1	2	3	4	5	
S. No.	Parameters of assessment	NA	BA	A	G	VG	O	Comments
1	Appearance and attitude (grooming, courtesy, appropriate dress)							
2	Personality (poise, bearing, rapport, method and manner)							
3	Communication (ability to adequately express himself)							
4	Education (appropriateness of degree and course work for job)							
5	Work experience							
6	Technical competence							
7	Ambition in line with anticipated job progression							
8	Potential (ability and motivation to grow or advance capable of developing scientific curiosity)							
9	Other (if any)							

(a) What other jobs (functional area/level) would he/she be suited for? ....

....

(b) Why does he/she seek a change? ....

....

Recommended for position	YES	NO

REMARKS

A. Positive:

....

B. Negative:

....

Interviewer's signature/date

Abbreviations	• NA: Not acceptable • BA: Below average	• A: Average • G: Good	• VG: Very good • O: Outstanding

ANNEXURE 6.6

Question Bank for Interviewers

Summer internship project (SIP)

1. How did you select the theme of your SIP?
2. Tell us about the methodology.
3. How did you select the sample and the sample size?
4. To collect data, have you used standard questionnaires or designed one of your own?
5. Explain validity and reliability of a questionnaire?
6. What statistical tools did you use?
7. Did you use any statistical package? Tell about the package.
8. Tell us about the findings of your SIP.
9. Have you put forth any recommendation to the organization?
10. Do you know about the reaction of the organization to your recommendation?

Achievements

1. Tell us something about the difficult projects you have handled.
2. Did you enjoy working on difficult projects?
3. Do you feel proud of your accomplishments?
4. Have you ever accomplished something you did not think you could?
5. Do you talk about your achievements to your spouse and close friends?
6. Of all the accomplishments, which one do you consider to be most important and why?
7. Do you feel that your achievements act like a health tonic?
8. Describe a significant risk you took to accomplish a task.

Motivations

1. Do you feel motivated to work harder?
2. How important is responsibility to you?
3. What challenges are you looking for in a job?
4. Have you identified your motives?
5. In which circumstances do you put forth your greatest effort?
6. What motivates you in a job and in your personal life?

Sense of self

1. Describe a situation in which you have been most successful.
2. How do you define 'success?'
3. How have your successes benefited your previous employer?
4. Tell us about some of your recent successes.
5. What are some of the reasons for your success?
6. Why are you better than your colleagues?
7. Would you rate yourself as an overachiever?

Weaknesses

1. Do you achieve all of the goals you set? If not, why?
2. Do you know your weaknesses?
3. How have you identified your weaknesses?
4. What weaknesses have you overcome when accomplishing difficult tasks?

Behaviour

1. Describe a conflict with an employee and how you handled it.
2. Describe a complex problem you have solved.
3. Explain a recent situation in which you approached others for help.
4. Describe a recent situation when you worked in a team environment.
5. Did you enjoy working in a team?
6. Describe how you would handle rude, difficult, or arrogant people.
7. After taking the help did you feel your image was undermined?
8. Explain how you could overcome a difficult situation.
9. Please tell us a situation where you succeeded though you were very stressed.

Creativity

1. Do you think you are creative?
2. What are some innovations you're particularly proud of?
3. Tell us some of the most creative things you have done?
4. How do you enhance creativity?
5. What do you prefer—routine or challenging tasks?

Aspiration for position

1. Why are you interested in our company?
2. Why are you interested in this position?
3. Why did you leave your last employer?
4. Why do you want to change positions?
5. Do you change jobs quite frequently?
6. What assurances do we have that you will stay with us?

Knowledge of company

1. Describe our company for us.
2. Describe our corporate environment for us.
3. How can you contribute to our company?
4. Do you know our product range?
5. How can we expand our business?
6. In which direction should we diversify?

Leadership

1. Do you feel confident while leading?
2. Are you more of a leader or follower?
3. Can you lead a group of employees without feeling intimidated?
4. Do you share information with team members?
5. Do you consider suggestions when you are busy?
6. Do you empower your junior colleagues?

Flexibility

1. Can you start in this new profession?
2. Do you like routine work?
3. How do you cope with change?
4. How do you handle change?
5. How important is job security to you?
6. What can you do to help adjust to a new job?

Organization

1. Do you prefer to work following a system?
2. Do you manage your time well?
3. How do you fix unexpected problems?
4. How do you organize your time?
5. How do you plan your day?
6. How do you plan your week?

Personal relations

1. How did you get along with your colleagues?
2. How do you deal with interpersonal conflict?
3. How do you resolve conflicts?
4. How would you pacify an angry colleague?

Inspirations

1. How did your boss help you to be your best?
2. What's been the greatest influence on your career plans?
3. Which person has had the most influence on your life?
4. Who has been an inspiration (or role model) to you?

Views of others

1. Do you feel comfortable while asking for help?
2. Do you get along with colleagues?
3. Have you ever worked with someone you didn't like?
4. How do you show interest in your peers?
5. How would you evaluate my interviewing skills?
6. What did you like most, least about your colleague?
7. What did you like most, least about your last boss?
8. What did you like most, least about your last job?

Perceptiveness

1. Do you know the postures people take if they agree with you?
2. Do you know what postures people take if they do not like your views?
3. What has been the biggest criticism of you?
4. What have you been most frequently criticized for?
5. What makes you angry?

Preferences

1. Do you like to work alone or with others?
2. How well do you interact with your colleagues?
3. What kind of people do you find it difficult to work with?
4. What kind of people do you like working with?
5. What are the factors you consider to identify least preferred coworkers?
6. Have you successfully dealt with difficult people?

Ability to persuade

1. How do you influence someone to agree with your ideas?
2. How do you persuade people to your point of view?
3. If your subordinates do not agree with you, how do you impose orders?

Progression

1. How did you move up within the company?
2. How do you feel about your career progression?
3. How has your job changed since you first joined your present company?
4. How would you determine progress in our company?
5. What do you see as your optimal career path?
6. When would you expect a promotion?
7. If you are not promoted, what will be your action plan?

Benefit to company

1. How can you contribute to this company?
2. How did the risks you took affect your company?
3. What can you bring to this company?
4. What can you do for us that no one else can?
5. Why should I/we consider you?

Disliking others

1. Do you frequently lose your temper?
2. Have you ever openly criticized someone else?
3. Have you ever accepted someone in your group whom you didn't like?
4. What did you dislike about your previous company?
5. What kinds of people do you have problems working with?
6. What types of people seem to rub you the wrong way?

Illegal and immoral dilemmas

1. Have you ever been discriminated against or treated unfairly?
2. Have you ever intentionally deceived someone?
3. How did you resolve the last moral dilemma you solved?
4. How do you react when your honesty is questioned?

Failures

1. Can you give me an example of one of your failures?
2. Have you ever missed a deadline?
3. How do you deal with failure?
4. Tell me about a situation that you just failed to manage?
5. What have been your greatest disappointments?
6. What was the greatest disappointment in your last job?

Accepts criticisms

1. How do you react when openly criticized?
2. Have you ever been reprimanded?
3. How do you deal with rejection?
4. When criticized, do you undertake a realistic analysis?
5. When has your work been criticized?

Areas of weakness

1. What types of decisions bother you?
2. What do you worry about?
3. Do your subordinates know your weaknesses?
4. What duties did you find the most troublesome?
5. What is your worst personality trait?

Self esteem

1. Do you think you are unique?
2. What are your greatest strengths as an employee?
3. What makes you unique?
4. Why are you better than your colleagues?

Introspection

1. Describe yourself.
2. On firing someone, how do you feel?
3. Do you classify yourself as a risk-taker?
4. Do you consider yourself a professional?
5. Do you consider yourself to be a kind person?
6. Do you see yourself as predictable?
7. Do you undertake a realistic analysis after you fail to achieve your goal?
8. What are the aspects that you would like to further improve on yourself?
9. What is your best quality?

Stress and work environment

1. Do you work well under pressure?
2. How do you cope with stress on the job?
3. How do you deal with tension?
4. Is there a lot of pressure in your current job?
5. What happens when two priorities compete for your time?

Intricate questions

1. Have you ever been in the position of firing anyone? Why did you fire that person?
2. How do you deal with pressure situations?
3. How well do you work under a deadline?
4. How well do you work under pressure?
5. What is your biggest professional challenge?

ANNEXURE 6.7

Credential Verification Format

Mr/Ms .... has applied to us for the post of ....

He/She claims to have been in your company from .... to ....

Having got an opportunity to observe the candidate's behavioural pattern (both in normal and stressed situations) your free and frank answer to the questions will be of immense value to us, and would be greatly appreciated. We assure you that your replies will be kept strictly confidential.

1. Mention the period of employment? From .... To ....
2. Positions held ....
3. What was the final salary (mention break-up)? .... PA
4. Was he/she regular in attendance? Yes/No.
   If not, kindly mention the cause of absence. ....
5. Was he liked by his peers? Well-liked, Acceptable, Often criticized, Isolated.
6. Rate of Progress (Slow, Average, Above average, Excellent)
7. Could he gain willing support of junior colleagues? Yes/No
8. Was he asked to resign or resigned voluntarily?
9. Would you re-employ him in a similar position? Yes .... No ....
   If not why? ....

10. Kindly comment on the following (Use 10-point scale.):
    (a) Personality (b) Technical/Professional/Clerical ability
    (c) Keenness and energy (d) Organizing ability
    (e) Initiative (f) Reliability
    (g) Tact (h) Self-reliance
    (i) Sobriety (j) Accepting changes

Reference check conducted by:

Name .... Title .... Date ....

ANNEXURE 6.8

Personality Inventory

Post .... Advt. reference ....

Instruction: Answer the listed questions as concisely and accurately as possible.
Use a maximum of 10 short sentences per question.

Name: ....

Contact details (local address, state, country, e-mail and telephone):

....

....

....

University degree: State your last two degrees.

Degree	University	Date completed	City	Comment

Professional work experience

Period (start and end date)	Company/ Organization	Position	City	Brief work description and accomplishments

Describe the kind of leadership positions you have held. What were your accomplishments and key learnings?

Describe a situation where you excelled in winning as a team. What actions did you perform and what was the outcome of the team's accomplishment?

Describe a situation where your creativity contributed to business advantage. What actions did you perform and what was the result of your accomplishment?

How open are you to an international career? What advantages and disadvantages do you see in relocating as a result of developments in your professional career?

Describe why you are interested in serving in this company. Explain why you should be the first to be chosen.

Describe your career objectives and specific areas of interest, for example, sales, marketing, sourcing, consulting, etc.

Do you have a valid work permit for the country you have applied for?

Do you want to be considered for countries other than the one you have applied for and do you have a valid work permit for these countries?

Languages spoken:

<u>For office use only</u>

All the information must be coded and inserted in the HRIS.

CHAPTER 7

Induction and Placement

LEARNING OBJECTIVES

After studying this chapter, you will be able to

- Appreciate the need for induction
- Understand various elements and processes of induction
- Distinguish the terms induction, orientation, and placement
- Develop checklists for induction
- Appreciate the role of HR in induction

OPENING CASE

Need for Behavioural Modification

Ramswarup was a non-resident Indian (NRI) based in New Jersey, US. He was an engineering graduate, and a post graduate in production engineering from an institute of international repute. He received lucrative offers from several organizations during campus interview but rejected them all, and decided to launch a consultancy firm so that he could be his own boss and remain independent. Within a short period, his firm, Ramswarup Technology Limited (RTL), gained reputation and had a thriving practice in New Jersey. However, Ramswarup harboured thoughts of returning to India. He married an Indian lady who had a master's degree in economics and a doctorate in Arts (Economics). After marriage, she visited India frequently and urged Ramswarup to settle in India. Additionally, Ramswarup too had been waiting to return to India.

During 1981–82, the Government of India appealed to NRIs to invest in various businesses in India. Many NRIs responded to this request, and Ramswarup viewed this as an opportunity. As the rate of return on investments was high, the idea appealed to him, and he invested a substantial amount in a few businesses that were flourishing in India. He discussed the business opportunity with an Indian businessman and having decided to return to India, conveyed his decision to some of his clients in New Jersey. The clients tried hard to persuade him to continue in New Jersey as he offered result-oriented advice and had a well-established practice. However, Ramswarup eventually returned to India after spending 15 years in the US.

Ramswarup set up close contacts with the companies in which he had invested, and studied their profit and loss statements, income and expenditure accounts, balance sheets, and other related financial documents in depth. Gradually, he became inclined towards starting a business of his own. During his stay in New Jersey, many firms had benefitted from his consultancy advice. A majority of his clients were producing special purpose hydraulic and pneumatic pumps. He provided advice regarding the design and manufacture of the components, assembly, and quality control parameters. The products practically never failed and as such, the clients never received any customer complaints. This showed Ramswarup's expertise.

Ramswarup decided to start an organization to design, manufacture, and sell hydraulic and pneumatic pumps. Accordingly, he selected a piece of land in an industrial area in his native state, applied for a trade license, registered his firm, and appointed both technical and administrative personnel. It took about six months to procure the machines, and another four months to erect and commission them. He appointed an expert mechanical engineer to look after the quality control department. Meanwhile, he secured many orders for the pumps. Thereafter, he gradually started production and sales, initially in the domestic market. He recruited salespersons, who were fresh diploma holders in sales management from a local management institute, to deliver the pumps directly to customers without the help of distributors or dealers.

After recruitment, Ramswarup organized a three-day orientation programme for the new recruits to learn about the company, and to make them comfortable with its practices. In this programme, he spent the first day with the new recruits and engaged them in formal and informal knowledge sharing. He discussed his achievements in the US but seldom talked about the means of achieving them. Over the next two days, his officers discussed about their products, technology, and the departments in RTL.

RTL followed the practice of sending a team comprising two or three persons under the leadership of an experienced person for the erection and commissioning of any project. In one such instance, the leader could not reach the customer's premises on time due to some unavoidable reason. He informed Ramswarup about his absence. While the work was in progress, the two team members expressed a difference of opinion. Gradually, their discussion lost professionalism and one member tried to dominate the other. The customer noted this with concern and tried to intervene, but failed to pacify the situation. Later, the two members were sent back to RTL.

On another such occasion, a salesman was deputed to a customer organization for demonstrating a particular product. In course of discussion, the customer inquired about another product. The salesman was not equipped with the information. In order to hide his ignorance, he provided a reply with which the customer was not satisfied. After this, the salesman became argumentative and showed domineering attitude.

In yet another situation, RTL received a complaint from a customer regarding a submersible pump. With this particular customer, they had concluded a contract with regard to comprehensive maintenance. On receipt of a complaint of the submersible pump from the customer, a mechanic was sent to attend the breakdown. The mechanic was not competent enough, and could not identify the fault. He said that he was not looking after submersible pumps, but as no other mechanic was available on that day, the company had sent him. He also added that the maintenance person concerned would come and attend to the problem the next day.

Following these incidents, RTL decided to strengthen its induction programme. The company wanted to engage Harish, an experienced employee, to train the recruits. He was expected to escort and guide the recruits during their visit, help them acclimatize with the departments, assist them , and lend a hand to their miscellaneous requirements on the second and third days.

Harish immediately agreed to do the tasks communicated by the HR manager. He joined the new recruits on the second day of induction as the syllabus of the first day contained only classroom sessions. However, he could not join the new recruits on the third day as he was bogged down by work pressure.

Learning outcomes

- A senior person must explain the organizational structure to juniors to develop them.
- New recruits must be alerted about behavioural disposition, particularly at the customer's premises.
- It is wise to confess rather than provide any information by guessing.
- New recruits should learn to protect the company's image. They must be inducted accordingly.
- A person should be relieved of other duties to the extent required.

INTRODUCTION

The induction process is carried out by almost all organizations. The new recruits of the company get an opportunity to meet the senior management as well as their peers. It is during induction that the new recruits are trained in the skills that should be mastered in order to perform their duties. It is important for the new recruits to fulfil all the tasks related to induction, such as attending induction workshops, conforming to the code of conduct, and executing all tasks (learn–meet–work) that may be defined in the induction plan of the organization. They also need to give feedback to the HR concerning all induction-related processes and materials.

Induction follows the recruitment and selection processes. It is the process that brings in new employees into an organization and engages them. The purpose of induction is to ensure that the employees know what is expected of them, and direct them on how they can add value to the company. The process begins with the first contact of the new recruit with the organization, and ends when the employees have been fully integrated into the organization. Induction is the process of receiving and welcoming an employee when he/she first joins the company, and giving him/her the basic information he/she needs, to settle down quickly and start work. Induction or orientation is a planned introduction of the new recruits to the organization, the job, and their colleagues. The process of induction helps an organization retain its talents.

Induction forms an important element of the recruitment process; it is not only a nice gesture, but if properly done, also ensures employee retention. Induction enables new employees to do the following:

1. Ramp up quickly with their new tasks. Therefore, the process also applies to those who are transferred within the company, and/or to other business units.
2. Obtain an in-depth understanding of the company's practices, guiding principles, values, and objectives.
3. Gain the knowledge and skills needed to perform their new role, and to accomplish the tasks efficiently and effectively.
4. Feel welcome in the company they have joined, thereby avoiding the stress of guessing what is expected of them.

This can be achieved by the following means:

1. Providing the new employee a welcome pack before or on the day of joining
2. Introducing the new employee to the team, peers, and key contacts, and ensuring competence development regarding values, systems, procedures, policies, and key strategic objectives
3. Providing the new recruits a buddy (Harish, mentioned in the opening case, is a buddy) or a mentor to ease the transition
4. Conducting the induction plan that contains tasks for the first three months
5. Conducting a planned induction workshop and other role-specific learning solutions

Induction familiarizes the new recruits to the organization's functioning so that they become more productive in the least possible time; it is a means of honing the workforce to greater efficiency, precision, and perfection.

Now, we shall focus on understanding the objectives of induction.

OBJECTIVES OF INDUCTION

The objectives of induction are manifold. The main purpose of induction is to provide the new employees with necessary information, resources, and motivation to ensure their effective integration into the new work environment. The employees should integrate well into his/her team and the organization, work according to the organizational values, and achieve optimum productivity. As a result, the new recruits will work to their full potential and obtain maximum job satisfaction. The induction process is designed primarily for the fresh recruits who join the organization from other companies, but relevant parts should also be applied to the new recruits who are transferred internally. A successful induction process has the following three broad objectives:

1. Aids the new joinees to settle in
2. Helps them understand their responsibilities and duties
3. Ensures that the employer benefits from the new recruits as quickly as possible

In particular, induction is designed to do the following:

1. To help the new recruits overcome timidity and nervousness in meeting new people in a new environment
2. To provide the new recruits with necessary information such as the location of a cafe, duration of rest period, etc.
3. To induce confidence in the new recruits in the organization
4. To reduce the probability of labour turnover, absenteeism, and employee attrition
5. To reduce confusion and promote healthy relations in the organization
6. To ensure that the new recruits do not form false impressions and negative attitude towards the organization
7. To develop a sense of belongingness and loyalty among the new recruits

NEED FOR INDUCTION

As companies work hard to recruit the right candidate for their organization, it is equally important for them to carry out a well-planned and organized induction session for the new recruits. Proper training sessions can make these recruits invaluable assets to the organization. The induction programme is an ideal occasion for the managers to influence the candidates positively, in order to extract the best possible outcome from them. An induction process is also conducted for the benefit of the experienced employees, who have been either transferred or promoted.

The prime aim of an induction session is to guarantee a successful integration of the employees and the management. Research has also shown that a well-planned induction programme increases staff retention. It is important for the new employees to get a proper idea of the organization's values and objectives, and the job they are required to do. Induction helps in reducing the time period required for these functions.

The advantages of a formal and well-designed induction programme are manifold, and are exhibited in Box 7.1.

Box 7.1 Advantages of formal induction

The advantages of formal induction of new recruits are diverse. Some of these are listed as follows:

1. Induction helps to build a two-way channel of communication between the management and the workers.
2. Proper induction facilitates informal relations and promotes teamwork among employees.
3. Induction, if meticulously planned and executed, helps to integrate the new employee into the organization and develop a sense of belongingness.
4. It helps develop good interpersonal relations.

(Contd)

Box 7.1 (Contd)

5. A formal induction programme establishes the interest of the company towards new recruits and gives them a good start.
6. Proper induction reduces employee grievances, absenteeism, labour turnover, and attrition.
7. Induction provides information about the organization, job, and employee welfare facilities.

Once the objectives of induction are clear, it is wise to plan the content and duration of sessions carried out during the induction programme in order to get the best from the employees.

CONTENT AND DURATION OF AN INDUCTION PROGRAMME

An induction programme ensures that all preparation is done before a new employee joins. These include system access, business cards, and necessary paperwork. The programme broadly includes an orientation of the company and its layout, facilities, and resources. The new recruits should be provided with a company booklet containing the history of the company, names and achievements of past chairmen or managing directors, its geographic spread, number of units in the country, various departments, technology, financial information, etc. A formal induction programme provides the information presented in Box 7.2.

Box 7.2 Content of an induction programme

1. Brief history, evolution, and operations of the company
2. Organizational structure of the company
3. Vision, values, norms, and organizational culture of the company
4. Introduction to the core business, business units, key people, and key products and services
5. Systems, policies, and procedures of the company
6. Instructions about the company's common computer systems
7. Details on major customers
8. Organizational layout—location of departments
9. Safety measures and personal protective equipment
10. Grievance-handling procedures
11. Benefits, compensations, and welfare services of the employee
12. Standing instructions and disciplinary procedures
13. Opportunities for training, promotions, growth, transfer, etc.
14. Employee suggestion schemes
15. Health and safety requirements
16. Introduction to generic legislation and compliance issues
17. Introduction to relevant HR policies and procedures

It is important for every organization, large or small, to have a well-thought out induction programme. However, designing an appropriate and cost-effective induction package is a complex task.

Socialization and on-boarding are processes related to induction. *Socialization* is a process by which a new recruit learns the values and behaviour expected of him, recognizes the organizational culture, gains abilities, appreciates working as a team member, and starts exhibiting organizational citizenship

> Socialization is a process by which a new recruit learns the values and expected behaviour, recognizes organizational culture, gains abilities, appreciates working as a team member, and starts exhibiting organizational citizenship behaviour.

behaviour. *On-boarding* includes the whole process from an individual's first contact with the organization to the time he/she formally joins.

The length and nature of the induction process depends on the complexity of the job and the background of the new recruit. One size does not fit all; a standardized induction course is unlikely to satisfy anyone. Proper commissioning is required to achieve the best results. We shall discuss about orientation, an important induction-related term, in the next section. In fact, orientation is done prior to conducting the induction program.

ORIENTATION

Employee potential and performance differ significantly. Employees' full potential must be utilized. They must know their organization, and follow its dos and don'ts. *Orientation* or *employee orientation* is the process adopted for providing new recruits the basic information and background about the organization. New recruits should feel at ease, understand the organization in a broad sense (its evolution, prevailing culture, climate, mission, and vision), and assimilate key organizational facts such as policies, systems, procedures, and so on. This information will help them socialize. The importance of orientation should never be underestimated. Employees can make serious mistakes due to lack of awareness of rules and regulations; hence, they may need more time to perform if they do not know the right way of working. New recruits must feel at home and work as members of a team. New employee orientation frequently includes carrying out a job that they would be responsible for, in the organization.

> Orientation or employee orientation is the process adopted for providing new recruits with basic information and background about the organization.

New employee orientation is the process of welcoming them into the organization. It contains information about the work environment, new job description, benefits and eligibility, company culture, company history, organizational chart, and all other details relevant to working in the new company.

> A good orientation programme answers the questions in the minds of new recruits and clarifies queries so that they can start working in the right direction.

Usually, employees who have many unanswered questions in their minds cannot perform to their full potential. A good orientation programme can answer many of these questions and clarify queries so that new employees can start working in the right direction. Depending on the number of new employees needed to be oriented, group or individnal orientations could be structured. If an employee's first day does not necessarily coincide with the orientation, consider how to make the employee's first day go smoothly, as first impressions can never be changed.

Orientation programmes can be organized in-house or off-site, preferably with audio-visual tools such as informational videos or slides. Inclusion of role playing, simulations, or simple discussion and question-and-answer time strengthens the learning process. In whichever manner an orientation programme is structured, it is important to make sure that it occurs during the employee's first week in the job. The programme must also cover the following aspects:

1. A welcome address to make new employees feel comfortable and motivated
2. An overview of the organization to cover activities, both inside and outside the employees' department to highlight the image, and convey a good sense of the company's products and/or services
3. A bird's eye view of where the firm fits into its industry so that the employees know the competition and are aware of the industry when handling customers, coworkers, and potential business contacts.
4. An insight into corporate culture to communicate union–management relations.
5. Availability of flexitime and telecommunication systems for employees.
6. The absence of status symbols (separate rest rooms for employees and officers, different entrance gates, etc.)
7. The company's history to ensure employee retention
8. Expected work habits and policies in regard to review hours, vacations, breaks, and dress code

Some companies also like to highlight the health-care benefits provided during orientation. Every company structures its orientation programme according to its needs. As mentioned earlier, new recruits should be encouraged to interact, discuss their issues, and learn from one another. It is good for employees to get to know coworkers from other divisions, and orientation can go a long way towards building bonds among departments. Finally, an employee handbook could be provided to the new recruits.

Induction vs Orientation

Induction is a formal training programme that acquaints new recruits with an organization's technology, processes, systems, and so on.

On the other hand, orientation refers to informal information sharing sessions on miscellaneous issues in an organization such as the facilities available, welfare issues, lunch time, location of crèche, facilities extended by the cooperative society, and so on, to the new recruits.

ELEMENTS OF INDUCTION

The rationale for induction is to ensure the effective integration of staff into or across the organization for their mutual benefit. Research has shown that tailor-made induction programmes help increase staff retention.

A well designed induction programme contains the following elements:

Orientation (physical) This describes the facilities available in a company and their location. A few examples of the facilities are recreation room, welfare bureau, cooperative society, medical dispensary, etc.

Orientation (organizational) This shows how an employee fits into the team and how his role fits with the organization's strategies and goals. A new recruit must know his/her role, the teams to which he/she is likely to be assigned, ways of improving performance learning opportunities, be aware of the career advancement system, etc.

Health and safety information Certain job profiles need information about possible health hazards and occupational safety. Employees are often required to work in an environment having toxic smells, high sound levels, dust, or other factors that may lead to health hazards. These employees must be informed about such issues prior to the commencement of their work. This is a legal requirement and hence, is obligatory for every company.

Explanation of terms and conditions This refers to the terms stated in the offer or appointment letter. The induction faculty members should explain these terms and conditions lucidly using examples to the employees.

Details about the organization Details of the organization's history, products and services, culture, and values must be provided to the employee. This information not only helps an employee understand the organization well, but also gives him a feeling of pride.

Job outline and role requirements One should know one's job and its importance, intricacy, and qualitative requirements. Moreover, it is very important for one to have clarity about his/her role.

Both full-time and part-time staff need an induction programme. Companies should have tailor-made programmes ready for groups with specific needs. It is wise for every company to make its new recruits or even the existing ones, go through it once in a while.

TYPES OF INDUCTION

Induction programmes are generally classified as organizational induction, departmental induction, job induction, and human induction.

Organizational induction This is used when a new employee is oriented to the evolution of the organization, its vision, mission, goals, strategies, and setup. In addition, new recruits are also briefed about the history of the current state of the organization, its financial position, and accounting ratios.

Departmental induction This is used when a new employee is oriented to the particular department where he/she has to work and the interdependencies of various departments, the suppliers, and the customers. In addition, they are told about related departments such as planning, store, quality control, and maintenance departments.

Job induction The new recruits are oriented to the job or tasks they are supposed to perform. They should learn the duties, responsibilities, working conditions, criticality of the job, the function of the component in the assembly, quality parameters, inspection criteria, etc.

Human induction The new recruits are introduced to all the personnel with whom they would have to interact frequently. In case of salespersons, they are introduced to customers. The major customers are invited to the organization when the new recruits are introduced.

Induction programmes are generally classified as
- organizational induction
- departmental induction
- job induction
- human induction

It is also important to remember that in any induction programme, certain prerequisites are required for its effectiveness and continuous use. Unless these prerequisites are fulfilled, the induction may not be effective. Some prerequisites of the induction programme are displayed in Box 7.3.

Box 7.3 Prerequisites of an induction programme

1. The induction programme must have clear objectives.
2. Assessment must be carried out to ensure that the objectives are met.
3. The programme should be evaluated for effectiveness by the staff and managers.
4. Organizations must take advantage of pre-employment enthusiasm.
5. The programme should readily be available to new staff members from the day of joining.
6. The programme should preferably be modular in nature.
7. The delivery methods may be versatile (e.g., online, selfpaced, on-job-training, and workshop).
8. It should cater to employees from all areas within the organization.
9. The programme design should be easy for managers to induct staff.
10. It should minimize the line and HR managers' time and resources.
11. The curriculum should be enjoyable and interesting for new recruits.
12. It should reflect the organization's desired image.
13. It should be conducted for every new recruit.
14. It should regularly be reviewed and updated for usefulness.

INDUCTION POLICY

All new employees/recruits who are appointed to positions within the organization, those who are transferred or promoted internally, or those returning after extended leave or lien services, should receive an appropriate induction.

An induction policy outlines the responsibilities and tasks related to the employees within the organization. It focuses on the personal development of the new recruits. With respect to the other tasks necessary for the on-boarding process, the policy fully relies on the general organizational processes for facility management, information technology, personal history, etc. Any issue with those processes need to be addressed with the process owners directly.

In a multinational organization, the policy applies to all the employees globally. However, implementation may be undertaken in accordance with the requirements of all local legislations and union, works council, or joint consultative machinery agreements. In the event of any conflict, the local legislative requirement takes precedence. The induction policy may also be organization-centric or employee-centric. These are discussed in the following sections.

Q 4 Organization-centric Induction Policy

The provisioning and maintenance of all induction-related material, in principle, is divided as follows:

1. Recruiting and engagement provides and maintains all materials needed before the first day. The materials include the recruitment policy, the contract, and the welcome kit.
2. The talent and leadership development department provides and maintains all the material needed thereafter. These materials include the induction policy, the induction plan template, and the induction checklist.
3. The training and development department or leadership development department of a national or multinational company maintains the national/global induction workshop materials.
4. The HR manager of an organizational unit bears the responsibility of implementing the induction process in that unit, taking the local organizational environment into consideration.

Employee-centric Induction Policy

An employee-centric policy concerns all tasks related to induction directly targeted towards the new employee. The relevant line manager should primarily bear the responsibility of the employee-centric induction process and explain the policies. This type of an induction programme focuses on providing a clear picture about the organization, its team, and job profile. This is to maximize the effectiveness and commitment of the new recruits.

Traditionally, induction programmes were considered more or less a casual exercise, which basically extended over a day or two. These were usually focused only on the vision and values, and were delivered by HR and senior managers. In today's changing times, there are structured, stimulating, and cost-effective ways of inducting new employees so that their journey in the organization is smooth.

Whether one needs to establish an induction programme, or review an existing one, designing a specific checklist as a guide is helpful to avoid any rework at a later stage.

DESIGN OF AN INDUCTION PROCESS

Most of the modern organizations follow the system theory of management. A system is a set of interrelated processes, whereas a process is a set of interrelated activities. Induction is also an organizational process. The term 'induction' is generally used to describe a process through which employees get acclimatized to their new jobs. The aim of the induction process is to facilitate new employees to make a smooth and positive adjustment at the workplace.

An induction programme is all about providing basic information encompassing working hours, holiday routine, leave policy, dress code, jargon, glossary, and definitions of local terms. Induction further includes information regarding location of the labour welfare office, cooperative society, dispensary, and other departments. The induction programme of the junior management level must also include highlights of disaster management, handling of unprecedented events, managing natural calamities, and so on.

In many organizations, the engagement with new recruits starts well before the first day. A candidate's experience during the recruitment process right from application to joining is the first impression that he/she gets about the organization. To support this engagement process with a new employee prior to his/her joining, there may be a welcome brochure containing a note summarizing some interesting aspects of the organization from the CEO to each new recruit. This brochure can be sent to the recruits as attachments to the employment contract. Availability of the same information in the organization's website may also be indicated in the print version.

As discussed earlier, a typical induction aids the new employees to be more acquainted with their work environment and organization functioning. It also helps them acquire a sense of belonging which can lead towards commitment to the organization. In other words, it can be considered as a means of honing the workforce to take them towards greater precision and perfection.

Every business, irrespective of its size, needs a well-planned induction process, which works towards the following:

1. Being flexible and interesting
2. Being employee-centered
3. Extending equal opportunities to all new recruits

The design of an induction programme is represented through Figure 7.1.

The first week of any new recruit is the most crucial time and it is imperative that the induction is efficient and presented appropriately to the recruits. The primary responsibility for this is generally

Purpose of induction
- Facilitate new employees to make a smooth, positive transition to the workplace
- Familiarize the new recruits to the organizational functions
- Make them productive in the least possible time
- Hone the workforce to greater efficiency, precision, and perfection
- Enable them to work in teams

↓

To define responsibilities of the faculty members and the mentor/buddy

↓

To define roles
- Line manager/supervisor
- HR personnel
- Safety officer
- Section supervisor
- Senior manager
- Training officer (or line manager)
- Representatives from trades unions, sports and social clubs, etc.
- Mentor or buddy

↓

To distribute
- Welcome brochure (If not sent as an attachment to the employment contract)
- Company booklet

↓

Make the induction process
- Flexible and interesting
- Employee-centered
- Extend equal opportunities to all new recruits

↓

To enlighten the new employees on the working hours, holiday routine, leave policy, dress code, jargon, glossary, and definitions of local terms.

↓

To inform the new employees about the location of the labour welfare office, cooperative society, dispensary, etc.

↓

To inform the junior management level about disaster management, handling of unprecedented events, managing natural calamities, etc.

Fig. 7.1 Flow chart design of an induction programme

vested with the line manager who needs to be supported by the HR organization. The respective roles and responsibilities of the employees should also be clearly described in the induction process.

ROLES AND RESPONSIBILITIES INVOLVED IN THE INDUCTION PROCESS

An induction programme that reflects the specific needs/roles of each employee is mandatory in any organization. While finalizing the structure of an induction course, it is important to consider the type of recruit, apart from the size and nature of the organization. For larger companies, this programme would be a combination of one-to-one discussions and formal group presentations, which may be given within an induction course.

Though a line manager is responsible for a new recruit's induction, he is not expected to cover all the elements personally. There are certain roles which other managers are responsible for, too. The different roles of various personnel in an organization are detailed in Exhibit 7.1.

Exhibit 7.1 Roles in induction

1. Line manager/supervisor explains his/her jurisdiction—the departmental organization, the requirements of the job, the purpose and operation of any probationary period, and the appraisal system.
2. HR personnel cover the general aspects of the day of joining for a new recruit such as completing employee formats, taking bank details, and explaining the induction programme.
3. Safety officer explains health and safety issues such as occupational diseases, precautionary measures, safety gadgets, and personal protective equipments.
4. Section supervisor provides an escorted tour of the department and introduces fellow workers; then gives day-to-day guidance in local procedures for the first couple of weeks.
5. Senior manager(s) and/or HR give an overview of the organization, its history, products and services, quality system, and culture.
6. Training officer (or line manager) describes available training services, and helps develop a personalized training plan. He/She also provides details of other sources of information during induction such as the company's intranet or interactive learning facilities.
7. Representatives from trade unions, sports and social clubs, etc., give details of membership and benefits.
8. Mentor or 'buddy' (or anyone from the personnel function) and not the immediate line manager, is sometimes allocated to a new recruit to help speed up the settling-in period, and hasten the familiarization process.

Source: http://www.chrmglobal.com

The responsibilities of different personnel involved in designing and execution of an induction programme also need a brief discussion. The main responsibilities should be discharged by the training manager, members of the faculty, and the buddies. These have to be carried out diligently in order to have a successful induction. Responsibilities of the different significant personnel are highlighted in Exhibit 7.2.

Exhibit 7.2 Responsibilities of personnel in induction

Manager of learning (training manager)—He/she has to design the curriculum of the induction programme after considering the nature of duties required to be performed by the new recruits. In addition, he/she has to consider the entire gamut of organizational activities.

Faculty members—They have to disseminate knowledge and share experiences with the new recruits.

Buddy—Though this role seems to be insignificant, buddies play a dominant role in projecting the image of the organization to the new recruits. As a playmate or companion, their statements carry a lot of weight to the new recruits. They can make or mar the organizational image.

PROBLEMS ENCOUNTERED DURING INDUCTION

The first hour and the first day of joining an organization is of paramount importance. It is equally important for the management to keep themselves thoroughly prepared, unless the process of induction suffers from certain impediments. Some of these problems are discussed here.

The person responsible for induction may be untrained. Thus, due to lack of preparedness, he/she may provide information in a manner that may confuse the recruits. Furthermore, overloading of information should also be avoided. Highlighting the company problems to the recruited employees might produce fear about employment. Employees must not be thrown into action soon after joining. Initially, difficult tasks should not be allocated to new employees. Only simple tasks should be assigned, so that on successful completion, they can gain confidence.

A cricket captain engages an inexperienced bowler in a match. If the bowler is beaten by a batsman, the captain withdraws the bowler and engages an experienced one instead. The experienced bowler will consider the strengths and weaknesses of the batsman, decide on the type of bowling that counters the attacking mood of the batsman. The captain takes such initiatives so that the bowler is not depressed at the start of his career. Thus, he protects and safeguards the talents.

It is important to keep in mind that problems may generate at any stage of the induction process. In addition, the consequence of ineffective induction may lead to an employee's underperformance.

Consequences of Ineffective Induction

If an induction programme is not organized effectively, the new recruits get off to a bad start and never really understand the organization or their role in it. This may lead the new recruits to exhibit the following characteristics:

1. Have the inability to work as member of a team, due to rugged individualism.
2. Exhibit an attitude that is not conducive to a healthy work environment, and make themselves fault finders rather than fact finders.
3. Suffer from low morale, particularly if the employee is a fresher.
4. Fail to contribute to the organization due to role ambiguity.
5. Suffer from loss of productivity on account of inadequate work knowledge.
6. Fail to work to their highest potential due to lack of motivation, commitment, and belongingness.

In extreme cases, the new employee leaves, either through resignation or dismissal; this results in a great loss to the company. Recruitment, retention, and turnover survey showed that 22% of the people who left the company had less than six months' service (up from 19% in the previous year's survey). Early leaving results in additional cost towards replacement and recruiting a substitute. It also leads to the following:

1. Wastage of time in the induction
2. Lowering of morale of the remaining staff
3. Damage to the employment record of the person who left
4. Having to repeat the unproductive learning curve of the person who left
5. Damage to the organization's reputation and image

An organization must meticulously plan the induction programme to avoid encountering such problems, and make it effective. Preparations to receive the new recruits, include determining in advance

A checklist is an ad memoir. It can be a vital source of reference later during employment for verification. Checklists support responsible persons to verify the complete coverage of all action items of the inductee.

the information they may ask for, establishing the technique of presenting the information, and completing the paper work. Some companies even provide a company booklet to the recruits.

CHECKLISTS FOR INDUCTION

While conducting an induction programme, it is wise to keep a checklist of the areas of induction training. Ideally, this should be prepared and signed by the induction programme designer and countersigned by the competent approving authority. The checklist helps ensure that nothing important for the new joinees gets missed out. Further, it can be a vital source of reference later during employment, for example, to check whether an employee has been briefed on the policies, or to produce evidence of training in the event of a health and safety inspection.

Checklists support the line manger, buddy, and new employee in the induction process by listing everything that the new recruits should be provided with, and enabled to learn or do. It is a generic list which should be customized to the local environment by the local HR department. To cover those specific needs, it can be easily extended and detailed to meet local and/or business requirements or regulations.

Four soldiers (what, how, who, and when), followed by a corresponding comment help to develop checklist on preparation, working environment, mandatory learning content, etc.

The four soldiers (what, how, who, and when), followed by a corresponding comment, help to develop checklists on preparation, working environment, mandatory learning content, location-/region-specific information, and business specific knowledge of an induction programme.

Checklist on Preparation

The activities of the four soldiers are specified in Table 7.1.

Table 7.1 Functions of soldiers in preparation

Soldier	Function
What	Facilitates concentration on the topic, contract, contents of the welcome pack, nominating a buddy, etc.
How	Helps decide on the method of conducting the induction, identifies the sources of information, considering the target participants (the new recruits, employees), following the welcome pack guidelines, and other related activities
Who	Provides details on the person in-charge, the HR personnel with specific responsibilities, the line manager concerned, and other persons of the induction squad
When	Directs to decide the time schedule, thus making the buddy free from his/her normal duties so that he/she can give undivided attention.

Checklist on Working Environment

The guidelines given by the soldiers are enumerated in Table 7.2.

Table 7.2 Functions of the soldiers in working environment

Soldier	Function
What	Facilitates knowing about office gadgets such as PCs, laptops, printers, copier machines, fax, office supplies in location, intranet, rights to access, databases and software required, read-write permission to files, desk phone/ mobile phone/ SIM card, office coupon for cafeteria, meeting rooms and their reservation system, virtual team work principles, and teleconferencing
How	Helps become aware of the information source, basic tools, role-specific applications, etc.
Who	Leads to the deploying person in-charge, the HR personnel, and the line manager
When	Decides the scheduling—during the first week; before the first day; by the end of the first week; or at the latest during the first month

Checklist on Mandatory Learning Content

Each soldier performs specific duties as listed in Table 7.3.

Table 7.3 Functions of the soldiers in mandatory learning content

Soldier	Function
What	Facilitates the new recruits to know the organization's ethics, code of conduct, e-learning facilities available, other learning facilities available such as EBSCO host, Springer link, etc.
How	Helps to know the venue or location of availability
Who	Details the persons responsible to organize or conduct the learning programmes including the target audience
When	Helps decide on the scheduling

Checklist on Location-/Region-specific Information

In different countries, the operational units of a multinational company may have different information needs. The activities of the four soldiers are depicted in Table 7.4.

Table 7.4 Functions of the soldiers in information

Soldier	Function
What	Facilitates the new recruits to know the principal customers/projects, country-specific rules and regulations, mobile phone policy, registration of working hours/absences (country specific), dress code, etc.
How	Helps to know the venue or location of availability
Who	Details the persons responsible for organizing or conducting the learning programmes including the target audience
When	Helps decide on the scheduling

Checklist on Business-specific Knowledge

Different strategic business units (SBUs) of a large organization operate in diverse ways. New employees need to know all the business aspects in order to acquire specific business knowledge. The functions of the soldiers in business-specific knowledge are discussed in Table 7.5.

Table 7.5 Function of the soldier in business-specific knowledge

Soldier	Function of the soldier
What	Tells the new recruits about the modes of operation, portfolios (products, solutions), processes, tools and technology, principal customers and projects, etc.
How	Helps to know the venue or location of availability of knowledge
Who	Details the persons responsible for organizing or conducting the learning programmes including the target audience
When	Helps decide on the schedule of collecting knowledge packages

Q 5 Comments in all the checklists are required to be endorsed for every soldier to verify its progress and execution according to the plan, identify deviations, and initiate remedial measures, in line with the PDCA (plan-do-check-act) cycle.

TRENDS IN INDUCTION

With the changing times, the content of induction programmes is also changing; it is gradually getting broader to incorporate the following emerging issues:

1. At present, organizations are going beyond induction to the broader 'on-boarding' process, keeping in mind the employee experience from their first contact with the organization.
2. Fewer chalk-and-talk sessions and more multi-media presentations, or active learning tasks, are practised. For example, giving the inductees a questionnaire where completion involves talking to people outside their normal scope.
3. Organizations are moving away from their practices to discuss prevailing culture and values.
4. Technology is widely used in the induction process. For example, an online induction and e-learning programme is developed to introduce the culture for new HR staff.
5. A wide range of personnel are involved in the curriculum development to ensure that the content continues to match the organization profile, as out-of-date or badly produced material is ineffective.
6. Socialization issues are stressed in the induction programmes and are organized for cross-functional team building which improve inter-organizational communication. Cultural issues are given great importance in such induction programmes.

Refer to Box 7.4 for a brief insight into induction software.

Box 7.4 Software on induction

With the advancement of information technology, organizations are performing managerial processes using various softwares. The induction process is no exception. Induction software mechanizes the entire process of induction and training. From orientation to shift timings, holiday routines to leave policy for all types of leave organization's goals to values and philosophy, personnel practices to job requirements; all functions are provided by the software.

These types of induction can be given online as well. They aid in adding comfort to the new employee by providing the information as and when they require. With online delivery, induction programmes

(Contd)

Box 7.4 (Contd)

can be made more interesting because one can present information and material more creatively in various forms using web-based delivery modes such as flash, animation, and powerpoint.

With this interactive software, induction can be conducted for individuals or groups on demand and online, thus eliminating the need for managers to disrupt their daily routine and conduct induction personally. However, the interactive software cannot replace human trainers totally. The body language, modulation of voice, understanding the receptive capacities of the new recruits, and specific interrogations can only be achieved by an instructor. Moreover, human touch, and ethnicity can only be transferred by a human being.

ROLE OF HR IN EMPLOYEE INDUCTION

The induction of a specific employee is the line manager's responsibility. The HR is responsible for the company's induction policy and for developing the induction programmes. There are certain personnel specialists also who implement some aspects of induction. Finally, the HR is responsible for the evaluation of the induction process.

The HR personnel are increasingly recognizing the value of employer branding and are instrumental in developing an employer brand. This involves careful consideration of the experiences of an employee from their first contact with the organization throughout their the employment lifecycle. In many cases, this leads to a focus on the on-boarding and induction process to ensure that it effectively reflects the brand name and the values of the organization.

This might mean, for example, reviewing pre-employment communications, to make sure the new recruits feel welcome and are engaged and that their potential is fully utilized. It could also mean thinking about opportunities to help the socialization process before people formally join the organization. For example, social networking technology may be used.

All induction programmes should be reviewed from the standpoint of auditing. However, auditing needs to done against a standard. The HR manager, as a manager of learning, should develop a 'facility time matrix,' in which each programme must have certain objectives. For each objective, the matrix should present a training method, time required for participants and trainers (the trainer time should further be split into time apportioned for preparation and training delivery), and the facilities required to achieve the objective. A format is shown in Table 7.6. The closing case of this chapter may be referred to, for detailed information.

Table 7.6 Objective-wise facility time matrix

Objectives	Training method	Time (Hours)			Facilities
		Participants	Trainers		
		Training	Preparation	Training	
Development	Lecture Quiz	2.00	4.00	2.00	Classroom, one case, powerpoint slides, LCD projector

The HR should design the feedback format to measure the effectiveness of the training. In the feedback format, the HR should also introduce columns on parameters such as achievement of course objective(s), following instructions, exercise/practical training facilities (whereever applicable), applicability of knowledge/skills, and topic and presentation grading. Participants will express their views on a five-point or 10-Likert scale. In a team meeting, the weightages of the parameters may be decided upon. The parameters and corresponding weightages are exhibited in Tables 7.7 and 7.8.

One can compute the quality of the course by processing the averages of each point grades (PG) and the corresponding weights. The average course grading (ACG) may be computed which will represent the conglomeration of the five parameters taken together.

Table 7.7 Average course grading

S. No.	Feedback from the participant	PG	W
1.	Achievement of course objective(s)	X_1	35
2.	Following instructions	X_2	10
3.	Exercise/Practical training facilities (wherever applicable)	X_3	10
4.	Applicability of knowledge/skills	X_4	30
5.	Topic and presentation grading	X_5	15

Table 7.8 Calculating average course grading

S. No.	Feedback from the participant	PG	W	PG × W
1.	Achievement of course objective(s)	X_1	35	
2.	Following instruction	X_2	10	
3.	Exercise/practical training facilities (whereever applicable)	X_3	10	
4.	Applicability of knowledge/skills	X_4	30	
5.	Topic and presentation grading	X_5	15	
PG: Point grading W: Weight			100	Σ PG × W

$$\text{ACG (in decimal)} = \frac{(\Sigma\,\text{PG} \times \text{W})}{\Sigma\,\text{W}}; \quad \text{Percentage ACG} = \frac{\text{ACG (Decimal)}}{5} \times 100$$

The ACG can be compared to the previous course and other courses. In case the value is low, the HR persons may identify the possible reasons or root causes behind that and can initiate corrective actions. Some of the possible reasons are alternate faculty, change of venue, shortage of time, non-administering of exercises, non-availability of pedagogical aids, poor performance of training gadgets, etc.

ORGANIZATIONAL PRACTICES OF INDUCTION

Organizations lay great emphasis on induction programmes. The practices that are followed by some reputed companies are described in Exhibit 7.3.

Exhibit 7.3 Organizational practices of induction

Indian Oil Corporation Limited (IOCL), Hindustan Petroleum Corporation Limited (HPCL), Tata Motors Limited, National Thermal Power Corporation (NTPC), and Moser Baer are some companies which organize induction programmes to achieve integration.

Indian Oil Corporation Limited The values of IOCL are to care and develop innovation, passion, and trust. IOCL is harnessing frontier technology, caring for environment and community, and pioneering the spirit of creativity and research. The induction begins with

(Contd)

Exhibit 7.3 (Contd)

a welcome by the HR director who conveys the core values, vision, and mission of the company. The induction programmes are organized at their own institute (Indian Oil Institute of Petroleum Management). In the micro lab, participants get to explore transitions, organize tasks, occupational choice, articulation of self, examining one's aspirations, etc. In other modules, the induction covers conflict management, assertiveness, managerial styles, etc.

Hindustan Petroleum Corporation Limited HPCL is a Fortune 500 company which recently designed a new induction programme called '*Samavesh*'. The programme seeks to provide seamless induction and integration of a fresher along personal, professional, and cultural levels into the HPCL family. *Samavesh* happens in three phases. The first phase focuses on 'What is HPCL?' and is spread over four days. In this stage, presentations are included from senior functionaries of various business units and the stalls of the business units detailing the various activities handled by the company are showcased. It also includes various informal events (as will be discussed in the next section). Stage two of the programme is designed around the theme of 'How HPCL works?', where joinees are taken on location visits and other practical inputs are provided through interactions with customers at petrol stations, storage points, etc. The third phase is themed, 'How the SBU works?'

Tata Motors Ltd Tata Motors Limited is India's largest automobile company. Tata Motors, the first company from India's engineering sector to be listed in the New York Stock Exchange (September 2004), has also emerged as an international player. The company is also expanding its international footprint that was established through exports since 1961. The company's commercial and passenger vehicles are already being marketed in several countries in Europe, Africa, the Middle East, South East Asia, South Asia, and South America. During its five-day induction programme, the company covers its history, values, and relevant HR policies and practices, quality, and work-related standards. For senior recruits, the induction is customized for each person based on the profile and requirements. There are specific departmental coordinators for induction of all new joinees.

National Thermal Power Corporation The mission of NTPC is to 'develop and provide reliable power, related products, and services at competitive prices, integrating multiple energy sources with innovative and eco-friendly technologies and contribute to society.' The core values of NTPC are business ethics, customer focus, organizational and professional pride, mutual respect and trust, innovation and speed, and total quality for excellence. At NTPC, there is an initial week-long induction programme which begins with an inaugural function. The initial induction process is followed by a 52-week induction training program, which has a mix of classroom learning and on-the-job training. The process is customized for different types of employees classified as executive trainee, diploma trainee, and artisans. NTPC provides interactive CD-ROMs containing the company's information to each inductee.

Moser Baer Moser Baer, headquartered in New Delhi, is one of India's leading technology companies. Established in 1983, Moser Baer successfully developed cutting-edge technologies to become the world's second largest manufacturer of optical storage media such as CDs and DVDs. Moser Baer believes in informal induction system. The induction programme is interspersed in informal sessions when employees are invited to talk about their experience of the overall culture in an informal and interactive mode. At the end of each day, a high tea session is organized with the director and leadership team to engage with them at an informal level. The new recruits get the unique opportunity of interacting with the top management.

Source: Best HR Practices (2009), Steel Authority of India Limited, New Delhi.

PLACEMENT

Q 1 Placement refers to the procedure followed by an organization wherein a new recruit is assigned a specific job. Placement is the process of assigning specific tasks to the selected candidates. This process involves assigning a precise responsibility to an individual. It implies matching the requirements of a job with the qualifications and attributes of the new recruit.

Every individual seeks a job and expects something from that job. The nature of the job satisfies certain intrinsic needs of every employee. The extent of satisfaction varies widely, depending on the nature of the job and the levels of expectations from the job. Occupational value usually guides a person's choice of career. However, in reality, expectations cannot always be fulfilled. An introvert who does not like to interact with unknown people, can never be happy if he/she is assigned to work in marketing, sales, or other tasks related to public relations. On the other hand, an extrovert (who is always expressive and successfully draws the attention of others to him/her) will soon be bored, if he/she is posted in research and development or a desk job. An introvert likes to isolate himself/herself from the mass, whereas an extrovert desires to interact with more people.

Thus, placement plays a vital role in determining employee job satisfaction, task accomplishments, absenteeism, turnover, productivity, and so on.

Placement is an important HR function, and if properly handled, it does the following:

1. Improves the morale of the employees
2. Reduces employee turnover
3. Decreases accident rates
4. Enhances labour productivity
5. Clarifies expectations

A person can contribute as per the predetermined objectives. Right placement improves employee morale, and the employee contributes more; lower absenteeism enables achieving delivery targets; reduced manpower attrition and turnover makes the recruitment cell, cost- and time-efficient. When the nature of duty and demands of the job are matched with the intrinsic needs of the employee, it enhances his/her job satisfaction which, in turn, promotes industrial relations. It helps the employee work and the objectives of the organization.

GLOBAL PLACEMENT

Recruitment for international placement, involving transfer from one country to the other, is a common organizational phenomenon for multinational companies. When a company operating in one country needs manpower, it floats job specifications through the company's website. It receives resumes from its overseas branches. Companies such as IBM, McDonald, and Coca Cola receive close to 50% of resumes from their overseas operations (Jyothi and Venkatesh, 2008).

While performing their regular assignments, managers exhibit some distinguishable skills and innovative leadership styles that produce excellent outcomes. The top management of multinational companies takes note of these aspects and decides to transfer selected managers to other countries where their abilities can be applied fruitfully if managers with the requisite abilities are not readily available in that country; or even if available, they are not identifiable.

> Managers with distinguishable abilities are transferred to other countries where they can fruitfully apply the skills if managers with the requisite abilities are not readily available in that country.

In a multinational company or the IT industry, project managers play a crucial role and are sent to attend projects developed in other countries as well. Off-shore placement is another kind of movement of employees that comes under the purview of global placement; sometimes, the employer sends the employees to handle or lead a project away from the home country or send them for overseas work. Very often, these kinds of transfers or offshore postings take place from a country in the East to a country in the West. Cultures of these two hemispheres differ significantly. Before transfer, they need to be introduced to cross-cultural issues and cultural diversity, to make their contributions fruitful and effective.

SUMMARY

Induction, orientation, and placement are functions which follow the recruitment and selection processes. These processes help new recruits to understand the organization and settle in. Formal induction has multifarious advantages and contains elements such as physical and organizational orientation, health, and safety information. The induction policy may either be organization-centric or employee-centric. Induction needs certain prerequisites for its effectiveness. The induction process should be flexible and interesting, employee-centered, and extend equal opportunities to all inductees. An induction programme should have typical allocation of tasks and defined responsibilities. Ineffective induction produces adverse consequences on the recruits. Specific checklists should be used for induction.

At present, many companies are using interactive software for induction. Orientation or employee orientation is the process adopted for providing new recruits with basic information and background about the organization. Objective-wise facility time matrix should preferably be used for effectiveness and a system of computing average course grading may be installed for the purpose of auditing. Many organizations have introduced innovations in their induction programmes. Placement refers to the procedure followed by an organization wherein a new recruit is assigned with a specific job. It implies matching the requirements of a job with the qualifications and attributes of the new recruit.

KEY TERMS

Buddy is a friend or playmate allocated to a new recruit who plays a key role in the induction process. He/she is an internal employee who acts as a guide in addition to the line manager, and should be identified and nominated on the first day.

Induction is the planned introduction of the new recruits to the organization, job, and colleagues; the induction process helps an organization retain its talents.

Orientation or employee orientation is the process adopted for providing new recruits with basic information and background about the organization.

Placement refers to the procedure followed by an organization wherein a new recruit is assigned a specific job. It implies matching the requirements of a job with the qualifications and attributes of the new recruit.

Socialization is a process by which a new recruit learns the values and behaviour, recognizes organizational culture, gains abilities, appreciates working as a member of a team, and starts exhibiting organizational citizenship behaviour.

EXERCISES

Concept Review Questions

1. Explain the term 'placement' and critically discuss its importance in organizational context.
2. Suggest a roadmap to make the induction programme effective. What documentation system do you find useful for successful induction?
3. Narrate the objectives of an induction programme. What are the important areas that need to be considered to make an induction programme effective?
4. Distinguish between organization-centric and employee-centric induction.
5. What do you mean by a checklist for induction? Discuss briefly the various types of checklists.

Critical Thinking Questions

6. You have been assigned the task of designing the curriculum of an induction programme. Write the data you would collect and steps you would follow to design the induction.
7. 'An induction programme needs certain prerequisites for its effectiveness and continuous use.' You have been asked to develop a checklist and use that to confirm the suitability of the prerequisites framed. How would you go about the same?
8. Develop a procedure to evaluate the effectiveness of an induction programme and design its format.

Assignments

9. With the help of your professor, visit two IT companies; meet the HR managers of the companies, and interview them to collect information regarding their placement criteria. Prepare an exhaustive list of factors.
10. Visit three organizations and discuss with the HR managers about their induction programmes. Collect the steps taken to improve employee induction. Develop a comparative chart and discuss with your professor.

MANAGER'S INSIGHT

Unique Management Consultants (UMC) recruited 12-high ranking engineering graduates from top institutes. As per UMC's policy, the new recruits had to attend a 12-week induction programme, and visit all the three units of the company in India.

The induction curriculum was meticulously designed and the programme was intensive. They even had to take up an examination and secure the qualifying marks. Soon after the induction process was completed and the new joinees secured qualifying marks in the exams, they were designated as junior managers, and were assigned tasks in their respective functional areas.

Harihar, one of the new joinees, was not interacting with the others during the induction. In fact, he even continued to remain isolated from others after completion of the induction. Looking at this problem, a team of three junior managers led by a senior manager, was deputed for carrying out a preliminary survey and collecting data from a client, Genius Exports. The employees and officers of Genius Exports also observed similar traits in Harihar's nature.

On one occasion, the manager of corporate social responsibility and ethics tried to answer Harihar's query about the values of UMC. However, Harihar still seemed unconvinced and distracted. The higher management of UMC became aware of this incident.

Questions:

1. What steps should UMC have undertaken in order to avoid such a problem?
2. What should UMC do to improve the situation?

BIBLIOGRAPHY AND WEB RESOURCES

Haldar, Uday Kumar, *Human Resource Development*, Oxford Higher Education, Oxford University Press, New Delhi, 2009.

Jyothi, P. and D.N. Venkatesh, *Human Resource Management*, Oxford Higher Education, Oxford University Press, New Delhi, 2008.

SAIL Best HR Practices, Steel Authority of India Limited, New Delhi, 2009.

Web Resources

http://www.chrmglobal.com/Replies/354/1/INDUCTION.html, last accessed on 19 May 2011.

INDUCTION OF CHARGEMAN AT OFILIS, ISHAPORE

About the organization

Ordnance Factories Institute of Learning (OFILIS), at Ishapore, West Bengal, is a training unit established under the HR division of Ordnance Factory Board (OFB), Ministry of Defence, Government of India. OFILIS receives guidance from the HR division of OFB, and functions accordingly. In 1997, the New Delhi-based Institute of Directors (www.iodonline.org), granted the Golden Peacock national training award to OFILIS and this boosted when the company received the award. OFILIS contested for the award in 2005 too and bagged it. Furthermore, OFILIS received the ISO 9001:2000 certification in 2003. The institute believes in 'getting more from people', rather than getting 'more people'. OFILIS conducts training courses and complies with a structured system that considers the feedback of participants. The institute conducts several short-term management development programmes. However, after considering various aspects of OFB, OFILIS developed the training curriculum that included designing the syllabus of the long-term induction and orientation course for 44 weeks for the post of chargeman, grade II.

Designing a training curriculum

The institute designs the syllabus of any course following an established, time-tested method, called 'Designing a training curriculum'. It includes the following steps:

1. Assessing customer's needs
2. Defining training objectives
3. Designing a repeat or new course
4. Consulting feedbacks for existing course
5. Benchmarking for new course
6. Estimating programme duration
7. Designing abridged syllabus
8. Designing course contents
9. Deciding methodology
10. Obtaining approval
11. Managing documentation

Step 1:Assessment of customer's needs The 'induction cum orientation' was a residential programme. OFILIS initially listed the nature of duties required to be performed by the chargeman by retrieving information from the OFB manual and through direct interrogation. A committee comprising experts from different fields was formed and it developed a draft curriculum for the course. In fact, the institute decided to convene training meetings twice a year, and invite all regular customers. The management development officer and training manager of each customer unit represented their units. OFILIS assessed the customer needs in detail.

Step 2: Defining training objectives The institute formulated and defined the training objectives aimed to fulfil customers needs.

Step 3: Designing a repeat or new course OFILIS searched as to whether this type of programme had been conducted earlier and it was revealed that it was a new one.

Step 4: Consulting feedbacks for existing course As the programme was new, no feedback was available.

Step 5: Benchmarking for new course To finalize the curriculum of this programme, OFILIS searched for similar programmes conducted by other institutes in line with the process benchmarking method. The institute could benchmark induction programmes with similar objectives.

Step 6: Estimating programme duration Having decided on the topics, the institute estimated the time required for them. This included time taken for knowledge dissemination, administering exercises, case study discussion, quizzes, pursuing projects (in team), presentation by trainees, etc.

Step 7: Designing abridged syllabus The institute drafted the abridged syllabus showing the topics adequate to meet the course objectives.

Step 8: Designing course contents The institute designed the course contents in detail showing time allocated for each topic. For example, part of the syllabus of training on 'internal audit - ISO 9001:2000' was appended.

Step 9: Deciding methodology The institute decided the methodology—use of lecture methods, industrial visits, practical demonstration, administering exercises and quizzes, syndicate tasks, and video display mentioning the time for each to achieve the stated learning objectives.

Step 10: Obtaining approval The programme director submitted the detailed curriculum along with the 'record of discussion' to the principal director, who was the competent authority for approval. After scrutiny, the principal director approved and authenticated the same by signing the curriculum.

Step 11: Managing documentation The training manager (programme director) endorsed revision number (0), revision date (Nil), and marked the document as 'master copy of syllabi'. He circulated the copies of the curriculum to all relevant persons maintaining a distribution list. He sent a copy to the technical library, as well.

Two phase—modular training

It was decided to conduct the induction programme in phases: phase 1 with a duration of 26 weeks, and phase 2 for 18 weeks, amounting to a total of 44 weeks. Details of the modules of phase 1 and 2 are as follows:

Phase 1

Module 1: Planning and material management (PMM)
Module 2: General factory administration (GFA)
Module 3: Man management and personality development (MMPD)
Module 4: Quality, environment, energy, and safety management systems (QESMS)
Module 5: Miscellaneous topics (educational and technical visits, library studies, review and discussions, and module-ending examination)

Phase 2 Posting in different departments of Rifle Factory, Ishapore (RFI), and concurrently pursuing project work (in teams) assigned to them.

Syllabus

Syllabi for each module were framed taking into account the assignable tasks, dischargeable duties, administrative manual of OFB etc. Each module had sub-modules.

Programme content

The knowledge and experience was shared over the entire syllabus of each module. External faculty members from organizations and academia were also engaged to bridge any possible gaps. Each topic ended with summarizing the delivery. Module directors summarized each module content followed by review and discussion.

Time and facility planning

The institute developed and used a matrix for the training method, time required for participants and trainers, and the facilities required against each course objective. For a small portion on quality management system (QMS) of the entire syllabus of QESMS, the matrix on time and facility planning is shown in Table 7.9.

Table 7.9 Time and facilities required for QMS

Objectives	Training method	Time (Hours)			Facilities
		Participants	Trainers		
		Training	Preparation	Training	
1. Development	Lecture Quiz	2.00	4.00	2.00	Classroom, one case, powerpoint slides, LCD projector
2. Understanding QMS	Case lecture Exercise	3.00	5.00	3.00	Classroom, two cases, powerpoint slides, LCD projector
3. Interpreting	Case lecture Exercise	11.00	20.00	11.00	Classroom, six cases, powerpoint slides, LCD projector
4. Auditing	Documents Lecture	3.00	3.00	3.00	Classroom, documents
5. Assessment test	Test paper	2.00	3.00	0.00	Hall
Total	- - -	21.00	35.00	19.00	Nine cases, classroom for 21 hours, LCD projector fixed

Faculty members need:	• 35 hours for preparing reading material, lesson plans, exercises, quizzes, power point slides, and assessment test papers • 19 hours of lecture sessions
Programme director and coordinator need:	• 25 hours for all arrangements

Note: For new induction programmes, the preparation time for faculty members, programme directors, and programme coordinators was longer than the time mentioned in the table.

Examination

The institute organized module ending examination for each module. Module directors, with the help of external experts, set the question papers.

Collecting feedback

Feedback was collected from the trainees in multiple stages and were subjected to analysis, on the basis of which, the institute incorporated minor changes in the curriculum.

Releases of the direct recruits

The direct recruits were released to join the respective OFL.

Post-training impact measurement

After a minimum of six months, OFILIS officials visited the OFL where the trained personnel were posted. The officials interacted with the trainees, the management development officer of the factory, and the training manager to interrogate the performance of the trainees as part of post-training impact measurement. The trainees were executing the assigned tasks confidently. The higher officials also provided positive feedback about their technical and behavioural disposition.

Discussion Questions

1. Discuss the importance of the post-training impact measurement adopted by OFILIS.
2. Mention the need for documentation, as stated in step 11, 'Managing documentation'.

HR MANTRA The ship and the radar

Radar is an object detection system that uses electromagnetic waves (particularly radio waves) to determine the range, altitude, direction, and speed of both moving and fixed objects. Marine radars provide distance of other ships and land targets (through the radar scanner) to avoid collision and assist in safe navigation in the sea. The radio waves are invisible to the human eyes. The captain views the readings and displays them on the monitor. The captain of the ship cannot work without viewing the readings in the radar.

Similarly, in organizations, a supervisor is responsible for extracting work from the workforce which reports to him. The workforce has certain strengths and weaknesses, desires and expectations, knowledge and ignorance, an innate urge to work or tendency to avoid work, inclination to accept or avoid risky and challenging assignments, and so forth. However, all these human attributes are invisible.

Familiarity with new people and getting acclimatized to organizational practices, policies and procedures and behavioural norms, facilitates behavioural modification and attitude building, and makes employees capable of contributing to the organization.

Therefore, employees must use observational skills and intuition to read the invisible, just as a radar does.

The mantra: Detect hidden attributes using observation and intuition.

DOUGLAS MURRAY MCGREGOR

Douglas Murray McGregor (1906–1964), a pioneer in management, was born in the bustling border metropolis of Detroit, Michigan. While in high school, McGregor worked as a night clerk at the McGregor Institute (originally set up by his grandfather), and also played piano at its services regularly. The institute was a family affair.

At the age of 17, for a brief period of time, he considered becoming a lay preacher, before choosing to enroll for a psychology degree at the college of the city of Detroit (now Wayne State University). After two years of the course, he tried a term at Oberlin, his uncle's old college in Ohio. However, at 19, McGregor dropped out of college altogether and started earning his living as a gas station attendant in Buffalo. By 1930, McGregor had risen to the rank of regional gas station manager.

Meanwhile, unemployment was soaring in the depression-hit Detroit, and the local department of public works had handed the McGregor institute a large subsidy to increase its facilities. McGregor decided that he could now afford to resume his studies if he also worked part-time at the muchexpanded institute. When he finally completed his first degree in 1932, he was also organizing mass soup kitchens for the unemployed, while helping with the management of the institute. Soon after his graduation, he chose to move to the academic tranquility of Cambridge, Massachusetts, to continue his education. For three years, he studied at Harvard and gained a post graduate degree and a PhD in psychology. The colour-blind McGregor chose the topic, 'The sensitivity of the eye to the saturation of colours' as the subject for his PhD. For the next two years, he stayed on at Harvard as a psychology lecturer. In 1937, he took a short trip down Massachusetts Avenue to set up an industrial relations division at the Massachusetts Institute of Technology (MIT).

He was the president of Antioch College from 1948 to 1954. He also taught at the Indian Institute of Management, Kolkata. Douglas has many publications to his credit; among them, *The Human Side of Enterprise* had a profound influence on educational practices. In this book, Douglas identified an approach to creating an environment within which employees are motivated by means of authority, direction, control or integration, which he called theory X, and self-control, that he called theory Y. Theory Y is the practical application of Dr Abraham Maslow's humanistic school of psychology, or third force psychology, applied to scientific management.

In addition to his teaching work at MIT, McGregor increased his consultancy work in the area of industrial relations. This work covered wage and salary administration, contract negotiation, foremen training, grievance handling, executive development programmes, union and management cooperation programmes, and problems of organizational structure and function. He was also much in demand as a speaker by both business and labour unions. In 1947, the president of the progressive Antioch College in Yellow Springs, Ohio, resigned; McGregor seized the opportunity and applied for the post. At the age of 41, McGregor commenced his presidential term at Antioch in 1948. It was vital to prove a pivotal point in his life and personal development. As he tried to put his cooperative style into practice, he could now appreciate the problems of leadership first hand.

At the forefront of what was to become the civil rights movement, Antioch was one of the first US mainstream colleges to welcome African-Americans. However, when they qualified as teachers, McGregor struggled to get them placed in local white schools. He also had to resist pressure from the powerful House of Un-American Activities Committee to expel student activists with left-wing views. There were the continuing problems of attracting enough new students and fee income to balance the college's books.

It took a couple of years for McGregor to realize that a leader cannot avoid the exercise of authority any more than he can avoid responsibility for what happens to his organization. Moreover, since no important decision ever pleases everyone in the organization, he realized the need to absorb displeasure, and sometimes severe hostility.

After trying for six years to reconcile the conflicting demands of leadership at Antioch College, McGregor decided to return to MIT, as a faculty member of the then recently established Sloan School of Management. He was a professor of management at the MIT Sloan School of Management. McGregor persuaded the former trade union accountant, Joe Scanlon, with whom he had worked at Dewey Almy, to join him at MIT. Scanlon had built an impressive reputation with his Scanlon plan for staff involvement, suggestion schemes, and profit sharing. Scanlon's work became an important source for Theory Y in McGregor's 1960 best-seller *The Human Side of Enterprise*. McGregor's compelling new vocabulary assured him of an almost instant global fame. However, for the rest of his life, McGregor tried vainly to dispel the simplified paradigm of 'Theory X = bad; Theory Y = good' that others had imposed on his analysis. At the age of 58, McGregor succumbed to a heart attack. However, even after his death, his work has stood the test of time. One small reflection of the contribution of McGregor is that the main Antioch campus at Yellow Springs is now called Antioch University McGregor, or more commonly just McGregor.

References

en.wikipedia.org/wiki/Douglas_McGregor, last accessed on 15 October 2011.

managers-net.org/Biography/mcgregor.html, last accessed on 15 October 2011.

www.google.co.in/imgres?q=Douglas McGregor, last accessed on 15 October 2011.

CHAPTER 8

Performance Management System

LEARNING OBJECTIVES

After studying this chapter, you will be able to

- Understand the link between system theory and human performance
- Identify different stakeholders in the performance system
- Appreciate the need for performance planning and review
- Realize the basics of performance appraisal and its need
- Define the benefits of appraisal
- Recognize various performance appraisal methods
- Distinguish between performance appraisal and performance review
- Empathize with an employee's performance appraisal problems
- Value the need for establishing performance criteria
- Welcome the utmost need for ensuring transparency
- Be aware of using computer software while appraising performance

OPENING CASE

Flaw in Performance Appraisal System

Albert Engineering Works (AEW), established in 1998, is into manufacturing mechanical engineering components and automobile spares. Until the year 2002, the company was giving annual increments to its employees. In 2001, AEW planned to introduce a system of linking pay with performance. It introduced a system of tracking employee performance, developed a form to assess the same, and implemented it in 2002. The appraisees were generally unhappy with the pay increments resulting from the performance ratings. The work environment gradually deteriorated on account of increasing dissatisfaction with the performance ratings. Once, an aggrieved employee asked his superior about his performance. He was not satisfied with the appraisal as he learnt that it was done on subjective aspects such as honesty, integrity, devotion to duty, etc. The manager confessed that he actually could not remember all the anecdotes of the employee. Later, the employee filed a law suit against the company. The court announced the verdict in favour of the employee.

AEW took the verdict of the court as a learning point. The company reviewed the entire appraisal system and redesigned the form to assess the employee's performance in a more efficient way.

In the year 2004, the company modernized its plants and machinery by purchasing some computer numerical control (CNC) machines, horizontal machining centers, and vertical machining centers. Some operators were selected from the existing workforce and were trained by the manufacturers of the machines. The period of training was considerably long and ranged from eight weeks to 14 weeks. The training programmes were intensive and the curriculum contained periodic evaluations. All the employees successfully completed the training programme. Thereafter, they were assigned tasks on the respective machines. Within two months, they were given two increments for working on sophisticated modern generation machines.

This decision was not viewed sportingly by a majority of the employees. The respective unions approached the management stating that the selection of employees to be trained to work on the modern machines was biased; the process of selection was based on nepotism and favouritism. The agitation affected the smooth working of the company. Later, the management also realized that the process of selecting employees was not transparent.

Learning points

- During appraisal, one performance feature should not influence other features or incidents.
- A company should establish performance standards of employees for the purpose of evaluation.
- Appraisers should maintain a chronicle of events with respect to the good work done, notable contributions, behaviours violating organizational norms, and acts that may jeopardize the image of the organization.
- There should be a standard documented system for ensuring transparency.

INTRODUCTION

The principal purpose of performance management is to develop and nurture talents in an organization. Job performance (also work performance or simply performance) was considered to be a special case of psychological measurement that provided a quantitative description of the extent to which individuals demonstrated certain characteristics, properties, or traits (Ghiselli 1964). Performance measurement involves the methods or procedures that quantitatively provide the extent to which employees demonstrate certain work behaviours and the result of those behaviours (Landy and Farr 1983). The work performance of a group of individuals employed in common jobs revealed considerable individual variation. McCormick and Tiffins (1980) reported that the ratio of the least productive worker's productivity to that of the most productive worker's varied from 1:2 to 1:3 for various kinds of productive jobs. Such a wide variation in work performance was attributable to multiple causes. Dwivedi (1990) defined performance appraisal as a continuous line function, which, if performed objectively, exerts motivational impacts on individuals.

Performance appraisal is different from performance management. This chapter contains discussions on the stakeholders of performance, facets of performance appraisal, methods of appraisal, performance appraisal problems, and need for establishing performance criteria, use of computer software, and related systems and subsystems.

PERFORMANCE

Performance is the ultimate outcome of any person's work, in the form of a product or service, which is essentially the most vital element of the tasks assigned to him/her to achieve a fraction of the business goals. It is also termed as the demonstration of work behaviours. The sum of performances of all the persons of a group is the group performance; that of a department is departmental performance; and that of an organization is organizational performance. Monitoring individual performances is vital to achieve organizational performance which is the business goal. Thus, it is the moral responsibility of every organizational stalwart to create a work environment in which people can contribute their maximum, both in quantitative and qualitative terms.

Performance has various dimensions such as output or result, input, time, quality, cost, and focus. These dimensions depend on the nature of the company, functional area, position in the organizational hierarchy, time, quality, and so forth. Some of these dimensions are presented in Box 8.1.

Box 8.1 Dimensions of performance

1. Output or result dimension refers to the ultimate outcomes from the efforts taken by a person.
2. Input dimension means the various types of resources used.
3. Time dimension is vital as any task should be achieved within a stipulated time.
4. Quality dimension emphasizes the conformance to specification.
5. Cost dimension refers to the expenditure associated with the various elements of performance.
6. Focus dimensions can be varied such as profit, sales volume, quantity, or new market. For example, the focus dimension for a sales director can be profit, market share, new areas, or any other parameter relevant to sales.

Various dimensions are interrelated and interdependent. Concentration on one dimension affects other dimensions. For example, quality of the output depends on the inputs, time utilized in processing, and technology employed which is associated with the cost dimension.

Apart from these dimensions, it is required to consider the business environment affecting performance and be familiar with the system theory.

SYSTEM THEORY AND HUMAN PERFORMANCE

The reign of owner–manager ended long before the economy was built upon mass consumption and mass production. Different operations within an organization were broken down so simply that novices could learn a job with little or no effort. However, this specialization, division of labour, emphasis on high speed machines, computer control machines, and flexible manufacturing systems, required a vast new pool of human resources. Tight discipline, close monitoring and controls, and constant pressure were the management tools of the early days. Performance systems never received attention; rather they were considered as a wasteful effort.

However, times have changed. The management of any organization tends to adopt a system theory and systematically approach any routine work. The system theory is an interdisciplinary theory about the nature of complex systems in nature, science, society, and organizations. A system is a set of interrelated processes and a process is a set of interrelated activities. Human performance management comprises a number of activities such as target setting, performance measurement, performance review, and performance management. Thus, system theory is applicable in performance management systems also.

People examine organizations from various standpoints. While on his rounds, an industrial engineer looks at the manufacturing systems, machine timing, queuing of in-process items, delays, and other things that anyone else belonging to another group might not notice. A production person looks at meeting the quantitative target; a quality control person takes account of conformance to the qualitative requirements; and an accountant looks for steps and procedures that ensure that material is being used as per the bill of material, and turns job cards to verify that wastages and rework costs were charged back to the originating department. The behavioural scientists study people and work groups; their mode of interaction, and other elements that indicate problems in the human side of the organization. Thus, different agencies view and judge the organization from different angles.

Most systems take something from the environment, change and transform it, and then release the changed product back to the environment. Thus, in order to manage performance, we have to study and examine practices followed by other organizations, identify the best practice, and benchmark them to enhance effectiveness.

> To deal with human performance problems, HR managers need a scientific technology, the characteristics of which are predictability, measurability, understandability, and controllability.

Behavioural scientists utilize a general system model to analyse human performance problems in organizations. A model is a useful tool, particularly for analysing and solving problems. In an organizational context, the model helps to analyse and predict what will happen when a change is made in one of the organizational elements. To deal with human performance problems, HR managers need a scientific technology, the characteristics of which are predictability, measurability, understandability, and controllability. Predictability refers to what will occur if a certain situation emerges in the work situation. Measurability follows predictability and emphasizes the need to measure the operational results or changes in employee behaviour. Understandability means identifying the cause-and-effect relationship between behavioural events that require measurement. Controllability is essentially the ability to change the organizational conditions or situations under which behaviour takes place and exercises to produce the outcomes we predict. Thus, system theory manifests its importance in performance management. Unless the influences are considered and steps are taken to control those, efforts to change human performance may not be effective.

The principal goal of any organization is to improve human performances and thereby, the organizational performance. Superior performance of both the people and the organization are of predominant importance. This topic will be discussed later in this chapter.

PERFORMANCE MANAGEMENT

Performance management is a process that enables the workforce by way of creation of an environment in which they can perform to the best of their abilities. Performance management begins with describing a job. Performance appraisal is often used as an alternate term to performance management. The process ends when an employee leaves an organization. A performance management system includes the following actions:

1. Developing clear job descriptions
2. Determining competency sets and selecting people through an appropriate selection process
3. Negotiating requirements and accomplishment-based performance standards, outcomes, and measures
4. Providing effective orientation, education, and training
5. Imparting on-going coaching and feedback
6. Conducting quarterly performance development discussions
7. Designing effective compensation management and recognition systems that reward people for their significant contributions
8. Providing promotional/career development opportunities for staff

STAKEHOLDERS IN THE PERFORMANCE SYSTEM

There are two stakeholders in the performance system—the employee and the organization. One must consider the viewpoints of both the stakeholders. One can look at the appraisal form from various views of the main stakeholders, employees, and organization, to be able to really appreciate the purposes of performance appraisal. The distinct views of the employees and the organization are exhibited in Box 8.2.

Box 8.2 Views of employees and organization

Employee viewpoints—From the employee viewpoint, the purpose of performance appraisal is manifold:

1. Tell me what you want me to do
2. Advise me how I should do that
3. Tell me how well I have done it
4. Help me improve my performance
5. Recognize my good performance
6. Reward me for doing well

Organizational viewpoint—From the organization's viewpoint, one of the most important reasons for having a system of performance appraisal is to establish and uphold the principle of accountability. Accountability refers to answerability. Accountability is the obligation of an individual, company, or institution to account for its activities, accept responsibility for them, and to disclose the results in a transparent manner; including the responsibility for money or other entrusted property.

PERFORMANCE PLANNING AND REVIEW

We all acknowledge the need for objective goal setting as an essential exercise for efficient performance management. Goal setting follows a top-down approach congruent with the organizational goal, getting cascaded down to the individual level. Performance planning and review at Jindal Steel and Power Limited (JSPL) is shown in Exhibit 8.1.

Exhibit 8.1 Performance planning and review

JSPL conducts performance management in the name of performance development and review (PDR) process. In the goal-setting phase, the officer and the employee hold a discussion to establish clear and specific performance expectations for the employee, for the year. In JSPL, PDR is a process of defining roles, discussing job requirements, answering employee's queries, and working together to reach a consensus on and commitment to performance standard. Obviously, the standard includes quantitative targets and qualitative requirements.

The primary objective of the PDR is setting the right direction. Discussions relating to goal setting thus aim to

1. Introduce the PDR process
2. Clarify the parameters on which the employee will be evaluated
3. Establish and agree upon performance expectations

Performance appraisal helps organizations to determine how employees can help contributing to achieve the goals of the organization.

Source: Best HR Practices, Steel Authority of India Limited, New Delhi, 2009.

PERFORMANCE APPRAISAL

Employees take efforts to accomplish the tasks assigned to them. They perform and hence their performance must be reviewed and appraised periodically to be improved. Performance appraisal is a system of reviewing and periodically evaluating an individual or team performance and giving feedback to the individual or team. Many organizations do not give feedback to the employees who have been apprised. In such cases, they treat the appraisal as an examination in their service life. Hence, appraisal system is not liked by the employees in these companies. However, performance appraisal, actually, is a vital and critical component type measurement, used by companies to achieve success.

Performance appraisal is a system of reviewing and periodically evaluating individual or team performance and giving feedback to the individual or team.

Corporate culture influences the process of appraising. It may either assist or hinder the process. A culture lacking from mutual trust cannot provide an environment conducive to smooth appraisal. An environment characterized by respect and trust for one another, information sharing, and socialization encourages high performance by individuals and teams. In such an environment, the appraisal system is welcomed. Let us now study the basic purposes of the appraisal system.

Appraisal—Basic Purposes

Performance appraisal refers to the evaluation or review of the accomplishment of a person in a specific period of time, say one year. Effective performance appraisal systems contain two basic systems operating in conjunction—an evaluation system and a feedback system.

Identifying the performance gap is the main objective of an evaluation system. This gap is considered to be the reason why performance does not meet the expected standard as set by the organization.

Similarly, the main aim of the feedback system is to inform individuals about their quality of work. The information flow, in this case, is two way. The management gives feedback to its employees and the employees give feedback to their appraisers.

These effective appraisal systems need to be structured to be effective. In the absence of any structured system, no one can be held accountable for anything, especially, in case anything goes wrong. Hence making employees accountable and responsible for their jobs is one of the tasks of appraisals. This system also helps in measuring an individual's performance vis-à-vis the organization's goals. Hence, one can say that this is an important system and must be present in every organization. The first recorded appraisal system in industry refers to Robert Owen's use of character books and blocks in his New Lanark Cotton Mills, in Scotland, around 1800 (Davis, 1980).

This system comprises an interview between the appraiser and an appraisee on a regular basis. In this interview, the performance of the employees is examined along with his accomplishments, and fall backs. It is a great way of assessing every employee and working towards their improvements.

Performance appraisals are also essential for career and succession planning. They are important for motivating, and attitude building of the employee. In some cases, behaviour modifications foster relationships between employees and management.

Appraisal is not daunting and time-consuming; it is an essential requirement of an organization. The process is seen as a difficult administrative chore and emotionally challenging. It is an important system for the human resource department, as it relies on evaluation results in determining the soundness of such developmental decision, which have a direct impact on the business surpluses.

Performance appraisal system, if properly structured, can achieve and contribute a lot to the organization. Appraisal is a tool of measuring performance; it should be objective and transparent for short, medium, and long terms. The purposes include the following:

1. Clarifying, defining, redefining priorities, and objectives
2. Motivating employees through acknowledging their achievement and sharing feedback
3. Guiding employees towards achieving their aims and targets
4. Identifying training needs and learning desires—assessment and agreement
5. Identification of personal strengths (including hidden strengths) and weaknesses
6. Career and succession planning—personal and organizational
7. Team roles clarification and team building
8. Appraisee and appraiser mutual awareness, understanding, and relationship
9. Resolving confusions and misunderstandings

The objective of performance appraisal is to align responsibility and accountability of all employees at every organizational level.

10. Reinforcing and cascading organizational philosophies, values, aims, objectives, goals, strategies, priorities, etc
11. Delegating additional responsibilities, employee growth, and development
12. Coaching, mentoring, counseling, and feedback
13. Managers' development enabling them to conduct appraisals objectively

The format of an annual performance appraisal and the format of apprising officers of middle management level are given in Appendix 8.1. Part 1 includes data about what needs to be appraised. Part 2 contains duties, targets/objectives (targeted and achieved), shortcomings, surpassing the target, and mandatory disclosure of immovable property.

Job performance appraisals, in whatever form, are vital for managing the performance of people and organizations.

Performance Appraisal—A Process Approach

Performance appraisal, as a process, encompasses activities such as preparing, informing, planning the venue, layout, introduction, review and measure, formulating action plan, and extending managerial support. Refer to Figure 8.1.

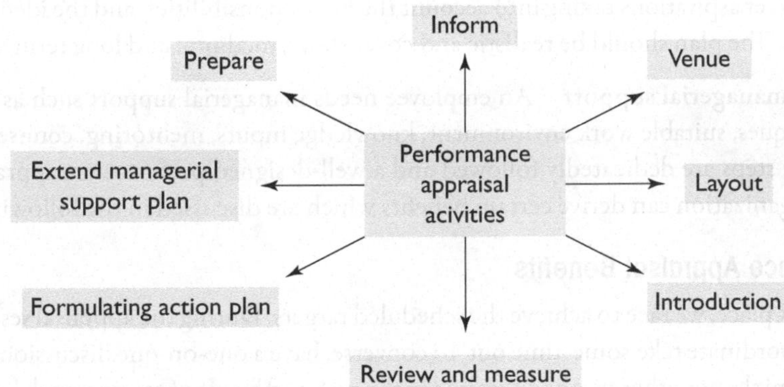

Fig. 8.1 Performance appraisal activities

Prepare Collate all the material, including a list of mutually-agreed tasks, current job description and records of performances, achievements, incidents, previous performance appraisal documents etc., and whatever material pertaining to performance and achievement. Remember that appraisals should focus on helping the 'whole person' to grow and attain fulfillment aimed at getting a 'total quality person.' Appraisals are not just about job performance and job skills training; they can go beyond the organizational boundary. One can get to know their good attributes outside of their normal work. People's natural talents and passions are often of significant use in the work place. Hence, these appraisals can become very useful.

> Appraisals are not just about job performance and job skills training; they can go beyond the organizational boundary.

Inform It is important for the management to give prior information to the appraisees. They should be informed about the suitable time and place and be allowed to gather all relevant data which can show records of their performance. In case the appraiser wants to follow a different order of discussion, appraisees must be informed.

Venue Plan a suitable venue, which is private and free from interruptions, where you and the appraisee can interact.

Layout You must create a relaxed situation, preferably at a meeting table or in easy chairs, sit at an angle to each other, at 90-degrees ideally, avoid face to face interaction, as it is very often treated as confrontational. Avoid sitting on your (boss's) chair with the appraisee sitting humbly on the other side of the desk.

Introduction Start with a formal introduction, offer a smile, be warm and friendly, and open with a positive statement. Enquire about his hobbies, areas of interest, and discuss the same. For example, you may discuss about a recently-concluded one-day international match if the appraisee is interested in cricket. It would be a good practice if you forecast the approximate length of the session.

Review and measure It is important for the appraiser to remember to review activities, objectives, and achievements of an individual, but not review the person. It is important for him not to be biased and be objective to the extent possible. This can be achieved by the manager if he concentrates on hard facts and figures, objective evidences, and avoids any guess work.

Formulating action plan You must formulate an action plan in consultation with the appraisee to fulfil his career aspirations taking into account the job responsibilities, and the identified strengths and weaknesses. The plan should be realistic and cover short, medium, and long term aspects.

Extended managerial support An employee needs managerial support such as aids to work, tools and techniques, suitable work environment, knowledge inputs, mentoring, counseling etc.

If these steps are dedicatedly followed and a well-designed performance appraisal system is used, then an organization can derive certain benefits which are discussed in the following section.

Performance Appraisal Benefits

In our work place, we race to achieve the scheduled targets. During the appraisal session, the supervisor and the subordinate take some 'time out' to converse, have a one-on-one discussion of important work issues that might not otherwise be addressed in the rush and bustle of routine work life. They can identify and correct the existing problems, which would lead to better future performances. Subordinates get uninterrupted access to their supervisor, an opportunity when they can vent out other related problems too, and hence, become very useful. During the appraisal session, the superior identifies the strengths and weaknesses of the appraisee. Recognition from the senior motivates the juniors. Similarly, weaknesses, if logically and convincingly expressed, enables the subordinates to accept them sportingly, and work towards improving them that would result in organizational gain.

Employees feel valued during appraisal; the appraisal program indicates to the employees that the organization is genuinely interested in their individual performance and development. Only this can have a positive influence on the individual's sense of worth, commitment, and belonging. Some organizations follow the documented procedure on 'training need identification'. However, the employee shortcomings identified during the appraisal session is the best way. This material can be used for designing training sessions too.

> Appraisal data can be gainfully utilized to monitor the success of the organization's recruitment, selection, and induction practices, and monitoring the effectiveness of changes in recruitment strategies.

Appraisal data can also be gainfully utilized to monitor the success of the organization's recruitment, selection, and induction practices. For example, the performances of the employees hired in the recent past can be tracked to discover any loopholes in the job specification, use of selection tools, coverage in induction methods, etc. The appraisal data further facilitates monitoring the effectiveness of changes in recruitment strategies. By analysing the yearly data related to new recruits, and applying vigorous analysis, it is possible to assess whether the general quality of the workforce is improving, staying steady, or declining with regards to the organizational needs.

Employees very often take the appraisal system as dehumanizing, demoralizing, and as a source of anxiety and distress. In order to do away with the negative feelings, management should instruct the appraisers to evaluate subordinates in a friendly and non-threatening manner, and highlight the benefits of appraisal system.

In summary, the benefits of performance appraisal are as follows:

1. One-on-one discussion on important work issues
2. Identifies and corrects existing problems
3. Better future performances
4. Psychological closeness
5. Motivates and satisfies juniors
6. Employees feel valued
7. Enhances employee's sense of worth, commitment, and belonging
8. Reduces absenteeism and turnover rates
9. Identifies training need for specific outcomes
10. Facilitates training need identification
11. Helps create a database on training and development need
12. Monitoring recruitment, selection, and induction practices
13. Helps in identifying loopholes in the job specification, use of selection tools, etc.
14. Helps to analyse the effectiveness of changes in recruitment strategies

Performance Appraisal Methods

The performance appraisal system has undergone a sea change. The performance appraisal systems refer to the systems that assess, evaluate, or review the performances of individuals with the ultimate aim of managing their performances.

The following are the various performance appraisal methods:

1. Management by objective (MBO)
2. 360-degree or multi-source assessment feedback system (MAFS)
3. Business scorecard (BSC)
4. Behaviourally-anchored rating scale (BARS)
5. Ranking (simple ranking, alternation ranking, and paired comparison ranking) methods
6. Forced distribution method
7. Annual confidential method

These methods are dealt with in the following sections.

Management by Objective

MBO covers a wide spectrum of thoughts. MBO can be applied to manage the national government, organization, or for personal development goals. Everyone is considered correct. The variation in perception about MBO is different as it can encompass any goal-setting procedure, from a highly structured corporate profit-target system to an individual's unstructured career plan.

There may be elephantine variations in the MBO systems. An MBO may be designed for just one sub-unit of a strategic business unit (SBU), for the whole SBU, or even for the whole organization. Emphasis can be laid on corporate planning, profit enhancing, individual motivation, and the like. Managers may also opt for different approaches.

MBO is 'a system of management whereby the superior and subordinate jointly identify the objectives, define individuals' major areas of responsibility in terms of results expected, and use these objectives and expected results as guides for operating the unit and assessing the contribution of each of its members' (Odiorne 1965).

Odiorne's definition may be examined for better understanding of MBO. Firstly, he points out that MBO is a system of management, an overall framework used to guide the organizational unit and outline its direction. Then, he points out that, 'the superior and subordinate jointly identify the objectives'; in other words, Odiorne has hinted that MBO is a participative management procedure that requires commitment and cooperation. Thirdly, the definition deals with identifying the results that are expected; thus, an MBO concentrates on the output of the organization, and evaluates people by assessing their contribution to this output.

Management by Objective—The Process

To understand the application of the MBO process, it is necessary to consider the parts of the process. MBO has three pillars: organizational objective setting, manager objective setting, and objective review.

Organizational objective setting The objectives are (a) to provide direction to the entire organization, and (b) to provide guidelines for junior level managers to formulate their objectives. As a result of this organizational objective-setting step, for example, air force managers should realize that a mission statement is a goal that defines the continuing purpose of air force organization. On the contrary, it is important to keep in mind that mission statements do not define the methods of accomplishing the goal stated. MBO helps in formulating these specific methods that are necessary to accomplish the mission.

Manager objective setting Each individual manager, of any unit or sub-unit in the organization, must know how to determine the objectives for his subordinates. This procedure takes place in three general steps—identifying key result areas, writing objectives, and negotiating with the boss.

First, the manager must identify the key result areas of responsibility assigned to his unit. In other words, just as the CEO reviews the whole organization in order to set organizational objectives, the manager needs to review his part of the organization in order to set his objectives. It is important for the individual office or shop managers to identify and lay emphasis on the areas of his unit where most of the results are obtained. In most of the cases, people find that 20 percent of their area of responsibility produces around 80 percent of their result.

Based on the area of responsibility identified, a manager can sit down and write his objectives. The criteria to be remembered while finalizing the objectives are that they should be specific, measurable, realistic, and result-oriented

Thereafter, the manager, with his written objectives, needs to enter the participative management phase of this technique, where he decides on his subordinate's objectives, with their consent.

> MBO has three pillars: organization objective setting, manager objective setting, and objective review.

Objective review A thorough review is conducted to manage the objectives by both the superior and subordinate officers. The subordinate manager bears the responsibility of managing this process. The process can only be interrupted, if

> Two types of objective reviews are
> 1. Intermediate review
> 2. Final review

both agree. In other words, MBO requires that each individual has the freedom to perform a well-defined task without interference.

There are two types of objective reviews that are carried out—intermediate review and final review. The purpose of the intermediate review is to determine the progress and identify the problems that emerge in the way of accomplishing objectives. The result of this intermediate session should be either to agree on a revised plan that resolves the blockage of objective accomplishment or to change the objectives.

The purpose of the final review is to evaluate the accomplishment of the preset objectives, that is, to find out the objectives that have been accomplished the whole year. This also helps in finalizing the objectives for the next year.

In addition to the three pillars discussed above, MBO programmes comprise six elements—commitment to the programme, top-level goal setting, individual goals, participation, autonomy, and performance review.

Commitment to the programme At the organizational level, managers must be committed to achieve personal and organizational objectives, and to the MBO process for programme effectiveness. Establishing congruency between personal objectives and organizational objectives are desired and essential.

Top-level goal setting This follows a top-down approach. The MBO programmes are finalized with the top managers who determine the unit strategy and set preliminary goals. These resemble the annual objectives in their content and terms. Some examples of these goals are—'No increase in overhead in the year 2010', 'To capture the new market (location)", and 'a 5per cent increase in profit in the next quarter'. Managers and their junior colleagues get a clear idea about the expectation of the top management, and accomplishment of the tasks becomes unambiguous.

Individual goals In an effective MBO programme, each manager and subordinate has his/her clearly defined objectives. The individual objectives are set in consultation with the person. Thus, the objectives (measurable) are realistic and achievable. The manager, however, helps the subordinates to 'raise their sights' toward higher objectives.

Participation The participation of subordinates varies from one organization to the other. While in some organization, the objectives are set in the presence of the subordinates; in some other organization, they are involved in the decision-making process. Yet, in some organizations, employees are completely free to set their individual objectives.

Autonomy in implementation of plans Employees get enough opportunities and a wide range of discretion to achieve the objectives. They are free, considering the constraints and resource availability, to develop, and implement programmes to achieve the organizational goals.

> Commitment to the programme, top-level goal setting, individual goals, participation, autonomy, and performance review are the six elements of MBO.

Performance review Performance needs to be reviewed objectively. Managers and their junior colleagues must meet for the review. During the review, they should discuss the problems that exist and methods of resolving them. The discussion must also include necessary modification of the objectives for the next period. The objectives and goals should be formulated in measurable terms. This facilitates managers to quantify the performance objectively.

All objectives must be measurable. Two examples are provided in Table 8.1 to understand how to formulate annual objectives in measurable terms.

Table 8.1 Examples of measurable objectives

Deficient or wrong objective	Measurable objective
1. To improve the quality of training programmes	(a) To adhere to course calendar (minimum 95 per cent achievement) (b) To provide training, for minimum 10 man-days, to 20 per cent employees of each department (c) To enhance the participant satisfaction by 3 per cent
2. To improve the morale of the divisions (plant, department, sections, and offices)	To reduce turnover (absenteeism, rejections, accidents, labour unrest, etc.) among salespersons by 5 per cent within three months. (Low morale bears causal relation with absenteeism, rejections, accidents, labour unrest, etc.)

MULTI-SOURCE ASSESSMENT AND FEEDBACK SYSTEM

Q 7 Multi-source assessment and feedback system (MAFS) is alternatively known as '360-degree feedback' or 'multi-raters appraisal system'. It is a long felt need by organizations. In this system, one person is assessed by his immediate superior, internal and external customers, suppliers, colleagues, seniors of cross-functional areas, and immediate subordinates. The all-round capability of a person can only be judged if the views of all the persons who are regularly interacting with him are gathered. MAFS enables the multiple raters to measure behaviours critical to performance using questionnaires designed by HRD department. External consultants are generally engaged to prepare the summary to eliminate any sort of any sort of bias.

In summary, the objectives include identifying developmental needs, generating data to serve as a more objective basis, reinforce change management efforts, buttress organizational effective dimensions and TQM efforts, customer focus, flat structure, quality improvement programmes, decision process changes, performance-linked pay or rewards, aligning individual and group goals with organizational vision, values, goals, culture building, leadership development and team building, potential appraisal and development, career planning and development, succession planning and development, role clarity and increased accountabilities, planning internal customer satisfaction improvement measures, etc.

Multi-source assessment and feedback system have multiple advantages over the traditional system as the spectrum of opinions received is broad as both internal and external customers offer feedback in structured questionnaires. The commitment of the top management of the organization to develop competencies on a continuous basis, and the willingness of top management to invest time, giving effort in developing subordinates to give feedback of seniors, making the organization free from politics, encouraging working in teams, making the organization value driven, and taking the number of HRD mechanisms seriously, are some essential prerequisites.

Philips Electronics India is one of the organizations using 360-degree appraisal, in addition to development centers, engagement surveys, and 4D surveys for their high-potential and senior managers in their performance management practices.

Implementation of the system needs the readiness of the candidate, which can be ascertained through the use of certain indicators. Before introducing 360-degree feedback system, one must address the benefits of the system to the employees. MFAS has many value orientations and is essential to improve self-esteem, in addition to how others view the appraisee. You will study all the topics in detail in Chapter 10.

Balanced Scorecard

Robert Kaplan and David Norton propounded the concept of balanced scorecard (BSC), and published a paper titled, 'Using the Balanced Scorecard as a Strategic Management System' in 1996. Since then, BSC has gone through an evolutionary change from performance measure ment to performance management. BSC has now become a globally recognized best practice for strategic management.

BSC suggests that we view the organization from the following four perspectives:

1. Learning and growth perspective
2. Business process perspective
3. Customer perspective
4. Financial perspective

Balanced scorecard suggests viewing the organization from four perspectives:
1. The learning and growth perspective
2. The business process perspective
3. The customer perspective
4. The financial perspective

Then, we need to develop metrics, collect data, and analyse it relative to each of these perspectives.

Learning and growth perspective This perspective highlights the employee training and corporate cultural attitudes related to improvement of both individual and the corporate scenario. In a knowledge organization, people are the only repository of knowledge and hence, the main resource. In the current business climate characterized by rapid technological change, it is becoming necessary for knowledge workers to be in a continuous learning mode. In knowledge organizations, both learning and growth contribute to the essential foundation for success.

Business process perspective This refers to internal business processes. Different metrics based on this perspective allows the managers to ascertain how well the business is running. These metrics must be carefully developed by those who are well acquainted with the processes and the unique business missions. External consultants cannot develop the business metrics.

Customer perspective This emphasizes the increasing realization of the importance of customer focus and customer satisfaction in today's management philosophy. A decrease in customer satisfaction is a leading indicator of future decline, even if the current financial picture may look good. The prime aspect of any business is whether its products and services conform to customer requirements.

Financial perspective This lays emphasis on timely and accurate funding data as top priority. However, Kaplan and Norton do not disregard the traditional need for financial data. Managers must do whatever necessary to provide the funding data. Financial measures are outcomes that represent the executive's success at achieving strategic performance goals.

Human resource can significantly contribute to the four perspectives of BSC. In the context of human resource initiatives, the learning and growth perspective encompasses hiring, training, developing, engaging, and retaining employees; the business process perspective needs design of business metrics to measure and promote the business. From the customer's perspective, the HR initiatives need customer relationship management, development of mechanisms to measure and enhance customer satisfaction; and optimal use of returns on investments to promote customer relationship.

BEHAVIOURALLY ANCHORED RATING SCALE

Behaviourally anchored rating scales (BARS), also called behavioural expectation scales, is extensively used to record and report performances. BARS is a method that combines elements of the traditional rating scales and critical incidents methods. BARS has been so named as it anchors behaviours and the scale represents a range of descriptive statements of behaviour varying from the least to most effective one.

BARS have the following features:

1. Area of performance to be evaluated is identified and defined by the users of the scales. The raters who will actually use the scales are actively involved in the development process.
2. The scales are anchored by description of actual job behaviours that immediate supervisor agree on and represent specific levels of performance. The result is a set of rating scales in which both dimensions and anchors are precisely defined.
3. All dimensions of performance to be evaluated are strictly based on observable or overt behaviours that are relevant to the job being evaluated, since BARS is tailor made for the job.

There are certain steps to be followed in order to construct BARS.

1. Examples of effective and ineffective behaviours related to job must be collected from people with knowledge of job.
2. These behaviours have to be converted into performance dimensions.
3. A group of raters are asked to reclassify the incidents. At this stage, only those incidents are accepted in which a minimum of 75per cent of the raters agree. The remaining observations are discarded as being too subjective.
4. These incidents are rated on a scale of 1 to 9.
5. Finally about six to seven critical incidents (incidents that demand requisite knowledge, skills, personal attributes, and are mainly responsible for the desired outcome) for each performance dimension must be picked up by observing the continuing duties and targets set for the job holder.

BARS is considered by far the best method used for performance appraisal. Some of its advantages are listed here.

Advantages of BARS

Conducting appraisals using BARS is time consuming. However, it has many advantages. Dessler and Varkkey (2009) mention five advantages of BARS.

1. *A more accurate gauge*—BARS is developed by people who know and perform the job and are familiar with the job requirements better than anyone else. They produce a good gauge of job performance.
2. *Clearer standard*—the critical incidents along the scale makes it clear as to what to look for in terms of superior performance, average performance, and so forth.
3. *Feedback*—appraisees can be convincingly explained about his/her ratings with the help of the critical incidents.
4. *Independent dimensions*—performance dimensions should be independent and mutually exclusive, but collectively exhaustive. Systematic clustering of the critical incidents into five or six performance dimensions helps them to be independent of one another.
5. *Consistency*—evaluations based on BARS seem to be relatively reliable. This helps in maintaining consistency in the appraisals of the same person by different raters.

RANKING METHODS

Ranking simply involves positioning of individuals from the highest to the lowest on a scale based on a predetermined definition of value or contribution. In some cases, you receive several reports from multiple assessors, which do not allow individuals to pinpoint their strengths or weaknesses for improvement. Simple ranking, alternation ranking, and paired comparison ranking are the three methods of ranking.

Simple Ranking

Of all the methods, simple or straight ranking method is one of the oldest and the simplest techniques of performance appraisal. In this method, the appraiser ranks the employees from the best to the poorest on the basis of their overall performance. It comes handy for a comparative evaluation.

Alternation Ranking

This method facilitates ranking employees from the best to the worst, based on a trait or a set of traits. As it is easier to differentiate between the best and the worst employees, alternation ranking method emerged as a very popular and widely adopted practice. For doing this, the following steps are used:

1. Deciding the characteristics on the basis of the ranking
2. Preparing a list subordinates to be rated
3. Deleting the names of those subordinates who cannot be considered
4. Identifying the best and the worst from the subordinates remaining in the list
5. Crossing out their names from the list
6. Identifying the best and the worst from the remaining subordinates
7. Repeating steps 5 and 6 till all the subordinates are exhausted

Generally, two simple formats are used for this ranking as shown in Tables 8.2 and 8.3.

Table 8.2 List of employees and designation

Alternation ranking method List of employees and designation	
Department:	Gang/Group:
1.	
2.	
3.	
...	...
n	

Table 8.3 List of ranked employees

Alternation ranking method	
Department:	Gang:
1.	
2.	
3.	
...	...
n	

Paired Comparison

Paired comparison method is a precise method of ranking employees. This method is a good way of weighing up the relative importance of employees for each trait pertaining to the quantity or quality of work. Each employee is compared against the remaining employees for a particular trait. Refer to Figure 8.2.

	Employee rated					
Rating when compared to	A Rama	B Hari	C Jadu	D Madhu	E Rishi	F Trisa
A (Rama)	X	+	+	-	+	+
B (Hari)	-	X	+	+	-	+
C (Jadu)	-	-	X	-	+	-
D (Madhu)	+	-	+	X	+	-
E (Rishi)	-	+	-	-	X	-
F (Trisa)	-	-	+	+	+	X
	1	2	4	2	4	2
Note: + indicates 'better than' and - indicates 'worse than'						

FIG. 8.2 Paired comparison method for the trait 'integrity'

Forced Distribution

Forced distribution or ranking is a method of performance appraisal to group employees in the order of forced distribution. The raters assign employees with a limited number of groups or categories such as 'best performer', 'moderate performer', and 'poor performer'. For example, the distribution is requested with 10 or 20 per cent in the top category, 70 or 80 per cent in the middle, and 10 per cent in the bottom. The distribution is done by the organization, based on the policy in their company. The distribution might be 20:70:10, 10:70:20, or 15:75:10. The underperformers categorized in the lowest group get the time and opportunity to improve.

Due to the increased focus of linking pay with performance, the forced distribution method is gaining increasing popularity. Nowadays, prestigious firms such as General Electric, Microsoft, and JPMorgan are using this method. However, the system is criticized as it is unpopular with many managers. Some believe this method fosters cutthroat competition, damages morale, and generates mistrust of leadership. One reason for opposition this method is the suspicion of employees towards the raters. Employees also suspect that these rankings are a way for companies to rationalize firings more easily.

Annual Confidential

Many organizations, mainly government organizations, use this method while appraising the employees. In this system, a subordinate does not know what the superior has endorsed in the report. He comes to know about the adverse points, if any, when they are communicated to him. Obviously, blind faith is placed in the subjective evaluation of the superior. As the name indicates, the juniors are never discussed while appraising. This method is criticized as seniors can use this report as a tool to control. Moreover, seniors can always offer biased opinion as the report is 'confidential.'

COMPARISON OF APPRAISAL TOOLS

Each appraisal tool has its own advantages and disadvantages. Dessler and Varkkey (2009) have narrated the important advantages and disadvantages of the appraisal tools. These tools are compared and contrasted in Table 8.4.

Table 8.4 Comparison of the appraisal tools

Tool	Advantages	Disadvantages
Management by objective	Performance objectives are jointly framed by the superior and subordinate.	Consumes appreciable time
Multi-source feedback system	All parties having regular contacts including peers and juniors rate the appraisee	Demands preparedness Need top management commitment
Behaviourally anchored rating scale	Overcomes rating errors Accurate gauge and clearer standards Considers six or seven critical incidents	Time consuming
Alternation ranking method	Simple to make the ranks Avoids central tendency	May cause disagreement among employees; find bias of superiors
Forced distribution method	Ends up with predetermined number of people in each group	The appraisal results depend on the choice of cut off points
Annual confidential method	The appraisal process takes less time	Appraiser can give highly biased ratings Employees remain in darkness

PERFORMANCE REVIEW

Performance appraisal is a formal process where the reports are documented, and referred to for multiple purposes. The appraisal is generally done once in year. But employees need continuous open communication for their development. The annual appraisal process does not affect development. Managers should review performance at close intervals, say every week, and keep records of discussion in their personal diaries for follow up. Additionally, managers must point out any lapses as soon as possible to facilitate continuous open communication.

> Performance review is a formal process of reviewing an employee's performance at frequent intervals, may be everyday, aimed at improving performance.

Managers can also conduct performance reviews informally on a weekly basis. This practice provides excellent opportunity for both the parties to freely exchange ideas. When managers follow this practice, performance review is viewed as a formal process about an employee's performance aimed at improving performance. Performance review facilitates to detect any error or omission in the appraisal, or an employee may disagree with the evaluation and want to challenge. Continuous employee performance documentation is vitally important for error-free performance appraisal.

Superior Performance

As discussed earlier, organizations look for superior performance of employees, thereby, to enhance organizational performance. Superior performance can be claimed through objective goal setting. Guidelines to setting specific targets, measurable targets, and time-bound targets are discussed.

SETTING GOALS

Q 6 Setting goals for self, a team member, or the team as a whole, needs experience, maturity, and pragmatism. If the goals are specific and the roles are clear and unambiguous, members can perform better. Specific goals lead to higher performance. Each goal must be split into its elements and time should be allotted. Completion of each element must be closely monitored.

Consider the objective of productivity enhancement. To achieve this objective, you are first required to consider the product range and logically segregate or stratify that. Consider a particular group of products, estimate the level to which you can enhance the output or reduce the resources required. You have to take into account all constraints you might encounter. The time you estimate to achieve an element or work package must be lesser than the time of the objective. This will enable you to initiate action if any element takes more time. In order to monitor the progress, you have to set the goal in measurable terms.

The goal should neither be more than attainable nor should it be less. If the goal is unattainable, the organization may run into losses. If the set goal exceeds the capacity of the team and remains unachieved, then it would simply lead to frustration of the leader and members, and the team's performance would become questionable. On the contrary, if it is less than the members' capacity, it would remain unutilized.

Moreover, a high-performing team with talented members prefers challenging tasks and innovative activities to derive intellectual joy. Such a team cannot prove itself, if a routine task is assigned. Targets must aim to produce superior performance, for which a considerable degree of stretch is required. But, they must also be realistic to motivate the manager. Highly unrealistic targets tend to demotivate members and also create a climate of 'fear of failure'.

Goals must be set in relevance to specific business objectives, making the target measurable, so that they can be accomplished within the time stipulated for them. Otherwise, even if the goal is completed within time, it will not lead to achieving a business objective. Targets must be measurable, even if not necessarily quantitative. A few examples of quantitative targets are as follows:

1. Improve sales by eight per cent in one year.
2. Achieve profit to the extent of ₹20 million in forthcoming financial year.
3. Improve yield to five per cent in one quarter.
4. Reduce costs by two per cent in six months.
5. Recruit 50 management trainees within four months.
6. Cut overtime to zero in two years.

Tables 8.5–8.7 provide guidelines for setting specific, measurable, and time-bound targets, respectively, in an automobile company.

Table 8.5 Guidelines for setting specific targets

How *not* to set targets	How to set targets
Initiate cost savings programmes.	Reduce transport rates by three per cent in the coming annual estimates.
Achieve 30 per cent market share for product 'roller bearing'.	Achieve average 'roller bearing' market share of 30 percent.
Liaise with information technology department to automate payroll.	Install the software on production, planning, and control in the second quarter; train people, and use in third quarter.
Conduct many staff training workshops.	Conduct quarterly workshops for staff focusing on selected parameters.

Table 8.6 Guidelines for setting measurable targets

How *not* to set targets	How to set targets
Successfully launch the product 'Front Axle' in second quarter.	Launch 'Front Axle' in second quarter and achieve exit value market share of five per cent.
Provide commercial support to business head.	Submit monthly commercial review docket within five working days.
Launch product 'Dove' if import rules are relaxed.	Launch product 'Dove' in second quarter (since imports are now allowed).
Sign a good welfare system with workers.	Sign a four-year welfare system before third quarter with 20 per cent productivity improvement.

Table 8.7 Guidelines for setting time-bound targets

How *not* to set targets	How to set targets
Increase market share to 20 per cent in product 'flange coupling'.	Increase exit market in product 'flange coupling' to 20 per cent by third quarter.
Advance target dates for accounts closing.	Complete accounts closing and audit by June 30 every year.
Reduce absenteeism in the factory.	Reduce absenteeism in the maintenance department from 12 per cent to eight per cent by October.

ACID TEST OF TARGET SETTING

'Acid test' refers to deciding the review mechanism at the beginning of the accounting period and periodic reviews of the targets. The acid test of target setting is—Will the deliverable and the level of target achievement be crystal clear at the end of the year to the manager to whom you report, the HR department, and to other relevant staff?

Exhibit 8.2 elucidates the review of targets (performance) and acceptance of the review mechanism at the beginning.

Exhibit 8.2 Acid test of target setting

Review of targets

1. Often, the most contentious and problematic aspect is review of performance.
2. Consideration of some of the common objections and pitfalls will help prepare the ground for success.
3. Advice: Start the exercise long before the review itself.

Acceptance of the review mechanism at the beginning

1. Clarify success criteria unambiguously
2. Description of the outcomes
3. Tendency to show leniency at the evaluation stage; this can be minimized if targets and success criteria are specific
4. Extra preparation needed especially when the target involves qualitative measures

USES OF PERFORMANCE APPRAISALS

Performance appraisal systems have undergone a sea change in the last two decades. There has been a realization that it is more important to focus on defining, planning, and managing performance than appraising it. However, the concept that has not changed is measuring performance and linking that with recognition and rewards. Most organizations use performance management system to monitor and improve employee performance, which is a welcome change. It is also said, 'stop appraising, start coaching'.

The need to develop employees is recognized and the development process has gained momentum. It is seldom said by managers that, 'we have good a performance management system.' Many surveys of Fortune 500 companies indicate a high degree of dissatisfaction with performance appraisal systems. It is presumed that the nature of performance is such that it can bring forth a satisfactory response from its users. Nevertheless, researchers pursue fundamental researches relating to performance appraisal too.

The use of performance appraisal in organizations is diverse. Empirical research in this area has been conducted to determine:

1. The extent to which performance appraisal is used in industry,
2. The extent to which appraisal data may be used for multiple and possibly conflicting uses within the same organization, and
3. The organizational correlation of these uses.

The uses of appraisal system are manifold and diverse. Organizations primarily use an appraisal system to improve individual performance, and in turn, organizational performance. Yet, the other purposes include linking appraisal with pay, identifying shortcomings, spotting special attributes, discovering and recording hidden potentials, etc. The problem associated with an appraisal plan is that a single plan cannot fulfil too many expectations. However, a properly designed system can help enhance employee performance and achieve organizational objectives. Performance appraisal reports are valuable for all human resource functional areas such as human resource planning, recruitment and selection, training and development, career planning and development, compensation management, employee relations, and assessment of employee potential.

Human resource planning Appraisal system helps in assessing an organization's human resources, and in utilizing data available in the human resource information system (HRIS). HR planning takes into consideration the credibility of employees for promotion. The performance appraisal reports help to discover shortage or excess manpower in relation to the targets. Management succession planning is a key concern for all organizations. A meticulously designed appraisal system depicts a profile of the management's human resource strengths and weaknesses, which contribute to HR planning.

Recruitment and selection Organizations always look out for manpower capable to perform and achieve the business goals. Manpower shows the capacity to achieve production target, and sustain productivity. Requirement of manpower by an organization depends on the workload, which varies from time to time. The requirement of manpower also needs periodic and meticulous planning. As the load of an organization fluctuates, at some point of time, it appears that the available manpower is adequate enough to achieve the target. Considering the consistency of the load, an organization goes for internal or external recruitment. Performance evaluation ratings also help in predicting the performance of job applicants in case of internal recruitment by way of promotions. The performance appraisal reports help to ensure the availability of human resource having the attributes essential to perform certain key tasks required in the organization. In order to make the recruitment and selection process perfect and to get the right man for the right job, an organization should model a competency framework discussed in Chapter 5. Mondy (2009) emphases that while validating selection tests, employee ratings may be used as a variable against which test scores are compared. Obviously, in such cases, the determination of the selection test's validity would depend on the accuracy of appraisal results.

Training and development Training is required to be imparted to fulfil specific skills or knowledge gaps, whereas development is generic in nature. Training refers to learning skills and knowledge for doing a particular job, and is job-centered in nature. Training helps to acquire specific operating skills among the workforce to accomplish the tasks successfully assigned to them. Training is concerned with maintaining and improving the current job performance. It produces short-term effects on the employee and to the organization. In the process of training, the trainer plays a vital role to impart the necessary knowledge and skills. On the contrary, development refers to the growth of an employee in all respects, and the overall growth cannot be attributed to any particular job, or task, or set of jobs or tasks. It shapes and moulds employee attitudes. Development is also considered to build up the competence of a career-oriented person. Development generates long-term effects both to the employee and the organization. However, an executive must have the urge to develop himself. Unless he is internally motivated for 'self-development', any amount of effort put in by the organization may be futile. More about training and development will be discussed in Chapter 9. Appraisers mention the training and development needs in their report, which becomes an input to the training system.

Career planning and development Career denotes all the jobs that are held in one's working life. Career planning is a process that fixes goals and lays down the path to meet these goals. The purpose of career planning is to provide continuity, order, and meaning to a person's work life, and hence, it is not an event or end in itself. It aims to integrate individual and organizational goals. Career counseling is a process of advising employees on setting career goals and assisting them find suitable career paths. Career development refers to the actions undertaken by a person to achieve the career goals. Dynamic appraisers mention about the requirement of career counseling and development.

Compensation management Presently, compensation management is a strategic issue. Employee compensation includes all forms of pay and rewards given to employees. Compensation includes both direct and indirect financial payments which employees receive during their employment period. Most organizations are linking compensation with performance. Performance appraisal results provide a basis for rational decisions with regard to pay, allowance, fringe benefits, and contingency rewards. Most managers believe that outstanding job performances must be rewarded. They believe that, 'the behaviours you reward are the behaviours you get' (Mondy 2009). Rewarding good performers contributing to achieving the business goals is the organizational and moral responsibility of top management and should be mentioned in the strategic plan. A company should develop and implement a system to objectively measure contributions of employees, design compensation programmes, and reward the most productive employees. The appraisal system manifests its importance in compensation programmes as well. Mondy (2009) highlights that according to a recent study, two-thirds of the companies use performance reviews to determine pay increases, and almost half of them use them to calculate bonuses.

Employee relations Employee relations encompass the set of work essential to maintain healthy employer–employee relationships that contribute to satisfactory productivity, motivation, and morale. It is concerned with preventing and resolving problems involving individuals that arise out of or affect work situations. In the prevailing business scenario, the management needs to be flexible to improve the employee relations.

Assessments of employee potential Employees are appraised based on their performances over a period. Past behaviours are considered as predictors of their future behaviours. Employees are promoted based on their performances and this enhances their job responsibilities. After promotion, a salesperson becomes a senior salesperson. At a later stage, he/she may become a sales manager responsible to look after a district. As a manager, he/she has to supervise many salespeople under his/her control. The tasks need a totally different set of competencies including man management skills. Thus, a successful salesperson may not be successful as a sales manager. In the arena of information technology, a data entry operator may not be successful as a junior programmer. The performance appraisal reports reflect only past behaviours which necessarily do not speak about the future behaviours. Organizations need to recognize these vital aspects, and should desist from promoting considering the excellent or very good reports. Mondy (2009) emphasizes that recognition of the problem has led some firms to separate the appraisal of performance, which focuses on past behaviours, from the assessment of potential, which is future-oriented.

All the functions mentioned in Figure 8.3 are HR functions and concentrating on them leads to improvement of the functions of both employees and the organization.

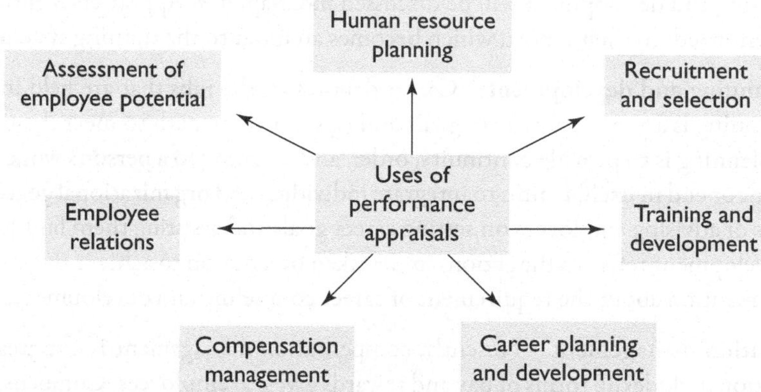

Fig. 8.3 Uses of performance appraisals

BUSINESS AND BALANCED SCORECARD

The performance of an organization cannot be accurately and precisely measured and evaluated only from the financial metrics, accounting ratios, profit and loss accounts, income expenditure accounts, balance sheet, etc. For any organization, there must be many non-financial performance measures that need proper consideration.

Managers and executives need a more 'balanced' view of the organizational performance. The balanced view can be provided by adding strategic non-financial performance measures to the traditional financial metrics. The concept of *business scorecard* (BSC) was originated by Robert Kaplan and David Norton as a performance measurement framework. The term *balanced scorecard* was coined in the early 1990s.

In short, the balanced scorecard is essentially a framework that attempts to collate measures across four areas as follows:

1. Financial
2. Internal process
3. Customer and (people) learning
4. Growth, rather than just the traditional financial measures

As the framework brings together measures across four areas, the term 'balanced' is used.

Uses of Balanced Scorecard

The scorecard is employed to understand the goal and strategy of the company, how they are measured, and how they influence critical indicators (activity or function which are critical to functioning of the organization). BSC is used by different companies for different purposes. For example, some companies use this to change behaviours of customer service representatives, some companies use to develop sales representative, and yet others use it for developing the production people. BSC is also used by the research and development department to analyse the business needs and research orientation.

The various uses of BSC are as follows:

1. Linking HRM activities to the business strategy of the company.
2. Evaluating the extent to which HRM functions facilitate the company to meet the strategic objectives.

Measures of HR practices relate to productivity, people, and process. Productivity measures encompass output per employee such as revenue per employee. For instance, for a sales department, BSC should be a measure of sales per employee in the sales department. Measuring people is a unique venture as it involves assessing employee behaviour, attitude, or knowledge.

Metrics of Balance Scorecard

BSC uses many metrics which facilitate measurement and evaluates parameters such as HR metrics, communications metrics, personal metrics, education metrics, customer relationship management metrics, marketing metrics, sales metrics, advertising metrics, etc. The elements under the purview of each metric are briefed.

Advertising metrics Web advertising, press advertising, TV advertising, outdoor advertising, cinema advertising, CD advertising, and any other innovative output.

Communication metrics Communication measurements, cell phones, internet access, and intranet usage.

CRM metrics Customer relationship, product knowledge management, customer profitability, customer profiling, customer value, customer conversion, customer loyalty, repeat customers, customer satisfaction, etc.

Education metrics Education and development, academic research, certification, university scorecard, school management, self assessment, etc.

HR metrics HR, HR hire, HR training, leadership development, motivating people, HR outsourcing, awards, retirement benefits, training pack, compensation management, reward and recognition system, etc.

Marketing metrics Marketing and personal relations in business, web investment, brand evaluation, presentation, marketing, direct mail, conference, word of mouth marketing, and exhibitions.

Personal metrics Productivity, innovations, time management, trade show, personal finance, leadership ability, etc.

Sales metrics Retail sales, sales, hypermarket, online retail and management.

Every company takes inputs from many functional areas, while designing a scorecard. The scorecard is designed following certain steps. Design of balanced scorecard is shown in Exhibit 8.3.

Exhibit 8.3 Design of a balanced scorecard

Preamble of the case study

This case deals with the design methodology of the balanced scorecard, choosing suitable parameters in each perspective, and measuring the parameters through an index. Colour coding norms were identified for each of the parameters. The dashboard was designed to give a bird's eye view of the departmental health to the top management. The templates were designed for calculation of all the parameters to give a practical insight on how the balanced scorecard could be put into operation.

Steps in designing a balanced scorecard

The design was completed in seven steps:

Step 1: Literature review for understanding the concept of balanced scorecard
Step 2: Understanding work and processes at the department
Step 3: Interviews with top management of the department for inputs on vision, mission, and strategic objectives
Step 4: Developing parameters for the scorecard with top management and leadership team. The process followed for the development of parameters was described in the flowchart. (Fig .8.1) The parameters have been categorized under the four perspectives: (a) financial, (b) customer, (c) internal process, and (d) learning and growth.

Financial perspective
1. Percentage variance from allocated budget
2. Staff HR utilization
3. Cost efficiency/process
4. Budget/employee
5. Percentage of expenses as per various heads

Customer perspective
1. Number of positive and negative customer feedback
2. Post-payment problems
3. Centre image
4. Customer relationship

Internal process
1. Competency synergy across activities in the department
2. Activity staffing process efficiency
3. Repetition of work
4. Time slip
5. Effort slip

Learning and growth
1. Number of people who have upgraded their technical skills
2. Number of training workshops on technological areas
3. Number of employees qualified for key jobs relative to anticipated requirement
4. Recognition for a job well done

Step 5: Developing colour coding norms through executive workshop with top management.

It is a snapshot for the management to look at the health of each of the measuring variables and then decide which variable needs immediate attention

(a) Black is an undefined parameter. The method to capture data needs to be determined.
(b) Orange is a parameter for not meeting the target and/or is high risk,
(c) Blue parameters are off target with moderate risk, or the parameter data is not available yet.
(d) Pink parameters are meeting the targets.

Step 6: Fixing the targets for all parameters
Step 7: Developing a balanced scorecard dashboard and measuring instruments

Templates for calculation of all the measuring variables were also worked out.

The dashboard with the list of parameters contained the following headings.

1. *Parameter:* In this column, the names of the parameters are mentioned.
2. *Definition*: In this column, the parameters are defined and described in detail. It also gives a view of the context in which a particular parameter is applied in the department.
3. *Empirical formula*: In this column, the formula for the calculation of the value of parameters is described.
4. *Target*: This column gives the target value of the parameters to be achieved
5. *Measuring frequency*: This column describes the time period in which a particular parameter has to be reviewed.
6. *Colour coding norm*: This indicates the health of a particular parameter at the time of its review.
7. *Template*: This describes the template for the calculation of the parameters with the help of some example numbers.
8. *Initiative*: This column indicates the initiative that the department should take to improve the health of a particular variable.
9. *Level*: This column explains the level or cluster at which the calculations will be done.

(*Contd*)

Exhibit 8.3 (Contd)

10. *Source of data collection*: This column contains the source in the department or in the organization from where the data will be collected.

Benefits of a balanced scorecard

The following outcomes could be derived from the design of the balanced scorecard:

1. The dashboard
2. The detailed table containing the parameters and their total description, which includes the formula, measuring frequency, colour coding norm, etc
3. The templates for the calculation of the parameters.

The dashboard contains all the parameters categorized into the four perspectives of the BSC and their health status.

The detailed table containing information on all the parameters completes the dashboard. It contains important information such as definition, formula, measuring frequency, colour coding norm, and source of data collection, level of drill down for data collection, targets and initiatives.

The templates were designed to reflect not only the data source but also the method of measurement that will go into the final calculation of the variable value.

Information table for balanced scorecard

The detailed table contains the parameters and their total description, includes the formula, measuring frequency, colour coding norm, etc. The columns for initiative are empty because most of the initiatives can be finalized only after one cycle of review were over. The information table for learning and growth perspective parameters is reproduced.

Information table for learning and growth perspective parameters

Parameter	Empirical formulae	Target	Measuring frequency	Colour coding	Level
Employee capability improvement	(0.4 × no of hours on lessons learnt) + (0.6 × no of hours on training workshops)		6 months	Pink—if final index is > = 0.9 Blue—if final index is between 0.7–0.9 Orange—otherwise	Department
Employee satisfaction	(0.3 × staff turnover rate rating) + (0.4 × perception of people) + (0.3 × employee suggestion)		6 months	Pink—if final index is >= 0.9 Blue—if final index is between 0.7–0.9 Orange—otherwise	Department

Source: Based on a paper titled, 'Process Mapping for the Finance and Business Administration and Design of the Balanced Scorecard,' submitted by Ashwini R. Reddy (graduate engineer trainee at Kirloskar Oil Engines Limited, Khadki, Pune) to the 47th National Convention at Pune from November 11 to 13, 2005, organized by Indian Institution of Industrial Engineering, Mumbai.

HRD SCORECARD

T. V. Rao (1999) introduced the concept of an HRD scorecard. Auditors assigned a series of four-letter grades in the scorecard on the basis of the HRD audit. In the audit report, the auditors assign letter grades for the four dimensions such as systems maturity, HRD competencies maturity, HRD culture maturity, and business linkages.

Systems maturity A department needs many structured systems. The training department must have procedures on training identification, training evaluation and validation, post-training impact measurements, etc. All the related procedures constitute the training system. Training is one of the many HRD mechanisms. The HRD system maturity indicates the extent to which the firm has mature (appropriate, well designed, and managed) systems in place.

HRD competencies maturity The HRD managers need to perform various functions to perform the tasks they need to do. Each task needs a few sets of competencies. The HRD competencies maturity indicates the extent to which the HRD managers have the required competencies to handle the HR function professionally and the extent to which line managers have the attitudes required to learn and grow. They also check HRD styles of top management which indicates the extent to which the top management styles are aligned to the HRD philosophy facilitate learning for all.

HRD culture maturity HRD initiatives significantly influence the organizational culture characterized by OCTAPACE (openness, confrontation, trust, authenticity, proaction, autonomy, collaboration, and experimentation). Also, HRD initiatives shape and mould the HRD culture in an organization and contribute to building the HRD climate. On the other hand, the HRD climate indicates the extent to which the firm has the required HRD culture. The maturity of HRD culture is a vital consideration of an HR scorecard.

Business linkages The purpose of any department is to contribute to achieving the business goals. Business linkages maturity indicates the extent to which the above three (systems, competencies, and culture) are aligned to the business goals or organizational objectives.

The letter grades range from an A+ to an F, where A+ indicates an extremely high level of maturity, and F indicates an extremely low or total lack of maturity. The HRD scorecard helps identify the areas that the firm needs to focus at a glance. Consider the scorecard of the following hypothetical company:

HRD scorecard			
Systems maturity	HRD competencies maturity	HRD culture maturity	Business linkages
B+	A	C	D

The scores clearly indicate that the firm has high competency levels of HR and line staff, and reasonably good HRD systems. However, the HRD culture has not yet been fully developed; or it may be that the impact of the HRD systems has not yet been evidenced. Nevertheless, the business linkages of all the systems are either weak or in the embryonic stage. The organization, therefore, should pay attention to ensure linkages of the HR systems with business goals. Obviously, the return on investment (ROI) on HR, in this case, is weak.

USE OF COMPUTER SOFTWARE

In the era of information technology, organizations extensively use computer software to capture appraisal data. The use of software reduces paperwork. Managers can customize the appraisal programmes. Customized software reflects the goals and values of the organization, enabling a more accurate and fair evaluation. The websites have the provision of viewing demo of the software. There are many softwares; some of which are displayed in Exhibit 8.4.

Exhibit 8.4 Use of computer software

1. KnowledgePoint (www.kpinfotech.com) delivers performance impact for intranet and web powered employee performance management. KnowledgePoint is a leading developer of knowledge-based human resource management solutions, and has released the intranet version of KnowledgePoint performance impact(TM). Based on new enterprise-class architecture, performance impact is designed to improve the performance review process and manage multiple facets of the employee lifecycle.
2. Halogen eAppraisal (www.halogensoftware.com) on performance appraisal helps organizations around the world take charge of their talent management practices and produces brilliant results. This software helps to conduct performance appraisals saving organizations from a dreaded task that yields a lot of paperwork, and little value for them. Further, the software transforms the appraisal process to deliver better business results and creates a more engaged and productive workforce.
   The website of Halogen eAppraisal software emphasizes that it lets the users easily (a) reduce the time and money spent in conducting and recording employee performance appraisals up to 85per cent, (b) improve the quality and completion rates of your employee appraisals, (c) align employee goals and development activities to business priorities, (d) easily track and manage the entire appraisal workflow from your HR control center, (e) free up employees, managers, HR, and IT to spend more time on strategic activities, (f) conduct appraisals your way, using your process, and employee appraisal forms, (g) create as many different appraisal forms and processes as you need, –all on your own, without vendor or IT involvement, and (h) reduce costs and improve employee engagement, retention, and overall performance.
3. Cornerstone Performance Appraisal Software by Cornerstone OnDemand (www.cornerstoneondemand.com/employee-performance-management). It provides comprehensive employee performance management tools, including automated performance reviews, SMART goals setting and alignment, competency assessments, and career development plans. Cornerstone Performance can be used to ensure that employee performance translates into organizational performance. Cornerstone also provides Team Manager which allows managers to optimize the daily performance of employees by automating important performance review and goal-setting. The software aligns key performances processes with departmental objectives and organizational goals, helps to identify and track high performing employees, increases performance review quality and reduce administrative costs, and cascade goals for increased opportunity.
4. TrakStar Professional by Promantek (www.promantek.com) is one of the most powerful and easy-to-use performance management system for businesses. Everything that is needed in an employee performance appraisal system is included at a very reasonable cost. The software provides a robust solution that offers unmatched value in the industry. Executives and HR professionals are achieving substantial bottom-line results. The software (a) is web-based, (b) helps to set well-defined expectations, goals, and directions, (c) facilitates creating competitive advantage, (d) assists to improve productivity, reduce costs, and save time.

PERFORMANCE APPRAISAL PROBLEMS

Performance appraisal is always flooded with criticisms, and is criticized in most of the organizations. Appraisees are generally unhappy with ratings of the appraisers. One of the reasons might be inadequate training of the raters or appraisers. Other reasons may be ascribed to appraiser discomfort, lack of objectivity, halo error, leniency or strictness, central tendency error, recent behaviour bias, personal bias (stereotyping), and manipulating the evaluation (Mondy 2009).

Appraiser discomfort It has been evidenced that many performance appraisal reports neither motivate the appraisees nor provide effective guidance to them. Rather, the reports create conflicts between the appraisees and appraisers that lead to dysfunctional organizational environment. It is also seen that appraisers do this job as an obligatory duty. But they should treat them as a tool for organizational development, derive pleasure, and love to do this. Organizational climate can effect this attitudinal change.

Lack of objectivity Some human characteristics or factors such as appearance, attitude, and personality cannot be measured as these are subjective in nature. Moreover, they have little to do with the performance of an employee. The subjectivity poses problem to the appraisal method, though it cannot be totally avoided. Mondy (2009) opines that employee appraisal based primarily on personal characteristics may place the evaluator and the company in untenable positions with the employee and equal employment opportunity guidelines. The firm may be hard-pressed to show that these factors are job-related.

Halo/Horn error During appraisal, one performance feature or incident often influences the other features or incidents. Generally, one positive feature results in high ratings of other features, thus making the overall rating very high. Halo errors mainly occur in immeasurable or subjective features such as obedience, sobriety, devotion, etc. Similarly, horn error occurs when the appraisee, considering one negative feature, rates other features or incidents at a lower level. In fact, no appraiser should mix up one feature with other features. Thus, generalization must be cautiously avoided.

Leniency or strictness Some appraisers, while appraising, compromise with strictness, and become very lenient and accordingly rate very high than the actual ranking. In fact, they intend to keep away from controversy. This sort of leniency makes an under performer equivalent to a good performer. Let us recall that, 'there is nothing so unequal as the equal treatment of unequals,' as 'different folks should get different strokes.' If the appraiser is lenient, he/she cannot identify some deficiencies that can otherwise be corrected after identification. Thus, leniency error leads to working with unidentified deficiencies and prohibiting a person from individual development.

Organizations cannot conduct training programmes for the underperformers for leniency errors committed by the appraisers. Again, some appraisers are unduly stricter than they should be. This results in strictness error, as appraisees get lower rankings than they should. Both leniency and strictness errors are chronic problems in performance appraisal. Many organizations follow a system of normalizing the ratings.

Central tendency error Many organizations design their appraisal forms seeking the appraisers to mark or tick against attributes. Generally, appraisers evaluate appraisees near the average or in the middle of the scale. Appraisers avoid controversy as employees are rated in the fully satisfactory range.

Recent behaviour bias Formal appraisal is conducted generally once in a year. During appraising the appraisers, remember any good work done, commendable behaviours exhibited, and remarkable contribution to the company only in the recent past. They cannot keep in mind the good or adverse behaviours exhibited in the beginning of the appraisal period, unless they are recorded. Recent behaviour bias is a natural happening as they flash in the memory easily; but it is difficult to recapitulate what happened in the distant past.

> Halo error occurs when the appraiser considering one positive performance feature of the appraisee rates other features high.

Personal bias (stereotyping) Similarities and dissimilarities between the appraiser and appraisee often influences the appraisal system. Pitfalls in the appraisal system occurs when gender, caste, creed, colour, race, and ethnicity of the appraisee influences the appraiser. Some appraisees may get favoured while someone else may not. Managers establish a high image about those who bear similarities, and rate them comparatively higher while the other group is rated lower than they should be. Mondy (2009) confirms that mild-mannered employees may be appraised more harshly because they do not seriously object to the results. But appraisers take care when they appraise out-spoken employees.

> Leniency error leads to working with unidentified deficiencies and prohibiting a person from individual development.

Manipulating the evaluation Nepotism and preferential treatment continue to influence the performance appraisal of employees. A supervisor having interest to promote or give a pay hike to a subordinate close to him can manipulate the entire appraisal. He rates the subordinate higher and gives high performance evaluation points/grades which the subordinate may not deserve at all. Similarly, the supervisor may not like another person who is argumentative, outspoken, and confronts often. In such cases, the supervisor evaluates him lower than the actual. If that person is close to an influential person and happens to be a member of any protected group, he exerts pressure and the smooth working of the department is disturbed. In either case, the system is distorted and the very purpose of performance appraisal remains unachieved. Mondy (2009) mentions a study in which it is revealed that more than 70 per cent of respondents opined that inflating or lowered ratings are 'unintentional'.

ESTABLISHING PERFORMANCE STANDARDS

Many organizations do not have established performance standards. The manager's appraisal is purely based on subjective concepts. In such cases, polite, submissive, and obedient employees get comparatively better reports than those who are truly excellent or very good but argumentative in their performances. To avoid such anomalies, organizations should identify performance criteria or standards to restore objectivity in the appraisal system. The most common criteria used in appraisal formats are trait, behaviour, competency, goal (target) achievement, and improvement potential.

Trait The common criteria used in evaluations include personality, keenness, and energy, initiative, tact, reliability, self-reliance, sobriety, attitude, appearance, inclination to accept changes, etc. The commonly-used characteristics or attributes are subjective and are difficult to define. They may also be unrelated to the task being performed. In such cases, inaccurate evaluations may occur and create legal problems for the organization as well (Mondy 2009). Traits such as adaptability, judgement, appearance, and attitude may be used when shown to be job related.

Behaviour Different tasks need different types of behaviours or competencies. A sales or a marketing director needs leadership skills such as involving and energizing members, encouraging teamwork, cooperating people, helping members, analysing problems, providing solutions, enhancing area of operation, etc. If the desired behaviours are exhibited by members, they must be recognized and rewarded such that they repeat same behaviours in the future. Such recognized behaviours should be included as performance criteria because these behaviours result in desired outcomes.

> Behaviours that are recognized and rewarded should be included as performance criteria because these behaviours result in desired outcomes.

Competency Competency is a bunch of related knowledge, skills, and attitudes that affects a major part of one's job that correlates with performance on the job, and can be measured against accepted standards, and improved through training and development. Competency set means a bundle of competencies in a particular category; for example, result-oriented competency comprises risk taking, decisiveness, business sense, energy, concern for excellence, tenacity, initiative, and customer orientation.

> Success in HR depends on competency and skills in five areas: strategic contribution, business knowledge, personal credibility, HR delivery, and HR technology.

Success in HR is dependent on competency and specific skills in the following five areas (Mondy 2007) (a) strategic contribution (connecting firms to their markets and quickly aligning employee behaviours with organizational needs), (b) business knowledge (knowing how businesses are run and translating this into action), (c) personal credibility (demonstrating measurable value; being part of an executive team), (d) HR delivery (providing efficient and effective service to customers in the areas of staffing, performance management, development; and evaluation), (e) HR technology (using technology and web-based means to deliver value to customers).

Goal achievement Many organizations consider the ends more important than the means. For organizations that consider the ends more important, an individual or a team should be able to achieve the slated outcomes. Also, the outcomes established by the organization should be within the control of the individual or the team. The nature of outcomes differs and is dependent on the level of employee. At upper levels, the goals generally deal with the strategy implementation, financial aspects, etc. At the lower levels, the outcomes might be meeting the quantitative targets, qualitative requirements, delivering according to the schedule, and so on. It is the responsibility of the supervising manager to help his/her juniors to achieve the goals and to develop them to achieve the specific goals. Both the senior and juniors should reach an agreement to the junior's goal for the forthcoming evaluation period. The supervising manager needs to provide both assistance and resources for the junior needs.

Improvement potential Performance appraisal is done based on the tasks assigned and the appraisal reports convey the qualities of the employees with reference to the task accomplishments. The reports never reflect anything about the future. At this juncture, firms should lay emphasis on the tasks or responsibilities likely to be assigned in future, the behaviours and outcomes needed, the competency sets essential to further the accomplishments, and develop employees to achieve the firms' goals. The process involves assessment of employee potential, which can be assessed using assessment centers. However, performance appraisal reports can also be used as an adjunct to the process.

ENSURING TRANSPARENCY

Q 8 Performance appraisal problems are manageable and can be achieved by way of ensuring transparency in the performance management system. Employees will have faith in the performance appraisal system, if transparency is maintained throughout the process. Details of the appraisal form should be made known to employees. Phillips Electronics India follows this practice. It percolates the targets achieved, targets set for the forthcoming period, performance and promotability ratings, development needs, assesses how an employee performs on values, competencies possessed and required, etc.

Schneider Electric India, in a joint venture with Tata in 1963, had implemented a system which the company is still following. The employees give comments about his/her performances which are reviewed by the manager (reporting officer), and manager's manager (the higher authority). Neither of the reviewers can modify the comments of the appraisee in the self-appraisal.

Sanghi Industries Ltd, having the world's largest lignite based cement plant at Sangipuram, Gujarat, allows the appraisee to see the ratings with comments of his/her immediate superior, head of department, peers, and also subordinates, if any. The company also allows an appraisee to view the ratings of his/her colleagues in the department. The access to view own and others' ratings makes the performance appraisal system transparent.

Q 10 TCG Lifesciences Ltd, one of the leading contract research organizations in India, with chemistry operations, is following a transparent appraisal system. The system includes enclosing a document in support of claims and comments by the appraisee and supervisor. The documentation system including critical incident records (CIR), makes the appraisal process transparent. Moreover, employees can access their appraisal form any time during their tenure in the organization.

The foremost need of making the appraisal system transparent is establishing the performance standards and specifying the documentation.

COMPARISON BETWEEN PERFORMANCE APPRAISAL AND PERFORMANCE MANAGEMENT

Agarwala (2007) has mentioned about the comparison of performance management and performance appraisal. There are certain characteristics such as types of objectives, types of performance measures, frequency, rating system, reward linkage, ownership, corporate alignment, focus of performance reviews, and questions asked. This is shown in Table 8.8.

Table 8.8 Comparison between performance appraisal and performance management

Characteristics	Performance management	Performance appraisal
Types of objectives	Emphasis on integrating organizational, team, and individual objectives	Individual objectives
Types of performance measures	Competency requirements as well as quantified measures	Quantitative and qualitative
Frequency	Continuous review with one or more formal reviews in a year	Annual appraisal
Rating system	Joint or participative process, ratings less common	Top down system, with ratings
Reward linkage	Does not have direct linkage to reward	Often linked to pay
Ownership	Owned by line management	Owned by human resource department
Corporate alignment	Integrated business driven system aimed at organizational and people development	Isolated system not linked to organizational goals
Focus of performance reviews	Focused on future	Focused on past
Questions asked	What can be done to help employees perform as effectively as possible?	How well was the work done?

RELATED SYSTEMS OR SUB-SYSTEMS

Performance management system has many other related systems or subsystems such as potential appraisal and assessment centre, career and succession planning, performance coaching and counseling, reward and compensation management, HR measurement and audit, which are briefly discussed in the following sections.

Potential Appraisal

Potential appraisal system is gaining increasing importance. The potential of an individual is assessed basically by the use of intuition. He is given a task of some other functional area. Then, his inclination to the work, devotion, and output is observed, measured, and/or evaluated. This is the basis of evaluation of potentiality and the undiscovered capabilities of the individual. Thus, the basic groundwork is done through an assessment centre approach. Potential appraisal will be discussed in detail in a succeeding chapter.

Assessment Centres

In recent times, organizations are investing in assessment centers, which map/diagnose competences. This, in turn, leads to job - person - organization fit and alignment to HR systems, which include talent management, recruitment and selection, retention, management development, and career and succession planning. American Telephone and Telegraph (AT&T) Company initiated the assessment center method in the year 1960 while promoting their line personnel to supervisory positions.

Assessment center is a procedural mechanism to identify the potential for growth. It is very often misperceived as a location. Assessment center is strictly a procedure (and not location) to evaluate employees for manpower planning and decisions. The procedure uses situational test to observe specific job behaviour. Assessment center procedure is used for suitability of a person for a specific job. As such, elements related to the job are simulated through a variety of tests. The assessors observe the behavioural disposition and make independent evaluation of the observation. This results in the identification of strengths and weaknesses of the attributes being studied. Assessment center, based on large bodies of academic researches, is treated as the most valid predictor of performance. It comprises a number of exercises such as group discussion; in tray; interview, simulation/role plays; and case studies/ analysis exercises.

Career and Succession Planning

Career planning, essentially, means helping the employees to plan their career, keeping in mind their capacities and aspirations. Career planning is a management technique to map out career movements and growth opportunities from the point of entry to the point of an employee's superannuating in skilled, highly skilled, supervisory, and managerial positions. A transparent organization does not keep the corporate growth plan secret from its workforce. In such organizations, the employees know the long-range plans and get help to prepare for the changes planned by the organization.

Succession planning is an ongoing process used by organizations to identify the necessary competencies required for significant positions. By doing so, an organization can develop and retain a talent pool of employees. This planning can prevent a generation gap and maintain continuity of leadership for all critical positions. Succession planning is an inescapable strategy, which spells out particular steps, to be followed to achieve an organization's missions and goals without any interruption. It is a plan that managers must follow, implement, and customize to the needs of any section, cost center, department, or the whole organization. The principal purpose of succession planning is to identify and develop people to replace current incumbents in significant positions for a variety of reasons such as superannuation, resignation, promotion, company diversification, and creation of new positions.

Performance Coaching

Performance coaching contributes to enhanced role performance. Coaching is collaborative, solution-focused, and result-oriented. It is a systematic process in which the coach facilitates the enhancement of work performance, sharing life experience that results in self-directed learning and personal growth of the learners, too. It is a popular means of professional development. The person being coached gets close attention, continuous feedback, and learns various methods of skill development. In an industrial organization, the master craftsman coaches his juniors or the trainees attached with him. Coaching is a focused conversation that facilitates learning and raises performance at work. The coach can be either a manager or an external consultant. The coach can help anyone, whoever wants to get better at his or her work. You can offer coaching

> Coaching is a focused conversation that facilitates learning and raises performance at work, and is a set of skills for managing employee performance to deliver results.

As a coach, a manager is required to perform the role of a transformational leader; one who challenges and develops the employees' skills, and abilities to achieve the best performance results.

in designated coaching sessions; many organizations use coaching as a style of management that takes place in a series of informal discussions between managers and their junior colleagues during performance review sessions.

In simple terms, coaching is a set of skills for managing employee performance to deliver results. As a coach, you are required to perform the role of a manager as a transforming organizational leader; as the one who challenges and develops the employees' skills and abilities to achieve the best performance results. Coaching is a valuable way of providing ongoing support for personal development plans. People enjoy participating in coaching, which is a popular and useful human resource development mechanism. The reasons for undertaking coaching, the methods used, and the results achieved are unique to every individual. It is a unique relationship designed and tailor-made in a way as to enhance the process of lifelong learning, effectiveness, and fulfillment. It provides support for other learning and development activities. A manager's task is simple—to get the job done and to develop his staff. Time and cost pressures limit the latter (letting the staff to develop and grow).

Coaching is an approach to management; enhancing the enabling capacity of a manager to help him discharge his roles effectively. As such, sharper attention is conferred on (a) focusing on goals rather than problems, (b) listening more than you talk, and (c) asking questions instead of giving advice or instructions.

Added to the above, coaching is meant for employee growth and development. There exists certain conditions on the part of the employee; the individual should be interested to develop himself, know the areas of his potential development, make a clear choice about the direction of growth, identify opportunities for development within or beyond the organization, make efforts to develop, and take help to get his progress reviewed, periodically. The management should create a positive and professional climate in the work place for the employees to progress and review their progresses in a non-threatening way. So, you should know the objectives, needs, and application area of coaching.

Objectives of Coaching

In the context of personal and organizational development, coaching has certain objectives. Any person has his own strengths and weaknesses, and the potential to contribute to achieving the organizational goals. You must be instrumental to facilitate your juniors to identify their inner potential. They should be able to acquire insight, develop problem-solving skills, understand the business environment better, enhance personal and interpersonal effectiveness, unearth the root causes behind a problem (the effect), generate alternatives, undertake techno-economic feasibility analysis, prioritize the alternatives, select the best alternative, develop an action plan, implement in the work area, visualize difficulties, and be prepared to face any anticipated problems. Juniors always try to progress but hindrances can always appear as roadblocks.

As their supervisor, you are required to review their progress, in a non-threatening manner, and help achieving various personal objectives. You have to provide them with an empathetic work atmosphere. You must share and discuss their tensions. You have to impart knowledge with regard to handling conflicts. You can now organize the coaching objectives as follows:

1. To help him to realize his potential as a manager while discharging his managerial responsibilities
2. To facilitate him to identify his weaknesses and strengths
3. To assist his to eliminate or reduce his weaknesses and enhance his strengths
4. To help him to better understand the environment
5. To provide him an opportunity to gain more insight and to develop problem-solving skills

6. To encourage him to set smart goals for himself for further improvement
7. To show him the way to increase his personal and interpersonal effectiveness
8. To review his progress, in a non-threatening way, such that he can achieve various objectives
9. To provide him an empathetic work atmosphere
10. To share success stories to develop him
11. To reduce his tension, concerns, and problems
12. To explain conflict resolution strategy and enhance his conflict handling skills

Coaching vs Other Developmental Tools

You must know how coaching differs from other forms of personal and professional development. If you ask yourself, 'what is coaching?,' you will get a series of explanations giving coaching a meaningful value highlighting the possible benefits. In fact, a lot many times, it is also misinterpreted as mentoring or counseling. You will evidence that the coaching jargon is very often used in a variety of professions to illustrate validity or spout and discharge old themes.

Counselling

Counselling refers to assisting, developing, and helping employees, workers, staff, and managers for their professional development. Counseling reduces the work role and stresses, and promotes quality of work life and, in turn, quality of life. The counsellor needs to build a trusting relationship with the counsellee, have warmth, and friendship. They need to contribute to the thought process of the counsellee and discuss about the solution to the problem with the ultimate aim to win the person in order to help him. Active listening, interest, compassion, acceptance, etc. are very much required to make the sessions fruitful, and the counseling process effective.

An employee should not be selected randomly for counseling. The supervisors should observe the counseling need through certain symptoms. Stress management intervention including stress and coping, coping strategies, and self-imposed behaviour modification methods are essential to prevent the employees from deterioration of mental and physical health. Counseling can go a long way in helping the employees to have better control over their lives, take their decisions wisely, and better discharge their responsibilities, and reduce the level of stress and anxiety.

Counseling of employees can have desirable consequences for the organization. It helps the organization when the employees know that the organization cares for them, and builds a sense of commitment with it. In other words, coping promotes job satisfaction, job involvement, and organizational commitment. It can prove to be of significant help to modify the behaviour of the employees, and more so, to reinforce achieving organizational goals too.

Reward and Compensation Management

At present, reward management is a tactical issue to keep the wheel of production moving. Organizational rewards include both intrinsic and extrinsic rewards. Organizations give a wide variety of financial rewards to employees depending on the contribution to the organization. Employee ownership, gain sharing, and profit sharing can all be useful practices for many organizations. The types of rewards that an organization offers to its employees play a crucial role in determining the level of motivation. The satisfaction that employees derive has an impact on their quantity and quality of output. Motivating one may demotivate several others. Rewards need tactful management. More about reward management will be discussed in a subsequent chapter.

Compensation management is a strategic issue. Employee compensation includes all form of pay and rewards given to employees. Direct financial payments include pay in the form of salary, wages, incentives, commissions, and bonuses. Indirect financial payments constitute pay in the form of insurances. Legal considerations in compensation management frequently use certain Acts such as: (a) Company Act, 1956 (sets the framework for remuneration of the top management of Indian companies), (b) Fair labour Standards Act, 1938 (provides minimum pay, maximum hours, overtime pay, and child labour protection. (This act has been amended many times, and covers most employees), (c) Equal Pay Act, 1963 (designed to ensure equal pay for women doing same work as men), (d) Social Security Act, 1935 (the amendment of the act provides for unemployment compensation for workers).

HR Measurement and Audit

Audit means verification of activities. Audit is intended for 'fact finding,' and not 'fault finding'. Human resource audit verifies and evaluates the HR activities in an organization with the purpose of improving those activities. An audit may be a part or full audit. Part audit refers to audit of some selected HR functions or some departments, whereas full audit means audit for the entire company. HR audit is pervasive and it envelops procurement function, development function, compensation function, maintenance function, and most importantly, integrating functions. HR measurement and audit will be discussed in a separate chapter.

HRD Audit as an Organizational Development Intervention

An organization invites auditors to audit the HRD system for the purpose of identifying loopholes in the system. The internal personnel cannot find the mistakes as it is established, implemented, and maintained by them. After auditing, the auditors submit the audit report highlighting the drawbacks in the system. The organization initiates corrective and preventive actions. These actions lead to organizational development (OD). Thus, HRD audit is a tool of organizational development, and an OD intervention technique.

HRD Audit Failures

HRD audits are organized for organizational development. But not all audits can fulfil the objectives of audit. The findings of the reports give scope for improvement. However, if the audit findings are not attended to and studied by the top management, the desired purpose of audit remains unachieved. The vital need is the commitment from the top management and initiative of the HRD manager. Customarily, the HRD audit team leader gives a presentation in front of the CEO, and other significant personalities. Unless they attend the presentation, they remain unaware of the shortcomings in the HRD practices, application of HRD mechanism, and measurement of analysis of the HRD outcome variables. This sort of apathy to HRD audit can make the initial initiatives futile which may amount to audit failure. In such situations, many times, auditors consider their sincere efforts as a waste of their time and energy.

PERFORMANCE MANAGEMENT PRACTICES

Having understood the performance system, we should now be acquainted with the performance management practices in India. The practices followed by some companies in manufacturing sectors in India (SAIL 2009) are discussed in Exhibit 8.5.

Exhibit 8.5 Performance management practices

Indian Oil Indian Oil Corporation Limited is India's largest commercial enterprise and the highest ranked Indian company in the prestigious Fortune 'global 500' listing. While planning for performance and goal setting, Indian Oil follows a top down approach where key result areas (KRAs) are cascaded down from the business scorecard with specific key performance indicators (KPIs). Indian Oil measures the indicators (HR metrics, communications metrics, education metrics, customer relationship management metrics, marketing metrics, sales metrics, etc) against time and gives specific weightages.

Honeywell Honeywell Turbo Technologies (India) Private Limited is a 100per cent subsidiary of Honeywell Technologies SARI, Switzerland, which is a part of Honeywell International Inc., USA. The company aligns the goals of individuals across the organization to the five Honeywell initiatives which include growth, productivity, cash, enablers, and people. In order to manage and develop performance, the 'growth file' is issued to all employees to maintain their performance. Employees keep track of their performance on a day to day basis, and record their performance and achievement in this growth file.

Moser Baer Headquartered in New Delhi, Moser Baer is one of India's leading technology companies that has developed cutting-edge technologies to become the world's second largest manufacturer of optical media. Moser Baer uses balanced scorecard approach and sets business goals on four perspectives—financial parameters, customer satisfaction, internal processes, and learning and development. The company derives the KRAs from organizational scorecard.

Tata Motors The company is India's largest public limited automobile company, and a leader in commercial vehicles in each segment, and ranks among the top three in passenger vehicles with winning products in the compact, midsize car, and utility vehicle segments. Tata Motors develops individual performance plans that are cascaded from the balance scorecard to the smallest work unit. The company does goal setting in the beginning of the financial year. The goal setting starts with company-level strategic plan which gets cascaded, and accordingly, the individual plans are prepared.

Schneider Electric India The company set foot in India through a joint venture with Tata in 1963, and became a private limited company in 1995. This company sets performance goals using human resource information system (HRIS). It is mandatory to include behavioural expectations based on Schneider values of POSE (passion, open, straightforward, and effective). These objectives are prioritized based on the business and departmental requirements, and the SMART objectives are required to mutually be agreed upon. The individual objectives are aligned with the functional/business unit objectives. The performance appraisal process is carried online. Performance objectives set up in People Soft are delivered using the HRIS. Managers create the performance documents in the system, and complete the performance evaluation online. Employees carry out self evaluation and comment on managers' evaluation.

Source: SAIL 2009

SUMMARY

The performance of the workforce is the ultimate need of any organization. Performance has various dimensions such as output or result, input, time, quality, cost, and focus dimensions. The principal purpose of performance management is to develop and nurture talents in an organization. Present day HR managers need a scientific technology to predict measure, understand, and control the employees. They also need to set goals objectively and then claim to get superior performance.

The organization and the employees are the two stakeholders of the performance system. Performance planning and review is essential for managing performance. Performance appraisal is a system of reviewing and evaluating individual or team performance periodically, and giving feedback to the individual or team. Appraisal data can be gainfully utilized to monitor the success of the organization's recruitment, selection, and induction practices, and monitoring the effectiveness of changes in recruitment strategies.

Various performance appraisal methods include management by objective (MBO), 360-degree or multi-source feedback system (MAFS), behaviourally-anchored rating scale (BARS), ranking (simple ranking, alternation ranking method, and paired comparison ranking) methods, forced distribution method, annual confidential method, etc. Performance appraisal reports are valuable for all human resource functional areas such as human resource planning, recruitment and selection, training and development, career planning and development, compensation management, employee relations, and assessment of employee potential. The balanced scorecard is employed to understand the goal and strategy of the company, how they are measured, and how they influenced the critical indicators.

Balance Scorecard uses many metrics such as HR metrics, communications metrics, personal metrics, education metrics, customer relationship management metrics, marketing metrics, sales metrics, advertising metrics, etc. The elements under the purview of each metric are briefed. Four dimensions of HRD scorecard are (a) systems maturity, (b) HRD competencies maturity, (c) HRD culture maturity, and (d) business linkages. Many organizations use computer software for online appraisal. Performance appraisal is always flooded with criticisms and problems which can be reduced by establishing performance criteria and making the system transparent. Performance appraisal and performance management are different. Performance management system has many related systems and subsystems.

KEY TERMS

Acid test refers to periodic reviews of the targets and deciding the review mechanism at the beginning of the accounting period.

Business scorecard is a strategic planning and management system that is used extensively in business and industry, government, and nonprofit organizations worldwide with the aim to align business activities to the vision and strategy of the organization.

Compensation includes all forms of pay and rewards, both direct financial and indirect financial payments, which employees receive during their employment period. Compensation management is a strategic issue.

Counseling is assisting, developing, and helping the employees for their professional development; reduces work role stresses, and promotes quality of work life and, in turn, quality of life.

Critical incidents are those incidents that demand requisite knowledge, skills, personal attributes, and are mainly responsible for the desired outcome.

HR audit verifies and evaluates the HR activities in an organization with the purpose of improving those activities and is pervasive in nature.

Multi-source feedback system (alternatively known as '360 degree feedback' or 'multi-rater appraisals system') is a method wherein a person is assessed by immediate superior, internal and external customers, suppliers, colleagues, seniors of cross-functional areas, and immediate subordinates as well.

Performance coaching is a collaborative, solution-focused, and result-oriented process that contributes to enhanced role performance.

Performance is the ultimate outcome, in the form of product or service, of any person which is essentially an element of the tasks assigned to him/her, to achieve a fraction of the business goals and is a demonstration of work behaviours.

Ranking method simply involves ranking of individuals from the highest to the lowest levels, based on a trait or predetermined definition of value or contribution.

EXERCISES

Concept Review Questions

1. Discuss the pros and cons of the performance appraisal tools.
2. Discuss the benefits of performance appraisal system. Discuss the steps one should follow during appraisal.
3. Explain in your own words how would you go about developing a behaviourally- anchored rating scale. Justify the critical incidents.
4. Explain the problems that are generally encountered in the appraisal system. How can the problems be eliminated or reduced.
5. As a HR manager, how would you use the alternation ranking method in a production section using computer control machines? Which trait would you like to choose for the ranking method?

Critical Thinking Questions

6. How can a manager, who supervises a few juniors, attempt and claim enhanced performance from them? Write your answer with examples.

7. A company wishes to implement 360-degree appraisal system. How should it go about? Discuss the steps involved.
8. Suggest few methods of ensuring transparency in performance appraisal system. Should employees be involved or discussed while developing the method. Justify your answer.

Assignments

9. Contact five medium-sized (say, employee strength is less than 2,000) companies. Discuss with the HR managers of the companies about the performance appraisal tools they are using. Take down the steps in detail and discuss with your subject professor.
10. Visit any five organizations; contact the HR managers to discuss whether they have established performance criteria. Further, inquire whether they are using computer software for online appraisal system. After spending some time in an organization, try to know how the organization is ensuring transparency in the appraisal system.

MANAGER'S INSIGHT

Gupta and Co. is a famous FMCG company based in Kolkata. The company has manufacturing units in Ahmedabad, Pune, and Noida, along with a distribution network across 12 tier 1 and tier 2 cities of India. The company has developed a system of conducting customer satisfaction surveys. The strength of the survey cell is 12 and is headed by a senior manager. The company approaches the principal customers (they are around 10 per cent, though they contribute to nearly 70–75 per cent of the company's total sales) every quarter. A specially designed feedback format is sent to the top management team of the customer organizations. On receipt of filled in forms, the company feeds the data into a software, which helps to calculate the customer satisfaction index (CSI).

A new manager, Mr Bhattacharjee, joined Gupta and Co as the head of the survey cell. On joining, Mr Bhattacharjee decided to compare the satisfaction indices of the past three quarters of a few customers (selected randomly). Astonishingly, for 10 companies, the CSI indices were the same. Mr Bhattacharjee desired to probe into the matter. After a discussion with his juniors and a few of the customers, he found that feedback format designed by Gupta and Co. is complex, and it takes time to fill the various sections. Since senior people from the customer organizations are either unwilling or are unable to devote more time, the same report is sent every year with minor or no changes. According to Mr. Bhattacharjee, this has misled the organization in getting a correct impression of its performance. He envisages serious repercussions, and decided to outsource the designing of an effective performance management system to a leading consultancy.

Questions

1. What repercussions of an incorrect PMS do you envisage in this case?
2. Can there be any shortcut in evaluating customer satisfaction?
3. Suggest ways through which a PMS could help in evaluating employee performance as well as customer satisfaction.

BIBLIOGRAPHY AND WEB RESOURCES

Agarwala, Tanuja., *Strategic Human Resource Management*, Oxford Higher Education, Oxford University Press, New Delhi, 2007.

Davis, K, *Human Behaviour at Work*, 5th edition, McGraw Hill, New York, 1980.

Dessler, Gary and Biju Varkkey, *Human Resource Management*, Dorling Kindersley (India), New Delhi, 2009.

Ghiselli, E.E., *Differentiation of Individuals in Terms of their Predictability*, Journal of Applied Psychology, pp 374–377, 1964.

Haldar, Uday Kumar, *Human Resource Development*, Oxford University Press, Oxford Higher Education, New Delhi, 2009.

Kaplan, Robert S., and David P. Norton, *Using the Balanced Scorecard as a Strategic Management System*, Harvard Business Review, p. 76, January–February 1996.

Landy, F.J., and Farr, *The Measurement of Work Performance: Methods, Theory and Application*, Academic Press, USA, 1974.

McCormick, E.J., and J. Tiffin, *Industrial Psychology*, 6th Edition, Englewood Cliffs, Prentice Hall, New Jersey, 1980.

Mondy, R. Wayne, *Human Resource Management*, 10th Edition, Dorling Kindersley (India) Pvt. Ltd, New Delhi, 2009.

Noe, Raymond A., John R. Hollenbeck, Barry Gerhart, and Patric M. Wright, *Human Resource Management Gaining A Competitive Advantage*, Tata McGraw Hill, New Delhi, 2008.

Odiorne, George S., *Management by Objectives; A System of Managerial Leadership*, Pitman, New York, 1965.

Reddy, Ashwini R., *Process Mapping for the Finance and Business Administration and Design of the Balanced Scorecard*, Convention Proceedings, 47th National Convention held at Pune from November 11 to 13, 2005, organized by Indian Institution of Industrial Engineering, Mumbai.

Rao, T.V., *HRD Audit, Evaluating the Human Resource Function for Business Improvement*, Response Books (A division of Sage Publications India Pvt. Ltd), 1999.

SAIL, *HR Best Practices Manufacturing Sector in India*, Steel Authority of India Limited, New Delhi, 2009.

Web Resources

www.learndirect.co.uk/media/pdfs/nurturing_talent.pdf, last accessed on 19 October 2009.

www.faqs.org/abstracts/Social-sciences/Multiple-uses-of-performance-appraisal-prevalence-and-correlates.html, last accessed on 17 June 2010.

www.kpinfotech.com, last accessed on 23 July 2011.

www.halogensoftware.com, last accessed on 23 July 2011.

www.cornerstoneondemand.com/employee-performance-management, last. accessed on 23 July 2011.

www.promantek.com, last accessed on 23 July, 2011.

PERFORMANCE MANAGEMENT SYSTEM AT TITAN INDUSTRIES LTD

About the organization

Titan Industries Ltd was incorporated in 1984 as a joint venture between Tata Group and TIDCO Ltd, a government of Tamil Nadu undertaking. The company is into manufacturing and marketing quartz watches since 1987. In 1995, the company diversified into manufacturing and marketing 18- carat studded jewellery. It expanded its business sphere entering into two more businesses that include (a) license brands and accessories to leverage the marketing and retailing skills by launching Fastrack Eye Gear and entering into an agreement for marketing Tommy Hilfinger watches; and (b) precision engineering division to leverage the precision engineering capabilities in Titan.

These business units attract customers in multiple areas such as automobile, clock and plastic components, precision engineered components, automobiles and aerospace solution. The company has its outlets for watches throughout the country. The divisions for watches and jewellery are the two main strategic business units.

Human resources

Titan Industries has a total strength of about 3,000 employees in its factories, regional offices, and corporate office. The members of the factory workforce are technocrats with a high level of technical skills, whereas the personnel of corporate and regional offices are from sales and marketing, retailing, finance, and administration background. The HR personnel perform support functions.

The tools

In order to make performance management system effective, the organization is mainly embarking on:

Management by objective (MBO) MBO is done on a half-yearly basis. The organization decides on the recognition and rewards as the central motivational tools.

Multi-source assessment and feedback system (MAFS) Titan Industry implemented a 360-degree feedback, way back 2001 for senior management as a development-focussed tool; for leadership development, team building, potential development, in addition to training needs identification and building relations with internal customers. The company implemented 360-degree feedback in 2001 for senior management as a development-focussed tool; for leadership development, team building, potential development, in addition to training needs identification, and internal customer relations building.

Business scorecard (BSC) Through the scorecard, Titan tracks the commitment of the senior management team (SMT) which is critical to successful implementation of a balanced scorecard. The BSC has created a dynamic environment in the organization. TITAN follows the

10,80,10 rule in this regard, which means 10 key result indicators (KRIs), up to 80 performance indicators (PIs), and 10 key performance indicators (KPIs).

The KPI team focuses sharper attention on the end product; do not try to identify 80 key performance indicators. But, it searches for the characteristics of a good KPI. The organization traps all performance measures in a database, make them available to all, and to make the system transparent.

Objectives of a performance management system

1. To create role clarity and clarify performance expectations, and measure at individual, group, and organizational levels
2. To provide job guidance, feedback, and counseling to build upon strengths and areas of improvements so as to bridge the gap between performance and expectations
3. To build up a positive work relationship between the appraiser and appraisee through a two way dialoguing communication process
4. To identify the training and development needs of employees
5. To unleash the creative capabilities of employees

Key result areas

The key result areas include

1. Areas of responsibilities in which an employee is expected to produce results.
2. Give directions to a person's job and help to focus on important job areas.
3. Provide a basis for appraisal, counseling, and feedback
4. Increasing mutual job understanding with superiors
5. These KRAs may change as priorities and responsibilities change. They are dynamic in nature.
6. Focus on new initiatives.
7. Implementing various organizational objectives.

Critical success factors

These are measures that focus on how the job is to be accomplished, and include skills, knowledge, and/or behaviour that improve job effectiveness or performance. Titan has currently identified 12 critical success factors based on required competencies. The critical success factors are attendance, quality of work, quantity of work, customer satisfaction, team work, time management, learning ability, communication, and ability to withstand pressure.

1. Attendance includes reaching the office in time, being comfortable with long working hours, and willingness to stay in office beyond normal duty hours for completion of daily assignments.
2. Quality of work comprises delivering high quality service and continuously striving for improvement of quality.
3. Quantity of work consists of handling large volume of activity and ability to go beyond normal activity as and when required.
4. Customer satisfaction embraces the parameters satisfying internal customer, satisfying external customer, and relationship with people.
5. Teamwork is perceived as the ability to work effectively in a team, cooperating with team members, and respecting suggestion of others in the team.
6. Time management refers to arranging various jobs to be done, according to priority and completion of work in time.
7. Learning ability takes in learning quickly and applying the gathered knowledge on the job.
8. Communication takes account of clarity in communication, sharing information with others, and listening to others' viewpoints.
9. Ability to withstand pressure signifies withstanding pressure situations, handling emergency situations effectively, and seeking new challenging assignments.

Rating by the appraisee

Against each of the nine items, the appraiser has to rate the appraisee as one of the following. The rating scale is as follows:

- Excellent = 5 points
- Very good = 4 points
- Good = 3 points
- Satisfactory = 2 points
- Below satisfactory = 1 points

KRA & CSF weightages

Up to the middle level executives, the points in key result areas carry 75 per cent weight and critical success factors carry 25 per cent weight. The critical success factors bring out the behavioural parts of an employee. For senior executives, area managers, and above, key result areas carry 50 per cent weights and critical success factors carry 50 per cent weights. However, for these levels, Tata Enterprises call the CSF as Tata leadership practices (TLP).

Level	KRA	CSF/TLP
Up to middle level	75 per cent	CSF – 25 per cent
Area manager and above	50 per cent	TLP – 50 per cent

Example of KRA

Job	Objective	Time line	Measure of achievement	Weightage
Recruitment	1. Meeting business needs of resource	30 days	Employer branding	W1 per cent
	2. Right purpose for right position	...	Job description/job satisfaction floated within due time	W2 per cent
	Using recruitment tools effectively	...	Database usage for reducing recruitment cost	W3 per cent
	Meeting the recruitment time line	...		W4 per cent

Note: The total of all the weightages = 100

Development plan

Titan is keen to equip its employees with the skill sets to perform and achieve in the respective key result areas, aims to fill the gap if any, and enables the development of employees. The organization draws development plan based on certain factors such as

1. The KRAs for the employees for the year under review.
2. The planned KRAs for the year to come.
3. Barriers to successful performance that have been identified.
4. Gaps identified in the critical success factors.
5. Any developmental need expressed by the employee during the performance review discussions.

The two-phase development plan includes (a) identifying training needs, and (b) and preparing a personal action plan (PAP). Training is offered in-house or from external sources. The appraiser does not choose the training course; rather, encourages and supports the employee to understand the skills, competencies, and experiences one may need for superior performance. In the PAP, the employee chalks out the list of actions he/she should undertake for performance enhancement and self-improvement.

Performance review

Titan lays a lot of emphasis on performance reviews. One HR representative is present at all appraisal meetings. While reviewing the key result areas and key success factors, the role of HR is to ensure consistency in the approach in the entire organization, and to constantly remind the appraisers about the rating errors such as (a) halo effect and (b) leniency error of harshness errors, (c) central tendency, and (d) personal biases.

In the performance appraisal process, the appraisee presents his/her contributions as against the agreed targets and the outcome of the process is evaluated. Both the appraiser and the appraisee reach a detailed agreement on the critical success factors. A five-point rating scale is used.

Categorization of employees

The organization divides employees into four categories based on their appraisal. The main purpose of dividing them is to initiate specific developmental measures and not disciplinary actions. In the appraisal process, it comes to the limelight as to who could meet the expectations, already communicated earlier, to what extent in regards to quantitative achievement, and conforming to qualitative requirements.

Category A: Exceeded expectations (EHP)
Category B: Met expectations (GP)
Category C: Somewhat met expectations (P)
Category D: Did not meet expectations (Poor)

The organization normalizes the categorized employees for each department. A maximum of 15per cent employees might be considered in category A, and 40per cent in category B, who are not very sacrosanct. The rest 45per cent fall in category C. The organization helps the low performers (category D) to come out with personal improvement plans (PIP).

Use of the outcome

Titan collects all the feedback across the organization, and each person's item-wise report is compared with the company's average for decision-making. The final ranking is used to determine the performance linked to pay, development opportunities, challenging assignments in various task forces, and promotions. During the process of reviewing, the appraiser is taken into confidence.

Building coaching and mentoring culture

The company believes that coaching strongly restores capacity to perform the tasks assigned. It also mentions some shortcomings of the appraisal. As such, coaching is often the by-product of performance appraisal. In an organization, coaching is an activity through which managers work with subordinates to foster skill development, impart knowledge, and inculcate values and behaviour, that will help them for more challenging assignments.

In Titan, mentoring, like coaching, is a means of developing human resources. Mentoring is about guiding others in their personal quest for growth through learning. A mentor acts as a trusted guide, offering advice when asked, and opening the doors to learning opportunities when possible and appropriate. Titan practices the principle of natural or informal mentoring; and on observing the relationship, the company formalizes the mentor-mentee relationship. The benefits of mentoring to the organization are four-fold:

1. It develops the human assets of the organization.
2. It helps to transfer important tacit knowledge from one set employees to another.
3. It aids in the retention of valued employees.
4. A web-based low-cost mentoring system is helpful to the organizations

[Case written based on an interaction with Mr Indranil Bhattacharya, Regional HR (East), Apeejay House, Kolkata, on 5 December 2009.]

Discussion Questions

1. Titan uses some performance management tools. Do you think the company can achieve the objectives stated above using the PMS tools mentioned?
2. Titan has specified some critical success factors. By appraising employee performances once or twice in a year, can the employees be evaluated with regard to the CSF? What should the organization do?
3. On the basis of this case, please devise a performance measurement system for the students of your institute.

HR MANTRA

While taking rounds in a department, a supervisor observed a junior colleague (Mr A) using a wrong approach to do a particular task. The supervisor criticized and reprimanded him using harsh language, to which Mr A reacted roughly.

On another day, the supervisor assigned a task to Mr A. After completion of the task successfully, the supervisor praised Mr A. However, the supervisor requested Mr A to see him in his office. When Mr A approached him, the supervisor explained the right way of performing the operation, and handed over the work instruction for the task assigned to Mr A. Mr A could follow the explanation, and accepted the advice of the supervisor.

The mantra: Praise in public, criticize privately.

AUBREY C. DANIELS

Aubrey C. Daniels, 'the father of performance management', was born on 17 May 1935, in Lake City, South Carolina, USA. A clinical psychologist by training, he was one of the first thinkers to make extensive use of the science of behaviour analysis in business. His rich history is proof of his dedication and devotion towards the science of behaviour. More than three decades ago, Daniels began pursuing and acting on his global mission—to help people and organizations apply the scientifically proven laws of human behaviour to optimize performance.

Daniels completed his bachelor's degree in psychology and speech in 1957 from Furman University; secured a master's degree in psychology and philosophy in 1963 from the University of Florida; and obtained his doctorate in psychology and philosophy (Phi Beta Kappa) in 1964 from the University of Florida.

Daniels started his career as a clinical psychologist. However, he was convinced that the work of B.F. Skinner and other behavioural scientists best enabled his patients to change their own behaviour. With this conviction, Daniels began to consider the impact of applying behavioural science at workplace. Daniels' ground-breaking impact in the workplace led him to coin the phrase 'performance management' and he began his company, 'Aubrey Daniels International'.

Daniels is an internationally-acclaimed and recognized author and speaker. He was the first editor of the *Journal of Organizational Behaviour Management* (JOBM) in 1977. He has authored several publications. His best known books are *Bringing Out the Best in People* (McGraw-Hill) and *Performance Management: Changing Behaviour That Drives Organizational Performance* (first and second edition In 1982 with Theodore Rosen, third edition in 1989, and fourth and current edition in 2004 with James E. Daniels, Performance Management Publications.)

Daniels has received many awards and acknowledgments for his excellent work. Most notably, he received the lifetime achievement award from the Organizational Behaviour Management Network (www.obmnetwork.com), the outstanding service award and the 2005 Fellow title from the International Association for Behaviour Analysis (www.abainternational.org). He has also been honoured as alumni of the year by College of Health Professionals in Furman University and University of Florida.

Daniels is a member in many prestigious boards, institutes such as Cambridge center for behavioural studies; John F. Kennedy School of Government, Harvard University; College of Health Professions, University of Florida; Georgia Association of Behaviour Analysis, and so on.

His contribution towards performance management system literatures is noteworthy. Some of his publications are as follows:

1. Measure of a Leader (2006)
2. Bringing Out the Best in People: How to Apply the Astonishing Power of Positive Reinforcement (1994, Revised 1999)
3. Performance Management: Improving Quality Productivity through Positive Reinforcement (Revised 1982, 1989)
4. Creating 'Above and Beyond' Performance
5. The Leader's Role in Pay Systems and Organizational Performance (2006)
6. Positive Reinforcement: Misunderstood and Misused; Management by Common Sense Is Not Management at All (1994)
7. Risky Rewards (1994)
8. Successful Rightsizing: The Organizational Challenge of the 90s
9. Performance Management Beyond the Workplace (1985)

Daniels interpreted performance as the sum of behaviour and results, which cannot be viewed as independent of either component. Daniels described performance management as a technology (science imbedded in application methods) for managing both behaviour and results. Performance management is an outcome of effective management. Performance management is applicable in many spheres such as schools, churches, community meetings, sports teams, health setting, governmental agencies, and even political settings.

Some of the universities and journals with which Daniels is affiliated are the following:

1. Journal of Organizational Behaviour Management, editorial board, since 1989.
2. Journal of Applied Behaviour Analysis, Editorial board, since 1986.
3. Florida State University, Psychology Department, Visiting Professor, since 1987.
4. Western Michigan, Psychology Department, Visiting Lecturer, since 1987.

References

aubreydaniels.com/aubrey-daniels-phd, last accessed on 21 October 2010.

en.wikipedia.org/wiki/ Aubrey_Daniels, last accessed on 8 October 2011.

APPENDIX 8.1

Annual performance appraisal

Part 1

(To be filled in by the administrative department of the factory)

Name of the officer:
Personal number:
Qualification (as on date):
Present designation:
Designation at entry:
Name of the factory where serving:
Name of the factories served:

Functional areas where he has worked (including present areas)

S. no.	Functional area (Name of the department)	Duration

Part 2

(To be filled in by the officer to be appraised)

1. Brief description of duties (describe your duties and responsibilities)

   1.1 1.2

   1.3 1.4

   1.5

2. Please specify the quantitative/physical/financial targets/objectives set for yourself or that were set for you is respect of eight to ten items of work, in order of priority, and your achievement against each target.

	Target	Achievements
1.		
2.		
3.		
4.		
5.		

3. (a) Please state briefly the shortfalls with reference to the targets/objectives referred to in column 2. Please specify constraints, if any, in achieving the targets.

1.		
2.		
3.		
4.		

3. (b) Please also indicate items in which there have been significantly higher achievements and your contribution thereto.

1.		
2.		
3.		

In your opinion, have you done any innovative work? YES/NO
If the answer is 'YES', give details: ....
....
....
....
....
....

4. Please state whether the annual return on immovable property for the preceding calendar year was filed within the prescribed date e.g. 31st January of the year following the calendar year. If not, the date of filing the return should be given.

....
....

Part 3

(To be filled in by the immediate higher officer)

Name of the reporting officer
Designation:
How long is the officer serving under your control?
Do you agree with the submission of the officer in Part 2 of this form? Offer point-wise reply.
Comment about the following:

	Attributes	X	1	2	3	4	5
1.	Honesty	X					
2.	Integrity	X					
3.	Loyalty	X					
4.	Initiative	X					
5.	Sobriety						
6.	Communication skill	X					
7.	Relationship with colleagues	X					
8.	Leadership style	X					
9.	Attend meetings timely	X					

10.	Responsive in meetings	X						
11.	Creative and innovative	X						
12.	Original in work	X						
13.	Can work under stress	X						
14.	Shares success with others	X						
15.	Analytical ability	X						
16.		X						
17.								
18.								
19.								
20.								

Write 1 for excellent, 2 for very good, 3 for good, 4 for fair, 5 for poor.
Note: If you want to highlight any attribute not covered between serial 1 and 15, use serial numbers 16 to 20.

Part 4

(To be filled in by the accepting officer to whom the reporting officer is responsible)

1. Do you personally know the officer?
2. Does he come to you in demanding situations?
3. Comment about the relationship between the officer and his senior.

....

....

....

....

....

4. Do you agree with the views express by the reporting office about the officer being reported upon? YES/NO
5. Justify whatever be your response to item 4.
6. Should the appraisal be communicated to the officer being reported upon? YES/NO

The appraisal report is acceptable.

Signature with date

CHAPTER 9

Training and Development

LEARNING OBJECTIVES

After studying this chapter, you will be able to

- Appreciate the need for designing training to achieve business goals
- Identify training needs to fill the knowledge gap
- Understand the science of training
- Explain the technique of training adults
- Describe the qualities of good trainers
- Understand the importance of training specifications
- Identify the impediments to designing a curriculum
- Estimate the time and facilities required
- Comprehend the importance of evaluating and validating the training process
- Discuss the evaluation models
- Understand the concepts of documentation and record retention
- Use the concept of 5S in preserving training documents and records
- Apply the concept of benchmarking to improve training practices

OPENING CASE

Importance of Training Design

The International Institute of Management and Technology (IIMT) came into existence in the year 1998, and has a total of 16 employees on its payroll. Mr S.K. Durani, its director, heads the institute. He was a faculty member in a training institute in Jaipur. He is also a member of several social clubs, and attends the social and cultural programmes organized by the clubs. Over the years, he has developed good contacts with many academicians and organizational stalwarts.

IIMT conducts the following short-term courses:

1. Production planning and control
2. Marketing management
3. Sales management
4. Quality management system
5. Environmental management system
6. Contract labour laws
7. Industrial safety and security
8. Computer courses (modules of MS Office)
9. Customized courses on specific request of companies

Elite Engineering is a medium-scale company, manufacturing mechanical components, sub-assemblies, and assemblies, and employs nearly 3,500 people. The company concluded a contract with IIMT in 2006. Elite Engineering recruited 12 assistant managers through campus interviews in B-schools and approached IIMT to conduct a two-week induction programme. This orientation programme was supposed to introduce the historical background of the organization, past chairmen, and managing directors of the company, technology in use, its principal products and regular customers, existing markets, potential markets, marketing strategy, etc.

In the contract, Elite Engineering specified the purpose of the induction programme and the requirements as follows:

1. Recognizing customer needs
2. Appreciating customer expectations

3. Valuing consumer psychology
4. Developing marketing skills
5. Learning use of statistical packages
6. Building and maintaining customer relationship
7. Gaining skills for identifying niche markets

The contract clearly stated that handouts covering all the topics must be given to the management trainees, and two sets of the same should be given to Elite Engineering.

The course was inaugurated in a grand manner. IIMT invited the vice chancellor of a university as the chief guest, the chief executive officer of Elite Engineering as guest of honour, the head of the department of business administration, and a few other dignitaries. The inaugural function motivated all the new recruits. IIMT distributed course material comprising a few pages photocopied from books in random order. The content of the pages included general marketing concepts, marketing mix, product mix, theories of motivation, leadership theories, etc. After a high tea session, the actual knowledge dissemination began. In the inaugural function, the director spoke highly about the institute, its clients, and the faculty members. During the course, most of the faculty members wanted to clarify the fundamental concepts of marketing management, such as the meaning of marketing, marketing mix, product mix, 4Ps and 7Ps of marketing products and services, respectively.

Out of the two LCD projectors in possession with IIMT, one had been lent to a nearby institute. The other projector was not in good working condition. Participants were unable to read the contents of the slides. Astonishingly, due to shortage of time, a vital topic (in the course routine) could not be discussed at all. At the end of the course, one participant noticed that a topic listed by Elite Engineering was not included in the routine. Some more irregularities were also noticed. Gradually, the attendance decreased. However, all the assistant managers of Elite Engineering attended the valedictory session. Participants did not hesitate to express their views in the feedback session, and endorsed their remarks in the feedback sheets of the company.

Mr Durani regretted the lapses. He explained that the errors occurred due to typing mistakes.

Three years have gone by since then. IIMT has not received any further enquiries from Elite Engineering. The institute is worried about the decreasing enquiries from many of its regular clients.

Learning points

- Pedagogical aids should be planned with adequate care.
- A training institute should plan the time and facilities required.
- Documentation, preservation, and retrieval of records is important.

INTRODUCTION

Hiring people and multiplying their talents over a period of time is a continuing responsibility of any organization. In the challenging world of business corporations, we often lose sight of the enormous benefits brought to organizations by means of enhancing capability and knowledge building among organizational members. Some organizations view training and development like other routine activities. But, for its employees to feel passionately about training, it is important to understand, assimilate, and leverage the true value that the training function brings to the surface. All the stakeholders need to align, be committed, and derive benefits from it.

Training is a tool of developing work culture. It is also important to select the right training methods to produce the desired results. To make training programmes effective and achieve business goals, the curriculum must be designed by following certain steps which shall be discussed later in this chapter. Successes of businesses are measured through four parameters—financial, operational, performance, and cultural. The financial parameter is an indicator of how well the sanctioned money has been spent, the operational parameter points out people development (refers to the people who have to be trained and have been trained), and the performance parameter refers to observing whether there has been observable changes at the operating and performance level. The cultural parameter encompasses measures of employees' attitude towards accepting changes to make those happen, participating in training, degree of organizational commitment, leadership encouraging working in teams, sharing success by leaders to enthuse team members, and so forth.

Training is the act of increasing knowledge and skills of employees. Training improves work culture.

Training manifests its importance in improving all the parameters; and in enhancing the value of organizational members. It is also wise to remember that expenditure incurred in training is investment and not expenditure. Training is an attempt to improve the current or future performance by increasing an employee's ability to act through learning, by increasing his/her skill or knowledge and/or changing the employee's attitude. The need for training and development is ascertained from the employee's performance deficiency, which is the gap between expected standard performance and actual performance. Every organization, irrespective of the size or nature of operations, needs to provide training to the organizational members at various stages of their career with defined objectives.

While developing a training programme, the training objectives must be designed considering the participant profiles and organizational needs. A new course may be benchmarked against similar ones offered by competitors; for repeat courses, the feedback given by participants of earlier courses must be considered.

Training is 'the systematic development of the knowledge, skills, and attitudes required by an individual to perform a given task or job adequately'. (Armstrong 2001). Training is 'the act of increasing knowledge and skills of an employee for doing a particular job' (Flippo 1984). Organizations offer training programmes to develop their people and achieve business goals effectively.

BUSINESS GOALS VS TRAINING

Training and development activities must be linked with business goals for survival and growth of the organization. In addition to achieving business goals, such alignment facilitates to evaluate any training and development effort from the standpoint of the rate of investment (ROI) approach. Furthermore, this makes the training efforts visible, draws attention of the managers functioning to achieve the primary goals of the organization, and obviously claim the admiration of the strategic apex of the organization.

Goals are specific, measurable, attainable, relevant, and time-bound (SMART). There can be many business goals:

1. Enhancing the market share by seven per cent in the forthcoming financial year
2. Adding new related products to the product range by three per cent within six months
3. Penetrating into five new markets in the north-eastern region in the forthcoming financial year
4. Identifying the market niche for 10 principal existing products in three months
5. Developing a procedure in three months to measure customer satisfaction
6. Developing a system in four months to develop (building bridges of) relationships with customers and other stakeholders

Apart from the goals already mentioned, building relationships with customers and other stakeholders in the present business situation is by far the most important goal, although it is not quantifiable (Haldar and Chatterjee 2007).

Training and development are strongly focused on talent management, and make a positive impact in the attitudes and mindsets of the members of the organization. The required training initiatives, if finalized in a structured manner and confirmed with documented procedure, lead to the solutions. Training efforts also contribute to the organization in decision-making processes such as

1. Formulation of business policy
2. Diversification and integration
3. Technical collaboration and cooperation
4. Product management

5. Undertaking cost control initiatives
6. Carrying out profitability analysis
7. Preparation of perspective plans

Frances and Bee (2000) have mentioned some common stimuli or triggers prompting business needs:

1. General external environmental factors over which the organization has no direct control, namely, economic, technological, social, demographic, cultural, and political factors
2. Specific environmental factors over which the organization might not exercise control but might exert some influence such as customers, suppliers, competitors, and pressure groups
3. Internal environment including employees, associations, trade unions, and shareholders

Achieving each goal needs certain strategies. One should know the various business strategy groups.

BUSINESS STRATEGY AND TRAINING

Defenders, prospectors, reactors, and analysers are the various business strategy groups.

Agarwala (2007) has categorized the business strategy groups as defenders, prospectors, reactors, and analysers.

The defenders' and prospectors' strategies are fundamental, distinct in their characteristics, and follow proactive actions. Defenders compete on the basis of low price and high quality, and a stable environment. This strategy is associated with the production and process efficiency. The skill types that lead to improved efficiency of the processes are also of vital importance. The strategists embark upon skill specialization, production and finance functions, and building skills.

On the other hand, the prospectors' strategy is associated with the preference to buy new and diverse skills from external sources. They compete on the basis of new markets and fresh products in unstable environments. Companies belonging to this category look for skill flexibility, multi-skilling, marketing and sales, research and development, and buying skills.

As the name indicates, the reactors' strategy is need-based to meet the consequences that emerge. The analysers' strategy is a combination of the two approaches—those of the defenders and prospectors.

The purpose of any business is achieving the objectives and goals, for which strategies are formulated. To keep up with a strategy, people need skills. If the skills are not available within the existing manpower, it must be imparted by way of training and workshops. Otherwise, it must be obtained from external sources.

Table 9.1 summarizes the difference between business strategy and training.

Table 9.1 Business strategy vs training

	Business strategy	**Staffing and training practices**
Skill type	1. Staff and train for narrow skills, need-based 2. Staff and train for production and finance functions	1. Internal staffing 2. Intensive in-house training 3. Intensive training from external sources
Skill source	1. Staff and train for marketing skills 2. Staff and train for research and development	1. External staffing 2. Less training to employees 3. Training from external source on as-required basis

TRAINING CONTENT TO ACHIEVE BUSINESS GOALS

Organizations conduct training programmes specific to their needs in order to achieve their defined business goals. Exhibit 9.1 is one of the formats used by organizations to plan their training modules, and has been compiled on the basis of the authors' interaction with training and HR executives.

Exhibit 9.1 Business goals vs training content

1. Enhancing the market share by seven per cent in the forthcoming financial year
   (a) Knowledge of consumer behaviour
   (b) Knowledge of consumer choices
   (c) Understanding intrinsic needs of people
   (d) Knowledge of customer relationship management
   (e) Managing distribution system
2. Adding three per cent new related products to the product range within six months
   (a) Knowledge of the market
   (b) Identifying market niche
   (c) Knowledge of input materials
   (d) Knowledge of facilities and utilities required
   (e) Scheduling and loading the new products
3. Penetrating into five new markets in the north-eastern region in the forthcoming financial year
   (a) Understanding demographic characteristics
   (b) Understanding intrinsic needs of people
   (c) Enhancing negotiation skills
   (d) Building relationship
4. Identifying the market niche for 10 principal existing products in three months
   (a) Applying strategy for market growth
   (b) Identifying target market
   (c) Understanding demographic characteristics of the market
   (d) Knowledge of choices of inhabitants
   (e) Assessing affordability of prospective customers
   (f) Positioning in mind
5. Developing procedure in three months to measure customer satisfaction
   (a) Understanding customer stated needs
   (b) Identifying implied (unstated) needs of customers
   (c) Knowledge of market survey
   (d) Developing and designing questionnaire for survey
   (e) Summarizing the observations
   (f) Developing the procedure to measure
   (g) Elucidating the procedure to market survey personnel
   (h) Implementing and maintaining the procedure
6. Developing a system in four months to develop (building bridges of) relationships with customers and other stakeholders
   (a) Understanding need and usefulness of socialization
   (b) Knowledge of relationship building
   (c) Means of relationship building
   (d) Technique of maintaining and strengthening the relation

TRAINING AND DEVELOPMENT

Both training and development help in enhancing the capabilities of employees. The planning methodology of both the processes should consider the following:

1. Experience of the people performing work contributing to quality of the product.
2. Tacit and explicit knowledge: Tacit knowledge is personal, context-specific, and therefore, difficult to communicate. Explicit knowledge or codified knowledge refers to the knowledge that is transmittable in formal, systematic language. (Refer to Chapter 16 for details.)
3. Managerial and leadership skills for smooth man management.
4. Planning and improvement tools for organizational effectiveness.
5. Team building to use synergy.
6. Problem solving is a part of mental process.
7. Communication skills and personal expressiveness are essential for conveying ideas, thoughts, opinions, etc.
8. Cultural and social behaviour are essential to improve quality of work life.

9. Needs and expectations of customers and other interested parties must be fulfilled to satisfy the customers, enhance customer base, and convert prospective customers to actual customers.
10. Business knowledge refers to acquisition of information about the current state of the company environment, what the company does, the user, and the place of the user, etc.
11. Benchmarking is a process of comparing parameters of one's business processes with the performance metrics of industry bests. If required, comparison is done with the best practices from other industries.
12. Creativity and innovation means thinking new things and implementing the thoughts.

To facilitate the involvement of people, training and development also includes understanding the points listed in Box 9.1.

Box 9.1 Organizational drives to involve people

1. The vision for the future of the organization
2. The organization's policies and objectives
3. Organizational change and development
4. The initiation and implementation of improvement processes
5. Benefits from creativity and innovation
6. The organization's impact on the society
7. Introductory and induction programmes for new recruits, and
8. Periodic refresher programmes for people already trained

Though both training and development build strengths and confidence of people, they differ on certain other dimensions as shown in Table 9.2.

Table 9.2 Comparison between training and development

Dimension	Training	Development
Definition	The process of affecting change in an individual's behaviour, often applied to the acquisition of limited operating job related skills	The process of growth, by which an organization expands the number or modernizes the nature of its activities. It results in overall growth
Purpose	Supplies the specific skill, knowledge, or attitudes needed to meet goals of organization (usually performing assigned task within specific productivity standards)	Assures organizations of available manpower, technology, and equipment to meet previously established goals
Expected outcome	A human being (or group of human beings) who can perform a specific task to specified standards in order to meet predetermined goals	The organization will engage in a new process or product; will also acquire systems, materials, and manpower to keep the process operative
Scope	Deals with specific tasks related to job performance	Complex sets of tasks; requirements of the entire economy of organization
Relationships	Consultative and administrative interfaces by goal setters, manpower planners, and sociologists. Learner/teacher relationships covering the stimulus response cycle. Interfaces with the immediate manager, trainees, and training specialists	Consultative and administrative interfaces by goal setters, manpower planners, and sociologists

(Contd)

Table 9.2 (Contd)

Responsibility	Leadership at all levels of the organization. Special burdens rest on all types of training specialists	Leadership of nation agency sector, or enterprise. Special burdens rest on manpower planners.
Timeframe	Deals with current needs and immediate application; short-term orientation is normal	Deals with projected needs on both long-term and short-term basis

PRINCIPAL LEARNINGS IN TRAINING

In the process of training, there should be specific and explicit stimulus to the learner. Some examples of stimuli are words used while disseminating knowledge, anything written on the board or flipchart, any picture projected, a demonstration, or video clippings. Trainees must be able to identify and relate to the relevant stimulus and respond to it. This is a part of the training process and it is the responsibility of the trainers and the curriculum of the training institute to make the stimulus understandable to the trainees in order to make the training effective. The response refers to the activities intended to be taught to the trainees.

The responses may vary from one trainee to the other. They may include a sequence of activities on a machine, a cluster of steps used in developing a programme, a string of words to convey a message, or an algorithm, etc. The trainee or the learner must be encouraged and motivated to practice the activity or series of activities.

Hence, the following aspects should be kept in mind by the trainer while planning a module (Bohlander 2002).

Goal setting The trainer should define the goals and formulate the training objectives clearly in short and simple language, and communicate it to the trainees. The trainees get motivated and make efforts to achieve the objectives, if they are clear about them.

Meaningful presentation, practice, and repetition While disseminating knowledge, the faculty member should lay stress on building upon the previous information. He should discuss in brief about what has already been taught and the other background knowledge required. In turn, trainees should be given the opportunities to present the knowledge gained by them in the training situation. Repeated practice leads to application of the knowledge in the work area and to enhancement of the job performance.

> The principal learnings in training are goal setting, meaningful presentation, feedback, and reinforcement, whole vs part learning, massed vs spaced learning, individual differences, and lastly, the transfer of learning.

Feedback and reinforcement The training institute must outline a system of collecting feedback from the trainees periodically during the training for long-term course programmes, and at the end of the training for short-term courses. The trainees should get an opportunity to share their views about the course content, achievement of the course objective, extent of applicability of the knowledge in the work area, and the delivery and presentation of the faculty members. Trainees need not necessarily write their names in the feedback form. In this manner, the trainees become enthusiastic knowing that their issues and doubts would be heard and clarified.

Whole vs part learning Complex jobs should be broken into parts. Training should be imparted in different modules separately, starting from the basic to the difficult ones. Going through all the modules in the correct sequence, the trainees gradually gain confidence on completing each module. After mastering all the parts through the modular training, the trainees should be taught on the assemblage of all the modules.

Massed vs spaced learning You may recall that practice makes one perfect, and practice is inescapable for learning new skills. As such, in a modular training system, the trainees should get the opportunity to practise new skills. Allowing some gap between two modules makes the training more effective, in contrast to continuous training without breaks, or what is called 'massed practice'.

Individual differences The grasping capacity differs from one person to another. People learn at different rates and in different ways. For example, some people learn by listening to faculty members or others, while some learn through observation; yet another group of people learn by actually performing the activity. Hence, the training module should keep all these aspects in mind before beginning the course.

Transfer of learning Applying knowledge and skills in the work area is the ultimate objective of the trainers and also the organizational need. The training process may be made effective by ensuring that the training situation has elements of the actual job context.

TRAINING AS A SYSTEM

Training is a mechanism and a system of the HRD because it is a set of several interrelated processes. Training manifests its importance whenever there is a change in the environment, for example, an amendment in the pension rules, income tax law, introduction of new systems, mechanization of office activities, and so on. Any change that is associated with a resistance produces a setback. Imparting training becomes inescapable if the dynamic equilibrium in an organization is to be maintained.

As a trainer, one is required to enhance reception, augment expectancy, facilitate retrieval, present the stimulus, provide learning guidance, provide feedback to reinforce, assess performance and enhance retention, and transfer to generalization in order to make the system effective. Thus, the keywords are reception, expectancy, retrieval, selective perception, semantic encoding, responding, reinforcement, retrieval, and generalization. These keywords and their meanings are summarized for reinforcement in Box 9.2.

Box 9.2 Training system keywords

1. Reception—gaining attention
2. Expectancy—informing learners of the objective
3. Retrieval—stimulating recall of prior learning
4. Selective perception—presenting the stimulus
5. Semantic encoding—providing learning guidance
6. Responding—eliciting performance
7. Reinforcement—providing feedback
8. Retrieval—assessing performance
9. Generalization—enhancing retention and transfer

TRAINING—A TOOL FOR DEVELOPING WORK CULTURE

An organizational leader is responsible for producing results, and must be aware of his personal values and prevailing organizational values. It helps if one's personal values are congruent with the organizational values. If not, the trainer's roles emerge to be predominant. Though values are enduring, a trainer can transform the personal values through HRD efforts—mainly training and development—making them appropriate and institutionalized as organizational values. Contextually, it is mentioned that the leader cannot escape examining the existing organizational values and redefining them.

In an organization, the groups should not work as isolated islands. The success of an organization depends on the concerted and orchestral efforts of various groups. The efforts put in by the organizational boundaries must not be independent of each other. In simple words, all the members should work cohesively towards a common goal. Development of work culture is a process of planned change and, as such, the trainer has a vital role to play. The trainer should work as an effective internal change agent. In addition, a trainer needs to ensure that training and development processes lead to empowering the participants to plan for, and implement the change in their respective work settings.

Agrawal (1991) argues that diagnostics is the first and by far, the most important step in ensuring that training and development leads to empowering and change. Through diagnostics, the trainer and the trainees become aware of the work-related problems and difficulties experienced by the trainees. This also becomes the learning needs of the participants in a training programme. The trainer can change the diagnostics data to redesign a need based training programme. The participants can concentrate and keep their focus in the programme to get answers to these diagnostics problems. The trainer must encourage the participants to keep a record of what they have learnt and how it can be used in their respective work situation. In addition, based on the diagnostics and learning from a programme, the participants would need to be helped to develop action plans for implementation.

Kurt Lewin (1947) proposed three phases of the change process—unfreezing, moving, and refreezing. Feedback about the action plan can be a way of refreezing the change. Thus the diagnostics, learning review, and action plan can link training and development efforts with plans for developing new work cultures comparable with unfreezing and moving stages. Lewin's model is given in Chapter 15 tilted 'Managing change'.

Agrawal (1991) further explains and elaborates the process of changing work cultures through training and development using five aspects, namely, awareness, empowering, planning for change, change, and refreezing. Refer to Table 9.3.

Table 9.3 Changing work culture through training and development

Awareness	Empowering	Planning for change	Change	Refreezing
Diagnostics	**Learning review**	**Action planning**	**Implementation**	**Feedback**
Identification of work-related problems and difficulties	Daily review of significant learning points and how this learning can be applied back in the work setting	Preparation of specific work-related action plans based on diagnostics and learning review	Implementation of an action plan after discussion and approval by one's superior	Feedback to the divisional management about implementation
Identification of learning needs to overcome diagnostics problems				Feedback to the training centre on implementation

Srivastava, et al. (2005) have highlighted the need and importance for training programmes to achieve changes in managerial mindsets. This was originally propounded by Gosling and Mintzberg in the year 2003, who mentioned five modules:

1. Managing self—the reflective mindset

2. Managing organization—the analytical mindset
3. Managing context—the worldly mindset
4. Managing collaboration—the collaborative mindset
5. Managing change—the action mindset

Training, particularly attitudinal change training, brings about changes in the mindsets of employees across the organization. The five perspectives mentioned earlier help managers to move from a confused, perplexed, and complicated mindset to a mindset that can ably synthesize insight, enhance capacity of exploration, augment problem solving skills, and perform realistic analysis, ultimately leading to a comprehensible whole. Training provides the knowledge skills and values needed for successful living with the culture, and offers the ability to deal effectively with new data and changing conditions.

COMPONENTS OF TRAINING

A training system comprises various components. Examining the job or task to be performed is the foremost requirement. While examining, you have to consider both the quality and quantity of the work. In order to produce the job to the desired degree of quality, accuracy, perfection, and finish, and to meet the set target, both knowledge and skills are required. Identifying the job-related knowledge, specific skills, and competency is an essential task. Thereafter, you are required to break down the knowledge and skills into smaller details. The gap between knowledge and skills required to perform a task, and those in possession of the person, determines the training need, and hence, the content of the training programme.

A training programme must have some objectives. For example, the objectives of a course on internal audit of ISO 9001 quality management system are that after successful completion of the course, the participants shall be able to (a) understand the quality management system and the scope of ISO 9001, (b) interpret the clauses of ISO 9001, (c) appreciate the importance of internal audit and gain auditing skill, and (d) perform the task of internal auditing fulfilling the requirements of clause on internal audit of ISO 9001. Box 9.3 gives some more examples of objectives.

Box 9.3 Training objectives—occupational health and safety

The following are the training objectives of a short-term course on occupational health and safety designed for junior managers and working personnel.

After attending the course, the participants will

1. Be aware of the Factories Act, 1948, and the rules made thereunder
2. Know the history of the safety movements in India and the role of the International Labour Organization
3. Understand the provisions relating to the manufacture, storage, and import of hazardous chemicals, as mentioned in Hazardous Chemicals Rules, 1989
4. Appreciate the principles of accident prevention
5. Realize the hazards in material handling and their prevention
6. Select and use personal protective equipment

A flowchart for designing the training curriculum, beginning from assessing customer needs, is exhibited in Figure 9.1.

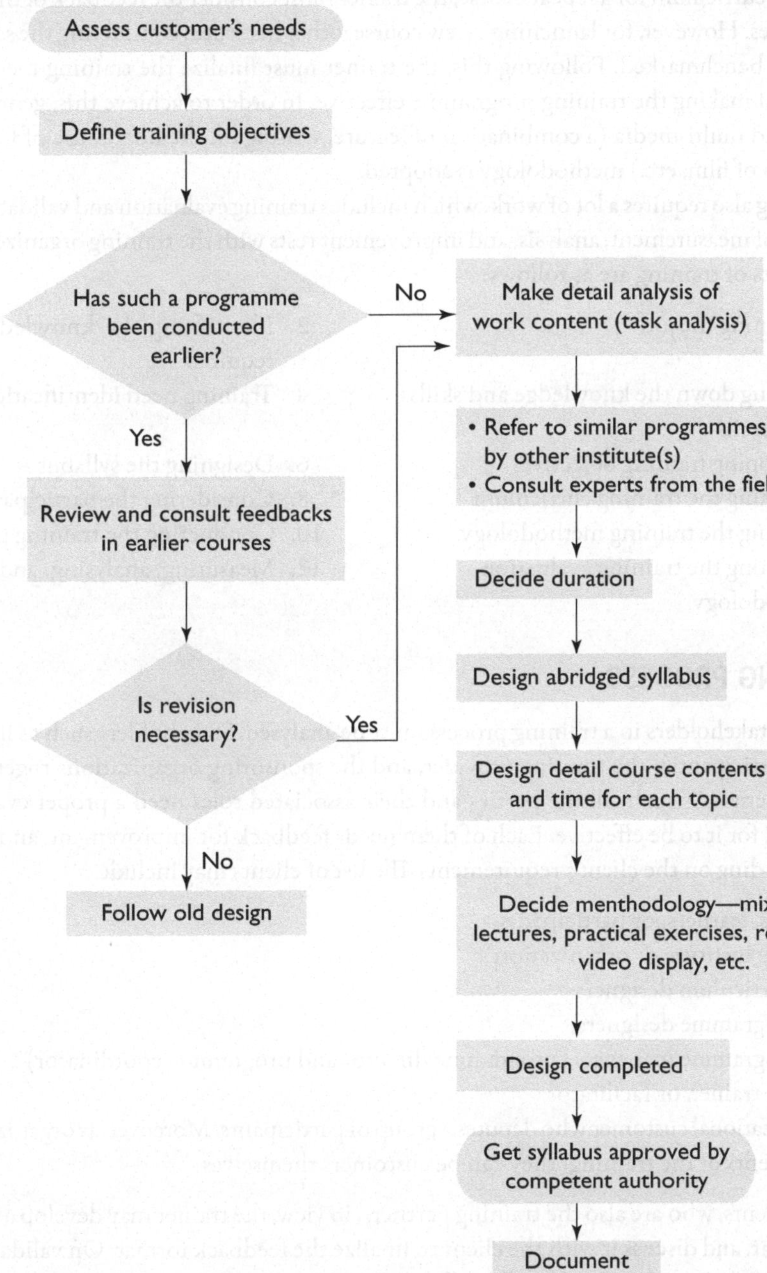

FIG. 9.1 Designing the training curriculum (Ordnance Factories Institute of Learning, Ishapore—OFILIS model)

After developing the course objectives, the trainer is required to design the syllabus considering the participant profiles and organizational needs. The course may be a repeat course or a new one. While developing the curriculum for a repeat course, the trainer must consider the feedback of the participants of earlier courses. However, for launching a new course, other institutes conducting the same or similar courses can be benchmarked. Following this, the trainer must finalize the training methodology for conducting and making the training programme effective. In order to achieve this, generally, a 4M—multi-mode and multi-media (a combination of lecture, writing on the board, use of OHP or LCD, showing a scrip of film, etc.) methodology is adopted.

Pre-training also requires a lot of work, which includes training evaluation and validation. Thus, the responsibility of measurement, analysis, and improvement rests with the training organizer. Summarily, the components of training are as follows:

1. Examining the job
2. Identifying the knowledge and skills required
3. Breaking down the knowledge and skills into details
4. Training need identification
5. Developing training objectives
6. Designing the syllabus
7. Designing the training curriculum
8. Considering the participants' profile
9. Selecting the training methodology
10. Conducting the training programme
11. Designing the training evaluation methodology
12. Measuring, analysing, and improving

CLIENTS IN TRAINING PROCESS

The clients or stakeholders in a training process must be analysed. Stakeholders such as individual customers (the participants), the training provider, and the sponsoring organizations together comprise the training clients. As such, all the parties and their associated roles need a proper evaluation prior to the training, for it to be effective. Each of them needs feedback for improvement, and the feedback will vary depending on the client's requirements The list of clients may include

1. Trainees, learners, or participants
2. Training institute or organization
   (a) Curriculum designers
   (b) Programme designers
   (c) Programme managers (programme director and programme coordinator)
3. Faculty, trainer, or facilitator
4. Organizational customer who deputes a group of participants. Moreover, as organizations receive the benefits of the training, they can be customers themselves.

Keeping the clients, who are also the training partners, in view, the trainer may develop a draft training feedback format, and discuss it with the client to finalize the feedback format. On validation, the final format is obtained. Coordination between all the clients is of paramount importance.

Role of Trainers

Q 5 Training programmes respond to both present and future needs. The current perspective is more operational and the futuristic perspective is strategic.

Trainers should perform
1. Training role
2. Research role
3. Consulting role
4. Change management role

The other dimensions, relevant to role of training, are 'content' vs 'process'. Apart from their training roles, the trainers are required to discharge perform roles with respect to research, consulting, and change management. These roles have been taken up briefly as follows:

Training role—This role facilitates in developing competencies needed by various role occupants. The trainers must consider the curriculum, content, training aids, and learners' receptivity. Trainers must keep themselves updated, and must have the relevant technical knowledge.

The Indian Institute of Social Welfare and Business Management (IISWBM) conducts a series of executive development programmes titled 'managerial excellence' for executives of Garden Reach Shipbuilders and Engineers (GRSE), Kolkata.

Research role—Trainers must identify the necessary competencies for accomplishment of the product range and what will be needed in the organization in future. This role is of great help to the organization.

Consulting role—Many organizations require the help of consultancy when they cannot find the solution of a problem. Organizations also need consultancy to improve the management process in certain aspects, and to get actions and steps reviewed by external agencies. Trainers with vast experiential backgrounds and a reservoir of knowledge should preferably discharge the consulting role, in addition to their other roles. The exposure gained contributes to enhancing the effectiveness of their respective organizations. While striving to accomplish tasks, various teams need consultation. The trainers should extend the requisite consultancy to keep the wheel of synergy moving.

Faculty members of IISWBM extend consultancy on many disciplines such as energy management, environment management, ground water treatment, pollution control, and many other disciplines.

Change management role—Changes are a part and parcel of present-day business scenario. In today's competitive world, training becomes a true strategic partner. Leadership emerges as the focal point and training appears inescapable to develop leadership at all levels. Training becomes essential to enhance the ability of strategic thinking, taking responsibility, feeling accountable, elevate creativity, and empowering others.

As a strategic partner, training serves to transform the organization. The trainer must be involved in the main business of the organization or trainers are to be drawn from within the organization having exposure in multiple functional areas. Faculty members share their knowledge and experience to the students and participants. The knowledge imparted brings attitudinal change to them; alters their thinking process of analysing a situation, and way of working. Faculty members also discharge the role of moderators while managing change. By way of disseminating knowledge, faculty members silently bring in attitudinal change from which an organization derives benefits. The change management role played by knowledge disseminators is vital to any organization.

Behaviour of a Trainer towards Learners

The behaviour of trainer towards learners should be cordial and modest. When a group of trainers get together, they often wonder what should be the ideal characteristics of a good trainer. This is a frequent question asked by those who aspire to be good trainers. Often, people with the necessary attributes are not sure about the qualities that make a good trainer. Contextually, Kozoll (1975), the associate director of continuing education and public service, Harvard University, identifies the significant qualities that essentially enhance the performance of a trainer. According to him, trainers must exhibit certain qualities in their behaviours such as empathy, honesty, patience, pace, democracy, purpose, listening ability, respect for experience, and prestige.

Trainers' qualities to be exhibited are empathy, honesty, patience, pace, democracy, purpose, listening ability, respect for experience, and prestige.

Empathy Empathy is the ability to put oneself in the shoes of another and understand one's problem from his perspective. It is the faculty who should recognize the fears and uncertainties in the minds of trainees when learning additional techniques or skills. For a trainer to be empathetic, he must be able to point out the difficulties that he faced, as a trainee in similar situation.

Honesty Any person will have individual strengths and weaknesses. Honesty is the courage to recognize personal strengths and weaknesses, and to be frank about these to the personnel being trained, for one's own benefit.

Patience Patience is shown in the willingness to compliment slow progress and refrain from anger when trainees make mistakes. It includes the techniques of repeating instructions, breaking down a task into small units, rephrasing questions or views, and allowing time for learners to understand, interpret, and experience.

Pace This is closely integrated with empathy and patience and is an external speed governor, which acts more to slow down than to speed up. It is far better to move slowly and attain complete mastery, than to push for rapid and sloppy completion. If the trainer starts the deliberation slowly, confidence will build up and he/she will be able to establish closeness with the participants and disseminate knowledge better and more effectively.

Democracy A trainer should be supportive and non-threatening in presentations followed by answering questions by the trainees. Receptivity and grasping powers differ from one person to another. From this standpoint, the trainer is required to create the kind of atmosphere where learning can take place. The tone of his/her voice and facial expression should lead the learners to feel comfortable in raising questions, offering suggestions, reinterpreting instructions, and generally feeling relaxed while learning.

Purpose This underlines the element of tenacity in achieving the training goals. A good trainer conscientiously moves a group of learners to a preset destination. There may be stops and shifts, but the eye is always fixed on the set performance standards and levels.

Listening ability A trainer has to be an empathic listener. He/She must listen to the questions raised by trainees, understand and interpret them, and answer them to the satisfaction of the trainees. In some cases, the questions could be from some other area. In such cases too, the trainer must explain accordingly.

Respect for experience Adults will learn more effectively if respect is given to the experience and qualifications they bring to a situation. This will encourage greater participation in the process of learning and activities.

Prestige The trainer must give respect to others for it to be reciprocated. A trainer should command respect from his colleagues in the organization through his behavioural disposition. If the trainer pays respect and shows deference to the trainees, the training programme will be strengthened by way of acceptance of his/her deliberations among older and experienced employees. Trainers with these qualities will be able to apply the training methodology successfully and make the learning effective, leading to organizational excellence. Trainers need not demand respect; they should command it.

Trainers need not demand respect; they should command it.

PLANNING THE TRAINING

Conducting a training session requires a lot of planning. It requires a lot of different individuals to take their task seriously and compile their findings together to understand the nature of training required.

During a direct market survey, the organizational people are able to gather the customer expectations; the design personnel is able and competent to include all features in the product as expected by the customers; people responsible for product realization and translation of ideas into actions and transformation of the raw material into finished products are able to produce products with zero defects, zero losses, and zero drift to make cost-effective and quality products.

But in most of the cases, people responsible for their jobs are not able to keep up to the organization's expectations. An organization is also concerned with quality of its products.

International standard (ISO 9001) on quality management systems emphasizes that, 'personnel performing work affecting product quality is competent on the basis of appropriate education, training, skills, and experience'. The standard further specifies that the organization determines the necessary competence required for personnel performing work affecting product quality. This helps in framing certain requirements to be fulfilled during the training.

On behalf of the organization, the HRD manager must be vigilant to observe and record the changes in the business environment. For instance, training needs must take the corresponding changes required in the organization's processes, the stages of development of people, and the culture of the organization into account, before planning a training session. The basic objective is to provide knowledge and skills to the members of the organization, together with experience to improve their competence, enhance their performance, and ultimately contribute to the organizational performance. The secondary objective is enhancing their level of confidence from the gained knowledge.

There are a lot of other aspects that should also be looked into, including the experience of the trainee. Obviously, an experienced person can definitely perform the tasks assigned to him, and meet the quantitative and qualitative requirements, better than an inexperienced new recruit. The experienced person knows the criticality, job contents, requirements, and the methodology of converting the raw material into a finished product and translating the ideas into actions for service offerings. Hence, the type of training required to be given to the trainee will also vary.

Similarly, tacit knowledge is personal, context-specific, and therefore, is also difficult to formalize and communicate. Example of tacit knowledge includes the knowledge base of an expert. Much of an expert's knowledge is tacit, and cannot be articulated in abstract contexts, such as interviews. Tacit knowledge is more valuable than explicit knowledge because it provides a context for people, places, ideas, and experiences. On the contrary, explicit knowledge refers to the knowledge that is transmittable in formal, systematic language. It can be articulated, codified, and stored in certain media. Knowing the tacit and explicit knowledge of an employee broadens the avenue of the trainer to plan accordingly to achieve and accelerate the achievement of the organizational policies, objectives, and goals.

For instance, a senior person should definitely have certain managerial and leadership skills other than the contextual knowledge. Through training and development, these enabling capacities of a person can be further enhanced.

Some other essential considerations for the planning process are listed in Box 9.4.

Box 9.4 Involving people

To facilitate the involvement of people, training and development should also include discussions on the following:

1. The vision for the future of the organization
2. Organization's policies and objectives

(Contd)

Box 9.4 (Contd)

3. Organizational change and development
4. The initiation and implementation of the improvement processes
5. Benefits from creativity and innovation
6. Organization's impact on the society
7. Needs and expectations of customers and other interested parties
8. Managerial and leadership skills

TRAINING POLICY

Apart from the planning, any training organization needs to have a defined training policy, training objectives, and strategies to achieve the objectives. A training manager needs to keep them in mind as well. Corresponding to the policy, there can be few objectives. However, all the objectives must be measurable and there should be a strategy; a way and means of achieving them. The training department of an organization should also have a training manual.

It is important for the organization to be able to address the client organization's viewpoints with regard to the training and answer certain questions such as:

1. What do you aspire to accomplish through training?
2. Is there any person responsible for organizing training programmes?
3. Should the training be formal or informal?
4. What are the training priorities?
5. What types of training are needed?
6. What should be the venue of the training?
7. Should training be one-time, continuous, or need based?
8. Who should identify the training needs?
9. Should external experts be invited in demanding cases?
10. Which outside agencies should be associated with training?
11. Should there be any system of evaluating the training programmes?
12. What should be the payment terms during the period of training?
13. How should training be related to labour policy?

TRAINING OBJECTIVE

The institute under reference prepares a draft course calendar based on the views of the heads of different functional areas, course calendar of the previous year, requests from regular clients, and inputs informally collected from conventions, seminars, and miscellaneous sources. The institute then sends this draft course calendar to their corporate office for approval. The corporate office further considers the training and development needs at national level and incorporates changes. The institute then finalizes the course calendar and circulates it to all regular customers.

The institute strives to adhere to the course calendar (the first objective). It collects feedbacks from the participants on the concluding day of each short-term course. Using a formula, it computes the course grading for everyone, and at the end of the year, it calculates the yearly course grading, which the institute wants to sustain and improve (the second objective).

The institute aims to keep a track of the application of the knowledge gained by the participants in their work area. After about six to eight months, it collects information (in well-designed formats) from the sponsoring units, to measure post training impacts (the third objective). At the planning stage of the course, the institute develops a programme displaying the topic of the course, the faculty, the time against each day of the course duration, and how it intends to perform conforming to the plan (the fourth objective). The corporate body remains vigilant to watch the course execution by all the institutes under its control and, as such, demands reports from the training institutes generally on a monthly basis (the fifth objective). The training policy (statement) and objectives of Ordnance Factories Institute of Learning, Ishapore (OFILIS) is given in Exhibit 9.2.

Exhibit 9.2 Policy and objective

Training policy

We commit to fulfil the training needs of regular and other customers by providing effective training services. We also commit to enhance customer satisfaction and continually improve the standard of training.

Training objectives

1. To adhere completely to course calendar (plan)
2. To sustain the annual course grading (ACG) and to further improve the quality of the courses by enhancing the ACG
3. To enhancing level of customer satisfaction by post training impact measurement for regular and repetitive courses by five per cent
4. To adhere 100 per cent to programmes for all courses
5. To adhere 100 per cent to monthly training report schedule

Source: OFILIS (2005).

TRAINING VALIDATION

Q 6 Validation of a training programme means corroboration, justification, or rationality of conducting the training. It directly refers and applies to the programme and its immediate results. Validation is categorized as internal validation and external validation.

Internal validation During internal validation, the focus is on the 'closeness and nearness' of the training and learning, thus resulting in the improvements, gaining knowledge, and enhancing the skills of the trainee. These, in turn, contribute to the enhancement of organizational performance.

External validation An organization has to objectively identify the training needs and provide the training to achieve the business goals. External validation involves a series of analysis designed to ascertain whether the objectives of an internally valid programme are based on accurate information, in relation to the criteria of training needs. This is to ensure the following:

1. Training is carried out in the most efficient and effective manner.
2. It is carried out at the lowest or most reasonable cost without compromising on the quality of training.
3. The training has a high implementation value.

DIFFERENT PHASES OF TRAINING

A training process starts with designing a curriculum. The different phases of organizing a training or management development programme include the following:

Training need identification The training needs of the people must be identified by following a structured procedure. The deficit of knowledge and skills required to perform the tasks assigned to people is of paramount importance. Identifying the training need, the tools, and identification checklist will be discussed in the subsequent section.

Developing the training curriculum A curriculum is a set of courses of actions and includes preparation of training specification, training methods, developing the syllabus, time and facility planning, etc.

Designing appropriate pedagogy Pedagogy generally refers to the strategies or a style of teaching instruction. Productive pedagogy is very comprehensive. Andragogy refers to the art and science of teaching or training adults.

Evaluating the training programme This is done to usually adjudge the effectiveness of a training programme.

Post-training work After the training is done, documentation helps in conducting courses in the future.

These five phases are also considered to be the checkpoints in organizing a training programme. Refer to Exhibit 9.3 for more details.

Exhibit 9.3 Planning an orientation and induction programme

Ordnance Factory Board, Ministry of Defence, recruited 56 chargemen (non-technical staff) through open advertisements in daily newspapers and the employment news. The board entrusted the tasks of designing the entire orientation and induction programme of about ten months to Regional Training Institute (RTI), Ishapore.

RTI planned the programme in two phases—phase I (26 weeks) and phase 2 (18 weeks). The first phase was designed to impart theoretical knowledge and practices followed in ordnance factories. This phase comprised five disciplines: (a) man management and personality development, (b) office management, (c) quality, environment, energy, and safety management systems, (d) material management, and (e) general management factory procedures. One competent course director was detailed for each discipline.

The draft syllabi were prepared based on the expressed need of client ordnance factories. The draft syllabi were submitted to the meeting of management development committee for scrutiny and comments. The syllabi of phase I were finalized.

Time and facility planning was carried out, the pedagogy was determined, and the infrastructure was settled by experienced faculty members.

At the end of phase I, absorption of knowledge was tested through written tests and viva voce. Industrial visits, and tours to places of historical and academic interests were organized. Faculty members of RTI escorted them during the tour programmes. Trainees were asked to maintain diary to record observations.

Phase 2 was aimed at the application of the knowledge in practices. Initially, they were posted in different sections and departments of Rifle Factory, Ishapore, and Metal and Steel Factory, Ishapore.

Some 56 management trainees (chargemen) were divided into eight groups and two projects were assigned to each group. The groups completed their projects, prepared power point slides, and offered presentation to faculty members. Thereafter, each trainee was interviewed individually and in groups, to further verify the knowledge they received and application of knowledge in the workplace.

Based on the results of phase ending examinations, continuous evaluation, and leadership skills exhibited, they were ranked.

IDENTIFYING THE TRAINING NEED

To make the training, development, and delivery easier, one has to have detailed knowledge about the requirements of the organization. The process must be focused, goal directed, and tuned with the achievement of business needs in a cost-effective way. Analysing the training needs provides a focus and direction for the investment that an organization must make to develop its people.

Four major approaches for collecting data relating to job performance are meeting managers, interviews, desk researches, and self-complete questionnaire.

Training need assessment helps to

1. pinpoint if training will make a difference in productivity and the bottom line,
2. decide what specific training each employee needs and what will improve their job performance, and
3. differentiate between the need for training and organizational issues.

There are many different techniques used for collecting data that needs to go into a training module.

Several basic training needs assessment techniques include meeting managers, questionnaires, review of company goals, focus group, records and report studies, and HR audit reports.

Meeting managers The trainer can meet the management to inquire about the achievement of business goals and involvement of the supervisors with the planning of projects and the future of the company. Managers will communicate where their employee's current abilities lie, and what is needed to get them to the next level for new projects on the horizon.

Questionnaires The trainer is required to design a questionnaire and administer that to the employees, and to the immediate supervisors, to be aware of the shortcomings of an employee. Consultation with persons in key positions, and/or with specific knowledge will help in decision-making.

Review of company goals A brief review of the company's past and where they are headed for in the future may also reveal valuable information for training sessions. A comparison should be made of what employees are currently doing, and what will be expected of them as the company continues to grow and change.

Focus groups You can also meet the employees to discuss what difficulties they may be facing in their day-to-day activities, and what would make their job easier and more efficient. Remember to keep them focused on what they need rather than on what they want. You should discuss with the line managers about the recorded points.

Records and report studies You can get valuable information from various records, for example, performance appraisal reports, performance review reports, HR audit reports, gap analysis records, and the like.

HR audit reports These reports (a) examine and pinpoint the strengths and weaknesses related to HR areas and skills, and competencies to enable an organization to achieve its long-term and short-terms goals, (b) increase the effectiveness of the design and implementation of human resource policies, planning, and programmes, and (c) help human resource planners develop and update employment and programme plans. Thus, you can assess the training needs referring to the audit reports.

Basic training needs assessment techniques include meeting managers, questionnaires, review of company goals, focus group, records and report studies, and HR audit reports.

There are certain other tools too that can be used for identifying training needs. Some of these are as follows:

Analysis of activity List the activities required in manufacturing a product or offering service or part thereof, in a logical sequence, and then determine what new competency, knowledge, or skill is required to successfully accomplish the product or service. This analysis also helps to find out necessary modification of present knowledge or skill.

Analysis of the problems If any task is performed without any problem or the problem remains hidden, then this analysis is not called for. But in case of emergence of any problem, this analysis is done to identify the root cause behind the problem and to ascertain the knowledge, skill, or both, in addition to the insights required.

Analysis of behaviour There are some potential employees who might behave differently at times. Analysis of these typical behaviours can help the management to be aware of all kinds of behaviours and their corrective action involving training.

Analysis of an organization Organizational diagnostics and analysis of organizational weaknesses provides clues to identify individual and group training needs.

Appraisal of performance Analysis of performance through formal performance appraisal or informal performance review helps determine whether someone lacks something, be it additional knowledge, skill, or understanding colleagues or the situation. These features could be included in the training sessions.

Brainstorming The unique technique of brainstorming is widely used in total quality management and many other disciplines. A group of homogeneous people from the work area meets at regular intervals to generate new ideas around a specific issue of interest. The issue may be with regard to solving a problem or for developing any system or procedure. Using brainstorming rules, which removes inhibitions; people are able to think more freely and move into new areas of thought and create numerous new thought-provoking ideas and solutions. The participants spell out ideas as they occur to them and also build on the ideas raised by others. One contributes the idea only when his turn comes in a systematic brainstorming session. All the ideas are noted down and are not criticized during the 'idea collection' stage. Only when the brainstorming session is over, the ideas are evaluated. Brainstorming helps to identify training needs from the answers to the 'how to' questions.

Buzzing This refers to interacting with the seniors, peers, and junior colleagues on 'what additional areas of knowledge do we need to handle the work better?'

Card sort Statemens or potential training needs are first written on cards, which are given to the participating members, whose ideas are sought. They arrange the cards in order of importance.

Checklist A whole job, process, programme, or area of responsibility is broken down into detailed parts or activities and arranged in logical sequence. Each person likely to be engaged in the job, checks the list to identify the additional inputs (knowledge or skill) that he/she needs to successfully accomplish the work.

Comparison This involves comparing what an individual is doing and what else he/she is being asked to do.

Conference This helps in decision-making on training needs identification.

Consultants If the task is critical and not so familiar, then an external consultant is engaged to identify the training needs.

Counselling It refers to discussions between a training practitioner and the person seeking guidance. A counselor listens attentively to what one says, works with him to define his goals with respect to his values and culture, appreciates the thoughts, feelings and worries about a situation, and helps to gain insight into how to act, think, and feel. He teaches, shows, and helps one to express emotions in one's own way and work out solutions to problems, and guides and supports the person towards his needs. Most importantly, he uses a variety of different techniques to help one to explore what is important and to become empowered to act in ways that are in ones best interest.

In-basket Managers are facing problems every day. The in-basket method is used to test the manager's ability to handle the problems. The problems come to his 'inbox' from various sources. The inbox may be electronic, say, intranet, LAN, WAN, or through e-mail.

Patra (2009) mentions the data source recommended and the corresponding training need implication. Refer to Table 9.4.

Table 9.4 Data source for training need implication

S. no.	Data source recommended	Training need implication
1.	Analysis of records and reports	A prolific source of information that is already available, hence, a time-saving device can enhance the objectivity of needs assessment.
2.	Inter-firm comparison	Enables a firm to compare its general performance and potential with other similar companies, find the areas where to look for improvement, and emulates performance.
3.	Management (diagnostic) survey	Provides information on main problems faced by the organization, including the indication of strengths and weaknesses, areas and units where training needs might be important.
4.	Management development audit	Managers' views and wishes are considered, and a comprehensive picture of management development within the organization is given.
5.	Attitude survey	Determines the opinions and feelings of a large group of individuals, and leads to a better understanding of the causes of different problems, anticipate undesired events, identify some training needs and improve the quality of decision making process and management style.
6.	Organizational goals and objectives	This is the place where training emphasis can and should be placed. It can highlight deviations from objectives and performance problem.
7.	Analysis of efficiency indexes	Cost accounting concepts may represent the ratio between actual performance and desired or standard performance.

Usually, organizations are well equipped with a definite structure to identify their training needs, but in some cases, they may miss a particular factor while finalizing the training curriculum. To overcome such problems, it is helpful for the organization to have a checklist suited as per their structure to be able to choose the best method for training.

The checklist (Box 9.5) should summarize the kinds of information discussed earlier.

Box 9.5 Checklist to identify training needs

The checklist to identify the training needs may include the following:

1. Increase/decrease in customer complaints
2. Loss/gain of customers
3. Higher/lower production than the target
4. High/low labour turnover and manpower attrition
5. High/low machine breakdown
6. Deviations in messages sent

(Contd)

Box 9.5 (Contd)

7. Excessive waste and scrap
8. Non-moving material increasing carrying costs
9. Deviation from the product specification
10. Errors in measuring tools
11. Flaws in measurement system
12. Undue acceptance or rejection
13. Lack of employee involvement
14. Faulty verbal instructions given by supervisors
15. High maintenance costs
16. Increase in accidents
17. Ignoring company rules
18. Declining markets
19. Employee complacency
20. Lack of a sense of belonging
21. Lack of challenging attitudes
22. Inability to solve problems
23. Deficient empowerment
24. Non-availability of data regarding customer requirements
25. Inability to meet customer expectations

One can group these checkpoints in categories such as human-related, machine-related, method-related, material-related, and measurement-related, in order to make decisions on the type of training or workshop to be organized.

DEVELOPING THE TRAINING CURRICULUM

A curriculum is a set of courses or a plan for a particular area of study. A curriculum includes a statement of an underlying philosophy or a learning theory, various assumptions, a program goal (short, concise, general statement of the overall purpose of a program), objectives, strategies to achieve the training objectives, instructional materials, programme timeframe, accountability, etc. It is important to develop the curriculum meticulously.

As discussed earlier, the curriculum of the training is designed, considering the initial behaviours (what a trainee knows in the area relevant, that is, the background knowledge in possession of the trainees at start of the training programme). The training designer develops the curriculum to elevate the knowledge of trainees to a level termed as, 'criterion behaviour'. The organizer of the training programme needs to pre-plan training specifications, methods, steps, syllabus, etc. and keep in mind the impediments that he could come across to get best results.

Haldar and Sarkar (2010) emphasize that, 'An organization has to design curriculum of training encompassing training specification (to meet specific business goal, participant profile, and training objectives and methods). The organization needs to consider the competencies of trainers, develop means of validating and evaluating results, and decide the pedagogical aids followed by training design. It must take into account the impediments to effective training, and specification of training methods. Most importantly, the organization must determine the time and facilities required before working on designing the curriculum.

TRAINING SPECIFICATION

The specification of training objectives and implementation of courses around objectives are becoming significant parts of instructional technology. Specification helps to finalize the training method that can be used, and the time required by the faculty members in preparing and developing the reading material, lesson plan, exercises, quizzes, and power point slides.

A training specification must invariably include certain information as follows:

1. Details of the business goals that have prompted the training to be conducted
2. Profiles of the participants undergoing the training
3. Training objectives
4. Training methods to produce the desired result
5. Competency levels of the trainers
6. Means of validating and evaluating the result
7. Training routine, showing the topic, duration, faculty, date, and time
8. Venue indicating the pedagogical aids available
9. Any other factors to be accounted for and constraints to be considered

To understand the specification of the training methods, the syllabus and objectives of a course entitled 'Internal Audit (ISO 9001:2000)' should be considered leading to the calculation of time and facilitaties required to achieve each objective. Refer to Exhibit 9.4 and Box 9.6 for details on internal audit (ISO 9001).

Exhibit 9.4 Syllabus of internal audit (ISO 9001)

The syllabus of the course entitled internal audit (ISO 9001:2000 quality management system—requirements) is reproduced to elucidate and explain the specifications of training module.

S. no.	Topic	Hours
1.	Course structure, contents, participant's requirements, examination, pass/fail criteria and other evaluation structure including continuous evaluation	0.50
2.	Quality philosophy	0.75
3.	Quality management principles, process model with cases	1.50
4.	Quality vocabulary (based on ISO 9000)	0.50
5.	Clauses of ISO 9001	4.00
6.	Case study (one for each for the clauses)	2.00
7.	Specific requirements of the current revision of ISO 9001 to other members of the ISO 9000 serie.	0.75
8.	Documented procedures and mandatory records	0.75
9.	Audit-related vocabulary based on ISO 9000	0.50
10.	Types of audits with examples: (a) system, process and product audit, (b) internal and external audit, (c) first party, second party, and third party audit, (d) compliance, pre-assessment, and certification/initial assessment and surveillance audit	1.00
11.	Role and responsibilities of auditor, team leader, auditee, process of certification of organization's quality systems	1.00
12.	Auditor's personal qualifications and conduct; do's and don'ts of conducting audit	0.75
13.	Individual exercises and discussion will follow all the above topics	1.00
14.	Case study on typical nonconformity	1.50
15.	Audit report (nonconformity) writing—individual exercises	0.75
16.	Group exercise on checklist preparation	0.75

(Contd)

Exhibit 9.4 (Contd)

17.	Review and discussion.	1.00
18.	Assessment test (100 marks) (#)	2.00
	Total course time in hours	21.00
(#)	Continuous evaluation—50 marks	

Box 9.6 Objectives of course on internal audit (ISO 9001)

After successful completion of the course the participants shall be able to

1. Develop quality system
2. Understand of quality management system and scope of ISO 9001
3. Interpret the clauses of ISO 9001
4. Understand the auditing of practice documents
5. Perform the task of internal auditing, fulfilling the requirements of the clause of ISO 9001

WAYS TO PRODUCE THE DESIRED RESULT

The training objectives, content of the training material, and the target trainees are the considerations while designing the training method. Conjointly, the three considerations can give the idea about how the training should be delivered.

For example, (a) training for the operating core of an organization needs practical demonstration, (b) junior level management personnel may be satisfied through computer- based training (CBT), (c) middle level managers prefer to learn through syndicate exercises involving decision-making and use/implementation of technology, market analysis, and deciding market penetration strategy, and (d) senior level managers shall be pleased with methods compatible with analysing business scenario, changing environment, technology selection, etc.

STEPS IN DESIGNING A TRAINING PROGRAMME

Reddy (2005) mentions that resources available, skills of the trainer(s), type of trainees, principles of learning, learning objectives and methods, and media for learning are the influencing criteria for the design of training. There are five steps in the design of a training programme.

Step 1: Choosing a strategy or usually a combination of strategies. The strategies, in turn, favour certain tools in the kit of training methods.

Step 2: Breaking the objectives into constituent parts. The rough breakdown may be classified into competent knowledge, understanding, and skills.

Step 3: Using the specifications of training methods with the aims to arrive at the total; adding the total to arrive at the rough grand total of time and facilities required by the programme as a whole.

Step 4: Deciding different packages or modules in which the programme could be offered and one can choose the acceptable alternative from these.

Step 5: Working out detailed training events into training sequences, and finally into the shape of the whole programme package.

TRAINING METHODS

There are multiple ways of organizing training and disseminating knowledge. The most commonly used methodologies are lectures, talks, discussions, in-basket (in-tray), business games, role playing, case study, sensitivity training (group dynamics), conferences and seminars, programmed instructions, computer-based training, exercises, projects, simulations and games, remote telecommunication, live teaching, laboratory training, managerial grid sessions, distance learning, etc. Each of these has its own advantages and application areas to achieve the objectives. Broadly, the methods are grouped in two categories, namely, informational and experiential.

Informational methods This method is primarily informational or transmittal in nature, and principally uses one-way communication to transmit the information (knowledge) to the learners (trainees or students). Examples include talks, lecture methods (gaining new knowledge), audiovisuals (gaining new knowledge and attention), independent study (gaining new knowledge, completing degree requirements, and continuous education), programmed instruction and e-learning. The programmed instruction method facilitates pre-training preparation to ensure that all trainees have similar backgrounds. The e-learning method, is an informational method, and uses electronic technology to deliver, support, and enhances teaching and learning.

Experiential methods In the experiential method, learners get the opportunity to interact with the faculty, which is distinctly different from academic learning. The faculty may, however, be replaced by a computer or simulator, customers, or other trainees. Experiential learning is the process of learning from direct experience. This is highly suited for the acquisition of practical skills, where trial and error, and the opportunity to practice practical techniques related to real tasks is essential. In many countries, experiential learning is integral to vocational education. This learning method is focused on the learner and his/her experience, as it focuses on the communicative relationship and exchange of information between teacher and learner. On-the-job training, equipment simulators, games and simulation, case study and analysis, role playing, behavioural modeling, and sensitivity (or t-group) training are a few examples of the experiential methods.

Some of the most common training methods come under both the categories. Some of these are as follows:

Application Project

Teachers are always seen to advice students to administer exercises at the end of, preferably every topic. These exercises ensure students to have a thorough understanding of the topics. Similarly, in application projects students get a greater opportunity to display their initiative and creative ideas. During the course of these projects, teachers lay down the task to be accomplished, whereas the students decide the lines of actions to achieve them. These projects are usually pursued out by a single student or by a group of students. The project reports help in providing feedback on a range of personal qualities of the trainees as well as their range of knowledge and attitude to the assigned task.

The trainees must be motivated by the trainer, stating that they have to pursue the project seriously in their own interest. The project topic and objectives must be relevant to their needs. If the trainee fails or feels that he has failed to pursue the project, there will be severe loss of confidence on his part. This might even result in antagonism towards the trainer. The trainer must be meticulous in saving the confidence of the trainees in both, his and trainees' interest. It is evidenced that trainees are generally hypersensitive to criticism of the project in which he/she has invested adequate efforts.

Apprenticeship

One important component of HRD is upgrading the knowledge and skills of its employees. It is important for trainings to happen at the actual work place other than what the training institutions provide. Apprenticeship is a system of training to impart knowledge, help acquire skills, and gaining competencies to meet the demand for skilled craftsman. The apprentice scheme includes on-the-job training, in addition to theoretical classes at industrial training institutes as well as factories.

The Government enacted the Apprentices Act, 1961, with the objectives of regulating the programme of training of apprentices in the industry, thus keeping in mind the need to conform to the syllabi, period of training, etc., as laid down by the central apprenticeship council. This would also help to utilize the facilities available in industry fully by imparting practical training with a view to meeting the requirements of skilled manpower for industry.

In India, the Department Of Education, which falls under the Ministry of HRD, is responsible for the implementation of this Act with respect to graduates, technical, and vocational apprentices. The Ministry monitors this through four boards of apprenticeship training located at Kanpur, Kolkata, Mumbai, and Chennai.

Behavioural Modelling

This is alternatively known as behaviour simulation games, and is used to impart knowledge on interpersonal skills, ways of working in a team, and cognitive teaching/training skills. Behavioural simulation games focus primarily on the processes of interpersonal relations, on how decisions are made, and with what consequences, rather than on the substance of the decisions (Lynton and Pareek 2007). The games consist of set rules and predictable results.

Instructors use such games to highlight a particular behavioural process appropriate for a particular situation and to dramatize the effect. It is important to note that the games should not be repeated with the same group, as they will simply be a meaningless attempt. Structured exercises are particular types of simulation that can be repeated until learning is assured. Thus, exercises provide scope for improvisation, adaptation, and redesigning, according to personal and situational needs.

Business Games

Business games or management games are suitable for giving trainee managers practice in dealing with management problems during the induction phase. Trainees are presented with detailed information about a company, its financial position, product range, customers, suppliers, markets, business status, competitors, etc. They are given different management roles to perform. One group may be concerned with production, whereas others may be concerned with maintenance, quality control, planning, purchase, marketing, sales, store, and so on. These groups then virtually run the company during the training sessions. They take decisions, plan actions, and compute probable results in terms of profitability.

This simulation of real-life situation aids the transfer of learning. This is necessary because if a trainee manager, after completion of his training, applies only broad theoretical knowledge to the work situation, it could cause major problems. This is a valuable way of assessing the performance of a trainee through his potential and decision-making ability.

The main difficulty lies in assessing the probable results of the decisions taken. Nowadays, computers are used for this purpose. The trainees may reject the decisions if they feel the assessment of the probable outcome of their decisions is unrealistic.

Career Counselling

Career counselling helps employees discover their true potential and interest in various tasks in order to help them progress in their career. Experienced employees help the trainees, new recruits, and other employees to identify the areas of improvement, and guide them on advancement in their professional career. Similarly, in academic institutions, career counselling helps students discover their true potential and interest in various subjects in order to help them choose the right career.

Several institutes, including schools and colleges, offer career counselling using a series of aptitude, EQ, and IQ tests. The tests usually have multiple choice questions, which do not have to be prepared in any way. Thereafter, the employee or the student, as the case may be, has a face-to-face interview with a career guidance counsellor. The interview provides the employee or the student with the opportunity to clear any doubts or queries he/she may have regarding career progression and career options. It also allows the counsellor to further judge the aptitude of the employee or student.

Case Study

A case is a written description of an actual business situation. Case studies fall into two broad categories in which the trainees (a) diagnose the causes of a problem and (b) set out to solve a particular problem. A case may illustrate diverse situations in an organization. These situations could be based on any financial position, market position, emerging competitors, planning of new technology, diversity management problems, human related issues, and so forth. The trainees need to examine the events, consider the business scenario, contemplate organizational culture, and devise a solution for implementation. It is important for the trainer to give proper instructions to the trainees before they go ahead with analysing a case.

The case must reflect the exact work situation; otherwise, the trainees may get a wrong impression of the real work situation. They should not feel that the decisions taken by them are only for practice in the classroom. The teacher's skill lies in convincing them that the decisions are applicable in live situations as well. The case study method enhances the power of realistic analysis, problem-solving ability, and capacity of exploration, decision-making skills, and analytical skills. The trainees should preferably be asked to present their findings to adjudge the communication skills. The trainer must be involved in the process, and be psychologically close to the trainees.

Coaching

The purpose of coaching is developing a person to fit him in a role. Coaching is a systematic process that is collaborative, solution-focused, and result-oriented. The coach helps the mentee to enhance his performance. The trainee gets close attention, continuous feedback, and learns various methods of skill development. In an industrial organization, the master craftsman coaches his juniors or the trainees attached to him.

Computer-based Training

Computer-based training (CBT) is usually conducted in classrooms with the facility of networked computers. An individual undergoes this training in a self-paced format. With the advent and advancement of computer facilities and networking, there can be an almost limitless interplay between instructor-led and individual-based computer training. Computer-based training is a unique approach to classroom training, a principal example of today's self-paced training approaches.

Computers and networking have produced an enormous impact on the delivery of training in organizations today. Interactive compact discs on educational topics provide the added advantages.

Today, it is estimated that 55 per cent of organizations use computer-based training via CD-ROM in their training programmes, with other multimedia-based efforts, thus pushing the number of computer-based approaches much higher (Werner, et al. 2007). Microcomputers and the rapid increase of their capabilities have further influenced the growth of CBT.

Conferences and Seminars

In conferences and seminars on selected themes and sub-themes, delegates present papers and the organizing committee publishes the proceedings, either on hard copy or on CDs, or both. Based on the sub-themes, the committee prepares a schedule of lectures. The speaker delegates present their papers and freely interchange knowledge, ideas, opinions, and findings on any of the sub-themes. They deliver the latest information citing examples from national and international businesses. Attending a seminar broadens, stimulates, and widens the spectrum of knowledge on the seminar theme and sub-themes.

Professional Courses

Universities, academic institutes, and other professional institutes organize course programmes relating to specific organizational needs. The objective of the programmes is to enhance the enabling capacities of the personnel to perform specific activities or work packages. Such courses are generally of short duration.

Discussion

While using this method, the teacher freely shares his knowledge, experience, opinion, and ideas on a particular subject with his students. This method manifests its importance when dissemination of information, attitudinal change, and behavioural modification is imperative. The teacher elucidates the aftermath of an incident due to the attitude of a person (perhaps one holding a managerial position) in a particular situation, particularly if the attitude is non-conducive to organizational effectiveness. This narration can impact the trainee's subconscious mind. This realization may result in attitudinal change and behavioural modification. As a manager of learning, the teacher should have the flair to offer positive direction in order to yield only positive results. The discussion has to be motivational as well as appealing.

Distance Learning

This is different from learning in a conventional classroom. Most distance learners, study in open universities after gaining some experience in the conventional face-to-face education system. Distance learning uses a variety of media and technology, where the learners primarily learn independently, from a distance.

The students are expected to read material supplied to them on their own. They are supposed to study at home, and do not readily get the opportunity of having their doubts and confusions clarified as in the conventional learning system. Such universities operate study centres in dispersed locations. Isolation from peer groups and irregular contact at the study centre may also become a major hindrance in learning.

Experience shows that learners need to develop effective learning strategies and discipline to succeed in distance learning. The Indira Gandhi National Open University (IGNOU, www.ignou.org) is the pioneer provider of distance learning in India. IGNOU provides reading material to the students and supplies them with a handbook to empower them in the learning process, and prepare them to make the best use of the facilities provided by the university. The handbook describes the steps that distance learners should follow to be effective learners. In the management programmes, IGNOU generally gives three assignments; two are tutor-marked, and one is computer-marked. Attempting the assignments ensures the students' involvement with the subject. The weightage allotted is 30 per cent for the assignments and 70 per cent for the term end examinations.

E-learning

Learning has moved from the classroom onto the desktop, and now into the pocket. E-learning refers to gaining new knowledge, being pre-trained to ensure that all training has a similar background, and to get into a homogenous group. Many companies are seen to be switching to e-learning. In simple terms, e-learning delivers better training to more people at the least training cost. This method is not only flexible, fast, and convenient, but also saves time, money, and resources.

E-learning also relates to knowledge management. The key to success is dissemination of knowledge (from the people who have it) to the people who need it. The knowledge transfer process delivers measurable and tangible results. Access, information, and speed occupy the driver's seat, and characterize today's world. These days, organizations want to make their employees aware of new information and technology. Learners, too, want a fast and suitable way to learn new skills and information. E-learning is a way to satisfy the individual and organizational needs.

Induction

Induction refers to the introduction of an employee to the job and the organization. The primary purpose is to 'sell' the company to the new recruit, so that he may feel proud of being an employee of the company. An employee has to work with fellow employees, comply with the policies and practices, work in teams, integrate with team members, and know them. Hence, it is always better to give an idea of the entire work frame to the newly employed. Further, inadequate induction may lead to higher manpower turnover, confusion and misunderstanding, wastage of time, and expenditure.

In an induction programme, the evolution of the company, its principal products, technology of production and major operations, organization structure, functions of the departments in brief, and the employee's own department, company policy and objectives, service conditions, employee welfare measures, working hours and overtime, reporting relationship, grievance and discipline handling mechanism, recreational facilities, career planning and promotion, and the like are discussed.

Internships

Management and technical institutes depute their students to organizations in order to familiarize them with real-life situations and gain experience. These organizations allot certain assignments to these interns to develop them. The duration for these internships is generally from two to four months. Some institutes call it a summer internship programme (SIP).

Intranet-based Training

Organizations have started using intranet for internal communication. HRD professionals are also seen to be using intranet to communicate with learners, identify training needs, impart training, transmit reading material, administer exercises and case studies, organize multimedia programmes, and miscellaneous administration activities. This is called intranet-based training (IBT). Conducting assessment tests through intranet is another very common feature.

In case of multinational companies, with branches in multiple countries, their geographical locations and dispersion are never a problem with IBT. The Indian Society for Training and Development (ISTD) is conducting diploma courses on training, and comprises eight papers in its curriculum. Paper 7 is on 'Electronic enabled training systems,' and paper 8 is on 'Electronic enabled training office and administration'. The objectives of the subjects are (a) to help the participants understand the concept, application, and evaluation of electronic-enabled training systems and (b) to help the participants understand the concept, practice, and management of electronic-enabled training office and administration. Many employed people, including senior executives from organizations, are pursuing the diploma programme to gain and utilize the knowledge in respective organizations.

Job Assignments

In this method, the employees are assigned particular tasks that are completely new to them. After completion they are asked to prepare a short report highlighting their observations, deficiencies felt, difficulties encountered, competency required in the process, scope of improvement in the process, developing the quality plan relating to the particular task, etc. This method greatly helps in discovering the credibility and inner potential of employees, and eventually helps the employees develop their potential.

Managerial Grid Sessions

Rapidly-growing large companies are choosing this method of training and requires considerable investment and time. Managerial grid sessions are generally five or six phased programmes extending over three to five years. The session starts with upgrading managerial skills, developing interpersonal relations, cultivating group dynamics, and several other managerial competencies. The sessions finally goes into corporate planning, strategic management, gaining visionary skills, business environment study and analysis, developing and designing implementation methods, etc. The programme ends with an evaluation phase.

Programmed Instructions

This is a technology aimed to improve the quality of teaching. It refers to self-teaching with the support of a specialized text book or teaching software. The device presents study material in a logical sequence. Programmed instructions encompass two essential elements—(a) a step-by-step series of bits of knowledge to build upon what has been done previously, and (b) a mechanism for presenting reviews and checking on the knowledge gained by the trainee.

Remote Telecommunication—Live Teaching

The faculty delivers lectures to groups of students in remote classrooms. The facility includes two-way voice communications where the students can address questions to the faculty. Through this teaching, the locations can be widely dispersed, say, the faculty may be located in the US and students in India, Pakistan, China, or elsewhere. The students or participants may belong to branches in different countries of a multinational company. Experienced and highly-skilled faculty members are assigned the responsibility of lecturing so that the topic content is delivered in a logical sequence with minimal gaps. This reduces the number of questions raised by the participants, thus trimming down the time, and economizing the session. Some faculty members use overhead or LCD projectors, too. The popularity of this method is ever increasing. Experts from Massachusetts Institute of Technology, Harvard Business School, or London School of Economics share their knowledge, experience, and research findings through this technology-backed method.

Role Play

A role is a set of interrelated behaviours, rights, and obligations as conceptualized by one in organizational or social situations. In role-play, participants are assigned specific roles of characters that may have personalities, motivations, and backgrounds different from their own. For example, after selecting a group, one trainee may be asked to play the role of marketing manager, the second trainee the role of finance manager, the third trainee the role of chairman and managing director, and so on. They may be asked to interpret their roles, and discuss among themselves, thus leading to decision-making for a given problem in a hypothetical situation. Role play is used for changing attitudes, practising skills, and analysing interpersonal problems.

Sensitivity (or t-group) Training

This methodology is widely used to enhance self-awareness, and to facilitate trainees to see how others see them. It is an experience of interpersonal relationships. This training encompasses learning and unlearning of certain things.

A situation is created and the trainees are virtually put into the situations in which the behaviour of each individual in the group is examined, along with the comments of other trainees. Generally, the group of trainees is unstructured. This is a vivid way for the trainee to learn the effect of his/her behaviour on other people, and vice versa. There may be difficulties if the trainee learns something distasteful about him. Occasionally, a participant may indulge in arguments when the facilitator will have to handle the situation. Others' comments must be taken sportively as this is the only scope when one can be aware about one's own shortcomings and weaknesses.

The trainer acts as a catalyst or a facilitator throughout the process. Having been given a task, the group members are motivated to express their feelings, which are analysed, and dealt with by the trainer spontaneously. The behaviour of the group or groups as a whole gets examined. The trainer or facilitator should have industrial experience or a psychological background. He has to analyse the behaviour and offer his comments in an acceptable manner to the participants. This enables one to understand why people behave as they do. It promotes communication skills, improves interpersonal relations, synergy, and working in a team.

Simulations of Real Life

Training in the field is a major venture, and effective roles for participants can take time to be established and performed. In order to reduce the associated costs and to provide practice of roles in a variety of situations, the training designer can move one step ahead towards real life by incorporating simulation. Simulation can range from simple to more elaborate methods. It includes role playing, games, and in-basket exercises.

Lynton and Pareek (2007) have emphasized that talking about people and talking with people is different. Role playing is a very flexible training method, and can be very real in these situations. To provide practice of in-basket exercises, you are required to rotate the participants through key roles. Management trainees are given the opportunity to work at an office desk with ringing telephones, read reports and give comments, study noting and give decisions, mark letters specifying action plans, and deal with whatever comes to the in-tray.

Fundamental research has established that (a) simulations and games are more effective at transferring learning to students than case studies, (b) students with non-convergent learning styles enjoy simulations more than those with convergent learning styles, (c) senior managers, say, over 40 years of age, prefer simulations that use real industry data over games that used fabricated data, and (d) younger managers who have used computer games in their childhood, enjoy simulations and games more than case studies; they also learned more from simulations and games.

This method is useful for group projects to enhance decision-making skills and requires integration of many factors. The method inspires salespeople, marketing personnel, and public relation officials. The subject should neither be too complex nor too simple. As such, only experienced trainers are engaged in simulation exercises. The students' motivation must be strong enough to carry out a self-development programme.

Simulations and games are widely practised on action plan, action replay, adult learning, building a great business, card sorting experiment, characteristic admired leaders, assertive communication, concern for customers, concern for employees, diversity management, conflict management, faster problem solving, influencing colleagues without authority, ice breaking, time management, goal setting, creativity, etc.

IMPEDIMENTS TO EFFECTIVE TRAINING

The presence of some impediments can make a training programme ineffective. However, if meticulously designed, the curriculum takes care of the impediments. The common impediments are as follows:

1. Lack of management commitment
2. Inadequate budget for training
3. Graduates with inadequate skills
4. Large-scale poaching of trained personnel
5. No help to workers displaced because of downsizing
6. Failure of employers and B-schools to develop close ties
7. Lack of assistance from organized labour unions

These points will now be discussed briefly.

Lack of Management Commitment

The management must be committed to impart three types of new skills—the ability to use new technology, the ability to maintain it, and the ability to diagnose system problems. The survival and growth of an organization becomes difficult when the management lacks commitment.

Inadequate Budget for Training

We often forget the adage—'training is costly; non-training is costlier'. Whenever the company's revenue is short, the finance personnel immediately look at the training budget. Companies usually allocate diminutive proportions for developmental purpose; particularly for developing people. The reason for this may be that in a company's balance sheet one will never find any head like 'human asset'.

Graduates With Inadequate Skills

Educational institutions enhance the generic knowledge base of students. In addition to educational base, organizations also need multiple skills. Various levels of management—senior, middle, and junior levels—need different types of skills. These include conceptual skills, human relation skills, and technical skills. An individual has to work as a member of team and requires team-playing skills. He should also have entrepreneurship skills, leadership skills, customer-orientation skills, and miscellaneous job-specific skills. Organizations have to invest funds to build these skills in the workforce at all levels.

Large-scale Poaching of Trained Personnel

After attending a training programme, the value of a worker enhances as he is equipped with additional knowledge and skill. Due to the enhanced value, the demand for such workers increases. Other local companies try to pull the trained worker. The worker also prefers to move to another company if he is offered an attractive salary package. In some countries, local business groups pressure companies not to poach on another company's manpower; and insist that they must be on ethical ground. In India, there is no such system. Indian companies insist on employees to sign 'bonds of tenure' before sending for a training where the cost of training is substantially high; particularly before deputing any person to undergo training abroad. Taking a bond is, of course, not effective, and is not a solution to the problem, as after the training, neither the person nor the poacher company hesitates to pay the bond amount. On paying the bond amount as compensation, the bonds are breached.

To avoid this problem, some companies do not conduct any training.

No Help to Workers Displaced because of Downsizing

On economic grounds, organizations are downsizing to trim the workforce. Different types of business process outsourcing are another reason behind downsizing. Whenever a particular process such as heat treatment or surface treatment is outsourced, all the employees from unskilled to highly skilled, and untrained and trained ones get displaced. The company thus looses carefully nurtured, skilled and trained workforce.

Failure of Employers and B-schools to Develop Close Ties

In recent years, there has been a mushrooming growth of B-schools. Getting a degree from a foreign university, without attending and receiving a single session there, is also evidenced. These B-schools are producing graduates in a large scale. Their course curriculum includes the structured syllabus. In B-schools, there is invariably a system of pursuing a 'summer internship project' (SIP) when the schools send students to business houses to understand the business by working there. But in many instances, the basic purpose of SIP remains unachieved. The responsibility does not end by just fixing a company, getting the offer letter, forwarding it to the students, and receiving the project report. Of course, exceptions are there. Many B-schools are often seen as not responding to the labour market demands. Business houses also are seen as not communicating its demands to the B-schools. This scenario must change.

The deans and heads of departments are required to sit across the table to discuss and structure the courses that would serve the purpose of the business. Now, the question arises as to who should take the lead. The deans and heads of the departments should take the lead to enhance the students' prospects and make the students easily marketable. B-schools should invite the industrial stalwarts to visit the schools, share their knowledge, experiences, and viewpoints with students. Otherwise, representatives of the schools should visit business houses to discuss, collect similar views, and reciprocate to the students. Anyhow, the need of establishing 'industry-academia partnership programme' exists for benefit of both and the growth of the nation as well.

Lack of Assistance from Organized Labour Unions

All organizations have educated, trained, skilled, and organized labour. They are also members of some trade unions. Major trade unions are inclined to protect the interests of the workforce, and look after the labour welfare issues such as wage revision, bonus, settlement of industrial disputes, working hours, promoting the working conditions, promotion of labour, and other similar issues.

Unions can organize training programmes using the educated and skillful workers. If this is done, the process of learning will be accelerated due to minimum psychological distance between the trainer and the trainees. However, unions are busy with their regular activities and have little time to impart training to their members. Of course, in some organizations training by trade unions is in practice.

Science and technology are rapidly advancing, competition is becoming stiff, customers are quality conscious and cost sensitive, and approaches to organizational redesign, technology management, and production management is changing. Employees of the organization must cope with the changes taking place in the company due to changes in the business scenario. Training and designing training curriculum need sharper attention. While designing a training curriculum, the impediments to effective training must be resolved for making the curriculum successful. The trainer has to strive to achieve the following:

1. Gaining management commitment
2. Communicating the importance of training
3. Getting the budget sanctioned to upgrade the people
4. Enhancing organizational belongingness
5. Preventing loss and attrition of trained personnel
6. Administering assignments, evaluating, and giving feedback to the students
7. Arranging knowledge sharing to workers by scheduled trainers and trade unions
8. Building industry–academia partnership programmes

TIME AND FACILITIES REQUIRED

Time and facility planning are essential tools to make a training programme effective. For each objective of a training programme, the curriculum designer should specify the training method, time required for participants and trainers, and the facilities essentially required to achieve the objective. Refer to Exhibit 9.5.

It is always wise for the trainer and the trainee to be adequately prepared for the training module, so that they can give their best, and learn the most. For example, with knowledge of the time and the facilities required, one can plan without disturbing their routine work.

Exhibit 9.5 Time and facilities required

Objectives	Training method	Time (Hours)			Facilities
		Participants	Trainers		
		Training	Preparation	Training	
1. Development	Lecture Quiz	2.00	4.00	2.00	Classroom, one case, powerpoint slides, LCD projector
2. Understanding QMS	Case Lecture Exercise	3.00	5.00	3.00	Classroom, two cases, powerpoint slides, LCD projector
3. Interpreting	Case Lecture Exercise	11.00	20.00	11.00	Classroom, six cases, powerpoint slides, LCD projector

(Contd)

Exhibit 9.5 (Contd)

Objectives	Training method	Time (Hours)			Facilities
		Participants	Trainers		
		Training	Preparation	Training	
4. Auditing	Documents Lecture	3.00	3.00	3.00	Classroom, documents
Assessment test	Test paper	2.00	3.00	0.00	Hall
Total	–	21.00	35.00	19.00	Nine cases, classroom for 21 hours, LCD projector fixed

Faculty members needed:	• 35 hours for preparing reading material, lesson plan, exercises, quizzes, powerpoint slides, assessment test papers, etc. • 19 hours for lectures sessions
Programme director and coordinator:	• 25 hours for all arrangements

Source: Adapted from the book *Human Resource Development* by Uday Kumar Haldar, published by Oxford University Press, New Delhi, 2009.

For new training programmes, the preparation time is more for faculty members, programme directors, and coordinators. However, for repeat training programmes the time is much lesser, as the specifications for the programme are more or less set.

DESIGNING APPROPRIATE PEDAGOGY

Pedagogy generally refers to the strategies or a style of instruction. It is the art and science of being a teacher. Critical pedagogy is a teaching approach that attempts to help the students and participants seeking clarifications through questions. Pedagogy is the theory and practice of helping students achieve critical consciousness that promotes inclination of reading, thinking, conceptualizing, writing, and speaking. A teacher works with students, disseminates knowledge, develops the students, attempts to eliminate or reduces differences, and manages diversity between the students who come from a variety of social and cultural backgrounds, national identity, and different languages. Pedagogy refers to the profession or function of a teacher and the methods he adopts while teaching.

Appropriate pedagogy brings success to a course programme. The Indian Institute of Technology, Kharagpur, (IITK) conducted a short-term course on 'managing stress at work'. IITK used pedagogy such as audio-visual presentations, group activities, role plays, structured exercises, and case studies.

Productive Pedagogy

Productive pedagogy is very comprehensive and requires attention to many essential aspects of classroom teaching, that comprise both existing aspects, and vital elements of student learning. The aspects are divided into four dimensions, namely, intellectual quality, relevance (or connectedness), socially-supportive classroom environment, and recognition of difference.

Intellectual quality A student or a trainee may be intelligent but unless he applies his intelligence, it remains invisible. A student, by virtue of his industrious trait, might have gathered profound knowledge or a fixed body of information. Intellectual quality emphasizes that having a fixed body of information does not necessarily characterize knowledge. Intellectual quality encourages students in higher-order thinking, using knowledge to solve problems, applying transferable ideas, and communicating logical arguments in demanding situations.

Relevance (or connectedness) This implies helping the students to establish connections between different aspects of school learning as well as connections to their past experiences, and the world away from the classroom, and beyond class hours. Similarly, a trainee has to apply the knowledge learned and the skills gained in his workplace. When he does this, the training inputs become meaningful and a connection is established between training and the work.

Socially supportive classroom environment The primary motto of any training programme is to develop the students and the students must get the opportunity to utilize their abilities. An institute should arrange educational events for the students in the forefront, and give them the scope of organizing, finalizing the programme, negotiating, raising funds, and similar responsibilities. Faculty members, as facilitators, should observe and tackle only unusual situations. In the process, students will learn self-management, self-control, self-regulations, and interaction with external parties. For instance, in Indian Institution of Social Welfare and Business Management, Kolkata (IISWBM), students studying for a masters' degree in human resource management (MHRM) organize an annual event called *Genesis*.

The students plan, organize, design the Genesis brochure, prepare the budget, contact business organizations, raise funds, invite dignitaries and students of other B-schools, and conduct the events. Faculty members are silent observers; though they extend support in times of need. Similarly, students of the MBA department organize an annual event called *Paradigm* and perform identical activities.

Q 4 **Recognition of difference** In any class or group of students or participants, you will find that some students or groups are more dominant and attempt to govern the rest. It is the noble duty of any knowledge disseminator to encourage all of them. As such, he must have the ability to identify and recognize the group identities and differential abilities, and initiate actions to develop those belonging to the non-dominant groups.

ANDRAGOGY—SCIENCE OF TRAINING ADULTS

Andragogy refers to the art and science of teaching or training adults. Andragogy focuses on the adult learner and the creation of an independent, adaptable individual. Wilson (2005) mentions that teaching adults should be substantially different from that of teaching children, as adults bring value in terms of more experience to the learning arena. Wilson (2005) further mentions three consequences for learning in the context of adults.

1. Adults have more to contribute to the learning of others; for most kind of learning, they are a rich source of information.
2. Adults have a richer foundation of experience to which they can relate new experiences.
3. Adults have acquired a large number of fixed habits and patterns of thoughts, and therefore, tend to be less open-minded.

Considering these points, one must appreciate that in case of training of employees with experience (for example, those sponsored by organizations); the modality has to be different. If one intends to train them by means of delivering lectures, it would amount to one-way communication, and may not be successful in effective learning of the trainees.

On the other hand, if the sessions are made participative, and trainees and encouraged to share their experiences, then the process of knowledge dissemination is likely to be more fruitful and effective. Adults must perceive the topics and dialogues as relevant to their daily activities. The trainer is required to ensure that the trainees are able to establish the link of the topics with their tasks and perceive the relevance to their everyday work lives. The central tenet of andragogy is the recognition of the trainees' personal agenda they bring from the workplace. The personal agenda must be attended to.

In andragogy, the development of training is based upon a process design.

1. Design and manage a process for facilitating the acquisition of content by the learners.
2. Serve as a content resource and provide what adult trainees want.

Werner, et al. (2007) have underpinned four aspects or assumptions one should consider while designing any programme for adults from the standpoint of andragogy.

1. Adults are self-directed.
2. During the course of their working, adults have acquired large amount of knowledge, skills, and experience that can be tapped as a vital resource of learning.
3. Adults show a greater readiness to learn lessons that are relevant to discharge the roles they have been assigned in their organizations.
4. Adults are motivated to learn in order to solve problems or address needs, and expect to immediately apply what they learn to these problems and needs.

Werner, et al. (2007) refer to seven issues when comparing pedagogy and andragogy from the standpoint of structure, atmosphere, leadership, planning, motivation, communication, and evaluation. While training adults, it should be kept in mind that (a) the structure should be flexible, open and broad, and responsive, (b) training atmosphere should be relaxed, trusting, mutually respectful, informal, and warm, (c) leadership must encourage creativity and innovation, high relationship orientation, mutual interdependence, coaching, counseling, mentoring, and risk taking propensity, (d) planning of training administration, faculty deployment, pedagogical aids, exercises leading to problem solving, (e) instilling motivation will develop curiosity, and launch incentives to energize the participants, (f) two-way communication, being expressed and supportive, is accepted, and finally (g) criterion-based evaluation is ensured both objectively and subjectively. The overall training atmosphere should be conducive to establish a win-win situation in favour of both the trainers and the trainees.

DEVELOPING TRAINING MODULES

Developing the training modules succeeds the training need identification. While developing the training module, one must consider the pedagogy and andragogy, and keep in mind that the training must produce the desired result. This can be done by performing an evaluation of the module. The trainer must follow the steps of designing a training programme, and initiate measures to prevent impediments in the process. Furthermore, while developing the module, the trainer must consider the profile of the trainees, the level of knowledge at the beginning of the training, expectations of the trainees, and the competencies of the trainers. Adequate care needs to be taken to ensure that trainers' competencies match the trainees and the specific purpose of the training.

The training institute designs the course curriculum conforming to the learning objectives of the course. At the course design stage, the institute or training organizer aims to raise the level of the trainees up to a particular level, termed as criterion behaviours. The level of knowledge with which a person comes to attend a training programme is the initial behaviour and the knowledge, after attending the training, with which he leaves, is the terminal behaviour. Criterion behaviour can be referred to the knowledge planned to be imparted to the participants through the training programme.

In order to achieve the criterion behaviours, you have to further consider the methods and techniques to be adopted, the level of the delivery of training, and the place to conduct the programme, keeping in mind the principles of learning. Measuring the gains of the participants after the training programme is within the purview of the organization's training policy. Similarly, post training impact measurement from a single source or multiple sources is done to conform to the training policy.

Answers to the questions listed in Box 9.7 help to develop the training module successfully.

Box 9.7 Questions to develop the training module

1. Who are the trainees?
2. What are the initial behaviours?
3. Who are the trainers?
4. What criterion behaviours have been finalized?
5. What are the methods and techniques?
6. What should be the level of training?
7. Where to conduct the programme?
8. What are the principles of learning?
9. Will the terminal behaviours be measured?
10. Is there any system of performing the post training impact measurement?
11. If so, who is/are responsible to initiate and collect it?
12. Is it collected from a single source (the person trained) and/or his supervisors also?

Thus, in short, the development of the training module comprises the following:

1. Deciding the course objectives
2. Designing a learning environment
3. Pre-conditioning of learning
4. Ascertaining the extent of achieving terminal behaviour
5. Gaining the support of the trainees and others
6. Conditioning of the learning environment

TRAINING FORMATS

Documents are generated in specific formats desired by the organization. Records are also required to be maintained in approved formats. A few examples are

1. Syllabus of the course or management development programme (MDP)
2. Bio-data of participants
3. Feedback format

4. Post-training impact measurement (from trained personnel)
5. Post-training impact measurement (from immediate supervisor or training manager)

Syllabus of the Course or MDP

A committee of experts designs the syllabus, considering the general needs of the employees. For a specific client organization, the institute customizes the syllabus to suit the specific training needs of the organization. The format of the syllabus includes the entry requirements, topics (knowledge module), description of the module, and hours allotted for coverage. The format also contains a faculty code to link and deploy the probable competent faculty. The syllabus is split, if necessary, in multiple modules. Refer to Table 9.5.

Table 9.5 Syllabus of the course

Course title: Required qualification: Diploma in engineering or B Sc

S. no.	Knowledge module	Module description	Time/ hours	Faculty code
1.				
2.				
3.				
4.				
5.				

Bio-data of Participants

The essential fields are title of the course, name in full, designation, personal number, section, department, sponsoring factory, date of birth, whether SC/ST/OBC (to identify reservation quotas), qualification (academic and technical), experience in the different grades and functional areas, the duration, and whether trained earlier on a similar topic/subject, etc. The bio-data format is annexed at the end of the chapter (See Annexure 9.1).

Feedback Format

A training institute must lay great importance on the participants' feedback as this is a vital document for improvement and a tool for decision-making for future courses. The fields one can incorporate in the feedback format are achievement of the course objective, follow the instructions, practical training facility or exercises, applicability of knowledge and skills imparted, quality of the topics and of their presentation, and remarks by the participants. The participants offer their views in a five-point Likert scale on the following parameters:

1. Achievement of the course objective
2. Follow the instructions
3. Practical training facility or exercises
4. Applicability of knowledge and skill imparted
5. Quality of the topics and the quality of their presentation

The feedback format is annexed at the end of the chapter (See Annexure 9.2).

Post-training Impact Measurement (from Trained Personnel)

It is also essential to keep a track of the trained personnel, sponsored by an organization, presenting the sessions. While giving the feedback, the participants express their immediate feelings about the course coverage. While filling the feedback format, some contextual factors, such as, for example, the accommodation, quality of mess arrangements, behavioural aspects of the hostel warden and attendants, transportation, and hospitality, etc. influence the feelings of the trainees. The feedback form should include these points. Without this, you may not get the feedback on the course content in a true sense. Moreover, you must attempt to find out about the application of the knowledge and skill in the workplace gained by the trainee. In other words, you must proceed with job- related evaluation to measure the impact of the course in their work area. Conducting a post- training survey aids improving the quality of the course.

Kirkpatrick (1994) developed a four-level model for measuring the impact of training. This form is tried, tested, and well-regarded by trainers. The trainer or the training organization must attempt to discover what the trainees thought and felt about the training. The impact can also be measured after about four to six months following the completion of the training. Contextually, it is mentioned that post training evaluation requires pre-training assessment (a benchmark against which to measure progress). Lack of resources, inflexible budgets, and organizational culture emerge as barriers to post training impact measurement.

A trained person may be able to apply his skill and knowledge while performing the tasks assigned in the workplace. He may perform them with greater ease, get more job satisfaction, and be more involved with the work. He may gain the attention of the supervisor and his colleagues. His qualitative and quantitative performance may be enhanced. The positive impact of the knowledge gained in his work area influences his personal life. These can be carefully assessed.

Moreover, he expresses his opinion about the training, reading material, shows the reading material to colleagues, and refers to the material when in need. You can develop a questionnaire and directly administer this to the trained employees after about five or six months. If you mail it and wait for the responses, you may not get a reply. Even if you do, it may not convey the true picture. It would be wiser to go to the trainees' organization for a group of trained persons. No doubt, the process will be costly, but the effort and cost will be justified by the value of the responses. The format you can use is annexed at the end of this chapter (refer Annexure 9.3). On the basis of this format, you can develop a tailor-made format for your own organization.

Post-training Impact Measurement (from Immediate Supervisor or Training Manager)

Fundamental research has established that the impact of a training course can be substantially increased, if the trainees get opportunities to embed their learning by applying it in the weeks following the training course attended by them. Training enhances the confidence level towards work, causes visible behavioural change in the work place, affects attitudinal change towards the work, augments capability to accept new types of work, improves job performance, enhances job involvement and job satisfaction, and develops a helping attitude towards peers.

After attending a training programme, an employee is seen to talk about the usefulness of the training, express his desire to attend further training, and show the training material to peers and his supervisor. Furthermore, the supervisor plans to depute his/her junior colleagues for training to the same institute with a view to boosting productivity. All these aspects can be interrogated through a questionnaire to the supervisor of the trained personnel.

By devising a suitable scale, you can attempt to measure the impact of the training through the supervisor or the training manager. A sample format is annexed at the end of this chapter (See Annexure 9.4).

The training department of some organizations develops documents and records as inputs to the training system. Some documents and records, though not course-specific, can be utilized for extending spectrum of information and manifest their usage for all courses are designed by organizations. Examples of few such documents and records are as follows:

1. Faculty database
2. Records of qualification and experience
3. Document amendment format
4. Training audit plan
5. Training audit schedule
6. Training audit report

Faculty Database

Any progressive institute does not hesitate to invite reputed consultants or faculty from other institutes or organizations to share their knowledge and experiences with the participants and internal faculty members. The institute may invite some of them frequently and the rest occasionally. Whatever may be the frequency of this process, the institute should maintain a faculty database. The institute may collect data such as name, address, mobile number, landline, e-mail, area of specialization, core topic, other topics, papers published, seminars or conventions (national and international) attended, etc. Refer to Table 9.6.

Table 9.6 Faculty database

Name	Mobile no.	Landline	Address	E-mail	Area	Core topic	Papers published

Records of Qualification and Experience

Qualified and experienced faculty members share their knowledge and experiences with the participants. A training institute should maintain a record of the same in its system and refer to it when assigning any training session. The record must be updated periodically, at least once in a year. However, on return of any institutional member after attending any training programme the training column should be updated immediately. Refer to Table 9.7.

Table 9.7 Records of qualification and experience

S. no.	Name	Personal number	Qualification	Training		Experience	
				Code	Years	Code	Years

Document Amendment Form

Documents are dynamic in nature. Any document issued may obviously need some changes or amendments for compatibility with the training process. You have to maintain the details of amendment using a document amendment format. The columns that can be included are document number, current issue number and date, page number or format number, past issue number and date, new revision number and date, brief description of the changes, document amended by, and document approved by columns. Refer to Table 9.8.

Table 9.8 Document amendment form

S. no.	Document no.	Current issue no./date	Page no./ format no.	Old revision no. and date	New revision. no. and date	Brief description	Amended by	Approved by

Training Audit Plan

The trainer should organize an audit of the training system to verify whether any deviation has occurred from the system laid down. He/She must plan the audit and mention the scope of the audit, the areas (training functions) to be audited, frequency of audit in a year, record management system such as training need identification methodology, compliance with business (institutional) needs, process approach to develop training objectives, measurability of the objectives, training objective analysis, etc. It is needless to mention that the trainer should design a format to record the audit plan. He/She should decide the frequency based on the importance of the area and relevance to the quality of training. The audit plan is the first-level audit document. Refer to Table 9.9.

Table 9.9 Annual training audit plan

Audit area	Freq-uency	Apr	May	Jun	Jul	Aug	Sep	Oct	Nov	Dec	Jan	Feb	Mar
A-1	3	#				#				#			
A-2	2		#						#				
A-3	4	#			#			#			#		

Table 9.9 shows the number of audits planned and the month of audit. Based on their importance, the frequency of audit in an area is decided.

Training Audit Schedule

The audit schedule is the second-level audit document. The trainer should comply with the audit plan. Corresponding to the training audit plan, he/she may prepare an audit schedule on a half-yearly or even quarterly basis. Compliance to the audit plan signifies that all the areas of training must be audited at the frequency decided in the plan. The institute might be conducting training courses and management development programmes in areas such as (a) human resource development, (b) human resource planning, (c) quality management system, (d) statistical quality control, (e) quality function deployment, (f) metallurgical processes, (g) general management, in addition to other customized courses demanded by the client organizations.

All the areas shall be reflected in the audit plan. In the audit schedule, the trainer is required to detail the auditor, and fix the date and time in consultation with the auditee and auditor, considering the convenience of both parties. Refer to Table 9.10.

Table 9.10 Training audit schedule

Audit area	Auditor	Auditee	Date	Time	Remarks

For all the areas, the director (HRD) or the training manager need not be the auditee. They have to establish and implement the system. They must oversee and ensure that the system is maintained. The trainer should empower his/her junior colleagues for system maintenance.

Training Audit Report

You can develop a checklist to make the audit effective. The purpose of audit is fact finding and not fault finding. You must scrutinize the findings of the audit and accept whatever you feel necessary for continual improvement of the training system. An auditor generally verifies the courses planned and actually conducted, whether all the planned courses have been conducted, if deferred, the reason behind the deferment, when else the course has been conducted, conformance of the participants with the course planned by the institute, feedback reports by the participants, analysis done, and actions taken by the institute. The auditors use the training manual as the primary reference document. They also refer to various connected documents and records, bring out the facts, and submit these to the training manager. Some examples of audit observations are highlighted in Box 9.8.

Box 9.8 Examples for audit

1. Sequence of the lectures in course titled ...., course number .... held from .... to .... does not conform to the programme of the course.
   Time allotted for topic serial no. .... of the syllabus for the course .... is three hours. In the programme only one and half hours has been allocated for the same topic. The programme has been used in two consecutive courses.
2. The programme for the topic .... in the course .... shows Mr ABC as the faculty but the record of lecture shows Mr PQR as the faculty.
3. The grading of one faculty member in three consecutive courses titled .... is less than 3 out of 5. The same faculty has been nominated for another course for the same topic. This does not conform to the point ...., section .... of the training manual.
4. One faculty Mr LMN has been nominated for the topic .... in the course titled .... But the faculty database does not include Mr LMN.
5. Six courses have been conducted during the period .... to .... Though there are seven classrooms, pedagogical aids (LCD projector, overhead projector) available are insufficient.

An auditor has to endorse his audit observations, as discussed in the audit report. The training manager or his authorized representative must consider the observations and initiate remedial measures. The training manager may authorize the programme director or the programme coordinator to undertake the scrutiny.

A deviation can occur in a compelling situation, but it should not recur. Refer to Table 9.11.

Table 9.11 Training audit report

Function:	Audit no.:	Date:
Auditor:	Auditee:	

Audit observations:

S. no.	Observation	Reference document
1.		
2.		
3.		
4.		

Responsibility of initiating remedial measures assigned to: ....

Actions to be completed by: (date) ....

Signature of auditor   Signature of training manager

EVALUATION OF TRAINING PROGRAMME

Of the many HRD mechanisms or instruments, training is by far the most vital mechanism. Training must be planned and evaluated using any standard model or combination of them, depending on the organizational needs and practices. The evaluation is required at many stages—before the implementation of the training, during conduction of the training or management development programme, immediately after completion of the programme, and even after a few months. Evaluation literally means the assessment of value or worth. In simple terms, it is the act of judging whether or not the activity to be evaluated is worthwhile in terms of the set criteria.

Indiana University's centre for research on learning and technology (CRLT) recently used seven principles to evaluate the four online courses being conducted in a professional school at a large mid-western university. These were principle 1—good practice encourages student–faculty contact, principle 2—good practice encourages cooperation among students, principle 3—good practice encourages active learning, principle 4—good practice gives prompt feedback, principle 5—good practice emphasizes time on task, principle 6—good practice communicates high expectations, and principle 7—good practice respects diverse talents and ways of learning (Charles, et al. 2000).

Lynton and Pareek (2007) have emphasized five sets of objectives and three main questions for such evaluation. The five sets of objectives include

1. evaluating the training programme (to improve the programme as a whole, to improve major components of the training programme, and to increase the effectiveness of specific modules or sessions),
2. evaluating the training process (to improve the training climate, to improve the training methodologies, and to improve the trainers team),
3. evaluating the training execution/conduction (to improve the training facilities and contextual factors),

Assessment and evaluation are different. Assessment is about the progress and achievements of the individual learners, whereas evaluation is about the learning programme as a whole.

4. evaluating training outcomes/impacts (to increase learning by individuals participants, to increase use of learning in work performance, to contribute data to organizational effectiveness, and to help the organizational change), and
5. evaluating programme factors (to maximize effectiveness, to ensure post-training support, and to identify helping and hindering factors).

In order to make a training programme effective, the training objectives must find answers to three questions—for whom, when, and how.

In a usual course of action, and as already discussed, an organization first identifies the training needs for its employees. Then, it designs the training programme, considers the pedagogy or andragogy, and thereafter, conducts the training programme. All the steps need evaluation for effectiveness of the programme. The evaluation is required from the training design stage, before conducting the training, during conduction of the training or management development programme, immediately after completion of the programme, and even after a few months to a year. Evaluation is an essential part of planning the training.

It is important to not confuse between evaluation and assessment. Assessment is about the progress and achievements of the individual learners, whereas evaluation is about the learning programme as a whole. Training evaluation constitutes the most systematic way of determining the strengths, weaknesses, and effects of training courses. Few trainers make use of this process on a continuing basis. Managers of training need to understand the practical benefits of training evaluation so that they will be motivated to support its use.

Allahabad Bank evaluates its training sessions based on the contents and coverage of the programme, methodology used, reading material provided for, presentation skills, utility of the contents, topics liked by the participants, infrastructure of the institute, etc. The format of 'programme evaluation form' of the bank is exhibited in Annexure 9.5.

Scope of Evaluation

The scope or areas of evaluation are manifold and include pre-training factors, training (an event), training management, training (a process), participant development, organizational development, and post training factors. Refer to Table 9.12. The scope of evaluation describes the area of evaluation, component, and dimension (stages of the training programme, such as planning, execution, post training, etc.)

Table 9.12 Scope of evaluation

Area of evaluation	Components	Dimension
Pre-training factors	1. Preparation 2. Learning motivation 3. Expectations	Context
Training	1. Curriculum 2. Specific events 3. Specific sessions	Events

(Contd)

Table 9.12 (Contd)

Training management	1. Area of satisfaction (or otherwise) 2. Training facilities 3. Allied facilities	Context
Training	1. Learning climate 2. Training pedagogy 3. Team management	Process
Participant development	1. Conceptual development 2. Learning of skills 3. Change in attitude 4. Change in behaviour	Outcome
Organizational development	1. Job effectiveness 2. Team effectiveness 3. Organizational effectiveness	Outcome
Post-training factors	1. Cost 2. Organizational support 3. Hindering factors 4. Helping factors	Context

Source: Lynton and Pareek, *Training for Organizational Transformation*, Sage Publications, New Delhi, 2000.

Purposes of Evaluation

Certain purposes guide and dictate the need for evaluation; the purposes behind training evaluation are wide enough. Evaluation will have at least one purpose as its primary focus. If the training cannot fulfil achieving the planned business need, then you are required to identify the root cause and take remedial measures. The purposes of evaluation are as follows:

1. To justify the role of training, considering budget availability and cutback situations
2. To improve the quality of training for employee development, training delivery, trainer deployment, duration, methodology, etc.
3. To assess the effectiveness of the overall programme, quality, and competency of the trainer
4. To justify the course through cost–benefit analysis and ROI approach

The evaluation data, once collected, takes many forms, and is highly valuable. It can also be used to do the following:

1. Provide feedback on whether the training or development activity is effective in achieving its aims
2. Indicate the extent to which trainees apply what they have learned back in the workplace (transfer of training), an issue which many organizations find they have problems with
3. Provide information on how to increase the effectiveness of current or later development activities
4. Demonstrate the overall value and worth of development activities

The purposes of evaluation further extends to gauging the effectiveness, effects of training on shaping attitudes, improving performance, reducing rejections, lowering machine downtime, enhancing job quality, enhancing the market share, penetrating new markets, increasing sales, improving quality of work life, promoting interpersonal communication, etc. The preceding factors speak about the complexity of any effort to evaluate training. These factors further emphasize the importance of being clear about the purpose and the process of evaluation.

In fact, effective evaluation must be carefully planned while designing the training. Obviously then, the evaluation plan should precede training and not follow it. Meticulously planned and well-conducted evaluation provides useful information to the institute, the trainer, participants, and sponsoring organizations. The output of evaluation will serve

1. To illustrate the real worth of a training
2. To pinpoint where improvement is required in forthcoming training programmes
3. To assess effectiveness of the overall course, trainer, and the training methods
4. To carry out cost–benefit analysis to justify the amount spent; to prove that the benefits outweigh the cost
5. To formulate a basis for making rational decisions about future training plans
6. To justify the role of training for budget purposes and in cutback situations of budget crunch

Summarily, you are required to improve the quality of the training, concentrating on the trainers' competency, training design, content of the course, participant profile, expected behavioural outcomes, methods used, length of training, achievement of the training objectives by means of improving the training delivery as a whole. Knowing the purposes of training evaluation, you will now be acquainted with the process through evaluation.

PROCESS OF TRAINING EVALUATION

Any training evaluation begins with the criteria, which depend on the training objectives. Some of these criteria could be the reaction of the trainees, their learning, behavioural changes, and impact on organizational changes. Thus, one may be required to evaluate the reaction of trainees to be aware of whether they liked or disliked the training programme. Check the learning by examining whether the trainee could assimilate the concepts, ideas, and principles of the training.

Training and development programmes are necessary for improving the quality of performance. As mentioned earlier, one of the important criteria for the evaluation of training incorporates behavioural changes, that is, whether the training has caused any alteration in the behaviour or not. Similarly, impact on organizational changes indicates if the modified behaviour has caused any positive results, such as increased output, and improved quality, supported by cost reduction.

The trainer can even group the criteria discussed as being subjective or objective. Subjective criteria can rely on the participants' verbal opinions—they are asked about their impressions of the training modality and effectiveness, on the concluding day of the training, whereas objective criteria relate to the effects of the training through measuring the specific outcomes, which can determine the quantity produced, number of rejections, time taken to produce a component, etc.

> The training evaluation process encompasses collection of data regarding training need identification, selection of training methodology, adoption of training aids, or modification of workplace learning activities.

The training evaluation process encompasses a systematic collection of data relevant to the training need identification, selection of training methodology, adoption of training aids, or modification of workplace learning activities. Despite organizations expending a great deal of effort and financial resources in setting up training and developing programmes, comparatively little attention is paid to evaluating their effectiveness. Organizations must be instrumental to evaluate the training programmes and in demanding cases, must initiate remedial measures.

Evaluation of training is 'any attempt to obtain information (feedback) on the effects of a training programme and to assess the value of training in the light of that information for improving further training' (Hamblin 1970).

Knowing the purpose and process of evaluation, you must now realize the principles of evaluation.

EVALUATION METHOD SELECTION

There are several evaluation methods that can be used. These range from learner feedback to discussions, surveys, and questionnaires, to more rigorous testing methods. The method must be appropriate to the learning objective. Time is also an important factor. The greater the time delay between the training event and evaluation, the less reliable the results are likely to be, as there will be factors other than the training, which may well have had an effect on the outcome. Method of evaluation is decided based upon on the learning objectives. Refer to Table 9.13.

Table 9.13 Evaluation method selection

Learning objectives	Possible methods
Acquisition of factual knowledge	Written or verbal tests
Application of knowledge	Practical tests, direct observation of the learner
Interpersonal skills	Direct observation of the individual interacting with others
Technical skills	Practical tests

TRAINING EVALUATION MODELS

You have studied various aspects of evaluation. Some points you must remember while studying or evaluating training performance are as follows:

1. Observations, interviews, and questionnaires are means of gathering data related to training and not evaluating the training.
2. Work samples are sources of data used in evaluation.

Job performance is a generic term for individual and group performance measures. These are measures that might help one to evaluate, provided the right measures are adopted, and if one gets the right data, he/she will be able to make the right analysis. There are different approaches to evaluate training, some of which are as follows:

1. Kirkpatrick's framework of four levels model (www.businessballs.com)
2. Jack Philip's ROI method (similar to but an extension of the Kirkpatrick model)
3. Stufflebeam's CIPP model (context, input, process, and product model)
4. Warr et al.'s CIRO model (context, input, reaction, outcome model)
5. Virmani and Premila model

Kirkpatrick's Framework of Four Levels Model

Kirkpatrick first published his ideas in 1959, in a series of articles in the US training and development journals. Over a period of time, the model has gained international acclamation and is now considered as a standard across the HR and training communities. The model suffices the needs of industrial and commercial organizations for training and learning evaluation aimed at ongoing people for development, planning, and managing training. Kirkpatrick (1998) himself redefined and updated his four levels of training evaluation model.

The four levels of Kirkpatrick's evaluation model essentially measure reaction, learning, behaviour, and results. Evaluation at the reaction level helps to understand what the trainees think and feel about the training, and their views about the training programme. This level measures the learner's perception (reaction) of the course.

Evaluation at the learning level attempts to answer the question, 'did the participants learn anything?' The evaluator finds what the trainees have learned from the training programme, and the resulting increase in knowledge or capability. The evaluation also includes their attitudinal changes, knowledge improvement, and enhanced skills. The learning evaluation requires post training testing to ascertain the extent of learning.

Evaluation of behaviour at the third level attempts to measure the effect on the job performance, or the extent of behavioural modification and capability of improvement, knowledge enhancement, or application in the work performance. However, you have to keep in mind that behaviour is the action which is exhibited, while the final results of the behaviour are the performance. This evaluation involves testing the trainees' capabilities to apply the learned skills on the job at the work place, rather than in the classroom. You can perform third level evaluation formally (by testing) or informally (through observing). The evaluation will help you to determine if the performance is correct by answering the question, 'do people use their newly acquired knowledge on the job?' Learning new skills and knowledge is no good to an organization unless the participants actually use them in their work activities.

Evaluations at the preceding three levels—reaction, learning, and behaviour—are focused on the individual trainees. The fourth level—result evaluation—is directed towards measuring the contribution of the training efforts on the organizational performance. Evaluation at this level answers the question, 'what impact has the training achieved?' The effects of the training programme on the business or environment resulting from the trainee's performance is measured at this 'behaviour evaluation' stage. These impacts can include such items as monetary, efficiency, moral, teamwork, etc.

Sometimes you may find it difficult to isolate the results of a training programme but you can definitely link contributions of training to organizational improvements. Data collecting, organizing, and analysing the data, and converting it into information can be difficult, time-consuming, and more costly than the other three levels, but the results are often worthwhile when viewed in the full context of its value to the organization.

Jack Phillip's ROI Method

Phillips' return on investment (ROI) approach is another internationally-acclaimed method to evaluate training and is endorsed by organizations such as The American Society of Training and Development (ASTD). This approach enables organizations to calculate the financial ROI from the training event.

Phillips (1997) added a fifth level to the Kirkpatrick model. He has included the same in his book *Return on Investment in Training and Performance Improvement Programmes*. Some experts argue that Kirkpatrick's model does not address anything about the worth of the training. After adding the fifth level, Jack Phillips (1997) called the Kirkpatrick approach, the ROI or return on investment, to get an answer to the question, 'did the training pay for itself?' Can the effort, time spent, and expenditure incurred for the training be justified? If it can, then the expenditure will be treated as an investment to enhance the potential of human assets.

Phillips' introduced the fifth level for the first time, considering the need for the evaluator to appreciate the finer workings of the organization and also employ some skill in determining costs and benefits.

Stufflebeam's CIPP Model

Daniel Stufflebeam developed the CIPP (context, input, process, and product) model of training evaluation in the 1960s. Obviously, from its name , it can be presumed that this model requires the evaluation of context, input, process, and product in judging the value of a programme. Stufflebeam developed this model as a means of linking evaluation with programme decision-making.

A training cycle comprises planning, structuring, implementing, reviewing, and revising decisions. The CIPP framework provides an analytical and a rational basis for programme decision-making conforming to the cycle. It is a decision-focused approach to evaluation. This approach emphasizes on the systematic provision of information for programme management and operation.

The information resource is viewed as the most valuable in this approach, as information helps programme managers to make better decisions. As such, evaluation activities should be planned to fulfil the decision needs of the programme staff. Obviously, a programme can always change during execution. Accordingly, evaluation activities should also be able to adapt to meet these changing needs as well as ensuring continuity of focus. The model further provides an analytical and a rational basis to evaluate all components of the training cycle (as stated earlier) for programme decision-making. This is based on a cycle of planning, structuring, implementing, and reviewing and revising decisions, each examined through a different aspect of evaluation—context, input, process, and product evaluation.

In order to the make the evaluation process successful, an organization should consider the following aspects of evaluation and take decisions. Gathering responses to some questions in this regard can also be helpful. Refer to Table 9.14.

Table 9.14 Model of evaluation

Aspect of evaluation	Type of decision	Kind of question answered
Context evaluation	Planning decisions	What should we do?
Input evaluation	Structuring decisions	How should we do it?
Process evaluation	Implementing decisions	Are we doing it as planned? And if not, why?
Product evaluation	Recycling decisions	Did it work?

Source: www.hub.col.org/2002/collit/att-0073/01 The_CIPP_approach.doc, last accessed on 8 March 2008.

Warr, et al.'s CIRO Model

Warr et al (1970) had propounded the CIRO model. It still remains one of the most widely used training evaluation models. The model strikes a chord with some of the key issues that trainers are still grappling with today—how to demonstrate the impact of training on organizational objectives, and in turn, how to make a strong business case for training.

In the CIRO evaluation approach, there are four components (context, inputs, reactions, and output) of evaluation and the evaluation can occur at two levels—at the organizational level and a single event level, such as a training programme. At the organizational level, the purpose of evaluation is to measure the success of the employee development strategy. This specifically assesses whether the planned objectives have been achieved. Employee development strategies depend on the size and the industry to which it belongs.

The basic purpose of training at organizational levels including induction programmes may be different. Whereas the aim of a large-scale industry may be to look at the wealth of schemes, that of a small-scale company may be its mere survival. Usually, it is advised that any programme that requires huge resources such as management time and cost should be regularly evaluated.

At the single event level, the purpose of evaluation is to assess how one particular event fits into the overall training cycle (business needs, identifying training needs, specifying training needs, translating training needs into actions, planning the training, and finally evaluating the training). This is a series of sequential steps that businesses need to go through in order to deliver effective training and development.

If a trainer adopts the CIRO approach to evaluate training, he/she will get the opportunity to follow a model while conducting training and development assessments. The trainer should conduct training evaluation in the following areas:

C—Context or environment within which the training takes place: The training management must objectively identify training needs through man, task, and organizational analysis. Here, evaluation is directed to pinpointing the reasons for the training or development event, and the system or strategy of need identification.

I—Inputs for the training event: This refers to evaluation at the planning and design processes, which leads to the selection of trainers, programmes, pedagogy, employees, and materials. It involves rethinking and determining the appropriateness and accuracy of the inputs, which are crucial to the success of the training or development initiative. If, for example, someone, without any flair and aptitude for teaching, attends a programme on 'training for trainers', they are likely to cause hindrance to the learning process. It is not just they who will not learn; they are likely to jeopardize the environment, ultimately leading to waste of time and money for the organization.

R—Reactions to the training event: The method of evaluation at this stage should be appropriate to the nature of the training undertaken. The management may want to measure the reaction of learners and assess the relevance of the training course. The assessment is directed to the content and presentation of the training event, to evaluate its quality.

O—Outcomes: The management may desire to measure the extent of learning transferred to the workplace. This is easier when the training is concerned with hard and specific skills.

For example, consider that a machine operator is trained on machine technology, selecting speed, feed and depth of cut relating to the material to be machined. Here, one can measure the outcome of the training programme from the average number of components produced over a period. Thus, the records of the pre-training and post training performance levels of the learners are the relevant objective evidences. The average production before and after training will directly indicates the outcome. However, softer and less quantifiable competencies including behavioural skills, cannot always be measured.

A key benefit of using the CIRO approach is that it ensures coverage of all aspects of the training cycle.

Virmani and Premila Model

In a study, Jiwani (2006) desired to find out the most effective training methods that help in ensuring learning and its transfer to real life situations based on Virmani and Premila's model of training evaluation. He based the training design of the programme on the research done by World Health Organization on the skill sets required to succeed in a competitive society. The broad objective of the programme was to equip the students with the skills required to deal effectively with the demands and challenges of the global environment. Jiwani (2006) mentions the three stages proposed by Virmani and Premila.

Stage I: Pre-training evaluation At this stage, he sent pre-training questionnaires to the trainees 15 days prior to the programme. Then, he discussed the components of the programme at the pre-programme meet. The objectives of the pre-training evaluation were (a) to ascertain the expectations of the trainees, and (b) to ensure goal congruence of objectives between the trainer and trainees.

Stage II: Context and input evaluation At this stage, he used the collated data of the pre-training evaluation questionnaire and documents of the pre-programme meet. He attempted to understand the background of each participant, and to get a direction of the pedagogical tools relevant to achieve the set objectives.

Stage III: Post training evaluation He embarked on the reaction evaluation and learning evaluation processes. The objectives were to capture the immediate feelings of the trainees with reference to certain parameters.

The manner in which Jiwani (2006) used Virmani and Premila's model is elucidated. Refer to Table 9.15.

Table 9.15 Application of Virmani and Premila's model

Stages	Process/ method used	Objectives
Stage I: Pre-training evaluation	• Sent pre-training questionnaire to the trainees 15 days prior to the programme • Called for pre-programme meet to discuss components of the programme [Gulzar (2006) used a pre-training questionnaire at this stage.]	• To know the objectives/ expectations of the trainees • To ensure goal congruence of objectives between the trainer and trainees
Stage II: Context and input evaluation	• Collated data of the pre-training evaluation questionnaire • Documents of the pre-programme meet [Gulzar (2006) used a programme evaluation questionnaire at this stage.]	• To understand the background, context of each participant • To get a direction of the kind of pedagogical tools relevant to achieve the set objectives
Stage III: Post-training evaluation	Reaction evaluation • Evaluation questionnaire circulated immediately after the programme • Informal descriptive comments were captured by the evaluation team • The data was collated and presented in graphical form [Gulzar (2006) used a pre- and post-test questionnaire at this stage.]	To capture the immediate feelings of the trainees with references to certain parameters • Knowledge of the faculty • Aids used • Relevance of the content • Utility and benefit • Time allotted • Objectives achieved
	Learning evaluation • Pre- and post-training questionnaires were administered before and after each session of the programme • Learning of each session was measured by applying the formula of learning index $\frac{\text{Pre-training score} - \text{Post-training score}}{100 - \text{Pre-training score}} \times 100$	To know degree of learning of each session at the end of the programme

(Contd)

Table 9.15 (Contd)

	• Learning index of each trainee was calculated and then average learning index was calculated by dividing the sum with the number of trainees [Gulzar (2006) used a follow-up questionnaire at this stage.]	
	Job improvement plan • Every trainee was asked to prepare an action plan based on his or her learning subsequent to the programme	• To provide an opportunity to the trainees to evaluate his own learning • To facilitate and guide the trainees in formulating the strategies of implementation
	On the job evaluation and follow up • Follow up questionnaire was sent to trainees after one year to know the usefulness and applicability of the concepts learned	• To assess the applicability of the concepts learned • To know the problems faced by the trainees in implementation process

TRAINING EVALUATION—A DIFFERENT APPROACH

Training can be evaluated at five levels—technology, reaction, skill acquisition, skill transfer, and organizational effect (Iyer, et al. 2009). They mention conceptually three different kinds of changes (alpha, beta, and gamma) that occur after a period of training and all the changes can be assessed following a particular methodology. In alpha change, the participant's report is unbiased between time one (pre-training ratings) and time two (post-training ratings) because it is based on an instrument that is continuously calibrated. Beta change refers to an apparent change where the measuring instrument has been recalibrated by the participants during the measurement intervals, that is, the individual perceptions about the response scale have changed. Gamma change refers to a situation where the participant redefines or reconceptualizes some relevant information about the training.

Some other models of training evaluation are the following:

1. Kaufman's five levels of evaluation
2. Bruce Aaron's V method (links needs, design, delivery, business results)
3. Tyler's objectives approach
4. Scriven's focus on outcomes
5. Robert Stake's responsive evaluation model
6. Robert Stake's congruence-contingency model
7. PERT (programme evaluation and review technique)
8. Alkins' UCLA model
9. Provus's discrepancy model
10. Eisner's connoisseurship evaluation models
11. Illuminative evaluation model
12. Robert Brinkerhoff's success case method
13. Martin Schmalenbach's five box model

Training evaluators often talk about two different types of evaluations—formative and summative.

Formative evaluation A formative evaluation is decisive; an organization usually conducts this in the early stages of a programme, and addresses questions about implementation and ongoing planning. This is used in the classroom as planned curriculum.

Formative evaluations manifest their importance for various purposes, for example (a) they may help catch problems at an early stage, while there exists scope for corrections and corrective actions, (b) they are an evaluation of the training process, so they may be useful in understanding why different outcomes emerge and improving the programme, and (c) they provide an opportunity to collect baseline data for future summative or collective training evaluations (like impact of the training).

Summative evaluation This is a method of judging the worth or value of a training programme at the end of training programme. Obviously, the focus is on the outcome. As such, summative evaluations assess programme outcomes or impacts. In order to explore and establish the relationship of different factors to outcomes, similar to formative evaluations, you are required collect some information used in summative evaluations at the early stage of a training programme such as primary data, test scores, etc.

Some advantages of summative evaluations are that (a) they can, if designed correctly, provide evidence for a causal relationship, (b) they assess long-term effects, (c) they provide data on impacts, and (d) they can provide data on change across time.

MANAGEMENT DEVELOPMENT PROGRAMMES

MDP is the process adopted to supply knowledge, skills, attitudes, and insights to managerial personnel, and help them manage their work effectively and efficiently. Management development is the systematic process of training and growth with the ultimate purpose of organizational growth. In management development programmes, the faculty members share their experiences in organizational context using anecdotes relevant to the development programmes.

Need for Management Development

In today's time, the survival of a business is not the only requirement. It has to grow, keeping pace with the global economy. 'Survival of the fittest' was the law of jungles. At present, in the industrial scenario characterized by acute competition, 'survival of the fastest' is the prevailing law. Organizations that are fast and consistent are likely to survive and grow.

Management development is necessary for the following reasons:

1. Rapid changes are taking place in the technological and industrial scenario. Managers are facing multifaceted problems arising out of automation, intense market competition, growth of new markets, rising customer consciousness, enhanced labour participation, and the like.
2. Organizational leaders are increasingly recognizing the company's social and public responsibility essential to be close to the society and customers.
3. Size and complexity of the organizations are ever increasing; a huge number of people are required to be managed, and the complexities have to analysed for solution.
4. Multicultural issues are emerging as vital considerations and the issues are crucial for multinationals.
5. Union-management relations are becoming more and more intricate, thus necessitating precise industrial relations
6. The socio-economic forces, effective market forces, changes in public policy and concepts of social, industrial democracy, ecological imbalances (smog or pollution), ekistics (problem of human settlements) and, ergonomics (human engineering), are changing.

Concept of Management Development

The important assumptions and concerns behind management development are as follows:

1. An executive needs development throughout his work life and his professional career. Thus, management development is an on-going activity.
2. There always exists a gap between 'required performance level' and the 'capacity' of an individual. Management must fill in the gap to provide an opportunity for improvement.
3. Some personal variables (such as age, habits, level of motivation, state of mind, etc.) retard the growth of an individual.
4. In work situation, growth involves stresses and strains. Development can seldom take place in a completely peaceful atmosphere.
5. Involvement and participation are inescapable for growth.
6. In addition to the methodology of achievement, there must be defined objectives and goals required to be achieved.
7. Shortcomings must be identified. Feedback and counseling to junior colleagues mentioning the shortcomings and applying suitable HRD instruments to overcome the shortcomings are essentially required.

Management Development Objectives

Management development programmes must aim to achieve the following objectives:

1. To provide the organization with the required numbers of managers having the ability to meet the present and future organizational needs
2. To inculcate a sense of self-dependency and achievement among managers
3. To encourage the managers to keep themselves up to date, and grow to meet the challenges, cope up with the changes, and handle complex situations and greater problems
4. To discharge their responsibilities with improved performance
5. To sustain good performance and gain distinctive competence

MANAGEMENT DEVELOPMENT TECHNIQUES

The techniques lay emphasis not on the skill but on the capacity of handling complex situations, dealing with tough-minded employees, and solving managerial problems.

The techniques that are generally used are as follows:

Planned progression It is a technique that gives managers an idea of their career path. From this idea, they develop understanding about the career anchors. A lower level manager can move up along the organizational hierarchy. Thus, the path of promotion is blue printed.

Job rotation Rotation is ensured in non-supervisory roles through work situations and changing assignments; and among managerial training positions by unspecified managerial positions.

Creation of 'assistant to' position The junior colleague can follow the activities of the senior. In turn, the senior colleague discharges teacher-like roles while judging the decision-making ability and leadership potential.

Temporary promotion The performance is tested at the elevated position.

Making member of junior boards of management: The behavioural dispositions of the junior managers are observed, and their views/decisions are very often implemented. This is done to instill a sense of responsibility.

Coaching and counselling These are done to transform the new subordinate, and to make him oriented in his job in order to accomplish better. Coaching is provided for developing the role; and counselling for managing and coping stress.

Syndicate Teams of people with mature judgement and proven ability drawn from different functional areas exchange and share their experiences and ideas. Large numbers of new recruits are divided into groups of sizes of eight to 10 people in a group.

POST-TRAINING WORK FOR MAKING TRAINING EFFECTIVE

The process of training and development should not end with conducting the training or management development programme. You have to learn this from your experience. You need to be aware of the characteristics of record management, comprising accessibility, speedy retrieval, the analysis and weeding of records, defining the retention schedule, and review of usage ratio, which are important characteristics of an efficient record management system. You must maintain records for future references which should comprise feedback received from participants, post-training impact measurement (from multiple sources), faculty database, knowledge repository, training management reports, HRD audit plan, schedule, and reports, non-conformity record sheets for courses conducted, attendance sheets, syllabi of training, and management development programmes, assessment test results, record of certificates, and many more records.

In addition, the organization has to maintain vital documents such as process analysis document, quality objective documents, and quality objective analysis relating to course conduction, course material management, and course administration.

TRAINING DOCUMENTS AND RECORDS

Training documents must be controlled and the training department should preferably develop a system of documentation. The training organization should approve documents for adequacy prior to issue, review, and update them whenever necessary, revise the documents, and make the relevant versions available at the point of use. Documents should be legible and readily identifiable. Obsolete documents (such as revised course material) must be removed. The nature and extent of documentation should satisfy the contractual requirements, if any, as in the case of course programmes for the clients to fulfil specific training needs. Training organizations must retain records for analysis and improvement. Formats of some of the records have been exhibited earlier in this chapter.

RECORD MANAGEMENT

No record without analysis; no analysis without feedback;
No feedback without corrective action; no corrective action without recording.

–Anonymous

A training institute receives many documents and records from several clients. These are obviously documents received from external origin. A training institute, in turn, generates good numbers of records for training administration purpose. All the documents and records should be controlled by record management.

Records management is the practice of identifying, classifying, archiving, preserving, and destroying records. Record management refers to the field of management responsibility for the efficient and systematic control of the creation, receipt, maintenance, use and disposition of records, including the processes for capturing and maintaining evidence of and information about business activities and transactions in the form of records of ISO.

Documents provide information and a supporting medium. Training documents include specification (document stating requirements), training manual (document specifying the training management system), training plan (document specifying the relevant procedures and associated resources for a particular training course), and records (document stating results achieved or providing evidence of activities performed). These records are special types of documents.

It is important to note that documents shall be under revision control but records need not be under revision control. 'Records are established and maintained to provide evidence of conformity to requirements and of the effective operations of the quality management system. Records shall remain legible, readily identifiable and retrievable. A documented procedure shall be established to define the controls needed for the identification, storage, protection, retrieval, retention time and disposition of records.' (ISO 9001:2000, clause 4.2.4, control of records). ISO 9001:2000, clause 6.2.2 (competency, awareness and training) specifies that organizations shall maintain appropriate records of education, training, skills, and experience.

In many organizations, including public sector organizations, the status of record management system is dismal. It will not be an exaggeration to say that most of the organizations are losing more than what they gain from the records they maintain. Some of the bills of the present system of records management are as follows:

1. Inordinate delay in retrieval
2. Records are not readily identifiable
3. Records are not legible
4. Unspecified retention schedule
5. Weeding out of old records
6. Absence of any system of record maintenance
7. Improper storage space
8. Preservation of records

Characteristics of Record Management

Review of usage ratio, accessibility, speedy retrieval, and retention schedule are important characteristics of efficient record management system.

Review of usage ratio As an HRD manager, you have to discharge the role of a 'manager of learning'. Records may be classified into three distinct categories: A- frequently used, B- sometimes used, and C- rarely used. You may install a system to periodically review the frequency of usage of the training records just to classify them in the categories.

The important characteristics of efficient record management system are review of usage ratio, accessibility, speedy retrieval, and retention schedule.

The holding of rarely used records simply occupies the storage space, and leads to shortage of storage. This category needs further investigation to sub-classify them as: C1 records that might be required afterwards and C2 records that would never be required. As such, the records belonging to the second category may be destroyed. But before destroying, you must prepare a list of the records and circulate to relevant personnel of your organization for information and comments on retention, if any. You may empower your junior colleagues to carry out the task of scrutiny, categorizing, and preparing the list of records in each of the three main categories and further classifying the third category. Removal of unnecessary records will make the record management system, including preservation of records, efficient.

Accessibility All records, particularly categorized A should be easily accessible and be available within the reach. Records of category C1 may be preserved at heights beyond the reach, up to the ceiling.

Speedy retrieval Each record must be classified, indexed, labelled, and numbered. This ensures proper identification of the records. The records must also be stored in separate storage devices according to the classifications. Within each class of records, one must arrange them by following an index. To warrant speedy retrieval, a system must be developed and complied with. One should preferably implement the concept of 5S for record management, and always remember, 'A place for everything, everything in its place.'

Retention schedule Each record has its own lifecycle. One has to decide the retention period considering the usage and nature of the record. The life of records may widely vary. For example, a record of attendance is useful during the period of training. However, for analysis and to prepare database of participants trained in an academic year or in the last five years, you may consider the life to retain the record for seven or even ten years. You have to decide the retention schedule for each record and review the schedule after three to five years for effectiveness.

In case of preservation of records in computers, you may plan a longer retention period as the question of occupying physical space does not arise.

Record Retention Time

You have realized the importance of retaining the record for defined period of time. You have to decide the retention period for each document and record, based on the nature of the document and contents of the records. You may finalize it once, and thereafter, you may revise them based on actual need and experience. The retention period of some commonly used training document and record are mentioned in Table 9.16.

Table 9.16 Record retention time

S. no.	Document or record	Format no.	Custodian	Retention period
1.	Assessment test result			Forever
2.	Attendance sheet			One year
3.	Audit plan			Two years
4.	Audit report			Two years
5.	Audit schedule			Two years

(Contd)

Table 9.16 (Contd)

S. no.	Document or record	Format no.	Custodian	Retention period
6.	Bio-data of participants			One year
7.	Continuous evaluation			One year
8.	Continuous evaluation summary			One year
9.	Corrective action sheet			Two years
10.	Document distribution list			Five years
11.	Document amendment form			Five years
12.	Faculty assistance from external source			One year
13.	Faculty hours assessment—external			One year
14.	Faculty hours assessment—internal			One year
15.	Feedback report			Two years
16.	Master list of formats			Forever
17.	Master list of training records			Forever
18.	Minutes of training review meeting			Three years
19.	Nomination of internal faculty			One year
20.	Participant registration sheet			One year
21.	Post-training impact measurement (from participants)			Continuous process
22.	Post training impact measurement (from supervisor)			Continuous process
23.	Preventive action sheet			Two years
24.	Programme			One year
25.	Record of attendance			Three years
26.	Record of education, training, and experience			Forever (three years after retirement)
27.	Record of lecture			One year
28.	Summary of feedback report			Two years
29.	Summary of participation			Two years
30.	Syllabus			Till updating

Source: Adapted from the book *Human Resource Development* by Uday Kumar Haldar, published by Oxford University Press, New Delhi, 2009.

Note: The retention periods of the records are based on the practices followed by Ordnance Factories, Institute of Learning, Ishapore. Table 9.16 is for your guidance. You are required to decide based on the characteristics of records in your own organization.

Training Records and Their Classification

In the previous section, we have discussed about classifying the records. Some training records are further classified based on their usage in various phases of training. Training records are obviously organization-specific. You must generate training records for analysis, decision-making, and improving the training efforts and results.

You can stratify the documents and records in two broad categories: (a) course-specific, and (b) independent of the courses, that is, similar to all the courses. You can further classify the course-specific documents and records into three classes; (a) required in the course planning phase, (b) during the conduction of the courses, and (c) after conduction of the courses. You are required to generate the documents and records in formats designed for the purpose. The formats may however be revised in view of the changing needs of the institute. A list of commonly-used documents and records are mentioned later in this chapter.

Documents Recorded at Planning Phase

It is required to generate or refer to some documents and records while planning a course. The syllabi for a course, programme, registration sheet etc. are examples of documents and records required to be developed before the start of the course. Although these are planning phase documents, they still need review after the conduction of the course as post training work. The review and identified lapses enable to make the training system more effective and ensure continual improvement.

1. Syllabus of course or MDP
2. Programme
3. Nomination of faculty
4. Reading material
5. Exercises
6. Books in library (course-wise)
7. Journals in the library (course-wise)

Documents Recorded During the Course

While conducting the course, you must concentrate on generating the following documents:

1. Registration sheet
2. Record of attendance
3. Bio data of participants
4. Continuous evaluation of participants
5. Feedback format

Documents Recorded after the Course

After conducting the course, you should perform certain post training work to make the training system effective. As such, you need to concentrate on the following documents:

1. Continuous evaluation summary
2. Assessment test result
3. Result sheet
4. Average course grading and yearly course grading
5. Post training impact measurement (from trained personnel)
6. Post training impact measurement (from immediate supervisor)
7. Summary of participation
8. Certificate number

Documents and Records—Not Course-specific

You have seen that the documents and records are grouped in three classes. Yet you are required to develop and use some of these documents and records, not specifically required for a particular course, and which you need for all the courses you conduct in your institute.

1. Faculty database
2. Topic-wise faculty
3. Faculty-wise topics
4. Records of qualification and experience
5. Training courses attended by internal faculty members

6. Annual calendar of training and MDPs
7. Corrective action sheet
8. Preventive action sheet
9. Distribution of list of documents
10. Document amendment form
11. Faculty hours assessment (internal and external)
12. Minutes of training review meeting
13. Training audit plan
14. Training audit schedule
15. Training audit report

Note: You are required to design formats for all the documents and records that you require in different phases of the training. All the formats must bear format numbers. Formats filled in with data must be under document control through a structured procedure, say, 'procedure for design and development of courses.'

Now, you will study designing of formats for the documents and records at each stage of the training and post-training phase to make the training system effective. Ideally, any training organization should develop and use two procedures—control of documents and control of records. These procedures would help to conform to uniform practices. The procedures are exhibited in Annexures 9.6 and 9.7.

Record Keeping—Concept of 5S

Record keeping is an integral part of record management. The application of 5S makes the record keeping systematic. 5S is a concept that primarily emphasizes on a change in the mindset. It is a systematic and rational approach to methodical housekeeping built on a sound economic base. It is a science as well as an art. It is a science in the sense that it is based on a logical approach and is analytical in nature. It is also an art in the sense that it contributes to decency, beautification, and esteem value. 5S should be a company-wide practice. It needs the support and commitment of top management.

This concept is applicable in any organization and in all functional areas. A training organization is not an exception to this concept. The concept originated from Japan. 5S stands for *seiri, seiton, seiso, seiketsu, shitsuke*. The meaning of these words and equivalent English terms are given in Table 9.17.

Table 9.17 Japanese terms and English equivalents for 5S

	Japanese term	English translation	Equivalent 'S' term
1.	*Seiri*	Organization	Sorting out or organizing (in order)
2.	*Seiton*	Tidiness	Systematic arrangement or neatness
3.	*Seiso*	Cleaning	Spic and span, cleaning, or inspection
4.	*Seiketsu*	Standardization	Serene atmosphere, standardization, or sanitizing
5.	*Shitsuke*	Discipline	Self-discipline

Application of 5S

You may have noticed that useful things, papers, and files get mixed up with unusable things, other papers, and files. Searching for some useful document or record takes a lot of time, causing inordinate delay. You can apply the concept of all the S's in your institute to enhance efficiency and effectiveness of preserving documents and record in a systematic manner. 5S facilitates quick retrieval of documents and records, however old they are. Both government and non-government organizations are widely using concepts of 5S. The 5S policy and 5S objectives of Regional Training Institute, Ishapore (RTIIS) are exhibited in Box 9.9. The benefits are listed in Box 9.10.

Box 9.9 5S policy and objectives

5S Policy

RTIIS commits to continually improve the quality of work place which in turn will enhance its productivity, through the practice of 5S.

5S Objectives

1. All employees of RTIIS shall maintain standard of records keeping, including weeding out unwanted/obsolete documents and records.
2. Shall ensure maintenance of clean and hygienic work environment.
3. Shall ensure reinforcement of self-discipline to provide better customer service.

Box 9.10 Benefits of 5S

1. Saves floor space
2. Helps to get rid of obsolete items
3. Gives a clear idea of study material in stock (useful for repeat courses)
4. Prevents incidence of unnecessary buying
5. Ensures utilization of available inventories
6. Makes workplace conducive to higher productivity and effective learning
7. Prevents blockage in workflow (conduction of training and workshops)
8. Controls the inventory levels of training inputs
9. Lessens production down time (like class hours)
10. Generates sense of achievement and accomplishment
11. Helps achieve higher product quality
12. Ensures system approach through standardized procedures
13. Restores confidence and minimizing errors
14. Reduces wastes and increases productivity
15. Improves working conditions
16. Provides opportunities to maintain improved quality in training system
17. Results in ownership and a sense of pride among employees
18. Reduced machine and system down time
19. Higher employee involvement

IMPROVING TRAINING METHODS

An organization should continuously review its training system, and work towards improving it. It should also put its best efforts to identify the state-of-the-art practices prevailing in the arena of training. In order to discover these practices, the organization needs to be able to determine and benchmark them.

BENCHMARKING OF TRAINING PRACTICES

Benchmarking is basically a process of determining which organization is following the best practice in the industry and what they are doing. In other words, the best ones set the standards. Benchmarking is essentially looking around and learning from others, and an exercise for identifying the best practices in the industry and emulating them. The practice of benchmarking enables an organization to accelerate its rate of improvement. It also helps in promoting a thorough understanding of the company's own processes. Thus, the company's own profile is well understood as well.

A thorough study leads to identification of non-value adding activities. Performance measures such as return on investment, lead time of designing a service product like a new training course or a management development programme, etc., can be compared for benchmarking. Generally, while benchmarking, focus is laid on the processes and performance measures. You should put your best intellectual effort into knowing what other institutes are doing with regard to finalizing their training syllabus, designing the curriculum, evaluating the training, record generation, and maintenance, etc. The benchmarking process begins with intensive research and preparation. Thus, you must first decide the objects to be benchmarked. This defines what is to be benchmarked and who will be the benchmarking partners with whom we will exchange benchmarking information.

Thereafter, you are required to collect data relating to specific processes, practices, and results. After collecting and analysing the information, stretch your goals, and develop an implementation plan to improve performance.

TRAINING WHEEL

Q 8 Training is a vital, and by far the most important mechanism of human resource development. It has already been discussed at the beginning of this chapter that the main purpose of training is to achieve the business goals where the training curriculum must be linked with business strategy. Evaluation and validation of any training are critical components of an organization's training system. The training cycle must start with defining and documenting the business goals, and end with training evaluation.

Planning, structuring, implementing, and reviewing and revising training, form a training cycle. The training wheel helps in achieving the business goals. Frances Bee and Roland (1998) propose that a training wheel unearths the business needs, identifies training needs, specifies the training needs, translates them into actions, plans, and evaluates the training. Refer to Figure 9.2. These steps are briefly discussed here.

Unearthing the business needs This refers to the consideration of the mission, policy, and targets of the business, as per the need requirements of the organization. The targets lead to formulation business strategies. As such, the business needs must be meticulously identified, documented, and communicated to significant personnel and all those who would strive to achieve those.

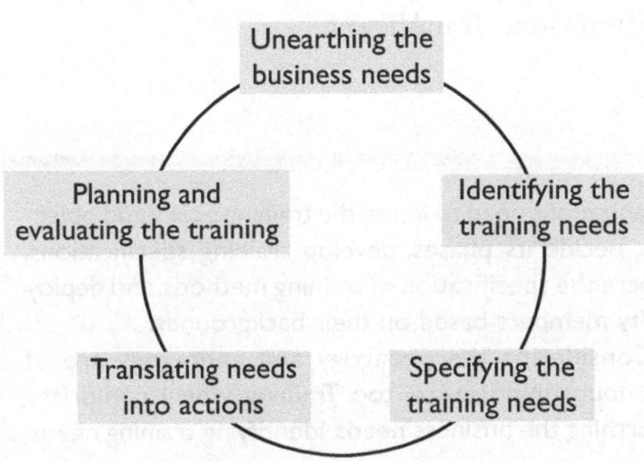

FIG. 9.2 Training wheel

Identifying the training needs The tasks must be identified and assigned strictly, considering the competencies required to perform those tasks and the competencies in possession of the workforce earmarked for the tasks. Keeping in mind these factors, the organization must identify the needs for which the employees need to be trained for.

Specifying the training needs On identifying the needs, they must be specified to the individuals participating in the training module. Employee-wise training needs should also be documented. The curriculum should be developed considering pedagogy and andragogy, and other factors of training discussed earlier. Thereafter, the training programmes should be executed.

Translating needs into actions The trained personnel need to utilize the knowledge gained and expertise obtained to translate the business strategies into actions, and perform the assignments. Any lapses in the design of the curriculum or the process of disseminating the knowledge and skills might hinder him in achieving the business goals. In order to eliminate this possibility, it is very important for any training programme to be evaluated.

Planning and evaluating the training Different phases of training, planning of training, and their evaluation have been discussed earlier. However, it is stated that evaluation constitutes the most systematic way of determining the strengths, weaknesses, and effects of training courses. The purposes behind training evaluation, as already discussed, are many and certain purposes guide and dictate the need of evaluation.

GLOBALIZATION OF TRAINING PROGRAMMES

The information revolution is characterized by an on-going process of economic, social, and political globalization. Education and training are not exceptions. The term, globalization, has become quite widespread and makes people to live, and function in global village. There are software that allows file-transfer applications, business collaborations, and accessing a second computer which is remotely placed. Some of these are as follows:

TeamViewer is a software that facilitates file-transfer applications, business collaborations, access a remotely-placed second computer, or help distraught relatives diagnose and cure computer problems. The software gives users precisely the tools they need to share screens securely, send files with a minimum of hassle, control access rights, and even flip which user has control.

TeamViewer breaks the boundaries of space and time using advanced information and communications technologies. The system adopted by TeamViewer permits application of a wide range of synchronous and asynchronous activities. These activities aid the professors and students in breaking the boundaries of space and time. Synchronous activities include real-time lectures (featuring audio, presentations, web sites, and even video), quizzes and group discussions; all of which can occur with the instructor being at the same location or even a different location from the learner. On the other hand, asynchronous activities can include archived lectures (in audio and video), and other archived course material that can be accessed at nearly any time or place.

For example, Prof. Buddhadip Mukherjee of the Indian Institute of Social Welfare and Business Management (IISWBM) shared his expertise on 'organizational behaviour' to working executives of United Kingdom, Malaysia, South Africa, Middle-East, Singapore, and India. The interactive classes is organized through the excellent screen-sharing software used TeamViewer.

SUMMARY

Organizations are seen to be making significant investments in their training and development programmes with the ultimate aim of meeting their business needs. Training motivates people, restores confidence in all the clients of the organization, and improves organizational culture. For any training to be successful,. its needs must be identified following a structured procedure, prior to the session. Organizations need to frame the training policy and objectives, decide its phases, develop training specifications, prepare the specification of training methods, and deploy faculty members based on their backgrounds.

Considering the pedagogy and andragogy are of paramount importance, too. Training wheel comprises unearthing the business needs, identifying training needs, specifying the training needs, translating them into actions, and planning and evaluating the training. For training to be effective and produce the desired result, at all stages the manager of learning must take care of possible impediments. Evaluating training programmes is of paramount importance. Record keeping system can be significantly advanced by applying the concept of 5S. Training methods can be continually improved by way of benchmarking. Role of trainers and their behaviours towards learners should be conducive to effective learning. Training system is now globalized by way electronic enabled training systems.

KEY TERMS

Andragogy refers to the art and science of training adults, focuses on creation of an independent, adaptable, and socially acceptable individual because training adults substantially differs from that of training children, and that adults hold considerably more experience to the learning arena than children.

Pedagogy is the science of disseminating knowledge; it refers to the strategies or style of instruction an educator is required to follow, and it deals with forming first impressions, dominant myths, traditional clichés and truisms, and understanding the deep meaning, root causes, ideology, and consequences of any personal action, event, object, and process.

Terminal behaviour is the level of knowledge with which a person leaves the institute after attending the training.

Training impediments are lack of management commitment and sanctioned budget, large-scale poaching of trained personnel, absence of tie-up employers and B-schools, etc.

Training objectives describe the performance or behaviours that you expect the trainees to exhibit after the completion of the training.

Training specification is a course of action—a blueprint for the programme required to bridge the gap between actual and expected performance.

Training validation is the attempt to determine whether the trainees have been benefited from the training programme and have learned what they needed to.

EXERCISES

Concept Review Questions

1. 'Business needs are the driving forces of a training programme'. Justify the statement citing examples of a few business needs.
2. Discuss various steps of developing the syllabus of a new course. Prepare an exhaustive list of information you would collect in this regard.
3. What is the importance of pedagogical aids in conduction of training programme? What might be the consequences if any particular aid is not available?
4. Differentiate between pedagogy and andragogy. What care would you take while training adults?
5. Discuss the roles and characteristics of a trainer. How can a trainer develop these characteristics?
6. What is training validation? Discuss the means of validating a training programme. Cite examples.

Critical Thinking Questions

7. If you have attended a training session, you must have evidenced the attitude a training personnel holds while the session. Identify some of the impediments that hinder in making the training effective. Also, narrate your action plans to take care of the roadblocks to organizational development through training.
8. 'Training evaluation is a process, and without the training wheel it can't move.' Do you agree with this statement? Justify your viewpoints.
9. Discuss the types of training evaluation design. As an HRD manager in a tourism industry responsible to develop the employees, which type training evaluation would you suggest for the employees deployed in the (a) front office (reception, public relations, information etc.) and (b) escorting the tourists.

Assignments

10. Visit the training department, collect the training calendar, and choose a training programme from the calendar. Also collect the syllabus, brochure, and prepare the objective-wise time and facility required. Approach the training manager, take his appointment,

and meet him to discuss what you have prepared. Request him to scrutinize and carefully observe his facial expression. Thereafter, collect his views about the usefulness of the same. Do you feel that you would succeed in getting this system implemented?

11. Visit an organization that has a training department. Find out how they evaluate their training programme. If the training department is using Jack Phillips's ROI approach, record the data they are collecting. Further note to what extent the organization is getting returns from training. Analyse all the information, finalize your findings, and suggest the training department suitably.

MANAGER'S INSIGHT

Alpha Consultancy is conducting general as well as customized training programmes on HR, quality management, industrial engineering, strategic management, etc. It has many customers. Alpha is conducting these programmes either in their own modern classrooms or in customer premises on request.

Magna Engineering approached Alpha Consultancy with a request to conduct a training programme, keeping in mind the following conditions:

1. Training to be imparted in the premises of Magna Engineering
2. Reading material to be handed over two weeks earlier
3. Course-ending evaluation is an essential need
4. Statement of marks, participant-wise, to be given to Magna
5. Specific weaknesses of the participants to be highlighted by Alpha

Alpha agreed to all the conditions as it had experience of conducting training for more than 20 years. Moreover, Alpha had conducted this particular training desired by Magna more than 120 times. The training material and exercises were time-tested as well. Alpha is also in a habit of reviewing and incorporating revisions immediately after the conduction of a course. Alpha lays lot of emphasis on the feedback of participants.

Alpha conducted the programme in Magna Seminar Hall. There were 22 participants. After five days, the six-hours per day course ended. Verbal feedbacks were excellent. Two participants emphasized about the applicability of knowledge transferred in the training in the work areas. All the participants were delighted as the sessions were interactive and they could get the doubts clarified. The HR director and manager of training of Magna were also present in the valedictory session. They also spoke high of Alpha. Alpha promised to hand over the statement of marks after evaluating within a week. Alpha was astonished to see that three out of 22 participants failed and secured less than the qualifying marks. However, the training administrator and one faculty member of Alpha visited Magna and enquired about the three participants who failed. Alpha also requested to refer to the record of attendance and the video that recorded movements of participants, faculties, and the happenings in the seminar hall.

The three participants were away from the seminar hall. On interrogation, they said that they were called by their respective seniors for some urgent work.

Questions:

1. Mention the records or documents a training organization must maintain.
2. What instructions should be communicated to the participants at the commencement of a training programme?
3. During negotiation of course at customer premises, what clause should be incorporated in the contract?

BIBLIOGRAPHY AND WEB RESOURCES

Agarwala, Tanuja, *Strategic Human Resource Management*, Oxford University Press, New Delhi, 2007.

Bee, Frances and Roland Bee, *Training Needs Analysis and Evaluation*, University Press (India) Limited, New Delhi, 1998.

Bohlander, George W. and Snell A. Scot, *Managing Human Resource,* Thomson Learning, New Delhi, 2002.

Charles, Graham, Kursat Cagiltay, Joni Craner, Byung-Ro Lim, and Thomas M. Duffy, *Seven Principles of Effective*

Teaching: A Practical Lens for Evaluating Online Courses, *The Technology Source*, 2001.

Hamblin, A.C., *The Evaluation and Control of Training*, McGraw-Hill (European Series in Management), UK, 1974.

ISO 9001:2000 Standard, Quality Management System - Requirements, issued by International Organization for Standardization and Adopted by Bureau of Indian Standards, New Delhi, 2000.

Iyer, Radha, Priya Pardiwalla, and Jimish Bathia, Training Evaluation Practices in Indian Organizations, *HRD Newsletter* (monthly publication of National HRD Network), Vol. 25, Issue 8, pp. 35–37, Hyderabad, November 2009.

Kirkpatrick, D.L., Evaluation of Training, in *Training and Development Handbook*, edited by R.L. Craig, McGraw-Hill, London, 1994.

Kozoll, Charles F., Characteristics of a Trainer, Harvard University, USA, in *Training & Development Journal*, Vol. 29, No. 7, July 1975.

Phillips, Jack J., *Handbook of Training Evaluation and Measurement Methods*, Elsevier, Australia, 1991.

Reddy, Dr Rathan B., *Effective Human Resource Training and Development Strategy*, Himalaya Publishing House, New Delhi, 2005.

Srivastava, V.N., M. Shafiq, and K. Ghosh, Higher Performance Management through Systematic Efforts, *Indian Journal of Training and Development*, Vol. XXXV, No. 4, October–December, 2005.

Warr, P.B., M. Bird, and N. Rackham, *The Evaluation of Management Training*, Gower Press, London, 1970.

Wilson, John P., Human Resource Development – Learning & Training for Individuals & Organizations, Kogan Page Limited, New Delhi, 2005.

Gosling and Mintzberg, The Five Minds of a Manager, *Harvard Business Review*, November 2003.

Patra, Rima, *Assessment of Training Needs in Allahabad bank*, Kolkata, prepared by and submitted to Indian Institute of Social Welfare and Business Management (IISWBM), Calcutta University, 2009.

Web Resources

www.ignou.org, last accessed on 23 December 2011.

www.knowledgeadvisors.com, last accessed on 23 December 2011.

ASSESSMENT OF TRAINING NEEDS IN ALLAHABAD BANK

About the organization

Allahabad Bank is one of the premier nationalized banks in India, and is the oldest joint stock bank as well. It was incorporated by a group of Europeans in the historic city of Allahabad on 24 April 1865. It was the time when the Indian economy had started shifting towards organized trade and business affairs. Thus, the history of the bank has spread over three centuries—19th, 20th, and 21st centuries.

Allahabad Bank is India's eighth largest bank in the terms of the assets, and provides services to over 26 million customers across India through its network of more than 2,200 branches. In 1923, Allahabad Bank shifted its headquarters to Kolkata. The bank got an entirely new identity when it was nationalized in 1969, along with 13 other banks in India. Since then, Allahabad Bank had a smooth journey towards progress. Today, it is one of the leading banks in India with a whooping business of over ₹10,00,000 million.

The goal of the bank is to further strengthen its position as one of India's premier commercial banks, and to increase the profitability by expanding the business, improving the spreads, and reducing its operating expenses.

At present, Allahabad Bank has 2,277 branches in India (as on 30 April 2009) and 46 zonal offices. Apart from general branches, the bank has also come up with specialized branches, such as industrial finance branches, international branches, finance branches, recovery branches, NRI branches specialized personal banking branches, specialized savings bank branches, quick collection service branches, trading finance branches, and service branches in many major cities of India.

Allahabad Bank offers a full range of the banking product services. The banking operations of the bank cater to corporate and commercial customers, as well as small and middle-market business and government entities.

The bank delivers its products and services through the extensive branch network, extension counters, ATMs, phone banking, and internet banking. The bank believes that it can use its large network of the rural branches to attract funds at a lower cost, by means of its saving bank deposit products, that have been a hit with the rural customers.

A study

A study was attempted to assess the training need identification system existing in Allahabad Bank. After nationalization, Allahabad bank has opened new branches in the unbanked areas to offer banking facilities to all sections of the society. This rapid branch expansion has led to the corresponding increases in deposits, credit, and employee strength. When such massive changes took place in business activities and manpower, the training system of the bank found it extremely difficult to cope with the increasing demands. Many educated people entered the bank at the levels of clerks and junior officers, thus changing the profile of the bank employees during post-nationalization era.

Special efforts for reorientation of these qualified employees were essential to leverage their skills, knowledge, and attitudes to meet business requirements of the banking industry. Therefore, the bank had to take up massive training activities through their training infrastructure all over the country. The impressive number of training institutions set up by the bank did not prove to be adequate to meet the increased demand. This widening gap led to the ineffective delivery of training inputs, in contrast to the reality of operational banking needs.

Over the years, unfortunately, the gap between the training needs and training efforts has gotten widened, and has resulted in a major criticism against the ineffective training activities. Therefore, there is a need to have a closer look at the existing training systems in Allahabad Bank, when it indicates that the real reason for ineffective training lays elsewhere.

Objectives

The broad objectives of the study were as follows:

1. To study the training system of Allahabad Bank.
2. To analyse the process of identifying training needs of the employees in the bank.
3. To study the extent to which the employees are able to transfer the inputs learnt from the training programmes (knowledge, skills, and attitude) to accomplish the tasks assigned at their workplace.
4. To suggest ways to further improve the procedure of training need identification in the bank.

Methodology

The present work in Allahabad Bank has been prepared in fulfillment of the broad objectives of the study on 'assessment of training needs' of the employees and the extent to which the employees are able to apply the inputs learnt from the training programmes at their workplace to alleviate their performance gap.

Sample size

The study was conducted with a sample size of 1,514 employees (primary as well as secondary), and the research work was carried out by an empirical method followed by analytical assessment. In order to get more reliable and detailed information, the entire population was further stratified into several sub-populations for homogeneity. Thus, heteroscedascity was avoided.

The size of the sub-population, which differs from each other according to the phases of analysis, is shown in Table 9.18.

Table 9.18 Sample size variation

S. no.	Steps of analysis	Sample size
1.	Questionnaire	155 employees
2.	KSA mapping (#)	570 employees
3.	Customers interviewed	30 customers
4.	Analysis of 'about me' form (##)	252 participants
5.	Analysis of program evaluation sheet (PES)	507 employees

Note:
(#) KSA mapping format is shown in Table 9.19.
(##) The bank collects personal details in the 'about me' form.

Table 9.19 KSA mapping format—Staff training centre

Programme name					From	To
S. no.	PF no.	Name	Zone	Qualification	Area of interest shown by the participants	Suggested area by the committee for future development

Tools used for collecting data

Both primary data and secondary data were collected for processing.

Primary data was collected through

1. Questionnaires
2. Direct interviews

Secondary data was collected through

1. Syllabi of internal training for staff colleges, taken from the bank
2. Program evaluation sheet, About-me form, and KSA report collected from the HRD department of the bank
3. Annual report (2008–09) of the bank

Steps taken

Data was collected through the following steps:

Step 1: A set of structured questionnaires were prepared and administered to the employees of various hierarchical level of the bank. Next, responses were obtained from them, and analysis was made in order to identify specific work and skill areas where training needs were realized.

Step 2: A thoroughly-developed list of the tasks linked to the KSAs was analysed to examine the true relationship between the employees and the actual training needs they have in order to accomplish the organizational goal. The KSA mapping was done from both organizational perspectives as well as from customers' view point. In this regard, a small Interview was held with the customers to get their opinion.

Step 3: Next, a study was carried out to evaluate the effectiveness of the training need identification of the employees. In this regard, a new devise was formulated, and was named 'summative assessment' to quantify the program evaluation sheet and the 'about me' forms of various training programs in order to understand the extent of fulfillment of the identified training needs exercise.

Step 4: The researcher pursued a small study on 'external training programme' as a live-case example to detect how those training programmes helped meet the training needs of the employees.

Step 5: After analysing all the data, the researcher submitted the recommendations to the bank for further enriching the procedure of identifying the training needs of their employees in a better manner.

Findings and conclusion

From the study and analysis of the data, the following points were revealed:

1. The superiors are not in a position to assess the training needs of the subordinates. Additionally, the feedbacks from superiors, trainees, and trainers provide a true picture that training need assessment in Allahabad Bank is not done scientifically.
2. After a careful study on various KSA reports of different training programmes, the results confirm that in most of the cases training attended by participants do not match with the organization's training need assessment.
3. The feedback from customers of the bank highlights the fact that the attitude of the staff affect the customers to a large extent.
4. Implementation of the 'summative scaling technique' (Likert scaling) clearly establishes the fact that the assessment of training needs in the bank is more of subjective importance rather than objective one.
5. System of review of 'external training programme' indicates that the outcome of training is evaluated. The evaluation results indicate that external training programmes are equally effective in fulfillment of training needs of the employees.

Limitations

Every research study is short of limitations and the following study is not an exception. The limitations are as follows:

1. Time was a constraint. Covering a very large area and large population of the bank was difficult in this tenure of two months in Allahabad bank. As the bank is largely spread out across the country, it was almost impossible to get access to all employees.
2. There was no access to the report of 'annual performance appraisal' of the employees.
3. There was limited access to the company documents and information.
4. Due to time constraints, the recommendations are framed based on comparative small sample size.
5. Most of the employees did not welcome filling up the questionnaire. They kept delaying it day after day. Some of them even did not want to reveal their identity.

Note: This case was prepared based on a project report titled Assessment of Training Needs in Allahabad Bank, Kolkata, prepared by Rima Patra, and submitted to Indian Institute of Social Welfare and Business Management (IISWBM) in partial fulfillment of master's degree course in Human Resource Management for evaluation by University of Calcutta.

Discussion Questions

1. The bank is carrying out KSA mapping and recording in a format. Do you feel that the format is adequate to

record knowledge, skills, and attitude of employees? If not, what additional columns should be added?

2. The bank is collecting information about a training programme from trained participants in its program evaluation sheet. The format has been exhibited at the end of this chapter. Study the format and comment whether the bank should collect some more information about the training programme.
3. How can the bank improve its training system? Explain with examples.

HR MANTRA Importance of training

ABC Limited came into existence in 1995 as a trader of basic chemicals. It used to purchase chemicals only from reputed chemical manufacturers. Thereafter, it added its profit, strictly based on its pricing policy. The company also used to supply its products to its customers well within the stipulated delivery time. The company gradually gained reputation and built an image in the minds of its customers, and turned them into its advocates.

The owner and founder director of the company planned and started a company to produce chemicals. The company initially engaged two chemical engineers who took keen initiatives to develop its manufacturing division. However, due to lack of attractive incentives, they left the company. The working class was not trained. During their stay in ABC Limited, the two engineers were repeatedly insisting for developing the workers by way of training. But the owner of the company expressed indifference and did not take any initiative. After the departure of the engineers, the workers could not produce the chemicals due to lack of knowledge. Subsequently, some of the customers of the company expressed their grievances with chemical manufactured and supplied to them.

The mantra: Training is costly; non-training is costlier.

PROF. B.R. VIRMANI

Prof. B.R. Virmani was born on 5 October 1939, in Bannu, a North West Frontier province (now part of Pakistan), in pre-independence India.

Virmani secured his postgraduate degree in social work from New Delhi. He obtained his MBA degree from Pittsburgh, and became a fellow at the Queen Elizabeth House, Oxford. He is also the Founder and Chairman of the Centre for Organization Research and Development in Management (CORD-M), Hyderabad, India. In addition, he was Professor of Strategic Management and Dean at the Administrative Staff College of India (ASCI), Hyderabad for over two decades. Prior to joining ASCI, he worked in the industry for 10 years. He began his career as a management trainee and rose to the position of chief executive of a large industrial group based at Kolkata.

He was a visiting fellow at the Manchester Business School, UK, and a Senior Research Fellow at the Friedrich Ebert Institute, Bonn, Germany. The Indian Society for Training and Development (ISTD), National Institute of Personnel Management (NIPM), and All India Management Association (AIMA) have conferred fellowship on Virmani. He was the National President of the ISTD in 1990–91 and the Chairman of ISTD's diploma programme. He also chaired the editorial board of the Indian Journal of Training and Development (IJTD).

Virmani has also been a consultant to several public and private sector organizations and government departments in India and abroad such as Indian Rayon, Ashok Leyland Limited, L&T, ITC, BPCL, IOC, ONGC, HPCL, University Grants Commission, National Institute of Agricultural Extension Management (MANAGE), and so on. He also worked as a consultant to the Government of Belize (Central America) for Reorganization of Civil Service on behalf of the Commonwealth Secretariat, London, USAID, and Centre for Financial Engineering and Development, Washington (DC) on their project on sustainable economic reforms project in India, and Overseas Development Administration (ODA) of British Government on their project on primary education. He was a resources faculty for programmes of the Asian and Pacific Development Administration Centre, Kuala Lumpur; Consortium for Oil Training, Baghdad; United Nations ESCAP for their programmes on Technology and HRD Policies in Korea; Asian Productivity Organization, Singapore; Dubai Institute of Business Management; ETA Escon group, Dubai; Chief Executive Forum of Sri Lanka etc.

Apart from his consultancy services, Virmani has published 15 books and over 60 articles, including research-based books on Indian management; evaluating management training and development; participative management vs collective bargaining; workers' education; economic development alternatives: Andaman and Nicobar Islands; economic restructuring, technology transfer and human resource development. Virmani's latest book, *The Challenges of Indian Management* (Sage Publications) is being translated and published in Indian regional languages such as Bengali, Tamil, and Marathi.

Virmani's widespread activities and contributions are directed towards the development of humankind in India and abroad. Moreover, he is keen to reach larger segments of Indians as evidenced through the translation of books to Indian regional languages.

References

www.indianmanagement.org/, last accessed on 8 October 2011.

E-mails from Prof. B.R. Virmani, dated 21 September 2011 and 24 September 2011.

ANNEXURE 9.1

Bio-data of Participants

Please fill in the form and submit it to the course coordinator.

Name of the course .... CS no.

1. Name in full (in capital letters) ....

2. Design. .... Per. no. .... Sec. ....

3. Factory: ....

4. Date of birth .... 5. SC/ST/OBC ....

6. Qualification (Academic) ....

   (Technical) ....

7. Experience—In the present grade (details required)

Name of the factory	Functional area (##)	Designation	Duration		Experience (In years)
			From	To	

Note: (##)—For guidance see functional area list.

8. Whether trained earlier on similar topic/subject: Yes/No
   If yes, give details.

Course	Institute	Period

Signature with date

Functional area and number

01. Production planning
02. Material
03. Tool planning
04. Material control
05. Industrial engineering
06. Production control
07. Product design
08. Design of tools (jig, fixture, gauge, cutting tool)
09. Production (press work, machining, CNC technology, etc.)
10. Computer services (information technology)
11. Purchase
12. TQM/quality management system/ISO: 9000
13. Administration (personnel industrial relations, finance, accounts, labour welfare, vigilance and litigation, secretariat, etc.)
14. Heat treatment
15. Surface treatment
16. Maintenance (electrical)
17. Maintenance (mechanical)
18. Maintenance (building)
19. Carpentry
20. Foundry
21. Smithy
22. Engineering office
23. Teaching
24. School administration
25. Medical services
26. Security
27. Safety and housekeeping
28. Fire services
29. Marketing
30. Pollution control
31. Library administration
32. HRD (training, etc.)
33. Miscellaneous (mention the nature of duty)

ANNEXURE 9.2

Feedback Format

(To be filled in duplicate)

Course title:		Course no.

Duration:	From:	To: ....

Objective—Please refer to next page.
Please offer your comments by ticking the appropriate box.

A. Achievement of course objective				
Excellent	Very good	Good	Fair	Poor

B. Were you able to follow the instructions?			
Fully	Satisfactorily	Moderately	Hardly

C. Practical training facility (Including exercise)				
Excellent	Very good	Good	Fair	Poor

D. Applicability of knowledge/skill imparted			
Fully	Satisfactorily	Moderately	Hardly

E. Which topic appeared most interesting to you (mention topic no.)?

F. Which topic in your opinion is not so relevant?

G. Please mention topics that you can apply in your work area.
- Immediately:
- Shortly (within three months):
- At a later stage:

H. Suggestions/comments if any, e.g., inclusion of any new topic, adequacy or shortage of time, or any other point not covered above.

Objective of the course: ....

Please offer your remarks about the quality of the topic and the quality of their presentation. Scores for grading are as follows:

Maximum: 5		Minimum: 1
Note: You can use any number including decimals, e.g., 1.5, 2.5, 3.5, 4.8		

TG: Topic grading PG: Presentation grading

S. no.	Topic	Day	TG	PG
1.	Topic 1	Day 1		
2.	Topic 2	Day 1		
3.	Topic 3	Day 1		
4.	Exercise 1	Day 1		
5.	Topic 4	Day 1		
6.	Topic 5	Day 2		
7.	Exercise 2	Day 2		
8.	Topic 6	Day 2		
9.	Topic 7	Day 2		
10.	Topic 8	Day 2		
11.	Group exercise 1	Day 2		
12.	Topic 9	Day 3		
13.	Topic 10	Day 3		
14.	Quiz 1	Day 3		
15.	Discussion (Group exercise 1)	Day 4		
16.	Topic 11	Day 4		
17.	Topic 12	Day 4		
18.	Presentation (by participants)	Day 4	–	–

Date: Signature of participants:

Name:

Designation: Factory: Section:

Note: Two copies of the feedback sheet will be prepared by participants. The first copy will be retained by the institute and participants will take the second copy.

ANNEXURE 9.3

Post-training Impact Measurement (From Trained Personnel)

1. Name of the employee: ....

2. Designation: .... 3. Department: ....

4. Course attended: ....

5. Duration: .... 6. From: .... 7. To: ....

Tick the appropriate box:

Poor Fair Good Very good Excellent

8.	Extent of knowledge you could apply in performing the tasks assigned to you	1	2	3	4	5
9.	Your feeling about ease of performing tasks	1	2	3	4	5
10.	Your level of job satisfaction after training	1	2	3	4	5
11.	Express the reaction of your supervisor	1	2	3	4	5
12.	Supervisor's impression toward your performance	1	2	3	4	5
13.	Report increase of your job involvement	1	2	3	4	5
14.	Encouragement received from colleagues	1	2	3	4	5
15.	Positive impact about the knowledge gained in the course in your personal life	1	2	3	4	5

16.	Have you told colleagues about the usefulness of the course?	Yes	No
17.	Do you want to attend other courses at this institute?	Yes	No
18.	Do you refer to the reading material when needed?	Yes	No
19.	Have you shown the reading material to your colleagues?	Yes	No

20. Any other indicative comments: ....

Signature with date: ....

ANNEXURE 9.4

Post-training Impact Measurement (From Immediate Supervisor or Training Manager)

1. Name of the employee: ....

2. Designation: .... 3. Department: ....

4. Course attended: ....

5. Duration: .... 6. From: .... 7. To: ....

Tick the appropriate box:

1: Poor 2: Fair 3: Good 4: Very good 5: Excellent

8.	Increase in confidence level towards work	1	2	3	4	5
9.	Visible behavioural change in work place	1	2	3	4	5
10.	Attitudinal change towards the work	1	2	3	4	5
11.	Sensitivity to accepting new types of work	1	2	3	4	5
12.	Improvement in job performance	1	2	3	4	5
13.	Improvement in job involvement	1	2	3	4	5
14.	Increase in job satisfaction (your view)	1	2	3	4	5
15.	Capacity of helping peers in augmenting their performance	1	2	3	4	5

16.	Has he/she told you about the usefulness of the course?	Yes	No
17.	Do you want to depute him/her to attend other courses?	Yes	No
18.	Have you seen the reading material given to him/her?	Yes	No
19.	Do you want to depute others to attend the same course?	Yes	No

20. Any other indicative comments: ....

Name, signature, and date: ....

ANNEXURE 9.5

Example of Post-training Impact Measurement (From Immediate Supervisor or Training Manager)

इलाहाबाद बैंक
ALLAHABAD BANK

कार्यक्रम मूल्यांकन प्रपत्र / PROGRAMME EVALUATION FORM

कृपया /Please (✓)

स्टाफ कॉलेज, कोलकाता Staff College Kolkata ☐	आइ.आर टी., पंचकुला IRT Panchkula ☐	स्टाफ ट्रेनिंग सेन्टर, पटना Staff Training Centre Patna ☐
स्टाफ कॉलेज, लखनऊ Staff College Lucknow ☐	स्टाफ ट्रेनिंग सेन्टर, भुवनेश्वर Staff Training Centre Bhubaneswar ☐	स्टाफ ट्रेनिंग सेन्टर, हैदराबाद Staff Training Centre Hyderabad ☐

कार्यक्रम का नाम Title of the Programme		
कार्यक्रम समन्वयक का नाम Name of the Course Co-ordinator	श्रीमती / श्री Smt. /Shri	
कार्यक्रम की अवधि Duration of the Programme	से / From	तक / To

कृपया अपने मूल्यांकन से सम्बन्धित बॉक्स में (✓) चिह्न लगायें
Please Tick (✓) in the Box matching with your assessment

	उत्कृष्ट Excellent	बहुत अच्छा Very Good	अच्छा Good	संसोषजनक Fair	अपर्याप्त Poor
1. कार्यक्रम की अन्तर्वस्तु एवं शामिल विषय Contents & Coverage of the Programme					
2. प्रशिक्षण प्रणाली का उपयोग /Methodology used					
3. उपलब्ध अध्ययन सामग्री जैसे बुकलेट, हैण्डआउट आदि Reading Material provided viz. Booklet, Handouts etc.					
4. अभिव्यक्ति दक्षता /Presentation Skill					

5. कार्यक्रम में शामिल विषयों को जोड़ने/हटाने सम्बन्धी आपका सुझाव
Your suggestions for inclusion/exclusion of topics covered during the Programme

जोड़ने हेतु To Include	जोड़ने का कारण Reasons for Inclusion	हटाने हेतु To Exclude	हटाने का कारण Reasons for Exclusion

	पूर्णतः उपयोगी Fully Useful	अत्यन्त उपयोगी Very Useful	उपयोगी Just Useful	आंशिक उपयोगी Somewhat Useful	अनुपयोगी Not Useful
6. कार्यक्रम की उपयोगिता Utility of the Programme क. व्यक्तिशः प्रतिभागी हेतु a. To the Participant in person					
ख. बैंक हेतु b. To the Bank					

7. कृपया कार्यक्रम से लाभान्वित न्यूनतम 2 महत्वपूर्ण बातों का उल्लेख करें
Please indicate atleast 2 important things you gained from the Programme

क/a. ______________________________

ख/b. ______________________________

8. कृपया आपके द्वारा पसंद किये गये चार सत्रों का (बरीयता क्रम में) उल्लेख करें
Mention names of four Sessions you liked most (in order of preference)

क/a. ______________ ग/c. ______________

ख/b. ______________ घ/d. ______________

/P.T.O.

(2)

9. आपके मूल्यांकन के अनुसार कार्यक्रम की अवधि होनी चाहिए
According to your assessment should the duration of the Programme be

	हाँ /Yes नहीं / No	
क. अवधि में वृद्धि / a. Increased		यदि हाँ, तो कितने दिनों तक / If Yes, for what period
ख. कोई परिवर्तन नहीं / b. Kept unchanged		
ग. अवधि में कमी / c. Decreased		यदि हाँ, तो कितने दिनों तक /If Yes, by what period

10. कालेज/केन्द्र की अन्य सुविधाओं के बारे में आपका अभिमत
Your views about other facilities at the College

	उत्कृष्ट Excellent	बहुत अच्छा Very Good	अच्छा Good	संसोषजनक Fair	अपर्याप्त Poor
क. आवासीय सुविधाएं / a. Hostel facilities					
ख. पुस्तकालय सुबिधाएं / b. Library facilities					
ग. मनोरंजन सुविधाएं / c. Recreation facilities					
घ. व्याख्यान कक्ष सुविधाएं / d. Class Room facilities					
ङ. भोजन की गुणवत्ता / e. Catering quality					

11. निम्न बिन्दुओं के अन्तर्गत आपका आभिमत
Your views about the following

	उत्कृष्ट Excellent	बहुत Very Good	अच्छा Good	संतोषजनक Fair	अपर्याप्त Poor
क. प्राचार्य / a. Principal					
ख. कार्यक्रम समन्वयक/ b. Course Co-ordinator					
ग. संकाय सदस्य / c. Faculty Members					
घ. अतिथि संकाय / d. Guest Faculty					
ङ. रखरखाव स्टाफ / e. Maintenance Staff					
च. भोजनालय स्टाफ / f. Catering Staff					
छ. स्वागतकक्ष स्टाफ / g. Reception Counter Staff					

12. कार्यक्रम का समग्र प्रभाव
Overall impression of the Programme

उत्कृष्ट Excellent	बहुत Very Good	अच्छा Good	संसोषजनक Fair	अपर्याप्त Poor

13. कोई अन्य सुझाव जो आप देना चाहते हैं
Any other suggestion you would like to give

___

___

___

समस्त वैकल्पिक
All Optional

हस्ताक्षर/Signature ___

नाम/Name ___

पदस्थापना स्थल/Branch / Office of Posting ___

मंडलीय कार्यालय/Under Zonal Office ___

तिथि/Date ___

कॉलेज/ केन्द्र के प्रयोजनार्थ / For College use only

कार्यक्रम समन्वयक की टिप्पणी, यदि कोई हो /Observations of the Course Co-ordinator, if any

___

___

___

ANNEXURE 9.6
Procedure for Control of Documents

1. Purpose—To define, establish, implement, and maintain a comprehensive system for control of training documents to achieve effectiveness of the training system and improve continually.

2. Scope—The scope of this procedure covers system related documents, for example, (a) training manual, (b) training procedure, (c) training instructions, and (d) related forms/formats referred to in the various documents mentioned.

3. Responsibility and authority—The preparing, approving, and issuing authority of the quality system related documents are defined in the 'authority matrix'. In the absence of a designated authority, the same exercises have to be carried out by a higher authority. The authority matrix is shown here.

Authority	Training manual	Training procedure	Training instruction	Training formats
Preparing authority				
Approving authority				
Issuing authority				

4. Definitions of terms—the abbreviations used are as follows:

TM:	Training manager
PD:	Programme director
PC:	Programme coordinator
CC:	Controlled copies (The recipients of CC get amendments done on any documents.)

5. References

1.	Training manual	Doc. no. ....
2.	Training instructions	Doc. no. ....
3.	Master list of training documents	Format no. ....
4.	Document amendment Form	Format no. ....
5.	Distribution list	Format no. ....

6. Procedure
   (a) The institute maintains a master list of all training related documents in format no. ....
   (b) The training manager maintains a master copy of the training manual and training procedures duly authenticated by the reviewing and approving authority with their signatures.
   (c) The training manager controls the training manual and records amendments through the amendment record sheet.
   (d) After revision, the obsolete page is withdrawn, and the revised page is issued to the recipients of controlled copies.
      (i) The revision numbers are incremented and dated.
      (ii) No amendment is implemented without its formal issue.
      (iii) If the complete quality manual undergoes change, a new issue is released.
   (e) The institute amends the training system related documents as per format no. ...., which are maintained by the training manager. Copies of formats are maintained along with procedures, if these are referred to.
   (f) Any user can propose the change of a document and submit the request through a change request form to the training manager. The training manager includes it in the agenda of training review meeting (refer to the authority matrix). On acceptance of the change, it is incorporated in the document, the revision number is advanced, superseded documents are withdrawn, and current versions are issued to the controlled copy holders.

The term 'issue number' is applicable for the procedures and formats (for all the pages).

(i) When a sufficient number of pages of the procedures or formats is revised, the issue number is increased by one and the revision number will be 00.
(ii) The amendments come into force provided the amendment is appropriately approved, the amendment is recorded, and the issue is registered by the training manager (the competent authority).
(iii) Whenever an issue/revision is made, the obsolete documents are withdrawn.

ANNEXURE 9.7

Procedure for Control of Records

1. Purpose—To establish and maintain a procedure for effective operation of the training management system, which provides evidence of conformity to requirements like identification, storage, protection, retrieval, retention period, and disposition of records.

2. Scope—All records referred to in the training manual, training procedure, and training instructions of the documented quality management system.

3. Responsibility and authority

   (a) Overall responsibility of maintaining and monitoring the procedure lies with the training manager.
   (b) Responsibility of maintaining each record lies with the person(s) responsible to generate the record(s) unless otherwise mentioned in the master list of training records.

4. Definition of terms

PD:	Programme director
PC:	Programme coordinator

5. References

A	Training manual	
B	Master list of formats	TF. ....
C	Master list of training records	TF. ....

6. Procedure

   (a) The institute identifies every training record through a unique number and name.
   (b) The institute generates legible records and maintains them at the appropriate functional area (refer to master list of training records).
   (c) The institute identifies the records with the unique name and keeps them in an indexed manner to ensure easy retrieval.
   (d) The institute mentions the retention period of any training record in the master list of training records.
   (e) The institute stores and maintains the training records in order to prevent loss, damage, or deterioration (till the expiry of the retention period). After the expiry of the retention period it destroys the records.
   (f) The institute makes the training records available to the customer and/or to his representative, if specified in the contract.
   (g) The institute evaluates the answer scripts or assessment test papers. The respective PD or PC of the programme preserves these till disposal.

The disposing authority initiates the disposal action of any training record on expiry of the retention period. The disposing authority is mentioned in the master list of records. If felt necessary, the record(s) are retained even after the expiry period in a separate place marking/mentioning boldly the reason, until finally disposed off. The custodian of the record is responsible for disposing off the records. He may however, retain them beyond expiry period after obtaining approval, mentioning the reason for this, from the head of the institute. He then intimates this to the disposing authority.

CHAPTER 10

Multi-source Assessment and Feedback System

LEARNING OBJECTIVES

After studying this chapter, you will be able to

- Describe multi-source assessment and feedback system (MAFS) and state its objectives
- Understand the prerequisites of MAFS
- Explain how to evaluate a candidate's readiness for MAFS
- Understand the Indian model of leadership development (RSDQ model)

OPENING CASE

Methodical Implementation of MAFS

Galaxy Limited has been in the business of manufacturing and marketing low-technology products, such as edible oils, detergents, and a few agro products, since 1960. During the early 1990s, the company decided to diversify into the production of basic chemicals—a high-technology area, where the government allowed foreign investments as per Foreign Exchange Regulation Act (FERA). With this changeover from 'low technology' to 'high technology' area, Galaxy ensured its future in India. The company had converted a threat into an opportunity.

Subsequent to the changeover, Galaxy decided to rejuvenate its management system. The company followed a system of performance-linked promotion. The personnel department was receiving a number of letters from its employees expressing grievances and complaints on promotion. Employees were not finding the performance appraisal system motivating. On investigation, it was revealed that most of the complaints mentioned bias in the performance appraisal. In fact, the company did not have a system of open appraisal; rather, comments about employee performance were recorded as apart of the 'annual confidential report' filled by the immediate supervisor. The higher authority authenticated the report just as a formality.

Some employees, being deprived of promotion, filed writ petitions in the court of law, challenging the system of appraisal. The personnel department is required to divert substantial time in representing the company in the court. On the other hand, the supervisors argued that they were endorsing the targets set and achieved, percentages of rejections, numbers of accidents, savings of indirect materials, etc. as major factors behind evaluation. They were not considering creativity, originality, innovation, teamwork, initiative, and similar other dimensions of work behaviour. The company's management was receptive, and paid serious attention to this problem. The board of directors decided to implement a multi-source assessment and feedback system (MAFS). Accordingly, the board empowered the manager—personnel management, Mr MPM, to implement the system within three to four months.

Mr MPM contacted a few managers from personnel management and industrial relations departments who were trying to implement MAFS in their organizations. He developed questionnaires to collect opinions of immediate supervisor and subordinates, colleagues, and some other organizational personnel. In the MAFS forum, he distributed the questionnaires to the invited raters, and requested them to fill in the format. When they completed the questionnaires, he collected and sorted them. From the next day onwards, he started analysing the responses. For each person evaluated, he prepared a summary sheet. In the summary, Mr MPM brought out the behavioural dimensions mentioning the name of the appraisers.

Later, he convened an interaction session, requested the evaluated employees to be present, and conveyed the salient points including the shortcomings, mentioning the name of the rater. He prepared a list of employees whose scores were very low as several raters expressed their negative feelings. Mr MPM forwarded the list of employees to the respective departmental managers for their review, enclosed the summary he prepared, and included his own feelings about the personnel. The departmental managers recommended disciplinary actions to the competent authority.

In this manner, multi-source assessment and feedback system was installed in Galaxy Limited. After about three months, the chairman and managing director (CMD) of Galaxy Limited invited one of his friends, who was a CMD of another company, for a visit. He explained to him about the implementation of MAFS in Galaxy Limited. He enquired in length about the company and offered his comments. In fact, his organization required little more than two years while preparing for MAFS, and they were practising MAFS for the preceding three years. The CMD of Galaxy Limited requested him to share his experience to the officers, and convened a lecture meeting. In his educative lecture, he highlighted many points and stressed upon the need of creating an environment for MAFS and readiness of the employees. The meeting ended with discussions. Finally, he requested Galaxy Limited's CMD and Mr MPM to visit his organization and study the system.

Learning points

- An appraisal system must have a defined purpose and should be motivating.
- The employee evaluation system must also lay emphasis on softer dimensions of performance.
- The identity of any feedback provider should not be disclosed.
- MAFS recommendations should not be used for initiating disciplinary actions.
- Analysis of feedback should preferably be done by some outsider.
- Readiness of employees of all levels is essential for making MAFS effective and deriving benefits.

INTRODUCTION

In today's world, the business environment is witnessing winds of change and the competition is getting stiffer. In such a scenario, organizations are constantly looking for ways to improve their performance in terms of their deliverables to the key stakeholders such as shareholders, customers, and employees. A key driver of building high performance in organizations is the performance management process, where an HR person plays a crucial role as a facilitator, coach, and process owner. He can truly add value to the business. While most organizations have a performance management process, they are not always satisfied by what it can deliver. Hence, they are constantly looking for ways to improve the process.

Successful organizations differentiate themselves from the rest by not only having a healthy and structured performance management process, but by creating a high performance culture, where employees are clear in terms of expectations and deliverables, and about what organizational behaviours will be rewarded or not. In simple words, a healthy performance management process is a tool used effectively to build high performing organizations to gain distinctive competence. Achieving organizational excellence by developing its people is an essential need. The best usable tool for doing so is, implementing and using a multi-source or 360-degree assessment and feedback system. But before that,

> Multi-source assessment and feedback system is also known as 360-degree or multi-rater feedback system.

you must refresh your knowledge relating to performance, performance management, and performance monitoring.

PERFORMANCE

The consideration of performance, performance indices, and performance appraisals is of supreme importance for successful performance management. Performance refers to effective and efficient working behaviour and has reference to personal data such as measures of accidents, turnover, absenteeism, and tardiness. A performance index helps to measure and determine if an employee's salary is commensurate with the organization's performance. In an organization, performance appraisal is a formal process whereby each employee is evaluated to determine how he or she is performing.

> Top individual strengths are ego strength, assertiveness, willingness to take risks, sociable and abstract reasoning, a healthy sense of scepticism, creativity, and empathy.

As discussed in Chapter 8, performance is a multidimensional variable and hence, people high on one measure may not be high on another, and such standings may change over time. The work performance of a group of individuals, with identical backgrounds, can also vary. The variation can be attributable to multiple causes. Employee performance is very much determined by the individual strengths and weaknesses of the employees. The strengths are contributors to their performance. Some of the top individual strengths identified are ego strength, assertiveness, willingness to take risks, sociable and abstract reasoning, a healthy sense of scepticism, creativity, and empathy. Effective performance depends on executing the roles (transformational and transactional), skills (managerial and non-managerial), delegation (leading to empowerment), and quality of performances in the right manner.

Performance Management

Performance management is a system through which the management can keep a check on the performance of their employees. They can also keep a track of whether the activities and output which the employees are producing are congruent with the organization's goals. Performance management is central to gaining competitive advantage. It comprises three phases, namely, defining performance, measuring performance, and giving feedback of their performance. It is important for the managers to keep in mind that for managing the performance, they need to manage the people well.

History is replete with examples of poor performance management. It has been evidenced that organizations cannot excel unless they focus on actions rather than results, define the long-term and short-term goals, rigidly apply a single doctrinaire approach, involve the use of jargon, and install suitable support measures. The goals and targets of successful performance management are very specific and quantifiable, easy to understand, and comprise continuous and ongoing activities concerned with the results.

Performance is a process. Performance management is an ongoing activity and the intention is continuous improvement for marching towards organizational excellence. The performance management process includes people orientation, quality of work life, benchmarking, measurement and monitoring, and use of techniques and tools. It is implied that the process leads to a healthy organizational environment and employee satisfaction (Baguley 2001). Drivers of the performance management process are people, quality, measuring and monitoring, goals, targets and benchmark, and techniques and tools.

There are 10 commandments (Box 1.1) to ensure successful performance management in an organization.

Box 10.1 Ten commandments

1. Successful performance management is no longer optional.
2. Successful performance management means accepting and embracing change rather than holding it at arm's length.
3. Successful performance management is a continuous and ongoing process, rather than a one-off project.
4. Performance management is a people-centred activity.
5. Successful performance management is done with the people and not without them.
6. Successful performance management is driven by the gap between 'where we are now' and 'where we want to be'.
7. Successful performance management measures are credible and understandable.
8. Successful performance management measures are about efficiency, effectiveness, and adaptability.
9. Successful performance management uses techniques that are relevant and effective, and are used logically.
10. The ultimate judges of the performance management are the customers and they deserve to be delighted.

PERFORMANCE APPRAISAL

Q 2 The process of measurement of the performance of employees at work is termed performance appraisal. It is a structured formal process of assessing an employee's performance based on a pre-decided set of standards. Each employee is appraised by his or her immediate supervisor. Workers are appraised by their line supervisors, directors are appraised by the managing director, and the managing director is appraised by the chairman or company owners. This varies and depends on the size and structure of the organization.

Performance appraisal system is essential for effective management and evaluation of the workforce. It involves a periodic (annual or semi-annual) interview between the subordinate and the appraiser. The interview helps in measuring the strengths and weaknesses of the appraisee. It also provides an opportunity to the subordinate to work on his weaknesses and improve as well. Today, the performance of every individual matters for any organization to succeed. In short, performance management has become a very critical area of the HR.

Performance appraisal, if performed objectively, develops motivational impacts for individuals. It enables the management to monitor the standards, achieve agreed expectations and objectives, and delegate responsibilities and tasks to the concerned employee. Whatever the nature of the job, it must be appraised and measured, because unless it is measured, it cannot be monitored. Performance appraisals are typically linked with the organizational annual pay and grading reviews. They commonly coincide with the business plans of the organization for the next trading year. Performance appraisals generally review each individual's performance against the objectives and standards set for the next financial year. This is usually agreed upon in a previous appraisal meeting.

It is also essential for career and succession planning—for individuals, critical jobs, and for the organization as a whole. Performance appraisals are important for employee motivation, attitude building, behaviour modification and development, communicating and aligning individual and organizational aims, and fostering positive relationships between management and employees. In general, they help in taking the organization towards success.

Appraisals should not be considered daunting or time-consuming, For many, it is also considered as a difficult and an emotionally-challenging process. It is an essential requirement of every organization, and it is for the HR to take this function seriously.

A performance appraisal system, if properly structured, can achieve and contribute a lot of information to the organization. It should be objective and transparent for short-term, medium-term, and long-term. The purposes of performance appraisal system are displayed in Box 10.2.

Box 10.2 Purposes of performance appraisal

1. Clarifying, defining, and redefining priorities and objectives
2. Motivating through agreeing helpful aims and targets
3. Motivating through achievement and feedback
4. Identifying training needs and learning desires, assessment, and agreement
5. Identifying personal strengths (including hidden strengths) and weaknesses
6. Installing career and succession planning system, both personal and organizational
7. Clarifying team roles and encouraging team building
8. Developing mutual awareness, understanding, and relationship of the appraisee and his manager
9. Resolving confusions and misunderstandings
10. Reinforcing and cascading organizational philosophies, values, aims, objectives, goals, strategies, priorities, etc.
11. Delegating additional responsibilities, employee growth, and development
12. Coaching, mentoring, counselling, and feedback
13. Developing the managers to enable them to conduct appraisals objectively and well

Appraisal—A Process Approach

A process is a set of interrelated activities. As a process, performance appraisal encompasses activities such as steps taken to prepare, inform, fix the venue and layout, introduce, review and measure, formulate action plan, and extend managerial support from the point of view of the appraiser. These are discussed here:

Prepare Prepare all materials, mutually agreed tasks, current job description, and records of performances, achievements, incidents, previous performance appraisal documents, etc., and all that is relevant to the performance and achievement. Remember that appraisals should focus on helping the 'whole person' to grow and attain fulfillment aimed at getting a 'total quality person'. Appraisals are not just about job performance and job skills training; it can go beyond the organizational boundary. Get to know what your people are good at outside of their work.

> As a process, performance appraisal encompasses activities such as steps taken to prepare, inform, fix the venue and layout, introduce, review and measure, formulate action plan, and extend managerial support from the point of view of the appraiser.

Sometimes, people's natural talents and passions often contain significant overlaps with the skills that are required for the job assigned to them.

Inform The appraisee must have prior information about the time and place of the appraisal. He should be given a chance to gather data related to his performance and achievement. The appraisee should also be informed if the appraisal form does not follow a natural order for the discussion.

Venue Plan a suitable venue that is private and free from interruptions, where you and the appraisee can interact.

Environment It is important to create a situation that is relaxing and comforting for the appraisee, preferably with a meeting table in between. It is believed that face to face sitting should be avoided. Avoid sitting on your (boss's) chair. Ideally, the appraisee should be sitting humbly on the other side of the desk.

Introduction Start the formal introduction with a smile, be warm and friendly, and open with a positive statement. Enquire about his hobbies, areas of interest, and discuss them. For example, you may talk about one-day international matches, if the appraisee is interested in cricket. It is a good idea to forecast the approximate length of the session.

Review and measure Review the activities, tasks, objectives, and achievements but do not review the person. As far as possible, be objective. The manager must concentrate only on hard facts and figures, and avoid any opinions.

Formulating an action plan An action plan should be formulated in consultation with the appraisee to fulfil his career aspirations, taking into account the job responsibilities, and the identified strengths and weaknesses. The plan should be realistic covering short, medium, and long-term aspects.

Extend managerial support An employee needs managerial supports such as aids to work, tools and techniques, suitable work environment, knowledge inputs, mentoring, counselling, etc.

Performance Appraisal—Different Approaches

The methods of appraising management performance are classified in two categories, the narrow interpretation and the broad interpretation. The narrow interpretation of performance appraisal includes a post-mortem of a subordinate's performance by his superior for a predetermined period of time. Broad interpretation, alternatively, is designated as accountability management, management by objectives, or management by end results, and embraces a continuing and ongoing process connecting the past, present, and future activities that purports to improve the entire management process.

A distinct shift has taken place in the performance appraisal system. The traditional performance rating system has completely changed to the result-oriented appraisal. The traditional performance rating procedurally stressed upon the individual personality traits by the superior, a procedure that is now almost abandoned. The present result-oriented appraisal is a new way of viewing performance. It involves setting of goals by superiors and subordinates together. This method had gained popularity.

The relatively new total quality management (TQM) approach is a unique approach to performance management, and advocates a system-oriented focus. The TQM approach advocates the evaluation of personal traits (for example, perfection, energetic, systematic, qualitative, risk-taking, cooperation, team player, tenacious, tolerant, etc.), which were difficult to relate to job performance, unless the company had been structured to work teams, in the early days.

A traditional appraisal system used to be one person's assessment of another, which could never be free from bias. Moreover, in the course of execution of duties and performing roles, an individual is required to interact with several people including his immediate superior, internal customers, external customers, suppliers, colleagues, seniors of cross-functional areas, and many subordinates. All of them cannot be biased. Considering this to be of supreme necessity, the most-talked-of system of appraisal has come into use. and is accepted as a principle system by many organizations.

MULTI-SOURCE ASSESSMENT AND FEEDBACK SYSTEM

Interpersonal relations play a dominant role in the process of assessment, and they can never be totally free from bias. A manager, in the course of executing his duties and performing his roles, is required to interact with many persons—his immediate superior, internal customers, external customers, suppliers, colleagues, seniors of cross-functional areas, and immediate subordinates. The all-round capability of a person can only be judged if the views of all the persons regularly interacting with him are gathered. This means getting information of the appraisee's performance from his seniors as well as juniors. This is the reason why the system is also termed as the 360-degree feedback system or multi-rater appraisal system. There has been a long-felt need by organizations to have an appraisal system that is free from bias and works effectively.

MAFS lays emphasis on measuring softer dimensions of performance such as leadership, creativity, originality, innovation, teamwork, initiative, emotional intelligence, entrepreneurship, etc. Today, organizations need information regarding softer dimensions along with multiple and objective assessment. As such, the use of MAFS has emerged as a crucial organizational need. Many websites confirm that almost every Fortune 500 company has implemented MAFS in in some form or the other.

Q 3 MAFS enables the multiple raters to measure behaviours critical to performance using questionnaires designed by HRD department. The questionnaires are designed differently for various appraisers. The raters' or appraisers' identity is kept confidential. Thus, in the anonymous MFAS 'what has been remarked' is important, and not 'who has offered the remarks'. To eliminate any sort of bias, external consultants are engaged to collect the assessment sheets and analyse the comments.

Objectives of MAFS

The objectives of MAFS are manifold. It provides insights into the strong and weak areas of the appraisee, in terms of the effective performance of roles, activities, styles, traits, qualities, competencies (knowledge, attitudes, and skills), impact on others, and the like. It helps to identify the developmental needs and prepare developmental plans more objectively in relation to current or future roles, and to plan performance improvements for an individual or a group of employees of managerial and other levels.

MAFS provides insights into the strong and weak areas of the appraisee in terms of the effective performance of roles, activities, styles, traits, qualities, competencies (knowledge, attitudes, and skills), impact on others and the like.

As human resource management functions include compensation management, incentive planning, management of rewards, placement and promotion, career growth, and so on, MAFS provides the means of generating data to serve as a more objective basis for rewards and other personnel decisions.

In the ever-changing business scenario, this system will also help to reinforce other change management efforts and organizational effectiveness directed interventions. These may include TQM efforts, customer focus, internal customer satisfaction enhancing interventions, flat organizational structures, quality enhancing and cost reducing interventions, decision process changes, etc. Pay and performance rewards should be based on certain criteria and the feedback analysis is the most appropriate basis.

An organization excels only when individual and group goals are aligned with organizational vision, values, and goals. The 360-degree system makes it possible by enabling and facilitating culture building, leadership development, potential appraisal and development, career planning and development, and succession planning and development. Furthermore, it aids team building, restores role clarity and increased accountabilities, and planning internal customer satisfaction improvement measures. Summarily, the objectives are listed in Box 10.3.

Box 10.3 Main objectives of appraisal

1. Identifying developmental needs
2. Generating data to serve on a more objective basis
3. Reinforcing other change management efforts and organizational effective dimensions such as (a) TQM efforts, (b) customer focus, (c) flat structure, (d) quality improvement programmes, and (e) decision process changes
4. Linking pay or rewards to performance
5. Aligning individual and group goals with organizational vision, values, and goals
6. Building organization culture
7. Developing leadership
8. Identifying top individual strengths such as ego strength, assertiveness, willingness to take risks, sociable and abstract reasoning, healthy sense of skepticism, and creativity and empathy building
9. Laying emphasis on role clarity and increased accountabilities
10. Planning internal customer satisfaction improvement measures

In most cases, 360-degree feedback is used as a developmental tool and many organizations use this system at senior management levels (Rao and Rao 2005). The most common dimensions on which organizations can seek feedback using this system include leadership ability, commitment to excellence, communication, initiative, team skills, commitment, customer orientation, ownership, and learning, etc.

Advantages of MAFS

It has already been discussed that multi-source assessment or 360-degree feedback system is not a substitute for a conventional appraisal system; rather it is in addition to the traditional system. MAFS aids the management to figure out the regular key performance area (KPA) or key result area (KRA) based on appraisal systems, which needs improvement. Most world-class companies are now promoting new organizational cultures such as participative culture, learning culture, quality culture, competency-based performance culture, teamwork culture, empowering culture, leadership culture, and so forth. To cope with the changes, we need to install MAFS for the advantages embedded in it.

This system has many advantages, some of which are as follows:

1. The entire feedback providers cannot be biased.
2. From the multiple inputs received, an employee gets the unique opportunity to improve his role, performance, managerial style, ideas, and most importantly, his acceptability to others.
3. Multi-source assessment and feedback system engulfs the basic purposes of traditional appraisal system—identifying developmental needs, managing a reward system, developing performance, pursuing compensation management, etc. It supplements the traditional system.

MAFS supplements the regular key performance area (KPA) or key result area (KRA) based on appraisal systems.

4. It has been evidenced that MAFS provides more acceptable feedback to employees.
5. It is more objective in comparison to the traditional system where one person identifies the traits and qualities of the appraisees.
6. It is more participative, which leads to quality HR decisions about the employee.
7. The spectrum of opinions received is broad, as internal and external customers offer the feedback in structured questionnaires.

Prerequisites of MAFS

In some situations, a 360-degree feedback system can be a very sensitive issue. If a person is not well prepared for the system, then it can throw him out of balance. At the same time, it can also create some new issues in an organization. If not properly designed and conducted, it can also have the potential danger of the candidate developing wrong perceptions or notions about one or more of his assessors, and developing new attitudes towards them. There are certain prime requirements for implementing a 360-degree appraisal system in an organization, the foremost being the top management support.

> In some situations, a 360-degree feedback system can be a very sensitive issue. It needs adequate preparedness. MAFS does not work in the presence of status symbols.

Top management has to build the confidence of employees in the appraisal methodology, create opportunities for employees, invest time and effort, take the current appraisal system seriously, conduct performance reviews, and agree to be assessed by juniors. In a lot of cases, it is seen that MAFS does not work well for senior management because seniors do not like to be evaluated by juniors. Top management also delegates the responsibility of preparing detailed plans, and formulating organizational philosophy, policy, and objectives to the head of HR department.

The first important step is to determine whether the organization is ready for it and then determine if the candidate is ready for the same (Rao and Rao 2005). Some other prerequisites required for a company to participate in a 360-degree feedback analysis are shown in Box 10.4.

Box 10.4 Prerequisites for successful MAFS

1. Commitment of top management of the organization for developing competencies on a continuous basis.
2. Considering the number of HRD mechanisms operating in the organization seriously, while implementing MAFS.
3. Willingness of top management to invest time and effort in giving feedback to their own subordinates.
4. Conduction of performance review sessions regularly by the top management and senior managers.
5. Acceptance of feedback by employees sportingly and using it for self-development.
6. Absence of politics in the organization, for the management to ensure that people are not inclined to use the feedback for playing politics.
7. Management to encourage employees to work in teams.
8. Employees to not view top management intervention with suspicion.
9. There should be a high degree of process-orientation in the organization.
10. The organization should be value-driven.
11. Management should be able to handle the softer issues such as professionalization, man management, and development well.
12. Work towards improving the organizational culture.

Indicators of Candidate Readiness

There are certain indicators to assess the readiness of a candidate for the multi-source assessment and feedback system. Rao and Rao (2005) specify the indicators of readiness which are reproduced here:

1. The candidate has a desire to know himself through the eyes of others. He is willing to receive feedback from others and does not become over-defensive.
2. The candidate intends to improve.
3. The candidate is receptive and respects the views of others.
4. The candidate is a learning-oriented individual.
5. The candidate has an aptitude for healthy competition.
6. The candidate has at least one-and-a-half years of experience (except in the case of managerial trainees).
7. The candidate has a direct relationship with at least six individuals who can rate him.
8. The candidate has no history of any previous psychological and psychiatric problems.

Source: Rao and Rao (2005)

Value of MAFS

MAFS adds value to the organization's HR initiatives. The set of feedbacks collected from different sources enables an organization to identify the improvement needs, and focus on the developmental efforts, at the individual as well as group level. In fact, MAFS is of great value to the organization in today's competitive world, as it is able to match an individual's doings with the organization's strategies. It adds value to the organization in different ways which are enumerated as follows:

1. The questionnaire must include questions relevant to the candidate's role, skill requirements, delegation, and quality of performance and help to identify his/her deficiencies.
2. All the raters must not be biased in a single direction.
3. Carefully-designed questionnaires help getting realistic feedback.
4. Layout of the questionnaire enables the raters to offer comments which are more important than the numerical ratings.
5. An appraisee learns self-management from the negative feedbacks received.
6. Confidentiality helps protect the interpersonal relationship of the appraisee with the raters like superiors, various colleagues, subordinates, and other stakeholders.
7. In a developed organizational culture, one sportingly accepts the remarks.
8. Feedback is essential to improve the self-esteem in addition to understanding how others view the appraisee.
9. Feedback from others reveals the true views of the appraisee.
10. An appraisee, on accepting the views of the raters, gains acceptance of the multiple stakeholders.
11. An appraisee gains new insights and more encouragement from feedback that reinforce the desired competencies of the business.

By studying the various sets of feedback, an organization can initiate specific developmental efforts.
The 360-degree feedback facilitates alignment of individual capabilities and behaviours with organizational strategies.

12. Identified individual strengths can be aligned with the organizational requirements for the best advantage to the business.
13. There is increased awareness of and relevance of competencies.
14. There is increased consciousness by senior management that self-development is an ongoing process, and has development needs.
15. Individuals get a broader perspective of how they are perceived by others. This was not possible in a traditional appraisal system.
16. Implementation of MAFS in an organization may be the starting point to improve the organizational climate and boost employee morale.
17. Senior managers get reliable feedback about their performance as different raters judge from different viewpoints.
18. Most managers are surprised and delighted by the amount of feedback, and feel positive on introspection.
19. A set of negative feedback makes it clear to the appraisee what to focus on. This can help him to work on his weaknesses and develop further.
20. A manager's effectiveness is enhanced by knowing what he is doing well, what he is not doing well, and how he can improve.
21. Feedback by different raters is perceived as objective and more valid. Hence, there is higher acceptance of the feedback and the remedial actions.
22. Provides a clearer picture to senior management of individual's real worth (although 'halo effect' syndromes cannot be totally eliminated).
23. It supports a climate of continuous improvement and leads the organization towards excellence.
24. The system identifies managers having low self-esteem.

Before introducing a 360-degree feedback system, you must address the benefits that the organization is likely to derive, and explain the perceived risks to all participants. The reviewers, particularly junior colleagues, may have concerns about issues with regard to the confidentiality of their identity and the usage of the completed reviews. The appraisee might also be worried about the comments that he is going to receive. It is important to communicate the purpose of the system to them so that they can appreciate the value of the 360-degree feedback system.

Indian Model of Leadership Development

T.V. Rao learning system (TVRLS, www.tvrls.com) is an expression of a few decades of experience, study, review, reflection, and action, combined with a desire to discover more about the behaviour of people in different settings, and ways of making them give their best. The advisory board of TVRLS consists of late Dr Udai Pareek, R.S. Ramnarayan, and other eminent personalities.

Q 4 TVRLS has developed a model for the top and senior management levels in Indian companies to measure the managerial and leadership competencies required by them in their fields. It is called the RSDQ model. This model of leadership and managerial effectiveness views effective management and leadership as a combination of four sets of variables—roles, style, delegation, and quality. TVRLS named it the RSDQ model of 360-degree feedback. These four variables will now be taken up for discussion one by one.

Roles

This means the extent to which an individual plays various leadership and managerial roles and activities. In order to discharge duties effectively, every manager is required to perform a number of roles.

The roles encompass both transformational roles (and leadership roles) and transactional roles (or managerial). Some of the roles are as follows;

1. Articulating and communicating vision and values
2. Formulating long-term policies and strategies
3. Introducing and managing new technology and systems
4. Inspiring, developing, and motivating juniors
5. Managing juniors, colleagues, and seniors
6. Culture-building
7. Managing internal customers
8. Managing external customers
9. Managing unions and associations

Standard base questionnaire generally covers nine dimensions of roles such as vision and values, policy formulation and goal setting, technology and system management, inspiring, developing, and empowering staff, culture building, team work and team building, management of colleagues/ internal customers, liaison with boss and top management, and external customer relations and client management (total 55 questions).

Style

Style is one element of McKinsey's 7-S framework. Effective managers are the ones who can recognize the demand of the situation, and apply the kind of leadership required. But, there are also cases where the managers may not be apt in identifying the leadership style required. In his research at Indian Institute of Management, Rao classified the styles into three categories—benevolent or paternalistic leadership style, critical leadership style, and developmental leadership style.

Benevolent or paternalistic leadership style The strategic apex believes that all his employees should be constantly guided, treated with affection like a parent treats his children, is relationship-oriented, assigns tasks duly considering likes and dislikes of the subordinates; extends uninterrupted guidance, and protects them. A benevolent leader attempts to understand their needs, salvages situations of crisis by personal active involvement, and distributes rewards considering characteristics like loyalty, obedience, and results achieved. He/she shares information with those who are close to him, etc.

Critical leadership style This style of leadership is characterized by its proximity to the Theory X belief pattern. Here, the manager believes that the employees should be closely and constantly supervised, directed, and reminded of their duties and responsibilities. As obvious from the previous discussion, such leaders cannot tolerate mistakes, and strictly work according to the standards. This type of leadership is short-term goal-oriented.

Developmental leadership style Managers possessing this style believe in empowering juniors and in developing the competencies of the staff. The manager treats his people as mature adults, leaves them on their own most of the time. Unlike the previous style, this one is long-term goal-oriented. It has been found that the developmental style is the most desired organization building style. However, benevolent and critical styles manifest their importance in times, and some situations to achieve the organizational goals. Research has also shown that some managers are not aware of the predominant style they tend to be used and the effect their style has on their employees.

Delegation

The RSDQ model considers level of delegation as an important part of a senior executive's effectiveness. A senior executive delegates not only to off-load his own work but also to divert the time to performing creative higher order tasks. Rao observed the weaknesses of many senior managers while delegating tasks. As such, Rao included this dimension after observing the difficulties of senior managers during delegation. The difficulties were also observed for the effective managers who quickly promoted during the course of their careers. On viewing phenomenon, Rao isolated delegation as an important variable of leadership. Unfortunately, those who do not delegate and continue to do lower level tasks, suppress their leadership qualities and managerial effectiveness.

Qualities

This model visualizes that managers should exhibit their leadership skills and qualities of in line with that of world-class managers (for example, proaction, listening, communication, positive approach, participative nature, quality orientation, etc.). Such qualities not only affect the effectiveness with which top-level managers perform various roles, but also have an impact on the leadership style and hence, are very critical.

MFAS Instruments

MAFS instruments play a crucial role in the entire feedback process. The success and the value addition of the feedback process depend on the tool that the organization uses (Rao and Rao 2005). The tools may focus on the general qualities of the individual or they may focus on traits and qualities that the individual is interested in. TVRLS has developed RSDQ-based instruments.

Roles 55-item questionnaire for senior level managers; 75-item questionnaire for top management levels

Style 51-item questionnaire

Delegation 10-item questionnaire to reveal the extent of delegation and non-delegation

Qualities 25 questions using semantic differential questions

It updates the instruments periodically, and positions them with the changing business scenario.

PHILIPS LEADERSHIP COMPETENCIES AND THE 360-DEGREE APPRAISALS

Philips uses a number of tools aimed at measuring the competency levels, focusing basically on the six competencies (www.ad.chinahr.com). These six leadership competencies define the behaviour that is required to achieve business success. Shortcomings in each competency and the actions to be taken to eliminate them are also identified. These competencies are as follows:

1. Show determination to achieve excellent results.
2. Focus on the market.
3. Find better ways.
4. Demand top performance.
5. Inspire commitment.
6. Develop self and others.

Show determination to achieve excellent results Effective managers can anticipate the business growth and they develop a vision of where their business should be going. They translate the business objectives into demanding and challenging goals, and take responsibility for moving the company towards achieving the vision.

The following six leadership competencies provide a solid basis for sustainable business success:

1. Show determination to achieve excellent results.
2. Focus on the market.
3. Find better ways.
4. Demand top performance.
5. Inspire commitment.
6. Develop self and others.

Focus on the market External inputs including information about business environment and excellent business knowledge are prerequisites to developing a focus onto the market. Other vital factors include profound market knowledge, knowledge of customer, insight to understand customer (consumer) behaviour, and a broad perspective on the business. Focusing on these aspects can help a manager plan his future actions strategically. Competitive advantage is essential to gain distinctive competence.

Find better ways There can always be a better solution. A managers' job is to value creation and for true value creation, a manager has to put his or her vision into organizational practices, putting the systems and processes in place, and managing them. They have to pursue profitability and champion change, utilizing every opportunity to continuously improve their business processes. Leaders optimize key processes by finding ways to get things done faster, more efficiently, and more effectively by collaborating with others, and securing cooperation from them.

Demand top performance Managers should turn their dreams into reality and vision into achievable targets within a planned time frame, while acting as a role model for top performance. They need to show direction and lead by personal example while addressing difficult people issues. Managers should not only demand high performance goals and ensure that standards are achieved; they have to also ensure that the standards are maintained. Furthermore, managers must clearly clarify employee expectations and actively manage performance to ensure success.

Inspire commitment True leaders get the willing support of team members, and are able to persuade their team to share the same vision. They do not demand support; they command support. They demonstrate excellent communication skills, win commitment at a rational and emotional level, understand the people to motivate and inspire colleagues and subordinates, and thus, get the best out of them.

Develop self and others Managers must develop themselves and then develop their organizations. Managers of world-class companies raise the capability of the organization by continuously developing both themselves and others, and by creating a learning organization in which knowledge is actively managed. Learning faster than other organizations gives a real competitive advantage. True leaders are masters in exchanging feedback, and helping others to improve through coaching, mentoring, and counselling.

The six leadership competencies exhibit a balance between the rational and emotional, between task and people, and thus, provide a solid basis for sustainable business development and ultimately success. The competencies such as 'display strength of mind, show determination and willpower to achieve excellent results', 'focus on the market', and 'find better ways' indicate that the emphasis is on the task aspects of the roles of the leaders. The other three competencies are 'demand top performance', 'inspire commitment', and 'develop self and others' and describe how results are achieved through people. Refer to Exhibit 10.1.

Exhibit 10.1 360-degree appraisal questionnaire in Philips

1. The instrument is called 'leadership assessment questionnaire'.
2. The high potential role holder who gets through the assessment chooses the 360-degree appraisers usu-

(Contd)

Exhibit 10.1 (Contd)

ally from his role set, namely, boss, colleagues, direct reports, and others.

3. The questionnaire is given to the assessors with clear instructions to complete it carefully, and making sure that the ratings of behaviours are a true reflection of actual behaviour seen in practice.
4. Assessors are assured that in the feedback sessions, only anonymous data is used.
5. Assessors complete the questionnaire, and hand it back to the assessee in a sealed envelope.
6. Basic data about the assessor is collected in terms of his/ her relation to the participant (assessee), how long he/ she have known the participant in his present position, etc.
7. The rating scale used is a five-point scale as follows:

   5: Behaviour is shown to very great extent.
   4: Behaviour is shown to a great extent.
   3: Behaviour is shown to some extent.
   2: Behaviour is shown to a small extent.
   1: Behaviour is not shown at all.

A few sample statements from the 360-degree assessment questionnaire are as follows:

(*Note:* Within the parenthesis, write the point grade. The range of point grade is 1–10.)

(___) Makes an overall plan, covering key aspects of assignment
(___) Encourages others to take initiatives and be involved in decisions
(___) Challenges others constructively
(___) Integrates information from various sources, interprets it, and identifies salient points
(___) Builds on the ideas and contribution of others
(___) Shows realistic appreciation of the broad business
(___) Gives feedback sensitively and constructively
(___) Secures effective cross-functional cooperation
(___) Shows resilience despite setbacks and challenges
(___) Makes efforts to discover and understand other views

There are 120 such statements that together constitute the 360-degree assessment. The feedback is to be analysed and kept ready when the participant is ready for the next logical step.

Source: www.ad.chinahr.com

LIMITATIONS OF MAFS

Multi-source assessment and feedback system has certain limitations too.

1. The organization may not be ready for the system.
2. Lack of top management commitment.
3. The organizational culture is not conducive to accept principle of being evaluated by juniors.
4. Managers do not believe that subordinates have the ability to identify strengths and weaknesses of seniors; as such, they are not willing to be evaluated by them.
5. Seniors do not like to involve customers and other stakeholders in the process.
6. Theory X managers are more in number and dominate Theory Y managers.
7. There is difficulty in organizing a common forum for such a voluminous task.
8. There is a feeling of being the market leader.
9. Most of the managers are suffering from complacencies.
10. The organization is not open and top management is not inclined to share information with juniors.
11. Strategic apex does not believe in the development of human assets.
12. The organization is not aware of the changes in the environment.
13. The organization is not ready to cope with changes in the environment.

This is only a short list of limitations. You can make more points from the prerequisites and indicators of candidate readiness.

ORGANIZATIONAL PRACTICES

Many organizations have successfully implemented the multi-source assessment and feedback system, and are deriving results from it. Generally, companies first implement the system for senior level employees. Some of the organizations that implement the system are Infosys, Titan Industries, Hindustan Unilever Limited, SKF India, Moser Baer Philips Electronics India, and many other companies.

Infosys uses nine pillars for leadership development which are (a) 360-degree feedback, (b) development assignments, (c) Infosys culture workshops, (d) development relationships, (e) leadership skills training, (f) feedback intensive programmes, (g) systemic process learning, (h) action learning, and (i) community empathy. MAFS emphasizes on the softer dimensions of performance and a company uses this method to gather information about its employee's performance. The most common source of collecting information is from co-workers, peers, and managers. This aids the employees to prepare their personal developmental plans. They are also assigned an ILI faculty member for their help.

Titan Industries implemented 360-degree feedback way back in 2001 for senior management as a development-focused tool, for leadership development, team building, and potential development, in addition to training needs identification and internal customer relations building. Keeping up the spirit of 360-degree feedback, it has been extended to middle management in 2004. The company launched the web-based application in 2004 for senior management, and in 2005, it was introduced to the middle managers too.

Titan is using the RSQ model where RSQ indicate role, style, and quality. With regard to role, Titan is trying to identify, 'How well the manager is able to exhibit Tata's leadership practices in the leadership and managerial roles he/she plays.' The company is actively engaged to locate critical managerial and leadership qualities among its employees. In order to identify the style, the company is collecting the manner in which managers carry out their roles as supervisor/boss. Titan has classified three styles—benevolent or paternalistic leadership (acts like a parent, relationship-oriented, tries to be partial , and guides and protects), critical leadership (theory X belief pattern, close and constant monitoring, short term goal orientation, does not share information, and high discipline, has low tolerance), and developmental leadership (empowering style, develops competencies, long-term orientation, open communication, and delegation). Qualities considered in Titan are factors relating to organizational commitment, interpersonal relations and teamwork, leadership and employee development, values, and strengths and weaknesses.

Hindustan Unilever Limited (HUL) is a pioneer in the field of leadership development in India and happens to be one of the first multinational companies in the country to have developed home-grown talents. The company strongly believes that the genesis of its very performance culture lies in its leadership behaviours. The behaviours are defined on the 'standard of leadership' (SOL) framework that is clearly aligned to the business needs and realities. HUL's executive director opines, 'leadership is fostered in a culture where individuals are provided a chance to grow in their own way. The foremost job of leaders is to produce more leaders.' As such, there is a sharp focus on six key leadership behaviours that need to be demonstrated by its managers. The behaviours are assessed through performance management process (line manager feedback). and 360-degree feedback (mandatory only for senior leadership).

SKF India is a leading global supplier of products, solutions, and services within rolling bearings, seals, and mechatronics, services and lubrication systems. The 360-degree appraisal is conducted using a CUBIKS tool designed on the basis of SKF competency clusters. The clusters include competencies relating to understanding, analysing, and making sound use of the strategic and business environment, competencies for influencing, leading and interacting with others, competencies required to constantly improve own performance and behaviour, and competencies specific to individuals' jobs and positions. At SKF, employees at all levels are part of this exercise, and it is optional and purely used for self development. The feedback is used for working on areas of development and the same is converted into action plans for improvement.

Moser Baer (a leading technology company in India that has developed cutting-edge technologies, and has become the world's second largest manufacturer of optical storage media) has employed 360-degree feedback process for levels from general manager and above, and for those who significantly contribute to the future growth of the organization. The 360-degree feedback process helps Moser Baer to identify stars and provide inputs for their career plans in terms of development, movement, and succession planning. Managers come to know about their shortcomings from everyone with whom they work.

Philips Electronics India exposes managers to 360-degree assessments and has improved their performance levels in the organization. The assessment at Philips is done for the management team and also for high potentials.

Source: SAIL (2009)

SUMMARY

As a one-man assessment, performance appraisal can be biased. Multi-source assessment and feedback system is a long-felt organizational need since all the raters cannot be biased in one direction about an appraisee. This system emphasizes the softer dimensions of performance such as leadership, creativity, originality, innovation, teamwork, initiative, emotional intelligence, entrepreneurship, etc. The feedback providers rate the candidate anonymously; generally one external person analyses and prepare the summary. The analysis provides insights into strong and weak areas, and identifies developmental needs.

MAFS also needs certain prerequisites but adds value to the organization's HR initiatives. It is a model of leadership, managerial effectiveness, and views effective management and leadership as a combination of role, skill, delegation, and quality. Many organizations use MAFS as a development tool, and a few others use it for promotion and reward as well. Many more organizations are in the process of adopting this system. TVRLS has devised instruments which play a crucial role in the entire feedback process.

KEY TERMS

Candidate readiness refers to certain indicators such as a desire to be seen through others' eyes, respecting others views, intention to be better, and possessing an aptitude for facing healthy competition.

Developmental need identification is an essential scope of multi-source assessment and feedback system.

Key performance area includes participative culture, learning culture, quality culture, competency based performance culture, teamwork culture, empowering culture, leadership culture, etc.

Process approach to performance appraisal system considers activities like prepare, inform, venue, layout, introduction, review and measure, formulate action plan, and extend managerial support.

RSDQ model of leadership and managerial effectiveness views effective management and leadership as a combination of four sets of variables, namely, role, skill, delegation, and quality.

EXERCISES

Concept Review Questions

1. What is the need for performance management in an organization? How can the performance management system be made more effective?
2. What do you mean by performance appraisal? Discuss the purposes of appraisal. What is a process approach to performance appraisal?

3. Discuss the essence of multi-source assessment and feedback system. What are the differences of this system from a traditional appraisal system?
4. Discuss the RSDQ model of 360-degree feedback system. Discuss the importance of instruments in the feedback process?

Critical Thinking Questions

5. Discuss the advantages of multi-source assessment or 360-degree feedback system. While implementing this system, you might come across some hurdles. Prepare a list of hurdles and suggest the means of overcoming them.
6. 'MAFS adds value to the organization's HR initiatives.' Do you agree with this statement? Can the values be enhanced? Justify your views.
7. Differentiate between role and style of RSDQ model. Establish a relationship between role and style. How can delegation and quality intervene in role and style?

Assignments

8. Take help from your teacher or placement officer and visit five organizations. Meet the HR manager or any other manager responsible for appraisal system in the organization. Interrogate him to ascertain the status of adopting MAFS. You may discover them in various stages—not planning to adopt in near future, in the process of implementing it, implemented for selected managerial levels, or implemented for all levels. Collect information relating to the roadblocks they are facing at the respective stages. Further, collect their action plans to get rid of the roadblocks.
9. Many organizations have implemented MAFS and are deriving benefits. Identify five such organizations. Prepare an exhaustive list of benefits, and discuss it with your teacher with your findings.

MANAGER'S INSIGHT

Mr Sethuram joined ABC Limited as assistant manager eight months ago. He has an excellent academic background, and has worked with a few companies prior to joining ABC Limited. Mr Sethuram is the controlling officer of three sections which have a total strength of 250 people, and reports to Mr Raman, the production manager. The junior staff and workmen occasionally come in contact with Mr Sethuram. They practically feel stressed when Mr Sethuram takes a round of the shop floor across the three sections. The heads of the sections, who report to Sethuram, find him a difficult man. They avoid meeting Mr Sethuram as they feel he is quite an erratic person. On the other hand, Mr Raman is satisfied with the performance and dealings of Mr. Sethuram. He was shocked to hear that the staff and workmen were unhappy with him.

Questions:

1. What steps can Mr Raman initiate?
2. How can MAFS be a better solution to record the feelings of majority of people in this situation?
3. Should MAFS be installed for the entire company?

BIBLIOGRAPHY AND WEB RESOURCES

Baguley, Phil.,. *Performance Management in a Week,* Hodder & Stoughton, London, 2001.

Dileep Kumar, M., *360 Degree-Performance Appraisals: Prospects and Pitfalls,* www.indianmba.com.

Rao, T. and Raju Rao, *The Power of 360 Degree Feedback – Maximizing Managerial and Leadership Effectiveness,* Response Books, New Delhi, 2005.

SAIL, Best HR Practices, *Steel Authority of India Limited,* New Delhi, 2009.

Web Resources

www.eurekaforbes.com/news/archive.aspx, last accessed on 29 August 2011.

www.indianmba.com/Faculty_Column/FC345/fc345.html, last accessed on 28 April 2008.

www.tvrls.com, last accessed on 22 March 2008.

ad.chinahr.com/jobads/philips/leadership.asp, last accessed on 13 April 2008.

MAFS AS A TOOL FOR LEADERSHIP DEVELOPMENT

Eureka Forbes Limited

Eureka Forbes Limited (EFL) has been following a system of preparing a consolidated feedback report, and receives inputs from three sources:

Performance appraisal

The primary focus is on evaluating performance. The company considers past three cycles of appraisal reviewing reports

360-degree feedback report

The primary focus is on capturing leadership competencies. Feedback is collated on various competencies from seniors, colleagues, and juniors of the person, customers (internal and external) having regular interaction with the appraisee. It measures frequency of behaviours (pertaining to the competencies) exhibited on the job as perceived by the raters.

Leadership development centres

The primary focus is on observing potential (ability to perform). The process objectively analyses leadership competencies through multiple simulations/exercises and trained assessors. It gives feedback on an individual's ability to display behaviours related to the competencies.

Competency framework of Eureka Forbes Limited

1. Communication
2. Interpersonal relations
3. Teamwork
4. Planning and organizing
5. Decision-making
6. Analytical/problem solving
7. Creativity
8. Influencing/leading
9. Initiative
10. People development
11. Stress management
12. Customer focus

EFL has clear explanations of the related terminology. For example,

Decision making

1. Brings cross-functional and cross-business knowledge to bear on issues
2. Considers alternative solutions before making decisions
3. Considers short-term as well as long-term impact of decisions
4. Anticipates and confronts problems before they get out of hand
5. Takes decisions without needing continuous guidance and is firm about the decision
6. Makes timely decisions

Creativity

1. Demonstrates ability to conceive ideas
2. Challenges the ways it has always been done
3. Constantly experiments and improves work systems, processes, and practices
4. Readily accepts changes
5. Stimulates creative ideas and experimentation in others

Behavioural dimensions at Eureka Forbes Limited

EFL has identified (a) five highest scoring behavioural dimensions (Table 10.1), and (b) five lowest scoring behavioural dimensions (Table 10.2) for each manager undergoing 360-degree feedback. Here is a sample taken from one manager's report which was supplied to the author during interview.

Table 10.1 Five highest scoring behavioural dimensions

S. no.	Dimension	Score	Competency
1.	Treats people with respect		Interpersonal
2.	Delegates effectively and empowers the team to function independently		People development
3.	Treats people fairly		Integrity and ethics
4.	Convenes enthusiasm and confidence in the ability of self and team to achieve goals and be successful		Influence
5.	Demonstrates the courage to do what is right despite personal risk or discomfort		Integrity and ethics

Table 10.2 Five lowest scoring behavioural dimensions

S. no.	Dimension	Score	Competency
1.	Constantly reviews progress against set goals/ key business indicators		Planning and execution
2.	Follows up tasks constantly and brings issues to closure		Planning and execution
3.	Makes timely decisions		Planning and execution
4.	Analyses and confronts problems before they get out of hand		Analysis and judgement
5.	Identifies and develops high potential employees		People development

Example of MAFS at Eureka Forbes Limited

Number of respondents: 10 (Immediate superior–1, related superior–1, peers–2, internal customers–3, and 3 junior colleagues having regular interaction with the appraisee).

Name of the appraisee: Mr XX YY ZZ

Designation: AAA BBB CCCCC

See Table 10.3 for an example.

Table 10.3 MAFS at Eureka Forbes Limited

Overall score	Self	Others				
		RL%	ST	MT	AT%	Score
Leadership factors	**8.6**	**–**	**7.8**	**67.4**	**24.7**	**7.5**
Vision and strategic thinking	10.0		8.2	60.9	31.0	7.7
Business acumen	9.0	–	11.3	66.1	22.6	7.4
Influence	7.8	–	7.1	58.9	33.9	7.8
Planning and execution	7.9	–	14.3	72.7	13.1	7.0
Collaboration and teamwork	8.1	–	2.1	67.3	30.7	8.0
People development	9.0	–	4.1	78.8	17.1	7.6
Thinking factors	**8.9**	**1.4**	**5.7**	**71.2**	**21.7**	**7.4**
Analysis and judgement	8.6	2.9	5.7	68.1	23.3	7.4
Innovation and continuous improvement	9.2	–	5.7	74.3	20.0	7.4
Relationship factors	**9.5**	**–**	**2.5**	**67.4**	**30.1**	**7.9**
Interpersonal	9.5	–	–	70.1	29.9	7.8
Communication	9.0	–	–	69.0	31.0	8.0
Customer focus	10.0	–	7.5	63.1	29.4	7.8
Self management factors	**9.3**	**–**	**5.7**	**71.3**	**23.1**	**7.6**
Initiative and drive	10.0	–	7.1	78.6	14.3	7.5
Result-orientation	9.6	–	14.3	65.7	20.0	7.3
Resilience	8.8	–	–	75.0	25.0	7.9
Integrity and ethics	9.4	–	4.1	65.5	30.3	8.0
Self development	8.6	–	2.9	71.4	25.7	7.6
Overall score	**9.1**	**0.4**	**5.4**	**69.3**	**24.9**	**7.6**

Legend

Ratings	Abbreviation	Score	
All the time	AT	9–10	Candidate clearly and constantly demonstrates all or most behaviours pertaining to the competency
Most of the time	MT	6–8	Candidate on many occasions demonstrates some behaviours pertaining to the competency
Sometimes	ST	3–5	Candidate on few occasions demonstrates some behaviours pertaining to the competency
Rarely	RL	1–2	Candidate on most occasions demonstrates behaviours that imply gaps in the competency
Do not know	–	N	–

(Based on discussion with Mr P.S. Sukumar, Deputy General Manager, Knowledge Management, Eureka Forbes Limited, Bangalore, and information given through e-mail dated 3 May 2008).

Source: www.eurekaforbes.com/news/archive.aspx

Discussion Questions

1. Eureka Forbes Limited has clarified its expectations from its managerial personnel. Expectations against aspects of decision making and creativity have been detailed. What might be other aspects?
2. The company has identified five highest scoring and five lowest scoring behavioural dimensions, and has mentioned the corresponding competencies. EFL is allotting scores to managers. How does EFL actually strive to get hold of from the scores of highest and lowest scoring dimensions?
3. Study the table exhibiting the overall scores of Mr XXYY ZZ; consider the scorings against each factor and its components, by self and others. Critically evaluate the scores and bring out the behavioural pattern of the manager.

HR MANTRA Performance appraisal system

A company with an employee strength of 2,000 introduced performance appraisal system ten years ago. Four years ago, the company decided to link pay with performance. This was severely resisted by the collective forums. However, the company developed and installed the system. Incentives and annual increments were linked with performance. After implementing the system, in the first year, none was affected. In the second year, annual increment of an employee was stopped for poor performance. All registered and recognized unions of the company protested, submitted a memorandum to management, organized gate meetings, and observed tool-down strike in the company. But the management did not change the decision. Later, the unions filed a law suit. After two hearings, the judge gave the verdict in favour of the petitioners.

The union representatives and their advocate highlighted several incidents emphasizing the appraisal report as biased. The verdict of the judge unequivocally stated lack of clarity, objectivity, and possibilities of bias in the appraisal system of the company.

The mantra: Evaluate one considering the views of many.

CLARK L. WILSON

Dr Clark L.Wilson, an American industrial psychologist, was born on 31 August 1913 in Winchester, Virginia. Wilson was renowned for introducing the concept of 360-feedback surveys for management training and development applications.

After completing his studies from Stanford University in 1935, Wilson joined the US Navy during World War II and served in the submarine force in the Pacific theater. He was awarded the Silver Star and Gold Star awards for his contribution. He earned a Ph D in applied psychology from the University of Southern California in 1948. He was a Fellow of the American Psychological Association and the Society of Industrial and Organizational Psychologists.

After the war years, Wilson studied under the famous psychologist J.P. Guilford in the University of Southern California. Guilford's work led Wilson to experiment with identifying important management and leadership skills through psychometrics. He eventually developed his task cycle assessment tools as an application of Guilford's statistical approach. It is also believed that Wilson borrowed the concept of multi-rater feedback from the field of psychological assessment, particularly as it was being applied by the US Army during World War II. He believed that managers and leaders could learn and improve if they knew how others perceived their skills and behaviour. He also believed that management skills can be learned, like any other skill, through a learning sequence. While Wilson named this system 'multi-level feedback', others eventually dubbed it '360-degree feedback'—the name by which it is now best known. It is also sometimes called multi-rater feedback.

By mid-1970s more companies, including Dow Chemical, Pitney Bowes and several other utilities were using the instrument and contributing data to the norm database. With wider use and accumulated data, Wilson could study and ascertain the reliability and validity of the instruments he developed. He also studied performance data on feedback recipients and was able to verify a mathematical basis for the task cycle learning sequence. He found that when a manager or an executive practised the task cycle skills with balance and in sequence, a measurable increase in effectiveness could be documented.

From 1970 to 1973, Wilson developed the Survey of Management Practices as a teaching tool for his management classes at the University of Bridgeport (Connecticut), Graduate School of Business, where he was the Warner G. Bradford Professor of Management. His students used the survey in their workplaces. He developed this survey based on a learning sequence that he called the task cycle theory. Today, 360-feedback surveys of many types are standard tools for management training and development worldwide.

The feedback comprised survey statements that were rated on a seven-point agree/disagree scale. The statements were strictly limited to observations about behaviour such as planning or communications, and avoided aspects of personality such as sociability or excitability. Each individual would rate him on the same survey as the supervisor, direct reports, and peers who were also providing ratings.

Until his last days, Wilson continued to develop and publish a full range of assessment tools. He published his last book in 2003 at the age of 89. The book *How and Why Effective Managers Balance Their Skills* offers conclusions based on 30 years of research. Wilson summarizes, 'After over 30 years of analysis, the problem of most managers is very clear. Too many managers try to exercise control without providing the technical and teambuilding skills needed to achieve their goals'. This imbalance derails individuals and undermines organizational performance while the presence of these skills—which can be learned—measurably improves business outcomes.

The Clark Wilson Group was formed in 1973 and currently publishes 13 surveys in the task cycle series. Dr Wilson died in August 2006.

References

en.wikipedia.org/wiki/Clark_L._Wilson, last accessed on 1 October 2011.

CHAPTER 11

Potential Appraisal, Career System, and Succession Planning

LEARNING OBJECTIVES

After studying this chapter, you will be able to

- Define career and discuss career development perspectives
- Recognize career paths
- Undertake achievement audit
- Understand career decision making

OPENING CASE

Unrealized Employee Potential Retards Organizational Growth

After completing her studies in a village school and securing good marks, Magnolia, a teenager, migrated to Kolkata to pursue further studies. Once she completed her graduation, she joined an industrial training institute (ITI) as a trade apprentice in trade electronics. Magnolia successfully completed the apprenticeship, and joined another multinational company in the city. Like many youngsters, she too had great career aspirations. In order to fulfil them, she joined and completed her master's degree in political science by attending evening classes. As years passed, Magnolia gradually came to know the culture of the organization.

She was aspiring for a position in the HR department. She even had a flair for HR activities. However, her dream did not materialize. To further strengthen her academic base and get an HR profile, she got herself admitted in a B-school. She completed her post graduation in business administration, with a specialization in HR. However, even after obtaining a degree relevant to the HR profession, she could not succeed in getting an HR profile.

Magnolia's frustration with her employer affected her morale. Her confidence declined and she could even sense a change in her behaviour. However, she kept working hard with the same vigour, and did not allow her performance get affected.

One day, she came in contact with an HR specialist who was a professor where Magnolia had studied. He had conversed with Magnolia on quite a few occasions and had discovered her potential. He requested Magnolia to become his co-author and write articles and papers. After thinking for a couple of days, Magnolia accepted the proposal. She also acknowledged the HR specialist as her academic mentor.

Both of them developed an article for the national convention of a reputed professional institute. The article was accepted for presentation during the convention. Their paper was published in a quarterly national journal. Consequently, both Magnolia and her academic mentor were invited by the management development centre of a reputed multinational company to contribute an article/paper for their annual journal on the specified theme. Another article was published in the prestigious journal. Magnolia slowly regained her confidence. In this manner, Magnolia realized her career anchors, by developing and publishing papers and articles on human resource development, organizational development, and so on.

Her dream to get an HR profile did not materialize in the company she was working in the She predicts that she would not get an HR profile in the near future as well. She revised her plan for growth and decided on her career anchors and is preparing accordingly. She is now planning to pursue her career in the academic field.

Magnolia is just one example whose potential was not identified by the organization, and hence remained unutilized. As a result, she got frustrated and the company also could not derive the best from her potential.

Learning points

- Organizations should develop systems to identify their employees' potentials.
- Unutilized employee potential leads to frustration.
- Employees need job rotation.
- Organizations should develop a career system.

INTRODUCTION

Potential appraisal, career system, and succession planning are crucial for advancing talent in any organization. Employees aspire to grow in their careers and expect this growth to take place at close intervals. Achieving organizational goals, enhancing productivity, and fulfilling corporate goals can only be possible if employees are able to derive satisfaction in their careers, and move up the organization ladder. An organization must be instrumental to avoid generation gap and needs to identify managers capable to fill in the possible gaps, whether they are predictable or unpredictable, in the managerial levels. This chapter has been developed to impart knowledge in potential appraisal, career system, and succession planning including the leadership pipeline.

POTENTIAL APPRAISAL

Potential refers to the 'latent but unrealized talent' in any individual. Potential appraisal is a process of identifying the potential or the capability of individuals to assign new tasks which also affects their promotions. Just by viewing the performance, the achievement of quantitative targets, and conformance to qualitative requirement, an appraising manager cannot comment about the potential of an appraisee. In fact, he/she needs to perform a potential appraisal in a holistic way for studying the wholesome qualities of an employee with a given intellect, personality, and character.

Across industries, the two widely-used approaches for potential appraisal are the 'helicopter' approach and the 'whole person qualities' approach (Bhattacharya 2006). The helicopter approach tries to measure the potential of a person with respect to broad as well as specific issues. The whole person quality approach, on the other hand, measures the wholesome qualities/potential of a person. Competencies of an employee to perform well in the current job are not automatic indicators of his potential for promotion or other purposes. An excellent production supervisor may not be able to prove his worth as an assistant production manager as the needs of the latter's assignment are much broader and, apart from other skills, needs man-management skills.

> Two widely-used approaches in industries for potential appraisal are 'helicopter' and 'whole person qualities' approaches.

Likewise, an excellent chief engineer may emerge as a poor or a mediocre engineering director. Potential appraisal data is extremely useful for career planning, succession planning, and promotion, as the identified latent abilities of an individual can be matched with the future roles and responsibilities. In the opening case, the company where Magnolia was employed, never tried to identify her potential.

Similar to the performance appraisal, potential appraisal is also done by the immediate supervisor of the employee who gets the opportunity of closely observing the appraisee. The performance appraisal format comprises some parts such as nature of duties, task achievement, reasons behind failure to achieve the target (if any), whether the target was surpassed for some of the tasks and if this is possible. Information relating to potential appraisal forms a part of the performance appraisal. Potential appraisal should be treated as an essential organizational need and done seriously; it should never be done inattentively.

Potential Appraisal vs Performance Appraisal

Q 1 Performance appraisal is a part of career development. Organizations across the world today follow the mantra, 'get paid commensurate to your contribution'. In organizations, the focus of performance management signifies finding ways and means to enhance an individual's performance. Performance appraisal helps to rate the performance of the employees and evaluate their contribution towards the organizational goals. Performance appraisal, similar to career development, leads to the recognition of the work done by the employees through rewards, appreciation etc. Performance appraisal system establishes the link between an organization and the employees' personal career goals.

Potential appraisal, as discussed earlier, helps to identify the hidden talents and potential of the individuals. Identifying the potential talent facilitates in preparing the individuals for higher responsibilities and positions in the future. Thus, identifying potential is the initial step of succession planning. The performance appraisal process in itself is developmental in nature.

Performance appraisal is also closely linked to other HR processes—facilitates identifying the training and development needs, decision-making regarding promotions or otherwise (demotions), reviewing the compensation, etc. A feedback based on the appraisal report communicated in a positive manner can go a long way to motivate the employees. It can also help the employee to identify his career development plans. On the basis of the evaluation, employees can develop their career goals, achieve new levels of competencies, and map their career progression. Performance appraisal encourages employees to reinforce their strengths and overcome their weaknesses. At this stage, the employers need to understand the categories and indicators of potential.

Categories of Potential

In this context, potential means a prospective employee who is capable to undertake different challenging assignments. Potential of employees need to be discovered for organizational effectiveness. Organizations must aim to utilize the full potential of the workforce, institute an environment to unleash the latent creativity, create conditions promoting innovation and team working, and so forth. Potential is actually a useful succession term if you filter it through the leadership pipeline model (to be described later in this chapter).

Three categories of potential (Ram Charan 2007) are turn potential, growth potential, and mastery potential.

Turn potential is the ability to do the work at the next level in an organizational hierarchy in the next three to five years, or sooner.

Growth potential refers to the ability to do work which is complex, more challenging, needs innovative skills, pioneering expertise, etc., at the same level in the near future.

Mastery potential is the ability to do the same type of work that is currently being done, in a better manner.

Indicators of Potential

Q 2 There exist some indicators of potential which managers meticulously observe and consider while making decisions about their potential. Some of the indicators are a sense of reality, imagination, power of analysis, breadth of vision, and persuasiveness. (Tom Phillip 1983).

Sense of reality People usually act based on their thought process. A sense of reality refers to the extent to which a person thinks and acts objectively, controls his emotional pressure, and continues to pursue realistic projects with enthusiasm and achieves business goals.

Imagination Imagination is the mind's eye. A man dreams by virtue of his imaginative power. It is the ability to let the mind range over a wide variety of possible causes of actions to achieve specific results. Imagination goes beyond conventional approaches to situations and does not remain confined to, 'this work is done in only one way'.

Power of analysis Power of analysis refers to the capacity to reformulate, innovate, break down, and transform an apparently complicated situation into manageable terms. People with power of analysis believe in, 'innovate or evaporate'.

Breadth of vision People need visionary skills and their breadth of vision should be wider. Breadth of vision means the ability to examine a problem in the context of a much broader framework of reference. People with breadth of vision can detect relationships with those aspects within a specific situation which could impact the situation.

Persuasiveness Persuasiveness helps one trying as long as it takes to produce results. It is the ability to sell ideas to others and gain a continuing commitment. Using managerial authority may not always produce results. Persuasion refers to using personal influence by way of negotiation.

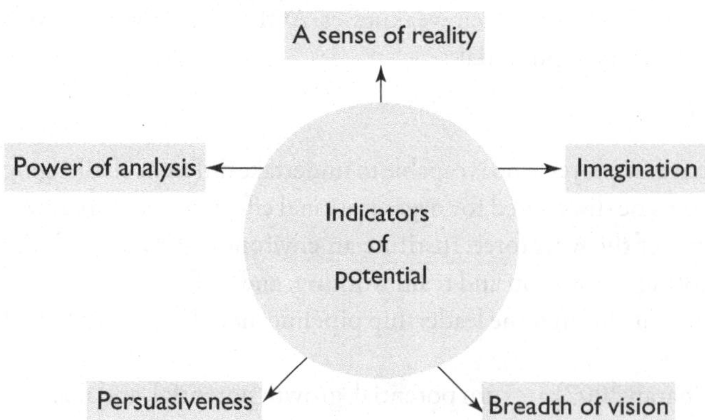

FIG. 11.1 Indicators of potential

These five indicators (Figure 1.1) are standard factors that are considered while judging the potential of any individual. These have helped many organizations in taking decisions.

Potential Appraisal Report

Organizations use appraisal reports to categorize employees. After categorizing, they plan developmental measures for each level and execute these measures. The curriculum of developmental efforts strictly specific shortcomings takes into account, and includes corresponding actions to advance their employees. Potential appraisal reports facilitate management to decide job rotation, assign challenging tasks, transfer higher responsibility, and so on. Titan Industries uses the reports of potential appraisal to develop them. Refer to Exhibit 11.1.

Exhibit 11.1 Categorization of employees by Titan Industries

Based on their appraisal reports, Titan Industries categorizes its employees into four categorizes. The main purpose of dividing them is to initiate specific developmental measures and some disciplinary actions. During the appraisal process, the status of all those could meet expectations and the extent to which they could meet the same were brought to the fore. The four categories are as follows:

Category A: Exceeded expectations (EHP)
Category B: Met expectations (GP)
Category C: Somewhat met expectations (P)
Category D: Did not meet expectations (Poor)

Further, the organization is also normalizing these categorized employees for each department. A maximum of 20 per cent employees might be considered in category A, and 40 per cent in category B. Even if the number of employees exceeds the limit of 20 per cent in category A, only 20 per cent is selected for the category. Titan classifies this process as normalization. The rest 45 per cent fall in category C. The organization helps the low performers (category D) come out with personal improvement plans (PIP).

Source: www.ignou.ac.in

Potential Appraisal at Maruti Udyog Ltd

Q 3 As already discussed, potential appraisal of an employee is done by the immediate superior as he gets the opportunity of observing the appraisee closely for a short span. Potential appraisal may be done periodically or whenever required. Generally, appraisal findings are recorded in a particular part of the performance appraisal form. Part III of the performance appraisal form of Maruti Udyog Ltd contains information to assess the future potential and ability of its L8 and above categories of workers to assume a position of higher responsibility (L13) in the following format. This format highlights three potentials—group effectiveness, ability to develop subordinates, and potential capability.

The format developed by Maruti Udyog Ltd is displayed in Exhibit 11.2.

Exhibit 11.2 Potential appraisal: Maruti Udyog Ltd

1. Group effectiveness: Maintaining and improving the morale of group and helping its identification with organizational objectives; optimal utilization of available manpower resources; directing and coordinating efforts, and effective follow-up actions to ensure accomplishment of planned objectives

☐	☐	☐	☐	☐
Outstanding	Very good	Good	Satisfactory	Unsatisfactory

2. Ability to develop subordinates: Sensitivity to develop subordinate's mental skills; ability to provide professional guidance to produce group results

☐	☐	☐	☐	☐
Outstanding	Very good	Good	Satisfactory	Unsatisfactory

(Contd)

Exhibit 11.2 (Contd)

3. Potential capability: Overall rating for managerial capability to head a department based on your assessment related to the earlier mentioned points

☐	☐	☐	☐	☐
Outstanding	Very good	Good	Satisfactory	Unsatisfactory

Source: www.ignou.ac.in

CAREER SYSTEMS

The term 'career' indicates all the jobs which an individual has held during his working life. In an organization, career planning of employees reduces the possibility of attrition. Career planning is a process that fixes the career goals and lays down the path to meet the goals, and provides answers to questions, 'where shall I be after 5, 10, or 15 years?' The purpose of career planning is to provide continuity, order, and meaning to a person's work life. It is not an event or an end in itself. It tells the employees/prospects about ways of advancing in the company. Career aims to integrate an individual's and an organization's goals.

Traditionally, doctors, engineers, lawyers, ministers, statesmen, musicians, and the like, were considered to have their respective careers. However, at present, the concept of career has been extended to include others' work-related roles too. There are a number of commonly held views with regard to a career. A career does not necessarily imply upward mobility. Doctors and lawyers do not lead to progression up a hierarchy. The careers of many doctors and lawyers are associated with an organization. Many people spend their entire working life in a single organization; many others are highly mobile, and pursue their careers in different organizations. While one person may aspire to earn money in his career to lead a lavish lifestyle, another may find the earning just enough to lead his life. Individuals are akin to career events differently.

The career planning system manifests its importance in attracting competent people, providing suitable promotional and advancement opportunities, providing challenging work, enabling to develop, boosting morale, increasing motivation, utilizing managerial reserves, and in retaining the talents. Career progression refers to making progress in one's career through a series of right moves. Career development means actions undertaken by a person to achieve the career goals.

Career counselling is the process of advising employees on setting career goals and assisting them to find suitable career paths. Career counselling helps employees to understand their careers more clearly, identify strengths and weaknesses, develop outlook, achieve and enjoy greater satisfaction, and realize the forces and dynamics in the career operating system. A career develops in various stages and follows multiple paths.

CAREER STAGES

What one wants from his/her career varies widely according to the stages of career. What was important in an early stage may not be important at a later one. Four distinct career stages are—exploration, establishment/advancement, maintenance, and late career. Each stage represents different career needs and interests of the individual.

> Four distinct career stages are exploration, establishment/ advancement, maintenance, and late career.

Exploration The exploration stage is actually a stage of investigation. This is a trial stage and begins with an individual's exploration of career-related matters. The stage usually ends when he/she attains the age of 25 or so with a commitment on the part of the individual to a particular occupation. Until he makes a decision to settle down, he may try diverse jobs in a number of organizations. Unfortunately, many organizations, at this trial and exploration stage, observe a high level of turnover among new employees. Employees in this stage need opportunities for self-exploration. The attrition rate may be reduced in this stage by providing a variety of opportunities and tasks for their career growth.

Establishment The establishment or advancement stage generally occurs when an individual crosses the age of 25. The stage continues for about 20 years, the individual makes his or her career choices, and is concerned with his/her achievement, performance, and advancement. The individual is motivated to succeed in the organization. Thus, this stage is marked by high employee productivity and career growth. He/she is not in any dilemma about the occupation chosen.

During this stage, an individual desires challenging opportunities in his job, where he/she could use some of his/her special competencies. The employee strives for creativity and innovation through new job assignments. Employees also need a certain degree of autonomy in this stage. They basically work towards succeeding and achieving their goals.

Mid-career crisis sub-stage This sub-stage occurs between the mid-thirties and mid-forties. At this stage, people often make a major reassessment of their growth, progress, and development in relation to their career ambitions and goals they had originally set for themselves.

Maintenance The maintenance stage, occurs roughly between the ages of 45 and 65.This stage is characterized by a continuation of established patterns of work behaviour. The person ceases to establish a place for him or her in the organization. Rather, they just seek to maintain their position. This stage is viewed as a mid-career plateau, in which little new ground is broken. In this stage, the individual may need some technical updation in his or her field. The organization should continue to encourage employees at this stage to develop new job skills. Otherwise, early stagnation and decline may occur.

Late career In this stage, the employees are on the verge of separation from the organization. Such employees are inclined to plan for retirement and seek to develop a sense of identity outside the work environment.

CAREER PATH

Industrial organizations provide a wide variety of task requirements to be carried out by employees, and this leads to diverse career opportunities for them. People move in and out of organizations, and often change their occupations. Career path may follow diverse routes. The four common paths can be transitory, steady state, linear, and spiral pattern.

Transitory Young people typically follow the transitory path, after entering the job market. There is no clear pattern as they seek jobs to enhance the salary package. Their loyalty to job or occupation is frequently little. They make lateral career moves, while some young prefer to be entrepreneurs.

Steady state The steady state is typical of many professionals, and indeed, is a craft-type occupation such as doctors, lawyers, tailor, carpenter, tradesman, etc. These professions take a long time to reach a steady state, undergoing training or through practices. They have to work hard for long periods to attain the role. They also need some more time to gain the confidence of respective customers. In some cases, it is also evidenced that the steady-state pattern may develop later in the work life.

Linear The steady pattern involves a balanced upward advancement or progression on a managerial/professional ladder, insatiable or voracious upward motivation, sacrifice of other interests, and plateau causes career crisis. The linear pattern is characteristic of high achievers, and usually requires significant sacrifices of other interests. An academician, eager to be an author and earn reputation, must sacrifice other common interests such as enjoying television, visiting relatives now and then, frequent tours and travels, and so forth. Family and other activities may often be orchestrated to support this career drive.

Spiral pattern The spiral career pattern offers great opportunity for diversity of experiences. This pattern involves lateral, diagonal as well as vertical moves. In an organization pursuing multiple projects, an individual gets the unique opportunity to be associated with a project for a long time, and on completion of the project, onto a linear track. This pattern is internally driven by a desire for self growth that propels the individual towards self-development and awareness. The two types of spirals are internal spiral and external spiral.

The term 'internal spiral' applies to those employees who stay in the organization or professional arena, but yet move around creatively in search of development. On the other hand, the 'external spiral' dramatically changes the field, and does not hesitate to switch over to other organization. It has been observed that internal spiral pattern is more appropriate for reaching top executive levels, than merely following the linear pattern.

In order to progress effectively through a career path, an employee needs to identify his/her strengths and weaknesses, talents, modify attitudes, apply creativity, etc.

CAREER ANCHORS

Q 6 Advancing in the career is a common desire. However, the advancement is not a factor of time. It needs sincere planning and directional efforts. One has to envisage the goal in advance, and decide the path through which he has to move to reach the goal. Career anchors are distinct patterns of self-perceived talents, attitudes, motives, and values that guide and stabilize a person's career. A few examples of such career anchors are given here:

Managerial competence In organizations, individuals are seen to be striving to manage situations and events, and also finding opportunities to manage. Most of them have a strong motivation to rise to the managerial positions. However, it is important for them to remember to also have the right emotional competence, to succeed.

Technical/functional competence Individuals with creative instinct search opportunities where they can innovate, as well as exercise their technical talents. The area may include functional area such as finance, engineering, marketing, sales, etc.

Security The individual is motivated by the need to stabilize his career, and thereby make his future stable and secure. The person does all that is needed he feels is required to maintain job security, a decent salary package, and the gain the potential of a good post retirement benefits.

Creativity The individual has an overarching need to create or build something that does not exist, that is entirely an outcome of his or her own originality. The creation may be related to product, process,

> Successful managers feel a high degree of competence in three areas—analytical competence, interpersonal competence, and emotional competence.

or system. The creation becomes an emblem of achievement which further results in adequate intrinsic motivation.

Autonomy and independence The dominant occupational value for some individuals is 'free from supervision by others'. They can execute the tasks assigned to them without supervision. They can solve problems; manage the hurdles, and roadblocks that emerge on the way. They use their knowledge and professional skills in the work place.

Technological competence There is a natural affinity for technology and a strong desire to work with technology, whenever possible. Individuals with high technological competence never hesitate to accept changes, and hence they are adaptable.

If the career anchor of a person is management competence, he will have an overriding interest in management, a capacity to bear considerable responsibilities, and an ability to influence and control others. He will emphasize priority on leading a team. The technical competence of a person drives him towards entrepreneurship. Creative thinking people are original in what they do and look for challenging work. They do unique things differentiable from general performers.

Schein (1978) mentions three specific areas in which successful managers feel a degree high of competence. The areas are analytical competence, interpersonal competence, and emotional competence. In this case, these three competencies are the career anchors.

Analytical competence refers to the ability to identify, analyse, and solve problems under a variety of conditions of incomplete information and uncertainty.

Interpersonal competence is the capacity to influence, supervise, lead, maneuver, manipulate, and control people at all levels of the organization, with the aim to ensure effective achievement of organizational goals.

Emotional competence is the aptitude to be stimulated by emotional and interpersonal crises, rather than being frustrated, exhausted, and weakened by them. Emotional competence restores the capacity to accept and bear high levels of responsibility without becoming dysfunctional, and the ability to exercise power assertively without guilt or shame.

Career anchors can be assessed by answering the questions (Dessler and Varkkey 2009) listed in Exhibit 11.3.

Exhibit 11.3 Questions to identify career anchors

1. What was/is your major area of concentration (if any) in high school? Why did you choose that area? How did you feel about it?
2. What was/is your major area of concentration in college? Why did you choose that area? How did you feel about it?
3. What was your first job after school? What were you looking for in your first job?
4. What were your ambitions or long-range goals when you started your career? Have they changed? When? Why?
5. What was your first major change in job or company? What were looking for in your next job?
6. What was your next major change of job, company, or career? Why did you initiate or accept it? What were you looking for? (Do this for each of your major changes of job, company, or career.)
7. As you look back over your career, identify some instances when you have definitely enjoyed. What was it about those times that you enjoyed?
8. As you look back at your career, identify some instances you have not especially enjoyed. What was it about those times that you did not enjoy?
9. Have you ever refused a job move or a promotion? Why?

(Contd)

Exhibit 11.3 (Contd)

10. Now, review all your answers carefully, as well as the descriptions for the five careers anchors (managerial competence, technical/functional competence, security, creativity, autonomy). Based on your answers to the question, rate, for yourself, each of the anchors from 1 to 5; 1 equals low importance, 5 equals high importance.

Managerial competence ....

Technical/functional competence ....

Security ....

Creativity ....

Autonomy ....

PEOPLE AND THEIR CAREERS

Traditional thinking says that people work in an organization as a means of making money, and for earning the livelihood. It is true that money is important. The pay package may comprise regular salary, fringe benefits, bonus, other compensations, and other elements as well. However, money is not the sole criteria. Apart from the salary package, you need something else. You will definitely consent that you have expectations about your career, from the work life, aspirations for getting a challenging position, utilize your capacities and potentials, desire personal development, and achieve what you want from your organization. Satisfaction is definitely the ultimate need.

In order to measure job satisfaction, Paul Spector (1994) developed a 36-item, 9-facet, 6-options per item scale, titled the 'job satisfaction survey'. The instrument is a summated rating scale that Spector developed and has six choices per item ranging from 'strongly disagree' to 'strongly agree'. The nine facets are pay, promotion, supervision, fringe benefits, contingent rewards (performance-based rewards), operating procedure (required rules and procedures), coworkers, nature of work, and communication. Spector originally designed the scale for human service organizations; though the scale is now used in all organizations.

It is evident from these facets that everyone looks for his/her pay (the salary package) and promotion. A person also considers the style of supervision and interaction pattern with the supervisor and takes into account the fringe benefits available, the performance-based contingent reward, the operating procedures comprising rules and regulations, and most importantly, the colleagues while pursuing a career and decide its worth.

Schein (1978) has also given a list of career anchors as follows:

1. Management and managerial competence
2. Technical/functional competence
3. Creativity and new wave thinking
4. Security/stability and clarity
5. Autonomy, independence, and delegation

Refer to Exhibit 11.4 to understand the need for importance and satisfaction for any individual while deciding on a career option.

Exhibit 11.4 Importance and satisfaction

Patricia and Edward (1978) worked with the staff of *Psychology Today* to find out the importance of satisfaction associated with the various aspects and concerns of jobs. In the following table, the sample size was large enough.

Importance and satisfaction with various aspects of jobs

Different people lay emphasis on different aspects. Importance and satisfaction are not the same. The view of a particular person is shown in this table:

(Contd)

Exhibit 11.4 (Contd)

Aspect	Importance	Satisfaction
Chances to do something that makes feel good about yourself	1	8
Chances to accomplish something worthwhile	2	6
Chances to learn new things	3	10
Opportunity to develop your skills and abilities	4	12
The amount of freedom you have in your job	5	2
Chances you have to do things you do best	6	11
The resources you have to do your job	7	9
The respect you receive form people you work with	8	3
Amount of information you get about your job performance	9	17
Your chances of taking part in making decisions	10	14
Information about job security you have	11	5
Amount of pay you get	12	16
The way you are treated by the people you work with	13	4
The friendliness of people you work with	14	1
Amount of praise you get for a job well done	15	15
The amount of fringe benefits you get	16	7
Chances of getting a promotion	17	18
Physical surrounding of your job	18	13

CAREER DEVELOPMENT PERSPECTIVES

Q 4 Every individual has his/her own choice regarding careers. However, one cannot decide one's career in isolation. He/She continuously tries to bring in a match between the organizational requirements and his/her own preferences. This match helps in characterizing the process of his/her career development.

Today, the business scenario, is highly competitive. An organization recruits, induces, places, trains, motivates, manages, and develops its human resources to maintain and sustain the effectiveness of the organization, keeping in mind the ways for its survival and growth. Employees, on the other hand, look for challenging job, security, and most importantly, opportunities for development throughout the work life cycle. Organizations attempt to provide what the employees want in order to prevent manpower attrition and to retain them. In the process, a psychological contract develops between the employees and the organization. Organizational outcomes include productivity, creativity, integration, market expansion, and effectiveness in all spheres. Factors such as job satisfaction, security, personal development, moving up the organizational ladder, and integration or involvement with the work are some of the ingredients of individual outcomes. Obviously then, this matching process leads to a mutually-beneficial long-term relationship of the employees and the organization.

Transitions and Choices

As discussed earlier, a career needs to be developed throughout the lifespan. Career development is not a one-shot process; rather it is an on-going one. While studying in an engineering college, you got selected in the campus interview. After completing your education and the academic curriculum, you joined an organization. After about two years, you have changed your organization. In the preceding two years, you have analysed 'what you wanted from the job' and 'what you were getting from the job'. The answers to these questions prompted you to change the organization. The reason for the change may be financial, non-financial, or both, based on self-analysis and self-assessment. At the end of the day, individuals transit to satisfy the pressing individual needs. They may need a change towards a different geographical location, organization, status, or even in the profession. This is a career transition for the individual.

Transitions are unavoidable in organizations that emerge as breakpoints distorting the relationships. For an individual, as one established relationship comes to an end, a new one gets forged. The individual forgets old behavioural patterns, learns new ones, abandons former responsibilities, and takes on new ones. You will agree, in a nutshell, that such breakpoints require an individual to discover, re-articulate, and re-shape certain assumptions about the work life. You face career transitions because of changes in yourself, your values and value system, motivation, preferred lifestyle, likes and dislikes, and so on.

External forces such as advertisements, changing technologies, and company takeovers or reorganizations play a major role in influencing career changes. Transition forces employees to make career decisions which are by far the most critical decisions people take during their lifetime. A few examples of such decisions and actions are listed in Box 11.1.

Box 11.1 Examples of career decisions

1. Deciding the career one should be in
2. Obtaining training and education necessary for career building
3. Opting for a beginning job to fulfil career aspiration
4. Planning a strategy to reach a desired position in an appropriate organization
5. Selecting a job offer from various available alternatives
6. Accepting assignments and pursuing them within the organization
7. Developing a career path, in the technical or managerial line
8. Preparing for the next position in the organizational hierarchy
9. Preparing for obtaining a position in another department within the organization
10. Continuing self-appraisal and development as per the selected career goal
11. Selecting the time for early retirement and strategy for disengagement

The four-stage process of job transition
1. Preparation
2. Encounter
3. Adjustment
4. Stabilization

Some organizations conduct career development seminars and discover a large number and a great diversity in career decisions. Each employee offers at least one issue; though many offer multiple issues. The issues offered are regardless of the level and or function in the organization. One will face career transitions and choices, and he/she needs to manage the decision-making process. Now, you need to study job transition and employee concern for careers.

The adjustment stage of job transition
1. Custodianship
2. Content innovation
3. Role innovation

Job Transition and Career Concerns

Every employee remains concerned for his/her career, especially when the work environment, in today's time, is often seen to be turbulent. This leads to the transition in job for the employees. The four-stage process of job transition is preparation, encounter, adjustment, and stabilization (Nicholson 1984).

Successful negotiation or compromise of one stage influences the outcomes of the next stage. The first stage of preparation occurs before the person starts the job and gets involved in a process of information exchange.

In the second stage of encounter, the employee essentially gathers information about the organization and the job, and 'how things get done around here'. The information is gathered explicitly by asking questions or consulting the written sources. During this stage, somebody gathers information simply by observing and listening to what is going on.

The third stage of adjustment occurs when people understand the new work environment, and consider how they are going to perform their jobs in that environment. There are three basic approaches which a person could adopt here—custodianship, content innovation, and role innovation.

Custodianship—The person accepts the role as given.

Content innovation—The person accepts the role/goals but finds his/her own way of implementing them.

Role innovation—The person redefines both the role and the methods to enact them.

Organizations prefer to reward the custodians most because they conform to the existing procedure and culture.

The fourth stage or stabilization phase evolves when the person is established in his job. Paradoxically, many employees spend the least time in this stage before moving on. Their careers are obviously a constant sequence of transition. These transitions may lead to happy or unhappy outcomes depending on the persons' capacity to deal with the kind of difficult transition effectively. The threat of this kind of 'dangerous transitions' increases people changing organizations frequently in search of career advancement.

Career Problems

Q 10 An employee's career may be associated with many problems. Organizational socialization is a process of the new recruit becoming an accepted member of the organization as an organizational citizen. Employees need to learn new values and appropriate ways of behaving, and understand what is expected by the organization. While employees move up the organizational hierarchy—from the entry levels into the managerial echelon—new career issues and problems develop. The exact timing of this move varies greatly. Graduate doctors are required to undergo internship. Most college graduates and MBAs are required to spend some time in learning, training and understanding the technical roles. They cannot directly go into managerial positions. The immediate superiors of young managers perform a great deal at their career development stage to orient them to the work, role, and the organizations.

> Underutilization of potential, insufficient performance evaluation and feedback, political aspects of organizations, feelings of dependence, loyalty issues, and ethical problems are some of the problems that young managers face today.

The skilled and supportive managers can provide excellent coaching, mentoring, and counselling to new recruits and his/her employees. If the superior manager has referent power by virtue of his knowledge and skills, he can influence others. But young managers or professionals rarely find a perfect superior. It has been evidenced that most successful executives have had mentors at their earlier work life who provided them with initial support, caused behavioural modification, developed a harmonious relationship, and behaved as a friend, keeping the status symbol apart. Even with continued support from a mentor and exemplary interpersonal relationship, young managers find a number of career problems.

The problems they generally encounter in careers are underutilization of potential, insufficient performance evaluation and feedback, political aspects of organizations, feelings of dependence, loyalty issues, and ethical problems.

Underutilization of potential Most of the young managers and professionals feel that their skills and talent remain unutilized or less utilized. In fact, young managers are assigned challenging tasks, empowered to make decisions, and asked to solve strategic problems. They are often motivated and aspire for early advancements in careers. In turn, the existing managers feel that young managers should prove themselves before they are given more important assignments.

Insufficient performance evaluation and feedback The feeling of underutilization of potential is associated with the syndrome of unused potential. Young managers seek feedback of their performances as they are eager to know how are they are doing and where they stand. They become anxious and frustrated when they do not get feedback. Employees with high achievement motive seek feedback of performance. On the other hand, existing managers feel that the young managers must have a good sense about their performance. As such, they do not mention about the feedback. We all know that good feedback not only motivates, but also helps any individual to learn and develop.

Political aspects of organizations An organization, by virtue of its nature, is a political system and cannot be free from political influences. The new managers do not believe this truth; they have difficulties in coming to terms with this universal reality. Their education system and background have tuned them to rational problem solving. When a young manager encounters the realities of a political problem, he becomes hypersensitive. Young managers hate to play power games; but desire to be evaluated purely on their merit. As a manager, one cannot remain outside the political arena. New managers and professionals need to face the political realities and learn to be induced with them.

Feelings of dependence Young managers generally prefer independence. The existing managers may not have up to date knowledge and may be unfamiliar with the state-of-the-art information. However, they are not completely aware of the organizational practices and systems. It is because of this fact that the young managers remain typically dependent on superiors for support and guidance, and acquaintance with the systems of the organizational practices. It is true that young managers join an organization with up to date knowledge, but it is the junior colleagues who possess all the technical skills and local knowledge. For this purpose, young managers need to depend both on existing managers and their junior colleagues. To be effective as a manager, it is vitally important for them to manage these dependencies through the acquisition of skillful use of powers.

Loyalty issues and ethical problems Top management continues to be concerned about issues on loyalty and ethics of young managers who should be loyal to superiors and colleagues, juniors, and most importantly to the organization. Often, issues of loyalty create ethical dilemma. Ethics does not only mean conforming to the system, obeying the law, adhering to the religious principles, being loyal to superiors, contributing to the organization, and so forth. Ethics also refers to obtaining greatest good for most of the people and goes much beyond this.

Career Development—Individual Strategies

Q 7 Organizations initiate efforts to develop their employees. However, they cannot take the sole responsibilities to develop each individual's career. Individual employees must also take initiatives themselves.

Career development is a joint responsibility of an employee and the organization. Organization imposes too much organizational control while developing an employee's career restricting the autonomy.

As discussed earlier, career results from the matching goals of the individual with that of the organization.

Career development is a joint responsibility of an employee and the organization. If an employee wants only the organization to develop his career, the organization is likely to impose too much organizational control restricting the autonomy of that employee. Therefore, it advised that you should be instrumental to manage your own career. The self management of your career will help you determine your own destiny and enhance your independence. In career decisions, the individual is the only one having appropriate information. He must be assertive to express his feelings so that he does not get deceived with regard to his career. Managing the self is of utmost importance. The steps involved in successful self-management of career are—do it now, know thyself, analyse career opportunities, establish career goal, obtain feedback, and manage your career.

Q 9 **Do it now** Suppose you have made decisions that will have an impact on your career. Do not delay in implementing the decisions. Do not wait for an auspicious day to come; for completing an academic activity, for settling down, and for any other reasons. Pursuing a career will always have uncertainties. Self management helps to reduce the uncertainties.

Know yourself You need to know your own strengths and weaknesses. Take the help of someone, whom you like and regard, to help you to identify your strengths and weaknesses. You must know how others see you; view your behavioural pattern, and opinions they possess. You must have the ear to hear what others are telling about you.

Analyse career opportunities Try and examine the sources of career opportunities. There are many sources of information concerning occupations and career opportunities. Many B-schools are publishing placement manuals or brochures containing information regarding career opportunities. You may also collect information from some of your friends or relatives who keep themselves informed. Spend few hours browsing the internet to determine what potential employers are seeking.

Establish career goals In the preceding three steps, you have learned that you should not delay in implementing decisions, you need know yourself, and you must analyse career opportunities. Using these as your arsenal, you should now develop your specific career goals. The goals should be measurable and attainable; may be for short-term or long-term. The self determined goals should stretch your performance. As success breeds success, meeting a short-term goal leads to even higher aspirations and improved performance.

Obtain feedback Feedback from relevant people help one correct his/her errors. You are required to think and plan how you will gather feedbacks from others with regard to your self-analysis and current career planning.

Steps for successful self-management of career are do it now, know thyself, analyse career opportunities, establish career goal, obtain feedback, and manage your career.

Manage your career Managing career is not just implementing your plan. It is not a one-shot operation; but rather an on-going process. The self-management spreads over your entire working life. You need to constantly look for opportunities, and take advantage of them. It is of utmost importance to build and maintain relationships. Evaluating and modifying career goals and plans should be a continual process. You must be flexible while taking decisions. You should not be tied up completely with a particularly job, department, or organization.

SELF-MANAGEMENT

Self-assessment is essential for self-management. Self-assessment is researching within you; finding who you are, what you like or love, what you have to offer, and so forth. Self-management enables you to take decisions about your career. Findings of self-assessment should be recorded on paper. Self-assessment includes some vital aspects such as achievements, skills and abilities, personal values, interests, disabilities (if known), personal and family circumstances, etc.

Achievements Thinking deeply and writing down your achievements enables you to rediscover yourself. The easiest way of reflecting your achievements is to start with your academic achievements at your school or university. Do not hesitate to include your achievements in co-curricular activities. Identify what led you to select a course of study. Think about the strengths you have developed along with specific knowledge gained. If you have got a job in an organization, think about the achievements, in terms of the responsibilities accepted. You must be deriving pleasure discharging certain responsibilities in your family or in the society. Recall those positive comments made by teachers, classmates, family members, friends in the society, colleagues, and organizational superiors.

Skills and abilities While pursuing self-analysis, never underestimate yourself; never say, 'I don't have any skills'. You must have many skills and abilities which are unknown to you. Skill is a vital element of Mckinsey's 7-S framework. Skills are the essence of what we contribute to the world. Skills bring perfection. Listening, memorizing, negotiating, persuading, inspiring, investigating, problem-solving, motivating, etc. are only few of the many skills one may have. A single person cannot have in his possession all the skills. In addition, a job does not need all the skills. Moreover, a job may need the required skills in varying degrees. Remember the skills and abilities you used to complete those achievements that you have already thought about. Highlight the skills that you would enjoy using on a regular basis as part of your ideal job.

Personal values Values guide a person to lay importance over things, turns him on and off, gives happiness in circumstances or otherwise, helps to decide the extent of integrity he needs in his work or life, exercise power and responsibility in the work place, and so on. Thus, the questions for self-examination are—what are the most important things to you? What turns you on and off? What are you committed to? What gives happiness to you? What degree of integrity do you need in your life and work? How much power and responsibility do you want in the work place? Your values further guide to your extent of devotion to work—do you want to live to work or work to live, and to strike a balance between them.

Interests There are many things that generate your interests. First, you make a list of 25 or 30 things you love to do. Thereafter, pick up the favourites and shortlist the interests. The job you are doing must have some of these. Give some thoughts to areas which fascinate and mesmerize you the most, that is, production, quality control, quality system, maintenance, purchase or planning, administrative, computational, scientific, indoor or outdoor work, etc.

Disabilities (if known) Your disabilities cannot stop you from achieving that you most aspire for. Your strong will always supports you to reach your goal. Be honest with your known disabilities or physical impairments that may impact upon what you want to do. You may have allergies, colour blindness, back problems, asthma, etc. The presence of anyone or two disabilities does not mean you cannot do a particular job. You need to be aware of how you would manage any roadblocks restricting you to achieve. Your strong will lead you to success.

Personal and family circumstances You now know your achievements, skills and abilities, personal values, interests, etc. Prepare yourself to face the impacts of these on your employment in terms of hours, financial commitments, limitations, etc. You will definitely be able to overcome the roadblocks.

SUCCESS OF CAREER PLANNING

The success of career planning depends on certain factors such as top management commitment, clearly-defined corporate goals, motivation level of the workforce, employee attitudes towards achieving the corporate goals, and stress-free work environment. The company should also maintain an age balance, and manage organizational role stresses, attempt to place right man for the right job, develop and implement fair promotion policy, install compensation management system including incentive schemes, and so on.

LIMITATION OF CAREER PLANNING

Though career planning leads an organization to expansion and growth, it has certain limitations. Career planning is not effective for a large number of employees, and cannot be applied for illiterate employees. The environment is ever changing. Therefore, career planning cannot be effective over a longer time, say more than 10 years. The growing expectations of family members, political intervention, and nepotism are some factors that negatively affect the career system.

CAREER DEVELOPMENT—ORGANIZATIONAL STRATEGIES

Being aware of the utmost need of employee career development, organizations are designing programmes for effective management of human resources. The aim of this effort is directly related to career issues such as reducing employee attrition, exploring potential and providing matching assignments, developing high-potential candidates, preparing for managerial positions, enhancing problem-solving abilities, reducing problems arising out of lack of knowledge and skills, providing ample opportunities for growth, ensuring upward movement for potential employees, and so forth.

Many organizations have instituted a system of career counselling through workshops, and have employed career guidance specialists. Literatures suggest a number of specific drives that organizations can take to make the career programmes effective.

Improving human resource planning and forecasting system Considering and analysing the targets of the organization, it should develop the job specifications and recruit personnel of the required quantity and requisite quality. Companies need to develop procedures to meet the target in fluctuating situations. They need to select the appropriate forecasting technique to assess manpower needs.

Improving dissemination of career option information Employees always remain impatient to know about their career and the various career options available. Companies having career planning system should share the information with the employees through administrative manuals, circulars, or other documents. The information calms their restless minds and they can concentrate on the work assigned to them. Organizations should develop instruments to keep employees informed about the career options.

Initial career counselling Career counselling is a way of periodic performance appraisal. In addition to appraising performance, counselling provides excellent opportunity to discuss career problems of employees; their goals, and opportunities available for developing in career.

Support of education and training Education and training system supports all levels of employees to improve their careers. The prerequisites for further career growth are first identified, and need-based training is conducted accordingly. Furthermore, for enhancing an employee's overall growth, education is imparted. It is important that the organization must have clearly-defined policies concerning time-off and the necessary financial supports.

Job posting Employees aspire to advance in their careers. In larger organizations, the aspirations are higher. Employees need to get information for advancement in their careers. Organizations must provide all employees with information concerning job openings. Moreover, a system of job posting helps an organization to attract talents from market. The system stimulates employees of all levels in career planning and development.

Special assignments and job rotation Doing the same job over a long period of time generates boredom. Employees should get the opportunity of gaining new experience by way of performing special assignments and through job rotation. These actions enable employees to learn new things firsthand and performing them in different settings. Simultaneously, management can also ascertain the capacity and potential of an employee to accept challenges, working in new settings, and with new people.

Career development workshops Considering the importance of employees' career development, organizations are arranging workshops and seminars as essential career development activities. These workshops clearly indicate organizations' concern for career development. However, the central assumption of these workshops is the joint responsibility of individual and the organization for career development.

Sabbatical, flexible working hours, and other off-work activities At present, people get engaged in multiple family and social activities. In spite of realizing the urgency of office work, they rush to perform the non-organizational activities considering the relative importance. Later, they repent thinking about the undone office work. This leads to the generation of organizational role stress on account of inter-role distance. Organizations need to develop sabbatical (time-off) leave, flexible working hours, and other off-work activities. Allowing employees, particularly middle-aged people, to avail sabbatical leaves provide the opportunity to develop new life interests. This organizational system may be a possible answer to boredom and apathy.

Flexible rewards and promotional system Organizations use both financial and non-financial rewards to recognize employees. The scope of rewards and determining success criteria are really limited; presumably due to limited thinking about them. Nowadays, in the financial arena, there is a growing trend toward giving employees a choice among several forms of financial rewards. In fact, organizations need to develop multiple ladders to consider promotion and rewards. The promotional system should reflect the desires for spiral as well as linear careers. The employees will definitely contribute their best to the organizations if flexible rewards and promotional system are installed.

Development and use of assessment system Many organizations use formal assessment centres and development centres in order to evaluate potential of employees to help them advance in their careers. Use of assessment centres have emerged as a practice while selecting people. Later, organizations use assessment centres for career planning as well. The terms assessment centre and development centre have been discussed later in this chapter.

CAREER DEVELOPMENT VS ORGANIZATIONAL DEVELOPMENT

When an organization takes initiatives to develop and document the career plans of its employees at all levels, it can derive several benefits.

Career system broadens the promotional avenues and employees can predict their scope of advancement. The system restores satisfaction among employees, and thereby reduces attrition.

Career system improves employee morale and motivation, and as a result, productivity enhances. The system enables organizations to fill vacancies through internal recruitment, thereby, providing opportunities to exercise control cost of managerial recruitment.

It ensures better utilization of employee skills and knowledge which provides enhanced job satisfaction, leading to increased job involvement and organizational commitment. Organizations get the best from its most valuable resources.

In the changing environment, career system makes employees adaptable to changes. Organizations can plan and implement changes without resistance. Most of the change efforts are likely to be successful. Career system reduces industrial disputes relating to work assignments, promotional matters, problems inherent to jobs, etc. Obviously then, career system provides a unique opportunity to the organization to sustain harmonious industrial relations.

Career system includes conduction of career development programmes; describes progression, and ensures equitable decisions regarding promotion, irrespective of gender bias and minority classes. The system assures affirmative actions for backward classes. In turn, the society benefits from the system too.

While recruiting from external sources, the presence of career system helps to attract new talents.

For all these reasons, organizational development is commensurate with individual career development.

ASSESSMENT CENTRE AND DEVELOPMENT CENTRE

In order to map/diagnose competences, organizations now invest in assessment centres. This, in turn, leads to a job–person–organization fit and alignment to HR systems, namely talent management, recruitment and selection, retention, management development, career, and succession planning. In 1960, the American Telephone and Telegraph (AT&T) Company initiated the assessment centre method while promoting their personnel line to supervisory positions.

Q 8 Traditionally, an assessment centre consists of matching a set of exercises designed to assess a set of personal characteristics. Assessment centre is a procedural mechanism to identify the potential for growth. It is very often misperceived as a location. Assessment centre is strictly a procedure (and not a location) to evaluate employees for manpower planning and decisions. The procedure uses a 'situational test' to observe specific job behaviour. Assessment centre procedure is used to determine the suitability of a person for a specific job. As such, elements related to the job are simulated through a variety of tests. The assessors observe the behavioural disposition and make independent evaluations of the observation. This results in identification of the strengths and weaknesses of the attributes being studied.

Assessment centre, based on large bodies of academic research, is treated as the most valid predictor of performance. It comprises a number of exercises such as the following:

1. Group discussion
2. In tray
3. Interview, simulation/role plays
4. Case studies/analysis exercises

Certain elements are essential if an assessment centre is to be considered as a process. The International Personnel Management Association (IPMA) identified these elements, some of which are listed in Box 11.1.

Box 11.1 Assessment centre elements

1. A job analysis of relevant behaviours is meant to determine attributes, skills, ability, etc., and is required for effective job performance, and to define the scope of evaluation of assessment centre.
2. One must validate the technique or techniques to assess the dimensions of skills and abilities.
3. One must not stick to a particular technique; rather use multiple techniques.
4. The assessment technique must include job-related simulations.
5. Multiple assessors must be engaged for each assessment to control any possible human errors.
6. Before assigning the task of assessment, the assessors should be thoroughly trained.
7. The observations must be classified into some meaningful categories of attributes, skills, and abilities.
8. The observations conforming to a systematic procedure must be recorded.
9. Assessors must prepare a report.
10. The information must be integrated through discussion or by applying statistical techniques.

Differences between Assessment and Development Centres

The type of centre can vary between the traditional assessment centre used purely for selection to the more modern development centre which involves self-assessment and whose primary purpose is development. Assessment and development centres are discussed together though they have different purposes for reasons such as (a) both of them involve assessment, and (b) it is impossible to draw a line between assessment and development centres because both the centres have naturally evolved to have a more developmental flavour.

A number of differences exist between assessment and development centres and are presented here:

1. Assessment centres have a pass or fail criteria while development centres do not have this type of criteria.
2. Assessment centres are geared towards filing a job vacancy while development centres are used for developing the individual.
3. Assessment centres address an immediate organizational need while a development centre addresses a longer term need.
4. Assessment centres have fewer assessors and more participants while development centres have a one-to-one ratio of assessor to participant.
5. Assessment centres involve line managers as assessors while development centres do not employ line managers as assessors.
6. Assessment centres have less emphasis placed on self-assessment while much greater emphasis is placed on self-assessment for development centres.
7. Assessment centres focus on what a candidate can do now while development centres focus on potential of the individual.

8. Assessment centres are geared to meet the needs of the organization while development centres are geared to meet needs of the individual as well as the organization.
9. Assessment centres assign the role of judge to assessors but development centres assign the role of facilitator to the assessors.
10. Assessment centres place emphasis on selection while development centres place emphasis on developmental feedback and follow up with little or no selection function.
11. Assessment centres use feedback and follow up; development centres give feedback immediately.
12. Assessment centres give feedback at a later date while development centres involve the individual having control over the information obtained.
13. Assessment centres have very little pre-centre briefing but development centres have a substantial pre-centre briefing.
14. Assessment centres tend to be used with external candidates while development centres tend to be used with internal candidates.

POTENTIAL ASSESSMENT PRACTICES

Finding the inherent potential in a company to make it competent is not a myth for the company's manager. Managers are practically adopting this practice to strengthen the bottom line, and thereby, stabilize their profit matrix. For example, Tata Motors Ltd, Schneider Electric India, Philips Electronics India, and others are practising this process as part of their organizational system.

Tata Motors Ltd In this company, an identified talent pool undergoes structured training and exposure to help broaden their perspectives. It also enhances key managerial skills for higher effectiveness as a step in leadership development. Potential assessment is done based on Tata leadership practices and development centre.

Schneider Electric India Potential assessment is done through talent acceleration programme (TAP), wherein people are identified as talent and undergo technical assessment such as personnel decision international (PDI) or local development centre, followed by an interview.

Philips Electronics India In this company, high potential senior managers are identified and subjected to the 360-degree appraisal, development centres, engagement surveys, etc.

SUCCESSION PLANNING

Succession planning refers to the process of identifying future potential leaders to fill in key positions in the organization. The developmental activities can also be identified and planned. It signifies searching for high potential managers capable of assuming higher managerial positions.

The traditional succession planning was purely based on organizational needs. To cope with the changing environment, at present, succession planning takes account of the growing recognition that people look for, in both men as well as women. Organizations also consider the need to make their careers and to balance their career and family responsibilities, to reduce stress due to inter-role distances, and to enhance their work life balance.

The succession planning process has undergone a sea change. Succession planning is perpetuating the enterprise by filling the leadership pipeline with high-performing people to assure that every level has an abundance of these performers to draw from, both now and the future (Ram Charan et al 2007). They designed the definition to provide the readers a way to use the pipeline model to increase the succession planning effectiveness. There are four rules to be followed to keep with the definition. The rules are (a) the focus should be on performance, (b) the pipeline demands continuous flow, (c) the pipeline turns must be fully understood, and (d) short-term and long-term needs must be simultaneously looked into.

The focus should be on performance Future growth and development depends on high performance at the present. Having many high-potential people in the leadership pipeline can cause damage because many individuals will be unable to perform at appropriate leadership levels. Full performance across all leadership levels is the objective of succession planning (Ram Charan, et al. 2007).

The pipeline should have continuous flow While carrying out succession planning all levels of leaders must be included. There must be a good supply of leaders developed at all levels. While not everyone aspires to be the chief executive officer (CEO), some people do. As such, a solid group of candidates should continuously be developed and moving up the pipeline. When the time of finding a CEO comes, there will be a number of internal candidates who have not skipped levels. This practice will avoid the disastrous consequences when people take the CEO's job being less than well prepared (Ram Charan, et al. 2007).

Four rules to keep with the definition of succession planning are (a) the focus should be performance,(b) the pipeline demands continuous flow, (c) the pipeline turns must be fully understood, and (d) short-term and long-term needs must be simultaneously looked into.

The pipeline turns must be fully understood People need to work at the right level, and the skills, time applications, and work values for each level must be clearly communicated to them and assessed. In order to take right decisions regarding who should be developed for key leadership positions, this understanding is central and crucial. Only concentrating on one parameter such as skills, the values might fail later under pressure (Ram Charan, et al. 2007).

Short-term and long-term needs must be simultaneously looked into Succession planning needs to be done to meet the immediate needs as well as to build a reservoir of leaders for the future. Both are critical to survive in business and ensure success in the future. Refer to Exhibit 11.5 for details about succession planning at Bharti Airtel.

Exhibit 11.5 Succession planning at Bharti Airtel

Bharti Airtel has a succession planning exercise for managers who are identified in a period of 12 months. The company looks for traits that include entrepreneurship and the ability to think big. Bharti Airtel empowers the leaders to the maximum. The company's leadership strategy is closely intertwined with its corporate mission. The company strongly focuses on building a unified culture to enable its leaders gain entrepreneurial zeal, and stretch themselves in terms of their execution capabilities. For succession planning, organizations use the multi-source assessment and feedback report.

Source: www.ignou.ac.in/edusat/mba/MS02/Unit-10.pdf

LEADERSHIP PIPELINE: AN OVERVIEW

The leadership pipeline comprises six passages (Ram Charan, et al. 2007). The passages are as follows:

1. From managing self to managing others
2. From managing others to managing managers
3. From managing managers to functional manager
4. From functional manager to business manager
5. From business manager to group manager
6. From group manager to enterprise manager

The six turns in the leadership pipeline are major events in the life of a leader (Ram Charan, et al. 2007). Each turn represents a significant passage, which needs adequate time to understand, and be mastered. Each passage demands familiarization with the skills, time applications, and work values. On understanding the need of each passage and the challenges involved in each transition, one can facilitate self-growth as a leader and can assess the organization's leadership pipeline. When a person moves through the passages, he/she takes up tasks of increasing responsibilities and complexities, and becomes emotionally stronger too.

Awareness of the six passages provides one with ideas and tools to achieve wholesome performance at all leadership levels in the organization. Ram Charan alerts that one may find a turn or passage in his/her organization not addressed in the leadership pipeline model. They say that the passage may not be a major one. Transition from team member to team leader is not worthy of a passage as this is usually a subset of the passage 'managing self to managing others'.

Furthermore, team leaders are also seen to lack the decision-making authority on selection and rewards that first-line managers receive. Team leaders usually focus on technical or professional matters (getting a project or programme completed) and are not interested in the general management areas.

STANDARD FOR JUDGING POTENTIAL

Q 5 Categories of potential have been discussed earlier in this chapter. Ram Charan, et al. (2007) elucidate the standard for judging potential of all the three categories.

1. Turn potential managers can be promoted to the next passage within three to five years. Any candidate belonging to this category
   (a) exhibits operating, technical, and professional skills that are extremely broad and deep
   (b) displays managerial skills that are expected at the next highest organizational level
   (c) demonstrates leadership skills that are expected at the next highest organizational level
   (d) regularly works at building new skills and abilities
   (e) aspires to higher level challenges and opportunities
   (f) demonstrates 'fire in the belly'
   (g) has a business perspective beyond current organizational level
   (h) is oriented towards total business results, not just focused on the success of own area
2. Growth potential managers can be promoted to a bigger job at the same leadership level within three years (Ram Charan, et al. 2007). A growth potential candidate
   (a) exhibits operating, technical, and professional skills that are high for current organizational level
   (b) showcases managerial skills that are high for current organizational level

(c) frequently demonstrates leadership skills that are high for current organizational level
(d) adds new skills when the job calls for it
(e) aspires to greater challenges but primarily at the same organizational level
(f) is motivated to do more than is expected
(g) has a business perspective beyond current position
(h) is focused on the current area and the team

3. Mastery potential managers can improve in current role with same effort (Ram Charan, et al. 2007). A mastery potential candidate
   (a) exhibits operating, technical, professional, managerial, and leadership skills that are acceptable for current organizational level
   (b) demonstrates little effort to build new skills
   (c) aspires to stay with the company, as opposed to assuming bigger challenges or higher personal challenges
   (d) is motivated to do what is needed in current job
   (e) understands the job
   (f) is focused primarily on the current job

Ram Charan, et al. (2007) adds that the individual has the desire, but has not yet demonstrated the ability, to progress to bigger jobs.

SUCCESSION PLANNING VS CAREER PLANNING

As already discussed, succession planning refers to identifying likely vacancies for higher level executives, and searching for high potential executives capable of assuming higher executives positions. Career development, on the other hand, takes care of employees at all levels including executives of the organization. Thus, succession planning is management development for the executives. Career development normally considers likely career progression (making progress in one's career through a series of right moves) in a given occupation. On the contrary, succession planning is a 'runner-up chart' for higher echelons such as managing directors, functional directors, general manager, etc. Succession planning refers to grooming of capable executives for different specialist positions such as marketing, sales, production, finance, personnel, production, and so forth. Please refer to Exhibit 11.6.

Exhibit 11.6 Succession and career planning at Rashtriya Chemicals and Fertilizers Ltd

Rashtriya Chemicals and Fertilizers Ltd (RCF) is a corporate body and a Government of India undertaking. It is responsible to the people of India the Government as owner, Government as Government, Consumers, Employees, the Society at large. The company is simultaneously accountable to all these agencies who have a stake in its successful operation, growth, and welfare.

Succession and career planning: Implementing a succession plan is important to the health of an organization as it ensures availability of future leaders at key positions and effective co-ordination. It also allows for creative development of personnel to "fit" within the organization at the middle and upper management level. RCF does not leave its leadership to chance. RCF meticulously works out "Succession Planning" for the top 3–4 layers of the organization and reviews at regular intervals for implementation.

Source: www.rcfltd.com/index.php/hr-hrd/108-hrd

Succession Planning vs Leadership Development at Philips Electronics India and ABB

Different companies are pursuing succession planning in different ways. Philips Electronics India identifies categories in two ways—short-term and long-term. Short-term successors refer to those who have the capability to take up one or two years' time frame, and long-term successor indicates the employees who can take up the responsibility in three to four years. Philips reviews this list every quarter, and tracks the 'talent leadership ratio'. The company treats the ratio 1:2 as the best possible scenario. For every key position, there is one short-term as well as one long-term successor available within the organization. (SAIL 2009)

In ABB, 41 per cent of all global positions are taken over by a planned successor. The succession planning policy of ABB for global key positions includes a review process comprising three levels. Potential leaders are identified through a combination of performance, verified potential, and recommendation of superiors. ABB decides the global key positions based on job/position grades which are assigned through the Hey Grading process taking into account impact, volume of business, etc. There is a customized three-day programme called 'leadership challenge' that operates the board for white and blue collar employees to identify potential leaders (SAIL 2009).

SUMMARY

Potential is unrealized employee talent and its appraisal is a process of identifying capability of individuals to assign new tasks, and also to effect promotions and other facilities. Potential appraisal is different from performance appraisal. A sense of reality, imagination, power of analysis, breadth of vision, and persuasiveness are some indicators of potentials. Career system is important in attracting competent persons, providing suitable promotional and advancement opportunities, providing challenging work and enabling to develop, boosting morale, increasing motivation, utilizing managerial reserves, and in retaining the talents. Career anchors are a distinct pattern of self-perceived talents, attitudes, motives, and values that guide and stabilize a person's career.

Career development is a responsibility of an employee and the organization. Employee's careers are associated with many problems. For any employee, self-assessment is essential for self-management. Career development and organizational development are intertwined with one another.

Succession planning refers to identifying future potential leaders to fill key positions in the organization. Objectivity in employee assessment makes succession planning effective. Succession planning is perpetuating enterprises by filling the leadership pipeline with high-performing people to assure that every level has an abundance of these performers to draw from, both at present and in the future. Organizations should develop standards for judging performance.

KEY TERMS

Career anchors are a distinct pattern of self-perceived talents, attitudes, motives, and values, which guide and stabilize a person's career.

Career cycle is the stage through which a person's career evolves. Career paths are flexible lines of progression through which an employees moves.

Career goals represent the future positions one may occupy.

Career paths are flexible lines of progression through which employees move in and out of organizations, and often change their occupations.

Career transition is a phase when individuals transit to satisfy pressing needs which may be financial or non-financial or both.

External spiral pattern applies to those employees who dramatically change the field of operation, and do not hesitate to switch over to other organizations.

Internal spiral applies to those employees who stay in the organization or in the professional arena, but move around creatively in search of development.This pattern is more appropriate for reaching top executive levels than merely following a linear pattern.

Linear careers refer to the steady pattern involving a balanced upward advancement or progression on a managerial or professional ladder through sacrifices of many other interests.

Persuasion refers to using personal influence by way of negotiation. Using 'managerial authority' may always produce results.

Spiral careers offer the greatest opportunity for diversity of experiences involving lateral, diagonal, as well as vertical moves. The two types of spirals are internal spiral and external spirals.

Succession planning refers to searching for high potential managers capable of assuming higher managerial positions.

EXERCISES

Concept Review Questions

1. Describe the concept of potential appraisal. How does it differ from performance appraisal?
2. Discuss various indicators of potentials of employees.
3. Discuss the needs, purpose, and objectives of career planning.
4. Explain the concept of career system and discuss the career development perspective using illustrations.
5. Discuss the categories of employee potential and the standard for judging potential.

Critical Thinking Questions

6. Review the description of five types of career anchors. Assess your own position in relation to them. Describe the organization in brief.
7. Explain the concept of career system and discuss the perspective of career development. Describe different strategies for career development being adopted in any organization you are familiar with.
8. Clearly distinguish between assessment centre and development centre in the context of organization. Describe the organization briefly.

Assignments

9. Form a team with one or two classmates who have similar career interests. Interview an individual in a position you aspire to be in 10 or 15 years. Ask him/her about the major career problems he encountered and his personal development strategies.
10. Take guidance from your professor or placement officer, and contact about five people who are working in their positions for more than ten years. They are also successful at their careers, could foresee problems with their careers ahead of time, and had achieved success by finding solutions before these problem surfaced. Interrogate them to know how they could foresee career problems. Share your findings with the professor of the subject.

MANAGER'S INSIGHT

Gaurav is a bright young man. He has a sense of reality, power of analysis, and other positive attributes. While studying in college, he aspired to become an engineer, but his dreams did not materialize. After completing his studies in physical sciences, he got a very good government job with an administration profile. Due to his tenacity and sharp analytical skills, he was appreciated among his peer group as well as his seniors.

During the initial years, he was very happy with the kind of work that he was involved in. He could find his ways with the challenging work, as it demanded innovative skills, and developed his expertise in emerging niche areas. If the challenges were greater, Gaurav's results were more efficient. Gradually, with the passage of time, his learning increased. The novelty of the work became a routine and he started losing interest in work. He felt that the work that he was getting now is only regular in nature and demanded no creativeness or experimentation of any sort.

Questions

1. Analyse the situation here. Could you identify the problem areas/situations with intelligent individuals such as Gaurav?
2. On the basis of the concepts learnt in the chapter, how do you see the role of career systems in organizations?

Bibliography and Web Resources

Bhattacharya, Dipak Kumar, *Human Resource Management*, Excel Books, New Delhi, 2006.

Dessler, Gary, and Biju Varkkey, *Dorling Kindersley* (India), New Delhi, 2009.

Nicholson, N., *A theory of work role transitions*, Administrative Science Quarterly, 29, pp. 172–191, 1984.

Patricia, A. Renwick, and Edward E. Lawler, *What You really Want from Your Job*, Psychology Today, pp. 54–65, May 1978.

Phillip, Tom, *Making Performance Appraisal Work*, McGraw Hill Ltd, UK, 1983.

Ram Charan, Stephen Drotter, and James Noel , *The Leadership Pipeline How to Build Leadership-powered Company*, Wiley India (Jossey-Bass, A Wiley Imprint), New Delhi, 2007.

Schein, Edgar, H., *Career Dynamics: Matching Individual and Organizational Needs*, Addison-Wesley Pub. Co., 1978.

Spector, P.E., 'Measurement of human service staff satisfaction: Development of the Job Satisfaction Survey', *American Journal of Community Psychology*, 13, pp. 693–713. (Copyrighted 1994) (www.shell.cas.usf.edu/~pspector/scales/jssovr.html, last accessed on 2 July 2011), 1985.

Web Resources

www.ignou.ac.in/edusat/mba/MS02/Unit-10.pdf, last accessed on 7 September 2010.

www.rcfltd.com/index.php/hr-hrd/108-hrd, last accessed on 29 July 2011.

CAREER DECISION-MAKING IN TURBULENT BUSINESS SITUATIONS

Vikram completed his postgraduation in aeronautical engineering from a reputed institute in India in 1965. He joined an aeronautical company (PQR Aeronautical Limited) as a junior engineer. The company was very successful in designing, manufacturing, and marketing aircrafts. Over the years, the company developed several models. Vikram had held a variety of engineering jobs in different departments of the company. By virtue of his inquisitiveness, Vikram could learn many aspects of commercial aircraft production and became multi-skilled. Within a time span of five years, he became more specialized in navigational systems. He was involved in his job and was a satisfied engineer. As such, he could trace his career with the company through the development of many new innovative aircraft models. He was proud of his own and the company's accomplishments.

Meanwhile, the oil embargoes and continuing crisis in the Middle East and a rise in aircraft fuel prices posed severe threats to the aircraft industry, and naturally affected all aircraft manufacturers. The dramatic increase in interest rates severely limited the ability of airlines to purchase new aircrafts. The aircraft industry was jolted by these adversities. The aircraft controllers convened a strike in the summer of 1981. However, the strike and the deregulation did not help the aircraft industry. Several airlines faced severe financial crises and straits. Several aircraft manufacturers including PQR Aeronautical Limited were forced into bankruptcy.

PQR Aeronautical Limited was hard-pressed for resources; it lost a major air force contract for military transport plane, and was finding very stiff competition in the commercial aircraft market from the European aircraft builder. The company had lost a number of large sales of different aircrafts from airlines in other countries. Vikram had been associated with the company during many of its ups and downs; however, the impact of this situation was grave. The company had already conducted a significant reduction in employment and things looked very bleak for the future. Rumours such as several other airlines might cancel their orders began spreading like wildfire, and Vikram knew that the projects he was working on were very likely to be terminated if things got any worse. He had spoken about the situation over to his superior, Mr Kirloskar. The boss assured him of the company's high regard for his abilities and performance. However, there was no guarantee that they would have a position for him.

Following the discussion with Kirloskar, Vikram quietly began looking for other career opportunities. He has no intention to leave PQR Aeronautical Limited at any cost. However, the situation compelled him to search for a job elsewhere, after spending 15 years with PQR Aeronautical Limited. His wife was employed as a district education officer in the board of higher education. He had two children who were studying at the local schools. He put his best efforts for a job in the nearby areas. His utmost endeavour for a job failed, due to general economic recession, and there was considerable unemployment in the area and good jobs were not easy to find.

Vikram had been involved in highly specialized work and there was not much demand for his skills. He was about 40 years old and had never searched for a job earlier. Finally, he could line up another opportunity with an electronic firm. The position did not offer as much as his current pay packet and opportunities for further growth were uncertain. There were risks involved in accepting the position in the electronic firm. However, there was certain risks in continuing at PQR Aeronautical Limited as well. Obviously, Vikram was in dilemma. He had always enjoyed the work with PQR Aeronautical Limited, and was loyal to the company. Had things gone well, he would have been satisfied to complete his career there. However, due to the strong likelihood of being laid off, and as he had an alternate offer, he faced a major career choice.

Discussion Questions

1. Do you feel Vikram took the right decision of pursuing a career than doing the current job? State reasons.
2. How do you see an employee's career planning system's role in such a situation?

HR MANTRA Career or job?

Two friends were brought up in the same locality, and studied together at the same institution for about 14 years. They had different ambitions which were influenced by their family backgrounds. One of them, Victor, desired to be a scientist, and the other, Joseph, always dreamt to be a journalist. Victor fell sick just before his graduate examination and could not prepare well. Unfortunately, he could not secure the marks essential to enter the master's degree course. Hence, Victor had to rethink about his career plans. However, Joseph studied two courses of his choice—(a) mass communication and journalism, and (b) creative writing in English.

More than a decade later, they met each other, with their families. As Victor could not pass the examination required to be a scientist, he appeared for the civil services examination, and cleared the same. He currently holds a senior position in the administrative discipline. He is happy with his present position and prospects in future. On the other hand, though Joseph was able to achieve his dream of becoming a journalist, he is unhappy with his career progression.

The mantra: Pursue a career, not just a job.

EDGAR HENRY SCHEIN

Edgar Henry Schein was born in 1928. Schein was a Professor Emeritus with MIT Sloan School of Management Alumnus of Harvard University, Stanford University, and University of Chicago. He has made a notable mark on the field of organizational development in many areas, including career development, group process consultation, and organizational culture.

Schien's research on career anchors in the mid 1970s showed that most people's self-concepts revolved around five categories reflecting basic values, motives, and needs: autonomy/independence, security/stability, technical-functional competence, general managerial competence, and entrepreneurial creativity. In 1980s, the follow-up research studies were conducted with a wider range of occupations and revealed three additional anchor categories: service or dedication to a cause, pure challenge, and life style.

In 2000, Schien received a lifetime achievement award from the Workplace Learning and Performance of the American Society of Training Directors and the Everett Cherington Hughes Award for career scholarship.

Schein developed a model on organizational culture in the 1980s. Schein (2004) identifies three distinct levels in organizational cultures: artifacts and behaviours, espoused values, and assumptions. The three levels refer to the layers of corporate culture.

1. Artifacts include any tangible or verbally identifiable elements in an organization. Architecture, furniture, dress code, office jokes, and history all exemplify organizational artifacts.
2. Values are an organization's stated or desired cultural elements. This is most often written or stated that the CEO or president hopes to exude throughout the office environment. Examples of this would be employee professionalism or a 'family first' mantra.
3. Assumptions are the actual values represented by the culture and they are not necessarily correlated to the values. These assump-tions are typically so well integrated in the office dynamics. As such, they are hard to recognize from within.

References

Edgar Schien, *Career Anchors Revisited: Implications for the Career Development in the 21st Century*, National HRD Network Journal, Vol. 1, Issue 4, August 2007.

www.google.co.in/imgres?q, last accessed on 15 October 2011.

CHAPTER 12

Compensation, Rewards, Incentives, and Wage Administration

LEARNING OBJECTIVES

After studying this chapter, you will be able to

- Analyse compensation and related issues
- Describe the determinants of executive compensation
- Understand the principles of compensation administration
- Understand the relationship between motivation and rewards
- Evaluate the role of reward systems in improving performance
- Identify the major components of wage structure in India
- Distinguish reward from compensation and incentives
- Explain the salient features of various Acts
- Understand social security benefits

OPENING CASE

Settling Compensation System in Precision Engineering Works

Precision Engineering Works (PEW), a family-owned company, manufactures small (up to five kg) and medium (above five kg and up to 25 kg) castings. Since its inception about three decades ago, PEW was able to supply castings and fulfil the qualitative requirements and ensure on-time delivery. Its management has multiplied the product range to a great extent, and is motivated to further increase the same. PEW has recruited operators, supervisors, and people in managerial cadres as well. The company has an unprecedented demand for its castings. The company has one registered and recognized union. About a year ago, the company reached an agreement with the union on a production incentive scheme. The management was hesitating to implement the scheme, anticipating the consequences. The union volunteered to implement the incentive scheme. The management was naturally pleased with the assurance of the union leader to personally undertake the task of implementing the scheme. Furthermore, the management promised to give them a free hand if they could assist in increasing production.

The leaders of the union put in their best efforts, closely monitored the production, and the average production of three months increased by about 40 per cent from the original level. As a result, the leaders gained importance. The union leaders were facing some problems. They could however sort the problems by direct access to the chief executive. At the time of incentives for the first quarter, the employees supporting the union benefited greatly from the incentive scheme. The leaders received disproportionately large incentives. Most of the workers raised a hue and cry, started tool down, and expressed dissatisfaction in many other forms. The incentive scheme was inequitable.

Another feature of the incentive scheme was that it was linked to the consumer price index (CPI) rather than the volume of production. The union members tried to misuse their power. The management evidenced the labour unrest and misuse of power by unions. The management struck back one day, and initiated disciplinary actions against all the leaders. All of a sudden, the union found that it was without a leader.

At this juncture, a second union emerged and arrived on the scene. The leaders had established a rapport with the chief executive. The second union faithfully followed the beliefs and tenets of the management. This union could extract some benefits for its members exclusively. The union, like the management cadre, took production and related activities as its exclusive responsibility. Most of the workers also got the message that the union has a hot line with the chief executive officer (CEO) for any problem resolution. However, the union leaders never exposed this to the workers. They spread this news of relationship with the CEO using the grapevine.

The management thought of delinking incentives from the CPI, and decided to make it performance-based. The union members did not agree to this proposal as some of the union members were earning incentives almost equal to their salaries. At the same time, workmen with no incentives were becoming aggressive. This mismatch resulted in discontentment and unhappiness amongst them. However, the dilemma could not be resolved and this led to an explosive situation.

To take advantage of the situation, a third union emerged on the scene, and this led to intense inter-union rivalry resulting in indiscipline, loss of production, and violence within the factory premises. As a result of these events, the company declared a lockout. Of course, the management had no alternative than declaring the lockout. The company reopened after four months. Unfortunately, the union in power lost its credibility. The workmen completely supported and favoured the third union. The third union expected the management to solve the problem of not having revised the wage scales for a long period. However, this was not an easy task as there were a lot of inequalities that the management wanted to set right.

To set things straight, the management wanted to revise the compensation system including wage administration to take out the inequalities, and hence, conducted series of meetings. The union unnecessarily anticipated a wage cut and became afraid and hostile. It not only wanted to cling to the beneficial aspects of the incentive scheme but also insisted that the management somehow give an increase in the basic wages.

The union drew the management to a vicious circle of the inequitable incentive scheme though the former was trying for high incentive categories. The management remained in a dilemma with regard to convincing the workmen. It also had to win over the constituency of workmen, make managers effective, and regain supremacy in production.

Learning points

- Any incentive scheme should be objective.
- The chief executive officer should maintain a distance from leaders.
- Management need to involve union and communicate to all.

INTRODUCTION

Compensation, its management, reward system, incentive schemes, and wage administration are critical for the smooth functioning of any organization. These systems together determine the industrial relations, quality of work life, union-management relations, labour unrest, satisfaction at the workplace, contribution to the organizations, and so forth. Designing of the systems, periodical reviews, and revising them in the context of changing business scenario need adequate attention of management. Faulty design can jeopardize an organizational functioning. Similarly, a carefully-designed system can help an organization to excel. In this chapter, the interrelated topics—compensation management, reward system, incentive schemes, and wage administration will be discussed in succession.

COMPENSATION

Compensation refers to the remuneration that an employee receives in return for his/her services to the organization. Compensation management is an integral part of human resource management and helps in motivating the employees and improving organizational effectiveness.

In organizations, determining the rates of monetary compensation is by far the most difficult functions of human resource management. It is not only complex, but significant both to the organization and its employees. Employee compensation decisions are crucial for the success of an organization. From a cost perspective, effective management of employee compensation is critical because of the existence of total operating costs. Another reason for studying compensation from the organization's perspective is to assess its impact on a wide range of employee attitudes and behaviours and, ultimately the effectiveness of the organization and its units. Some of the organizational outcomes such as job satisfaction, attraction, manpower retention, job performance, skill acquisition, cooperation, and flexibility are directly influenced by compensation.

At present, in any organization, compensation management is a strategic issue. Employee compensation includes all forms of payments and rewards given to the workforce. Compensation includes both direct financial payments as well as indirect financial payments which employees receive during their tenure of employment. A sound compensation management system is the key driver of motivation, employee retention, and enhanced quality of work life. The term compensation refers to reimbursement, disbursement of incentives, and a strategic issue with regards to salary and wage administration. Direct financial payments include pay in the form of salary, wages, incentives, commissions, and bonuses. Indirect financial payments are given in the form of insurances.

As we have been studying in all the earlier chapters, human resource is the most vital resource for any organization. Like every other function, it also needs to take care of the remuneration and compensation of every employee to get the best out from them. It is needless to mention that lucrative compensation will also serve the need for attracting and retaining the best employees. Now, one needs to understand executive compensation and strategic compensation.

Executive Compensation

In organizations, executives play pivotal roles, hold key positions, and their contribution becomes significant to the organizations for sustenance, growth, success, and profitability. They are keen to look after the health of the company. In order to make the executives happy to the extent possible and check attrition, in recent years, companies have been offering bigger and more frequent raises in salaries and perquisites. For the top management, the salaries are influenced by the size of the company, the industry to which it belongs, and the contributions of the incumbent to the process of decision-making. Bigger companies pay more compensation. Straight salaries, bonuses, stock option plans, profit sharing, etc. are used to compensate executives. Companies compensate executives reimbursing various expenditures incurred by them as tax relief takes away a major portion of their salaries. The perquisites are in the form of the following:

1. Medical care and health benefits
2. Professional service in legal and financial matters
3. Facilities for entertaining significant personalities and dining
4. Cost of self-development
5. Cost of education of children
6. Allowances for professional magazines, and books
7. Free and furnished accommodation, and conveyance and servants

Executive compensations should be lucrative for a number of reasons such as the following:

1. To attract and retain competent personnel in the company
2. To motivate significant contributors
3. To extract the best from all employees in the face of competition

Executive compensation practices are based on factors such as tradition, technology, management beliefs, and executive acceptance.

Executive compensation packages typically comprise the following components:

1. Basic salary
2. Annual incentives
3. Long-term capital accumulation
4. Deferred compensation arrangements
5. Supplemental benefits and perquisites
6. Special severance and retirement arrangements
7. Employment and change of control agreements

In organizations, there should not be any disparity between compensation patterns, and the absence of internal equity leads to dissatisfaction. Dissatisfaction among executives can lead to organizational jeopardy. Compensation survey brings to limelight dissatisfaction with regard to compensation. Executive compensation practices are based on factors such as tradition, technology, management beliefs, and executive acceptance.

The foremost responsibility of top management is to develop an approach to compensation that accounts for both internal and external equity (external equity refers to relative wage fairness compared to wages with other farms or businesses). However, the success of executive compensation depends on the packages and their characteristics. These are as follows:

1. Establish sufficient levels of pay.
2. Provide internal and external competitiveness.
3. Supply opportunity, security, and status.
4. Maximize after-tax earnings.
5. Invest maximum effort.
6. Make the executive a much better performer both as an individual and as a team member, now and in the future.

Strategic Compensation

Achieving the business objectives and goal is the primary target of any company. Hence, the company should plan their compensation schemes in a manner so as to link components of compensation packages with the business goals and objectives. This is referred to as strategic compensation. In today's competitive business scenario, organizations have to take special measures regarding compensation of the employees so that they can retain their valuable assets. Today, one can see a lot more organizations with strategic compensation systems.

COMPENSATION DOMAIN

Compensation basically represents an employment contract. It is important to employees, organizations, and the economy. Therefore, it is important for us to understand the theories applicable to compensation. Compensation has two vital domains—economic concept and psychological concept.

Compensation has two vital domains—economic concept and psychological concept.

Economic Concept

To employers, compensation is the price paid for labour services. Compensation is a price for a factor of production. Compensation serves to assign scarce human resources to productive uses. As an economic concept, compensation is governed by the same logic as the purchase function by a firm. An organization strives to get the maximum quantity and the highest quality for its money. By the same logic, the worker is selling labour services to obtain income and holds out for the highest price obtainable. The actions of these buyers and sellers are supposed to set the price and to allocate labour, and offer services, to its most productive use. The market for labour services and for commodities differs in many ways. Labour service is perishable and as an inherent characteristic of service, it is to be noted that current labour requirements have to be procured today, as it will not have any value tomorrow.

Labour service may vary from hour to hour and day to day because it varies with the ability of a person to work. As a labourer is producing services, he/she can change the quality and quantity of those services. In the labour market, the pay for similar work tends to be equal. Organizations need labour in different occupations. In some occupations, there can be scarcity of labour due to the skills needed. Differences in pay among occupations arise from the scarcities in those occupations.

Obviously then, economic analysis is inescapable in any study of compensation. However, studies in the differences between labour markets and other markets suggest that economic analysis alone is not sufficient.

Psychological Concept

A good compensation system satisfies the employees. The system may generate dissatisfaction as well. Compensation actually represents a psychological contract between an individual and the organization. An organization's reward practices can only have positive or negative impact consequences through this contract. The extent of satisfaction depends on the perception of individuals about the pay or compensation. Thus, pay or compensation, as a psychological concept, is how individuals view it.

The situation and the needs, perceptions, and attitudes of the individual, and values are determinants of behaviour. A situation is perceived by different individuals differently. Thus, situation and individual are interdependent. Maslow propounded the need hierarchy model. Needs are felt states of an organism. Needs influence perceptions and also influenced by perceptions. An organism cannot relax till the needs are satisfied. The various means adopted for satisfying needs are those that individuals perceive and interpret through attitudes. One need may be satisfied by multiple means, and also one means may satisfy a number of needs. The psychological concept complements the economic perspective of compensation by emphasizing the perceptions of individuals.

COMPENSATION SYSTEM—BEHAVIOURAL ISSUES

From the standpoint of the psychological concept, compensation management is interwoven with various behavioural issues of the employees; it is an application of motivation theory. The level of motivation influences the behavioural issues. That is why motivation theory is interrelated with a form of compensation theory. At this stage, it would be wiser to establish the link between motivation and compensation administration.

Human relations encompass important reactions of a person to other people's action and behaviour in the society, club, organization, or anywhere else. The relations between individuals, between individuals and groups, and between groups constitute a critical phase of industrial psychology. Motivation transcends all topics in industrial psychology. Employee motivation and attitudes to an event may be positive or negative. An employer wishes to hire positively motivated people who want to work and will continue to work hard throughout the years of employment. People work for various reasons. Some work for money, while a few other people like the power associated with the position, an attractive position in the organization, or enhanced self-respect as a result of executing a useful or a difficult job.

There are four phases in the process of motivated behaviour—a need is aroused in the organism, behaviour is directed towards satisfying the need, the need is satisfied, and the organism relaxes (Pestonjee 1991). During the period between arousal and satisfaction of the need, the organism is in a state of tension, a condition of unrest, or uneasiness. The organism can only relax after the need is satisfied because the equilibrium has been restored. Equilibrium is the state or condition in which no pressure (needs) is compelling the organism to become active. Motivating the employees should be an ongoing activity though during good times when a company is growing and energy is high, this often seems unnecessary. Employees show up for work, work is done, activities progress, and business is good. However, if people start suffering from complacency, then the results may be serious, and invite disaster for the organization.

In times of uncertainty, however, employee motivation becomes not only more important as a general principle, but is often critical to survival. In reality, employee motivation underlies success during all market cycles but problems with employee motivation become even more apparent in times of uncertainty and change (Kennedy 2001). Motivating the employees should be a continuous process in an organization.

People come to work in an organization from different cultural, social, and economic backgrounds. They come with diverse aspirations and work because their needs differ and expectations from the organization vary. Some people work to support their family financially, while some people need power, social status, and prestige, and few more people need self-respect for accomplishing work in an exemplary way. For the same person, the needs change from time to time. A person is considered to be an organism in this context. First, a need is aroused in the organism. Then, the organism's behaviour turns towards satisfying the need. When the need is satisfied, the organism relaxes. Needs occur when there is perceived discrepancy between an actual state and a desired state of being.

Motivation is an activated state within a person that leads to goal-directed behaviour. Motivation comes in many forms and what motivates one individual is not necessarily the same for their team members. Therefore, it is important to understand how motivation differs among individuals, and how these differences affect the overall drive and determination of a team toward a goal. Motive is a construct representing an unobservable force that stimulates and compels a behavioural response, and provides specific direction to that response.

People are the functional instruments of an organization, and they always need motivation to exert their best. Unless their behaviour and elemental attributes are fully understood, it will become difficult to plan and execute any action. We may make gross mistakes if we desire a particular behaviour from a particular person for a particular cause, all the time. There is no better method of understanding human nature than by actually handling the person. However, it takes a long time to understand human behaviour.

From the standpoint of psychology, compensation designing acts as an operant conditioning, as employees show two types of behaviours—respondent and operant—while their behaviour gets reinforced. Respondent behaviours are controlled by instincts and direct stimulation. Operant behaviours are released in the absence of any apparent external stimulation.

Respondent behaviours are controlled by instincts and direct stimulation. Operant behaviours are released in the absence of any apparent external stimulation.

Sociological Concept

In the society, the style of living and the organization pay is a status symbol. The style of living depends on the pay packet. In less complex societies, the status of individuals is a product of many standards of judgement. For example, their families, friends, occupations, education levels, and religious and political affiliations depend on pay. In large societies, many of these standards are harder to measure and become less significant. Income, as a symbol of status, does not present any significant problem. Organizations create status structures of jobs by way of pay and compensation. Status differences are measured by both organizations and by individuals in terms of pay and pay differences. In fact, employees learn to place associates in the status structure of the organization on the consideration of how much they are paid. Compensation, as a sociological concept, focuses on the relationships of the organization and the individuals, and society and the inhabitants. The mutual influence of individuals, organizations, and of groups within and outside constitutes another important dimension of compensation decision-making.

Political Concept

Unions, associations, and joint consultative machineries form the collective bargaining forum. The collective bargaining forum always tries to exercise influences and uses power derived from the political parties to which they are affiliated. Compensation, as a political concept, refers to the use of power and influence. Organizations, unions, groups, and individual employees use their power to influence pay. Unions exert influence at the time the contract is concluded, and during the lifespan of the contract, by means of the grievance procedure. Similarly, compensation, in unionized organizations, influences that of non-union organizations in that locality. A political perspective stresses on accommodating the influence of all parties.

Equity Concept

Equity concept in compensation is like distributive justice. Discussions on compensation can never proceed without appealing to fairness. Phrases such as 'a fair day's pay' or 'the just wage' are very common in organizations. The fundamental embedded concept is that returns in the form of compensation should be proportionate to contributions, and should be free from any sort of bias. Compensation should be so designed that employees perceive them as 'fair' and 'equitable'.

Communication Concept

The electronic age, through the proliferation of the internet, has paved way to easily access gather information. Employees can browse and come to know to some extent about the compensation package in other organizations. Particularly, they can gather the competitive rates commonly paid for their positions within any given geographic area. If the functions of the companies are similar, employees will make that a point and put forth through collective bargaining forum. It is evidenced that employees know some of their interests more than their employers; especially about the value of their positions in the competitive marketplace.

Multi-disciplinary Concept

Economists, psychologists, sociologists, political scientists, philosophers, management researchers, and teachers have focused on different aspects of pay and compensation. Experts from different disciplines have studied compensation selectively. Economists have focused on the price (wage) of a factor of production, and considered employee behaviour in terms of labour units employed (typically in terms of working hours). Psychologists have focused on the needs of individuals and the means by which they may be met by organizations. Psychologists, however, laid less emphasis on the needs and difficulties of the organization. Sociologists, political scientists, and philosophers have developed concepts relating to other purposes which may be usefully applied to the study of pay and compensation. Management researchers and teachers have focused on more aspects of compensation. Organizational stalwarts have focused on the ability to control costs and the capacity to afford attractive compensation.

> Decisions are based on three primary core aspects involving pay level, pay structure, and pay system. Three secondary or supporting decisions concern the pay form, pay treatment for special groups, and pay administration.

ELIGIBILITY FOR THE REWARD

Compensating executives requires a series of decisions that ends after finalizing a pay rate for each executive in the organization. Through job analysis and from the job descriptions, skills, efforts, and responsibility are recorded. The jobs also are evaluated from which pay determinants are obtained.

Decisions are based on three primary core aspects involving pay level, pay structure, and pay system. Refer to Figure 12.1. Three other secondary decisions are pay form, pay treatment for special groups, and pay administration, and these support the three core decisions. A number of environmental and organizational variables influence these decisions. The variables are economic, social, cultural, and legal environments, as well as the organization's structure and work force.

> Major considerations in pay level decisions are public policy, pay for comparable work in the industry ('going rate'), and the company's response to economic, political, and social issues.

Of all the primary decisions, the pay level decision is the broadest. The pay level decision determines how much the organization will pay for labour services, or what would be the average pay. Pay level refers to the average pay for jobs, for departments, or for the entire enterprise.

An average pay must be set to keep the work force productive. The major considerations in pay level decisions are public policy, pay for comparable work in the industry (usually called the 'going rate'), and the company's response to economic, political, and social issues. These considerations may be weighed unilaterally. However, for better organizational health decisions may be taken involving the union(s). Some of these decisions are directed towards individuals (salaries), and some are directed towards groups (medical insurance).

> Pay structure decision focuses on the interrelationships of jobs in the organization, arranging them in a hierarchy, and fixing pay for them relative to their status.

The second core decision is the pay structure decision, which focuses on the interrelationships of jobs in the organization. Pay structure decisions generally involve arraying or arranging jobs in a hierarchy and fixing pay for these jobs relative to their status within the hierarchy, involving decisions by the organization regarding the amount, and the type of benefits to provide.

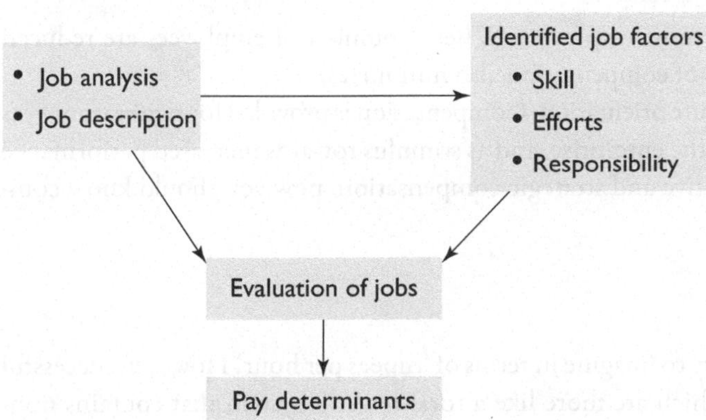

FIG. 12.1 Compensation decision-making

The pay level and pay structure decisions conjointly determine the pay. In addition, external and internal standards are considered. Seemingly, pay level decisions ensure that the organization is in line with the requirements of the external environment, and pay structure decisions ensure that the pay for jobs is internally consistent.

The third core decision involves determining individual pay of employees engaged in accomplishing similar types of jobs. Of course, it is possible for all employees on the same job to get the same pay, wherein no decision is needed. However, once a decision of differential payment is made for employees on the same job, two further decisions are required—(a) the factors behind differentiation among employees, and (b) whether to pay for time or for output. The first decision on differential payment is labeled as individual pay determination while the second as the pay method decision. Adopting the designation of pay system for both decisions makes sense.

The first supporting decision is pay form which entails the composition of the pay an individual receives. The major part is money or take-home pay. However, a large proportion constitutes benefits of several kinds. The second supporting decision is pay treatment and relates to some special employee groups. Although the organization expects similar behaviour from all employee groups, compensation policies and practices may obviously differ to some extent for market personnel, salespeople, professionals, and managers. The final supporting decision and pay administration involves ensuring that pay achieves organizational as well as individual objectives and meets public policy goals. The process of compensation planning and control seeks answers to questions of efficiency, effectiveness, and legality. Discrimination in pay is a particularly important issue today.

COMPENSATION AND ORGANIZATIONAL EFFECTIVENESS

A compensation system contributes to the organizational effectiveness. The four basic ways are as follows:

1. A good compensation can serve to attract qualified and competent applicants to the organization. Other things being equal, an organization offering a higher level of pay can obviously attract a larger number of qualified applicants in comparison to its competitors.
2. Compensation helps to retain competent employees in the organization. Retaining competent workers depends on many factors. One major factor is compensation policies which help by maintaining a fair internal pay structure and by providing attractive benefits. Thus, turnover and the costs associated with recruiting, selecting, and training replacements are reduced.
3. Compensation motivates employees as it serves as an incentive to them. Employees put forth their best efforts to achieve organizational goals. Manufacturing and sales organizations, for example, use monetary incentives to attain higher levels of production or sales without hiring additional employees. Investing the best efforts enhances average productivity of labour. Thus, fewer employees are needed to achieve the same level of output which, in turn, reduces costs and increases organizational profitability.

Compensation is a significant cost for most employers. When a number of employees are reduced without affecting the output, then costs of compensation also minimizes.

Compensation has both past and future orientation. Compensation is provided for two reasons—as a reward for significant contribution to the enterprise, and as stimulus towards increased performance in the future. Having understood executive and strategic compensation, now you should know compensation package and its worth.

COMPENSATION PACKAGE

While discussing compensation, it is easy to imagine in terms of 'rupees per hour'. However, successful compensation packages are the ones which are more like a total rewards system that contains non-monetary, direct, and indirect elements. Refer to Figure 12.2.

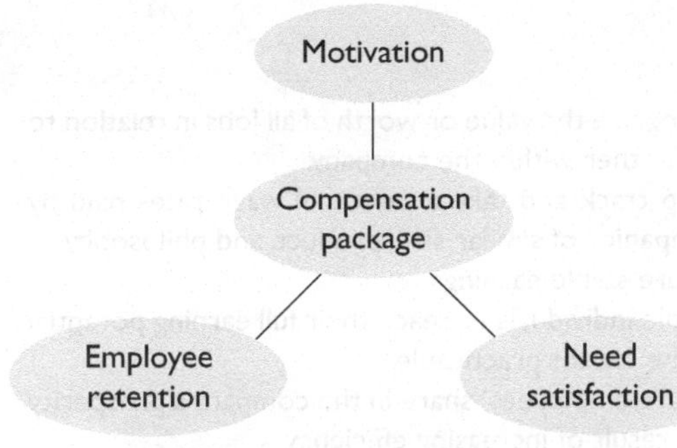

FIG. 12.2 Compensation package

A significant change has come into the compensation management system over the last few years. As a result, the very definition of compensation has been reconceptualized. The modern definition considers both intrinsic (intangible) and extrinsic (tangible) components of compensation. While extrinsic compensation covers both the monetary and non-monetary rewards, intrinsic compensation reflects employee's emotional satisfaction through job accomplishment. Presently, more organizations are seen to be using this pattern.

Non-monetary compensation includes career and social rewards such as job security, flexible working hours, working from home, and opportunity for growth, praise and recognition, task enjoyment, and avenues of warmth and friendships.

Direct compensation is an employee's base wage. It can be a monthly or annual salary, hourly wage or any performance-based pay that an employee receives, such as profit-sharing bonuses.

Indirect compensation varies widely from one organization to another organization. Indirect compensation includes everything from legally required public protection programmes such as social security to health insurance, post-retirement benefits, paid leave, child care and maternity benefits, housing facilities, etc.

In some organizations, employees can choose compensations suitable to them from a wide variety of compensation elements designed by the employer. Progressive HR mangers can create compensation packages by combining many of these compensation alternatives to make them employee-friendly.

Recent studies reveal that pay should be tied to performance for organizational effectiveness. Of course, business performance cannot always be ensured by compensation. Successful managers must search and innovate to influence employees and their performances. Your organization may benefit from the tenure bonuses for long-time employees, equipment repair incentives to encourage good equipment maintenance, or bonuses for arriving at work on time. Levels of employee motivation, need satisfaction, and employee retention are directly linked with designing and practising compensation packages. Exhibit 12.1 describes the worth of a compensation package. Exhibit 12.2 shows the ideal aims of the compensation policy. In order to design the policy, an organization must formulate both primary and secondary objectives.

Exhibit 12.1 Worth of a compensation package

Compensation packages need to be designed for multiple purposes:

1. A good compensation package motivates the employees to contribute more to the organization, and thereby to increase the organizational productivity.
2. Compensation helps in running an organization effectively and accomplishing its goals. When a company needs and advertises for experienced persons, prospective applicants consider compensation packages prior to changing organization.
3. Salary alone cannot satisfy employees. Salary is just an element of the compensation system, the employees have other psychological and self-actualization needs to fulfil. Thus, compensation serves the purpose.
4. The most competitive compensation will help the organization to attract and retain the best talent. Other organizations cannot poach talented employees from an organization having an exemplary compensation system. The compensation package should be as per industry standards.

Exhibit 12.2 Compensation policy

Similar to the quality policy, environment policy, safety policy, and administrative policy, an organization should also have a compensation policy. Organizations must develop a compensation policy statement. The aim of compensation policy statement is to set down the policy of company with regard to salary. It is the responsibility of all concerned to implement the compensation policies and to explain the same fully to their subordinates. The compensation policy should aim for the following:

1. Recognize the value or worth of all jobs in relation to each other within the company
2. Keep track and take account of wage rates paid by companies of similar size, product, and philosophy
3. Ensure stable earnings
4. Enable individuals to reach their full earning potential to the extent practicable
5. Ensure employees' share in the company's prosperity as a result of increasing efficiency

Primary Compensation Objectives

The primary objectives of compensation or wages are classified under four broad categories—equity, efficiency, macro-economic stability, and optimum allocation of labour.

Primary objectives of compensation are equity, efficiency, macro-economic stability, and optimum allocation of labour.

Equity

The first category is equity, and may take several forms. Equity includes income distribution through narrowing down of inequalities, increasing the wages of the lowest paid employees, protecting real wages, and the concept of equal pay for work of equal value. Compensation management strives for internal and external equity. Internal equity requires that pay should be related to the relative worth of a job such that similar pay is assured for similar jobs.

External equity refers to making comparable payments, that is, paying workers what other firms in the labour market pay comparable workers. Compensation differentials, based on differences in skills or contribution, are all related to the concept of equity. Internal equity actually means employees and their contribution are treated fairly with a pay programme in relation to other jobs in the organization.

Efficiency

Efficiency is often closely related to equity. These two concepts are not adverse. The objectives of efficiency are evidenced in attempts to link a part of wages to productivity or profit, group or individual performance, acquisition and application of skills, and so on. Preparations to achieve efficiency are also seen as being equitable, provided they fairly reward performance. The preparations are treated as inequitable if the reward is viewed as unfair.

Macro-economic Stability

Companies try to achieve macro-economic stability through high employment levels. Low inflation helps to achieve macro-economic stability. For instance, an inordinately minimum wage would have an adverse impact on the levels of employment, though at what level this consequence would occur is a matter of debate. Although compensation and compensation policies are two of the many factors which influence macro-economic stability, they do contribute to or hinder balanced and sustainable economic development.

When employees move from declining to growth industries, an efficient allocation of labour due to structural changes takes place.

Efficient Allocation of Labour

Employees consider the net gain. Efficient allocation of labour refers to the concept of labour/employee moving out of a situation to another for a net gain. Such movement may be from one geographical location to another, from one job to another, and within or outside an enterprise. The provision or availability of financial incentives causes such movement.

For example, workers are likely to move from a labour surplus or low-wage area to a high-wage area. On acquiring new skills, they may be tempted to derive benefit from moving to jobs with higher wages. Employee attrition is more when an employer's wages are below market rates. Again, an employer attracts job applicants when his wages are above market rates. When employees move from declining to growth industries, an efficient allocation of labour due to structural changes takes place. Figure 12.3 illustrates the primary compensation objectives.

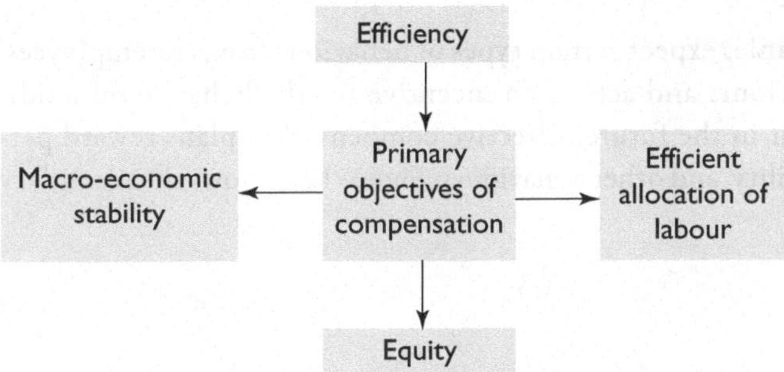

FIG. 12.3 Primary compensation objectives

Secondary Objectives of Compensation

From the standpoint of human resource management, a well-designed compensation package helps an organization to achieve additional objectives which are the secondary objectives of compensation. The secondary objectives include acquiring competent personnel, complying with regulations, controlling costs, enhancing administrative efficiency, facilitating understanding, retaining employees, and rewarding desired behaviour.

Acquiring competent personnel Good compensation helps an organization attract competent applicants. As everyone has become aware of their value in the market, it is only wise for the management to provide suitable compensation packages to the employees for their retention.

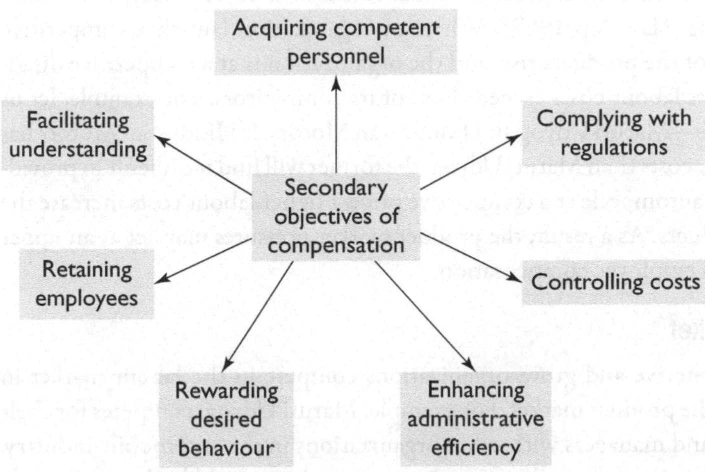

FIG. 12.4 Secondary compensation objectives

Complying with regulations A sound wage and salary system considers the legal challenges imposed by the government and ensures the employer's compliance.

Controlling costs A rational compensation system helps the organization obtain and retain workers at a reasonable cost. Without effective compensation management, workers might be over-paid (when product costs go up) or under-paid (which reduces employee motivation).

Enhancing administrative efficiency Any organization desires and attempts to optimally use the human resource information systems (HRIS). A well-designed sound wage and salary programme helps to manage HRIS efficiently.

Facilitating understanding The compensation management system should have a high level of clarity. In addition to the human resource specialists and operating managers, the employees also should understand the compensation management system easily.

Retaining employees Attrition may increase when compensation levels do not fulfil employees' expectations. They quit due to the feeling that compensation is not competitive.

Rewarding desired behaviour Companies expect certain types of behaviour from the employees. Pay is likely to reinforce desired behaviours and acts as an incentive for the behavioural modification, and for the behaviour to occur in the future. Effective compensation plans reward performance, loyalty, experience, responsibility, and other behaviours. Figure 12.4 shows the secondary compensation objectives.

DETERMINANTS OF COMPENSATION

> As compensation determinants, education, experience, performance, and other individual differences play dominant roles. In addition, product market and labour market play a crucial role in pay determination.

In the field of compensation determinants, the question that is most commonly encountered by the compensation designers is that of the factors that account for individual differences in pay within organizations. A broad literature suggests that education, experience, performance, and other individual differences play dominant roles. In addition, the product market and labour market play a crucial role in pay determination. Pay levels of labour market and product market competitors play an important role in determining pay levels.

Let us try to understand how both markets affect designing of appropriate compensation packages.

Product Market

Competitors in the product market are always instrumental in designing competitive compensation packages. It is also argued that product market competition places an upper boundary on pay level because organizations in a particular industry, 'encounter similar constraints of technology, raw materials, product demand, and pricing' (Dunlop 1957). When an organization launches competitive compensation packages, the price of the products rise, and the organization is at a competitive disadvantage in the product market if its labour costs exceed those of its competitors. For example, let us consider two vehicle manufacturers—Maruti Udyog and Hindustan Motors. If Hindustan Motors has higher labour costs than Maruti Udyog, the former will find it difficult in providing a quality automobile at a competitive price. Higher labour costs increase the costs of products. As a result, the product market pressures may act as an upper boundary on employee compensation.

> Product market pressures may act as an upper boundary on employee compensation.

Labour Market

> Labour market competition can be seen as placing a lower boundary on pay level.

In order to survive and grow, organizations compete in the labour market in addition to the product market. For example, Maruti Udyog, competes for their technicians and managers with other organizations in the automobile industry. A pay level that is too low relative to these competitors could lead to difficulties in attracting and retaining sufficient number of quality employees. As such, labour market competition can be seen as placing a lower boundary on pay level. In order to avoid such a situation, many companies emphasize that their total compensation is equal to or better than other companies in the market.

TYPES OF COMPENSATION

Two types of compensation, direct and indirect, are provided to employees. Direct compensations are in the form of monetary benefits and indirect compensations are in the form of non-monetary benefits generally termed as perks or perquisites, time off, etc. Compensation does not include only salary but it is the sum total of all rewards and allowances provided to the employees in return for their services. If the compensation offered is effectively managed, it contributes to employee satisfaction and high organizational productivity.

1. Direct compensation includes pay in the form of salary, wages, incentives, commissions, and bonuses.
2. Indirect compensation encompasses financial payments such as medical insurances, travel insurances, and so forth.

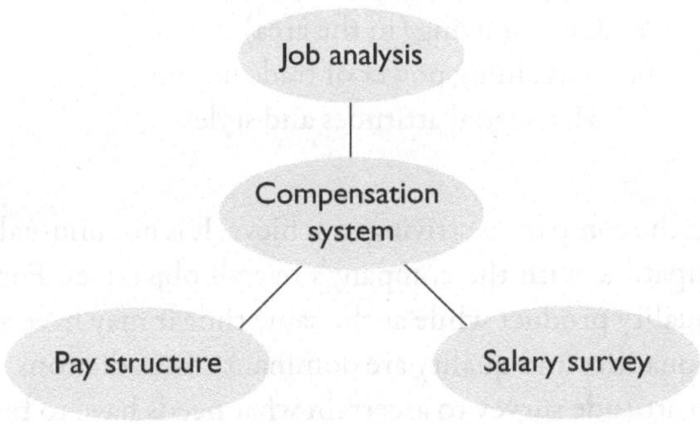

FIG. 12.5 Components of compensation system

COMPONENTS OF COMPENSATION SYSTEM

Compensation systems are designed keeping in mind the strategic goals and business objectives, and on the basis of certain factors after analysing the job work and responsibilities. Components of a compensation system are (a) job analysis, (b) pay structure, and (c) salary survey. Figure 12.5 illustrates these components.

COMPENSATION ISSUES

The main problem faced by any organization is the designing of a fair and equitable compensation system. The objective is simple, but the process is complex. For instance, the employer will be concerned primarily with productivity. The employee's emphasis may be on higher compensation to offset their increased cost of living. An employee may perhaps like to equate the price that his skill will fetch in a competitive job market. Discussions on compensation issues are likely to continue in future that will centre on questions of compensation levels and compensation structures. Obviously, this will raise questions concerning the level of compensation rates in the plant or firm, industry, region, nation, or crossing the boundary of the country. The broad question of the determinants of compensation relationships is also related to this to this issue.

A decision about compensation rates in a given situation must be reconciled with a variety of considerations such as when pay rates should be revised and by how much, how they should be distributed among the different employees, and what departments should be covered. Many industrial disputes stem from wage and salary administration. Several conflicts between employers and unions are generated from disputes over wages and salaries than other diversified matters. Quantum of take-home pay is a major consideration while formulating a pay package. Take-home pay is the net packet that an employee receives after all deductions. Some of these deductions are savings for post-retirement leisure life, general or contributory provident fund, pension schemes, etc.

The balance between what is received now and what he will get on retirement is something that varies from one organization to another. Employees generally require a higher pay in earlier years of employment. In the normal course, he/she needs to spendfor children's education, medical treatment, and recreation. However, at later years, an employee will need to provide for his old age, in terms of a house, and a steady income to maintain his habituated life style.

Another issue related to the context is salary and tax planning. In this context, organizations are seen to take recourse to fringe benefits, some of which are taxable. The incidence of tax, either on money incomes or on the total taxable income including perquisites, has to be worked out.

DETERMINANTS OF COMPENSATION STRUCTURE

We have studied job evaluation, manpower planning, recruitment and selection in Chapter 6. A sound compensation structure must be based on job evaluation programme in order to establish fair differential in payments depending upon differences in job contents. While designing compensation structure, basic factors provided in job description and job evaluation are primarily considered. In addition, the following factors are taken into consideration:

1. Organization's ability to pay
2. Supply and demand for labour (in the area)
3. Prevailing market rate
4. Cost of living (in the area)
5. Productivity
6. Bargaining power of trade unions
7. Job requirements
8. Managerial attitudes and styles
9. Psychological and sociological factors

The compensation structure must be linked to what the company is striving to achieve. It is not unusual to find a company with a wage structure not compatible with the company's overall objectives. For example, a company may plan to produce a high quality product while at the same time it may have a direct incentive geared to quantity. We know that quantity and quality are dominant contradictions.

It would be wiser for a company to conduct an attitude survey to ascertain what needs have to be satisfied through a compensation structure. What are the employees' attitudes towards the current pay structure and what are their deeper expectations? The pay structure, to a large extent, determines and reinforces attitudes. Two of the areas a survey ought to highlight are the reasons why employees work for a particular company, and what motivates them. An attitude survey helps to unearth the level of satisfaction. Compensation structure can only be successful if the compensation system is administered in line with achieving the goals. Refer to Exhibit 12.3.

Exhibit 12.3 Compensation package of NHPC

National Hydroelectric Power Corporation (NHPC) offers one of the best pay packages in the industry. A trainee engineer/officer, on successful completion of the training period, is placed as an engineer/officer in the pay scale of ₹10,750–₹16,750 (IDA) (E-2A) with a probation period of one year. Medical officer and assistant Hindi officer will also placed with probation period of one year in their respective pay scales. Besides basic pay, candidates will also be paid industrial dearness allowance. Other allowances and benefits such as house rent allowance, conveyance reimbursement, leave travel concession, leave encashment, gratuity, employee provident fund, group insurance, employees' pension, medical reimbursement, children education assistance, newspaper/magazine allowance, and special compensatory allowance etc will be admissible as per company rules in force from time to time. The pay scales are due for revision with effect from 1 January 2007.

Source: www.nhpc.co.in

COMPENSATION ADMINISTRATION

The primary purpose of compensation administration is to assure the management of a sound compensation system for its employees. The objectives of a sound compensation administration programme are classified into specific sub-goals.

1. Ensuring equitable payments in proportion to relative work to the organization
2. Providing uniform payments between comparable occupations
3. Reviewing and adjusting payments in relation to changes in the labour market
4. Recognizing individual capability and proficiency
5. Establishing procedures to solve compensation problems rationally

Principles of Compensation Administration

Compensation administration is guided by certain principles. Beach (1975) propounded seven principles of compensation administration.

1. Different jobs need different types of skills, effort, responsibility and working conditions. An enterprise should have a clear-cut plan to determine differential pay level in terms of divergent job requirements.
2. An enterprise should attempt to keep the general level of wages and salaries of the enterprise in line with that prevailing in the labour market or industry.
3. People and jobs should never be mingled. Adequate care should be taken to distinguish people from the jobs.
4. The compensation system should be designed with objectivity. Irrespective of individual considerations, care should be taken to ensure equal pay for equal work, depending upon the flexibility of jobs. However, variations may be permitted within a pay range.
5. There should be a plan to implement equitable measure for recognizing individual differences in ability and contribution.
6. Attempt should be made to establish some procedure for handling wage grievances.
7. Adequate care should be taken to inform the employees and the union, if any, about the procedure followed in determining wage rates.

Perceptions of employees about compensation play a vital role in attracting capable employees to the organization. Employees must perceive if the compensation offer is fair and equitable. In order to ensure equity, an enterprise should establish consistent and systematic relationship among base compensation rates for all jobs within the organization. The process of such establishment is termed 'job evaluation'.

Similar to compensation administration, compensation formulation also depends on certain principles.

Principles of Compensation Formulation

The main factors which affect wage or compensation levels of an organization are external relativities, salary relativities, and individual worth.

1. External relativities comprise market rates as affected by supply, demand, and general movements in pay levels.
2. Salary relativities between jobs within the organization depend on the values attached to different jobs.
3. Individual worth refers to the value of the individual's performance to the organization.

COMPENSATION SURVEY

Compensation survey should essentially be undertaken while designing or reviewing a compensation system. A compensation survey is a process of collecting data and facts about compensation policies, practices, and programmes of companies in some labour market. It provides information that is used by many organizations. This information is particularly relevant to the problem of establishing and adjusting salary levels. It may also be used to validate the compensation structure. The objectives of compensation survey vary from one organization to another. Before conducting a compensation survey, an organization should study the compensation data already available within the organization. If such information is not available, a company may either conduct its own survey or participate with other organizations in a cooperative effort for benefit of both the organizations. Employees of different companies are discussing about the compensation system in their companies. It is wiser to design a comparable system. That is why data on compensation should preferably be collected from local companies in the area, whatever be the nature of the organization.

In addition to direct salary, the data should include key jobs and their comparisons, information on benefits, bonuses, and other methods of compensation. If these data are not considered, the total compensation package will have loopholes. It is also useful to collect information on the characteristic of the surveyed organizations to ascertain the similarity with the organizations for the compensation being developed. In either case, great care must be given to compensation survey procedures.

Compensation survey is a complex procedure which must be meticulously undertaken. Carrying out this survey is an expensive and time-consuming process. Hence, employers need to thoroughly examine the existing compensation survey from secondary sources before planning to conduct one of their own. In case any of availability of any standard survey, employers should consider a number of factors before using them. Some of the factors are

1. Does the survey report provide information to suit the organization's needs?
2. If a single survey does not meet an employer's needs, several surveys need reference to gather the information needed.
3. How representative are the surveyed organizations? Can the organization make pay comparisons?
4. Does the existing survey provide detailed job descriptions to permit detailed comparison with the jobs in the organization developing compensation system?

Personal interview is the most reliable method of conducting a compensation survey. The other two methods are mail questionnaires and telephone interviews. Of course, personal interview is time consuming as well as expensive. Compensation administrators need to gather useful and necessary information concerning industry pay structures and practices. As such, they are using compensation survey serves as a valuable tool.

> Three basic methods of conducting a compensation survey are personal interviews, mail questionnaires, and telephone interviews.

Castrol India compensates its employees by way of a deferred cash bonus scheme. It is one of the long-term incentives offered by the company. Under this scheme, managers could get as high as 50 per cent of annual basic salary (approximately 15 per cent of the individual cost of company) as grant of leave travel insurance. Castrol India is compensating only those employees who have completed three years of service. If the business performance exceeds certain targets, employees could get as high as 150 per cent of the grant (approximately 22 per cent of cost to company for superior performers) as leave travel insurance payouts.

Organizations design compensation system to suit their organizational needs. Thus, individual organizations may have differences in their compensation system based on factors best suited to their perceived organizational needs. However, from close analysis, some general compensation trends are evident, as given in Exhibit 12.4.

Exhibit 12.4 General compensation trends

1. Allowances are linked to the salary as a percentage of the basic payment or by slabs, though preference continues for flat amounts. In the slab system, allowances do not increase automatically.
2. In the fast changing business scenario, compensation systems are generally reviewed annually, and sometimes at closer periodicity.
3. The basic or consolidated salary continues to be the major component of compensation system.
4. Benefits comprise mostly unfurnished company-owned or leased accommodation, use of company-owned or leased vehicle, medical coverage, retirement benefits covering provident fund, pension or superannuation or gratuity, post retirement medical assistance, and easy loan schemes at subsidized or no interest rates for house building.
5. Compensation is somewhat tailor-made for experts or key contributors to the organizations to prevent attrition in the very volatile job market.
6. Emphasis on variable performance pay or bonus as a reward is increasingly becoming important and popular, and is emerging as a growing component of the compensation system.
7. Employee stock option plan (ESOP) has gained popularity in IT industry. ESOP is not yet used extensively due to their comparatively lesser share values, especially in the well-established older companies. Retirement benefits are important to many; but the younger generation and specially, information technology professionals, do not consider it as an advantage. As mobility of information technology professionals is more, they look for the benefits if available to them on moving to a new job.
8. Few payments are made annually such as bonus or commission, and leave travel concession. These are common features of compensation.
9. Reimbursements of expenses incurred on company work will become limited, and in line to conform to the prevailing tax laws. As reimbursements are the actual expenditure incurred, they will not be considered as part of the compensation. However, any reimbursement may be treated as compensation provided that is towards personal benefits.

There are certain salient features of employee compensation in India, which can be highlighted from corporate practices. Some of the practices are given in Box 12.1.

Box 12.1 Corporate practices on compensation

1. Existence of substantial difference in gross compensation for managers and their junior colleagues.
2. Dissimilarity in gross compensation and in compensation structure are often practised between the project and support functions.
3. There is selective design of personalized salaries from a basket of options for top management levels.
4. There has been a significant increase in basic salary, and hence in deferred benefits.
5. Companies have restricted non-tax perks in the form of reimbursement under various heads to certain top levels of management.
6. Differential higher annual increments and average increments vary from 50 per cent to 100 per cent, for different levels of management provided by companies.
7. A significant shift in the incentives system from the individual-based incentives to the group/team incentives. Incentives, such as performance incentive, commission, performance payment, and performance bonus, are not always individual-specific. They are usually team or level-based. Individual-based cash incentives are declining.

(Contd)

Box 12.1 (Contd)

8. A soft furnishing allowance is being provided towards the purchase of curtains, carpets, cutlery, and crockery, and this is usually paid as an annual, non-taxable allowance.
9. Abolition of components, by most companies, such as servants' wages and utilities allowances, as they are no more non-taxable any longer.
10. There is a lot of scope for variations in the area of conveyance. This category includes practices with regard to provision of car, driver, and reimbursement of expenses on car, parking, cleaning, petrol, and maintenance.
11. The practice of providing company-owned cars to employees is declining. Instead, the company encourages employees to buy the cars themselves through hire-purchase schemes, and the installments are then paid by the company. This system relieves companies from the problem of accumulation of used cars.
12. The common practice is to sanction loans to buy two-wheelers and four-wheelers. Interest rates may vary, with the repayment period generally varying from three to five years.
13. Companies have tie-ups with insurance companies and hospitals to extend medical benefits to employees. Companies organize annual medical check-ups for all employees. In some companies, though rare, hospital expenses are also entirely reimbursed by the company, based on grade or age-level slabs.
14. Some companies encourage and assist employees in their higher education by sponsoring evening classes or providing sabbaticals at the cost of the company. Interest-free loans up to ₹0.3 million are sometimes extended to employees.
15. Companies are reimbursing expenditures towards books, periodicals, newspapers, journals, etc., against a pre-determined limit. Subscriptions to professional bodies are also reimbursed.
16. An attractive perk for senior management is reimbursement of the one-time joining fee for one club plus the monthly or annual subscription to one or more clubs. Now a day companies also go for bulk corporate club memberships.
17. Housing loan or interest subsidy is also provided.
18. Soft loans are approved for purchase of furniture, appliances, and computers are also extended to employees by some organization.
19. Many corporate bodies reimburse travel expenses for holidays including accommodation in guesthouses and transit flats. Corporate bodies are now extending this facility to cover holidays abroad for senior management personnel and their families. In most cases, this is used as a discretionary reward for exemplary performances rather than as a perk.
20. There is a trend of providing pre-employment benefits for attracting talent, including coverage of all relocation expenses for the family, transport of personal goods, assistance in locating housing, schooling, etc.
21. Several compensation components such as long-term paternity or maternity leave, as well as part and flexi-time employment options, working from home, are also available.
22. The trend has shifted to making components direct and taxable. There is a distinct shift towards schemes for asset creation.
23. Under profit-sharing schemes, senior executives sometimes share accrued profits when the company earns profits beyond a certain fixed level. The average share is 20 to 25 per cent of the excess profit.
24. Companies also provide employee stock options (ESOP) to employees.

COMPENSATION PRACTICES IN INDIA

It is worthwhile to go through the findings of salary surveys in India for successive years which confirm that employee compensation is still not being considered as a major strategic issue, regardless of its cost and added value aspects. Mercer/Hewitt Associates release compensation survey reports periodically. Some of the parameters organizations generally considered, while designing compensation, are internal equity, industry trend, retention, organizational performance (usually in terms of profits), market conditions, employees' performance, and finally market positioning.

Annexures 12.1 and 12.2 illustrate the trends in employee compensation practices in India using some sample employment contracts (restricted only to the compensation part). Both the examples are drawn from corporate practices. However, in reality, it may vary. While calculating cost-to-company (CTC), we find wide variation in corporate practices.

The elements of the salary, with regard to CTC, normally include basic pay, house rent allowance (HRA), contributory city allowance (CCA), other allowances (mobile reimbursement, medical reimbursement, PF contribution, and ESI contribution), any fixed portion of compensation (usually paid as ex-gratia), food coupons, holiday package, furnishing items, etc. Thus, CTC can be defined as the annual total cost of compensation to the company, which employees may not get in hand.

FAULTS IN COMPENSATION DESIGN

While designing compensation packages, three common mistakes generally occur:

1. Failure of the organizations to distinguish between a bonus and an incentive. An incentive is linked with some measurable outcomes. Nevertheless, in India, we make payment of bonuses to meet statutory requirements and avoid labour unrest. The Indian Railways, Ordnance Factories, Post and Telegraph departments pay productivity-linked bonuses. In compensation management literature, we view bonus as a price for the best efforts, which contributes to organization outcomes. It is more productivity-linked and performance-driven. Bonus is never based on individual performance; it is the collective output of all the employees. Hence, including bonus as compensation component encourages employees to expect it as a right.
2. Organizations often attempt to solve compensation claims on an adhoc basis. The second mistake in compensation design occurs due to this inclination of organizations. Moreover, organizations create an imbalance in internal pay equity when they try to compromise with their talent by overpaying. Thus, it is better for the organization to adopt a strategic approach, while designing compensation for their employees.
3. The equity compensation plans should be simple without any ambiguity. Additional mistakes are likely to occur if the compensation design is complicated.

While planning compensation, adequate care must be taken to avoid the faults described here.

COMPENSATION PLAN

A compensation plan is explained considering the perspectives of organizational compensation. From both statutory and strategic perspectives, each component of a compensation plan has different connotations and implications. The plan optimizes the cost of compensation and simultaneously helps the organization achieve its strategic objective.

The definition of compensation extends to the amount of benefits accrued in a deferred benefit plan. The definition further extends to incorporate the amount of contributions allocated to accounts for a deferred contribution plan. A well-designed compensation plan helps ensure equity within the organization. Any compensation plan has two important statutory implications (a) qualified compensation plans and (b) non-qualified compensation plans.

> From a strategic perspective, a compensation plan should emphasize and promote employee retention, ensure cost efficiency, and promote a performance-driven culture.

Qualified compensation plans are tax-exempt and non-qualified compensation plans attract tax burdens. Hence, even while designing deferment or rearrangement, the organization must look into these aspects. Similarly, from a strategic perspective, a compensation plan should emphasize and promote employee retention, ensure cost efficiency, and make sure a performance-driven culture. The best way to set up compensation plans is to tie them directly to the costs of running the company.

SIGNIFICANCE OF EMPLOYEE COMPENSATION

Obviously, to any employee, pay is the most important reason for working to earn livelihood. For some individuals, it may be the only reason. For most of us, it is the means by which we provide for our own and our family's needs.

Compensation represents a large proportion of the expenditure. In manufacturing firms, it is seldom lower than 20 per cent; in service enterprises, it is often as high as 80 per cent (www.eridlc.com). More importantly, organizations try to accomplish many goals with compensation. These goals include attracting and retaining people, and motivating them to perform more effectively to achieve business goals. Compensation is also significant in the operation of the economy. Salaries and wages are the largest contributing factors to the national income of many countries in the world and India is not an exception.

As a large proportion of expenditure is incurred under compensation, you must know the compensation domain, which we have already discussed.

There are certain other ways of attracting employees. Creative compensation (Exhibit 12.5) is one such method and it is important to carefully plan the same.

Exhibit 12.5 Creative compensation

With regard to employee compensation, most managers remain busy in asking juniors, 'What is your expectation?' Answering this question is not easy. A better approach might be, 'We are reviewing employee compensation packages. What do you think should be your compensation package?' Compensation packages can be versatile. It is a matter of realization of employees. Organizing a party with family members at the end of a busy business season lets the employees and their families know that the company appreciates contribution of employees. The images and the value of each employee are enhanced to family members. If you give a long service award on employment anniversaries, the self-esteem of employees is enhanced.

(Contd)

Exhibit 12.5 (Contd)

At the same time, the company gives a signal that it recognizes continuing commitment of employees. Employees realize that the company values the employees. Education allowances take away the worries of needy families. Companies can demonstrate that it values the family by extending child care and health benefits. The examples are matters of realization. Whatever the compensation elements, each element carries a message. If the messages create a positive impact, you are successful. If the creative compensation package developed by one organization is found to be highly successful, and if it is imitated by another organization, it might not be successful.

Creative compensations are designed considering the intrinsic need, the geographic location, the industry to it belongs, the organizational culture and climate, and so forth. Creative compensation packages are organization-specific. Compensation packages can be linked to business structure, employee recruitment, retention, motivation, performance, feedback, and satisfaction. While changing organizations, potential employees duly consider the compensation package. Creative compensation packages can attract creative people from the job market.

DIRECT COMPENSATION

Wages are direct compensation; paying wages is obligatory, and hence, is a standard practice in organizations. Competitive advantage can only come by paying a higher amount. There are many alternatives to direct compensation:

Incentive pay A bonus paid on meeting specified performance objectives which are likely to inspire employees to set and achieve a higher performance level and is an excellent motivator to accomplish company goals.

Stock options A right to buy a part of the business which may be given to an employee to reward an excellent contribution to the company. An employee, who owns a share of the business, is far more likely to go an extra mile getting this indirect compensation.

Bonuses A gift given periodically or occasionally to reward exceptional performance or in special occasions. Giving bonuses show that an employer appreciates his/her employees and ensures that good performance or special events are rewarded so that employees repeat the performance. Some indirect compensation elements are required by law, such as, social security, and unemployment and disability payments. Other indirect elements are up to the employer and can offer excellent ways to provide benefits to the employees and the employer as well. For example, a working mother may take a lower-paying job with flexible hours or work from home. These facilities allow the employee to be home when her children get home from school.

Small businesses can gain competitive advantage by providing creative compensation alternatives that they can afford.

In a competitive business scenario and scarce labour market, indirect compensation becomes increasingly important. Businesses that cannot compete with high cash wages can offer very individualized alternatives that meet the intrinsic needs of the people you want to employ. Small businesses can gain competitive advantage by providing such creative compensation alternatives which they can afford.

INDIRECT COMPENSATION

Some items are categorized as part of indirect compensation. A short list is provided for reference.

1. Clothing
2. Cellular phones/pagers
3. Child care
4. Company parties
5. Farm produce/foods/meals
6. Flexible working schedules

7. Insurance (health, dental, eye)
8. Laundry service
9. Magazine and newspaper subscriptions
10. Travel expenses
11. Old age care
12. Paid leave (sick/holiday/personal days)
13. Retirement programs
14. Subsidized housing
15. Subsidized utilities
16. Tickets to events (ball games, concerts, and other recreational events)
17. Use of farm pastures and gardens
18. Use of farm trucks and machinery

PAY EQUITY

Companies pay incentives to workers. Obviously, pay differentials become sufficiently large. These differentials are often misinterpreted. In such cases, perceived inequity in pay structures may result in detrimental effects such as turnover, grievances, and decreased motivation to perform. Organizations may also face a conflict between the goals of internal consistency and external competitiveness. Out of these two goals, organizations need to focus greater attention on external competitiveness. (Lawler 1986) Internal focus encourages employees to compare themselves with others within the organization and results in competition within the organization. Internal focus further results in employees focusing on promotions rather than performing well. The internal focus retards the need and preparation of competitions with other organizations. There is some belief that conflicts between external and internal equity and may be resolved by increasing the pay scales of all jobs, irrespective of their competition in the labour market.

Various steps for creating pay equity are enumerated here.

Step 1: Categorize employees by job. Compensation system will be cumbersome and difficult to administer if you focus on too many jobs at a time. Fewer jobs are better.

Step 2: Collect data of the labour market and compare pay levels of your company with them. There are many compensation survey reports available.

Step 3: Manage internal equity carefully as it is crucial and more important than external equity. Dissimilar internal equity causes more dissatisfaction.

Step 4: Link pay with job performance. Employees performing better should obviously receive larger salary increases than those who do not.

Step 5: Explain the working of the compensation system to everyone.

In order to get an idea of appropriate pay levels, companies often conduct formal or informal surveys of their competitors. This survey report helps them achieve external pay equity by comparing the probable differences that may exist among similar operations in a particular labour market. While developing a compensation plan, external considerations lay emphasis on labour market conditions, cost of living, and economic factors.

COMPENSATION BENCHMARKING

Benchmarking is a process of determining the very best who sets the standard, and what that standard is. It is an exercise involved in the identification of the best practices in the industry and to emulate them. The practice of benchmarking enables an organization to accelerate its rate of improvement. Benchmarking promotes a thorough understanding of company's own processes. Thus, the company's profile is well understood. In order to retain key employees, good organizations always practice compensation benchmarking. Unnecessary attrition enhances human resource costs due to the expenses involved in replacing manpower, and also badly affects the organizational brand image. If the compensation package is less than the market trend, then attrition is likely to be more, and the reason is attributable to less-than-competitive pay. Refer to Exhibit 12.6.

Exhibit 12.6 Compensation benchmarking—Xerox Corporation experience

In the United States, Xerox Corporation adopted a compensation benchmarking process comprising four phases—planning, analysis, integration, and action. In each phase action there were action items that needed to be accomplished.

The planning phase

1. What are the issues required to be addressed that would be benchmarked?
2. Which company should be benchmarked?
3. How will the data be collected?

The analysis phase—analysing the choices made about the companies.

1. Are the benchmarked companies better?
2. If so, in which parameter and by how much?
3. Why are they better?
4. How can we apply the lessons learnt to our business?

The integration phase—integrates decisions taken in planning and analysis phases.

1. Have the results been accepted by management?
2. Do goals have to be changed or modified based on the benchmarking results?
3. Have these new goals been communicated to all affected parties?

The action phase

1. Have the steps required to achieve the desired goals been identified?
2. Have the steps been implemented?
3. Is progress being tracked?
4. Is there a plan for recalibration of the benchmarks?

The first two phases, planning and analysis phases, were identified by Xerox Corporation as the most important phases in the benchmarking process. They need to be carried out with utmost care to have a greater chance of success in the next two implementation phases and make the benchmarking more effective.

Source: Singh (1996)

BROADBAND PAY PLANNING

Companies often need to restructure the pay into fewer, but wider, pay grades. This is done to establish and use much fewer but broader bands with relatively wide salary ranges consolidating a large number of pay grades and salary ranges. Broad banding is a process of reviewing and restructuring pay structures into fewer but broader bands for administrative ease and effectiveness. These ranges may typically have wider differences between minimum and maximum.

Broad banded pay plan simplifies the classification of positions, increases the emphasis on market-based pay, and promotes competency-based human resource systems including compensation. This plan also provides the flexibility for the adoption of other job components and employee-based pay components. The plan is finalized by combining different grades of pay. Thereafter, employees are fitted to a particular pay level based on their performance criteria.

COMPENSATION AND VIE THEORY

Vroom (1964) formulated the VIE (valence, instrumentality, expectancy) theory in the context of compensation. Valence is the indicator of value, instrumentality refers to the belief that if one does something, it will lead to a consequence, and expectancy is the probability that the action or effort will lead to an outcome. The compensation system encompasses incentive or bonus schemes. The schemes work if and only if the link between effort and reward is clear to the employees. Furthermore, the value of the reward should be worth of the effort put by the employees. In line with the VIE concept, Porter and Lawler (1968) developed a model and suggested that two factors determine the effort that people put into their jobs.

1. The value of the rewards to individual employees needs to satisfy their needs for security, social esteem, autonomy, and self-actualization.
2. The probability that rewards depend on effort and this is perceived by individual employees. Additionally, they have some expectations about the relationships between effort and reward.

The influencers of motivation and performance are the following:

1. The perceived link between effort and performance
2. The perceived link between performance and outcome
3. The significance (valence) of the outcome to the person

Efforts (motivation) depend on the likelihood that rewards will follow the efforts and that the reward is worthwhile. The key emphasis of the VIE theory is that there must be a link between the effort and reward; the reward should be achievable, and should be worthwhile to develop continuance commitment.

An organization can take various steps for enhancing welfare of the employees and improvement of the organization. However, to make the steps successful, ethics emerge as an indispensable issue.

ETHICS IN COMPENSATION

A profession is an 'open declaration or avowal of a belief or opinion' (Webster's dictionary). Professions are distinct from simple collections of people engaged in performing similar types of work. A profession or professional behaviour refers to a high degree of specialized knowledge, expertise, social responsibility, self-management, and self-monitoring of high ethical behaviours through a code of ethics. For members of a profession, 'ethical standards are central to understanding what constitute proper conduct as well as expectations of virtues professionals should possess' (Gellerman et al 1990). Ethics is the science (study) of morality. Ethical behaviour defines what is right or good. It is often called moral philosophy. It emanates from the value theory. Other aspects of ethics are aesthetics, metaphysics, epistemology, and logic.

In any organization, compensation management practices need to be ethical. As many organizations align their incentives and variable pay components with performances, both at the individual and organizational level, it is often seen that organizations try to manage their performance metrics without considering ethical issues. While it may be imperative for organizations to optimize compensation cost to remain competitive in the market, resorting to such practices is considered unethical. Even world-class organizations face this dilemma.

For instance, Wal-Mart often faces this dilemma. In order to deal with this problem, organizations are now adopting separate codes of conduct for compensation management practices. At the outset, building a value-based organizational culture is the foundation of compensation ethics. Organizational values permeate workplace practices, letting people share such values in their day-to-day performances. Ethical organizations care about their people and even go beyond statutory limits when paying compensation and benefits. For example, in India, Tata Steel pays compensation and benefits beyond the statutory limits. Government organizations also are following ethical practices and developing codes. Developing and using an organizational code is worthwhile. Contextually, DeGeorge (1987) emphasizes, 'The very exercise of developing a code is in itself worthwhile; it forces a large number of people...to think through in a fresh way their mission and the important obligations they as a group and as individuals have with respect to society as a whole'.

BASES FOR ETHICS IN COMPENSATION

The vision of an organization encapsulates its values, which are ultimately translated into the long-term goals of the organization. Vision essentially guides the behaviour of the employees working in the organization; and shapes and moulds the style of interactions. Vision helps formulating the organization's current purpose, or mission. Vision and mission conjointly influence the routine and other decision-making and practices of the people working with the organization. Therefore, for every organization, core compensation ethics emerge from its vision and mission. Organizations must have documented vision statements. Ethics in compensation also depend on the actions taken and choices of the significant people of the organization. Organizations may choose to be proactive in their human resource management practices, or reactive and traditional. With proactive choices, organizations become ethical in managing people issues, as well as compensation. On the contrary, reactive practices focus on individuals acting in a self-defined direction, and ethical issues are often violated.

Ethics in compensation also need to be aligned with the strategic choices of the organization. Strategic choices may differ from employee to employee, primarily on hierarchical level, performance criteria, the nature of the job, and the type of skill sets. Many Indian organizations, particularly in the information technology sector, indulge in discriminatory compensation practices that lead to labour unrest, increased attrition, and ultimately to the jeopardy of the organization.

If the organization embraces ethics in the compensation system in the form of a structured code of conduct, it will inevitably ensure certain positive changes in the behaviour of its employees. Tata has documented and published 'Code of Conduct'. More about ethics will be discussed in Chapter 22. Some of the distinct behavioural modifications are as follows:

1. Work-related behaviour, decision-making style, managerial styles, and interpersonal interactions reflecting ethical values.
2. Organizational decisions based on values and ethics will help make people to develop and be more cooperative.
3. Compensation and rewards will become more structured and free from bias.
4. Organizational goals get aligned with ethical practices.
5. Regular performance feedback to people will facilitate continuous development.
6. Human resources practices become more congruent with values.

Ethics in compensation facilitates ensuring that the work environment is free from all forms of harassment, intimidation, or coercion; and ultimately improves the quality of work life. From mass media, we have evidenced that serious charges were framed against few global companies such as Citigroup and Merrill Lynch for unethical compensation practices. The CEOs of both these companies had to quit because of a drop in business, but both received huge accumulated benefits (even without their severance pay). Obviously, unethical compensation payouts, especially disproportionately large payouts to senior executives, have now become common in many organizations.

Many organizations are now setting up their own ethics committees to monitor compliance with the prescribed ethics in the day-to-day activities of the organization. The monitoring group systematically conducts ethics audits, ethics training, and even sets up ethics hotlines to ensure that employees follow the ethics and values of the organization.

JOB EVALUATION SYSTEM

Job evaluation is a method used to describe, analyse, compare, and evaluate jobs within a unit, a branch, or an industry on the basis of the work content and the job requirements in order to place them under particular wage or salary grades. Various facets of job evaluation have been discussed in Chapter 6. It is a systematic attempt which provides the basis for comparing jobs and determines the relevant worth of different jobs in an organization. It has two basic objectives: (a) to compare jobs and determine their level within each occupational group, and (b) to compare jobs between occupational groups.

A number of specific goals may be derived from the basic objectives:

1. Providing a basis for more objective and rational wage structure
2. Correcting wage inequities, resulting from personal acquaintance, bargaining pressures, change, customs, and so forth
3. Providing the means for the ranking of new and changing jobs
4. Reducing pay dissatisfactions by providing procedures for appeals and forgrievance and their redressal
5. Presenting basic information to facilitate wage negotiations and wage determination

Job evaluation approaches are probably the most prevalent methods ofestablishing base pay. Similar to the usefulness of any management system, their worth depends on how well they achieve their objectives. Nevertheless, they have a role to play in the administration of compensation. It can provide, at least, an internally justifiable wage structure for organizations.

Hay Job Evaluation System

Many corporates and organizations use Hay job evaluation methodology to map their job roles in the context of the structure on their organizations. A job is a daily activity which the workforce performs in exchange for payment or wages. The time taken to perform jobs varies widely depending on the work content involved, complexity, and type of machines used. A person trained for a certain type of job takes lesser time in comparison to an untrained person. The general purpose for carrying out job evaluations using Hay system is that it enables the organizations to map or plan all their roles in a manner that delivers the certain key benefits some of which are

1. Recognizing equivalent levels for the purposes of salary and benefit grading/pay banding
2. Improving succession planning
3. Creating more useful and focused job descriptions

Application of the Hay methodology to a role results in the generation of two profiles which are called long profiles and short profiles. The long profile offers a view on aspects of the role and the score. The short profile refers to a broadbased approach of grouping of job types that would fit the profile. As such, the short profile acts as a check on the long profile.

Job evaluations using Hay system are carried out in a number of steps within an organization.

Delegates from main operational departments and from HR functions are selected. They are trained on the use of the method. The training curriculum includes practical exercises where participants (a group of people) are required to evaluate some trainer-provided job specifications. In case of customized training, particular company specifications of some real jobs from their own company are drawn.

All the job descriptions in the company are revised under the guidance of the HR personnel. The system calls for a single standard. In case of non-existence of such a standard, it must be established. Data are captured in a particular form enabling the job board to analyse the roles more easily.

Job boards—The leader of the job evaluation initiative allocates the trained personnel into job boards of about four people in a small group. They are given reporting lines (related jobs) and each member is required to rate the jobs as they see them prior to being presented before the board. At the job board, the group members discuss the final scoring; examine the differences and agree on a short and long profile for each role. Initially, the task can take a long session to rate jobs. However, as the members work together, they become more productive.

The HR personnel works with senior management to put together a suggestion for banding or grading staff wherein the benefits that will be attracted by each band are described.

Board review is essentially done after rating all the jobs, and after the completion of organizational mapping. The company board or any equivalent committee reviews the summary, the banding proposals, and the associated cost, if any. On approval of the banding proposals, the overall project manager initiates implementation.

LEGAL CONSIDERATIONS IN COMPENSATION

The following are the legal considerations involved in deciding the compensation structure:

1. Designing and administering compensation need certain legal considerations, such as, acts relating to framework for remuneration of the top management of Indian companies
2. Conformance to minimum pay
3. Maximum hours
4. Overtime pay
5. Child labour protection
6. Ensuring equal pay for men and women doing the same work
7. Unemployment compensation for workers

The Acts that must be taken into account for compensation system design are as follows:

1. The Payment of Wages Act, 1936—This Act emphasizes timely payment of wages and deductions from wages and fines.
2. The Minimum Wages Act, 1948—This Act aims to extend the concept of social justice to the workmen employed in certain scheduled employments by statutorily providing minimum rates of wages.
3. The Payment of Bonus Act, 1965—The object of this Act is to maintain peace and harmony between labour and capital by allowing the employees to share in the prosperity of the establishment reflected by the profits earned by the contributions made by capital, management, and labour.
4. The Equal Remuneration Act, 1976—The object of this Act is to provide for the equal remuneration to men and women workers and for the prevention of discrimination, on ground of sex, against women in the matter of employment. This Act further seeks to provide increasing opportunities for women in the specified employments.

REWARDS

In the context of compensation, the term 'reward' is generally applied at the managerial levels. Reward systems and their role in organizations have been studied from many perspectives and by multiple disciplines. Economists, sociologists, and psychologists, in particular, have contributed to the growing literature on reward system. Reward systems, like compensation system, have a wide-ranging impact on organizations, and their impact is greatly affected by their design and by the organizational context in which they operate.

Thus, to understand reward systems in organizations, it is necessary to focus on the characteristics of both the organizations and the pay system. Often, new lines of businesses require a different approach, and therefore, a different reward system. Simply put, the old reward system in the new business sphere is often not good enough, and indeed, can lead to failure. On the other hand, developing a new reward system for one part of an organization can cause problems in other parts because of comparisons made between different parts.

Reward management is about the development, implementation, maintenance, communication, and evaluation of reward processes. A substantial literature review focuses on the relationship between reward systems and the degree to which participative management is practised in the organization. If an organization encourages participative management, it needs to change all its systems, including its rewards system. It stands established that effective participative management demands a different approach to pay for performance.

It is also seen that the correct approach is to pay bonuses based on group-wise or plant-wise performance. The argument for this essentially rests on the point that traditional pay plan supports individual excellence at the cost of team performance. However, modern approach emphasizes working in teams and using collective wisdom. Team performance needs to be rewarded for success of participative management. Reward system practices are changing as they keep pace with participative management. For example, gain sharing has become increasingly popular in the last two decades, and skill-based pay plans have replaced job-based plans in many manufacturing organizations practicing participative management.

Reward system influences the attraction and retention of employees. Organizations that given the most rewards are seen to be successful and attract and retain the most people (Lawler 1971). These obviously occur because high reward levels lead to high satisfaction, which, in turn, leads to lower turnover and create more job applicants. The best performers of an organization are generally prone to leave the organization for better prospects and rewards. Of course, if the continuance commitment of any performer is more, he is unlikely to leave. To prevent or reduce possibility of attrition, a reward system must work on a par with those received by individuals performing similar jobs at a similar level in the same or other organizations. The emphasis here is on external comparisons because turnover refers to leaving an organization for a better position at some other organization. Reward systems have been demonstrated to motivate performance. However, the extent of motivation depends on the situation and how it is perceived. One vital matter must be considered. Rewarding and motivating employees may be a cause of demotivation to others. Rewards should be given based on an objective evaluation of performances. One way to accomplish this is to reward everyone at a level that is above the reward levels in other organizations. The connection between performance and rewards must be visible. A climate of trust and credibility enhances the visibility in an organization.

> High reward levels lead to high satisfaction, which, in turn, leads to lower turnover and creates more job applicants.

Marchetti (1999) observed compensation and reward to have a major impact on the motivation and performance of the salespeople, and opined that while rewriting the pay plan for the sales force, management must bear in mind four principles—know your goals, stick to the basics, get from involved line managers, and communicate the facts to the sales force.

PSYCHOLOGICAL BASIS OF REWARDS

Expectancy refers to the subjective probability of an outcome. Expectancy theory provides the basis of reward system. When a student feels that through devotion and by working hard there is a good chance (high subjective outcome) of getting the top position, and an offer of attractive salary package in the placement interview, he works hard. The psychological basis of rewards is the 'expectancy theory'.

Expectancy explains the subjective probability of efforts resulting in the outcome (the first level outcome). Instrumentality is a related concept. When the first level outcome is seen as leading to a second level outcome, the instrumentality is said to be high. A production manager may feel that strenuous efforts on his part may lead to higher production (high expectancy), and that higher production beyond scheduled target will result in getting a reward (high instrumentality).

> Expectancy theory provides the basis of the reward system. Instrumentality is a concept related to the reward system. Valence means the strength of an individual's preference of a particular outcome.

Work motivation is a result of high expectancy, high instrumentality, and high attraction and magnetism of the second level outcome (a reward). If any one of the three factors is zero, the resulting motivation is zero. Valence is term related to motivation and reward system. Valence means the strength of an individual's preference of a particular outcome.

AIMS OF EMPLOYEE REWARDS IN INDIA

The aims of employee rewards in India vary widely from one organization to the other. The presence of business priorities is the main reason for the variation . Keeping in view the organizational requirements, the overall aims of employee rewards are as follows:

1. Contributing to added value
2. Contributing to competitive advantage
3. Managing compensation and reward
4. Integrating individual employees' aims with the compensation and reward systems in the organization
5. Optimizing employee costs

The prime aim of employee rewards in India is to help attaining organizational, strategic, and short-term objectives. Attainment of these objectives helps to ensure the availability of skilled, competent, committed, and self-motivated people. Objectively- designed employee reward systems focus on the improvement of individual employees. It further facilitates in developing a team. As a result of the process, organizational performance improves, and organizations are better-equipped in value creation, thus achieving a competitive advantage. Added value is the difference between the incomes arising out of sales (organizational output) and the amount spent on materials and other inputs. Of all the resources that utilize other resources, only the human resources can make certain sustainable value additions because of its inimitable character.

People at various hierarchical levels, create visions and values, translate them into missions, set goals and objectives, develop strategies, and plan action plans. All these actions add value to organizations.

Efforts to enhance added value, through effectively designed employee reward system, benefit the organization by way of promoting a culture of mutual trust, openness, collaborative efforts and teamwork, and in turn, high performance.

It stands established that innovation, quality, and cost effectiveness are the three pillars and essential prerequisites of added value from employees. As organizational citizens, people can construct the pillars and ensure added value through their performances. People need something in return for their contribution. Organizational reward strategies are linked with performance results and integrated with overall goals and objectives through effective performance management systems. Effective employee rewards motivate people and keep them satisfied, which ultimately improves performances. It is not always true to view rewards as the only way to reinforce performance improvement though many organizations consider so. There are many examples of corporate failures despite the higher level of employee rewards. While deciding on a reward, generally the industry average is considered. Consider the following example. Bata India was offering high rewards to motivate employee. The rewards were much higher than the industry average. However, the company failed to improve its performance, and was ultimately forced to scale down its manufacturing facilities and start outsourcing to ensure cost efficiency.

> Innovation, quality, and cost effectiveness are the three pillars and essential prerequisites of value addition for employees.

PURPOSE OF REWARD SYSTEMS

One cannot advance in life unless one dreams big. In the organizational context, the outcomes are collectively achieved. The only way employees will fulfil your dream is to share the dream with them. Reward systems are the mechanisms that make this happen. However, reward systems go beyond bonuses, bonus plans, and stock options. They can also include awards and other recognition, promotions, reassignment, non-monetary bonuses (like vacations), or a simple thank-you. As Steve Jobs said, 'The journey is the reward'.

SKILLS AND REWARDS

As employee gains skills, his/her performance increases, and this, in turn, enables him/her to fetch rewards. Learning specific skills and valued rewards are linked to each other. The linkage has to be visible to all employees. Just as reward systems motivate performance, they can motivate the learning of skills and the development of knowledge. Climates of some organizations encourage learning and skill development. In such organizations, employees perceive that they must develop their skills in order to perform effectively. Pay for performance systems work well. Sometimes, pay for performance systems may dishearten individuals from learning new skills or motivate them to learn the wrong skills. This is likely to happen when the skills that should be learned are not directly related to present assignments and, hence, performance. The reward systems in hierarchical organizations act as a strong motivator and employees learn those skills that are perceived to lead to promotion. To counter this tendency, some organizations are using skill-based pay when they want individuals to add new skills that do not involve promotions.

> Reward system may influence the degree to which culture is seen as an HR-oriented, entrepreneurial, innovative competence-based, and participative culture.

Reward systems also contribute to the overall culture and climate of an organization. Depending on the methodology of developing, administering, and managing the reward systems, the cultures of organizations vary quite widely. For example, the reward system may influence the degree to which it seen as a human resources-oriented culture, an entrepreneurial culture, an innovative culture, a competence-based culture, and a participative culture.

Reward systems are often a significant cost factor in organizations. Indeed, the pay system alone represents about 40 per cent of an organization's operating cost. Pay systems involve direct pay and benefit costs, as well as the costs associated with managing and operating the system.

REWARD SYSTEM—A DEFINITION

The reward system of an organization is a tool of recognizing talent. Reward system includes 'group incentive plan' which means giving bonuses to workers in a team. The group incentive schemes are designed to promote teamwork, encourage synergy, and making the team work effectively. The performance and output of the team as a whole determine the rewards to be given to the team.

TOTAL REWARDS—THE MEANING

Total rewards emphasize collection of all the tools available to the employer that may be used to attract, advance, develop, motivate, and retain employees. Total rewards include everything the employee perceives to be of value resulting from the employment relationship. Organizational history is replete with examples where employers have been challenged with attracting, motivating, and retaining employees. From the simplest barter systems of the ancient past to the complex incentive formulas of today's competitive business scenario, the organizational premise has been the same. Offer your productivity and results to our enterprise and we will provide you with 'something of value' that is a 'total reward'.

ELEMENTS OF TOTAL REWARDS

Total rewards embrace five elements which are both financial and non-financial in nature. Each of the elements includes programmes (curriculum), practices, elements and dimensions that collectively define an organization's strategy to attract, motivate, and retain employees. These elements are the following:

1. Compensation
2. Benefits
3. Work-life
4. Performance and recognition
5. Development and career opportunities

Organizations decide on elements to create value, and align a value proposition to both the organization and the employee. The total rewards strategy, if effective, results in satisfaction, employee engagement, and productive employees, who, in turn, create desired business performance and results.

Compensation As discussed earlier, compensation is the pay provided by an employer to an employee for services rendered (time, effort, and skill). Compensation comprises four core elements—fixed pay, variable pay, short-term incentive pay, and long-term incentive pay.

Benefits Benefits are programmes or actions that an employer uses to supplement the cash compensation given to employees. These programs are designed to protect the employee and his/her family from financial risks, and can be categorized into the following three elements—social insurance, group insurance, and pay for time not worked. Table 12.1 illustrates these elements.

Table 12.1 Employee benefits

Social insurance	Group insurance	
1. Unemployment 2. Workers' compensation 3. Social security 4. Disability (occupational)	1. Medical 3. Vision 5. Mental health 7. AD&D insurance 9. Retirement	2. Dental 4. Prescription drug 6. Life insurance 8. Disability 10. Savings
Pay for time not worked These programmes are designed to protect the employee's income flow when not actively engaged at work. 1. At work (breaks, clean-up time, uniform changing time) 2. Away from work (vacation, company holidays, personal days)		

WORK–LIFE BALANCE

Employees of an organization must perform the organizational role and at the same time, pursue a happy family life. They need to achieve success at both work and home. A specific set of organizational practices, policies, programmes, and a defined sound philosophy actively supports efforts to help employees to achieve both the goals. Organizations can extend support for work-life effectiveness in the workplace. The support can be classified into seven categories. These categories encompass compensation, benefits, and other HR programmes. The seven categories encompass the key aspects of the workers, their families, the community and the workplace.

The seven major categories are the following:

1. Workplace flexibility
2. Paid and unpaid time off
3. Health and well-being
4. Caring for dependents
5. Financial support
6. Community involvement
7. Management involvement/culture change interventions

Employees must maintain work-life balance and yet perform for the organization.

PERFORMANCE AND RECOGNITION

Rewards are given to recognize exemplary performance beyond the scheduled assignments, when employees perform the assignments in a cost-effective manner, or develop a newer way to complete faster without compromising with the qualitative requirements. Performance concerns the behaviours directed toward achieving the organization's missions and business goals, and manufacturing the products or services resulting from those behaviours. It refers to only those behaviours related to production of goods or services maintaining the qualitative requirements. Performance differs from effectiveness, which generally involves making judgements about the adequacy of behaviour with respect to certain criteria such as work group or organizational goal (Hughes, et al. 2008).

Performance

Performance involves the alignment of organizational, team, and individual effort toward the achievement of business goals and organizational success. Performance planning, performance, and performance feedback are all essential for organizational success.

Performance is the manner of demonstrating skills or capacities to achieve the assigned tasks. Performance planning is a process whereby organizational expectations are established and organizational goals are linked with individuals and team efforts. Adequate care needs to be taken to ensure that goals at all levels are aligned to achieve the organizational objectives and strategies set at the highest levels of the organization.

Performance feedback is a mechanism to communicate to the employees how well people do a job or task compared to expectations, performance standards, and goals. Feedback should comprise both quantitative and qualitative aspects of the assignments. Performance feedback can motivate employees to improve performance.

Recognition

Recognition is a strong tool of motivating people. Acknowledgements or giving special attention to employee actions, efforts, behaviour, or performance meet an intrinsic psychological employee needs. Acknowledgements reinforce certain behaviours (like more devotion, extraordinary accomplishments) that contribute to organizational success. Whether formal or informal, recognition programmes acknowledge employee contributions after the fact. Immediate recognition impacts more. Awards can be monetary or non- monetary (verbal recognition, trophies, certificates, plaques, dinners, tickets, etc.). Organizations recognize and reward exemplary performances on versatile fields as you will see in the exhibit at the end of this chapter.

The values of recognition are manifold as follows:

1. Reinforce the urge of performance improvement.
2. Foster continual improvement.
3. Modify behavioural disposition.
4. Improve work environment and restore positive culture.
5. Foster communication of valued behaviour and attitudes.

Development and Career Opportunities

Workers of an organization need all round development—technical, general, moral, and other types of development. Organizations should carefully attempt to develop the inner potential of the workforce. HRD efforts, mainly career opportunities, for workers are essential to help them to lead a productive life. A person needs developmental supervision. They need development and career opportunities.

Development Opportunities

A set of learning experiences must be designed to enhance skills and competencies of employees. Development facilitates employees to perform better. They should be able to lead a productive life. In order to help them, you have to provide them with certain information. Some of the information you should share with employees is as follows:

1. Make them aware of the available resources.
2. Let them know the business environment.
3. Make them aware of the company's strategy.
4. Recognize the achievements of the worker in all possible ways.
5. Identify the occupational competencies that an employee should possess.
6. Develop the occupational competencies using HRD mechanisms.

7. Develop self-management skills.
8. Help them to broaden their inner potential.
9. Develop psychological contracts, and social and cultural bonds.

Career Opportunities

Career denotes all the jobs that are held in the working life of a person. An employee looks for career goals which represent the future positions that he may occupy. Career planning is the process of selecting career goals and the path to achieve the career goals. Employees need career opportunities and career counseling as a process of advising employees on setting career goals and assisting them find suitable career paths. A responsible person of an organization can be career counselor. The organization supports career opportunities internally so that talented employees are deployed in positions that enable them to deliver their greatest value to their organization. Development and career opportunities include the following—learning opportunities, coaching and mentoring, and advancement opportunities.

Learning opportunities Any employee needs self-growth and advancements. An organization may extend facilities to extend

1. Sponsoring to attend course programmes to corporate universities
2. Providing training on new technology
3. Allowing attending external seminars, conferences, virtual education, etc.
4. Self-development tools and techniques
5. Conducting opportunities of on the job learning; rotational assignments at a progressively higher level
6. Approving sabbaticals with the express purpose of acquiring specific skills, knowledge, or experience.

Coaching/mentoring The purposing of coaching is to gain expertise to perform work roles effectively, and that of mentoring is to gain confidence and capacity of technically leading a work group in the workplace. Employees need

1. Leadership training
2. Access to experts/information networks—association memberships, attendance and/or presentation at conferences outside one's area of expertise
3. Exposure to organizational experts
4. Formal or informal mentoring programs, inside or outside the organization

Advancement opportunities Apart from learning opportunities and availing coaching and mentoring facilities, employees further need

1. Internships
2. Apprenticeships with experts
3. Overseas assignments (having knowledge of managing cross-cultural issues)
4. Internal job postings
5. Job advancement or promotion
6. Career ladders and pathways
7. Succession planning, providing defined and respectable 'on and off ramps' throughout the career life cycle

INTEGRATED TOTAL REWARDS STRATEGY

An integrated total rewards strategy encompasses and emphasizes the culture, organizational environment, approach to attract people, line of action to retain them, and keeps them motivated.

Role of Culture

The culture of organization refers to the collective attitudes and behaviours that influence behavioural disposition of employees. Culture determines how and why a company operates the way it does. Typically, culture comprises a set of often unstated expectations, behavioural norms, and performance standards to which the organization has become accustomed. Changing culture calls for changing attitudes and behaviours by altering their fundamental beliefs and values. Hence, a changing culture is difficult to achieve. Organizational culture is subject to internal and external influences; thus, culture is depicted as a contextual element of the total rewards model, overlapping within and outside the organization (Schein 1990).

Role of Environment

Environment refers to the total collection of observable physical, psychological, and behavioural elements in the workplace. Work environment or organizational climate is the tangible manifestation of organizational culture. Any new recruit should be accustomed to the environment prevailing in the workplace. They may react to the environment either consciously or unconsciously. Environment is directly observable and often measurable, and specific elements of the environment can be deliberately manipulated or changed. The external environment in which an organization operates is likely to influence the internal environment. Obviously, the environment is portrayed as a contextual element of the total rewards. The external environment also overlaps within and outside the organization.

Need for Talent Attraction

Organizations need to fulfil the manpower needs either through internal promotions or recruitment from external sources. When an organization needs experienced persons in a requisite area, it advertises the requirement in mass media. Attracting manpower refers to the ability of an organization to draw the right kind of talent to achieve organizational success. Attraction of an adequate and everlasting supply of qualified talent is essential for the organization's survival. Acquiring and retaining qualified talent is the key plank of a business strategy. The organization can obviously use AIDA (attention, interest, desire, action) model in the advertisement to fill the vacancy. The AIDA model has been discussed in Chapter 6 of this book. A deliberate strategy to attract the quantity and quality of employees needed to drive organizational success is one of the key success factors of business strategy.

> Integrated total rewards strategy encompasses and emphasizes the culture, organizational environment, approach to attract people, line of action to retain them, and keeping them motivated

Need to Retain Talent

An organization should initially identify its valued contributors to achieve the business objectives. Thereafter, the organization needs to adopt ways and means to retain them in the organization for its overall success. Total rewards package can be well-utilized to promote retention and keeping them in the organization. However, it is desirablethat the organization must develop a formal retention strategy with appropriate steps.

Motivating the Talent

Human relations encompass the important reactions of people to one another in the society, club, organization, or anywhere else. The relations among individuals, between individuals and groups, and between groups constitute a critical phase of industrial psychology. Motivation cuts across all topics in industrial psychology. Employee motivation and attitudes to an event may vary from being positive or negative. Motivation is the ability to cause employees to behave in a way that achieves the highest performance levels. Motivation is classified as intrinsic motivation and extrinsic motivation.

Intrinsic motivation relates to work content and is linked to factors that include an employee's sense of achievement, respect for the whole person, trust, and appropriate advancement opportunities. Intrinsic motivation consistently results in higher performance levels.

Extrinsic motivation is most frequently associated with rewards that are tangible and given for doing an activity. Extrinsic motivation relates to work context.

Satisfaction, commitment, and engagement are the three defined levels of intensity with regard to motivation.

1. Satisfaction—how much you like your job, nature of duty, colleagues, communication, supervision, etc.
2. Commitment—how long you want to continue here.
3. Engagement—how much you are involved with the assignments entrusted and you will actually do to improve business results.

REWARD SYSTEMS IN THE 21ST CENTURY

In view of the complex business scenario, acute competition, globalization, and other factors, the compensation system is rapidly changing.

Pressed forward by competitive forces, organizations are laying far more emphasis on variable compensation. The use of incentive pay to motivate performance (individual, team, and company-wide) continues to grow and become more sophisticated. Many companies are moving to broad-based ownership designing creative compensations. The design of sales, management, executive, and board of director's compensation plans are becoming more innovative. Organizations are in spree to design and launch creative compensation packages. Fundamental transformations are occurring in aligning rewards with organizational change. Moreover, computer and communication technologies have radically altered the compensation landscape.

PERFORMANCE-BASED REWARDS

Many organizations have developed a system of linking rewards with performance. Some performance-linked reward schemes are (a) schemes based on individual performance (IPW), (b) schemes for performing the whole job, (c) schemes based on small group performance (GPW), and (d) schemes based on productivity (PLB) of the whole organization.

Schemes based on individual performance In the production department, employees are paid based on piece work rate. The industrial engineering department, based on time study, is recording the observed time. Then, it is multiplied by the factor. Thereafter, considering fatigue allowance and other permissible allowances, the standard time is calculated.

Schemes for performing whole job The whole job is first is split into elements. The, the time for each element is calculated. This is followed by summing the time for each element and the total time of the whole job is calculated.

Schemes based on small group performance Maintenance jobs cannot be generally done individually as they necessitate collective efforts. Maintenance department assigns a task to a group of mechanics. The group is paid for the jobs they do. This system is also termed as 'gang piece work'. In such departments, the activities of persons cannot be separated.

Schemes based on productivity In this scheme, a base year is fixed. Organizations consider the production of number of years, find the average, and ultimately decide on the base year. Then, the organization calculates the ratio of production in the current year and the base year. Bonus is calculated considering productivity in both base year and the current year.

In addition to the schemes discussed here, there exist schemes based on productivity bargaining, and employee stock option plan (ESOP).

DESIGNING THE REWARD SYSTEM

Rewards are symbols of recognition. It is primary importance for an organization to decide on what it must reinforce through rewards. Organizations generally like to reinforce performance, effort, process, credibility, teambuilding, loyalty (retention), sincerity, punctuality, etc., as employees need clear communication about the parameters that the organization is interested for. Employees should preferably be involved in such decision-making process.

Extrinsic and intrinsic rewards are the two broad types of rewards. Extrinsic rewards can be monetary and non-monetary. Examples of extrinsic rewards are bonuses, paid holidays, flexible work hours. Intrinsic rewards include empowerment, providing more responsibilities, more freedom in the workplace, allowing using discretion, assigning interesting and challenging tasks, diversity of activities, opportunities for personal growth, and so forth. Examples of monetary rewards are performance bonus, profit sharing, stocks, etc. Non-monetary rewards include holidays, gifts, facilities, and so forth. At present, organizations prefer employees to work in teams to enable collective wisdom. So, it is necessary to reward both individuals and teams.

As already discussed, an organization should first develop consensus involving organizational citizens. Consensus is needed on values, norms, and behaviour that an organization wants to reinforce. In other words, the effort is directed to creating or changing the organizational culture. The significant points that need consideration while designing reward system are as follows:

1. Employee representatives should be involved in reward design.
2. Rewards should be given to both individuals and teams.
3. Multi-dimensional and wider reward system reduces possibility of attrition.
4. Variable components of compensation may be part of the reward system.
5. Rewards should be so designed that they enhance organization belonging.
6. Lumpsum rewards are liked more by employees than extra increments.
7. Rewards design must consider the findings of annual or half-yearly survey done by the HRD department.
8. Employees must be informed about the factor that is emphasized in the reward system.
9. Organization may think of raising funds for rewards, like 'reward corpus' from managers' wage bill.

10. Transparency and fairness should be ensured in the reward system.
11. Basis of selecting persons for the rewards should be objective.
12. Persons selected to receive the reward should be communicated to all employees.

Reward Design—Role of the Internet

Compensation is partly an economic concept; compensation decisions are made considering a number of environmental and organizational variables. It is important to consider how unions view the compensation packages and wage structure. During collective bargaining, they give examples of similar, local, and other companies. Social environment impacts the compensation decisions. Members of a society possess ideas about the worth of different jobs, and these ideas need to be taken into account. Subsequent to the entry of women into the workforce, the social environment has been changing dramatically. This change is compelling to value the diversity while taking compensation decisions.

The dynamics of a particular organization affect compensation decisions. Employee's pay must be consistent within the organization's structure. The organizational culture helps determine the priority to be given to various compensation goals. The organization's workforce characteristics influence the success of different compensation programmes.

Furthermore, compensation decisions are affected by the worldwide information highway. Internet facilitates collection of data relating to compensation and benefits. Availability of this information produces a significant impact on the compensation design. One can expect severe communication conflicts relating to competitive practices.

E-mail, chat boards, and dotcom companies attract visitors to their site by giving employees compensation data. Larger organizations are now administering their stock, salary, and incentive plans on a worldwide basis through the internet. Smaller organizations will also gain by this capability over time. The internet is about to give benefit and compensation administration a new identity.

DETERMINING THE CASH WAGE

If you interrogate 10 different people about fair wage, you will get 10 different answers. While there are no hard and fast rules in determining a fair wage, the importance of the task is obvious. Academic research findings indicate that employees expect wages to (a) cover basic living expenses, (b) keep up with inflation, (c) provide some funds for savings or recreation, and (d) increase of overtime. Collecting employee views about wage expectations can help determine what their compensation package should look like.

> In case of existence of internal and external inequity, employees with begin to balance their performance through a variety of ways ranging from decreased productivity to absenteeism, and eventually to leaving the business.

A compensation package should be fair. While developing a package, the first aspect that employers should consider is fairness. It is absolutely vital for businesses to maintain internal and external equity. (Internal equity and external equity have been discussed earlier in this chapter). No matter what the compensation level, if either internal or external equity is violated, a business will most likely experience employee dissatisfaction. In case of such imbalances, employees will begin to balance their performance through a variety of ways ranging from decreased productivity to absenteeism, and eventually to leaving the business.

It is difficult to constitute a fair wage. Even if it is constituted, ascertaining the fairness emerges as the next difficult task. One good approach to determine fair wage is a direct market survey. These are typically fast and easy ways to establish compensation guidelines for many businesses. Skills required for some professions and sectors such as agricultural sector are difficult to gather. However, operating a forklift or battery truck in a shop floor, an overhead crane in a factory, and driving a tractor may require similar skills and, therefore, can be compensated similarly.

Broad banding was used in a Cornell University study. Five competency levels were developed to classify employees according to three criteria—authority to make decisions, skill level, and supervisory capacity. By using a competency scale, each employee can be cross-referenced by title and competency level or studied solely within either category. Employees of similar skill levels or competency are taken together in compensation 'bands', regardless of job title. These bands then compensate similar employees at related rates across the entire organization, and serve to maintain both internal and external equity.

FRINGE BENEFITS

There must be certain principles to govern the use of fringe benefits and managing them.

1. Employees need protection and promotion of their well-being. Benefits and service must be provided to meet both the needs. The management should never feel that the fringes are thrust upon them. Rather, they should have a genuine interest in protecting and promoting the workers' well being.
2. Any benefit that interests the employees need to be used. If any benefit is not liked, employees continue to remain indifferent to that. In fact, the benefit must satisfy a real need.
3. The benefits must be cost-effective.
4. The benefits should be as broad-based to the extent possible.
5. Sound planning is essential prior to administering the benefits.
6. Employee sentiments must be honoured considering their aspirations expressed through the representatives of their unions. In addition, the bargaining power of the union must be considered.
7. Employees should be educated and developed to make use of the benefits.

REWARD SYSTEM IN INDIA

Processes, practices, structure, schemes, and procedures are the five components of the reward system. The components (Figure 12.6) are briefed here.

Processes This component facilitates measurement of the value of jobs and the worth of individuals in those jobs. Processes further guide to evaluate the range and level of employee benefits to be provided. Job evaluation, market rate analyses, and performance management system are the processes.

Practices Organizations motivate people by the use of financial and non-financial rewards. The financial rewards consist of basic and variable pay, employee benefits, and allowances. Organizational culture and values, managerial and leadership styles, work assignments, opportunities to develop skills, prospects of career growth, etc. are some of the non-financial rewards used by organizations.

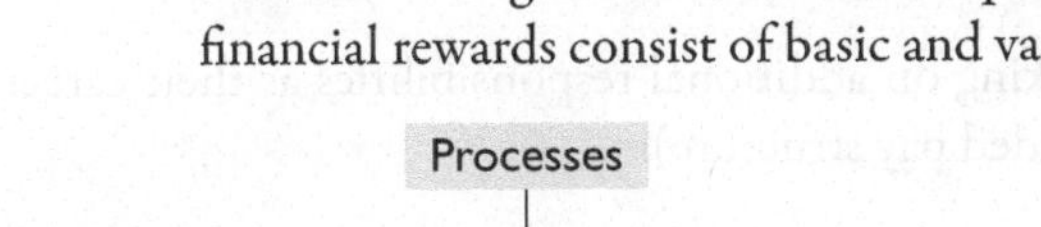

FIG. 12.6 Reward system in India

Structure These are used to link pay and benefit levels to the value of positions in the organization. Structure further provides the scope for rewarding people based on their performances, competence, skills, or experiences.

Schemes These are methods to provide financial rewards and incentives to people according to individual, group, or organizational performance.

Procedures These are modus operandi used to maintain the system and to ensure that the same operates efficiently and flexibly and provides value for money.

ELEMENTS OF EMPLOYEE REWARDS IN INDIA

The base or basic pay is the level of pay, the fixed salary or wage, which constitutes the rate for the job. The basic pay acts as a datum for determining additional payments related to performance, competence, or skills. It may also govern pension entitlement and life insurance. Base pay may be expressed as an annual, weekly, or hourly rate. It may be adjustable to reflect increase in the cost of living or market rates by the organization unilaterally, or by agreement with a trade union.

Additions to basic pay Additional financial rewards are provided and are related to performance, skill, competence, or experience. Special allowances may also be paid. The main types of additional pay are individual performance-related pay, bonus, incentives, commissions, etc.

Individual performance-related pay Increases in basic pay or cash bonuses are determined by performance assessment and ratings. Some organizations use the term merit pay.

Bonus It refers to rewards for successful performance, which are paid as cash and is related to the results obtained by individuals, teams, or the organization. Bonuses are linked to productivity for the whole organization.

Incentives These payments are linked with the achievement of previously set targets. Incentives are designed to motivate people to achieve higher levels of performance. The targets are usually quantified in such terms as output or sales.

Commissions It is a special form of incentive in which sales representatives are paid on the basis of a percentage of the sales value they generate.

Service-related pay It increases by fixed increments on a scale depending on service in the job. Sometimes, there may sometimes be scope for varying the rate of progress up the scale according to performance.

Skill-based pay This is also known as knowledge-based pay; it varies according to the level of skill the individual achieves.

Competence-related pay It varies according to the level of competence achieved by the individual.

Career development pay It rewards people for taking on additional responsibilities as their career develops laterally within a broad grade (a broad-banded pay structure).

Allowances Elements of pay in the form of a separate sum of money for aspects of employment such as overtime, shift work, or call-outs, etc.

Employee benefits These benefits are also known as indirect pay and include pension, sick pay, insurance cover, and company cars. Benefits comprise elements of remuneration in addition to the various forms of cash pay, and also include provisions for employees that are not strictly remuneration, such as annual holidays.

Total remuneration It is the value of all cash payments or total earnings and benefits received by employees.

Non-financial reward It includes any reward that focuses on the need that people have in varying degrees for achievement, recognition, responsibility, influence, and personal growth.

Employee stock options Stock options are common in executive compensation. By offering stock options to managerial employees, companies try retain their talent and move ahead of the competition. It is a significant component of compensation.

Please refer to Exhibit 12.7 for some reward-related practices being followed by organizations.

Exhibit 12.7 Reward practices in various organizations

Schneider Electric India offers various awards for promoting behaviour deemed as valuable to the organization's success. Some of the behaviours are

1. Cost consciousness—for conscious and optimum utilization of the resources provided
2. Time management—efficient and effective management of time
3. Workspace management—management of the workspace assigned
4. Responsiveness—the quality or state of being responsive
5. Customer satisfaction—giving good services in a pleasant manner and meeting the customers' expectations
6. Accessibility—easy to approach, reach, and speak with
7. Adaptability and flexibility—able to adjust oneself readily to different conditions or being responsive to change

Moser Baer, one of India's leading technology companies, has developed cutting-edge technologies to become the world's second largest manufacturer of optical media, and has been awarded for specifically promoting organizational values.

Moser Baer has a novel TIPS award that stands for their values. TIPS is the acronym for teamwork, integrity, passion, and speed.

The main objective of this award is to celebrate the spirit in upholding and role modeling. Moser Baer's values by rewarding those who consistently live out the core values of teamwork, integrity, passion, and speed in their day to day behaviour. The company gives the award once a quarter, across the organization.

Schneider Electric India offers an 'office etiquette' award for employees who best adhere to basic courtesy, and also to the code of conduct as defined in the HR policy of the company.

Crystal Phosphate is awarding employees who are most punctual, most energetic, and most methodical in the organization.

Hindustan Petroleum Corporation Limited (HPCL) is a Fortune 500 company and has instituted a safety award for accident-free operations for refineries.

Jindal Steel and Power Limited (JSPL) has a 'best safety man award' for serving as an exemplary employee in maintaining highest standard of safety. JSPL has also initiated a 'bravery and courage' award for recognizing those exhibiting outstanding bravery and courage deeds.

Tata Motors has a safety award for safe working throughout the year.

Source: SAIL (2009)

INCENTIVES

Incentives are monetary benefits paid to workmen to recognize their outstanding performances. Incentives are defined as 'variable rewards granted according to variations in the achievement of specific results.' The international labour office refers to incentives as 'payment by result'. However, it is also appropriate to call them 'incentive systems of payment emphasizing the need of motivation, which is, giving incentives to workers for higher production and productivity'. Unlike wages and salaries, which are relatively fixed, incentives generally vary from individual to individual, and period to period for the same individual. Now you need to be acquainted with the role of incentives. The term 'incentive' has been used both in the restricted sense of participation and in the widest sense of financial motivation. It is used to signify inducements offered to employees to put forth their best in order to maximize production results.

FEDERAL WAGE SYSTEM

The federal wage system (FWS) is a uniform pay-setting system that covers federal appropriated fund and non-appropriated fund for blue-collar employees who are paid by the hour. The system's goal is to make sure that federal trade, craft, and laboring employees within a local wage area who perform the same duties receive the same rate of pay. The FWS includes 132 appropriated fund and 125 non-appropriated fund local wage areas. Successful labour-management partnership is the hallmark of the FWS, and labor organizations are involved in all phases of administering the pay system.

Under this uniform pay system,

1. Your pay will be the same as the pay of other federal jobs like yours in your wage area.
2. Your pay will be in line with pay for private sector jobs like yours in your wage area.

ROLE OF INCENTIVES

Incentives recognize employee contributions with pay. Pay level and benefits influence the so-called membership behaviour. Employees take decisions about whether to join or remain in the company considering the pay level and benefits. On the contrary, incentives influence the behaviour and attitudes of current employees.

However, it is getting increasing recognition that individual pay programmes may also affect the nature and composition of an organization's workforce. In some organizations, the pay may remain delinked from performance. Organizations that have linked pay with performance are likely to attract performers or talents from those organizations where these two are not linked. The reason is that performers will get more pay in return for their contribution. There may be a similar effect with respect to job retention. Different pay systems are likely to attract people with different personality traits and values. Moreover, at present, many organizations believe in team performance. These organizations implement a system of rewarding teams to attract people inclined to and habituated to work in teams.

The implication is that the incentive programme design needs close coordination with the business strategy and also with the human resource strategy. Linking pay with performance has become a common practice in many organizations in India and abroad. Incentive programmes are unique and have critical areas for consideration.

INCENTIVE PROGRAMME

In most of the industries, the labour cost significantly contributes to the operation cost. Flexibility of labour cost is timely and relevant, and needs consideration. Multiple aspects of incentive design could effectively improve the flexibility of labour cost structure. The possibilities and limitations of flexibility need evaluation. Research on performance management effectiveness emphasizes that the most challenging areas for most of the organizations were the need to improve the ability to link organizational performance and incentive, and provide direct feedback to employees on individual performance. Incentive pay programs are also termed 'variable pay programs'

There are two critical questions that could improve the effectiveness of incentive programmes. These are (a) how can changes to the incentive programme design facilitate better line of sight to business performance and (b) what changes could help increase differentiation of incentive payouts by performance.

Linking organizational performance to incentives could be a function of two critical factors—(a) the use of organizational performance metrics in the design of incentive compensation and (b) effective ongoing communication of organizational performance to the employees. Box 12.2 provides examples of HR metrics in organizational performance.

Box 12.2 HR metrics in organizational performance

1. Turnover (number of employees who leave the organization)
2. Cost of turnover
3. Separation including voluntary turnover
4. Safety as evidenced through accident rates
5. Hiring cycle—the periodicity at which the company recruits
6. Select error—candidates actually selected though they should have not been selected. An error that happens due to use of wrong selection tools
7. Cost of employee training and development

INCENTIVE PROGRAMME COMPONENTS

Noe, et al. (2008) mentions an overview of the programmes for recognizing employee contribution. Each programme shares a focus on paying for performance. Based on three design features, four consequences, and two contingencies, the programmes differ. Apart from incentive pay, employee contributions can also be recognized by way of merit pay, profit sharing, ownership, gain sharing, and skill-based pay.

The three design features are payment method, frequency of payout, and performance measures.

The four consequences are performance motivation, attraction, culture, and costs.

The two contingencies are management style and type of work.

Incentives may be given in the form of bonus (payment method) payable weekly (frequency of payout), and based on individual output or productivity sales (performance measures). Incentives can generate a clear performance-reward connection (performance motivation), relying of the philosophy of 'pay higher-performer more' (attraction) creating competition among individuals (culture) who are obviously conforming to the set and maintained standards to reduce wastage (costs). Incentives should be under control (management style) for a stable individual and output of efforts is easily measurable (type of work).

Employees at all levels in the organizational hierarchy are motivated through incentives and rewards and the chief executive officers are not an exception.

CEO INCENTIVES

The economic downturn and global financial crisis have focused new attention on long-term incentives or executive compensation schemes. The main purpose behind this is to align the interests of owners and the executives. Research findings suggest that a long-term compensation structure could be better and effective from the standpoint of company's future rather than the common practice of providing short-term incentives or rewards. Alex Edmans, finance professor at Wharton, and a group of colleagues propose linking an executive's compensation to the performance of the firm over a longer horizon. Their method also takes into account changing conditions within the firm.

In a working paper titled, 'Dynamic Incentive Accounts,' Edmans, along with Xavier Gabaix and Tomasz Sadzik of New York University, and Yuliy Sannikov of Princeton University, outline a system that escrows compensation for a given period of years stretching into the executive's retirement. The longer time frame is designed to prevent the executive from taking short-term actions that may enrich the manager at the expense of the firm's future profits. The plan reduces the probability of attrition and also provides a rebalancing mechanism to maintain a constant percentage of compensation in cash and stock. In this system, the executive always has sufficient equity in the firm to provide performance incentives, even if the stock price falls.

At present, linking compensation to the share price is viewed as a way to make sure the interests of the CEO and other senior managers are aligned with those of shareholders. In recent years, however, the system has encouraged executives to take actions that boost share price in the short term. Placing incentive compensation in escrow accounts with a longer-term horizon of around five years would help prevent destructive short-term actions.

Another problem identified with the current system is that it fails to adapt to changing conditions in the firm and its share price. If the firm is in trouble and the share price falls, the stock options are worth little. Consequently, the executive loses an important incentive to perform just at the time when it is most important to be working at full swing. Thus, to keep managers working hard at troubled times, boards typically give the executives more shares for free or they reprise the existing options. Edmans opines this as controversial because, in effect, the CEO is being rewarded for failure.

Incentive programmes need funds which need to be raised by some means following certain protocol.

SELF-FUNDING INCENTIVE/REWARD SCHEMES

Companies can consider three different types of funding options while designing an incentive programme—fully funded, self funded, or a hybrid approach.

Fully funded programme In this type of programme, the amount required for distribution is effectively budgeted and there is very little impact on the quantum based on the performance of the organization. This means that there is no risk function applied to the programme funding.

Self-funded programme In a self funding approach, the quantum is linked to few critical performance measures of the organization. The fund gets accrued as the organization reaches pre-defined levels of performance. Typically, most of the companies anchor these metrics on revenue and profits with equal or differentiated weights. The design aspects of the funding curve could vary, with a composite index that factors the differentiated weight of the performance parameters or a model based on prioritization of the performance metrics.

> Three types of funding options while designing an incentive programme are fully funded, self funding, or a hybrid approach.

Hybrid programme This approach is a combination of both fully-funded and self-funding programmes. The primary contribution in a hybrid design could be the self funding with a discretionary fund to address situations that may arise from unforeseen events or vice versa. The advantage of this approach is that it facilitates addressing the better performing employees during periods with significantly higher levels of uncertainty. At the same time, the cost of operations has limited exposure to the extent the programme is funded externally.

If organizations intend to create a stronger linkage between the business performance and individual performance through the incentive or reward mechanism, it should be either a self-funding program or a hybrid-funding approach which is significantly anchored on self funding.

DESIGN OF SELF-FUNDING PROGRAMME

In funding design, the key aspects that should be considered are threshold performance, funding leverage, and funding limits.

Steps involved in designing any self-funding programme are as follows:

Step 1: Defining the key performance metrics

Step 2: Establishing a correlation between the key performance metrics and the profitability of the organization

Step 3: Converting available surpluses from the operations to available funds for distribution as incentives

It is essential to understand the historical data and the changing cost structure of the organization in step 2 while establishing the co-relationship.

In a self-funding design, the key aspects that should be considered are—threshold performance, funding leverage, and funding limits.

Threshold clarifies and establishes the minimum expected level of performance by the organization to effectively fund any incentive programme. The threshold level of performance can always exceed. In such instances, the relationship between the determinant metrics and the funding amount should be defined.

The performance of an organization may increase or decrease. The incentive fund amount will naturally increase with a marginal increase in performance. This is defined as funding leverage. The higher the leverage, there is a faster increase in fund size with a marginal increase in performance of the organization. The funding leverage is evenly balanced at the target performance.

Some of the funding models will also have 'funding caps' to limit the undesired impact due to windfall business scenarios. Effectively, all these design elements are integrated to balance the labour and operations cost structure of the organization within pre-defined parameters.

COMMUNICATION

Performance expectations and its impact on incentive pay funding must be communicated to the employees. This is as critical as the funding design. Each of the elements in the funding design can be fully translated as expectation of the organization from the employees. Similarly, the funding leverage and the growth in incentive fund in relation to the performance of the organization should be communicated in the context of the business environment. Communication should also include the amount of money that will be available, in absolute value, to be distributed as incentive pay and how this could be translated to individual incentive payouts. The improved understanding of this linkage to the business performance will help reinforce incentive/reward relationship with organizational performance.

In organizations, all employees contribute to the outcomes. However, salespeople specifically communicate with the customers, try to understand their intrinsic need, face hassles, and remain calm during testing times. The incentive plan should be designed carefully.

SALES INCENTIVE PLAN

Some companies design a sales incentive plan (SIP) to reward eligible sales people for achieving or surpassing predefined objectives based on their contribution to company's success. An SIP should preferably be designed involving employees to obtain their views and harmonize the process with the employee needs.

An SIP is intended for people who formally join the plan, either during the harmonization process or when accepting a new role.

Interim sales incentive is extended to people who are eligible for SIP and are located in specific countries. According to the work council, the plan needs approval by competent authority.

Short term incentive is sanctioned for employees who did not opt to join the SIP during the harmonization. Refer to Box 12.3 for the objectives of an SIP.

Box 12.3 Objectives of a sales incentive plan

1. To align with the company values and sales culture
2. To be financially responsible implying that SIP should be 'self funding' in nature
3. To be simple in facilitating all employees to understand transparency
4. To be specific, measurable, and practical, and be able to implement and administer the plan
5. To recognize individual performance, and reinforce pay-for-performance culture
6. To recognize the right people, with objectively defined eligibility criteria to determine the roles that should be included
7. To remain competitive in market; SIP supports the organizational desire to attract and retain the talents and performers
8. To support sales that are aligned with the company strategy
9. To support the necessary team work through complementary plan design

WAGES—AN INTRODUCTION

Among the major factors in the economic and social life of any community, wages play a significant role. They have ethical, social, economic, political, psychological, and legal consequences in an organizational life. The international labour organization (ILO) has conducted various conventions and recommendations laying down the principles and methods of payment and fixation of wages. The Constitution of India protects the concept of social justice as one of the objectives of the state. The legal framework on wages in our country includes certain Acts discussed earlier in this chapter. Under different social security enactments, the employers are also required to provide various benefits to the employees both in cash and kind.

In most organizations, wage and salary administration is performed in the personnel department, although larger organizations often have a separate payroll or wage and salary administration department. The department or group of an organization needs to maintain employment records, the set of job classifications, finalize wage brackets, overtime policy, salary review plans, and monitor administrative procedure of establishing and supervising wage levels and operations in an organization.

DEFINITIONS OF WAGE

From a financial perspective, wages are defined as the cash paid for some specified quantity of labour, in contrast with salaries. Wages are paid based on the wage rate (based on units of time), while salaries are paid periodically without reference to a specified number of hours worked. Given an established job description, wages can often be negotiated by workers through collective bargaining.

Economists define wages more broadly than just cash compensation and include any return on labour, such as goods that workers might create for themselves, returns in kind, or even the enjoyment that some derive from work. Even food hunted or gathered is considered wages and any return resulting from an investment in tools (such as an axe or a hoe) is deemed interest (a return on a capital investment).

WAGES AND COMPENSATION

Wage rate is the compensation for labour per period of time. It is a basic compensation for labour. The two terms, compensation and wage, are often interchangeably used. Payment per unit of time (typically an hour) or earnings representing payment accrued over a time period (week, month, or year) and is also alternatively used for wages. Total compensation represents earnings and other benefits for labour. Total compensation, including unearned income, refers to wage income. Wages are also referred to as economic rent spent for getting the efforts and services of the labour.

The payment of wages to workers should be based on the optimal allocation of cooperative human labour. Optimization here does not indicate only a technical variable, because workers are not considered just as a factor of production. Workers' participation in the production process can either be oppressive, irrational, and exploitative or can be beneficial, rational, and effective. With regard to wage, the interests of workers and employers are bipolar. Thus, the most desirable form of labour organization in the workplace is the one where workers manage themselves collectively, and elect managers where necessary.

The term labour cost is best understood from the ILO's 11th international conference of labour statisticians (Geneva 1966). Labour cost is the cost incurred by the employer in the employment of labour. The statistical concept of labour cost comprises remuneration in return for the work performed. This also includes payments in respect of time, including paid holiday or time-off, bonuses and gratuities, the cost of food, drink, and other payments in kind, the cost of workers' housing borne by employers, employers' social security expenditures, the cost to the employer for vocational training, welfare services, miscellaneous items, such as the transport of workers, work clothes, and cost of recruitment, and taxes paid *by* the employers on employment. From the perspective of employers, the compensation of employees consists of all payments (in kind or in cash), and all contributions to employees' social security, pension, insurance, etc.

Labour cost and employee compensation are closely-related concepts, with many common elements. The major part of labour cost comprises compensation of employees. However, definitions of labour cost and the compensation of employees differ from country to country. For example, some items of labour cost, such as social security and vocational training, are borne not by employers but by the respective governments. In India, the central board for workers' training and the regional labour institutes provide either free or subsidized training for industrial workers. Similarly, the regional provident fund commission now marginally contributes to employees' pension along with the employers. The state's contributions to wage-related social security schemes are not included in the cost of compensation for employers. In some countries, payroll taxes or employment taxes are considered labour costs.

Operationally, both compensation and wages are intended to price the efforts of employees. However, the term compensation is more holistic and is used to acknowledge the strategic importance of wages. Theoretically, compensation means something, such as money, given or received as payment for some damage. However, in human resource management literature, we consider the term from a broader perspective, and refer to the strategic use of wages paid to employees.

Strong bargaining strength gives the worker a fair share, and direct participation of the state in the economic life of the nation enlarges this share.

Wage issues are no longer purely analytical issues. In a given case, the wage structure should take industrial adjudication as well as considerations of right and wrong; and fairness and unfairness into account. The collective bargaining is now the most dynamic form of negotiation to decide wage structure in a particular organization. It was with this perspective that the framers of the Constitution drew up a declaration in Article 43 (as part of the directive principles of state policy) which states that, 'The state shall endeavour to secure, by suitable legislation or economic organization or in any other way, to all workers—agriculture, industrial, or otherwise—work, a living wage, conditions of work ensuring a decent standard of life and full employment of leisure and social and cultural opportunities' (Bhattacharyya 2009).

By this declaration, the state acknowledged its role in directly promoting social welfare. In addition, it also recognized the inadequacy of market forces to determine a wage level that is consistent with any welfare standard of a living wage. The declaration, in effect, assured labour that where they were not able to secure a living wage for themselves, the government, through legislation or other means will come to their aid. Two aspects of the state's role prevent employers from taking undue advantage of the workers—(a) strong bargaining strength and (b) direct participation of the state in the economic life of the nation. Strong bargaining strength gives the worker a fair share and direct participation of the state enlarges this share.

WAGE COMPONENTS

In a broader sense, the term 'wages' is all encompassing and includes any form of financial support and benefits extended to workers for their services rendered. In a narrower sense, wages are the price paid for the services of labour. There are two wage components—the base or basic wages and other allowances. The basic wage is the remuneration, and by way of basic salary and allowances, it is paid or payable to an employee in terms of the contract of employment for the work done. Allowances are paid, in addition to the basic wage, to ensure that the value of basic wages does not fall over a period of time. Some allowances are statutory, while others are voluntary. Most organizations pay allowances such as holiday pay, overtime pay, bonus, and social security benefits. Theoretically, these are not included in the definition of wages.

NON-WAGE COMPONENTS

Employers make some payments which do not form a part of the contract of employment. These are excluded from wages.

1. Bonus or other payments under a profit-sharing scheme.
2. Value of any house accommodation, supply of light, water, medical attendance, travelling allowance, or payment in lieu thereof or any other concession.
3. Any sum paid to defray or settle special expenses entailed by the nature of the employment of a workman.
4. Any contribution to pension, provident fund, or a scheme of social security and social insurance benefits.
5. Any other amenity or service excluded from the computation of wages by a general or special order of an appropriate governmental authority.

A wage level is an average of the rates paid for the jobs of an organization, an establishment, a labour market, an industry, a region, or a nation. A wage structure is a hierarchy of jobs to which wage rates have been attached.

WAGE DETERMINATION METHODS

Wages are determined by methods such as job evaluation, job design, job assessment, job analysis, job description, or job specification.

1. Job evaluation—the process of systematically determining the value of a job. Pair comparison introduces more rigour by comparing jobs in pairs, However, in reality, it is a more structured way of building a basic rank order.
2. Job design—work arrangement (or rearrangement) aimed at overcoming job dissatisfaction, reducing operator's fatigue, etc. with the ultimate intention of enhancing productivity.
3. Job assessment—collecting information about a job. The assessor asks questions to the operator and the supervisor to collect information about job content.
4. Job analysis—examining a specific job, determining the job factors, skills required, experience, etc.
5. Job description—giving title to a job considering the job content.
6. Job specification—qualities (physical, mental, emotional, behavioural, etc) essential to perform a job correctly.

DETERMINANTS OF WAGE RATES

The economy of a country dictates the system of determining wage rates. Wage rates depend on the structure and traditions of different economies. Wage rates either depend on the product of market forces (supply and demand), or they may be influenced by other factors such as tradition, social structure, and seniority. In the United States, market forces determine wage rates. In Japan, seniority is still the dominant factor for wage determination. Several countries, including India, have enacted a statutory minimum wage rate that fixes the price of certain kinds of labour. While market forces determine the wage rate in most developed countries, workers often negotiate their wage rate through collective bargaining wherever unions are present. Often, we use the term 'benefit' to indicate wages. Theoretically, benefit refers to something which someone is entitled to receive. Workers' benefit component is the non-monetary part of the compensation.

Many organizations often confuse unearned income with wages. Theoretically, unearned income includes interest, dividends, or realized capital gains from investments, rent from land, or property ownership, as well as any other income that does not derive from the work. It means that even the interest earned on the provident funds of workers (in cases where the employers themselves are the trustee) cannot be interpreted as wages. Some parts of the unearned income are taxable, while some other parts are not (interest on provident fund is an example). Economists, however, have a differing point of view, as they consider unearned income as compensation for deferring consumption.

> Wage rates either depend on the market forces (supply and demand), or they may be influenced by other factors such as tradition, social structure, and seniority.

The consideration of opportunity costs is one of the key differences between the concepts of economic cost and accounting cost. Assessing opportunity costs is fundamental to assessing the true cost of any course of action. In case where there is no explicit accounting or monetary cost (price) attached to a course of action, ignoring opportunity costs may produce the illusion that its benefits cost nothing at all. The unseen opportunity costs then become the implicit hidden costs of that course of action.

THEORIES OF WAGE DETERMINATION

Two key theories to determine wages are—the traditional theory of wage determination and the theory of negotiated wages.

Traditional Theory of Wage Determination

This theory assumes that market forces—demand and supply—determine wages. In the arena of information technology, system analysts are in short supply, so they are able to command higher salaries. In India, many organizations pay very high salaries to entry-level IT professionals, who sometimes get more than senior managerial level employees in other sectors. This is because of the demand-supply gap.

Theory of Negotiated Wages

Employees of organized sector having unions and collective bargaining forum can negotiate salaries. Generally, in any unionized organization, collective bargaining fora periodically submit their memorandum to the management, asking for wage raises to keep pace with market standards and organizational profitability. Then, wages are negotiated in a collective bargaining meeting attended by the unions and the management nominees. However, in collective bargaining, many other employment-related issues can also be negotiated. For non-unionized employees, wages can be negotiated through individual bargaining. In some cases, there may even be regulatory intervention by wage boards in wage determination. The wage boards are tripartite in nature and represent the workers, employers, and independent members. Wage boards finalize wage recommendations. Wage boards are not statutory. They are now less important because of the rising bargaining power of workers and employees.

PRINCIPLES OF COMPENSATION DETERMINATION

Wage determination, apart from the statutory aspect, is influenced by different theories (Bhattacharyya 2009). These theories—subsistence theory, wages fund theory, surplus value theory, residual claimant theory, marginal productivity theory, bargaining theory of wages, and behavioural theory of wages are discussed in brief.

Subsistence Theory

Subsistence theory, propounded by David Ricardo (1772–1832), advocates that workers should be paid, 'to enable them to subsist and perpetuate the race without increase or diminution'. The theory is based on the assumption that if the workers were paid more than subsistence wage, their numbers would increase, and this would bring down the rate of wages. If the wages fall below the subsistence level, the number of workers would decrease, as many would die of hunger, malnutrition, disease, cold, etc., and many would not marry. In this situation, wages would increase again due to short supply of labour. In economics, the subsistence theory of wages states that, in the long run, wages will be reduced to the minimum level needed to keep workers alive.

Wages Fund Theory

This theory, developed by Adam Smith (1723–90), rests on the assumption that wages are paid out of a predetermined fund of wealth, the surplus savings of the wealthy. This fund could be utilized for employing labourers for work. If the fund was large, wages would be high; if it was small, wages would be reduced to subsistence level. The demand for labour and the level of wages were determined by the size of the fund.

Surplus Value Theory

The surplus value theory of wages owes its development to Karl Marx (1818–83). According to this theory, labour was an article of commerce, which could be purchased on the payment of the 'subsistence price'. The price of any product was determined by the labour and the time needed to produce it. The labourer was not paid in proportion to the time spent on work, but was paid much less, and the surplus was utilized for paying other expenses.

Residual Claimant Theory

The residual claimant theory, advocated by Francis Walker (1840–1897), assumes that four factors of production/business determine wages. The factors are land, labour, capital, and entrepreneurship. Wages represent the amount of value created in the production, which remains after payment has been made for all these factors of production. In other words, labours get the residue as residual claimant.

Marginal Productivity Theory

The theory assumes that wages are based upon an entrepreneur's estimate of the value that will probably be produced by the marginal worker. In other words, it assumes that wages depend upon the demand for, and supply of, labour. Consequently, workers are paid what they are economically worth.

Bargaining Theory of Wages

This theory considers that wages are determined by the relative bargaining power of workers, trade unions, and employers. When a trade union is involved, basic wages, fringe benefits, job differentials, and individual differences tend to be determined by the relative strength of the organization and the trade union.

Behavioural Theory of Wages

This theory was pioneered in succession by several psychologists and sociologists, such as Marsh and Simon, Robert Dubin, and Eliot Jacques. Based on their various research studies, we can identify the following areas of interest in behavioural theories of wages.

1. The employee's acceptance of a wage level: Individuals believe in employment stability and prefer to stay on with the same organization, pacing with their salary level. There are, however, several other factors to be considered such as size and prestige of the company, trade unions' power in the organization, their level of knowledge and competencies, etc.

2. The internal wage structure: Employees value internal pay equity. Moreover, some jobs also command social status (such as the job of a journalist). Organizations design wages for different cross-sections of employees, while considering maximum and minimum wage differentials, norms of span or control, and demand for specialized skill-sets. Balancing of wages with such internal equity also keeps employees more motivated.

TYPES OF WAGES

The various types of wages are minimum rate of wages, living wage, and fair wage. This section discusses the various types of wages in India.

Minimum Rate of Wages

Any minimum rate of wages fixed or revised may comprise a basic rate of wages and a special allowance; a basic rate of wages with or without a cost of living allowance and the cash value of concessions in respect of supplies of essential commodities at concessional rates; or an all inclusive rate allowing for the basic rate, the cost of living allowance, and the cash value of concessions, if any. Every employer is required to maintain registers and records giving particulars of employees, the work performed by them, the wages paid to them, the receipts given by them, and any other required particulars. The appropriate government may, by notification in the official Gazette, appoint inspectors for the purpose of this Act and define the local limits for their functions.

The appropriate government may, by notification in the official Gazette, appoint the labour commissioner or commissioner for workmen's compensation or any officer not below the rank of labour commissioner or any other officer with experience as a judge of a civil court or as a stipendiary magistrate, to hear and decide for any specified area, all claims arising out of the payment of less than the minimum rates of wages as well as payment for days of rest or for work done.

All establishments covered under the Act are required to furnish to the concerned authority (central or state) an annual return in prescribed form as per the rules framed under the Minimum Wages Act, 1948. The centre/state governments, in turn, send a consolidated return to the labour bureau which compiles an all-India report based on the data contained in these returns. Besides, quarterly returns sent by these agencies to the bureau are also made use of in compiling information at all India level.

From normative perspectives, the committee on fair wages indicated that the minimum wages provide 'not merely for the bare sustenance of life but for the preservation of the efficiency of the worker by providing for some measure of education, medical requirements, and amenities'. This recommendation was further stretched to the concept of need-based minimum wages by the Indian Labour Conference (1957).

For the calculation of the minimum wage, the Conference accepted the following norms and recommended that they should guide all wage-fixing authorities, including the Minimum Wage Committee, Wage Boards, and adjudicators.

Living Wage

Living wage is defined by the committee on fair wages as 'one which should enable the earner to provide for himself/herself and his/her family not only the bare essentials of food, clothing, and shelter but a measure of frugal/careful comfort, including education for his children, protection against ill-health, requirements of essential social needs and a measure of insurance against the more important misfortunes, including old age'. In other words, a living wage was to provide for a standard of living that would ensure good health for workers and their family, a measure of decency, comfort, and education for their children; and protection against misfortunes. This obviously implied a high level of living.

Such a wage is determined by keeping in view the national income, and an industry's capacity to pay. The committee was of the opinion that although the provision of a living wage should be the ultimate goal, the present level of national income did not permit the payment of a living wage on the basis of standards prevalent in more advanced countries. The goal of a living wage was to be achieved in three stages. In the first stage, the wage to be paid to the entire working class was to be established and stabilized. In the second stage, fair wages were to be established in the community-cum-industry. In the third stage, the working class was to be paid the living wage. The living wage may be somewhere between the lowest level of the minimum wage and the highest limit of the fair wage, depending upon the bargaining power of labour, the capacity of the industry to pay, the level of the national income, the general effect of the wage rise on neighboring industries, the productivity of labour, the place of industry in the economy of the country, and the prevailing rates of wages in the same or similar occupations in neighboring localities.

Thus, a living wage should maintain a worker's health and decency, a measure of comfort, and some insurance against the more important misfortunes of life. The Supreme Court has laid down some principles for wage fixation as follows:

1. There is a minimum wage, which must be paid in any event, irrespective of the extent of profits, the financial condition of the establishment, or the availability of workers at lower wages.
2. The wages must be fair, which is, sufficiently high to provide a standard family with food, shelter, clothing, medical care, and education of children appropriate to the workers.
3. A fair wage lies between minimum wage and the living wage, which is the eventual goal.
4. Wages must be paid on an industry-wise and region basis, having due regard to the financial capacity of the unit.

Fair Wage

According to the committee on fair wages, fair wage represents the wage above the minimum wage but below the living wage. Further, it believes that the lower limit of the fair wage is obviously the minimum wage; the upper limit is set by the 'capacity of the industry to pay'. Between these two limits, the actual wages should depend on the following considerations:

1. Productivity of labour
2. Prevailing rates of wages in the same or neighbouring localities
3. Level of the national income and its distribution
4. Place of industry in the economy of the country

Thus, fair wages is an adjustable step. It increases according to the capacity of the industry to pay, and the prevailing rates of wages in the area or industry.

WAGE BOARDS

After independence, for about two decades, the organized labour sector was at a nascent stage of its development without adequate unionization. Trade unions were not as powerful as they are now, and unions had inadequate bargaining power. The government, aware of the problems which arise in the arena of wage fixation due to the absence of bargaining power, constituted various wage boards. The wage boards are tripartite in character having representatives of workers, employers, and independent members participate and finalize the recommendations. The utility of such boards in the present context is debatable. Except for the wage boards for journalists and non-journalist newspaper and news-agency employees, which are statutory wage boards, all other wage boards are non-statutory in nature. Therefore, recommendations made by these wage boards are not enforceable under the law.

The importance of non-statutory wage boards has consequently declined over a period of time and no non-statutory wage board has been set up after 1966, except for the sugar industry, where such a wage board was constituted in 1985. The trade unions, having grown in strength in these industries, are now capable of negotiating their wages with the management. This trend is likely to continue in the future.

WAGE POLICY

Subsequent to globalization, international competition has been increasing. Wage policy issues have now become more important in India. Globalization of market and competition has now increased the heterogeneity of organizations, in terms of size, business practices, and culture. This has given rise to a wide variation in wage or compensation design practices. International competitions are now forcing organizations to focus on cost and profitability. In the organized manufacturing sector in India, wages constitute approximately nine per cent of the total input costs. Another reason for the study of wage policy has been due to reason that wage rates and jobs are not exactly like other prices and quantities.

In India, the government used to play a crucial role in wage determination. This is primarily because of the presence of relevant articles of the Constitution and the report of the committee on fair wages. In line with the constitutional convention, a tripartite committee, the committee on fair wages (1948), provided guidelines for wage structures in the country. The concepts of living wage, minimum wage, and fair wages have emerged in India based on these guidelines.

A wage policy guides organizations in taking decisions on wage-related matters. At the organizational level, wage policies are framed, keeping in mind various regulatory requirements and the organization's own strategies. Whatever wage policies are framed, the organization should consider the recommendations of the committee on fair wages, which provides the basic approach for tribunals, wage boards, and other stakeholders to fix wages of workers. Within the boundaries of the fair wage concept, every organization must strive to ensure fair growth in workers' remuneration.

1. Firstly, the current purchasing power of workers should be maintained against any price rise by providing for adequate neutralization of the rise in cost of living. Thus, there should be no erosion in total emoluments in terms of their purchasing power.
2. Secondly, the organization should aim for a reasonable growth in the real earnings of workers, and an improvement in their living standards, commensurate with their level of productivity, firms' profitability, and other factors.

OBJECTIVES OF SOUND WAGE POLICY

The objectives of a sound/ideal wage and salary policy are manifold. A sound wage policy promotes industrial relations, protects against price rise, and serves many more purposes:

1. Establish good labour relations
2. Decide on appropriate wages

3. Decide wages based on the individual's capability
4. Develop a pre-determined scheme for payment of wages
5. Establish linkages of wage payment with performances
6. Maintain parity of wages with other organizations
7. Provide for incentive payment
8. Guarantee minimum wages
9. Provide for neutralization of price rise
10. Develop wage structures that can attract talent

A sound wage policy should adopt a job evaluation programme in order to establish fair differentials in wages based upon differences in job content. Besides the basic factors provided by a job description and job evaluation, those that are usually taken into consideration for wage and salary administration are as follows:

1. Organization's ability to pay
2. Supply of and demand for labour
3. Prevailing market rate
4. Cost of living
5. Living wage
6. Productivity
7. Trade union's bargaining power
8. Job requirements
9. Managerial attitudes
10. Psychological and sociological factors
11. Levels of skills available in the market

ACTS CONCERNING WAGES AND SALARY

The following are the Acts concerning wages and salary (labour.nic.in).

1. Payment of Wages Act, 1936
2. Minimum Wages Act, 1948
3. Payment of Bonus Act, 1965
4. Equal Remuneration Act, 1976
5. Statutory social security benefits

Payment of Wages Act, 1936

The Royal Commission on Labour in its report (1931) recommended, among other things, that legislation on timely payment of wages, and deductions from wages and fines, was necessary and desirable. In the light of its recommendations, the Government of India introduced a bill in 1936, and the Act came into force from 28 March 1937.

The Payment of Wages Act is divided into three parts. Part I deals with the regulation and payment of wages by the employer. Part II specifies the heads under which deductions can be made from wages. Part III provides the machinery for enforcing specific claims arising out of delayed payments, deduction from wages, appeals, etc. It is a self-contained Act and provides its own machinery for the disposal of the claims. The Act contains 26 sections.

Object of the Act

The object of the Act is to regulate the payment of wages to certain classes of persons employed in industry in a particular form and at regular intervals; and to prevent unauthorized deductions from the wages. The Act is concerned merely with the fixation of wage periods and not with the fixation of wages.

Applicability

The Act is applicable to persons employed in any factory, railway, and to such other establishments to which the State Government may, by notification, extend the provisions of the Act after giving three months' notice to that effect. In the case of industrial establishments owned by the central government, the notification can be issued with the concurrence of the central government. Employees whose average wage is less than ₹1,600 a month are covered under the Act. The Payment of Wages (Amendment) Bill, 2002 provides for the enhancement of the wage ceiling to ₹6,500 per month.

Definitions

'Wages' means all remuneration (whether by way of salary, allowances or otherwise) expressed in terms of money or capable of being so expressed which, if the terms of employment express or implied were fulfilled, would be payable to a person employed in respect of his employment or of work done in such employment. It includes

1. Any remuneration payable under any award or settlement between the parties or order of a court.
2. Any remuneration to which the person employed is entitled in respect of overtime work or holidays or any leave period.
3. Any sum which by reason of the termination of employment of the person employed is capable under any law, contract or instrument which provides for the payment of such sum whether with or without deduction but does not provide for the time within which the payment is to be made.
4. Any sum to which the person employed is entitled under any scheme framed under any law for the time being in force.

However, it does not include

1. Any bonus (whether under a scheme of profit sharing or otherwise) which does not form part of the remuneration payable under the terms of employment or which is not payable under any award or settlement between the parties or order of a court
2. The value of any house accommodation or of the supply of light, water, medical attendance or other amenity or of any service excluded from the computation of wages by, a general or special order of the state government
3. Any contribution paid by the employer to any pension or provident fund and the interest which may have accrued thereon
4. Any travelling concession
5. Any sum paid to the employed person to defray special expenses entailed on him by the nature of his employment
6. Any gratuity payable on the termination of employment

The term 'establishment' includes

1. Tramway service or motor transport engaged in carrying passengers and goods or both by road for hire or reward
2. Air transport service other than such service belonging to, or exclusively employed in the military, naval or airforce of the union, or the civil aviation department of the government of India
3. Dock, wharf, or jetty
4. Inland vessel mechanically propelled
5. Mine, quarry, or oil field

6. Plantation
7. Workshop, or other establishments in which articles are produced, adapted, or manufactured, with a view to their use. transport or sale
8. Establishment in which any work relating to the construction, development or maintenance of building, roads, bridges or canals or relating to transmission, or distribution of electricity, or any other form of power is being carried on
9. Any other establishment or class of establishments, which the central or a state government may notify in the Official Gazette

Wage Payment

The responsibility for the payment of wages under the Act is that of the employer or his representative. In the absence of the employer, a person who employs the labourers and with whom they enter into a contract of employment will be regarded as the employer.

No wage period shall exceed one month in any case. The main purpose of this provision is to ensure that inordinate delay is not caused in the payment of wages and that a long time does not elapse before wages are paid for the period for which an employee has worked.

Wages may be payable daily, weekly, and fortnightly and monthly. However, the payment thereof must not extend over a period longer than one month (month means a solar month; a period of four weeks or 30 days).

Where less than 1,000 persons are employed, wages shall be paid before the expiry of the seventh day, and in other cases, before the expiry of the 10th day, after the last day of the wage period. If for instance, the wage period fixed is the first day of January to the 31st day of January, an employed person working in any railway, factory, or industrial establishment in which less than 1,000 persons are employed would be entitled to receive his wages before the seventh day of February, and in other cases, on the 10th day of February in respect of the wage period of January.

In case the employer terminates the services of an employee, the employee is entitled to receive the wage earned by him before the expiry of the second working day from the day on which his employment has been terminated. The weekly or other recognized holiday is to be excluded in computing the second working day.

All wages shall be paid in current coin or currency notes or in both. After obtaining the written authorization of the employed person, the employer may pay the wages either by cheque or by crediting the wages into his bank account.

Deductions from Wages

Wages shall be paid to an employed person without deductions of any kind except those authorized by or under the Act. Withholding of increment or promotion (including the stoppage of increment at an efficiency bar); reduction to a lower post or time scale or to a lower stage in a time scale, and suspension are not deemed to be deductions from wages.

The term 'deduction from wages' has not been defined in the Act. However, the Act specifies the heads from which deductions from wages may be made.

Deductions may be made by an employer, with the written authorization of the employed person, from the wages payable to such an employed person, for payment of contribution to any welfare fund constituted by the employer for the welfare of employed persons and the members of their families, and also for the payment of the fees payable by the employed person for membership of any registered trade union.

There are also certain deductions peculiar to railways, such as deductions for recovery of losses sustained by railway administration on account of certain omissions and commissions on the part of the employees.

The total amount of deduction which may be made in any wage period from the wages of an employed person shall not exceed 75 per cent of such wages in cases where such deductions were wholly or partly made for payment to co-operative societies; and in any other case, 50 per cent of such wages. There are certain conditions and limitations subject to which fines may be imposed:

1. A fine can be imposed only for such acts or omissions as are specified by the employer and previously approved by the state government.
2. A notice specifying such acts or omissions must be exhibited on the premises in which employment is carried on.
3. A person involved must be informed in writing on the reasons for imposing fine.
4. No fine shall be imposed on an employed person who is under the age of 15 years.
5. No fine shall be recovered from an employed person by installments after the expiry of 60 days from the day on which it was imposed.
6. The total amount of fine in one wage period shall not exceed an amount equal to three per cent for that wage period.
7. All realizations by way of fine have to be recorded in a register and must be applied only for such purpose as are beneficial to the persons employed in the factory or establishment as are approved by the prescribed authority.

The Act authorizes deductions for actual absence from duty. However, if 10 or more employed persons acting in concert absent themselves without due notice and without reasonable cause, such deductions may be made for a maximum period of eight days.

Deductions from wages for damage or loss caused to the employer by the neglect or default of the employed person have been laid down under the Act. Such deductions can be made only after giving the person concerned an opportunity of showing cause against the deductions. All such deductions and realizations are to be recorded in a register. Exhibit 12.8 lists the authorized/permissible deductions.

Exhibit 12.8 List of authorized or permissible deductions

1. Deductions for fines
2. Deductions for absence from duty
3. Deductions for damage or loss
4. Deductions for house accommodation
5. Deductions for amenities and services
6. Deductions for recovery of advances or for adjustment of over payment of wages
7. Deductions for recovery of loans made for the welfare of labour
8. Deductions for recovery of loans granted for house building
9. Deductions for payment to co-operative societies and insurance schemes
10. Deductions of income tax
11. Deductions made under orders of court
12. Deductions for contributions to provident fund
13. Deductions for the welfare of the employed persons
14. Deductions in respect of fees payable for the membership of trade union
15. Deductions for payment of insurance premia on fidelity guarantee bonds
16. Deductions for recovery of losses sustained by railway administration
17. Deductions for contribution to the Prime Minister's "National Relief Fund"
18. Deductions for contributions to any insurance scheme

Authorities

The Act makes provision for the appointment of inspectors. The inspector of factories is also the inspector under this Act.

The Act also provides for the appointment of a person to be the authority to hear and decide, for any specified area, claims arising out of deductions from wages or delay in payment of wages.

The authority under the Act can only adjudicate upon claims regarding deductions and delay in payment of wages and not upon any dispute in respect of wages.

An appeal lies against the decision of the authority to a court of small causes in a metropolitan town and before the district court elsewhere within a period of one month.

The Act prescribes penalties for offences committed under the Act. Any contract or agreement whereby an employed person relinquishes any right conferred by this Act shall be null and void.

Obligations of Employers

1. To fix the wage-period not exceeding one month.
2. To pay wages in cash or by cheque after taking written authorization of the employed person.
3. To pay wages on any working day.
4. To make deductions permissible from the wages of the employed person.
5. To ensure that deductions do not exceed 75 per cent where payment to a cooperative society is to be made, and in other cases, deductions do not exceed 50 per cent.
6. To seek, before imposing fines, approval of list of acts and omissions from the prescribed authority.
7. Not to impose fines exceeding three per cent of the wages on the employee.
8. To give show-cause notice to the employed person before imposing fines.
9. To recover fines within 60 days of the date of offence.
10. To afford facilities to inspectors for entry, inspection, supervision, examination, or inquiry under the Act.
11. To display abstract of the Act and the rules in English, and in a language understood by the majority of workmen.
12. To maintain following register in the prescribed forms:

    (a) Register of wages
    (b) Register of fines
    (c) Register of deductions for damage or loss
    (d) Registrar of advances

Apart from maintaining the necessary records and registers, the employer is required to display an abstract of the Act at a conspicuous place.

Obligations of Employees

Every employee is entitled to the following (http://labour.nic.in):

1. To receive his wages in the prescribed wage period in cash or by cheque or by credit to his bank account.
2. To refuse to agree to any deductions and fines other than those authorized under the Act.
3. To approach within six months the prescribed authority to claim unpaid or delayed wage, unauthorized deductions and fines along with compensation.
4. To appeal against the direction made by the authority if the amount of wages claimed exceeds rupees one hundred.

Minimum Wages Act, 1948

The genesis of the Minimum Wages Act is traceable to the minimum wage fixing machinery convention, 1928 (No. 28) of the ILO. This convention has become one of the most widely accepted instruments of the ILO. The minimum wages bill was introduced in the central legislature in 1946, and was passed in 1948. The Act contains 31 sections.

Object of the Act

The Act aims to extend the concept of social justice to the workmen employed in certain scheduled employments by statutorily providing for them minimum rates of wages. It is a piece of social legislation which provides protection to workers in employments in which they are vulnerable to exploitation by reason of the lack of organization and bargaining power and where sweated labour is most prevalent.

Applicability

The Act is not applicable to all employments or industries. A schedule appended to the Act gives a list of employments covered by the Act. It covers an establishment regardless of the number of workers actually employed. Some of the employments are listed in Part I of the schedule. Part II of the schedule contains employment in agriculture and other allied activities.

The appropriate government may add to the schedule any other employment in respect of which it is of the opinion that minimum rates of wages should be fixed.

The contract labour, falling within the purview of the contract labour (regulation and abolition) Act, 1970, has to be paid minimum wages under the Minimum Wages Act.

Definitions

The Act contains a number of definitions. Some of the important ones are the following:

Appropriate government In this Act, the term 'appropriate government' means
Central government—for any scheduled employment carried on under the authority of central government or railway administrations and for a mine, oilfield or major port or any corporation established by a central act
State government—for any other scheduled employment carried on within its territory

Wages Wages means all remuneration capable of being expressed in terms of money, which would, if the terms of the contract of employment, express or implied, were fulfilled, be payable to a person employed in respect of his employment or of work done in such employment, and includes house rent allowance but does not include

1. The value of any house accommodation, supply of light, water, medical attendance; or any other amenity or any service excluded by general or special order of the appropriate government;
2. Any contribution paid by the employer to any pension fund or provident fund or under any scheme of social insurance;
3. Any traveling allowance or the value of any traveling concession;
4. Any sum paid to the person employed to defray special expenses entailed on him by the nature of his employment; or
5. Any gratuity payable on discharge.

Employer The term 'employer' means any person who employs one or more employees in any scheduled employment in respect of which minimum rates of wages have been fixed under the Act. The term 'employer' also includes

1. Manager of a factory as defined under the Factories Act, 1948
2. Head of department or any person appointed for the supervision and control of employees or chief executive officer of a local authority, in case, the scheduled employment is carried on under central government or a local authority
3. In any other case, the person responsible for supervision, control, or payment of wages

Employee The term 'employee' means any person who is employed for hire or reward to do any work, skilled or unskilled, manual or clerical, in a scheduled employment.

Fixing of Minimum Rates of Wages

When, in respect of an employment, the appropriate government has fixed and notified the minimum rates of wages, the employer is bound to pay every employee engaged in that employment at rates not less than the rates notified.

The appropriate government may review wages at such intervals as they think fit but not exceeding five years, and revise them, if necessary.

The appropriate government may refrain from fixing minimum rates of wages in respect of any scheduled employment in which less than 1,000 employees are employed in the whole state. The minimum rates of wages may be fixed

1. For different employments
2. For different classes in the same employment
3. For adolescents, children and apprentices
4. For different localities.
5. The rates of wages may be
   (a) A time rate
   (b) A piece rate
   (c) A guaranteed time rate
   (d) An overtime rate

The rates may be fixed by the hour, by the day or by the month or by any other longer period as may be prescribed. The rate fixed may consist of the basic rate of wages and cost of living allowance and the cash value of concessions in respect of supply of essential commodities at concessional rates. In fixing or revising the minimum wages, the appropriate government shall either:

1. Appoint as many committees and sub-committees as it considers necessary to hold enquiries and advise it in respect of such fixation or revision, as the case may be; or
2. By notification in the official gazette, publish its proposals for the information of persons likely to be affected thereby and specify a date, not less than two months from the date of the notification, on which the proposals will be taken into consideration.

After considering the advice of the said committee or representations received, the appropriate government will, by notification in the gazette, fix or revise the minimum rates of wages. Unless otherwise provided, the decision shall come into force on the expiry of three months from the date of notification. When fixation is made on the basis of representations, the appropriate government shall consult the advisory board as well. The government is not bound to accept the committee's recommendations.

The Act also empowers state governments to constitute advisory boards to coordinate the work of different committees and sub-committees, and advise the government on the fixation of minimum wages. Similarly, the central government is empowered to constitute a central advisory board to advise the central and the state governments, and to co-ordinate the work of the advisory boards. These bodies consist of an equal number of employers' and employees' representatives, and of independent persons not exceeding one-third of their total strength. The non-official members hold office for a period of two years, while others hold office during the pleasure of the government.

The minimum wages payable under the Act are to be paid in cash. However, they also provide for authorization of payment in kind where the appropriate government considers it necessary. It may direct the supply of essential commodities at concessional rates by notifying it in the official gazette. Authorized deductions are allowed under the Act. The appropriate government may fix the number of hours of work, rest day, and payment of overtime in respect of scheduled employments.

Registers, Notices, and Returns

Every employer is required to maintain

1. Register of wages
2. Register of overtime payment
3. Muster roll
4. Register of fines
5. Register of deduction

Every employer is required to

1. Put up a notice containing the minimum rate of wages fixed
2. Exhibit an extract of the Act and rules
3. Send annual return to the labour commissioner as prescribed

Inspectors

The appropriate government appoints inspectors for the purposes of this Act, and defines the local limits within which they exercise their functions. The inspectors are public servants. Any person, who is called upon to provide any relevant information, is legally bound to provide information to the inspectors under the provisions of Indian Penal Code.

Authorities under the Act

The appropriate government appoints, by notification in the Official Gazette for any specified area, an authority to hear and decide claims arising out of payment of wages at less than the minimum rates of wages and other incidental matters. The authority so appointed has powers of a civil court.

An employee or any legal practitioner or any other official of a registered trade union, authorized in writing, or any inspector can apply to the authority for settlement of disputes with respect to non-payment or payment of less than the minimum wages. The Act prohibits civil courts from entertaining any suits for the recovery of minimum wages payable under the Act.

Enforcement

The central government is the appropriate authority for the enforcement of the Act in relation to any scheduled employment carried on by or under the authority of the central government, railway administration, a mine, an oilfield, a major port, or any corporation established by a central act. The chief labour commissioner (central) is in charge of implementation of the Act in the central sphere. In the state sphere, officers of the industrial relations machinery are entrusted with the enforcement of the Act, in addition to the enforcement of other labour laws. In some states, a small number of whole-time inspectors are appointed exclusively for the enforcement of the Act. In some states, in addition to the officers of the labour department, officials of the revenue department, panchayat departments, and agricultural departments have been authorized to work as inspectors for the purposes of the Act.

Offences and Penalties

The Act lays down penalties for violation of the provisions of the Act.

Any contract or agreement whereby an employee relinquishes or reduces his right under this Act shall be null and void. However, the Act does not prevent an individual from entering into an agreement which is more advantageous or beneficial to him.

Obligations of Employers

Under the Act, employers have the following obligations:

1. Once the minimum wages are notified and become effective, the employer must pay to every employee engaged in a scheduled employment under him wages at a rate not less than the minimum rate of wages fixed by such notification for that class of employees.
2. The employer may make deductions out of wages as may be authorized.
3. The employer shall pay overtime at double the ordinary rate of wages for the period of work done beyond nine hours on any day or 48 hours in any week or for days of rest.
4. The employer must pay minimum wages in cash unless the appropriate government authorizes their payment wholly or partly in kind. The government may direct the supply of essential commodities at concessional rates by notifying them in the official gazette.
5. Every employer shall issue a wage slip to every employee in a prescribed form containing prescribed particulars.
6. Every employer shall get the signature or the thumb impression of every person employed on the wage group and the wage slips.
7. The employer or his agent should authenticate the entries in the wage books and the wage slips.
8. The employer shall allow a rest day with wages to the employees every week which ordinarily should be a Sunday or any other day. No employee shall be required to work on a day fixed as rest day, unless he is paid wages for that day at the overtime rate and is also allowed a substituted rest day with wages.
9. The employer shall not make deductions from wages except those authorized by or under the rules.

Source: http://labour.nic.in/wagecell/mwact.pdf

Payment of Bonus Act, 1965

In pursuance of the decision taken at the 18th session of the Indian labour conference, the Government of India constituted the bonus commission on 6 December 1961. The government accepted the recommendations of the commission with slight modifications, and promulgated an ordinance on 29 May 1965. The Act came into force from 25 October 1965. Subsequently, there were a number of amendments to the Act. The Act consists of 40 sections and four schedules.

Object of the Act

The object of the Act is to maintain peace and harmony between labour and capital by allowing the employees to share the prosperity of the establishment reflected by the profits earned by the contributions made by capital, management, and labour.

Applicability

The Act applies to all factories and establishments employing 20 or more persons on any day during an accounting year. Such an establishment continues to be governed by the Act, notwithstanding that the number of persons employed therein falls below 20. Establishments also include departments, undertaking, and branches.

Definitions

Employee: The definition of 'employee' includes any person (other than an apprentice) employed on a salary or wage not exceeding ₹3,500 per month in any industry doing any skilled or unskilled, manual, supervisory, managerial, administrative, technical, or clerical work for hire or reward. The Payment of Bonus (Amendment) Bill, 2002 provides for omission of the ceiling of ₹3,500 for applicability of the Act. If this provision comes into force, then all the employees in an industry will be entitled to get bonus irrespective of their salaries/wages. The term of employment may be expressed or implied. There must, however, be a contract of service between the person employed and the employer.

Appropriate government The term 'appropriate government' means

1. in relation to loan establishment in respect of which appropriate government under the Industrial Disputes Act, 1947 is the central government;
2. in relation to any other establishment, the government of the state in which that establishment is situated.

Employer The term 'employer' includes

1. in relation to an establishment which is a factory, the owner or occupier of the factory, including the agent of such owner or occupier, the legal representative of a deceased owner or occupier and the manager of the factory;
2. in relation to any other establishment, the person who, or the authority which, has the ultimate control over the affairs of the establishment. Where the said affairs are entrusted to a manager or managing director, such manager or managing director is the employer.

Accounting year The term 'accounting year' means

1. in relation to a corporation, the year ending on the day on which the books and accounts of corporation are to be closed and balanced;
2. in relation to a company, the period in respect of which profit and loss account is laid before the annual general meeting (first day of April or 31st March).

Salary or wage The term 'salary or wage' includes

1. basic pay and dearness allowance but not any other allowance,
2. It excludes the value of any house accommodation or of supply of light, water, medical attendance or amenity or any service or of any concessional supply of food grains or other articles, any travelling concession, any contribution paid or payable, by the employer to any pension fund or provident fund, retrenchment compensation, and gratuity.

Calculation of Bonus

If an establishment consists of different departments or undertakings or branches, whether situated in the same place or in different places, unless a separate balance sheet and profit and loss account are prepared and maintained in respect of them, all such departments or undertakings or branches should be treated as parts of the same establishment for the purpose of computation of bonus, and once they are treated as parts of the same establishment, they should be continued to be treated as such.

The determination of gross profit is the first step towards calculating the amount of bonus. From the gross profit, certain prior charges arc to be deducted to arrive at the available surplus. However, the bonus is to be paid out of the allocable surplus. In case of a company, the allocable surplus is 67 per cent of the available surplus, and in other cases it is 60 per cent.

Eligibility for Bonus

Every employee shall be entitled to be paid bonus by his employer in an accounting year, provided that he has worked in the establishment for not less than 30 working days in that year.

An employee will be disqualified from receiving bonus if he is dismissed from service for the following:

1. Fraud
2. Riotous or violent behaviour while on the premises of the establishment
3. Theft, misappropriation, or sabotage of any property of the establishment

Amount of Bonus

The Act imposes a statutory obligation on the employer to pay bonus at the minimum rate of 8.33 per cent of the salary earned by an employee or ₹100, whichever is higher, in an accounting year. It shall be paid irrespective of profits and loss or whether there is allocable surplus or not in an accounting year. The maximum is fixed at 20 per cent.

Where the salary or wage of an employee exceeds ₹3,500 per mensem, the bonus payable to such employee shall be calculated as if his/her salary or wage was ₹2,500. There is also a provision under the Act for proportionate reduction in bonus where the employee has not worked for all the working days in any accounting year.

The excess of allocable surplus, if any, after distributing the maximum bonus as provided shall be set-on and taken into account up to the fourth accounting year. In the case of any shortage or want of allocable surplus, the amount distributed as bonus shall be carried forward for set-off and adjusted out of the allocable surplus. The Fourth Schedule illustrates the method of distribution and set-off or set-on of the amount available for bonus out of the allocable surplus.

Newly set-up establishments get exemption from payment of bonus for a period of six years following the accounting year in which the goods produced or manufactured are sold for the first time and, in other cases, up to the year when the new establishment shows profits, whichever is earlier.

Under the Act, adjustment can be made towards payment of customary or *puja* bonus against bonus payable under the Act.

If an employee is found guilty of misconduct causing financial loss to the employer, then the employer can deduct the amount of loss from the amount of bonus payable to the employee for the year in which he was found guilty of misconduct.

Time Limit for Payment of Bonus

The bonus shall be paid within a period of eight months from the close of the accounting year. If there is a dispute, it shall be paid within one month from the date on which the award becomes enforceable. The appropriate government may extend the said period up to a maximum of two years.

Claim for Bonus

If any bonus is due to an employee under a settlement, award or agreement, the employee himself, or any other person authorized by him in writing in this behalf, or in the case of death of the employee, his assignee or heirs, may make an application for its recovery to the appropriate government. The government, if satisfied, may issue a certificate to the collector to recover the same as arrears of land revenue. The application must be made within one year. However, the mode of recovery prescribed shall be available only if the bonus sought to be recovered is "under a settlement or an award or an agreement". It will not apply to the recovery of bonus which is payable under the Act.

A dispute about bonus payable under the Act will have to be raised by the employees concerned in accordance with the provisions of the Industrial Disputes Act, 1947, or any corresponding state law applicable to them.

If accounts are audited by duly qualified auditors of a company or by the comptroller and auditor-general of India, then the statements and particulars contained in such balance sheets and profit and loss accounts will be presumed to be accurate. It shall not be necessary for the corporation or the company to prove the accuracy of such statements. If the trade unions require any clarification, the court may direct the employer to furnish necessary clarification.

The Act provides for the appointment of inspectors and for the maintenance of registers and records. It also provides for different offences and corresponding penalties.

Mode of Payment

Employees can enter into an agreement or a settlement with their employer for grant of bonus under a formula different from that under the Act, i.e., bonus linked with production or productivity; but subject to the provisions of the Act in respect of payment of minimum and maximum bonus.

Exemption

The Act does not apply to the following establishments:

1. Newly set up establishments, units, or branches of existing establishments for six years from the date of starting production unless such establishments make profit
2. Government institutions
3. Reserve Bank of India
4. Deposit Insurance Corporation
5. Industrial Development Bank of India
6. Agricultural Refinance Corporations
7. Unit Trust of India
8. State Financial Corporations
9. Employees of insurance companies and the Life Insurance Corporation
10. Seamen
11. Stevedore labour
12. Universities and other educational institutions
13. Hospitals, chambers of commerce, and social welfare institutions
14. Inland water transport
15. Employees employed through contractors on building operations

If the appropriate government, having regard to the financial position and other relevant circumstances of any establishment or class of establishments is of the opinion that it will not be in public interest

to apply all or any of the provisions of this Act thereto, it may, by notification in the official gazette, exempt for such period as may be specified therein and subject to such conditions as it may think fit to impose, such establishment or class of establishment, from all or any of the provisions of the Act.
Source: http://labour.nic.in/wagecell/mwact.pdf

Equal Remuneration Act, 1976

To give effect to Article 39 of the Indian Constitution, on 26 September 1975, the Government of India promulgated the Equal Remuneration Ordinance. The ordinance was replaced by the Equal Remuneration Act, 1976, which received the assent of the President of India on 11 February 1976. It came into force from 11 March 1976 throughout India in the employments notified for the purpose. In exercise of the powers conferred under Section 13 of the Act, the Central Government framed rules known as the Equal Remuneration Rules, 1976.

Object of the Act

The object of the Act is to provide for the payment of equal remuneration to men and women workers and for the prevention of discrimination on the ground of sex, against women in the matter of employment. It also seeks to provide increasing opportunities for women in the specified employments.

Definition

The term 'remuneration' includes basic wage or salary and additional emoluments payable, either in cash or kind, to a person employed in an employment, or work done in such employment, if the terms of the contract of employment, express or implied, were fulfilled.

Equal Remuneration

It is the duty of the employer to pay equal remuneration to men and women workers for the same work or work of a similar nature.

No discrimination shall be made while recruiting for the same work or work of a similar nature between men and women workers, except where the employment of women in such work is prohibited or restricted by or under any law for the time being in force. The Act prohibits discrimination against women not only in recruitment but also in relation to the conditions of service subsequent to employment, such as promotions, training, and transfers.

Administration

For the purpose of providing increasing employment opportunities to women, the appropriate government may constitute one or more advisory committees.

The appropriate government may appoint an authority, not below the rank of a labour officer, to hear and decide on the claims and complaints. The authority appointed for this purpose shall have all the powers of a civil court under the Code of Civil Procedure, 1908. The aggrieved employer or worker may prefer appeal to the appellate authority within 30 days from the date of the order.

It is the duty of employers to maintain prescribed registers and other documents in relation to the workers employed by them.

The appropriate government may appoint inspectors for the purpose of enforcing the provisions of the Act.

The Act provides for penalties for violation of provisions of the Act.

Exemption

The requirement of equal treatment for men and women will not apply in certain special cases in so far as:

1. The terms and conditions of a workmen's employment are, in any respect, affected by compliance with the law regulating the employment of women
2. Any special treatment is accorded to women in connection with the birth, or expected birth, of a child

If the appropriate government is satisfied that the differences with regard to the remuneration of men and women workers in any establishment or employment are based on a factor other than sex, it may, by notification, make a declaration that any act of the employer attributable to such a difference shall not be deemed to be a contravention of any provision of this Act.
Source: http://labour.nic.in/wagecell/mwact.pdf

Statutory Social Security Benefits

The social security legislation in India consists of the following enactments:

1. Workmen's Compensation Act, 1923
2. Employees' State Insurance Act, 1948
3. Employees' Provident Funds and Miscellaneous Provisions Act, 1952
4. Maternity Benefit Act, 1961
5. Payment of Gratuity Act, 1972

Table 12.2 lists the benefits of the social security legislation in India.

Table 12.2 Benefits under social security legislation in India

Laws	Objectives	Benefits
Workmen's Compensation Act, 1923	To provide compensation for workmen in cases of industrial accidents occupational diseases resulting in disablement or death	Compensation for death. permanent total disablement, permanent partial disablement, temporary disablement, and occupational disease
Employees' State Insurance Act, 1948	To provide for health care and cash benefits in the case of sickness, maternity, and employment injury	Benefit for sickness and extended sickness benefit, maternity benefit, disablement benefit, dependants' benefit, medical benefit, funeral benefit, rehabilitation benefit
Employees' Provident Fund and Miscellaneous Provisions Act, 1952	To provide compulsory provident fund, pension, deposit-linked insurance	Refundable withdrawals, provident fund, pension, and deposit-linked insurance
Maternity Benefit Act, 1961	To provide for maternity protection before and after child birth	Payment for actual absence up to 12 weeks on average daily wages or minimum wage. Additional benefit for miscarriage, and illness arising out of pregnancy

Source: http://labour.nic.in/wagecell/mwact.pdf

DETERMINING THE CASH WAGES

The first thing employers should consider when developing compensation packages is fairness. It is absolutely vital that businesses maintain internal and external equity. Internal equity refers to fairness among employees in the same business while external equity refers to relative wage fairness compared to wages with other businesses. If these systems are not followed, the employees will be dissatisfied and the efficiency will come down automatically.

So, what constitutes fair wage? One approach that helps in determining a fair wage is a market survey. These are typically fast and easy ways to establish compensation guidelines for many businesses. A few phone calls to other employees in similar businesses can determine the 'market' value for a specific job. Unfortunately, this technique is not necessarily well-suited for agricultural producers. An agricultural manager can do informal surveys of other agricultural producers to determine the 'going rate' for labour or modify existing studies of non-agricultural businesses to compare employees not by job title but by skill sets. For example, operating a forklift in a factory and driving a tractor may require similar skills and, therefore, can be compensated similarly.

Another useful approach is broadbanding. Broadbanding was used in a Cornell University study. Five competency levels were developed to classify employees according to three criteria—authority to make decisions, skill level, and supervisory capacity. By using a competency scale, each employee can be cross-referenced by job title and competency level or studied solely within either category. Employees of similar skill levels or competency are taken together in compensation 'bands', regardless of job title. These bands compensate similar employees at the same rates across the entire organization and serve to maintain both internal and external equity.

CHECKLIST FOR MAKING WAGE STRUCTURE

Agricultural managers face several decision-making problems every day. Finding the time to build and implement an equitable wage structure can be difficult. To make the process easier, consider the following checklist:

1. Decide what you want your compensation package to do.
   - (a) Recruiting new employees
   - (b) Motivate current employees
   - (c) Rewarding well-performing employees
   - (d) Minimizing risk of violating federal laws
   - (e) Build employee loyalty
   - (f) Any combination of above
2. Determine your internal wage structure by
   - (a) Evaluating the job
   - (b) Evaluating the employee
   - (c) Creating competency groupings
3. Talk to your employees about their indirect compensation needs regarding
   - (a) Health insurance
   - (b) Paid vacation
   - (c) Housing
   - (d) Child care
   - (e) Retirement planning
4. Structure your total rewards system, including
   - (a) Indirect compensation based on your employee's needs and your compensation objectives
   - (b) Direct compensation based on labor market information and your compensation objectives
5. Implement your new system, while remembering to
   - (a) Communicate with your employees about their needs
   - (b) Review your compensation package regularly; make sure it is fair, equitable, and competitive
   - (c) Be flexible and innovative to maintain a competitive advantage
   - (d) Maintain both internal and external equity

Successful agricultural producers rely on common sense when it comes to management decisions. Employee compensation should be no different. If you want employees to be innovative, reward them for new ideas. If you want employees to stay for a long time instead of training new employees every season, offer bonuses or tie their wages to their tenure. If you need employees that show up on time, work hard, and can be trusted with the most challenging of tasks, recruit, reward, and promote those people. The future of your business could depend on it.

PRODUCTIVITY AND WORK STUDY

In numerical terms, productivity is equal to the ratio of the amount of output to the amount of input. The purpose of compensation including reward, incentives, and wages is to enhance productivity. The time required to perform an activity is ascertained using work study.

Definition of Work Study

The following are four different ways of defining work study:

1. An analysis of a specific job in an effort to find the most efficient method in terms of time and effort
2. An investigation of the most efficient way of doing a job, especially with regard to time and effort
3. The systematic examination of the methods of carrying out activities so as to improve the effective use of resources and to set up standards of performance for the activities carried out
4. A generic term for those techniques, particularly method of study and work measurement, which are used in the examination of human work in all its contexts, and which lead systematically to the investigation of all the factors which affect the efficiency and economy of the situation being reviewed, in order to effect improvement. It has to do with productivity improvement but not at the cost of quality and safety

Work Study Elements

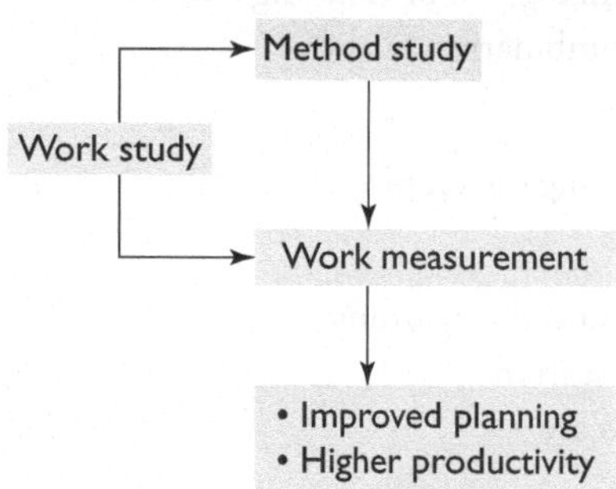

FIG. 12.7 Work study elements

Work study comprises method study and work measurement.

Method study is 'the systematic recording and critical examination of existing and proposed ways of doing work, as a means of developing and applying easier and more effective methods of doing work and reducing costs.' It is used to simplify the jobs and to develop more economical methods of doing the jobs.

Work measurement is the 'application of techniques designed to establish the time for a qualified worker to carry out a specified job at a defined level of performance.' It enables to determine how long the job should take to carry out. Refer to Figure 12.7.

PIECE WORK RATE CALCULATION

In piece work rate (PWR) calculation, the time required to perform an operation is first observed. On a particular day, a man can work slowly or fast. In addition, a particular piece may take more or less time for completion. For this purpose and to avoid any discrepancy in job rate, the time taken is observed over a number of items and over few days.

Moreover, a worker can work slower or faster. In order to nullify this effect, the rating factor is considered. If the rater (observer) perceives that a worker is performing faster than average workers, say 120 per cent, the observed time is to be multiplied by 1.2 (= 120/100) to arrive at the standard time. Again, if the rater perceives that a worker is slower (at 90 per cent) than the average worker, the observed time to be multiplied by 0.9 to calculate the standard time.

Fatigue allowances and personal need allowances are added with the standard time to calculate the allowable time from which the piece work rate is determined.

Piece work rate = Adjusted hourly rate/Average production per hour.

Let us illustrate the piece work rate with the help of the following problems.

Problem 12.1 The basic hourly rate of a worker, working on a multi-spindle automatic machine, is ₹60. Considering all allowances, the rate of the worker is increased by 25 per cent. He is expected to produce 800 units per hour. On a particular day of eight hours shift, he could produce 7,000 components. Calculate the earnings for the day.

Solution:

Basic hourly rate: ₹60; Increase in rate: 25 per cent; Adjusted hourly rate: ₹60 × (1.25) = ₹75
Expected/standard hourly output: 800 units
Expected production in eight-hour shift: 800 × 8 = 6,400 units
The worker produced 7,000 components.
Earnings = (7,000/6,400) × 75 × 8 = ₹656.25

DIFFERENTIAL PIECE RATE

Customers often enhance the ordered quantity and demanding the supply as early as possible. In order to fulfil customer satisfaction, companies revise the target and strive to achieve the same. To enthuse the workers and to meet the target, companies follow 'differential piece rate' system in times of emergency.

In this system, workers performing at higher than standard speed are given more incentives. Conversely, workers performing at lesser speed are given lesser incentive.

Problem 12.2 A company has two differential rates for determining piece work earnings of workers. It gives workers 80 per cent of the standard piece rate below average performers. However, the company gives 120 per cent of the standard piece rate to above average performers. According to structured system, it calculates earnings on day-to-day basis. Calculate earnings of the day for two workers using the following data:

(a) Length of shift: eight hours (excluding lunch break and tea time)
(b) Labour rate per hour in rupees: 20
(c) Standard output per hour in numbers: 125

In a particular day, worker A produced 1,200 numbers and worker B produced 900 numbers. Calculate the earnings of the two workers.

Solution:

Standard output per hour in numbers: 125
Expected standard output per day = 125 × 8 = 1,000 units
Standard piece work rate: ₹20/125

Normal rate for 900 units: (20/125) × 900 = ₹144
Normal rate for 1,200 numbers: (20/125) × 1,200 = ₹193
Worker A is a below average performer as he has produced less than standard output.
Worker A will earn at 80 per cent = ₹144 × 0.8 = ₹115.20
Worker B is an above average performer as he has produced more than standard output.
Worker B will earn at 120 per cent = ₹193 x1.2 = ₹231.60

Problem 12.3 If 360 pieces are produced at a standard price of ₹1,000 each, with a manufacturing cost of ₹4,000, material cost of ₹20,000, and overhead of ₹12,000, find the multifactor productivity.

Solution:

$$\text{Productivity} = \frac{\text{Quantity at standard price}}{\text{Manufacturing cost} + \text{Material cost} + \text{Overhead}}$$

$$= \frac{360 \times 1{,}000}{4{,}000 + 20{,}000 + 12{,}000} = \frac{3{,}60{,}000}{36{,}000} = 10$$

Problem 12.4 The workers of a modern television manufacturing organization are entitled to productivity-linked bonus to the extent of 10 per cent of savings arising out of productivity improvement as compared to the targeted budget. The productivity is measured in terms of production of component of television per man-hour in the department. The budgeted target for a month is 10,000 components in 1,000 man-hours.

During a particular month, 15,000 components were produced in 1250 man-hours. Assuming the budgeted contribution as ₹20 per component, calculate the amount of bonus payable per man-hour for the previous month.

Solution:

Budget level of productivity = 10,000/1,000 = 10 components per man-hour
Actual level of productivity = 15,000/1,250= 12 components per man-hour
As per unitary method, components that could have been produced in 1,250 man-hours = (10,000/1,000) × 1250 = 12,500
Extra production due to incentive = 15,000 – 12500 = 2,500 components
Saving due to increased level of productivity
= increase in production of components × budgeted contribution rate per component
= 2,500 components × ₹20 per component = ₹2,500 × 20 = ₹50,000
Total incentive payable to workers = 10 per cent of ₹50,000 = ₹5,000
Incentive payable per man-hour = ₹5,000/1,250 = ₹4 per man-hour

SUMMARY

Compensation and its management, reward system, incentive schemes, and wage administration are critical to the smooth functioning of an organization. These systems together determine the industrial relations, quality of work life, union-management relations, factors contributing to labour unrest, and satisfaction at the workplace. Companies need to define compensation policies and compensation objectives, and adhere to them to make the compensation system effective which, in turn, will contribute to the company. Compensation should be designed carefully to avoid any fault in its execution. The compensation domain includes many concepts including behavioural issues. Valence, instrumentality, and expectancy theory contribute to the compensation system. While designing a compensation system, ethical issues must be considered. Compensation including reward, incentive, and wage rests on certain legal considerations. An integrated total rewards strategy encompasses and emphasizes the culture, organizational environment, the approach to attract people, line of action to retain them, and keeps them motivated. Wages and salary administration is a major human resource management function today. While compliance with procedures and regulations is one aspect, cost to the organization, and employee motivation are other aspects which also need to be considered.

Human resource managers need to consider the trade-off between these considerations. In percentage terms, salary, wages, and bonus taken together are still the major causes of industrial disputes in India. Wages should be determined based on certain defined methodologies. Linking wages to performance is again a major issue. Suitable incentive schemes need to be identified to reward good performers. Organizations can be innovative in designing employee compensation, considering various aspects. Organizations need to emulate the best practices, continuously benchmark their compensation designs, and understand what works for them. Decisions on fixed and variable components of compensation need to be taken, while considering numerous factors—the nature of the job, company's business goals, product life-cycle, performance management systems, etc. There are various short-term and long-term incentive schemes available for organizations. Taking into account human resource strategy, the organization should choose from different alternatives, which meet the test of cost-benefit. Right incentive plans visibly contribute to organizational outcomes.

KEY TERMS

Compensation is pay provided by an employer to an employee for services rendered (time, effort, and skill). Compensation comprises four core elements—fixed pay, variable pay, short-term incentive pay, and long-term incentive pay.

Compensation benchmarking is an exercise to study the degree of competitiveness of the compensation rate of an organization, emulating best practices.

Dearness allowance is meant to protect the real wages of employees from falling in value, while keeping pace with the price rise.

Employee stock options (ESOPs) are offered as incentives by the organization to ensure an increased level of motivation and enhance probability retention of employees.

External equity refers to relative wage fairness compared to wages with other farms or businesses.

Fair wage is the wage that is above the minimum wage but below the living wage. Thus, the lower limit of the fair wage is the minimum wage, and the upper limit is set by the capacity of the industry to pay.

Fixed pay or base pay is nondiscretionary compensation that is independent of performance or results achieved, and is usually is determined by the organization's pay philosophy and structure.

Funding leverage is the increase in incentive fund with the increase in marginal increase in performance.

Going rate refers to the pay for comparable work in the industry.

Internal equity refers to fairness between employees in the same business.

Job evaluation is process of measuring the relative worth of a job to decide the wage rate.

Key result areas (KRAs) indicate the performance target of individual employees of an organization, aligning with business goals.

Leaving wages not only provide the bare essentials of food, clothing and shelter but are a measure of careful comfort for the worker, including education for his children, protection against ill-health, requirements of essential social needs, and a measure of insurance against the more important misfortunes, including old age.

Long-term incentive pay is a form of variable pay that is designed to recognize and reward performance over a period longer than one year, and includes stock options, restricted stock, performance shares, performance units, and cash.

Method study is used to simplify the jobs and to develop more economical methods of doing the jobs.

Minimum wages are need-based and statutorily decided, both by the central and the state government; the payment of minimum wages is obligatory for the organization.

Pay administration involves ensuring that pay achieves organizational as well as individual objectives and meets public policy goals.

Pay treatment for special groups is a supporting decision in compensation management.

Performance management systems are a system of integrating individual employee performance with the performance of the organization.

Reward management deals with the development, implementation, maintenance, communication, and evaluation of reward processes.

Short-term incentive pay is a form of variable pay that is designed to recognize and reward performance over a period of one year or less.

Time study is carried out to decide the standard time required to perform a job and then base the wage and incentives on the same standards.

Variable pay is also known as 'pay at risk', and changes directly with the level of performance or results achieved. It is a one-time payment that must be reestablished and earned again in each performance period.

Wage level is an average of the rates paid for the jobs of an organization, an establishment, a labour market, an industry, a region, or a nation.

Wage structure is a hierarchy of jobs to which wage rates have been attached.

Work measurement is the application of techniques designed to establish the time for a qualified worker to carry out a specified job at a defined level of performance. It enables to determine how long the job should take to carry out.

EXERCISES

Concept Review Questions

1. Explain the concept of employee compensation management. What is its significance?
2. What are the important compensation domains? Which domain do you feel influences compensation design in India?
3. Explain a compensation decision model and its determinants.
4. Define the term 'executive compensation'. What are the important components of executive compensation?
5. Discuss different theories of executive compensation.
6. Discuss the salient features of employee compensation in India.
7. Discuss the important elements of employee rewards.
8. Discuss the main features of reward system. How do the behavioural science theories influence reward management?
9. What is the rationale for job evaluation? Discuss the various methods of job evaluation.
10. What are the requirements of the Payment of Wages Act, 1936 in respect of payment of wages? Give an account of various deductions under the Act.

Critical Thinking Questions

11. Manpower attrition continues to be a burning problem in the information technology and telecom industry. Do you feel that a well-designed compensation system can take care of this problem? Mention few measures to eliminate or reduce this continuing problem. Enumerate the role of HR managers of companies belonging to a particular industry.
12. An organization engaged in manufacturing electronic components has to recruit a large number of both skilled and unskilled workers. These workers are easily available. The company believes there is no need to pay the workers above the minimum wage set by the state government. However, you personally feel that as the company is capable of paying more (due to high profit margins and a sound financial position), fair wages should be paid to the workers. Provide your arguments accordingly. As an HR manager, how would you attempt to convince the board of directors?

Assignments

13. Suppose after completing your MBA degree you joined an organization and worked there for three years. Your organization has recently completed the compensation survey which clearly shows that remuneration levels of several executive positions were either less than or more than what they should be. How would you bring these positions 'on line', and establish pay equity?
14. Visit five companies and discuss with the HR managers regarding various allowances and fringe benefits paid to industrial employees as an integral part of their compensation package. In addition, discuss the various components of a compensation structure. What are the factors they usually consider in determining the compensation structure? Prepare a comparative study and show it to your professor for his/her comments.

BIBLIOGRAPHY AND WEB RESOURCES

Beach, D.S., *The Management of People at Work*, Macmillan Publishing Company, New York, 1975.

Bhattacharyya, D.K., *Compensation Management*, Oxford University Press, New Delhi, 2009.

Chary, S.N., *Production and Operation Management*, Tata McGraw-Hill Companies, New Delhi, 2007.

DeGeorge, Richard T., *Military Ethics: A Code of Ethics for Officers*, National Defense University Press, Washington, 1987.

Gellerman, W., M.S. Frankel, and R.F. Ladenson, *Values and Ethics in Organizations and Human System Development: Responding to Dilemmas in Professional Life*, Jossey-Bass, San Francisco, 1990.

Hughes, Richard L., Robert C. Ginnett, and Gordon J. Curphy, *Leadership Enhancing the Lessons of Experience*, Tata McGraw-Hill Publishing Company Limited, New Delhi, 2008.

Kennedy, Kevin, Manager as Motivator, *Executive Excellence*, 18(6), p. 13, June 2001.

Lawler, Edward E., *Pay and Organizational Effectiveness: A Psychological View*, McGraw-Hill, New York, 1971.

Noe, Raymond A., John R. Hollenbeck, Barry Gerhart, and Patrick M. Wright, *Human Resource Management: Gaining A Competitive Advantage*, Tata McGraw-Hill, New Delhi, 2008.

Pestonjee, D.M., *Motivation and Job Satisfaction*, Macmillan, New Delhi, 1991.

Porter, L.W. and Lawler, E.E. III, *Managerial Attitudes and Performance*, Dorsey Press, Homewood, 1968.

Porter, L.W., and Lawler, E.E. III, *What Job Attitudes Tell About Motivation*, Harvard Business Review, January–February 1968.

Prakash, Ravi, *Correlation between Performance and Incentive released in State bank of India*; submitted to Indian Institute of Social Welfare and Business Management (IISWBM) for evaluation by University of Calcutta.

SAIL, *Best HR Practices*, Steel Authority of India Limited, New Delhi, 2009.

Schein, E., Organizational Culture, *American Psychologist*, February, Vol. 43, No. 2, pp. 109–119, 1990.

Schein, E., *Organizational Culture*, American Psychologist, February, Vol. 43, No. 2, pp. 109–119, 1990.

Singh, D., *Special Report: Benchmarking the Compensation System for Executive Staff, Research and Practice in Human Resource Management*, 4(1), pp. 115–124, 1996.

Vroom, V.H., *Work and Motivation*, Wiley, New York, 1964.

Web Resources

www.eridlc.com/onlinetextbook/chpt01/text_main.htm, last accessed on 6 August 2011.

www.nhpc.co.in, last accessed on 6 September 2011.

CORRELATION BETWEEN PERFORMANCE AND INCENTIVES IN STATE BANK OF INDIA

About State Bank of India

The origin of the bank can be traced back to early 1800. In 1921, three banks (Bank of Bengal, Bank of Bombay, and Bank of Madras) were merged to form The Imperial Bank of India. This bank was very important from the view point of the growth of the State Bank of India (SBI). The present state, functioning, structure, and operation of SBI were basically inherited from The Imperial Bank of India. The Imperial Bank was the only governmental bank till 1935. It was the custodian of the government bonds and performed the treasury work of the government free of charge. They were entrusted to handle public debt of the Government of India, provided the machinery for the issue of government bonds, and kept a watch on the exchange rate of the country. The commercial banks, including Imperial Bank, were prospering in the urban areas. Thus, SBI was formed by the passage of the State Bank of India Bill, 1955. The bank was formally constituted on the model of its predecessor. SBI has seven subsidiary banks—State Bank of Bikaner and Jaipur, Hyderabad, Indore, Mysore, Patiala, Saurashtra, and Travancore. SBI has an extensive coverage and has electronically networked most of its metropolitan, urban, and semi-urban branches under the core banking system (CBS). The bank has the largest ATM network in the country with more than 12,000 ATMs. SBI has had grown steadily over the years.

About the research objectives

The study was undertaken by SBI in West Bengal. The objectives of the study were the following:

1. To find out the correlation between performance and incentive of SBI employees of Bengal circle for the years 2005–06, 2006–07, and 2007–08
2. To find out how the existing incentives schemes at SBI influence its core sector employees

3. To find out the analytical relationship between performance and the incentive allocated so that the amount of incentive given on the basis of any level of percentage achievement can be easily and accurately predicted
4. To find out ways to boost employees to perform their work spontaneously by getting acquainted with their grievances, if any

Parameters for incentives

SBI listed the incumbents and decided the parameters based on which the incentive would be sanctioned. The traditional parameters are deposit, advances, non-performing assets (NPA), and net profit. Miscellaneous parameters considered by the bank are fee income, new accounts and customers, NEFT/RTGS, internet usage, ATM cards, and average CASA deposits.

The parameters for evaluation were decided to be reviewed and changed every year so as to keep an element of challenge therein. The managing director and group executives, in consultation with the chairman, were to decide these parameters and the eligibility criteria for their respective groups.

SBI developed an equation to calculate the amount of incentive which can be given to the different branch managers on the basis of different percentage achievements of the traditional parameters (advances, deposits, NPAs and net result) complying with the incentive allocation scheme of SBI for the year 2006–07.

The bank also decided the incumbents and amount of incentives for achieving the parameters. Most interestingly, SBI tabled the amount of incentive for achieving (a) three of four parameters, and all the four parameters. For information, one table is reproduced.

The bank also introduced system of differential incentives for branch managers and managers of the division.

Incumbency of branch	Branch manager Budget achievement			
Incumbency	75 per cent to less than 100 per cent in three out of four parameters	75 per cent to less than 100 per cent in all four parameters	100 per cent or more in three out of four parameters	100 per cent or more in four parameters
TEGS VI	₹50,000	₹55,000	₹60,000	₹60,000
SMGS V	₹40,000	₹45,000	₹50,000	₹55,000
SMGS IV	₹35,000	₹40,000	₹45,000	₹50,000
MMGS III	₹30,000	₹35,000	₹40,000	₹45,000
MMGS II	₹25,000	₹30,000	₹35,000	₹40,000
JMGS I	₹20,000	₹25,000	₹30,000	₹35,000

Incumbency of branch	Branch manager Budget achievement	Manager of division Budget achievement
	100 per cent to 110 per cent in three out of four parameters	100 per cent to 110 per cent in three out of four parameters
TEGS VI	₹45,000	₹35,000
SMGS V	₹35,000	₹30,000
SMGS IV	₹30,000	₹25,000
MMGS III	₹25,000	₹20,000
MMGS II	₹20,000	₹15,000
JMGS I	₹15,000	₹10,000

These incentives were subjected to the following conditions:

1. For achievement in deposits and advances, budgeted growth and actual calculated as quarterly averages for the entire year were to be reckoned. For profit, year-end achievement of the budget was taken.
2. Branches which were dropped to 'B' or 'B(-)' ratings in the central office inspection and audit report held between April, 2005 and March, 2006 were not eligible for the incentives.
3. Branch managers of branches which were loss-making as on 31 March 2006 in metropolitan and urban centers were not eligible.
4. The concerned functionary remained in that position as on 31 March 2008 for at least nine months or more.
5. Annual NPA reduction budget for 2005–06 was fully achieved.
6. DGMs of modules and AGMs of regions were rendered ineligible, if any one the following criteria is applicable in their cases:
   (a) 10 per cent or more of their branches have B or B(-) ratings in the central office inspection and audit as on 31 March 2006.
   (b) Less than 75 per cent of branches are profit-making as on 31 March 2006.
   (c) 25 per cent or more branches had achieved 25 per cent or less of budget in P segment deposit as on 31 March 2006.

As a sequel and to follow up the incentive scheme for the managers, SBI introduced two schemes (effective from the financial year 2005–06.

Scheme I: Team incentive scheme for the staff at a branch which achieved certain benchmarks in the areas of deposits, advances, net profit, and NPA reduction.

Scheme II: Individual incentive scheme for those staff members (officers/ employees) who exhibited individual brilliance but were posted at branches which were not eligible for 'team incentive' under scheme I.

The objectives of the incentive schemes were the following:

1. Inculcating performance culture.
2. Providing right motivational impulses on an ongoing basis.
3. Recognition to team efforts/individual efforts regardless of the category of staff members.

The scoring model for team incentive was a weighted average-based model. The weightings given to the traditional parameters were as follows:

Parameter	Weightage
Average deposits (excluding C & I deposits)	0.3
Average advances	0.3
NPA reduction	0.1
Profit	0.3

The incentives were proposed to be given to all the branches which achieved at least 100 per cent of their budgeted growth during the year 2005–06. However, branches achieving more than 150 per cent of the average budget in respect of average deposits and average branches were not given any weightage in score card beyond 150 per cent.

The incentive was in cash and was proposed to be given to those who met the preset requirements. A format was devised in which the branch managers, Managers of divisions and assistant general managers (region/branch), deputy general manager (module/region) were to submit the details of their performance for the year to the sanctioning authority to claim the incentive. The controlling authority (AGM—region/DGM—module) was the sanctioning authority for grant of incentive to managers of division/ branch managers. Similarly, the DGM of module was the sanctioning authority for AGMs (region/branch) and the concerned general manager was the sanctioning authority for DGM (module/branch). For mid-corporate levels, SAM, and CAG branches, the respective chief general manager of the group was the sanctioning authority.

Statistical tools used

For carrying out the data analysis, simple as well as multiple correlations was used. in addition, coefficient of determination, F-statistic, degrees of freedom analysis and multivariate analysis using linear regression method were employed.

Simple and multiple correlations were used to find out the degree of correlation between the traditional parameters (deposit, advances, NPA, and net profit) and the incentive amount given to the branch managers as well as the employees of the branch.

Summary of results and findings

The results of the statistical tests and interpretations are interesting and useful. Some of the findings are briefed as follows:

1. There is a measurable relationship between the performance of the employees of SBI, and the incentive amount given to them.

2. Incentive scheme of the financial year 2007–08 has motivated the branch managers of the various branches of SBI in Bengal Circle to work even harder.
3. The correlation of team incentive with the traditional parameters of budget achievement (deposits, advances, NPAs, and net results) is significant.
4. Managers are motivated by incentive and this is evidenced from the multiple correlations between the manager's incentive and the traditional parameters.
5. Team incentives motivate (employees below the rank of branch manager) to a large extent to work even harder to increase the traditional parameters. The correlation is far strong than that between the manager's incentive and the traditional parameters.
6. Variation between the actual value and the predicted value for manager's incentive or team incentive and traditional parameters can be well explained from the coefficient of determination.
7. Linear regression analysis establishes that amount of incentive given on the basis of any level of percentage achievement of the four parameters can be predicted.
8. If recognition is added as a variable along with the other variables then the coefficient of the various correlations would almost be equal to unity implying a perfect linear relationship between the performance and the incentives.

Incentive and performance

There is a measurable relationship between the performance of the employees of SBI and the incentive amount given to them. The correlation between the managers' incentives and the traditional parameters show that the employees of SBI in Bengal circle do get motivated by the presence of the incentive programme introduced by the bank.

If the data regarding the team incentive and the traditional parameters is seen carefully, then it can be observed that those employees of the Bank in Bengal circle who are not the branch managers are motivated by a large extent to work even harder if they are rewarded with incentives for their performance. Incentive programme of SBI helps a lot in enhancing the performance of the employees which in turn helps to increase the revenue of the bank.

Suggestions

The researcher offered several suggestions, some of which are listed here:

1. Incentives should include both reward and recognition.
2. Recognition is more important as compared to monetary reward.
3. Communicate to employees through suitable media.
4. Proper implementation of the schemes such as 'The Best Employee Award'.
5. Felicitating with a bouquet and a gift in the meeting to further enthuse.
6. To introduce awards such as 'Best Effort Award'.
7. Timely incentive to boost the morale of the employees.
8. Maintaining record of the work performed by the employees for objectivity in team incentive.

(Case study written based on the a project report prepared, in partial fulfillment of master of human resource management degree by Ravi Prakash, and submitted to Indian Institute of Social Welfare and Business Management (IISWBM) for evaluation by University of Calcutta.)

The following is a questionnaire used for collecting primary data.

Questionnaire

Branch name: ______________

Code: ______________

Incentives: An HR Initiative in SBI

1. Are you a pro-incentive employee? (Please tick.)

Yes	No	Can't say

2. To what extent do you like the incentive programme introduced by SBI? (Please tick.)

Strongly like	Like	Neutral	Dislike	Strongly dislike

3. Do you work hard to get the incentives? (Please tick.)

Yes	No	Indifferent

4. What should be the level of the incentive? (Please tick.)

High	Moderate	Low

5. Are incentives necessary to perform better? (Please tick.)

Yes	No	Can't say

6. (a) What should be the mode of the incentive? (Please tick.)

Cash	Real Term	Both

(b) If other than cash, then please specify.

___

___

___

7. Does recognition serves as a better means than the incentive? (Please tick.)

Yes	No	Can't say

8. Is the present incentive programme up to the mark? (Please tick.)

Yes	No	Can't say

9. Do incentives motivate the employees to work even harder? (Please tick.)

Yes	No	Can't say

10. Does the incentive scheme de-incentivize the employees in any manner? (Please tick.)

Yes	No	Can't say

11. What at present is the degree of correlation between incentive and performance? (Please tick.)

Yes	No	Can't say

12. Do you think that there exists a negative correlation between the two? (Please tick.)

Yes	No	Can't say

13. What is the rating procedure adopted by you for selecting the employees for team incentive?

___

___

___

14. How do you motivate those employees who do not get the incentive to work hard?

___

15. What changes has this scheme brought about in the performance of your branch?

16. Please make suggestions for improving the present performance linked incentive programme.

Date: ....

Signature: ....

Name: ....

Mobile no.:

Email address:

HR MANTRA Importance of incentives

People join organizations to earn their livelihood. Some may be sincere and dedicated to work, some may focus on achieving the set target, and some may be complacent and smug. The first group strives to excel doing something innovative. The management has to reward them to keep them motivated.

The management must reward good and exceptional performers. It has to design a compensation system for taking care of performance parameters, so as to keep the wheel of production moving. Incentives and benefits facilitate achieving the organizational goals.

The mantra: Compensation facilitates company growth.

MICHAEL ARMSTRONG

Michael Armstrong is an honours graduate in economics from the London School of Economics, and a companion of the Chartered Institute of Personnel and Development (CIPD). He has had over 25 years of experience in personnel management, of which he spent 12 years as a personnel director. He has also been a management consultant for many years and is a former chief examiner for the CIPD.

His career comprises his hands on experience within the engineering industry. Initially, Armstrong specialized in employee relations, and later as a learning and development specialist in the aerospace and food industries.

He was the executive director and was responsible for managing human resources in a publishing firm for 12 years (he was a general manager for three years). This was followed by heading the consultancy division of Coopers & Lybrand for 10 years. Armstrong is a managing partner of e-reward.uk and also practices as an independent consultant.

Armstrong has published several books, of which three books are related to reward management. His book *Employee Reward*

(2002) sets out the competences that all practitioners need in their portfolio. Another book, *A handbook of employee reward management and practice* (2007) provides updated guidance on the various approaches to use in developing and managing reward strategies, policies, and processes, while *Reward management: a handbook of remuneration strategy and practice* (2007), co-authored by Helen Murlis, explains reward management. The latter is concerned with formulating and implementing policies and strategies that aim to reward people fairly, equitably, and consistently in accordance with their value to the organization.

Michael's other distinguishing publications are *Performance management: Key Strategies and Practical Guidelines* (2000), *A Handbook of Human Resource Management Practice* (2006), *Strategic human resource management: a guide to action* (2008), *How to Be an Even Better Manager: A Complete A-Z of Proven Techniques and Essential Skills* (2008).

References

www.google.co.in/imgres?q, last accessed on 14 October 2011.

ANNEXURE 12.1

Best Practices—Functional Managers in HR/Finance

HR head	Finance head
Qualification: Postgraduates, preferably MBAs	Qualification: CA/MBA (finance)
Experience: More than 5 years	Experience: 7–8 years
Responsibilities: 1. Manage the HR functions of the SBU 2. Frame strategies of sourcing 3. Develop and retain people 4. Play a crucial role in business strategy formulation and implementation	Responsibilities: 1. Manage the finance of SBU/division/region/zone 2. Contribute to sourcing funds 3. Mobilization of resources 4. Financial management, working capital management, planning, and control
Benefits: HRA (50 to 60 per cent of basic), house lease of ₹10,000 to ₹15,000 per month, or leased accommodation	Benefits: Same as HR head
Conveyance: Company buys a car within the sanctioned limit, with compulsory buy back after five years. In this case, the company maintains the car. However, when the cost of care is above the sanctioned limit, the company funds the difference and charge interest on such amount.	Benefits: Same as HR head
Medical: Group medical for self, wife, and two children not exceeding ₹2,00,000	Medical: Same as HR head
LTA: One to two months' basic pay	LTA: Same as HR head
ESOP: Share scheme for more than one year service. Company deposits the ESOP equivalent amount in bank to earn interest and pays a sizable amount at the end of three years.	ESOPs: Same as HR head
Incentive schemes: Performance incentive: Six–twelve months' salary on a four-scale rating Annual performance incentive: 40–50 per cent of basic salaries Bonus: 20 per cent of basic Travel: Free two-year air ticket to anywhere in the world	Incentive schemes: Same as HR head

HR head	Finance head
Co-curricular activities: 1. Cultural programmes, sports, etc. 2. In-house magazine 3. Picnic with family 4. Open chat with MD 5. Annual ball	Co-curricular activities: Same as HR head
Other benefits: Credit cards, club membership, and telephones (not part of CTC)	Other benefits: Same as HR head
Loans: 1. General loan: After six months, with a subsidy of 2–4 per cent 2. House loan: ₹3,00,000 – ₹5,00,000 with 6 per cent interest 3. Car loan: Up to ₹,00,000 at 6 per cent interest 4. Furniture: Up to ₹90,000 5. White goods: AC and other amenities at only 10 per cent value charged 6. Soft furnishing: Provided 7. Deferrals: Provident fund (12 per cent of basic plus DA), gratuity (4.8 per cent), and superannuation (15 per cent).	Loans: Same as HR head

Source: Bhattacharyya (2009).

ANNEXURE 12.2
Best Practices—Compensation in Call Centres

Levels	Assistant manager and section manager
Entry procedure	Graduate/post graduate (Technical background in IT essential)
Requirements	1. Three to five years of experience 2. Team player 3. Excellent managerial and supervisory capabilities 4. Analytical 5. Excellent communication skills 6. Handle a team of ten to fifteen people 7. Coordinate their activities and schedule projects implementation 8. Plan
Responsibilities	Two to three shifts, five days a week
Working time	*Induction:* Three to seven days *Periodic training:* Three to four days per year person
HRA	50–60 per cent of basic pay
Conveyance	₹800 per month
Medical	Group medical insurance for parents, spouse, and two children up to ₹2,00,000

Levels	Assistant manager and section manager
Deferrals	Provident fund—12 per cent, gratuity—4.8 per cent, superannuation—13 per cent
LTA	One month's basic pay
Loans	• General loans after six months of service • ₹10,000 per year interest free
Rewards	• Cash award for consistent performer • Cash award, certificate, and medal once a month for the best team • Yearly best team award
ESOPS	• share scheme for more than one year service • Company deposits the ESOP equivalent amount in the bank to earn interest and pays sizable amounts at the end of three years
Incentive schemes	• Annual performance incentive 10–15 per cent of basic salary • Free two-way airline ticket, to anywhere in the world

Source: Bhattacharyya (2009)

CHAPTER 13

Separation and Beyond

LEARNING OBJECTIVES

After studying this chapter, you will be able to
- Understand the meaning of separation
- Analyse the various types of separation
- Appreciate the essence of separation management
- Realize the utmost need for conducting an exit interview
- Identify the benefits of an exit interview
- Design an exit interview questionnaire

OPENING CASE

Angst of a Separated Official

After rendering his services for 40 years in an organization, Adams retired. He was holding a senior position and was active in the discharge of his duties, with a high degree of achievement and motivation. By virtue of his dynamism and energetic, dutiful, inquisitive, perfectionist, and persuasive nature, he was treated as an asset to the company. Adams had contributed many innovative ideas and changes in the processes and the company had driven significant benefits from them. All his contributions were recorded. Immediately after his retirement, Adams became a different man who always seemed to be deep in thoughts. He was also gradually losing his health.

To feel better, he joined some social clubs and began playing cards and chess to kill time. However, this diversion did not help him to a great extent. He was still found very indifferent by most of the club members.

One day, about three months after his retirement, he desired to visit the company from where he had retired. At the entrance, Adams was greeted with an indifferent welcome. The security personnel, who had joined recently, did not know Adams. However, Adams proceeded to his department. He spoke about the treatment meted out to him and desired a rectification. The operator approached his immediate supervisor and informed him about Adams' request. The supervisor who was much junior to Adams greeted Adams, but instructed the operator to carry on with his usual routine. Adams felt hurt.

Learning points
- One needs to forget his/her attachment with the company that he/she worked in.
- After retirement, one should not try to exercise control in the workplace that one retired from.
- After retirement, one should not expect to be treated with the same warmth by one's juniors as during the tenure of service.

INTRODUCTION

Separation is a common phenomenon in an employee's social as well as organizational life. The foreseeable separation occurs when a person superannuates from service. In organizations, separations also occur due to lay-off, resignation, dismissal or discharge, retrenchment, and voluntary retirement schemes. It is seen that in knowledge business industries, manpower attrition is higher. Separation, for any reason, is painful not only to the employees, but for their colleagues and the management. Separation cannot be avoided, and hence, needs to be managed carefully.

Employee exits are a natural part of the employee life cycle. Whether caused by voluntary resignation, retirement, or company-induced termination, employee separations need to be efficiently managed, and the HR department must discharge the vital role. Let us analyse the various grounds of separation.

SEPARATION

Separation happens on many grounds such as lay-off, resignation, dismissal or discharge, retrenchment, voluntary retirement schemes, transfer, and attrition. We will now discuss these concepts:

Lay-off

A lay-off cannot be avoided in certain situations. A lay-off is a temporary separation of an employee from his/her employer at the instance of the latter, without any prejudice to the former. Lay-off is initiated as the failure, refusal, or inability of an employer to continue employment of a worker whose name is in the rolls but who has not been retrenched. Lay-off may occur as a result of the occurrence of the following:

1. Major breakdown of machinery
2. Shortage of coal, power, or raw material
3. Accumulation/accrual of stock, thus increasing the inventory of finished items

> A lay-off, caused by major breakdown of machinery, shortage of input materials, etc., is a temporary separation of the employee from his/her employer.

One of the major stress triggers for human resource professionals is bearing the bad news of layoffs. In addition, losing a trusted colleague all of a sudden, is a major shock and one's reaction is quite similar to losing a loved one. Some companies arrange for re-engagement of their laid-off employees through outplacement agencies. Refer to Exhibit 13.1 for more details about the outplacement of laid-off employees.

Exhibit 13.1 Outplacement of laid-off employees

Some organizations offer outplacement services through companies such as Insala, Right Management, KPGM India, BTI Consultants, Ayers Group, etc., to the laid-off employees. These companies deal with career transition and outplacement services. The outplacement cell is a support system consisting of assessment centers that evaluates a person's competencies freshly, and comprises occupational therapists and psycho-analysts who aid the laid off employee to cope with the change and direct them towards new career possibilities. Such support systems make layoffs more acceptable and less painful for individuals and organizations. This kind of service is prominent in

(Contd)

Exhibit 13.1 (Contd)

the UK markets where organizations take responsibility for their laid off employees.

Tata Consultancy Services, IBM, Motorola, and Microsoft are a few companies that are utilizing the services of outplacement agencies to train their laid-off workforce and find appropriate placements for them.

Source: Human Capital (2009)

Resignation

Resignation or early retirement refers to termination based on the employee's discretion to discontinue employment. Generally, an employee resigns on securing better employment elsewhere. Sometimes, female employees may have to resign after marriage, if the company does not have a branch in the city where she has to move to. The administration of separation caused by resignation is simple, as this is initiated by the employee.

Dismissal or Discharge

Dismissal or discharge is a drastic step initiated by the employer; this step should be taken after careful analysis and thought. A dismissal needs to be supported by sufficient reasons and documentary evidences. Initially, departmental enquiry is instituted by engaging an inquiry officer and a presenting officer. The role of the inquiry officer is similar to the judge, and the role of the presenting officer is similar to that of a prosecution officer. The accused may opt for a defender. Some of the reasons for a departmental inquiry are excessive absenteeism, serious misconduct, fake statement of qualification at the time of entry, theft of company property, etc. Based on the findings, the delinquent employee can be dismissed. A worker or even a union leader can be dismissed if he uses filthy language or creates a scene that stops regular production. A court verdict is explained in Exhibit 13.2.

Exhibit 13.2 Uttarakhand high court verdict

Dismissal of union leader justified for yelling, using filthy language, and abusing the management. He tried to snatch papers from officers and disrupted production for one and a half hours. Labour court pronounced him guilty.

Verdict of the high court: Labour court's verdict upheld.

Justification: Dismissal of the workman, even though he was a union leader, was rightly upheld since he had indulged in shouting of abusive slogans and filthy language towards his seniors and disrupted the production, causing loss to the management.

The fact that the enquiry report was not supplied to the workman along with show-cause notice would not mean that the enquiry had to be vitiated, since no prejudice had been caused.

Source: *Ravindra Sharma* v. *Labour Court* and others (2011 LLR 495), *Business Manager*

Retrenchment

Retrenchment refers to an employer giving a termination to a workman for any reason whatsoever, otherwise than a punishment inflicted by way of disciplinary action. It is important to remember that it does not include the following:

1. Voluntary retirement of the workman
2. Retirement of the workman on reaching the age of superannuation
3. Termination of the service of the workman as a result of non-renewal of the contract of employment between the employer and the workman

4. Termination of the service of a workman on the ground of continued ill-health (The Industrial Disputes Act, 1947)

Retrenchment also results in the separation of an employee from his/her employer. It differs from lay-off and dismissal. In case of lay-off, the employee continues to be in the pay-role of the organization and is assured of being called back after the expiry period of lay-off. However, in case of retrenchment, an employee is sent for good, and his/her connections with the organization completely end.

Retrenchment differs from dismissal, too. It means the discharge of surplus labour or staff in the continuing industry, and the removal of dead weight of uneconomic surplus. An employee can be retrenched even if a company operates at a level of profits. As per Industrial Disputes Act, 1947, employers must fulfil conditions precedent to retrenchment. Dismissal, on the other hand, refers to separation on account of gross misconduct.

A retrenched employee can approach the court of law for justice. If an employee is retrenched illegally and the employer cannot produce supporting documents to the court, the employee becomes eligible for reinstatement with back wage.

The verdicts of Rajasthan High Court and Uttarkhand High Court on retrenchment are provided along with the case numbers. Refer to Exhibits 13.3 and 13.4.

Exhibit 13.3 Rajasthan high court verdict

Verdict of the high court: In case of illegal retrenchment, reinstatement with 50 per cent back-wages granted by the labour court held proper.

Justification: Reinstatement has been rightly awarded by the labour court when the municipal council did not comply with provisions of Section 25F of the Industrial Disputes Act providing for payment of retrenchment compensation and one month's notice or pay in lieu thereof at the time of termination, whereas considering the peculiar facts and circumstances, 50 per cent back-wages are awarded instead of full wages.

Source: *Municipal Council* v. *Chhotalal* and another (2011 LLR 517), *Business Manager*

Exhibit 13.4 Uttarakhand high court verdict

Verdict of the high court: Retrenchment without following the principle of 'last come first go' held illegal. Reinstatement without back-wages held proper.

Justification: Reinstatement without back-wages would be appropriate even when a workman has worked for more than 240 days in a calendar year but the principle of 'last come, first go', stipulated by section 25G for effecting retrenchment, has not been followed.

Source: Mussoorie Dehradun Development Authority v. *Shri Rameshwar and others* (2011 128 FLR 1030) *Business Manager*

Voluntary Retirement Schemes

Companies launch voluntary retirement schemes (VRS), which can be exercised optionally or mandatorily. Over the last few decades, companies have gotten into the practice of cutting surplus manpower. VRS, unlike retrenchment, is a noble or righteous scheme, and is alternatively known as the 'golden hand shake' plan.

VRS is actually a painless and time-saving method of trimming employee strength. The collective bargaining fora cannot object to this mode, as the scheme is attractive and voluntary. Employees who opt for this scheme get handsome compensation. In other words, management pays a hefty amount to attract employees to opt for this scheme rather than retaining surplus manpower, resulting in recurring expenditure. Voluntary retirement schemes are also termed 'separation incentive program' for employees.

Transfer

In companies, employees are transferred from one department to another of the same unit, or from one unit to another unit. Though transfers are usually ordered without any change in the job responsibilities or remuneration, sometimes they may also involve a change in the job role. In the latter case, they are often accompanied by a change in the place of the job. In some cases, the senior employees working in multinational companies are even transferred to serve in units in other countries.

A transfer is different from a promotion which involves a significant change in responsibility, status, and income. Transfers are regular and frequent organizational phenomena. In banks and in government organizations such as ordnance factories, transfers in gazetted ranks are frequent. Some of the common reasons behind transfers are listed as follows:

1. Frequent disputes between an employee and the controlling manager
2. Frequent complaints about one employee by his/her colleagues
3. A change expressed by an employee with regard to his/her interest or capabilities to perform other tasks
4. Declining productivity of an employee over a period of time; may be due to monotony of the assignments
5. Work environment not suiting an employee's health following some ailment
6. Family-related issues such as marriage (of a women employee), continued sickness of parents

In case of shortage of manpower in one department, due to explosion of demands from the customers, the management tries to deal with the situation by working extra time or multiple shifts. Furthermore, if any department has surplus manpower, the management neutralizes the same by way of inter-departmental transfers. People are transferred from one department having surplus resources to another department where the demand is more. In order to avoid industrial disputes, there are certain principles behind transfers that must be followed.

Principle of Transfer

Transfers must be ordered based on certain company-specific principles or dogma. Transferring an employee without adhering to policies or norms may lead to deteriorated industrial relations. The management might think of issuing transfer orders, treating each case on its own merit. Even if management takes the right decisions, some employees may take exception to them. Thus, management must frame a transfer policy and follow the same. Some principles of a transfer policy are as follows:

1. In a usual phenomenon, a transfer causes some disturbance to the transferee. Hence, a minimum period between transfers and the frequency of transfer must be decided upon by the HR department and made known to all the employees. A company should develop its administrative manual to endorse the policies and objectives relating to administration.
2. Authorities of the manager who will handle transfer must be earmarked and responsibilities must be defined. In an organization, the authority to handle transfers should be centralized to ensure uniformity in practices.

> Transfer is different from promotion; the latter involves significant change in responsibility, status, and income.

3. Transfers on individual employees' requests should be based on documented transfer system.
4. Transfer orders must clearly specify whether the transfer is of permanent or temporary nature.
5. Prior to transfer, the performance of an employee needs to be assessed. The assessment helps management to assign new tasks to the employee as per the job description.
6. While developing the transfer policy, the interest of the organization must always be remembered.

Types of Transfer

Aswathappa (2006) proposed the following five types of transfers:

Production transfer Employees are posted in different departments, based on their interests and qualifications. This also depends on the work load that a department possesses. However, this load keeps fluctuating, and the demand for manpower keeps changing with time.

For departments with surplus manpower, lay-off is a solution. However, a better solution is the interdepartmental transfer to balance the manpower allocation. In simpler terms, production transfer refers to the transfers ordered to avoid such unavoidable lay-offs.

Q 4 **Replacement transfer** When an employee leaves a department for a particular reason, the department needs a replacement. In such scenarios, especially in demanding situations, a senior employee might have to function in place of the junior employee, till the time a replacement is found. Senior employees are required to work in place of junior employees even in situations of decling production. Thus, replacement transfer also helps in reducing the organizational need for lay-off; particularly for long-service employee.

Versatility transfer Some organizations believe that the workforce needs to have multiple skills capable to perform multiple tasks. People can achieve multiple skills only by working in different departments. In learning organizations such as ordnance factories, banks, and many private companies, people get the scope of working in different departments and can learn different systems, procedures, and rules and regulations. They gain the necessary skills to attend to the activities in the departments, and ultimately become versatile. People who pick up their tasks quickly emerge to become the company's assets. During rush periods, they are able to contribute greatly to achieve business goals. Versatile transfer may comprise production transfer or replacement transfer.

Shift transfer In order to enhance capacity utilization, industrial organizations, operate in multiple shifts—generally morning, evening, and night shifts. Some organizations allot employees to staggered shifts as well. Employees are engaged in all the shifts on a rotational basis. Requests of employees for transfers on a particularly shift are also entertained, considering the importance of ground of requests. However, conformance to law and administrative procedures are essential requirements to avoid employee unrest.

Remedial transfer After induction, employees are placed in a department and jobs are assigned to him/her, and their performance and behavioural dispositions are recorded. Some employees may emerge as good performers, while many others may emerge as underperformers. In course of time, an employee's inclination to work is also observed. The objective of remedial transfer is therapeutic in nature, that is, to rectify the wrong placement.

In other words, remedial transfer is an act of transferring an employee to a more suitable job after they have failed to perform well in their present position. Poor performance could be attributed to reasons such as an employee being uncomfortable in his job as he may not possess good relations with his senior or suffer from ill health.

ATTRITION

Attrition of manpower is also an important reason for separation. This phenomenon is seen to be affecting knowledge industries in particular and continues to be a problem that challenges HR managers and the human resource management function. Companies are experiencing difficulties in retaining experienced manpower due to high rate of manpower attrition. Manpower turnover is present due to higher aspirations of employees, especially in information technology companies.

Key Attrition Factors

From the studies of many industrial stalwarts and academicians, and also through personal interactions with HR and IT personnel, a set of factors which can be treated as the key attrition factors is listed.

1. Inability to use one's competencies
2. Lack of challenge
3. Boss and his/her management style
4. Lack of scope of growth in terms of salary, status, and other factors
5. Lack of role clarity
6. Lack of sense of belongingness
7. Rust out stress syndrome (ROSS) develops when an employee does not get the opportunity of utilizing his capacity or potential
8. Burst/burnt out stress syndrome (BOSS) develops when a performer is assigned more and more work as the management is confident of getting the work done by the employee
9. Lack of learning opportunities
10. Levels of motivation
11. Unfulfilled 'occupational values'
12. Life style inventory—unmatched with the task
13. Lack of excitement and innovation in the job

An employee can be separated for many reasons. It must be noted that not all separations are the same; some are more 'regrettable' than the others. It is important to understand the cases when it is worthwhile to go an extra mile to keep the separating employee unhurt. To understand it better, one must understand the concept of separation management.

SEPARATION MANAGEMENT

Employee separation needs to be handled with sensitivity, discretion, and speed so that exits can happen without injuring the sentiment and burning bridges with the employee. It should not be forgotten that the employees are the most effective brand ambassadors for the company. At the time of the separation, employees of an organization present an opportunity to glean and assemble a wealth of valuable feedback and insights on the organizational strengths and weaknesses during the process of engagement between the employer and the employee. Hence, it is important for the personnel concerned with the separation management to carefully gather all this information. These valuable insights about the organization can be collected from the departing employee through exit interviews that would help the organization to reduce future attrition.

The separating employee has to return all property of the company that was under his/her custody. The entire separation process should happen smoothly and the separating employee should never feel harassed though he/she can become emotional at times. Soon after the exit interview, employees are bid farewell. After separation, one can pursue his/her life in multiple ways of his/her choice; such as joining another company, a social or philanthropic organization, work as an author of a reputed publishing house, and so on.

Transition takes place after separation. Exhibit 13.5 highlights an incident after separation.

Exhibit 13.5 Transition after separation

Devanathan, 68, was a mechanical engineer by profession, and had worked in various capacities with Tata Steel. He retired close to eight years ago. His transition to post-retirement life was not very tough, as he was always involved equally with his family and his profession. While he was heading the maintenance team for Tata Steel, one of the vendors of Tata Steel, GE, was interested in getting help from Devanathan in understanding their client needs better. While assisting GE, he started interacting with the chemical engineers there to have a better understanding of the company's operations. In this process, Devanathan soon got in touch with many other clients of GE in specific areas of mechanical engineering operations. This also got him in touch with JSW steel as well. Soon, they wanted him to be a consultant for them.

Devanathan did not hesitate to move to JSW steel as an advisor, after his retirement. According to Devanathan, 'These assignments made me a pure professional. I could voice my opinions. In addition, my suggestions invariably get accepted. I no longer have any worries regarding formal designations or higher compensation.'

The next move was much more interesting for him. He took up a role with a small company which was planning to set up a plant as a joint venture with a German steel plant equipment supplier. This called for a more focused approach from his side and he agreed to work for them, mostly from home. He set up his own office at home and conducted a series of planned meetings with the clients. Some of the key challenges that Devanathan had to face in his second career were to balance the work-life demands, move into a purely advisory role, set expectations of an advisory role, and manage networks. The key was to not disturb the balance that he wanted from the second career.

Source: Based on an article in Human Capital (2009)

EXIT INTERVIEW

An exit interview is organized for separating employees to collect vital information from them. Generally, separating the employees is an emotional process. Exit interviews have always been conducted with employees leaving the organization to understand the reasons behind their leaving, to obtain feedback on their experiences during their period of work, and to get inputs for improvement, with the ultimate aim of strengthening the company's retention strategy. It is believed that exit interviews have evolved from feedback interviews and have now become knowledge management tools.

During the exit interview, the separating employee may respond well to the questions asked; but may not prefer an official recording of the same. Thus, confidentiality should be ensured or at least, anonymity must be maintained, in order to obtain factual, true, and candid information. The interviewer must assure that his/her identity will not be disclosed and that the remarks will only be used as part of a general consensus. It is also opined by experts that all information obtained from exit interviews should not be taken literally as true, as an employee who is leaving the organization may sometimes be experiencing a gamut of negative emotions. Thus, the information must be filtered. Box 13.1 provides sample questions for an exit interview.

Box 13.1 Exit interview questions

During exit interview, many questions may be asked and it is always an unstructured interview. However, there are some common questions which can be asked. Some of these questions are displayed here.

1. Narrate the reason for your leaving the organization.
2. During your tenure, what did you like or dislike about your job?
3. Did you have the training and developmental support to do your job? If not, what did you need?
4. Were the responsibilities of your job clear to you?
5. Did you get adequate feedback for your performance?
6. Did you discuss any specific issues you were having with a manager before deciding to leave?
7. What do you like or dislike about the company?
8. How is your relationship with your colleagues?
9. How is your relationship with your manager (immediate superior)?
10. How could your manager improve?
11. What is your opinion about managerial styles?
12. For the position falling vacant, would you like to recommend to us some friend?
13. Comment about general employee morale.
14. How can we make this company a better place to work?
15. What qualities should we look for in your replacement?

Q 5 Benefits of Exit Interview

Information received from exit interview benefits the HR department, employees, and managers, and the organization as whole.

Benefits to HR Personnel

Some organizations face problems in formulating policies relating to employee separation. Through these exit interviews, the HR department can obtain benefits as follows:

1. Formulating policies for employee separation mentioning the notice period
2. Establishing policies for termination on account of unauthorized absence conforming to the Legislative acts
3. Creating a smooth process for updating employee data and correcting them, especially for payroll

Benefits to Employees and Managers

Employees of all levels can take proactive actions conforming to the notice period, getting dues cleared, etc. They can also take steps towards the following:

1. Manage leave against notice period
2. Get timely clearance of dues
3. Get access to build bridges of relationship and join the alumni community for business and social networking

Benefits to the Organization

Organizations pursue succession planning for their senior positions. Moreover, organizations need to build bridges of relationship by way of networking and partnering. From the responses in exit interviews, an organization can derive the following benefits:

Manage succession planning All organizations, private or public sectors, initiate proactive action to find people with the right skills to fill their key and top leadership positions, whenever any vacancy is created due to separation. This process needs to be managed effectively. Traditionally, large companies always plan the leadership pipeline. They use highly-structured, mechanistic, secretive, and top-down schemes to keep the pipeline aimed at identifying internal successors for key posts. Organizations plan their career paths to provide the necessary range of experience. These schemes work reasonably well in a stable business environment where structures were fixed and careers were intended for the long-term.

Create an alumni community This refers to the creation of a strong and a vibrant professional network. In case of sudden separation, the gap in the expertise can be filled by selecting one with a requisite background and proven track record. This helps to reduce the searching time.

Guidelines for Exit Interviewers

While conducting the exit interview, the interviewers should follow certain guidelines so that they proceed smoothly. One important aspect is that the interviewees should not be hurt. Some other points are mentioned here:

1. Questions and topics that require exploration must be carefully designed and be kept ready.
2. Interviewers should not conduct the interviews in a hurry; they must allocate about 45 to 60 minutes for the interview. Further, they should aim to conduct face-to-face exit interviews. Interviewers should be keen to analyse responses and vulnerable feelings of the separating employee about the company.
3. Some employees may be shy and reserved. It is advisable to administer them through the feedback questionnaire form.
4. The employee should get adequate time to think and respond to the questions.
5. The employee can obviously throw some overpowering, bitter, offensive, and defamatory remarks or accusations; sometimes even against any interviewer. The interviewer needs to remain calm and composed in such cases. Any sort of provocation should be avoided courteously and be handled with maturity.
6. In order to gain more factual information, interviewers should ask open-ended questions.
7. The exit interview can flow in multiple directions that cannot be predicted earlier. As such, interviewers should change the style and approach based on the nature of the exit interview. The interview conducted can be for any type of separation such as for a resigned employee, terminated employee, retired employee, or retaining the employee, or for a laid-off employee.
8. The separating employee should 'feel good' during and after the interview. Therefore, he/she must be thanked for the feedback at the end of the interview session.
9. After the interview, responses should be checked, analysed, and implemented as per company guidelines and policies.
10. In some cases, the separating employees become violent during the course of the interviews. Interviewers should take out the right tools from the arsenal and use them to manage the

situation while the exit interview is in progress, so that they control the outburst and emotions of the employees. There are instances when the employees were not able to control their tears, when they remember their association with the company and get reminded of past moments.

Exit Interview Questionnaire

An exit interview questionnaire generally contains a brief on separation, a request to respond to the questions, personal details, reasons for leaving the company, work environment and managerial styles, objective questions on supervision, and opportunity for learning and self-development. The questionnaire ends with an emotional question attempting to retain the employee or to facilitate his return. Questionnaires of some organizations contain questions on planning or spending time after retirement or about the new company in case of attrition. A typical exit interview form is shown in Annexure 13.1.

BEYOND SEPARATION

A separation has many more dimensions than just cessation of a regular job, and marks the end of a long chapter in one's life. Obviously, for an individual, this is the time for quick change, especially for those who were at the peak of their careers and power status. For some, it might be a time of confusion, uncertainty, and planning. One of the choices for leaving the company could be to pursue purely life-related aspects, and have an understanding of moving away from the professional realm or monarchy. Many options exist for a professional after separation. Sometimes, individuals desire to be reengaged in same profession or change tracks.

On the other hand, many prefer to lead a post-retirement life by sacrificing professional competence. Studies in the West show that as many as 70 per cent of people would like to continue in some profession or another to keep them busy. Many even wish to continue their regular jobs.

The course of action depends on the preparations that enable the transition, life attitude, and perceptions. Psychologically, retirement is one phase in the occupation, which leads either to personal satisfaction and self-fulfillment with contribution to organization, society, family and self or job discontentment, sense of low self worth, or negative outlook to organization and society. This ultimately leads either to positive or negative orientation to life. Either way, it reflects the life cycle and the options possible for post-retirement life. The happiness one experiences or the attitude towards others would largely depend on the outcome when one retires or separates from the career. It is usually seen that positive people go for better options, while the not-so-happy ones either opt out or become frustrated.

There exist two distinct aspects or phases after separation—the life aspects and the professional aspects.

LIFE ASPECTS

The most common life aspects are the following:

1. Catching up with friends and relatives
2. Concentrating on one's health
3. Devoting more time for oneself and with the family
4. Developing social networks
5. Engaging in more domestic and social roles
6. Engaging in spiritual pursuits
7. Planning for exploring various leisure pursuits
8. Resting and relaxing

PROFESSIONAL ASPECTS

The most common professional aspects are as follows:

1. Accepting that regular salary income might cease
2. Continuing professional credibility
3. Developing different equations with the professional networks that has developed earlier
4. Fading away of status with designation and roles
5. Feeling of frustration of lack of avenues to exhibit one's talent and knowledge or freedom from job demands
6. Moving out of operational roles
7. Moving out of regular professional networks
8. Sensing that more time is available and activities have declined

SUMMARY

Separation is a typical phenomenon in one's social and organizational life. In organizations, separation happens on many grounds such as lay-off, resignation, dismissal or discharge, retrenchment, voluntary retirement schemes, transfer, attrition, and so on. Some organizations arrange outplacement services through companies. Companies launch voluntary retirement schemes paying hefty amount to the employees. Transfer of employees causes separation from the department or unit he/she is working in. The reasons behind transfer could be multifarious and vary from organization to organization.

Transfers must be ordered based on certain documented principle to prevent industrial disputes. Production transfer, replacement transfer, versatility transfer, shift transfer, and remedial transfer are the five types of transfers. Manpower attrition occurs for certain key attrition factors.

Employee separation needs to be handled with sensitivity and utmost care without injuring the sentiment of the separating employees. Organizations can collect vital information through exit interviews which should be carefully conducted preferably using preset questionnaires. After separation, the life aspects and the professional aspects for an individual becomes distinctly visible.

KEY TERMS

Exit interview is a means of collecting views of the separating employees about various aspects of the organization.

Lay-off is a temporary separation of the employee from his/her employer at the instance of the latter without any prejudice to the former. Lay-off is ordered in case of shortage of inputs to the organizational processes.

Separation is a usual phenomenon in social as well as organizational life, and it occurs on many grounds such as lay-off, resignation, dismissal or discharge, retrenchment, voluntary retirement schemes, transfer, attrition, and so forth.

Separation management is a crucial process to save an employee, departing on any ground, without injuring his/her sentiments.

Voluntary retirement scheme (alternatively known as 'golden hand shake' plan) is a noble or righteous scheme; a painless and time-saving method of trimming employee strength.

EXERCISES

Concept Review Questions

1. How can organizations reduce the difficulties of laid-off employees?
2. Distinguish between retrenchment and dismissal.

3. Discuss the possible reasons for which employees are transferred. What are the various types of transfers.
4. What is the relationship of versatility transfer with production transfer or replacement transfer?
5. Discuss the benefits that can be derived from the process of exit interview.

Critical Thinking Questions

6. How can organizations discharge social responsibilities to their employees who are separated from the organization?
7. Do organizations really get vital information from the separating employees through exit interviews? What course of actions should organizations initiate to fetch the right answers from interviewees?
8. An employee can become emotional or indulge in making offensive remarks during the exit interview. How can the situation be managed?

Assignments

9. Contact any company to inquire about the exit interview process. Does the company have any structured questionnaire for interrogating the separating employees? How do the personnel attempt to reason with the separating employee about him leaving the company and how is the information used for development?
10. Visit three companies and enquire whether they have identified the reasons for attrition. In addition, attempt to know the measures they have taken to manage attrition.

MANAGER'S INSIGHT

Tapashi worked in a software company for more than four years as a senior software engineer. She got a better offer in terms of salary package as well as designation in another internationally reputed software company and tendered her resignation. As always, the company organized an exit interview and it ended well.

At the end of the interview, Tapashi hosted a lunch party. During the post-party chat, she spoke high of the company. She also emphasized on the friendly environment and her learning experience in the company.

All of a sudden, a senior marketing manager asked her, 'If this company is really good, why are you leaving?' This question changed the environment of the party.

Tapashi could not control her emotions. She asked for the bill, and immediately left after paying it, citing urgent work.

Questions

1. Tapashi spoke high of the company on her last day. Was there anything wrong in it?
2. Should the senior marketing manager have asked the question?

BIBLIOGRAPHY AND WEB RESOURCES

Aswathappa, K, *Human Resource and Personnel Management*, Tata McGraw-Hill, New Delhi, 2006.

Business Manager, Vol. 13, No. 12, Alwar, Rajasthan, June 2011.

Kunhikrishan, Prof. K., and Dr Sandip K. Krishnan, *Second Innings*, Human Capital, New Delhi, Vol. 12, No. 12, May 2009.

Shikari, Arva, *Involuntary Exit HR at the receiving end*, Human Capital, Vol. 12, No. 12, New Delhi, May 2009.

Human Capital, 12 (12), May 2009.

Ravindra Sharma vs Labour Court and others, (2011 LLR 495), *Business Manager*, Vol. 13 No. 12, Alwar, Rajasthan, June 2011.

Municipal Council vs. Chhotalal and another (2011 LLR 517), *Business Manager*, Vol. 13 No. 12, Alwar, Rajasthan, June 2011.

Mussoorie Dehradun Development Authority vs Shri Rameshwar and others. 2011 (128) FLR 1030, *Business Manager*, Vol. 13, No. 12, Alwar, Rajasthan, June 2011.

Involuntary Exit: HR at the Receiving End, *Human Capital*, New Delhi, Vol. 12, No. 12, May 2009.

MANAGING THE MIND AFTER SEPARATION—NHPC LIMITED

About the organization

NHPC Limited, formerly known as National Hydroelectric Power Corporation, is a Government of India enterprise. It was incorporated in 1975 with an authorized capital of ₹2,000 million and with an objective to plan, promote, and organize an integrated and efficient development of hydroelectric power in all aspects. Later, NHPC went ahead to expand its objectives to include development of power in all its aspects through conventional and non-conventional sources in India and abroad.

Mission of NHPC

1. To achieve international standards of excellence in all aspects of hydro power and diversified business.
2. To execute and operate projects in a cost-effective, environment-friendly, and socio-economically responsive manner.
3. To foster competent, trained, and multi-disciplinary human capital.
4. To continually develop state-of-the-art technologies through innovative research and development and adopt the best practices.
5. To adopt the best practices of corporate governance and institutionalize value- based management for a strong corporate identity.
6. To maximize creation of wealth through generation of internal funds and effective management of resources.

A man waiting for separation

Mr Chowdhury, 65 years, retired as the chief engineer of NHPC. Prior to retirement, he had worked in various capacities of the corporation and got promoted as the vice president. He was pleased about the balance that he had been able to maintain between his professional and personal life. The transition to retirement was not tough for Mr Chowdhury. He had a son and a daughter, who were both employed and married. The son was working in NHPC as well. While the son was located in New Delhi, the daughter was located in Mumbai.

Organizational drive

The corporation organized a camp for some senior management personnel whose retirement was due in a short duration. About a year before retirement, Mrs and Mr Chowdhury were invited to attend the camp in a star hotel. All the invitees and their spouses travelled in executive class in flights at the cost of the corporation. NHPC organized a programme to prevent depression after retirement for employees who rendered services to NHPC for several decades.

About the programme

The main objective of the programme was to prevent the occurrence of depression among NHPC executives after separation.

In the sessions, the participants were repeatedly reminded on the utmost need of forgetting the past—their working life and associated responsibilities. They were told that during the work life, they have performed the organizational roles assigned to them, discharged the duties to achieve organizational goals, expressed opinions, and offered suggestions for growth of the organization. However, that chapter would be closed after retirement and they should not think about it. It goes beyond doubt that it not easy to forget the attachment of decades. It is essential to control the mind, reduce one's ego, and engage in socially-utilizable activities.

As a tool, the faculty members advised meditation to keep the mind calm and composed. Retired persons must feel proud on knowing about the company's significant achievements. However, they must desist to ponder about their contribution to the achievement during their tenure in the company. This sort of pondering would simply aggravate their feelings of disassociation, thus giving pain.

Discussion Questions

1. Do you feel that NHPC initiated a noble drive for its employees? Justify your response.
2. Propose a method of evaluating the effectiveness of such a programme.
3. What essential features you would suggest if entrusted with designing a similar separation programme?

HR MANTRA A story of three friends

In an interval of about four months, three close friends retired from their respective services. One of them joined a community club to engage in social service. He also started playing card games and chess. The second friend started spending more time with his family. His wife was very pleased and would sometimes say, 'You should have retired a few years ago. I could have given more time to the women's welfare association'.

The third friend used to contribute articles/papers to reputed journals and magazines while in service. He used to attend seminars/conventions organized by professional engineering and management associations. In the post-retirement stage, he started reading and writing more, and obtained membership of a few more professional associations.

After about five years, the three friends met at a distant, lonely place. They were very happy to see each other. The first friend said, 'I have come here to introspect on whether the activities I am doing are really needed by the society.' The second friend confessed that his wife was unhappy as she wanted to devote more time to her association. So he had come there to think about how to make her happy. The third friend, by then an established academician and author said, 'I have come here to utilize my creativity and think something out-of-the-box. I want to gain distinctive competence'.

Although the three were friends and retired at about the same time, each had a different approach to his post-retirement life.

The mantra: Plan ahead for your post-retirement life!

SANJEEV HIMACHALI

Sanjeev Himachali was born on 7 September 1976 in Himachal Pradesh. He completed his MBA from Bangalore University. Sanjeev is a certified global professional in human resource (GPHR) and a certified MBTI (Myers Briggs type indicator) assessment practitioner.

Sanjeev began his career in human resources in 1999 and has worked in various facets of HR across multiple industries such as BFSI (banking, financial services, and insurance), information technology, IT enabled and entertainment in India, Mauritius, South Africa, and Hong Kong. He has successfully completed various assignments and projects on talent acquisition, talent management, employee relations, and strategic alliance of HR with core business, performance management, succession planning, career coaching, mobility and relocation, compensation and benefits, and HR research. Having worked in start-up companies for five years, he gained expertise in green-field operations and new setups.

Since 2010, Sanjeev has been working as HR vice president at CyberTech International Holdings Limited. The company develops software for online games such as Casino, Poker, and Bingo and licenses them to gaming operators across the globe. These games are developed by using technologies such as C, C++, Java, J2ME, and QT.

Sanjeev's areas of specialization are versatile and include employee relations, HR operations (generalist role), policy reviews and formulating and implementing various HR policies, processes, procedures, and forms; performance coaching; skill inventory management; career planning; competency mapping; mobility and relocation; green-field operations; compensation and benefits; HR research, and performance management.

Sanjeev has published articles on a variety of topics and themes encompassing loyalty of employees, challenges for HR professionals, the PCMM model, report on human issues in call centers and BPO industry, workplace politics and the role of HR department, talent acquisition and management in the new economy, six myths of effective communications, 'You…Your Appearance… Your Profession and Your Selection or Rejection', etc., in leading journals and dailies.

Sanjeev views employee separation as an important process which does not involve unilateral decisions; however, he suggests, 'be accurate, be professional'. He adds that the separation process, if not handled in an efficient manner, can lead to various legal complications.

References

Emails from Sanjeev Himachalli, dated 20 October 2011 and 24 October 2011.

Himachalli, Sanjeev, *Retention Strategies in ITES-BPO Industry,* (in *Global Business Process Outsourcing – Concepts and Practices*), ICFAI University Press (www.icfai.org), June 2007.

ANNEXURE

Exit Interview Questionnaire

Preamble

You are leaving us and this company after rendering loyal and trustworthy services for several years. It is unfortunate that the day of separation has come. We would have been delighted had you been with us till natural separation or superannuation. We acknowledge your association with the company, your contributions, and many eventful moments in the office and during social gatherings.

At the juncture of your separation, the company needs your help to make it a better place to work in. Your frank and open responses are extremely important to help the colleagues you are leaving here. The responses would get utmost attention of the strategic apex in reviewing the policies and practices, to attend to the intrinsic needs of the employees at all levels.

The company assures that the HR department will maintain confidentiality and your responses will not affect your future references or prospects for reemployment here or elsewhere.

Part 1 of the questionnaire has been filled in by the HR department. You may verify the correctness of the entries. You are requested to express your views for the rest of the parts.

Part 1: Personal information

Name: Mr/Mrs/Ms/Dr ....

Personal no. ....   Date of joining: ....

Designation: ....   Department: ....

Age: ....   Date of joining: ....

Service rendered in functional areas (use code):

Code: .... Years ....   Code: .... Years ....

Code: .... Years ....   Code: .... Years ....

Award or appreciation received with details:

Disciplinary action taken (if any):

Part 2: Reasons for leaving

(a) ....

....

(b) ....

....

(c) ....

....

Part 3: Work environment and managerial styles

Please select the response that best describes your feeling. The scale is in the range 1–5. The point grades are described here:

1	Strongly disagree (If you never or rarely feel this way)
2	Disagree (If you occasionally, only a few times, feel this way)
3	If you sometimes feel this way
4	Agree (If you frequently feel this way)
5	Strongly agree (If you very frequently or always feel this way)

Flow of information in the company was good	1	2	3	4	5
Relationship with peers, senior/junior colleagues was harmonious	1	2	3	4	5
Transportation system of the company was satisfactory	1	2	3	4	5
Work pressure on you was unmanageable	1	2	3	4	5
You had role clarity and responsibilities	1	2	3	4	5
You never felt resource inadequacy to work	1	2	3	4	5
You were receiving infrastructural supports whenever needed					
You were receiving communication about business plans in time	1	2	3	4	5
You were satisfied with the compensation package and reward system	1	2	3	4	5
You were satisfied with the job and roles	1	2	3	4	5
Your efforts were recognized and rewarded for notable contributions	1	2	3	4	5
Your were satisfied with your career progression in the company	1	2	3	4	5

Part 4: Comment on supervision

Please select the response that best describes your feeling. The scale is in the range 1–5. The point grades are described here:

1	Strongly disagree (If you never or rarely feel this way)
2	Disagree (If you occasionally, only a few times, feel this way
3	If you sometimes feel this way
4	Agree (If you frequently feel this way)
5	Strongly Agree (If you very frequently or always feel this way)

Clarifying work assignments and responsibilities	1	2	3	4	5
Communication of policies and procedures	1	2	3	4	5
Conducting employee development programmes	1	2	3	4	5
Demonstration of unbiased treatment	1	2	3	4	5
Encouraging and accepting feedback from juniors	1	2	3	4	5
Encouraging cooperation and working in team	1	2	3	4	5
Percolation of business plans	1	2	3	4	5
Resolving issues promptly	1	2	3	4	5

Taking decisions and actions promptly	1	2	3	4	5
Valuing suggestions and innovative ideas	1	2	3	4	5

Part 5: Opportunity for learning and self-development

Please select the response that best describes your feeling. The scale is in the range 1–5. The point grades are described here:

1	Strongly disagree (If you never or rarely feel this way)
2	Disagree (If you occasionally, only a few times, feel this way
3	If you sometimes feel this way
4	Agree (If you frequently feel this way)
5	Strongly Agree (If you very frequently or always feel this way)

The company utilized your talents and abilities well.	1	2	3	4	5
The guidance provided helped you perform better.	1	2	3	4	5
You found most of the task assignments challenging.	1	2	3	4	5
You got the unique opportunity to use a variety of skills.	1	2	3	4	5
You had the opportunity to apply your creativity and originality in the workplace.	1	2	3	4	5
You received adequate technical and purposeful inputs to accomplish the tasks effectively.	1	2	3	4	5
You received learning inputs on time.	1	2	3	4	5
You received regular feedbacks which brought about a positive change.	1	2	3	4	5
You were able to apply the learning inputs at your workplace.	1	2	3	4	5
You were getting adequate scope of learning.	1	2	3	4	5
You were happy with your career progression and development.	1	2	3	4	5
Your learning needs were correctly identified.	1	2	3	4	5

Part 6: Any other point you want to mention

....

....

....

....

Thank you very much.
You have once again helped the company by expressing your views.
The company shall benefit from your thoughtful responses.

Signature of the employee: ....

Date of interview: ....

Name and signatures of interviewers

1. ....
2. ....
3. ....

CHAPTER 14

Developing Workers and Subordinate Staff

LEARNING OBJECTIVES

After studying this chapter, you will be able to

- Understand the objectives of HRD for workers and subordinate staff
- Appreciate the need of preparing for human resource development
- Help develop the inner beauty of the workers and subordinate staff
- Consider the factors that influence performance
- Understand the state of mind of knowledge workers
- Discuss the reasons behind retention of knowledge workers
- Describe the process of developmental supervision

OPENING CASE

Solve Problems and Develop

Sutapa was working in the finance and accounts department of a multinational company since 2001. She was a commerce graduate and had studied accountancy as her honours subject. Her superiors in the company were satisfied with her work.

When Sutapa got married, there was a change in her work culture. Her parents-in-law were conservative. The problem started as a result of the distance of her new residence from the workplace. Employees were required to overstay in the office on the last four or five days of every month. After completion of duty, they would return home in a pool car arranged by the company.

One day, her parents-in-law spotted her chatting with her colleagues in the car after the pool car dropped her at home. Her parents-in-law thought this unnecessary and discussed the matter with their son. The son explained to his parents that this was a normal occurrence among office colleagues. However, his parents were stubborn and did not want their daughter-in-law to work late. After this incident, Sutapa approached her seniors to allow her to leave office after normal working hours throughout the month. At about the same time, Sutapa was asked to attend a training programme in another metro city, which also she refused.

Soon, her relationship with the department management gradually deteriorated. She began spending most of her time in isolation. Her colleagues speculated about what could be wrong with her and rumours spread. Sutapa did not disclose her problems to her superiors. All of a sudden, she submitted her resignation stating personal grounds.

Her head in the finance and accounts department referred the matter to the HR department. The senior HR manager, SS, collected background information about Sutapa's change in attitude. Thereafter, he discussed the incidents with Sutapa and understood her dilemma.

In the past, Sutapa had contributed immensely to the growth of her company. On many occasions, the management had recognized her efforts and rewarded her as well. Keeping this in mind, SS discussed Sutapa's issue with the senior management. He projected the views of the department manager, Sutapa's work efficiency, and her personal problems. He also submitted the following set of recommendations, which the management approved.

- Sutapa would not be asked to overstay in office.
- The company would give her a laptop, an Internet connection at home, and any other facilities that she may require.
- Sutapa would be permitted to work from home beyond duty hours.

Sutapa was informed about the decisions taken by the company. She expressed her delight and extended her gratitude to the company, particularly to the HR manager. After a long time, she appeared relaxed and her colleagues could spot a smile on her face.

Learning points

- HR managers must identify the root causes of stress in employees and initiate suitable remedial measures.

INTRODUCTION

Human resources are the most valuable assets of an organization and are responsible for the utilization of other resources. Their knowledge, skill, experience, expertise, maturity, and wisdom define the way an organization works. Hence, human resource needs to be nurtured, inspired, motivated, and developed continuously for deriving organizational benefits.

Many organizations do not pay attention to the development of workers and subordinate staff because they believe that they can achieve their desired results just by developing the managers. Some other reasons could be as follows:

Developing workers and subordinate staff helps in advancement of business.

1. Lack of integration between HRD and industrial relations (IR) in many organizations
2. The prevailing IR climate in the organization
3. HRD is treated as a non-bargainable domain
4. The traditional belief that 'workers' work for wages only and not for developing the organization
5. The urge to keep the workers and their unions away and hence neglecting their participation in the decision-making process
6. The belief that each worker has two hands to work with and a worker's job is 'to do'
7. The mindset that 'only managers can think' and 'it is the management's task to decide'
8. The prevailing laws and their intervention in process
9. Inability and the feeling of 'powerlessness' in managing the workforce, which is diverse in terms of languages spoken, religion, region, belief systems, etc.

Some organizations have developed a set of technical competencies (Box 14.1) that the workforce must possess, along with other competencies.

Box 14.1 Technical competencies in organizations

Technical competencies that organizations must focus on are as follows:

1. Competency identification skill—essential to assign tasks to juniors
2. Computer competencies—inescapable in the era when organizations are trying to be paperless
3. Career development theories and techniques understanding—vital to develop people in the right direction and bestow intrinsic satisfaction
4. Electronic system skill—important in the information technology age and modern computerized numerically controlled (CNC) machines

(Contd)

Box 14.1 (Contd)

5. Facilities selection skill—critical to enhance productivity and facility utilization ratio
6. Objectives preparation skill—necessary to pin-point the needs
7. Performance observation skill—crucial to monitor and develop subordinates
8. Training and development theories and technical skill
9. Research skill—indispensable to unearth causal relationships

DEVELOPING TECHNICAL COMPETENCE

People have to perform a job assigned to them by fulfilling the quality standards and quantitative requirements. This task needs knowledge, skills, intelligence quotient, and the right aptitude. Based on the job specification, the present level of knowledge and skill of an employee, and the tasks assigned, an organization can identify his training needs and provide the required training. Competency refers to the attitude, emotional quotient and underlying feelings, and behaviour to perform a job effectively. For an internal auditor (quality management system), technical competence includes his knowledge about the clauses of the international standards, verifying compliance of an organization's structured system with the requirements of the international standard, attributing the clause to non-conformity, etc.

Similarly, for a workman working on machines, the technical competence includes handling the machine, observing safety, and protecting the machined items from deterioration. For a marketing manager, the technical competence encompasses understanding consumer psychology, market demand, marketing mix, product mix, pricing strategy, salesperson identification, etc. Again, the technical competence of a faculty member embraces depth of knowledge, communication skill, selection of pedagogical aids, preparing transparencies, developing slides, designing exercises, administering case studies, class management, responding to students' queries, setting papers, objective evaluation of answer scripts, and so forth. One can develop technical competence through training, workshops, management development programmes, or other means. Please refer to Exhibit 14.1.

Exhibit 14.1 Developing the workforce at Grasim Industries

The textile division of Grasim Industries comprises three units—BTM spinning, elegant spinning, and weaving (Rao 2006). Grasim's effort towards workers skill development started with specific individual identification through administering a skill assessment format. The survey included six parameters, namely basic knowledge, workshop skill, housekeeping, maintenance of machines, quality consciousness, and reduction of wastage. The assessment system included the use of responses on a five-point scale. The company identified the training needs with full involvement of the departmental heads and line managers, using the line managers as internal faculties.

The training programmes were organized and followed by observing and recording the on-the-job skills on a regular basis. Grasim, thus, evaluated the training outcome linking it with performance, such as quality and productivity improvements. The company identified the performance parameters (knowledge and skills) for each section (work units) in each division. The massive programme motivated the workers and brought about a change in their mindset. The workers were inclined to learn and develop them. The line managers were also delighted, primarily because of the improved labour productivity, and secondarily, through their involvement in the process. It also helped

(Contd)

Exhibit 14.1 (Contd)

to reduce wastage. Through the orchestral efforts of the organizers, Grasim moved one step ahead in building a quality culture in the organization.

Today, the profile of the working class has significantly changed. Enhancing technical competence alone could not have solved the problem. Workers need multidimensional development. Of course, the thought process has changed; organizational stalwarts have realized the utmost need for developing workers concurrently with the managerial personnel, as neglecting the workers may generate counterproductive business results. Furthermore, when the developmental efforts are directed on a particular segment of the members of the organization, the effort would be inadequate and produce marginal impact on the organizational growth and development.

It is good to remember that it is impossible for any developed manager to achieve the corporate objectives with the help of undeveloped workers, the operating core responsible to transform the raw material into a finished product. To be successful in development, the management has to do some background work.

Source: Indian Journal of Training and Development (2006)

PREPARING TO DEVELOP WORKERS

To develop the working class, one needs some background knowledge about their evolution.

In order to develop the working class, one needs some background knowledge about the evolution of the working class from earlier times to the present, the utmost need for empowering them, and the barriers associated with empowerment, forming cross-functional teams, and reorganizing the work place for the benefit of the workers, subordinate staff, and the organization.

MANAGING GENERATIONS OF WORKERS

The principal aim of HRD interventions and efforts is to promote the welfare of labour and improve the quality of work life, in addition to labour productivity. The history of workers is as old as the history of civilization. Workers were totally unorganized and had no labour organization to look after their interests. The workers' revolution had started, with a significant rise before the First World War. Every year, May 1, is observed as international labour day globally, and May Day in India. Labour welfare refers to 'all those efforts of employers, trade unions, voluntary organizations, and governmental agencies, which help employees, feel better and perform better.' Labour welfare 'is understood to include such services, facilities, and amenities as may be established in or in the vicinity of undertakings to enable the persons employed in them to perform in healthy, congenial surroundings, and to provide them with amenities conducive to good health and high morale' (ILO at the Asian regional conference).

The operating core of the organization was termed 'workers' and not employees, having two hands given to them only to work. They were treated as docile and dumb. As they had to execute the orders of seniors, information sharing with the workers was forbidden and prohibited. Times have changed and many statutory provisions such as Industrial Disputes Act, 1947, Factories Act, 1948, Minimum Wages Act, 1948, Employees State Insurance Act, 1948, Payment of Bonus Act, 1965 have come into force. The constant feeling of insecurity and helplessness stand abolished. The attitudes and values of the workers have been shaped and moulded by various generations and as an HR personnel, one has to consider the same while investing efforts to develop the workers.

EMPOWERMENT

Empowerment is the process of passing the authority and responsibility to individuals at lower levels in the organizational hierarchy. This is essential to enhance their decision- making skills, level of

Empowerment is the process of passing authority and responsibility to individuals at lower levels in the organizational hierarchy to ensure a greater of degree involvement.

confidence, and leadership ability and expertise. Empowerment does not mean delegation of power; rather, it means bringing the balance of power. After the successful completion of a task, great leaders say,' we have done it ourselves'; this is the characteristic of great leaders. Conger and Kanungo (1988) show empowerment as a motivational concept associated with 'enabling' rather than 'delegating'. Empowerment ensures a greater degree of involvement and a higher degree of responsibility among employees. However, junior colleagues cannot be merely empowered. Managers must be sure that employees at lower levels of the organizational hierarchy possess the right mix of information, knowledge, power, and reward to carry out a particular task. (Lawler et al. 1989, Lawler 1992)

Information is related to process, quality, customer feedback, and events. Knowledge refers to understanding about the work, the business, the total work system, and their interactions. Power enables one to act, take decisions about the work, and apply discretion in exceptional cases. It is seen that empowerment ensures involvement. If one is empowered, higher quality products and services will be delivered. Other benefits include less absenteeism, lower turnover, effective decision-making, and better problem solving abilities, which in turn, result in greater organizational effectiveness (Dennison 1984). Empowerment is not an end state, but a process that all human beings experience. An empowerment process involves change. Sometimes, the process appears painful and frustrating. Henkel, et al. (1993) designed an empowerment readiness survey consisting of 10 statements that addressed six dimensions of empowerment (Pattanayak 2006). These are communication, value of people, ambiguity, concept of power, information, and learning. Refer to Figure 14.1.

1. Communication—What mechanism does the organization use for communicating information? Is it communicating assertively? How much information is communicated?
2. Value of people—Does the organization value the people and their suggestions? How do the people respond to any new and innovative ideas?
3. Ambiguity—How does the organization ensure role clarity? Does any problem arise due to possible overlapping roles?
4. Concept of power—How do people perceive power in the organization? What type of power do the managers generally wield?
5. Information—Are people willing to disseminate knowledge and share information with others? Is there trust among the people?
6. Learning—Is the organization a learning organization or it is a business as usual?

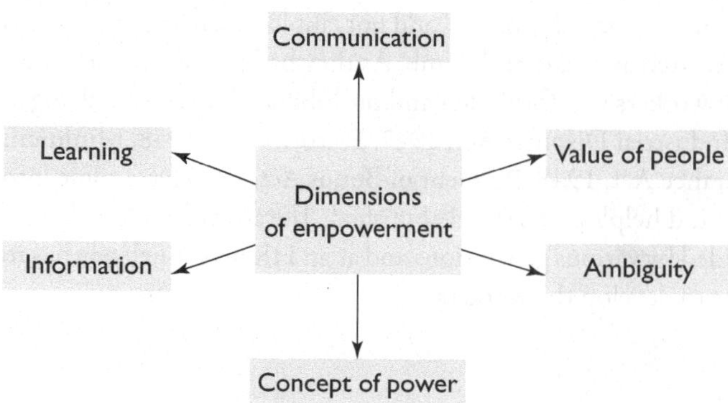

Fig. 14.1 Dimensions of empowerment

Barriers to Empowerment

Certain factors prohibit empowerment in an organization:

1. The organizational culture of holding power and foregoing delegation prohibits empowerment.
2. Managers are not readily willing to distribute powers on account of bureaucratic attitudes.
3. Inhibition due to negligence and lack of top management participation.
4. Top management seldom pays attention to the problems of the operating core relating to their development.

To overcome these barriers, organizations can adopt two ways, namely, information sharing and restructuring. Employees feel frustrated and irritated when they do not know what is happening to the company they are working in. Information sharing fades most of the barriers when management starts communicating information such as market share, product selling, new products planned to be launched, benchmarking results, competitors in the market, emerging threats and opportunities, growth plan, market penetration results, etc. On receiving such valuable information, employees, in turn, share sensitive information about the work place with seniors. The reciprocation of information helps growth of empowerment. In the process, a 'feel good' attitude is established and employees feel responsible and accountable.

Managers may also empower employees to operate performance planning comprising goal setting, knowing, and adopting leadership style, work scheduling, and finding alternate methods of working to enhance productivity. Thus, restructuring influences empowerment. Being empowered, the employees understand the goals they have to reach and the ways to achieve them. Employees themselves come out with better ideas, solutions to problems, suggestions, and proposals. In this way, a culture of self-management develops in the organization, thus promoting the organizational culture as well. The involvement of employees enhances their participation in management and the organization becomes healthy. With the empowered workforce, one can think of forming cross-functional teams. For instance, before the independence of India, the example of empowering workforce could be related to freedom fighters empowering their followers.

FORMING CROSS-FUNCTIONAL TEAMS

Q 2 A cross-functional team is a small group of interdependent employees from various functional areas of the organization—research, planning, production, maintenance, marketing, sales, finance, human resources, and operations. It is not that each group has representatives from all the functional areas. The members are chosen depending on the problem and specific objectives. For example, the members are chosen with respect to their focus on a specific objective and whether they are responsible enough to work as a team to improve coordination and innovation across divisions and resolve mutual problems.

In today's organizations, which are constantly facing complex challenges, one needs to incorporate a wide range of strategies, systems, styles, skills, and perspectives. Cross-functional teams are regarded as the means to manage social collaboration and concept creation. They work, operate, or communicate across different functions within an organization. Neither can a salesperson blame the marketing personnel nor can the marketing personnel blame the salesperson. Neither can production blame maintenance nor can the maintenance people hold production responsible for machine breakdowns. Team building is an essential element for improving the awareness and effectiveness of small groups. The cross-functional teams must be given the freedom to work and be empowered. Such teams become essential when the organization

1. struggles with a problem that impacts many sections of the organization;
2. needs to improve the operation, system, or process demanding close coordination from more that one section or department;
3. reveals that multi-skilled persons cannot take up the work; and
4. requires simultaneous application of multifarious skills, expertise, and judgement of persons from different sections (crossing the boundaries) to accomplish the goal.

One has to think of teaming beyond the domain.

REORGANIZATION OF WORK

In the changing business scenario, some interventions to look after work performance includes work life programmes, motivation design, job redesign, work reorganization, etc. In order to sustain competitiveness and meet the new demand of knowledge there is no substitute to reorganizing the work. Cross-functional job design and forming cross-functional teams are merely a trade-off between motivational work design and mechanistic work design. Reorganization of work is a broad and a comprehensive concept with no structured definition.

> Reorganizing the work is essential to sustain and meet the new demand for knowledge. It aims at cost reduction, waste elimination, morale boosting, problem solving, enhancing quality of work life, increasing productivity, and influencing the work culture.

However, reorganization refers to changes in different aspects of the workplace; it aims at cost reduction, waste elimination, morale boosting, problem solving, enhancing quality of work life, increasing productivity, influencing the work culture, etc. The degree of effectiveness of such intervention depends on the top management's commitment and the success of involvement of the employees in the reorganization process. The extent of involvement is a major determinant in the change implementation process. It is pertinent to recall the words of Rosabeth Moss, Professor, Harvard School of Business, 'Changes are exciting when done by us and threatening when done to us'.

Reorganization of work rejuvenates the workers. Preferences of customers, employees, employer, and changes in the physical capital are the drivers of the reorganization process.

Purposes of Reorganization

Q 3 A good number of personnel are engaged in the reorganization process for

1. keeping the organization structure compatible with each other and with the business environment;
2. developing a match between organizational change and skill change;
3. considering the health of the employees and their requirements;
4. improving the quality of life;
5. producing innovation-driven growth rather that input-driven growth;
6. delivering quality of products and service offerings, keeping in mind that quality is what the customer wants and not what the organization can give;
7. encouraging creativity and originality in the processes;
8. increasing effectiveness as well as efficiency; and
9. playing a key role in coping with challenges through cooperation and collaboration.

Human beings are unique creations of the Almighty and the human body is an epitome of vastness. Every person has 'something' within him/her, either known or unknown, and it needs exploration. It is extremely essential to know what these are and develop them.

Developing Virtues

Q 5 Virtues constitute the 'inner beauty' of a person. Virtues are exhibited in the way one does things. It is believed that an individual may not have money, but if he has virtue, he/she will always be rich, for everything that is close to him/her will be filled with quality (Brahma Kumaris 1996). There are several thoughts on inner beauty but only a few will be discussed here to help readers develop their workers and subordinates.

Benevolence Benevolence means kindness, compassion, and generosity.

Contentment It refers to the pleasure, gratification, and happiness that one gets with what one has.

Cooperation Collaboration, support, teamwork, and mutual aid are some synonyms of cooperation. Cooperation is perhaps the least recognized but is the most valuable of human virtues. It is to do with the process of achieving something and its greatness lies in the fact that it is expressed through ordinary everyday action. If one extends cooperation to someone else, he/she will get it back directly or indirectly.

Courage Courage helps a man to take a step forward into an area of difficulty without a solution in mind, but yet feeling that victory is ahead. Courage is similar to starting a venture empty-handed, but knowing that the 'will' will help to achieve success. One must have the courage to initiate.

Determination Determination means willpower, fortitude, and refers to the strength of mind. It develops from involvement and intrinsic satisfaction.

Humility Humility signifies modesty. Humility dismisses nothing; rather it takes into account every small thing seriously. It teaches us to respect everything in front of us.

Tolerance Tolerance means broadmindedness, acceptance, and patience. It develops from the feeling of 'forgive and forget'. A tolerant person can accept any challenge and work in any situation, however adverse and unpleasant it may be.

Wisdom Wisdom is knowledge supported by intuition and experience. Intuition and deep insights are the key prerequisites for wisdom. Wisdom is making the best of what one has.

There are many other elements of virtue such as accuracy, cheerfulness, cleanliness, gentleness, introversion, lightness, mercy, obedience, truthfulness, and so on. Developing virtues does not need money or great effort. Knowledge workers need contentment, courage, determination, tolerance, and wisdom in order to achieve success.

Workers constitute 70–75 per cent of the total strength. They are no more a dumb entity; rather they protest to protect their rights. Organizations will develop if workers also are developed along with managers.

HRD FOR WORKERS

For workers, HRD attempts to change the profile of their class. In the presence of unions, associations, and collective bargaining fora, workers today are no more a dumb entity; rather they are vocal and protest to protect their rights. Workers constitute 70–75 per cent of the total strength of the organization. In many organizations, they are now considered to be an significant segment of the manpower. Their contribution is the soul of the organization and if the organization succeeds in directing and unleashing the latent talent, it will bloom with energy. Organizational stalwarts, both professionals as well as academicians, have recently felt the need for developing workers.

Some HRD mechanisms include performance appraisal, potential appraisal, review discussions, feedback and counselling sessions, role analysis exercises, potential development, training, communication, formulating HR policies, job rotations, job enlargement, and job enrichment. There is a need to identify the mechanism suitable in a particular situation and apply that to develop the workforce.

HELPING WORKERS LEAD PRODUCTIVE LIVES

Q 6 In any organization, workers need to lead a productive life. They must be assisted and provided with certain information. Some of the information to be shared with workers is as follows:

1. Make them aware of the available resources and the business environment.
2. Create awareness about the company strategy.
3. Recognize the achievements of the worker in all possible ways.
4. Identify and develop the worker's occupational competencies.
5. Develop the 'achieve orientation' and self-management skills.
6. Help them identify and broaden their range of virtues.
7. Develop psychological, social, and cultural bonds with the workers.

Refer to Exhibit 14.2 to understand ways of developing employees.

Exhibit 14.2 Developing organizational personnel—Eureka Forbes Limited

Eureka Forbes Limited (EFL) has a unique means of developing its personnel at various levels. EFL is instrumental in developing the technical competence of its employees. It is important to note that people are working in a stress-free work environment. Apart from imparting technical competence, EFL takes all-round steps to develop those who can undertake any challenge, never fear to accept new tasks, and exhibit positive behaviour towards one another and to any external party who is visiting EFL for any purpose—whether business associates or academicians to study EFL practices.

EFL has tied up with Narsee Monjee institute of management studies (NMIMS) University, Mumbai, for imparting management training to the managerial personnel.

Eureka Forbes has also established the EFL academy of learning to develop the frontline salespeople. The academy periodically conducts self-learning programmes utilizing the concept of experiential learning. EFL has a leadership development centre (LDC) to impart leadership skills and conduct programmes such as 'seven habits of highly effective people'. When managers report to the LDC, it administers instruments such as 'Myer-Briggs type indicator' (MBTI), 'fundamental interpersonal relations orientation—behaviour' (FIRO-B), and other psychometric instruments. The LDC considers the scores in the tests and conducts the leadership programme to make it effective and result-oriented.

In order to develop its salespeople, EFL recognizes their contribution using non-financial motivational tools such as

1. exclusive club membership for top 100 salespeople (Club 100);
2. membership of 'Silver Circle Club' (SCC) for selling 26 units for seven continuous cycles;
3. 'Crest of Honour' if someone retains the position in SCC for three consecutive years;
4. 'Living Legend' for salespeople retaining the position in SCC for five consecutive years; and
5. 'Pioneer Legend' if anyone retains the position in SCC for 10 consecutive years.

Other motivational tools include

1. three-day special holidays when the winners can stay in star hotels with their family;
2. meeting with the dignitaries of Eureka Forbes; and
3. observance of a 'fun day' once a month to facilitate knowing one another.

EFL believes that success breeds success. In order to encourage the subordinate staff and workers, it displays its victories and mistakes in the EFL 'Hall of Friendship' (the company's archives). In addition to achievements, EFL also displays its failures and the reasons responsible for the failure, along with remedial initiatives. EFL has exhibited the products of all generations in the Hall Of Friendship to let visitors know how they have grown over the years.

(Contd)

Exhibit 14.2 (Contd)

The company addresses its employees as 'eurochamps' to inculcate a sense of belonging to the organization and pays tribute to their champion-like qualities, which helps all the eurochamps to

1. develop and perform their roles efficiently through coaching;
2. develop leadership through mentoring; and
3. cope with organization role stress through counseling.

EFL has established SOUL (School of Universal Leadership) at Ahmedabad, Bangalore, Chennai, Cochin, Delhi, Jaipur, and other major cities. Each SOUL conducts induction programmes, on-the-job training, and organizes a graduation ceremony for qualified trainees. SOUL also organizes learning management systems for its employees—from salespeople to senior managers.

Each eurochamp receives mentoring for 10 hours in six months. In the mentoring sessions, the regional head (mentoring) grooms, identifies leadership potential, nurtures talents, etc.

[Based on an interview with P.S. Sukumar, Deputy General Manager, Eureka Forbes Limited, Bangalore on 17 March 2008.]

DEVELOPMENTAL SUPERVISION

All employees, workers, knowledge workers, and other subordinate staff need developmental supervision. Supervision is a fundamental managerial function. It is a process of facilitating and monitoring individuals and teams to achieve business goals, and concurrently facilitating the development and growth of the individuals and teams. The traditional concept of supervision embedded the concept that the supervisor will plan while the workers will execute the plan. The concept of developmental supervision (Figure 14.2) is radically different from the traditional concept of supervision. It embraces hierarchy and responsibility, tasks and personal growth, individuals and teams, and task accomplishment and boundary management.

Hierarchy and responsibility Developmental supervision relies heavily on the belief that responsibility is well spread amongst all the levels of the organizational hierarchy and that, managers and workers are equally reliable and trustworthy in their respective work areas. If an employee's sense of responsibility is less developed then the supervisor must develop it. In addition, if the sense of responsibility is less developed in a group of employees, the supervisor is accountable as he is responsible for the deficiency. The task of identification and initiating remedial measures are within the purview of developmental supervision.

Tasks and personal growth Developmental supervision also concentrates on organizational tasks and development of employees, work groups, and teams as it treats the efforts in accomplishing tasks and developing the workforce as being complimentary and reinforcing to each other. The supervisor helps to enhance knowledge and skills, improves problem solving capacities, and thereby integrates both task accomplishment and personal growth.

Developmental supervision embraces hierarchy and responsibility, task and personal growth, individual and team, and task accomplishment and boundary management that is radically different from the traditional concept.

Individuals and teams A team has it own dynamics. The characteristics of a team are that it operates with clearly defined goals and expectations, members are given a great deal of personal freedom, makes decisions, shares information among team members, and sets high standards, its members are disciplined, possess a sense of commitment, and share successes. A developmental supervisor needs to encourage its members working in a team due to the synergistic effect of inputs. Members mostly solve the problems on their own.

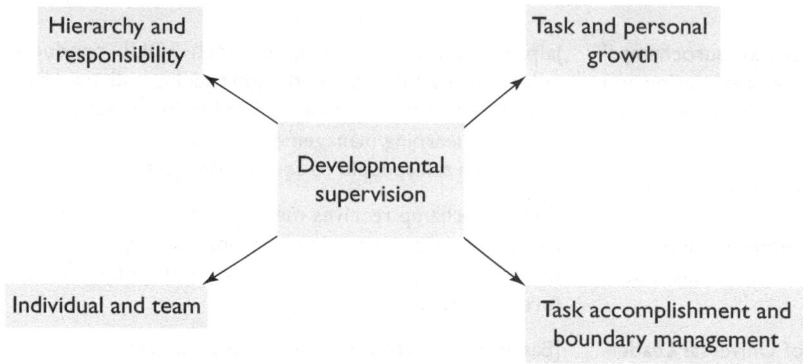

FIG. 14.2 Developmental supervision

Task accomplishment and boundary management A developmental supervisor delegates, empowers, and transfers the planning process to the team; he works as a member of the team keeping aside status symbols and gets involved in the task accomplishment. He never says 'go and work,' and rather says 'let us work'. Due to his involvement, he can read the pulse and never allows the work to slow down. Thus, a developmental supervisor views his task as boundary management, that is, facilitates the work of his junior colleagues and procures the resources needed to progress the task complying with the plan.

DEALING WITH KNOWLEDGE WORKERS

A knowledge worker's task is to work with the information available or develop new information. His primary job is to make use of the intangible assets such as knowledge and talent to create, distribute, and apply the assets. Knowledge workers are responsibility-bound and not time-bound. They prefer to go to office even on holidays, get satisfaction for the extra time spent, and complete the tasks within or even before the estimated timeframe. They are dedicated and their affective commitment (emotional attachment and identification with the organization) is of a high order.

In today's scenario, it is difficult to grow without the contribution of a knowledge worker. Knowledge workers provide benefits to the company; the benefits could be in multiple forms such as developing business intelligence, enhancing the value of intellectual capital, gaining insight into customer preferences, fulfilling customer expectations, converting customers into advocates of the company, or a variety of other important gains in knowledge that aid the business. Due to the constant global industrial growth, there is an increasing need for an academically capable workforce. The professional knowledge workers were identified as employees whose jobs require high levels of knowledge input in a non-routine manner, where the subsequent output results in a product or service within which their knowledge is embedded. Knowledge workers derive intrinsic satisfaction unearthing something new. They often apply highly developed theoretical frameworks to solve practical problems (www.cipd.co.uk/research).

Knowledge workers read, write, and spend a lot of time in meetings. Increasingly, knowledge workers also process information and knowledge—on paper, in telephone conversations, and voice messages, and electronically. This subject is much newer than the conventional mode of communications such as reading, writing, and preparing minutes of meeting. There is relatively little information available about how to do it well—better and faster, and ease in retrieval. Certain distinct characteristics of knowledge workers are that they

1. rely heavily on knowledge;
2. believe that knowledge is a very powerful weapon in their arsenal;
3. prefer to follow a hectic life and continuously strive for achievement;
4. tend to be carried away by intellectual achievements;

5. view life and career progress linearly;
6. decide on the right actions, take logical steps, and remain conscious throughout the journey;
7. analyse the external environment, try to perceive threats therein, and exert to convert threat into opportunity; and
8. tend mostly towards 'enlightened' self-interest.

Information workers are usually left on their own to finish their tasks without any support. The technologies used for handling personal information and knowledge, have been largely separated and non-integrated. Thus, their PCs, laptops, landlines, and cell phones, handheld communicators, and other assorted technologies—not to mention the paper-based tools, have largely been unconnected. This makes it difficult for the managers to manage personal information and knowledge.

The other problem that one faces is that only a handful of these managers actually know how to use the latest technologies and tools. Technology and information have become closely integrated with one another. Better use of these can easily make the organizations more effective and efficient.

Dilemmas Faced with Knowledge Workers

The Chartered Institute of Personnel and Development (CIPD) mentions certain dilemmas faced with the knowledge workers relating to retention and employability, skills, and value appropriation.

Retention and employability Retention of knowledge workers continues to be a problem for organizations, particularly in a knowledge-intensive organization. In knowledge industries, it is important for the employers to be up to date with the latest technology to be able to be efficient and to have a high market value. However, the managers have a different take on this, as they do not want to have their employees joining other companies, they do not get into the cycle of development of an employee. They do not want to make their employees too attractive to the competition. However, at the same time, without developing them, an organization cannot expect and extract quality output from them.

Skills The innate desires of the knowledge workers widely differ from the desires of employers. Employers want to develop organization-specific skills whereas knowledge workers possess desires of gaining transferable knowledge, for obvious reasons.

Value appropriation Organizations use their employees' knowledge and skills for production of goods and services to sell for a profit. In most cases, this happens smoothly. However, in knowledge industries, workers are seen to hold on to as much of their value as possible. This helps them ensure that they intend to trade themselves at the highest rate.

Knowledge workers do not like to be told how to do things; they find the best way of doing the tasks. They prefer autonomy while doing a task. Exhibit 14.3 provides ways of managing the careers of knowledge workers.

Exhibit 14.3 Managing careers of professional knowledge workers

The main findings of CIPD research on managing the careers of professional knowledge workers include the following vital points:

1. As professional knowledge workers have a number of distinct characteristics, in knowledge-intensive organizations, people management issues emerge as critical to firm performance.
2. The success of knowledge-intensive organizations depends on their ability to convert their human assets such as the knowledge base, skill sets, and wide experiences of their employees—into intellectual capital. The intellectual capital needs to be

(Contd)

Exhibit 14.3 (Contd)

utilized in developing and design the products and services that have value in the marketplace.

3. The effectiveness of this conversion process depends on the successful management of the knowledge-intensive situations and professional knowledge workers.
4. There are three key knowledge-intensive situations:

   (a) Creation and development of knowledge
   (b) Sharing of knowledge within the organization
   (c) Sharing of knowledge between organizations

5. Professional workers have the following specific characteristics:

   (a) They need to apply highly structured technical knowledge to ambiguous client demands
   (b) They work in an autonomous fashion within fluid leadership structures
   (c) They are normally ambitious and upwardly mobile, and their key focus is the development of their own careers

6. Careful attention must be paid to developing people management policies and processes that allow these identities to be managed in ways that are well suited to conditions for the success of these organizations.
7. This emphasizes the need for mutually reinforcing processes for managing knowledge-intensive situations and professional knowledge workers within these organizations.

CIPD advocates that organizational success depends on having the right mix of HR policies in place. The AMO (ability, motivation, and opportunity) model supports the theory that business success is based on the capacity of organizations

1. to recruit people with the right ability;
2. to motivate them; and
3. to provide them with the opportunities to use their skills in well-designed jobs;

Source: http://www.cipd.co.uk/research/_mancarrspkw.htm

RETENTION STRATEGY VS DEVELOPMENT

Kinnear et al. (2000) identifies the top 10 most preferred strategies of retaining knowledge workers in organizations. He further identified the top 10 least preferred strategies. These strategies are linked with the development of the knowledge workers, directly or indirectly. A consideration of these strategies enhances organizational belongingness, exerting for the organization, finding the best for the company, etc.

Most Preferred Retention Strategies

The most preferred strategies are focused on salary package linked to performance, development, challenging assignments, competent colleagues capable of disseminating knowledge etc. Thus, it is obvious that most of the strategies are non-financial. They comprise the following:

1. A competitive remuneration package
2. Opportunities for development in the area of expertise
3. Incentives linked to performance
4. Challenging work assignments in the area of expertise
5. Freedom to plan and execute work independently
6. Colleagues from whom one can learn
7. Growth potential of the industry
8. Access to leading edge technologies and products
9. Progressive leadership, which allows one to do things differently
10. Share in the profits of the business

Consider some of the retention strategies for developing knowledge workers. For example, knowledge workers need opportunities for development in their area of expertise, challenging work assignments, freedom to plan and execute work independently, access to leading edge technologies and products, and progressive leadership, which allows to do things differently.

Obviously, with the advancements along the organizational hierarchy, they need a competitive remuneration package, incentives linked to performance, and a learning environment facilitating self-development from colleagues. They further look for growth potential of the industry as otherwise all means of development shall be blocked.

Least Preferred Retention Strategies

Kinnear et al. (2000) further identify ten least preferred retention strategies.

1. Healthcare benefit
2. Utilization of education, skills, and expertise directly to the job
3. Clearly-structured promotional progress
4. Pension scheme
5. Well-defined job descriptions with clear responsibilities
6. Availability of jobs in the market
7. Time for socializing and relaxation at work
8. Need for a change
9. Encouragement to associate with institutionalized professional bodies
10. Contractual obligation due to educational assistance received from the company

These strategies might be least preferred but still need consideration of the organization. Healthcare benefits to employees and dependents make them free from worries, scope of applying education directly to the job gives intrinsic satisfaction, and structured promotional progress ensures career progression. A knowledge worker might not save a huge amount during the service period; however, in the dwindling economic environment, pension schemes ensure social security. All workers and staff prefer to have responsibilities and seek job availability.

However, at the same time, the company should provide time for socializing and relaxing at work. Changes in the work assignments restore pleasure to knowledge workers. Membership of professional bodies helps one interact with others and enables an employee to achieve the objectives and work in same conditions and exchange information for mutual benefit. Knowledge workers are frequently deputed to gather knowledge from various fora on product development, languages, and other aspects. They consider the contractual obligation due to educational assistance received from the company, the least.

SUMMARY

Workers of an organization need all round development—technical, general, moral, and other types of development. Before initiating any developmental measure, the organization has to consider the evolution of the working class, need for empowering them, and the associated barriers, and the usefulness of forming cross-functional teams and reorganizing the work. Organizations should carefully attempt to develop the inner beauty of the workforce. HRD efforts for workers are essential to help them to lead a productive life. The days of traditional style of supervision are over. At present, a person needs developmental supervision.

Knowledge workers differentiate themselves from others presumably due to the fact that they have received education from a reputed institute and acquired skills, apply knowledge and skills fruitfully in the workplace, have elevated themselves to a respectable position, and have gained the confidence of seniors. They have gained distinctive competence. Dealing with knowledge workers needs vision and diplomacy. Organizations face certain dilemmas with knowledge workers relating to retention and employability, skills, and value appropriation and have identified three key knowledge-intensive situations and specific characteristics of knowledge workers. CIPD has suggested that careful attention must be paid to developing people management policies and processes for organizational effectiveness.

Key Terms

Developmental supervision is radically different from the traditional supervision in that it embraces hierarchy and responsibility, task and personal growth, individual and team, and task accomplishment and boundary management.

Empowerment motivates, enables, and ensures a greater degree involvement and a higher degree of responsibility. It is a process of passing authority and responsibility to individuals at lower levels in the organizational hierarchy.

Information sharing fades most of the barriers to empowerment when management communicates information such as profits, product selling, new products launched, emerging threats and opportunities, growth plan, market penetration results, etc.

Retention strategy encompasses competitive remuneration package, scope for development, performance-linked incentives, providing challenging work, freedom to plan and execute work independently, growth potential of the industry, etc.

Wisdom is knowledge supported by intuition and experience. Intuition and deep insight are the key prerequisites for wisdom.

Exercises

Concept Review Questions

1. Discuss the various considerations while developing workers. Why do you feel the considerations are appropriate? If you abruptly initiate the developmental measures, what might be the consequences?
2. What do you mean by a cross-functional team? How does it help to achieve organizational objectives and goals smoothly? Cite examples.
3. Discuss the purposes of reorganization of work. How does reorganization help in achieving effectiveness?

Critical Thinking Questions

4. Highlight the essence of inner beauty. How can you develop the inner beauty of knowledge workers?
5. Give an example of developing a subordinate in the organization where you are working. Mention the developmental tools used. Narrate the steps of application of the developmental initiatives.
6. What are the tools available to promote quality of work life? What are the correlations of developmental supervision?
7. 'Manpower attrition is high in information technology sectors.' Design a plan to eliminate or reduce the rate of attrition. Justify your views.

Assignments

8. Visit any three organizations and inquire about the retention strategy used by them. Let them comment about the effectiveness of the strategy used.
9. Visit any two information technology companies and collect information on how they are managing careers of their professional knowledge workers.

Manager's Insight

Mr Singh worked in a company that belonged to the knowledge industry. He had a brilliant educational record and used to receive pay hikes more frequently than others in the company. In addition to his qualification, he possessed some positive personality traits to his credit. He used to always engage in developmental work and successfully completed them. The company recognized the brilliant work done by him that brought substantial profits and raised its image.

One fine morning, he submitted his resignation. On

receiving his resignation, the management seemed puzzled and requested Mr Singh to withdraw his resignation. In fact, the company even promised him a promotion and offered a further hike in salary. However, Mr Singh refused, and ultimately left the company.

Questions:

1. Specify the reason behind Mr Singh tendering his resignation.
2. Which retention strategy could the company have employed in order to retain him?

BIBLIOGRAPHY AND WEB RESOURCES

Brahma Kumaris, *Inner Beauty*, Brahma Kumaris Ishwariya Vishwa Vidyalaya, Pandav Bhavan, Rajasthan, 1996.

Conger, J.A. and R.N. Kanungo, 'The Empowerment Process: Integrating Theory and Practice', *Academy of Management Journal*, 13, pp. 471–82, 1988.

Dennison, B., 'Bringing Corporate Culture to the Bottom Line', *Organizational Dynamics*, 13, pp. 22–24, 1984.

Farooquie, Dr Jamal A., 'Productivity-oriented Development of Employees, Measuring Organizational Intangible Assets—Human Capital', *Indian Journal of Training and Development*, Vol. XXXVI, No. 2, pp. 79–90, April–June 2006.

Haldar, Uday Kumar, *Human Resource Development*, Oxford University Press, New Delhi, 2009.

Henkel A.G., C. Repp-Begin, and J.F. Vogt, *Empowerment-readiness Survey—Foundations for Total Quality in Developing Human Resources*, pp. 147–161, Pfeiffer and Company, San Diego, 1993.

Kinnear, Lisa and Margaret Sutherland, 'Determinants of Organizational Commitment Amongst Knowledge Workers', *South African Journal of Business Management*, 03789098, Vol. 31, Issue 3, September 2000.

Lawler, E., *The Ultimate Advantage*, Jossey-Bass, San Francisco, 1992.

Lawler, E. and G. Ladeford, *Employee Involve in America: A Study of Contemporary Practice*, American Productivity and Quality Centre, Houston, 1989.

Pareek, Udai, *Organizational Behaviour*, Oxford University Press, New Delhi, 2007.

Pattanayak, Biswajeet, *Human Resource Management*, Prentice-Hall of India Private Limited, New Delhi, 2006.

Rao, Srinivas A., 'Workers Skill Development: A Case Study of Grasim Industries, Measuring Organizational Intangible Assets—Human Capital', *Indian Journal of Training and Development*, Vol. XXXVI, No. 2, pp. 166–170, April–June 2006.

Shantaram, M.R., 'Measuring Organizational Intangible Assets—Human Capital', *Indian Journal of Training and Development*, Vol. XXXV, No. 4, October–December, pp. 133–136, 2005.

Warier, Sudhir, 'Measuring Organizational Intangible Assets—Human Capital', *Indian Journal of Training and Development*, Vol. XXXVII, No. 1, January–March, 2007, pp. 48–55, 2007.

Web Resources

www.cipd.co.uk/research/_mancarrspkw.htm, last accessed on 23 April 2008.

DEVELOPING WORKERS AND SUBORDINATE STAFF

A leading multinational company (XYZ), engaged in the production of food and beverages including cold drinks and snacks, has been in business for more than five decades. It has been selling its products in 72 countries. XYZ uses certain developmental tools that have proved to very effective over the years.

The organizational culture has developed gradually during its lifetime. XYZ has its training and development centres set up in several countries. The company believes that expenditure incurred in developing people is an investment. Workers have autonomy and freedom at work. Quite surprisingly, most workers in XYZ solve workshop problems themselves. In rare cases, they approach their supervisors for guidance.

XYZ is developing the competency level of its employees; in addition, the company is constantly endeavouring to develop employee commitment to the organization and employee motivation. XYZ believes in getting more from people rather than getting more people to accomplish tasks. In XYZ, employees worked in a stress-free environment.

So how does XYZ make this possible? The simple answer is that apart from imparting technical competence, XYZ takes all-round steps to develop those who can undertake any challenge, never fear to accept new tasks, and exhibit positive behaviour towards one another and to any external party visiting XYZ—whether business associates or academicians wanting to study XYZ practices.

The company is utilizing many developmental tools as well as motivational tools, including the following:

1. Career planning
2. Potential identification and development
3. Training and development
4. Monthly appreciation programme and internal award
5. Man of the month award
6. Promotion linked with performance
7. Coupons for dinner with family in hotels

Discussion Questions

1. How did XYZ initiate all round development of its workforce? Critically evaluate them.
2. XYZ is keen to use motivational tools along with developmental tools. Do you feel this is the right approach?

HR MANTRA Right place, right time

An employee was not in the good books of the department he was working in. Even the head of the department had issues with him regarding his inability to achieve the target, indifference to work, and conservative attitude. He was even issued warning letters for his faults.

Following a particular incident, the head of the department prepared a strongly-worked letter mentioning the charges framed against him and forwarded it to his superior for a counter signature. The superior (a divisional manager) was new and wanted to interrogate the worker. While discussing the matter, he felt that the worker was good but for some reason, maintained a conservative attitude and failed to achieve his targets.

One day, the superior met the worker and his wife in a busy market place. The worker politely introduced his wife to the superior. The superior, who was an engineer and an HR expert, interacted with the worker's wife and began collecting information about the employee's family background. He found that all the family members were in senior positions and his wife was a teacher in a higher secondary school.

Following this meeting, the superior was sure that the employee was suffering from an inferiority complex and needed a change. He transferred him to another department though the head of that department was not willing to accept such a poor worker. In the course of time, the worker emerged as an indispensable asset to his new department. He was seen to be accepting challenging assignments and getting them right in the first attempt. The head recommended the worker for a lucrative award that was to be handed over to the worker during the celebration of 'Company day'.

The superior was delighted to see the proposal, called the head of the department, and took the necessary steps to ensure that the award went to the worker.

The worker received the award in presence of his colleagues, including the head of the department where he worked earlier.

The mantra: Understand the background and needs of your people.

SHARU S. RANGNEKAR

Sharu S. Rangnekar was born on 1 November 1928 at Sawantwandi, Maharashtra. Rangnekar studied chemical engineering in Mumbai and secured an MBA degree from the USA. He carried out research in mathematical economics at the Carnegie-Mellon University, Pittsburgh. He undertook management training with Imperial Chemical Industries, UK, and computer training with IBM and Union Carbide Corporation, USA.

He started his management career in 1951 as a consultant in Ibcon and subsequently worked in several multinational companies till he took early retirement from Searle (India) as the managing director at the end of 1978. He worked as visiting faculty at Tata Institute of Social Sciences and other management institutes from 1979 to 1986.

Rangnekar received many awards including the following:

1. Fulbright-Fellow, University of Kansas, 1954
2. Office of Naval Research Fellow, Carnegie-Mellon University, 1955–56
3. Escorts Award for the best book on management in India, 1975
4. Bombay Management Association award for contribution to management movement, 1977
5. Lillian Gilbreth Award, for contribution to industrial engineering, Indian Institution of Industrial Engineering, 1980
6. The Pillar of Hindustani Society award from TACCI (Trans Asian Chamber of Commerce and Industry), 2007
7. Indian Society for Training & Development, President Emeritus, 1996
8. Lifetime achievement awards from several associations and institutes

He has been a popular lecturer and a writer on management topics. His books, *In the Wonderland of Indian Managers* and *In the World of Corporate Managers* have become management classics. He has also published books in Indian regional languages to reach a greater segment of people. His lectures on management topics have been issued in audio CDs. He has been featured in diverse management development video CDs and also participated as a faculty in nearly 5,000 management development programmes in India and abroad since 1966. Rangnekar has earned global reputation as a management educator.

Rangnekar's website, www.sharurangnekar.com, gives details of his programmes, books, and training material.

References

Email from Prof. Dr Sharu S. Rangnekar dated 19 September 2011.

www.sharurangnekar.com, last accessed on 19 September 2011.

PART THREE

Overview—Contemporary Issues in HRM

Human resource management is dynamic, and changes continuously, with the business environment. In keeping with the changes in the business environment, the government of India has changed its policy for transformation of the national economy. Liberalization has allowed foreign companies to carry out business in India. The government has also allowed foreign direct investment. Changes in the environment are compelling business houses to modify their way of functioning by making internal changes. Any change is accompanied by resistance due to the fear of the organizational personnel. The sources of resistance are several. The utmost need for change must be communicated to persons who are likely to be affected by the changes, so as to reduce resistance.

Business houses try to derive competitive advantage through the use of knowledge. Organizations and individuals alike are trying to gain the upper hand by knowledge accumulation. Organizations should have customer knowledge to understand their stated and implied needs and serve them better. Adequate knowledge in products and services is essential to strengthen the marketing strategy. Networking, partnering, and building bridges of relationship are of principal importance to deal with suppliers, employees, and stakeholders such as customers, shareholders, regulatory bodies, and obviously the community. Organizations need to mobilize hidden knowledge; trace, transfer, and integrate internal and external knowledge; and develop new knowledge and make it available. Creation of knowledge is followed by preservation and use at the right time.

Human resource functions (recruitment and selection, induction and placement, training and development, compensation management, etc.) are many. While executing the functions, mistakes take place inadvertently. Periodical verification of activities, called HR audit, is considered inescapable to get rid of mistakes in HR functions. HR audit is a fact-finding task; it is never about fault finding. If the audit report is minutely studied, the management may like to review its management style, identify cost-effective training to enhance organizational effectiveness, streamline various management practices, identify key performance areas and indicators, restore effectiveness of training, and so forth.

Industries are in a mode of fortifying good governance practices and reinforcing ethical values in business conduct. Corruption in present businesses has probably reached its

threshold limit. Ethics is not new subject. But the concept of ethics has now assumed a great deal of importance. Ethics in the work place is as significant as ethics anywhere else. It is rightly said that work makes a man and a man is known by his work. Work gives a man his identity, recognition, and status. Ethics is a value orientation concept. In a wider sense, ethics may be defined as a positive attitude towards work. Organizations are now establishing and documenting booklets on 'code of conduct', 'ethical conduct', 'code of ethics', and so on to instill a sense of ethics. Ethics is needed in all spheres of life and in business as well. A business house operates in society. The society expects something from the business houses and the expectations are ever increasing. Organizations also are feeling the importance of discharging social responsibilities. Corporate social responsibility (CSR) is an analytical tool that can be used in the field of business management to facilitate different business practices both from an ethical angle and a utilitarian perspective. From the standpoint of CSR, an enterprise is accountable for its impact on all relevant stakeholders. Through CSR, companies are affirming social and territorial cohesion, quality, and environment.

The advancement of science and technology, information technology in particular, has given rise to a global village. Geographic distance is more a hindrance in business performance. It is not surprising today if an organization has its board of directors in Canada, manufacturing department in Spain, warehouse in Korea, and accounting division in Bolivia. The spread of globalization is quite large and it has powerful economic, political, cultural, and social dimensions. As an offshoot of globalization, two companies, one manufacturing products and the other offering services, can work in partnership for the benefits of each and expand the businesses of both. Globalization is now an integral part of the recent economic progress of many countries, including India. Managing culture is a vital component of globalization. Intercultural transitions are the need of the day for global organizations.

With the emergence of new technology, especially the Internet, companies are feeling the need to change across multiple dimensions. As a consequence, the roles of HR managers are changing. They need to develop people, transform their mindsets, and ensure seamless integration of new technology into the work routines of employees.

With advancements in technology, processes, and systems, employees are having to invest more time at work, understanding and implementing the new systems and processes. This results in a work–life imbalance and consequent stress. Striking a balance between professional and personal priorities is a big challenge for any employee in today's world characterized by high competition, advanced technology, fast pace, and commercialization in every aspect of life. Both achievement and enjoyment are significant facets of lives. One of them cannot be sacrificed at the cost of the other. Everyone must pay attention to the four life quadrants—work, family, friends, and self—for overall satisfaction.

Customers today are quality conscious. Therefore, quality levels are not to be compromised at any cost. Otherwise, it would be difficult to fulfill consumer expectations. Both product quality and service quality must be assured at costs affordable by the consumers.

There must be a well-designed strategy for successful accomplishment of any task. A human resource strategy is a desired course of action planned by an organization to achieve its goals. An organization must have a strategy to recruit from the market or internal resources, finalize selection tools, empower the people, improve the quality of work life, compensate the employees, link rewards to performances, deal with unions, settle grievances, enhancing corporate image, etc. Organizations fulfill a large variety of our societal and personal needs. Whatever be the type, an organization strives to achieve the goals that it sets for itself.

Organizations are classified as manufacturing and service organizations. Companies of various types are present in each type of organization. HRM strategies deal with various dimensions. Some of the dimensions are as follows: What are the HRM goals? What are the major purposes behind the use of a particular HRM strategy? What are the functions likely to be used? What must be the order of use of the functions? What are the ways in which the HRM functions are envisaged to be implemented? It is thus obvious that HRM is applicable equally across all sectors and is essential for the successful functioning of all organizations.

In view of the above, this part of the book has been divided into ten chapters:

15. Managing Change
16. Knowledge Management
17. Human Resource Development Audit
18. Ethics and Corporate Social Responsibility
19. Managing Globalization
20. Technology and HRM
21. Work–Life Balance
22. Quality Management and HRM: JIT, 5S, Kaizen, Six Sigma
23. HRM Strategies
24. HRM in Various Sectors

CHAPTER 15

Managing Change

LEARNING OBJECTIVES

After studying this chapter, you will be able to

- Understand today's business scenario
- Appreciate change management as a collaborative effort
- Recognize the sources of resistance
- Identify the coping mechanisms
- Recognize the significance of culture in change initiatives
- Initiate a proactive approach in traditional culture

OPENING CASE

Reducing Machine Breakdown at Elite Press Works Limited

Elite Press Works Limited (EPWL) owned many sophisticated hydraulic and pneumatic press machines, which made the company one of the best in the business.

One particular season, owing to the breakdown of some of its critical machines, EPWL could not deliver its products on time. To overcome this problem, EPWL desired to introduce an intensive preventive maintenance policy during the holidays and weekends, in order to reduce the mean time between failures. The company brainstormed and analysed all documents, facts, and figures to decide the direction of change, and decided that the operators needed to undertake repair of their respective machines. It was also planned that the machine operators would be trained, enabling them to undertake the repair of their own machines.

When the workers came to know about the decision, they raised a furore, assuming that they would be overloaded and may not get the necessary maintenance gadgets; the unions took up the matter and collectively objected. This lead to large scale disturbance of normal work and a fear of work overload. The management however identified HRD mechanisms such as job enrichment, job rotation (machine operator to maintenance, maintenance mechanic to production department, etc.), role clarity, trust building, etc. The management engaged internal experts and educated union leaders to conduct a series of training programmes, and used the HRD mechanisms to ultimately overcome the resistance.

EPWL implemented the system in 2007 and since then, the company has seldom faced the problem of delayed delivery due to machine breakdown.

Learning points

- Any change is initially opposed, but with the right stimuli, people ultimately learn to accept and welcome changes.
- Changes must be implemented slowly and steadily.

INTRODUCTION

'It is wise to ride a horse in the direction it is going'. This saying implies that we should study the changing environment and change ourselves accordingly, and not oppose the changes. In the organizational context, it means that we should accept and adapt to organizational development. A change could refer to an alteration in the existing field of forces such as structure, strategy, system, budget, inter-department synergy, new technology, and related aspects inside or outside the organization. A planned change tends to affect the equilibrium. Sometimes, change initiatives and implementation might be a blessing to an organization. In other cases, an organization might have to implement the change keeping with the changing trend of the industry. Changes are necessary to protect an organization from the clutches of the 'static' syndrome.

> 'It is wise to ride a horse in the direction it is going'. We must change to keep pace with the changing environment.

> To derive benefits, we have to analyse the changes in the environment to modulate and transform through active change management initiatives.

Change is an inevitable process in any organization and it is important for organizations to cope with these changes in order to sustain themselves. It has been seen that many organizations have perished as they did not or could not adapt to the changes. Some organizations have perished as the change points were wrongly decided upon. The direction and speed of change are important to understand for any organization to succeed. It is also important to remember that change does not just happen. It is driven by a reason, a thought, and an idea. The cause of the change comes either from 'outside'—the business environment, or from 'within'—the organization.

Every organization has its own internal environment, and is a part of the external environment. To derive benefits from these changes, we have to analyse them in the environment to modulate and transform through active change management initiatives. An organization needs to consider the current state (where it is today), identify the desired state (where it wants to move), and ascertain the gap between the current state and desired state which is referred to as 'delta state'.

BUSINESS SCENARIO

Business organizations are seen to be operating more in uncertain environments in the global village. As a result of this phenomenon, the majority of the modern industrialized world is unable to extract the best from the available human inventory. To a large degree, achieving business goals are constrained by the level of employee productivity. Similarly, as huge investments are centered around technological upgradation, process improvement, structuring system, and so forth, collaterally, improving human productivity must be a never-ending effort as well.

The majority of the modern industrialized world is focusing on the available human inventory. This organizational fact permeates through every aspect of the business. It is believed that performance excellence can lead to business excellence. This refers to doing simple things such as concentrating on the performance of a single employee, so that more time and money can be spent on the more complex issues.

It also needs to be mentioned that with the onset of globalization, we are witnessing integration or commonality in the context of business, economics, and societies in the unified global system. This has been possible due to the numerous social, economic, and cultural convergences, notwithstanding divergent consumer preferences, varied business perspectives, and atypical geopolitical conditions among nations. We need to look at the business scenario, particularly from a 'down to earth' perspective, and initiate steps to survive. Let us take a brief look at the prevailing business scenario.

INSTANCES OF CHANGING BUSINESS SCENARIO

In this section, a few examples of some businesses which were affected due to recession (including those from the retail industry, aviation industry, information technology sector, outsourcing services, and academia) are highlighted (Majumdar and Dmonte 2008).

Until the worldwide recession, retailers such as Shopper's Stop were busy chasing headhunters to find candidates willing to join them. Later, the company decided to be very selective in filling up new vacancies and to recruit only when new stores came up. It was evident that the tables had turned. Future Group said that companies owning large retail chains such as Pantaloon and Big Bazaar had cut people cost by one per cent by linking salaries with performance. It further emphasized, 'human capability is infinite and multi-tasking is the order of the day'.

In the aviation sector, Jet Airways laid off 800 employees and announced a further lay-off of 1,150 employees. However, the laid off employees were reinstated within 24 hours after public and political outcry. The company was reeling under pressure and was experimenting with various alternatives. In the same sector, Kingfisher Airlines slashed the salaries of its co-pilots by 90 per cent.

Wipro Technologies put four to five per cent employees under the scanner for non-performance. However, it mentioned that the exercise was a regular annual feature. Bangalore-based IT service provider, MphasiS, reduced hiring plans by almost 50 per cent. It had earlier announced that it would recruit 8,000 people; however, later, the company planned to recruit only 4,000 people. Teamlease, the largest staffing solution company of India, was earlier recruiting people without laying much emphasis on job specifications. Now, it has changed its recruitment strategy. It is obvious that we have moved from 'plenty' to 'paltry'.

All these changes pose threats and challenges to the organizations that are now finding ways and means 'to get more from people'. As a means of encouraging teamwork, they are looking for leaders who are capable of uniting, motivating, driving, and produceing results.

REASONS FOR CHANGE

There are a number of reasons which lead to change. Apart from the economic recession, there are some common reasons that generally affect organizations. Refer to Box 15.1.

Box 15.1 Common reasons leading to change

1. Multiple and fast-paced technological innovations—products, processes, and 'know-hows', are fast becoming obsolete
2. Scarcity of natural resources
3. Increasing costs of basic resources
4. Cost sensitivity and quality consciousness of customers
5. Sharp increase in competition

(Contd)

Box 15.1 (Contd)

6. Frequent changes in regulatory mechanisms
7. Changes in socio-economic structure
8. Growth and popularity of information technology
9. Proliferation of environmental and consumer interest groups
10. Liberalization, privatization, and globalization

All the reasons mentioned in Box 15.1 are external to the business. To survive and sustain, it becomes imperative for the companies or businesses to change. It would not be over emphasizing to say that change is an indispensable part of our lives, central to our work lives, and is completely unavoidable in today's business environment. Individuals, managers, and companies are left with two choices:

1. Be reactive to the changes in the environment.
2. Be proactive and manage the change processes to maximize benefits, and eliminate or reduce negative impacts.

Changes may be required in the whole organization; however, broadly, there are four dimensions or kinds of changes—process change, system change, structural change, and organizational change.

Process change This deals with incremental planning, action research approach, modelling, mentoring, process awareness and orientation, counselling, and organizational norms.

System change System refers to a set of interrelated processes. In an organization, there is an administrative system, material management system, quality control system, maintenance system, etc.

Structural change Structural change considers elements such as stability of the business structure, temporary systems, linkage binding mechanisms, information systems, rewards, regular budgets, and guidelines or standing instructions.

Organizational change Organizations need to adapt to the continuous changes taking place in the environment; otherwise they may become obsolete and extinct, no matter, how big or established it is or what the market share is. Continuous scanning to adapt to changes is as essential as any other important function in organizations.

Four dimensions or kinds of changes are
1. Process change
2. System change
3. Structural change
4. Organizational

Irrespective of the kind of change, affected people exhibit certain patterns of response. The change agents need to anticipate these patterns. Change agents can initiate planned and proactive steps by understanding these patterns. It helps them avoid crisis management and smoothen the change process. Thus, changes are manageable and must be tackled in a rhythmic way. Let us now discuss the scope of change management.

CHANGE MANAGEMENT

Q 4 Change management is the systematic process of applying the knowledge, skills, and resources needed to effect a change.

Basically, any change is initiated to bring certain positive outcomes; however, the most common obstacle, as is usually experienced, is human resistance. If we are able to control human resistance and convert it human support, the changes will be faster, smoother, and more successful.

Understanding the reasons for people's resistance and discovering the means to overcome the resistance, are the core concerns of change management. However, most interestingly, converting the human resistance to human support is also a kind of change. Leaders must have the competence to anticipate and respond to employees' concerns and feelings. The feelings may be expressed in terms of practical concerns or emotional responses. An effective change agent identifies the kind of reactions and questions that employees have, and prepares the responses. Remember that the success of any change rests with the ability of the leaders to address both the emotional and the practical issues.

Effective change management can help one to successfully implement the change necessary for an organization's future prosperity and profitability. However, one must plan, analyse, and communicate effectively to get the best results.

Planning and Analysis

Planning is the first and the most significant step in effective change management. Before communicating the changes to the workforce or the public, organizations should always draw a road map and proceed accordingly. Leaders must assess the readiness of the organization to participate in the change. Organizational climate and mutual trust are essential determinants of effective change management. They should mull over a few points: what is the level of trust within the organization? Do people feel generally positive about their work environment? Have the organizational stalwarts created a history of open communication? Have they communicated the organization's mission, policy, objectives, targets, and strategies to the workforce? Is the organization disclosing its financial statement to the public?

These factors have a tremendous impact on people's acceptance and willingness to change. If firms can start building this positive and supportive environment prior to the change, then they can have a great head start on the change implementation. For accomplishing this, organizations must gather information and determine ways to communicate the reasons for the changes. Further, they have to assess each potential impact to organizational processes, systems, employees, customers, suppliers, vendors, and other stakeholders, and assess the risks. In addition, it must develop specific improvements or mitigation plans for each risk. People need to understand the context, the reasons for the change, and the benefit to the organization and individuals. Any change is associated with amendments to the roles and responsibilities. People must know the organization's clear expectations in the post-implementation phase.

Effective Communication

Communication is the key to effective change management. Organizations must develop the mode of communication and communicate consistently and frequently through multiple channels. They must communicate the present state, the desired state, and the necessity of moving to another state. It is also essential to highlight the benefits and the possible consequences if the change is not implemented. It is important to communicate all that is known about the changes, whenever the information is available, and as quickly as possible. Further, providing significant amount of time for people to think, allowing generation of doubts, asking questions, requesting clarifications, and providing inputs is another charge not to be forgotten. It is essential to clearly communicate the objectives of the change management effort, and help people to understand how these changes will affect them personally, ease out the work, and task accomplishments. Emphasize the utmost need of their involvement and their spontaneous help in the change process. Otherwise, people will make up their own invalid conclusions based on assumptions and the change process will be in jeopardy.

Communication should not be a presentation or monologue; rather it should be a conversation or a dialogue. The change agents, leaders, or sponsors need to devote ample time conversing in a one-on-one manner or in small groups, especially with people involved in the change and those likely to be affected by the implementation. The management needs to be proactive and provide credible answers to questions of the employees, based on valid facts and figures. Lastly, change agents should provide opportunities for people to network with each other, both formally and informally, to share ideas about change and change management.

Change is all about perceiving, learning, and making people respond more to effective change leaders, rather than being controlled by influential good managers. Effective change agents use appropriate dialogue, consultation, and employ a principle of empowerment, or a combination of these, while leading. Change cannot be easily imposed upon people; rather people willingly accept the changes if the change process is methodically designed. During the change management process, it is essential to understand that a supporting and leading nature wins over attempts to managing them. The persons likely to be affected by the change should be taken into confidence.

PROCESS OF ORGANIZATIONAL CHANGE

Successful management of change demands an in-depth study of the process of organizational change. Kurt Lewin (1947) lucidly discussed the process of organizational change using three stages in the process—unfreezing, moving, and refreezing. Refer to Figure 15.1 for an illustration of this process.

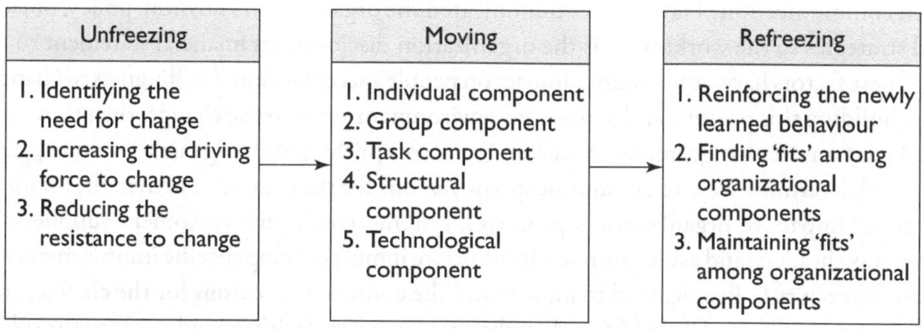

Fig. 15.1 Process of organizational change

Unfreezing The stage of unfreezing refers to loosening emotional as well as intellectual forces, recognizing, and enhancing the driving forces for the people to develop keen sensitivity towards the external and internal forces, and reducing the resistance to change.

The strategies used to enhance driving forces for change are (a) express the need for changes, (b) communicate the potential benefits, (c) protect the interest of people concerned, (d) get people involved, (e) periodically communicate the progress of change, (f) use an internal change agent who is respected by the organizational citizens, and (g) reinforce earlier changes. There are certain techniques to reduce resistance, which will be discussed later.

The process of organizational change involves three stages:

1. Unfreezing
2. Moving
3. Refreezing

Moving After the unfreezing stage, the individual is ready for the new behaviour and a change in perspective. He/she must get an opportunity to build new patterns of behaviour. This stage typically needs monitoring and mentoring by an expert. Traditionally, attention is paid to only one area; say the sub-system technology, under change. At present, a much broader view is taken by focusing attention on all the organizational components comprising task, structure, technology, and the people.

Refreezing This is the final phase of the change process, leading to the reinforcement of the new desirable behaviour. The new parts of one's total perspective are now established and integrated, and are capable of fitting into the whole. At this period, the individual or group begins to enjoy the rewards for the new behaviour in the changed situation. The reward may be extrinsic in the form of social approval, monetary reward, organization's recognition, or the likes or intrinsic in the form of work satisfaction, sense of mastery, achievement and self-fulfillment. At this stage, one might even enjoy work satisfaction that derives from accomplishing a complex task, sense of mastery which develops from acquiring new skills.

Dynamics of the Change Process

IGNOU (1994) quotes the dynamics of the process of organizational change. Refer to Table 15.1.

Table 15.1 Dynamics of process of change

Stage of adoption	Psychological (cover) process	Behavioural outcomes
Initiation	Arousal	Readiness: Dissatisfaction with the present state
Motivation	Selectivity and stimulus perception	Seeing or hearing about innovation
Diagnosis	Orientation and exploration	Gathering information and data
Information collection	Exploration	Collecting more relevant data
Deliberation	Cognitive reorganization and reinforcement	Discussion and planning
Action proposal	Expectancy	Presenting one proposal with pay off and detailed planning acceptance by the group
Implementation	Acquiring new learned drives	Extended use of the innovation
Stabilization	Generalization of the learned behaviour and inhibition of the older modes of behaviour: consummatory response	Change of attitude and acceptance as a part of the total behaviour complex with secondary changes in other forms of behaviour: communication reinforcing adoption

The stages of adoption are as follows:

Initiation Initiation is the stage of vocalization of the need for change. A change is initiated when there is a feel of dissatisfaction with the present state of affairs. The idea may be routed to the corporate management for consideration and approval.

Motivation Motivation is the stage of involving and motivating people to work and think of ideas towards the change, especially those who are likely to be affected by the change.

Diagnosis Diagnosis is an attempt to search for the main cause of the symptoms encountered.

Information collection Based on the diagnosis, in this stage, detailed information is collected.

Deliberation While finalizing a change, various alternatives are generated. Deliberation refers to evaluation of the alternatives.

Action proposal Action proposal is framed including the derivable benefits, current stage, desired stage, plan of moving, and so forth.

Implementation Translating the proposal into action is implementation.

Stabilization Any change must be a part of the organizational life. This must be kept in mind in the various process of organizational change. Stabilization is the stage of internalizing the change.

RESISTANCE TO CHANGE

The success of a change management process is more probabilistic than deterministic. The uncertainties associated with an expected change and the likelihood of non-equilibrium sometimes result in resistance to change. The resistance may result in decline in production and productivity, increase in absenteeism, low turnover, strikes, etc. Resistance largely develops from misperceiving the effects of change, and hence it arises from individuals' problems. A majority of people assume that introduction of change factors are likely to disrupt the basic cultural fabric and core values of a group or various groups. Resistance to change is similar to dissent which stimulates the individuals and group to consider many factors that should otherwise be ignored. To make a change programme better and smooth, attention should be paid as soon as dissent is diagnosed.

Outsiders or external change agents are often engaged to design and implement changes. They cannot have microscopic details about the organization. As such, they lack ownership of the change programme and may fail to make the programme participative. Resistance often develops due to lack of awareness and non-participation of employees. Managing resistance to change requires instilling ownership, responsibility, and involvement in the affected people during the process of change. When affected people feel they need the change, and the change is seen as reducing problems, burdens and worries, then resistance will be less likely. Resistance can also be greatly reduced by designing changes as a participative forum by involving juniors in the diagnosis of the problems, and in the decision-making process.

On the flip side, resistance has positive aspects too. When people offer resistance, the top management gets an opportunity of getting a signal to a problem area and needs to pay attention to relook into an issue. It has been evidenced that resistance has helped reveal some organizational issues those were hidden otherwise.

SOURCES OF RESISTANCE VIS-À-VIS COPING MECHANISMS

Some sources of resistance and their coping mechanisms are described below:

Perceived superficiality of change When executives perceive that the change introduced will not benefit them, they resist. If they are involved in the diagnosis of the issues, they may appreciate the change; their attitude towards the innovative change may be positive. The coping mechanism here is, 'participation in diagnosis'.

Perception of imposition When managers or executives feel that the national headquarters or the corporate office is introducing a change and imposing these changes on them, they generally resist. Moreover, they apprehend that they would be overburdened due to some additional work; and become stressed. Stressed employees must be helped to cope, handle a potential stressor, and the resulting stressful situation to minimize their harmful consequences (Sarkar 2010). The foundation can be created by conducting seminars and/or work group meetings, and by forming task forces to work out the details of implementation in a phased manner. The coping mechanism here is, 'participation and involvement'.

Indifference of top management Attitude and behavioural disposition of top management always impacts change implementation. People at the lower level offer more resistance when they observe a lack of enthusiasm or interest in the top management in the change implementation drive. The top management should be committed, involved in the process which should be visible to the lower levels. This coping mechanism is termed 'active support from the top'.

Complacency and inertia People are accustomed to work in a place, amidst known colleagues, and in a familiar environment. Any proposed change of state produces discomfort due to addiction, love, and affinity to the existing set up. People initially tend to concentrate only on the problems at the new place. However, once they move and become involved, they find the new place enjoyable and see many more positive aspects in it. To reduce the resistance, one can share experiences about the new set up, and they can be informed about the dislocation in advance; prior to issuing the formal order. This coping mechanism is called 'fait accompli'.

Fear of large-scale disturbance People become afraid of unpredictable consequences of the forthcoming change. This is a common fear in large organizations having multiple units in different locations. If the proposed station is a sensitive area and demands special skills and competencies, information about the change, highlighting the job requirements at the new area, and phasing the change programme may reduce the resistance. Resistance is an indicator of the potential difficulties and points out potential failures or problems. This coping mechanism is 'phasing of change'.

Fear of inadequate resources A new assignment or an assignment in a new place may need additional resources and capabilities in the form of additional human resource, special materials, budgets, etc. Procurement and organizing these resources may be difficult. If the additional resources are estimated and the availability is reasonably assured, then resistance reduces. This coping mechanism is 'support of resource'.

Fear of obsolescence Research and development initiatives unleash modern and state-of-the-art technologies, making traditional technologies obsolete. Resistance on account of obsolescence can be reduced by way of providing orientation and imparting training in the new skills and competencies. This coping mechanism is 'development of skills and competencies'.

Fear of loss of power The power motive is generally high among senior managers. Changes arising out of diversion of responsibility or creation of new roles for organizational effectiveness produce tension among seniors who are seen to offer pseudo resistance. Redefining and redesigning the roles help one overcome the fear of loss of power. The coping mechanism is, therefore, 'redefining and redesigning roles'.

Fear of overload Many managers resist assignments related to new functions as they feel that they will be overburdened. If their roles are defined clearly with opportunities for prioritizing their tasks and delegating authorities, they will not feel overwhelmed in the new role and resistance can be reduced. This coping mechanism is 'role clarity and definition'.

KEY TO CHANGE MANAGEMENT

Change management process needs planning and decisions on system, structure, and technology-related aspects. When compared to the difficulty emanating from resistance, estimating the budget, preparing the justification, and obtaining approval are less complicated.. Resistance is the single most hindering factor in any change management process. To smoothen the process, the change agent must have the competency to do the following:

1. Identify the source and volume of the resistance to change
2. Design ways to reduce the resistance

3. Formulate action plan to implement the change
4. Sustain the change

METHODICAL APPROACH TO CHANGE MANAGEMENT

Corresponding to the change in the environment, an organization has to identify its direction of change needs. Analyses must be done mainly from four angles: structure, process, culture, and people.

In order to cope with the need of delivering services to the customer promptly, the structural change might demand modern and state-of-the-art technology, reorganizing the communication system, extensive use of information system, and so forth. This change may also call for a change in the reporting relationship in the organization or launching an innovative incentive scheme. Every aspect of structure—from the point at which things have gone wrong to the aspect that needs to be changed—have to be analysed.

The component process needs analysis of the flow of work. In order to gather information about the workflow, answers to certain questions are sought. Some of the questions are: Is the work flow process efficient? Are there any bottlenecks, which slow down the workflow? Does a single item hold the delivery of the whole consignment?

The culture and feeling of belongingness is assessed from responses to questions such as: Does the workforce have a sense of belonging and feeling about the organization? What is view of the workforce about the organization's products? Did the workforce welcome changes earlier?

In order to make out how the people function, the relevant questions are: Does the workforce currently in operation have the knowledge? What HRD mechanisms may be used?

A close analysis of the structure, process, people, and culture reveals a lot about what needs to be changed, why, and what strategy to be followed. The whole organization will appreciate the possible consequences of 'not changing' and why the 'current-status' cannot be allowed to continue. A clear picture of the problem, where it lies, and how bad it is, will emerge.

To effect the change successfully, it is absolutely necessary to ascertain the volume of changes, pinpoint the direction of changes, determine the speed of change, and identify the anticipated source of resistance to change.

To gather further information, one has to ask certain questions to oneself and the employees. Gather all the information and obtain answers to the structured questions. Some examples of questions are: Why is the change required? What has to be changed? Who ordered the change? Will the change be handled in the same way as the previous one? Who is going to deliver the change? By gathering information in this way, through questionnaire, it is possible to identify who might resist and to what extent, and how serious the problem of potential resistance might be. By gathering all the information, one is definitely better prepared to face the resistance.

KEY ROLES IN ORGANIZATIONAL CHANGE

Roles refer to the expectations of significant personnel and peers of the organization. Roles include both external and internal roles. To initiate organizational change, six main roles are (a) corporate management, (b) consultant, (c) internal resource person, (d) implementation team, (e) chief implementer, and (f) task force. The functions of each role occupant are briefed here.

Six main roles for organizational change are
1. Corporate management
2. Consultant
3. Internal resource person
4. Implementation team
5. Chief implementer
6. Task force

Corporate Management

The corporate management of an organization comprises the chief executive officer, chief operating officer, members of the board, etc. They perform three distinct functions—legitimizing function, energizing function, and gate-keeping function.

Corporate management legitimizes the need for the change being planned. They are instrumental to implement the follow-up, so that the change efforts do not slow down. This is referred to as the energizing function. Corporate management energizes the slackening pace and interest by taking up problems for discussion and by exhibiting their concerns. Corporate management convenes meetings and group discussions to establish the relationship between the consultant and various groups in the organization to discharge their gate-keeping functions.

Consultant

The role of a solitary consultant or a team of consultants is that of an expert. External consultants come with vast knowledge. Internal employees may have vast knowledge but they are likely to be inhabited to have their own perception of the problem. Thus, their decisions are likely to be biased. The functions that are performed by the consultants(s) are—implanting function, transcending function, alternative generating function, process facility function, shock absorbing function, resource sharing function, resource building function, self-liquidating function. All these functions are briefly discussed as follows:

Implanting function The consultant provides the team with internal expertise and never replaces it.

Transcending function Organizational constraints cannot limit the drives of a consultant. He coordinates various units and departments of an organization together to capture an idea of the organization. He further gets the willing support of the people and as time passes, brightens the future of the organization.

Alternative generating function A consultant takes people, organizes small group meetings, brainstorms to generate alternative ideas, and ultimately solves problems.

Process facility function A consultant, as a process facilitator, helps the people of the organization to take over their roles as the change management initiatives advances.

Shock absorbing function Consultants often need to give unpleasant feedback to the organization and encounter distasteful situations as well. They need to perform the activities in a calm and quiet manner. They have to absorb some shocking moments at times.

Resource sharing function Consultants need to mobilize resources and share them with internal people to accelerate the change process and make the change effective.

Resource building function Consultants help to develop internal people by sharing knowledge and experience, and thus generates people from within.

Self-liquidating function A time comes when the consultant has to withdraw after the expiry of the consultancy period. By building internal expertise and resources, he has already broadened the avenue. His expertise is evidenced when people do not feel his absence after his departure.

Internal Resource Person

A consultant needs the continuous support from selected employees of the organization. These employees are generally termed as 'internal resource persons' or 'facilitators' and represent the same expertise as that of a consultant. As an internal change agent, they help in implementing the policies and activities leading to organizational change. Without the spontaneous support of the facilitators, it is practically impossible for an organization to effectively implement a change. They get support from the organizational members and maintain linkage with the consultant.

> Internal resource persons, in a broad sense, are actually internal OD facilitators.

Support from employees They are required to communicate the need for the change, process, benefits, etc. to organizational members to reduce or eliminate resistance to change.

Linkage with the consultant They have to act as a buffer between the consultant and the organization. They are actually linkmen with expertise.

Stabilization of the role The top management should share the successes and failure of the change with these internal resource persons. Their performances need periodical reviews. In this way, their role may be stabilized in the system.

Professional development The internal resource persons, in a broader sense, are actually internal organizational development (OD) facilitators. They need professional development.

Implementation Team

In an organization, various departments or functional areas are assigned the responsibilities to monitor, deliberate, communicate, and make necessary recommendations whenever needed. They form the implementation team. They execute the collaboration building function, gate-keeping function, reviewing function, policy formulating function, etc.

Collaboration building function Collaboration among various departments is essential for the synchronization of activities. Members should work in a team and use 'collective wisdom'.

Gate-keeping function The implementation team helps to keep the communication going relating to planning and change implementation within the members. This is achieved by way of developing liaison between the departments and sections.

Reviewing function Periodical reviews facilitate identification of any drawback, decide corrective action, and make adjustments so that the implementation becomes effective.

Policy formulating function The programme should be smooth and effective. Based on the reviews, the implementation team makes recommendations, and prepares a 'draft policy'. The top management, in consultation implementation team, finalizes the policy. This makes the change programme more realistic.

Chief Implementer

The chief implementer heads the implementation team as the chairman. He scrutinizes all the recommendations, gives directions, receives feedback, and ultimately ensures proper implementation. The main functions of this role are monitoring function, diagnostic function, and executive function.

Monitoring function To perform this function better, the chief implementer needs to stick to the schedule, and relentlessly put effort to keep the change programme on the schedule to end that in time.

Diagnostic function Some hurdles always emerge during implementation. The chief implementer needs to collect information through tailor-made questionnaires or other means. Based on the information, he has to take actions to tackle the hurdles. For example, if he feels the requirement of providing additional inputs, resource allocation or smoothing or resource leveling, he goes ahead with it.

Executive function Recommendations by the implementation team must be translated into actions. Through systematic approach, the chief implementer achieves this. He should neither be rigid nor flexible; he should be flexibly rigid. He must take feedback from various sources about the change programme and analyse them. It has been evidenced that personal prejudices of a chief implementer might result exorbitantly in delaying a change programme.

Moreover, prejudice may guide a chief implementer to a wrong direction. He has to use his creative potential and originality. He must imagine and dream; then realize the dream into actions. This role requires high acceptance in the organization. He should have rapport with various persons at various levels in the organization. He must not demand respect; rather he should command respect.

Task Force

A task force is formed for a specific purpose. The task force dissolves after the task is over. In an organization, there can be many task forces simultaneously working to achieve their respective assignments. Each task force prepares the material, collects data, processes them into information, generates ideas/alternatives, and undertakes specific responsibilities. The task forces make use of various kinds of expertise and skills available in the organization.

The functions of each role occupant (corporate management, consultant, internal resource person, implementation team, chief implementer, and task force) are presented in Table 15.2.

Table 15.2 Key role and functions of role occupants

Role	Function
Corporate management	1. Legitimizing function 2. Energizing function 3. Gate-keeping function
Consultant	1. Implanting function 2. Transcending function 3. Alternative generating function 4. Process facility function 5. Shock absorbing function 6. Resource sharing function 7. Resource building function 8. Self-liquidating function
Internal resource person	1. Support from employees 2. Linkage with the consultant 3. Stabilization of the role 4. Professional development
Implementation team	1. Collaboration building function 2. Gate-keeping functions 3. Reviewing function 4. Policy formulating function
Chief implementer	1. Monitoring function 2. Diagnostic function 3. Executive function
Task force	Any combination of the above functions

CHANGE AGENT

A change agent is a person who can motivate and alter human capabilities or organizational systems to achieve a higher degree of organizational output. Change agents may be internal or external. They may even be consultants hired temporarily by the organization to implement the changes. They have expertise in behavioural sciences and the intervention technology. They begin with the end in mind; the goal of a change agent is obviously to make changes that sustain. Effective change agents enable people to do more, or find a new and better perspective on work life, which, at times, is the foundation for future change. They ultimately transform various aspects of the organization to achieve outcomes that were apparently not attainable.

A change agent uses visionary skills and can foresee what could or should be the goal for the

Change agents have expertise in behavioural sciences and in the intervention technology, and begin with the end in mind. The goal of a change agent is obviously to make sustainable changes.

future. Generally, a change agent is dissatisfied with what they see around them in favour of a much better vision of the future. A change agent is driven by passion, and inspires passion in others. Change implementation is hard work and consumes a lot of time and energy. A change agent is self-motivated; he/she must have the inherent ability to understand people. If one can change everything but the people, one may not be effective as a change agent. Change will happen when people like and support it. Therefore, change implementation involves sales, counselling, and encouragement. It is all about people, and hence, changes are possible only by involving them.

Manager vs Change Agent

Can every manager be a change agent? A manager can be an agent of change, provided he has certain characteristics. The characteristics of a successful change agent include empathy, linkage, proximity, structuring, openness, energy, and synergy.

The skill of understanding the feelings and thoughts of another person is empathy. Linkage is the degree of collaboration between a manager and his people. Proximity refers to the accessibility of a change agent to others; the more the proximity, the more will be the collaborative linkage. Structuring refers to the ability to meticulously plan and organize activities with regard to the change efforts facilitating implementation of the change approach in a straightforward step-by-step manner. Openness is a characteristic that refers to the degree to which the change agent is receptive to ideas, needs, and feelings. Energy refers to the amount of effort or liveliness that a change agent has to his/her credit to complete the change process. Consequently, it must be mentioned that Jack Welch, former chairman of General Electric, also strongly emphasized that energy, energize, edge, and execution (4Es) are important for a leader's mission. Synergy is the positive reinforcing effect that each of the preceding six factors (empathy, linkage, proximity, structuring, openness, and energy) have upon one another.

SIGNIFICANCE OF CULTURE

In the course of introduction and implementation of changes, both societal and organizational cultures play a dominant role. Values, attitudes, and rituals play predominant roles in the change management process. Understanding of and respect for a culture are important for those who are involved in envisaging, planning, implementing, and managing the changes. Changes in the larger context need the consideration of the culture prevailing in the society and the organization.

Values, attitudes, and rituals play predominant roles in the change management process.

Culture also dictates the use of time in relation to certain rituals or affairs. It shapes and moulds an individual's behavioural patterns. Certain human responses to significant issues and phenomena are also influenced by culture. Generally, a team undertakes the responsibility of planning, designing, and implementing a change. The members come from certain cultures, dictated by their social and economic backgrounds. They possess a variety of values and attitudes. In an organization, certain prevailing values must be preserved. If a change agent, as an impatient reformer, attempts to introduce a change in a society or an organization disregarding the prevailing values, problems will definitely arise. This necessitates a proactive approach to change.

The following incident (Exhibit 15.1) will reinforce the utmost need for considering societal culture and the consequence of ignoring it, even while attempting to do something good for the society.

Exhibit 15.1 Burning of school by tribal people

A few years ago, the government of a particular state felt the necessity to impart education to its tribal communities. Officers of the Department of Public Instruction (DPI) were assigned the task of establishing schools in tribal areas of the state. The government further directed the DPI to provide the schools with identical facilities as those in urban areas and arrange for school uniforms.

Anticipating that the tribal people may resist, some initial discussions were organized with the tribal population. The DPI did their best to construct the schools, assigned teachers to each school, and arranged school uniforms. One such school in the tribal region was inaugurated in the presence of important personalities including the Tribal Education Officer. During the inauguration, much was spoken about the uplifting of backward communities and tribal areas, the necessity to emancipate them, the need for them to progress, their contribution to the country, etc. Nevertheless, the people of one particular tribe in the area were hesitant to send their children to the school.

The Tribal Education Officer and a few other officials went to visit the school and found the school burnt to the ground. The officer was annoyed and feared that he would be held responsible. An in-depth investigation into the cause revealed the following facts:

The tribal people had formulated their own indigenous system of educating their children. The system was complete with organized study, special dresses, educational games, and ceremonies at different stages to motivate the children. The tribal people were very loyal to the system. They realized that if the children were sent to the government school, they would not be able to attend the traditional education system. In addition, the tribe resented the school uniform which they believed would be unfit for the children to wear. In addition, they believed that the teaching might not educate the children to be good tribal citizens.

Obviously, they thought of the government school as a bad initiative and resorted to burning it down.

PROACTIVE APPROACH TO MANAGING CHANGE

The demands of modern organizational management and traditional cultures might be conflicting in many cases. There exist two extreme views on this aspect—some advocate that change management practices should be designed to suit the culture, while the other group opines that modern management practices should be uniformly adopted to achieve the goals of the organization. A proactive strategy must be initiated. The following steps are essential to successfully manage a change.

Determine the direction of change The goal of the organization must be clearly defined in terms of specific system and process movement. Systems include performance feedback, potential appraisal, coaching, mentoring, counselling, career planning, etc. Process movement encompasses more openness, more collaborative actions, consulting with one another, and the like. By determining the direction of change, one can be better prepared to handle resistance or any foreseen situations.

Share possible consequences The consequences of change efforts are mostly probabilistic and seldom deterministic. The journey is unlikely to be pleasant; this should be made clear to all people concerned. An external consultant often prefers to communicate the possible consequences in writing. The change agent, however optimistic he/she is, must avoid giving only rosy pictures. When a system is at its commencement stage, people test the limits of openness to some extent. It must be kept in mind at the beginning; any system might give problems, which are part of the 'teething problems'.

Start from the base of the delta state An organization, whatever be the age, must have a tradition and elementary forms of a specific system. Some systems can obviously be designed for an organization to reach the business goals. The system analyst must carry out an 'as-is' analysis and then design the new system keeping in view the 'to-be' needs. Alternatively, the analyst has to consider two aspects: 'where we are' and 'where we want to go'.

Take only one step at a time The delta state defines the total task content. The change agent needs to plan various steps, according to the task content. Multiple tasks can obviously be planned concurrently. However, it is not advisable to undertake multiple changes concurrently.

For instance, the task could be introduction of ISO 9001 quality management system in a manufacturing organization. The logical steps for this could be launching company-wide awareness programme conforming to training curriculum, asking each department to develop the draft procedures. The management representative (MR) should then study the procedures to verify completeness and correctness, compatibility with other procedures, and so forth. The total task should be split into interlinked components.

Plan and prepare for the journey A new system requires to bring about changes in the orientation and attitude of the people in the organization. People may need to acquire new set of skills and competencies, which must be identified at the planning stage. Otherwise, the total project of change will be delayed. If a person lacks a skill essential to perform a task, either the task will remain unachieved or the task will have errors. Training must be conducted to abridge the skill and competency gaps. Thus, training must precede introduction of new system.

Involve people Involving people of various levels primarily enhances the strength of a team and secondarily broadens the ways of managing resistance to change.

Be prepared for reversals Introduction of a new system will have its own consequences. The new system may create confusion, doubts, and suspicion, and few unforeseen problems, thus jeopardizing the normal flow of work. There might be some mistakes in the preliminary planning work. For example, the feedback and counselling sessions have not been as effective as was expected. In such situations, reversals emerge as essential. However, such reversals should not generate anxiety as they are likely to occur. Organizations should be prepared to deal with them in demanding situations and move forward.

Develop internal expertise While designing and implementing a system, enough internal expertise should be available. A professional external change agent can obviously provide adequate expertise in certain dimensions generally at the beginning and the end of the change process. Continuous work needs to be executed by the internal experts, as they know the people, culture, and the organization. Enough attention must be paid in developing internal experts; otherwise the system may remain incomplete and goal unachieved.

Continue moving towards the goal Persistence is the key to success. Short-term plans need to be designed along with long-term plans. Each short-term plan must be continuously monitored through predetermined yardsticks. Coordination of all the short-term plans, keeping in view the long-term plan, is of paramount importance.

Review periodically Periodic review helps to track the progress to initiate remedial measures, if necessary.

Use a compass and a speedometer Data need to be analysed for decision making. Information obtained from data analysis helps to evaluate direction and speed of changes, and take actions.

S-P-S-T MODEL

Q 3 In order to bring about a change in organization culture, the management needs to concentrate on four dimensions: structural elements (S), process (P), strategy (S), and tactics (T).

Structural elements The structural elements include stability of the structure, temporary systems, the mechanism of building linkages with influencers, information system, compensation and rewards, regular budget, standing instructions and guidelines, etc.

Process The process dimension comprises incremental planning, action research programme, modeling and mentoring, counseling, process awareness and orientation, and organizational norms.

Strategy This refers to the process of identifying and using the strengths, building the organization's competencies, developing key institutions, sanctions, and support of significant agencies, and most importantly, system ownership.

Tactics It emphasizes diplomacy to prepare in advance, moving one step at a time, mobilizing resources, going together in teams, reviewing progress and initiating remedial measures, reinforcing, perseverance, and persuasion.

Positive Approach

Q 5 As discussed earlier, delta state is the space between the current state and the desired state. The change agents vary widely in their mindset and initiate different approaches. Some of them may find the change interesting, for others; the path might be challenging but energizing while some others may find the task meaningless and confusing, and the journey stressful. However, all change agents face resistance to change. Those who view the change efforts as positive can plan and take a proactive approach. This group of persons can anticipate roadblocks and remove them. On the contrary, those who find the assignment meaningless, can never be proactive enough to anticipate and remove the hurdles, and ultimately fail to achieve the goals of the organization. Hence, it is important for a change agent to always face the tasks ahead of him/her with a positive approach so as to be able to achieve the best from it.

SUMMARY

The business scenario is continuously changing due to multiple reasons such as social, economic, and cultural forces. These are forcing organizations to change in order to survive and grow. The organizations need to anticipate the speed and direction of changes and initiate appropriate actions to cope with the changes. Organizational change management needs planning, and communicating effectively. These provide project managers with a systematic process for managing the business changes required and managing resistances to those changes for achieving its business benefits. Resistances develop within people, and can be managed. For organizational change, six main roles are corporate management, consultant, internal resource person, implementation team, chief implementer, and task force. Change agents may be internal or external. Each has its own advantages and disadvantages. Culture also impacts the process of change but proactive steps facilitate managing change. HRD interventions smoothen out the change management process. Selected HRD mechanisms make the people fit to contribute to the organization for overall development. We should remember that managing organizational change mainly needs attitudinal change of people.

KEY TERMS

Change is an alteration in the existing field of forces such as structure, strategy, system, budget cuts, and inter-departmental changes, introduction of new technology, a desire for continuous improvement and many other internal causes.

Change agent is a person who can motivate, alter human capability or organizational systems to achieve a higher degree of organizational output; who can be either external or internal to the organization.

Change management is a systematic approach to dealing with change, both from the perspective of an organization and on the individual level. It incorporates different aspects, including adapting to change, controlling change, and effecting change. Change management, in an organizational context, means defining and implementing procedures and/or technologies to deal with changes in the business environment and to profit from changed opportunities.

Delta state is the space between the current state (where we are today) and the desired state (where we are planning to move) where change happens.

Resistance to change generates due to uncertainties associated with an expected change and likelihood of inequilibrium which may decline production and productivity, increase in absenteeism, turnover, tool down, strikes, etc.

EXERCISES

Concept Review Questions

1. Explain the importance of social and organizational culture in bringing about a change.
2. Discuss the various key functions in organizational change.
3. Explain how the S-P-S-T model can help in developing culture-change management?
4. Discuss the role of a change agent in implementing a change.
5. What do you mean by 'delta state'? Explain with examples.

Critical Thinking Questions

6. Define and describe the nature of change and briefly discuss categories of changes in the business environment. Explain with suitable examples (IGNOU June 2009).
7. Describe the skills a manager is expected to possess for managing change. How can a manager scan the business environment to monitor external drivers of change? Discuss with examples.

Assignments

8. Visit two organizations; inquire about the key functionaries in a change process. Record the roles peformed by them.
9. Visit an organization and find out about the employees' resistance to change and how the management could overcome those resistances. Inquire about the time frame.

MANAGER'S INSIGHT

The top management of Innovative Engineers Limited (IEL) decided to upgrade its technology by switching over to computer numerical control machines. The decision was finalized in a meeting of the Board of Directors. IEL decided to implement the change in phases and take up the departments one by one. Initially IEL planned to upgrade three production departments.

The company carried out a cost–benefit analysis. IEL also engaged a consultant for this purpose. Within about eighteen months some of the new-generation machines were received at the factory premises. As per contract, the workforce from the respective suppliers of the machines arrived at IEL for erection and commission.

During the erection, the workers of the production department expressed their resentment and started offering resistance. The 'Works Committee' member elected from that department discussed this issue with the department manager, but the latter was not convinced. Soon, all the labour unions joined hands and protested the switch over to the new technology. The unions organised a few 'gate meetings' also. Production suffered and the management was in a quandary.

Questions:

1. What was the type of change IEL was interested in?
2. Enumerate the other change management mechanisms that IEL could have used.
3. Did culture play a role in change resistance at IEL?

BIBLIOGRAPHY AND WEB RESOURCES

Cook, Sarah, Steve Macaulay, and Hilary Coldicott, *Change Management Excellence: Using The Five Intelligences For Successful Organisational Change*, Kogan Page Publication, 2005.

Haldar, Uday Kumar, *Human Resource Development*, Oxford University Press, New Delhi, 2009.

Haldar, Uday Kumar, *Leadership and Teambuilding*, Oxford University Press, New Delhi, 2010.

Haldar, Uday Kumar, *Total Quality Management Text and Cases*, Dhanpat Rai, New Delhi, 2007.

Haldar, Uday Kumar, and Juthika Sarkar, *Change Management, Crossing the Delta State*, Larsen & Toubro, Journal of Management, MDC, Issue No. 3, 2010.

Lewin Kurt, Frontiers I Group Dynamics – Concept, Method, and Reality in Social Science, Social Equilibria and Social Change, *Human Relations*, 1(1), pp. 5–41, 1947.

Majumdar, Shyamal and Lesliy Dmonte, Down to Earth, *Indian Management*, November, Volume 47, Issue 11, pp. 22–30, 2008.

Managing Change in Organizations, *Indira Gandhi National Open University*, New Delhi, 1994.

Nilakant, V., *Change Management*, Sage Publications, New Delhi, 2006.

Paton, Robert and James McCalman, *Change Management: A Guide To Effective Implementation*, Sage Publications, New Delhi, 2000.

Rebecca, Potts and Jeanenne Lamarsh, *Managing Change for Success*, Duncan Baird Publishers, 2004.

Sarkar, Juthika, *A New look to Industrial Relation in Perspective of Role Stress, Kolkata Kindle* (E-journal of National HRD Network, Kolkata Chapter), 2010.

DEVELOPING QUALITY CULTURE IN EUREKA HOSPITAL

Since its inception, Eureka Hospital (EH) has introduced key innovations that have made healthcare services more accessible and affordable for customers (patients). They have improved the quality and coordination of healthcare services, and helped individuals and their doctors make more informed healthcare decisions. The hospital now has nearly 700 beds and is planning to further expand its facilities. The hospital conducts allied courses as well. In addition to OPD (out-patient department) services, the hospital has a speciality clinic, mobile clinical unit, telemedicine services, trauma care, senior citizen care, etc.

EH believes in continuous improvement. It continuously analyses its quality culture through the quality parameters such as customer (patient) orientation, number of repeat customers, complaints, customer satisfaction, etc.

To promote quality culture, it introduced behavioural modifications of employees at all levels, and developed 'total quality people'. EH formed a team of seven comprising a medical superintendent, an HR manager, two members from board of governors, and three customers who objectively and logically expressed their grievances and suggested improvement measures. The hospital authority decided to co-opt some other members depending on the specific needs that might emerge. The team carried structured brainstorming sessions to identify the factors relevant to quality culture.

Competitive environment, customer quality awareness, non-demanding customers, technology upgradation, non-challenging employees, dormant strength of employees, fund restriction, mutual trust, lack of confidence, conflicts among managers, etc. were some of the identified factors. Thereafter, the team classified the factors as hindering factors (restraining forces) and helping factors (driving forces), and then represented the finding through a force field diagram (Figure 15.2).

Helping factors (Driving forces)	Hindering factors (Restraining forces)
Competitive environment	Fear psychosis
Customer health consciousness	Non-demanding customers
Cost consciousness	Non-challenging employees
Modern equipment	Monopoly
Quality image	Low aspirations
TQM environment	Happy-go-lucky attitude
High morale	*Chalta hai* attitude
Dormant strength of people	Fund restriction
Awards and prizes	Inter-union/association conflicts
Posters, banners, and badges	Satisfaction with present status
Observation of quality month and quality week	Difference in opinion among managers
Seminar, lectures, and competitions	Lack of confidence
Mutual trust	Mutual mistrust
HRD mechanisms	

FIG. 15.2 Force field diagram—developing quality culture

The team leader circulated the findings to all the departments of the hospital, brainstormed to identify the ways and means to eliminate or reduce the hindering factors and strengthen the helping factors. A hospital-wide drive was taken to achieve the goal. The changes involved job redesign, task reallocation, interdepartmental transfer, etc. The persons who took the leading roles encountered resistances in many steps. Few employees in the senior positions perceived the change efforts as imposition of some burden on them, some anticipated they are about to lose power, and yet another group could foresee that in the changed state where they would not get adequate resources to discharge responsibilities. The core group could discover the persons likely to oppose the change and the sources of resistance. The core group formed a task force including those possessing exceptional views about the changes, ensured resource availability, and emphasized on the creation of new roles accompanied with responsibilities. The concerted efforts of the core group helped to overcome all the barriers and resistances.

Discussion Questions

1. The hospital identified some helping factors. Can you propose a few more factors that might help the hospital to further develop quality culture?
2. Prescribe the coping mechanisms the hospital could have used.
3. Comment about the top management role in developing and improving the quality culture.

HR MANTRA Embracing change for growth

A family owned a *vidyalaya* that offered courses such as M Tech, MCA, MBA, and biotechnology. It was located in a remote place. The *vidyalaya* was highly reputed and was considered to provide quality education. Students who passed out from this *vidyalaya* were placed in big organizations with high remuneration. Teachers exhibited ethical behaviour and were very affectionate with the students. The *vidyalaya* had excellent hostels, mess facilities, but only vegetarian food was served. Moreover, it did not allow students to use mobile phones. This, in particular, generated considerable displeasure among the parents and students.

On one occasion, while visiting other institutes in India and abroad, the director of the *vidyalaya* realized the difficulties encountered by the students and parents of his school.

He desired to change the orthodox system in his school. He discussed the issue in the meeting of governing body to which he faced resistance, but eventually overcame it and made the *vidyalaya* rules more lenient and rational.

Now, the *vidyalaya* students are allowed to use mobile phones in the hostel, enjoy television in the common room, and make use of other facilities when required. The change has made both students and parents happy.

The mantra: Changes have many motivations—understand and analyse them, and then take your stand.

JOHN PAUL KOTTER

John Kotter was born in 1947 and is a professor at the Harvard Business School. Kotter is an eminent author, and is regarded as an authority on leadership and change. He graduated from Massachusetts Institute of Technology (MIT) with a bachelor of science in electrical engineering and computer science in 1968. In 1970, he earned a master's degree in science from MIT, and obtained his doctorate in business administration from Harvard Business School in 1972. He is an alumnus of the Sigma Phi Epsilon fraternity. He joined the Harvard Business School faculty in 1972 and was given tenure and a full professorship in 1980.

Kotter has published 17 books, 12 of which have been business best-sellers, and six of which have won awards. His books have been translated into more than 90 foreign language editions, and their total sales have exceeded two million copies. Other books on change management by Kotter include *Leading Change* (1996), *The Heart of Change* (2002), and *A Force for Change* (1990). His international bestseller, *Leading Change*, outlined an actionable, eight-step process for implementing successful transformations. Over the past 20 years, Kotter's articles in the Harvard Business Review have become classics, and are still among today's most popular reprints.

Kotter outlines eight steps that organizations need to implement to successfully change:

1. Create a sense of urgency.
2. Develop a guiding coalition.
3. Develop a vision for change.
4. Communicate the vision.
5. Empower broad-based action.
6. Generate short-term wins.
7. Do not let up.
8. Make it stick in the organizational culture.

In 1996, *Leading Change* was named the #1 management book of the year by *Management General*. In October 2001, the Business Week magazine rated Kotter as the #1 'leadership guru' in America, based on a survey they conducted among 504 enterprises.

Kotter's educational articles in the Harvard Business Review have sold a million and a half copies, more than any of the hundreds of distinguished authors in the last 20 years.

His latest work, *Our Iceberg Is Melting*, was released in September 2006, and emphasizes the eight-step process within an allegory. This work is also provided as the basis for an in-depth leadership training program called 'Leading Bold Change—Creating Leaders at All Levels'. The program is offered in cooperation with Dr Kotter by ISB Worldwide Corporate Learning Management. He has received the Exxon Award for innovation in graduate business school curriculum design, and the Johnson, Smith & Kinsley Award for new perspectives in business leadership.

References

en.wikipedia.org/wiki/John_Kotter, last accessed on 1 January 2011.

www.harvardbusiness.org/corporate/demos/change-center/Bio_Kotter.html, last accessed on 3 October 2011.

CHAPTER 16

Knowledge Management

LEARNING OBJECTIVES

After studying this chapter, you will be able to

- Understand the concept of knowledge
- Appreciate the need for managing knowledge in organizations
- Learn ways of framing a knowledge strategy
- Identify and understand ways to use knowledge management tools
- Mobilize knowledge
- Understand the benefits derived by organizations from knowledge management

OPENING CASE

Knowledge Management at Perfect Engineering Works

Perfect Engineering Works (PEW), established in 1988, has modern plants and machinery, with a heavy workload. Since its inception, PEW has been producing critical mechanical engineering products. PEW imports most of the machines from renowned manufactures in Switzerland, Sweden, and Germany. It has five production engineering sections, heat treatment and surface treatment plants, and a painting shop, in addition to mechanical, electrical, and electronic maintenance departments. It also has a mechatronics department that undertakes maintenance (both preventive and breakdown) of all the new generation machines, as well. PEW has a well-equipped tool room with all types of machines, gadgets, and appliances required to produce special purpose tools.

It is worthwhile to mention that the proprietor, Hareram, possesses a high degree of entrepreneurial zeal and passion for achievement. He has revitalized the company, increased its product range, acquired land, and procured the latest generation machines with state-of-the-art technology. With the increase in business, the strength of the company has risen from 15 in the first year to 1,200 at present.

The company invests a huge amount in training and development as it believes that unless the human resources are developed, a company cannot develop and grow. The company recruits engineers mostly from the Indian Institutes of Technology (IITs) and trains them at the Central Machine Tool Institute (CMTI), Bangalore. PEW also deputes these engineers to the Central Toolroom and Training Centre (CTTC) and places them in the design department. It recruits assistant managers from the Indian Institutes of Management (IIMs). However, in demanding situations, the company also recruits people having experience in the relevant field.

PEW also deputes young and new recruits to IIMs, XLRI, IISWBM, or other institutes of repute to attend management and executive development programmes. There exists a system of submitting a training report mentioning the training coverage, field of application of the knowledge gained, or delivering a lecture during the weekly officers' meeting or a similar gathering in PEW. The industrial employees are trained. While recruiting, PEW insists on proficiency in computers related to documentation, spreadsheets, project planning, etc., and familiarity with simple programming languages.

PEW has a well-defined quality policy and quality objectives. So far, they have not received any customer complaints. PEW started its export venture in 1999. Within a few years, it has gained an enormous reputation and has become a major player. The huge number of knowledge workers is behind the advancement and growth of the company.

The company has seven employees who have joined from other organizations. Ramamurthy is one of them. He completed his BTech degree in the US and then acquired an MTech in production engineering. He also obtained a distinction in aerospace engineering and has a flair for aerodynamics. He was working in the US, but left his job and returned to India. He is dynamic, active, and a perfectionist with reasonably high motivation for achievement.

On one occasion, PEW received an order for manufacturing a huge quantity of aerospace components from a UK-based aerospace company. The planning department convened a meeting and invited a few senior managers from the production department, design office, and tool room. PEW has a practice of notifying the time of the meeting and the approximate duration of the meeting, that spans from an hour, to an hour and a half. The meeting continued for about three hours without arriving at any decision regarding the acceptance of the order. The members were required to study the blueprint received from the aerospace company. Another meeting was convened. The planning department carried out a techno-economic feasibility analysis; however, it could not finalize the process plan due to the lack of expertise and prior experience in the field of aerospace. Ultimately, PEW sent a regret letter expressing their inability to manufacture the components. Needless to say, the aerospace company was surprised at the reply from PEW. It was the first time PEW had sent this type of a letter to anyone.

Later, it came to light that the aerospace company had floated the order to PEW after taking their machinery, facilities, excellent workmanship, dedicated supervision, and stringent quality control, and other factors into account. In fact, they had already enhanced the production of aircrafts and attempted to develop new vendors capable of supplying components meeting all qualitative requirements. The aircraft producer even tried contacting PEW who had the quality plan of all the components of the aircrafts under production. Before expressing their inability, PEW did not interact with the aerospace company.

The chairman and managing director (CMD) of PEW was indifferent. He was afraid that the image and reputation of the company might be damaged. After a couple of days, a meeting was convened with a different agenda. In course of discussion, the CMD lamented about refusing the huge export order. Ramamurthy reacted immediately and wanted to see the blueprint. After studying this and on further interrogation, Ramamurthy declared that it was possible to produce and execute the order. He needed jigs and fixtures, one key way broach, position gauges, and some standard tools that were available in PEW. He also emphasized that the tool room could produce these parts. Mr Ramamurthy explained the operation layout and quality plan required to undertake mass manufacture of the aerospace components. Other personnel had the technical skills and the required human relation skills. When the decision to refuse the order was taken, Ramamurthy was out of station on official duty. The other officials were not aware of Ramamurthy's background although his credentials, including his past experience, were mentioned in the files maintained by the personnel department. PEW contacted the aerospace company and accepted the order. For the first time, PEW felt the need to create a database containing the details of all employees, their past experiences, and fields of specialization.

PEW discussed this issue at length and decided that all employees must be aware of the company's details, and finally decided to use the intranet in all its offices, production sections, maintenance, store, etc. The company discussed this issue with an HRD consultant who, in turn, advised them to contact a knowledge management expert.

Learning points

- Knowledge is required by all people in the organization.
- Everybody should know what others know.
- An organization must have knowledge of customers and their potential.
- Information technology plays a dominant role in knowledge management.
- Innovative use of information technology is vital.
- Organizations need to use intranet, collaboration tools, e-learning tools, enterprise portals, etc.

INTRODUCTION TO KNOWLEDGE

In today's business environment, companies are trying to derive competitive advantage through the use of knowledge. Interests in knowledge management are increasingly growing. Employees must understand the value of knowledge and the utmost need for sharing knowledge and expertise. Human resource management should increase the awareness and the interest of people in gaining and sharing knowledge,; treat knowledge sharing as an integral part of every employee' s daily function, and establish a compensation/reward system in place to recognize and promote employees who adopt that new behaviour. Thus, knowledge management is becoming indispensable in HRM for enhancing the overall organizational growth.

The concept of knowledge management has become the latest management buzz and has generated a lot of interest in recent years. Knowledge is an asset that enables sustainability of competitive advantage. It is the integration of experiences, values, lessons learnt, contextual information, intuition, and expert insight that provides the potential for making decisions and improving actions. Knowledge originates, and is applied, in the mind of the learner. The information required to acquire knowledge is available through published works, websites, laboratory notebooks, company files and filing cabinets, departmental record rooms, discs, archives, museums, and data banks. Knowledge can be shared to multiply its value. It is a scarce resource, and its refinement and reproduction creates wealth. Knowledge is considered to be the key resource of the post-industrial era where telecommunication is the key technology.

In organizations, knowledge often becomes embedded not only in documents or repositories, but also in the organizational routines, processes, practices, and norms (Davenport and Prusak 1998). Knowledge can be used to enhance the value of a product; it can be embedded as a part of the product or used to surround the core product with complimentary services. Contextually, the question that often comes to one's mind is, 'what is knowledge?' Consider the following observations made by Fleming (www.systems-thinking.org) as the basis for answering this question:

1. A collection of data is not information.
2. A collection of information is not knowledge.
3. A collection of knowledge is not wisdom.
4. A collection of wisdom is not truth.

One's understanding of knowledge is based on one's life experience. Hence, knowledge creation is a natural phenomenon. When a task is performed, the need to change the process in some way is felt. The process is fine-tuned and adapted to suit unique contexts. Some individuals even mould the process of their doing this according to their convenience. So, one may say that people develop new knowledge at all possible times.

Morey, et al. (2001) proposed the following points relating to the significance of knowledge (Exhibit 16.1):

Exhibit 16.1 Significance of knowledge

1. Human beings create knowledge—'Necessity is the mother of invention.' One undertakes problem solving whenever faced with a problem. One has to work with knowledge to attend to human needs and dynamics.
2. Human needs and motivation lead us to create knowledge—A number of fundamental researches have established that people want their work to provide opportunities for growth, recognition, meaning, and good relationship. In a society, employees are associated with many people and situations, and strive for an improved quality of life. One may want to get along with others because of the affiliation motive, may contribute to them, and ultimately learn about the various societal incidents. A person may get involved in the societal decision-making process, grow, enjoy the work, and become more productive. People reinvent

(Contd)

Exhibit 16.1 (Contd)

themselves, learn to trust and respect others, and rely on them.

3. Everybody is a knowledge worker—This learning is gained from Japanese experience. The words 'knowledge worker', are applicable in all functional areas, in all organizations, and in any industry. Knowledge is omnipresent in the organization. It is untrue that knowledge is merely present in a few functions or with some special people. Employees, at all levels, are knowledge workers.
4. People choose to share their knowledge—A debate exists with regard to knowledge management that, individuals do not share their knowledge and that people share knowledge only when they think it is important to the work. Morey (2001) contributes to the second opinion. People share knowledge when they feel encouraged to learn, that is, when they feel that it would help them in their work. There are certain conditions that make people willing to learn and share their learning. This happens when an individual understands the importance his work which adds value to the overall objective. In these situations, people feel connected with their work.
5. Knowledge management is not about technology—Humans bring success to an organization. Leaders gain energy and energize people so that they achieve the organization's objectives. By just creating and installing the intranet, or providing video cameras on people's desks, one may not succeed in implementing knowledge management in the organization. The creation of an organizational culture is important to recognize the members of the organization, value their values, and empower them. Technology does not connect us, but relationship does. Once connected by relationship, technology can be used for knowledge sharing.
6. Knowledge is born from chaotic processes that take time to get organized. 'Insights and innovation are the results of nurturing; they cannot be commanded to appear instantly, no matter how desperately we want them' (Morey 2001). Creativity is the ability to create and use knowledge to solve subject-specific problems that are worth-solving. Creativity involves bringing something into existence that did not exist before, either as a product, a process, or an analysis.

It is also important for one to have the urge, drive, or motivation to create something new, and have the talent to carry out and materialize those urges and drives. Many talented persons cease to create something new and original due to a lack of motivation. Instead, they devote themselves only to performing, teaching, studying, reviewing, or criticizing the creations of others.

FORMS OF KNOWLEDGE

There are two main types of knowledge—tacit and explicit.

Tacit Knowledge

Tacit knowledge is subjective (Morey 2001) and refers to knowledge gained from experience. It is also known as analog knowledge. Tacit knowledge refers to the kind of knowledge that is personal, context-specific, and hence difficult to formalize or communicate. People carry knowledge in their minds, and it is therefore, difficult to access it. An example of tacit knowledge includes the knowledge base of an expert. A majority of an expert's knowledge related to his expertise is tacit in nature. Often, people are not aware of the knowledge they possess or how it can be valuable to others.

Tacit knowledge is considered more valuable because it provides a context for people, places, ideas, and experiences. It is a subtle conception rooted in cognitive schemes and is referred to as, mental models. Tacit knowledge of the workforce is a source of competitive advantage. However, knowledge acquisition schemes cannot hope to capture all the knowledge possessed in the mind of an individual. Extensive personal contact, faith in one another, and good relationship can help in transferring the tacit knowledge effectively. It is also important to keep in

> Tacit knowledge is personal, context-specific, and therefore difficult to formalize and communicate.

mind that in order to transfer tacit knowledge, it must first be converted into explicit knowledge and then shared.

Explicit Knowledge

Explicit or codified knowledge is transmittable in formal and systematic language; it can be articulated, codified, and stored in certain media. It can be readily transmitted to others.

Explicit knowledge, also referred to as codified knowledge or digital knowledge refers to the knowledge that is transmittable in a formal, systematic format. Explicit knowledge can be articulated, codified, and stored in certain media. It can be readily transmitted to others. Transfer of explicit knowledge is relatively straightforward. The most common forms of explicit knowledge are manuals, documents, procedures or audio-visual. Explicit knowledge is objective and includes knowledge of rationality, sequential knowledge, and digital knowledge.

Some other forms of knowledge are discussed in Box 16.1.

Box 16.1 Some other forms of knowledge

Apart from tacit and explicit knowledge, there are many other forms:

1. Known knowledge—This is knowledge that every individual is aware about.
2. Unknown knowledge—There is some knowledge which an individual knows, but is not aware that he knows. This is because such knowledge is embedded in the way he works and performs.
3. Shallow knowledge—Some individuals and organizations are not aware of what they know. Shallow knowledge is information that can be easily retrieved from the organization's database using a suitable tool such as a structured query language (SQL) script.
4. Multidimensional knowledge—This is information that can be analysed using online analytical processing tools. OLAP or online analytical processing is a tool with the scope to rapidly explore all sorts of clustering and different orderings of the data. It facilitates the knowledge discovery in databases (KDD) too. Structured query language (SQL) can do most of the things that OLAP can do.
5. Hidden knowledge—Tacit knowledge is hidden knowledge; hidden even from the consciousness of the knower. A person with tacit knowledge knows more than what he/she can tell. One's organizational superior can somehow capture this knowledge, even though it is unknown to the employee (inaccessible to the consciousness of the knower).
6. Declarative knowledge—This is a type of explicit knowledge that describes something for information of others similar to a declaration.
7. Procedural knowledge—This knowledge helps in finding the cause–effect relationships between various factors.
8. Casual knowledge—This information helps individual identify the reason for something to occur.
9. General knowledge—This type of knowledge has a broad scope, and is largely independent of a particular event or a context.
10. Specific knowledge—This is information is directly related to an issue or a context.
11. Deep knowledge—Organizations create a database to store information. Essentially, deep knowledge embodies (a) organizational processes that seek a synergistic combination of data and information processing capacity of information technology and (b) the creative and innovative capacity of human beings.

A more precise definition of knowledge might be that it is a true justified belief that is acquired by a method that is, in the context, reliable. A subject's belief counts as knowledge when he has good reason to believe that the belief is true (Bah Humbug 1997).

SEVEN KNOWLEDGE LEVERS

Organizations commonly use seven knowledge levers to exploit knowledge. Of these, the main ones are knowledge of people, products, and processes (Morey 2001). However, the seven levers are as follows:

1. Customer knowledge to know their tacit needs and serve them better
2. Knowledge of people to understand their expectations
3. Knowledge of products and services to strengthen the marketing strategy
4. Knowledge of processes to make products right in the first time
5. Organizational memory database, reading material in sharing mode
6. Knowledge of relationships to deal with suppliers, employees, and stakeholders such as customers, shareholders, and regulatory bodies, and obviously the community
7. Knowledge assets that refer to intellectual capital of the workforce

These points are elaborated here.

Customer knowledge International standards on 'quality management system—fundamentals and vocabulary' (ISO 9000:2000) states that the first principle on 'quality management is customer focus. Since customer focus enables an organization to move towards growth and increase the revenue, it becomes an important responsibility of the organization to understand and keep the market requirements and their expectations in mind. The main strategy for many companies today is to be able to identify and meet the implied and unstated needs of the customers to gain competitive advantages.

Knowledge of people Imparting knowledge to people is considered as a pay back. In simpler terms, it is believed that training is costly but non-training is costlier. One must share knowledge at individual levels as well as at organizational levels. A knowledgeable workforce forms the backbone of an organization. Organize innovation workshops, train the people on expert and learning networks, make people adaptable to change, encourage them to work in teams to derive the benefits of synergy, and so on.

Knowledge of products and services Organizations are seen to produce and market goods to their customers, along with a user booklet/guide. Morey (2001) advises to surround products with knowledge, such as the user guide/booklet or operation manual incorporating tables on 'troubleshooting', 'do and do not', 'take care of your own item', etc. These are examples of knowledge intensive services. One benefit with this is that most of the customers are able to maintain their consumer durable items. For example, BPL provides its customers with a user manual that provides details on installation (guide to install), maintenance, precautions to be observed, handling the remote, connecting other equipment, and most importantly, preliminary troubleshooting for its TV. The points on troubleshooting are of great help to customers.

Knowledge of processes Process is a set of interrelated activities, irrespective of the nature of goods or services. Any process has its inputs (tangible and intangible) to get the desired output. Hence, it becomes very important for an organization to embed the knowledge into business processes and managerial decisions in all functional areas, for example planning, purchase, material control, production and maintenance, quality control, storage, preservation, and delivery for the best results.

Organizational memory Examples of organizational memory include course materials in sharing mode, computer databases on intranet, etc. The Camellia School of Business Management (CSBM) offers a variety of course programmes and has reputed faculty members with enriched industrial experience from multiple disciplines. The faculty members develop course notes and allow them to be shared by other interested members of faculty. This practice, within the purview of organizational memory, helps anyone in the institute to gather knowledge. This knowledge lever further extends with the display of mission, vision, policy, objectives, targets/goals, and strategies of the organization.

An employee's database includes several parts, for example static information (such as date of birth, designation at entry), dynamic information (such as age, present designation), performance details, achievement records, behavioural aspects (non-conforming with the rules, norms), and human dimensions (personality traits, motivation, lifestyle inventories, occupational values, etc.). An individual at any particular time can look into the complete details of any employee. It can also be used to look for other employees.

Knowledge of relationships Knowledge flows between an organization and its suppliers (vendors), employees (internal customers), and stakeholders such as customers, shareholders, regulatory bodies, community, etc. All the parties benefit from the flow of knowledge. An organization needs to communicate with its suppliers about its requirements and places purchase orders for raw materials. An organization receives purchase orders for finished goods from its customers.

In today's time and age, organizations must create online facilities so that the suppliers can know about the load on the organization arising out of the demands from customers. The supplier will then be ready to deliver the items as per the bill of materials. This will reduce the time taken by the organization to prepare and place orders.

Knowledge assets Intellectual capital is an intangible asset of an organization. The intellectual capital of an organization includes human assets (knowledge, skill, experience, pragmatism, maturity, etc.), its capital (system, procedure, process, work instructions, databases), intellectual asset or property (patents, copyrights, logo, emblem, trademarks, research findings), and customer assets (quality and depth of relationship). The intellectual capital or intangible assets of the organization need to be identified and measured. This is important because unless one measures, it becomes difficult to monitor and improve. As an HR expert, one has to add value to the intangible assets. To bring about the value addition, one must develop an able and energetic team to initiate a dynamic role to manage the patents and other intellectual capital.

RELATIONSHIP AMONG DATA, INFORMATION, KNOWLEDGE, AND WISDOM

Data represents facts, figures, images, or values of results. Data is crude in nature. Information is processed, formatted, filtered, and summarized data. The type of relations between data and information, and other patterns has the capacity to represent knowledge. Information backed with reasoning, abstraction, relationship, and application is knowledge. Examples of knowledge include cases, rules and procedures, process, model, instincts, ideas that guide actions, and decisions. In organizations, knowledge often becomes embedded not only in documents or repositories but also in routines, processes, practices, and norms. Thus, knowledge is highly contextual information enriched with individual interpretation and expertise. It is an applied product—used and analysed information. Wisdom is knowledge supported by intuition and experience. Intuition and deep insight are the key prerequisites for wisdom.

Suppose we have the information that sales started at ₹2,00,000 about a year ago and has been rising by 20 per cent each quarter. We are confident that sales are around ₹4,14,720 per quarter. We can further forecast that the sales after a year will be around ₹0.86 million. Here, we have used the data, processed the data to information, and then into knowledge with the help of mathematics, by compounding the interest. If someone asks what the sales will be after two quarters, it can be answered that it will vary as it will depend on many factors. This indicates that although one has the data and information, there is no knowledge.

Now, one must appreciate that data does not predict trends of data. It is important to estimate the sales for the next quarters. One needs information about the competition, emergence of new competitors, market size, market demand, extent of market saturation, current backlog, customer satisfaction levels associated with current product delivery, current production capacity, the extent of capacity utilization, and a whole host of other things. We have to create value for the data to get a reliable level of predictability of the future. We need to consider the data that defines past results, the data and information associated with the organization, its market, its customers, and the organization's competitive initiatives.

Knowledge management emerges at this stage and manifests its importance by way of capturing, retaining, and reusing data, information, and knowledge. The value of knowledge management relates directly to the effectiveness with which the managed knowledge enables the members of the organization to deal with today's situations and effectively envision and create their future.

Bah Humbug (1997) represented the relationship between data, information, knowledge, and wisdom, and schematically placed them in relation to 'understanding' along abscissa, and 'connected' along the ordinate. Refer to Figure 16.1.

From the figure, we see that data is the source that lies at the origin. On understanding the relations, the connection gets established and we get information. When we further understand the pattern of relationship between various data, we get knowledge. We are now required to apply intuition and experience to this, in order to gain wisdom.

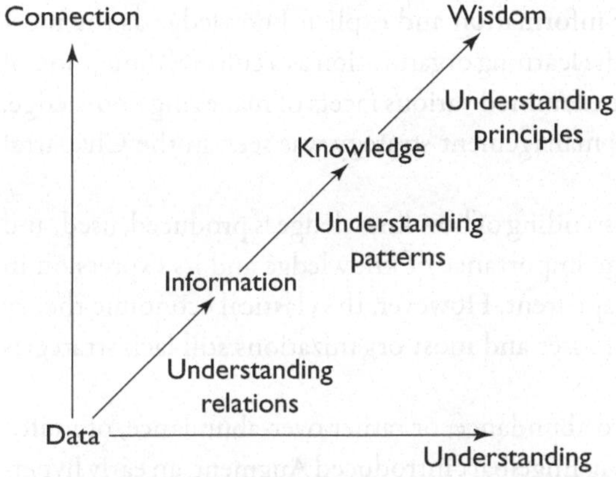

Fig. 16.1 Understanding vs connection

KNOWLEDGE MANAGEMENT

After understanding the concept of knowledge, different forms and levers of knowledge, and its relationship with data, information, and wisdom, one should now study how knowledge management has developed in the last four decades and its importance in today's business scenario.

Box 16.2 lists the characteristics of a knowledge organization.

Box 16.2 Characteristics of knowledge organization

The characteristics of a knowledge organization are distinctive. Liebowitz and Beckman (1998) identified some characteristics of knowledge organizations. Chaudhary (2005) has highlighted the following characteristics:

1. Customer driven
2. High flexibility and adaptive attitude

(Contd)

Box 16.2 (Contd)

3. High levels of expertise, knowledge, learning, and innovation
4. Self-directed and managed
5. Proactive and futuristic
6. Innovative use of information technology
7. High-performance oriented
8. Improvement-driven
9. Excellence-driven
10. Value expertise and sharing knowledge

Brief History of Knowledge Management

Barclay and Murray of Knowledge Praxis (www.media-access.com) highlighted the history of knowledge management step-by-step, very lucidly. Chaudhary (2005) has reproduced the history.

American management theorists such as Peter Drucker, Paul Strassmann, Peter Senge, and several others have significantly contributed to the evolution of knowledge management. Drucker and Strassmann have stressed on the growing importance of information and explicit knowledge as the most vital organizational resources. Senge has focused on the learning organization as a cultural dimension of managing knowledge. Chris Argyris and others have examined various facets of managing knowledge. Leonard-Barton mentions that effective knowledge management strategy was seen in the Chaparral Steel Company in the mid 1970s.

Everett Rogers has also contributed to our understanding of how knowledge is produced, used, and diffused within organizations. By the mid 1980s, the importance of knowledge and its expression in professional competence as a competitive asset was apparent. However, the classical economic theory ignores the value of knowledge as an organizational asset and most organizations still lack strategies and methods for managing it.

Computer technology has heavily contributed to abundance, or rather over-abundance, of multidisciplinary information in a variety of domains. Doug Engelbart introduced Augment, an early hypertext/groupware application capable of interfacing with other applications and systems, for augmenting human intelligence, in 1978.

Systems for managing knowledge were developed in the 1980s. These systems relied on the work done in artificial intelligence and expert systems. They gave us the concepts of knowledge acquisition, knowledge engineering, knowledge-base systems, and computer-based ontology. Gradually, knowledge management emerged as a phrase and secured a place in the dictionary and glossary of management terms. Companies in the US took the initiative for managing knowledge assets in 1989. Academicians and organizational stalwarts started writing articles on knowledge management. Sloan Management Review, Organizational Science, Harvard Business Review, and others journals published the articles. Among the books on the subject, Senge's *The Fifth Discipline* and *The Knowledge Value Revolution* by Sakaiya, are worthy of mention.

A number of management consulting firms had begun in-house knowledge management programs by 1990. Concurrently, US, European, and Japanese firms had instituted focused knowledge management programmes. In 1991, Tom Stewart published 'Brainpower' in *Fortune* magazine. Ikujiro Nonaka and Hirotaka Takeuchi published *The Knowledge-creating Company: How Japanese Companies Create the*

Dynamics of Innovation in the year 1995. This book is by far the most widely read work on knowledge management.

With the advent of the Internet, management initiatives flourished in the mid–1990s. The International Knowledge Management Network (IKMN) was instituted in Europe in 1989. It went online in the year 1994. The US-based knowledge management forum and the other KM-related groups and publications joined IKMN. Organizations were focusing on managing and leveraging explicit and tacit knowledge resources, in order to achieve competitive advantage and distinguished competence. This had paved the way for a number of knowledge management conferences and seminars.

In 1994, the IKMN published the results of a knowledge management survey conducted among European firms, and the European community began offering funding for KM-related projects through the ESPRIT (Esprit Project 311: Advanced data and knowledge management system, (portal.acm.org/citation) program in 1995.)

Many organizational leaders believed knowledge management to be a highly desirable alternative to the failed total quality management (TQM) and business process reengineering (BPR) initiatives. The main reason behind the failure of TQM and BPR was that the human aspects were ignored. Knowledge management has become a big business for major international consulting firms such as Ernst & Young, Arthur Andersen, and Booz-Allen & Hamilton. A number of professional organizations are on the spree to correlate knowledge management with related areas such as benchmarking, best practices, risk management, and change management.

Some academicians believed that knowledge management emerged when TQM and reengineering endeavours failed in industries. However, they do not have adverse ideas about the TQM and reengineering endeavours and techniques. Academicians simply say that the ground was not prepared for implementing TQM and BPR. These organizations did not really understand where the key emphasis should be; they became wandering generalities rather than meaningful specifics.

Value of Knowledge Management

The growing importance of organizational knowledge, in today's time, is a known fact. Organizations are sensing the need to increase the available knowledge exponentially. They are concerned over how to deal with the exponential increases in the amount of available knowledge accompanied with the recognition of the growing importance of organizational knowledge. Knowledge is essential for the increasingly complex products and processes.

Some of the tasks related to knowledge management are the following:

1. Mobilize the hidden knowledge.
2. Trace, transfer, and integrate internal and external knowledge.
3. Develop new knowledge and make it available.
4. Establish the culture of experimenting and learning in the organization.
5. Reflect and evaluate knowledge processes.

Knowledge management manifests its importance for certain reasons:

1. The world is changing at a faster rate.
2. Markets are increasingly competitive and the rate of innovation is rising.
3. There is diminution and depletion in manpower.
4. Reductions in staffing create a need to replace informal knowledge with formal methods.
5. Competitive pressures reduce the size of the work force that holds valuable business knowledge.

Knowledge management can cure all organizational ailments such as manpower attrition, cultural contrast, failing to achieve organizational objectives, lack of growth, and innovation stagnation.

6. The amount of time available for experiencing and acquiring knowledge has diminished.
7. Early retirements and increasing mobility of the work force lead to loss of knowledge.
8. There is a need to manage increasing complexity, as small operating companies are trans-national sourcing operations.
9. Changes in strategic direction may result in the loss of knowledge in a specific area.

Knowledge management, in simple terms, refers to transferring knowledge of every employee to a pool from which the entire organization will be benefited. If this is done in the new knowledge economy, the organization will win. Knowledge management provides the answer to the question, 'how can the organization update and use its knowledge more effectively?'

Knowledge management is nothing new, but needs application to key areas of focus in organizations. Many organizations intend and endeavour to make knowledge management a participative, enjoyable, and integral part of their culture. These organizations believe in deriving strategic advantage in the 'butterfly effect'. This effect emphasizes that organizational knowledge and innovation on one side helps to attract good customers, provides challenging projects, provides learning opportunities, and promotes innovation. On the other side, the intelligent workforce attracts corporate image, which, in turn, helps building the organizational knowledge.

Knowledge management is the answer to all organizational problems. It can cure all organizational ailments such as manpower attrition, cultural contrast, failing to achieve organizational objectives, lack of growth, and innovation stagnation. Knowledge managers were earlier trying and testing only one measurement system. However, now they are utilizing a whole range, combining different measures, and developing newer and better methods for measuring intangible assets. Periodic review enables the knowledge managers to analyse the successes and failures of knowledge management implementation within the organization. Box 16.3 lists the elements of knowledge management in business.

Box 16.3 Knowledge management in business

A *Business Intelligence* report reveals that the following elements are a part of knowledge management:

1. Detailed coverage of all the key issues—the main developments in measurement thinking, methods, and practical applications. Why should one measure the intangible and knowledge assets—external influences and recognition of the value of intangibles?
2. How can macroeconomic measures can guide business practices?
3. How are the different methods and models compared with one another?
4. How does one use performance systems to manage intellectual capital performance—a practical guidance on scorecards?
5. What are the different types of intellectual capital measurement systems?
6. How do knowledge leaders justify their investment in knowledge management—making the case for knowledge management?
7. What separates the winners from the losers—key success factors and practicalities?
8. What are the future developments in both the accounting arena and management practices within organizations?

Knowledge Management Practices

Traditionally, knowledge processing included 'creation, dissemination, and utilization'. Raman (2003) argues that there are a number of other ways and a considerable variety of formats for processing knowledge in stark contrast to the traditional classification. Raman gives some examples of processing knowledge:

1. Identification of knowledge that may be useful
2. Capturing or retrieval of knowledge
3. Altering the format, for example, codifying knowledge by transferring onto paper of IT systems, and having various other formats ranging from fields to hypertext
4. Validation of knowledge by way of discussion with peers within or outside the organization
5. Contextualizing or re-contextualizing—for example, looking for common aspects and differences between the original context of the knowledge and the intended context
6. Achieving closure—for example, agreeing on the common definitions, as for instance between research and development practitioners and patent attorneys, or between different project disciplines

Knowledge management is a process that starts with identifying the knowledge assets in possession of an organization, followed by analysing the knowledge assets capable to add value, specifying necessary actions to promote the value addition, periodically reviewing the use of the knowledge assets, and finally to convert the organization into a learning one that would interact with the environment to gather feedback. Interrogations help one to identify the action plan in each area. Please refer to Exhibit 16.2 for the checklist.

Exhibit 16.2 Checklist of knowledge management action plans

1. Identifying what knowledge assets an organization possesses
   (a) What is the location of the knowledge asset?
   (b) What are the broad contents?
   (c) What is the use?
   (d) What is the form of the knowledge—tacit or explicit?
   (e) How can the knowledge be accessed?
2. Analysing how knowledge can add value
   (a) What are the opportunities for using the knowledge asset?
   (b) What would be the benefits of its use?
   (c) Is there any obstacle to its use?
   (d) Can the knowledge be used in some specific areas?
   (e) What would be the enhanced value to the organization?
3. Specifying what actions are necessary to promote value addition and usability
   (a) How to prepare the actions plan to use knowledge assets?
   (b) How to ratify the actions?
   (c) How to monitor the actions?
4. Reviewing the use of knowledge to ensure added value
   (a) Has the knowledge management action produced the desired added value?
   (b) How can the knowledge assets be further strengthened?
   (c) How can the knowledge assets be maintained?
   (d) Has the use created new opportunities?
5. Organizational learning—a powerful tool to improve the performance of an organization
   (a) How does an organization collect/receive feedback from the environment?
   (b) How does it process the feedbacks?
   (c) How does it create knowledge from the processed feedback?
   (d) What actions does it formulate from the knowledge?
   (e) How does the organization implement and follow up the actions?

> Information technology plays a vital role in knowledge management and the infrastructure must provide a seamless pipeline for the flow of explicit knowledge through the five stages.

All knowledge management systems involve a common process model—identifying, capturing, retrieving, sharing, and evaluating data. From this standpoint, the checklist facilitates a methodical approach to knowledge management implementation.

Though it is a known fact that knowledge management is a popular and useful concept for organization, there still lies a few myths associated with it. Please refer to Exhibit 16.3.

Exhibit 16.3 Knowledge management: Myth vs reality

Knowledge and knowledge management facilitate an organization to progress by utilizing the knowledge in any form—be it captured, distilled, and systematically organized. However, there are some myths are associated with knowledge management. It is interesting to distinguish between the myths and the reality.

Q 12 Myth 1 : Knowledge is the only or the most important resource of a company.

Reality 1 : However intensive knowledge may be, a company may not survive on knowledge alone. The human capital must be harnessed through organizational structure and processes. Knowledge is one critical component of the human capital. Organizations ultimately achieve success by properly harnessing the human capital.

Myth 2 : Knowledge management has a perfect solution. Organizations can perfectly codify knowledge and organize knowledge sharing.

Reality 2 : Knowledge is nebulous, intangible, most often tacit, and difficult to bring out.

Myth 3 : Knowledge management is all about technology.

Reality 3 : Technology is essential but technology alone cannot be the sole consideration. Organizational culture and human aspects matter most.

Myth 4 : Only a few individuals or groups in the organization own knowledge.

Reality 4 : All departments or groups in the organization own knowledge. However, specifically in the research wing, training, and development division, MIS (management information system) group, and even the strategic apex, the top management own knowledge. It is the responsibility of all the wings or departments or divisions.

Myth 5 : In organizations, knowledge grows monotonically.

Reality 5 : Similar to other resources, knowledge grows selectively. Some knowledge grows, some becomes obsolete, and some loses it relevance in view of the changing environment.

Role of Information Technology in Knowledge Management

Q 4 Information technology plays a vital role in knowledge management. The information technology infrastructure provides a seamless pipeline for the flow of explicit knowledge through the following four stages:

1. Capturing knowledge
2. Defining, storing, categorizing, indexing, and linking digital objects corresponding to knowledge units
3. Searching for (pulling) and subscribing to (pushing) relevant content
4. Presenting content with sufficient flexibility to render it meaningful and applicable across multiple contexts of uses

Information technology provides a very useful environment within which a multimedia repository for rich and explicit knowledge can be built. One needs to capture inputs in different forms to assign various labels, categories, and indices to each unit of knowledge. The structure must be flexible enough and reflect the composition of contextual knowledge and the content of factual knowledge of the organization. To use information technology to communicate knowledge, an organization requires sharing of interactive context. When communicators share similar knowledge, background, and experience to a greater extent, more knowledge can be communicated effectively through the electronic media.

At one point of time, the dissemination of explicit and factual knowledge within a stable community includes a high degree of shared contextual knowledge. The process can be accelerated with access to a central electronic repository. Many companies have identified the use of information technology as an inevitable means to manage and share organizational knowledge to improve business performance. Tapping the knowledge and experience of individuals within an organization and sharing that expertise across a company has long been one of the most strategic goals of IT and business managers.

Role of Organizational Culture

Human beings and human dimensions play second fiddle to information technology. As already mentioned, information technology plays a vital role in knowledge management. To effectively utilize knowledge management, technology must be accompanied with organizational culture, particularly knowledge-compatible culture. Knowledge management involves soft issues such as organizational culture as well. Organizational stalwarts must help people realize how vital knowledge is to their organization's future.

Davenport and Prusak (1998) have emphasized time-sharing in the context of knowledge management. According to them, organizations should spend a maximum of one-third of their time thinking about technology. They should utilize the rest of the time in building a healthy corporate culture, organizational roles, and responsibilities, focusing on knowledge content, finalizing strategy, reviewing the status, and so forth. It stands established that a bureaucratic culture suffers from a lack of trust and cannot promote collaboration and cooperation. Critical success factors for knowledge management are a trusting work environment, a self-motivated workforce willing to share knowledge, the use of expertise available elsewhere within the organization, good interpersonal relationships, and organizational transparency.

In reality, it is universally acknowledged that people are the biggest stumbling blocks to successful leveraging of knowledge in the organization. Thus, it becomes even more important for the HR managers to be more alert and manage people better for them to be able to think more creatively and come out with many ideas.

Tools of Knowledge Management

Knowledge management requires certain tools such as intranet, Internet, groupware, e-mail, and synchronous interaction tools; document, records, or knowledge repositories; collaboration tools; tools to capture, distil, and present knowledge; staff directory, expertise directory, yellow pages, personal and enterprise portals; data warehousing; etc., to work smoothly.

Some of the tools of knowledge management are as follows:

1. Internet—It refers to the WWW technology. It is a global network.
2. Intranet—Organizations can easily communicate, distribute information, and facilitate project progress through collaboration, keeping unauthorized users out of the picture.
3. Groupware—It is a collaborative software with built-in calendars, scheduling, e-mail, and web navigation tools that supports the collaborative activities of various work groups. Microsoft's MS exchange server is an example.

4. E-mail and synchronous interaction tools—E-mail or electronic mail is the method of composing, sending, storing, and receiving messages over electronic communication systems.
5. Document, records, or knowledge repositories—Document is information and its supporting medium. Record, specification, procedure, drawing, report, contractual agreement, standard, etc., are all documents. Records are special types of documents. The knowledge repository is a kind of data warehouse having the computational mechanism to handle and manage various data that occur in the e-learning process. The knowledge repository is utilized for any information referencing, diagnosing/evaluating of learners' activities, consulting, and so on. It also tackles problems of knowledge sharing, knowledge retrieval, and various types of collaboration in the learning environment.
6. Collaboration tools—These types of tools include networking tools for shared information, conversations, etc.
7. E-learning tools and applications—It refers to computer enhanced learning methodology. It is commonly associated with the field of advanced learning technology (ALT), which deals with both the technologies and are associated with methodologies in learning, using networked and/or multimedia technologies.
8. Staff directory, expertise directory, yellow pages—These have a variety of information which people refer to depending on their requirements.
9. Personal portals—This is a data communications network that comprises of a number of sites. This means that a portal is displayed in the same way on a large computer. The user profile generally comprises a private part that is accessible only by the user, and a public part accessible by the public.
10. Enterprise portals—This is a framework for integrating information, applications, and processes across organizational boundaries.
11. Data warehousing—Means reporting and query tools to store historical and current data, extracted or mined from various operational systems. The tools consolidate the data for management and reporting analysis.

Knowledge Management Terms

Knowledge allocation This process element, on the one hand, describes the distribution of knowledge within the organization (refers to which employee needs what type of knowledge and to what extent), and on the other hand, it describes the ways in which individuals in an organization share knowledge.

Knowledge assessment Knowledge assessment controls whether the steps (or measures) in the knowledge management framework are successful.

Knowledge base This is an organized structure of information, which facilitates the storage of intelligence in order to be retrieved in support of the knowledge management process.

Knowledge goals There are three levels associated with goals that include (a) normative knowledge goals or the creation of knowledge-based entrepreneurial culture, (b) strategic knowledge goal or programs and concepts that help reach the entrepreneurial objectives (e.g., introduction of appropriate organizational structure, and the determination of which kind of knowledge should be preserved and created), and (c) operational knowledge goal or the realization of the strategic knowledge goal.

Knowledge identification This element of the process provides internal and external transparency. The key question relates to 'what kind of knowledge exists or does not exist?' The more clarity that exists in defining knowledge goals, the easier it is to identify the knowledge sources. Specifically, several aspects are distinguished: (a) internal transparency (knowledge exists)—individuals' knowledge (e.g., skills, proficiencies, abilities, capabilities, specific experience, etc.), and collective knowledge (e.g., order of events, rules, networks, connections, relationships to others, etc.), (b) external transparency (knowledge does not exist)—this element deals with the survey of information suppliers that are not related to the individual organization (data banks, partners, news, etc.).

Knowledge management system Organizations undertake design of knowledge management systems (KMS) to provide a single interface for a range of text processing functions:

1. Creating repositories of texts (frequently based on integrated web searches)
2. Creating a single XML representation of texts for several types of analyses (incorporating full parsing, discourse analysis, discourse entity analysis, and XML tagging of text elements)
3. Characterizing document contexts through automatic keyword generation and headline creation
4. Answering natural language questions
5. Creating general and topic-based summaries (where a topic can be described by a single word or a full paragraph)
6. Semantic category analysis of major text elements (nouns and verbs)
7. Creating single or multiple document ontology (Ontology is a data model that represents a set of concepts within a domain and the relationships between those concepts. It is used to reason about the objects within that domain.)

Knowledge management It is the system process of finding, selecting, organizing, distilling, and presenting information in a way that improves an employee's comprehension in a specific area of interest.

Knowledge preservation This process addresses the maintenance of knowledge basis by selection, retention, and updation of appropriate libraries, databases, information, and accumulated experience. The objective is to guarantee the preservation and dissemination of high-quality knowledge and prevention of any potential losses in the valuable organizational knowledge base. It would be desirable to establish an organization that could set standards for knowledge preservation, and to serve as a qualification/certification body in Europe.

Knowledge utilization This process element guarantees the application of the newly introduced knowledge basis within an organization. Acceptance barriers will have to be overcome. Examples include introduction of new concepts (for example, risk-informed versus traditional deterministic approach), and/or technologies within the organization. The user is considered as a customer in this process.

After understanding knowledge and knowledge management, one should now know how to frame a knowledge strategy.

Framing a Knowledge Strategy

A knowledge strategy, if framed meticulously, improves the potentiality of the people, helps them to utilize the knowledge in the work area, and enhances the productivity and organizational effectiveness. Organizations use a number of instruments and mechanisms to support their collection and sharing of knowledge resources. There are some mechanisms such as data warehousing, knowledge mapping, and electronic library that are particularly useful for explicit knowledge management. Organizational knowledge initiatives typically include creation of knowledge bases, activation of process management, and development of knowledge centres, nurturing of communities of

practices, introduction of collaborative technologies, and appointing a knowledge manager or chief knowledge manager for an effective knowledge management (Morey et al 2001).

1. Creation of knowledge databases—Identify the best practices, create expert directories, develop strategy of market intelligence, etc.
2. Active process management—Gather, classify, and store knowledge.
3. Development of knowledge centres—Knowledge centre personnel shall play key roles. The centre will be the nodal department for knowledge skills and facilitating knowledge flow.
4. Nurturing of communities of practices—Refers to the networks of individuals with common interests who informally share knowledge. The knowledge webs often go beyond organizational boundaries.
5. Introduction of collaborative technologies—Collaborative technologies include intranets, and groupware for rapid information access and exchange.
6. Appointment of a knowledge manager or chief knowledge officer (CKO)—The CKO (or KO) is generally a person from the strategic apex of the organization. The CKO is assigned the task and responsibility of initiating new knowledge practices within the organization and developing knowledge sharing. A creative and innovative CKO performs the task better.

> Mechanisms such as data warehousing, knowledge mapping, and electronic library are particularly useful for explicit knowledge management. Organizational knowledge initiatives typically include creation of knowledge bases, activation of process management, and some more activities.

Knowledge Business

A knowledge business is one that leverages knowledge to create value for customers. In knowledge businesses, the main input is knowledge; the businesses convert the knowledge into products or services useful for the customers. At present, information technology companies and information technology enabled services are predominantly engaged in knowledge businesses. Consulting, training, education, and research are classic examples of knowledge businesses.

Knowledge is seen to be becoming central to organizations and giving managements the signal to undergo changes in the coming years. Organizations must make knowledge and knowledge workers central to their business strategy. Reformulation of the business strategy enables the organizations to generate sustainable competitive advantages. To facilitate this, the change must start from the role of managers. The role will change from supervision to facilitation, organizing a hierarchal defined structure to organizing communities, hiring and firing workers to recruitment, and from learning and evaluating tangible performance on the job to assessing intangible knowledge achievement. Companies must create the right organizational structure and environment conducive to building a knowledge edge. Here, the role of the HR department responsible for making the employees adapt to these changes, comes to the fore.

In an organization, where tangible assets are increasingly becoming unimportant, companies must appreciate the role that knowledge can play in driving their business (Vedpuriswar 2007). Moving knowledge to the centre of business demands the right mindset.

There are four levels of knowledge and achievement management in knowledge-driven organizations, namely industrial, learning, teaching, and coaching organizations.

Industrial organization Everybody needs knowledge. Industrial organizations study structure and boundaries between the organization and the market to initiate proactive measures to survive and grow, as part of their economics.

Learning organization Everybody is learning. The management of these organizations extends ample opportunities to employees to learn to promote organizational transformation. Learning organizations develop as result of pressures from the environment. Systems thinking, personal mastery/expertise, change mindset, shared vision, and team learning are the main features of learning organizations.

Teaching organization Everybody is learning, teaching, and being taught. In the process of teaching organizations, all the members are inclined to share their knowledge and experience. Everyone is a teacher and a further learner as well. In teaching organizations, reciprocal teaching and learning are built in into everyone's daily activities.

Coaching organization Everybody is learning, teaching and being taught, and coaching and being coached. Coaching organizations believe in the maxim, 'stop appraising-start coaching'. Coaching organizations are keen to create an environment in which the behaviour is directed and practices are aligned to continuous learning. Self-leadership development are also actively encouraged and facilitated.

Consequently, sustained growth and value creation are the results that follow these processes.

Mobilizing Knowledge

Knowledge plays a crucial role in knowledge businesses such as information technology companies and information technology enabled services and a central role in other businesses too. Such businesses have to keep mobilizing knowledge in a planned and systematic way. This involves identifying and tapping various sources, which may be internal or external.

Internal knowledge, which is latent in employees, often remains undiscovered, and hence unutilized. One can access external knowledge through publications, libraries, universities, government agencies, professional associations, and personal contacts. The other sources of capturing knowledge from external sources include consultants, vendors, knowledge brokers, customers, and strategic alliances. Identifying the right source of knowledge can help companies to move in the right direction.

Similarly, it is also important for the knowledge managers to follow a proper system for smooth functioning. In organizations, knowledge becomes embedded not only in documents or repositories, but also in the organizational routine, processes, practices, and norms. In such an organizational scenario, the role of facilitation instead of supervision of the knowledge managers, emerge as a predominant prerequisite.

Davenport and Prusak (1998) conducted a research and came up with the following report (Exhibit 16.4).

Exhibit 16.4 Role of knowledge managers

The role of the knowledge managers must incorporate the following:

1. Recognizing the role and potential in the knowledge management agenda.
2. Networking informally with peers, inside and outside their own company.

(Contd)

Exhibit 16.4 (Contd)

3. Benchmarking their personal efforts and their company's competitiveness, making the best use of resources.
4. Learning from the best practices.
5. Fostering collaboration to accomplish improved outcomes.
6. Investing in people and bringing them into a 'community of practices' to solve problems.
7. Responding much better to being pulled in problem areas, rather than being pushed.
8. Making available the knowledge embedded in the organization by identifying and capturing the intangible assets that exists.
9. Accomplishing more, driven primarily by the pride of success.
10. Making certain that information is easily accessible to those who desire it.
11. Facilitating the process of unlocking information that is created internally and externally.
12. Linking the investment in research learning and teaching with the outcomes.
13. Ensuring that employees have the skill to use the information and knowledge well throughout their professional and personal lives.
14. Identifying themselves primarily with their profession, and being more sensitive to the kudos and esteem they receive from their peers than those they receive from management.

On similar lines, Jack's model of knowledge management in organizations was also developed. Vedpurishwar (2007) details the following steps necessary for any knowledge manager:

1. Define the organization's mission and purpose in terms of knowledge.
2. Define the industry in which the organization belongs and the position of the organization, in terms of knowledge within the industry.
3. Formulate the strategy with knowledge in mind.
4. Implement knowledge management processes and structures that directly support the company's key knowledge requirements.
5. Transform the company into a learning organization.
6. Segment the company's customers and market, not only on the basis of products and services, but also according to how much can be learned from them.
7. View learning as an investment and not as an expense.
8. Rethink the business model.
9. Take human resource management seriously.
10. Reinforce the organization's mission through internal and external communication.

Q 7 Barriers to Knowledge Management

There have been many roadblocks to the adoption of formal knowledge management activities. Managing knowledge very often emerges as an unmanageable problem—an implicitly human, individual activity. Cultural resistance, technological immaturity, cost of technology and process, social impediments, and certain human attributes cause hindrances to knowledge management. However, it is not necessary to throw up one's hands in despair. There is nothing that is unmanageable. Problems will arise and employees will be able to manage the problems. We do know a lot about how people learn and the steps taken by organizations to develop and use knowledge.

> Cultural resistance, technological immaturity, cost of technology and process, social impediments, and certain human attributes cause hindrances to knowledge management.

It must be kept in mind that the nature of business itself has changed and knowledge-intensive work is fundamentally different in character from physical labour. The knowledge worker is almost completely immersed in a computing (PC, laptop, palmtop, etc.) environment. This new reality has dramatically altered the methods by which we must manage, learn, and represent knowledge, interact and solve problems, and act accordingly.

People come into the organization from a variety of cultural backgrounds, social structures, work practices, and environmental factors. This leads to cultural resistance. Though not all, some environmental factors affect the industry, and the economic and social pressures on the organizations. Added to this, the historical, personal, and social perspectives of the owner or group of owners also affect the functioning of the organization. All these factors taken together emerge as the source of cultural resistance.

Practically, the cost of technology also prohibits many organizations from implementing knowledge management. These organizations cannot go ahead due to non-availability of adequate funds. In addition, the workforce comprises employees from different social and economic backgrounds that emerge as social impediments in knowledge management practices in an organization.

Benefits of Knowledge Management

One can achieve organizational mission, policies, objectives, and goals using the concepts of knowledge management. One must appreciate that knowledge management helps to significantly improve performance and to achieve the organizational mission. Knowledge management encourages innovation and creativity, free flow of ideas, streamlines response time, generates and speeds up a feedback loop, and eliminates redundant activities. Customers, both internal and external, seek response for any proposal, suggestion, confirmation, verification, authentication, etc., within a short time. Knowledge management also helps to attend the customer needs by attending to their needs. It facilitates in simplifying the processing and streamlining the response time. Refer to Exhibit 16.5.

Exhibit 16.5 Measuring benefits

Infosys Technologies developed an approach to quantitatively express the benefits. The approach includes staged introduction of metrics and phased data analyses.

1. Staged introduction of metrics—Health, participation, performance, effectiveness, and self-sustenance
   (a) Knowledge management surveys administered every year
   (b) Acceptance, acculturation, participation, interest, potential, and benefits
   (c) Average effort savings through knowledge management practices
   (d) Pain points to be remedied through knowledge management
2. Phased data analyses
   (a) Health and participation
   (b) Conformance and performance
   (c) Knowledge management effectiveness and business benefits

Metrics to assess knowledge management performance

Infosys has defined responsibility for the four levels, namely organizational level, practice unit, delivery unit, and project. This makes it easy for them to access their knowledge performance.

Level	Metrics	Responsibility
Organizational level	1. Knowledge management contribution and usage metrics 2. Knowledge management effort metrics 3. Correlation between knowledge management metrics and project performance measures (Q&P metrics)	Knowledge management group
Practice unit	1. km contribution and usage metrics 2. Knowledge management effort metrics 3. Correlation between knowledge management metrics and project performance measures (Q&P metrics)	1. Knowledge management group 2. Delivery managers

(Contd)

Exhibit 16.5 (Contd)

Level	Metrics	Responsibility
Delivery unit	1. Knowledge management contribution and usage metrics 2. Knowledge management effort metrics 3. Correlation between knowledge management metrics and project performance measures (Q&P metrics)	1. Knowledge management group 2. Process consultant 3. Delivery manager
Project	1. Knowledge management contribution and usage metrics 2. Knowledge management effort metrics 3. Qualitative benefit measures	1. Knowledge management group 2. Project manager 3. Process consultant

Annual knowledge management survey

Infosys Technologies also undertakes an annual knowledge management survey. The result of an annual survey on the perceived benefits from knowledge management over a sample size of 400 includes comments of respondents.

1. Some 79 per cent said that knowledge sharing environment in the company encouraged the documentation of knowledge for future use.
2. About 87 per cent asserted that they tried to reuse existing organizational knowledge rather than start from scratch, whenever possible.
3. More than 80 per cent believe that the quality of work and productivity of their team has improved.
4. About 70 per cent said good knowledge sharing practices had helped in delivering tangible benefit to customers.
5. About 73 per cent felt they saved more than one person-day in the last six months by using the existing knowledge architecture, with 14 per cent saying they saved more than eight person-days.
6. Some 75 per cent approximately said that when needed, they were easily able to tap organizational knowledge in doing their work.

Source:

1. Presentation by Dr J.K. Suresh, Principal Knowledge Manager and Associate Vice President, Infosys Technologies, Bangalore, India on 30 September 2005 in the 48th National Convention of Indian Institution of Industrial Engineering held at Bangalore.
2. Suresh, Dr J.K. and Kavi Mahesh, *Ten Steps to Maturity in Knowledge Management Lessons in Economy*, Chandos Publishing, Oxford, England, 2006.
3. http://www.infosys.com/, last accessed on 7 October 2007.

Hence, knowledge management paves the way for the following in an organization:

1. To achieve the organizational mission, policies, objectives, and goals
2. To accelerate the advancement of organizational mission
3. To improve organizational performance
4. To innovate and create, thus encouraging free flow of ideas
5. To streamline response time and to generate a feedback loop
6. To eliminate redundant activities, processes, and systems
7. To delight customers—both internal and external—considering their proposals, suggestions, confirmations, verifications, authentications, etc., within a short time.

SUMMARY

We are familiar with designations such as chief executive officer (CEO), chief operating officer (COO), chairman and managing director (CMD). However, designations such as knowledge officer (KO) or chief knowledge officer (CKO) have come into existence only recently. It is needless to mention that knowledge sharpens our intuition and helps us cope with situations, which we may have or have not, encountered before. While

implementing knowledge management, organizations have to develop their ability to accumulate knowledge, unlearn a few practices if applicable, then relearn, and reapply. This ability will be a critical success factor.
Knowledge management has generated much interest in recent years and has become the latest management buzz. Many people wonder whether knowledge management is here to stay or it is just another consultancy fad.
To effectively use knowledge management, organizations need to take a hard-nosed perspective. Knowledge management activities will build momentum only if the activities generate business value for the organization.
Knowledge-based competitive advantage is sustainable because it has the potential to create a virtuous circle.
Organizations need distinctive core competence to emerge as market leaders in the industry. Knowledge generated within the company and embedded within its system tends to be unique.
The role of managers will change from supervision to facilitation. It will organize a hierarchically-defined structure to organize communities; hire and fire workers to recruitment; and assist people from learning, developing, and evaluating tangible performance on the job to assessing intangible knowledge management.
Companies have invested a lot of effort in creating a knowledge organization. However, they have to do much more in order to make an organization conducive to knowledge management. Organizations that make knowledge and knowledge workers central to their business strategy will generate sustainable competitive advantage. It is easy to predict the state of other organizations.

KEY TERMS

Explicit knowledge refers to the knowledge that is transmittable in formal, systematic language; can be articulated, codified, and stored in certain media.

Knowledge is familiarity, awareness, acquaintance with facts through study or investigation, or understanding of truths and principles through experience and general learning.

Knowledge business is one where the main input is knowledge; it leverages knowledge to create value for customers; it uses knowledge as the principal weapon to win customers.

Knowledge levers help to develop knowledge and surrounds customer knowledge, knowledge in people, knowledge in products and services, knowledge in processes, organizational memory, knowledge in relationship, and knowledge assets.

Knowledge organizations are distinct and customer-driven; highly flexible and adaptive; rely on learning, innovation, and expertise; are proactive and futuristic; value expertise and sharing knowledge; and make innovative use of information technology.

Knowledge repository is a collection of information stored in a database of any type.

Knowledge workers differ in their relationships to their organizations compared to general employees and the organizations make them central to the organizations' business strategy.

Organizational memory is a knowledge lever and includes intellectual assets such as course materials in sharing mode, computer databases on intranet, etc.

Tacit knowledge is the personal, context-specific, knowledge base of an expert that an employer carries in his mind and is not accessible; it cannot be articulated in abstract contexts. This knowledge is more valuable because it provides a context for ideas and experiences.

Wisdom refers to business acumen and knowledge supported by experience, intuition, and deep insight.

EXERCISES

Concept Review Questions

1. What kind of knowledge has to be stored in an organizational memory?
2. How is knowledge made available to the employees?
3. Explain the seven knowledge levers in the context of the organization you are working in or in any other organization you are familiar with.
4. Specify the role of information technology and organizational culture in a knowledge organization.
5. What do mean by value of knowledge management? Discuss with examples.

6. Mention some of the characteristics of knowledge organizations. Are the characteristics unique for knowledge organizations? Offer comments.
7. Discuss the various roadblocks to knowledge management. How can the effects of the roadblocks be reduced?
8. Elaborate the benefits of knowledge management.

Critical Thinking Questions

9. What are the knowledge-intensive business processes that may be supported and improved by a knowledge management approach?
10. Discuss the best and most economical approaches for generating and keeping the contents of the organizational memory up-to-date.
11. Discuss the human dimensions in knowledge management. How can cooperation and coordination between different employees or different departments be enhanced for the success of knowledge management efforts?
12. Some myths are believed to be associated with knowledge management. What are your viewpoints in this regard?
13. Suppose you have been assigned the task of knowledge management in your organization. How would you frame the knowledge strategy? Justify your answer.
14. How would you mobilize knowledge and plan to manage the knowledge workers?

Assignments

15. With the help of your professor, take an appointment from a company that has implemented a knowledge management system in their organization. Inquire about the steps followed. Record the steps and show it to your teacher.

MANAGER'S INSIGHT

A manufacturing company desired to introduce knowledge management practices in its system. It engaged a consultant for this purpose. In an introductory lecture, the consultant elucidated the concepts of knowledge management, seven knowledge levers, values, practices, process, tools, and benefits of knowledge management. Contextually, he also highlighted the difficulties in managing people employed in knowledge industry. In his deliberation on knowledge levers, he also discussed various aspects of knowledge in products and services, processes, organizational memory, building and maintaining relationships, and knowledge assets. He further narrated the utmost need of knowledge sharing among managerial levels, and finally concluded stating, 'This is all about knowledge management'.

Questions:

1. Which vital point of knowledge levers did the consultant miss?
2. Was he right in mentioning about knowledge industry in a manufacturing company?
3. He conveyed a wrong concept. Try to identify the concept.

BIBLIOGRAPHY AND WEB RESOURCES

Bah, Humbug, *Knowledge Management,* San Jose, 27 February 1997.

Barclay, Rebecca O. and Philip C. Murray, *What is Knowledge Management?,* Knowledge Management Associates, Austria.

Barclay, Rebecca O. and Philip C. Murray, *What is Knowledge Management?* Knowledge Praxis, www.media-access.com, 1997.

Bellinger, Gene, *Knowledge Management—Emerging Perspectives,* http://www.systems-thinking.org/kmgmt/kmgmt.htm, 2004.

Bernardin, John H., *Human Resource Management—An Experiential Approach,* Tata McGraw-Hill Publishing Company Limited, New Delhi, 2007.

Chaudhary, Harish Chandra, *Knowledge Management for Competitive Advantage,* Excel Books, New Delhi, 2005.

Davenport, T.H. and L. Prusak, *Working Knowledge: How Organizations Manage What They Know,* Harvard Business School Press, Boston, 1998.

Fleming, Neil, *Coping with a Revolution: Will the Internet Change Learning?* Lincoln University, Canterbury, New Zealand.

Hamel, Gary and C.K. Prahalad, *Competing for the Future*, Harvard Business School Press, 1996.

Knowledge Management: Communities for Knowledge Sharing, pp. 78–82, November 2006.

Liebowitz, Jay and Tom Beckman, *Knowledge Organizations: What Every Manager Should Know*, St Lucie/ CRC Press, Boca Raton, FL., 1998.

Morey, Daril, Mark Maybury, and Bhabani Thuraisingham, *Knowledge Management*, University Press, Hyderabad, 2001.

Prusek, Laurence, *Knowledge in Organizations*, Butterworth-Hainemann, Singapore, 2001.

Raman, Thothathri A., *Knowledge Management: A Resource Book*, Excel Books, New Delhi, 2003.

Review, H.B., Harvard Business Review on Knowledge Management, *Harvard Business Review*, Boston, 1998.

Skyrme, David J., Measuring the Value of Knowledge Metrics for the Knowledge-based Business, *Business Intelligence*, www.skyrme.com/pubs/measures.htm, 1998.

Suresh, J.K. and Kavi Mahesh, *Ten Steps to Maturity in Knowledge Management Lessons in Economy*, Chandos Publishing, Oxford, England, 2006.

Vedpuriswar, A.V., 'Knowledge as a Competitive Edge: How can Companies Align Knowledge Management with Corporate Strategy?', *Indian Management*, Vol. 45, Issue 12, pp. 166–176, December 2006.

Vedpuriswar, A.V., 'Knowledge Management: Communities for Knowledge Sharing', *Indian Management*, Vol. 45, Issue 11, pp. 78–82, September and November 2006.

Vedpuriswar, A.V., 'Managing a Knowledge Business', *Indian Management*, Vol 46, Issue 2, February 2007.

Zack, Michael. H., 'Managing Codified Knowledge', *Sloan Management Review*, Vol. 40, No. 4, pp. 45–58, web.cba.neu.edu/~mzack/articles/kmarch/kmarch.htm, 1999.

Web Resources

www.eurekaforbes.com/press, last accessed on 23 February 2008.

www.infosys.com/, last accessed on 7 October 2007.

www.kmstrategy.ed.ac.uk, last accessed on 7 July 2008.

www.media-access.com/whatis.html, last accessed on 14 July 2008.

www.systems-thinking.org/kmgmt/kmgmt.htm, last accessed on 14 July 2008.

PARTNERSHIP IN BUSINESS OBJECTIVES AT EUREKA FORBES LIMITED

About Eureka Forbes

Eureka Forbes Limited (EFL) commenced its operations in 1982 and has since then grown from a single product, single channel company to a multi-product, multi-channel corporation with a turnover of ₹8,575 million, with over six million satisfied customers. It is a part of the Shapoorji Pallonji (SP) group. It has an array of channels which reach out to 450 cities and includes Asia's largest direct sales force, dealers, institutional networks, a channel to access the lower end of the market, as well as a rural channel. As one of the largest service networks in India, it assures customers prompt doorstep service. It recently began international operations that spanned across 39 countries in a joint venture with the brand, Lux International, Switzerland, the global pioneer in direct selling.

EFL's products are dominant leaders in water cleaning, air purification systems, and security systems. The company has established a strong manufacturing base, adhering to stringent standards of reputed Indian and international bodies. This includes the largest UV water purification plant in the world. It also has a strong research and development department including Aqua diagnostics, a world-class water research and technology centre, which is one among the seven centres across the globe recognized by the prestigious Water Quality Association, USA. This is supported by a nationwide network of laboratories, as well.

Concerned about the rapidly dwindling natural resources for future generations, EFL created the Eureka Forbes Institute of Environment (EFIE) to propagate the cause of safeguarding the environment. To further its vision of 'unpolluted water and air is the birthright of every Indian', the institute has undertaken numerous initiatives.

Awards won by Eureka Forbes

Eureka Forbes has received numerous accolades in its exciting history. It has been inducted as a case study in the curriculum of the respected Harvard Business School, USA. The legendary marketing guru, Philip Kotler, has cited the company as a reference in his famous book *Marketing Management*. The Eureka Forbes story has been featured in the 'Asia's Top 50' issue of the Asian edition of *Forbes*, the leading international business magazine.

Both its leading brands, Aquaguard water purification systems and Euroclean vacuum cleaners have been accorded with the super brand status. They have also been voted as the consumers' brands of choice through a nationwide poll for the *Mera* brand awards (thrice and twice respectively).

Maintaining employee relationships

Eureka Forbes believes that its people, whom it has christened Eurochamps, are at the heart of its success. Through a novel philosophy, summed up as 'earning, learning, pride, and fun', it instils in them a sense of belonging and commonality of purpose, infuses pride, trains them, gives them a chance to earn and learn, as well as enhance their lifestyle, honours, and rewards their efforts in every facet of its business, nurtures their careers, and helps them fulfil their dreams. Learning has been institutionalized through the Eureka Forbes academy of learning and the sharing of knowledge and experiences is fostered through the internationally lauded Euroshare knowledge management programme.

Many Eurochamps who joined as salespeople have risen to senior management positions such as vice presidents, and have been associated with prestigious Indian and global organizations. Direct selling has been professionalized and elevated to the status of a fruitful career. The company has become a virtual nursery of direct selling; it is the single largest institution of its kind in the world. Over 20,000 people and 500 business leaders have started out as Eurochamps.

Recently, Eureka Forbes created corporate history by giving new meaning to the empowerment of people with the launch of the euro senate, which is a body 'of the Eurochamps, by the Eurochamps, for the Eurochamps'. Comprising Eurochamp representatives (senators and counselors) and elected by Eurochamps in each strategic business unit (SBU) through a secret ballot to be their voice in the decision-making process of their company, the euro senate has proved to be an effective forum for knowledge networking and application.

Promoting customer relationships

The customer has always been at the centre of the EFL's business. The company firmly believes that a relationship only begins with a sale. The company remains deeply committed to being a 'friend for life'—its corporate slogan—to its customers. It religiously adheres to this *mantra* in every facet of its business. This unwavering customer focus has been crucial to its progress. Thus, it makes a special effort to let the bonds of friendship endure through service, post purchase training, and a host of other customer care initiatives such as gift-a-smile (a courtesy call merely to enquire if all is well with the customer and her/his machine).

An important barometer of its success in building enduring bonds with customers is that a significant part of its revenue comes from relationship marketing including service contracts, spares, and accessories sales, product up-gradations, and references of new customers. A well-equipped and expensive service network helps uphold the promise of always being there for the customer. It comprises over 4,000 company-trained technicians operating from over 1,000 service points, supported by call centres, customer care representatives, and mobile service vans. A customer finance scheme, eurovalue, has been added so that customers can easily obtain the means to live healthier lives. A customer relations management team keeps in constant touch with customers and seeks to enhance relationships.

To strengthen its focus on the customer, Eureka Forbes has rechristened its offices as customer response centres (CRCs), making them the hub of all its customer-centric efforts and facilitating teamwork. Every individual in the company assumed responsibility for customer satisfaction. As other business channels were developed to reach out to the customer, it became important for the company to harmonize these multiple avenues of interaction to present a single face to the customer. Hence, the organization was restructured to seamlessly integrate all its functions. Under 'convergence', any customer becomes everyone's customer and everyone's objective is to weave the magic of friendship around them.

The Economic Times Avaya Global Connect Award for customer responsiveness (consumer durables) is a fitting recognition of its customer relationship management strength for the company.

Knowledge levers used

There are various online and offline programmes for capturing and disseminating knowledge to its various users. These innovative programmes are time-bound and linked to the business goals of the various divisions. Many seek to capitalize on topical events to heighten excitement and participation. A synopsis of some of the key programmes such as (i) Knowledge Olympics, (ii) Eurobiographies, (iii) Euro Ambassador, (iv) Passport to SMART, (v) Work-book on best practices, (vi) Expedition Everest, etc., are well explained in their brochure, titled *Knowledge@Eureka Forbes*. Mega programs such as Knowledge Olympics and Expedition Everest have also been presented as case studies at various leading fora such as KM Asia and World Knowledge Forum. A short brief of one such program which was presented as a case study in KM Asia, a gathering of key knowledge professionals from worldwide, is detailed here.

Knowledge Olympics was a landmark programme and was inspired by the Athens Olympics. It was created to tap the experiences and capabilities of the Eurochamps, enabling them to contribute to the key organizational facets, feel part of the decision-making process, and thereby, pool together a wealth of knowledge.

Launched in 157 locations across India (more venues than Athens) and spread over 15 consecutive days to coincide with the Athens games, 2,800 Eurochamps in 18 teams with cross-functional members (named after participating countries) sent 1,350 entries for 34 events (branded after Olympic events) in this festival of challenges that was supervised by Olympic marshals and judges. At the rousing opening ceremony, the respective country's flags and participants' badges were handed over, the oath was taken, and the commemorative stamp was released. The Knowledge Olympics mascot was also unveiled—a cute elephant (elephants being renowned for their memory) wearing a scholar's cap, and holding a pen and a mouse (symbols of offline and online communication, as the event was run using both these means). Finally, the Olympic torch was lit and solemnly relayed.

The events exceeded their objectives and left a considerable positive impact on their business. New benchmarks of performance were set. A wealth of competitive and market information poured in; amazing customer profiles and testimonials were elicited. Several existing customers strengthened their relationship with the company by purchasing additional products. Customers who had experienced a demonstration but not purchased any product were revisited and converted into actual customers. Precious service tips were captured first-hand on video. Incisive water maps were drawn up. Easy-to-implement ideas to neutralize parallel operators, reduce transportation costs, make good defective stock, and enhance the customer experience, were pooled. The best practices of leading companies in a broad spectrum of categories were gathered. Archival material of key promotion activities flowed in. A national catalogue of resources emerged and the euroshare library that was painstakingly built over two years was doubled.

The winning submissions were compiled in a CD and were widely disseminated so that this knowledge could be assimilated and productively utilized. High performers at the Olympics were constituted into five dream teams, in order to nurture tomorrow's leaders. Each team was entrusted with planning, implementing, and institutionalizing an Olympics project deemed vital to organizational excellence. Soon 104 gold, 96 silver, and 83 bronze medals and 98 certificates of merit were presented at an awards ceremony that also became India's biggest video conference, spanning across 15 cities and 18 centres.

The Knowledge Olympics became probably the single biggest knowledge management initiative in the world and was even featured on the home page of the KNOW network website.

The most recent event was the knowledge world twenty 20 challenge 2007 that rode on the astonishing success of young Team India at the inaugural ICC twenty 20 world cup in South Africa. In typical tournament format, the participating divisions and Eurochamps faced 20 exciting matches—a variety of challenges across a wide spectrum of business activities, that amounted to a judicious blend of individual and team events.

Steps taken in implementing knowledge management

The implementation was undertaken in two phases. In the first phase, Eureka Forbes used the traditional route of creating a portal and inviting as well as encouraging users to visit it. Realizing the vast numbers of employees in the organization and the fact that most of them did not have access to a computer, the company understood the constraints of this approach. Hence, the company decided to expand its approach and infused a lot of innovative activities, both online and offline, to generate excitement and consequently, stimulate the sharing of knowledge. Immensely successful results have ensued.

Mobilizing knowledge

One mega event along with numerous other activities are organized annually. Each knowledge-sharing programme was treated as a competitive event and extensively marketed, using a multimedia approach, and capitalized on a topical and popular theme. This included a national live video hook-up for the launch of the key event of the year. The vice chairman and managing director inaugurated the programme and challenged the leaders. The activities were simplified in the process and a fun element was incorporated so that the learning became more exciting and meaningful.

Team spirit in knowledge management process

The knowledge management team decided on the structure of the programmes scheduled for the year, in keeping with the business objectives of the organization. These are finalized at the beginning of the financial year and presented to the leaders (the key drivers) at the company's annual managers' meet known as SMART. In the same forum, the awards for excellence in knowledge management are presented to the previous year's winners in various programmes. Well-defined awards criteria are formulated at the beginning of every year and circulated amongst the users so that they are clear about what it takes to win the respective awards and then aim to be winners all year through. Every function in the organization also has a domain, and a domain head who controls the contribution and content flow into the programme. Domain recognition is accorded for the best domain at the end of each year. This procedure is well explained in their awards booklet which is released every year.

Role of information technology

EFL is making use of all the knowledge levers through information technology. The company has adopted the innovative tool called EuroSMS for knowledge sharing using information technology and many knowledge management tools. Some of the innovative tools are Mindstores and Mindcircles which form a part of Euroshare—the company's knowledge portal repository wherein all employees have an opportunity to share and learn from experiences. The knowledge portal has also integrated a system of net meetings through a chat module called 'K-Chat', which is a platform for not only internal meetings, but also for knowledge experts to come online and give solutions to certain key and vital issues. This system has thus brought in a speedy method of addressing matters of routine and internal nature.

The 'mindstore', a central repository of information, has a collection of over 40,000 files which can be accessed by users through a very powerful and advanced search engine capable to give out information either by word, or user, or date. This tool helps users to get to the relevant information needed, thus saving time and facilitating quick execution. There are also links provided to various useful sites which can be of help to users.

Information technology, which plays a key role in today's environment, has also helped Euroshare to develop an internal 'learning management system', through which users can take online tests on various modules which are developed by experts to enhance their productivity and knowledge at work. These competency tests are administered on a regular basis to all levels of employees at frequent intervals and the results of the same are shared with the users and their superiors for further improvement of the individual.

Euro SMS for knowledge sharing

The company has adopted an innovative tool, Euro SMS, that facilitates knowledge sharing communication between individuals and groups. The euro SMS system keeps them abreast with the latest information as well as enables instant access and quick transfer of data as it is connected to the central management information system. The Eurochamps retrieve data and information and respond to the customers' queries. Euro SMS has revolutionized knowledge management at EFL by providing knowledge at the fingertips, even when one is on the road or travelling in his car or in general transport where one cannot use a personal computer or laptop.

Role of organizational culture

Every eurochamp is aware of the knowledge management activities and looks forward to, as well as participates enthusiastically in the various programmes all year round. In addition, the core leadership team (comprising the senior-most leaders in the organization) actively supports every initiative. Besides, each senior vice president heads a domain and drives all the activities of their respective division. This is summarized as 'know, share, grow—knowledge grows when shared'. The pillars of operation are earning, learning, sharing, and fun, inspired from the pillars of EFL's philosophy of managing its eurochamps—earning, learning, pride, and fun. Recognizing the contribution of every Eurochamp and every activity is a celebration of learning and sharing. This makes the whole concept truly fun-filled.

[Based on (a) information given by Mr P.S. Sukumar, Deputy General Manager (Knowledge Management), Eureka Forbes Limited, Bangalore, India, through e-mail dated 31 October 2007, and (b) Euroshare booklet, (c) paper presented by Mr Sukumar at the Seoul Convention on knowledge management (2007), (d) website www.eurekaforbes.com/press, last accessed on 23 February 2008, and interview of Mr Sukumar on 17 March 2008.]

Discussion Questions

1. Eureka Forbes Limited is concentrating on promoting employee and customer relationships. How does it contribute to the knowledge management implementation process?
2. The company initiated certain steps while implementing knowledge management. Do you feel that the steps are adequate enough to achieve the purpose of knowledge

management practice in an organization? Justify your findings.

3. Identify the unique knowledge management tool devised by the company. Mention the specific benefits the tool gives to the employees. How does the tool help the company to get knowledge from external experts and contribute to customer relationship management?

HR MANTRA Improtance of awareness

A company excelled in manufacturing quality products. In a period of only seven years, it earned a very good reputation. Soon the company also became involved exporting its products. Customers abroad are seen to be appreciating their products as well. One day, the company received a major order from an aircraft manufacturing business for one of its critical components. After studying and researching about the technical aspects of the component that was supposed to be delivered, the company came to the conclusion that it did not have anyone suitable or capable to supervise the manufacture of this component. Hence, for the first time, the company had to respond negatively to an order. The proprietor and chairman of the company began lamenting about the loss of the order. When he heard of such a situation, he called for a meeting. During this meeting, the chairman came to know of a dynamic young engineer, who was away on study leave for about six months. Apparently, he had worked in an aeronautical company for 11 years. After the meeting, he was asked to visit the planning department, study the drawing, and get back to the chairman regarding ways of delivering the order.

The mantra: Be aware of the knowledge in your organization.

IKUJIRO NONAKA

It is a well-known fact that Japanese companies develop innovative products and services with consistently superior results. Ikujiro Nonaka is a Tokyo-based business scholar. Nonaka is professor emeritus at Hitotsubashi University in Tokyo, and is recognized as the nation's most significant management scholar. Nonaka is the coauthor (with management researchers Ryoko Toyama and Toru Hirata) of *Managing Flow: A Process Theory of the Knowledge-based Firm*. In this book, the authors have explored the methods by which Japanese companies manufacture consistently by 'harnessing the power of knowledge creation'.

Nonaka and his coauthors illustrate examples from companies such as Toyota, Honda, Canon, Seven-Eleven Japan, Eisai, the pharmaceutical company, Mayekawa Manufacturing, and the educational institute, Kumon. They divulge the underlying dynamics for building knowledge in these companies. For example, Eisai follows a practice of sending its researchers to work with the elderly in hospital wards so that they can develop a stronger feel for the way patients use medications, and lead to the development of better medicines.

Nonaka's perception of the knowledge creating company refers to a kind of community in which people communicate intensively and interact, transforming tacit knowledge to explicit knowledge. In his paper, Nonaka summarizes and extends a body of work that could change the prevailing view of knowledge management in most companies from a branch of information technology to an enabler of in-depth learning. Nonaka has been developing this work for more than 40 years.

Besides his scholarly work, Nonaka is the president of the Japan–America Institute of Management Science (JAIMS) in Honolulu, a visiting scholar at the Helsinki School of Economics and at the University of California at Berkeley. He is the Drucker Scholar in Residence (a position named after the late management author Peter Drucker) at Claremont Graduate University in Los Angeles.

David Teece, the director of the Institute of Management, Innovation, and Organization at Berkeley's Haas School of Business, equated Nonaka's stature with that of Drucker. 'Both integrated knowledge from across many disciplines, and both had the early experience of conducting a lot of interviews in which they listened to real managers talking about real problems, which kept their theories grounded in the real world,' said Teece.

Nonaka's work first came to the attention of those within US management circles in 1986 with an influential *Harvard Business Review* article titled, 'The New Product Development Game,' coauthored with Hirotaka Takeuchi, who is presently the dean of the Graduate School of International Corporate Strategy at Hitotsubashi University and a visiting professor at Harvard Business School. Nonaka's first article to explore organizational knowledge creation was followed in 1991 with another Takeuchi-coauthored *HBR* article, 'The Knowledge-Creating Company.' Their 1995 book, *The Knowledge-Creating Company: How Japanese Companies Create the Dynamics of Innovation* (Oxford University Press), laid out a comprehensive theory on developing collective intellectual capability.

'Jiro is quite simply the father of knowledge management,' says Takeuchi. 'His research over the last 20 years opened up a whole new field and set the stage for how the best organizations understand human capital today.' Although Nonaka cites mostly Japanese companies in his research, Takeuchi opines that his model is universal. Hence, he is the only Asian on the *Wall Street Journal's* May 2008 list among the 20 most influential business thinkers.

Most companies allocate the task of knowledge management to the information technology departments, which focus on codifying best practices that can be captured, stored, indexed, and retrieved as efficiently as possible. Nonaka views all this data management as a minor, almost incidental aspect of the capability development that enables business success. Thus, Nonaka's perspective also runs counter to conventional corporate practice.

'Companies and leaders who treat knowledge management as just another branch of IT do not understand how human beings learn and create,' says Takeuchi. Unlike land, capital, energy, labour, and technology—the conventional inputs into business practice—knowledge is innately self-renewing. He emphasizes, 'It is produced and consumed simultaneously. Its value increases with use, rather than being depleted as with industrial goods or commodities. Above all, it is a resource created by humans acting in relationship with one another.'

References

www.urenio.org/2009/02/15/managing-flow-a-process-theory-of-the-knowledge-based-firm/, last accessed on 4 October 2011.

CHAPTER 17

Human Resource Development Audit

LEARNING OBJECTIVES

After studying this chapter, you will be able to

- Understand and define human resource development (HRD) audit and its objectives
- Appreciate the need for an HRD audit and human resource information systems
- Understand the auditing process

OPENING CASE

Compensation System Review at United Dairy Limited

United Dairy Limited (UDL) manufactures and markets milk, ice cream, curd, butter, ghee, *khoa*, and other dairy products in many cities in West Bengal. UDL is an ISO: 9001 certified company that follows a quality management system. Additionally, it is also an ISO: 14001 certified company and employs an environment management system. UDL distributes its products using modern dairy business vehicles. A majority of the working class in the company comes from below the poverty line and the downtrodden segment of the society.

Following the emergence of a competitor, UDL observed attrition of experienced and key employees. UDL noted this incidence of attrition with great concern and desired to revamp the compensation management system and appointed a consultant. The consultant developed his plan, made a presentation to the UDL management, and on receiving the green signal, started his job as per the plan.

However, neither the management nor the consultant felt the necessity to review the existing compensation system. The consultant did not collect data from the local areas and companies in the surrounding localities, nor did he speak with any representative of the beneficiaries of the existing compensation system. It is important to realize that a company operates in a society; people of one company mix with people working in other companies. Thus, a parity or equivalence is preferred to avoid labour unrest.

Much later, the consultant considered looking into the compensation practices in advanced countries. The consultant also took into consideration compensation measures in leading business houses in India. He collected data from both the sources.

Ultimately, the consultant designed a new compensation management system covering rewards, incentives, and the wage system. The management perceived the system as thought-provoking and innovative, as it encompassed performance-linked bonus, medical benefits after retirement, interest-free education loans for higher education of children, and many such initiatives. Funds were sanctioned to the departmental heads and the system was implemented.

However, even after the implementation of the new system and easy availability of funds, it could not satisfy the beneficiaries of the compensation system.

Note: The case is based on a reputed manufacturer of dairy products who endeavoured to revamp the compensation management system but failed due to inadequate data. The name of the manufacturer has been changed.

Learning points

- Review of an existing system reveals its faults and strengths.
- The beneficiary of a system can discover the inherent loopholes better.
- The points of reference should be judiciously selected.

INTRODUCTION

Human resource management, as the name implies, is people-intensive, and hence needs a lot of managerial time. Merely concentrating on technology or sophisticated machinery may not be helpful for the survival and growth of an organization. Today, the world is enormously competitive and the inner potential of the employees has to be fruitfully utilized to gain a high degree of competitive advantage and distinctive competence.

During the last three decades, many organizations have instituted a human resource development (HRD) department. Some of these organizations are Larsen and Toubro Limited (L&T), Crompton Greaves Limited (CGL), L&T Construction Group (L&T ECC), State Bank of India (SBI), Indian Oil Corporation Limted (IOCL), and Steel Authority of India Limited (SAIL). These organizations have made some structural changes in terms of differentiating HRD from the human resource functions, even while integrating both. The organizations have also derived substantial benefits from the structured HRD efforts.

In order to derive the best out of the human capital, human resource functions, strategies, structures, systems, styles, and skills must be aligned with the business and its goals. If they are not aligned properly, then delivering the human resource functions could become a big liability. The synchronous efforts of the human resource personnel, the line managers, and the top management are of utmost importance. The skills and styles of all employees at all levels must produce synergy. All these factors are reviewed and the HR personnel are kept on their toes by the auditors.

HR FUNCTIONS

As discussed earlier, HR functions include human resource planning, job analysis and design, recruitment and selection, placement and induction, training and development, job evaluation and merit rating, performance appraisal, remuneration, motivation, participative management, employee welfare, safety and health, industrial relations, industrial disputes and resolution, trade unionism, and customer relationship management. Due to the immense responsibilities involved, HR personnel need certain specific competencies to build an organizational climate conducive to effective working.

Some of the required competencies for a successful HR manager are positive, proactive, and helpful attitude, keen desire to learn, and good communication skills. The HRD department must be formed with competent HR personnel. The department should develop a HR philosophy for the entire organization and endeavour to get the top management committed to the policy. Some of the other tasks include the following:

> HR management functions have reached a good degree of maturity. Systematic evaluation of HR functions and related activities is called HR audit.

1. Continuously inspire the line managers and inculcate the willingness to learn and develop further

2. Plan and design new, innovative methods and systems of developing and strengthening the HRD climate
3. Be aware of the business, social, and economic goals and direct their HRD efforts to achieve the goals
4. Remain vigilant and monitor the implementation of HRD mechanisms and sub-systems effectively
5. Work with unions, associations, and collective bargaining fora
6. Organize human resource researches, organizational health surveys, and renewal of exercises
7. Formulate personnel policies by providing the necessary inputs to the personnel department and the top management

At present, many academicians view corporate social responsibility as an HR function. They believe that employees can perform interdependent and interrelated activities in furtherance of certain personal, functional, and societal objectives. The HR management functions, such as procurement, development, compensation, and maintenance, have reached a good degree of maturity. Now, the functions need verification to assess the continuing suitability.

Procurement

Procurement refers to acquisition of manpower. The HR personnel need to consider the existing manpower, estimate the manpower required to meet the forthcoming business objectives, anticipate attrition, etc. The auditor verifies the actions. The information required to carry out this function effectively includes the following:

1. Present human inventory
2. Future manpower needs
3. Possible changes in manpower (due to attrition) and its effects
4. Means adopted to cope with the attrition (particularly in information technology and information technology enabled services).
5. Available and required skills
6. Valid measures of testing, recruiting, and selection
7. Cost of recruitment and selection

Development

As an HR manager, one must continuously upgrade and develop the manpower of the organization. Their performance needs constant monitoring. At the same time, the new recruits need placement and induction. The auditor will seek information regarding the execution of the development function. The information must be updated. The information required in this case includes the following:

1. Measuring employee performance and comparing it with company standards
2. Linking individual capability with the organization needs
3. Cost–benefit analysis relating to training and development
4. Career and succession planning

Compensation

An organization offers statutory benefits to its employees under various social security enactments. It plans the compensation determinants, structure, strategy, and administration. Regulatory bodies observe the compensation allowed to the employees by the employer. The compensation packages, if not carefully designed, deteriorate the HR climate. Auditors meticulously audit this function. They examine the following:

1. Relationship among wages, salary, and productivity
2. Relationship between bonus and productivity
3. Turnover per employee
4. Unit employee cost
5. Effect of inflation on wages
6. Effect of inflation on productivity
7. Value of collective bargaining and fringe benefit systems

Maintenance

Once the employees are procured, they need maintenance. Unless the employees are maintained, their retention becomes a critical task. It is the duty of the HR department to take care of situations such as employees going on long leaves, strikes, etc. All these functions are part and parcel of organizational life and are indicators of organizational health. The HR auditors examine how the organization maintains its manpower. To be able to make a correct judgment, they need to look at the following:

1. Absenteeism, number of accidents, disciplinary measures taken, and man-days lost
2. Ergonomical issues relating to illumination, noise, smell, sizes of work benches and stools, operating levers of machines, and material-handling devices
3. Causes and costs of employee separation
4. Incentives for voluntary separation, whenever it occurs

Integration

The management is instrumental in maintaining harmony among various groups at all levels. The management integrates all the processes and functions to ensure delivery of quality products to its customers. To perform an audit, the auditors need to seek information on relevant aspects such as the following:

1. Organizational climate of the company
2. Communication and leadership styles
3. Impact of environmental changes
4. Causes behind variation in the level of production
5. Impact of changes in technology and the market

GOOD HR PRACTICES

The motto of any organization is to enhance its three Cs—competencies, commitment, and culture. In order to function well, organizations need all the three Cs. Competency refers to the accumulation of proficiency, aptitude, fitness, expertise, capabilities, etc. It is essentially required to accomplish a task cost-effectively and with optimal efficiency. Competency is related to an individual and also to a team or a group of individuals. This includes divisions, cost centres, departments, task forces, and other formal or informal groups or teams that have come into existence on temporary, quasi-permanent, or permanent basis.

> To function well, organizations need three Cs:
> 1. Competencies
> 2. Commitment
> 3. Culture

A competent person can also be very often guided by his emotions. He has to use his competencies to achieve the organizational goals. In other words, he has to be committed to his/her work. Work efforts, zeal, involvement, connection, and contribution to work are all indicators of commitment.

Culture provides the sustaining force and spirit for any organization to live and grow. It gives a sense of pride and identity to individuals and teams. A strong culture helps in the sustenance of the organization. Good HR practices such as these distinguish an organization from others.

Elements of Good Human Resource Development

Rao (2007) mentions a few elements of good HRD:

Corporate strategy and business-linked HRD An organization may opt for merger and acquisition, technology upgradation, market penetration, launch of new products, internationalization of business, quality improvement, etc. Irrespective of the corporate strategy, HR initiatives should be aligned with it.

Systems-engineered and systems-driven HRD Udai Pareek and T.V. Rao (1992) developed a HRD system framework comprising a career system, work-planning system, development system, self-renewal system, and cultural system. The career system encompasses manpower planning and recruitment, potential appraisal and promotions, and career planning and development. Work planning includes role analysis (goal setting), contextual analysis, and performance appraisal. Training and development includes performance coaching or counseling, staff development, job rotation and other means. Role efficacy, organizational development, and action-oriented research come within the purview of the self-renewal system. The culture system includes consideration of HRD climate, values, quality orientation, reward and recognition, information, communication, and empowerment.

Appropriately-structured and competently-handled HRD To improve the productivity, organizations are seen to be thinking and paying attention to technology, systems, and procedures. The concept of diverting attention towards developing human resources was felt in the early seventies, when Pareek and Rao introduced the concept of HRD in L&T. The diffusion and institutionalization of the concept spread at the national level. Pareek and Rao also developed a paper titled, *From a Sapling to the Forest—The Saga of the Development of HRM in India*.

The concept has now grown and many organizations have formed an HRD department. Though it has grown, HRD needs must be appropriately structured and competently handled. The functions performed by the HR departments need evaluation. These evaluations may begin with the HR managers and HR professionals, and extend to HR orientations of line managers, top management, union leaders, and all categories of stakeholders.

HRD framework comprises career system, work-planning system, development system, self-renewal system, and cultural system.

Evaluation of an HR function may begin with the HR managers and HR professionals, then extend to HR orientations of line managers, top management, union leaders, and all categories of stakeholders.

Appropriately rooted (in terms of culture and values) HRD The capability of an organization to achieve excellence greatly depends on the culture of the organization. Rao and Pareek in their paper, shared 15 guiding principles for designing the HR function of L&T in the early 1970s. Some of the guiding principles include focus on enabling capacity, integrating the development of people with organizational development, maximizing individual autonomy, growth through increased responsibility, etc. (These principles have been discussed in Chapter 3). The principles are roots of organizational culture. HR initiatives should have long-term enablers, in addition to short-term objectives.

The culture determines the managerial styles and their effects on juniors, inculcates a sense of mission, and promotes organizational health. All the characteristics, HR functions and activities need a proper corroboration periodically.

VERIFICATION OF HR ACTIVITIES

The primary purpose of any organization is to deliver a certain output, which may be products or service offerings, to meet the various kinds of customer needs. Quality is considered to be the most important factor that justifies the purposeful existence of any organization. The quality is to be controlled, maintained, and upgraded. The tool of verifying the system and all related activities is known as audit.

As per ISO 8402 1994, quality audit is 'a systematic and independent examination to determine whether quality activities and related results comply with planned arrangements and whether these arrangements are implemented effectively and suitably to achieve objectives'. To achieve quality, the organization has to be efficient (relationship between the result achieved and the resources used) and effective (extent to which planned activities are realized and planned results achieved). HR functions are not exceptions and should be brought under the purview of periodic verification. The verification process helps to reveal whether

1. the HRD strategy is aligned with the business strategy,
2. the strategic contribution made by HRD has achieved the expected business/corporate objectives,
3. the role played by HRD was appropriate,
4. the extent to which HRD issues had been delegated to line managers was appropriate,
5. the HRD efforts ensured organizational, ethical, and legal obligations,
6. the objective evidenced that HRD efforts are contributing to the business, and
7. the HRD efforts of other organizations are used as benchmarks.

The verification process extends to an analysis of the following:

1. Contribution of HRD emphasizing quantitative measures such as value addition per employee, safety and accidents rates, absenteeism, and attrition.
2. Role of HRD with reference to service delivery in the areas such as induction of new recruits, compensation and reward management, health and safety, enhancing employee engagement, managing diversity due to cultural differences, preventing or reducing attrition, establishing and implementing human resource information system (HRIS), etc.
3. Role of HRD in corporate social responsibility and ethical considerations, improving organizational culture and climate, employee attitude modification, trust building, humanizing industrial relations, and promoting work-life balance
4. Contribution of HRD in customer relationship management

HRD AUDIT

In simple terms, audit means verification of activities. HR audit refers to the evaluation of the HR activities in an organization. The audit is required to periodically review the HRD functions and the effectiveness of implementation of HRD. As such, a systematic and a comprehensive audit of all the HR functions is essential. The audit findings facilitate renewal of the HRD system in the organization, whenever required.

The main objective of HR audit is to assess the effectiveness of the human resource functions and to ensure compliance. Anyone with sufficient HRD experience can conduct this audit. HR audit manifests its need and importance primarily in auditing the functions of HRD department and the competencies possessed by the personnel of the department. Both the internal and the external HR auditors can do the audit. However, there is an advantage with the external auditors as they are designated for the

said purpose. The internal auditor may suffer from a 'halo' effect. In this regard, TVRLS (T.V. Rao Learning System) conducts a certificate education programme in HRD audit that aims to prepare the participants to be internal or external HR auditors.

Apart from the functions mentioned here, HRD audit also verifies if the department is properly staffed with qualified and suitable professionals and if the related functions are organized and performed well at the requisite periodicity. The systematic evaluation of HR functions and related activities is termed as HR audit.

Human resource audit is a systematic assessment of the strengths, limitations, and developmental needs of an organization's existing human resources in the context of organizational performance (Flamholtz 1987).

The audit can be a part audit or a full audit. Part audit may include audit of HR functions in one or few departments while a full audit refers to audit of all the departments, that is, the entire organization.

Similar to quality management system audit, HR audit is also 'fact finding' and not 'fault finding'. One must accept the audit findings in the right spirit. The audit process finds the loopholes, and based on the audit report, the HR functionaries initiate necessary corrective actions. As an HR personnel, one must find the most suitable corrective action and implement them. It is important to be vigilant to oversee the effectiveness of results from the action taken. HR audit aims to provide feedback about the HR functions to the HR professionals, analysts, and operating managers.

CHARACTERISTICS OF HRD AUDIT

Rao (2007) defines the notion, thought, and salient features of HRD audit:

1. HRD audit is comprehensive,
2. it examines linkages with other systems, and
3. it is business-driven.

Comprehensive An audit team must consider the business plan and its corporate strategies from the very beginning. The HRD auditor needs to take into account where the company intends to be after a definite period of time. The top level management needs to discuss these issues with the auditor. The auditor needs to examine the objective evidences such as long-term documents as well. Thereafter, the auditor needs to assess the skill base required to perform the new roles and the current skill base of HRD staff in the company in relation to various roles and role requirements.

Following this, an auditor should verify the effectiveness of the existing HRD mechanisms in developing people and ensure that human competencies are available in adequate levels in the company.

HRD audit does not always provide solutions to organization-specific problems related to industrial relations, discipline, performance, etc.

An HRD audit examines linkages with other systems. The HRD structure existing in the company should be adequate enough to manage the company's HRD functions. Top management and senior managerial styles of managing people need to promote a learning culture. The managerial styles should facilitate the creation of a learning environment. Auditors need to examine this difficult task.

Linkages with other systems There is a linkage between HR and other functions such as production management, maintenance management, total quality management, personnel policies, strategic planning, etc., in any organization. An audit examines these linkages between HRD and other systems. On the basis of evaluation, HRD auditors suggest future HRD strategies required by the company. The suggestions further include (a) the structure the company needs to have for developing new competencies, (b) the systems that need to be strengthened, (c) the ideal managerial styles and work culture conducive and compatible with HRD processes in the company. The managerial styles of the top management should also be emphasized.

Q 5

Business-driven HRD audit is business-driven and primarily focusses on fulfilling the objectives. Along with meeting objectives, HRD audit evaluates HRD strategy, structure, system, staff, skills and styles, and their appropriateness.

HRD audit is not a problem-solving exercise. HRD audit does not always provide solutions to organization-specific problems involving industrial relations, discipline, performance, etc. However, it throws some insights into the sources of the problem. It never gives feedback about any specific individuals. However, it gives feedback about the HRD department, the structure of the HRD departments, competency levels of the personnel manning, leadership styles, processes practiced, interrelationships of HRD system with systems, influence of the HRD on the other systems, etc.

HRD audit is one of the five systems used to measure the effectiveness of HR practices, the other systems being (a) benchmarking, (b) HR accounting, (c) HR information system, and (d) HR researches. These will be discussed later in this chapter.

HRD AUDIT FOR BUSINESS IMPROVEMENT

HRD audit gives many insights into a company's affairs. It is time-consuming, but cost-effective. The auditors come together for a period ranging from three days to two weeks, stay at the organization, and give a report generally within a fortnight or a month's time. The auditors generally offer a preliminary presentation on the last day of the audit. HRD audit can lead to several benefits (Rao 2007) as underlined in Box 17.1.

Box 17.1 Benefits of HRD audit

1. Getting the top management to think in terms of strategic and long-term business plans
2. Changes in the styles of top management
3. Clarifying and distinguishing the role of the HRD department and line managers in HRD
4. Improvements of HRD systems
5. Increased focus on human resources and human competencies
6. Better recruitment policies and adding more professional staff
7. More planning and more cost-effective training
8. Strengthening accountability through appraisal systems and other mechanisms
9. Streamlining of other management practices
10. Providing emphasis on quality of products and services
11. Enhancing the return on investment (ROI) of the HR functions

As evident from Box 17.1, the benefits of HRD audit are diverse and manifold. Apart from improving the organization's practices, it creates a more professional image of the department among managers. In addition, it helps to project an elevated image of an organization to its stakeholders. Exhibit 17.1 lists some of the private and public sector companies which have benefited from HRD audit.

Exhibit 17.1 Benefits derived from HRD audit

The organizations that have derived benefits from the findings of HRD audits include public sector, private sector, and multinational organizations.

Public sector

- Steel Authority of India Limited
- National Thermal Power Corporation
- Indian Oil Corporation
- Hindustan Petroleum Corporation Limited
- Bharat Petroleum
- National Aluminum Company Limited
- State Bank of India
- State Bank of Baroda
- State Bank of Indore
- State Bank of Patiala
- Reserve Bank of India
- Neyveli Lignite Corporation
- Indian Farmer Fertilizer Cooperative Limited
- Bharat Earth Movers Limited

Private sector and multinational companies

- Larsen & Toubro
- Voltas Limited
- Sundaram Fasteners
- E.I.D Parry, Bangalore
- TI Group Automotive
- Crompton Greaves
- NOCIL Limited
- Mahindra and Mahindra
- Tata Cummins Limited
- Hindustan Lever
- KPMG

SCOPE OF HRD AUDIT

The scope of HRD audit is decided only when audit is taken up. However, the approach to be followed while conducting an HRD audit and the objectives to fulfil remain more or less the same.

The scope of the audit includes the following:

1. Human resource inventory
2. Current competencies
3. Organizational structure
4. HRD instruments (or mechanisms or sub-systems)
5. Organizational climate assessment
6. HRD outcome variables

The scope of HRD audit extends over the following functions:

1. Procurement function
2. Development function
3. Compensation function
4. Maintenance function
5. Integration function

The spectrum of a full HR audit generally includes the following:

1. Performance and potential appraisal
2. Legal compliance
3. Compensation, reward, incentive, and salary administration
4. Recruitment and selection
5. Induction and placement
6. Training and development
7. Separations such as terminations, dismissal, lay-off, etc.
8. Employee relations
9. Communications
10. Files/record maintenance/technology
11. Policies and procedures (including employee handbook)
12. Communications

An audit needs a considerable amount of data relating to all the functions. Human resource inventory contains all the details about the employees, which include name, addresses (present and permanent), designation (at entry and present), date of birth, family details, qualification, training courses attended, and papers published. Some organizations use personnel information system (PIS) in place of human resource inventory. Some industries also include psychological bases, occupational values, dominant motives, personality traits, life styles, aptitude, etc., in the inventory.

The auditor verifies the data structure of the HR inventory, which comprises the column variables. He attempts to verify the adequacy of the variables to meet the stated HR objectives. The auditor focuses sharper attention to assess the capability of the organization to achieve the future business goals, linkages between the HR practices and organizational goals. Unlike quality audit, in HR audit, the external auditor offers suggestions to overcome the weaknesses. The HR audit is contextual and is aimed at helping the organization achieve its goals. For example, HR audit finds how an organization identifies the customer requirements and endeavours to meet the identified customer requirements, which amounts to customer satisfaction.

The auditors mainly examine the effectiveness of the functions relating to human resources. In order to carry out the task, as an auditor, one must be ready with a checklist so that the audit can bring out the salient facts and figures. The auditor prepares the checklist depending on the functions to be audited. However, a generic set of questions is given as a guideline in Exhibit 17.2. The checklist is provided in Exhibit 17.3.

Exhibit 17.2 HRD audit—generic set of questions

1. What activities does the department perform?
2. Who are the persons responsible?
3. What are the purposes of the activities?
4. How were the HR policy, objectives, and targets formulated?
5. What are the strategies to meet the targets, objectives, and policy?
6. How many procedures are used to meet the targets?
7. To what extent does the company adhere to procedures?
8. How does the company review the objectives and policy?
9. What are the communication and promotion policies?
10. How does the company handle employee grievances?
11. Does the company have any open forum for employees of all levels to interact?

Exhibit 17.3 HR audit checklist

There are various HR aspects such as legal compliance, procuring human resources, and maintaining and developing human resources. An audit checklist is developed to carry out the audit effectively.

1. **Legal compliance**
   (a) Equity in employment opportunity
   (b) Immigration reforms
   (c) Unsettled grievances
   (d) Suggestion schemes and other guidelines
   (e) Uniformity of decisions—based on documented company system
   (f) Displaying employment law posters in appropriate places

2. **Procuring human resources**
   (a) Recruitment strategy
   (b) Job descriptions and specifications
   (c) Recruitment process and procedures
   (d) Use of selection tools
   (e) Making employment decisions based on applicable employment laws and compliance thresholds

3. **Maintaining human resources**
   (a) Wage and salary structure
   (b) Climate surveys and studies of organizational culture
   (c) Exit Interview guidelines and data

(Contd)

Exhibit 17.3 (Contd)

(d) Diagnostic and evaluation studies
(e) Compensation and reward system- policies and guidelines
(e) Career system
(f) Opportunity of advancements and growth

4. **Developing human resources**

(a) Identification of appropriate HRD mechanism
(b) Performance and potential appraisal system
(c) Job rotation, enlargement, and enrichment
(d) Training policy guidelines
(e) Developmental tools in practice
(f) Coaching, mentoring, and counselling

HR AUDIT METHODOLOGY

An auditor can conduct the audit in many ways. As an auditor he/she may interview the auditee with a checklist. An auditor most commonly adopts this methodology and while auditing he verifies all the related records and documents. The auditors also develop questionnaires on the relevant areas such as the methodology of audit; verify, and analyse the secondary data generated by the organization. The audit proceeds with the examination of HR policy, objectives, goals/targets, strategy, etc. Summarily, HR auditors conduct audits through the following means:

1. Interview of the auditee (HR personnel or other functionary)
2. Questionnaires on the relevant areas
3. Observation of records and documents
4. Secondary data verification and analysis
5. Examination of HR policies, objectives, goals/targets, strategies etc.

Irrespective of the methodology used by the auditors, customarily, the audit team has to meet the CEO of the organization, where the presence of the chief of HR is solicited. The CEO gives a brief about all the HR practices being followed and this interaction starts with details of the plans, their execution, formulation of future plans, outline of the competencies requirements etc. Generally, the CEO discusses only about the macro aspects while the chief of HR covers the micro aspects. The chief of HR also prepares a schedule of the audit in consultation with the audit team leader.

MEASURE OF EFFECTIVENESS OF HR PRACTICES

It has been discussed earlier that HR audit is one of the five systems used to measure the effectiveness of HR practices in an organization. The other four systems are benchmarking, HR accounting, HR information systems, and HR research. These are discussed here for complete understanding of ways to ensure complete effectiveness of the HR practices.

BENCHMARKING

Q 4 The term benchmarking is dynamic and means several things. Benchmarking essentially refers to looking around and learning from others. The pioneer of benchmarking is Xerox Corporation, USA. They coined this term while their market shares declined. Engineers and designers of Xerox Corporation took their competitor's product, dismantled, and studied the components. Whey they found a better component, they incorporated in their own product. Added to this, the managers also studied some of the best management practices. They believed that if a company intends to benchmark performance measures such as, customer satisfaction, it has to first identify a competitive company having a good reputation of high customer satisfaction. Next, the attributes supporting this reputation need to be identified.

Products, as well as services can be benchmarked. Performance assessment, including effectiveness of HR functions, can also be benchmarked. Benchmarking is a methodology adopted to identify the best in class wherever it is found. 'Best-in-class benchmarking' implies comparison one's practices with that of the best practices prevalent in an organization, irrespective of products or services.

Performance includes both quantitative and qualitative (less tangible) features. Benchmarking should include both quantitative and qualitative measures of performance. One department can benchmark another department (internal benchmarking) and one organization can benchmark another organization (external benchmarking). These are discussed here:

Internal benchmarking This kind of benchmarking refers to the comparison that an organization makes between various departments and then benchmarks the standards. To accomplish this, one is required to measure the performances. Unless it is measured, performance cannot be monitored. After measuring the performances, compare them with the preset company standard, or the laid down targets. The performance of department in one's control may or may not conform to the expectations. If not, make an effort to improve the same.

The need for benchmarking, is mainly internal, and evolves from this point. While benchmarking, one may want to compare the performances of two individuals, two teams, or two departments. First of all, decide upon the performance parameters, such as production (against targets), sales (against forecasting), financial performance (against the budget), training offered (against the planned development programme), and machine breakdown (against number of breakdowns and mean time before failure). This is the only way it is possible to adopt to discern whether the performances are in line with expectations. It is needless to mention that expectations must be congruent with the organizational objectives and goals.

External benchmarking External benchmarking refers to selecting points of reference from other industries. The backbone behind the success of benchmarking is the state-of-the-art processes, effective management system backed by organizational culture, management commitment, empowerment, transparent administration, self-motivated workforce, and so on. It is needless to mention that reward system, incentive schemes, and non-financial tools accelerate the process of benchmarking. This benchmarking engrosses identifying the dimensions of the company to be compared with other companies, spotting other companies to be benchmarked, and finally choosing ways and means of information collection. Collection of information from other companies or industries always poses series of problems. As such, very often, two companies exchange their know hows and know whys, and both the companies progress. After gathering the know hows and know whys, the company must critically ascertain the suitability of the information. Abrupt acceptance and application may lead to disaster. Refer to Exhibit 17.4.

Exhibit 17.4 Benchmarking by Xerox Corporation, USA

Xerox Corporation, USA, the pioneer in benchmarking, recommends a ten-step methodology for successful benchmarking:

Step 1 : Identify the parameters you want to benchmark. The parameters may include the ability to deliver items within the contractually agreed time period, capacity of producing with minimal errors, delivering undamaged products, attending service calls promptly etc.

Step 2 : Spot the companies you want to benchmark.

Step 3 : Establish the data collection methods and collect data.

Step 4 : Determine your current performance levels.

Step 5 : Project your future performance levels.

Step 6 : Communicate benchmark results and gain acceptance.

Step 7 : Establish your functional goals.

Step 8 : Develop your action plans.

Step 9 : Implement action plans and monitor progress.

Step 10 : Recalibrate benchmarks.

The benchmarking process yields positive results and HR is no exception.

Process Benchmarking

In process benchmarking, phrases such as 'know where', 'know how' and 'know why' are of paramount importance. In addition to knowing 'where' a company is, it is important to know 'why' the company wanted to reach there, and 'how' it reached that stage. It is important to recall that 'a process is a set of interrelated activities' and 'a system is a set of interrelated processes'.

The process adds value to the item with the ultimate goal of ensuring 'user satisfaction'. Process benchmarking helps one to open one's eyes, provide one with a more effective, and efficient process. This type of benchmarking contains all the elements of an ideal benchmarking process, which includes analysis, comparison, and synthesis. The national productivity council proposed a model called process benchmarking methodology to be carried out by a team of process experts. The following steps are initiated:

Step 1: Identify the object or process to be redesigned.
Step 2: Map and measure the existing process in its entirety in terms of relevant critical dimensions.
Step 3: Identify the partner where the same process is known to be better performed.
Step 4: Analyse the partner's process and find out the differences. This often requires collection of checklist/questionnaire and/or physical visit to the partner's site.
Step 5: Redesign the process and put up the proposal for management approval.
Step 6: Implement the redesigned process.
Step 7: Monitor the performance of the redesigned process.

HUMAN RESOURCE ACCOUNTING

Material resources depreciate, whereas, human resource appreciates. Human resource is the most important asset in an organization. Their knowledge, skill, experience, maturity, and wisdom increase with time. The value goes on increasing with the right placement. Their concerted efforts can take the organization out of danger and help the organization survive and sustain in the competitive market. Analytical approaches by the manpower also help to gain customer goodwill and augment the market share. Human resource accounting, at present, is receiving enormous attention from organizational stalwarts.

Koley (2005) has applied accounting to human resource management. The three major reasons behind human resource accounting are as follows:

1. Genuine need for reliable and complete management of human resources
2. Accounting of human resource management is gaining more importance in modern business parlance
3. People are the most important assets of an organization, and yet the value of this asset does not appear in the book of accounts.

It is important to recognize the values of all organizational resources including human resources; and manage the human resources for quantity and quality of the goods and services. The need for HR accounting originates from here.

Objectives

The principal objective of HR accounting is managing the human resources to enable them to enhance the quality and quantity of goods and services. Human resource accounting, through the use of cost benefit analysis, facilitates to take decisions regarding direct recruitment versus promotion, and transfer versus retention. In addition, an organization assesses the impact on budgetary controls of human relations and organizational behaviour. Some of these objectives are as follows:

1. Acquiring, developing, and maintaining the manpower
2. Enhancing the enabling capacities of the people with regard to decision-making, and developing generic potential
3. Monitoring the human resources efficiently and effectively by establishing good management practices
4. Analysing the psychological bases of the human assets and identifying the necessary remedial measures, wherever necessary
5. Facilitating valuation of human resources, documenting the valuation, recording in the book of accounts, and disclosing the information in the financial statements
6. Preparing and furnishing cost value information relating to human resources

Advantages

1. Enables the organization to initiate developments of employees and advancement in their career
2. Enhances employee contribution headed for increased organizational productivity
3. Facilitates the management to foresee the change in value, attitude, and aptitude of human resources, and formulate the techniques of interpersonal management
4. Guides the management to deploy the right person for the right job at the right time
5. Assists the management to increase employee job satisfaction
6. Promotes employee involvement and organizational health
7. Triggers the management to analyse the requirement and availability of manpower
8. Directs the management to procure more manpower or otherwise, revise the corporate plan

After understanding the objectives, advantages, and disadvantages, it worth studying the practices in a few organizations (Exhibit 17.5).

Exhibit 17.5 Organizational HR accounting practices

In India, very few companies, such as Bharat Heavy Electrical Limited (BHEL), Infosy,s and Reliance Industries, have implemented HR accounting, and a few more companies are working on it. Infosys, which started showing human resource as an asset in its balance sheet, has been reaping high market valuations. National Institute of Information Technology (NIIT) has been following a similar method called economic value addition (EVA), which also helps in assessing the real value that an employee can fetch for the company.

Experts possess the view that companies can derive many benefits by implementing the HRA system. HRS facilitates measuring the return on capital employed on total organizational assets (including the human assets).

Organizations can track HR accounting by means of two methods—cost-based analysis and value-based analysis. The cost-based approach focuses on the cost parameters, which may relate to historical cost, replacement cost, or opportunity cost. The value-based approach suggests that the value of human resources depends upon their capacity to generate revenue.

Limitations

The system of HR accounting has not fully grown in organizations so far. Many organizations have not been able to derive benefits from the HR accounting. It is vital to appreciate that persons working in the same department at the same level greatly differ in their knowledge, skills, experiences, motivations and intellectual capabilities. The limitations of HR accounting are mainly due to the following factors:

1. The methodology of accounting has not been proposed/established
2. No laid down procedure or guidelines to find the cost and value of human resources
3. Valuing the people may be full of uncertainty
4. HR accounting may dehumanize many employees
5. Not much research work in HR accounting as a tool of HRM
6. Unvarying fear from trade unionists
7. Human resource differs from material and other resources
8. Human resource cannot be owned, retained, and utilized similar to physical resources
9. Tax laws do not recognize human resource as company assets

HUMAN RESOURCE INFORMATION SYSTEM

Human resource information system (HRIS) is a system used to acquire, store, manipulate, analyse, retrieve, and distribute information related to the company's HR. HRIS supports strategic decision making to avoid litigation, to evaluate programmes or policies, or to support daily operating concerns.

Issues While Adopting HRIS

Some of the issues associated with adoption of HRIS are need assessment, type and size of the organization, developing or buying the software, and decisions relating to implementation—whole organization (total) or any select department (part).

The need assessment includes deciding whether HRIS would be implemented in the entire organization or in a few departments. This must be meticulously decided duly considering the type and size of the company. To suit the exact need, the HRIS software may be developed internally or customized software may be purchased. The cost aspect must be taken into account. Another important decision is to decide the phases of implementation. Thus, the following four points need to be taken care of:

1. Meticulous need assessment
2. Determine type and size
3. Decide on developing or buying the software
4. Decide on total or part implementation

Sub-systems of HRIS

HRIS has the following sub-systems:

1. Recruitment information: Includes placement databank, job specification, advertising media, etc.
2. Personnel information: Includes data regarding transfer, designation when joined, present designation, present and permanent address, family information, and increment and promotion details.
3. Manpower planning information: Comprises human resource mobilization system.
4. Training information: Seeks to provide information for training need identification, designing training curriculum, framing the syllabus, training execution, evaluation of training programme, associated cost analysis, and finally feedback and post training impact analysis.
5. Health information system: Includes data on physical status (height, weight), occupational diseases (if any) and information on maintenance of health related to the activities.
6. Appraisal information: Employees are promoted based on their contribution to the company, performance and merit. The related data and information serves as input for promotion, periodic increment, pay hike, succession planning and career planning.
7. Payroll information: Deals with wages, salaries, incentives, date of joining, stoppage of increments, advanced increments, and other similar information.
8. Personnel statistics information: includes historic data and current data for various types of analysis.
9. Psychological data: Provides psychological data e.g. assertiveness, job satisfaction, job involvement, organizational commitment, personality traits, motivation, life style inventory.

Steps in Designing HRIS

The design of HRIS comprises five distinct steps:

Step 1: Preliminary system analysis involves defining the problem, stating the objectives and operational needs, conducting a feasibility study, and submitting the report.

Step 2: System design entails describing the problem in detail, brainstorming to identify the alternatives to meet the objectives, evaluating each idea, and ascertaining the effects of the alternatives on people.

Step 3: System engineering necessitates detailed study of engineering components and associated activities, and pursues cost effectiveness study followed by recommendations.

Step 4: System testing and implementation refers to deciding whether HRIS will be implemented in the entire company or on experimental basis in a few departments. Running and installing the system are also a part of this step.

Step 5: System monitoring and evaluation incorporates measuring performance, continuous evaluation and modification, assessing contribution of HRIS to strategic needs, evaluating the role of HRIS in competitive scenario, and most importantly, making the people aware of the benefits HRIS.

Advantages of HRIS

The various advantages of HRIS are as follows:

1. HRIS defines the HR goals clearly and unambiguously.
2. It helps to store the HR data in a logical manner.
3. It reduces the cost of storing HR data.
4. It makes information available timely and accurately.
5. It contributes to setting performance standards of HR division.
6. It develops individuals linking reward and training with performance.
7. It enables quick problem solving.
8. It guides systematic training programmes.
9. It enhances the enabling capacity to cope with changes.
10. It keeps the status of HR functions up-to-date.

HUMAN RESOURCE RESEARCH

Research is a systematic and scientific process of collecting data, applying statistical tools, getting results, and interpreting in organizational context. Five types of applied human resource research are:

Comparative approach This approach may be applied to the entire organization or to any specific department. The approach compares the performance one organization or department with another to identify the poor areas where scope of improvement exists. Comparison is done on specific activities or HR programmes.

Outside authority approach Engaging an external consultant is a common practice. Often, research findings on similar areas are taken for consideration. The existing standards are compared with recommendation in the research findings. The external consultant or the research findings help diagnose the causes of problems or shows the direction for improvement.

Statistical approach Often, companies need prediction of employee turnover, absenteeism, incentive schemes, etc. In such cases, statistical measures are developed based on the company's existing information. Data are collected and processed to predict the future course of action.

Compliance approach In this approach, the researcher or the research team collects sample from the HRIS elements and searches for any deviations that may be found in the company policies or procedures or law. Thus, in this approach, the researcher verifies compliance of practice with the legal regulations and documented company policies.

Management by objectives approach Management by objectives (MBO) is a system of performance management whereby the superior and subordinate jointly identify the objectives; define individuals' major areas of responsibility in terms of results expected. When an MBO approach is applied to the human resource area, the researcher compares the actual results with the predefined objectives. This approach enables to identify and report poor performance from the non-achievement of target.

HR AUDITING PROCESS

The auditing process varies widely across organizations. The process includes briefing and orienting the employees to develop the plan and programme of audit, scanning/scrutinizing material information, surveying and interviewing the employees, synthesizing the current situation, prioritizing, identification of issues, etc. The last stage comprises reporting wherein results of the audit are discussed with managers and staff specialists, in several rounds. Further, important issues are identified for inclusion in the formal report. The steps taken in this regard are as follows:

Determine the scope and type of audit To decide upon the information sought leading to the areas to be audited.

Develop the audit questionnaire In order to carry out a comprehensive audit or an audit of a specific practice, a questionnaire or checklist is designed for use during an audit.

Collect the data This is the phase of the actual process of reviewing specific areas to collect the data about the company and its HR practices

Benchmark the findings The audit findings are compared with other similarly-sized companies. For example, the ratio of HR personnel to the total strength of the workforce is often compared.

Provide feedback about the results During a closing meeting conducted by the auditors at the end of an audit (on the last day of audit to brief the findings), feedback is verbally provided and followed by a written audit report. Remember that audit is a fact-finding exercise and not a fault-finding one. The company needs to analyse and develop a roadmap to determine the order in which the issues should be addressed. In addition to the top management, the auditor(s) should discuss the results of the audit with employees in the HR department.

HR Auditor

HRD audit is generally conducted by a team, comprising an internal responsible person representing a cross-section of the organization including line personnel, junior, middle, upper management, and those responsible for HR functions. Organizations prefer to engage an external consultant to assist them during an audit.

An auditor should have diverse capabilities, some of which are as follows:

1. Faith in HR and positive approaches to people
2. Thorough knowledge of concepts
3. Knowledge of dynamics in organizations such as personal, interpersonal, and team dynamics
4. Knowledge of andragogy (dealings with adults)
5. Knowledge of HRD mechanisms/sub-systems, processes, and methods of evaluating the same
6. Strategic thinking and knowledge to verify the linkage of HR strategies with business goals.
7. Specialization in any HR function with an understanding of how people provide competitive advantage to organizations
8. Ability to behave in a friendly manner, empower and motivate people to collect information be involved in the audit process
9. Faith in participative, positive approach
10. Benchmarking skills for setting standards
11. Communication, questioning, listening, and sensitivity
12. Presentation and report-writing skills
13. Desire to learn and grow in the organization

HRD Audit Documents

Audit proceeds with an interview of organizational personnel and verification of objective evidences, that includes documents and records. Documentation enables communication of intent and consistency of action. It also contributes towards the achievement of conformity with customer requirements and quality improvement; provision of appropriate training, traceability, evaluation of the effectiveness, and continuing suitability, etc.

The commonly used documents and records employed in an HR audit are displayed in Box 17.2.

Box 17.2 HR audit: Documents and records

1. Previous HRD audit reports	2. HR manual
3. Manpower planning guidelines	4. Succession planning guidelines
5. Career planning guidelines	6. Recruitment policy
7. Promotion policy	8. Transfer policy
9. Performance appraisal manual	10. Total quality management manual
11. Suggestion schemes	12. Training policy guidelines
13. HRD department activities	14. HRD department—organizational structure
15. Training identification methods	16. Training pedagogy
17. Training evaluation, validation and improvement methods	18. Communication system
19. Small group activities	20. Attrition rate
21. Measures adopted to prevent/reduce attrition	22. Exit interview guidelines
23. Worker education and training programmes	24. Welfare schemes
25. Residential colony facilities	26. Climate survey and culture study

HR Audit Outcomes

T.V. Rao Learning System, (TVRLS, www.tvrls.com), is an outcome of a few decades of experience, study, review, reflection, and action combined with a desire to discover more about the behaviour of people in different settings and ways of making them give their best. The company was floated in 1996 and is a unique institute with the philosophy of networking with prominent behavioural scientists and HRD practitioners. TVRLS is a pioneer in the world of HRD audit.

When conducting audit in an organization, TVRLS identified that the employees were unaware of their future in the company. They wanted to be aware of the vision, strategy, and future plans of the company. The HR strategies were not linked with business strategies and careers of individuals. On pointing out this gap, the CEO of the organization took the issue seriously and impressed their head office in another country with his corporate plan. Thereafter, in a period of three years, the company grew by three times in terms of turnover, and became a ₹3,000 million company from a ₹1,000 million-company. In simple words, it could be said that a small HRD audit led the top management to think in terms of the strategy involving many employees and consequently, resulted in business development.

In another company, certain quality issues, cost issues, empowerment issues, and leadership issues were listed in the HR agenda. The company redefined the role of the HRD and got some line managers involved in various HR interventions. This changeover paved the way for a distinct shift in the HR and its activities began to be owned by the line managers.

An IT company got its People Capability Maturity Model (PCMM) level certified. However, the company possessed some of the most unreliable HR managers who did not keep up their promises and did not have any commitment to the company. PCMM is systems-sensitive and not role sensitive, and does not examine any kind of issues. This lapse compelled the company to increase their return on investment on their HR departments and interventions.

Table 17.1 displays the tools used and the corresponding action plans.

Table 17.1 Guide to HR action plan

Tools of audit	Observation—audit finding	Action plan suggested
Interrogation	Three employees of the maintenance department do not know the duties they need to perform.	Role clarity should be achieved.
Interrogation	Two senior employees of the training department could not lucidly explain the training policy.	Policy should be communicated and explained.
Document (HR manual)	In the HR manual, potential appraisal and development are not adequately addressed.	Potential appraisal and development system should be incorporated.
Document (Training register)	Staff members are sent to attend training but there is no system for identifying the training needs.	Procedure on training need identification must be framed.
Observation	Mechanics of the maintenance department are not confident about identifying the root cause behind failure.	Training is required to be conducted, based on training need identification procedure.
Observation	The company sends employees for training; however, on their return, they do not keep any track of learning inputs from the training	Establishing, implementing, and maintaining procedures on training effectiveness is necessary.

HRD Audit: Research Findings

M.G. Jomon (1997), a member of the advisory board of TVRLS, studied four organizations using four different audit processes. He discussed the benefits derived by the organizations as follows:

1. Organizations have initiated HRD audit intervention with specific reasons. To highlight the glimpse of professionalization of the organization, they initiated the audit to assess the organizational health, to benchmark against international organization, to see the unit in relation to its sister concerns, for a formal take off of HRD, etc.
2. Audit findings in all the four organizations pointed out the strengths and areas of improvement. Thus, the report served as a mirror. Audit findings included views about top management as well. Hence, reports were opened up to all the employees. Out of the four organizations studied, in three organizations, the 'audit report' was treated as confidential and made available to the top management and HR chief.
3. Implementation of the HRD audit inputs were done selectively by the HRD department without much involvement of line managers. However, in one organization, line managers implemented the audit inputs.
4. They could see visible changes in various activities ranging from all spheres of organizational activities. There were some specific changes also seen in HRD systems, people-competency development, and culture-development activities.

5. The most important factors influencing HRD audit intervention and utilization of HRD audit inputs are enumerated:

    (a) CEO/top management's commitment to HRD
    (b) HRD chief's commitment to HRD
    (c) Management style of the organization
    (d) Organizational characteristics
    (e) HRD department profile

Jomon concludes that all the four organizations studied benefited out of the HRD audit intervention and used the audit as a tool for organizational development.

SUMMARY

Organizations perform many HR functions. The execution of the functions is often accompanied by several difficulties. Thus, the activities need verification; this is called HR audit or HRD audit. HRD audit is a comprehensive evaluation of the current HRD strategies, structure, systems, styles, and skills in the context of the short and long-term business plans of a company. It attempts to find out the future HRD needs of the company after assessing the current HRD activities and the available inputs. The scope of HRD audit is pervasive and encompasses multiple lapses in HR practices. HRD audit can give several insights into a company's affairs, leading to business improvement, as well. HRD audit examines the linkages with other systems and is business-driven. It is one method of measuring the effectiveness of HR practices in an organization while the other four systems are benchmarking, HR accounting, HR information system, and HR research. The benefits of HRD audit are versatile. These days, auditors are seen to be using checklists while auditing. HRD audit methodology includes interviewing of the auditee, using questionnaires on the relevant areas, observing records and documents, examination of HR policy, objectives, goals/targets, strategy etc.

KEY TERMS

Andragogy refers to the art and science of training adults, and focuses on the creation of an independent, adaptable, and socially acceptable individual.

Compensation function means conferring statutory benefits to employees under various social security enactments, which include rewards, incentives, and other compensation determinants, structure, strategy, and administration.

Cost-based approach focuses on the cost parameters, which may relate to historical cost, replacement cost, or opportunity cost.

Development function means upgrading the existing manpower, organizing orientation, and inducting new recruits.

Maintenance function emphasizes the need for retaining, and is important to enhance the probability of retaining.

Procurement function refers to acquisition of manpower to meet forthcoming business objectives.

Value-based approach suggests that the value of human resources depends upon their capacity to generate revenue. It is further classified into two broad categories: non-monetary and monetary.

EXERCISES

Concept Review Questions

1. Describe HRD audit and explain why it is required in organizations.
2. How can HRD audit be used as an intervention mechanism?
3. Discuss the need for following a structured HRD audit methodology.

4. What do you mean by benchmarking? Discuss benchmarking in the context of HRIS.
5. Discuss the characteristics of HRD audit. Cite examples for the characteristics.

Critical Thinking Questions

6. 'The HR functions comprise procurement function, development function, compensation function, and maintenance function'. If any one of the five functions is not verified/ audited, what might be the consequence? Discuss critically.
7. 'Human resource audit is a systematic assessment of the strengths, limitations, and developmental needs of an organization's existing human resources in the context of organizational performance.' Do you subscribe to this view? Provide justification in favour of and against the statement.

Assignments

8. With the help of your professor, take an appointment from a voluntary organization. Collect data on HRD practices and make a comparison of HRD practices between the voluntary organization and any other organization. Briefly describe the organization you are referring to.
9. Visit two organizations and collect the information regarding objective evidences they are generating and retaining for HRD audit. Show the lists of objective evidences to your teacher for his/her comments.

MANAGER'S INSIGHT

Sharma and Sons is a well recognized small and medium enterprise (SME), engaged in the business of printing greeting cards. For the last few years, their market share and profit had been declining. This got the management of the company thinking and they decided to assess each department and discuss the problems that they could be facing. After a proper survey and research, it was found that the HR department had failed to provide job specifications and responsibilities to its employees. The HR audit committee was immediately contacted; however, they did not have a proper answer to this situation.

Questions:

1. How important do you think an HR audit is for a company's growth?
2. What should be the necessary actions for the company?

BIBLIOGRAPHY AND WEB RESOURCES

Aswathappa, K., *Human Resource and Personnel Management*, Tata McGraw-Hill Publishing Company Limited, New Delhi, 2006.

Banardin, John J., *Human Resource Management*, Tata McGraw-Hill Publishing Company Limited, New Delhi, 2007.

Bhattacharya, Dipak Kumar, *Human Resource Research Methodology*, Oxford Publishing House, New Delhi, 2007.

Koley, M.K., *Accounting Applied to Human Resource Management*, Allied Publishers, Pvt. Limited, New Delhi, 2005.

Ramnarayan, S., T.V. Rao, and Kuldeep Singh, *Organization Development—Interventions & Strategies*, Response Books, New Delhi, 1998.

Rao, T.V., *Evaluating the Human Resource Function for Business Improvement*, Response Books, New Delhi, 2007.

Web Resources

www.titanindustriesinc.com, last accessed on 29 August 2011.

HR EFFECTIVENESS—THE TITAN PRACTICE

About the organization

Titan Industries Limited was incorporated in 1984 as a joint venture between Tata Group and TIDCO Limited, a government of Tamil Nadu undertaking. The company is engaged in the manufacturing and marketing of quartz watches since 1987. In 1995, the company diversified into manufacturing and marketing 18-karat studded jewellery as well. It expanded its business sphere by entering into two more businesses—(a) license brands and accessories to leverage the marketing and retailing skills by launching Fastrack eye gear and entering into an agreement for marketing Tommy Hilfinger watches; and (b) precision engineering division to leverage the precision engineering capabilities in the company.

These business units attracted customers in multiple areas such as automobile, clock and plastic components, precision-engineered components, automobiles and aerospace solution. The company has established its outlets for watches throughout the country. The divisions for watches and jewellery are the two main strategic business units.

Titan conducts annual or half-yearly surveys to evaluate vital HRD pillars:

1. Organizational development—OD is an applied behavioral science approach that is focused on the organization as a system. Using this tool, Titan assesses the health of the organization, effectiveness, capacity to solve problems, ability to adapt, change, or of self-renewal, and ability to create a high quality of work life for its employees.
2. Training and development—Titan treats training and development as the backbone for progress; it has gained distinguished competence, and enhanced its competitive advantages.
3. Manpower planning—Manpower planning is a process of developing a set of decisions for action with regard to manpower. This planning process comprises putting the right number of people, right kind of people at the right place, at right time, doing the right things for which they are suited for to achieve business goals. Titan assesses the competency required to perform key functions and deploy employees with those competencies. It develops competencies by way of training and development and hires employees through competency-based interviews.
4. Human resource information system (HRIS)—Titan has a well-established HRIS to acquire, store, manipulate, analyse, retrieve, and distribute information to company's HR; the system supports strategic decision making.
5. Compensation management—Titan believes in compensating employees for their outstanding achievements. It has a structured compensation system and periodically reviews the system for continuing suitability.
6. Employee satisfaction—Employee satisfaction refers to whether employees are happy, contented, and are fulfilling their desires and needs at work. Many measures purport that employee satisfaction is a factor in employee motivation, employee goal achievement, and positive employee morale in the workplace. Titan is keen to assess the level of employee satisfaction and uses psychometric tools as part of the process.

Performance and potential appraisal

Titan appraises performance and potential twice a year. It identifies the strengths and weaknesses of employees. It brings the weaknesses to the notice of the employees and also suggests the remedial actions. The company considers the potential for new assignments and initiates proactive and not reactive measures.

Titan carefully observes the situations and identifies the appropriate HRD mechanism to solve problems or further the development of employees. Titan has many employee-related foci and changes its focus every year. The focus of the year 2009–10 was 'people first'.

Discussion Questions

1. Titan used some HRD pillars for development. Do you feel that there was an inadequacy in their implementation?
2. Should Titan use any psychometric scale to measure employee satisfaction? Discuss critically.

Source:

Case based on an interaction with Mr Indranil Bhattacharya, Regional HR (East) Manager, Apeejay House, Kolkata, on 5 December 2009.]

www.titanindustriesinc.com, last accessed on 17 January 2012

HR MANTRA Role of management

Employees join an organization with some aspirations. Some prospective job seekers dream of employment in a particular company. Companies develop HR systems and practices to keep the wheel of production of goods or services moving. Some employees derive intrinsic satisfaction from their jobs. They become committed to the organization and continue there. The another category of employees look for extrinsic satisfaction; this is where management needs to play its role. Drives undertaken by the management may or may not fulfil their need for extrinsic satisfaction. However, the third category of employees never feels satisfied. They do not get what they want from the job. The demands of the job do not match their personality attributes. In this case, the role of the management emerges as central and crucial.

To get the best from its employees, the management needs to understand its employees and help to nurture and develop them.

The mantra: Understand, nurture, and develop your employees.

T.V. RAO

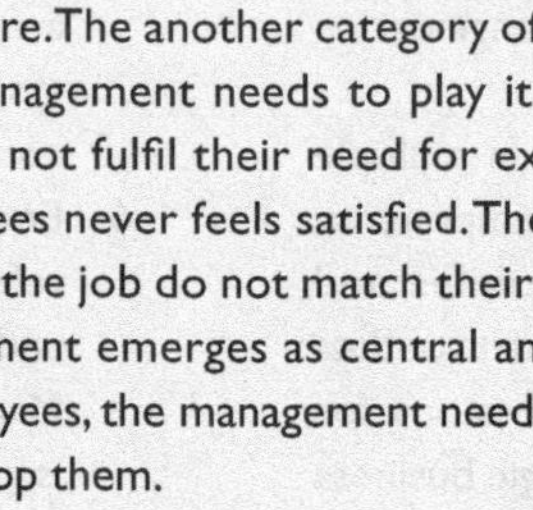

Dr T.V. Rao was born on 14 March 1946, in Akunuru, Andhra Pradesh. Rao secured his B Sc from Andhra Pradesh; B Ed from Mysore University; MA from Osmania University; and also possesses a doctoral degree. He is currently the chairman of T.V. Rao Learning System (TVRLS), Ahmedabad, and an adjunct professor at the Indian Institute of Management Ahmedabad (IIMA). He was professor at IIMA for over 20 years since 1973. He set up the TVRLS in 1996, two years after he left IIMA. During his tenure at IIMA, he was chairman of various programmes such as post graduate programme, Fellow programme, public systems group, Ravi Matthai center and had also coordinated the PGP review. In 1994, he served the Academy of Human Resources Development, Ahmedabad as its first honorary director. Since 2006, he is a visiting professor and adjunct professor at IIMA.

Rao has also worked as professor of HRD at XLRI, Jamshedpur from 1983 to 1985. He is the founder and first president of the national HRD Network. He was also president of the Indian Society for Applied Behavioral Science (ISABS). He worked with David McClelland of Harvard University (the initiator of the competency movement) and had conducted joint research projects with him in 1970s. Rao was a visiting faculty at the Indian Business School, Hyderabad and also worked as HRD advisor to the Reserve Bank of India. He assisted the administrative reforms commission in reviewing the personnel management practices for civil services, and also served as member of the HRM Review Committee of nationalized banks set up by the ministry of finance in 2009–2010.

Rao worked as a short-term consultant to UNESCO, ministry of health, Indonesia, National Entrepreneurial Development Association, Malaysia and the Commonwealth Secretariat, London. He has designed and assisted in implementing performance appraisal and other HRD Systems for a number of organizations in India and abroad.

Rao's consulting work is involved in areas of designing and managing HRD systems of various corporations in India and other Asian countries. He has assisted several organizations on various HR themes. Some of them include: SAIL, NTPC, Indian Oil Corporation, HPCL, Bharat Petroleum, NALCO, SBI, Bank of Baroda, Neyveli Lignite, MRL, BEML, Reserve Bank of India, Larsen & Toubro, Voltas, Sundram Fasteners, EID Parry, TI Group, Crompton Greaves, Transpek Industries, BILT, NOCIL, IL&FS, Mahindra and Mahindra, Escorts, Tata Finance, Titan, Taj Group of Hotels, Tata Cummins, KPMG, ICI, Hindustan Levers, Pfizer, Chanrai Group (Nigeria),

Indorama, Indonesia, Godfrey Phillips India, Amway, Nestle, Wockhardt, Wyeth, Fulford, Galfar (Oman), Ministry of Health, Indonesia; FAO, Rome; Commercial Bank, Sri Lanka; Hemas group Sri Lanka, CHR Oman etc.

Rao and Dr Udai Pareek are credited to have established the first dedicated department of human resources development at L&T in the mid 1970s much before HRD was known. Rao has been working on HRD for the last 40 years.

Rao is the first thinker to start a leadership development methodology in the mid-eighties in India and used what is later termed in the USA as 360 degree feedback in India. His HRD audit methodology is the first of its kind across the world and he started and created a HRD score card based on the same concept. Rao has authored, coauthored and edited over 30 books dealing with HRD, education management, health and population management, entrepreneurship development and so on. He has also won several awards for his outstanding contributions to HRD.

Rao has several publications to his credit including over 50 books on various themes relating to education, health and population management, behavioural sciences, and HRD. His recent publication is, *Managers Who Make a Difference* (IIMA Books, Random House, New Delhi, October 2010).

Some of the forthcoming books authored by Rao include *Hurconomics* (Pearson Education, 2011) and *Nurturing Institutional Excellence* (IIMA Books, edited by Vijaya Sherry Chand and T.V. Rao, MacMillan India, 2011).

Among the various titles authored by Rao, the title HRD audit is not only first of its kind but also unique. With the changing business scenario, HRD, that was initially a responsibility of the CEOs and top management in the eighties; a business necessities in the nineties; has become a principal need in the present decade. Rao's title presents the utmost need of HRD audit, discusses in detail about the various aspects of HRD that should be looked at for a comprehensive evaluation, and presents an in-depth methodology to assess HRD. The purpose of HRD audit is developmental and leads to leadership development.

Source:

Email from Prof. Dr T.V. Rao dated 11 September 2011.

CHAPTER 18

Ethics and Corporate Social Responsibility

LEARNING OBJECTIVES

After studying this chapter, you will be able to

- Understand ethics and its role in business
- Recognize the need for developing and documenting a code of conduct
- Appreciate the role of corporate social responsibility (CSR) and be aware of the spectrum of CSR initiatives taken by various organizations

OPENING CASE

Preaching Ethics

One day, a little boy's mother spotted a fancy-looking pencil in his pencil box. She interrogated her son and found that he had stolen it from a classmate. She reprimanded him and reported the matter to her husband when he got home from work that evening.

Her husband lectured the boy on good versus bad behaviour, principles, and morals. The boy listened to his father's advice attentively and promised that he would never steal again. The father finished his sermon by saying, 'If you ever want a pencil or any other stationery, don't hesitate to ask me. I will bring as many as you want from my office.'

Now, will the little boy ever learn to be ethical?

Learning points

- Practice what you preach.
- Good manners should be instilled from childhood.
- Lead by setting examples.

INTRODUCTION

Ethics is very significant in the world of business. It is the study of morally appropriate behaviour and decisions, and examining what should be done. Ethics helps to mould and shape human behaviour. It aids employees to perform their roles. However, ethics cannot be instilled unless we 'practice what we preach'. Otherwise, the effect of preaching will last only as long as a house of cards.

Corporate social responsibility (CSR), on the other hand, is the process by which businesses negotiate their role in the society. The two terms—ethics and CSR—are intertwined. In fact, in many firms, ethics and CSR are interlinked. In some cases, CSR is also considered to be a guarantee of ethical behaviour.

CSR has now become a global issue and has gained prominence in the language and strategy of every business. Today, the image of an organization is judged by the CSR activities that it performs. Governments and many international organizations are increasingly encouraging CSR and forming CSR partnerships.

In this Chapter, ethics and its various facets, code of ethics or conducts practised by professional bodies and organizations, including knowledge business, and CSR initiatives/ and practices adopted by reputed organizations will be discussed.

ETHICS IN THE WORKPLACE

The concept of ethics, though not altogether new, has now assumed a great deal of importance. The subject is now widely discussed at all levels. It is even said that human life without ethics would mean nothing. It is also rightly said that work makes a man and a man is known by his work. Work gives identity, recognition, and status. Ethics has been defined in many different ways and there is a wide diversity in opinion. It is a value orientation concept. In a wider sense, ethics may be defined as a positive attitude towards work, a belief that work itself is supreme, important, and that doing a particular job is essential.

Unfortunately, people do not talk about ethics when engaging in ethical behaviour on a daily basis. It is spoken about only in the case of occurrence of an unethical event. Today, organizations are seen to be framing 'code of ethics' encompassing the ethical system, moral values, and moral judgements.

Employees perform roles to achieve business goals, and their performance is based on the code of ethics. While performing their roles, they make decisions and choose between the right and the wrong. Some of the instances where they, consciously (with vested interest) or unconsciously (on account of carelessness), do something that may cause harm to the organization are highlighted in Exhibit 18.1.

Exhibit 18.1 Instances of violation of ethics

1. The top management of your organization has requested you to host a dinner party to visiting officials (potential supplier) in a hotel. You have received a very expensive gift of a holiday with your family in a posh resort while price negotiations were going on during the dinner.
2. Your office is attempting to switch over to paperless office. All communications will be through intranet. As such, it has extended Internet facilities through proxy server. You are browsing the office Internet to book flight ticket for your wife who will go to meet her mother. You are frequently checking out latest movie updates.
3. You are sharing confidential information such as business strategies of your company against a negotiated amount with your competitors in a party hosted by them.
4. You have met your friend after a long time. You are telling him/her about the action plans finalized by your company, forgetting that your friend is an employee in your competitor's house.

Employees at all levels should behave in a culturally appropriate manner in their companies. They should behave ethically and conform to the company's standards. Some companies have developed a 'code of conduct' which is circulated to all employees. For example, the code of conduct of the Tata group prescribes that every employee should conform to the rules in the code of conduct (Exhibit 18.2).

Exhibit 18.2 Ethical conduct at Tata

Every employee of a Tata company, including full-time directors and the chief executive, exhibit culturally appropriate deportment in the countries they operate in, and deal on behalf of the company with professionalism, honesty and integrity, while conforming to high moral and ethical standards. Such conduct will be perceived by the third parties as fair and transparent.

Every employee of a Tata company preserves the human rights of every individual and the community, and strives to honour commitments. Every employee is responsible for the implementation of and compliance with the code in his/her environment. Failure to adhere to the code could attract severe consequences, including termination of employment.

Source: www.tatamotors.com, last accessed on 3 May 2010.

IMPORTANCE OF ETHICS

From the perspective of business, ethics matter because it makes good business sense to be socially right. Additionally, good corporate ethics result in the following:

1. Acquiring talent from the job market and retaining them
2. Retaining customers and increasing customer base
3. Improving quality of work life
4. Ensuring a positive effect on return on investment (ROI)
5. Creating a positive effect on corporate reputation

It is no surprise that corporates strive to build a lasting image on all stakeholders who come in contact with them, regularly or occasionally. Corporates formulate their ethical standard, and develop a 'code of ethics' or a 'code of conduct'. Contextually, the code of ethics of a few significant professional bodies and companies are discussed here.

Code of Ethics: The Institution of Engineers (India)

The Institution of Engineers (India) is the largest professional body in India, formally inaugurated in Chennai in 1920. In 1935, the Royal Charter granted the Charter of Incorporation to this institution by His Majesty George V, the King and Emperor of Great Britain. It is headquartered at Kolkata. The code of ethics for the corporate members of this esteemed professional body is given in Exhibit 18.3 (www.ieindia.org).

Exhibit 18.3 Code of ethics for corporate members: The Institution of Engineers (India)
(Effective from 1 March 2004)

1. Engineers serve all members of the community in enhancing their welfare, health, and safety by a creative process and utilize the engineers' knowledge, expertise, and experience.
2. Pursuant to the avowed objectives of The Institution of Engineers (India) as enshrined in the presents of the royal charter granted to the institution, the council of the institution prescribed a set of 'professional conduct rules' in 1944 replacing the same with the 'code of ethics for corporate members' in 1954 which was revised in 1997.
3. In view of globalization, concern for the environment and the concept of sustainable development, it has been felt that the prevailing code of ethics for corporate members needs review and revision in letter and spirit. The engineering organizations world over have updated their code of ethics.

(Contd)

Exhibit 18.3 (Contd)

4. The council of the institution vested with the authority in terms of the present 2(j) of the Royal charter adopted at its 626th meeting held on 21 December 2003, at Lucknow the 'code of ethics for corporate members' as provided hereinafter.
5. The code of ethics is based on broad principles of truth, honesty, justice, trustworthiness, respect and safeguard of human life and welfare, competence and accountability which constitutes the moral values every corporate member of the institution must recognize, uphold and abide by.
6. This 'code of ethics for corporate members' shall be in force till the same is revised by a decision of the council of the institution.

Source: www.ieindia.org

Code of Ethics: National HRD Network

The National HRD Network (NHRDN) is an association of professionals committed to promoting the HRD movement in the country and enhancing the capability of human resource professionals in order to enable them to make a significant contribution for enhancing competitiveness and creating value for society. NHRDN has chapters in various cities.

The code of ethics of NHRDN is displayed in Exhibit 18.4.

Exhibit 18.4 Code of ethics: National HRD Network, Kolkata chapter

1. I will always strive to meet the highest evolving standards of competence in the profession and add value to organizational success.

Dos

(a) I will keep myself updated regularly by reading the latest management books, HR publications, and related literature with time targets.
(b) I will network professionally to build my competencies through right emulation.

Don'ts

(a) I will not wait for my employer to provide me the opportunities to learn.
(b) I will not be afraid to acknowledge gaps in my knowledge, skill, and competence actions and decisions and foster fairness with firmness.

2. I will deal with all stakeholders with utmost integrity and create an environment of trust leading to ethical success of my organization.

Dos

(a) I will have a completely open and transparent relationship with all, and be clear of each stakeholder; expectations from me, my organization and also my expectation from them.
(b) I will uphold and respect the confidentiality imposed on me by other individuals / the organization.
(c) I will be authentic in my words and actions and always stand by what I have said.

Don'ts

(a) I will not indulge in or encourage or be a bystander to any negative talk or rumours about anybody or such related behaviour.
(b) I will not divulge any information of the organization to any unauthorized person for any reason or purpose.

3. I will ensure that I am always reliable and consistent in all my actions by accepting responsibility for my decisions and actions, thereby creating credibility for my profession and myself.

Dos

(a) I will deliver results consistently and in tune with my promises.
(b) I will own all my mistakes and take action to rectify them at the very earliest.

Don'ts

(a) I will not blame others for my mistakes.
(b) I will not overestimate what I can do.
(c) I will be result-oriented rather than fault finding or blaming others.

4. I will be objective in all my actions and decisions and foster fairness with firmness.

(Contd)

Exhibit 18.4 (Contd)

Dos

(a) I will investigate situations and get all the facts before I take any action or arrive at conclusion.
(b) I will take decisions as quickly as possible and be firm in my actions.
(c) I will consistently communicate transparently to all concerned with a personal touch.

Don'ts

(a) I will not take snap or hasty decisions.
(b) I will not hide behind someone else's decision making authority.
(c) I will not take biased or prejudiced decisions based on gender/community/religion/minority.

5. I will conduct myself in a way that facilitates growth and development of all those I am responsible for.

Dos

(a) I will always listen to people and relate to them with openness and fairness.
(b) I will foster development in my staff, my team and for those whom I am responsible for.
(c) I will delegate, coach. and mentor as appropriate.
(d) I will meticulously plan for my succession and prepare concerned persons.
(e) I will provide a training and development budget for my team.
(f) I will attempt to counsel/teach/coach the HR student community.

Don'ts

(a) I will not make assumptions about what others are capable of.
(b) I will not decide their future without asking their inputs.
(c) I will not cut the training budget as the first step toward cost reduction.
(d) I will not imagine that I am too old / experienced to learn from others.

6. I will strive to be a role model for all others and champion exemplary practice of the HR profession.

Dos

(a) I will set an example in all my actions.
(b) I will understand the influence I have over the perceptions of those around me.
(c) I will prudently mix fun and work.
(d) I will stand up for what is right.
(e) I will always be driven by long term interests rather than short term gains.
(f) I will understand and comprehend the core beliefs from which I derive my ethics.
(g) I will be clear on what my values in life are.

Don'ts

(a) I will not participate in inappropriate joke or story telling just to be 'in'.
(b) I will not be afraid to speak up when it is necessary.
(c) I will not have double standards in values like one in personal life and one in professional life or a set of values for myself and another for others.

7. I will respect the rights of privacy, will not use my position for personal gains and ensure that there is no conflict of interest in what I do with any of my stakeholders.

Dos

(a) I will be very objective and diligent in giving references of my employees to others.
(b) I will respect their rights of privacy and keep their information in utmost confidence.
(c) I will keep the employees interest above all else when dealing with different stakeholders.

Don'ts

(a) I will not pass on confidential personal information regarding employees to others.
(b) I will not give out information on my employees to competitors, search firms, and other vendors under any pressure.
(c) I will not share any privilege information I have regarding employees either with their supervisors or peers or any other group of employees which might compromise their interest.

Source: www.nhrdn.org

BUSINESS ETHICS AT ERICSSON

Lars Magnus Ericsson started the company Ericsson in 1876. Over the years, the company has grown multidirectionally. The founder had envisioned the great potential of phones, and also saw the need to improve their technical quality.

Ericsson contributed to the making of Stockholm, the world's most telephone dense city. His foresight has led to the company positioning itself at the forefront of the industry, ever since the dawn of telecommunications. The company firmly believed that communication is a basic human need.

Ericsson also set out how the company would achieve and maintain high ethical standards in its 'code of business ethics'. The code summarizes the company's basic policies and directives, which is translated into more than 20 languages, and is accessible to all employees. It covers the importance of following the laws and statutes that concern the operations and financial reporting. It also gives details on how to protect information about their operations, customers, and suppliers.

The Ericsson code of business conduct sets the standard for the way it does business. Refer to Exhibit 18.5.

Exhibit 18.5 Code of business conduct: Ericsson

1. Honest and ethical conduct, including ethical handling of actual or apparent conflicts of interest between personal and professional interests
2. Full, fair, accurate, timely, and understandable disclosure in reports and documents that we file with or submit to government agencies and in other public communications
3. Protection of confidential and proprietary information about Ericsson, our employees, contractors, customers, partners and vendors
4. Compliance with applicable governmental directives, laws, rules, and regulations
5. Prompt internal reporting of any violations of the code

Source: http://www.ericsson.com/article/life_at_ericsson_553969845_c

Every employee is required to observe the Ericsson code of business conduct, and the company asks them to acknowledge their commitment to these shared values. Ericsson periodically reviews the code.

ETHICS IN KNOWLEDGE BUSINESS

Educational institutes belong to the knowledge business category. Some educational institutes have earned a reputation over the years by imparting quality education to students. Ethics are vital in the knowledge business as well. Refer to Exhibit 18.6 for incident in which the actions of an engineering college appear to be unethical.

Exhibit 18.6 Diversification drive of an engineering college

A reputed engineering college in India is known to produce quality engineers every year. A major portion of graduates from the college pursued management education from other institutes. Considering the emerging trend of engineering graduates pursuing management courses, the institute planned to diversify from purely engineering to engineering-cum-management. In spite of the presence of several B-schools in the country, the institute aimed to play a pioneering role in management education. It made efforts to provide management education to fresh graduates as well as working executives.

The dean of the department of management studies was given a free hand for rolling out the course as per the laid down standards of the college (Mathur and Das 2009). A new course for executives was launched with the same entrance examination as that of post graduate diploma in business administration courses. The college named the course 'post graduate diploma in management' to give it a different identity. In order to meet the demanding academic requirements, the college hired external lecturers on interim and casual terms.

(Contd)

Exhibit 18.6 (Contd)

The gaps in the two levels of educators (experienced, full-time faculty and external, interim faculty) became evident and paved the way for the development of discontent among students. The students felt uncomfortable and dissatisfied. However, there were some dynamic students who put in efforts to convince a few multinational companies to form an industry–academia alliance in order to enhance their hands-on experience. Nevertheless, this proposal was rejected by the college. The flash point of all these disparities emerged when the students had to choose their subjects of specialization and summer projects had to be decided. The college washed off its hands regarding summer projects saying that the students should find companies themselves.

It was evident that a great idea had to be succumbed to bad planning and unacceptable execution. The question that remains is whether a reputed college should run a new course in the backdrop of its reputation, without possessing the right infrastructure and means of implementation. As education should not be treated commercially, another question that evolves in this context is whether it is ethical or not to make education a business.

FACTORS INFLUENCING BUSINESS ETHICS

There are certain factors that influence ethics in businesses. The factors can be both internal and external (Gupta and Gupta 2010). Figure 18.1 portrays these factors.

Factors influencing business ethics

Internal

1. People—individual characteristics
2. Vision statement—policies and procedures
3. Measure and follow up
4. Strategies and transaction of business financial rewards—direct and indirect reward and punishments
5. Targets and budgets
6. Profits
7. Ethical guidelines and standard of business
8. Crisis management
9. Working conditions
10. Leadership
11. Corporate culture
12. Ethical analysis, training, and guidelines

External

1. Society
2. Religion and culture
3. Government
4. Laws
5. Market
6. External events
7. Technology
8. Competition
9. Public perception of laws
10. Role of ethical values in society
11. Reputation quotient (RQ) (RQ is defined in terms of better reputation in business. A higher RQ gives better financial performance. Johnson and Johnson reaps financial benefits from being ranked the most reputable company globally for its social responsiveness.)

Fig. 18.1 Factors influencing business ethics

INSTILLING ETHICS

Q 3 Fraud is a major concern among business executives. One needs to ensure that employees and the management team practice ethical behaviour. Anyone could be involved in a scam; a person may have vested interests or a situation may compel one to commit the act. Whistle blowing may be necessary in a variety of business situations—when a senior or a junior is seen to be indulging in an unacceptable practice or when the boss orders something unacceptable with regard to the environment. In order to instill ethics among employees in organizations, there are two methods that can be used—whistle blowing and fraud hotline.

Whistle blowing In a football match, whenever there is a forward in off-side or a defender fouls, the referee uses his whistle to correct the fault done immediately. Similarly, in organizations as soon as a fault or unethical action is done, someone should blow the whistle to alert the erring employee.

Whistle blowing means calling attention to a wrongdoing at the instance when it occurs within an organization. The accountability project lists some ways to blow the whistle. Some of them are as follows:

1. Reporting an unlawful activity or a violation of the law to the proper authorities
2. Refusing to participate in workplace wrongdoing
3. Testifying in a legal proceeding in a departmental inquiry or a court of law
4. Leaking evidence of wrongdoing to the media by a person other than the spokesperson

Fraud hotline The fraud hotline is a process for reporting concerns about improper, illegal, or any thing that may violate the company's image. The most important and common hotline is the telephone for reasons of convenience. The manager responsible to maintain ethics may be accessible through a 24-hour hotline system. The hotline is the most effective system that a company can allow for employees, customers, and even vendors to give information anonymously. The witness or observer of an unethical incident will have to convey the message and the voice will be recorded at the other end. The recipient of the message, a trained live interviewer at the other end of the line, may like to seek some more information for probing the extent of gravity of the information.

For example, being an employee of a large company, if one has information about a fraudulent incident happening in the company, one may not feel like talking to the senior. The superior may be committing the fraud. In such cases, one should bring the matter to the notice of his/her senior's senior. However, this may be a dangerous step as the senior also might be entangled in the fraud chain. Furthermore, one may not want to talk to other employees because he/she may not be sure how they would react. By protecting oneself, an employee may access the information without disclosing his name and contact details. If the identity is revealed, the experienced interviewer may ask pertinent questions to get all the relevant information they need, so that they can get the take up matter to the company. The hotlines operate 24 hour/365 days a year and are equipped to handle different languages spoken within a company.

Organizational Drives

It has already been established that the code of conduct should be laid out in a formal document. Concurrently, organizations should educate the new recruits and existing employees, create an environment conducive to promoting ethical conduct, and demonstration by the leadership team. The measures that can be adopted are as follows:

1. Business conduct process should be an integral part of the induction programme for new recruits. Management needs to send frequent messages to them, keeping in mind that 'it is easier to make the doll when the clay is soft'.

2. Employees should be aware of the business conduct policies. The legal department should design a 'legal compliance course curriculum' and the course should be conducted by experienced personnel. These courses should be mandatory and the employees must be evaluated.
3. Management–employee interaction session is a great platform to raise employee awareness and is of paramount importance where the management can share certain dos and don'ts with regard to behaviour disposition. These interaction sessions promote employee relations.
4. Internal communication plays an important role in conveying business conduct policies informally in a non-instructional manner, citing examples of actual situations to communicate acceptable form of behaviour (Sasikar 2010).

Organizations can definitely derive benefits by adopting these practices in a planned manner.

Instilling Ethics through Culture

An organization needs to create a culture of ethical conduct. The processes must be well defined so that the decision-makers can take the right decisions from amongst available alternatives. The organizational culture should develop employees so as to evaluate them through self-questioning. Sasikar 2010 suggests three dimensions of self-questioning:

1. Is my action consistent with the company's corporate values of uncompromising honesty and integrity?
2. Can my action stand public scrutiny?
3. Will my action protect the company's reputation as an ethical company?

ETHICS AND VIRTUE

It is as important to be virtuous as it is to be ethical. As discussed in Chapter 14, some of the virtues that one must possess are benevolence, contentment, cooperation, courage, determination, humility, tolerance, and wisdom. Other virtues include mercy, obedience, cleanliness, and introversion.

CODE OF CONDUCT

Q 2 A code of conduct is a set of rules. It outlines the responsibilities of or proper practices for an individual or an organization. Compliance with the documented code is ascertained through observation. In case of deviation, solutions such as whistle blowing are used to sort out the differences. Today, it has become mandatory for every company to formulate a code of conduct for compliance of its employees. Exhibit 18.7 lists the clauses in the Tata code of conduct.

Ethics practised in business is often blended with individual codes of ethics. Within the business framework, businesses are expected to have good ethical values and act in a socially responsible manner. This is why it is important to have good individuals in the company's bus. It is also equally important that while at work, it is imperative to share the values of colleagues. Ethics does not mean just talking about the right thing; it also includes taking the right move in every decision that is made in the organization.

Exhibit 18.7 Tata code of conduct: Clauses

Tata is a rapidly growing business group based in India with significant international operations. The business operations of the Tata Group comprise operations in every major international market.

The Tata code of conduct (TCoC) enunciates the values, which govern the conducts and activities of the companies using the name of Tata and of their employees. The employees strive to create a culture that promotes compliance, encourages employees to raise their questions and concerns, provides for counseling, and prohibits retribution.

The TCoC is very exhaustive and has 25 clauses.

1. National interest
2. Financial reporting and records
3. Competition
4. Equal opportunities
5. Gifts and donations
6. Government agencies
7. Political non-alignment
8. Health, safety, and environment
9. Quality of products and services
10. Corporate citizenship
11. Cooperation of Tata companies
12. Public representation of the company and the Group
13. Third party representation
14. Use of the Tata brand
15. Group policies
16. Shareholders
17. Ethical conduct
18. Regulatory compliance
19. Concurrent employment
20. Conflict of interest
21. Securities transactions and confidential information
22. Protecting company assets
23. Citizenship
24. Integrity of data furnished
25. Reporting concerns

Social responsibility is an example of ethical behaviour by corporate personnel. A corporate gets recognition in the society when it goes beyond legal minimums, introduces innovative ideas to benefit the public, and forces its competitors to follow suit by consistently upping the ante for what it takes to be an ethical leader. Discharging social responsibility brings a corporate psychologically closer to the community.

As discussed earlier, ethics reflect a positive attitude towards work, garner a belief that work itself is supreme, and becomes a value-orientation concept. Ethics has assumed a great deal of importance and ethics at the workplace is as significant as any other vitue.

CORPORATE SOCIAL RESPONSIBILITY

Q 4 Corporate social responsibility is an analytical tool that can be used in the field of business management to facilitate different business practices, both from an ethical angle and a utilitarian perspective. From the standpoint of CSR, an enterprise is accountable for its impact on all relevant stakeholders. Through CSR, companies affirm social and territorial cohesion, quality, and environment. This affirmation helps business managers to establish networks of trust, loyalty, and cooperation within and outside their organizations.

CSR is a concept whereby companies integrate social and environmental concerns into their business operations and in their interaction with their stakeholders (employees, customers, shareholders, investors, local communities, and government), on a voluntary basis. Furthermore, CSR is also associated with the principles of sustainability. This principle argues that every organization should make decisions based on their immediate and long-term impact on the social and environmental factors, rather than only the financial factors.

When an organization only concentrates on maximizing its profits, the profit becomes probabilistic. If the sense of ethics of the people of the organization, particularly of the top management, is not adequate enough, it is believed that the CSR orientation will also be less.

The management of human values and corporate trust is a long, arduous, and unpleasant journey that requires out-of-the-box thinking matched with the capacity to relate to the empathy of individuals, society, and other stakeholders. Hence, rapport-building is a crucial requirement in the context of trust management.

CSR is particularly important in today's age of decreased product differentiation and heightened competition. CSR initiatives are innovative and a less imitable means of strengthening customer relationship and loyalty. In this context, it is relevant to mention that 80 per cent of the world's 250 largest companies have filed CSR reports in 2008. In addition, there has been a heated debate around the Companies Bill, 2009, which required all employers earning a net profit of more than ₹100 million to contribute at least two per cent of their income towards CSR. CSR ratings play a significant role in the rankings of the 'most admired companies' by magazines such as *Forbes* and *Money*.

CSR CONTINUUM

CSR refers to the act of balancing profits and social objectives. If a company diverts its funds towards CSR initiatives, it is not treated as expenditure; it is an investment. The CSR gamut is pervasive and some of salient points of CSR are as follows:

1. Divert funds to CSR and activities and yet maximize the firm's profit.
2. Identify and execute social responsibility initiatives.
3. Cross the normal domain of thinking on CSR.
4. Innovate or 'evaporate'.
5. Understand the society and give more than what is expected.
6. Integrate social objectives and business goals.
7. Ensure compliance with legal requirements.
8. Articulate socially valuable objectives.
9. Lead the industry with the best practices.
10. Allow other companies to benchmark one's company.

CSR INITIATIVES

The range of CSR activities is wide. The CSR spectrum includes helping the visually challenged, conducting affirmative action programmes (AAP), organizing medical camps for a variety of purposes, educating and developing rural people, abolishing child labour, and teaching art and craft, dance, etc., in addition to providing education to promote literacy.

Irrespective of their nature of business, organizations are investing substantial funds in CSR activities. These activities are scheduled and executed by organizations such as Infosys Technologies, NHPC Limited, Tata Motors, Dr Reddy's Laboratories Limited, Anand Corporate Services Limited, and Aptech Limited and help one understand the diverse initiatives taken by organizations. In turn, CSR initiatives contribute to the nation.

CSR Initiatives of Infosys Development Centres in 2009

Employees of Infosys actively participate in the welfare of the local community. The development centres (DCs) make a difference through several CSR initiatives. Their employees organize and contribute to welfare programmes, especially for underprivileged children. They support the activities of institutes and non-government organizations (NGOs) dedicated to healthcare and education, and undertake campaigns for skills development and community welfare. Infosys has established several DCs at Bengaluru, Bhubaneswar, Chandigarh, Chennai, Hyderabad, Mysore, Pune, Thiruvananthapuram, etc. Contributions of all the developmental centres are exemplary and worth benchmarking. Some of these will be discussed in this chapter.

Bengaluru development centre

1. *Rakum school for the visually challenged*: Mitr, the Infosys local CSR team, visited the Rakum school for the visually challenged. Mobility, an exercise in which team members walked blind-folded using canes, helped them empathize with the children. The team organized games and distributed chocolates and stationery to the children.
2. *Notebook distribution*: The Infynite Smiles CSR team has been distributing books and stationery to underprivileged children across Karnataka since 2001. In 2009, the team touched more than 45,000 lives, including the tribal community. They collected donations amounting to ₹10,00,000. The drive has been actively supported by the Dream School Foundation, Ramana Clinic, Sri Vivekananda Youth Movement, Chrysalis, and other NGOs.

Bhubaneswar development centre

Project genesis: This initiative of the Infosys affirmative action programme (IAAP) prepares students for a career in the business process outsourcing industry. The project was launched in Orissa in 2007 along with the state government to enhance the skills of academicians. Till date, 515 professors have been trained to make learning more focused by combining traditional teaching methods with modern education. In 2009, 70 professors underwent a 12-day training programme.

Chandigarh development centre

1. *Behaviour and social skills development*: Prayaas, the local CSR team, organized a programme where 60 children from the Panchkula slum showcased their creativity in group activities. The children were imparted training in social etiquette.
2. *Medical camp and cleanliness drive*: Prayaas adopted Tanda village to drive the need for social transformation in the region. The volunteers engaged residents in a cleanliness drive to prevent malaria. A free camp for eye and general medical check up was organized. Medicines and spectacles prescribed by doctors at the camp were distributed free of cost. The team collected data on health and sanitation-related issues to address them.

Chennai development centre

1. *Educare*: Sneham, the local CSR team, managed a dedicated intranet portal to help employees support education of the children of the company's housekeeping and security staff. In 2009, 1,500 members contributed approximately ₹14,00,000 to support more than 370 students. Meritorious students were awarded for their performance. A special award was presented to a girl child with exceptional recitation skills.
2. *Helping the visually challenged*: Infoscions partnered with Nethrodaya, an NGO that works with visually challenged children. The volunteers regularly conduct weekend reading sessions.

In 2009, they organized a south India inter-state sports festival with modified versions of cricket, volleyball, and chess.

3. *Facilities for rural schools*: Volunteers constructed a water tank to supply drinking water to 1,000 students of the Avanippoor government higher secondary school. They have been donating notebooks to the Anoor school since 2005. In 2009, they donated a water tank to the school and also distributed notebooks to the children of Infosys' support staff.

Hyderabad development centre

1. *PC donation drive*: Mamata, the local CSR team, donated more than 105 computers to institutions that undertake non-commercial and public activities. They have already invited requests for the next list of beneficiaries.
2. *Day of change*: Every Wednesday, drop boxes are placed at the campus entrance and exit points, food courts, and parking areas to collect coins from Infoscions for social welfare activities.

Mysore development centre

1. *Notebook distribution*: The company's local CSR team distributed 57,000 books, 36,000 pencils, and 3,600 erasers in the notebook distribution drive in 2009. Underprivileged students from various schools have been benefiting from this drive since 2002.
2. *Language and computer education*: Basic computer education was imparted to the security and housekeeping staff of the DC. The team also helped 10 guards improve their English-language skills.
3. *Summer camp*: A month-long workshop was conducted in May 2009 at Karunya Mane, a child rehabilitation centre. Around 30 children were taught art and craft, dance, math, English, environment awareness, traffic rules, health and fitness, and social etiquette. Quiz contests helped the children assess their general knowledge.
4. *Blood donation*: More than 80 Infoscions donated blood in a special camp conducted in collaboration with the Mysore Rotary and Chandrakala Hospital.
5. *School for dropouts*: The team works with Kaliyuva Mane, an informal school for dropouts run by the Divya Deepa trust. They also interact with children in open classrooms through painting competitions and games.

Pune development centre

Sparsh, the local CSR team, is a registered NGO. In 2009, it conducted several programmes:

1. *Eye donation camp*: More than 330 Infoscions pledged to donate their eyes in a special camp organized by the Ruby Hall clinic and the eye bank association of India.
2. *Play and live (PAL)*: Sports is used as a tool to boost the confidence of underprivileged children, teach them various skills, and change their outlook. The company donated sports equipment including carom and chess boards, and offered prizes such as watches, perfumes and chocolates.
3. *Blood donation camp*: Around 700 volunteers donated blood during a two-day camp in June 2009. Three blood banks—ISIS blood bank, KEM, and Janakalyan—participated in the drive. Doctors highlighted the need for safe blood donation at the camp.

Thiruvananthapuram development centre

Notebook distribution: Infosys CEO and Managing Director, Kris Gopalakrishnan, inaugurated a notebook distribution drive, which benefited 4,000 students in 2009.

Source: http://www.infosys.com/sustainability/Pages/corporate-social-responsibility.aspx

CSR Initiatives by NHPC

NHPC Limited (formerly known as National Hydroelectric Power Corporation Ltd), is a Government of India enterprise. NHPC has been committed towards CSR and ethical behaviour, and has contributed to the economic development and improving the quality of life of internal as well as external stakeholders and the society at large. The CSR aspects are mentioned in the mission statement of the company: 'To execute and operate projects in a cost effective, environment friendly, and socio-economic responsive manner'. With this focus, a full-fledged scheme on CSR-community development (CSR-CD) initiatives at the power stations has been put in place.

NHPC has undertaken a number of CSR-CD initiatives in the areas of health, education, peripheral development, sports and culture, development of employment opportunities, preservation of nature etc. for the community living in and around the power stations and construction projects. Various other initiatives include creating herbal parks, large scale afforestation, catchment area treatment (CAT), fisheries management, development of tourism in the region, infrastructural developments such as construction of roads, bridges etc.

NHPC has empowered millions of rural poor in the surrounding communities through education, vocational training programmes, adult education programmes, health care, promoting sports and culture etc. These initiatives have led to a large scale socio-economic development in the vicinity of various NHPC power stations and projects.

NHPC's CSR initiatives has become a matter of folklore with reputed awards and recognitions such as SCOPE (standing conference of public enterprises) meritorious award for corporate social responsibility and responsiveness, power HR forum award for best practices as a corporate citizen, AMITY award for best CSR practices, golden peacock award for environmental excellence, GreenTech environmental excellence award, SRISHTI awards for good green governance etc.

Source: www.nhpcindia.com/english/Scripts/CSR_Home.aspx

CSR Activities by Tata Motors

Tata Motors (TM) has always followed the golden words of its founder, JRD Tata: 'No success or achievement in material terms is worthwhile unless it serves the needs or interest of the country and its people and is achieved by fair and honest means'.

Social responsibility is inherent in Tata's DNA. Tata has been contributing to society for the last half-century. The CSR activities of TM spread over sectors as wide as healthcare, education, environment, employability, etc.

TM offers preventive and curative health care services, including provisions for sanitation and safe drinking water. The company provides opportunities for students to get quality education at different levels, protects and preserves the environment by adopting green practices, enhances employability of youth and women by providing a training in income generating activities and improving the quality of technical education.

In 2008–09, TM extended its preventive and curative healthcare services to more than 104,000 community members, built 1,900 low-cost toilets, and organized cleanliness drives involving 4,000 villagers. TM has helped 100 schools in infrastructure development, faculty upgradation, and offered donations. It initiated extracurricular activities for 4,167 students to enhance their overall personality. Moreover, TM sanctioned scholarships to 734 students for higher studies. In order to boost employability, TM organized vocational training (for 1,048 youth) and technical training (for 1,542 youth in mechanic motor vehicles (MMVs), refrigeration and electrical work, etc.). In the realm of entrepreneurship development, TM created 200 entrepreneurs in 2008–09 who were focused on areas such as mid-day meals, garages, honey making, tailoring, garage ownership, etc.

The concern for environment is evidenced from the planting of 30,000 trees in 2008-09, creating 132 ponds to increase irrigational facilities for agricultural development, and constructing 107 biogas plants through alternate sources of energy to reduce CHG (http://www.tatamotors.com).

CSR Initiatives at Dr Reddy's Laboratories Limited

Dr Reddy's Laboratories (DRL) has two projects: CAP (child and police project), and LABS (livelihood advanced business school). Under the CAP project, DRL picks up underprivileged children, who are ragpickers , and are deprived of basic education. They impart teaching in 'bridge schools' which help them to get acclimatized to the academic rigour of customary schools before they are shifted to regular schools to complete their high-school education under company's sponsorship. The idea of involving police is that organizations/groups/vendors which employ such juvenile ragpickers may be reluctant to dispense with their services and are subject to subtle pressure from the police so that they release such childworkers. Once such children complete their high-school education, the company puts them into the LABS project which imparts vocational training such as garment-stitching, automobile-repairing, vending, and so on, so that they can earn their respective livelihoods independently.

Anand Corporate Services Limited

Anand has a longstanding commitment in addressing the needs of the society, and believes that for any economic development to be meaningful, the benefits from the business must trickle down to the society at large. Anand is of the firm view that the corporate goals must be aligned with the larger societal goals. Around 25 years ago, the SNS Foundation, an expression of Anand's CSR, was born. The objective of SNS foundation was comprehensive community development. The foundation has created programmes in the fields of health, education, natural resource management, and life skills training, and ensures that fellow humans could breathe easy.

The long term goal of Anand's CSR is to implement concepts such as zero tolerance zone for child labour, zero waste zone using strategies such as reduce, recycle, and reuse. These practices are extended to Anand residential areas as well.

Aptech Limited

Aptech Limited, a leading education player with a global presence, has played an extensive and sustained role in encouraging and fostering education throughout the country. As a global player with complete solutions-providing capability, Aptech has a long history of participating in community activities. The company has provided computers to schools, facilitated education to the underprivileged, and conducted training and awareness-camps in association with leading NGOs.

Aptech students donated a part of the proceeds from the sale of their art work to NGOs. To propagate education among all sections of the society, especially the underprivileged, Aptech fosters tie-ups with leading NGOs throughout the country. The drive also included Udayan, the Barrackpur-based NGO, a residential school for children of leprosy patients in Barrackpur, established in 1970.

The company strongly believes that education is an integral part of the country's social fabric and works towards supporting basic education and computer literacy amongst the underprivileged children in India.

Summary

Ethics is the study of morally appropriate behaviour and decisions, and examining what should be done. Society should attempt to implant ethics among children during their formative years. In organizations, new recruits may be briefed about the importance of ethics during their induction. Organizational stalwarts need to plan programmes to instill ethics to existing employees through structured courses such as legal compliance course designed by the legal department. Violation of ethics should be pointed out as and when noticed. An organization operates by the people, of the people, and for the people; and functions in a society. It should fulfil some of the needs of the society. Realizing and fulfilling the needs enhance the image of the company. Employees of the organization are people in the society. Identifying and satisfying the societal need are comparable to employee welfare programmes. The workers can identify the needs of the society from their involvement with the masses. Their involvement will enable discharging social responsibilities better. The funds spent in discharging CSR activities is classified as investment. Profits and social responsibilities must be balanced for the benefit of both the organization and the society. Further, CSR initiatives by organizations contribute to the nation.

Key Terms

Code of ethics encompasses ethical system, moral values, and moral judgements established, documented, and communicated to employees of all levels.

Corporate social responsibility refers to the act of balancing profits and social objectives while operating a business.

Ethics is the study of morally appropriate behaviour and decisions, and examines what should be done in a business scenario.

Fraud hotline is a process for reporting concerns about improper, illegal, or any thing that may violate the company image to the person responsible.

Whistle blowing refers to pointing out an ethically unacceptable practice or mistake to a person at the instant when it is committed or when the consequence comes to limelight.

Exercises

Concept Review Questions

1. Why should ethics be defined? Explain whether ethics can be taught. What is more important—ethics or law? Give reasons.
2. Why do companies formulate code of conduct? Discuss the benefits.
3. How should a company attempt to instill ethics in employees? Discuss the means with example.
4. Discuss the main issues in corporate social responsibility? How can companies become sensitive towards the community? Discuss with examples.
5. How should a company identify the CSR issues? How can the CSR issues be tackled by a company?

Critical Thinking Questions

6. What do you mean by ethics in advertising? How should an advertiser evaluate the ethical values in the society?
7. Why should finance be within the purview of ethics? If accounting is an objective science, what is the role of ethics in accounting?
8. 'Corporate values and managerial stress are reciprocally dependent.' Critically discuss the statement citing examples.

Assignments

9. Analyse the family wages of a bank clerk employed in the State Bank of India and verify whether the present wages justify as family wages. Your response should be in the context of ethics and morals.
10. Take help from your professor to get an appointment from three companies including one producing chemicals. Visit the organizations and collect information regarding their drives to instill ethics among employees. In addition, identify their CSR initiatives.

MANAGER'S INSIGHT

Sreechala, a software company, is located in a small town in Maharashtra. As a socially responsible organization, it has adopted a school in a nearby village. The company contributes books and other reading material to the school. However, due to the lack of availability of good teachers, the students of the school have not been able to benefit much.

In order to overcome this problem, the HR circulated a newsletter amongst its employees, trying to convince them to devote some time to the school.

Questions:

1. What are the other ways through which the HR can try to encourage its employees for this noble cause?
2. How well do you think the newsletter will work?

BIBLIOGRAPHY AND WEB RESOURCES

Gupta, Deepa and Mukul Gupta, *The Concept of Welfare State & Corporate Sector's Social Responsibility*, Indian Journal of Training & Development, Indian Society for Training & Development, Vol. XXXX, No. 2, pp. 61–73, New Delhi, 2010.

Jha and Steven Kirn, Restoring Values, *Indian Management*, Vol. 50, Issue 1, January 2011.

Jyoti, P. and D.N. Venkatesh, *Human Resource Management*, Oxford Higher Education, Oxford University Press, New Delhi, 2008.

Mathur, Prashant K. and Anju Das, Ethics of the Knowledge Business, *HRD Newsletter* (Monthly Publication of National HRD Network), Vol. 25, Issue 8, Hyderabad, November 2009.

Sasikar, Nathaniel, *Instilling Ethics Among Employees*, Business Manager, Vol. 13, No. 3, Alwar, Rajasthan, September 2010.

Toffler, Alvin, *The Third Wave*, Pan Books, London, 1980.

Web Resources

http://www.ericsson.com/article/life_at_ericsson_553969845_c, last accessed on 14 October 2010.

www.bkwsu.com/whoweare/headquarters/gyansarovar, last accessed on 19 August 2011.

www.ieindia.org, last accessed on 14 October 2010.

www.infosys.com/sustainability/pages/corporate-social-responsibility.aspx, last accessed on 3 May 2010.

www.nationalhrd.org, last accessed on 14 October 2010.

www.nhpcindia.com/English/Scripts/CSR_Home.aspx, last accessed on 14 October 2010.

www.nhrdn.org, last accessed on 14 October 2010.

ww.pepsicoindia.co.in/purpose/environmental.../replenishing-water.htm, last accessed on 12 January 2011.

www.tatamotors.com/CSR-09/pdf/impact-social-developement.pdf, last accessed on 3 May 2010.

CORPORATE SOCIAL RESPONSIBILITY AT PEPSICO INDIA

PepsiCo was founded in 1965 by the merger of Pepsi Cola and Frito Lays. PepsiCo is a world leader in convenience foods and beverages with a turnover of US $60 billion and has more than 285,000 employees. PepsiCo brands are available in nearly 200 countries.

PepsiCo entered India in 1989 and has grown to become the country's largest selling food and beverage company. PepsiCo has a wide range of products from 'treats to healthy eats', which are nutritious as well as tasty.

PepsiCo India's expansive portfolio includes iconic refreshment beverages including Pepsi and other drinks. PepsiCo's foods division, Frito Lays, is the leader in the branded salty snack market and all its products are free from transfat and monosodium glutamate (MSG), which includes Lay's potato chips, Kurkure, Cheetos, Uncle Chipps, Aliva, and many more salty snacks.

PepsiCo has 36 bottling plants in India and the Frito Lay foods division has three state-of-the-art plants. PepsiCo's business is based on its sustainability vision of making tomorrow better than today. The company is committed to living by this vision every day and this is visible in its contribution to the country, consumers, and farmers.

The company believes that its performance is fundamentally connected to its agenda, which represents the commitment to give back to the society as the company grows. PepsiCo's responsibility is to continually improve all aspects of the world in which they operate—the social and economic environment, thus creating a better tomorrow than today.

It is a continuing journey that articulates PepsiCo India's 'performance with a purpose' initiatives in three major areas of focus—human sustainability (that comes from healthy kids and supporting the community), talent sustainability (through the use of innovative development and retention strategy), and environmental sustainability (ensured by replenishing water, partnerships with farmers, and converting waste to wealth).

Human sustainability

Human sustainability is a key element in PepsiCo's agenda. It refers to nourishing consumers not only with healthy products, but rounding out the equation by promoting active lifestyles.

Nourishing consumers is PepsiCo's fundamental commitment. It begins with product innovation and transformation, extends to marketing, and continues with support for research and development programmes to advance public health around the world.

The various tools and techniques for achieving human sustainability are as follows:

1. *Making healthy and easy choices:* PepsiCo's portfolio reflects its commitment to nourish consumers with a diverse range of fun and healthy products, making healthy eating an easier choice. As PepsiCo grows, the portfolio transformation continues with a systematic plan to reduce added sugar, sodium, and saturated fats in its products. Today, the portfolio includes several healthier treats and some hydrating and nourishing products such as Quaker Oats, Gatorade sports drink, Tropicana juice, Aquafina packaged water, products with reduced sugar or calories such as Diet Pepsi and Pepsi Max. It also comprises food products cooked in rice bran oil to significantly reduce the saturated fat in these brands by 40 per cent, such as Lays, Kurkure, and Cheetos Whoosh.

   Under the same agenda, PepsiCo also has a wide range of initiatives to support human sustainability through community programmes. The basic objective of the community initiative programme of PepsiCo is to act as a socially responsible corporate citizen by working as a partner in developing the community and the nation as a whole. PepsiCo partners with different stakeholders in facilitating its community initiatives programmes. Thus linkages built with the government, panchayat functionaries, NGOs, and community-based organizations (CBOs), involve the community at large and pay special importance to women.
2. *Healthy kids:* As part of its initiative in building 'tomorrow better than today', PepsiCo's 'get active' logo programme is committed to promoting good nutrition and active lifestyles among school kids. 'Get active' has seen robust growth and implementation in schools in partnership with NGOs such as Swashrit and Hriday, and till date has reached more than half a million children across 10 cities.

   'Get active' programmes have the central objective of raising awareness on the importance of balanced nutrition and regular physical activity for a healthy lifestyle among school children.

   Starting with a 'Breakfast makes me smart' module in 2008 that emphasized the importance of healthy breakfast, to the 'My pyramid' module launched in April 2009, 'get active' school programmes have been promoting healthy lifestyles for children by means of helping them learn about nutrition and actively engaging them in the process. 'Get active' believes in combining simplicity with enjoyment. The basic principle is simple and establishes the fundamentals of 'calories in = calories out' which help the children to stay fit and lead a healthy lifestyle. After launching the programme in schools in collaboration with the NGOs and the Indian Medical Association, it received positive response from school children and has yielded great results.
3. *HIV/AIDS:* India embarked on the HIV/AIDS awareness journey in 2005 in collaboration with the International Labour Organization (ILO). With the purpose of spreading awareness, the company has focused on the 'each one teach one' approach. The programme was kicked off by creating a pool of master trainers and peer educators who could cascade the programme across all work locations. Besides this pool, PepsiCo also got four regional NGO representatives trained along with the former's employees to partner in the initial years of the journey. PepsiCo started the programme by spreading awareness about HIV/AIDS awareness amongst its own employees. This was progressively enhanced to cover other stakeholders including spouses of employees, business partners,

distributors, contractual workers, and bottling partners. It further strengthened the impact of PepsiCo's efforts through community outreach programmes conducted by master trainers and peer educators.

Today, PepsiCo has 64 master trainers and 175 peer educators across both businesses and the endeavour is to continue to create more master trainers and peer educators. PepsiCo has been awarded the TERI Corporate Award for outstanding business response to HIV/AIDS in 2009. It also received a certificate of appreciation from ILO in 2009 in recognition of the contribution made in successful implementation of the HIV/AIDS programme in collaboration with ILO.

4. *Women's empowerment:* It must be kept in mind that women are one of the major stakeholders in the betterment of the society and play a major role in its development. Empowerment of women is necessary to empower the nation as a whole. PepsiCo is engaged in awareness generation among women on social development issues as well as on income generation programmes, and facilitating self-help groups (SHGs), establishing market linkage, and skill development training in tailoring, *kantha* stitching, *batik*, embroidery, knitting, etc.
5. *Health:* PepsiCo has stayed committed to the health and wellbeing of children and the community as a whole. The company's health initiatives include general health check-up camps for children as well as women and other citizens. It also conducts eye check-up camps, blood donation camps, and acts as a partner to the government in conducting the intensified pulse polio immunization programme (IPPI), care and support programme for people living with HIV/AIDS, various awareness generation and training programmes with women on health-related issues, etc.

Talent sustainability

PepsiCo's commitment to talent sustainability means continual working to develop and retain exceptional people. This is founded on PepsiCo's belief that cherishing its extraordinary group of people is crucial to building an empowered workforce. PepsiCo pursues diversity and creates an inclusive environment which encourages associates to bring themselves to work. PepsiCo has increased the women and minority representation in the management ranks and has encouraged employees to participate in community service activities and has continued to create rewarding job opportunities for people with different abilities. By valuing its employees, supporting their abilities to work effectively together, and providing them with the tools they need to succeed, it is ensuring that PepsiCo is the kind of company where talented people of all backgrounds would prefer to work.

Environmental sustainability

Environmental sustainability is based on PepsiCo's commitment to be responsible stewards of our planet's resources and delivering its best to the society as a responsible corporate citizen. PepsiCo's responsibility is to continuously improve all aspects of the world in which it operates and aims to create a better tomorrow for future generations.

This initiative is based on PepsiCo's commitment to strive to replenish the resources used wherever possible, and minimize the negative impact on the environment. PepsiCo continues to work to further reduce its water and electricity consumption, and improve its packaging sustainability. Across the world, PepsiCo has reused water from its processing plants, worked with local communities to provide access to clean water, and supported farmers in delivering 'more crop per drop' and generating wealth from waste.

Environmental sustainability is ensured through replenishing water, building partnerships with farmers, and converting waste to wealth.

1. *Replenishing water:* PepsiCo India has pioneered several major initiatives to replenish water in communities. PepsiCo's goal is to conserve and replenish water through community and in-plant water recharge projects and water conservation projects in agriculture. The year 2009 was a year of immense joy and pride for PepsiCo. PepsiCo was able to give back more water than it consumed, by means of various initiatives of recharging, replenishing, and reusing water. This meant that PepsiCo achieved a positive water balance. For example, PepsiCo launched community water projects. PepsiCo's CSR team has pioneered and initiated several sustainable water resources management projects with the dual goals of positively impacting quality and quantity of water supply around PepsiCo's manufacturing plant, and providing clean water access to rural neighbourhood communities.

Approach of PepsiCo

(a) Sustainability and community ownership are at the heart of PepsiCo's approach. It works with the local panchayat or municipality and engages the community in planning and executing the project right from inception. One of the key elements of sustainability is that the local panchayat and community members—strongly represented by women—assume ownership of the maintenance of the projects. Community user groups were trained on the maintenance of the check dams. Awareness sessions were conducted to help the community understand the long-term advantages of check-dams and drip irrigation demonstration projects executed.

(b) The ripple effect caused by improved water availability and the resulting impact on agriculture patterns, income levels, health, and overall standard of living is monitored.

Achievements of PepsiCo

(a) Contribution to positive water balance: Community water projects conserve and recharge water, and thus offset water used in manufacturing process and contribute significantly towards the goal of 'positive water balance'.

(b) In 2009, CSR interventions such as check dams and recharge ponds created a recharge potential of 1,159 million litres towards positive water balance.

(c) The initiatives provided rural communities around its neighbourhood with access to clean water. In 2009, water projects benefited nearly 35,000 community members.

PepsiCo's initiatives

Community check dam project, Paithan, Aurangabad: PepsiCo's check dam project has transformed the lives of 12,000 villagers. The water levels have visibly risen for the first time in several years; old, and dry wells have been filled with water; barren fields have become fertile; and farmers have started earning incremental incomes.

Beneficiaries: The construction of 13 check dams and 100 recharge wells have recharged more than 719 million litres. The project benefits nearly 12,000 community members through improved access to water, additional crops, increase in yield of rain-fed crops, and the opportunity of a second cultivation cycle during the rabi season due to improved availability of water.

Water conservation in agriculture

One of the most effective initiatives is PepsiCo's work with farmers is to reduce water intensity in paddy, and cultivation through a unique method called direct seeding. The agriculture team has become a leading proponent of direct seeding of rice as against transplanting seedlings from nurseries to paddies that are then flooded.

PepsiCo has been experimenting with direct seeding for four years. It has been testing various herbicide combinations to reduce weed growth and developing a tractor-mounted direct seeding machine, adjustable for seed variety, planting depth, and plant-to-plant spacing.

After carrying out initiate trials of direct seeding on its Rand D farms, trials have been conducted in farmers' fields to confirm the results. In 2008, direct seeding was extended to more than 1,000 acres in five states and it saved close to 1 billion liters of water. In addition to saving water, it also reduced costs by ₹1,400/acre for farmers.

2. *Building partnerships with farmers*: PepsiCo India continues to strengthen its partnership with farmers across the country to provide access to the latest varieties and agronomic practices, facilitating insurance and financial assistance to boost their productivity and income. PepsiCo now has a partnership with over 22,000 farmers.

   Apart from these initiatives, PepsiCo also brings farmers and their families into the purview of their CSR initiatives with the objective of ensuring greater inclusion in the company's CSR programmes.

   The company has initiated measures towards the socio-economic development of its farmers, vendors as well as their families. and acts as a facilitator and catalyst and partners with the government, panchayats, and NGOs, CBOs, and other voluntary organizations for the development of farmers and their families.

3. *Converting waste to wealth*: PepsiCo has been strengthening its solid waste management initiatives by partnering with Exnora, an environmental NGO. This award-winning, and income-generating partnership benefits more than 4,50,000 people across seven cities in India. These initiatives include a community waste management proposal that converts waste to wealth by means of community awareness, segregation, and recycling of waste.

   A four-way partnership has been followed and comprises PepsiCo's tie-ups with Exnora, municipality, and the community.

   In this process, it recycles 80 per cent of the household waste. Community members also enjoy benefits of a clean environment and are educated on recycling of waste, and not just relocating it. This initiative provides a clean environment to more than 4,50,000 people across Pammal, Chennai,

Nagapattinam, Tenkasi, Cuddalore, Sangareddy, and Panipat.

Solid waste management initiative by PepsiCo's Kolkata plant is conducted in collaboration with municipalities and includes making vermi composting/ anaerobic manure from the biodegradable nonhazardous wastes consisting of potato wastes and effluent treatment plant (ETP) sludge.

Source:

1. Sanjoy Shaw, General Manager (HR), PepsiCo India (Frito Lays, Kolkata Plant), vide his email dated 21 September 2010, and his seniors, Ayan Das, Rikhia Basu, Devraj Sharma, Vivek Bharati, and Rohini Seth.
2. www.pepsicoindia.co.in/purpose/environmental.../ replenishing-water.htm

Discussion Questions

1. To achieve 'performance with purpose', PepsiCo lays major focus on three areas—human sustainability, talent sustainability, and environmental sustainability. What should be the role of leadership in achieving this?
2. The various tools and techniques of achieving human sustainability are making healthy and easy choices, keeping kids healthy, eradicating HIV/AIDS, empowering women, and maintaining good health. Which of these need an extensive awareness programme? Suggest suitable measures to raise the awareness of the beneficiaries of PepsiCo's drives.
3. Do you feel the means adopted by the company are adequate enough for talent sustainability? Discuss.

HR MANTRA Humpty Dumpty had a great fall

Humpty Dumpty sat on wall, Humpty Dumpty had a great fall
All the king's horses and all the king's men
Could not put Humpty together again

A manufacturing company began its operations in 1982. Over the years, it expanded its operations and gained strength with respect to various business metrics. The reputation of the company grew in leaps and bounds.

Consumers of the company's products were faithful to the products, to the extent of being obsessed. In fact, the company followed the skimming strategy to price its products. Irrespective of the price of the products, the consumers remained faithful to the company's products.

In 2004, the company could not procure the requisite raw materials from the market due to unavailability following government regulations. Hence, it purchased alternative materials from unregistered suppliers and used them to produce the products.

Initially, the consumers did not react strongly. However, over time, with word-of-mouth publicity, consumers stopped buy the company's products. Along with its customers, the company lost several distributors and its position in the market. All its efforts to recoup failed miserably.

The mantra: Unethical practices lead to irrevocable loss.

IMMANUEL KANT

Immanuel Kant (1724–1804) is the central figure in modern philosophy. Kant was born into a modest artisan family. Kant's father was a master harness maker; his mother was the daughter of a harness maker, and she was better educated than most women of her social class. His family was never destitute; however, his father's trade was in decline during Kant's youth and his parents had to rely on extended family for financial support occasionally.

Kant attended college at the University of Königsberg, also known as the Albertina. His early interest in classics was quickly superseded by philosophy. The subject was studied by all first year students and encompassed mathematics, physics, logic, metaphysics, ethics, and natural law. (Metaphysics a branch of philosophy concerned with explaining the fundamental nature of being and the world).

Kant synthesized early modern rationalism and empiricism, set the terms for much of 19th and 20th century philosophy, and continues to exercise a significant influence in metaphysics, epistemology, ethics, and other fields. The fundamental idea of Kant's 'critical philosophy' is human autonomy. Kant argued that human understanding is the source of the general laws of nature that structures all our experience; that human reason gives itself the moral law, and that the moral law is our basis for belief in God, freedom, and immortality. Therefore, scientific knowledge, morality, and religious beliefs are mutually consistent and secure as they all rest on the same foundation of human autonomy. Contextually, Kant attempted to unify the theoretical and practical parts of his philosophical system by emphasizing that human autonomy is the final end of nature according to the teleological worldview of reflecting judgement.

According to Manfred Kuehn, Kant's biographer, his parents probably influenced him much less through their piety (stress on the emotional and personal aspects of religion) than through their artisan values of 'hard work, honesty, cleanliness, and independence,' which they taught him by example.

It is worth mentioning that Kant was an unsalaried lecturer at the Albertina. He was paid directly by the students who attended his lectures. Obviously, he needed to teach more to attract many students in order to earn a living. Kant held this position from 1755 to 1770; during the same period, he would lecture an average of 20 hours per week on logic, metaphysics, ethics, and few other subjects.

Kant stands as a milestone in the history of Western philosophy, with respect to his viewpoint, way of life, thinking, belief, and values. Kant was quite skillful and proficient at discussing many aspects of moral philosophy in the courses that he taught. Kant's writings on ethics should be seen in the context of his larger projects. Thematically, Kant's ethical theory represents the classical formulation of deontological ethics (an approach to ethics that judges the morality of an action based on the action's adherence to a rule or rules). For deontologists, right action consists solely in the conformity of an action to a justified rule or principle. For Kant, this becomes equivalent to the rational and autonomous conformity of one's will to maxims that abide by the Categorical Imperative (Moral Law).

In the book *Foundations for the Metaphysics of Morals* (1785), Kant tried to express how his position provided a philosophical foundation for what is already commonly understood by 'morality' and 'moral action.' He embarked onto the analysis of three concepts: the good will, the notion of duty, and the nature of imperatives.

1. The good will: A good will is the only thing that is 'good without qualification.' Other 'goods,' such as intelligence and health, can be qualified. The good will is good by virtue of the fact that it is 'the will to follow the Moral Law.'
2. The notion of duty: There is a distinction between 'I want' (self-interest) and 'I ought' (ethics). Moral actions are not 'spontaneous' actions. That is, if I see someone in need of help, I may be inclined to 'look the other way' and attend to my own busy day, but I would recognize that I should assist in some way. For example, an elderly woman falls and is bleeding badly... I may be on my way to work, but I recognize that I should at least seek assistance and call the emergency. Kant further elucidated the distinction among duties: duty in mere accordance (conformity) and actions are done 'from a sense of duty'.
3. The nature of imperatives: Imperatives are commands. Among commands, some command hypothetically while some command categorically. A categorical imperative has the general form. For Kant, there is only one imperative that commands us unconditionally and is the Moral Law.

An excerpt from Albuquerque (2010): 'Immanuel Kant, the German philosopher who gave to the world a new metaphysics, the theory of knowledge, and the most comprehensive understanding of moral theory. His advocacy of duty as the principle of moral obligation compares and synthesizes well with the concept of duty in the *Gita*. His clarion call, *sapere aude*, meaning dare to use reason and be wise, is a challenge to moral behaviour. He advocated the idea of world citizenship.'

Today, some organizations are committed to providing a work environment that is free from discrimination, exploitation, or harassment of any kind. For example, companies under the Tata group, Ericsson, Lubrizol Corporation, and many more are keen to develop and maintain ethical standards and code of conduct. However, more than two centuries back, the foundation was laid by Kant.

References

Albuquerque, Daniel, *Business Ethics – Principles and Practices*, Oxford Higher Education, Oxford University Press, New Delhi, 2010.

www.phil.cmu.edu/Cavalier/80130/part1/sect4/Kant.html, last accessed on 7 October 2011.

www.plato.stanford.edu/entries/kant/#MorFre, last accessed on 7 October 2011.

CHAPTER 19

Managing Globalization

LEARNING OBJECTIVES

After studying this chapter, you will be able to

- Understand globalization, its benefits, threats, and premises
- Appreciate the role of global companies
- Appreciate the role of IT in multinational corporations
- Comprehend the utmost need for managing culture

OPENING CASE

Cross-border Failure

ABCL is an Indian engineering company and has been in the business of manufacturing products since 1992. Its products were widely accepted in the Indian market. Due to the steady rise in its volume of sales, ABCL decided to acquire a company abroad that was engaged in manufacturing similar products.

After completion of the deal, ABCL posted functional heads of the Indian unit in the offices of the acquired company abroad. In the Indian offices, each unit head would define the mission of the unit; however, the mission statement was complex and could not be readily understood by employees of all levels. The same style of functioning was followed abroad as well. Gradually, the employees started working in the same manner as those in the Indian unit.

Soon, regular production commenced. Concurrently, the marketing and sales executives started performing their respective tasks. However, they could not reach out to the local people. The functional heads of planning, purchase, and production did not attempt to understand the local culture. The managers did not understand the requirements and were using leadership styles that they were using in the Indian units.

The top management of ABCL was concerned, and looked into the matter. They found that what was deemed to be good quality in one location was not necessarily suitable for other locations. The management recruited talented locals, but soon discovered that mere talent did not suffice to become a good team member. Messages sent to the employees were misinterpreted; publicizing efforts also went astray. On the whole, ABCL could not harvest benefits out of this takeover to the extent it had planned.

Learning points

- The mission statement should be clear to all employees.
- Products should suit the local conditions.
- Cross-cultural issues must be studied and understood.
- Internal and external communications should reach the intended recipients.

INTRODUCTION

Q 1 Globalization has become the buzzword of the business world. Today, we witness unprecedented examples of mass customization at international standards. Barriers in doing business in foreign countries no longer exist, and the obstacles that foreigners while doing business in India have also been removed.

The withdrawal of these barriers has led to the generation of free trade, giving an impetus to globally distributed work (GDW). Today, we can say that the world is borderless and the differences across continents, regions, and countries are melting. Advancement in science and technology has also made the world better linked with the chains of innovation and creativity. This transformation in the business environment is called 'globalization'. Several organizations are now on a globalization spree.

This chapter discusses the various aspects of globalization, themes, benefits, and threats, and ways of managing international businesses.

GLOBALIZATION—A CONCEPTUAL FRAMEWORK

Globalization can be defined as a process of interaction between various companies and the governments of different nations. This interaction is mostly economical in nature. The international trade and investment department drives this process and has a massive impact on the business and other aspects of the society.

Multinational companies (MNCs) are functioning in different nations, facilitating economic integration, and interacting with people of different countries. Thus, MNCs are helping the process of globalization and globalization is also aiding MNCs in their growth stories. Hence, we can observe a reciprocal dependency or facilitation between globalization and functioning of MNCs.

Globalization is also defined as the development of extensive worldwide patterns of economic relationships among nations. Globalization has been successful in aggravating many of the region's most chronic problems, such as the pronounced degree of economic exploitation and social inequality. It is also viewed as a set of processes leading to the integration of economic, cultural, political, and social systems across geographical boundaries. The term combines two aspects of work, namely, internationalization and localization. Internationalization helps the product or the service to work even with culture barriers present, and localization helps in translating the product or the service suitable for a specific environment.

> Information technology, Internet, and aviation industries have demolished geopolitical boundaries, thus making globalization possible.

> Indian companies have started to reach out to international markets. In fact, some prominent leading IT multinationals have been around for the last 20 years.

Society has always felt the need for having a single unified community. Information technology and aviation industries have fulfilled this long-felt need by demolishing the geopolitical boundaries. Covering a wide range of distinct political, economic, and cultural trends, the term 'globalization' has also quickly become one of the most stylish buzzwords of contemporary political and academic debates which are influencing the global business scenario. In popular discourse, globalization is more than 'classical liberal' or 'free market' policies in the world economy. It is restated that with the proliferation of information technologies along with the 'internet revolution', the globalization trend has intensified and has unified the world.

Globalization has also emerged as a key idea for business theory and practice, and found its place in academic debates. Today, globalization is also commonly used to describe the interaction of economic and cultural activities along with

> Living in a global village and an experiential global economy, where there has been globalization of markets, products, and production, and thinking of isolated survival will be suicidal to a company.

the interaction among different departments. As mentioned earlier, the need for this process and dialogue has been felt for centuries.

Different industrial stalwarts are interpreting globalization differently. For example, 'globalization has a special meaning within Procter and Gamble. It means that we will continue to change from a United States-based business into a truly world company. A company that thinks of everything it does in terms of the entire world' (Edwin Artzt, Chairman and CEO, Procter and Gamble, 1990).

Today, we are living in a global village and an experiential global economy. There has been globalization of markets, products, and production. It is not surprising today if an organization has its production department in Spain, warehouse in Korea, accounting division in Bolivia, and the board of directors in Canada. At this juncture, thinking of isolated survival will be suicidal to a company.

Globalization can also be schematically represented. Figure 19.1 clearly depicts the networked locations of a global company—its warehouse, production department, and accounts department, though its customers are spread throughout the globe. It also shows the global players.

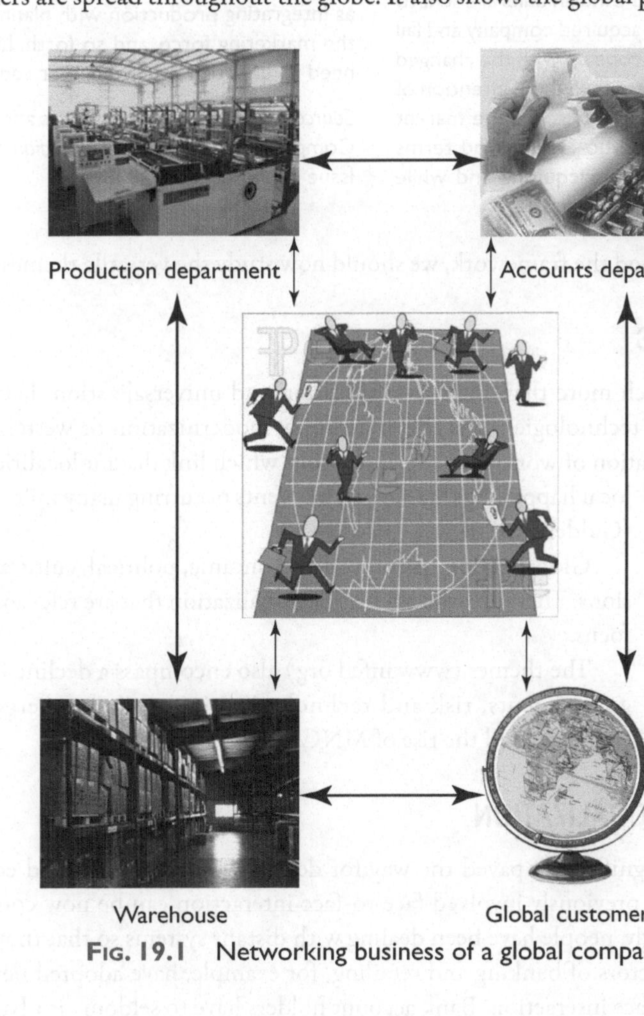

FIG. 19.1 Networking business of a global company

Many companies are trying to go global. However, only a few have been able to be so. Indian companies are in the early stage of globalization. Refer to Exhibit 19.1 for more details.

Exhibit 19.1 Few companies are truly global

The initiatives taken by Indian companies on their path to becoming global are highlighted here.

Many Indian companies are trying to be more global in their outlook. However, they are at an early stage of the development curve. They have only started to reach out to international markets. Of course, some prominent leading IT multinationals have been in the scene for the last 20 years.

When Indian companies are seen to acquire any company in the international markets, usually only two extremes are found—either people from the Indian units are sent to take over the operations of the acquired company and fail miserably as they are unable to cope up with the changed working conditions. In such a case the whole intention of acquiring the market gets defeated because the market is held by only by local people who are in good terms with the local sellers. In fact, after acquiring and while operating in another country, one must understand the local people and the market. On the other extreme, it is found that while making acquisitions, Indian companies make no attempt to drive any synergy.

Indian companies go global not only for market access but also for gaining access to knowledge, and global capital markets. However, they also need to understand the people and identify those who know the local market to procure the best benefits. The fundamental mistake which the Indian companies make while going global is that they take a lot of time to integrate operations such as integrating production with planning, sales force with the marketing force, and so forth. Likewise, brands also need to be integrated, wherever required.

Source: Interview of Jeffrey Watts and Joydeep Dutta, Few Companies are truly Global, *Indian Management*, Vol. 47, Issue 11, November 2008.

Having understood the framework, we should now study the versatile themes of globalization.

GLOBALIZATION THEMES

Globalization is much more than internationalization and universalization. It involves diffusion of ideas, practices, and technologies. It is also not simply modernization or westernization. Globalization is 'the intensification of worldwide social relations which link distant localities in such a way that local happenings are shaped by events occurring many miles away and vice versa' (Giddens 1990).

> Globalization involves the diffusion of ideas, practices, and technologies that are much more than internationalization and universalization

Globalization has powerful economic, political, cultural, and social dimensions. There are four themes of globalization that are relevant and need a sharper focus.

The themes (www.infed.org) also encompass a decline in power of national governments, risk and technological innovation, emergence of knowledge economy, and the rise of MNCs and branding.

GLOBALIZATION VS DELOCALIZATION

Globalization has significantly paved the way for delocalization in social and economic exchanges. Many activities that previously involved face-to-face interaction can be now conducted across great distances. Increasingly, people have been dealing with distant systems so that they may live their lives comfortably. The sectors of banking and retailing, for example, have adopted new technologies that involve less face-to-face interaction. Bank account holders have to seldom visit banks; rather they can withdraw money from automatic teller machines (ATMs).

There are also cases when one buys goods on the Internet and the only person with whom one might interact is the delivery driver. From this example, it is obvious that we have moved beyond simple notions of distance and territory into a new realm or area of borderless communication. Delocalization has been possible only because businesses houses are organized around networks of production, management, and distribution. In this world of dynamism, firms, and more importantly, the people, need to be prepared to respond to the changes around them. This shows the importance of the HR department in every organization.

In the last two decades of the 20th century, a new economy has emerged in the world. This economy is a new brand of capitalism that has three fundamental features—productivity and competitiveness, firms and territories, and core economic activities. Productivity and competitiveness are mostly a function of knowledge generation and information processing. Firms and their core economic activities are global and have the capacity to work as a unit in real time, or chosen time, on a planetary scale. The third feature refers to globalization.

SPEED OF GLOBALIZATION

Technological innovations are taking place at a fast pace. These innovations are accelerating the globalization process. The decline in the power of national governments is a prime aspect of globalization. At the same time, it is also influencing the image of the national economies directly; especially with regard to macroeconomic management. Countries such as Japan and the United States have made their presence felt in countries all over the globe. Hence, governments have to think twice before framing an economic policy in the context of globalization.

Some of the features of globalization are the momentum and power of the change involved. Extraordinary and surprising technological innovations clubbed with worldwide reach have given specific complexions to the ongoing changes. Developments in technology have resulted in newer possibilities. Innovations such as the internet have made it possible to access information and resources across the world, and to coordinate activities in real time.

For countries in the frontline of the world economy, the balance between knowledge and resources has vastly shifted towards only knowledge, which has become the most important factor in determining the standard of living. It is also believed that the importance of knowledge is even more significant than land, than tools, and labour. Most technologically advanced economies are truly knowledge-based.

Economists were looking at labour and capital as central factors of production. However, the rise of the so-called 'knowledge economy' has challenged economists to look beyond labour and capital.

GLOBALIZATION AND RISE OF MNCS

One central aspect of globalization is the growth of MNCs. Such companies now account for over 33 per cent of world output, and 66 per cent of world trade (Gray 1999). Significantly, about a quarter of world trade occurs within MNCs. For example, car manufacturers typically source their components from plants situated in different countries.

Following globalization, multinationals are turning, on a large scale, to transnational companies. However, some international businesses are still largely confined to their home territory in terms of their overall business activities.

Multinational Corporation vs Transnational Corporation

A multinational corporation (MNC) is a business that manages production or offers services in more than one country. MNCs are often termed as multinational enterprise. MNCs are also referred to as international corporations. As defined by the international labour organization (ILO), an MNC is a corporation having its management headquarters in one country, which is its home country, and operates in several other countries, known as host countries. Thus, MNCs are traditional national companies with foreign subsidiaries.

On the contrary, a transnational corporation (TNC) differs from a traditional MNC in some aspects. A TNC does not identify itself with one national home. TNCs are companies having investments in other countries without having coordinated product offerings in those countries. They spread out their operations in many countries and sustain high levels of local responsiveness. Nestlé is an example of a TNC. Nestlé employs senior executives from many countries and attempts to make decisions from a global perspective rather than from one centralized headquarters.

Instability and Division

Globalization has created free global markets. There is significant and diverse impact of MNCs on communities. MNCs initially look at establishing or contracting operations (production, service, and sales) in countries and regions where they could exploit cheap labour and resources. Obviously then, the flow of additional wealth into the communities produces significant inequalities. It can be interpreted that communities where these industries were previously located would suffer from large scale unemployment. One reason for unemployment is that the wages paid in new settings following globalization would be minimal. For example, a 1998 survey of special economic zones in China showed that manufacturers for companies such as Ralph Lauren, Adidas, and Nike were paying as little as 13 cents per hour while the 'living wage' in that area was around 87 cents per hour at that time. In the United States, workers doing similar jobs might expect $10 per hour. It is also worth mentioning that multinationals have often intended to increase sales by trying to create a new set of needs among different target groups. They were constantly seeking out for new markets or under-exploited markets. In fact, multinationals have utilized the child and youth markets to become their profitable and influential sectors.

The growth of multinationals has revolutionized the concept of branding. Companies such as Nike, Levis, Coca Cola, and others are spending huge sums of money in promoting and sustaining their brands (www.infed.org). Multinationals are trying to study the way people understand, or would like to see themselves. Accordingly, they are following diverse strategies to try and establish particular brands. Of course, expanding the market is the fundamental objective of any businessmen.

Contextually, economist Amartya Sen (2002) has argued that 'the market economy does not work by itself in global relations; indeed, it cannot operate alone even within a given country.' He says that in the view of some proponents of globalization, the aim is to expand market relations, push back state and interstate interference, and create a free global market.

According to Prof. Sen, many public policies influence the development of markets, the expansion of economic activities, and the extent to which growing prosperity is experienced by populations as a whole. For example, education, land reforms, and the legal framework are few public policies. Sen argued that 'public action can radically alter the outcome of local and global economic relations'. It has been evidenced that when power of multinationals grows or appears to have grown significantly, neither the multinationals nor individual national governments have control over macro-economic forces.

Multinational Companies and Global Business

Today, MNCs are operating their respective businesses in a global village. Global customers are also seen to be demanding global products. Moreover, customers have become quality-conscious and cost-sensitive. Further, multinational businesses can obviously realize cost advantages in traditional input factors such as labour and raw materials. At this juncture, MNCs endeavour to leverage their investment in knowledge and technology on a global basis.

For example, global pharmaceutical companies operate research and development laboratories in Europe, Asia, and North America. Irrespective of their location, they develop new drugs with the best scientific expertise, and share the data throughout the world. Let us study the case of the Unilever–Accenture deal (Exhibit 19.2).

Exhibit 19.2 Unilever–Accenture deal

Unilever is a leader in the food and personal care brands, with 12 brands that generate more than US$1 billion each in revenues. As a global leader and a fast-growing company, Unilever has faced two mega-trends—managing the multinational workforces within acquired companies in emerging markets, and vicious brand competition. Adjusting rapidly in this environment is essential for survival.

Accenture is a global management consulting, technology services, and outsourcing company. Accenture collaborates with clients to help them become high-performance businesses and governments by combining unparalleled experience, comprehensive capabilities across all industries and business functions, and extensive research on the world's most successful companies.

Accenture signed a seven-year contract with Unilever to provide application outsourcing including applications development, implementation, and support across Europe. The contract was part of Unilever's 'One Unilever' program, which was designed to deliver annual savings of €700 million (US$ 927.633) through the implementation of a unified and streamlined operating model for the company. The contract covered the provision of information technology services to Unilever's operations in 25 European countries. As a part of this programme, the team deployed a unified European IT platform. Accenture expected to deliver the services from six countries—the United Kingdom, Germany, the Netherlands, France, Spain, and Hungary.

Unilever's Chief Information Officer, Neil Cameron, opined that the deal allowed the company to create a simpler and a more agile European IT function to better support Unilever's growth agenda.

Building on this relationship, Unilever also teamed with Accenture HR services to provide a broad range of human resources services—including payroll administration, reward administration, performance management, workforce reporting, and core HR administration—in 100 countries under a seven-year business process outsourcing pact. In addition, HR services are provided to more than 200,000 Unilever employees in more than 20 languages from delivery centers in Bangalore, Manila, Dalian, Bucharest, Prague, and Curitiba. Unilever's global HR staff (approximately 3300 employees)are expected to be a part of this transformation process. It is expected that less than half of the staff will be affected by the transition of roles and services to Accenture.

Unilever Senior Vice President, Reg Bull, opined that Unilever's selection of Accenture's HR Services hinged on meeting the operational people and possessed the depth to deliver, rather than just a wild set of aspirations.

(Contd)

Exhibit 19.2 (Contd)

Leading companies know that human and organizational performance are the key determinants of high performance—more organizations are using outsourcing to help them gain business advantage from their HR functions.This seemed to be a strategy adopted by Unilever.

The outsourcing agreement of the HR deptartment extends an existing relationship between the two companies under which Accenture has been providing business consulting and IT services to Unilever for more than 10 years.

Source: accenture.com/us-en/Pages/success-unilever-application-hr-outsourcing-summary.aspx

Information technology has played a vital role in globalization. In fact, the contribution of information technology has become an inevitable aspect of the globalization process.

The entire world has witnessed the recent economic turmoil in Asia and Latin America. Regardless of the turmoil, there has been a sharp increase in global business activities. This is one of the most significant business trends during the 1990s. Moreover, there is no sign that this growth will abate. Following the tremendous advancement in science, we are also observing the explosive growth of the Internet and the world wide web. This growth has paved ways to modern and state-of-the-art technologies that are inherently global in character. These trends create unprecedented challenges, as well as opportunities for MNCs.

In order to respond to the changes on account of globalization, information managers of MNCs need to be fully conversant with important issues related to the international aspects of document technologies and business recordkeeping. The HR needs to plan training sessions for employees to get fully acquainted with these technologies.

We will now discuss the benefits of globalization.

BENEFITS OF GLOBALIZATION

Q 4 Globalization results in economic progress and poverty alleviation.

Economic Progress

Globalization is an integral part of the recent economic progress made by India. In fact, it plays a major role in the export-led growth. In India, one of the major forces of globalization has been evident in the growth of outsourced information technology and business process outsourcing (BPO) services.

In order to understand the process better, consider the banks located at USA, UK, Canada, and other countries. The customers (account holders) are also present in those countries. When customers raise a query, they receive the responses from 'call centers' in India. Competent and skilled professionals employed by both local and foreign companies extend their service to customers in the USA, Canada, and Europe in particular.

In India, the last few years have seen an increase in the number of skilled professionals employed by both local and foreign companies to service customers in the US and Europe. Companies are taking advantage of India's low cost of labour and its educated and English-speaking work force. They are utilizing global communications technologies such as voice-over Internet protocol (VOIP), the email, and the Internet. Foreign companies have outsourced and the international enterprises have been able to lower their cost base by establishing outsourced knowledge-worker operations in India.

Poverty Alleviation

Through the use of IT, BPO industries have brought a new consumer base into India. International companies are also expanding their operations in India to serve this massive growth opportunity.

Notable examples of international companies that have done well in India in the recent years include Pepsi (www.pepsicoindia.co.in), Coca Cola (www.coca-colaindia.com), McDonald's (www.mcdonaldsindia.com), and Kentucky Fried Chicken (www.kfc.co.in), whose products have been well accepted by Indians at large.

Many foreign companies are seen to be venturing in the Indian markets as globalization has been advantageous for them. By simply increasing their base of operations, expanding their workforce with minimal investments, and providing services to a broad range of consumers, large companies entering the Indian market have explored many profitable opportunities. Indian companies are rapidly gaining confidence and are now major players in globalization through international expansion.

The effects of globalization are pervasive and tend to assume all-encompassing forms. The effects are visible in industries such as steel, automobiles, information technology, and so forth. Even Bollywood is no exception.

Indian companies and industries are setting themselves up as powerhouses of tomorrow's global economy. Globalization initiatives are accompanied with common hurdles such as problems arising out of cross-cultural diversity. With so many companies setting up in India, the rate of employment is definitely set to go up, thus alleviating poverty.

CROSS-CULTURAL DIVERSITY

Corporate culture is defined as the act of developing intellectual and moral faculties, especially through education in any organization. Culture is also the moral, social, and behavioural norms of an organization based on the beliefs, attitudes, and priorities of its employees. The difference in culture among different groups comes under the purview of cross-cultural diversity. Cultural diversity deals with cultural differences within the nation. The way in which things are done in one culture may not hold good for another. Further, the same activity performed in two cultures may convey different meanings and generate different results. Obviously, managing people across different cultures forms a part of cross-cultural management.

To effectively manage an organization, cross-cultural issues must be understood, interpreted, and managed effectively to harvest benefits. A good example is that of Hewlett Packard's (HP) operations. HP proclaims and demands that cultural diversity gives it competitive advantages and strengths. Due to diversity, HP gets the best creative solutions and is able to be more innovative with divergent ideas from people across cultures. Wherever HP operates, it absorbs the local culture prevailing in that country. HP relooks and reinvents the best suitable management practices.

Globalization gives a unique opportunity of operating in different countries, with employees of diverse cultures in a particular unit, and so forth. Cultural diversity should never be viewed as a menace. Analytical thinking helps to convert the threat into an opportunity. The prime necessity in a global company, at any stage of globalization, is managing the culture.

MANAGING CULTURE IN A GLOBAL COMPANY

Culture is a set of values, beliefs, languages, and norms that guide human behaviour in a country. Culture is a learned behaviour that develops as individuals grow from childhood to adulthood

(Mondy 2009). In India, religions and religious beliefs are additional determinants of culture. Asian cultural norms promote loyalty and teamwork among citizens working in corporates or organizations. Hence, it becomes very important for a manager to understand the cultural differences present in the organization. Understanding and recognizing the cultural differences present in the workplace gives adequate leverage to maximize managerial effectiveness.

The characteristics of a company's culture differ from one country to another. Some common characteristics of company cultures are enumerated here. These characteristics must be identified with particular companies:

1. Clarity of the mission statement
2. Employee engagement and commitment
3. Freedom to use discretion
4. Extent of empowerment
5. Integrity and cohesion among employees in the workplace
6. Interpersonal trust and relationships
7. Effective leadership styles
8. Structured and documented systems and processes
9. Performance-based compensation, reward, and incentive system
10. Customer orientation
11. Internal and external communications
12. Commitment to learning and skill development
13. Laying emphasis on recruiting and retaining outstanding employees
14. High degree of adaptability to changes
15. Defining accountability standards
16. Encouraging and demonstrating support for innovation

Having identified the set of characteristics of the company, there is a need to transform and align them to achieve the business goals of the company that are so far unachieved. For this purpose, certain actions are essential.

1. Develop a specific action plan to leverage whatever is good.
2. Identify the wrong actions and find remedial initiatives.
3. Conduct brainstorming sessions (preferably systematic and not random) to review shortcomings in different policies and regular practices.
4. Develop a model representing all the actions and behaviour, showing their interdependencies.
5. Communicate the new culture to the employees in a language they understand easily.
6. Communicate the new culture objectively and elaborate on the step-by-step actions required by each individual.

> Overcoming geopolitical issues and maintaining common corporate culture should be the chief concern for global executives.

Sometimes, geopolitical issues also emerge as hindering factors in globalization initiatives. Thus, overcoming geopolitical issues, and maintaining a common corporate culture should be the chief concern for global executives.

HR practices may not run smoothly in several countries. For example, the multi-source (360-degree) feedback and assessment system is a long-felt need in organizations. However, in any Thai company, the implementation of 360-degree feedback system may be extremely difficult due to the differing cultures and beliefs of subordinates and managers. Thai managers do not think that their subordinates are in any way eligible to evaluate them; this is the prevailing attitude of Thai managers. On the other hand, Thai workers do not see it as their business to evaluate their bosses. Hence, the system that is welcome in many organizations in different countries has restricted applications on the grounds of cultures and beliefs.

The organizational climate is also characterized by a separation between seniors and juniors. Contextually, Mondy (2009) quotes the views of Arab businesspeople regarding their perception of Westerners. In view of the Arab businesspeople, Westerners act as superiors, as if they know the answer to everything and are not willing to share credit for joint efforts. They seem to be unable to or are not willing to respect or adjust to local customs and culture, and prefer solutions based on their home culture rather than meeting local needs. They resist working through administrative and legal channels and procedures, and manage in an autocratic and intimidating manner. Obviously, this way of working prohibits the willing participation of juniors.

Culture Management Elements

A company striving to manage culture needs to pay attention to four dimensions: structural elements, processes, strategy, and tactics to be employed (Pareek 2008). Culture change must be built into the system such that the new culture becomes a part of the organization. This necessitates paying attention concurrently to the processes underlying the structural elements and plan of action (strategy). Both the processes and strategies must be broad and clearly thought out. The strategy must be split into specific action steps, known as tactics. The four-fold S-P-S-T model emphasized and proposed by Pareek (2008) helps to smoothen out the process of culture management. The model is displayed in Table 19.1.

Table 19.1 Four-fold S-P-S-T Model

Structural elements	Processes	Strategy	Tactics
1. Stable structure 2. Temporary system 3. Linkage bondage mechanisms 4. Information system 5. Rewards 6. Regular budget 7. Guidelines	1. Incremental planning 2. Action research approach 3. Modelling 4. Process awareness and orientation 5. Counselling 6. Organizational norms	1. Anchoring in and using strength 2. Sensitivity to stone walls 3. Competency building 4. Critical concentration 5. Developing key institutions 6. Sanction and support 7. System ownership	1. Prepare in advance 2. One step at a time 3. Prepare for the journey (resources) 4. Go together 5. Stop and review progress 6. Keep up the spirit (reinforcement) 7. Keep going (perseverance)

Intercultural Transitions

Intercultural transitions are the need of the day for global organizations. Highly effective corporate cultures have three people-related key traits.

Vision, mission, and values among employees Enterprise needs to percolate the vision and mission to all the employees. The management must take adequate care to ensure that the vision and mission statements are unambiguous.

Understanding interdependent roles While striving to achieve business goals that lead to achieving corporate vision, employees need to work individually as well as in teams. Enterprises need to promote interpersonal understanding, keeping cultural differences aside. A strong urge to achieve team goals is likely to eliminate or reduce the diversity arising from cultural differences.

Aligning employee attitudes Enterprises have to initiate to establish strong alignment of employee attitudes and strategic goals and objectives.

On identifying the key factors, the leaders can begin to alter them to manage the company's culture as part of the ongoing culture and management purposes. Ongoing development of employees by way of education is the foundation of culture management. Education transforms the thinking process and facilitates to work in unison, thus ensuring harmony.

Considering the extreme importance, the Interchange institute, a non-profit research organization, conducts research on the process of intercultural transition, produces publications to assist newcomers to the US, designs and delivers specialized cross-cultural training workshops, and trains and consults professionals in the field. Brands such as Coca Cola, Nike, Sony, and a host of others have become part of the fabric of vast numbers of people's lives.

THREATS OF GLOBALIZATION

With regard to the consequence of globalization for India, it is seen that globalization is based on a western world view, which has been universalistic and positive, generalized and total in all aspects (Pareek 2008). Any venture, in spite of having opportunities, is accompanied by a few threats as well and globalization is not an exception.

Globalization has opened up opportunities for products, services, and people to different parts of the world. It has been promoted by primarily western and mainly US-based MNCs. Globalization has also created problems for developing countries. Due to advancement in science and technology, developed countries can afford new generation technologies and are now producing goods and services at comparatively lesser costs. The same products are manufactured by local cottage, small, and medium-scale industries. These industries contribute a major portion of India's GDP and are going out of business, resulting in multiplying unemployment.

With the emergence of global village or the unipolar world under the domination of Western capitalism, the cultural impact of market and trade relations has further intensified. Of course, culturally, globalization involves some homogenization that basically means Americanization (Pareek 2008). The developing world believes that gains from globalization are going to be negligible.

Globalization is a step towards standardization. In India, we enjoy different varieties of tastes in different states. For example, we eat the *idli-dosa* of South India, and also the *chhole-bhature* of North India. In the name of hygiene, globalization may standardize the cooking process on a large scale, leading to similar tastes of *idli-dosa* at Delhi and *chhole-bhature* in Chennai!

Let us now analyse the competencies required and considerations needed in executing globalization projects.

DEFINING COMPETENCIES: THE P-A-C-T MODEL

Q 5 We have studied various aspects of globalization such as including benefits, culture management, threats, and so on. Globalization needs a variety of competencies and considerations to make the attempt successful. Jain and Mehta (2010) proposed the P-A-C-T model which described the various competencies required to fulfil work norms and criteria across borders. To work in and for the global teams, we need to consider certain aspects of the psychological, analytical, communication, and technological facets of work. The acronym P-A-C-T has been derived from the four aspects of globalization—pillars of difference, wheeling the globe, power scenario, and outcomes. The model is explained through a tabular presentation. Refer to Figure 19.2.

<table>
<tr><td>P</td><td>1. People
2. Policies
3. Procedures
4. Political ideologies</td><td rowspan="4">1. Trust
2. Values
3. Control
4. Communication
5. Understanding
6. Cooperation
7. Collaboration
8. Leadership
9. Negotiation
10. Human rights
11. Exchange</td><td rowspan="4">1. Power of the global
2. Power of the local
3. Individual power</td><td>Transformation</td><td>T</td></tr>
<tr><td>A</td><td>1. Attitude
2. Assertion
3. Aggression
4. Analysis</td><td>Through
1. Cooperation
2. Competition</td><td>C</td></tr>
<tr><td>C</td><td>1. Communication
2. Culture
3. Collaboration
4. Characteristics</td><td>For Ascending</td><td>A</td></tr>
<tr><td>T</td><td>1. Technology
2. Talent
3. Time
4. Traits</td><td>Progress rates</td><td>P</td></tr>
<tr><td></td><td>Pillars of difference</td><td>Wheeling the globe</td><td>Power scenario</td><td colspan="2">Outcomes</td></tr>
</table>

Fig. 19.2 P-A-C-T model

The model brings out the elements of each pillar. The model depicts that the human actions are essential for wheeling the globe. Nothing can move or can be created without power (individual power being the prime source). The model also helps in portraying the outcomes. The outcome encompasses transformation through cooperation and competition for ascending the progress rate.

The model proposed by Jain and Mehta (2010) is just a glimpse of the whole requirement which suggests that if all the key words of P-A-C-T are considered intelligently, the outcome will be targeted and we will be fair enough at transforming competitions to cooperation for 'ascending progress and profits at a global level.' Multiple aspects such as psychology, economics, technology, and social factors are also very sensitive issues and depict the real pillars of difference when it comes to border function.

Let us now have a cursory view of human resource management practices in international companies.

HRM IN INTERNATIONAL COMPANIES

> India has unique features of culture, employment law, and regulation of the labour market. The global economy is enormously diverse.

HRM has diverse facets. Different types of human resource management practices are needed in different companies. HRM practices depend on the nature of business (producing goods or offering services), type of company (general or knowledge industry), management styles (task orientated or relation oriented), leadership (autocratic, supportive, situational, etc.), geographic location (region, country), class of the country (underdeveloped, developing, developed), and other organizational structures.

The cultural background, as an approach for managing people, is evidenced in North American organizations. Hofstede (1980) says that in North America, the work culture is individualistic and more achievement-oriented than other countries, and this is reflected in the employment practices and employee relations legislation. The European Union is unique in having its members committed to an international level of legislation which affects the employer-employee relationship (Henderson 2009). India, on the other hand, has unique features of culture, employment law, and regulation of the labour market and requires an all together different style of HRM to be followed.

The global economy is enormously diverse. Companies need to adopt specific HRM practices considering various influencing factors. Henderson (2009) has quoted the definition of international HRM as, 'the process of employing and developing people in international organization which operate... globally.'

A company going global needs to lay emphasis on various approaches to HRM, ways of managing culture, preference for certain leadership behaviour, selection process of expatriates, etc. (Henderson 2009). Considering these in advance not only helps the organization to attain its goal but also move smoothly towards it. Some pointers to be kept in mind are as follows:

Approaches An ethnocentric, polycentric, region-centric, geocentric approach, or a combination of all these, should be followed, on careful consideration of the need.

Culture The culture of a nation gets a distinctive profile based on four basic distinctive dimensions—power distance, uncertainty avoidance, individualism/collectivism, and masculinity/femininity.

Leadership behaviour The preference for certain leadership models (benevolent autocratic, autocratic, consultative, participative, etc.) is reflected within organizations. Cultures influence the preference of leadership.

Selection process of expatriates In managing international businesses, management of expatriate employees emerge to be very challenging. The failure rate of expatriate assignments is high. Henderson (2009) quotes that multinationals of UK experience lower failure rate than the multinational of US. UK managers tend to have more international outlook than the US managers.

SUMMARY

As a result of globalization, the world is becoming borderless, and the differences across the continents, regions, and countries are melting. Globalization has become the fruit of advancements in science and technology.

Globalization yields benefits such as generation of economic progress and poverty alleviation. Managing cross-cultural diversity is required in global companies. Structural elements, processes, strategies, and tactics are the culture-management elements which must be taken care of. Intercultural transitions are the need of any global organization. Globalization is often accompanied by threats. It needs a variety of competencies and considerations as well. A company going global needs to lay emphasis on managing culture, preference for certain leadership behaviour, and selection process of expatriates along with other initiatives.

KEY TERMS

Cross-cultural diversity refers to the multiplicity of beliefs, attitudes, and priorities of employees of an organization; managing the diversity is essential to effectively manage an organization

Delocalization means performing activities remaining across great distances in place of conventional face-to-face interaction

Globalization refers to the transformation in business environment when the world becoming borderless; melting of differences across the continents, regions, and countries

Intercultural transitions means the smoothing out of individual differences arising out of cultural differences considering people-related key traits

Internationalization is enabling the product to be used without language or culture barriers

Localization is translating and enabling a product for a specific environment or conditions.

EXERCISES

Concept Review Questions

1. Define globalization. Write an essay on the present global business environment.
2. Discuss the various themes of globalization in detail.
3. What is meant by cross-cultural diversity in a global company? Discuss the various ways and means of managing culture.
4. Discuss the benefits and threats of globalization citing examples.
5. Clearly bring out the essence of P-A-C-T model in the context of globalization.

Critical Thinking Questions

6. In the last decade, there were a few Indian companies that had gone global. Why do Indian companies prefer to go global? Discuss critically.
7. How can an Indian company perform better and survive longer abroad? Anlayse the steps logically.

Assignments

8. With the help of your professor, identify a company that attempted to become global about ten years ago. Visit the company and try to collect, (a) the steps the company followed, (b) the hurdles faced, and (c) tools used to overcome the hurdles. Produce your notes/records to your professor.
9. In the same company or elsewhere, inquire about the threats encountered and benefits gained by the company.

MANAGER'S INSIGHT

TNN International is a global manufacturer and supplier of air conditioning systems, headquartered in Canada. Due to the predicted expansion in the overseas markets, it has realized the need for appointing a sales manager to manage the sales of the same in the southeast Asian countries. The person would report to the managing director of eastern region.

The position has been advertised internally. The company wants to recruit from within its existing employees because it believes that training would be cheaper and faster in such a case. However, very few applications were received. There have also been talks about some of these applicants having some reservations about working under a boss of a different origin. To overcome this problem, they even hiked up the compensation package to almost double to what was originally planned.

Questions:

What is the role of the HR department in such a case? What strategy must be applied to find a suitable candidate for the post?

BIBLIOGRAPHY AND WEB RESOURCES

Castells, M., *Information Technology and Global Capitalism* in W. Hutton and A. Giddens (Eds), *On The Edge:. Living with Global Capitalism,* London: Vintage, 2001.

Henderson, Lain, *Human Resource Management,* University Press, Hyderabad, 2009.

Hofstede, G., *Culture's Consequence,* Sage, London, 1980.

Interview of Jeffrey Watts and Joydeep Dutta, Few Companies are Truly Global, *Indian Management,* Vol. 47, Issue 11, November 2008.

Jain, Samta and Namrata Mehta, The Global Corporation and Societies in Global Competition: The Challenge of Globally Distributed Work, *HRD Newsletter* (National HRD Network), pp. 45–48, September 2010.

Mondy, Wayne R., *Human Resource Management,* Dorling Kindersley India Pvt. Ltd, Pearson Education, New Delhi, 2009.

Pareek, Udai, *Understanding Organizational Behaviour,* Oxford Higher Education, Oxford University Press, New Delhi, 2008.

Web Resources

web accounting.smartpros.com/x36880.xml, last accessed on 16 April 2011.

www.economywatch.com/economy-articles/globalization-in-india.html, last accessed on 18 October 2010.

www.economywatch.com/economy-articles/globalization-in-india.html, last accessed on 18 October 2010.

www. erricson.com, last accessed on 18 October 2010.

www.infed.org/biblio/globalization.htm, last accessed on 14 November 2010.

www.interchangeinstitute.org/html/cross_cultural.htm, last accessed on 16 April 2011.

www.newsroom.accenture.com/article_display.cfm?article_id=4493, last accessed on 18 October 2010.

www.prospect.org/print/V13/1/sen-a.html, 2002, last accessed on 18 October 2010.

GLOBALIZATION INITIATIVES BY ERICSSON

About the company

Ericsson was started in 1876 by Lars Magnus Ericsson. It has grown in multiple directions over the years. Ericsson contributed to making Stockholm the world's most telephone-dense city. However, his foresight has led the company to position itself at the forefront of the industry since the dawn of telecommunications. The company had firmly believed that communication is a basic human need. Ericsson is the only company in the world offering systems for all major mobile communication standards and actively promoting standardization and open systems. It is worth knowing that 40 per cent of the world's mobile calls pass through Ericsson's networks, and that Ericsson has 27,000 patents. Ericsson provides communication networks, telecom services, and multimedia solutions to operators and service providers all over the world. Mobile and fixed networks, multimedia solutions, and telecom services of the company make a real difference to people's lives and the world we live in, and are an essential part of a sustainable society. Ericsson believes that once a social change begins, it cannot be reversed. Sometimes the industry is limited, not by the abilities, but by the vision. Today, Ericsson does not see all the opportunities available in telecom industry. The company envisages that the vast possibilities of a great future will only become a reality if it makes the people responsible for that future.

Ericsson and its people

Ericsson empowers people, business, and society by means of its innovative practices. The company encourages all unique employees to develop and build their lives and careers within the global organization. The core values of the company are: respect, professionalism, and perseverance. The values are reflected not only in the workplace but also in the business the company does with the customers and while dealing with society. The human resource philosophy believes in treating every individual equally and with fairness. The report of the annual employee survey shows that 90 per cent of the employees feel the core values of the company are relevant to them. This attitude significantly contributes to the company's culture. It is also supported by the managers, who make sure the core values are part of everyone's work every day.

Globalization initiatives

The company has been in conducting its operations across 175 countries and had 23 market units. All the units were not performing at the same pace. Some of the market units were weak, while others were strong. Various steps were taken to increase organizational effectiveness at a global level.

1. Considering the heterogeneity of their functioning and differential capabilities, the company reduced the numbers of market units to 10 to enable close monitoring of the units. Each unit is headed by a business head. So, the first step was organizational restructuring.
2. Ericsson has defined its HR policy. The policy needs to be followed by all units of the company. In India, the compliance with the policy was automated

through SAP in 2008. The same software was installed in other countries. The principal aim was to uniform the policies of the company. So, the second step was standardization of practices.

3. Since its inception, the international head office of Ericsson is located at Stockholm, Sweden. Decisions were being taken by strategic apex of the company, who were mainly Swedish. The company apprehended this as a hindrance in the globalization venture, and decided to introduce diversity in the leadership team by appointing people from other countries at top management positions. Another intention behind this decision was to promote multicultural views in the board meeting and convey to the world, in true sense, that Ericsson is a global organization. For example, Ericsson has recently appointed an Indian by birth as its global HR head. The opening up of organizational culture and the allowing of non-Swedish people in decision making process was a unique venture of the company. So, the third step initiated by the company was policy redefining.
4. Ericsson looks for speed and perfection to serve world-wide customers better. Ericsson was taking software supports from other vendors. To some extent, this was a barrier in its march ahead. As a counteractive measure, the company formed Ericsson global services to design its software requirements. This initiative not only ensured the desired speed in achieving its business objectives, but also, has been beneficial from a financial standpoint. So, the fourth step initiated by the company was, integration.

The timely intervention measures helped Ericsson grow faster and be more effective as well. With these multifarious initiatives in good management practices, Ericsson has gained distinguished competence, derived competitive advantages, and has been able to render excellent services to the mankind.

Discussion Questions

1. Identify the factors responsible behind the aforementioned initiatives by Ericsson.
2. In what ways do you think Ericsson proactively took initiatives to achieve greater success globally?
3. Study a similar move by an Indian multinational organization and analyse its initiatives. Comment on the success/failure of the initiatives.

Source: www.ericsson.com

HR MANTRA Frog in the well

A frog was born in a well. He grew up inside the well and had not seen the world outside. He was in awe of the size of the well and believed that it was the biggest home one could have! One day, a frog born in the sea, was thrown ashore by high tides and wandered into the well. The frog residing in the well welcomed the second frog. They got talking, and the first frog asked complacently, 'Is your home as big as mine?'

The second frog, amused by the first frog's question, tried to describe the sea, but the latter would not believe him. Nothing the second frog said could convince the first frog about the vastness of the sea! Sighing, the second frog gave up and said with a resigned shrug, 'This well is certainly big enough'!

The mantra: Understand your environment and the world outside.

BINA CHAURASIA

Born in 1962 in Kolkata, India, Bina Chaurasia holds a master's degree in management and human resources from the Ohio State University and a masters degree in philosophy from the University of Wisconsin. She gained rich experience in the various facets of human resources after working in many companies.

Prior to joining Ericsson, Chaurasia served in Hewlett Packard for three years where she was the vice president of global talent management, learning and development, executive development, diversity, and staffing. Chaurasia also held senior HR leadership roles at Gap where she was responsible for driving HR strategy for the company and leading international and corporate HR, worldwide supply chain, and the outlet and online divisions. Chaurasia worked in Sun Microsystems and PepsiCo/Yum. She has a varied experience across different industries, including IT and retail.

Chaurasia assumed the position of senior vice president and was appointed head of human resources and organization at Ericsson on 15 November 2010.

'With presence in 175 countries, Ericsson is a truly global company working in an exciting industry, which impacts billions of people,' said Chaurasia. 'I am looking forward to joining the company.'

Hans Vestberg, president and CEO at Ericsson, 'We are a knowledge-based company with people being our core assets. To maintain our leading position, we have to attract, develop and retain the talent, and Bina's experience will be crucial in this effort.'

Reference

www.ericsson.com/news/1446270, last accessed on 25 September 2011.

CHAPTER 20

Technology and HRM

LEARNING OBJECTIVES

After studying this chapter, you will be able to

- Understand the real meaning of technology
- Appreciate the need for procuring intellectual capital
- Recognize the skill mix required for technology management
- Value the role of HRM in implementing total quality management

OPENING CASE

Managing Technology Upgradation

Magna Engineering Works (MEW) came into existence in 1988 and is engaged in the business of manufacturing aerospace components. Since its inception, it has steadily developed and has gained the confidence of customers for delivering products of good quality. The company has also been maintaining its documents and records systematically. Five years ago, MEW began exporting its products.

The chief executive officer of the company is dynamic and believes in continuous development. He expects performance of a high order at every level, especially at the managerial and senior supervisory levels. MEW recruits people of high calibre through open advertisements to meet the personnel requirements at all levels, specifically at higher levels. However, it fills up the junior level vacancies by recruiting local people and providing extensive in-house training.

MEW employs an HR manager who looks after the management and development of employees of all levels. Presently, he is keen to design training programmes for all the existing employees and new recruits. MEW has structured a system of identifying their training needs.

Recently, MEW purchased a 3D coordinating and measuring machine for inspection of aerospace and other critical components. The machine is sophisticated and the reports are computer-generated. MEW also purchased a few computer numerical control (CNC) machines and replaced the conventional machines to enhance productivity. The supplier and manufacturer of the CNC machines also conducted customized training for the production personnel. Training was also conducted for persons of the research and development (R&D) department to enable them to design technically feasible and economically viable components and spare parts.

The unions were not in favour of replacing conventional machines with new generation machines. The union leaders also projected the need for wage and bonus protection, which was ignored by the management.

Despite resistance, CNC machines were commissioned and regular production commenced. The manufactured components were submitted to the quality

control department for inspection. Customers of aerospace components wanted a self-surveillance certificate along with computer-generated inspection reports. However, neither the operator nor his supervisor knew how to print reports using the CNC machines. Ultimately, the supplier of the machines was contacted and the company requested him to send his engineer. This caused unnecessary delay in delivery.

Learning points

- Management should not disregard any wage-related issue.
- People need extended skills while working on new generation machines.
- Organizations must groom their people to undertake new tasks.
- Organizations should be instrumental in enhancing employee confidence.

INTRODUCTION

The world has crossed the stone age and the iron age. Many centuries have elapsed and we now live in a civilized world. The world is changing at a faster pace as a result of the contribution of science and technology. In addition, intellectual capital is getting increasingly recognized.

These technological changes seem to be impacting the economies of all countries substantially. Organizations are switching over from conventional machining system to new generation CNC machines, flexible manufacturing systems, and fully automated plants. They are implementing quality management and using quality management tools, total productive maintenance, just-in-time concept, supply chain management, enterprise resource planning, and so forth. All these are boons of advancements in science and technology. Consequently, customers are becoming quality conscious and cost sensitive, and look for products and services of improved quality at competitive prices. To keep updated with all the technological changes happenings around the world and in order to meet the customer demands, there is a need to change one's mindset towards accepting new and advanced technology.

TECHNOLOGY

A century ago, in manufacturing industries, operators worked using general engineering methods such as hand tools, based on their experience and skills. There is now a sea change in technology management across industries. A distinct shift has taken place from 'person dependence' to 'system dependence' and 'technology dependence'. The market has also shifted from 'sellers market' to 'buyers market'. Consequent to technology development, product quality has improved as well. As customers have become quality conscious and cost sensitive, companies need to cope with customer's requirements. Quality is not 'what manufacturer can produce'; quality is 'what customers want.' Thus, technology and quality are intertwined.

Now, let us study the present status of technology. Technology refers to the application of knowledge that leads to production and marketing of goods and services. Technology develops business by providing technical knowledge for the goods and services that a firm produces. Advanced technology facilitates faster production of defect-free output.

> Technology refers to application of knowledge that leads to production and marketing of goods and services.

Contextually, technological innovation implies creating new technology, developing new products and services, and opening new opportunities to launch innovative products and services.

TECHNOLOGY TODAY

Q 1 Videoconferencing facility and Internet are the two prime gifts of technology that have made global communication faster and more effective. A massive amount of information and ideas are constantly moving from one part of the globe to the other. The challenge for managers is to make the best use of what technology offers. They need to select the appropriate technology that is likely to add value to their organization. In the years to come, they will even need to figure out ways to make technology a viable and productive part of the work setting. Managers will have to think ahead when delivering information about business results.

Managers must have the adequate appetite to gather ideas and not restrict themselves to merely accumulating data. To make the best use of technology, management would need to identify intellectual capital in the organization. It is needless to recapitulate that in the mid 20th century, human beings had achieved a mastery of technology that would be sufficient to leave the atmosphere against the force of gravity of the Earth for the first time and explore the outer space.

Intellectual Capital

Let us recall the maxim, 'knowledge is power'. In today's competitive world, knowledge has become a direct competitive advantage for companies selling ideas and building relationships. In fact, knowledge seems to indirectly give a competitive advantage to all industries. In the era of technological explosion, successful companies are the ones that are the most adept or skillful at attracting, developing, and retaining talents capable to drive a global organization that is responsive to widespread customers and mushrooming opportunities of technology. The challenge to the HR manager is to find, assimilate, develop, compensate, and retain capable talents in the organization.

> The challenge to the HR manager is to find, assimilate, develop, compensate, and retain capable talents in the organization.

Intellectual capital is unparallelled and incomparable with other types of capital.

TECHNOLOGICAL CHANGES

Technological change is broadly defined as the process by which economies change over time with respect to the manufacture of the products and services and the processes used to produce them. The nature of technological changes may comprise incremental innovation, radical innovation, new technological systems, and technological revolutions.

Incremental innovation This refers to small and marginal improvements brought about by individual units through *kaizen* (small group) activities. Incremental innovation needs very less or negligible costs. Incremental innovation comes from the efforts of voluntarily formed small groups.

Radical innovation Radical or major changes are outputs of the efforts of the R&D department. Examples of radical changes include invention of a 'jumbo aircraft', a life saving drug, etc., which have not been in existence earlier.

New technological systems Any radical innovation undergoes incremental development over the years. A series of radical innovations are interconnected with one another, both technologically and economically, thus leading to the development of a new technological system.

Technological revolutions These are technological changes that are all-pervasive and affect many branches of economy.

Each type of innovation needs a set of HRD intervention which will be discussed later in this chapter. Having understood the different types of innovations, we proceed to understand the impact of technology.

IMPACT OF TECHNOLOGY

In addition to the effects on competitiveness and factor endowments, technological changes have impacted the economy of a country substantially. Among the most commonly perceived impacts are increasing knowledge intensity and greater mismatch of employee skills.

Increasing Knowledge Intensity of Production

Industries need knowledge for conducting R&D. They also need knowledge for design, engineering, manufacturing, maintenance, advertising, marketing, sales, and administrative management. In short, knowledge input emerges as the primary factor behind the success of any department. This has forced the training and developmental department to become more instrumental in keeping the workforce and their knowledge updated. The radical innovations and innovating capabilities provide competitive advantage to any commercial organization. This can be evidenced from the deployment of engineers and scientists in R&D departments. The tireless efforts of these personnel are enabling the launch new products.

> Radical innovations and innovating capabilities provide competitive advantage to any commercial organization.

Following globalization, more products and a growing number of services are available. High R&D costs have increased the risks in knowledge generation through planned innovation. The competitive advantage derivable from enhanced knowledge along with access to global markets provides high returns to successful innovators as knowledge is the backbone of success. Refer to Exhibit 20.1.

Exhibit 20.1 Technology advancement

The telecom industry plays a vital role to connect or communicate with people. The slogan, 'anytime, anywhere', is relevant to the telecom industry. Without the aid of the communication industry, the functioning of other industries is likely to be paralysed. In India, the communication industry has a significant role to play in the development of its economy.

About two years ago, it was foreseen that the telecom sector might see a great change if service providers could opt for something beyond 3G. Today, the dream has been realized. In fact, a shift from voice to data including MMS on the mobile environment was driving mobile operators to move towards new wireless technologies. These technologies offered new opportunities in service capabilities, significantly improved data rates and latency performance. The 3GPP's (third generation partnership project) organizational partners include standard bodies such as ETSI (European telecommunication standards institution), ARIB (association of radio industries and business of Japan), etc. The partners have evolved a single common specification for future wireless networks that would provide default global roaming facilities. The introduction of 3G by BSNL and MTNL, initially deploying the release of 99 specifications and moving over to release 4 and release 5, marked a transition from 2G to 3G. All the facilities add value to mobile networks by increasing data rates and enhancing functionalities such as video calls, etc.

The third generation (popularly known as 3G) of mobile telecommunications is a higher generation of standards for mobile phones and mobile telecommunication services. It fulfils the international mobile telecommunications-2000 (IMT-2000) specifications developed by the international telecommunication union. The application services of 3G includes wide-area wireless voice telephone, mobile internet access, video calls, and mobile television. All the facilities are available in a single mobile environment. To meet the IMT-2000 standards, a system is required to provide peak data rates of at least 200 kilobits per second. Recent 3G releases, often denoted as 3.5G and 3.75G, also provide mobile broadband access of several megabits to smartphones and mobile modems in laptop computers.

Research and development is a continuous process with the constant advancement of technology. To cope with the changes in technology, upgrading human resource management and development is the need of the day.

Source: Technology Update, LTE: The Future of Wireless Technology, IEI News, Published by the Institution of Engineers (India), Kolkata, Vol. 60, No. 4, 1 July 2010, p. 5.

Greater Mismatch of Skills

The general effect of technological changes is that it has led to replacing labour (the workforce) with capital (the technology). Contextually, it must be mentioned that advancement of technology has replaced pottery making, horse carts, and many age-old practices.

The introduction of new and advanced technologies has produced two-fold effects: (a) reduction in number of employees engaged in production and distribution, and (b) enhanced skills to work with new generation of technological changes. The former effect affects the employment pattern negatively and the latter affects the skill-mix of employment. To cope with the latter, the training and development department needs to play a dominant role.

Introduction of advanced technology produces two-fold effects—reduction in the number of employees engaged in production and distribution, and enhanced skills to work with new generation of technology.

Many companies have been technologically transformed into departments with a new generation of sophisticated machines. These companies are trying to impart the requisite knowledge and skills to the existing employees. However, the older generation workforce is primarily resisting the changes and is not inclined to learn new technology, gain new skills, and prefers to work utilizing their existing skills. Thus, despite acquiring new technology, the skill gap is hindering the productivity levels. Therefore, even when technology is developed to ease the burden of the work load and derive benefits, a mismatch can result in a disaster.

Increasing knowledge intensity and greater mismatch of employee skills make the task of managing technology difficult.

TECHNOLOGY MANAGEMENT

While planning technology upgradation, the management must consider managing culture, resistance, stress, and people development.

Keeping pace with the technological revolution, organizations are replacing conventional machines with new generation CNC machines. The use of new generation machines has facilitated the manufacture of defect-free products. The working class may view technology upgradation differently, as it might lead to unemployment due to downsizing of human resources. Therefore, while planning new generation machines, management must take into account the need for managing culture, resistance, and stress, in addition to developing the people.

Technology management includes some key functions or elements such as technology forecasting, technology generation and development, technology transfer, absorption, evaluation and assessment, and diffusion of technology.

Technology has made it possible to manufacture and deliver zero-defect products to customers. Thus, organizations are able to ensure customer satisfaction and, in turn, are able to convert customers to advocates of the company's brand.

Technology: Impact of Globalization

In Chapter 16, we have studied the various facets of globalization as a process of interaction and economic integration among people, companies, and governments of different nations. In the business scenario, globalization is driving companies towards viewing quality as a necessary tool to compete successfully in world markets. A direct outcome of this new emphasis is the philosophy of total quality management (TQM).

Essentially, TQM is a company-wide perspective that strives for customer satisfaction by seeking zero defects in the entire gamut of products and services. Hence, technology needs to be studied in conjunction with quality of goods and services as against aspiration of people.

TECHNOLOGY AND QUALITY

Technology has enhanced the aspirations of people with regards to quality. People have become more quality conscious. During the early days of industrialization, the market was dominated by producers and sellers. With the increase in the number of producers, the demands easily match the supplies. Presently, supply exceeds the demand, the markets are customer driven, and this trend signifies the concept of a 'buyer market'. Customers have become quality conscious and consider the cost effectiveness of the product before buying it.

During the early 1920s, manufacturers were dependant on the skills of the craftsmen and the absence of a particular skilled person jeopardized smooth production. Organizations were 'person dependent' at that time. In the following decade, batch and mass production systems were introduced in the industry. This system developed the concept of 'inspection' to prevent defective products from reaching the customers. In 1940, different statistical methods were adopted in the production systems, and were termed 'system control'. They aimed to reduce the cost of inspection and associated rejections (quality cost).

In 1950s, production systems were further developed with the introduction of process control and led to the development of 'process design'. The concept of 'employee participation' was initiated in 1960s in order to enrich the quality of work life of employees along with the improvement of quality of product and enhancing productivity of the organization. This was the beginning of the introduction of 'quality circle' in the industry. In the decade starting from 1970, the concept of 'total quality management' prevailed in organizations. TQM emphasizes a complete involvement of all employees.

At this point, let us study the concepts associated with introduction of new technologies.

TECHNOLOGY AND WORK

We are acquainted with the concepts of learning, unlearning, and relearning. During the introduction of a new technology, an organization needs to employ concepts of deskilling, reskilling, and multiskilling.

Deskilling Deskilling refers to fragmentation of a work or task done by an individual. Thereafter, the individual is assigned only part of the work when he loses the integrated skills and the comprehensive knowledge. Deskilling is the process by which division of labour and technological development leads to the reduction of the scope of an individual's work to one, or a few, or specialized tasks.

Reskilling Reskilling is categorized as horizontal and vertical reskilling. Horizontal reskilling refers to the extension of skills required at an equivalent level of the existing job. Vertical reskilling means addition of skills of higher level than what a worker has been accustomed to. Vertical reskilling solves the purpose of job enrichment. The overall effect of a new technology in the factory may demand removal of some skills and the addition of others. For example, managers see the importance of quality flexibility, or job flexibility across a range of tasks. This demands redefining the work roles. One example of potential vertical reskilling is adding programming task to the job of a production worker.

Multiskilling Multiskilling means acquiring the skills or undertaking multiple jobs at a time when the demands arise. Multiskilling is instilled by providing training and assigning different jobs on a rotational basis. Building multiskilled capabilities of middle level people allows organizations to loop in talent for new business initiatives or ventures. Multi-tasking allows them to gain diversified knowledge, competencies, and maintain high levels of motivation and enthusiasm. Multiskilling obviously emphasizes gaining multiple skills. Those who resist, and intend to continue in his/her existing domain, can never be multiskilled.

Deskilling, reskilling, and multiskilling are essentially required during the introduction of new technology or technological revolution.

The role of human resource management needs a relook while upgrading technology, keeping in mind the concept of TQM.

TQM IMPLEMENTATION: ROLE OF HRM

Q 4 Improving quality is an important task in an organization. Making quality improvements was once assumed to be the sole responsibility of specialists such as quality engineers, product designers, and process engineers. Today, developing quality across an entire firm is an important function of the human resource management department. However, it is not their sole responsibility. The principal role of HRM division is to identify the training needs and to provide appropriate need-based training.

The HRM function acts as a senior management's tool in implementing TQM in two fundamental phases. The first phase emphasizes the need for developing the TQM philosophy and principles within departmental operations. Thereafter, with the support of HR department, the quality managers take up the TQM processes across the company by way of developing and delivering long-term training and development necessary for the major organizational culture shift required by TQM.

The TQM theme encompasses five basic principles focusing on customer needs; concentrating on problem prevention but not correction; making continuous improvements, seeking to meet customer requirements immediately; training employees in ways to improve quality; and applying the team approach to problem solving.

The second phase is called the simultaneous need of human resource management and development and is prevalent at this juncture of TQM in the context of technology upgrading. The HR department needs to manage culture, resistance, and stress.

Managing culture Corporate culture is the act of developing intellectual and moral faculties, especially through education. The culture of an individual includes the moral, social, and behavioural norms of an organization based on the beliefs, attitudes, and priorities of its employees.

Managing resistance Management may develop tools to understand why people resist and study the means to overcome resistance. This is the core concern of change management and attempts to convert the human resistance to human support (Haldar and Sarkar 2010).

Managing stress Management needs to identify the organizational role stresses and initiate remedial measures such as problem solving and counselling.

HR INITIATIVES

The HR initiatives commonly adopted by organizations are discussed here.

Developing HR policy The HR policy guides the HR department and the whole organization towards achieving the goals.

Formulating HR strategies The strategies set clear directions for long-term development management and provide the foundation for building a coherent approach to human resource management.

Managing culture Culture management has been discussed in the previous section, on the role of human resource management in implementing total quality management.

Managing commitment Commitment refers to the dedication and loyalty of the employees towards the company. Management needs to introduce tailor-made educational programmes to increase identification with the company's mission and values, and to develop attitudinal change and influence behavioural modification which support their achievement.

Ensuring flexibilities Strategies must be formulated for systematic working. However, as business scenarios keep evolving, one must consider the need to develop and implant strategies that would allow flexibility so that strategies are aligned as per the changing environment. Sincere employees should be allowed to use discretion in demanding cases. Employees should be motivated to be a part of an autonomous work group.

Encouraging teamwork People can work individually and also as members of a team. Enhancing the ability of people to work as a team member, making the best use of team spirit, and enjoying increased intrinsic motivation by being a part of an autonomous work group are the moral responsibilities of management.

Implementing quality management It refers to lending a hand to the introduction of TQM approaches, accepting the principles through a series of educational and training processes, and involving people in quality improvement programmes.

Resourcing This function invólves the need to match human resource capabilities with the changing requirements of the organization.

Managing performance This refers to introducing systems clarifying expectations and measuring the achievement against those expectations. The systems lead to employee development.

Installing reward management This is an objective reward management system that motivates employees by rewarding them according to their contribution,

Promoting employee relations Developing a cooperative climate characterized by mutual trust promotes employer-employee relations, allowing direct communication to employees and recognizing the roles played by the unions.

In addition to these common HR initiatives, management of technology involves a change in the mindset. Developing a change in the mindset is essential for overall organizational effectiveness.

DEVELOPING A CHANGE IN MINDSET

Change is one aspect of life that never seems to change. Employees in the organization should seek, create, and even love change. It is believed that one cannot survive without change because the world and business scenarios are constantly changing. Changes are taking place at a rapid pace in multiple directions. At this juncture, HR personnel have to discharge their roles as their leading duties are aimed at building a culture that can accept and promote changes.

A manager must be aware of his managerial responsibilities. A manager must know the essence of the term, 'management', which involves risking oneself in the mobilization of resources and building relationships.

A manager must take decisions and calculated risks. He should not expect that everything will follow as a set pattern in the changing business environment.

One may need to sell some produced goods, services, or ideas, and need several types of resources which may not be readily available. Even if they are available, they may not of the right quality and quantity. It is important to make the best use of the available resources. When one starts working towards it, the process will be successful. On the other hand, worrying and blaming will only aggravate the worries. Mobilizing relationship emphasizes on building bridges of relationship with internal and external agencies. Networking and partnering helps in enhancing the strengths. Networking also helps to accommodate changes and succeed in change implementation. Right relationship will facilitate in getting good suppliers, customers, shareholders, and establish cordial relations with the community.

Value addition is a primary duty of a manager irrespective of whether the company is a government enterprise or a voluntary public sector where the duty involves serving the community effectively and economically. In these cases, the activities must be run outside the normal market domain or mechanism. It is emphasized that value addition encompasses all kinds of business activities.

If one's senior is not keen to empower the employee, the principle of self-empowerment must be used. An employee must strive to be forceful, thrusting, innovative, creative, and enterprising. He can further strengthen these qualities if he has the will. Recall the maxim, 'I am the master of my fate and commander of my soul.'

A change in one's mindset cannot be instilled or developed by a law or an act of the Parliament. It is up to the person to develop it.

CHANGING ROLE OF HRM

Q 4 An organization comprises people. Despite physical differences found among employees, it is their knowledge, skill base, and attitude which must be closely monitored. Even within each category, there are enormous individual differences. The attributes may also widely differ based on level of intelligence, capacity of work, commitment to the work assigned, devotion to the organization, and so forth. The differences can never be eliminated. The point is that the differences need attention so that each individual can maximize his/her potential, and contribute his/her best leading to enhancement of organizational effectiveness. The challenge of the HR managers today is to identify and recognize talent, nurture them carefully, and achieve a significant boost in productivity over a period of time.

The role of HR managers is shifting from a protector and a screener to a planner and a change agent. HR professionals are required to play key roles in planning and implementing downsizing, restructuring, and other cost-cutting activities. At present, they are further required to work integrating HR initiatives with the business goals. With the change in technology, the businesses goals are frequently revised. As such, HR managers must keep themselves updated with the latest changes in their fields.

> The role of HR managers is shifting from protectors and screeners to planners and change agents.

With technological innovations taking place, an organization must develop its people to welcome new technologies. Building a change in the mindset is primarily required and people must be provided with knowledge inputs. For instance, many telecom companies have conducted a series of training programmes to welcome 3G technologies.

HRM PRACTICES TO COPE WITH CHANGES

Q 8 We have studied four types of innovations earlier in this chapter. HRM practices will be different in various situations.

In case of incremental innovation training, the HR interventions comprise communication, enhancing presentation skills, encouraging team working, etc. These interventions may be for a short duration.

To promote radical innovations, apart from projecting the requirement of fund and getting them sanctioned, the HR needs to conduct a series of management development programmes on technology, motivation, interpersonal skills, networking and partnering, liaison, and so forth. For instance, while switching over to 3G technology, different types of training programmes were conducted by mobile service providers.

For new technological systems, the essential HR interventions are training, communication, enhancing presentation skills, negotiation skills, technology evaluation skills, encouraging team working, management development programmes on technology, motivation, interpersonal skills, liaison, etc. of short as well as long duration.

Technological revolution demands visionary skills, change management skills, and initiating prior actions to cope with the anticipated changes.

PRESCRIPTIONS FOR BETTER HRM

In recent times, during selection interviews, many organizations ask, 'What can you contribute to this company?' On the same line, new recruits are seen to often ask, 'What can you do for me and how can you develop me?' In the prevailing business scenario, managing human resources management practices needs a relook. Organizational employees need continuous development, future talents must be groomed, and there must be deployment and engagement of employees, an attempt to build employee communities and participatory culture, and ability to turn managers into coaches. Summarily, the prescription emphasizes the following HRD interventions:

Developing people Organizations create opportunities for the employees, to monitor if they are working hard. It is essential to give them learning opportunities, empower them to apply discretion and gain leadership skills and confidence, help them to come out from routine thinking, encourage them to innovate, and so forth to facilitate their development. These are the duties of an organization. In a knowledge industry, the question, 'what the organization is doing for me?' is increasingly gaining more importance. At some places, it can be observed that the subordinates are performing the tasks that are assigned to them but the managers can give them certain special skills and tools to do the tasks even better.

> Steps to be taken for better HRM:
> 1. Developing people
> 2. Grooming future talents
> 3. Deploying and engaging the employees
> 4. Turning managers into coaches
> 5. Building employee communities
> 6. Satisfying psychological needs

Grooming talent It is necessary to groom the talent to enable them to reach greater heights to add them in the leadership pipeline, and to extract the best performance. Analytical and communication skills, and a boosted morale give graduates and post graduates an edge to work effectively and move up the organizational hierarchy. Training needs analysis for skill enhancement and plotting career growth paths for employees, particularly the performers.

Deploying employees Employees with transferable skills may be deployed in diverse areas. By doing so, an organization becomes more agile. Moreover, employees feel satisfied from the standpoint of handling multiple projects, gaining manifold learning platforms, more exposure to people both inside and outside the organization, and, apart from intellect commitment, they become emotionally attached with assignments which, in turn, contribute to the organization's growth. Thus, employee and organization gain mutual benefits.

Employee communities Organizations should put efforts to build high quality internal talent communities through segmentation. By doing so, an employer will be able to cultivate relationships with the segmented employees on their terms. The employer will also be able to consistently demonstrate value to the employees through opportunities for internal mobility. This practice will reduce the probability of employee turnover.

Participatory culture Organizational culture is an important factor that may facilitate or inhibit participatory management. Participatory culture enhances assertive communication; encourages expression of views and thoughts without any fear; facilitates communicating opinion without trampling others interests, and without encroaching his/her interests (Haldar 2003). If organizational hierarchy is valued, implementation of participatory culture would certainly be a difficult task. In such circumstance, restoring participatory culture improves managerial effectiveness.

Turning managers into coaches 'Stop appraising, start coaching,' has emerged as a popular maxim. When an MBA degree holder joins an organization, he/she is a fresher with almost no experience. The annual appraisal is a common practice in organizations. The appraisal contains the strengths and weaknesses of an appraised. He/she can definite develop initiating remedial measures. However, coaching by the immediate superior is obviously a stronger tool for developing juniors. The immediate superior can offer penetrating insights. The implementation and maintenance of this system is a duty of the HR department.

Satisfying psychological needs Matching psychological needs and job requirements generates huge enthusiasm among employees as their job involvement and commitment are enhanced. Moreover, an employee must have some dominant personality traits. If the job requirements match the traits in his/her possession, then the output will be maximized. In such cases, the role of the supervisor becomes irrelevant as the employee is self-propelled. Motive is another psychological factor that needs consideration. One who possesses affiliation as a dominant need, and one whose personality trait is that of an extrovert, is seen to perform well in areas where he/she gets the scope of working with new people. On the other hand, an introvert is likely to perform well in research and development where he/she gets the suitable opportunities with work.

SUMMARY

Rapid advancement of science and technology is changing the world. The advancement of technology is being welcomed, considering the qualitative requirements. In the competitive world, human assets such as intellectual capital have been able to give a competitive advantage to an organization.

Technology explosion is also increasing knowledge intensity and point to greater mismatch of employee skills. Globalization has an impact on technology upgradation as well. Technology and quality are interrelated. HRM plays a vital role in TQM implementation. Apart from taking traditional HR initiatives, we also need to develop a change in the mindset of people for organizational benefits.

KEY TERMS

Deskilling refers to fragmentation of a work/task done by an individual and then assigning only part of the work to him when he loses his integrated skills and comprehensive knowledge.

Reskilling (horizontal) refers to the extension of skills at an equivalent level of the existing job.

Reskilling (vertical) means addition of skills at a higher level than what a worker has been accustomed to; vertical reskilling solves the purpose of job enrichment.

Multiskilling refers to acquiring the skills of undertaking multiple jobs and the skills instilled by providing training, assigning different jobs on rotational basis, and allowing a person to become diversified and maintain high levels of motivation and enthusiasm.

EXERCISES

Concept Review Questions

1. Define the terms technology and technology management.
2. Discuss the types of technological changes. Cite examples.
3. How is technology related to quality of products and services?
4. Discuss the role of HRM while implementing TQM in an organization.
5. Explain and discuss the role of technology in the overall business strategies of a firm.
6. What should be the 'HR Mantra' in the context of change implementation? Discuss in brief how to develop a change in mindset.

Critical Thinking Questions

7. In your opinion, what has been the role of technology at enterprise level in India? What are the factors that may affect the management decisions concerning technology?
8. 'During introduction of new technology, an organization needs to utilize concepts of new skill sets.' Discuss the statement critically.

Assignments

9. Take help of the professor teaching technology management or strategic management to get an appointment from an enterprise that has recently upgraded its technology. Collect information about the role of HRM while implementing TQM and analyse how they are planning to produce an impact on the employee mindset. Show your notes to the professor who helped you to get the appointment and your professor teaching HRM and HRD.

MANAGER'S INSIGHT

Shaan Strings has been into manufacturing brake and clutch wires for various two and four wheelers. Its client list included Indian as well as the foreign companies in the automobile industry. The delivery of product quality and delivery schedules through established quality standards and inventory norms has helped Shaan become one of the most reliable providers of auto accessories in India today. With the advent of nanotechnology, there has been a demand in the auto industry to engage partners who have adopted the new technology. This would mean the majority of existing machines may become obsolete or would require upgradation, which would not be financially viable for the company. The top management at Shaan is also worried about the existing skills of its employees as it would require extensive training if such changes are done. The HR head had been asked to provide a proposal for skill upgradation of the employees after consulting the production head.

Question:

Highlight the role of the HR department in such situations.

BIBLIOGRAPHY AND WEB RESOURCES

Haldar, Uday Kumar, *Job Performance of the Operational Agents of L.I.C.I in relation to some Specific Job behaviours: A Case Study of 24 Parganas (North),* West Bengal, Unpublished doctoral thesis submitted to the University of Burdwan, Burdwan, West Bengal, 2003.

Haldar, Uday Kumar and Juthika Sarkar, *Change Management: Crossing the Delta State,* MDC Journal of Management, Larsen and Toubro, Issue 3, Mumbai, 2010.

HRM INITIATIVES DURING TECHNOLOGY UPGRADATION

About the organization

OFDC is a public sector enterprise, located in north Kolkata. It was established in 1846 as Ammunition Factory, and following restructuring, it changed its name to OFDC in 1964. The organization manufactures high precision engineering components. It received an ISO 9002:1994 certification in 1996, and renewed it in 1999. Thereafter, it switched over to ISO 9001:2000 within the period of transition permitted by the International Standards Organization (ISO). OFDC had a structured system of working.

While preparing for the ISO certification, OFDC also developed its quality manual, quality procedures, quality instructions, and quality formats to maintain records. It also defined its quality policy and formulated its quality objectives, and communicated them to all levels of employees in the organization. OFDC conducted a series of training programmes on quality awareness, quality control tools, and quality management systems. The management representative (MR) took the initiative of motivating the people and delivered lectures, shared views followed by a question and answer session. The MR was keen to conduct such programmes in various manufacturing sections, maintenance departments, and offices, and used examples from the respective locations. This venture helped raise the quality awareness at a faster space. After the compliance audit, the audit team was satisfied and recommended the company to the national head office for certification.

Considering the various merits of CNC machines, OFDC planned to switch over from conventional machining system to CNC machines. The other reason for the switchover was its depleting manpower on account of natural retirement or superannuation. It formed a separate section, 'high tech machining center,' where people handling the higher generation machines were trained to part programming, fault detection, rectifying minor defects, etc.

OFDC duly considered the increasing knowledge intensity of production, quality aspirations of customers, skills and other human attributes required to run the sophisticated CNC machines, the essential deskilling and reskilling, and the financial impact with regard to wages. Workers were paid on the basis of individual piece work (IPW) and gang piece work (GPW) system. IPW and GPW were finalized by the industrial engineering department's rates and estimates section.

OFDC wanted to analyse the prevailing culture, and anticipated the possible resistance and stress that might generate among the workforce. The enterprise believed in participative management and hence, took the unions and associations in confidence; explained the utmost need for modernizing the plants and switching over to new-generation machines. The management also emphasized the need for manufacturing high quality products, and enhancing the productivity. The general manager was highly committed towards the same and offered a presentation to the audience comprising senior officers and decision-makers, significant union representatives, and invited dignitaries from the corporate headquarters.

OFDC formulated the HR strategies, framed procedures keeping scope of flexibility in demanding cases, reviewed and revised the reward management system. The uniqueness of this organization was that management made the system transparent by way of rigorous internal and external communication.

The management was instrumental in developing a change in the mindset of the people. It conducted a series of lecture programmes to people of different levels. Most interestingly, it educated union representatives, and shared knowledge about the new technology and its need to union cadres. Their deliberations were well appreciated and well taken. Ultimately, CNC machines were erected and commissioned in the 'high tech machining center'. The new shop was inaugurated, and production commenced.

Discussion Questions

1. OFDC meticulously planned and took adequate measures to switch over to the new technology. Discuss what else OFDC could have done to make the switch over more flawless.
2. Production commenced in the 'high tech machining center'. Discuss what OFDC should have done to keep the wheel of production moving.

HR MANTRA Manpower for machines

Rama International, which came into existence in the early 1990s, has grown in size and product range. The company has diversified, adopting both backward and forward integration. Now, the top management of Rama International was keen to get rid of the conventional machines and install new generation machines, for the company fund was not a problem. To intensify the distinctive competence and gain competitive advantage it wanted to welcome technological advancements and modernize the plants at the earliest. The decision, taken at a meeting of the board of directors, was recorded and circulated to all departmental managers, with a mention of the timeframe. The process of modernization involved huge tasks in various levels in each department. Numerous problems and hassles crept into the process. However, the commitment of the top management made it possible to modernize the plants.

Quite naturally, after investing a huge amount on the new machinery, the top management expected an increase in quantitative targets and qualitative improvements. Accordingly, the industrial engineering department was advised to revise the material and manufacturing estimates.

Indentifying matching human resource capabilities emerged as a mammoth challenge. Even though acute skill mismatch was observed, the management was not keen on investing in the appropriate manpower. Try as it may, the HR department could not convince the top management to hire appropriately skilled manpower.

The mantra: The right people are as important as the right technology.

SAM PITRODA

Satyanarayan Gangaram Pitroda, popularly known as Dr Sam Pitroda, was born in Titilagarh, Orissa, on 4 May 1942. His parents, originally from Gujarat, migrated to Orissa. As they were deeply influenced by Gandhi and his philosophies, they sent Pitroda and his brother to Gujarat to study the Gandhian philosophy.

Pitroda completed his schooling from Vallabh Vidyanagar in Gujarat and completed his masters degree in physics and electronics from Maharaja Sayajirao University in Vadodara. After completing his masters degree, he went to the US to complete his masters in electrical engineering from Illinois Institute of Technology in Chicago.

Pitroda is an inventor, entrepreneur, and a policymaker. All through the late 1960s and early 1970s, Pitroda was involved in the cutting-edge technology research work in telecommunications and hand-held computing. Pitroda is particularly known for having introduced microprocessors in telephone switches leading to early digital switching.

Pitroda is currently advisor to the Prime Minister of India on public information infrastructure and innovations. He is also widely considered to have been responsible for India's communications revolution. As an advisor, he creates information infrastructure for enhancing delivery of services to the citizens in various areas and also worked on creating a roadmap for a 'decade of innovation' in India.

Pitroda has spent four decades in the world of telecommunications helping bridge the global communication technology. His professional career has been partitioned across the continents of North America, Asia, and Europe. His strategy of using telecommunications in nation building has been internationally acclaimed.

In the 1960s and 1970s, he was involved in developing digital switching systems in the United States, which went on to become the key to global networks to integrate voice and data. In the 1980s, Pitroda, in his role as advisor to then Prime Minister Rajiv Gandhi, helped in the transformation of Indian's telecommunications and information technology infrastructure. He was the first founding chairman of the Telecom Commission in India. He also oversaw national technology missions related to drinking water, literacy, immunization, oil seeds, and dairy. While performing those roles, he helped transform India's developmental policies and philosophy.

In 1975, Pitroda invented the electronic diary that is presently regarded as one of the earliest examples of hand-held computing. Pitroda has more than 100 patents to his credit, and is a leading name in telecommunications and information technology for more than three decades. The latest set of patents relate to mobile phone-based transaction technology, which cover the entire range of financial and non–financial transactions through mobile phones.

In the 1990s, Pitroda worked out of Europe where he collaborated with the International Telecom Union (ITU) to help develop telecom infrastructure in developing countries to reduce the global telecom gap. Pitroda believes in using telecommunications as means to expediting the process of development and nation building.

Pitroda was the founder of Wescom Switching. The company was acquired by Rockwell International, and Pitroda eventually became its vice president. In 1983, Pitroda designed his own computer-themed card game called Compucards, which incorporated binary numbers (1, 2, 4, 8, ...) instead of decimal and had a computer bug as the 'joker'.

In 1984, Pitroda responded to the request of the then prime minister Indira Gandhi, returned to India, and established the Center for Development of Telematics (C–DOT), an autonomous telecom research and development organization.

In 1987, Pitroda became advisor to Rajiv Gandhi and was responsible for shaping India's foreign and domestic telecommunications policies. Pitroda is largely considered responsible for the telecommunications revolution in India and specifically, the yellow–signed public call offices (PCOs) that quickly brought cheap and easy domestic and international public telephones all over the country.

Pitroda is the chairman of World-Tel Limited, an ITU initiative. As he was holding many key technology patents, Pitroda has been involved in several startups, and lectures that were extensively started around the world on management, governance, and the implications of communications and information technology. Pitroda is the founder and CEO of C–SAM Inc, which has developed a group of patented mobile business technology called 'One Wallet'. The company has offices in London, Tokyo, and offshore development centers in India in Mumbai and Vadodara.

In 1993, Sam Pitroda established the Foundation for Revitalization of Local Health Tradition (FRLHT) near Bengaluru, India. The aim of the foundation is to make full use of India's rich and diverse medicinal knowledge. Presently, Pitroda is a Governing Council member. Pitroda cited an example of the importance of telecommunications in every kind of development. By 2000, India had about 30 million telephones or one telephone for every 34 people. In comparison, Americans have one telephone for every 1.5 people.

In order to provide greater accessibility to telephone services, Pitroda prepared ordinary telephones with small meters. This equipment was sold to local entrepreneurs who set up manual PCOs on makeshift tables in *bazaars*, at street corners, or in shops whose owners use them to attract customers to make calls. Pitroda revolutionized the telephone entrepreneurs who were paying bills only six times per year, and earn a 25% discount as their commission and the income from one telephone is enough to support an entire family.

In 2002, Pitroda was awarded the Dataquest IT Lifetime Achievement Award. In the subsequent decade,

Pitroda continued his business interests in computer manufacturing and software.

For the 2004 elections, Rahul Gandhi, member of Indian parliament, asked him to help with regard to a small committee that he was founding to advise him on policy issues. When the United Progressive Alliance government came to power after the 2004 general elections, prime minister Dr Manmohan Singh invited him to lead the National Knowledge Commission.

In January 2008, Andhra University honoured Pitroda with a doctorate of science. Pitroda is also the recipient of prestigious Canada India Foundation (CIF) Chanchlani Global Indian Award in 2008 for his outstanding performance as an Indian who has established global leadership, vision, and personal excellence.

Pitroda received this award in presence of the prime minister of Canada, Stephen Harper, and former president of India, Dr A.P.J. Abdul Kalam. Pitroda has been awarded the Padma Bhushan in 2009 by the Indian government for his contribution to science and engineering.

As an entrepreneur, he has owned and run several companies in the US and Europe. He is widely featured in print and television media worldwide for his contribution to telecom development.

Considering the need to roll-out a national optic fibre network, capable to take high-speed internet to the hinterlands, a team has been formed. The chief executives of leading mobile phone companies, industry associations, and all key government departments have been roped to oversee the implementation of the ₹20,000 crore project, the largest project of the Ministry of Communication. The project is the first of its kind for the communications ministry. Pitroda had been asked to oversee this project of building 25 lakh kilometers of optic fibre cable. Chief executives of companies such as Bharti Airtel, Reliance Communications, Tata Communications, Hathway Cable, Tikona Digital and You Telecom, are part of the advisory body.

This panel will also comprise the Chairman of the Unique Identification Authority of India (UIDAI), Nandan Nilekani and representatives from ministries such as education, rural development, health, *Panchayati Raj*, and the Planning Commission. The project involves setting up a special purpose vehicle (SPV) comprising state-owned telcos such as BSNL and MTNL and other public sector undertakings such as RailTel, Gail, and Power Grid Corporation that already own optical fibre cable.

Pitroda has always favoured an open and transparent e-auction system for all government auctions and tenders, including the sale of spectrum bandwidth to telecom providers, in order to avoid any legal hassle and bad name to the government.

References

Economic Times, dated 14 June 2011.

en.wikipedia.org/wiki/Sam_Pitroda, last accessed on 6 October 2011.

www.knowledgecommission.gov.in/about/profile.asp?id=sp, last accessed on 5 October 2011.

www.winentrance.com/general_knowledge/sam-pitroda.html, last accessed on 6 October 2011.

CHAPTER 21

Work–Life Balance

LEARNING OBJECTIVES

After studying this chapter, you will be able to

- Understand the concept and the importance of work–life balance
- Identify the means of maintaining work–life balance
- Appreciate work–life balance issues and various life quadrants
- Understand work–life balance practices in organizations
- Estimate the scope for research on work–life balance

OPENING CASE

Problems of a Nuclear Family

A girl from a middle-class family, with an M Tech degree, was employed in a foreign firm. After two years, she married one of her colleagues, who had a B Tech degree. The couple had joined the company on the same date and in equivalent positions. Within two years, the lady got promoted and thereafter, she got promotions every alternate year. However, the husband did not get any promotion. On their domestic front, after a year of marriage, they were blessed with a baby. Her career took the backseat, and she started losing the balance that she had so far maintained between work and home. After her maternity leave, she joined duty. The company had no system of day care for the children. They arranged a caretaker to take care of the baby during her hours of work. One day, the caretaker did not turn up. The wife insisted that her husband take leave, but the husband had a meeting in office. Though she had an urgent meeting as well, she had no other option but to take leave from work. Later, employees of the company felt that the meeting could have been held by means of a teleconference. However, the office had not installed the required facilities.

Learning points

- Organizations should have a crèche for babies of young mothers, as part of their welfare measures.
- Companies should install modern gadgets and have state-of-the-art technology.

INTRODUCTION

Interference between work life and family life is a common phenomenon. People differ in their perceptions, lifestyles, expectations, likes, dislikes, societal and cultural backgrounds, and so forth. They differ widely in their attitudes towards their professions and responsibilities for family including children and other members of the family and society. A person performs a variety of roles throughout a day, and while performing them, he/she is likely to get more involved in some roles. However, he/she must execute all the roles. Thus, striking a balance among all these roles emerges as an inescapable need. Balance can be achieved in different ways by different people. Hudson (2005) defines work–life balance (WLB), in its broadest sense, as a satisfactory level of involvement or a 'fit' among the multiple roles in a person's life.

'Our lives are becoming increasingly complex with every passing year. We have more choices, more opportunities, and more demands placed on us,' says Clutterbuck (2003), author of *Managing the Work-Life Balance*. One's work life and personal life are interconnected and interdependent. The conflict begins when the burdens, obligations, and responsibilities of work or the family roles become incompatible. Sometimes, complying with an obligation or favouring the other also results in a strenuous situation. There are various reasons for this imbalance and conflicts in one's life. The reasons may be individual career ambitions, pressure in the work place, demands from the family, or any other reason. Broadly, these reasons could be situation specific or individual specific.

As age advances, the increasing responsibilities on the personal front can also create stress on personal and professional fronts.

Constant struggles in the effort to maintain a balance between work and personal lives can have serious implications on an individual. This gets aggravated because of the use of technology and the increasing competition among organizations. Work–life balance, thus, is a dynamic phenomenon; it is not a simple structure but an ongoing process. By nature, it is also individual based, although there are several common issues across different types of people.

IMPORTANCE OF WORK–LIFE BALANCE

It stands established that jobs affect and create stress in the personal lives of the job holders. The pressures of work or personal lives can lead to stress. It has been found that stressful situations can take a toll on a person's health, both physiologically and psychologically. Pressure, stress, or tension in work life can also lead to bad social life and vice versa. Employees should maintain a healthy balance between work and their private lives.

Work–life balance is a dynamic phenomenon; it not a simple structure but an ongoing process.

Maintaining this balance can help them achieve their personal goals, professional goals, and organizational goals smoothly. Programmes to support work–life balance fall into categories of alternative work arrangements, benefits, support programs, and health programs.

Contextually, Sekar (2009) quotes Bryan Dyson, the Chief Executive Officer of Coca Cola: 'Imagine life as a game in which you are juggling some five balls in the air. You name them—work, family, health, friends and spirit. You are keeping all of these in the air. You will soon understand that work is a rubber ball. If you drop it, it will bounce back. However, the other four balls—family, health, friends, and spirit—are made of glass. If you drop one of these; they will be irrevocably scuffed, marked, nicked, damaged, or even shattered. They will never be the same. You must understand that and strive for balance in your life.'

Table 21.1 summarizes the opinions of respondents in a survey conducted to collect opinions of marital status and differential earnings along four dimensions.

Table 21.1 Views of respondents

Dimension	All workers	Married	Unmarried	Earning $20,000–$40,000	Earning $100,000+
Satisfied with work–life balance	36 per cent	42 per cent	26 per cent	28 per cent	46 per cent
Employer encourages balance	61 per cent	65 per cent	53 per cent	57 per cent	67 per cent
Has fun at work	70 per cent	74 per cent	64 per cent	67 per cent	75 per cent
Typically works 40+ hours every week	39 per cent	41 per cent	37 per cent	36 per cent	56 per cent

Source: www.hudson-index.com/documents/us-hudson-index-081705.pdf

> Work–life balance is time variant, depends on one's marital status, number of children, stage of one's career, and is person specific. There cannot be any perfect and one-size work–life balance that fits all.

Work–life balance does not necessarily mean an equal balance. Trying to schedule an equal number of hours for each one's work and personal activities can never be rewarding or realistic. Life is and should be more fluid than that.

The best individual work–life balance of any person varies over time, and often on a day-to-day basis. Today's right balance will probably be different from tomorrow's. Again, the right balance for a person also differs before and after marriage, childbirth, starting a new career, and retirement. Thus, work–life balance varies with time, marital status, number of children, stage of one's career, and is person specific. There cannot be any perfect and one-size work–life balance that fits all.

As mentioned earlier, work–life balance does not mean an equal sharing of time between work and personal life. Two terms—achievement and enjoyment—play a dominant role in balancing the two. We will study these terms later in this chapter.

Striking a balance between professional and personal priority is a big challenge for an employee in today's world, which is characterized by high competition, advanced technology, fast pace, and commercialization in every aspect of life. An employee's personal and professional wellbeing is fully dependent on how well he balances his work and life. Employers cannot afford to neglect this aspect in their own interest of getting maximum return on their investment on employees. Table 21.2 lists the importance of work–life balance from the perspectives of both employees and employers.

Table 21.2 Importance of work–life balance

For employees	For employers
Taxation on the person's health, both physiologically and psychologically It might lead to heart ailments, cardiovascular problems, sleep disorders, depression, irritability, jumpiness, insecurity, poor concentration and even nervous breakdowns	Organizations need to manage increased expectations of employees without compromising on business needs
Lack of concentration, low productivity, lesser quality of work, conflicts at workplace	Organizations face problems such as enhanced absenteeism, less productivity, low quality of work, employee turnover, failure to attract the best talent
Affected family life	Management needs to spend increasingly more time on counselling, motivation, conflict management etc.
Strained social life	More investment on additional resources
Financial problems due to ill health, poor management of personal finance issues	Low return on investment

MEASURES FOR WORK–LIFE BALANCE

Work–life balance cannot be achieved by a single party, that is, by the employee or employer, without the support of the other. Employees will have to initiate the balance while employers need to extend their helping hand. Table 21.3 lists some measures for ensuring work–life balance.

Table 21.3 Measures for work–life balance

By employees	By employers
Adopt time management through task prioritization, activity planning, and delegation, considering the feasibility	Regular and direct communication with workforce to clarify business priorities and encourage them to be equally clear about their personal priorities
Negotiating and using facilities such as work-sharing, flexi timing, job rotation, delegation, telecommuting, work from home, onsite childcare, eldercare assistance, online wellness assistance	Help employees in their pursuit of balancing personal commitments and organizational duties by providing them with necessary support and resources which are feasible
Employees use gadgets to perform routine jobs such as washing, cleaning etc., and their use helps in spending quality time with family	Flexi working arrangements includes 1. job sharing 2. part time work 3. shift work 4. telework 5. flexi hours
Employees are energized to indulge in creative hobbies and voluntary service which helps to de-stress	Counselling and guidance help to take away relationship problems and manage workplace conflicts
Continue education in the subject of interest either on part-time or online basis. Though knowledge of all techniques is important, employees need to have an understanding of stress management tools, time management techniques, and the importance of children's education.	Training and education on topics such as health, hygiene, stress management, time management, parenting, personal finance, usage of technology/gadgets, children's education, retirement planning etc.
Employees must take care to remain healthy for the benefit of self and the organization.	Childcare centers in or near the workplace, assistance for the elderly, facilities/training for health and fitness, work from home option
Access to information and help required from management from time to time	Home care and home services–allowance for elders' care

National and multinational organizations are helping their employees in various ways to discharge some of their family roles, which cannot otherwise be managed beyond office hours. Exhibit 21.1 illustrates one such measure.

Exhibit 21.1 Role of organization in work–life balance

AH is working in a multinational Internet service company and holds a fairly high position. AH's son is 3 years old and is studying in the preparatory class in a school in California. School timings are 9.00 am to 1.30 pm. However, children can stay up to 6.00 pm in case the parents of the child are working.

AH's parents went to California to visit their son. They desired to have their grandson home immediately after normal school hours. So every afternoon, AH picked his son up from school and dropped him at home. One day, AH's father asked him how he managed to leave office

(Contd)

Exhibit 21.1 (Contd)

during the afternoon every day to pick up the child and drop him home.

AH replied that several of his colleagues also did the same thing for their children and that the company, keeping in mind the employees' needs, did not schedule any meetings during that time of the afternoon.

Assisting employees perform essential family-related duties during office hours helps to avoid stress, and facilitates work–life balance.

REASONS FOR IMBALANCE

Some of the reasons for work–life imbalance are discussed here.

Work–life balance is critically important for working women to ensure sound physical and mental health.

Societal drivers Agricultural society is giving way to the industrial and knowledge societies. Consequently, we can observe major shifts in societal forms and structures. This shift is leading to conflicts between work and life activities. In the past, husbands used to earn livelihood while wives were responsible only to manage the domestic issues. In other words, men were responsible for working outside the family while women were the homemakers. The centuries-old traditional gender roles have changed now.

Women are pursuing higher levels of education. Added to this, double income has emerged as a prime necessity. Societal perceptions have changed and it is now appropriate for both men and women to pursue paid employment outside home and also share responsibilities within the home (Barnett and Hyde 2001).

The Indian society is male dominated and has traditionally granted a favoured status to men as the chief breadwinners (Awasthy and Gupta 2001). The employment rate of women has also increased worldwide. Women's increased wish for autonomy and social recognition is quite justified. Work–life balance is critically important for working women to ensure sound physical and mental health.

Organizational drivers Employee-oriented organizations believe that if employees' work–life balance is well achieved then organizational effectiveness will be high. It is evident from literature survey that most multinationals from Scandinavian and western countries take initiatives to promote work–life balance. On the other hand, the inclination towards the same in Korean and Indian organizations are low.

HR initiatives such as job description, role clarity, flexi time, no meetings after core working hours, forced annual leave, maternity and paternity leave, shopping at work, crèche, disincentives to overtime, gym and good food facility, no late sitting culture, help in achieving work–life balance.

HR initiatives play a vital role in promoting work–life balance practices in an organization. Work load, working hours, stress at work, and organizational reasons are the grounds behind experiencing difficulty in balancing work life. Organizations should formulate HR practices such as job description, and role clarity to reduce role stress due to overload, role ambiguity, and role conflict. Effective organizational design and systems and processes further facilitate achieving work–life balance. Progressive organizations develop a variety of work–life balance practices, such as flexitime, no meetings after core working hours, forced annual

> The life philosophy can focus either on 'being' or 'becoming' or a balance between the two.

leave, maternity and paternity leave, shopping at work, crèche, disincentives to overtime, gym and good food facility, no late sitting culture, and so on.

Individual drivers Individuals hold differing views about life. The philosophy of life is a major determinant of work–life balance. All of us have a life philosophy that affects of work–life balance. However, philosophy is generally implicit and people cannot articulate it concisely in a few words. One's philosophy of life can focus either on 'being' or 'becoming' or strive to attain a balance between the two (Singh and Awasthy 2009).

The state of *being* is concerned with human endeavour for self actualization, contentment, harmony, and enjoying what one is. However, the state of *becoming* is related to material achievement, money, power, and social status, etc. 'The greater the conflict between *being* and *becoming* within an individual, the lower is the WLB' (Singh and Awasthy 2009). Individuals must learn to prioritize between and professional and personal goals while companies cannot afford to neglect the need for work–life balance.

CONSEQUENCES OF IMBALANCE

Work life, if not properly balanced, leads to a range of physical and psychological strains, such as irritability, depression, anxiety, diminished self-confidence, inability to relax, lack of sleep, increased susceptibly to a number of illnesses, a number of psycho-somatic disorders, burnout, low productivity, high employee turnover, safety hazards, increase in divorce cases, high blood pressure, ulcer, migraine and many psychosomatic disorders. Karatepe and Tekinkus (2006) found that the work–family conflict has increased emotional exhaustion and decreased job satisfaction.

The consequences of work–life imbalance are also categorized as societal, organizational, and individual consequences. Figure 21.1 shows the reasons and consequences of work–life imbalance.

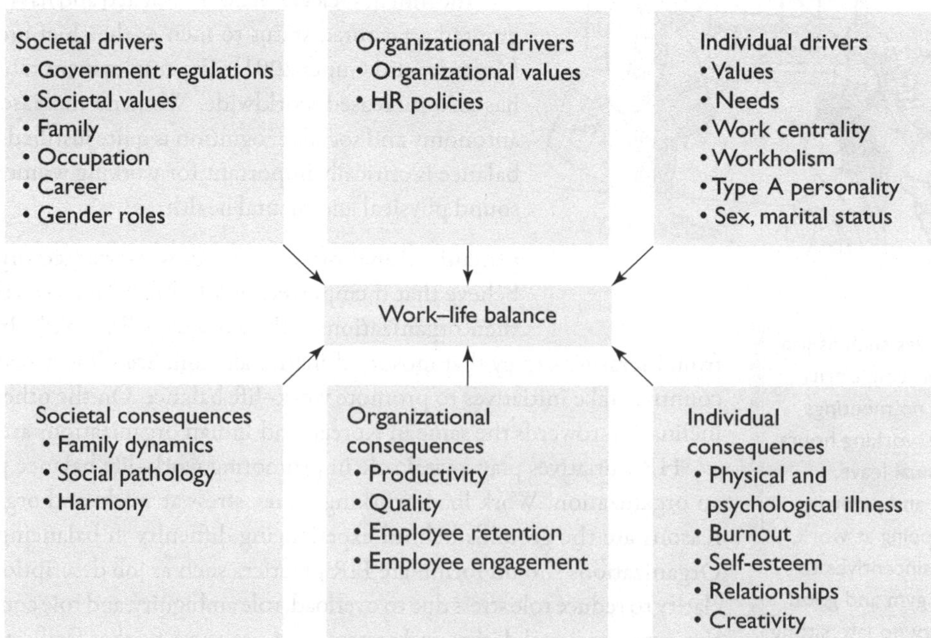

Fig. 21.1 Causes and consequences of work–life imbalance

Societal consequences Societal consequences include family dynamics, social pathology, and harmony. People with poor work–life balance cannot do justice with family members. In such conditions, the family is likely to be unhealthy characterized by exchange of hot words, misunderstanding between husband and wife, and so forth. This unhealthy family environment gets reflected onto the society. A family lives in a society and hence, it is a subset of the society. To improve the societal life and make it healthier, it is of utmost importance to put all-round efforts to balance the work life.

Organizational consequences The direct consequences are poor productivity, high employee turnover, accidents, etc. The indirect consequences are low involvement, serious interpersonal conflicts at work, apathetic attitude towards work and so on.

Individual consequences Lack of work–life balance affects family dynamics indirectly and negatively. The child may not get proper guidance. In many cases, it results in marital discord, divorce, child abuse, and neglect of old parents. All these affect societal functioning and harmony.

The drivers and consequences are well represented through the model presented in Figure 21.1.

CHOICES INVOLVED IN IMPROVING BALANCE

The direction and degree of work–life balance differs from one individual to another because each individual is unique. People desire different life goals, and vary in their values, needs, and career aspirations. What is a desirable work–life balance to one can be totally irrelevant and unacceptable to another person. It may also alter an individual over a period of time. As one moves from one stage of life to another, work–life balance issues must be readdressed. If the dynamic nature of work–life balance is not understood or appreciated by individuals, they suffer from its consequences.

People make two types of choices to achieve the desired degree of work–life balance—the choice about selecting a situation and the choice about responding to the situation.

People make choices continuously to achieve the desired work–life balance. These choices can broadly be divided into two categories—the choice about selecting a situation and the choice about responding to the situation. Both types of choice are important. Refer to Table 21.4.

Table 21.4 Choices of work–life balance

Dimension	First type	Second type
Choice	Selecting a situation	Responding to the situation
Nature	Responsible for the direction of work–life balance	Conducive to the management of the dynamics of work–life balance
Time	Long-term implications	Short-term but vital consequences
Importance	More important	Less important

An individual has to be aware of both types of choices while making decisions. People generally opt for the second choice. Exhibit 21.2 highlights the choices of work–life balance.

Exhibit 21.2 Choices of work–life balance

After completing MBA from a reputed B-school, Paromita got an offer from a multinational organization for the post of deputy manager. She also received an offer for the post of assistant manager with a public sector organization.

She analysed the pros and cons of both job offers and chose the job offer from the public sector organization. Despite being a financially less attractive option, she believed that it would provide a better work life, which she would be able to balance with her personal life.

The decision, as is apparent, was centered on the consideration of work–life balance.

The dynamic nature of work–life balance needs intervention at both the organization level and the individual level.

ORGANIZATION-LEVEL INTERVENTION

The system to identify work–life balance should be an integral constituent of an HR policy. Organizations should communicate openly, their work–life balance philosophy, policies, and practices.

Different organizations may adopt different policies and practices. Common practices include working from home, working flexi-time, not scheduling meetings after core working hours, not working on Sundays and holidays, child career counselling, child care, elder care, maternity and paternity leave, forced annual family vacation, etc. An organization could benchmark the practices of other companies and organize a work–life balance audit. This gives them sufficient data to plan for various other interventions. Once these interventions are implemented, organizations should conduct employee perception surveys to measure their effectiveness. It would provide them with important information about the relative success of various interventions and also help improve organizational effectiveness. Continuous learning about the employees' work–life helps to identify ways of addressing them.

INDIVIDUAL-LEVEL INTERVENTION

The most important step that an individual should take, in order to maintain work–life balance, is to do a thorough self-analysis, and make a choice about the situation by asking a host of questions. The questions may be: What is my life's vision? What are my needs? From what do I derive satisfaction? What do I wish to get from my career? What are my priorities? The answers to these questions will prompt him/her to decide about an occupation. Finalizing the decision is a major situational choice. Thereafter, he has to make a choice about responding to the situation by negotiating his roles within the family and organization. He has to also analyse his family structure and aspirations, because they determine the degree of work–life balance.

> Individual-level interventions need self-analysis by asking a set of questions, so as to make a choice about a situation.

For instance, a dual career family has to put more efforts to achieve work–life balance in comparison to a single career family. Similarly, greater role negotiation is required in a joint family as compared to a nuclear family. A family with high financial aspirations may have to compromise on its work–life balance. Therefore, the involvement of family members and role exchange with them forms an important part of the balancing.

> A family with high financial aspirations may have to compromise on work–life balance.

A lifestyle that stresses on a high degree of work–life balance may be decided upon on the basis of self-analysis and family analysis. In order to achieve the same, individuals knowingly decide to forego excellence in certain work areas. They do understand the trade-offs between self and the family, and welcome both positive and negative outcomes of a high degree of work–life balance. Of course, there are certain work–life dilemmas that cannot be resolved by oneself; hence, counselling and external help become important. Individuals need to seek counselling from seniors, mentors, elder family members, and professional counsellors to identify and overcome barriers to work–life balance.

FOUR LIFE QUADRANTS: WORK, FAMILY, FRIENDS, AND SELF

The life component of work–life balance includes family, friends, and self. Work–life balance is not just a concern of the people within the family but of everyone associated with that individual. A man cannot live alone; he needs the company of his family members to be able to share his joys and sorrows. Obviously, he also has to move along a career path. Any person, irrespective of gender, cultural background, social status, and income level, needs leisure and satisfaction, when he/she interacts with members of the family and society.

An effective manager has to continuously deal with the different priorities and needs of the four domains of work and life. A tug of war exists perpetually between achievement and enjoyment.

Both achievement and enjoyment are the prerequisites of life. Defining a positive work–life balance requires an understanding these two concepts in a wholesome manner.

Achievement It refers to fulfillment of a goal. The goal may be getting a promotion, an attractive pay package, a furnished office accommodation, a position in a social club, or anything along these lines.

Enjoyment It means pleasure, pride when a goal is fulfilled, satisfaction, happiness, celebration, eternal peace, and a sense of wellbeing.

If we cannot attain these quadrants, then traces of imbalance will start emerging. If we ignore them at the initial stage, then it might lead to stress. A stressed person can never contribute effectively to the society.

PRIORITIES OF EMPLOYEES AND EMPLOYERS

Work and personal life, the two sides of the same coin, are mutually dependent and an integral part of an individual's life. Striking a balance between professional and personal priorities is a big challenge for an employee in today's world marked by high competition, advanced technology, fast pace and commercialization of every aspect of life. His personal and professional well being is fully dependent on how well he balances them.

Q 3 Employers cannot afford to neglect this aspect in their own interest of getting maximum returns on their investment on employees. The impact of work–life balance is very significant for organizations as the employee's attitude, loyalty to the organization, and productivity are directly dependent on how well he balances his time between these two lives. Hence, organizations have to extend the needed support to the employee in achieving work life balance to get the maximum out of him in workplace. Employees also have to understand their role, expectations out of them, and prioritize their time and efforts. Accordingly, they can seek the help of management and family members as required to achieve the best of both worlds. This combination, if judicially done, can help to receive both achievement and enjoyment.

FAMILY-FRIENDLY WORKPLACES AND WORKFORCE

Nowadays, companies are regarding themselves as great places to work as they take care of some of the responsibilities of workers along with responsibilities of their families. The companies have created family-friendly policies and practices. Workers try to know the extent of sensitivity of the employers towards work, life, and family concerns. Keeping in view this aspect, companies are launching the best HR practices. As employers are paying attention to work–life balance, most individuals realize that 'they do not live to work, but they work to live'. For them, life and family occupies the central space.

Q 7 Work-family and family-work conflicts are pervasive. To a large extent, they can be managed. Management is a function of an individual's own sense of role-goal clarity and personal decisions about life's choices. They plead for reducing the work hours; argue for non-regular employment needs to be better, and launching of more family-friendly policies. They also advocate promoting the status of women both at home and at work.

In general, larger companies and those in more modern or emerging sectors (such as information technology and IT-enabled industries in comparison to the older industries such as mining and construction) typically adopt more family-friendly policies that can moderate the level of tension between work and life/family (Ferrer and Gagne 2006).

Public sector is known for townships and celebrating festivals, and for encouraging cultural and sports and recreational events. Nokia's 'volunteering programme' and 'helping hands' give employees a chance to contribute their time and effort to worthy causes in their community. Employees can use up to two days of working time in a year for the purpose.

Tung (2009) concludes that community can play a supportive or complementary role; however, ultimately one's work–life balance is a function of how the individual assesses and makes appropriate choices.

Family-friendly Policy

The International Labour Organization (ILO) recognizes that 'families need financial resources which come from the work to provide for members. At the same time, families must ensure that dependents, such as children or the elderly, are looked after during working hours. Recent trends in both the labour market and the family are making it increasingly difficult for families as they are caught in 'time money squeeze' between family-caring responsibilities and the demands of work.' The ILO provides an illustrative checklist concerning family friendly policies/workplaces (Chandra and Venkata Ratnam 2009). The checklist is displayed in Box 21.1.

Box 21.1 Checklist concerning family-friendly policies

1. Promote family-friendly strategies in the organization.
2. Survey the business needs.
3. Survey the workforce to find out their needs.
4. Identify and obtain agreement on the aim of the family-friendly program.
5. Engage employees at an early stage in the process and listen to their views.
6. Collaborate with trade unions to encourage family-friendly policies.
7. Demonstrate/document both business and employee benefits.
8. Include a long-term perspective when weighing benefits against costs for implementation.
9. Provide relevant information so that everyone can take part in the policies.

(Contd)

Box 21.1 (Contd)

10. Clarify and agree eligibility criteria, for example, which staff have a priority claim on the provisions made?
11. Establish channels for open and ongoing communication.
12. Make sure that information on practices is available to everyone in the organization.
13. Ensure that top management sets the example.
14. Provide support and relevant training to managers throughout the organization.

Roles of Different Stakeholders

Governments, employers, trade unions, the community/civil society organizations, and individuals are the various stakeholders who have started recognizing and responding to work-life issues. For instance, persons suffering from HIV/AIDS are losing family support. There are many other issues at both workplace and families. The range of measures which the stakeholders can initiate and need to take care of are unlimited.

They should specifically be careful about

1. creating a family-friendly workplace,
2. addressing gender equality through work family measures, and
3. developing individuals to realize their own responsibility through education and counselling, among others.

Government Through legislation and other measures, the Government of India has provided for minimal facilities and benefits with a view to secure a better work–life balance. The Shops and Establishments Act, Factories Act, and various other legislations contain several such measures.

Employers The employers may adopt many initiatives such as

1. Facilities for child care (maternity/paternity leave, creche/kindergarten, and long leave without adverse affect on career)
2. Home care and home services (allowance for elders' care)
3. Flexi working arrangements (job sharing, part time work, shift work, telework, and most importantly flexi hours)
4. Benefits and services (as par family circumstances)
5. Dual career (spouse posting, residence at employees' choice, accommodation near place of work if both reside in different cities/locations)
6. Pay and employment equity (older workers, workers with family responsibilities, and part time workers)

Employers may further adopt organization-specific work–life balance initiatives.

Trade unions Trade unions are playing vital roles in ensuring work–life balance. The roles include many aspects some of which include the following:

1. Educating and encouraging their members about the need for role/goal clarity and cultivating habits and attitudes conducive to promotion of better work life balance,
2. Counseling employees about ways of dealing with trade offs/compromises concerning time-money squeeze in terms of their approach to converting work life balance amenities into cash,

3. Advocating influencing public policy and policy at industry/enterprise level,
4. Taking up work life balance issues in work committees and on the collective bargaining agenda, and
5. Directly undertaking work–life balance measures themselves either on free or fee-paying basis, depending on resources from within and outside with or without partnership with other stakeholders.

Community/civil society organizations Community-based organizations can primarily help to build awareness. They should further provide collaborative, supportive, and supplementary as well as complementary facilities through the mobilization of local resources. In fact, child care and elderly care are the facilities that are easily accessible and affordable. Researchers, academicians, and educational institutions should focus on the emerging issues relating to work–life balance, undertake studies to make impact assessment, suggest measures to mitigate or alleviate the problems, and develop appropriate metrics to measure, monitor, and rectify the situations appropriately. Together, they can also use the information and knowledge to promote dialogue and advocacy to adjust public policy and action at other levels aligned to meet the emerging challenges.

CURRENT PRACTICES AND TRENDS

Exhibit 21.3 shows the highlights of a report that shows that while the flexible work timings option is in, long work hours are also the norm of today.

Exhibit 21.3 Current practices and trends

A report from the UK Department for Education and Employment (DFEE) Work–Life Balance 2000 paints a mixed picture. It shows growing awareness of work–life issues, quite widespread flexible working practices, and also a dominant long-hours culture.

The highlights of the report include the following:

Flexible work

1. The most common type of 'flexible' work is part-time work.
2. Some 25 per cent of employees work in workplaces which offer flexitime.
3. About 20 per cent of employees work from home occasionally.
4. About 24 per cent of men and 16 per cent of women work from home occasionally.
5. About 35 per cent of managers work from home occasionally.
6. About 80 per cent of those who work from home are managers.
7. A third of employees not currently working from home said they would like to do so.
8. The most frequently cited reasons for working from home given by employees were work-related. Few employees cite factors related to caring as a reason.

Long hours

1. Most workplaces have staff working in excess of standard hours.
2. Almost half of all employees work additional hours.
3. Those who work extra hours do so by an average 9.6 extra hours per week.
4. Almost 11 per cent of full-time employees work 60 hours or more per week and belong to professional or managerial jobs.
5. The employees most likely to work long hours are men in households with dependent children.

Measures to create a balance

1. The majority of women returning from maternity leave switch to part-time work.
2. More women (56 per cent) prefer greater flexibility on return rather than longer leave.
3. Very few employers provide workplace crèches (two per cent) or subsidized nursery places (one per cent).
4. Employers are more willing to pay for facilities to relieve symptoms of stress than to prevent it in the first place.

The website points out that the figures are part of a baseline study and future research shows if the government's

(Contd)

Exhibit 21.3 (Contd)

WLB campaign is making a difference. The figures need comparison with earlier surveys of working hours and of flexible working practices.

The picture that comes through is that progress is more in some areas than others—flexi-time and part-time works have become well-established ones.

Long hours continue and there is little evidence that flexible working has been actively introduced in order to achieve work–life balance.

Source: www.flexibility.co.uk/issues/WLB/report.htm

BEST PRACTICES IN INDIVIDUAL COMPANIES

As discussed earlier, there has been a considerable amount of innovation with respect to work–life balance policies and practices in the fields of IT and IT enabled services in multinational and Indian companies. This is because of the preponderance of gender balance and the resultant increased awareness and concern about family responsibilities. The companies' employee referral programmes encourage spouses, relatives, and friends to opt for a job in the company. Interestingly, as Wipro's website puts it, the emphasis is on 'work balance towards life' rather than 'life balance towards work.'

Several companies focus on the life after work and put in place several programmes to connect. These programmes also include the younger workforce who does not have any family responsibilities. Some of these practices are mentioned in Exhibit 21.4. In contrast, in the Indian public sector, the emphasis is predominantly on employee and family welfare through statutory and non-statutory benefits, while many private sector companies in India are generally paternalistic in their approach. Refer to Table 21.5.

Table 21.5 Work–life balance rating across companies

Company	Rating	Company	Rating
Nokia	4.3	PepsiCo	3.5
Agilent Technologies	4.2	HSBC Holdings	3.5
Microsoft	4.0	Evalueserve	3.2
Procter & Gamble	4.0	Cognizant Technology Solutions	3.0
GlaxoSmithKline	3.8	Tech Mahindra Limited	2.8
Nestlé	3.8	Wipro Infotech	2.8
HP India	3.7	Tata group	2.8
GE	3.7	Infosys Technologies	2.7
IBM India	3.6	Aditya Birla	2.1
Citigroup	3.6	Hyundai	1.5

Source: www.glassdoor.com

Note: Glassdoor.com provides company ratings and reviews, employee satisfaction, and CEO approval ratings. All company reviews are posted anonymously by employees.

Exhibit 21.4 Organizational practices

Different organizations have installed a variety of measures to enhance work–life balance. The measures are briefed here.

Nokia developed a work–life balance tool, Nokia E71, a sleek mobile device that is designed for smooth life-in-balance. The tool empowers work and leisure connections

(Contd)

Exhibit 21.4 (Contd)

in a stylish way and its work-play mode allows users to easily switch between personal and work home screens to access one's favourite functions when one wants those most. It developed a complete list of 'get your (work) life in balance' check list (http://www.nokia-americas-press.com/lifeinbalance).

Microsoft's work–life programs include flexible work arrangements, grocery services, adoption assistance, backup child-care, child-care assistance, commuting and public transportation assistance, dinners-to-go programme, disease management programme, dry cleaning and laundry service, employee affinity groups, employee development courses, employer-sponsored discount programmes, ergonomics programme, financial planning, fitness benefits, legal assistance, long-term care for extended family members, maternity and paternity leave programme, new mothers' rooms; on-campus convenience shopping, on-line parenting resources and seminars, resources and referrals for counselling and education, school programmes, smoking cessation programme, tuition assistance programme, and weight management programme.

IBM's mobility program, launched in 2003, enables employees to access information and perform work from anywhere and at anytime. It gives employees an opportunity to enhance their effectiveness by providing tools to use at any location, whether it is a customer office, airport, IBM mobility workstations, or home.

Nestle offers pre-retirement classes. Additionally, it offers facilities for retiree activities. It has probably the largest retiree club in Vevey, Switzerland, which is home to a large number of ex-employees. With more than 950 members, it organizes a regular programme of events ranging from climbing, skiing, and cycling to foreign travel, fitness, and computer classes. Several of them also take part in local volunteer projects such as delivering meals to other Nestle retirees in the region.

Tata Consultancy Services (TCS) started *Maitree*, with an objective to strengthen the relationship between employees and their families as well as to provide a platform to encourage the talents of children. It 'strives to encourage the hidden aspirations and talents through cracking quizzes to conquering tall peaks, from shaking a leg to bending it like Beckham. It also conducts workshops on theatre, yoga, flower arrangement, chocolate making, and a host of others that allow employees to learn and know about things they always wanted to'. *Maitree* provides opportunities to establish relationships that extend beyond work and thereby, help build bonds that make work so much more fun.

Infosys's health assessment and lifestyle enhancement (HALE) initiative focuses on enhancing the emotional value of employees by optimizing their health, quality of life, and work environment. It has created world class gymnasiums, swimming pools, aerobics centres, tennis courts, etc.

Tech Mahindra's *Josh* programme enables people to enjoy with parties, picnics, yoga and salsa classes, musical events, sporting events, quizzes, adventures, social activities, etc.

Source: Chandra, V. and C.S. Venkata Ratnam (2009)

WORK–LIFE BALANCE ISSUES: INFLUENCE ON CHILDREN

Many children are being raised by a childcare provider or someone other than a parent. This figure is ever increasing. It is disheartening to note that older children are more likely to come to an empty house and spend time with video games, television, and the Internet.

According to a study by the National Institute of Child Health and Human Development (US), the 'more time that children spent in child care, the more likely their sixth grade teachers were to report problem behaviour.' The findings are the results of the largest study of child care and development conducted in the US, and the analysis tracked 1,364 children from birth.

RELATIONSHIP BETWEEN FLEXI-TIME RETENTION

In the knowledge business, manpower attrition continues to be a problem. The management is trying to develop retention mechanisms to retain workforce. Flexi-time system is just one retention tool. It is a work-family practice that allows employees to have flexible start and finish times, without changing the total number of hours worked. In Indian workplaces, the standard weekly working hours remain

The flexi-time system promotes retention; flexible working may alternatively be referred to as work–life balance or work–life integration.

the same. Employee retention is linked to flexi time (Gordon and Whelan 1998). Compensation packages, flexible work schedules, and training are important tools for retaining employees; employers should not underestimate the power of these benefits package. It is also established that work-family practices such as flexi time lead to positive job outcomes.

Smithson and Stokoe (2005) emphasize that flexible working may alternatively be referred to as work–life balance or work–life integration. In a study, 73 per cent of employees with availability of flexi-time system reported that there was a high likelihood that they would stay with their current employer for the next year as well.

FLEXI-TIME AS A RETENTION TOOL

Many organizations have adopted flexi-time as a retention tool. In the IT sector, companies such as IBM, Intel, Accenture, Cummins, and Hinduja TMT have implemented flexi-time systems. Companies such as Tata have tried to adopt many retention tools including helping employees achieve a healthy work–life balance by providing flexible work practices along other with initiatives (Baral Bhargava 2006). These work–life initiatives are most highly sought by employees. Companies who allow for work–life balance through flexi-time system attract more prospective talents from the market.

A study at IBM, for example, found that the ability to balance work and life was a key driver for the top performers of the company; and the company was most eager to retain them. IBM India offers options such as flexible workweek schedules, working from home, part-time employment, dependable child care, family counselling, and leave of absence programmes etc. which can be labelled as family-friendly programs. IBM is committed to providing employees with an attractive and comfortable working environment to maintain a healthy and productive lifestyle. In times of hectic schedules and work pressure, this initiative helps employees deal with the demands of home and family better.

IBM India offers options such as flexible workweek schedules, working from home, part-time employment, dependable child care, family counselling, and leave of absence programmes, etc.

Work–life balance is a strategic initiative that helps IBM attract, motivate, and retain the very best talent in the technology industry. 'Intel India claims to provide work-life benefits (family-friendly policies) to help its employees manage work and personal life commitments realizing the fact that managing a job and personal responsibilities is not easy. The range of options includes flexible work schedules, compressed workweeks, alternate work schedules, telecommuting, home office, part-time employment, childcare assistance, resource and referral services, and health and wellness benefits etc.

RESEARCH FINDINGS

The concept of work–life balance is not new; it is only now that the issue has started receiving a great degree of attention. Researchers are engaged in pursuing fundamental investigative work to establish relations between work–life balance and other related organizational phenomena such as balance practices, flexi-time working, working from home, employee retention measures, etc. Some interesting findings are presented here.

1. In a research to collate responses of the question, 'How important do you think are work–life balance practices?', 25.3 per cent ranked it as extremely important, 34.7 ranked it as important,

11.7 per cent felt neutral, 14.3 per cent felt it is slightly important, and 14 per cent felt it is not at all important.

2. For the research question, 'I would be less likely to quit a job that allowed flexi-time' the responses were as follows: 25.7 per cent strongly agreed, 35.3 agreed, 12.7 felt neutral, 12.7 per cent disagreed, and 13.7 per cent strongly disagreed.
3. The correlation coefficient between 'employee retention' and 'flexi-time' was 0.648 ($p = 0.000$) and indicated a high degree of dependence of the variables. The study was conducted on 300 managerial personnel.
4. Analysis of variance (ANOVA) between 'employee retention' and 'flexi-time' generated $F = 264.533$, which indicated significant dependence of 'employee retention' on 'flexi-time' system.
5. Nielsen pursued a global online consumer survey in April 2008. Internet users from countries in Europe, Asia-Pacific, North America, and West Asia participated. It revealed that Indians are more concerned about their work–life imbalance than the slowing economy. Most Indians consider work–life balance as their biggest concern since demanding careers are taking a toll on their family lives.

Benefits of Study of Work–Life Balance

The study of work–life balance unearths many truths, and brings to light many hidden facts. Major findings can be implemented for organizational benefits. The major factors that contribute to the interest in work–life balance practices in India are as follows:

1. Greater participation by women in the labour market
2. The culture of working long and odd hours
3. Work intensification
4. Adaptation of new technology
5. Global competition
6. Interest shown by companies in personal lives/family values
7. Development of a young workforce

SUMMARY

Complexity is growing in the workplace. Interference between work life and family life is a common phenomenon and the two are interconnected and interdependent. Ignoring one cannot lead to effective functioning of the other. It is seen that jobs are affecting and creating stress in the personal lives of job holders. Improving work life and personal life is essential for all of us. It is the primary responsibility of an employee to ensure work–life balance. Organizations can only extend a helping hand to the employees.

Employees strive for achievement in the work place and want to build careers. However, employees, as member of a family and society, need enjoyment at the same time. The revenue of human life is enjoyment. Achievement and enjoyment are complimentary and supplementary. work–life balance has societal, organizational, and individual drivers. It produces consequences of three types—societal, organizational, and individual. In the arena of work–life balance, both organizational and individual interventions are prevalent. The people factor is a vital driver of competitiveness in the knowledge economy; and work–life balance practice can play a significant role in the engagement, motivation, and retention of people.

Key Terms

Flexible work means a facility of working from home; at irregular hours (before or after the normal working time or in staggered shift). Flexible work or flexi-time working helps the work force; particularly the women employees.

Individual drivers are related to demographic variables, social, and psychological factors; they are major factors of work–life balance.

Organizational drivers regulate the behaviour of people, create structures, choices for work –life balance, and can be improved by HR interventions.

Societal drivers refer to societal forms and structures; a shift in these forms and structures lead to conflicts between work and life activities.

Exercises

Concept Review Questions

1. Define the terms 'work life' and 'family life'.
2. Discuss the four life quadrants—work, family, friends, and self.
3. What is the role of the employer to maintain work life balance?
4. Discuss the role of employee while implementing work–life balance in an organization.
5. What should be the 'HR *mantra*' in the context of work–life balance?

Critical Thinking Questions

6. Explain and discuss the need for maintaining work–life balance in the overall business strategies of firm.
7. 'Women employee suffer work life imbalance.' Discuss critically.
8. 'Maintaining balance between work and family is the critical issue to employee.' Discuss the statement critically.

Assignments

9. Take the help of a professor teaching work–life balance to get an appointment from an enterprise that practices work–life balance. Collect information about the method of maintaining work–life balance and its impact on the employee mindset. Show your notes to the professor who helped you to get the appointment and your professor teaching HRM and HRD.

Manager's Insight

A person joined a private company about seven years back. He joined as an assistant manager; was promoted twice, and is now designated as a marketing manager. He is a manager with proven track record. He is likely to be promoted within a year as senior manager.

Recently, he married a lady who was an English teacher in a higher secondary school. Her mother's house and the school are at distance of about 120 kilometres from her husband's company quarters. After marriage, she continued teaching and stayed with her husband in the weekends. To pursue her family life, she tendered her resignation to the school. The problem stemmed from that time.

Being a career-oriented husband, he stayed in office for long hours and returned home late in the evening. He was in pursuit of 'achievement'; while his wife insisted him to come home after normal office hours. His inclination to 'enjoyment' was minimal. Consequently, he could not strike a balance between the two roles.

Questions:

1. How can this problem be solved?
2. Will you suggest the need for the intervention of a career counsellor?

BIBLIOGRAPHY AND WEB RESOURCES

Awasthy, R. and R.K. Gupta, *The balancing Act: how to balance between work and family,* Human capital, March: 22–24, 2001.

Baral, Rupashree and Shivganesh Bhargava, *Family-Friendly Policies: Prospects For Indian Organizations,* 14th International Employment Relations Association Conference on 'Family-Friendly Employment Policies and Practices: An East-West Perspective on Work-Life Balance', 19–23 June 2006, Hong Kong, 2006.

Barnett, R.C. and J.S. Hyde, *Women, men, work, and family,* American Psychologist, pp. 781–96, 2001.

Chandra, V. and C.S. Venkata Ratnam, *Model Guidelines and Best Practices for Family Friendly Workplaces and Workforce,* NHRD Network Journal, July 2009.

Clutterbuck, David, *Managing work-life balance: a guide for HR in achieving organisational and individual change,* CIPD, London, 2003.

Ferrer, Ana and Lynda Gagne, *Housing and Canadian Children Development Outcomes,* Canadian Public Policy, 32(3), pp. 275–300, 2006.

Gordon, J.R. and K.S. Whelan, *Successful professional women in midlife: how organizations more effectively understand and respond to the challenges,* Academy of Management Executive, Vol. 12, No.1, pp. 8–27, 1998.

Hughes, J. and N. Bozionelos, *Work-life balance as source of job dissatisfaction and withdrawal attitudes,* Personnel Review, 36(1): pp. 145–154, 2007.

Karatepe, O.M. and M. Tekinkus, *The effects of work-family conflict, emotional exhaustion, and intrinsic motivation on job outcomes of front-line employees,* International Journal of Bank Marketing, 24(3): pp. 173–193, 2006.

Krishnaveni, R. and B. Sripirabaa, *Achieving Work-life Balance: Women Perspective,* Quarterly Journal of Indian Society for Training and Development, Vol. XXXVIII, No. 1, New Delhi, January-March 2008.

Sekar, N., *Work-Life Balance — A Priority for both Employee and Employer,* NHRD Network Journal, July 2009.

Singh, Arup Kumar and Richa Awasthy, *Work-life Balance: Causes, Consequences and Interventions,* NHRD Network Journal, July 2009.

Smithson, J. and Stokoe, E. *Discourses of work-life balance: negotiating 'gender blind' terms in organisations,* Gender Work and Organisation, Vol. 12 No.2, pp.147–68, 2005.

Tung, Rosalie. L., *Perspectives on Work-Life Balance: Implications for the Indian Context,* NHRD Network Journal, July 2009.

Unpublished report on 'Work Life Balance of IISWBM Faculty and Staff', Abhishek Banerjee, Kolkata, 2009.

Web Resources

www.psier.qld.gov.au/publications/docs/wlb-definition.pdf, last accessed on 11 November 2009.

WORK–LIFE BALANCE OF IISWBM FACULTY AND STAFF

About IISWBM

Indian Institute of Social Welfare and Business Management (IISWBM) was established in 1953. This institute is the first management institute in the country. IISWBM offers three master degree courses (MBA, MHRM, and MPSM), and various diploma courses.

Preamble of the project

IISWBM faculty members perform a variety of roles such as teaching, research, consulting, and so forth. In addition to performing all the roles and completing the specified tasks within time frame, they spend time in the institute beyond office hours. As a result, they might be neglecting societal and domestic roles. This observation prompted the researcher to pursue this project under the guidance of Dr Sumati Roy and Prof. Ram Konar.

Aim of the research

The researcher aimed

1. to find the work–life balance of IISWBM faculty members and staff
2. to find the obstacles in achieving it
3. to suggest better ways and strategies to improve work–life balance

Methodology

The methodology comprised sampling, questionnaire design, data collection, preparation of charts and tables, etc.

Sample size: 56 (28 faculty members and 28 staff members)

Data collection: The survey is conducted in IISWBM and data have been collected through interviews with the help of a questionnaire. Each interview lasted for about 15 to 20 minutes. The questions had to be explained to the staff and faculty for their clear understanding. The interviews were conducted face to face.

Age profile in years: Under 30 (6 per cent), between 30–50 (55 per cent), and over 50 (39 per cent)

Number of children: No child (18 per cent), one child (20 per cent), and two children (57 per cent)

Findings

The research findings were multifarious. Some important findings are presented here.

Balancing the work life: For the question, 'whether the staff and faculty members are able to balance work and family life', 43 per cent responded positively and 57 per cent responded negatively. They are unable to take the burden, and fulfil obligations and responsibilities to family members. The inability to achieve work–life balance affects their attitude.

WLB policy: It is customary to know whether the institute has any documented policy regarding WLB. Out of the total respondents, 95 per cent confirmed that no WLB policy was documented. In absence of a WLB policy, balance can only be achieved by chance.

Flexi-hours: Employees were not aware of the availability of flexi time working. However, out of the total sample, the staff members were better able to manage their family commitments as compared to faculty members.

Obstacles to WLB: The staff members are engaged in monotonous routine jobs and feel as if they were working for longer hours. When they are offered overtime, they felt more frustrated. The frustration is the main hindrance in attaining WLB.

Support: The faculty members are getting adequate support from others in maintaining the WLB. This happens because of a greater sense of belongingness, a strong team spirit, and bonding. Moreover, there is no negative attitude prevalent in the workplace which hampers the faculty and staff members in attaining WLB.

Time with loved ones: About 57 per cent of the sample is able to spend time with loved ones.

Time spent on important aspects: About 21 per cent spend time in doing whatever they feel important in whichever work it might be. They do so from a sense of accomplishment.

Working at home: About 78 per cent faculty work at home for preparing lectures, evaluating reports, etc

Overall satisfaction: About 80 per cent respondents are happy and satisfied with their work in spite of the fact that they are unable to attain WLB.

Recommendations

The researcher recommends the following course of action:

1. Using commute time wisely to allow mental transition from home to work, and from work to home.
2. Preparing for lectures or question papers at the institute itself, through effective planning so that workload is not carried back to home
3. Setting priorities at work place and home and sticking to them by (a) prioritizing the tasks and planning the activities, and (b) monitoring the workload and time sharing.
4. Observing 'bring-your-kids-to-work' day as a means to get families of employees involved in their work lives. The opportunity to share a day of work with children is a benefit that many employees appreciate and gives a sense of belongingness to children and families.
5. Sponsoring family-oriented activities to employees to combine the work and life. The activity can be a cultural event on the foundation day of the institute; a monthly social gathering in case of any achievement of an employee and thereby, felicitating the employee and the recognizing the contribution of family members.
6. Formulating a documented policy regarding attainment of WLB for faculty members. It should be made aware to every employee of the institute so that they can avail of the policies.
7. Introducing flexible work system to help respondents meet conflicting needs without compromising the amount of hours they work; training the employees, both faculty and staff. Prior to implementing flexi hour system, it is important to enable them to make the best use of time
8. Sanctioning 'time off' to employees on their birthdays, marriage anniversaries, or other memorable special occasions.
9. Introducing 'paternity benefit' system to look after one's wife.

Source: Work–Life Balance of IISWBM Faculty and Staff, unpublished project report submitted by Abhishek Banerjee to IISWBM for evaluation by University of Kolkata, 2009.

Discussion Questions

1. How can the flexi-hour working system facilitate maintaining a work–life balance? Discuss in the context of the academia.
2. How can the management of an academic institution extend support to its faculty members to maintain work–life balance?

HR MANTRA Work–life imbalance

The incident is about a poor Bengali lady. Her family included her parents-in-law, husband, and a daughter.

Due to long duty hours and the hectic nature of job, she was not able to afford adequate time for her parents-in-law, who wanted to live out of her money. The house rent, electric bill, and telephone bill, as also other household expenditure, such as purchasing vegetables and provisions, were paid from her salary. Her parents-in-law also insisted on buying a refrigerator, colour television, and even a new house, all from her salary.

In addition, her parents-in-law are guided by her sister-in-law, who indirectly influences all her activities. In essence, her work life was hectic, and her personal lime traumatic.

To make things worse, her parents-in-law also started plotting ways to eliminate her, so as to enjoy the sum assured through her life insurance policy!

The mantra: Help the breadwinning members of your family achieve work–life balance.

DR ROSALIE L. TUNG

Professor Rosalie L. Tung, Ph D, is Fellow of several institutions such as the Royal Society of Canada, Academy of Management, Academy of International Business, British Academy of Management, and The Ming and Stella Wong Professor of International Business, Simon Fraser University, Burnaby, Canada.

With regard to work–life balance, Rosalie (2009) provides a conceptual paradigm and highlights the role of environmental and moderating factors in facilitating WLB or exacerbating and aggravating family work conflicts. Rosalie argued vociferously that paying attention to WLB can have favourable outcomes, both at personal and organizational levels.

She was formerly a Wisconsin distinguished professor and was associated with the University of Wisconsin system. She has served as faculty member of the Wharton School, University of Pennsylvania; University of Oregon, and worked as a visiting professor at Harvard University; University of California, Los Angeles; the University of Manchester Institute of Science and Technology, England; the Copenhagen Business School, Denmark; the Chinese University of Hong Kong; Peking University; and the China Europe International Business School, Shanghai, China.

She was the president of the Academy of Management in 2003–04, and had been elected as Fellow of institutions such as the Academy of Management, the British Academy of Management, the International Academy for Intercultural Research, and the Royal Society of Canada.

Rosalie has significantly contributed to theory development and had developed practical applications of cross-cultural understanding and communication in the context of economic collaboration among entities from around the world in two important approaches. In the field of human resource management, she has conducted ground-breaking research in the area of expatriate assignments. She developed a theoretical framework for selecting and training of people for international assignments and tested this model on samples of Canadian, US, West European, Japanese, and Australian multinationals. Secondly, her analysis into the mindsets of east Asians as they affect management thought and practices has contributed to the development of theories of comparative management.

Rosalie won the 1998 Vancouver YWCA Woman of the Year Award in management, professions, and trades. In 1997, she won the American Society for Advanced Global Competitiveness Research Award.

Rosalie is also involved in management development and pursues consulting activities around the world. Chinese brush painting and meditation are her hobbies and in her spare time and is able to balance her work life with personal life.

Rosalie has published widely on the subjects of international management and organizational theory. She is the author and editor of dozen of books and papers. Her publications include *Female Expatriates: A Model for Global Leaders, Organizational Dynamics* (2004), *Building Effective Networks* (2002), *Learning from World Class Companies* (2001), *International Encyclopedia of Business and Management: Handbook of International Business* (2001) in her capacity as an editor.As coauthor, Rosalie has published *Toward the Boundaryless Career:A Closer Look at the Expatriate Career Concept* and *Perceived Implications of an International Assignment* (2002).

References

Tung, Rosalie. L., *Perspectives on Work life Balance: Implications for the Indian Context*, National HRD Network Journal, Volume 2, Issue 3 2009.

www.beedie.sfu.ca/profiles/RosalieLTung, last accessed on 16 October 2011.

www.aib.msu.edu/fellow.asp?FellowID = 59, last accessed on 16 October 2011.

CHAPTER 22

Quality Management and HRM: JIT, 5S, Kaizen, Six Sigma

LEARNING OBJECTIVES

After reading this chapter, you will be able to

- Understand the concept of just in time (JIT), its benefits, and limitations
- Recognize the considerations needed to finalize JIT suppliers
- Appreciate the role of people and need for people management
- Realize the utility of 5S in any functional area, including audit
- Explain the concept of *kaizen*, appreciate the contribution of *kaizen* towards organizational improvement, and identify the areas where it can be applied
- Use brainstorming sessions to collect ideas for problem solving
- Understand and identify the role and use of six sigma

OPENING CASE

Application of JIT, 5S, and Kaizen in a Medium-Sized Company

Albert Engineering Works (AEW), established in 1998, manufactures mechanical engineering components and automobile spares. The organization comprises a few thousand employees, and is headed by a chairman and a managing director. All the departments in this company—production, maintenance, finance and accounts, and personnel—are headed by a vice president.

The company recruited three assistant managers through campus interview. After prolonged induction, one of them, Ratan, was inducted to the material management department. He took over the responsibility of the department in the middle of the financial year. The material management software was implemented two years ago. Ratan, a dynamic manager, considered the trend of customer demands. He further referred to the bill of materials (part list) of all the assemblies, sub-assemblies, and individual finished components. He visited the industrial engineering department and studied the manufacturing warrants and the rejections allowed by industrial engineering department.

Using these data as input, Ratan calculated the raw materials required in the forthcoming financial year. He placed purchase orders for the raw materials to meet the annual requirements. His intention was to save the cost of order and to get rebate over the bulk purchase. The suppliers confirmed acceptance of the orders and started delivering the ordered quantities.

Once, AEW received supplies of full quantities of the material ordered a few months ago from four suppliers. After a lengthy inspection process, it was detected that the storage of the materials posed problems due to the inadequacy of space. Partial quantities had to be stacked outside which was not the normal practice.

Moreover, many small items got mixed up; rubber seals, gaskets, O-rings, and so on perished and had to be thrown. Many raw materials were not drawn from the store by the production department. After looking into all these aspects, the store manager prepared and submitted a list to the higher authority.

The manager of the store requested a small group of the store department to undertake the task of storing the small items. The group collected some iron sheets from the scrap yard, prepared boxes with lid, painted the boxes, marked the name of the items and their ledger folio (LF) numbers, segregated the items, and put them in the respective boxes. The group also devised a method of locating the boxes from the LF numbers of the items.

At the end of the financial year, the senior material manager undertook an analysis. He classified the raw materials into non-moving items, slow moving items, and moving items, based on their periodical demand by manufacturing section from the store. Finally, he calculated the holdings or carrying cost of the items. He further calculated the loss incurred from the expiry of life of perishable rubber items and chemicals. On analysis, it was also revealed that a few regular customers did not place their purchase order on AEW. Ratan was involved in the execution of the entire exercise.

On a friendly note, the senior material manager advised Ratan to consider all activities pertaining to materials such as planning, procurement, inward inspection, preservation, storage, and so on, in totality for organizational effectiveness.

Note: This case is based on a reputed company that gained huge popularity in the 1980s, and expanded business, but could not sustain and lost market share substantially. The name of the company has been changed.

Learning points

- A company should consider an economic ordering quantity.
- Overstocking of items blocks a company's capital.
- Small items should be stored in bins with identification marks or labels.
- A small group can significantly contribute to departmental effectiveness.
- The lives of perishable items and items with a long shelf-life must be considered while ordering.
- Companies should use an integrated material management system.

INTRODUCTION

Quality refers to the degree to which a set of inherent characteristics fulfil the requirements (ISO 9000:2000). It is the totality of characteristics of an entity that bear its ability to satisfy the stated and implied needs. The needs may include aspects relating to usability, safety, availability, maintainability, reliability, economics, and environment. Quality is undefined without specifications of features and characteristics.

Quality is not a result of instructions or exhortations (ISO 8402:1994). It is the result of a mindset and the need for developing an attitude that is committed to production and delivery of quality goods.

Quality management refers to coordinated activities to direct and control an organization's need to upkeep quality. Quality improvement is part of quality management and is focused on increasing the ability to fulfil quality requirements.

Quality system is 'the documented plans, organizational structure, and activities that are implemented to control the conformance of a product or service to specified requirements and to provide evidence of such conformances.' (ISO 8402:1994)

In simple terms, quality management system refers to the organizational structure, procedures, processes, and resources which are needed to implement quality management. It encompasses four main components—quality planning, quality control, quality assurance, and quality improvement.

Quality has to be viewed from two distinct perspectives—customer perspective and manufacturing perspective. From the customer's perspective, quality is the summation of performance, features, reliability, conformance, durability, serviceability, aesthetics, and perceived quality. In other words, it is a set of dimensions of quality. From the manufacturing perspective, quality refers to conformance of design to customers' specifications and conformance of product specifications to design specifications.

Customers evaluate products as well as service quality. Service quality is ascertained over certain dimensions such as credibility, security, access, communication, customer focus, tangibles, reliability, responsiveness, competence, and courtesy. Dimension-wise definitions and evaluation questions are given in Annexure 22.1.

The operational view about quality is the degree to which the customer requirements are addressed. We classify a product as a 'quality product' when the customer expectations are met and there are no complaints.

Generally, an organization seeks to accomplish three objectives with regard to quality:

1. To achieve and maintain the quality of its products and services to meet its customer needs.
2. To gain confidence of its customers that the quality has been, or will be achieved and maintained.
3. To support management's confidence that the quality system has been installed and is effective.

There are certain tools that are used for problem solving related to quality. Some of the common and simple quality control tools are check sheet, cause and effect diagram, Pareto analysis, histogram, stratification, scatter diagram, control chart, etc.

Quality management also needs several tools, of which just-in-time (JIT), 5S, *kaizen*, and six sigma concept are discussed in this chapter.

JUST-IN-TIME

Q 1 Companies spend funds in procurement of raw materials, transportation, stocking them, manufacturing parts and semi-finished items, handling damages, payment towards insurance and taxes, etc. The finished goods should ultimately reach the customers. Thus, money is invested in the organization/business for return on investment (ROI). Unless the raw material is converted into finished goods and sold to the customers, they cannot get their returns. Money (investments) gets blocked instead of being circulated.

For instance, industries purchase raw materials to produce finished goods. They incur costs for purchasing them. After purchasing the material (be it casting, forging, bar material, a basic chemical, etc.), if it is not readily utilized, then the holding cost or carrying cost increase.

Elements of Cost

The terminologies associated with material management are procurement cost, material cost, ordering cost, and carrying or holding cost. If a company plans to purchase in small quantities, the carrying cost will decrease, the number of orders will increase, and consequently, the ordering cost will increase. Companies try to balance these two costs. Let us analyse these two costs individually.

Procurement cost This refers to the cost of obtaining goods through purchasing system. It includes

1. cost of processing the requisition, (floating enquiry, preparing CST (comparative statement of tenders), vetting, placing the purchase order after TPC (tender purchase committee) meeting
2. cost of following up and expediting,
3. cost of receiving the material and inspection for conformance,
4. cost of processing vendor's invoice, and
5. cost of the material.

Ordering cost Ordering cost refers to the cost of placing an order. It includes searching and deciding on the suitable supplier, floating tender inquiry, and placing the order involving all related formalities. If items are purchased in small quantities, then this cost will be more but carrying will reduce.

Cost of carrying/holding cost This includes money spent on handling, storage, packing, preserving, delivery, insurance, taxes, etc. Carrying costs are more if the store has slow-moving and non-moving items. Unnecessarily, storage space will remain occupied.

Total expected cost The total expected cost (TEC) is the sum of ordering cost and carrying/holding cost.

$$\text{TEC} = \frac{DC_c}{Q} + \frac{QC_o}{2}$$

C_c = Cost of carrying/holding one unit for unit time
C_o = Ordering cost = Number of orders × Cost of placing a single order
D = Total requirement in time t

$$\text{TEC} = \sqrt{D \cdot C_c \cdot C_o}$$

The objective of the management is to reduce the TEC to the extent possible. It is important to know that there is less scope for reducing the procurement cost; however, the carrying/holding cost can be greatly reduced. This should be kept in mind when trying to minimize the TEC. Thus, control is required to be exercised and concerted efforts are required to be directed to eliminate or minimize the holding or carrying cost.

Purpose of JIT

Big companies are seen to be facing difficulties while manufacturing or managing their large inventories in terms of the work-in-process (WIP) queue. Over a period of time, slow moving and non-moving items in inventories can contribute to carrying costs. Chief executive officers are always seen to be launching massive reorganization plans, known as the business process reengineering (BPR). To smooth the entire system, the whole plant is even bifurcated into individual cost centers and profit centers. Some of these problems include shortages, long lead time, huge storage area, high movement of materials, very low stock turn ratio, first piece introduction, low productivity, rejection/rework, discrepancy in design, material non-availability, high throughout time etc.

To get rid of most or some of these problems, big companies, today, are seen to be introducing the JIT system. JIT is a concept which is aimed towards reducing the holding or carrying cost. Thus, in a perfect JIT system, the carrying/holding cost is zero. The prime goal of JIT is the achievement of zero inventories throughout the entire supply chain.

Prerequisites of System

For a JIT system to function efficiently, it needs a lot of discipline in the production system. A JIT system can fail due to the failure of the suppliers/vendors/sub-contractors not being brought under the JIT umbrella. If JIT is considered as a game, the suppliers need to be considered the most important players. If the players do not perform well, the game may be lost, and the sustenance of JIT system may become difficult. Consciousness and role of suppliers are of paramount importance in JIT system.

JIT system obviously imposes certain conditions on the production system and its environment. It requires discipline in the following areas:

1. Demand on production facilities
2. Maintenance of production facilities
3. People associated with production
4. Quality of the products
5. Feeding materials (in any form) by the suppliers to the production system

JIT is a pull-system unlike the conventional job-shop/batch type push-system. It is weak when it comes to deal with variations and uncertainties in the quantitative and qualitative characteristics of the market.

ABC Analysis

While implementing JIT, a purchase manager needs to carry out ABC analysis to be able to monitor the total range of purchased items effectively. These bought out items can be classified into three categories, namely, A (high usage value), B (moderate usage value), and C (low usage value). The company also differentiates 'significant few' from 'insignificant many'. Generally, it is seen that 20 per cent or less number of items cost 80 per cent or more of the total amount spent for purchase. These items are obviously 'A' class items, which need maximum attention.

Table 22.1 ABC analysis

Class of item	A	B	C
Holding time	2 hours to 10 days	10 days to 20 days	20 days to 45 days

It is not at all advisable to attempt to bring all the items under JIT umbrella together. In respect of inventory holding, a differential policy related to ABC classification may be formulated. Based on thumb rule, the holding time of the three classes of items is tabulated in Table 22.1

With the achievement of perfection in JIT system and gaining experience, improved performance of the JIT suppliers and inventory holding time may be planned for further reduction.

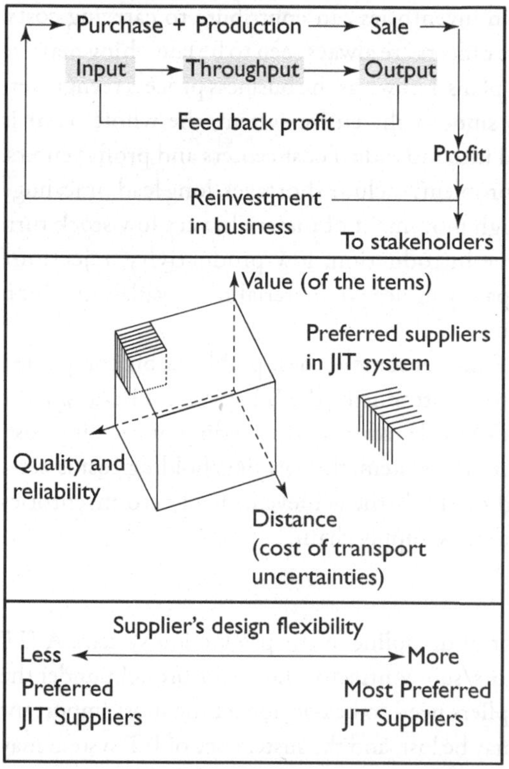

FIG. 22.1 JIT parameters for preferred supplier in JIT system

JIT Parameters

Let us take it for granted that there is a match in the supplier–client environment. It has already been pointed out that low value items are not brought under JIT system from the standpoint of economic sense. Only high value items are considered. The quality and reliability of the products from the suppliers, are also important to be of high order. Thirdly, if the distance between the supplier and the client is short, it is advantageous, as the transportation cost would be less and meetings could be organized across the table. Refer to Figure 22.1 for an illustration of this concept.

Thus, the three parameters of JIT are as follows:

1. Value of the item

2. Quality and reliability
3. Distance

To be a good JIT supplier, a company must be able to supply its product to its client in the best possible condition, as per the client's requirement. The supplier also needs to keep adequate stock of the finished goods to meet the fluctuating demand. In such cases, the supplier's inventory holding becomes high (cost of items supplied goes up) and needs serious cost consideration.

JIT and Design Flexibility

Very often, the JIT clients seek outputs of varying specification to suit their fluctuating needs (product range) from their suppliers. In other words, the customer company looks for design flexibility from the supplier company. This desire is not unusual, as different designs would be available to the buying organization with the least loss of time. JIT is involved in promoting design integration of the supplier with the customer companies. If the parameter of design flexibility is introduced in Figure 22.1, it will become a four-dimensional concept.

A large level of design flexibility and JIT supplier are difficult to achieve simultaneously. Still, to sharpen the competitive edge, suppliers strive to affect JIT supplies having design flexibility.

People Management

Systems are designed and operated by people. So people management is extremely imperative for JIT systems. The following is a detailed analysis of why people management is imperative for JIT systems:

Continuous improvement through people The integrated/synchronized efforts of all—from top management to hourly operators are essential in JIT environment. To achieve the best results, people of all levels must be assigned responsibility to suggest improvements and authority to implement them in practice.

Total employee involvement JIT demands involvement of everyone in the company. Attitudinal change towards the very concept of JIT needs to be improved.

Multi-skilling This concept insists on the aspect of an individual taking care of a multitude of work. Thus, the enabling capacity of a man increases as he acquires a variety of skills. He can perform his task efficiently and effectively with an innovative approach.

Please refer to Box 22.1 for an idea about the companies in India using JIT.

Box 22.1 JIT companies in India

1. Maruti Udyog uses the JIT system. After the ABC analysis, they fix their inventory holding time class-wise and also fix the courses of actions.
2. Larsen & Toubro is currently operating on a system that is a typical combination of JIT and MRP (material requirement planning) 'A' class items have been brought under JIT umbrella, while 'B' class and 'C' class items are procured based on EOQ (economic order quantity) and reorder levels (material requirement planning or MRP).
3. Lucas TVS and Sundaram have also progressed way ahead in implementing JIT systems and have developed JIT vendors.

ROLE OF HR IN JIT

JIT companies need strong relationship building with customers and suppliers. The suppliers, organization, and customers must be professional experts and close to each other. The success of the company depends on promptness and mutual understanding among the company and the suppliers and customers. Often, a company may be required to plan and execute a purchase order before receipt of the formal purchase order. The suppliers of the company should know the fluctuating demands. Suppliers must have access to the material database for their preparedness. Trust is of paramount importance. The relevant company personnel also need to have analytical skills as they have to behave like businessman yet try to understand others feelings and problems. They have to take calculated risks systematically.

At the time of recruitment, HR needs to make sure that all employees possess these qualities. They also need to make sure that everyone works together with the same focus of implementing the JIT successfully. So, in short, the dominant personality traits required in JIT are: calculative, definitive perfection, empathetic, enterprising, inquisitive, optimistic, perfectionist, persuasive, and risk-taking but systematic. (A list of personality traits and the situation is provided in Annexure 22.2).

Persons whose dominant motives are affiliation, achievement, and activity are likely to be successful.

INTRODUCTION TO 5S

Some visitors prefer to take rounds in an organization to assess the management's general attitude to work place and good housekeeping. In addition to impressing any outsider, it is needless to mention that a good workplace also results in higher productivity and cleanliness. Creativity, common sense, and professionalism are the success factors for a good organization. Some of the benefits of 5S are as follows:

1. Service efficiencies
2. Better quality system
3. Safer workplace
4. Higher employee morale
5. Workplace layout
6. Improved material handling

Q 4 5S is a concept that emphasizes a change in the mindset. It is also the first step towards continuous improvement. Using the concept of 5S, workplace organizations can reduce the cost of production. It is basically a systematic and rational approach to methodical housekeeping built on a sound economic base. It is a science in the sense that it is based on a logical approach and is analytical in nature. It is also an art in the sense that it contributes to decency, beautification, and esteem value. 5S should be a company-wide practice which needs top management's support. This concept is a well applicable and implementable in domestic situation as well.

The concept originated from Japan. 5S stands for *seiri*, *seiton*, *seiso*, *seiketsu*, and *shitsuke*. The meaning of these words is listed in Table 22.2.

Table 22.2 5S and its meaning

Japanese term	English translation	Meaning
Seiri	Organization	Sorting out/organizing (in order)
Seiton	Tidiness	Systematic arrangement/neatness
Seiso	Cleaning	Spic and span/cleaning/inspection

(Contd)

Table 22.2 (Contd)

Japanese term	English translation	Meaning
Seiketsu	Standardization	Serene atmosphere, sanitizing, standardization
Shitsuke	Discipline	Self-discipline

Now, let us discuss each of the five terms individually.

Seiri or Sorting

This refers to sorting, arranging, and organizing items in different categories such as items that are critical, important, frequently-used, useless, or items that are not needed presently. Critical items should be kept for use in place nearer to the work station. Things that are not likely to be used in near future should be stored in another place. Unwanted items can be salvaged. To carry out this step, the worth of the item or its place should be decided based on its utility and not cost. As a consequence, the search time is significantly reduced.

The theme of this step is, 'stratification management and dealing with the causes'. It is a natural tendency to retain things, which might not be required at all. However, obsolete and rejected items make the floor and surrounding look untidy and clumsy. Added to this, we often face difficulty to trace and locate a useful thing amidst lot of useless things. Hence, sorting them is an important task.

There is a general practice which is followed to carry out *seiri*. Please refer to Table 22.3.

Table 22.3 Means of arranging/stacking things

Priority	Frequency of use	How to deal with it
Low	Less than once a year	Throw away, store away from the workplace
Average	May be used within three to six months, once per week or once per month	Store together but near the workplace
High	Once a day	Locate at the workplace

Steps for sorting The steps involved in sorting are as follows:

1. Remove all garbage and tools, rejects from shop floor.
2. Remove unnecessary papers from file.
3. Discard old files, stationery not in use.
4. Give a horizontal and vertical look on the floor and wall to remove all unnecessary items.
5. Clean walkways.

Benefits of sorting Some of the benefits or sorting are that it

1. saves floor space,
2. helps to get rid of obsolete items,
3. gives a clear idea of material in stock,
4. prevents incidence of unnecessary buying,
5. make certain that bin card balances conform to actual, and
6. ensures better utilization of existing material.

Seiton or Systematic Arrangement

Seiton follows the theme of 'functional storage and eliminating the need to look for things'.

> Slogan of *seiton*:
> 1. Each item has a place and only one place.
> 2. A place for every thing, everything in its place.

This step emphasizes on, 'a rational, orderly, and methodical arrangement of all items we use, rework, or write off'. The concept is that, 'each item has a place and only one place'. To identify items easily, they should be placed back from where they were picked up after their usage. Tools such as name plates and coloured tags should be used for arranging the items. Vertical racks can be used for this purpose, where heavy items can occupy the bottom position in the racks.

The slogan of the step Seiton is 'a place for everything, everything in its place'.

Placement of items There should be a basis for the positioning of items. The possible answers are as follows:

1. Things regularly used (hourly, daily, weekly) placed close to the machine or workplace
2. Things occasionally used (say monthly) placed near the work area
3. Things seldom used but still needed (say once in a quarter) placed in store

Brainstorming sessions can be organized to finalize matters regarding the place where things should be easily stored, ensuring identification, making them retrievable, and enabling them to be returnable to original position.

Benefits of systematic arrangement The following are some of the benefits of systematic arrangement:

1. No wastage of time in searching
2. Material easily available and retrievable
3. Lesser production downtime
4. Fast handling of machine breakdown

Seiso or Spic and Span

This involves cleaning the work place, making components free from burns, grease, oil, waste, scrap etc. along with no loosely hanging wires or oil leakage from machines.

The theme of this approach is, 'cleaning not for beautification alone but with a sense of purpose.'

Tools such as brain storming, problem-solving techniques, and cause-effect diagrams may be used.

Benefits of *seiso* The following are some of the benefits:

1. Workplace conducive to higher productivity
2. Fast corrective action
3. Tools well laid out
4. No blockage in material flow
5. Inventory levels can be found visually
6. Lesser production down time
7. Sense of achievement
8. Pride to employees

9. Greater confidence of customers
10. Higher product quality achieved

Shiketsu or Serene Atmosphere/Standardization

The theme of this step is, 'visual management'. Standardization of work procedures, and maintenance of safe and hygienic conditions at workplace are believed to contribute greatly to a 'serene atmosphere'. Employees should discuss together and decide on standards for keeping the work place/machines/pathways neat and clean. These standards should be implemented in the whole organization and inspected randomly.

Steps to create serene atmosphere These are some of the steps for creating a serene atmosphere:

1. Wear neat and clean uniform and protective clothing.
2. Ensure ergonomically-suitable standards.
3. Provide adequate lighting, exhaust, and ventilation.
4. Check electrical wiring, cables, and switches.
5. Maintain sanitary/hygienic conditions.
6. Earmark smoking and eating areas.
7. Indicate godowns containing inflammable items.
8. Provide indications for silence zones.
9. Earmark garbage area.
10. Look for heavy noise, vibration, and heat, and find root causes.

Typical indicators Some typical indicators of serene atmosphere are listed:

1. Danger zones
2. Colour-coded pipes
3. Voltage levels
4. Thermal level indicators
5. Okay marks
6. Warning colours
7. Belt size levels
8. Direction marking

Benefits of serene atmosphere The following are some of the benefits:

1. Standardized procedures emphasize system approach and reduce person-dependence
2. Standardized procedures restore confidence and minimizes errors
3. Productivity increases as defects go down
4. Easier and safer working condition
5. New problems get exposed and solved
6. Easier to initiate corrective and preventive action
7. More opportunities to maintain improved quality
8. Easier to adhere to quality system
9. Ownership and sense of pride among employees

Shitsuke or Self-discipline

The theme of this step is, 'habit formation and disciplined workplace'. The step emphasizes training, sincerity, and constancy of purpose by following the rules and standards developed in the earlier 4S. 5S may be considered as a way of life that brings about self-discipline among the employees of the organization. This includes wearing badges, following work procedures, punctuality, dedication to the organization etc.

Steps to self-discipline The following are the steps to inculcating self-discipline:

1. Create awareness of 4S.
2. Prepare a 5S manual.
3. Develop action details for maintaining standards.
4. Make them easily understandable.
5. Give specific directions.
6. Display correct and formal work procedures on the floor near the work station.
7. Correct deviation on the spot.
8. Manage public space.
9. Define responsibilities.
10. Maintain punctuality.
11. Organize 5S audits.
12. Demonstrate sincerity in following rules.
13. Share success to enthuse others.
14. Practice what you preach.

Advantages of 5S If all the steps are followed, the following advantages can be derived:

1. A clean and beautifully organized workplace
2. Time taken to retreive things minimized
3. Lesser time required for material handling
4. Problems detected quickly
5. Machine production downtime reduced
6. Lower cost of production
7. More usable space
8. Better preventive maintenance
9. Higher employee morale
10. Consistent better quality of products
11. Higher productivity
12. Lesser accidents
13. Higher employee involvement
14. Sustenance of quality system
15. Reduction in error/defects due to standardized procedure

Audit of 5S

Audit means verification of activities, as per the prescribed standards. However, there is no standard process available for 5S as it is merely a concept. Hence, there cannot be any standardized check list for auditing. In such a case, an audit checklist can be developed by a trained personnel of an organization, its zones, and sub-zones.

For the purpose of auditing, auditors must be selected from the same zone (functional area). However, one member may belong to another zone to maintain impartiality. The strength of an audit team should preferably comprise four to five members.

The following points need to be considered while following 5S:

1. No standard checklists are available for 5S auditing (since it is merely a concept)

2. Audit checklists have to be developed by trained personnel of the organization, its zones, or sub-zones (the checklist is organization-specific)
3. For auditing, auditors have to be selected from the organization
4. Auditors are to be deployed in a zone, and are not associated with the zone to maintain impartiality
5. In certain cases, if one auditor is selected from the home zone, then one or two auditors must be selected from other zones (to maintain impartiality)
6. The size of an audit team should preferably be two or three members
7. The team may develop an audit checklist, suitable for that zone, with relevant points and weightages
8. Such checklist will be of immense use to the audit team members

Auditor's checklist

Auditors prepare a checklist with relevant points and its relative weightage to ease out the 5S audit. An audit checklist developed for auditing and used during audit is furnished in Table 22.4.

Table 22.4 Audit checklist

S. no.	Activity	Points
1	Documentation maintained as per retention plan	10
2	Items are retained at their assigned places	10
3	Innovative methods of storage, visual display system, etc	5
4	Cleanliness/hygiene	5
5	Space released	5
6	Reporting of waste reduction	5
7	Aesthetic aspect	10
8	Safety aspect	15
9	Auditee' s personal appearance	5
10	Shop floor layout	5
11	Lighting level	5
12	Noise level	5
13	Temperature/humidity	5
14	General ergonomics	10

Note: This is merely a guideline. The organization has to decide upon its checklist by considering its product range, space, manpower, etc.

The checklist is meant for a shop floor. Safety aspects and general ergonomics have received a higher degree of importance in an audit checklist. Aspect-wise points are to be finalized by the audit team who may, however, take consent of the auditee to finalize the checklist. The company periodically reviews the checklist. The zonal coordinator should retain a copy of the checklist.

Display of 5S status The auditee may like to use a display board for presenting information.

Section: Zone

Date	Marks/Points obtained					
	Sorting	Systematic arrangement	Spic and span	Serene	Self-discipline	Total

The auditee may also include the auditor's signature in one column.

5S Manual

An organization should develop their 5S manual in line with the quality manual or environmental manual. However, this is generally much shorter in volume and extends to about 35 to 50 pages. The contents of the 5S Manual may include the following:

1. 5S policy and objectives
2. Brief history of the organization
3. Product range
4. Types of input materials and their classifications
5. System of handling, storage, packing, preservation, and delivery
6. Methodology to ensure identification and traceability
7. 5S organization structure (responsibility)
8. Audit of 5S
9. Rewards and recognition with regard to 5S

5S Policy and Objectives

For the benefits of students and other readers, the 5S policy and objectives are detailed for a company (say, PQR limited). Please refer to Exhibit 22.1.

Exhibit 22.1 5S policy and objectives

5S policy

PQR Ltd is committed to improve the quality of workplace which, in turn, will enhance its productivity through the practice of 5S.

Date: dd.mm.yyyy.

Signature
CEO

5S objectives

All the employees of PQR

1. shall maintain standard of recordkeeping, including weeding out of unwanted and obsolete documents, and records,
2. shall maintain clean and hygienic work environment, and
3. shall ensure enforcement of self-discipline to provide better customer service.

Date: dd.mm.yyyy.

Signature
CEO

Role of HR in 5S

5S is an art because it makes the workplace look good; it is also a science as there must be a rationale behind it. The person responsible to initiate and promote 5S should have a sense of aesthetics. Implementation of 5S needs some expenditure. The relevant persons have to strike a balance between expenditure and derivable benefits. They need to be calculative and proceed with perfection and be esteemed. They have to be enduring and patient to see that things are happening in various departments. Qualitative attribute is of immense importance to them. To keep a check on all these requirements for the concept of 5S to excel, HR needs to take the responsibility to manage the people.

The dominant personality traits should be initiator, esteemed, frank, calculative, perfectionist, patient, qualitative, etc. (A list of personality traits and the situation are provided in Annexure 22.2).

People with high degree of achievement, affiliation, and activity motives are likely to establish, implement, and maintain 5S and derive benefits from the applied concept.

INTRODUCTION TO KAIZEN

Q 8 The term 'kai' means change, and 'zen' means good (for the better). Basically, *kaizen* is a Japanese concept and refers to small improvements that are carried out on a continuous basis and involves all people in the organization. *Kaizen* differs from big spectacular innovations. It requires no or little monetary investment. The principle behind the concept is that 'a very large number of small improvements are more effective in an organizational environment than a few improvements that give significant impact.' *Kaizen* is aimed at reducing losses in the workplace that reduce our efficiencies. *Kaizen* activities extend over production, maintenance, quality control, store, and also in offices such as planning, purchase, design, industrial engineering, administrative, vigilance, etc.

Kaizen helps management to ensure on-time delivery of items at competitive costs, satisfying both their stated and implied needs. *Kaizen* is also a means to continuous improvement. *Kaizen* solutions and suggestions can be implemented and maintained without any resistance as they are done only in small groups associated with work and from the work area. However, it is wise to keep in mind that maintenance of *Kaizen* to derive benefits needs intensive persuasion.

In offices, kaizen is popularly known as 'kobetsu kaizen' and facilitates

1. Inventory reduction
2. Lead time reduction of critical processes
3. Motion and space losses
4. Retrieval time reduction
5. Equalization of work load

Kaizen has been effectively applied in the following areas:

1. Operation
2. Quality
3. Productivity
4. House Keeping
5. Energy
6. Delivery
7. Energy
8. House keeping
9. Morale building

Benefits of *Kaizen* Methodically-implemented *kaizen* facilitates an organization to derive benefits such as

1. Improving the office efficiency (eliminating the time loss)
2. Tending to achieve zero breakdown
3. Enhancing employee satisfaction and improved morale
4. Making jobs easier, simpler, safer, and faster
5. Increasing efficiency

> *Kaizen* is used
> 1. whenever there is a problem and
> 2. whenever there is an opportunity for improvement.

6. Ensuring overall improvement of organization
7. Generating a satisfied and delighted customer

Kaizen is generally undertaken in an organization to solve a problem. Depending on the type of the problem, a particular segment of the workforce volunteers takes up the problem. in other cases, *Kaizen* is also done whenever there is an opportunity of improvement though there is no problem.

Kairyo

Kairyo refers to a major innovation or breakthrough, and is based on new technology or management concept. It involves considerable investments.

Kaizen* versus *kairyo The biggest difference between the two concepts is that *kaizen* requires little or no investment while *kairyo* requires a great deal of effort (motivation). There are some other distinct differences between *kaizen* and *kairyo*:

1. The effect of *kaizen* is long lasting and is meant for the long term but is not dramatic. *Kairyo* has a dramatic effect.
2. *Kaizen* appears in small steps but *kairyo* is executed in big steps.
3. *Kaizen* is continuous and incremental, while *kairyo* is intermittent and non-incremental.
4. The change is gradual in *kaizen*, while it is abrupt in *kairyo*.
5. Involvement of all levels of employees is necessary in *kaizen*; only a selected significant few employees are needed for *kairyo*.
6. *Kaizen* encourages collective approach, group efforts, and teamwork. On the other hand, strong 'individualism', individual ideas, and efforts are associated with *kairyo*.
7. Maintenance and improvement of existing utilities and facilities are ensured in *kaizen*; *kairyo* emphasizes on 'scrap and rebuild'.
8. *Kaizen* signifies conventional knowledge, while *kairyo* calls for (a) technological breakthrough, (b) new inventions and new theories, and (c) new management systems.
9. *Kaizen* is people orientation and *kairyo* is technology orientation.
10. The evaluation criteria for *kaizen* is, 'process and effort for better result' and for *kairyo*, it is 'results for more profit'.
11. *Kaizen* works well in low-growth economy while *kairyo* is better suited for fast-growth economies.

***Kaizen* implementation** *Kaizen* may be effectively implemented in an organization by following these steps:

1. Formulation of the *kaizen* policy
2. Defining the objectives and goals
3. Demarcation of zone or functional areas
4. Develop a structure to facilitate idea generation and idea evaluation
5. Train facilitators of each functional or work area
6. Deploy facilitators to design *kaizen* documentation format. The facilitators should design the promotional material
7. Top management and facilitators are required for the following

   (a) To design recognition and reward system
   (b) To launch *kaizen* programme
   (c) To train all employees on *kaizen*
   (d) To start implementing *kaizen*

Cause–Effect Diagram

The cause–effect diagram is also known as '*Ishikawa* diagram', 'fish bone', or 'herringbone diagram'. Irrespective of the name, this diagram depicts the various 'causes' responsible to produce the 'effect'. The first level causes, called the primary causes, include man, machine, material, method, and environment (4M + 1E). The primary causes may also include person, material, process/methodology, and equipment. For each of these primary causes, there is a secondary cause too.

Brainstorming The causes responsible to produce an effect are listed by a simple popular technique known as brainstorming. A small group (say 5 or 6 persons) participates in the brain storming session. The group is required to have a leader. The leader may be chosen on a rotational basis. The steps are as follows:

1. The problem is first defined.
2. Each person gets his turn to express his view in rotation.
3. In case no idea is contributed, the member has to say 'pass'.
4. Each point is listed under 4M + 1E in the cause–effect diagram.
5. No idea is assessed or criticized at this time—idea collection stage.
6. The idea generation and listing continues till all the group members say 'pass' in one round.
7. Inputs and contribution of all members are thus considered. Brainstorming without data should be avoided.
8. Members should be informed beforehand of the problem so that they can come prepared.

Checklist: Broad areas Checklists are used for detecting deviations from whatever is desired and documented. They ensure coverage of all aspects such as

1. Man (operator)
2. Machine (including facilities or utilities)
3. Material (inputs)
4. Method (operation
5. Measurement

Checklist to Generate Kaizen Ideas

There are certain questions, which help us generate ideas in *kaizen*. A few questions, likely to stimulate the idea collection stage of the brainstorming session, are listed here.

1. Can I reduce the strain in the operation?
2. Can this Improvement be applied elsewhere?
3. Is there an alternative way to do this task or operation?
4. Can the time taken to perform this task be reduced?
5. Can the output or productivity be increased?
6. Can the defect be identified at source?
7. Can the operator identify it?
8. What are the non-value adding operations?
9. Can this be done in a faster, cheaper, safer, and easier way?
10. Can I reduce the variation and deviation?

Remember that there can always be a better solution.

The Kaizen Environment

It is possible to effectively create an environment conducive to implementing *kaizen*. Organizational culture and climate are the main highlights of the environment. The following points are relevant.

1. Success breeds success—create small islands of successes.
2. Promote teamwork and collective wisdom.
3. Do not ridicule or criticize.
4. Be patient.
5. Need-based training is essential.
6. Do not be complacent with present status.
7. Do not hide problems (maintain openness).
8. Be honest with your mistakes.
9. Have respect for individuals.
10. Appreciate openly (where deserved) but criticize privately.
11. Ensure group consensus before implementing ideas.
12. Find out what is wrong rather than who is wrong.
13. Do not hesitate to take internal and external help form others.
14. Always standardize.
15. Emphasize on systems more than results.
16. Be proactive.
17. Do it now.
18. Do not give up.

Box 22.2 lists the *kaizen* policy and objectives that need to be focused.

Box 22.2 Focus of policy and objectives

1. Practice concepts of zero losses in every sphere of activity.
2. Relentless pursuit to achieve cost reduction targets in all resources.
3. Un-compromising pursuit to improve over all plant equipment effectiveness.
4. Comprehensive use of preventive maintenance analysis as a tool for eliminating losses.
5. Focus on easy handling of operators.

Prohibited expressions in *kaizen* *Kaizen's* philosophy restricts the use of certain expressions as it believes that these expressions can demotivate spontaneous involvement in the concept. Any person, even higher authorities, must be cautious about the uses of these expressions. In addition, the higher authorities have to ensure that employees are not using these. Some of these expressions are listed in Box 22.3.

Box 22.3 Prohibited expressions

Q 17

1. Everybody knows that.
2. We tried this before; I know this won't work.
3. It is impossible and absurd.

(Contd)

Box 22.3 (Contd)

4. Your idea is not up-to-date enough.
5. You are offering high-level ideas.
6. I am overburdened with suggestions.
7. We will talk some other day.
8. There are rules. Your suggestion won't be accepted.
9. So, you are also an engineer.
10. Your idea is far away from the ideal one.
11. This idea may work in Japan, but this is India.
12. Your level of understanding must improve.
13. Idea is good, but what about budget?
14. This will create another problem.
15. Why do you want a change? Everything is fine.

Role of HR in Kaizen

The traits and motives have been stated for JIT and 5S. In addition, persons responsible for establishing and promoting *kaizen* should have the personality traits of being inquisitive and innovative. *Kaizen* may not produce distinct results immediately. As such, tolerance is essential for effectiveness. (A list of personality traits and the situation are provided in Annexure 22.2).

The most important task of the HR manager is to build the right culture, as organizational culture plays a vital role in *kaizen*'s implementation and maintenance.

INTRODUCTION TO SIX SIGMA

Q 13 The present business scenario is characterized by acute competition. The concept of six sigma is applicable in many companies, though it has wide application in manufacturing companies. There is a lot of pressure on manufacturing organizations to become more productive and efficient. Brilliant and highly innovative approaches and ideas are replacing the conventional techniques and these are essential to survive in the global competitive market. Manufacturing organizations need to improve quality, while controlling and reducing cost, and boosting productivity with limited resources.

Motorola propounded the six sigma principles, which, in quality literature is called the 'zero defects (ZD)' programme. The concept of 'zero defects' is a philosophical benchmark or a standard of excellence in quality. ZD is aimed at stimulating each employees to care about accuracy.

The six-sigma technique provides mathematical precision to everything we do. This rational approach for solving any problem also leads to reduction of the irrelevant procedures to complete an activity so that the product or service is nearer to perfection. In simple terms, six sigma stands for 'six standard deviations', (σ:sigma is the Greek letter used to represent standard deviation in statistics). Six sigma is the methodology that combines the gradual and continuous improvement and promotes radical design. It is a statistical tool used for problem solving which reduces the defects by streamlining various processes.

Six sigma ensures 'value enrichment' of the products or services for the customers. This approach can directly enable an organization to remain competitive, if implemented judiciously. It is a highly disciplined process that helps us to focus on developing and delivering quality products and services.

'The best six sigma project begins not inside the business but outside it, and is focused on answering the question—how can we make the customer more competitive? What is critical to the customers' success? One thing we have discovered with certainty is that anything we do that makes the customer more successful inevitably results in a financial return to us,' Jack Welch, former CEO of GE.

Motorola started six sigma to implement in its manufacturing division, and millions of parts are made using the same process. Six sigma has been successfully applied to other nonmanufacturing processes, too. Today, Six sigma is applied to many fields such as services, medical and insurance procedures, call centers. Following Motorola's success with the concept, General Electric, Allied Signal, Honeywell, Ford, etc. also followed suit and realized the powerful bottom-line results in their organization.

Six Sigma Process

In manufacturing organizations, tools such as templates, jigs, and fixtures are used for production. Organizations having present generation computer numerical control (CNC) machines make part programming (programmes to produce a component on a particular CNC machine) where they are not required to use the tools. Whatever be the type of machines used, dimensions of manufactured components vary slightly. Product designers allow tolerance on the basic dimensions of components within which components are required to be manufactured. Tolerances are deviations allowed; where basic dimension and the allowed departure is the 'upper specification limit' (USL) and basic dimension minus the allowed departure is the 'lower specification limit' (LSL). Whatever be the technology, dimensions of some components go beyond the specification limits (USL and LSL).

Companies take several measures to reduce variations. They train employees on statistical techniques to enable them to identify critical factors responsible for variation. Trained workers reduce mistakes on their part. Processes are reviewed and redesigned for better performance, and maintenance of machines are improved. The standard deviation of the process also gets reduced. In the process, the twelve sigma spread may be achieved within the LSL and USL. Six sigma relies heavily on statistical techniques to reduce defects and measure quality. Six sigma strives for perfection and allows for only 3.4 defects per million opportunities for each product or service transaction.

Companies train employees on statistical techniques to enable them to identify critical factors responsible for variations of products from the basic dimensions.

For example, the higher the σ level, the better the capability of the process to produce defect-free work and vice versa. To elucidate the differences in a printed book, 3σ would be equivalent to one misspelled word per 15 pages of textbook and 6σ would be equivalent to one misspelled word over 300,000 pages of the book.

Six Sigma and Value Enrichment

If a company strives to produce the highest quality products or services at the lowest possible costs and gains competitive edge over its competitors in markets, then it leads to 'value enrichment' for the company. It is a measurement-based approach which also enables us to find out the ways and means to pursue 'value enrichment' for the company and the customer. Obviously, for customers, 'value enrichment' is the right to purchase high quality products or services at the lowest cost. The companies need to identify the parameters important to customers and proceed accordingly.

In any business, there are vast areas of activities; there are many activities in the multiple functional areas and we may not have adequate knowledge about all of them. When we do not know about the parameter important to customers, we do not value it.

It implies that unknowingly we do not consider the value of a parameter and we do not measure it. If we do not measure, we cannot improve. This leads to the question, 'unless we measure, how can we improve?' Six sigma helps in overcoming this problem.

SIPOC Diagram

SIPOC stands for 'supplier-input-process-output-customer'. It is a tool used to identify all relevant elements of a process improvement project before the commencement of work. SIPOC is highly effective to apply six sigma in non-manufacturing processes. Please refer to Figure 22.2.

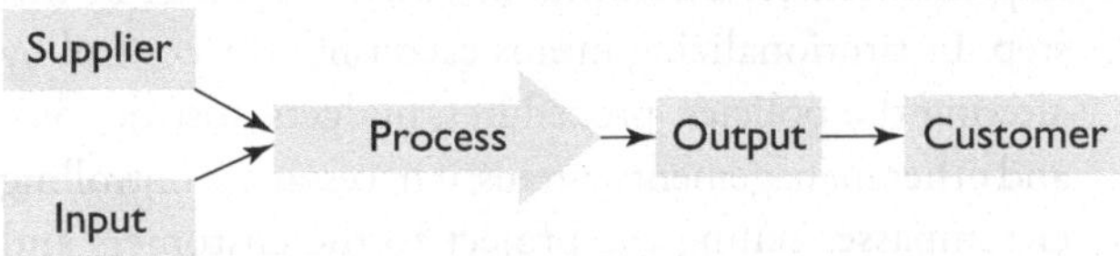

Fig. 22.2 SIPOC diagram

Organization as an Adaptive System

To survive in the buyers' market, it is very much essential to understand the requirements of customers on a continuous basis and meet the demands with an edge over the competitors. To gain competitive edge, an organization is required to work as an adaptive system. Everything done inside the organization is cost to the company. Only when a company goes outside it, can it make money from profit.

Thus, businesses have to be adaptive to customers. A six sigma organization is supposed to remain adaptive to external factors. Focusing for improvement inside the organization without considering external factors may not result in profit.

Six Sigma DMAIC Methodology

Six sigma methodology improves an existing business process by constantly reviewing and retuning the process by involving the use of a methodology known as DMAIC (define, measure, analyse, improve, and control).

D: Define opportunity.
M: Measure performance.
A: Analyse opportunity.
I: Improve performance.
C: Control performance.

Define opportunity Defining the goals and objectives of an improvement project, derived from 'critical to quality characteristics' based on 'voice of customer' (VOC) are included in this step. A problem statement, milestones, scope of project, improvements required in project, and a high-level road map of the process (the steps/ways of completing a process) are also developed in this phase.

Measure performance Measuring the process to find the current level and future level of performance, and to gauge the improvements, forms the next important step. Measures cover gathering and sampling data, and determining when to count it. Calculate the σ level as a measure against customer requirements and for comparison with other processes.

Q 14 **Analyse opportunity** Analysing the data collected in the measurement phase to identify any problems in the process and to find the root causes behind the variation is carried out in this phase. Viable causes are determined using experience, data, and a process review. These are repeated for refinement or rejection of possible causes, until the root cause is found and verified with data.

Table 22.5 Tools of six sigma

No.	Phase	Tools used
1.	Define	(a) Team charter (b) Knowing voice of customer
2.	Measure	(a) SIPOC - 'Supplier-Input-Process-Output-Customer' (b) Data collection (c) Rejection trends (d) Rejection cost (e) Defect matrix (f) Measurement system analysis
3.	Analyse	(a) Process stratification (b) Pareto analysis (c) Root cause analysis (d) Why–Why analysis
4.	Improve	Action plan
5.	Control	(a) Training of the workforce (b) P charts

Improve performance Improving the system by finding ways to do things better, safer, cheaper, or faster and satisfying customers should be the next step. This phase needs testing, refining, and implementing a solution to the root cause. It is necessary to implement the new approach and validate the improvement in this phase.

Control performance Controlling the improvement implemented on a continuous basis is the crux of this step. Institutionalizing means exercising the control by altering the policies, procedures, budgets, instructions, and other management systems, if necessary. Controlling encompasses selling the project to the customers and securing management support, and giving final ownership to those working with it on a day-to-day basis.

At each phase of DMAIC of six sigma, specific tools are used. Refer to Table 22.5 for a list of six sigma tools used.

Steps to Achieving Six Sigma

Motorola prescribes six steps to achieve six sigma:

Q 13 *Step 1:* Identify the product or service provided.
Step 2: Identify the customer(s) for the product or service and determine what they consider important.
Step 3: Identify the needs to provide the product or service that satisfy the customer.
Step 4: Define the process for doing the work.
Step 5: Mistake-proof the process and eliminate waste effort.
Step 6: Ensure continuous improvement by measuring, analysing, and controlling the improved process.

Many companies are frequently adopting measure-analyse-improve-control (MAIC) cycle to use six sigma. They adopt the following steps:

1. Select critical to quality characteristics (CTQ).
2. Define performance standards (the targets to be achieved).
3. Validate measurement systems (to ensure that data are reliable).
4. Establish product reliability (how good are the products).
5. Define performance objectives (to verify the extent of achievement).
6. Identify sources of variation (use seven quality control tools).
7. Screen potential causes (apply correlation studies etc.)
8. Ascertain relationship among variables (causes or factors and the output)
9. Establish operating tolerances for input factors and output variables
10. Validate the measurement system (without validation, one cannot be sure)
11. Determine the process capability (expressed as process capability index C_{pk} or C_{pm})
12. Implement process controls (a discipline for maintaining the output of specific process within a desired range).

Steps for Implementing Six Sigma

Bedi (2008) proposes the following five steps while implementing six sigma in organizations.

Step 1: Define the priorities of the customers with respect to quality. In this step, attributes of the product that are considered the most important by customers in evaluating the quality of the product are identified. These attributes possess critical to quality (CTQ) characteristics. The customers' perception of quality attributes is periodically updated by way of customer survey.

Step 2: Measure the processes and defects arising in the product due to process. The important processes influencing/affecting the CTQ characteristics are identified through the performance measurement techniques that are established for these processes.

Step 3: Analyse the process to determine the most likely causes of defects. The key variables most likely to responsible for variation in the process are identified to find the reason for defect generation.

Step 4: Improve the process performance and remove the causes of the defects. Specification limits of the key variables are fixed and a system for measuring the deviations of the variables is established and validated. The process is improvised in order to keep the variables within specification limits.

Step 5: Ensure that the improvements are maintained over time. The modified process is subject to vigil at regular intervals of time to ensure that the key variables do not show any unacceptable variations (beyond specification limits).

Translating VOC into CCR

The voice of the customer (VOC) must be translated into critical customer requirements (CCR). Table 22.6 will help convert VOC to key customer issues and then to CCR.

Table 22.6 VOC to CCR

Voice of customers	Key customer issue	Critical customer requirements
Student: Unable to win in national competitions	Students need adequate preparedness.	Provide guidelines and prepare students based on the competition themes and evaluate them, point out deficiencies.
Student: Unable to obtain placement through campus interviews	Students need good placement in campus.	Prepare students though interviews by faculty members and invited experts from organizations.
Customer: Large number of piston rods rejected due to reverse threads in piston rod	Customers want defect-free threads in piston rod.	Reduce rejection PPM (parts per million) due to reverse thread.
Customer: Defective piston rod may lead to slippage.	Customers want to prevent the slippage of defective piston rod.	Reduce setting time.

Six Sigma in HR

Of all the industries, the manufacturing industry has applied six sigma in improving processes using DMAIC methodology (Gupta 2011). Some larger companies have integrated six sigma well into the corporate culture. In such companies, the six sigma concept can be considered the DNA of the company.

HR has a significant effect on every business. In creating the six sigma culture, this department is the best suited to facilitate management of change.

HR people are now looking to benefit from Six Sigma initiatives. It is evidenced that many strategies fail and get lost in the middle layers of management. But, HR can definitely help execute the profit and growth strategy through the use of Six Sigma.

The challenge in implementing six sigma in HR includes questions such as

1. What should I do?
2. What should I measure?
3. How would I improve the HR process?
4. How can HR be at 3.4 parts per million as it does not deal with a million people?

Though not a huge part of any business, HR has a significant effect on every business. Human resources are actually the human capital of an organization. HR department must ensure that there is good return on investment in human capital. Typical HR functions include recruitment and selection, induction and placement, compensation management, employee skills development. At present, in the changing environment, innovation and change management have also emerged as key functions in the HR department. Added to this, managing these functions well, managing the idea to innovation, improving HR functions, and ensuring the accountability of employees and executives must also be implemented. HR department plays an important role in driving business strategy through six sigma and in creating the six sigma culture. This department is the best suited to facilitate management of change. An organization needs HR to integrate the six sigma methodology and a business scorecard to achieve growth and profitability.

A proper map should be created for the HR to function efficiently and smoothly and prepare them for implementing the concept. Some questions could be kept in mind while preparing such a map. Answering these questions help the management to identify the output (unit), measures of reliability, and elements that can go wrong (opportunities for error). After this, they can even formulate their own indicators for improvements such as HR responsiveness, employee involvement, idea and innovation for improvement, and HR effectiveness in fulfilling its intended functions. The questions are as follows:

1. What is the purpose of the HR function or sub-function?
2. What are the expected deliverables (people, skills, services, value, reports, etc.)?
3. What are the measures of goodness of key deliverables?
4. What are the error opportunities for key deliverables?
5. What improvement activities are carried out in the HR function?

HR departments of some companies have successfully completed six sigma projects which include reduction in overtime, reduction in time and cost to hire an employee, reduction in employee retention or turnover, reduction in safety violations, reduction in cost of employee separation, and HR response to internal inquiries for benefits, payroll, promotion and fairness (Gupta 2011).

Six sigma differs from total quality management in various aspects (Table 22.7).

Table 22.7 Six sigma versus TQM

Six sigma	Total quality management
Executive ownership	Self-directed work teams
Business strategy execution system	Quality initiative

(Contd)

Table 22.7 (Contd)

Six sigma	Total quality management
Truly cross functional	Largely within a single function
Focused training with a verifiable return on investment	No mass training in statistics and quality with return on investment
Business result orientated	Quality orientated

Six Sigma Certification

Organizations are increasingly recognizing the need for implementing six sigma. Training institutes have also become instrumental in organizing general and customized training programmes. They are categorizing six sigma experts based on their involvement and expertise.

Champion The champion establishes the roles and roadmap of the six sigma implementation. He/she selects projects and allocates the necessary resources, reviews progress and offers assistance, assists in quantifying efforts, keeps the projects moving ahead and in harmony, shares the best practices, both within the organization and with suppliers and customers, if applicable, and applies the lessons learnt.

Black belt The black belt works on six sigma full time and possesses the expertise in statistics and change management. A black belt leads, manages, inspires, coaches, and delegates to other team members. He/she gets six sigma project teams started, builds their confidence, participates in their training, manages team dynamics, and ensures successful results.

Master black belt A master black belt is an expert in six sigma statistical tools, coaching, and mentoring black belts. He/she acts as a team consultant. They may also become involved in special six sigma projects, such as establishing key measures.

Green belt Green belts often receive training similar to black belts. They only work on six sigma projects on a part-time basis, retaining their former role in an organization. In some organizations, green belts are team leaders, but they are usually six sigma project team members. Green belts form an important link between the six sigma implementation and the everyday operations of the organization.

Role of HR in Six Sigma

An organization applies the six sigma concept for value enrichment, and for reduction of defectives practically to zero level. The concept needs mathematical precision for all tasks. Operators are required to be trained on statistical tools to the process within the specification limits. HR needs to organize intensive training programmes for operators. Management needs to appreciate and encourage training for attaining tangible benefits. The ground work demands adjusting with the changing organizational needs, making tireless efforts, establishing a directional approach to achieve the goal, being well prepared, communicating ideas in most subtle form, stopping only after achieving the goal, considering real life problems, remaining optimistic and original, exploring possibilities, working with junior colleagues keeping ego aside, and so forth.

The personality traits of the six sigma team members should include adaptability, analytical, energetic, calculative, definitive, diplomatic, finisher, materialist, salesman, team member, etc. The HR needs to identify persons with these traits from the workforce. People may have all the traits in their possession. (A list of personality traits and the situation is provided in Annexure 22.2). Thus, training emerges as inescapable to identify the traits and enhance the essential requirements.

For senior employees, achievement and affiliation motives are helpful. However, juniors need activity and affiliation motive. All the people need sense of organizational belongingness.

Six Sigma in Technical Education

The quality in education has been perceived as an ideal, an absolute, relative, and apparently complex phenomenon (Rajeswari, et al. 2010). The concept of six sigma is well applied in technical education (Exhibit 22.2).

Exhibit 22.2 Six sigma in technical education

In a technical institute, six sigma stresses on the following characteristics:

1. Focus on the customer.
2. Data and fact-driven management with effective management systems that track results, outcomes, processes, inputs, and other predictive variables.
3. Process focus, management, and improvement, for growth and success. Process in six sigma is documented, communicated, measured, and redefined on an ongoing basis.
4. Proactive management, involving habits and practices that anticipate problems and changes, apply facts and data, and question assumptions about goals and 'how do we do things.'
5. Boundary-less collaboration featuring cooperation among internal groups and customers, suppliers, and supply chain partners.
6. A drive for perfection and yet a tolerance for failure, that gives the freedom to take risks and learn from mistakes to the people in a six sigma organization, thereby 'raising the bar' of performance and customer satisfaction.

Model of Six Sigma in Technical Education

Six sigma is represented in a variety of models as the organizational philosophy. The model emphasizes on the customer, processes, data, statistics, teams, and continuous process improvements in an individual institution. The model of six sigma is built on the basis of experiences of quality management practices adopted in institutions.

First, an organization takes the decision for applying six sigma. A top level quality management team is formed. Thereafter, quality mission and objectives are formulated. This is followed by identification of customers and quality specification, and establishing quality standards and benchmarks are finally done. Subsequently, major internal quality processors (QP) are identified. The measurement of sigma level of each process is undertaken by the analysis of defect and PPM from data. The last two steps involve deciding the strategy for improving sigma level and problem solving, and measurement of new sigma level, review, and analysis. Whenever any developmental measures are initiated, resistance is generated. Resistance is encountered while implementing the six sigma quality change. The necessary steps must be taken to manage resistance. The model given in Figure 22.3 will elucidate the six sigma steps in technical education.

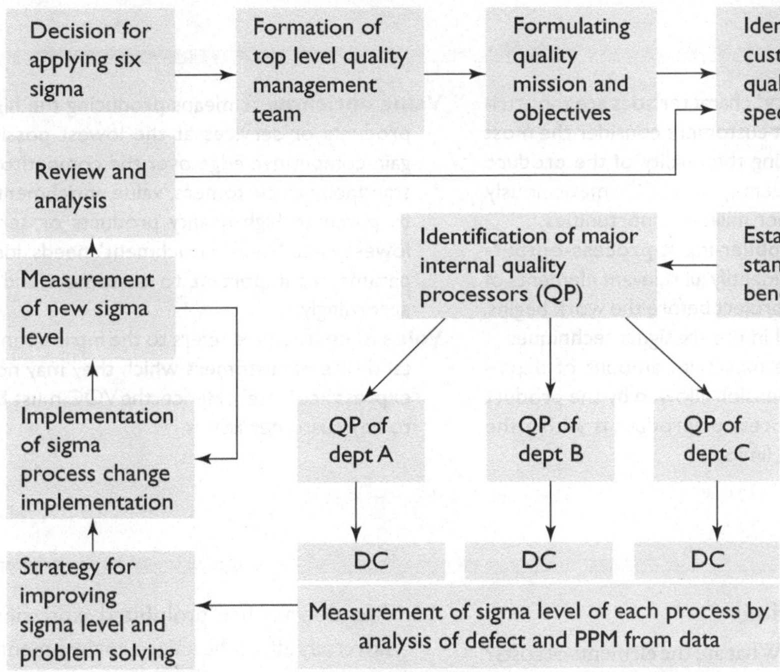

FIG. 22.3 Model of six sigma in technical education

SUMMARY

JIT is a concept that refers to operating a business with zero inventories, and is practically impossible to achieve. However, an attempt to implement this concept with planned integrated effort helps to reduce the inventory to a great extent. Partial achievement in the JIT system also ensures quick ROI.

The concept of 5S necessitates a change in the mindset. It is also the first step towards continuous improvement. 5S is an art as it makes the workplace look beautiful. It is also a science because there must be a rationale behind it. Using the concept of 5S, workplace organizations can reduce the cost of production. It is basically a systematic and rational approach to methodical housekeeping built on a sound economic base. Application of 5S can be audited. 5S are very effectively applied in offices, production, maintenance, quality control, or any other department.

Kaizen is a small group activity and is based on the philosophy that a very large number of small improvements are more effective than a few numbers of large improvements that give significant impact. This philosophy is true in any organizational environment. *Kaizen* activities extend over production, maintenance, quality control, store, and offices such as planning, purchase, design, industrial engineering, administrative, etc. As it is done by internal people associated with the work, no resistance is faced during implementation.

Six sigma techniques provide mathematical precision to every thing we do in an organization. This rational approach for solving any problem leads to the reduction of rejections due to defects and in turn, reduces production costs. Six-sigma technique needs intensive training on statistical tools to keep the manufacturing process within control. The unit of defectives in the six sigma concept is referred in parts per million (PPM). This technique facilitates producing highest quality products or services at the lowest possible costs and helps to gain competitive edge over the competitors in markets. Thus, it leads to 'value enrichment' for that company.

KEY TERMS

CTQ or 'critical to quality' characteristics are the attributes of the product that customers consider the most important while evaluating the quality of the product. Organizations need to identify the CTQs meticulously.

DMPO means defectives per million opportunities.

SIPOC indicates the 'supplier-input-process-output-customer' chart used to identify all relevant elements of a process improvement project before the work begins. SIPOC is a planning tool in the six sigma technique.

Specification limit is the maximum amount of departures from the basic dimension allowed by the product designers in which a process or product is within the acceptable performance limits.

Value enrichment means producing the highest quality products or services at the lowest possible costs to gain competitive edge over the competitors. From the standpoint of customers, 'value enrichment' is the right to purchase high quality products or services at the lowest cost. 'Value enrichment' needs identifying the parameters important to customers and to proceed accordingly.

Voice of customers refers to the intrinsic and fundamental desire of customers which they may not be able to express accurately. Hence, the VOC must be translated to key customer issues.

EXERCISES

Concept Review Questions

1. What is 'just in time'? What are the elements of costs? Explain the total expected cost (TEC) equation.
2. Does the concept of JIT have any limitation? Elucidate the limitations.
3. Mention the various JIT parameters. How are they linked with the selection of suppliers?
4. What do mean by 5S? Explain the significance of each 'S'. How does the fifth 'S' differ from the earlier 4S?
5. What do mean by 'audit of 5S'? What is the necessity of this audit?
6. Can there be any standard checklist for audit of 5S? Justify.
7. 'The 5S checklist is generally organization-specific'. Does it retard the organization's drive to maintain 5S?
8. What is *kaizen*? Can everybody follow *kaizen*? Justify your answer.
9. Do you agree that the concept of kaizen has limited application? Mention the fields of application of kaizen. Take up one area you are familiar with and discuss in detail.
10. How should an organization implement kaizen? Elucidate the various steps essential to establish and maintain kaizen.
11. How can a healthy kaizen environment be created in an organization? Mention the special efforts essential to maintain the environment.
12. Mention any five 'prohibited expressions' that may adversely affect the kaizen environment and jeopardize the organization. Discuss citing examples from your work area. Briefly describe your work area.
13. What is 'six sigma'? Explain the process model for six sigma. Mention few application areas.
14. Six sigma methodologies require the use of DMAIC. Elaborately discuss the meaning of DMAIC and explain each of the elements.

Critical Thinking Questions

15. Should an organization try to bring all its suppliers under the umbrella of 'Just in time'? If not, why? Which suppliers should be considered initially?
16. 'There are certain rules to be observed for brainstorming'. Do your feel that rules are essential? If the rules are not observed, what may be consequences?
17. Some work environment prohibits the promotion of *kaizen*. Name any five such expressions. Suggest the actions needed to keep wheel of *kaizen* moving. Discuss the specific roles of the HR personnel and department in such situations.

Assignments

18. Design a scheme for launching kaizen programme in your establishment. Your project proposal should contain the following;
    (a) Policies, objectives, and strategies for kaizen
    (b) *Kaizen* structure
    (c) Methodology for kaizen documentation

(d) Recognition and reward system
(e) Various stages required for launching kaizen etc.

Prepare a write-up for presentation to your organization.

19. With the help of your professor, identify an organization that has implemented six sigma techniques and take appointment from a responsible person in the organization. Approach him/her and try to collect information regarding
(a) use of SIPOC diagram
(b) six sigma methodology (DMAIC) used by the organization
(c) tools used in the six sigma process
(d) how the organization collected VOC and translated the VOC into CCR

MANAGER'S INSIGHT

Quality management systems at Kara pipes Ltd had been institutionalized, and practised by all the employees. The company had adopted JIT for inventory management, *kaizen* for continuous process improvement, and six sigma for product quality and error-free processes. Kara has also received ISO 9001, ISO 14001, and OHSAS 19001 certifications. The huge investments during initial years has paid off and Kara has now emerged as the most dependable manufacturer and supplier of alloy pipes across the globe today.

Question:

Highlight various quality management practices in a similar company of international repute and suggest how other companies can adopt various quality management systems.

BIBLIOGRAPHY AND WEB RESOURCES

Bedi, Kanishka, *Production and Operations Management*, Oxford Higher Education, Oxford University Press, New Delhi, 2008.

Haldar, Uday Kumar, *Total Quality Management Text and Cases*, Dhanpat Rai & Co., New Delhi, 2007.

Rajeswari, C.S., Ganga Agnihotri, and Geeta Agnihotri, *Relevance of Six Sigma in Technical Education System*, Indian Journal of Training and Development, (Monthly Journal of Indian Society of Training and Development), Vol. XXXX No. 3, July–September 2010, pp. 11–19, New Delhi, 2010.

ISO 9000:2000 Quality Management, Definitions and Vocabulary, International Organization for Standardization, 2000.

Web Resources

Gupta, Praveen, *Six Sigma in Human Resources*, www.accelper.com/pdfs/Six%20Sigma%20in%20Human%20Resources.pdf, last accessed on 29 April 2011.

www.amrihospital.com, last accessed on 29 August 2011.

VOICE OF CUSTOMERS TO CRITICAL CUSTOMER REQUIREMENTS

AMRI Hospital, Salt Lake

About the hospital

Advanced Medicare and Research Institute Limited (AMRI), the first state-of-the-art hospital in Kolkata, is a joint venture in collaboration among Emami Group, Shrachi Group, and the Government of West Bengal. The hospital is NABL accredited. In the healthcare sector, AMRI has gained confidence of customers for its quality of treatment, systematic documentation system, and public relation approaches. It has gained distinctive competence for its dynamic leaders and leadership styles. AMRI has its branches in different locations of Kolkata and a branch at Bhubaneswar, too. Every branch has multifarious facilities of diagnosing and treatment and families feel relieved after admitting patients in AMRI hospital. Today, it has 800 beds available for patients and is planning to expand further to 2,000 beds by 2015.

The hospital is ISO 9001:2000 certified and has tie-ups with many leading corporates. AMRI has collaborated with the government for establishing AMRI CT scan center at Coochbehar and MRI scan center at Bankura and Siliguri medical colleges.

AMRI hospitals were rated Kolkata's leading hospitals on the basis of opinions of general physicians and specialists. The hospital was also adjudged as possessing the fastest front desk by *India Today* (15 June 2009)

Eight Cs of AMRI

AMRI hospital believes in 8 Cs which include collaboration, convenience, comfort, care, commitment, coverage, concern, and community. The 8 Cs differentiate AMRI hospital from others.

Collaboration: AMRI is the first joint venture collaboration in healthcare among the Emami Group, the Shrachi Group, and the Government of West Bengal. It is the first group in eastern India to be accredited with the prestigious International Hospital Federation (IHF) of France.

Convenience: It is conveniently located, and serves a large population.

Comfort: It is centrally air-conditioned with 540 beds, 18 operation theatres, ICCU, ITU, HDU units, and an in-house pharmacy.

Care: The hospital employs renowned doctors and specialists with international expertise and is also supported by experienced consultants, trained nurses, paramedical staff, and technicians.

Commitment: The hospital aims to strengthen transparency, and has introduced a 'patient charter', where all inpatient, outpatient, and treatment-seeking customers can ascertain their rights, expectations, and responsibilities during their treatment period.

Coverage: It is equipped with a range of sophisticated equipments in the field of cardiology, neurosciences, nephrology, oncology, critical and trauma care, paediatrics, gynaecology, and gastroenterology.

Concern: To strengthen security, AMRI recently implemented barcode solutions for all inpatients and outpatients to ensure identity, convenience, safety, and security. A tamper-proof barcode wristband is provided to all new inpatient admissions. The band comprises a barcode, patient's name, identity, age, and date of birth.

Community: AMRI hospital is committed to the cause of helping the underprivileged in Kolkata through an initiation of various schemes (free treatments, economy package for surgery, and 15 per cent discount for senior citizens, based on investigations and neighborhood card scheme) among others.

Voice of customers

AMRI interprets the voices of customers (VOC) as the intrinsic and fundamental desires of customers that they may not be able to express accurately. To collect the VOC, AMRI has developed a feedback form comprising patient's details (name, age, sex, address, email ID, contact numbers, date of admission, bed number, doctor's name, reason behind choosing AMRI hospital, etc.), front office, floor coordination, and feedback information of other departments and functionaries. The feedback form is reproduced here.

Feedback form of AMRI hospital

1. Front office	**Excellent**	**Good**	**Average**	**Poor**
Accessibility of our telephone numbers (If applicable)	☐	☐	☐	☐
How do you rate us for our admission process? Staff greeting/courtesy/efficiency/professionalism	☐	☐	☐	☐
How long did we take for your admission?	☐ < 10 mins		☐ 10–20 mins	
	☐ 20–30 mins		☐ > 30 mins	
How long did we take for your discharge?	☐ < 15 mins		☐ 15–30 mins	
	☐ 30–45 mins		☐ > 45 mins	
How did you find our billing process?	☐	☐	☐	☐

2. Floor coordinator				
Staff greetings/courtesy/efficiency/professionalism	☐	☐	☐	☐

3. Senior doctors/consultants				
Promptness/professionalism/interaction/courtesy	☐	☐	☐	☐
4. Junior doctors				
Professionalism/responsiveness/interaction/courtesy	☐	☐	☐	☐
5. Nursing services				
Staff greetings/courtesy/efficiency/professionalism	☐	☐	☐	☐
6. Food services				
Quality/quantity/presentation/variety	☐	☐	☐	☐
Timely service	☐	☐	☐	☐
7. Dietician				
Staff greetings/courtesy/efficiency/professionalism	☐	☐	☐	☐
Attention paid by the dietician	☐	☐	☐	☐
8. Cleanliness				
Cleanliness of public area/floors/rooms/toilets	☐	☐	☐	☐
9. Ward boys/housekeeping				
Courtesy/promptness	☐	☐	☐	☐
10. Other services (security/liftman)				
Staff greetings/courtesy/efficiency	☐	☐	☐	☐
11. Dental and physiotherapy services				
Staff greetings/courtesy/efficiency/promptness	☐	☐	☐	☐
12. Blood collection/lab services				
Staff greetings/courtesy/efficiency/professionalism	☐	☐	☐	☐
13. Radiology/imaging services (X ray, CT, MRI, USG)				
Staff greetings/courtesy/efficiency/professionalism	☐	☐	☐	☐
14. Cardiology service (Cath lab, echo, ECG.TMT, PFT, Holter, Till table)				
Staff greetings/courtesy/efficiency/professionalism	☐	☐	☐	☐

15. Neurology services (ECG, EMG, NCV, VEP)				
Staff greetings/courtesy/efficiency/professionalism	☐	☐	☐	☐

16. Pharmacy				
Staff greetings/courtesy/efficiency/professionalism	☐	☐	☐	☐

Overall experience at AMRI

17. Please rate your total experience with AMRI.	☐	☐	☐	☐

Would you like to recommend us to others? Please tick (✓) Strongly/Casually/Hesitantly

Any comments or observations to help us to improve our services

....

....

....

Please help us to recognize anyone whom you think provided exceptionally good service at AMRI.

....

....

....

Please mention anything that you were particularly impressed with, at AMRI.

....

....

....

Analysis of the feedback items

As a provider of medical service, AMRI acts as a JIT supplier to its ailing customers.

From the Likert scale points for items on cleanliness and ward boys/housekeeping, it is obvious that AMRI is inclined to the 5S concept. Further, when the authors visited AMRI, they observed application of all the 5Ss in the hospital.

The endorsements in the feedback forms are transferred to computers to generate reports. Medical superintendents, senior doctors, hospital management personnel, and the HR department study the endorsements. They encourage juniors to solve problems and thus, AMRI promotes *kaizen*.

AMRI is keen to capture VOC from multiple angles and follows a 360-degree approach, as shown in the 16 items.

AMRI is dedicated to identifying the parameters important to customers, produce the highest quality medical services to the citizens, and accordingly, enrich value of its intangible products. The hospital is instrumental in discovering the attributes of the service offerings that customers consider the most important.

Translating VOC to critical customer requirements

AMRI is in a position to move from VOC through key customer issues to critical customer requirements (CCRs).

Voice of customers	Key customer issue	Critical customer requirements
Consultant was busy in emergency with another patient.	Needs prompt medical service	Reduce waiting time
The corridor had a little dirt and after request, staff took some time to clean.	Desires prompt cleanliness	Need to be more responsive
Though quantity and quality of food is good, I need a change in taste.	Wants variations in taste	To ensure supply of variety of food

Discussion Questions

1. AMRI has a well-designed feedback system. How can AMRI use the filled-in feedback forms to develop its services?
2. How does the term 'value enrichment' apply in the case of AMRI Hospital?

(Case developed based on the feedback form of AMRI hospital and knowledge inputs provided by Dr T.S. Kuckrejja, president, AMRI hospital, Salt Lake, Kolkata. Authors are grateful to Dr Kuckrejja)

Source: www.amrihospital.com

HR MANTRA *Seiton* begins at home

More than a decade ago, Madona married Samuel. They were blessed with a beautiful daughter, who is now seven years old and studies in Kendriya Vidyalaya. She studies well and is in the good books of most of her teachers. Samuel is employed in a US-based MNC and Madona works for an export organization.

They are leading a happy family life, but for one constant nag. Every weekday morning, when Madona is busy in the kitchen, Samuel shouts, 'Where is my watch?'. She finds the watch and gives it to Samuel. Then her daughter cries, 'Mom, where is my pencil box?'. Madona finds the pencil box and gives it to her. Next her daughter says, 'I don't know where my diary is', and so on. Madona solves this nagging problem by allocating two separate cupboards for father and daughter and earmarking specific shelves for each of their items.

The mantra: A place for everything; everything in its place.

JOSEPH JURAN

Dr Joseph Juran was born on 24 December 1904 in Braila, Romania. He moved to the United States in 1912 when his age was eight. Juran's teaching and consulting career spanned more than seven decades, and he is known as one of the foremost experts on quality in the world.

After completing his BS in electrical engineering, Juran joined the inspection branch of the Hawthorne Co. of Western Electric (a Bell manufacturing company) in 1924. Juran was a quality professional from the beginning of his career. In 1934, he became a quality manager. He worked with the US Government during World War II and afterward became a quality consultant. In 1952, Juran was invited to Japan. Dr Edward Deming helped arrange the meeting that led to this invitation and his many years of work with Japanese companies.

Juran founded the Juran Center for Quality Improvement at the University of Minnesota and the Juran Institute. His third book, *Juran's Quality Control Handbook*, published in 1951, was translated into Japanese. Other books include *Juran on Planning for Quality* (1988), *Juran on Leadership for Quality* (1989), *Juran on Quality by Design* (1992), *Quality Planning and Analysis* (1993), and *A History of Managing for Quality* (1995).

With regard to quality Juran opined, 'Prepare quality-costing reports on an ongoing basis (say once in year) as management control tool'.

Juran's concepts are well used to establish a traditional quality system, as well as to support strategic quality management. Among other things, Juran's philosophy includes the Quality Trilogy and the Quality Planning Roadmap.

Juran's major contribution to society was in the field of quality management and he is often called the 'father of quality'. Most importantly, Juran is recognized as the person who added the managerial dimension to quality and broadened it from its statistical origins. Considering the importance of his contributions to quality he is referred to in many publications, such as the Harvard Business Review, Business Week, the Financial Times, and many quality-related journals.

Professor Kano of Japan recalls, 'He impressed top executives here with his managerial aspect of quality and contributed to the quality development in Japan by helping to establish the reputation of made-in-Japan products.'

Of the various publications, Juran's Quality Trilogy and Quality Planning Roadmap are unique.

In the Quality Trilogy, Juran emphasizes the roles of quality planning, quality control, and quality improvement and their integration.

Juran's Quality Planning Roadmap can be used by individuals and teams throughout the world as a checklist for understanding customer expectations/requirements, establishing measurements based on customer needs, optimizing product design, and developing a process that is capable of meeting customer requirements. The Quality Planning Roadmap is used for both product and process development.

In the past, under the concept of 'little q' the quality department was responsible for quality. At present, under the 'big Q' concept, all people and departments are responsible for quality. The 'big Q' allows workers to regain pride in workmanship by assuming responsibility for quality.

References

en.wikipedia.org/wiki/Joseph_M._Juran, last accessed on 6 October 2011.

Haldar, U.K., Total Quality Management—Text and Cases, Dhanpat Rai & Co., New Delhi, 2007.

www.juran.com/about_juran_institute_our_founder.html, last accessed on 6 October 2011.

ANNEXURE 22.1

Generic Dimensions Used by Customers to Evaluate Service Quality

Dimension	Definition	Evaluation questions
Credibility	Sincerity, trustworthiness, believability, honesty of the service provider	1. Does the hospital have a good reputation? 2. Does the repair firm offer after-sales service? 3. Does the stock broker pressurize to purchase?
Security	Free from danger, risk, or doubt	1. Is it safe to use the equipment? 2. Will the private insurance company give the amount due based on sum assured? 3. Does the travel insurance company have coverage for luggage loss and delayed arrival of flight?
Access	Ease to contact, approachability	1. How easy is it to contact the customer service manager? 2. Does the airlines service have 24-hour tool free number?
Communication	Listening to the customers, considering the 'voice of customers'	1. Does the TV service center send an engineer/mechanic after receiving the complaint? 2. Does the customer service manager of the private listen with attention and record the complaints? 3. Does the hospital intimate the relative if a patient turn serious?
Customer focus	Making efforts to collect customer expectations	1. Does the company undertake market survey? 2. Does the insurance agent propose a policy after consider customer (the insurant) desire?
Tangibles	Esteem values of physical facilities, appearance,	1. Is the reception of the hotel attractive? 2. Are the classrooms of the B-school air conditioned? 3. Are the monthly statements legible?

Reliability	Innate ability to perform the promised services consistently and dependably	1. Does the B-school take care of placements of student? 2. Does the hotel serve food of consistent quality? 3. Does the TV service center provide spare parts of old models?
Responsiveness	Tendency to provide prompt service to customers?	1. Does it take long to get reply from the customer complaint department? 2. Does the mobile internet provider react quickly when any problem is lodged?
Competence	Having the requisite skills and knowledge in possession	1. Do the call center people fumble while giving answers to queries? 2. When I visit the information counter of the hospital with questions, does the person reply confidently?
Courtesy	Civility, politeness, respect to unknown visitors	1. Does the aircraft crew have pleasant manners? 2. Does the electrician take off his shoes while entering the house for repair? 3. Do the telephone exchange personnel respond in a decent way?
Source: Bhat, K. Shridhara, *Total Quality Management,* Himalaya Publishing Company, Mumbai, 2007.		

ANNEXURE 22.2
Personality Traits

Personality traits and the situation
Adaptable: You normally adjust yourself very well and perform as usual in different playing conditions, with different captains or different forms of game, easily.
Argumentive: You are the first man to be seen contesting a point about anything on and off the field.
Authoritative: Whatever you do in the game has an extraordinary stamp on it.
Energetic: You are a tireless horse, which keeps galloping whether its sun or moon up in the skies.
Calculative: You normally set a field in a way that the ball goes where the fielder is placed.
Gentleman: If cricket is called a gentleman's game, then your game is an ideal personification of the same.
Definitive: You never move your feet unless you have prepared for an intended act.
Democratic: Your action always follows from a general opinion of your other team members.
Diplomatic: You have the capacity to communicate ideas in most subtle form.
Dramatic: You are most likely to bring showmanship to everything you do.
Dutiful: You love responsibilities and you perform them diligently.
Egoist: Your sense of self-pride always affects your acceptance by others
Empathetic: Your usual priority to understand other's feelings goes beyond team members and extends to a general human class.
Enterprising: Your purchase of listener's time and the effect you create is businesslike.
Esteemed: Irrespective of many compulsions, you never sacrifice your sense of self-esteem in any situation.
Experimental: You try varied combinations as a matter of habit to reach targets.

Extrovert: You are always in an expressive mood and successfully get the attention of others to whatever you are doing.
Finisher: You always finish the task you have taken in hand before starting another one.
Follower: You keep following a school of thought and keep flowing in the river stream.
Frank: Nobody needs to take any trouble to find out what you think.
Gamesman: You can use many soft means to derive an advantage.
Initiator: You are always at the forefront of initiating an action.
Inquisitive: You always have an enormous ability to ask questions in any given situation.
Innovative: In any given situation, you can find stunning ways to make good the situation.
Just: Your sense of justice remains undeterred despite most testing situations.
Loyal: Your loyalty to the team is undisputed.
Man-leader: Your ability to bring people together and make them perform to the fullest is remarkable.
Materialist: Your commitment to an act is in proportion with the rewards.
Mature: You speak and understand things beyond your age.
Moralist: Your adherence to values is strict and undefeated.
Negotiator: You seldom give up anything unless you see a larger gain in doing so, at present or in future.
Opportunistic: You see and identify opportunities from miles away.
Open: You are always a person who looks forward to suggestions from one and all.
Optimistic: You always imagine your future to be a bed of roses.
Original: In your most natural form, you are the one who cannot be compared to anyone.
Parent: You love to nurture children.
Patient: You seldom mind waiting irrespective of how long you have done that already.
Peace-loving: You avoid confrontation, quarrels, and conflicts at all costs.
Perfectionist: You always strive for meeting the results in a purist way.
Persuasive: You keep trying as long as it takes to produce results.
Philosophical: You are capable of amalgamating many truths and making greater, wider, and larger sense.
Positive: You are always committed to accepting the brighter side of life.
Qualitative: Your class is apparent through every mannerism and action.
Rational: You are unstoppable when it comes to use of logic to understand most mundane things.
Realistic: You accept only that which you see and experience.
Risk-taker: You love to explore even against heavy odds.
Romantic: You have uncurbed tendency to possess, feel, touch, and think about something all the time.
Salesman: You love to explore possibilities to do business with everyone every moment.
Selfish: You always want everything to happen for you and never worry about others.
Sensitive: You are very easily affected by the smallest changes in the surroundings.

Shy: You are extremely conscious of yourself and ensure you are seen by others as little as possible.
Shrewd: You always use varied tricks to meet to your objective.
Social: You always think of benefits for masses in all your plans.
Sophisticated: You care a lot to maintain up-market looks and lifestyle.
Spiritual: You have a firm belief that hands are yours but wishes are His.
Sporting: You appreciate your opponents even when you are losing.
Systematic: Before you attempt to undertake any work, you create a system of work.
Teacher: You love to help people understand the subject in totality.
Thought leader: You love ideas and strive to popularize them.
Team member: You always exist as a part of the whole human entity you belong to and never insist on your personal presence.
Tenacious: When the going gets tough, you get going even stronger.
Tolerant: You have an incredible capacity to stand to something much against your own taste.
Trendy: You are always on the lookout for something new and take to following that soonest.
Trendsetter: You have an innate desire to start a new system, culture, or a trend.
Truthful: You chase the truth all the time and use truth all the time.
Unbiased: You rarely have an extreme feeling for anything.
Visionary: You are capable of seeing far into the future.
Wise: You always look at the long-term repercussions of every event that takes place.

CHAPTER 23

HRM Strategies

LEARNING OBJECTIVES

After studying this chapter, you will be able to

- Understand the importance of HRM strategies
- Learn common HRM goals and strategies
- Understand strategies of some organizations
- List some common strategies that organizations should adopt

OPENING CASE

Failure to Achieve Goals due to Inadequate Planning

Albert, the managing director of Albert Engineering Works, decided to launch three new products and market them in both existing and new markets. He expressed his desire in a meeting with the important employees of the company.

The R&D department designed three innovative products, and gave a presentation explaining the utilitarian aspects of each product. After obtaining the green signal from Albert, the products were designed. Around 25 prototypes were manufactured and tested for accuracy and perfection.

As there were no discrepancies in the products, bulk manufacturing was undertaken; the products were inspected, and ultimately dispatched to the respective markets for sale. The company estimated the expected sales of each product. However, over a period of one year, the company could actually sell only 17 per cent of the estimated sales. Albert constituted a team to investigate the reasons behind the low sales and directed the team to submit their findings. He also asked the team to present recommendations for making the situation better.

The team consulted an external expert having profound knowledge in this regard. Based on his guidelines, the team collected all facts and figures, and reached a conclusion.

The findings comprised the following:

1. Market survey was not undertaken to ascertain the need of the markets.
2. Demographic characteristics of the people of new markets were not collated.
3. The affordability of the prospective customers was not considered.
4. Presence of competitors' products and the choice of the market were not evaluated.
5. Marketing efforts were inadequate.

The team recommended the following:

1. Identify the target customers in each market.
2. Advertise in appropriate magazines/journals to reach the target customers.

3. Collect views regarding fitness.
4. Gather the extent of fulfillment of customer expectations through questionnaires after using the product.
5. Ensure prompt and intensive after-sales service to enhance market share.

Note: This case has reference to the opening case of Chapter 8 titled, 'Flaw in performance appraisal system'.

Learning points

- A company should have documented procedures and a step-by-step approach to implement a plan.
- Business expansion needs the involvement of the relevant personnel.

INTRODUCTION

Organizations strive to achieve goals, and require strategies to accomplish them. A strategy is a course of action planned to be undertaken to achieve the decided business goals. Strategy is of great importance to every organization and is decided by the top management. Strategy refers to basic directional decisions, and consists of the important actions necessary to realize these directions, and the means of translating the desires into action.

HRM strategy indicates the desired course of action planned by an organization to achieve HRM goals or HRM outcomes. The course of action may deal with a specific choice of action derived out of various means to achieve the desired goal and plans for implementing the chosen action or activity. Most successful organizations treat human resource as their key asset and make the most effective use of this resource.

Human resource management involves recruiting capable, flexible, and committed people, managing and rewarding their performance, and continuously developing their capabilities. Therefore, the important embedded issues comprise selection procedures including proper selection tools, pay and incentives, performance and potential assessment, grading structures, training and development, welfare and communication, employee relations, separation procedures, personnel administration, and legislative requirements.

Strategy indicates the desired course of action planned to achieve HRM goals or outcomes. Strategies and tactics bridge the gap between ends and means.

People generally work within a culture of compliance or a culture of commitment. People working within a culture of commitment are generally prepared to work longer, apply greater initiative, and originality to resolve a problem and try much harder to achieve goals. In the knowledge industry, people prefer to work within a learning environment because knowledge acquisition and skill development are of paramount importance. Many organizations have foregone the system of piecemeal training of individual employees and they have either become 'learning organizations' or emphasize on continuous learning.

People working within a culture of commitment are prepared to work longer and apply greater initiative and originality to resolve a problem, and try much harder to achieve goals.

This chapter discusses the goals and strategies of human resource management to achieve the goals and organizational practices. Application of these strategies will be discussed in Chapter 24.

COMMON HRM GOALS

Organizations fulfil a large variety of our societal and personal needs and affect a larger segment of our lives. Parsons (1979) perceives organizations as 'a social unit which is deliberately constructed and reconstructed to seek specific goals'. In order to achieve business goals, organizations frame HRM goals. Goals of human resource management are multiple and diverse. Some of them are mentioned in Box 23.1.

Box 23.1 Examples of HRM goals

1. Acquiring and retaining competent manpower
2. Converting the organization into centres of learning
3. Effecting attitudinal change
4. Reinstating behavioural modification
5. Developing a changed mindset
6. Instilling organizational values
7. Formulating new dimensions of business expansion
8. Enhancing visionary skills
9. Augmenting leadership potential
10. Ensuring achievement of individuals' career goals
11. Relieving work stress and role stress
12. Linking HR practices with corporate goals

To achieve these goals, it is very important for the organizations to formulate and follow well thought-out strategies.

STRATEGY

Q 1 A strategy is a route to a destination, which may be an objective or a goal to be achieved within a definite timeframe. In simpler terms, objectives and strategies must be intertwined in an organization in order to characterize effective management for the best results.

Naturally, HRM strategy paves the direction for achieving the HRM goals. To achieve the same goals in similar situations, organizations may adopt different strategies based on the organizational philosophy.

HRM STRATEGIES

HRM strategies are manifold and widely differ based on the organization's philosophy. They are manifested in beliefs, faith, management styles, governance, etc. In simpler terms, HRM strategies are an organization's plans for managing people, culture, structure, and development, and for determining how people fit into the organization's future growth.

> HRM strategies are an organization's plans for managing people, culture, structure, and development, and for determining how people fit into the organization's future growth.

People In the context of people, HRM strategy refers to determining the type of people needed to work in the organization for survival and growth. In the same context, strategy is not just a matter of mere personality, but also of the personalities and work styles that are essential to help an organization achieve its overall business strategy.

Culture Strategy also relates to the overall organizational culture. One should take the time to determine the leadership and management style of the organization that would be best suited for it. The management style is manifested through the manner in which an organizational leader strives to achieve the task

(mission, objective, or goal). While doing so, he has to build his team as a cohesive group and develop every individual in the team to give his/her very best.

Consequently, he has to harmonize and integrate the needs related to the accomplishment of the task with those of the group he leads and the individuals in the group. These are the functions of leadership. For example, Infosys Technologies is keen to develop leadership potential of its people in various tiers. It has identified

1. nine leadership pillars,
2. six leadership traits, and
3. nine dimensions of leadership.

These have helped them identify a suitable management style which they follow. These aspects will be elaborately discussed in Chapter 24.

Structure In addition to people and culture, HRM strategy also relates to the organization's structure. One must decide the jobs and functions to be carried out, and decide the connection between jobs and departments and also formulate the persons who will be managing those departments. It is important for people to carry out these jobs sincerely.

Individual and organizational development Developing individuals and the organization are by far the most important strategies. This is important to the people and assists them in deciding the plans for training in the long run. Leadership training may be decided as part of the overall development plan in line with the tier system of Infosys Technologies. Employees must be empowered to choose courses for their development enabling them to map out their future career. A procedure may be established to identify the training needs objectively. Organization development (OD) is a conceptual, organization-wide effort to enhance the effectiveness of an organization and gauge its viability and feasibility.

OD is a response to change; it is a complex educational strategy intended to change the beliefs, attitudes, values, and structure of an organization to enhance the adaptability to new technologies, markets, and challenges. OD is a particular kind of change process. It is not merely 'an effort to better an organization' or a 'set of training functions of an organization'. OD demands a change in the mindset of the people which relates to the culture of the organization. Individual development and organizational development must go hand to hand.

Human behaviour is complex and each individual is different from another. Challenges of OD are intertwined with individual development. Individuals have to be developed and the tactics must be aligned with in the direction of OD efforts.

Please refer to Box 23.2 for some examples of the common human resource management strategies.

Box 23.2 Examples of common HRM strategies

1. Inhibition or restraining influence of trade unions
2. Recruiting the best talent available in the market
3. Recruiting people conforming to structured recruitment policy
4. Controlling the costs without compromising on the quality

(Contd)

Box 23.2 (Contd)

5. Becoming flexible and flexibly rigid
6. Empowering people and allowing them to take decisions and apply discretion
7. Developing people by providing them with the best training
8. Improving the quality of work life
9. Compensating and rewarding employees to keep them motivated
10. Developing a culture within the organization which enhances enabling capacity
11. Encouraging creativity and innovation
12. Identifying members who can contribute creatively and competitively with their best efforts and abilities
13. Becoming a learning organization
14. Conducting training and development for everyone to be competent in their present job and gain mastery over skills
15. Downsizing by changing the relationship between the organization and those who are providing with services—buy in rather than employ our own
16. Linking rewards with measurable performances
17. Staying clear of the pitfalls and difficulties offered by employment laws
18. Being an equal opportunities employer by implementing behavioural approaches and not imposing expensive systems of control
19. Building a corporate image such that employees and others view the organization with high regard

HRM STRATEGIES IN VARIOUS ORGANIZATIONS

Different organizations adopt different strategies to achieve their organizational goals. Let us study the HR strategies of some select organizations/industries.

Strategies of Rashtriya Chemicals and Fertilizers

The strategies of Rashtriya Chemicals and Fertilizers (RCF) are pervasive and encompass all aspects of human resource development. The organization's HR managers work towards vision building, innovation, structuring and restructuring of the organization, systems development, managing change, succession and career planning, employee training and development, employee involvement and commitment, manpower audit, and commercialization of HR services. The strategies of RCF are collectively exhaustive; hence, the company is consistently marching towards excellence.

Strategies of HAL

In the manufacturing sector, Hindustan Aeronautics Limited (HAL) intends to strategize total alignment of HR along with the corporate strategy. Some of the other strategies of HAL are as follows:

1. Be in total alignment with the corporate strategy.
2. Maintain human resource at an optimum level to meet the objectives and goals of the company.
3. Be competent in mapping, analysis, and upgradation of knowledge and skills including training, re-training, multi-skilling, etc.
4. Cultivate leadership with a shared vision at various levels in the organization.
5. Focus on development of core competence in high-tech areas and build cross-functional teams.
6. Create awareness of mission, values, and organizational goals throughout the company.

7. Introduce/implement personnel policies based on performance that would ensure growth, rewards, recognition, and motivation.

The human resource management practices of HAL will be discussed in detail in Chapter 24.

Strategies of ONGC

Oil and Natural Gas Corporation Limited (ONGC) is dedicated to excellence by leveraging competitive advantages in research, development, and technology with people who are involved in their work. ONGC strives to

1. instill high standards of business ethics and organizational values among its employees,
2. abide by health, safety, and environment norms for its employees to enrich quality of community life,
3. foster a culture of trust, openness, and mutual concern and work towards stimulating and challenging experience of people, and
4. delight customers through quality products and services.

Strategies of the Knowledge Industry

Due to the explosion of information technology, the knowledge industry has developed in multiple directions. Human resource attrition continues to be a major problem in this industry. The strategies to overcome recruitment challenges in the knowledge industry include

1. Attracting people with multidimensional experiences and skills
2. Introducing fresh blood in the organization
3. Developing a culture that attracts people
4. Designing entry pay that competes on quality and not quantum
5. Anticipating and finding people for positions that do not exist yet

Strategies for Common Organizational Aspects

There are certain strategies that are required to be developed for some common organizational aspects such as change management, conflict management, instilling ethics, empowering people, delegating tasks, discharging corporate social responsibility (CSR), linking HRM initiatives with business goals, and so on. These strategies could be used by various organizations. Some of them are mentioned here.

STRATEGIES TO MANAGE CHANGE

Changes are taking place at a fast rate and organizations need to absorb and manage changes at a much faster rate than they did in the past. Moreover, organizations need to develop a more focused and coherent approach in managing people. Just as a business requires a marketing or information technology strategy, it also requires a human resource or people strategy. While developing such a strategy, organizations must address two critical questions:

Q 3

1. What are the kinds of people needed to manage and run the business to meet the strategic business objectives?
2. What are the programmes and initiatives required to be designed and implemented to attract, develop, and retain staff to compete effectively in the ever-changing business environment?

An organization has to cross the delta state which is the space between the current state and the desired state. It must develop its strategies to manage changes. The strategies that may be adopted by an organization are as follows (Haldar and Sarkar 2010):

Determine the direction of change Knowing the direction of change an organization must clearly define the specific system and process movement to cope the change.

Share possible consequence The consequences of change efforts must be clearly communicated to the relevant personnel. The change agent should never present only rosy pictures. Change management efforts are always probabilistic. It must be kept in mind that in the beginning, any system might give problems, and these are considered part of the 'teething problems'.

Start from the base of the delta state The system analyst must carry out an 'as-is' analysis and design the new system, keeping in view the 'to-be' needs. Alternatively, the analyst should consider two aspects: 'where we are' and 'where we want to go'.

Take only one step at a time Organizations should not undertake multiple changes concurrently. Adverse consequences of one change effort may jeopardize and endanger few others.

Plan and prepare for the journey People may need to acquire a new set of skills and competencies, which must be identified at the planning stage. Otherwise, the total project may be delayed. Thus, training must precede introduction of new systems.

Involve people Involving people of various levels primarily enhances the strength of a team, and secondly, broadens the ways of managing resistance to change.

Be prepared for reversals Introduction of a new system has its own consequences. It may be revealed that the new system may create confusion, doubts, and suspicion, and a few unforeseen problems, jeopardizing the normal flow of work. In such situations, reversals to the original state may emerge as essential. Hence, one must always be prepared for reversals.

Develop internal expertise A professional external change agent can obviously provide adequate expertise in certain dimensions, generally at the beginning and the end of the change process. Continuous work needs to be executed by the internal experts, as they are aware of the people, culture, and the pulse and vein of the organization.

Continue moving towards the goal Persistence is the key to success. Short-term plans need to be designed along with long-term plans. Each short-term plan must be continuously monitored through predetermined yardsticks.

Review periodically Review helps to track the progress to initiate remedial measures, if necessary.

Use a compass and speedometer Information helps to evaluate direction and speed of changes, and take actions. Data need to be analysed for decision making. The speed at which environment is changing needs a speedometer that must be calibrated.

STRATEGIES TO MANAGE CONFLICT

Conflicts are a part and parcel of organizational life and must be managed efficiently. There are some tools available for resolving conflicts and the selection of these tools depends on the organizational culture and climate. There are several dimensions and determinants involved in this stage. Different taxonomies have been given by difference authors. Four major strategies are briefly discussed—conflict avoidance strategy, conflict diffusion strategy, conflict containment strategy, and conflict confrontation strategy.

Conflict avoidance strategy The conflict can either be ignored or a solution can be imposed. The strategy actually depends on the gravity and nature of the conflict.

Conflict diffusion strategy This strategy attempts to keep the conflict in abeyance. The emotions of both the parties are allowed to precipitate down. Smoothing or appealing to super ordinate goal are choices.

Conflict containment strategy In this strategy, the issues are selectively discussed through mediators or through representatives of collective bargaining forum, or by restructuring the interaction patterns.

Conflict confrontation strategy This particular strategy has been designed in such a way so that all the issues are first 'uncovered' and then, a solution acceptable to the conflicting parties is realized. This strategy deals with the conflict more openly and thoroughly.

ETHICS

Ethics help to mould and shape human behaviour and help employees perform their roles. Ethics matter because it makes good business sense to 'do socially right things'. Whistle blowing and fraud hotline strategies are used to protect organizations from scams and assist in developing ethics. These have been discussed in Chapter 18. An organization opts for any one of the strategies or both of them.

For example, Mumbai-based Lubrizol India Limited, a public sector undertaking under the administrative control of the Ministry of Petroleum and Natural Gas, Government of India, follows a structured system of inculcating ethics. Lubrizol has earmarked responsible persons in many countries depicting the name of the country, the 'ethics leader', and his/her contact numbers in the company's website.

CORPORATE SOCIAL RESPONSIBILITIES

Corporate social responsibility (CSR) is the process by which businesses help the society and obviously make their presence felt in the society. The terms ethics and CSR are intertwined. In many firms, ethics and CSR are interlinked. However, it is believed that CSR activities guarantee ethical behaviour. CSR has now become a global issue and CSR organizations have grown globally. Various facets of CSR have been discussed in Chapter 18.

Q 5 PepsiCo India discharges its CSR functions in three major areas—human sustainability (that comes from healthy kids and supporting the community), talent sustainability (through the use of innovative development and retention strategy), and environmental sustainability (ensured by replenishing water, partnership with farmer, and converting waste to wealth).

> Empowerment is not enhancing power; it is creating an environment or situation in which an employee can utilize the power effectively.

EMPOWERMENT

Empowerment is the process of increasing the enabling capacity of individuals or groups, allowing them to make choices and to transform those choices into desired actions and outcomes to advance the business. Empowerment signifies enhancing the spiritual, religious, political, societal, or economic strengths of individuals and communities. Empowerment gradually increases confidence among individuals. Empowerment is not enhancing power; it is creating an environment or situation in which an employee can utilize the power effectively.

DELEGATION

Delegation refers to transferring authority from a higher organizational level to a lower level, allowing junior colleagues to make decisions that enable the senior person to manage time more effectively. Delegation is a four-step process and comprises allocation of duties to subordinates, delegation of authority, assignment of responsibility, and creation of accountability.

> Delegation is basically a four-step process: allocation of duties to subordinates, delegation of authority, assignment of responsibility, and creation of accountability.

Allocation of duties refers to the charter of activities and tasks that one desires to get done by junior colleagues. Allocation of tasks precedes delegation of authority. Delegation of authority refers to passing on tasks, empowering one to carry out tasks acting on behalf of his/her senior. Delegation is a formal right step that helps developing the juniors. Assigning the person a corresponding obligation to perform follows the delegation of authority. From this obligation, responsibility is developed. The delegation process completes on creation of accountability of the person delegated. Delegation helps increasing the decision-making ability of juniors.

Purpose of Delegation

Delegation helps developing juniors and enables them to make decisions. In addition, delegation provides time for a senior and helps him/her utilize the time in doing creative activities. The juniors can consider all inputs meticulously and the quality of decision improves. It is needless to mention that subordinates get stimulation and energy, which in turn enhance their commitment.

Determinants of Delegation

Organizational culture is a powerful influencing factor of a managers' delegation. Tolerance for risk, support for employees, high degree of autonomy, system of working, and extent of decentralization are few organizational characteristics in which managers feel more comfortable to delegate. On the other hand, in risk-aversive situations and non-supportive and high control cultures, managers hesitate to delegate. Juniors hesitate to accept the higher responsibilities, too.

Principles of Effective Delegation

The principles behind effective delegation include deciding what to delegate; whom to be delegated; making the assignment clear, specific, and measurable; assigning an objective; give credit but share blame; allow autonomy, but monitor performance; and share success to enthuse others.

> The principles of delegation are what to delegate; who to delegate to; make the assignment clear, give credit but share blame; allow autonomy but monitor performance; and share success to enthuse others.

Decide what to delegate Seniors should perform very urgent and important tasks on their own. Other tasks may be delegated to juniors, considering their sincerity and regularity, and extent of urgency and importance.

Decide who to delegate to Any team comprises excellent, good, and fair performers. Delegating only to excellent performers makes them overburdened. There has to be a balance in the developmental opportunities among all followers, considering their capabilities. A good leader delegates to all team members considering individual competencies.

Make the assignment clear, specific, and measurable Having decided the two steps, the next duty should be to ensure clarity of the assignments to be delegated. A good leader invites and welcomes questions to ensure whether the communication interpreted by the team members conforms to what actually has been communicated.

Assign an objective Assign the tasks to be performed by them; do not tell the procedure they need to follow. Revealing the procedure will curtail their creativity and they will never brainstorm. It will not help them grow and their growth vector will come to a standstill.

Give credit but share blame Recall the old proverb, 'to err is human'. Sincere and dedicated team members can also commit mistakes. If they do something commendable, praise them to motivate to continue good contribution. However, if anyone does any mistake, criticise the work but not the person; rather share the blame such that he feels your greatness as a leader. This will definitely pay back. Follow the practice, 'praise in public; criticise privately'.

Allow autonomy, but monitor performance Empowering juniors and giving subordinates a degree of autonomy in carrying out their new responsibilities must also include the freedom to make certain mistakes. Punishment for doing mistakes suppresses initiative and innovation. As a leader-manager, remember that mistakes are important sources of development. Create an organizational environment conducive to learning from mistakes.

Share success to enthuse others A manager might be the main architect behind an achievement. However, sharing the success with team members results in transmitting a silent message to them and upholding one's image among them. Remember that image building is an essential prerequisite for successful accomplishment. The sharing will not only motivate them, but will also enhance the leader's charisma.

LINKING HRM INITIATIVES WITH BUSINESS GOALS/STRATEGY

Many organizations are shifting functional responsibilities to line functions. As a result, line managers are assuming new roles. The exact shape of the transformation differs across companies. The most noticeable change is that many functions traditionally performed by a human resources department are shifted to the line. This shift has a plausible result, as the line managers are psychologically closer to the frontiersmen of the organization. Companies such as Oticon and Johnsonville Foods have shifted many traditional human resources functions, such as hiring, reviewing, firing, training, career development, and program development to line managers and employees. Human resources are now being treated as business partner. HR department is finalizing HR initiatives strictly considering the business goals. Career and competency development are planned based on the business goals required to be achieved. HR is no more a staff function; rather it is becoming line function.

SUMMARY

Organizations fulfil a large variety of our societal and personal needs. Whatever be the type, an organization strives to achieve the goals that it sets for itself. Strategies, the route to the destination, are required to be formulated to achieve the goals.

HRM strategies are organization's plans for managing people, culture, structure, and development, and determine how people fit into the organization's future growth. Different organizations, whatever be the nature, adopt different strategies to achieve their goals. For the same goal, the strategies may differ depending on the organizational philosophy. Strategies are required to be developed for some common organizational aspects such as change management, conflict management, instilling ethics, empowering and delegating, discharging corporate social responsibility (CSR), linking HRM initiatives with business goals, and so on.

KEY TERMS

Conflict confrontation strategy In this strategy, all the relevant issues are first uncovered and then a solution is identified that is acceptable to the conflicting parties. This strategy deals with the conflict more openly and thoroughly.

Conflict diffusion strategy This strategy attempts to keep the conflict in abeyance to allow the emotions of both the conflicting parties to precipitate down.

Empowerment refers to the process of increasing the enabling capacity of individuals or groups allowing them to make choices and to transform those choices into desired actions to advance the business. Empowerment is not enhancing power; rather it is creating an environment or situation in which an employee can utilize the power effectively.

Strategy This is a route to the destination, which may be an objective or a goal to be achieved within a definite timeframe.

EXERCISES

Concept Review Questions

1. Define strategy. Discuss the importance of strategy in an organizational context.
2. Narrate the essentials of recruitment strategy in the knowledge sector.
3. While developing a strategy, organizations generally address two critical questions. What are these questions and the reasons behind self questioning? How do these answers guide the course of actions for the company?

Critical Thinking Questions

4. 'Changes are part and parcel of organizational life.' Which strategy can an organization adopt to cross the 'delta stage'? Discuss it in the context of an organization.
5. Had you been the HR manager of a company, how would you handle issues relating to ethics, empowering, and delegation?

Assignments

6. Find out a few companies that have implemented some changes for organizational benefits. Interrogate them about the steps followed by the company on how they manage the resistances encountered.
7. Visit two small or medium-sized companies and try to understand the strategy which they have followed in recent past while revising the compensation packages.

MANAGER'S INSIGHT

Woodward Machines Ltd is planning to integrate and restructure the entire organization. After the takeover of Grain Systems Inc. seven months ago, the top management faced severe challenges not only in retaining its sales but also integrating the new workforce. The parent company had predominantly Swedes while Grain Systems had a mix of Chinese, Indians, South Americans, and Canadians.

Question:

Suggest strategies for the HR department to tackle this situation. (Assumptions regarding the market, product lines, and sales strategies could be made and outlined before formulating the HR strategies.)

BIBLIOGRAPHY AND WEB RESOURCES

Goel, S.L. and Gautam, P.N., *Human Resource Development in the 21st Century,* Deep & Deep Publications Pvt. Ltd, New Delhi, 2005.

Haldar, Uday Kumar, Conflict Management, *Defence Labour (Special Issue),* 1992.

Haldar, Uday Kumar and Juthika Sarkar, *Change Management: Crossing the Delta State,* Larsen & Toubro, Journal of Management, MDC, Issue No. 3, 2010.

Parsons, Talcott, An Approach to the Theory of Organizations, *Organizational Science,* Vol. 13, No. 1, April 1979.

Web Resources

www.hal-india.com, last accessed on 10 October 2007.

www.ongcindia.com/idt.asp#e, last accessed on 20 May 2011.

www.rcfltd.com/website_red/mission.html, last accessed on 29 September 2007.

GROWTH STRATEGY FOR ABC LIMITED

ABC Limited follows a policy of ensuring that its annual growth at the rate of 10 per cent over business turnover is generally measured in terms of sales figure.The company meticulously plans the strategy of this growth in the previous financial year. It decides to adopt the strategies/ tactics such as

1. Modifying the marketing mix
2. Entering a new market with existing products
3. Initiating crash marketing drives
4. Launching of new products to multiply the product range

In order to implement the strategies systemically and derive the best, the company decided to develop its people. It took up the exercise to identify the competencies essential for each of the strategies. As such, the company referred to the employee database to examine the personality traits and identified the people to assign the tasks.The company also believes in continuous development of people and that organization development is interlocked with people development.

For strategy 1: Modifying the marketing mix—by adding more products in the product range, revising the price to penetrate in new market, and enhancing market share in existing markets; to initially adopt push strategy and enjoy benefits of pull strategy at a later stage; exploring new markets.

For strategy 2: Entering new markets with existing products—the company collected information about similar products (two wheelers) used by the inhabitants of the areas.The market personnel selected were trained on sales promotion, understanding the customers, and enhancing communication skills with emphasis on listening skills. Another group was engaged to cram the consumer behaviour.

For strategy 3: Initiating crash marketing drives—the company decided to (a) consider the demographic characteristics opt for market penetration strategy by selling at a lower price than competitors to take hold of the market; and (b) adopted Internet marketing as the principal marketing strategy.

For strategy 4: Launching of new product to multiply the product range—the company pursued direct market survey, interviewed some customers, prepared an exhaust list of spares, analysed the make and model numbers of the two wheelers, and compiled other related information.

Discussion Questions

1. Identify the HR initiatives essential to make the implementation of the strategies successful.
2. Suggest how the results derivable from the strategy can be measured.

HR MANTRA Dealing with problems

Once, an ailing man went to a doctor. The doctor simply measured his body temperature, blood pressure, and prescribed nine medicines. The patient's relative went to a pharmacy to buy the medicines, when the pharmacist told him that four of the nine medicines listed in the prescription were very expensive, and that the entire prescription was actually meant for three (suspected) diseases. The pharmacist suggested that the patient consult the doctor once again, and ask him to prescribe only the most essential medicines.

In an organization, taking decisions without diagnosing the cause of the problem is much like what the doctor did in this incident.

The mantra: Diagnose, then strategize.

MICHAEL E. PORTER

Prof. Dr Michael E. Porter was born in Ann Arbor, Michigan. Porter is widely recognized as the father of modern strategy; he has been identified in a variety of rankings and surveys as the world's most influential thinker on management and competitiveness. Porter is the leading authority on competitive strategy, the competitiveness and economic development of nations, states, and regions, and the application of competitive principles to social problems such as health care, the environment, and corporate responsibility.

Porter's ideas are the foundation for courses on strategy and competitiveness, and his work is taught at virtually every business school in the world. At Harvard, Porter's course, 'Microeconomics of Competitiveness' is a graduate course open to students from across the university. The course is also taught in partnership with more than 80 other universities from every continent using curriculum, video content, and instructor support developed at Harvard. Porter speaks widely on strategy, competitiveness, health care delivery, and related subjects to business, government, non-profit, and philanthropic leaders.

Porter is the Bishop William Lawrence University Professor, based at Harvard Business School. A university professorship is the highest professional recognition that can be awarded to a Harvard faculty member. In 2001, Harvard Business School and Harvard University jointly created the Institute for Strategy and Competitiveness, dedicated to advance Porter's work.

Porter developed the new CEO workshop for newly appointed CEOs of the world's largest and more complex corporations. He chairs this Harvard Business School programme. The programme is held twice in a year and participation is based solely on invitation. The workshop focuses on the challenges faced by new CEOs in assuming leadership. Porter's *Harvard Business Review* article, 'Seven Surprises for New CEOs' coauthored by Jay Lorsch and Nitin Nohria (October 2004), describes some of the learnings from this ongoing body of work.

Porter is the author of 18 books and over 125 articles. He received a BSE with high honours in aerospace and mechanical engineering from Princeton University in 1969, where he was elected to Phi Beta Kappa and Tau Beta Pi. He received an MBA degree with high distinction in 1971 from the Harvard Business School, where he was a George F. Baker scholar and received his Ph D in business economics from Harvard University in 1973.

Porter has pursued extensive research on strategy, competitiveness of nations and regions, competition and society, health care delivery, and many other themes. However, his core field is competitive strategy, which remains a major focus of his research. His book,

Competitive Strategy: Techniques for Analyzing Industries and Competitors, is being printed for the 63rd time and has been translated into 19 languages. His second major strategy book, *Competitive Advantage: Creating and Sustaining Superior Performance,* was published in 1985 and is being printed for the 38th time. His book, *On Competition* (2008), contains his most influential articles on strategy and competition, including the award-winning Harvard Business Review article 'What is Strategy?' (1996) and 'The Five Competitive Forces That Shape Strategy' (2008). Porter's next major book on strategy is being developed.

Porter's 1990 book, *The Competitive Advantage of Nations,* submits a new theory of how nations and regions compete and examines their sources of economic prosperity. Motivated by his appointment by President Ronald Reagan to the President's Commission on Industrial Competitiveness, the book has guided economic policy in countless nations and regions. Successive articles have expanded on the concept of clusters (geographic concentrations of related industries that occur in particular fields) and other aspects of the theory. Porter has published books on national competitiveness covering New Zealand, Canada, Sweden, and Switzerland. His book *Can Japan Compete?* (2000) challenged long-held views about the Japanese economic miracle.

Porter's efforts are not limited to organizations. His efforts extend over society, poverty alleviation, natural environment, and philanthropy. Porter's another major body of work has addressed the relationship between competition and important social issues such as poverty and the natural environment. For example, Porter offered a new approach to revitalizing economically distressed urban communities. With regard to the natural environment, Porter introduced a controversial theory that environmental progress and economic competitiveness were not inconsistent but complementary to one another. Porter has devoted growing attention to philanthropy and the role of corporations in society. He has devoted considerable attention to competition in the health care system, with a focus on improving health care delivery.

Porter has served as a strategy advisor to top management in numerous leading US and international companies including Caterpillar, DuPont, Procter & Gamble, Royal Dutch Shell, Scotts Miracle-Gro, SYSCO, and Taiwan Semiconductor Manufacturing Company. At present, Porter serves on the board of directors of two public companies—Thermo Fisher Scientific Corporation and Parametric Technology Corporation. Porter advises national leaders in numerous countries on competitiveness including Armenia, Colombia, Ireland, Nicaragua, Russia, Rwanda, Saudi Arabia, Singapore, Taiwan, and the United Kingdom. He has personally led major studies of economic strategy for the governments of countries such as Canada, India, Kazakhstan, Libya, New Zealand, Portugal, and Thailand.

Porter has been widely recognized for his work. Some of these honours include Harvard's David A. Wells Prize in economics (1973) for his research in industrial organization. He received the Graham and Dodd Award of the Financial Analysts Federation in 1980. His book, *Competitive Advantage,* won the George R. Terry Book Award of the Academy of Management in 1985 as the outstanding contribution to management thought.

Porter is a fellow of several institutions such as the International Academy of Management (1985), the Academy of Management (1988), and the Royal Swedish Academy of Engineering Sciences (1991). Porter was honoured by the Massachusetts State Legislature in 1991 for his work on Massachusetts competitiveness. Porter has received many awards and honours for his stupendous contributions in different areas.

Porter has lived and travelled throughout the world as the son of a career Army officer. He was an all-state high school football and baseball player in the state of New Jersey where he attended high school. At Princeton, he played intercollegiate golf and was New England champion. After graduating from college, Porter served through the rank of captain in the US Army Reserve. He maintains a long-time interest in the aesthetics and business of music and art, having worked on the problems of strategy with arts organizations and aspiring musicians. Porter has two daughters and resides in Brookline, Massachusetts.

Reference

http://drfd.hbs.edu/fit/public/facultyInfo.do? facInfo=bio&facEmId=mporter, last accessed on 7 October 2011.

CHAPTER 24

HRM in Various Sectors

LEARNING OBJECTIVES

After studying this chapter, you will be able to

- Understand the scope of human resource management (HRM) and recognize its various premises
- Know the functions of HRM in various companies
- Understand HRM practice in various sectors
- Appreciate the role of HRM in the knowledge industry and education sector
- Value the benefits of HRM practices

OPENING CASE

Understanding Sentiments of Juniors Pays

PQR Works, a medium-sized engineering organization, received a huge order from a British company. Initially, 300,000 units were ordered. The quantity ordered was required to be supplied over several years at the rate of 60,000 units per year. During negotiation, PQR highlighted the high initial cost of tools including jigs and fixtures, broaches, press tools, and other miscellaneous production items.

PQR carried out a techno-economic feasibility analysis for all its machines and skill availability. The HR manager confirmed availability of workers with requisite skills to the industrial engineering department. The average age of skilled workers at PQR was 56. At the end of the second year, PQR faced problems on account of shortage of skilled manpower. Two skilled master craftsmen were retiring and PQR deployed other highly skilled workers to continue production. In the middle of the third year, the company received confirmation for an order for a higher quantity, spanning across a period of six years. During that time, two other skilled craftsmen retired. Consequently, the company was not able to continue smooth production. To overcome this problem, PQR engaged retired workers on contractual agreement.

One day a retired and reengaged worker approached a newly recruited supervisor and expressed the need for going home early to discuss the marriage of his daughter. The supervisor turned down the request. Following this incident, the worker approached his higher authority with a request of premature termination of contract with immediate effect. After gathering the details, the higher authority was able to solve the worker's problem.

Soon, the supervisor realized his fault but could not build a rapport with the worker. The retired worker was regarded as exceptionally skilled and indispensable by all seniors. Even after the incident, he was seen to be behaving modestly and gently with all his colleagues and seniors.

Learning points

- Organizations should consider and protect the emotional needs of its employees.
- The management should have a personal touch with its employees to reduce any kind of psychological barriers.

INTRODUCTION

In Chapter 23, we have discussed HRM strategies. In this chapter, we will study some HRM practices which involve application of these strategies in manufacturing and service companies. This chapter includes discussions on HRM practices in versatile organizations such as Ordnance Factories, Ministry of Defence, the knowledge sector including IT companies, educational institutions, non-government organizations (NGOs), life insurance, and *Panchayati Raj*.

Even though we consider *Panchayati Raj* as a rural concept, villagers possess considerable knowledge about the functioning and practices of HRM. With this in consideration, the closing case has been developed on *Panchayati Raj* to enhance awareness among the readers. Let us take a quick glance of the scope of HRM.

As we have been studying in previous chapters, the scope of HRM is pervasive. It includes human resource planning (HRP), job analysis and design, employee hiring, induction and deployment; training and development, appraisal, remuneration, and incentives; motivation, participative management, and employee communication; employee welfare, safety and health, and promotion and transfer; industrial relations, trade unions, industrial disputes, and conflict resolution; and ethical issues, corporate social responsibilities, and human resource audit. Keeping the scope of HR in mind, we will now try to look at various strategies that are being used by various companies in multiple sectors and their effects in the organization, on the people, and the society at large.

STRATEGIES—CHALLENGES AND APPLICATIONS

McKinsey's 7S framework speaks about strategy, structure, system, staff, skill, and style having super ordinate goals or shared values at the core. Thus, it can be said that similar to all the other S's, an organization cannot survive without a strategy. A strategy is the methodology of achieving the planned objectives and goals. Thus, a strategy is a course of action that deals with various means to achieve the desired goals.

HRM strategy deals with the following dimensions:

1. What are the HRM goals? What are the major purposes behind the use of a particular HRM strategy?
2. What are the functions likely to be used? What must be the order of use of the functions?
3. What are the ways in which the HRM functions are envisaged/ visualized prior to implementation?

Having refreshed the scope of HRM and discussed the challenges and applications of strategies, let us discuss HRM in various sectors.

HRM IN EDUCATION

Education aims at the generic development of human resources. Therefore, when we talk of HRM in education, we are talking about the broad development of those human resources involved in education.

The scope of HRM in education takes account of teachers, headmasters, principals, support staff working in educational institutions, heads of university departments, and university vice-chancellors.

Furthermore, the scope extends over educational administrators at the local, district, state and central levels, planners, and policy-makers. People belonging to all these categories must perform their roles efficiently. As such, it is extremely important to develop all these categories of people for the effectiveness of education. People at different levels require diverse competencies to perform various roles in order to be effective in their performance. These competencies also vary because the environment is changing, knowledge base is continuously improving, and the needs are changing. For example, with the advent of information technology, computer competency is inevitable. Such a dynamic and changing environment requires an equally or even faster developing human resources to cope with it. Hence, there is a need to continuously develop the capabilities of people involved in education.

The primary competencies required for teachers include subject matter competencies and pedagogic skills. As we go up the hierarchy in education stream, the competency requirements become much complex. For example, the headmasters of schools require leadership skills, ability to work under stress, human management skills, interacting with external agencies, building the image of the schools, and so on. These are more sophisticated competencies than what a teacher requires.

As one goes still higher up to the level of district education officer (DEO), the competency requirements become even more complex. A DEO is required to deal with a large number of institutions and guide them; he/she is required to be familiar with the region and its educational problems and should have the competency to guide the headmasters of a large number of schools. DEOs should further be able to establish management systems to maintain information, monitor school performance, suggest innovative schemes to the schools, involve the community for improving educational facilities in the region, etc.

Thus, the complexity of the capability requirements changes for different roles. As all these roles are equally important for the effectiveness of the education systems, it becomes essential to ensure the continuous development of the human resources occupying these roles.

> Principals of schools require some leadership skills, such as working under stress, man management skills, taking initiatives, interacting with external agencies, and building the image of schools, and so on.

Training has always been used as a vital component of the HRM function for developing human resources in the education sector. We need to identify other mechanisms of human resource development for successful role accomplishment. The limitations of training in developing complex capabilities have not been adequately recognized in the past. The country is now facing a shortage of skills and knowledge among graduates from engineering and management institutes. They are not capable of efficiently contributing to any company immediately after graduation. The educators and educational administrators need complex skills to design the curriculum, impart the knowledge required by industries, and produce graduates who are readily employable. For example, it is easier to develop subject matter competencies in teachers through classroom instruction. However, teaching skills cannot be developed only through classroom instruction; these skills develop through actual practice. Higher level competencies required by headmasters, principals, DEOs, etc., cannot be developed in the classrooms alone.

> Activities of district education officers include dealing with several educational institutions, establishing systems, monitoring school performances, improving educational facilities, etc.

There is a need to identify alternate mechanisms for developing skills among the human resources. Experience from other sectors indicates that HRD can be affected through performance appraisal systems that are designed to promote employee development in their present roles. Potential development system is also used for keeping one prepared for the future. Organizational development (OD) exercises could be undertaken to create self-renewal capabilities in educational institutions.

Educational institutions and agencies need a development climate. As such, career opportunities and rewards are vital. An educational institution may be facing slow growth in situations where there is no good development climate, pressure, or compensation including rewards and incentives.

HRM IN THE KNOWLEDGE INDUSTRY

Q 2 There are many HRM theories. In this era of explosion of information technology, knowledge management, dwindling business scenario, and acute competition, the need for young and energetic individuals is challenging several time-tested theories of employee recruitment, staffing, motivation, and general HR practices. Organizations are facing a lot of challenges while recruiting fresh talent.

The recruitment challenges include attracting people with multidimensional experiences and skills, developing a culture that attracts people, designing entry pay packages that compete on quality and not quantum, and so forth. Companies also need to anticipate future vacancies considering their strategy and future needs. Human resources are required to be searched and recruited such that their services can be utilized immediately after such a need arises.

The role of the HR manager is

1. to develop fully self-expressed and self-propelled individuals
2. to involve and engage them in organizational activities
3. to enable and facilitate their effective participation in teams
4. to empower them to innovate

> In this millennium, time-tested theories of employee recruitment, staffing, motivation, and general HR practices are facing challenges.

However, to develop fully self-expressed and self-propelled individuals, involving and engaging them, enabling and facilitating their effective participation, and making them innovative, some careful steps must be pursued. These individuals primarily need challenging jobs, growth, intrinsic satisfaction, and so forth. Designing attractive compensation management system is only secondary. People working in the knowledge industry need to be supported more than to be managed. In order to derive their best performance, the HR needs to care for their emotional needs. People of higher levels mostly remain engrossed in office work and can seldom discharge family responsibilities. HR must make sure that their work and family lives are well-balanced. Some added responsibilities of HR with regard to managing employees in the educational sector include the following:

> Self-expressed and self-propelled people working in the knowledge industry need to be supported more than managed.

1. Caring for their emotional needs
2. Balancing work and personal life
3. Advocating change
4. Being a strategic partner
5. Providing a human touch

> In organizations, effective people are no more the ones with only high intelligence quotient (IQ); they are the ones with high emotional quotient (EQ) as well.

Caring for emotional needs In order to get the best from the employees, we must take care to identify and fulfil their emotional needs. The first step is to enhance the emotional intelligence of people. A person can have the best training in the world, a penetrating and insightful brain, and an analytical mind with an endless supply of smart ideas. In spite of having the positive attributes, he can never be a good leader if he does not possess high emotional stability. Effective people are no longer the ones with only high intelligence quotient (IQ); they are the ones who also possess high emotional quotient (EQ).

A high correlation between emotional intelligence and effective performance has already been evidenced by many academicians and research scholars. People with high emotional intelligence help in establishing good interpersonal relations, guided by dominant independence motive, are self-propelled, self-motivated, and emphatic.

Balancing work and personal life Balancing work and personal life is a significant area as achieving the right balance between the work place and home is crucial to the efficient running of any organization. Incidentally, the findings of a recent survey on 2,500 highest-ranking MBAs from B-schools in Europe and USA conducted by management graduates identified balancing personal life and work life as their top most career objective (en.allexperts.com, last accessed on 7 February 2012).

Advocating change HR managers and professionals should be able to develop and change the mindset of the employees. Therefore, they should work as a change advocate who is responsible for bringing about changes in individual behaviour patterns. For being a better change advocate, one has to be an extrovert, possess considerable interpersonal skills, have to be creative, take risks, and be good in organizing activities.

The change advocate should also be close to employees, understand their feelings, emotions, and thoughts, possess good communication skills, be accessible to all, plan activities systematically, evaluate objectively, and reward people for outstanding performance.

Being a strategic partner Human resource plays a substantial role in achieving the business goals. In order to perform this role effectively, HR professionals should have thorough knowledge of business and human resource functions, the ability to lead any change process, innovation, problem solving, the leadership ability to influence the members and organization, be able to work in stressful conditions without being frustrated, and view the brighter side of any situation.

Providing a human touch Employees should be close to one another for creating a healthy work environment and improving their quality of work life. The work environment should be conducive to performance without generating unwanted stress. Good interpersonal relations and highly motivated employees can create such an environment. Both monetary and non-monetary benefits are required to motivate the workforce. Organizational systems such as job restructuring, job redesign, career development, promotional opportunities and so on are also essential.

Some motivational tools comprise celebrating achievements of teams and individuals, offering birthday gifts, gifting dinner coupons on marriage anniversaries, installing flexi-time work systems, offering paid vacations, giving cards/mails and appreciation letter to recognize personal achievement, going on an outing with project team at the end of the successful completion of a project, ensuring services such as free health check-ups, canteen facility, recreation room and so on.

There is a need to increase the credibility of HR within the organization and this can be accomplished by being accurate in HR tasks, being predictable and maintaining consistency, being committed and sticking to specified budget, and being personally comfortable with peers, subordinates, and superiors.

Most of the time, talent remains underutilized and untapped. It is important to understand people and provide them with the appropriate environment to harness the latent power within them. This initiative will make a difference between success and failure in the future and lead to the realization of the power of the human spirit.

Source: Based on 'Challenges for HR Professionals in the Knowledge Industry' by Rahul Sharma, executive HRD, Datamatics Limited'. www.humanlinks.ws, last accessed on 5 February 2012.

HRM IN INFOSYS TECHNOLOGIES

Q 3 Infosys Technologies is a significantly known company in the knowledge industry. The company believes in the power of talent and follows the maxim, 'Aspiration is the main fuel for progress. Aspirations transform a set of ordinary people into extraordinary achievers'. Infosys has become a role model for many companies as it possesses value-based leadership, exemplary corporate governance, one of the best-in-class processes, a caring and development-oriented attitude, commendable wealth creation, and delivery of world class products and services.

Strategies of Infosys

Infosys relies heavily on leadership development. The vision of Infosys is to create an organization that is 'built to last' and has the agility and liveliness to manage ambiguity and uncertainty under all circumstances. Irrespective of hierarchy, Infosys gives the employees an equal opportunity to shape the future of the company. Infosys undertook an assessment to look at all aspects of its business and its performance. After introspection, it discovered that one of the areas that required improvement was that the company needed to have a structured way of developing leaders.

The company developed a three-tier leadership model. This model is based on their belief that the company is the campus, the business is the curriculum, and the leaders shall teach. Senior members of the Infosys management conduct courses on leadership at the institute, and share their experiences. This drive helps the company to attract, retain, and motivate the best and the brightest talent pool from India and abroad. The company grooms about 700 to 800 employees annually.

The strategies of Infosys towards leadership development are adopted through nine leadership pillars that identify leadership traits, and create a leadership funnel through nine dimensions of leadership.

Leadership Development in Infosys

Infosys is keen to develop its leadership potential methodically at its own institute, Infosys Leadership Institute (ILI) at Mysore. It invites applications from employees from middle and senior-level management to participate in leadership programmes. The leadership competency department evaluates these applications on the basis of the nine leadership competencies formulated by the company and selects employees for different sets of programmes. The entire initiative starts with identifying the competencies that organizational leaders require. Apart from these leadership pillars, Infosys looks for six leadership traits in its employees.

Leadership pillars The nine pillars for leadership development are as follows:

1. *360-degree feedback:* Multi-source assessment and feedback system, a long-felt organizational need, emphasizes the softer dimensions of performance such as leadership, creativity, originality, innovation, teamwork, initiative, emotional intelligence, entrepreneurship, and so on. This is a mechanism through which the company gathers data about an individual's performance and abilities. The information is collected from co-workers, peers, subordinates, managers, and customers. Personal development plans are prepared on the basis of the feedback. The employees are assigned an ILI faculty member to help prepare and follow a personal development plan.

2. *Development assignments:* Infosys identifies high-potential employees, called Infoscions, at various events of the company, and trains them through job rotations and cross-functional assignments. This helps employees acquire new leadership skills outside their own areas of expertise and experience.
3. *Infosys culture workshops:* These tailor-made workshops help to fortify and strengthen the Infosys culture among participants, instill better communication skills through sustained interaction, and assists in identifying the values and processes involved in leadership development.
4. *Development relationships:* The company believes in developing healthy relationships among various levels of personnel. This includes fostering a one-on-one interaction in the actual on-the-job work climate and leads to better sharing of knowledge and camaraderie and companionship among people. Mentoring forms an integral part of this exercise and strengthens the camaraderie.
5. *Leadership skills training:* The company conducts 'Leaders Teach Series' workshops wherein its tier 1 members share their knowledge and rich experiences to acclimatize the next rung with leadership roles and groom them. Dr Narayana Murthy, Chairman emeritus and Nandan Nilekani, former chief executive officer and managing director were also engaged in developing leadership skills.
6. *Feedback-intensive programmes:* These programmes are similar to 360-degree feedback, but are based on formal and informal feedback from employees that an individual interacts with.
7. *Systemic process learning:* Infoscions gain an overall view of the company and its diverse and complex systems, businesses, operations, and processes through systemic process learning. It is a continuous process and helps improve the individual and the systems.
8. *Action learning:* Infosys believes and encourages teamwork. Action learning is an exercise constituting solving real problems in real-time conditions as part of a team.
9. *Community empathy:* A company functions in a society. Infosys stresses the need to give back to society by engaging in various developmental, educational, and social causes. This programme helps nurture social conscience among its leaders.

Leadership traits The company examines the following six leadership traits:

1. *High penetration for self and organization:* Self-assessment is a process that assesses what one is doing, why he/she is doing it, and what he/she must do to improve the organization's performance. A leader can penetrate deeper through this process. There are five essential questions to the process:
   (a) What is our mission?
   (b) Who is our customer?
   (c) What does the customer value?
   (d) What are our results?
   (e) What is our plan?
2. *Passion for excellence:* Without enthusiasm and excitement of its employees, an organization cannot gain excellence, become a role model, display value-based leadership, exhibit exemplary corporate governance, and so forth.
3. *Team player:* Each team player must possess clarity of role, and should know how his/her job fits in with others. Each team member must perform the assigned work and not be affected by office politics. If each person of a team makes a point to treat other members with respect, they can work as team players to achieve team goals, irrespective of their personal differences.

4. *Desire in learning:* Infosys, believes in continuous learning, and inculcates the spirit of knowledge among Infoscions and develops organizational commitment to continuous personal and professional development. These ideas place Infosys at the forefront in a fast-changing industry.
5. *Courage to take risk:* One cannot avoid taking risk in the work place. A person with high risk-taking propensity ultimately wins the game even if the playfield is the work area. However, one should take calculated risks and be aware of the organizational environment. A good leader has the courage to take risk.
6. *Focus on results and attention to detail:* The result or outcome and the process of any project are important. Understanding the approach to an activity helps in completing the project with perfection.

Leadership dimensions Infosys believes that leadership must drive the creation of a leadership funnel at different levels of the organization, must be centered on Infoscions, and be rooted in the organizational context. There cannot be any single mantra to develop leadership as it needs multiple methods in several directions. Infosys focuses on nine dimensions of leadership. These are strategic leadership, change leadership, operational leadership, talent leadership, relationship/networking leadership, content leadership, entrepreneurial leadership, transactional leadership, and adversity leadership. These nine dimensions are explained for in-depth understanding, irrespective of the nature of business.

Strategic leadership This is about unique positioning; it explains how one can create a unique position of the company in the market. Strategic leadership is based on creating an agile and a flexible organization, which can cope with changes in the business environment and suitably respond to them.

Change leadership This is about changing the context and making the change effective. A leader, particularly a top-level leader, must have the vision to anticipate the direction and speed of changes in the business environment. Accordingly, he/she has to finalize steps to set up changes in the organization, and communicate the reasons behind the internal changes at various levels of personnel. While incorporating the changes, several issues may emerge, and he/she must handle them by combining firmness with flexibility.

Operational leadership It is about achieving a high degree of effectiveness and productivity. This leadership dimension refers to defining the operational excellence in the organizational context, considering the framework used to achieve the operational excellence, and judging the used parameters for rightness.

Talent leadership It is about creating a top-quality leadership team, that is the best in the relevant area globally. A top-level manager must understand the need for nurturing talent and he/she has to develop a system to identify talent of the middle and junior level managers and provide them with required inputs so that their potentials are realized. A top-level organizational leader has to see him as a teacher or coach and devote time to develop the next levels of leaders.

Relationship/networking leadership It is about building bridges of relationship, and developing, maintaining, and leveraging long-term internal and external relationship networks. In fact, relationships operate at different levels in an organization and are accompanied by various influential agencies that can impact the business. A leader must understand the difference between the breadth and depth of a relationship framework. A suitable communication strategy needs to go hand in hand with the relation-building strategy.

Content leadership This dimension emphasises that leadership must be based on content (knowledge) and not merely on process skills. Process skills refer to the consistent and efficient use of core communication skills and strategies to achieve the intention. Leaders need process skills, in addition to a thorough knowledge about the tasks, to achieve the goals. These skills definitely help an executive to move up the organizational hierarchy. While doing so, they also help develop content leadership. Content leadership facilitates gaining competitive advantage for continuous innovation and helps in assessing the level of domain expertise of the business. The domain can be banking, insurance, advertising, software development, etc. If the domain is banking technology, the content includes core banking, internet banking, and customer relationship management.

Entrepreneurial leadership It is about having an entrepreneurial zeal and concentrates on taking ownership or responsibility for business outcomes. The entrepreneurial zeal of a manager takes him/her from a humdrum and monotonous state to a state in which he/she can contribute effectively to the organization. This skill encompasses the power of imagination and commitment in the face of challenges.

Transactional leadership It is about acquiring and integrating new lines of businesses. Even when it is clear as to what is required of their subordinates and the rewards that they get for following orders, transactional leaders create clear structures and roles for their employees. They do not always propose punishment for non-conformance when things go wrong. A transactional leader often uses management by exception methodology and works on the principle that if something is operating to the expected and defined performance level, it does not need attention. Exceptions to expectations require praise and reward for exceeding expectations, while some kind of corrective action is applied for performance that is below expectation.

Adversity leadership Adversity may arise from multiple types of differences in region, religion, language spoken, gender, belief system, cultural, and social background, and so on. Adversity is a part and parcel of any business organization. It can be small or big and is likely to impede the functioning of a business. As a leader, one has to handle the adversity, irrespective of its intensity. A leader learns from his/her experiences and initiates steps to prevent recurrence of such situations. However, Infosys has an adversity center to manage problems arising out of diversity.

Source: Based on a discussion with Dr Shushant Tharappan, Associate Vice President and part of the senior leadership of Infosys Leadership Institute, on 13 October 2009, and used as case study in *Leadership and Team Building* by Dr U.K. Haldar, published by Oxford University Press, New Delhi, 2010.

HRM IN LIFE INSURANCE CORPORATION OF INDIA

Life Insurance Corporation of India (LIC) was set up in 1956 by the Government of India, following the nationalization of life insurance business. Until 1956, the entire life insurance business scene was being transacted by private companies. The nationalization changed the scenario and LIC took over the entire business. The fund (assets and liabilities) and employees pertaining to this business were automatically transferred to the LIC. Since 1956, LIC has been vested with the sole authority to transact life insurance business in India, subject to special authorizations for some government schemes, which are allowed to operate outside the purview of the LIC. LIC has its central office at Mumbai, five zonal offices, 64 divisional offices and branches in over 800 centres.

> Life insurance is a contract that pledges payment of an amount to the person assured (or his nominee) on the happening of the event insured against.

Following the implementation of the liberalization policy by the Government of India in 1991, private insurers were allowed to run insurance businesses in India. The Insurance Regulation and Development Authority (IRDA) was formed to regulate the businesses of insurance companies. Though LIC does not have monopoly in insurance, it is continuing its march towards excellence.

In 1980, LIC launched a major exercise for organizational restructuring which led to key decentralization of responsibilities of the branches. LIC recognized each branch as a profit and growth centre. The number of positions in the branches was considerably enhanced along with the level of responsibility in the positions. Each branch was equipped with microprocessors. The new structure provided for consultation processes and joint decision-making in planning and other operations.

The new systems also included data being generated about the socio-economic conditions of the area under the jurisdiction of the branch for planning purposes and developing strategies for operations on the basis of such data. Consequent to the restructure of work, there was a need to enhance the skills of the personnel to operate these new systems. It was recognized that in order to successfully adapt to the serious challenges from the complex turbulent environment, organizations need long-term strategies with regard to the social systems. Being aware of bureaucratic procedures, narrowly defined jobs, and the tight supervision that could wreak havoc on human motivation and that excellent performance comes when individuals are committed to using full capacities to solve problems, there was a need to develop strategies that would meet the needs for learning, development, belongingness, variety, and creativity. LIC documented its human resource related philosophy.

HRD Philosophy

Way back in 1987, LIC stated its beliefs about HR issues as follows:

1. That human potential inherent in every employee is vast; it can be further enhanced by various interventions such as training, job rotation, counselling, organizational action, and so on.
2. That people are major assets and that an organization can foster full realization of individual potential by providing a developmental environment and opportunities, by encouraging and rewarding innovativeness, etc.
3. That such people who are not able to contribute to the organization fully due to reasons beyond their control can also give their best if they are taken care of, and proper environment and conditions are provided.
4. That competencies can be developed in people at any point of time; as a model employer it is desirable that we encourage competency enhancement.
5. That HRD provides for higher quality of work-life through opportunities for a meaningful career, job satisfaction, and professional development.
6. That HRD philosophy emphasizes human well-being and organizational growth, that HRD policies are relationship-centred and the extent of relationships under the ambit of HRD is lifelong and not merely for eight hours.
7. That as a model-employer, the corporation must provide for employee growth; if an employee perceives a nurturing environment, there would be a positive response to matching individual aspirations with organizational needs.
8. That in order to be effective, HRD processes have to be planned and continuous.

Defined HR Goals of LIC

In order to achieve the business objectives, LIC defined certain HR goals. These are as follows:

1. Ensuring that adequate number of persons with sound insurance background and experience, both as generalists and specialists, are available at different levels, to facilitate enhancement of standards of service to customers and fast growth
2. Providing human resource policies that are not only fair and just but also perceived in the same manner
3. Providing employees with equitable opportunities to move up in the organizational hierarchy on the basis of their performance and ability
4. Ensuring that responsibility for results is provided right from the lower levels so that employees can develop a sense of independence and self-confidence
5. Extending opportunities to employees to learn new and varied skills, thus, making work more satisfying and meaningful
6. Providing opportunities for training and development of employees with special potential

Several HR strategies were developed, to achieve the stated objectives and goals, in consultation with experts in the field of insurance. LIC circulated and discussed new strategies among groups of employees. It also formulated the new strategies as the organization needed a comprehensive HR approach.

Source: www.licindia.in, last accessed on 7 February 2012.

HRM IN ORDNANCE FACTORIES, ORDNANCE FACTORY BOARD, MINISTRY OF DEFENCE

The department of defence protects our country from intruders. Human resource management, in its entire parlance, is especially relevant in the defence services. Organizationally, the defence sector represents one of the largest, most differentiated, and geographically dispersed systems of the country. Efficient coordination of defence activities for the common purpose of maintaining the security and integrity of the country can, therefore, only be brought about when appropriate skills, attitudes, and behaviours are inculcated among people. As there is a high degree of unpredictability in the events which may call for action on the part of the defence services, people have to be kept physically, mentally, and morally prepared at all times.

The Indian defence comprises the army, navy, and air force. These are termed as three arms of Indian defence. The Indian ordnance factories organization is a family of 40 ordnance factories under the aegis of its corporate headquarters, Ordnance Factory Board (OFB), Kolkata. OFB possesses the unique distinction of over 200 years experience in defence production. OFB is engaged in production, testing, logistics, research, development, and marketing a comprehensive product range in the area of land, sea, and air systems.

OFB receives patronage from residents of India and foreigners who speak highly of the quality of its products and services. Undoubtedly, OFB is the force behind armed forces, and as such is termed as the fourth arm of Indian defence.

Integrity, transparency, fairness, and trust are the values of OFB. Its mission is 'production of state-of-the-art battle field equipments'.

OFB prepares people by developing strategies and tactics, and trains officers and employees in the latest techniques of production technology. They are simultaneously trained on devising more and better methods of motivating people to ensure their commitment to the objectives of the organization. Another factor which increases the importance of human resource management activities is the absence of lateral induction of personnel at any level of the hierarchy of the defence services. Unlike other organizations, the defence services cannot fill vacancies by inducting persons from outside at all levels. Hence, grooming people from the lower levels for positions at higher levels is a regular practice. However, both technical and non-technical chargemen are recruited and are required to undergo an intensive long-term of 44 weeks.

The Ordnance factories' training system commenced way back in 1920. OFB has its own training and development mechanisms. Senior and top-level managers attend management development programmes at the National Academy of Defence Production (NADP), formerly Ordnance Factories Staff College (OFSC) at Nagpur. Junior managers, non-gazetted officers, and staff members are trained at Ordnance Factories Institute of Learning (OFIL). There are eight institutes of learning and factory training institutes under the control of each factory for training trade apprentices. NADP and all OFILs are ISO 9001 certified units. The training system is structured and training needs are identified by following a documented procedure.

The terminal human resource objectives are:

1. Creating self-awareness within participants through introspection, retrospection, and self-study
2. Improving their knowledge of individual differences relating to personality such as values, attitudes, and motives, as well as developing the cognitive side of personality such as reasoning ability, judgement, conceptualization, and problem solving
3. Improve their understanding of the process of communication with emphasis on transactional nature involved in personal and organizational communication
4. Developing their decision-making ability by developing emotional maturity and tolerance for ambiguity and empathy
5. Enhancing their skill of engaging human resource in a better manner for increasing overall organizational effectiveness
6. Helping the human resource to create a work environment characterized by mutual trust, cooperation, collaboration, team work, etc.

The pedagogical features used by the department includes all modern methods of imparting training including role playing exercises, case studies, films, diagnostic instruments, syndicate and panel discussions, brain storming, visits to industrial organizations, conducting projects, etc. It lays special emphasis on experiential learning which has proved to be very effective with the officers, particularly at the senior management level (ofbindia.nic.in).

HRM STRATEGY IN RASHTRIYA CHEMICALS AND FERTILIZERS LTD

Rashtriya Chemicals and Fertilizers Ltd (RCF) is a corporate body and a Government of India undertaking. The company is simultaneously accountable to all agencies that have a stake in its successful operation, growth, and welfare, namely the government, consumers, employees, and the society at large. Keeping these aspects in view, RCF has set certain corporate goals as follows:

1. To help increase the national agricultural productivity by providing agricultural inputs and services
2. To provide input and services with the least consumption of resources and at minimum cost
3. To obtain for its employees a decent standard of living and as good a quality of life as possible, consistent with the general socio-economic conditions in the country
4. To secure as high a return on the rate of investment as possible, keeping in view the requirements of other competing objectives

5. To promote self-reliance in all activities in relation to the company's operations including process of know-how, design and engineering, erection, commissioning, operations, maintenance of plants, and marketing of products
6. To manufacture and market industrial chemicals related to agricultural inputs and also to others based on similar technology and intermediates, by-products, co-products, and waste from the main operations
7. To promote, organize, and perform research and development in products, technology, engineering, soil science, and agronomy in furtherance of various corporate objectives
8. To improve the environment and reduce all harmful emissions, atmospheric discharges, and effluents to the maximum technologically possible extent
9. To continuously upgrade the quality of human resources, and promote organizational and management development.
10. To cooperate nationally and internationally in exchange of information and services of personnel
11. To achieve corporate growth at a pace consistent with the availability of resources and the developmental needs of the economy
12. To promote specific social objectives such as development of entrepreneurs, ancillary industries, special assistance to SC/ST, and other backward classes

Implementation of Strategies at RCF

The strategies of RCF include HRD, vision building and innovation, structuring and restructuring of the organization, systems development and managing change, succession and career planning, employee development, training and development, employee involvement and commitment, manpower audit, and commercialization of HR services. The strategies of RCF are collectively exhaustive and facilitate RCF towards its march to excellence.

Human resource development At RCF, human resources management is linked to its corporate vision and goals. The HR approach of RCF is focused completely on employee development. While RCF strives to achieve the heights of business and customer satisfaction, quality of management, innovativeness, employee talent, and dynamism, it is equally keen to discharge corporate social responsibility. RCF treats CSR initiatives to be as important as effective operations, and aims to save costs and ensures product quality. HRM sub-systems are very well established in terms of design, infrastructure, and continuity.

Vision building and innovation RCF treats vision building and innovation as one of the powerful tools for taking the organization forward in leaps and bounds. The company considers vision building and innovation to be of top relevance in today's dynamic business situation. RCF has engaged its executives across all levels, from the shop floor and frontline executives to senior strategy makers of the organization, in fruitful vision building exercises and idea sharing for overall business growth.

Structuring and restructuring of the organization RCF continuously reviews and revamps at appropriate junctures in order to keep away from imbalances in organizational structure that might lead to inefficiency and delays. RCF has always reviewed the need for internal restructuring and also engages external expertise on an occasional basis for retaining a balanced and efficient structure.

Systems development and managing change Considering the crucial role of HRM in development and implementation of systems in an organization, RCF has entered into enterprise resource planning (ERP) by networking its major functional areas. This move will drastically reduce the manual administrative work. RCF treats HRM as a powerful catalyst in managing change in the organization.

Succession and career planning Implementing a succession plan is important for maintaining organizational health as it ensures availability of future leaders at key positions and effective coordination. Succession plan allows for creative development of personnel to 'fit' within the organization at the middle and upper management levels. RCF does not leave its leadership to chance. It meticulously works out succession planning for the top three to four layers of the organization and reviews it at regular intervals for implementation.

Employee development In this era where employability has taken priority over the old promise of secure employment, organizations that support employee development are better able to attract and retain talented people. RCF adopts the HRD sub-systems, namely, training and development, employee involvement and commitment, manpower audit (rightsizing/redeployment/retraining needs/recruitment), and commercialization of HR services. RCF has established these sub-systems well in order to attract and retain employees.

Training and development RCF identifies training needs for all levels of employees; it aptly designs training curriculum for all levels on a continuous basis. The company has developed modular training concept to provide uniform inputs at different employee levels, leading to positive change in organizational performance, overall quality of manpower, and most importantly, organizational culture.

Employee involvement and commitment RCF makes continuous efforts to encourage employee involvement at different levels and ensures the enhanced commitment of the workforce. OD interventions such as quality circles, suggestion schemes, total quality management, 5S, best employee awards, are implemented. Additionally, RCF has the following systems in place:

1. Performance-linked compensation (profit sharing)
2. Best employee retention
3. Counselling services for employees

Manpower audit The scope extends over rightsizing, redeployment, or identification of training and retraining needs and recruitment and selection systems. In view of the competitive environment that is forcing organizations all over the world to review their structures and manpower strength, RCF systematically takes an internal review of the need to restructure in order to maintain a balanced and efficient structure. The organization gives priority to manpower redeployment and retraining, rather than inviting the possibilities of retrenchment. RCF carries out a study of the present status of manpower allocation and an analytical study of optimum manpower in various departments such as

1. identification of redeployable manpower
2. retraining scheme for employees identified for redeployment
3. developing scheme for non-redeployable employees (VRS, etc.)

Commercialization of HR services RCF believes in mutually beneficial networking and offers HR services relating to infrastructure, faculty expertise, and resources to other organizations. Designing, developing, and implementing need-based HR interventions is RCF's strength (www.rcfltd.com).

HRM IN HINDUSTAN AERONAUTICS LIMITED

Hindustan Aeronautics Limited (HAL) came into existence on 1 October 1964. The company was formed by the merger of Hindustan Aircraft Limited with Aeronautics India Limited and Aircraft Manufacturing Depot, Kanpur. The company traces its roots to the pioneering efforts of late Seth

Walchand Hirachand, an industrialist with extraordinary vision. He had set up HAL at Bangalore, in association with the erstwhile princely State of Mysore, in December 1940. The Government of India became a shareholder in March 1941 and took over its management in 1942.

Today, HAL has 16 production units and nine research and design centres in seven locations in India. The company has an impressive product track record—it has manufactured 12 types of aircraft with in-house research and development (R&D) and has produced 14 types under license. HAL has manufactured 3,550 aircrafts (which includes 11 types designed and produced indigenously), 3,600 engines, and has overhauled over 8,150 aircraft and 27,300 engines. HAL has been successful in initiating numerous R&D programs for both defence and civil aviation sectors. It has made substantial progress in its following projects:

1. Dhruv—advanced light helicopter (ALH)
2. Tejas—light combat aircraft (LCA)
3. Intermediate jet trainer (IJT)
4. Various military and civil upgrades

In March 2002, HAL delivered Dhruv to the Indian army, navy, air force, and the coast guard, in the very first year of its production, and this was considered a unique achievement.

It has played a significant role for India's space programs by participating in the manufacture of structures for satellite launch vehicles such as

1. PSLV (polar satellite launch vehicle)
2. GSLV (geo stationary launch vehicle)
3. IRS (Indian remote satellite)
4. INSAT (Indian national satellite)

There are three companies who have joint ventures with HAL:

1. BAeHAL Software Limited
2. Indo-Russian Aviation Limited (IRAL)
3. Snecma HAL Aerospace Pvt. Ltd

Apart from these companies, other major diversification projects are industrial marine gas turbine and airport services. There are several co-production and joint ventures with international participation under consideration.

HAL's supplies and services are mainly directed to Indian defence services, coast guards, and border security forces. Transport aircraft and helicopters have also been supplied to airlines as well as state governments of India. The company has also achieved a foothold in export in more than 30 countries, having demonstrated its quality and price competitiveness.

Vision

To make HAL a dynamic, vibrant, value-based, learning organization with exceptionally skilled, highly motivated, and committed human resources to meet the current and future challenges. This will be driven by core values of the company fully embedded in the culture of the organization.

Mission

To enable all those who work for HAL to give their best in order to ensure their all-round growth as well as that of the organization.

Awards for Achievement

HAL has won several international and national awards for achievement in R&D, technology, managerial performance, exports, energy conservation, quality, and fulfillment of social responsibilities.

1. HAL bagged the international gold medal award for corporate achievement in quality and efficiency, at the international summit (Global Rating Leaders 2003), at London by M/s Global Rating, UK, in conjunction with the International Information and Marketing Centre (IIMC).
2. It was awarded the International Arch of Europe Award in the gold category in recognition for its commitment to quality, leadership, technology, and innovation.
3. At the national level, HAL won the gold trophy for excellence in public sector management, instituted by the Standing Conference of Public Enterprises (SCOPE).

In the financial year 2004–2005, HAL scaled new heights with a turnover of ₹45,340 million and export over ₹1,500.5 million.

Strategic HRD Goal

The goal of HAL is directed towards creating an atmosphere of technological and managerial excellence to become a globally competitive aerospace industry. The strategic human resource development (HRD) goal of HAL emanated from the company's mission statement.

With the changing environment, rapid technological changes characterized by a paradigm shift from licensed production to R&D-based production duly balanced with co-development/co-production, technological up-gradation, etc., greater customer demand, and focused diversification to civilian and export markets, the overall objective of the human resource development plan is to build a vibrant and learning organization. This will help meet the challenges of quality and excellence, recruitment and retention of competent human resources, and develop high commitment and a sense of belonging to the company.

Objectives

The objectives of HAL are

1. to ensure availability of total quality people to meet the organizational goals and objectives
2. to have a continuous improvement in knowledge, skill, and competence (managerial, behavioural, and technical)
3. to promote a culture of achievement and excellence with emphasis on integrity, credibility, and quality
4. to maintain a motivated workforce through empowerment of the individual and team building
5. to enhance organizational learning
6. to play a pivotal role directly and significantly to enhance productivity, profitability, and improve the quality of work life

Focus of Human Resource Policy

HAL focuses its HR policy through

1. Competence building
2. Commitment
3. Motivation
4. Employee relations

HRD Initiatives

HAL treats training and development as the most important HRM function. In the backdrop of this discussion, the focus of HRD efforts at HAL emphasizes the following:

Manpower planning This comprises the following sub-functions:

(a) Outsourcing of low-tech and medium-tech jobs
(b) Inducting fresh talent only in critical and highly specialized areas based on requirements, in case of an increase in workload and superannuation profile. In the workmen cadre, induction will be restricted to direct workmen
(c) Improving the existing qualification profile by focusing on induction of professionally qualified personnel and diploma holders

Hence, the focus of recruitment would be to recruit people with a combination of knowledge, skill, experience, and attitude in line with the organizational requirement through an appropriate manpower plan, and short-term (contract appointments) and long-term recruitment programmes.

Training and development Training is one of the most important tools for developing human resources. Hence, identification of training competency profile in terms of vision and mission of the company would be the strategic point of the training and development strategy of the company. The following objectives have been set in this regard:

1. To provide training to all employees at regular intervals in a plan period of five years
2. Training to become an integral component of individual professional evolution by
   (a) updating knowledge to avoid obsolescence
   (b) enhancing professional creativity
   (c) enabling employees to shoulder higher responsibility
   (d) creating a business trend and strategic thinking to take up new business challenges (creation of centres of excellence, etc.)

The goals of training will be to progressively achieve seven days training per employee per year with a budget of two per cent of the annual wage bill.

Keeping in view the organizational requirement and goals and objectives of training, the following have been identified as the key focus areas of training:

1. Technology
2. Tooling
3. Quality
4. Information technology

Further, to facilitate the development of soft skills (change of mindset, managerial development, etc.) training would be imparted on a continuous basis. Tie-ups with centres of excellence such as Indian Institutes of Technology, National Defence College, Foreign Investment Advisory Service (FIAS) France, and so on, for imparting training, would be given prime importance.

Performance appraisal Appraising people for meeting the company's goal is the prime focus of performance management. The new performance appraisal system based on work planning and commitment (mutually-agreed tasks), self-review, and performance analysis, performance review, and feedback ensure that the focus would be on value adding activities rather than on routine activities, which bear no relationship to the organization's goals and objectives.

Identification of low performers and initiating corrective action throughout the company are in practice. Similarly, faster career growth opportunity is provided for high performers.

Reward system The focus of reward system is to promote teamwork and cultivate a sense of achievement and excellence in the organization. This is in addition to the existing scheme of reward for an individual who makes exemplary contributions innovatively and creatively in key thrust areas of the company that would lead to its achieving overall excellence. Coupled with these traits, schemes such as interdivisional competitions and profit-sharing schemes have been institutionalized in the company for team reward.

Scheme for learning and certification for executives In the present era of liberalization, privatization, and globalization, the presence of a learning organization is essential for survival. Therefore, knowledge is the only core competence of organizations for coping with changes. As individual knowledge is the starting point for organizational knowledge, employees can convert knowledge into efficient actions.

In line with this philosophy, other initiatives such as institutionalizing learning centres in divisions, and so on, HAL has also introduced the scheme for learning and certification for executives as a starting point for building individual knowledge. The scheme inter alia provides an opportunity for junior and middle management cadre executives to broaden their perspectives. This is achieved not only by learning about all functions and procedures in their respective disciplines but also in related areas and gaining overall knowledge about the organization and its environment. So far, approximately 45 per cent (both for 'O' and 'A' levels) of executives have been certified. It is proposed to expand the coverage of this scheme further, if required, by linking the scheme to some kind of reward mechanism.

The HRD efforts also include time-to-time OD interventions to address specific requirements of the company (www.hal-india.com).

HRM IN VOLUNTARY ORGANIZATIONS

More than six decades have elapsed after independence. However, the need for socio-economic transformation of the country is still widely prevalent. Nevertheless, the efforts of the government, government-sponsored organizations, and agencies have been inadequate to achieve the enormous task.

Over the years, the role of non-profit voluntary organizations has increased to a very great extent in a variety of arenas such as rural development, community development, health and rehabilitation, vocational training, consumer organization, and so on. In fact, the seventh five-year plan acknowledges the need for establishing voluntary organizations. The seventh plan can be implemented successfully only with the involvement of the masses. The plan proposes to accomplish this by increasing the involvement of voluntary agencies in the implementation of plan programmes.

There is an extensive range of voluntary organizations in India. Voluntary organizations range in size from small groups of only five or six individuals to large organizations employing hundreds of people and are engaged in varied operations scattered throughout the country. There are around 10,000 voluntary organizations in India. These organizations enjoy a number of advantages which make them potentially effective change agents. As they are usually small in size, they can be flexible and, obviously, organizationally more adaptive.

They possess a strong ideological commitment to social justice, economic opportunity, and empathy for the underprivileged and downtrodden sections of society. These organizations are, by and large, autonomous, independent and dynamic by nature of their functions. As such, they are able to take on risks and undertake controversial activities which government and corporate bodies find difficult.

There are many illustrious of voluntary organizations. Refer to Exhibit 24.1 for an example.

Exhibit 24.1 Maliwada rural development project

The place Maliwada signifies 'gardener's village'. It is located approximately midway between the growing industrial city of Aurangabad and the ancient rock-hewn temple caves of Ellora. Maliwada is 15 kilometres north-west of Aurangabad and the village is situated at the foot of Deogiri (the original name of Daulatabad fort). Its proximity to Daulatabad fort places the village at a cross-roads where both local travelers and international tourists pass.

The history of the Maliwada village is full of glory. In India, many village movements have taken place. The Maliwada Human Development Project (MHDP) might be of significant value as a pilot effort in India's new village movement.

The MHDP was carried out by a group of young men who were working for the institute of cultural affairs, a non-profit international group involved in research, training, and demonstration relating to the human factor in world development. The institute adopted Maliwada as a demonstration village.

The group of young men settled in the village, lived and worked with the rural folk, and was able to remove many long-standing obstacles in social and economic development of the village within 10 to 12 months. The project became popular because of the use of some unique methods and approaches in achieving the remarkable results. These young men gave the villagers a measure of self-confidence.

We have been acquainted with the nature of activities of voluntary organizations and their characteristics. Now we can make some generalizations regarding the kind of HR interventions. These interventions are likely to be useful in voluntary organizations.

HRM Interventions

1. Voluntary organizations may be more effective in participative management culture where each employee will be able to contribute ideas. These organizations need to be flexible.
2. It is essential to conduct a periodical organizational climate survey. As the flexibility and extent of participation tend to reduce with the growth of the organization, the survey is required to be undertaken.
3. In addition to team development, culture-building or culture changing interventions have particular relevance to voluntary organizations.
4. Many voluntary organizations are engaged in educational training and consciousness-generation activities with various client groups. The members of the organization often suffer from the neglect of these aspects among themselves. As such, systematic mechanisms of performance and potential appraisal are essential. The design and development of appropriate HRD systems and procedures can strengthen these organizations. Members' need for training and development should be satisfied.
5. The organizational climate of voluntary organizations should be characterized by a high degree of achievement orientation, one of the 12 motivational climates of organizations proposed by Pareek (2002).
6. Open communication, warm interpersonal relations, and mutual respect are critical prerequisites. As such, there is a need to address organizations about the kind of systems and interventions required to build and foster such climates. This is the responsibility of HRD practitioners.

7. The issue of compensation in voluntary organizations is also crucial. In most of the organizations, people work under conditions which are usually less attractive and less rewarding, when compared to mainstream workplaces. Compensations of people working in business and governmental organizations are on the higher side. This imbalance leads to manpower attrition. Unless they get competitive salaries and facilities, attrition is likely to continue.
8. Members working in voluntary organizations derive intrinsic motivation. In most organizations, the working condition is not conducive to effective working. Target-based performance appraisal systems, activity analysis and task design, organizational development activities, and other HRM activities would be useful in these situations.
9. In voluntary organizations, the most crucial HRM function is training and development as they need to build human resources who are motivated and capable of working in them. Similar to other organizations, voluntary organizations also need people with skills and competencies.
10. The attitudes, values, and motivational needs for people of voluntary organizations need to be distinctly different from those working in corporate houses. HRD may need to reorient many of its conventional tools to suit the specific human resource needs of voluntary organizations.

SUMMARY

Organizations may belong to the education, knowledge, insurance, manufacturing or service industries. Irrespective of their type, organizations need to formulate strategies and implement them to achieve the organizational goals. HRM strategy deals with multiple dimensions. While implementing the strategies, organizations encounter problems and solve them using human resource management functions. The scope of human resource management is pervasive. To achieve the same goal, different organizations finalize diverse strategies, and follow varied tactics.

KEY TERMS

HRM intervention refers to improving the wellbeing of an organization and enhancing workers' performance. It is vital for organizational effectiveness.

Knowledge industry organizations mainly deal with information or development of information technology.

Leadership traits refer to qualities of leaders such as possessing high penetration for self and organization, having a passion for excellence, being a team player, having desire in learnability and the courage to take risk, focusing on results, and paying attention to detail.

Strategic leadership is about unique positioning; it deals with the methods by which one can create a unique position of the company. Strategic leadership is about creating an agile and flexible organization, which can cope with changes.

Voluntary organizations refer to non-profit organizations which function in a variety of arenas such as rural development, community development, health and rehabilitation, vocational training, consumer organization, and so on.

EXERCISES

Concept Review Questions

1. Discuss the importance of performance appraisal in the education industry. How do the roles of functionaries differ depending on their levels?
2. What are roles of HR in the knowledge industry? How is it different from the role of the HR manager in a different industry?
3. How does Infosys involve people, particularly new recruits, and get their opinions in formal meetings?

Comment on the action plans of the company to develop them.

Critical Thinking Questions

4. 'People working in knowledge industry need to be supported more than be managed'. Do you agree with the statement? Discuss critically citing examples.
5. One of the nine pillars of Infosys Technologies is community empathy. Does this pillar contribute to leadership development? Critically discuss.

Assignment

6. Visit any two companies by taking prior appointment from the HR managers. Discuss how they collect data for business goals, and how the corresponding HR strategies are formulated and implemented. Discuss with them how they encounter and solve problems.

MANAGER'S INSIGHT

Technological upgradation

The chief executive officer (CEO) of a company invited senior managers to an urgent meeting in his office. He expressed his long-standing desire of upgrading the technology in the company. Accordingly, he constituted a task force with managers from the departments of strategic planning, production, and finance. He directed them to scan the external environment, study the technology available, consider the lead time of procurement, identify the suitable technology, estimate the benefits, and finalize and implement the new technology.

While implementing the technology, the operating core could not understand the ongoing process. The junior management was not clear about the changes and did not have any confidence in it. Initially, a section of the operating core resisted. Gradually, the disturbance spread towards all departments. Apart from rumours, the work force started suffering from fear of uncertainty, loss of job security, and reduction in payments and compensation. In effect, there was total chaos jeopardizing the smooth working of the organization.

At this juncture, the HR manager was co-opted as a member of the task force. The CEO directed the HR manager to study the situation from the HRM's perspective and submit recommendations including possible remedial measures.

Questions:

1. As an HR manager, how would you go about solving the issue?
2. What actions would you plan?
3. Would you explain the benefits derivable from the new technology?
4. Would you keep the CEO informed of the progresses?

BIBLIOGRAPHY AND WEB RESOURCES

Sharma, Rahul, *Challenges for HR Professionals in the Knowledge Industry*, humanlinks.ws/manres/articles/challenges_hr.htm, last accessed on 20 May 2011. (Rahul Sharma, executive HRD, Datamatics Limited)

Web Resources

en.allexperts.com/q/Human-Resources-2866/2010/8/Challenges-HRM.htm, last accessed on 7 February 2012.

www.hal-india.com, last accessed on 10 October 2007.

www.humanlinks.ws/manres/articles/challenges_hr.htm, last accessed on 20 May 2011.

www.infosys.com, last accessed on 16 August 2011.

www.licindia.in, last accessed on 16 August 2011.

www.ofbindia.nic.in, last accessed on 16 August 2011.

www.rcfltd.com/website_red/aboutus.html, last accessed on 29 September 2007.

FUNCTIONING OF THE PANCHAYATI RAJ IN WEST BENGAL

Inception

More than six decades have elapsed since India gained independence. However, till date, India is predominantly a village and rural-based country. Despite rapid urbanization, around three-fourths of our population continues to live in villages despite the fact that the rural situation in the country is still plagued with social and economic problems.

Mahatma Gandhi, India's visionary leader, recognized the utmost need for development of rural areas. Gandhi further desired the needs to be vested largely in the hands of people by setting up appropriate socio-political institutional mechanisms. Later, after independence, Pandit Jawaharlal Nehru ventured to realize the dream of Mahatma Gandhi. The institution of village *panchayat* is the outcome of the thought process of visionary leaders.

According to Article 40 (organization of village *panchayats*) of the Directive Principles of the Constitution of India, 'The State shall take steps to organize village *panchayats* and endow them with such powers and authority as may be necessary to enable them to functions as units of self government.' The Balvanta Raj Mehta Committee of 1958 had attempted to translate the principles into action. The committee recommended the introduction of the *Panchayati Raj* system and expected the system to establish a linkage between local leadership that enjoys the confidence of people and the government. It was also required to translate the policies of the government into action.

Democracy flourishes in India today largely because it has always existed in some form at the macro level for a long time. The *gram panchayat* functions as a village council and consists of elderly people in villages. *Panchayat* means grass-root democracy which is essential for long survival of the rural populace. The system is also referred to as village democracy, village council, or village republics. India has the widest democratic base in the world with more than three million elected local representatives in the *panchayat*. Of these three million, the law requires that one-third be constituted by women. The involvement from chosen representatives ensures effective participation in both the preparation and execution of development schemes. *Panchayati Raj* helps in purposeful understanding of the masses and articulation of their responses. It is perhaps the best means of spreading democracy at the grass-root level. Now, we should know the roles of the *Panchayati Raj*.

Roles of Panchayati Raj

The roles that *Panchayati Raj* was expected to fulfil were as follows:

1. To encourage participative decision making at the micro social level by involving people in decision-making relating to various activities affecting them
2. Look after day-to-day administration of local areas by mobilizing resources and administering day-to-day facilities
3. Formulating micro-level plans on the basis of constraints of development
4. Taking care of local physical infrastructure
5. Working for awakening of the people and making them aware of their plight (difficulty) and rights

Performing the role

In order to perform the role, the enabling capacities of the people of the Panchayats need enhancement. *Panchayati Raj* institutions (PRI) rely heavily on capacity building. Capacity building policies include both training and non-training interventions for PRI functionaries. These interventions include developing focus on attainment of adequate knowledge, overall awareness, appropriate attitude, adequate skills, and self-confidence. Use of principles of adult learning or andragogy is the prerequisite behind capacity building. Further needs include emphasis on values, motivation, and commitment.

Responsibility of capacity building

The responsibility for overall training policy development is vested on the training cell of the *panchayats* and rural development department, West Bengal. The training cell is accountable for organizing different training programmes though it does provide any direct training. There are certain training institutions in the state to cater to the training needs.

The training institutions

The institutions are state institute of *panchayats* and rural development (SIPRD) at Kalyani; five extension training centres (ETC) at Cooch Behar, Burdwan, and Raigunj in Uttar Dinajpur district, Rajarhat in 24 Parganas (North), and Midnapore; and district training centres (DTC) across the state.

Organizing the training

Based on the mandate of Government of India, all PRI members need to attend at least three days training in each year. Accordingly, the National Capacity Building Framework, ETCs, and DTCs have been preparing the training calendar.

For implementing the capacity building policies of the department, 849 trainers were identified. Of them, 820 were trained on several issues in multiple phases. There are two kinds of trainers: (a) full time contractual staff working under state/district programme management unit or working under administrative control of the directorate of Panchayat and rural development offices (DPRDO), and (b) 225 trained resource persons from working offices in the district.

Training infrastructure

Training infrastructure for PRI functionaries were restricted to

1. One SIPRD
2. Five ETCs for off-campus sessions of SIPRD
3. District training centre
4. Extension training centres

Training modules

Training for capacity building is organized on various modules. Some of modules are

1. Capacity building for state level trainers on training and non-training interventions
2. Refresher of trainers of state level trainers on training and non-training interventions
3. Capacity building of district and region level trainers on training methodology
4. Refresher of district and region level trainers on training methodology
5. Training of *zilla parishad sapadhipatis*
6. Training of *sapadhipatis* and *sahakari sapadhipatis* of *panchayat samitis*
7. Training of *pradhans* and *upapradhans* of *gram panchayats*
8. Training of chairpersons of standing committees of *zilla parishads* and *panchayat samities* (nine categories)
9. Training of chairpersons of sub-committees of *gram panchayats* (four categories)
10. Training of general members of *gram panchayats*
11. Training of general members of *panchayat samitis*
12. Training of general members of *zilla parishads*
13. Refresher training of *pradhans* and *upapradhans* of gram panchayat
14. Refresher training of *sapadhipatis* and *sahakari sapadhipatis* of *panchayat samitis*
15. Training on mentoring and handholding support to PRIs.

This calendar clearly signifies that the training modules are pervasive and the target audience (levels of participants) covers all the strata of functionaries.

The training calendar is developed in a documented format reproduced as follows:

No.	Name of training module	Topics covered	Who are the intended users for the module	Languages	Month of publication	No. of copies distributed

Policy/strategy

A large number PRI members (to the tune of 51,000) are required to be trained in a year. However, the department has limited capacity. A strategy was undertaken that elected members of *panchayati samitis* and zilla parishads would be taken care of by SIPRD.

Training package

Training modules were prepared following the training-need assessment (TNA). Further modules are likely to be incorporated by to cope with the changes and changing needs.

Preparation of course material

Faculty members of the institute develop the course material for training, workshops, seminars, etc. PRI members, subject matter specialists, and institutions are involved in the process of course material development.

Faculty development

PRI perceives faculty development as predominantly important to achieve the objectives. Faculty members and officials are deputed to reputed institutes including IIMs to attend workshops, seminars, management development programmes, etc. in addition, there is participation in in-house workshops, round-table discussions, and miscellaneous knowledge dissemination forums on emerging issues as part of capacity building.

Subject matter of training

Training PRI members—main areas of training programmes

1. Roles and responsibilities of PRIs
2. Transparency and accountability
3. Good governance
4. Rural development programmes implemented by PRIs in West Bengal
5. Financial management
6. Computer literacy
7. Social audit

Training for block level/*panchayat samiti* officials—main areas of training programmes

1. Roles and responsibilities of PRIs
2. Office management
3. RTI Act
4. Rural development programmes implemented by PRIs in West Bengal
5. Transparency and accountability
6. Financial management
7. Social audit
8. Management information system
9. SMS-based reporting system
10. Rural engineering

Training to district level officials—main areas of training programmes

1. Roles and responsibilities of PRIs
2. Office management
3. Rural development programmes implemented by PRIs in West Bengal
4. Transparency and accountability
5. Financial management
6. RTI Act
7. Management information system
8. Rural engineering

It is worth noting that some areas of training are common for all levels as knowledge on those areas are needed by all associated with *panchayat* developments

Training evaluation

Considering the utmost need of training for developing people, the ministry of rural development decided to evaluate the training programmes conducted by SIPRD. Accordingly, measures were initiated by administering questionnaires of respondents at multiple levels, different departments, and comprised both genders. The evaluation was done on manifold aspects through training and the findings were satisfactory.

Research projects

Research is of extreme importance for *panchayats* in West Bengal. Accordingly, SIPRD has embarked upon the following research projects. SIPRD has specified a researcher for each project. Considering the gravity and complicacy, SIPRD has engaged multiple researchers for some projects. It is worth mentioning that some research projects are funded by the department for international development (DFID).

The titles of the research projects are:

1. Study of capacity building of self-help groups in SGSY
2. Payment of wages to workers under MGNREGS through different financial institutions in West Bengal: Its problems and probable solution
3. Gender justice: A comparative analysis between West Bengal and Kerala
4. Comparative analysis of the progress of SGSY in the state of West Bengal over a decade (1999-2010)
5. A pilot action research for finding out a workable methodology of district plan with special emphasis on women component plan
6. Understanding *Panchayat* and health initiatives: present status and future condition
7. Changing gender relations through MGNREGS
8. Impact of MGNREGS on SCs
9. Study of self-help groups in *Siliguri Mahakuma Parisad*
10. Decentralized public rural delivery service

Research completed

Studies on MGNREGS in collaboration with NIRD, Hyderabad, were undertaken and completed in 2009–2010.

Abbreviations

DFID	Department for International Development
DPRDO	Directorate of *Panchayat* and Rural Development Offices
DTC	District Training Centre
ETC	Extension Training Centre

MGNREGS	Mahatma Gandhi National Rural Employment Guarantee Scheme
PRI	*Panchayati Raj* institutions
PS	*Panchayat samitis*
RTI	Right to Information
SGSY	*Swanajayanti Gram Swarojgar Yojana*
SHG	Self-help group
SIPRD	State Institute of *Panchayats* and Rural Development
SRD	Strengthening Rural Development
ZP	*Zilla Parishad*

Source: Mr Biplab Biswas, an official of Directorate of Panchayat and Rural Development Offices, West Bengal, and a master trainer of the department, who has helped contributing the entire source material and also extending motivational support.

Discussion Questions

1. Identify the weak areas in the functioning of the *gram panchayat* in West Bengal. Suggest remedial measures for eradicating the weakness.
2. The public's impression about *gram panchayat* and its functioning is not very high. Suggest ways and means of 'image building' that PRIs and associated functional agencies can adopt.
3. Compare activities of *gram panchayat* departments in West Bengal with those of the state you belong to. Prepare a comparative analysis and share with your professor.

HR MANTRA Assessing individual strengths

A reputed social club of south Kolkata, having around 3,000 members on its rolls, recruited two people who possessed a bachelor's degree in business administration. Considering their backgrounds, the club posted one of them, Mr A, in the reception counter of the club, and the other, Mr B, in the finance cell.

Mr A was trying to perform the duties to the best of his abilities. However, the visiting members were not happy with his dealings. A few members brought this issue to the knowledge of the club secretary. One day an old member of the club, Dr Sanyal, came to the club with his family. Dr Sanyal was a professor of psychology and had retired about three years ago. He worked as a consultant in clinical psychology, had his own office in the ground floor of his residence, and was a well-known doctor.

Dr Sanyal had some queries regarding a forthcoming event in the club. Mr A answered his queries regarding the same and Dr Sanyal had made his own observation about him. Before leaving the club he met the secretary and casually discussed with him about Mr A. In his view, Mr A was diligent with exceptionally brilliant skills and high analytical abilities. Dr Sanyal identified Mr A as an introvert and this was his dominant personality trait. He further advised the secretary to assign tasks which he would be required to do on his own. He further commented that Mr A could not work in a group and deal with many people and that as an individual worker, Mr A was extremely able.

The mantra: Assign roles according to individual strengths.

KUMAR MANGALAM BIRLA

Kumar Mangalam Birla, chairman of Aditya Birla Group, was born on 14 June 1967. He spent the early years of his life in Kolkata and Mumbai. A chartered accountant, he completed his MBA from the London Business School. Kumar Mangalam took over as chairman in 1995, at the age of 28, after sudden demise of his father and noted industrialist Aditya Birla, after whom the group is named. The Birla group is India's third largest business house. Other companies of the Group are Grasim, Hindalco, UltraTech Cement, Aditya Birla Nuvo, and Idea Cellular. Aditya Group's joint ventures include Birla Sun Life (financial services) and Birla NGK (insulators). The group also has its presence in various countries such as Thailand, Indonesia, Malaysia, Philippines, Egypt, Canada, China, and Australia.

When Kumar Mangalam assumed the position at the Aditya Birla Group, doubts were raised from various corners about his ability to handle a giant business house with interests spanning viscose, textiles, and garments on the one hand, and cement, aluminium, and fertilisers, on the other. However, Kumar Mangalam proved his sceptics wrong. He brought in radical changes, changed business strategies, professionalized the entire group, and replaced internal systems. He reduced his group's dependence on the cyclic commodities sectors by foraying into consumer products. Kumar Mangalam has exhibited his leadership skills in driving the Group forward. Apart from consolidating the group's position in existing businesses, Kumar Mangalam has also ventured into sunrise sectors such as cellular telephony, asset management, software, and business process outsourcing (BPO).

Kumar Mangalam seems to have umpteen tools, techniques, and weapons in his vast arsenal which he has very efficiently utilized in planning and managing the human beings of the group. Without having unique and distinctive human resource management strategies, it would have been impossible to effectively install the changes.

Kumar Mangalam opines that, 'Transformation is the end result of a highly energized process that combines human ingenuity with its indomitable spirit to make new things happen and create value.' His mantra is: 'The creation of new alchemists from ordinary people.'

In addition to his efforts in the Birla group, Kumar Mangalam also holds several key positions on various regulatory and professional boards, including chairmanship of the advisory committee constituted by the Ministry of Company Affairs for 2006 and 2007, membership of the Prime Minister of India's advisory council on trade and industry, chairmanship of the board of trade reconstituted by the Union Minister of Commerce and Industry, and membership of the central board of directors of the Reserve Bank of India.

Kumar Mangalam implemented innovative, breakthrough management practices, built meritocracy and a learning organization, espoused highest corporate governance principles in his companies in India and overseas, established operations in more than 25 countries across the globe, and has taken India to the world. As Chancellor of Birla Institute of Technology and Science (BITS), Pilani, and as member of the London Business School's Asian Regional Advisory Board, Kumar Mangalam has nurtured tomorrow's leaders through his role as an inspirational educationist. He has instituted the Aditya Birla India Centre at the London Business School and stoked up interest in Indian managerial success stories as case studies. In the process, he has weaved India Inc. into the texture of that world-renowned institution. In order to satisfy his passion in taking education to the interior regions, Kumar Mangalam has established more than 40 schools. He has spearheaded changes without losing continuity; has been global in vision but remaining Indian at heart and holding noble values.

Kumar Mangalam believes that 'making talent' must be a strategic priority; solving the talent paradox is not an impossible task as it just requires new and innovative ways to hunt, acquire, and retain talent. He quotes John Gardener who says, 'There are those who perform great deeds and those that make it possible for others to perform great deeds. There are pathfinders and path preservers. There are those who nurture and who inspire. There are those whose excellence involves doing something well and those excellence lies in being the kind of people they are, lies in their kindness or honesty or courage'. He says that the term 'talent' has a broad connotation; views talent in terms of the capabilities of people needed to the agenda of the particular organization, and believes that talent entails having those skills that provide the edge and the difference to the organization.

While delivering the J.R.D. Tata Memorial Award lecture at the All India Management Association (AIMA), New Delhi, on 21 February 2009, Kumar Mangalam Birla addressed four issues of leadership: Why does Aditya Birla Group need global leaders? What are the common competencies common to all global leaders? What initiatives must Aditya Birla Group take to develop global leadership talents? What are the challenges that Aditya Birla Group faced in creating a global leadership pool?

Kumar Mangalam has been recognized by different for and has won several honours. Some of them include titles such as The Business Leader of the Year (2003) by The Economic Times, Business Man of the Year 2003 by Business India, and The Ernst & Young Entrepreneur of the Year India in 2005.

References

Haldar, Uday Kumar, *Leadership and Team Building*, Oxford Higher Education, Oxford University Press, New Delhi, 2010.

www.adityabirla.com/the_group/km_birla_profile.htm, last accessed on 25 October 2011.

www.aima-ind.org/AIMA-Managing-India-Awards-2010.html, last accessed on 25 October 2011.

PART FOUR

Overview—Research in HRM

The ultimate objective of any organization is to grow and expand its business and functions. The present-day business environment is unpredictable and companies have been seen to increasingly leverage the strengths of their employees to survive, grow, and gain competitive advantage.

Research in HR involves conducting a thorough and systematic investigation of an effect to identify the various causes (independent variables) responsible for the effect (dependent variables). From the viewpoint of behavioural science, it is assumed that there are various contingency variables that influence the effect. Job satisfaction, job involvement, assertiveness, commitment, stress, organizational climate, occupational values, managerial styles, personality traits, lifestyles, communication styles, extent of work–life balance, creativity, and innovation are some examples of the contingency variables. Organizations focus on effects that are not conducive to organizational growth and pursue fundamental research to recognize their causes and identify the influencing contingency variables.

It is important to remember that the collective performance of employees at all levels contributes to organizational performance. The various HR features are performance management; performance indicators and metrics; career and succession planning; assessment and measurement; leadership development; talent management system; change management, culture assessment; and recognition, award, and incentives. Each aspect is expected to have a causal relationship with individual performances and, in turn, with the organizational performance.

In the current scenario, research in HR has gained importance and can be undertaken by an internal research cell where the researchers are well acquainted with the organization and the industry climate. Internal researchers can interpret the independent and the contingency variables better.

This part of the book comprises Chapter 25, Research in HRM.

CHAPTER 25

Research in HRM

LEARNING OBJECTIVES

After studying this chapter, you will be able to

- Recognize the need and importance of research in the field of human resource management (HRM)
- Realize the motivation behind pursuing a research
- Be familiar with the types of research and their uses
- Acquaint well enough with statistical tools and their usage
- Select and use user-friendly and economically statistical packages
- Organize material for a thesis or project report methodically

OPENING CASE

Pursuing Research

Anjela is a smart girl from an educated family. She passed her higher secondary examination with flying colours. She scored first division in her undergraduate examination and secured admission for MBA at a nationally acclaimed institute. After completing her education, she got placed in a highly reputed company through campus interview. However, she chose not to join it; instead, she planned to pursue her doctoral research and join the academia. She always dreamt of being a teacher, and sharing her knowledge with the future managers of the nation. She was looking for the right guide who could supervise her research work. On one occasion, she came to know of Dr Sharma and approached him with all her gathered information. Anjela wished the professor and started conversation, which is presented here.

Anjela: Sir, I want to pursue doctoral research under your guidance.
Guide: What is your background?
Anjela: I have completed my MBA with 76% marks.
Guide: Why do you want to pursue research? Why don't you take up a job?
Anjela: My friends are also pursuing research.
Guide: Alright, that's fine. Why are they pursuing doctoral research?
Anjela: I do not know exactly, but they are pursuing research.
Guide: Pursuing doctoral research takes time and the journey needs a lot of tolerance. It is also important for you to identify the reason why you want to pursue Ph D.
Anjela: Sir, I am eager to pursue research.
Guide: I appreciate your eagerness. Tell me whether you want to work with primary data or secondary data.
Anjela: What are primary or secondary data?
Guide: I will tell you later. From which organizations do you want to collect data?
Anjela: I will go by your decision.
Guide: Alright. Have you articulated an area of interest for your research?

Anjela: You are my guide. Tell me what should I find out and from where I should gather data.

Guide: Which type of research do you want to pursue?

Anjela: I want to pursue research work of any type.

Guide: Are you interested in statistics?

Anjela: Not at all, Sir. It was quite difficult for me to clear that paper.

Guide: However, to pursue research and prepare the thesis, you need fairly good knowledge in statistics.

Anjela: Sir, tell me the chapters. I will read and come prepared.

Guide: You also need adequate knowledge on research methods.

Anjela: I am not very comfortable with that subject as well.

Guide: Without knowledge of statistics and research methods, it would be extremely difficult to complete your doctoral thesis. It would be better if you think again and decide. I do not want any scholar to leave half way.

Anjela: Sir, I would not like to rethink. It is my final decision that I will pursue and complete my doctoral journey. For accomplishing it, I will read, gain the essential background knowledge, and I am committed to starting my doctoral journey immediately. In fact, I have refused a job offer which I got through our college placement. I want to get my doctorate degree and join the academia. That is my coveted career and dream. I need your blessings.

Guide: Now I understand; my blessings will always be with you. I have now decided to supervise your research work. Come next Friday as I do not have any class on that day. I will tell you some salient points of research methodology. Take my card and remind me on Thursday. I will introduce you to our registrar and person in-charge of research section. I will take you to our library which has a huge stock of books and journals, including e-journals.

The research episode thus began. Anjela got registered, started her research work steadily, worked diligently, and completed her doctoral journey. She submitted her thesis after three and a half years and received her degree in the university convocation.

Learning points

- Any research process requires a defined intention and objectives.
- For a researcher to complete his research, he must have knowledge about research methods and statistics and a pre-set timeline.

Author's note:

The case has been written based on a discussion with the supervisor during dinner in a social gathering when he narrated many anecdotes. On contacting Anjela, she highlighted her relationship with the guide. In her words, 'My guide is showering paternal affection on me; I am now treated as a member of his family. I send emails to his son and daughter and receive motivational replies from them.'

INTRODUCTION

The modern business environment is characterized by acute competition. Companies are increasingly leveraging the strengths of their employees to survive, grow, and gain competitive advantages over their competitors. Human resource issues have become significant and companies are relying on the results of systematic researches for finalizing any strategy that they would want to use for growth. The intention is to manage the organization effectively.

It is for these reasons that human resource has been classified as the most valuable asset and is gaining immense importance. HR issues, decisions, and initiatives are gaining prime attention in all organizations. The motives, occupational values, managerial styles, personality traits, lifestyles, communication styles, creativity, and innovation of human resources make them unique, and hence, HR research has become important. Before going deeper into HR research, one must understand the objectives and the motivation behind a research work, along with its various types.

PURPOSE OF RESEARCH

The purpose of research work may be versatile. Some may pursue it to discover answers to questions through the application of scientific procedures and statistical tests. The main aim of research is to find out the truth that is not yet discovered. Refer to Box 25.1. Though each research work has its own specific purpose, research objectives may be grouped as follows:

1. Exploratory or investigative research refers to gaining familiarity with a phenomenon or to achieve new insights into it.
2. Descriptive research portrays the characteristics of a particular individual, situation, or a group accurately.
3. Diagnostic research is aimed to determine the frequency with which something occurs or its association with something else.
4. Hypothesis testing research undertakes tests of hypothesis to ascertain a causal relationship among variables.

Box 25.1 Objectives of a study

The objectives of a study titled 'Training need assessment in the Indian power sector' were

1. To examine a typical power sector organization
2. To investigate the various functions and jobs involved
3. To explore the competencies required
4. To determine the training requirements

MOTIVATION BEHIND RESEARCH

There are numerous objectives for conducting research and people undertake research for variety of reasons. There can be versatile motives behind undertaking research. The possible motives for doing project work may be either one or more of the following:

1. Desire to face the challenge in solving unsolved problems, that is, concern over practical problems initiating the research work
2. Desire to derive intellectual joy out of doing some creative work
3. Desire to be of service to society
4. Desire to get respect and credibility in the society or organization

Students pursue dissertations or project work in partial fulfillment of a course curriculum and gain from the consequential benefits, which is also a motivation for them. The curriculum of B-schools or colleges/institutes includes submitting a dissertation and project report.

This is not an exhaustive list of factors that motivate people to undertake research work. Many other factors such as directives of government, employment conditions, curiosity about new things, desire to understand and investigate causal relationships, social thinking and awakening, emerging issues, and so on may also motivate people to undertake project or research studies.

TYPES OF RESEARCH

There are many types of research. The four paired types of researches are discussed here.

Applied vs Basic

Q 3 Applied research is mostly referred to as research aimed at finding a solution for an immediate problem faced by a society or a business organization. This type of research is designed and undertaken only in particular circumstances. An example of applied research is finding the reason for high absenteeism in an organization in a particular period. Finding the causes behind deterioration of quality or frequent machine breakdown is also classified as applied research. Thus, the central aim of applied research is to discover a solution for some pressing practical problem.

> Applied research aims at finding a solution for an immediate problem faced by a society or a business organization.

Basic research is fundamental and generic in nature. Basic research is directed towards finding information that has a broad base of application and adds to the already existing organized body of scientific knowledge. For example, as a researcher, one may be interested in investigating the factors that motivate people to work hard at their job.

Descriptive vs Analytical

Descriptive research includes survey reports and fact-finding enquiries of different kinds. Descriptive research work is used to portray the state of affairs as they exist in the present. In social science and business research, we quite often use the term ex-post facto research work, for undertaking descriptive studies. The main characteristic of this method is that the research worker has no control over the variables; he can only report what has happened or what is happening at present. In most ex-post facto research (finding causes corresponding to something that happened; a fact-finding research), the researcher uses descriptive studies in which he seeks to measure parameters such as, frequency of shopping, preferences of people, or similar data.

> Descriptive research portrays the state of affairs as it exists at present and includes different kinds of survey reports and fact-finding enquiries.
> Analytical project work uses facts or information already available, and analyses them to make a critical evaluation of the material.

Ex-post facto studies also include attempts by researchers to discover only the causes corresponding to an effect. Various kinds of survey methods are utilized in such research work.

On the other hand, in analytical project work, the team members have to use facts or information already available, and analyse them to make a critical evaluation of the material.

Quantitative vs Qualitative

Quantitative research work is based on the measurement of quantity or amount. It is applicable to events, attributes, or personal variables that can be expressed in quantitative terms. For example, we might measure a person's height and weight to draw a conclusion, or we might construct a survey to measure how many employees like their company's HR policy and to what extent (say, using a five-point scale). A researcher might be interested to measure the job satisfaction scores to categorize the respondents as high, medium, or less satisfied. Similarly, after measuring role stress, the respondents can be classified in groups as less, medium, and highly stressed. The classification may be done on the basis of the mean score and standard deviation.

> Quantitative research is applicable to phenomena that can be expressed in quantitative terms.
> Qualitative research is concerned with qualitative phenomena relating to or involving quality of objects which are immeasurable.

Q 1 Qualitative research is concerned with qualitative phenomena relating to or involving the quality of objects. For example, we may be interested in investigating the reasons for human behaviour (such as why people think or do certain things). We often talk of motivation research, an important type of qualitative research work. This type of research uses in-depth interviews to ascertain the underlying motives and desires causing an effect. Other techniques of qualitative research are word association tests, sentence completion tests, story completion tests, and other projective techniques.

Attitude or opinion research is designed to find out how people feel or what they think about a particular subject. Through such research, we can analyse the various factors which motivate people to behave in a particular manner or which make people like or dislike a particular thing.

Conceptual vs Empirical

Conceptual research work relates to abstract ideas or theories. Philosophers and thinkers develop new concepts or reinterpret existing ones.

Empirical research relies solely on experience or observation. It is data-based research and comes up with conclusions that are capable of being verified by observation or experiment. This can also be called experimental research. In this research, it is necessary to get all the facts firsthand, from their source, and actively apply statistical analysis to get the desired information. While pursuing such research, the researcher must formulate the hypothesis, collect enough facts (data), and subject them to statistical analysis to prove or disprove the hypothesis.

> Conceptual research work relates to new concepts or reinterprets existing ones. Empirical (or experimental) research is data-based research where conclusions can be verified by observation or experiment.

Following this step, the researcher sets up experimental designs to bring forth the desired information or otherwise. The research is characterized by the experimenter's control over the variables under study and his deliberate planning of one of them to study its effects. Empirical research is appropriate when proof is sought that certain variables (the set of independent variables) affect other variables (the dependent variable). At present, empirical studies are considered the most powerful while dealing with a hypothesis.

HR RESEARCH

Research concerning HR issues must be exclusively discussed in a book on human resource management. The findings will help us develop relevant approaches for successful human resource management in organizations and thereby, for successful management of the organizations.

The research can be centered on human resource guiding principles, human resource administration/management, human resource development, and industrial relations which are discussed in detail in Chapter 3.

> HR research is undertaken to find ways and means to exercise influence on human beings to the extent possible. HR research helps us to develop relevant approaches for successful management of the organization.

In organizations, different people behave differently in a group in various situations. Moreover, the same person behaves differently in identical situations on different days. Why do they do so? Why do their behavioural dispositions vary? To get the answers to these questions, we rely heavily on fundamental research relating to human issues. In fact, inquisitiveness, interest, devotion, dedication, enthusiasm, etc., vary widely from person to person.

Psychological science conducts scientific study in the behavioural context. The need to pursue research is perhaps embedded in the basic assumptions of science. In scientific research, we perform experiments, control certain parameters such as temperature, pressure, and so on, and move to find out the effect. In behavioural research, we observe the effect and endeavour to identify the causes behind the effect. Thus, the directions of scientific research and behavioural research are different. Moreover, in case of behavioural science, we have no control on the parameters. These uncontrollable parameters are called the intervening variables. Kerlinger (1995) says, 'constructs have been called intervening variables, and this is a term invented to account for internal and directly unobservable psychological processes that take into account behaviour.' HR research may be undertaken to unearth the unobservable psychological processes, and find ways and means to exercise influence on them to the extent possible. HR research helps us develop relevant approaches for successful management of the organization.

Similar to any other research, HR research is a rigorous scientific activity which requires statistical analysis. It needs systematic development and acquisition of knowledge tailored to a specific management function to answer specific research questions within a given or pre-selected timeframe, with the ultimate aim of meeting organizational needs and achieving organizational effectiveness.

Types of HR Research

There are many types of human resource research. The three types that are of particular importance in classifying types of research are explained here (Bhattacharyya 2007):

1. Exploratory versus confirmatory
2. Applied versus basic
3. Quantitative versus qualitative

Exploratory versus confirmatory: Exploratory research refers to investigating the unknown. It is aimed at entering the unknown horizon to broaden the known horizon of knowledge. It is used to investigate issues that are not understood, as the causes behind the effects are unknown.

Let us consider the case of the sale of a book, say, on human resource management, by author A. The book has gained popularity and is purchased by management students in most Indian states. Another book on the same subject by author B has similar content with more material on case analysis, class and field assignments, concept review, critical thinking questions, etc.; the sale of this book is still limited. A researcher undertakes research to study the readers' psychology in the context of management books. He has undertaken this study as findings established in researches on consumer psychology could not satisfactorily explain the psychology of the readers. The researcher may search for causes without really knowing how to proceed and what to look for in particular.

> Exploratory research is used to study issues that are not understood and the causes behind the effects are unknown. Confirmatory research allows the researcher to start with a fairly good idea about the research problems based on previous works.

Confirmatory research, on the other hand, allows the researcher to start with a fairly good idea about the research problems. The researcher is likely to possess relevant theories, findings of previous researchers, etc. He can formulate the objectives, research questions, hypotheses of the research, based on earlier research and publications, and proceed to pursue the research.

Applied versus basic, and quantitative versus qualitative researches have already been discussed in this chapter.

Approaches to HR Research

The research approaches may widely differ from one situation to another. These approaches could be academic, theoretical, or action-oriented. Depending on the situation, the researcher needs to select the exact approach to satisfy his/her research needs. The five most commonly used approaches in HR research (Bhattacharyya 2007) are the following:

Pure basic approach The approach tends to resolve, illuminate, and exemplify theoretical issues. It facilitates enhancing knowledge, gaining insights, and understanding the reasons behind an effect. Most core management concepts have been developed from pure basic research.

Objective research It focuses on the ways to overcome a general problem in the application of established knowledge. It is, however, not intended to solve a specific management problem. For conducting objective research, the researcher needs to frame certain clear objectives and hypotheses. Thereafter, he tests the validity of established knowledge in a given situation.

Evaluative research This research is aimed to analyse issues relating to the effectiveness of an organizational function. For example, the effects of performance-linked pay over fixed pay on workers' motivation, or the study of changes in the organization culture before and after implementing a major change such as a quality management system are examples of evaluative research. Evaluative research helps managers to develop scientific neutrality when looking into certain issues. This research leads to formulation of a framework for future management issues.

Applied research Applied research refers to the application of appropriate knowledge to solve a particular problem in another organization. It can be used as a benchmark by organizations. In the knowledge industry, the attrition rate of knowledge workers is appreciably high. Similarly, in the IT industry, attrition of talented workers continues to be high and is posing a problem. A researcher can put efforts to identify the root causes and thereby, reduce the turnover of talented workers. This research attempts to solve a problem existing in an organization or industry.

Action research It refers to a particular kind of research where the solution of a problem is both an outcome and a part the research process (Bhattacharyya 2007). The main purpose of this approach is to improve the stock of problem while tackling a problem. This methodology combines action and research in order to examine specific questions, and issues, through observation and reflection, and deliberate intervention to improve practice.

Refer to Box 25.2 to get an idea about the top ten popular areas of HR research.

Box 25.2 Top ten areas of HR research

Bhattacharyya (2007) mentions a global survey that identified the top 10 areas of interest and current popular topics in HR research. The top 10 areas of HR research and the percentage priority clearly connotes that performance management and leadership development are the first and second preferred issues in organizations.

1. Performance management
2. Leadership development
3. Career and succession planning
4. Change management
5. Talent management
6. Assessment and measurement
7. Indicators and metrics
8. Culture assessment
9. Talent management system
10. Recognition, award, and incentives

RESEARCH ON EMPLOYER BRANDING

> Employer branding refers to development and communication of an organization's culture to the labour market with the prime objectives of affecting the perception of potential employees about the organization and enhancing the opportunity of poaching talents from the market.

Bhattacharyya (2007) emphasizes employer branding as another important emerging area in HR research. Employer branding refers to the development and communication of an organization's culture in the labour market. The prime objective of employer branding is to improve the perception of potential employees about the organization, and enhance the scope and opportunity of poaching talents from the market. To conduct research on employer branding (table 25.1), it is essential to first understand the underlying concept and develop ideas for implementation of the strategies step-by-step.

Some important steps are required to develop measurable and attainable objectives, retain the services of a recruitment advertising agency, launch an information collection process, create a branding strategy, execute the branding strategy, and monitor the progress of the branding strategy periodically (Bhattacharyya 2007).

Table 25.1 Popular topics in HR research

Area of research	Percentage
Compensation and benefits	
1. Healthcare cost containment	38
2. Executive compensation	34
3. Job analysis, evaluation, and grading	25
4. Employee benefits	23
5. Benefits outsourcing	17
6. Retirement and pension	15
Employment selection/staffing	
1. Pre-employment and employee testing	28
2. Job boards, online media, and print media	20
3. Background investigation	18
Human resource information system	
1. Workforce analysis	20
2. Employee self-service	15
3. Benefit administration and communication tools	13
Organizational planning and development	
1. Employee surveys	35
2. Mergers and acquisitions	20
Training and development	
1. Assessment	38
2. Mentoring	31

(Contd)

Table 25.1 (Contd)

Area of research	Percentage
3. E-learning	24
4. Diversity	24
5. Distance learning	18
6. Learning management systems	15
Others	
1. Research and best practices	38
2. HRM	30
3. International and global HR	14
4. Labour relations	14

STATISTICS

Having gained knowledge on general research and HR research, let us try to understand statistics and its tools. For analysing the data, either descriptive statistics or inferential statistics can be used.

Descriptive Statistics

Quantitative descriptions can be presented using descriptive statistics in a manageable form so as to be able to interpret them easily. In a research study, there will be several measures or the researcher may gauge a large number of people on any measure. Descriptive statistics are procedures for organizing and summarizing data so that the important characteristics of the data can be described and communicated (Heiman 1992).

Each descriptive statistic reduces a large amount of data into a simpler summary. For instance, consider the case of a batsman who has scored an unbeaten 150 runs playing only 113 balls in a one-day international cricket match. The opponent coach and captain will be interested to know how many strokes crossed the boundary from the position. We can now see the strokes made—cover drive, on drive, late cut, etc. The captain of the opponent party decides his fielding strategy using the information. The descriptive statistics give frequencies, percentiles, and measures of central tendency, namely, the mean, median, and mode. They also measure variability such as the range, variance, and standard deviation.

The respondents of a study are first grouped into different categories depending on specific requirements. Then, descriptive statistics are used to describe the demographic characteristics of the data. Descriptive statistics provide simple summaries about the sample and the measures. Along with simple graphical analysis, they form the basis of virtually every quantitative analysis of data. With descriptive statistics, it is possible to simply describe what the data are or what the data show.

In his doctoral thesis titled, 'Job performance of the operational agents of Life Insurance Corporation of India (LICI) in relation to some specific job behaviour: a study of 24 Parganas (North), West Bengal', Haldar (2003) classified performance levels, job behaviour (assertiveness, job satisfaction, and job involvement), and distribution of the respondents based on the demographic variables. Quantitative descriptions of distributed data from the arena of descriptive statistics are presented for easy understanding. Refer to Tables 25.2–25.5 for these statistics.

Table 25.2 Distribution of sample based on their performance scores

S. no.	Classification	Frequency *n*	Percentage
1	High performer	30	13.7
2	Moderate performer	141	64.4
3	Low performer	48	21.9

Table 25.3 Assertiveness scores of low, moderate, and high performers

Performance grade	Frequency *n*	Mean	Standard deviation
Ass_JP_low	30	1.033	15.544
Ass_JP_mod	141	16.567	13.380
Ass_JP_high	48	37.333	12.205
Ass_JP_total	219	8.99	17.36

Ass = assertiveness; JP = job performance

Table 25.4 Job satisfaction of low, moderate, and high job performers

Grade	Frequency *n*	Mean	Standard deviation
JSS_JP_low	30	143.567	13.325
JSS_JP_mod	141	149.461	13.470
JSS_JP_high	48	165.688	10.225
JSS_JP_total	219	152.21	14.76

JSS = job satisfaction score

Table 25.5 Distribution based on demographic variables

S. no.	Variable	Classification	Frequency	Percentage
1.	Gender	Male	182	83
		Female	37	17
2.	Age	Less	45	20
		Middle	124	57
		Aged	50	23
3.	Experience	Less	45	20
		Moderate	124	57
		High	50	23
4.	Educational qualification	Undergraduate	79	36
		Graduate	116	53
		Post graduate	24	11
5.	Region of engagement	Urban	113	52
		Rural	106	48

Inferential Statistics

Data are statements of facts or figures. We analyse data and get information based on which we make inferences and take a decision. Irrespective of whether the inference is statistically significant or not, it is termed inferential statistics. Inferential statistics enables researchers to use data collected from samples to make inferences about the nature of the population from which the samples are drawn (Crowl 1993), while descriptive analysis does not provide such a basis for generalizing, beyond the particular study or sample (Rubin and Babbie 1993). Inferential statistics helps to check if any difference or relationship that is observed in a sample is due to sampling error or chance, or if it is due to the intervening factors being studied.

Inferential statistics involves testing for statistical significance. Statistical significance involves calculation by using complex formulae, the probabilities of finding due to chance, a difference, or a relationship as strong as the one that is observed in the sample (Rubin and Babbie 1993). If the calculated value of the statistic is higher than the tabulated value, the test becomes statistically significant at that level of significance. It is then interpreted that the observed difference or relationship is not due to chance but there are assignable causes to that effect. The null hypothesis, of no difference, is rejected, and the alternate (research) hypothesis is accepted. We will discuss about null and alternate hypotheses later in this chapter.

The dividing line between high probability and low probability for an observed difference or relationship to occur due to chance is drawn by the researcher. In other words, the researcher is the one who fixes the significance level at which he or she will reject the null hypothesis. This means that any calculated level of significance lesser than or equal to 0.01, will result in the null hypothesis being rejected. Conversely, any calculated level more than 0.01 will support the null hypothesis and hence the test fails to reject the null hypothesis. The significance level for this study has been fixed at 0.01. Researchers decide the level of significance considering the context of the research and its importance in real life. However, Rubin and Babbie (1993) opined that the significance level of 0.05 is an appropriate level for most social and educational research.

PARAMETRIC TESTS AND NON-PARAMETRIC TESTS

There are many alternative ways to calculate statistical significance. The prime criteria influencing the selection of a statistical significance test are

1. the level of measurement of the variables (nominal, ordinal, interval, or ratio),
2. the number of variables included in the analysis (bivariate or multivariate) or the number of categories in the nominal variables,
3. the type of sampling methods used in data collection, and
4. the way the variables are distributed in the population, which the study seeks to generalize.

Depending on a study's attributes regarding these criteria, a selection is made between two broad types of significance tests, namely, parametric tests and non-parametric tests (Rubin and Babbie 1993).

Parametric tests assume that at least one of the variables being studied has an interval-level or a ratio-level of measurement, the sampling distribution of the relevant parameters of those variables is normal, and that the different groups being compared have been randomly selected and are independent of one another (Rubin and Babbie 1993).

In the research (Haldar 2003) referred to in the beginning of this section, the independent variables were assertiveness, job satisfaction, and job involvement, and the dependent/criterion variable was job performance; and all the variables were continuous data. It was evidenced that the population was distributed normally and hence only parametric tests were used. The general opinion is that parametric tests are more powerful than non-parametric tests.

However, Elifson, Runyon, and Haber (1990) had a different opinion. They said that parametric techniques are usually preferable because of their greater sensitivity. However, this generalization is not true when the underlying assumptions are seriously violated. Indeed, under certain circumstances, a non-parametric test may well be as powerful as its parametric counterpart.

INTRODUCTION TO STATISTICAL TOOLS

It is necessary to be acquainted with a few statistical tools for processing the data to be collected. There are a number of statistical tools but only some of them—such as test for homoscedasticity, correlation coefficient, chi-square tests, analysis of variance (ANOVA), and regression analysis—are discussed.

Test for Homoscedasticity

Q 6 Data can be collected from widely dispersed geographic regions such as rural, semi-urban, and urban areas. While pursuing a research, say, on the effect of attitudes on human performance, data can be collected from some units in different countries of a multinational company. The units may be situated in developed, developing, or undeveloped countries. In such cases, perform a test for homogeneity of the samples. It is also important to perform a test for 'equality of two variances' if data is collected from respondents of two geographically dispersed areas. The statistical tool to be used is the F-test for equality of variances (homoscedasticity—a test carried out when samples are drawn from two or more dissimilar and divergent population).

Suppose two random samples ($x_1, x_2, \ldots\ldots\ldots, x_m$) and ($y_1, y_2, \ldots\ldots\ldots, y_n$) are available from two independent normal populations. Let σ_1^2 and s_2^2 be the respective population variances. Consider $H_o: \sigma_1^2 = \sigma_2^2$ against $H_1: \sigma_1^2 \neq \sigma_2^2$. Let s_1^2 and s_2^2 be the corresponding sample variances based on ($x_1, x_2, \ldots\ldots\ldots, x_m$) and ($y_1, y_2, \ldots\ldots\ldots, y_n$) respectively. In the spirit of likelihood ratio principles, we consider the F-test, which rejects H_o at level α if

$$\frac{s_1^2}{s_2^2} < F_{1-\frac{\alpha}{2};m-1,n-1} \quad \text{and} \quad \frac{s_2^2}{s_1^2} < F_{1-\frac{\alpha}{2};n-1,m-1}$$

Otherwise, the F-test accepts the H_o at α.

H_o is the null hypothesis and H_1 is the alternate hypothesis.

In a study, Haldar (2003) collected samples from rural as well as urban areas. These samples could have significantly varied due to different geographic, demographic, socioeconomic, and psychographic behavioural patterns exhibited by the population of the respective areas. This is precisely the reason behind carrying out the F-test; to measure any statistically significant difference (heteroscedasticity) in variances of the populations (Goon, Gupta, and Dasgupta 2000).

Correlation Coefficient

Correlation coefficient indicates the extent of the relationship among the values in ordered pairs and is reported in large quantities in research journals. To be statistically significant, for example, a coefficient of correlation calculated between pairs of measures has to be approximately 0.31 at the 0.05 level and 0.42 at the 0.01 level. With 100 pairs of measures, the problem is less accurate and the law of large number manifests (Kerlinger 1995). The law of large numbers signifies that the larger the sample size, the less will be the chance of error due to individual variation.

Chi-square Test of Independence

Chi-square test is the most frequently used statistical test for the analysis of frequency (Rubin and Babbie 1993). This test can be used on just one variable as a one-way chi-square or on two sets of variables (Heimann 1992). It tests whether the values taken by one variable are independent of the values taken by the other variables (Kenkel 1989).

Haldar (2003) used two-way chi-square tests after cross-partitioning the variables to study the interrelationships between the two sets of variables. χ^2 (chi-square) measures the departure of observed frequency from the frequency expected by chance. Larger χ^2 indicates more departure, while $\chi^2 = 0$ indicates no departure. In chi-square test, the degrees of freedom means the latitude of variation a statistical problem has. χ^2 only indicates the statistical significance but tells us nothing about the magnitude of the relationship.

From the value of chi-square, the strength of the relation is calculated by computing the coefficient of contingency, $C = \text{sq.rt.}\,[\chi^2/(\chi^2 + N)]$. C is a rough and conservative index of the 'strength of relation' that cannot get the value 1.00. C is a measure of association that is useful if used with circumspection (Kerlinger 1995). Haldar (2003) used two-way chi-square tests after cross-partitioning the variables to study the interrelationships of the dependent variable with each of the independent variables.

In order to carry out analysis of frequency (chi-square test), the respondents (with a size of 219) of market survey were distributed based on their scores of job performance (JP) and level of job satisfaction (JSS) in a 3 x 3 matrix. Please refer to Table 25.6.

Table 25.6 Chi-square—job performance grade by job satisfaction grade

Job performance grade	**Job satisfaction grade**			
	JSS_low	JSS_mod	JSS_high	Total
JP_low	14	11	6	30
JP_mod	51	73	13	141
JP_high	5	24	22	219
Total	70	108	41	219

Analysis of Variance (ANOVA)

This important statistical technique is an extension of the independent group t-test for two variables. ANOVA is used for more than two independent groups to compare their means. As defined by its originator, Sir R.A. Fisher, 'the separation of variance ascribable to one group of causes from the variance ascribable to other groups' is accounted for in this test. The test statistic is F in ANOVA test with (K-1) and (N-K) degrees of freedom, where N is the total number of subjects, and K is the number of groups.

In this test, the p-value indicates evidence to reject or not to reject the null hypothesis in favour of the alternative. The statistic F, when compared to the table on critical values of F distribution, signifies whether the difference between two groups is significant or not. Critical values of F distribution are shown in Table 25.7 (Bhattacharyya 2007).

Table 25.7 Critical values of F distribution

P value	Wording	
>0.05	Not significant	P: Theoretical level of significance In the context of HR issues, p < 0.001 is extremely significant
0.01 to 0.05	Significant	
0.001 to 0.01	Very significant	
<0.001	Extremely significant	

ANOVA on job performance scores: In a research (Haldar 2003), the total sample (size 219) was divided into three groups—low, moderate, and high performers based on percentile cut-off of the job performance scores.

Table 25.8 ANOVA—the F statistic

Source of variation	Sum of square	Degree of freedom	Mean square	F	p
Among groups	10662.4	2	5331.2	395.37	<0.0001
Within groups	2912.6	216	13.5		
Total	13575.0	218			

Table 25.9 ANOVA pair wise

Contrast	Difference	LSD–99% CI	Remarks
JP_Low versus JP_mod	−11.5	−13.37 to −9.5	(significant)
JP_Low versus JP_high	−23.5	−25.73 to −21.3	(significant)
JP_Mod versus JP_high	−12.1	−13.65 to −10.5	(significant)

Regression Analysis

Regression analysis is a test for agreement between two methods or two sets of values of variables, for example, between performance and assertiveness of the same objects, which are a sample of the study. This test is used to predict values of a response variable, say performance, based on a predictor variable say, assertiveness. Regression analysis has been widely adopted in research with psychological variables. In this research study (Haldar 2003), multiple regression analysis was done for the response variable performance, based on the predictor variables, assertiveness, job satisfaction, and job involvement. Job performance had been expressed as a function of assertiveness, job satisfaction, and job involvement.

General Model of Regression Analysis

The general model is a mathematical equation of the form:

$$Y = \beta_0 + \beta_1 x_1 i + \beta_2 x_2 i + \ldots + \beta_k x_{ki} + \varepsilon_i,$$

where $i = 1,2,3, \ldots, n$. The model describes the relationship between the dependent variable Y and K independent variables. $x_1, x_2, \ldots, x_k$: The parameters β_0 is the intercept and other parameters, β_1 to β_k, are the slopes associated with each independent variable.

In all these cases, the null and alternative hypotheses may be treated as

Null hypothesis (H_0): $\beta_1 = \beta_2 = \ldots = \beta_k = 0$, and $\beta_0 \neq 0$

Alternative hypothesis (H_1): $\beta_1, \beta_2, \ldots, \beta_k \neq 0$.

MEASUREMENT

We have discussed nominal, ordinal, interval, or ratio types of variables pertaining to measurement of objects. In fact, to process the collected data using statistical methods and make an inference, some fundamental idea on measurement of data is required. Measurement is the assignment of numerals to objects or events according to some rules. Numerals are symbols of the forms 1, 2, 3, ..., I, II, III, ... or alpha, beta, gamma, ... etc. They have no quantified meaning unless we give them such a meaning. After being assigned the quantitative meaning, numerals become 'numbers'. There are four levels of measurements, namely, nominal, ordinal, interval, and ratio.

Nominal Scale

This is the lowest level of measurement. The numbers assigned to objects are numerical without any number meaning. They cannot be ordered or subjected to arithmetical operations such as addition, subtraction, multiplication, division, averaging, and so on. Numerals can merely be names assigned to objects, for example, hockey team players, football players, telephone sets, and so forth. These symbols constitute the nominal scales used to facilitate identification of objects in a team, set, cell, etc. For computing a median or performing a chi-square test, nominal data can be used.

Ordinal Scale

Ordinal measurement requires that the objects of a set can be rank ordered on an operationally-defined characteristic or property. The hypotheses 'if A > B and B > C, then A > C' must be satisfied. Most measurements in behavioural research depend on this postulate. Ordinal numbers indicate rank order and nothing more. Ordinal data can be used to compute Spearman correlation coefficient, median, etc.

Example of ordinal measurement: In order to clarify ordinal measurement, a list of top B-Schools published by Indian Management, monthly journal of AIMA, Business Standard publication, Volume 48, Issue 10, October 2009, is reproduced. Refer to Table 25.10.

Table 25.10 B-School scores

Institute category (super league)	Location	Overall score	Intellectual capital	Admissions and placement	Infrastructure	Industry interface	Governance
Faculty of Management Studies, Delhi University (FMS)	Delhi	**95**	95	95	90	85	70
Indian Institute of Management	Ahmedabad	**95**	95	95	95	95	95
Indian Institute of Management	Bangalore	**95**	95	95	80	95	90
Indian Institute of Management	Kolkata	**95**	90	95	90	95	90
Indian Institute of Management	Lucknow	**95**	90	95	80	90	85
Indian Institute of Foreign Trade	New Delhi	**95**	95	95	95	85	90
Institute of Management Technology	Ghaziabad	**95**	95	90	90	90	95
Management Development Institute	Gurgaon	**95**	95	95	95	95	80
National Institute of Industrial Engineering	Mumbai	**95**	95	95	85	90	95
Xavier Labour Relations Institute	Jamshedpur	**95**	90	95	80	95	95

Interval Scale

Interval or equal interval scale possesses the characteristics of nominal and ordinal scales, specially the rank order characteristics. Numerically equal distances on an interval scale represent equal distances in the property being measured. Here, distance is the key word. Intervals can be added or subtracted. If five kilograms represent one unit, then the distance between the marks 7 and 9 will indicate 10 kilograms. Interval data permits all types of univariate and multivariate analysis. An example of interval measurement is a centigrade and fahrenheit thermometer. For both thermometers, the key word is temperature.

Ratio Measurement Scale

This is the highest level of measurement and is ideal for physical or behavioural scientists. This scale has an absolute or natural zero that has an empirical meaning. All econometric and statistical analyses can be processed using ratio data. A ratio variable has all the properties of an interval variable but also has a clear definition of zero. Numbers on the scale indicate the actual amounts of the property being measured. If a measurement is zero on a ratio scale, then there is a basis for saying that some objects have none of the property being measured. When a variable becomes zero, it becomes nonexistent. Variables such as height, weight, etc., are ratio variables.

STATISTICAL PACKAGES

The collected data is further processed for getting information that could be applied to suitable statistical tests. Generally, the volume of data is huge and compels us to use statistical packages. For effective research and more accurate inference, data analysis, and decision-making, we have to use user-friendly and time-saving software. Software packages that are commonly used by researchers and help HR researches are listed in this section along with a brief description. However, it also wise to keep in mind that not all the packages are user-friendly. Some packages that are commonly used by researchers are analyse-it.com (www.analyse-it.com), Statistical Package for Social Sciences or SPSS (www.spss.com), Winks (www.texasoft.com), Statistica (www.statsoft.com), Lisrel, etc. Of all the software, analyse-it.com appears as most user-friendly and affordable.

Analyse-it.com

The software Analyse-it (Leeds, England, UK) is excellent, student-friendly, and affordable even to an individual researcher. This software can be purchased online for a period of one, two, or three years.

The company has been a leading developer of software packages for statistical analysis for the last 25 years. Its flagship product, Analyse-it, was released in 1997, and has supported Excel 5, 95, 97, 2000, 2002, and 2003 versions. It now fully supports and embraces the new features of Excel 2007. Analyse-it is used by well over 15,000 users in countries worldwide, from large multinational pharmaceutical and diagnostic companies to small businesses, start-ups, and individual researchers.

Building on the industry standard spreadsheet, Analyse-it extends Excel with statistics and charts for visualizing, describing, and testing hypotheses on data. The ease-of-use of Analyse-it, combined with the power of Excel, makes it a formidable statistics package. The 'getting started' tutorials of Analyse-it help one to grasp the use of the software.

Some of the salient features are as follows:

1. Describes samples, distributions, correlations, and relationships
2. Visualizes relationships, distributions, and differences with new Excel charts
3. Tests difference, change, correlation, agreement, or prediction hypotheses

4. Integrates into Microsoft Excel 97, 2000, 2002, 2003, 2007
5. Provides accurate, reliable statistics, not built on Excel functions
6. Facilitates ready-to-print publication quality reports
7. Provides jargon-free statistical reference, help, and tutorials

Analyse-it's standard edition provides statistics to describe and test hypotheses, with powerful charts (not available in Excel) to visualize data.

1. Describe: Visualize and describe a sample, or test hypotheses about the mean, proportion, or randomness of a sample.
2. Compare: Visualize and describe differences between samples, or test hypotheses about the difference between means, variances, or proportions.
3. Correlation: Visualize and describe associations between variables, or test hypotheses about the strength of association.
4. Regression: Visualize and describe the relationship among variables, or test hypothesis about which model fits your data best.
5. Agreement: Visualize and describe agreement among methods.

The software facilitates working within the familiar Excel environment.

Analyse-it integrates from Excel 97 to 2007 and analyses data directly from the worksheet. The researcher is not required to export data to another package, and will not end up with his data locked into an inaccessible, proprietary file format. With data in Excel, data can be easily exchanged with guide, co-researchers, and colleagues.

The analysis results can be printed immediately, or copy-paste charts and statistics into documents or presentations can also be done. Chart look is based on the most popular formats used in published research, and charts are immediately ready for inclusion into research.

The analysed data can be saved as a standard Excel workbook, re-opened later, and updated. Data can be added, corrected, included, or excluded.

SPSS

SPSS (www.spss.com) was founded in 1968 and is headquartered at Chicago. It is the world's leading provider of predictive analytics software. SPSS helps administration and institutional research by providing business solutions. The management of educational institutions, hospitals, not-for-profit organizations, and government agencies requires continual and careful monitoring. It offers a wide range of solutions that help institutions to monitor both day-to-day operations and progress towards achieving strategic objectives. Any combination of SPSS advanced analytical software and any of their consulting services may be used.

The most commonly used SPSS module for organizational research is 'Dimension'. With Dimension, a company can centralize not only the creation and fielding of surveys in any mode and language, but also perform data analysis and reporting. Most importantly, Dimension is a platform on which customized tools and branded applications can be created. Branded applications include use of innovative data collection methods such as virtual environments and text or instant messaging. Dimension can conduct more sophisticated analyses (Bhattacharyya 2007).

Some of the benefits that an organization can get using Dimension are as follows:

1. Streamline processes and eliminate costly bottlenecks.
2. Deliver results in easy-to-use formats quickly and automatically.

3. Develop unique, customized offerings more rapidly.
4. Optimize staff skills.
5. Leverage IT infrastructure investments.
6. Deliver high quality results meeting clients' demands.

Statistica

Statistica suite of analytics software products is StatSoft's flagship product line. Statistica provides the most comprehensive array of data analysis, data management, data visualization, and data mining procedures. Its techniques include the widest selection of predictive modelling, clustering, classification, and exploratory techniques in one software platform.

Statistica is a tried and true analytics platform with a history of more than two decades in delivering successful business results for its customers, and with a global user base of more than 600,000 users (www.statsoft.com).

Statistica is provided in four basic categories of product lines.

1. Enterprise: Statistica products are designed for use by multiple users across a site or an entire organization, including the use of Statistica through thin client (web browser) architectures access across a wide area network.
2. Web-based analytic applications: Statistica products are deployed in a highly scalable, web-based architecture for customized, turnkey, web-based analytic applications.
3. Data mining solutions: This contains the most comprehensive and effective system of user-friendly tools for the entire data mining process, from querying databases to generating final reports.
4. Desktop: Statistica products are designed for use on a single workstation.

Statistica continues to be applied across countless industries and applications, including (a) research and development, quality control, and process monitoring in chemical, petrochemical, pharmaceutical, and heavy equipment manufacturing industries, (b) warranty analysis and remote monitoring applications in the manufacturing industry, (c) six sigma applications across all industries including manufacturing, healthcare, and business process analysis, and (d) risk analysis, customer segmentation, and credit scoring in the financial services and insurance industries.

Statistica offers the statistical functionality available in any or all of the Statistica products. Some features of Statistica include the following:

1. Integration with data warehouses
2. Intuitive query and filtering tools
3. Easy-to-use administration tools
4. Automatic report distribution
5. Alarm notification

Winks

Winks (www.texasoft.com) is yet another popular statistical package that helps one to analyse research data. The two versions are Winks Basic and Winks Professional. Once the data is organized, this package allows processing of the huge research data quickly. Winks helps to obtain descriptive statistics including mean, standard deviation, variance, median, minimum, maximum, standard error of the mean, percentile calculations, confidence intervals, and detailed C_P and C_{PK} calculations. Winks allows the performance of different types of non-parametric tests as well.

Winks Statistical Data Analysis (SDA) Basic Edition has the following features:

1. Enter data from Excel, comma separated files, directly into Winks (Winks will use raw or summary data on many analyses).
2. Winks explains the hypothesis tested and takes one through the decision-making process to get an answer for most analyses.
3. Winks provides graphs for most analyses.
4. Winks shows how to write up the conclusions on many of the procedures.
5. A Winks diagram in the manual helps to select the correct procedures to analyse the data.

Report results in Winks help researchers prepare write-ups by providing sample write-ups using the APA format to help in describing the results. Most analyses include a graph that explains and supports the conclusions.

Lisrel

Lisrel is a statistical software used for estimating the coefficients in a set of structural equations. Prerel is the pre-processor of Lisrel (Bhattacharya 2007). Prerel does a fair amount of data screening before processing (including tests of univariate and multivariate normality). It is also used to compute a specified matrix for reading into a Lisrel session. A fairly high level of statistical sophistication is required to use Lisrel or Prerel effectively. Lisrel can be used for the following functions (Bhattacharya 2007):

1. Measurement models and confirmatory factor analysis
2. Causal models for directly observed variables
3. Structural equation models for latent variables
4. Analysis of ordinal and other non-ordinal variables
5. Multi-sample analysis
6. Linear and non-linear constraints
7. Fit measures
8. Path diagrams

Even though it is very reliable, this software is not user-friendly and is used more in scientific research (Bhattacharya 2007).

RELIABILITY AND VALIDITY OF INSTRUMENTS

Q 4 Consistency is the foremost requirement of any questionnaire or instrument. If there is more consistency, reliability would be high. A questionnaire or an instrument is designed to meet a particular purpose. Validity is the term that is used to indicate that the purpose would be fulfilled administering the questionnaire.

Reliability

It is a measure of dependability or trustworthiness of an assessment instrument. Reliability refers to the degree to which a test consistently measures whatever it intends to measure. It is expressed numerically in terms of a coefficient. A high reliability indicates minimum error variance. Depending on the methodology adopted, reliability is categorized as test-retest reliability, split-half reliability, and odd-even reliability. Examples of reliability of three instruments are given here:

The most common instrument used to measure assertiveness of a person is RAS or Rathus assertiveness schedule. The schedule is shown to have high test-retest reliability ($r = 0.78$, $p < 0.01$), split-half reliability ($r = 0.77$, p, 0.01) and validity in terms of the impression and respondents made on other people ($0.33 \leq$ r's ≤ 0.62, p's < 0.01) and in terms of an indicator of how they would behave in specific situations.

Lodahl and Kejner (1965) developed the 20-item scale to measure job involvement. This scale is widely used by researchers. The split-half reliability of the scale was obtained by calculating the product-moment correlation coefficient, between the two halves of the scale, using odd-even items as the split.

Spector developed the job satisfaction survey to measure job satisfaction. The split-half reliability of the scale is obtained by calculating the product-moment correlation coefficient, between the two halves of the scale, using odd-even items as the split. As per manual of the test, reported reliability for three norming groups which includes nurses, engineers, and students is shown in Table 25.11. As per the manual of the test, reported reliability for three norming groups, namely, nurses, engineers, and students are shown in Table 25.11.

Table 25.11 Reported reliability for three norming groups

S. no.	Norming group	Reliability coefficients
1.	Nurses (N=137)	0.72
2.	Engineers (N=70)	0.80
3.	Students (N=46)	0.89

Validity

Validity is a characteristic of measurement concerned with the extent to which a test measures what the researcher actually wishes to measure. The differences found with a measurement tool reflect the true differences among participants drawn from a given population (Cooper and Schindler 2007). In words of Kerlinger (1995), the most common definition of validity is epitomized by the question, 'are we measuring what we think we are measuring?' The emphasis in this question is on what is being measured. After giving the most popular definition of validity, Kerlinger also emphasizes that there cannot be a single validity. Bhattacharya (2007) argues that validity is quantified by comparing our measurements with values that are as close to the true values as possible. Poor validity degrades the accuracy of the measurement, and reduces our ability to characterize relationships between variables in descriptive studies. A test measure is designed keeping in view specific purposes. Hence, validity can be evaluated only in terms of test purpose. Validity is categorized into content, construct, concurrent, and predictive validity.

Content validity It is the degree to which a test measures an intended content area. Content validity has two areas—item validity and sampling validity. Item validity measures the intended content area that is determined by experts from the field. The sampling validity, on the other hand, tests samples in the total content, and judges them in the context of statistical tests.

> Validity is categorized into content, construct, concurrent, and predictive validity.

Construct validity This validity measures the degree to which a test measures a hypothetical construct. To establish credibility, one is required to carry out a series of independent studies. Construct validity requires a thorough understanding of various statistical tests and matching the tests in the context of the hypothesis constructs. We may like to test whether the results of students studying in a particular class depend on the time devoted in study. To do this, we need to frame a hypothesis to test the dependence or otherwise.

Therefore, it is necessary to use Kendell's test to measure the degree of concordance. Similarly, we may be interested to measure the degree of indifference by using ANOVA, a strong statistical test, which measures the degree of indifference.

Concurrent validity Concurrent validity compares scores on an instrument with the current performance on some other measure. It shows that the test is valid by comparing it with an already valid test. High validity coefficient indicates that the test has good concurrent validity.

Suppose there is a training curriculum to impart technical skills as well as communication skills to a group of selected employees. Technical skill enhancement gets translated into increased performance both in terms of quality and quantity, and improved communication skills promote interpersonal relations. In this situation, one can simultaneously measure both dependent variables, that is, job performance and interpersonal relations through the same training curriculum.

Predictive validity It measures the degree to which a test is successful in predicting the success of individual samples for a future situation. It is determined with a validity coefficient by establishing the relationship between the test scores and some predetermined measures of success in a situation of interest. When the validity coefficient is high, the predictive validity is good (Bhattacharya 2007). For example, to predict the job performance of its employees, an organization may assess employee capability to learn the relevant technique.

Having understood different aspects of a research, it is necessary to be acquainted with a few research findings.

RESEARCH FINDINGS ON HR

Inquisitive minds are intrigued by events around them. People formulate hypotheses, pursue research, select statistical tools, apply statistical packages, consider results, and ultimately interpret observations. Many people observe but do take the observations to explore the possible reasons behind any untoward or exceptional behaviour. However, among all organizational issues, managing human resources is by far the critical task. In order to manage them, recordings of behaviour followed by analysis are essential for organizational effectiveness. Managing human resource needs consideration of personal attributes. Few research findings are briefed.

1. In a study titled, 'Occupational values and managerial styles: study in central government departmental enterprise,' Haldar (1995) identified a close correlation and dependence between occupational values and managerial styles of junior management levels.
2. In a study titled, 'Effect of leadership styles on followers'satisfaction and perceived effectiveness,' Mukherjee (2004) observed the leadership style that provides maximum satisfaction to the followers and generates worthiness to an individual in terms of being able to contribute effectively to the attainments of organizational goals and objectives. The leadership style that provides maximum satisfaction, appears to be 'intellectually stimulating.' More specifically, these types of leaders encourage followers to take up new challenges, search for newer and better ways of doing things, instead of demanding unquestionable obedience from them.
3. Ghosh (2009) undertook a research on small business houses to identify most popular and widely used behaviour among five core leadership behaviour namely directive, supportive, participative,

reward and punishment, and charismatic. Ghosh developed a questionnaire based on Howell and Costley (2008) for this investigative study. He observed that it is common to find leaders exhibiting supportive, participative, and 'reward and punishment' behaviour. Leaders displaying directive styles are not uncommon. However, followers or subordinates do not identify any leader as charismatic in small business houses. In the study extended on followers' satisfaction,

Ghosh (2009) observed that subordinates or followers prefer to work under 'supportive' leaders; do not hesitate to work under leaders exhibiting 'participative style' of behaviour, and do not have aversion to work with leaders with 'reward and punishment' style. However, they are not inclined towards leaders who exhibit 'directive behaviour' styles. Most interestingly, the researcher did not find any leader with charismatic styles in small business houses.

4. Sen (2008) formulated a hypotheses to identify whether leaders' behaviour vary on (a) organisational hierarchy and (b) functional area, and concludes that the styles are neither dependent on the organisational hierarchy nor necessarily on the functional area. Sen (2008) further attempts to investigate whether the styles identified through questionnaires match with the behaviour actually exhibited by the managers. He observes that the objectively identified style does not match with the exhibited behaviour based on observational analysis.
5. Sarkar (2011) formulated 19 hypotheses including hypotheses relating to organizational role stress (ORS), and age and experience of respondents from manufacturing companies, telecom companies, and academia. The findings confirm that (a) ORS is negatively correlated with age, implying that elderly persons, by virtue of their maturity and pragmatism, can reasonably manage their stress levels than younger generation; and (b) ORS is negatively correlated with length of experience, implying that while working in organisations, people learn various organisational characteristics and can manage their stress to reasonable extent than younger generation.

PREPARING THESIS

Research work is conducted to discover answers to questions through the application of scientific procedures and statistical tests with the main aim of finding the truth that is hidden and has not yet been discovered. Though the journey is long, academicians pursue it to obtain intellectual joy.

Having acquainted with objectives, motivation, types of research, various types of measurement of data, statistical tools and packages, and reliability and validity of measurements, a student is ready to write a thesis.

Now we will discuss and gain some knowledge on how to structure and sequence the thesis.

Introductory Pages

A thesis may be structured in several ways. However, the most popular way of arrangement is discussed here.

The introductory pages include title page, foreword, preface, acknowledgement, table of contents, lists of tables and illustrations, and an executive summary. The page numbers of these preliminary pages are written in lowercase Roman numerals (for example, i, ii, iii).

Foreword This is a prologue or a preamble written by an expert in the respective field. It is not an essential inclusion; but if it is included, the gravity of the thesis gets enhanced. Do not number the first page of the foreword but count it for numbering subsequent pages.

Preface It is the gateway to the contents of the thesis and therefore, it is important that it gives the reader a good initial impression. Apply undivided attention to write the preface with a punchy style. Do not number the first page of the preface but count it for numbering subsequent introductory pages.

Acknowledgement In the course of pursuing the research, the researcher must have taken help from many persons including the supervisor. Acknowledge them briefly by highlighting their contributions. Remember that someone else might need their help as well. Acknowledgement is generally included at the end of the preface.

Table of contents This helps the reader to read the thesis.

Lists of tables and illustrations Lists of tables and illustrations should follow the table of contents. Each list should preferably start on a separate page. If there are only a few items in each list, both the lists may be put on the same page but under different headings.

Executive summary This section is required to introduce the reader to the overall contents of the thesis with special emphasis on the findings and discussion.

Main Chapters of the Thesis

The thesis generally comprises the following chapters:

1. Introduction
2. Review of literature
3. Operational definition
4. Research methodology
5. Results and discussion
6. Summary
7. Applications and limitations
8. Scope for future researchers
9. Recommendations
10. Acknowledgement
11. Bibliography

Introduction

This is the first chapter of the thesis and the researcher should discuss the motivation for the work, state and define the problem that the findings are trying to address or solve, state the aims and objectives of the work, give an indication of how the work has been progressed, and finally provide a brief overview of each of the main chapters that any reader will encounter.

Review of Literature

Literature review is a critical examination, summarization, interpretation, or evaluation of the existing literature in order to formulate hypotheses in their context. There might be difficulty as there may be a huge amount of published work on the subject area, which dates back many years. At the same time, in the era of internet, it is possible to get a great deal of information online. The researcher can pick up those that are relevant to his study and rephrase what he wants to include in the thesis. The literature review will have several chapters under properly designated titles.

Operational Definition

An operational definition assigns meaning to a construct or variable by specifying the activities or operations necessary to measure it. Alternatively, an operational definition is a specification of the activities of the researcher in measuring a variable or in manipulating it (Kerlinger 1995). If the term 'moderate performer' is used in the thesis, then define in which sense it has been used the particular category.

For example, in a study on job involvement, the scores of the respondents ranged from 47 to 76. Percentile cut-off three grades were decided as shown in Table 25.12.

Table 25.12 Scores of respondents

Job involvement: Scale range (20 to 80)		Measured score range	
Job involvement level	**Grade**	**Minimum**	**Maximum**
Low job involvement	JI_low	47	56
Moderate job involvement	JI_mod	57	66
High job involvement	JI_high	67	76

From the Table, it is obvious that the respondents who scored between 47 and 56 are low job involved, those who scored between 57 and 66 are moderate job involved, and high job-involved respondents are those whose scores range from 67 to 76. Thus, from the standpoint of operational definition, moderate job involved persons are those whose job involvement scores lie between 57 and 66. Obviously then, there can not be an absolute range since it is study-specific.

Research Methodology

Research methodology is the structural heart of a thesis and should generally include statement of the problem, research questions, hypotheses, etc.

Methodology is the structural heart of a thesis and should generally include the following:

1. The researcher is required to briefly discuss the problem that prompted him to undertake the research.
2. Research questions are prepared based on the statement of the problem. The questions help in initiating directional efforts. A few examples of research questions are cited in Box 25.3.

Box 25.3 Examples of questions

This research aims to find answers to the following research questions:

1. Are the respondents' performance homoscedastic (variances are equal) in regards to rural and urban areas?
2. Can the performance be taken as the classificatory variable?
3. Are behavioural styles of the respondents influenced by psychological factors such as assertiveness, job satisfaction, and job involvement? If so, what is the extent of the influence on job performance?
4. Are their performances influenced by socio-demographic variables such as gender; age of the agents, length of experience, level of education, and region of engagement?

3. Specific objectives of the study: It is necessary to describe the investigation and exploration that are essential to get the answers to the research questions.
4. Statement of hypotheses: There are two types of hypotheses: null hypothesis and alternate hypothesis. A hypothesis is a statement describing the relation between two or more variables. Hypotheses are always presented in a declarative sentence form such as (a) the performance of the respondents is independent of their assertiveness, and (b) there is no difference amongst the high, moderate, and low performing respondents with respect to their job satisfaction scores. There will be many such hypotheses, in any thesis.
5. Methods: In this section, specify and discuss the selection of the area for study, sampling procedure, and provide justification for selecting the area of study.
6. Statistical tools used: In this section, it is essential to discuss the statistical tools along with the reliability and validity of the tools.
7. Scales used and scoring techniques: The research might be concerned with job performance and its determinants. The researcher might have decided to explore the effects of assertiveness, job satisfaction, job involvement, and organizational commitment on the job performance of respondents. So, he must measure the independent variables using suitable psychometric scales. He has to describe the scales and the scoring technique.
8. Justification of using the scale: In this section, the researcher is expected to justify the selection of the measuring instruments. He can justify by mentioning the scales used by previous researchers whose area of study were similar to research.

Results and Discussion

The researcher should display the results of the statistical tests, whether descriptive or inferential, as shown earlier in this chapter. Thereafter, he is expected to discuss the results and provide inference. Readers of the thesis look for his interpretation of the results in the study's context.

An example of ANOVA test is as follows:

The value of F (= 395.3) and p (< 0.0001) prompted to reject the null hypothesis, signifying that the three groups, namely, high performing (HP), moderate performing (MP), and low performing (LP) respondents differed significantly. Job performance could be well taken as a classificatory variable.

Summary

The researcher should utilize this chapter for providing short summaries of all the chapters in the thesis.

Applications and Limitations

Here, the researcher is required to specify the areas where the findings are best applicable. It would be wiser if he also specifies the limitations of the application since he knows this better than anyone else.

Scope for Future Researchers

Before the start of a study, a prospective researcher looks for the topic or theme he/she should undertake. One source for the same is a university library where theses are carefully preserved. Someone may like to pursue a study in line with the researcher's work. Therefore, it is advised that he should mention about a few areas that have the scope, are in line with the work, and which can guide others.

Some examples are (a) a similar study may be undertaken to explore the conglomerate effect of assertiveness, job satisfaction, and job involvement along with other job behaviour such as achievement, motivation, organizational commitment, risk-taking propensity, personality, and so on, (b) separate studies on the impact of extrinsic and intrinsic satisfaction on job performance might be undertaken, (c) the job attitudes, significant to the organization, such as pursuing ideas, feedback, autonomy, skill, challenge, creativity, reputation establishment, and professionalism may be taken as the set of independent variables influencing sales performance, (d) the effects and impact on performance, of the work environmental factors—such as job incentives encompassing salary, advancement opportunity, directing and communicative supervisors, clear rules and procedures, and easy to get along with colleagues—might be considered to build up a separate research study.

Recommendations

If the researcher has conducted research in a particular company, the recommendation will be of immense help to the company. If he has surveyed the market, and drawn conclusions, then the recommendations will be helpful to the manufacturers of the products which are considered in the study. Thus, researchers' recommendations are useful to manufacturers, consumers of the products, and the society as a whole.

Bibliography/References

The researcher may have referred numerous books, journals, magazines, and websites. All the sources of information must be mentioned. This exhaustive list will help future researchers.

Appendices

Long tables, questionnaires, and instruments should not be included in the main thesis. The researcher must mention them, highlight their contents, include them in the appendix, and identify them with unique reference numbers. Suppose he has mentioned the Rathus assertiveness schedule or job satisfaction survey in the research methodology. Then he must number the instruments as they appear in the chapter. Reproduce the instruments in the appendix. In such cases, after the table of contents in the preliminary pages, the list of appendices should be included.

SUMMARY

Organizations and the society face a number of problems in managing their human resource issues for multifarious reasons—capability building, responsibility sharing, extending autonomy, managing change, balancing internal and external help, balancing differentiation and integration, balancing quantitative and qualitative decisions, manpower attrition, empowerment, and many such aspects. Organizations search for stability that is opposed by the variability of human behaviour at work. To solve this, organizations depend on HR research to obtain organization-specific solutions.

Academicians, research scholars, and organizational stalwarts pursue research to gain familiarity with a phenomenon, to achieve new insights, and to portray the characteristics of a particular individual, group of individuals, or situation. Motivation of researchers includes a desire to face the challenge in solving unsolved problems, concern over practical problems, deriving intellectual joy from doing some creative work, rendering service to the society, establishing credibility, and so on. Few organizations have implemented HR research recommendations and have been able to get more from men rather than getting more men.

The right approach for conducting HR research largely depends on the specific requirements of an organization. Having selected the right approach, the researcher needs to decide the sample from which he will collect data and select the right statistical tools or tests, followed by choosing the right statistical package for data processing and getting the result in readily usable form. Finally, in case of organizational research, there is a need to prepare a structured report and in the case of a doctoral research, it is necessary that the researcher writes the thesis methodically.

KEY TERMS

Construct Also called intervening variables, is a term invented to account for internal and directly unobservable psychological processes that take behaviour into account.

Employer branding Refers to the development and communication of an organization's culture to the labour market with the prime objective of influencing the perception of potential employees about the organization, and enhancing the scope and opportunity of poaching talents from the market.

Homoscedasticity Refers to the homogeneous characteristic of a population, that is geographically widely dispersed, and from where the researcher has drawn samples. It may be established using the F-test for 'equality of variances'.

Reliability Is a measure of dependability or trustworthiness of an assessment instrument and refers to the degree to which a test consistently measures whatever it intends to measure and is expressed numerically in terms of a coefficient.

Validity Is a characteristic of measurement concerned with the extent to which a test measures what the researcher actually wishes to measure, and that the differences found with a measurement tool reflect the true differences among participants drawn from a given population.

EXERCISES

Concept Review Questions

1. State the need and importance of HR research. How does quantitative research differ from qualitative research? Cite examples.
2. Discuss the guiding principles for designing the HR functions in an organization. What are the motivations behind pursuing an HR research?
3. Distinguish between pure basic research and applied research. Are these two types complementary to each other? Justify your answer.
4. Elaborate the concept of reliability and validity of instruments. What are the types of reliability? What is concurrent validity?

Critical Review Questions

5. Discuss critically the importance of literature review in HR research. What might be the consequences if the literature review is inadequate? Justify your views.
6. In what circumstances does a test for equality of variances become essential? Would the conclusion drawn from other statistical tests bring out the real life scenario?

Assignments

Visit any university library and take out few theses on HR or social science. Study the statement of the problem, research questions, hypotheses, results and discussion, limitations, scope for future researchers, and recommendations.

1. Examine whether the recommendations encompass answers to the research questions.;
2. Observe the objectives of the research and try to understand how the research methodology was structured.

BIBLIOGRAPHY AND WEB RESOURCES

Bhattacharyya, D.K., *Human Resource Research Methods*, Oxford University Press, New Delhi, 2007.

Cooper, Donald R. and Pamela S. Schindler, *Business Research Methods*, 9th Edition, Tata McGraw Hill Companies, New Delhi, 2007.

Crowl, T.K., *Fundamentals of Educational Research*, WCB Brown & Benchmark, Iowa, 1993.

Elifson, K.W., R.P. Runyon, and A. Haber, *Fundamentals of Social Statistics*, 2nd Edition, McGraw Hill, Singapore, 1990.

Ghosh, Lipi, *Leadership and Team Building*, Dissertation report submitted in partial fulfillment of master degree in business administration (specialization—human resources), submitted to the Indian Institute of Social Welfare and

Business Management (IISWBM), for evaluation by University of Calcutta, Kolkata, 2009.

Haldar, Uday Kumar, *Occupational Values and Managerial Styles: A Study in Central Government Departmental Enterprise*, unpublished project report submitted to Indira Gandhi National Open University, 1995.

Haldar, Uday Kumar, *Job Performance of the Operational Agents of LICI in Relation to Some Specific Job Behaviours: A Study of 24 Parganas (North), West Bengal*, unpublished doctoral thesis submitted to University of Burdwan, West Bengal, 2003.

Haldar, Uday Kumar, *Human Resource Development*, Oxford Higher Education, Oxford University Press, New Delhi, 2009.

Heiman, G.W., *Basic Statistics for the Behavioural Sciences*, Houghton Muffin Co., Boston, MA, 1992.

Kenkel, J.L., *Introductory Statistics for Management and Economics*, PWS–Kent, Boston, 1989.

Kerlinger, Fred N. , *Foundations of Behavioural Research*, 3rd Edition, Harcourt Brace College Publishers, Prism Book Pvt. Ltd, Bangalore, 1995.

Lodahl, T.M. and M. Kejner, 'The Definition and Measurement of Job Involvement', *Journal of Applied Psychology*, 49, pp. 24–33, Washington D.C., 1965.

Mukherjee, Kum Kum, 'Effect of Leadership Styles on Followers' Satisfaction and Percieved Effectiveness', *South Asian Journal of Management* (ISSN 0971 5428), Vol. 11, No. 1, pp. 7–19, January–March 2004.

Pareek, Udai and T.V. Rao, *Pioneering Human Resources Development: The L&T System*, Academy of Human Resource Development, Hyderabad, p. 165, 1998.

Rao, T.V. and Udai Pareek, *From a Sapling to a Forest*, Larsen & Toubro, T.V. Rao Learning Systems, 1971.

Rathus, A.S., 'Assessing Assertive Behaviour', *Behaviour Therapy*, 4, pp. 398–406, USA, 1973.

Rubin, A. and E. Babbie, *Research Methods for Social Work*, (2nd Ed.), Brooks/Cole Publishing Co., California, 1993.

Sarkar, Juthika, *Study of Organisational Climate and Organisational Role Stress Across Industries in Kolkat*a, Doctoral thesis (unpublished) submitted to Singhania University, Pacheri Bari, Jhunjhunu (Rajasthan), 2011.

Sen, Sureeta, *Leadership and Patterns of Leadership Behaviour*, Dissertation report submitted in partial fulfillment of master degree in business administration (specialization—human resources), submitted to Indian Institute of Social Welfare and Business Management (IISWBM), for evaluation by University of Calcutta, Kolkata, 2009.

Web Resources

www.analyse-it.com, last accessed on 27 April 2008.

www.hr.com, last accessed on 25 April 2008.

www.spss.com, last accessed on 27 April 2008.

www.statsoft.com, last accessed on 27 April 2008.

www.texasoft.com/Describe_Basic6.htm, last accessed on 27 April 2008

www.texasoft.com, last accessed on 27 April 2008.

STUDYING A THESIS

Author's note: For this chapter, no closing case is furnished; rather students are recommended to treat any doctoral thesis on human resource management as the closing case. A student is advised to study a thesis in the following way.

Firstly, read the preface and foreword. Read the introduction chapter that defines the problem, examine why it is important, what other researchers have done, what the central idea(s) of the thesis is, how the rest of the thesis is organized, and similar other aspects. Thereafter, meticulously go through the chapter's research methodology (comprising statement of the problem, aim of the study, research questions, statement of hypotheses, selection of the area for study, justification of selecting the area of study, sample size, sampling procedure, statistical tools used, brief description of the tools including reliability and validity, the statistical package used, etc). At any point of time, one should analyse as to why the researcher did in this way. This self questioning will greatly enhance conceptual understanding.

The researcher should take a glance of the review of literatures to be familiar with how the review had prompted the researcher to formulate the statement of the problem. He should also be acquainted with sections and sub-sections of the literature reviews and note the logical arrangement of the chapters.

The researcher must have selected certain statistical tools and to process the data, he/she must have arranged the data to use the tools. This is a point that must be studied with adequate care. It is important to be acquainted with the tool to be used as against arrangement of the data. The statistical packages display the results in a tabular form or otherwise. The results prompt to accept or reject the null hypothesis that are framed and stated in the chapter 'research methodology', and interpret the data. The chapter 'findings and conclusion' is of paramount importance.

While pursuing research, a scholar may face some hurdles. He/she may like to include a short chapter on 'hurdles faced' mentioning the various hurdles and how could he/she resolve the hurdles one by one. This may help a future researcher of being careful and well prepared to face those hurdles.

A copy of thesis is retained in the university library so that anyone intending to pursue a research in an area can refer to the thesis. Therefore, a researcher includes a chapter on scope for future researchers. The researcher will pursue a research among many constraints, and it may not be possible to consider all the factors that he wanted to. Accordingly, narrate the limitations in the doctoral thesis for which guidance may be taken from the chapter, 'limitations' of a similar thesis. Additionally, take into account how the material (chapters) has been organized in thesis to gain insights.

PAUL E. SPECTOR

Paul Spector was born in New York in 1949. He moved with his family to Sarasota, Florida in 1958. He attended the University of South Florida (USF) in Tampa from 1968 to 1975 where he earned a BA in psychology, an MA, and Ph.D in industrial/organizational (I/O) psychology. He held a variety of diverse jobs in his early career, including teaching in the USF College of Business Administration, being a programme evaluator/planner for Northside Community Mental Health Center, and working as director of research for the Florida Mental Health Institute. In 1982, he returned to the USF Psychology Department as an assistant professor of I/O psychology. Presently, he holds the title of distinguished professor. He is also the director of the USF Occupational Health Psychology (OHP) program. The OHP program is funded through a training grant from the National Institute of Occupational Safety and Health, and is part of the USF Sunshine Education and Research Center, headquartered in the College of Public Health. Spector has extensive professional experience to his credit.

Spector has developed several tools relating to research which are used by several researchers as arsenals while pursuing research. Among the tools developed by Spector, the 'Job Satisfaction Survey'—a nine-faceted instrument to assess job satisfaction—is widely used.

Spector has varied research interests in both content and methodology. His content interests concern employee health, safety, and well-being. More specifically, he has studied workplace aggression and counterproductive work behaviour (with Suzy Fox, Loyola University Chicago), occupational stress, violence exposure, and work-family conflicts. Spector and Cary Cooper of Lancaster University founded the Collaborative International Study of Managerial Stress (CISMS) in the mid 1990s by collecting data from over 14,000 managers. Spector's work has appeared in a number of refereed journals such as Academy of Management Journal, Applied Psychology: An International Review, Journal of Applied Psychology, Human Resources Management Review, Journal of Management, Journal of Occupational Health Psychology, Journal of Organizational Behavior, Journal of Occupational and Organizational Psychology, Journal of Vocational Behavior, Organizational Behavior and Human Decision Processes, Organizational Research Methods, Personnel Psychology, and Work & Stress. His work has also received several distinctions for the impact that it has generated. A 1991 study by ISI Thomson Reuters listed him among the 50 highest impact psychologists worldwide. According to a 2008 study conducted by Philip Podsakoff and colleagues, published in Journal of Management, he was the 27th most cited author in management-related journals between 1981 and 2004. In 2009, the editors of Journal of Organizational Behavior chose two of his articles as among the eight most influential ones in the journal's history.

In 1991, the Institute for Scientific Information listed him as one of the 50 highest impact contemporary researchers in the world among over 102,000 researchers in psychology.

Spector has an outstanding expertise in issues such as health and wellbeing/wellness, overwork/ workload, resiliency and stress, global economy/global focus, and work-family conflict.

Spector has served on the editorial boards of Human Resources Management Review, Journal of Applied Psychology, Journal of Management, Organizational Research Methods, and Personnel Psychology. He has been an associate editor for Journal of Occupational and Organizational Psychology, Journal of Occupational Health Psychology, Journal of Organizational Behavior, and Work and Stress. His I/O psychology textbook, *Industrial and Organizational Psychology: Research and Practice* has been translated into several languages, including Chinese, Korean, Portuguese and Spanish, and is now in its sixth edition.

Spector is member of several professional bodies such as Academy of Management (Organizational Behavior Division and Research Methods Division); American Psychological Society, Fellow; and International Association of Applied Psychology.

Spector has published several books; of which only a few are mentioned here. Some of them are *Research Designs* (1981), *Summated Rating Scales* (1992), and *SAS Programming for Researchers and Social Scientists* (1993). He has authored more than 100 journal papers/articles in journals.

Spector is member of editorial boards of many journals such as Human Resources Management Review, Journal of Applied Psychology, Journal of Management, Journal of Organizational Behavior, Journal of Occupational and Organizational Psychology, Journal of Occupational Health Psychology, Organizational Research Methods, Personnel Psychology, and Work & Stress, as well.

References

Email dated 14 October 2011 received from Dr Paul Spector, (pspector@usf.edu).

psychology.usf.edu/faculty/pspector/, last accessed on 14 October 2011.

APPENDIX A

Stress Management

INTRODUCTION

Stress is a part and parcel of work life. In the work place, stress develops through pressure or work load, anxiety, constant worries, daily hassles, and so on. Stress can never be totally eliminated although it can be substantially reduced. Excessive stress causes mental and physical problems. On the other hand, some amount of stress helps to keep the wheels of action going. Stress is a natural phenomenon in all types of organizations. In order to be effective in human resource management, managers need to take into account stress factors irrespective of the functional area and levels of management hierarchy.

WORK STRESS

Work-related stress is of more concern today than it was two decades ago. Different people have different views about stress as it can be experienced from a variety of sources (Pestonjee 1999). Businessmen view stress as frustration or emotional tension; air traffic controllers see it as a problem of alertness and concentration; and biochemists perceive it as a purely chemical event. Stress has become a major problem for individuals working in an organization as well as the organization itself. Cooper and Marshall (1978) suggested the classification of stress in terms of six different stressors.

Stress is a person's response to his/her environment. It is the pattern of emotional states and psychological reaction occurring in response to demands from within or outside organizations. Each person has his/her own normal (homeostatic) level of alertness at which he/she functions best. Stress in itself is not so negative or harmful. It can, in fact be very positive as well. Stress becomes a problem when we do not understand and manage it skillfully. Stress becomes distress or disease when individuals lose touch with their physical limits of stress tolerance. This often results in a breakdown of physical and psychological health. Therefore all stresses do not lead to distress. A certain amount of stress or pressure is necessary to make a positive adaptation in a person. Bad or negative stress is called 'distress'. It is the negative psychological and emotional response by a person when stress is intense or unresolved.

Cooper and Marshall (1978) have identified the following six major sources of stresses at work:

Factors intrinsic to the job These factors include working conditions, shifts, and the two types of work overload (quantitative and qualitative).

Role in the organization When a person's role in the organization is clearly defined and understood, and when expectations placed on the individual are clear and non-conflicting, stress can be kept to a minimum.

Relationship at work This refers to the working relationship one has with colleagues and others.

Career development Job security, fear of loss of job, obsolescence, retirement, and numerous performance appraisals are the various organizational issues that can create pressure.

Organization structure and climate Employees desire freedom and autonomy at work. Supervision, in excess than required, tends to reduce the sense of belonging. Lack of adequate opportunities to participate and unduly restricted communication can lead to overall poor health, drinking, depression, low esteem, and absenteeism.

Non-work factors There are other various factors apart from work that cause stress in an individual such as family problems, economic, and health problems. Political uncertainty also falls in this category.

Whatever be the source of stress, management needs to take care of burnout.

BURNOUT

Burnout is the response to interpersonal stressors on the job, wherein an overload of contact with people will result in changes in attitude and behaviour among them. Burnout stress syndrome (BOSS) is the consequence of a high level of job stress, personal frustration, and inadequate coping skills. All these result in major personal, organizational, and social costs. BOSS is a weakening psychological condition and can lead to the following:

1. Depletion of energy reserves
2. Lowering of resistance to illness
3. Increased dissatisfaction and pessimism
4. Increased absenteeism and inefficiency at work

Burnout is defined as the end result of 'stress experienced but not properly coped', resulting in symptoms of exhaustion, irritation, ineffectiveness, inaction, discounting of self and others, and heath problems (hypertension, ulcers, heart ailments, etc.). Burnout occurs at the individual level and is a negative psychological experience.

STRESS LEVEL AND CONSEQUENCES

Stress influences the reaction of a person to stimuli. The reaction directs his/her behaviour and performance. Table A.1 lists various stress levels and their respective health effects.

Table A.1 Stress levels and consequences

Stress level	Reactions	Behaviours	Performance	Health effects
Low	Boredom/Apathy	Low motivation, psychological withdrawal	Low	Dull, inactive state
Optimum	High energy	High motivation, heightened perception, high involvement	High	Good, healthy state
High	Exhaustion	Anxiety and nervousness, incisiveness, bad decision making	Poor	Insomnia, psychosomatic disease

Stress Levels vs Performance

An employee will perform to full capacity under an optimum level of stress. The individual will be bored and apathetic, if the stress is below this optimum level. As far as behaviour is concerned, the person is likely to withdraw psychologically from work. Psychological withdrawal will result in frequent careless mistakes, poor memory, and poor concentration. In addition, at low stress levels, one may physically withdraw, leading to increased rates of tardiness and absenteeism, which may ultimately result in high employee turnover.

Similarly, if the level of stress is high, employee performance will be adversely affected. The employees will suffer from BOSS. Errors will increase due to anxiety and nervousness, and ineffective decisions will be made; the individual may experience insomnia, and psychosomatic illnesses such as peptic ulcer and asthma. Organizational performance and individual health are at their peak only at optimum levels of stress.

The management needs to identify the causes of stress and implement suitable coping strategies.

COPING STRATEGIES

Coping means handling a potential stressor or a stressful situation by minimizing the harmful consequences. Coping comprises efforts, both action-oriented and intra-psychic, to manage the demands and conflicts (Lazarus and Launier 1978). When coping is effective, the potential stressor does not result in a stressful situation. Pestonjee (1999) has discussed cognitive restructuring and cognitive-type coping strategies, and has quoted certain strategies to cope with the stress that frequently arises in organizations. The following are some of the strategies:

1. Consider difficulties, adverse or demanding job situations, as inevitable parts of job life.
2. Perceive stressful job situations as a temporary phase of the job.
3. Try to rationalize stress situations and their consequences.
4. Take excessive demands as a challenge.
5. Assess the severity of your job stress with reference to others who are facing similar or more severe stress in their jobs.
6. Believe that time itself will take care of such situations.
7. Accept the situation of stress, thinking that there is nothing you can do to change it.
8. Simultaneously, think about the positive outcomes of successfully dealing with the situation of stress.
9. Believe that every problem has some remedy—always remember that a problem develops with its solution, and you are required to identify that solution.
10. Realize that no one is free from stress and that every stress is of different nature and severity
11. Accept the situations of stress as a reality of life.
12. Remind yourself that work is not everything.
13. Believe in the philosophy that 'your right is only to do your job, not to expect its results'.

The counsellor needs to explain these coping strategies and advise the stressed person accordingly, in a very convincing manner so that the individual remembers the counsellor's words especially during times of stress. During counselling, a counsellor has to provide people with a better understanding of the coping strategies, and elucidate the ill effects of stress. The counsellor should propose the most suitable (considering the situation) method from his/her knowledge and experience.

Dimensions of Coping Strategies

The three coping strategy dimensions are internality, externality, and mode.

Internality This dimension reflects the extent to which the stressed person engages himself/herself with the problem causing stress, either to confront or avoid it.

Externality This dimension reflects the extent to which the stressed person involves or engages others with the problem causing stress, either to confront or avoid it.

Mode This dimension reflects the intention of the person. The intention may either be avoidance or approach. If the person concerned runs away from the problems creating stress, that is 'avoidance' mode. On the other hand, if the intention is to solve the problem, it is called, 'approach' mode.

The dimensions internality, externality and mode coexist in varying degrees, and each can be low or high.

Based on the binary or twofold nature of the three dimensions, eight types of coping strategies evolve.

Types of Coping Strategies

The eight types of basic coping strategies or styles (Pestonjee 1999) for dealing with stress are the following:

Impunitive This is a dysfunctional style resulting from low internality, low externality, and avoidance mode. It is characterized by fatalistic thinking and denoted by the letter, *M*. Problems are accepted believing that they are inevitable and nothing can be done about them.

Intropunitive This is a dysfunctional style resulting from high internality, low externality, and avoidance mode. It is characterized by blaming the self, and is denoted by the letter, *I*. The person concerned resorts to blaming himself/herself for the problems and doing nothing about solving them.

Extrapunitive This is a dysfunctional style resulting from low internality, high externality, and avoidance mode. It is characterized by blaming others, and is denoted by the letter, *E*. The persons resort to blaming others for the problems and do nothing about solving them.

Defensive This is a dysfunctional style resulting from high internality, high externality, and avoidance mode. It is characterized by denial or rationalization and denoted by the letter, *D*. Problems are either denied or rationalized by pointing out their benefits.

Impersistive This is a functional style resulting from low internality, low externality, and approach mode. It is characterized by wishful thinking, and is denoted by the letter, *m*. The person concerned believes that problems will be solved eventually due to change in circumstances.

Intropersistive This is a functional style resulting from high internality, low externality, and approach mode. It is characterized by self-effort and denoted by the letter the letter, *i*. The individuals put in efforts to get a solution.

Extrapersistive This is a functional style resulting from low internality, high externality and approach mode. It is characterized by external efforts, and is denoted by the letter, *e*. The person concerned gets the problem solved by others.

Interpersistive This is a functional style resulting from high internality, high externality, and approach mode. It is characterized by team effort, and is denoted by the letter, *n*. The person concerned shares the problems causing stress with others and makes joint efforts along with others to solve the problems. Table A.2 lists the features of these eight types of coping strategies.

Table A.2 Eight types of basic coping strategies or styles

Coping strategy	Denoted by	Style	Internality	Externality	Mode
Impunitive	*M*	Dysfunctional	Low	Low	Avoidance
Intropunitive	*I*	Dysfunctional	High	Low	Avoidance
Extrapunitive	*E*	Dysfunctional	Low	High	Avoidance
Defensive	*D*	Dysfunctional	High	High	Avoidance
Impersistive	*m*	Functional	Low	Low	Approach
Intropersistive	*i*	Functional	High	Low	Approach
Extrapersistive	e	Functional	Low	High	Approach
Interpersistive	*n*	Functional	High	High	Approach

Coping Strategy Focus

Coping strategies can also be classified on this basis of their focus (Taylor, et al. 1998):

1. Problem-focused coping strategy
2. Emotion-focused coping strategy
3. Functional coping strategy
4. Dysfunctional coping strategy
5. Proactive coping strategy
6. Reactive coping strategy

Problem-focused coping strategy This strategy aims at managing or changing a stressful situation by 'confrontive coping' or 'planned problem solving'. Confrontive coping involves aggressive, rash, and risky efforts to change the stressful situation. This strategy is used when the situation in uncontrollable such as the death of a near relative or the sudden loss of service). On the other hand, planned problem solving is carried out when the problem is controllable; it comprises systematic analysis of the situation, identification of most suitable solution, and its implementation.

Emotion-focused coping strategy This strategy aims at regulating the psychological responses to potential stressors or stressful events in order to minimize their harmful consequences. Attempts are made to change the ways of thinking of the individual concerned. Such strategies are used when the situation is uncontrollable. The stressful situation may seem confronting in the short run, but harmful in the long run, and cause depression and anxiety.

Functional coping strategy These are positive strategies for managing stress as they provide lasting solutions for handling potential stressors or stressful situations, while promoting individual well-being and effectiveness.

Dysfunctional coping strategy These strategies provide only temporary relief from stressful encounters. As such, these types of strategies are termed as negative or dysfunctional coping strategies.

Proactive coping strategy These strategies are modern and forward looking. The strategies are multi-dimensional in nature; integrate quality of life with self-regulatory goal accomplishment (Greenglass 2001). Proactive coping strategy is the result of perceiving the internal and external demands as challenging opportunities.

Reactive coping strategy These strategies are traditional, as the coping strategy is initiated after the stressful event has developed. The strategy is aimed at minimizing the harm and loss created by the stressful event. When people find the internal or external demands threatening, they generally adopt the reactive coping strategy.

STRESS MANAGEMENT INTERVENTION

Researches have established that the management of stress influences the nature of family interactions, reduces violence, and promotes quality of life. Stress interventions have been successfully used on bio-behavioural processes in breast cancer patients undergoing medical treatment for reduced mood disturbance before surgical operations. Stress management interventions are frequently used in organizational life. Stress management intervention, including stress and coping, coping strategies, and self-imposed behaviour modification methods, are discussed here.

Self-imposed Behaviour Modification Methods

It is the responsibility of the counsellor to develop certain temperamental qualities and adopt specific behavioural patterns or habits, which could help in preventing, mitigating, or effectively coping with the situations of work role stress (Pestonjee 1999). A few behavioural modification methods are listed here:

1. Increase self-esteem and the levels of tolerance and patience.
2. Do not be rigid in your ways of functioning, attitudes, and decisions—you should neither be rigid nor be flexible; instead, be flexibly rigid.
3. Do things at work in a planned and systematic manner.
4. Try to separate and maintain coordination between your job and other roles.
5. Avoid doing many things simultaneously.
6. Set your priorities on job activities.
7. Discuss the problems with your supervisors, and/or other superiors, or even competent colleagues.
8. Avoid time pressure and role overloading—be regular, and make proper distribution of your time to your job activities.
9. Do not try to reach the highest level of perfection all the time in your routine work.
10. Work sincerely, but do not be overenthusiastic all the time in discharging your duties.
11. Frankly communicate your limitations and capabilities—do not hide your inability.
12. Try to nip the problems in the bud.
13. Be a realistic manager—aspire within the framework of your capabilities and resources.
14. Try to overlook rather than react to the irritating situations or behaviour of people at work.
15. Before doing something that is new, challenging, creative, or original, you must consider all possible consequences.
16. If there is no way out, do your best to get out of the situation gracefully.
17. Set SMART (specific, measurable, attainable, realistic, and time bound) goals for self and junior colleagues.
18. In case of role overloads, apply the concept of time management.

Managing Job Stress

Job stress is the leading cause for chronic stress. While managing the stressors, we develop 'on the job' and 'off the job' stresses. Whatever be the source, stress can be reduced significantly, thus leading to greater wellness and happiness. It is important to take steps to take care of oneself and one's body. One should never feel that the stress in life is beyond control as he/she can always control the responses. Managing stress is all about taking charge of thoughts and thought processes, and most importantly, emotions. One has to take charge of the time schedule, environment, and ways of handling problems. Stress management involves changing the stressful situation when you can, changing your reaction when you can't, taking care of yourself, and making time for relaxation. Thus, the key is already in your hand, and all you need to do is to turn it.

The following strategies can help one stay healthy, and possibly, reverse many of the negative effects of stress:

Reduce daily stressors One can reduce stress by suitably changing the lifestyle; becoming more organized in managing time, and making other changes at work. Maintaining a positive outlook is also important to overall health. Positive thinking helps one get enough sleep.

Learn stress-reducing practices Learning and practising a stress management technique or two can also help in activating the body's relaxation response (the mechanism in the body that counteracts the fight or flight response to stress). The stress management practices return hormone levels and other systems to normal; they are an important part of your life, and a valuable tool to stay healthy.

Find ways to reduce stress at work and enjoy the job more Part of job stress relief involves making changes at work that can increase satisfaction and cut down factors that cause stress and burnout. You can learn more about this by reading articles in managing job stress with specific reference to finding greater satisfaction at your current job. Creating suitable fun activities at work place helps eliminate burnout and stressors.

Make changes that become habits These practices may help one in making appropriate changes that will soon be ingrained as habits, thus leaving that person feeling less stressed, and increased physical and psychological well-being for years to come.

Strengthen your relationships Remember the fundamental truth that a strong support network (from family and friends) is your greatest protection against stress. When you have trusted friends and family members, share the causes of stress with them. So, spend time with the people you love and don't let your responsibilities keep you away from having a social life. If you do not have any close relationships, or your relationships are the source of your stress, make it a priority to build stronger and more satisfying connections. You will get relief. The following tips can be used for building relationships:

1. Help someone in need voluntarily
2. Have lunch or coffee with colleagues (may be in the office canteen)
3. Call an old friend and talk about some events when you were associated with him/her
4. Send emails and share jokes to a few old friends; ask them to send jokes in return
5. Go for a walk with a workout buddy
6. Schedule a weekly dinner with family (may be in local restaurants)
7. Take a class you can, or join a club you like

Learn to relax Stress can be reduced and can't be totally eliminated from one's life. But, anyone can exercise control over the stresses strictly considering the causes. Relaxation techniques such as yoga, meditation, and deep breathing activate the body's relaxation response. If these are practised regularly, they will lead to a reduction in everyday stress levels, and boost the feelings of joy and serenity. These practices will further increase the ability of the individual to stay calm and quiet under pressure.

Invest in emotional health Do not ignore your emotional health to the extent of a problem. Both time and energy are required to build or maintain your physical health. Similarly, time and energy must be spent to build emotional health and well-being. People with stable emotional health possess an ability to bounce back during stresses and adversity. This ability is called resilience. They remain focused, flexible, and positive in bad times as well as good. The good news is that there are many steps you can take to build your resilience and overall emotional health.

STRESS-FREE LIVING

Stress-free living gives us an opportunity to learn what we have to change, and how to expand our personal capacities and find ways to respond. We live in a world of exponential change, constantly demanding us to increase our ability to respond. We are flooded with more information than any other generation earlier. There are, therefore, two challenges which every human being faces in this 21st century. The first one is to be able to continue to respond effectively and positively to people and the world around us, and the second is to be able to manage ourselves and the world inside us. In both these worlds, everybody experiences stress every day. A majority of people are still trying to absorb or live with stress, but are clueless to decide upon what can be done. We see a high rate of divorce, crime, and substance abuse in all spheres of life.

Stressed people have to be ready to explore and make changes in their lives before it becomes painful. Through continuous learning, they will become stronger, calmer, and enlightened. They will be able to manage themselves, their relationships, and their life journey in a conscious and focused way.

If one practises the practical methods of stress-free living, he/she will receive important insights and self-inspiration. The vision of the person will change.

In this world where so many of our needs and desires are met almost instantly, many goals still remain unachieved. As the owner of the key to stress-free living, only the stressed person can turn the key to enter into the psychological world of mental freedom.

Principles of Stress-free Living

Stress is a part of work and social life. In order to lead a stress free life we need to adhere to some principles.

Be conscious It is advisable to listen deeply to your reactions and responses inside. Just by listening, one will be able to find out what is going on and realize at once what needs change.

Observe It is wise to simply observe what is happening around oneself. This will provide numerous insights to the stressed person.

Practice detached involvement Despite having a bad experience; one can detach himself/herself from the person, but still stay involved, perhaps in helping them. That way, he/she will get enormous peace.

Recover from failures One should not blame oneself for failing. Failures are pillars to success. One should perform realistic analysis, and use failures to learn. Going into retreat helps one recover, and that relieves stress.

Accept others One should accept others as they are; and accept failures as natural phenomena. From acceptance, comes forgiveness and compassion. Without these abilities it will be difficult to prevent stress. In fact, wrong actions of others have their root causes in some kind of disease in their minds. Freedom and peace comes from acceptance.

Understand time When we give attention to managing ourselves; managing our thoughts and feelings, the resulting clarity and foresight helps us to plan better and prepare ahead of time. This creates a feeling of control over time and work. In contrast, if our thoughts are disorderly, we constantly experience the feeling of 'running out of time' and being overloaded with work.

Manage expectations Watch others' expectations, but do not allow your lives to be ruled by them, because ultimately you cannot meet the standards of everybody's expectations. When you are unable to meet your own expectations, be wise enough to know that it will be difficult to meet others' expectations. Thus, you need to learn and expand your knowledge in order to meet their standards next time.

Cultivate personal mastery Try to be the master of your self – the mastery that we had given away to other people and situations. It is therefore necessary to rebuild self-esteem and get back total control over every creation within your own consciousness. This will greatly enhance your self-esteem.

Practice daily meditation Stress-free living is only possible when one can learn to manage one's thoughts, emotions and behaviour in such a way that one's creation is based on his/her innate qualities and values. Hence, it is essential to give oneself the gift of time everyday, for his personal meditation. In world of constant and frenetic change, meditation is not a submissive or passive activity. It is the most important action of effective self- management.

Be patient These skills do need practice before they become your natural power or ability to respond. Expect occasional failure. But do not blame yourself when you do not achieve instant perfection. Perfection and determination take some time. But be sure that you will win them.

Benefits of Meditation

Meditation is the method to rediscover and access one's true values that lie hidden in him/her. The benefits of meditation are pervasive and wide spread. Meditation does the following:

1. Helps one to reinstate the balance between being and doing and to achieve his/her goals
2. Helps one to experience inner silence—the silence of the mind. Without inner silence, one can never accomplish creativity.
3. Inner silence brings energy. Without this energy, life is only noise.

Maintaining a Diary

It is wise to maintain a dairy. In this diary, note down your stress levels and how you feel throughout the day. Particularly, record the stressful events. At regular intervals, for example, every hour, record routine stress. Note the following points in the diary.

1. The time
2. The amount of stress that you feel (on a scale of 1 to 10)
3. How happy you feel
4. How efficiently you are working

When stressful events occur, write down the following:

1. What was the event?
2. When and where did it occur?
3. What important factors made the event stressful?
4. Were you expecting to please everyone?
5. Were you reaching or viewing things as absolutely critical and urgent?
6. How stressful was the event? How exactly did you feel?
7. What was the nature and quality of your thinking at that time?
8. How did you handle the event? Did you tackle the cause or the symptom?
9. Could you have handled it in a better way?
10. Was it really a problem at all?

You should later refer to the diary when you feel the need to. You may simply feel that you should not have been stressed.

MANAGING STRESS IN KNOWLEDGE SECTOR

People in knowledge sectors like IT and BPO experience higher stress levels, due to the pressure of deadlines and acute global competition. IT major Wipro has started a campaign among employees, called 'fit for life' to manage stresses. Cycling Clubs have been formed as part of the stress management initiatives, and employees are encouraged to cycle within the campus; Green Clubs help de-stress through gardening, and Music Clubs allow employees to express themselves through performances. Nutrition and health camps have specialists providing guidance (Gangjee 2010). Organizations (WHO) are investing substantial amount to counter mental illness.

BIBLIOGRAPHY AND WEB RESOURCES

Gangjee, Zahid *Fun at Work De-stresses Employees*, Economic Times dated 21 May 2010.

Greenglass, E.R., *Proactive Coping, Work Stress, and Burnout*, Stress News, April, Vol. 13, No. 2, 2001.

Lazarus. R. and R. Launier, *Stress-related Transactions between Person and Environment* in A. Pervin and M. Lewis (Eds), *Perspectives in International Psychology*, Plenum, New York, pp. 284–327, 1978.

Pestonjee, D.M., *Stress and Coping—The Indian Experience*, Sage Publication, New Delhi, 1999.

Sarkar, Juthika, *Study of Organisational Climate and Organisational Role Stress Across Industries in Kolkata*, Doctoral thesis (unpublished) submitted to Singhania University, Jhunjhunu, Rajasthan, 2011.

Srivastava, A.K., *Achievement in Quality Assurance—An Empirical Study on Relationship with Stress, Coping, and Personal Variables*, Indian Journal of Training and Development, Indian Society for Training and Development, Vol. XXXVI No. 1, New Delhi, January–March, 2006.

Taylor, S. and Psychological Working Group, Coping Strategies (Summary), in D. John and C.T. MacArthur (Eds), *Research Network on Socioeconomic Status and Health*, July 1998.

Web Resources

articles.timesofindia.indiatimes.com/2011-10-16/holistic-living/30242111_1_stress-personal-reasons-diary, last accessed on 27 October 2011.

stress.about.com/od/stresshealth/a/jobstress.htm, last accessed on 27 October 2011.

D.M. PESTONJEE

Dr D.M. Pestonjee was born on 18 April 1939 at Aligarh, Uttar Pradesh. Pestonjee served the Indian Institute of Management, Ahmedabad for over two decades (1979–2001) as professor of organizational behaviour.

In November 2000, he was conferred the title of Honorary Professor of the Albert Schweitzer International University, Geneva (Switzerland). He was Chairman, Organizational Behaviour Area for three terms and also L&T Chair Professor of Organizational Behaviour (1992–99). He is a psychologist by training having obtained his MA in psychology with first class, and Ph D in industrial psychology from the Aligarh Muslim University. He has been conferred the D Litt (*Honoris Causa*) by the Banaras Hindu University in April 2003. He was awarded the Albert Schweitzer Medal for Science and Peace in April 2004.

He has over four decades of teaching experience and has so far successfully supervised eighteen Ph D Candidates. He is the author/co-author of ten books and over 100 research articles. Among his better known works are: *Organization Structure and Job Attitudes* (1973), *Behavioral Processes in Organization* (1981), *Second Handbook of Psychological and Social Instruments* (1988), *Third Handbook of Psychological and Social Instruments* (1997), *Studies in Organizational Roles and Stress and Coping* (1997), and *Studies in Stress and Its Management* (1999).

Professor Pestonjee has been active as a trainer and consultant in non-business sectors of education and health. He has been a temporary advisor to international organizations such as World Health Organization (WHO), United States Agency for International Development (USAID), and Oxfam. He was also an individual category elected member of the International Social Science Council of the UNESCO to represent management sciences for three terms, 1980–83; 1983–86; 1986–89. He was also a member of executive of the International Sociology Association (1986–90). He served as a regional representative of the International Association of Applied Psychology.

He has served on several national bodies such as the Indian Council of Social Science Research (ICSSR), the All India Council of Technical Education (AICTE), and the Indian Council of Medical Research (ICMR) and the University Grants Commission (UGC).

He has conducted a large number of management development programmes for executives on the theme of 'executive stress and coping' and also helped organizations with 'stress audit' to analyse and understand their role stresses with a view to incorporate relevant development inputs. He has been associated with public and private sector organizations, NGOs, MNCs, and joint sector organizations. His current areas of interest are executive stress, coping and issues related to executive health, job satisfaction, and morale.

He is presently Dean, Faculty of Technology Management, CEPT University, Ahmedabad and GSPL Chair Professor at School of Petroleum Management, Pandit Dindayal Petroleum University, Gandhinagar.

Source: Mails received from Prof. D.M. Pestonjee, dated 19 and 29 September 2011.

APPENDIX B

Organizational Climate and Organizational Role Stress

INTRODUCTION

In Appendix A we have been acquainted with work stress and its consequences, the effects of stress on performance, basic coping strategies or styles, and most importantly stress management interventions and means of stress-free living.

Businesses are operating in dwindling environments due to sporadic changes in the business environment. Businessmen are trying to gain distinctive competence and derive competitive advantages. Organizations are paying sharper attention to various aspects of HRM embracing industrial relations (IR). IR is influenced by leadership styles and strategies adopted by managerial personnel and plays a vital role in maintaining peace and harmony. Industrial democracy gives workers a sense of belonging, enhances their commitment, encourages involvement, contributes to boosting productivity, and so forth. Organizational climate plays a significant role in ascertaining the quality of industrial relations and magnitude of industrial democracy in any organization. Organizational climate is contributing to the industrial relations in organizations. Furthermore, managers and employees at any level of an organization are required to perform various roles. Performing multiple roles leads to stress build up.

Studying the motivational climates of an organization, finding out role stress levels, and their interrelationships in the industries is essential for organizational development. In addition, inter-organizational differences in climates and stress levels, ascertaining possible variations of stress on auxiliary variables such as age, sex, organizational hierarchy, education level, and management levels, and so on should also be studied. The possible reasons and grounds behind the differences should also be unearthed. The ultimate aim is ensuring a stress-free work environment where employees can invest their efforts to smoothly achieve the organizational goals.

ORGANIZATIONAL CLIMATE

Organizational climate is the perceived attribute of an organization and its subsystems, as reflected in the way an organization deals with its members, groups, and their issues (Pareek 1989). The personality of the employees of an organization is influenced by the organizational climate. Organizational climate depends on the perception of the organizational members about various dimensions, working, and problems in the organization. Pareek (1989) reviewed various studies, discussed with many managers, and proposed 12 processes with regard to organizational climate. Accordingly, in his psychometric scale titled, Motivational Analysis of Organizational-Climate popularly known as MAO-C scale, Pareek (1989) first proposed the dimensions of organizational climate which are orientation, interpersonal relationships, supervision, problem management, management of mistakes, conflict management, communication, decision making, trust, management of rewards, risk taking, and innovation and change. Achievement, expert influence, extension, control, dependency, and affiliation are the six motives. Each motive has its own indicators.

Indicators of Motives

The generic indicators of the six motives are

Achievement A concern for excellence; the employee is active and works hard, sets high goals for self, derives pleasure from work, works hard, prefers new tasks, and accepts challenging assignments. These employees possess a high standard of achievement in mind with which they keep comparing themselves. They dream about accomplishing tasks and strive to realize their dreams.

Expert influence This motive refers to an inherent desire to be driven by knowledge. The people try to gain knowledge consulting specialists. They are attracted by knowledgeable personalities, enhance capabilities through continuous learning, and contribute positively to the organization.

Extension A desire to be helpful to others, or to provide services to the external agents, organization, and the nation. People dominated by this motive are eager to help others in need, such as by collecting cash and materials after a natural calamity. They generally get willing support from juniors, peers, and seniors in the organization.

Control A concern to influence others and gain control over many. The people having this motive try to lead and influence, seek opportunities for leadership, look out for being in the limelight, and enjoy having followers. They cannot tolerate another person with a similar attitude.

Dependency People with this motive prefer to consult many before undertaking any work, or making decisions. They seek direction for all the tasks. They lack initiative and want to be protected by someone.

Affiliation A concern for establishing and maintaining affectionate and warm relationships. People whose dominant motive is affiliation, build emotional relationships with colleagues, join groups, become members of social clubs, and feel depressed in isolation.

ORGANIZATIONAL ROLE STRESS

A role is defined as a set of functions, which an individual performs in response to one's as well as others' expectations. While performing various roles, if the outcome is uncertain, but important, the employees feel stressed. The stresses relating to a person's role is termed as *role stress* (Pareek 1993). Therefore, it is of utmost importance both for the individual and the organization to work in the area of role stress management.

More stresses upset the mind and hinder the logical thinking process, making people argumentative and irritating, which results in an unhealthy work environment. Many researchers have opined that stress leads to wrong decision-making. Due to the economic downturn, all sectors (especially IT and BPO) have experienced higher stress levels due to the pressure of deadlines and global competition (Ganjee 2010). There exists traditional ways of handling IR. However, we can give a re-look and view the root causes behind IR in different ways through a different lens (Sarkar 2011). Organizational role stresses should be measured and managed to promote IR to ensure industrial democracy in true sense.

Stress generated due to complexity of the work content can be dealt with by providing training and strengthening supervisory instructions. In comparison to work stress, role stress is considered very important as it negatively impacts the organizational outcomes and successes and its management is not so easy.

Pareek has developed an organizational role stress (ORS) scale to measure organizational role stress that has mentioned ten variables. They are inter-role distance (IRD), role stagnation (RS), role expectation conflict (REC), role erosion (RE), role overload (RO), role isolation (RI), personal inadequacy (PI), self-role distance (SRD), role ambiguity (RA), and resource inadequacy (RIn).

Of the above ten most prominent organizational role stresses, an individual role occupant can take appropriate measures for addressing frequently encountered problems (while performing his/her role) that create high stress, jeopardizing his/her well-being, performance, and effectiveness (Srivastava 2007).

ORS Variables

The ORS variables are briefly described here. ORS is experienced while performing roles. The ORS scale measures the following ten types of role stresses:

Inter-role distance IRD arises when there are difficulties in balancing between organizational and non-organizational roles.

Role stagnation RS develops when there are difficulties in taking over the new role responsibilities due to lack of preparedness. The role occupant keeps stagnating in the old one, which is secure, familiar, and comfortable.

Role expectation conflict REC appears when there are conflicting role expectations.

Role erosion RE results when some of the important functions of one's role are performed by others or when the credit for one's role performance is given to others.

Role overload RO generates from too high or too many role expectations.

Role isolation RI results when the role occupant feels isolated due to lack of communication.

Personal inadequacy PI develops when there is lack of competencies for the role.

Self-role distance SRD develops when (a) the role occupant has to do what he/she dislikes, (b) his/her main skills are not utilized, or (c) he/she perceives a conflict between the self and the role.

Role ambiguity RA results from unclear and indistinct role expectations.

Resource inadequacy RIn generates when the role occupant perceives that role performance is suffering due to lack of external resources.

RECIPROCAL DEPENDENCIES

Reciprocal dependency of organizational climate and organizational role stress has been observed in different types of companies and in different places. Organizational climate determines the behaviour of the workforce and influences role stress. Obviously, organizational climate correlates and significantly influences the experience of stress in an organizational role, that is, organizational role stress (Pestonjee 1999). Organizational climate is one of the prominent factors behind organizational role stress in an organization (Srivastav 2006).

Based on a review of literature, Sarkar (2011) proposes a conceptual model depicting reciprocal dependency of organizational climate (determined six motives) and organizational role stresses (concluded by ten variables) shown in Figure B.1.

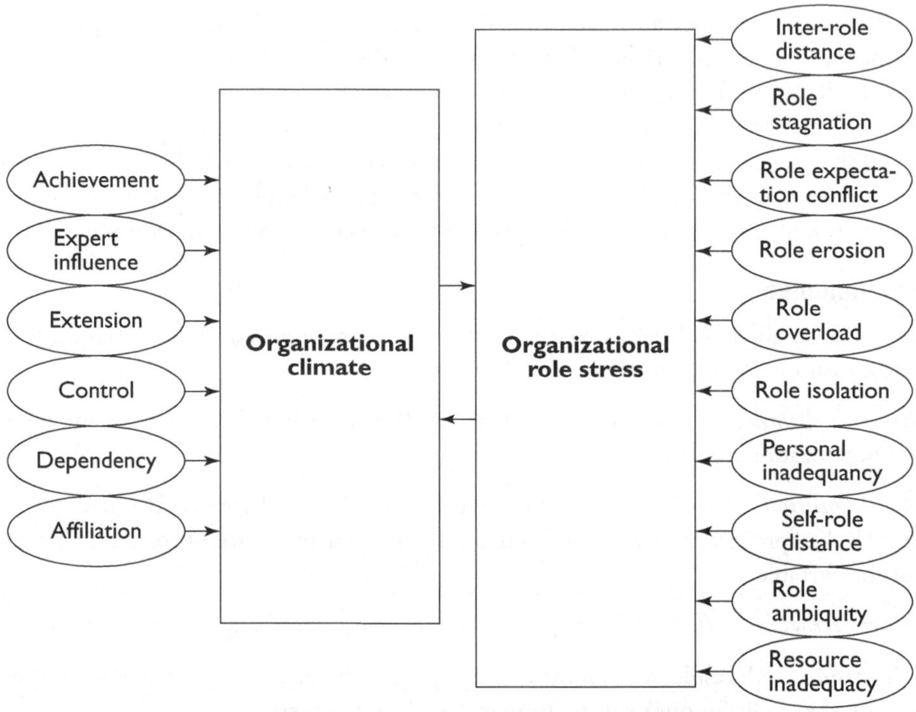

FIG. B.1 Conceptual model of reciprocal dependency of organizational climate and organizational role stress

CONSEQUENCES OF ORS

It has been previously discussed that stress causes change in motivation, cognition that can result in an altered relationship to environmental and social stimuli. Stress stimulates a surge on the physiological system which makes ones sleep and relaxation moments worthless, forces one to use unusual language, and behave in exceptional manner. As a result, a stressed person feels headaches, moodiness, and memory loss, inability to concentrate and even aggressive behaviour. Organizational role stress causes change in motivation and effectiveness of an individual, role, and organization. Continuance of role stress causes burn out, reduces problem-solving ability, disturbs rational thinking, hinders in synergistic drives to achieve business goals and hampers accomplishing production target smoothly, etc. leading to profit. If many people suffer from role stresses then marching organization towards excellence is greatly blocked.

MANAGING ORS

Role stresses are manageable and hence they must be managed. Two distinct strategies (emotion focused strategy and problem focused strategy) can be utilized. Organization can help stressed employees to cope. Coping means handling a potential stressor or the resulting stressful situation to minimize their harmful consequences. Coping comprises efforts, both action-oriented and intra-psychic, to manage the demands and conflicts (Srivastav 2006). The following coping strategies (discussed in Appendix A) can be used to manage ORS:

1. Problem-focused coping strategy
2. Emotion-focused coping strategy
3. Functional coping strategy
4. Dysfunctional coping strategy
5. Proactive coping strategy
6. Reactive coping strategy

Strategy of Managing ORS

Organizational role stresses are manageable for which organizations adopt functional strategies. However in some instances, dysfunctional strategies are also adopted. Pestonjee (1999) elucidates both the functional and dysfunctional strategies.

Table B.1 Strategies of ORS—avoidance vs proactiveness

Organizational role stress	Dysfunctional strategies (avoidance)	Functional strategies (proactiveness)
Inter-role distance	• Role partition • Role elimination	Role negotiation
Role stagnation	Role fixation	Role transition
Role expectation conflict	Role taking	Role making
Role erosion	Role visibility	Role development/enrichment
Role overload	Role reduction	Role slimming
Role isolation	Role boundedness	Role linkages
Personal inadequacy	Role shrinkage	Role linkage/relearning
Self Role Distance	• Role rejection • Self rejection	Role integration
Role ambiguity	Role prescription	Role clarification
Resource inadequacy	Role atrophy	Resource generation

The functional strategies for each role stress variables are described as follows:

Inter-role distance This variable interferes with the work life balance. An individual has to find ways to perform the non-organizational roles (mainly family role) without affecting the organizational roles. Time management and time sharing emerge as the solution. Thus role negotiation is the functional strategy of managing stress.

Role stagnation This stress develops when a role occupant finds difficulties in taking over new role responsibilities due to lack of preparedness or competency. But he should not stagnate. Management should develop an individual for a new role prior to assigning the role. The job demands must be considered and skill imparted. This will prevent or reduce generation of stress due to role stagnation. The functional strategy is role transition.

Role expectation conflict If an individual is receiving assignments from two superiors then this stress may arise as the expectations of the superiors may differ. They may lay emphasis on different organizational goals. In line management system the principle, 'one man, one boss' prevail. The probability of generation of role expectation conflict almost disappears. Otherwise, organizations must clearly define and document the role which is 'Role making'.

Role erosion Depending on the competencies, an individual can execute many assignments at a time. Management needs to consider the work ability of the employee and do not reassign part of the work to others. It is evidenced that a fellow colleague, other than the scheduled role occupant, is credited for doing the part work only. Management need to adopt role development strategy or job enrichment strategy. This practice will take care of generation of role erosion strategy.

Role overload The capacity of any individual is not unlimited. In organizations expectations from good role performers are more than their capabilities. Over expectations from an individual create illegitimate burden onto him leading to generation of stress on account of role overload. Justified work expectation from subordinate is a good management practice. So management needs to match expectation with individual capability adopting role slimming strategy.

Role isolation Communication are internal and external. Employees seek essential information in time. Stress naturally develops if they do get that. Lack of authentic communication in regards to role performance impacts the role occupant negatively. Role linkages are the functional strategy to prevent role isolation of employees.

Personal inadequacy The root cause behind personal inadequacy is lack of competency essential to execute the role. A person may not have the competency required to perform the role. Organizations can identify the competency required and the competency in possession of individuals; organizations can conduct training programmes to impart the necessary knowledge and skills. Identifying the training need is a joint responsibility of the individual and the management (immediate supervisor of the individual). Role linkage/relearning is the functional strategy organizations need to follow.

Self role distance This role stress develops when the role occupant has to do what he/she dislikes and main skills remain utilized. The conflict between the self and the role generate stress. Management should consider this point and assign tasks, to the extent possible, matching the individual job demands and the likes/dislikes and skills in possession. Role integration is the functional strategy of managing stress.

Role ambiguity Role is expectations of significant personality and also peers. In organizations a role occupant often remains unclear about the role required to be performed. Management need to develop system to ensure role clarity to reduce this stress. The functional strategy is role clarification.

Resource inadequacy A role occupant may find it difficult to perform the role due to non-availability of requisite resources. It is management's responsibility to provide the resources. But, the role occupant must project the exact resources with the corresponding specifications duly considering the lead time to procure. Resource generation is also a joint responsibility.

RESEARCH FINDINGS

On intensive review of literature, Sarkar (2011) observed that individual performance as well as organizational performance are affected by role stresses generated within employees and its management can positively contribute to achieving smooth functioning of the organization, reduced labour unrest, less attrition, improved quality of work life, etc. Sarkar (2011) undertook a research relating organizational climate and organizational role stress in select industries (manufacturing, telecom, and academia) in Kolkata city.

The objectives of the research were identifying dominant and back up organizational climate, identifying the influence of significant organizational climate behind generation of role stresses, recognizing the prominent role stresses in companies of the select industries, exploring the influence of dominant organizational climate on the personal correlates of organizational role stress and role stress variables.

Some significant findings are enumerated as follows:

1. Role stresses are more in manufacturing companies than telecom companies and least in academia.
2. In improved functional climates (achievement, expert influence, and extension) stress generation is lesser.
3. In dysfunctional climates (control, dependency, and affiliation), stress generation is more.
4. ORS is negatively correlated with age implying that elderly persons can manage their stresses reasonably better than younger generations.
5. ORS is negatively correlated with length of experience implying that while working in organizations people learn various organizational characteristics and hence people with more experience can manage their stresses better than younger generations.
6. Mean ORS score is highest for the middle income group. This value is even higher for those who did not disclose their income.
7. Mean ORS is more for those males whose wives are unemployed than those whose wives are employed.
8. Mean ORS is the highest for the junior management group than the middle management and senior management groups.

Social Benefits

The social benefits of study on organizational climate and role stress take account of identifying the climate, finding the root cause behind generation of stresses, eliminating or reducing the root causes adopting suitable methods including counselling, helping to cope with the stresses and disaster, etc. The findings give way to multiple benefits to the employees and in turn to the company. The following are some of the benefits of stress management interventions:

1. Increasing morale and self-esteem
2. Enhancing problem-solving ability
3. Providing an improved quality of work life, in turn quality of life
4. Applying synergistic drives to achieve goals
5. Reducing possibility to burn out

Research Cell

Progressive companies may plan to have its own research cell manned by competent personnel to accelerate its progression. The research cell personnel should have fundamental knowledge of behavioural science, organizational behaviour, contingency variables of organizational behaviour, research methodology, acquaintance with statistical tools, selection of tools for results leading to decision making, etc. They also should have knowledge of organizational culture and organizational climate survey and interpreting the results. External consultants might have widespread expertise but they do not and cannot be acclimatized with the organization is short period of time. As such, internal research cell under the direct supervision of the CEO is strongly recommended.

The salary of the research cell personnel will obviously call for additional cost; but their salary must be treated as investment and not as expenditure. This is because their efforts would help the company to diminish the 'hidden cost' due to stressed persons. Needless to mention that stress reduces productivity, enhances absenteeism, leads to manpower attrition, raises interpersonal mistrust, invites unwanted problems in the work place, lowers the quality of work life leading to quality of life, and so forth.

CONCLUSION

Stress is a hidden cost to companies. Managers and employees face the problems of stress despite changing technologies that have made their lives easy. Organizational climate and organizational role stress are reciprocally dependent. Managers, in addition to traditional roles, need to execute stress management role encompassing measuring levels of job satisfaction, conducting climate survey, organizing HR audit, matching qualification and job assignments, ensuring work–life balance, trimming down brain drainage, employee counselling, etc. Cost incurred in stress management initiatives should be treated as investment and not as expenditure.

As a change agent, an organizational leader must know the people well and understand their stress and tolerance level. The change agent has to develop a strong inventory of stress management skills. This is necessary to maintain a sense of mastery and control over themselves and life/work to avoid feeling victimized, overwhelmed, or controlled by pressure and demands.

Role stress is inevitable. Some amount of stress induces dynamism in the work flow. One cannot eliminate it. One can only manage it functionally, so that optimum individual performance will be achieved to fulfill the organizational as well as the personal goals.

BIBLIOGRAPHY AND WEB RESOURCES

Gangjee, Zahid, 'Fun at Work Destresses Employees', *Economic Times*, 21 May 2010.

Pareek, Udai, *Training Instruments in HRD* and *OD*, Tata McGraw-Hill, New Delhi, 1989.

Pestonjee, D.M., *Stress and Coping—The Indian Experience*, Sage Publication, New Delhi, 1999.

Sarkar, Juthika, *Study of Organizational Climate and Organizational Role Stress Across Industries in Kolkata*, Doctoral Thesis (unpublished) submitted to Singhania University, Jhunjhunu, Rajasthan, 2011.

Srivastav, Avinash Kumar, *Coping with Stress with Organizational Roles*, Indian Journal of Industrial Relations, Vol. 42, No.1, July 2006.

AVINASH KUMAR SRIVASTAV

Born in Jhansi, Uttar Pradesh, India on 17 July 1945, Dr Avinash Kumar Srivastav holds a Ph D in management in the area of organizational behaviour and an MS in electronics and communication engineering. He was admitted as a Senior Member of the Institute of Electrical and Electronics Engineers, Inc., USA in 1977 and a Fellow of All India Management Association in 1989.

After a highly successful and promising career in engineering spanning over two decades, he changed his profession from telecommunications engineering to organizational behaviour and development after attending the Tenth Advanced Management Programme for Public Enterprises at Indian Institute of Management, Ahmedabad in 1988.

Dr Srivastav has 37 years of rich and diverse experience in the government, public, and private sector industries in India and Indonesia followed by 8 years of experience in Indian business schools. He has worked in top-level executive and advisory positions including Assistant Director, Telecom Research Center, New Delhi; Executive Director, ITI Limited, Bangalore; HRD Director/Change Management Adviser/Organization Development Adviser/Corporate HR Director in Indonesian industries at Jakarta; Dean (Research) of ICFAI Business School, Director of Management Research and Director of Business School in Dayananda Sagar Institutions at Bangalore. He has served as an external consultant to the International Labour Organization.

As a member of the development team at Telecom Research Centre, he successfully contributed for the development of India's first Stored Program Controlled Electronic Telephone Exchange in early 1970s. Dr Srivastav set up Electronic Switching Research Division in ITI Limited in 1973 and contributed to development of a variety of electronic switching systems. He was actively involved in setting up India's first two digital switching systems manufacturing units. He was a recipient of Award for Meritorious Invention from National Research Development Corporation of India in 1984 for the development of Microprocessor Controlled Road Traffic Signaling System.

He turned around a sick manufacturing unit in the most difficult industrial relations climate of Kerala in 1989.

Dr Srivastav has developed principles of ISO 9000 to facilitate the understanding of international standard for quality management system and a novel model for its implementation which was used for successful ISO 9000 certification of several units of ITI Limited—a public sector industry with formidable resistance to change. He has conducted research studies on the impact of ISO 9000 on organizations and demonstrated how ISO 9000 can be employed as an organization development intervention. The work resulted in the National Quality Award for ITI Ltd from The Institute of Directors in 1992 and Lal C. Varman Award for outstanding achievements in the field of quality and standards by The Institution of Electronics and Telecommunication Engineers, India to Dr Srivastav in the same year.

Dr Srivastav had the fortune of working in close association with human resource and organization development guru: Late Dr Udai Pareek for human resource development and corporate restructuring of India's premier public sector industry: ITI Limited in 1993–94. Following up Dr Udai Pareek's research publications, he completed his doctoral thesis: Study of Organizational Climate, Role Stress and Coping Strategy amongst Public Sector Executives that earned him a doctorate in management in 1994.

His postdoctoral research on role stress led to the identification of *role underload* as the 11th type of role stress and scope for improvement of Dr Udai Pareek's classic invention, the ORS scale. Dr Srivastav had the honor of publishing this work jointly with Dr Udai Pareek in 2008 Pfeiffer Annual in USA. He also developed New Organizational Role Stress Scale for measuring eleven types of role stress.

Dr Srivastav has been ardently working for taking the knowledge of organizational behaviour and development to operational managers. He was privileged to have conducted a workshop for operational managers on harnessing the potential of organizational behaviour jointly with Dr Udai Pareek at Bangalore in 2008. He has been conducting organization development workshops for the operational managers of Hindustan Aeronautics Limited.

He has developed practical organization development interventions: role stress audit for individual and organizational improvement and process-based role analysis and design for enhancing the effectiveness of organizational roles.

Dr Srivastav developed a comprehensive system for promoting research and intellectual capital generation among business school faculty. He conducts workshops on writing high quality research papers. He has developed process based organization structure for business schools. He has done extensive research on organizational climate, role stress, coping strategy, ISO 9000 implementation and has published more than 60 research papers in refereed journals, annuals, edited books and conference proceedings in Australia, Europe, India, UK and USA. His research interests include individual and organizational effectiveness, learning effectiveness, change management, practical organization development and progressive human resource development system. He has been the consulting editor for ICFAI Journal of Organizational Behaviour.

Source: Mail received from Dr Avinash Kumar Srivastav on 12 September 12 2011.

APPENDIX C

Leadership Styles in Organizations

INTRODUCTION

HRM functions are manifold encompassing human resource planning, recruitment and selection, induction and placement, performance management system, training and development, multi-source feedback, potential appraisal and career system, compensation management, managing change, knowledge management, HRD audit, installing CSR activities and instilling ethics, managing globalization, managing technology, promoting work-life balance, initiating stress management drives, etc. Leadership plays a predominant role in all HRM functions and manifests its importance in achieving success.

The nature of good leadership is that it provides an important direction to an organization. However, for effectiveness, leaders must understand their followers. People unconsciously start to follow a leader on observing certain characteristics and willingly become followers. Such leaders never demand respect; rather they command it. The four parameters of leadership are—follower, leader, communication, and situation. Leadership principally refers to organizing a group of people to achieve a common goal. All functions in an organization are performed by the people in various levels of organization. It is the leadership style that can make or mar an organization.

LEADERSHIP STYLES IN ORGANIZATIONS

The role of HR functions is changing. In view of this changing role and to achieve the common themes which characterize and ultimately shape the process of organizational transformations, managers need to exhibit certain leadership styles in different situations for organizational effectiveness. The contemporary leadership styles practiced in organisations are transactional, transformational, and charismatic. Value-based leadership, ethical and servant leadership, and boundary spanning and team leadership are common in effective organizations. In organizations, one will find leaders using various types of styles. They all try to achieve the organization's mission, policy, and objectives. The styles of leaders are identified from the component behaviours, and are mostly used to influence the subordinates or followers. As an influencer, each style impacts the followers' response and determines their performance.

Transactional Leadership

Transactional leaders rely on eventuality, that is, they treat rewards or punishments as determinants of performance. Transactional leaders conform to rules and regulations, structured systems and procedures, and they treat any deviation from them as nonconformity. When people have agreed to do a job, a part of the deal is that they admit to the authority of their manager. Transactional leaders determine what employees need to do to achieve their own and organizational objectives, classify those requirements, and help employees become confident to achieve their objectives by expending the necessary efforts (Stoner, et al. 2006). The transactional leader works through creating clear structures by which it is clear as to what is required of their subordinates, and the rewards that they get for following the instructions. Penalties are not always mentioned, but they are also well understood and formal systems of discipline are usually in place. This leadership style rests on the belief that social systems work best with a clear chain of command and that the prime job of a subordinate is to do what their managers tell them to do. They possess the belief that people are motivated by reward and punishment.

Transformational Leadership

Transformational leadership is a behavioural process that encourages change, innovation, and entrepreneurship. The leadership process is systematic, comprises purposeful and organized searches for changes, methodical analysis, and has the capacity to utilize resources to enhance productivity. The underlying assumptions of transformational leadership are the following:

1. People will follow a person who inspires them.
2. A person with vision and passion can achieve great things.
3. The way to get work done is by injecting enthusiasm and energy.

Transformational leaders inspire followers, gain their trust, exhibit the kind of behaviour that contributes to the achievement of organizational goals, and perform at high energy levels. Transformational leaders

1. increase awareness among subordinates of the importance of their tasks and the significance of performing them well
2. alert the subordinates regarding the need for personal growth, development, and accomplishment
3. inspire and stimulate the subordinates to work for the good of the organization

They influence their followers by intellectually stimulating them to become aware of problems in their teams and the organization as a whole; they also view their problems from a new perspective that is consistent with the leader's vision. A transformational leader encourages the followers to view problems differently and feel some degree of responsibility in helping to solve them. Transformational leadership is a discipline with a set of predictable steps: revitalization (recognition of the need to change), creating a new vision, and institutionalizing the change. A transformational leader positively contributes to productivity enhancement, manpower retention, and higher employee satisfaction as it instils feelings of confidence, admiration, and commitment in the followers.

Transformational leaders are flexible and innovative, and today's changing business environment needs such leaders for overall growth. It is of utmost importance to have leaders with the appropriate orientation, defining tasks and managing interpersonal relationships. However, it is even more important to have leaders who can convert an organization into a truly global one in terms of quality. Transformational leadership is the essence of creating and sustaining competitive advantage. 'Leaders are truly transformational when they increase awareness of what is right, good, important, and beautiful; when they help to elevate followers' needs for achievement and self-actualisation; when they foster in followers high moral maturity; and when they move followers to go beyond their self-interests for the good of their group, organisation, or society' (Bass 1997). Kumar Mangalam Birla in his nine important learnings mentions about transformation.

Charismatic Leadership

Charisma is synonymous with charm, appeal, magnetism, allure, and it means the divine gift of grace. It is a type of authority or influence based on exceptional characteristics of an individual. It is also an important social influence that pulls people, irrespective of caste, creed, or colour, to a person. Some leaders have exceptional qualities and almost magical powers that inspire people to devote and commit to them. Followers of one such leader identify themselves with the leader, become emotionally involved in the leader's mission, ideology, and thought process. Being associated with such a leader for some time, the followers experience increased self-esteem. Such leaders are called charismatic leaders. A charismatic leader does not demand attention rather he/she commands it. This quality matters for the success of a leader though it can also let one down. People are ready to tread the path of a charismatic leader even if the path is ridden with difficulties. These leaders do not demand attention, rather they command it. They possess some unique qualities, which may be absent in many other leaders. Messages from these leaders produce much-needed effects in the followers. The spinning wheel that Mahatma Gandhi often used symbolized self-reliance, the value of cottage industries, and the demand for Indian independence. The message 'Give me blood, I will give you freedom' by Netaji Subhash Chandra Bose produced tremendous impact on his followers. Messages of Mother Teresa attracted her followers to join her in the voluntary efforts. Howell and Costley (2008) define charismatic leadership as an attribution made by followers about leaders who exhibit certain personal traits, abilities, and behaviours, and who have unusually strong influences on followers' emotion, values, beliefs, attitudes, and behaviours. In all walks of organizational life, one finds gifted charismatic leaders who advocate radical solutions to critical problems. They are able to see things from another person's perspective. Charismatic people speak emotionally about placing themselves in the line of fire. Obviously, followers are unquestioningly and magnetically attracted to these leaders.

Naturally, a charismatic leader can easily induce huge doses of enthusiasm in his/her team, and is very energetic in driving others forward. The departure of a charismatic leader can create a risk to a project or even an entire organization. In the eyes of his/her followers, success is tied up with the presence of the charismatic leader. Such a leader demonstrates creativity, innovative behaviours, risk-taking propensity, and self-sacrifice to project their courage, compassion, credibility, and convictions about achieving the mission. Charisma matters enormously in start-up companies, turnaround contexts, or whenever a business is ripping through rapid and unpredictable change. Howell and Costley (2008) identify certain leadership behaviours of a charismatic leader that are listed as follows:

1. Makes inspirational speeches
2. Builds own image in the followers' eyes
3. Uses and frames modus operandi to guide followers
4. Distils complex ideas into simple messages
5. Role models of behaviour for followers with high expectations and confidence
6. Takes risks to achieve mission
7. Advocates moral mission and vision

All the behaviours tend to generate loyalty, dedication, trust, devotion, and commitment to the leader, emotional involvement in the leader's mission, increased self-esteem, and belief in the leader's values.

By distilling complex ideas into simple messages these leaders stimulate, challenge, prod, push, and poke. Robert House, a Wharton School professor who has studied charisma for 20 years, says that when conditions are uncertain, charismatic bosses spur and stimulate subordinates to work above and beyond the call of duty.

Visionary Leadership

Leadership and shared value shape and mould the individual, group, and organizational behaviours. Vision includes the broader sense of mission. A leader must have a vision and should develop strategies for translating the vision into reality. The foremost needs of visionary leaders are insight and foresight. A visionary leader must have spontaneous dynamism, respect for others, willingness to make sacrifices for team-mates, creative thinking to make the work environment conducive for effective working. In addition to these, the leader must have qualities such as communication skills, decision-making skills, human relation skills, and commitment to achieving goals. Using leadership with these principles, prerequisites, and preconditions in mind, a vision must be articulated for the future of the organization that should fit TQM in the organization. The leader shows the need and sets the vision, defining the basic purpose, goals, and parameters or requirements of TQM. He/she must be able to get willing support from team-mates and motivate others to adhere to the process during the early stages when resistance and obstacles may seem insurmountable. The leadership must be a participative one, using the intervention approach. An intervention approach is a purposeful process extensively used to change peoples' thoughts, feelings, and bring about behavioural modification. Use of this approach ultimately leads to organizational effectiveness. Visionary leadership embraces core spiritual values and visionary leaders are those with a commitment to these values.

Inspiration and a practical vision of the future are the basis of visionary leadership. The vision encourages and invites others to participate as partners. They glow with a sense of vigour, energy, and optimism that influences and motivates others. They are also creative, innovative, and go beyond the limits of conventional thought in their efforts. They survive to truly serve the common good. The leader must have the skills of building a strong team of people, understanding the middle management, creating a learning environment, monitoring and reviewing periodically, ensuring that team members are open to problems, enhancing their problem-solving skills, attracting and retaining talents, preventing manpower attrition, sharing ideas regarding organizational growth, recognizing innovative work done, and the like. The leader has to discharge interpersonal, informational, and decision-making roles for sustenance and growth of the organization. Visionary leaders can effectively induce enthusiasm and energy to juniors.

Ethical (Spiritual) Leadership

Spiritual leadership is distinctly different from other leadership styles. Leadership in this millennium needs a new style for motivating, inspiring, and engaging a critical mass of committed and capable people whose concerted efforts would lead to business success smoothly. Of course, achieving success has always been a criteria and concern of business leaders. But in today's business parlance characterized by downsizing, restructuring, cost reduction, business process reengineering, flat organization structuring, de-layering have posed a threat to the organizations. Spiritual leadership comprises the values, attitudes, and behaviours required to intrinsically motivate self and others in order to have a sense of spiritual well-being (International Institute of Spiritual Leadership [IISL]). The purpose of spiritual leadership is to create vision and value congruence across the strategic, empowered team and individual levels and, ultimately, to foster higher levels of organizational commitment and productivity. Spiritual leadership deals with workplace spirituality and spiritual survival. Spiritual leadership strongly aids organizational transformation to create an intrinsically motivated and learning organization.

Organizational leaders with spiritual values make a difference, and feel understood and appreciated. It stands established from the findings of many research reports that organizational commitment strengthens motivation and reduces turnover, and that organizational productivity is at the heart of the total quality movement. Obviously technology is essential for progress as much of industrial change revolves around technology.

Fry (2003) pursued a research to examine leadership as motivation to change and review motivation-based leadership theories. He noted the accelerating call for spirituality in the workplace. He describes the universal human need for spiritual survival through calling and membership, and distinguishes between religion and spirituality. He also reviewed religious and ethics and values-based leadership theories and conclude that to motivate followers, leaders must get in touch with their core values and communicate them to followers through vision and personal actions to create a sense of spiritual survival through calling and membership. Fry (2003) argues that spiritual leadership theory is not only inclusive of other major extant motivation-based theories of leadership, but that it is also more conceptually distinct, parsimonious, prudent, and less conceptually confounded. Effective human performance and success in the work area need vision, efforts needs hope and faith, and whereas rewards are associated with altruistic love. Spiritual leadership contributes to performance, efforts, and altruistic or selfless love. Spiritual leadership philosophy is needed for organizational executives to articulate, communicate, and implement truly meaningful and authentic core values. Spiritual leaders can develop mutual trusts between people which lead to organizational effectiveness.

Servant Leadership

Robert Greenleaf coined this term in 1970s to describe a leader who does not formally recognize oneself as a leader. He/she is someone, at any level within an organization, who leads simply by virtue of meeting the needs of the team. It is a form of democratic leadership, as the whole team tends to be involved in decision-making. In some organizations, values are valued. There the organizational leaders, as servant leaders, achieve power on the basis of their values and ideals. On the contrary, others believe that in competitive leadership situations, people practicing servant leadership will often find themselves left behind by leaders using other leadership styles. They treat their key roles as those of developing, enabling, and supporting their team members, helping them fully develop their potential and deliver their best. The 'adjective' of this style emphasizes that one has to work, listen, search something, give feedback, provide service, and offer service whenever desired. With this analogy, a servant leader has to work with the members, search better ways of doing work, give feedback of team activities, provide guidance to members, and so forth. On the contrary, a servant leader cannot have separate status than the members though a servant has to maintain a safe distance from his/her masters. As a servant leader, you need to listen carefully. You need to be attuned to people around you and empathically understand what they are thinking. You need to tune into what inspires and motivates them. You need to help remove barriers and help people be the best they can be. Followers like the idea of servant leadership—there is something immediately attractive about the idea of having a boss who's a servant leader. And people without responsibility for results may like it for it is obviously democratic and consensual approach.

Value-based Leadership

Human values also play a dominant role in continuance in one's career, satisfaction, performance in the position held. When a person chooses his/her occupation, he/she believes there is something good in it. The concept of good is a part of an internalized mental structure, which establishes priorities regarding what he/she wants out of life. Organizations today are realizing a need for change in their management practices. Whatever be the leadership style of a manager, effectiveness is possible only if the leader's values emanate from the heart and not just from what he/she preaches. This is value-based leadership.

Value-based leaders do not use authority or exercise power with his/her people. This voluntary relationship of the leader with work becomes the guiding and driving force for the followers in pursuing their tasks and assignments as a challenge for the organization. By virtue of the values, these leaders can foresee the direction and speed of changes, understand the people, and gain confidence of supporters. Value-based leadership goes beyond transformational and charismatic leadership.

In today's business environment characterized by acute competition, intrusion of foreign players, increased customer demands, for an organization to create and sustain high performance is a major challenge. In the days of growing global competition, excellence can be achieved through value-based leadership. Adopting value-based leadership is also an instance of transformation where the role of a transformational leader is essential to bring about change and a paradigm shift in the organization.

Values, ethics, and trust are the keys to the growth of the organization and the societal capital in business. An organization carries out business in a society having its own culture, belief, and tradition. For sustainable growth, the business organization cannot ignore the social, cultural, global realities of the present times. There must be congruence between societal needs and organizational practices. For leaders, some skills are innate and some are learned.

Good management is a skill and leadership is an art. To be on top of the craft, an organization needs socially conscious organizational leaders. This consciousness integrates leadership skills in a value-based system. Obviously then, value-based leadership involves vision, motivation, organization, and action of the leader. All these inculcate sense of power and hope, provide guidance, direction and inspiration, and empower people to realize their potential.

Information technology has created possibilities for communication unimaginable in its absence. This tremendous change has altered the avenues to promote ideas and the path of doing business. The reality is that an artisan-driven organization has changed to a knowledge-driven one. It is being increasingly realized to cope with the challenges, organizational leaders of the new economy need wider knowledge, a broader perspective, and vision, newer skills and greater understanding of people, process, and technology. Leadership may prove to be a strategic tool to achieve organizational excellence. Value-based corporate leaders with human values, enhanced confidence and professional commitment possess the ability to transform and revitalize organization with vision, foresightedness, ensure trusting environment and healthy organizational culture, and promote human touch, which are essential elements for an organization to survive and grow in any economy including a downturn. Both value creation and living the values are important for leaders to be successful. Inspiration, innovation, and communication and collaboration help create values. Inspired employees generate passion and commitment, resulting in them taking on leadership roles. Innovative employees generate competitiveness and sustainability. Narayana Murthy expresses his views on leadership and values.

Boundary Spanning Leadership

Boundary spanning and leadership is defined as leader actions that establish and maintain a group's integrity through negotiation with non-group members, resolving disputes among followers and subgroups, obtaining resources, establishing influential networks, and helping followers deal with the external environment (Howell and Costley 2008).

Boundary spanning incorporates performing representative functions and linking-pin functions of leaders. Discharging the role of spokesperson is an example of a representative function where one's loyalties remain entirely with the group. On the contrary, linking-pin roles refer to interacting with two or more groups, with loyalties in both, fulfilling liaison functions. Thus, performing intra-group functions are representative roles, and inter-group functions are linking-pin roles. They discharge the roles of figurehead, liaison persons, monitors, disseminator, spokesperson, disturbance handler, and negotiator.

As a figurehead they perform symbolic acts, such as, representing the organization in social gatherings. As a liaison they build and maintain networks with members of their own group and other groups, developing new contacts, keep touch with significant outsiders, and reciprocate helps. They gather relevant information that might be helpful to the whole organization as monitor. As a disseminator they are sharing information on to units, subunits, and other insiders helping decision-making. Towards discharging the role of spokesperson they are transmitting information and expressing value statements to outsiders to promote company image. They are handling disturbance; identifying conflicts of any nature that may lead to loss of organizational members, closure, strikes, or other industrial disputes. As a negotiator they bargain logically for the unit demanding resources, constraints, interfering problems; buffering the unit and its members from higher-ups and outsiders. The locus of control of boundary spanning leaders should be high, have effective communication and political and negotiation skills in addition to conflict management skills. They should have expert, referent, legitimate, and reward and coercive power for organizational effectiveness.

LEADERSHIP STYLE VS STRESS

Transactional leaders rely heavily on rewards or punishments to get the job done by juniors. Less competent juniors get stressed while working with such leaders.

Transformational leaders influence their followers intellectually and stimulate them. Transformational leaders follow some predictable steps. As such, juniors are not much stressed as they know the consequences of actions. Another reason is the flexible or flexibly rigid style of the leaders.

Charismatic leaders easily induce huge doses of enthusiasm into their team. The team members are self-propelled. Members can conveniently achieve the goals in presence of the charismatic leader. As such, the stress levels are low. But, when the leader departs, the members feel greatly stressed from the sense of helplessness.

Visionary leaders develop strategies based on both their insight and foresight and as such very less stress develops within them.

Organizational leaders with spiritual and ethical values make a difference, and feel understood and appreciated. They are never the cause of stress to their followers.

Servant leaders, as they have termed, listen carefully and empathically understand what the juniors are thinking; inspire and motivate them; and involve team members in decision-making. For the democratic style of leadership, the juniors or followers remain reasonably unstressed.

Value-based leaders do not use authority or exercise power onto their juniors and people around; simply treat them team members. This voluntary relationship of the leader established with juniors becomes the driving force for the followers in pursuing their tasks and assignments. As such, stresses are minimal.

Boundary spanners negotiate with non-group members and maintain a group's integrity. In order to perform the variety of roles, they and their followers need diverse personality traits. They need to have expert, referent, legitimate, and reward and coercive power for organizational effectiveness. The followers remain moderately stressed.

Each person has a different style of leading; reacts in a different way to followers and others. Their style differs by a very little extent when faced with stress. Natural reactions to stress also alter their style of dealing with people. However, any leader can equip oneself with leadership qualities that are essential in stressful situations. This ability to adapt a leadership style to exemplify stability, control, and transparency will aid in successfully leading through stress.

BIBLIOGRAPHY AND WEB RESOURCES

Bass, B. M., Does the Transactional–Transformational Paradigm Transcend Organizational and National Boundaries? *American Psychologist,* 52, pp. 130–139, 1997.

Haldar, Uday Kumar, *Leadership and Team Building*, Oxford Higher Education, Oxford University Press, New Delhi, 2010.

Howell, Jon P. and Dan. L. Costley, *Understanding Behaviours for Effective Leadership*, Prentice-Hall India, New Delhi, 2006.

Louis, W., *Towards a Theory of Spiritual Leadership*, Tarleton State University, Central Texas. Killeen, USA, 2003.

Stoner, A.F., *Management* (Eastern Economic Edition), Prentice Hall India, New Delhi, 2006.

The Sunday Indian, dated November 01 2011.

Web Resources

en.wikipedia.org/wiki/Jayaprakash_Narayan accessed on October 29 2011.

www.google.co.in/search jayaprakash+narayan, last accessed on October 29 2011.

www.liveindia.com/freedomfighters/JayPrakashNarayan.html, last accessed on November 01 2011.

www.tarleton.edu/~fry/SLTTheory.pdf, last accessed on February 27 2009.

JAYAPRAKASH NARAYAN

Jayaprakash Narayan (JP), popularly known as Loknayak, was born 11th October 1902 in Sitabdiara village of Suremanpur, Ballia disctrict, Uttar Pradesh. His father Harsudayal was a junior official in the canal department of the State government and was often touring the region. JP, affectionately called Baul, was left with his grandmother to study in his home town.

There was no high school in the village, so JP was sent to Patna to study in the Collegiate School. He excelled in school. He participated in competitions. His essay titled, 'The present state of Hindi in Bihar', won the best essay award. He entered the Patna College with a government scholarship. He later joined *Bihar Vidyapeeth*, founded by the first President of India, Dr Rajendra Prasad, for motivating young meritorious youth, and was among the first students of eminent Gandhian Dr Anugrah Narayan Sinha who was a close colleague of M.K. Gandhi.

JP was practically a committed Marxist and he was convinced that the communists in India must join the main stream of the struggle for national liberation even if it was under the hegemony and domination of the so-called bourgeoisie. JP had met some communist leaders in London and discussed with them the issue of India's freedom and revolution. JP had read Lenin's famous Colonial thesis calling upon the communists in the 'slave' countries to take active part in the national freedom struggle. Later JP joined the nationalist freedom movement. However, he could not understand the rationality of the fight against the Indian National Congress which was fighting for the freedom of the country. JP was jailed in 1932 for civil disobedience against the British rule.

In the Nasik prison, JP had the opportunity to meet thinkers such as Ram Manohar Lohia, Ashoka Mehta, Minoo Masani, P. Dantawala, Achyut Patwardhan, and others. They were all impatient for the freedom of India and agreed to steer the Congress towards the goal of socialism. JP was released from prison in 1933.

In 1934, JP and his friends formed the Congress Socialist Party under the leadership of Acharya Narendra Deva (President) for which JP was the secretary. The group intended to function as the socialist wing within the Congress party and aimed to make socialism the goal of the Congress. In a book titled *Why Socialism?*, JP (1932) explained why socialism would be right for India. He was adored by the youth for his idealism.

During the Quit India Movement of 1942, when senior Congress leaders were arrested in the early stages, JP along with Ram Manohar Lohia and Basawon Singh (Sinha) were at the forefront of the agitations.

Initially a defender of physical force, JP was influenced by Mahatma Gandhi's position on nonviolence and advocated the use of satyagraha to achieve the ideals of democratic socialism. Furthermore, he became deeply disillusioned with the practical experience of socialism in Nehru's India.

JP's role in reinstating social life to the dacoits of Chambal is exemplary. Though six decades has elapsed after India's independence, the guns continue to reverberate in Chambal. Way back in 1970s, JP attempted and partially succeeded in changing the face of Chambal. He was also the key person in acquiring the surrender of dacoits in the Chambal valley. This incident speaks of one of the glorious chapters of JP's life.

JP was an Indian independence activist and political leader. He is especially remembered for leading the opposition to late Prime Minister Indira Gandhi in the 1970s and for giving a call for a peaceful revolution. A nationalist friend of JP and an eminent writer of Hindi literature, Ramavriksha Benipuri wrote the biography of JP.

The great socio-political leader expired on 8th October 1979. In 1998, JP was posthumously awarded India's highest civilian award Bharat Ratna in recognition of his social work. Prior to this he had received the Magsaysay award for Public Service in 1965. The airport of Patna is also named after him. After his death, Vinoba Bhave said that JP considered himself only a *lok-sevak*, or servant of the people.

Index

About the Authors

Uday Kumar Haldar, C.Eng , B.Sc, MISTE, MISTD, MIMA, MBA, FIIE, FIE, Ph.D, D.Lit., was formerly Director, Indian Ordnance Factories, post which he served as the Principal of Swami Vivekananda Institute of Management and Computer Science, Narendrapur, and retired in 2014. Now, he is engaged as Advisor and Strategic Skill Consultant, Skill Consultancy Services, Kolkata and Chief Editor and Author, Skill Hub Publication, Kolkata. He has authored 12 books on management, 4 of which are published by Oxford University Press. He has edited proceedings, and authored 50 papers/articles in national and international conferences, seminars, and congresses. He bagged the 'Bharat Jyoti Award' and 'Glory of India Award'. He also mentors doctoral (Ph D) scholars registered with 5 universities.

Juthika Sarkar, MISTE, MISTD, MIMA, MIC, MA, MBA, Ph.D, has more than 16 years of industry experience in Siemens and Nokia Siemens Network and has worked in telecom manufacturing, SAP ERP system, logistics and supply chain management and many other departments. Now she is engaged as Skill Consultant, Skill Consultancy Services, Kolkata; proprietor and author of Skill Hub Publication. She has authored 15 books on management and skill development, including 2 by Oxford University Press. She has published and presented 16 papers/articles in reputed journals and conventions. She has conducted management development programmes in prestigious corporate houses and is a qualified assessor of skill development initiatives under the Ministry of Skill Development and Entrepreneurship. She has a vast experience in assessment of modular employable skills. Dr Sarkar has received the 'Mother Teresa Excellence Award' and 'Bharat Gaurav Award' in 2017.

Related Titles

UNDERSTANDING ORGANIZATIONAL BEHAVIOUR, 3/E

9780198070733 | Udai Pareek, Sushama Khanna

The third edition of *Understanding Organizational Behaviour* is a comprehensive textbook specially designed to meet the needs of post graduate management students. The book explores the core concepts of organizational behaviour and provides in-depth coverage of the issues faced by Indian organizations.

Key Features

- Provides in-depth coverage of the issues and challenges faced by Indian organizations in the areas of traditional culture and modern management
- Includes numerous case studies on major organizations including Mumbai *dabbawalas*, McDonalds, BHEL, and Cisco
- Includes self-assessment tools to help students analyse various concepts and theories of OB

ORGANIZATIONAL CHANGE AND DEVELOPMENT

9780198066460 | Dipak Kumar Bhattacharyya

Organizational Change and Development is aimed at postgraduate students specializing in human resources (HR) and strategy. Providing a strong conceptual foundation of the subject, the book takes the readers through all the processes and stages of change, as seen and experienced worldwide.

Key Features

- Discusses OD experiences in several Indian and international organizations such as Walmart, Lehman Brothers, Godrej, and Indian Ordnance Factories
- Provides appendices on guidelines for organizational change, sample of a dashboard, and organizational health survey

CROSS-CULTURAL MANAGEMENT

9780198066293 | Shobhana Madhavan

This is a comprehensive textbook designed for postgraduate degree/diploma students of business management and practising managers. It explains how culture impacts international management in the areas of communication, negotiations, organizational behaviour, and human resource management.

Key Features

- Discusses cross-cultural management in today's corporate India with a wide variety of Indian/Asian examples—making this text relevant to today's global India
- Provides important tips on business etiquette and key information regarding doing business in several countries, ranging from Brazil to Nigeria

INDUSTRIAL RELATIONS

9780195671087 | C.S. Venkata Ratnam

The text provides an in-depth coverage of the four key components of industrial relations: the conceptual foundations, the institutional structure and policy framework, the role of government, and industrial relations in unionized organizations.

Key Features

- Explores the emerging issues in industrial relations, such as labour law reform, employment security and management of redundancies, and technological change and industrial relations
- Examines the challenges faced by business organizations in industrial relations

Other Titles by the Same Author

- 9780195698718 Haldar: *Human Resource Development*
- 9780198062578 Haldar: *Leadership and Team Building*

Other Related Titles

- 9780195676945 Jyothi and Venkatesh: *Human Resource Management*
- 9780195683592 Tanuja Agarwala: *Strategic Human Resource Management*
- 9780195693379 Deb and Kohli: *Performance Management*
- 9780195698374 Bhattacharyya: *Compensation Management*